Data-Driven Computational Neuroscience

Data-driven computational neuroscience facilitates the transformation of data into insights on the structure and functions of the brain. This introduction for researchers and graduate students is the first in-depth, comprehensive treatment of statistical and machine learning methods for neuroscience. The methods are demonstrated through case studies of real problems to empower readers to build their own solutions. The book covers a wide variety of methods, including supervised classification with non-probabilistic models (nearest-neighbors, classification trees, rule induction, artificial neural networks, and support vector machines) and probabilistic models (discriminant analysis, logistic regression, and Bayesian network classifiers), metaclassifiers, multidimensional classifiers, and feature subset selection methods as well as unsupervised classification. Other parts of the book are devoted to association discovery with probabilistic graphical models (Bayesian networks and Markov networks) and spatial statistics with point processes (complete spatial randomness and cluster, regular, and Gibbs processes). Cellular, structural, functional, medical, and behavioral neuroscience levels are considered.

Concha Bielza is a professor in the Department of Artificial Intelligence at Universidad Politécnica de Madrid. She has published more than 120 impact factor journal papers and coauthored the book *Industrial Applications of Machine Learning* (2019). She was awarded the 2014 UPM Research Prize and received the 2020 Machine Learning Award from the Amity University in India.

Pedro Larrañaga is a professor in the Department of Artificial Intelligence at Universidad Politécnica de Madrid. He has published more than 150 journal papers and coauthored the book *Industrial Applications of Machine Learning* (2019). He is Fellow of the European Association for Artificial Intelligence and of Academia Europaea. He received the 2020 Machine Learning Award from the Amity University in India.

Data-Driven Computational Neuroscience

Machine Learning and Statistical Models

CONCHA BIELZA

Universidad Politécnica de Madrid

PEDRO LARRAÑAGA

Universidad Politécnica de Madrid

CAMBRIDGE
UNIVERSITY PRESS

University Printing House, Cambridge CB2 8BS, United Kingdom

One Liberty Plaza, 20th Floor, New York, NY 10006, USA

477 Williamstown Road, Port Melbourne, VIC 3207, Australia

314–321, 3rd Floor, Plot 3, Splendor Forum, Jasola District Centre, New Delhi – 110025, India

79 Anson Road, #06–04/06, Singapore 079906

Cambridge University Press is part of the University of Cambridge.

It furthers the University's mission by disseminating knowledge in the pursuit of education, learning, and research at the highest international levels of excellence.

www.cambridge.org
Information on this title: www.cambridge.org/9781108493703
DOI: 10.1017/9781108642989

First published 2021

Printed in the United Kingdom by TJ Books Limited, Padstow Cornwall

A catalogue record for this publication is available from the British Library.

Library of Congress Cataloging-in-Publication Data
Names: Bielza, Concha, author. | Larrañaga, Pedro, 1958– author.
Title: Data-driven computational neuroscience: machine learning and statistical
    models / Concha Bielza, Universidad Politécnica de Madrid, Pedro Larrañaga,
    Universidad Politécnica de Madrid
Description: Cambridge, United Kingdom ; New York, NY : Cambridge University Press,
    2020. | Includes bibliographical references and index.
Identifiers: LCCN 2019060117 (print) | LCCN 2019060118 (ebook) |
    ISBN 9781108493703 (hardback) | ISBN 9781108642989 (epub)
Subjects: LCSH: Neurosciences–Data processing. | Neurosciences–Statistical methods.
Classification: LCC QP357.5 .B54 2020 (print) | LCC QP357.5 (ebook) | DDC 612.8–dc23
LC record available at https://lccn.loc.gov/2019060117
LC ebook record available at https://lccn.loc.gov/2019060118

ISBN 978-1-108-49370-3 Hardback

Contents

Color plates can be found between pages 366 and 367

Preface

This book describes statistical and machine learning methods to build computational models learned from real-world neuroscience data. These methods cover supervised and unsupervised classification with probabilistic and non-probabilistic models, association discovery with probabilistic graphical models, and spatial statistics with point processes. Chapters with necessary basics of statistics are also included.

Rationale and Scope

Neuroscience is living a historical moment of an intense growth, with increasingly large-volume, high-dimensional, multimodal experimental data gathered by many research groups. Computational neuroscience is a fact of life, but the field needs a new twist based on data, and that is *data-driven* computational neuroscience. The methods of this book conform to this spirit. They can definitely help in exploiting such data to gain insights into the brain understanding, one of the greatest challenges in the twenty-first-century science. Data-driven computational neuroscience allows this transformation, from data to knowledge.

The map of the world is full of brain research initiatives (the Human Brain Project, the Brain Research through Advancing Innovative Neurotechnologies Initiative, the China Brain Project, etc.) that can be regarded as neuroscience's equivalents to the ground-breaking Human Genome Project. A revolution in neuroscience must go hand in hand with statistics and machine learning, forming the data-driven computational neuroscience alliance. Our experience in closely working with top neuroscientists shows that they generally use very basic analytical tools and are reluctant to share data. However, data-driven models are going to trigger a cultural (and indispensable) shift in neuroscience, in particular, educating neuroscientists to be more experienced in modern analytical tools and more open to data sharing. This is a challenge that this book addresses.

Beyond neuroscientists, given the breadth and depth of the data-driven methods covered in the book, an additional motivation is to reach other disciplines that can benefit from them in their application domains.

Special Features

The book's approach is holistic, coherent, and systematic. Fundamentals of data preprocessing and visualization are first reviewed. Then models covering all data mining tasks (supervised and unsupervised classification, association discovery, and spatial statistics) are thoroughly presented. This is hardly found within a single book.

An introductory summary is provided at the beginning of each chapter. As hands-on support, contents are illustrated with examples, tables, graphs, plots, images, flowcharts, pictures, and other kinds of figures. Mathematical rigor is sought, yet we make things easier by accompanying textual explanations. Mathematical proofs are given when they are constructive and provide deeper insights. The notation is consistent throughout. Algorithms are preferred to be given in intuitive and plain words, but sometimes pseudocode is included. Although there is standard material, we also add our own original specialized material that is the fruit of our work. Each chapter includes a variety of published applications on any neuroscientific field here and there. In addition, there is a specific section in every chapter that elaborates on model building from a real data set, thus motivating the chapter with a neuroscientific question. All these data sets, detailed in Chapter 1 and used throughout the book as case studies, cover many neuroscience levels: neural morphology, functional connectivity networks, and neurological diseases. Each chapter is rounded off with bibliographic notes. They contain insights into more complex topics for additional reading and open issues. An extensive list of references and a useful subject index are located at the end of the book.

Organization of the Book

The book is divided into six parts. Parts I–II provide background material, whereas Parts III–VI form the core content of the book.

Part I includes Chapter 1 on computational neuroscience, describing the multilevel organization of the brain, main brain research initiatives, recent neurotechnologies for data recording, and the statistical and machine learning approach to data-driven computational neuroscience. The seven data sets used as case studies in Parts III–VI of the book are described in detail.

Part II contains a thorough review of statistics, with examples from neuroscience. It covers exploratory data analysis (Chapter 2); probability theory, random variable distributions, their simulation, and information theory (Chapter 3); and probabilistic inference, including parameter estimation and hypothesis tests (Chapter 4).

Part III is about supervised classification, with six chapters. Chapter 5 contains information on how to evaluate a model: performance measures, their honest estimation methods, and statistical significance tests to compare multiple classifiers. Chapter 6 is related to feature subset selection techniques – filter, wrapper, and embedded – an essential topic for high-dimensional data. Chapter 7 explains non-probabilistic classifiers (nearest neighbors, classification trees, rule induction, artificial neural networks, and support vector machines), whereas Chapter 8 focuses on probabilistic classifiers (discriminant analysis, logistic regression, and Bayesian network classifiers). Chapter 9 covers metaclassifiers, with ensembles of classifiers given in Chapters 7 and 8. Chapter 10 deals with multidimensional classification, where multiple class labels are simultaneously predicted.

Part IV covers unsupervised classification, with a chapter on non-probabilistic (Chapter 11) and a chapter on probabilistic (Chapter 12) clustering. The former introduces hierarchical clustering and 11 methods for partitional clustering. The latter covers methods based on the EM algorithm for finite-mixture models and Bayesian networks.

Part V on probabilistic graphical models is devoted to Bayesian (directed) and Markov (undirected) networks, Chapters 13 and 14, respectively. Exact and approximate inference methods are presented for both types of graphical models. We also explain learning algorithms for discrete and continuous models.

Part VI (Chapter 15) deals with the foundations of spatial point processes (exploratory data analysis, modeling, and simulation).

We have organized the book guided by our expertise in statistics and machine learning over the last 25 years and in data-driven computational neuroscience over the last 10 years, as researchers, PhD trainers, and teachers. While Parts III–VI in the core content can be read in any order, we cover supervised classification (Part III) before unsupervised classification (Part IV) because students find it conceptually easier that way. The rationale for this is that the presence of a ground truth enables defining clear performance measures. Part V on probabilistic graphical models is mainly concerned with the discovery of associations. Although some specific Bayesian networks are already used in previous parts (in Section 8.4 about Bayesian classifiers and Section 12.3 on clustering with Bayesian networks), we provide pointers therein to the necessary readings. Part VI is at the end of the book because spatial statistics is a very specific topic, less used, although important in neuroscience.

Using the Book in a Course: How and Whom?

The book can be used as a textbook. Concise explanations of the relevant statistical and mathematical background make the book self-contained. Because the mathematical level ramps up slowly, the book is suitable for both STEM advanced undergraduate and graduate students. For STEM advanced undergraduates, the syllabus would include Parts I and II (basics) and then Chapters 5–8 of Part III (supervised classification) and Chapter 11 of Part IV (unsupervised classification). For STEM graduates, the syllabus could follow the whole structure of the book and skipping the introductory Part II (expected to be known by the students). The material could be covered in a one-semester course if not getting depth, as it is our experience in the Computational Biology Master at our Universidad Politécnica de Madrid. Courses only devoted to classification (Parts III–IV), probabilistic graphical models (Part V), or spatial point patterns (Part VI) are also possible if more in-depth teaching is provided.

The book conveys practical content because we aim at solving real problems, and it is our wish that neuroscience practitioners understand, dare, and use these techniques. We provide the examples with R/WEKA open source software, giving details on the functions/packages used for the results to be reproducible. Interweaving programmable languages (R) and menu-driven interfaces (WEKA) aims at reaching out to a broad range of readers.

The seven neuroscience data sets used as case studies are accessible at the dedicated website `cig.fi.upm.es/books/CUP`. R scripts for reproducing some figures and a list of errors that readers or ourselves may find are also there. Working throughout from those real-world-use cases empowers readers to build their own solutions.

Theoretical content is also strong, however. Therefore, the book is also targeted for researchers in computational neuroscience ranging from any level (bachelor's students, master's students, post-doctoral researchers, and also senior researchers). People working in disciplines like neuroscience, bioinformatics, biology, medicine, cognitive science, computer science, engineering, applied mathematics, and physics may find the book of interest.

This book brings statistical and machine learning techniques to the neuroscience community by introducing the most complete and in-depth collection of data-driven computational intelligence methods. The combination of a broad topical coverage, comprehensive and up-to-date style, and rigor and practicality of this book are expected to fill a real need within the neuroscience community.

Acknowledgments

This book has been a long journey in our lives, starting back in 2013. Much effort in our busy day-to-day schedule, but always with enthusiasm, determination, and persistence.

We are grateful to our PhD and post-doc students of the Computational Intelligence Group at the Universidad Politécnica de Madrid, especially Sergio Luengo and Mario Michiels, for their support with some figures.

We thank different institutions for their financial support of this work: the Spanish Ministry of Economy and Competitiveness through the Cajal Blue Brain project (C080020-09; the Spanish partner of the Blue Brain initiative from EPFL), TIN2016-79684-P and PID2019-109247GB-I00 projects, the European Union's Seventh Framework Programme under grant agreement no. 604102, and the European Union's Horizon 2020 Framework Programme for Research and Innovation under Specific Grant Agreements no. 720270 (HBP SGA1), no. 785907 (HBP SGA2) and no. 945539 (HBP SGA3).

Finally, we would like to acknowledge with gratitude the love, understanding, and support of our families; without them this book would not have been possible.

Acronyms

ACO	ant colony optimization
AD	Alzheimer's disease
ADALINE	ADAptive LInear NEuron
ADNI	Alzheimer's disease neuroimaging initiative
AIC	Akaike's information criterion
ALS	amyotrophic lateral sclerosis
ANN	artificial neural network
ANOVA	analysis of variance
AODE	averaged one-dependence estimator
APOE	apolipoprotein E
AQR	AQ rule-generation algorithm
AUC	area under the ROC curve
BAN	Bayesian network augmented naive Bayes
BD	Bayesian Dirichlet
BDe	likelihood-equivalent Bayesian Dirichlet
BIC	Bayesian information criterion
BN	Bayesian network
BOLD	blood-oxygen-level-dependent
BRAIN	Brain Research through Advancing Innovative Neurotechnologies Initiative
Brain/MINDS	Brain Mapping by Integrated Neurotechnologies for Disease Studies
CAIM	class-attribute interdependence scheme maximization
CART	classification and regression trees
cdf	cumulative distribution function
CFS	correlation-based feature selection
CHAID	chi-square-automatic-interaction-detection
c.i.	conditionally independent
CI	confidence interval
CIQR	circular interquartile range
CLARA	Clustering LARge Application
CLG	conditional linear Gaussian network
CLL	conditional log-likelihood
CML	classification maximum likelihood
CPDAG	completed partially directed acyclic graph
CPT	conditional probability table

CRF	conditional random field
CSF	cerebrospinal fluid
CSR	complete spatial randomness
CV	coefficient of variation
DAG	directed acyclic graph
DARPA	Defense Advanced Research Projects Agency
DBSCAN	density-based spatial clustering of applications with noise
DTI	diffusion tensor imaging
ECoG	electrocorticography
EDA	estimation of distribution algorithm
EEG	electroencephalography
EQ-5D	European Quality of Life-5 Dimensions
EM	expectation-maximization
EMA	expectation model averaging
FAN	forest augmented naive Bayes
FDA	Food and Drug Administration
FDG	fluorodeoxyglucose
FDR	false discovery rate
FIB	focused ion beam
fMRI	functional magnetic resonance imaging
FN	false negative
FoG	freezing of gait
FOIL	first-order inductive learner
FP	false positive
FPR	false positive rate
FSS	feature subset selection
FWER	familywise error rate
GA	genetic algorithm
GAN	generative adversarial network
GES	greedy equivalence search
GRASP	greedy randomized adaptive search procedure
GS	grow-shrink
GSIMN	grow-shrink inference-based Markov network
HBP	Human Brain Project
HD	Huntington's disease
HMM	hidden Markov models
IAMB	incremental association Markov boundary
IARPA	Intelligence Advanced Research Projects Activity
IBL	instance-based learning
ID3	iterative dichotomiser
i.i.d.	independent and identically distributed
iMaGES	independent multiple-sample GES
IQR	interquartile range
IREP	incremental reduced error pruning
IRLS	iteratively reweighted least squares
JPD	joint probability distribution

k-**DB**	*k*-dependence Bayesian classifier
k-**NN**	*k*-nearest neighbors
K2-AS	K2-attribute selection
LBR	lazy Bayesian rule
LDA	linear discriminant analysis
LiNGAM	linear non-Gaussian acyclic model
M2	secondary motor cortex
mad	mean absolute deviation about the mean
MAD	median absolute deviation about the median
MAP	maximum a posteriori
MAR	missing at random
MARS	multivariate adaptive regression splines
MB	Markov blanket
MB-MBC	Markov blanket MBC
MBC	multidimensional Bayesian network classifier
MCAR	missing completely at random
MCI	mild cognitive impairment
MCMC	Markov chain Monte Carlo
MDL	minimum description length
MDLP	minimum description length principle-based discretization
MEG	magnetoencephalography
MICrONS	Machine Intelligence from Cortical Networks
mle	maximum likelihood estimate
MLE	maximum likelihood estimator
MLP	multi-layer perceptron
MMSE	mini-mental state examination
MNAR	missing not at random
MoPs	mixture of polynomials
MPE	most probable explanation
MR	magnetic resonance
MRI	magnetic resonance imaging
mrMR	minimal redundancy maximal relevance
MS	multiple sclerosis
MSE	mean square error
MTEs	mixture of truncated exponentials
MWST	maximum weighted spanning tree
NBTree	naive Bayes tree
NC	normal control
NIF	Neuroscience Information Framework
NIH	National Institutes of Health
NIRS	near infrared spectroscopy
NSF	National Science Foundation
ODE	one-dependence estimator
OPTICS	ordering points to identify clustering structure
PAM	partitioning around medoids
PCA	principal component analysis

PCMB	parents and children based Markov boundary
PD	Parkinson's disease
pdf	probability density function
PDQ-39	39-item Parkinson's Disease Questionnaire
PET	positron emission tomography
pmf	probability mass function
PPA	primary progressive aphasia
PPRS	people-powered research science
PROCLUS	projected clustering
QDA	quadratic discriminant analysis
QUEST	quick, unbiased, efficient, statistical tree
RAkEL	RAndom k-labEL sets
RBF	radial basis function
R-fMRI	resting-state functional magnetic resonance imaging
RIPPER$_k$	repeated incremental pruning to produce error reduction
ROC	receiver operating characteristic
ROI	region of interest
RSA	random sequential adsorption
S2	secondary somatosensory cortex
SEM	scanning electron microscope
SICE	sparse inverse covariance estimation
SMO	sequential minimal optimization
SMOTE	synthetic minority oversampling technique
SNP	single nucleotide polymorphism
SOM	self-organizing map
SPECT	single-photon emission computed tomography
SPODE	superparent-one-dependence estimator
SVM	support vector machine
TAN	tree augmented naive Bayes
TN	true negative
TP	true positive
TPR	true positive rate
t-**SNE**	t-distributed stochastic neighbor embedding
V2L/TeA	lateral secondary visual cortex and association temporal cortex
VC	Vapnik–Chervonenkis
VNS	variable neighbor search
WEKA	Waikato Environment for Knowledge Analysis
WHO	World Health Organization

Part I

Introduction

1 Computational Neuroscience

Neuroscience is a scientific area that aims to understand the nervous system, in particular, the brain. The brain is studied by researchers from different disciplines, such as anatomy, physiology, medicine, physics, biology, biochemistry, genetics, psychology, mathematics, and computer science. The challenging field of neuroscience must cross boundaries, and a multidisciplinary approach with the combined efforts from multiple scientists is necessary to understand the brain. Neuroscience has also given rise to other disciplines, including neuroeducation, neuroethics, neurolaw, neuroaesthetics, and neuromarketing, to name a few.

Computational neuroscience is an increasingly important branch of neuroscience that employs mathematical models, theoretical analyses, and abstractions of the brain. Computational neuroscience develops and tests hypotheses of brain mechanisms. Models are often analytically intractable. Models are compared to experimental data using carefully designed numerical experiments. **Data-driven computational neuroscience** employs statistical and computational models learned from data, obtained from disparate sources, such as the electrical activity of a neuron or a confocal microscopy image of a neuron, a recording of a neuronal population, magnetic resonance imaging of the whole brain, or microarray data from a patient with Parkinson's disease (PD). Models are evaluated and can be used to make predictions that must be experimentally verified.

This chapter starts with a basic introduction of the multilevel organization of the brain in Section 1.1 and some figures from the human brain in Section 1.2. Section 1.3 presents the main brain research initiatives worldwide. Section 1.4 covers helpful and recently developed neurotechnologies to understand the brain and record data. Data-driven computational neuroscience is elaborated in Section 1.5 from a statistical and machine learning perspective, in which data-sharing and bidirectional brain–computer benefits are described. Finally, the data sets employed throughout the book are described at length in Section 1.6.

1.1 The Multilevel Organization of the Brain

1.1.1 Multiscale Organization

The brain is a complex system whose functional and structural organization is characterized by a hierarchy of spatial and temporal scales (Bassett and Gazzaniga, 2011). The relationship between the mind and brain is far from being understood (Ascoli, 2015), but characterizing the structure of the brain and its organizing principles is a necessary first step. Different levels of organization range from the molecular and cellular levels to networks, systems, and behavior. All of these levels form the physical and biological bases of cognition. Moreover, the structure within any given scale is organized into modules.

Neuroscientists – and hence societies, jobs, conferences, and publications – are usually categorized according to the organizational level they primarily address. However, these levels do not define independent domains, and their conceptual integration should be targeted. Therefore, all neuroscientists should have a basic understanding of the functions of the brain at different scales. Although the dependence on specialized and expensive equipment is a reason to investigate a single level of organization in experimental approaches, homogeneous computational tools are also available for theoretical approaches. Thus, integrative multilevel concepts addressing how one level constrains or informs another are lacking. For example, it is unknown how a mechanism at the genetic level influences the characteristics of large-scale systems, such as the behavior of an organism. An exception is the Hodgkin–Huxley formalism, which explains how the properties of membrane components determine the electrical behavior of entire neurons.

Nevertheless, cross-level integration is a difficult task. Relationships between phenomena at different levels are nonlinear and highly complex. These relationships are difficult to articulate in mathematical terms, and scientists have achieved the first step by investigating how variables at one level influence variables at another level. Unlike experimental approaches with technical or ethical limitations used to study some variables, computational approaches benefit from the free manipulation of parameters and complete reproducibility. Computational models can foster multilevel investigations. A multilevel computational model might integrate elements from compartmental neuron models, microcircuit representations of neuronal populations, and activity propagation in large-scale neuronal networks.

1.1.2   Spatial and Temporal Scaling

In the spatial domain, the brain has many levels of organization, ranging from the molecular level of a few Angstroms ($1\text{Å} = 10^{-10}$m), to the whole nervous system of over a meter. The **neuron** is a cell that is specialized for signal processing. Neurons generate electric potentials to transmit information to other cells via special connections called **synapses**. Mechanisms operating at the subcellular level play a role in information-processing capabilities. Neurons use cascades of biochemical reactions that must be understood at the molecular level, including the transcription of genetic information. The complexity of a single neuron makes computational models essential, and substantial progress has been achieved at this level.

Minicolumns are vertical columns that extend through the cortical layers of the brain. Minicolumns are the anatomical basis of columns, contain approximately 100 neurons and are 30 microns in diameter. More complex constructs include subareas (e.g., S2), areas (e.g., the somatosensory cortex), lobes (e.g., the temporal lobe), and the complete cerebral cortex.

Neurons connect to each other to form **neural circuits**. Networks of interconnected neurons exhibit complex behaviors and enable additional information-processing capabilities that are not present in a single neuron. This unique property of **emergence** of neural computation extends beyond the mere multiplication of single-processor capabilities. The brain is also organized into higher-order levels. Networks with a specific architecture and specialized information-processing capabilities are included in larger structures or systems that interact and enable more complex information-processing tasks and new emergent properties. The central nervous system depends on the dynamic interaction of many specialized subsystems and the interaction of the brain with the environment.

In the temporal domain, the organization of the brain dynamically changes over multiple temporal scales. Inherent rhythms of brain activity vary in different frequencies (the highest frequency gamma band is >30 Hz, whereas the delta band is 1–2 Hz) and relate to different cognitive capacities. Learning and memory change neuronal connection patterns (through synaptic plasticity) on both short (seconds to minutes) and long (hours to days to months) timescales.

1.1.3 Modular Organization

Organization within a given scale is modular. Thus, the brain is decomposed into subsystems or modules. For example, anatomical modules in the spatial domain are present in cortical minicolumns or columns, whereas short- and long-term memory are the modules in the temporal domain. Within-module elements are more highly connected than between-module elements. This organization provides a compartmentalization that reduces the interdependence of modules and enhances robustness. Hierarchy and modularity together allow the formation of complex architectures of subsystems within subsystems with a high degree of functional specificity. Furthermore, modularity enables behavioral adaptation because each module functions and changes its function without negatively affecting the rest of the system.

The modular architecture has been more formally described by **complex network theory** applied to neuroimaging data (Sporns, 2010). The functional and structural hierarchical modularity of the connectivity of the human brain has been reported. Within these modular structures, brain regions perform different roles, as hubs with higher connectivity or as local processors. These regional roles are evident in both structural and functional connectivity networks and might have neurophysiological correlates. Each region displays different patterns of energetic activity and maintains different trajectories of synaptic development and redevelopment or plasticity. Hierarchical modularity is compatible with the minimization of energy consumption in developing and maintaining wiring, where most of the energy is used for the function of synapses. Physical constraints of wiring are also compatible with the spatial configuration of the observed connectivity (close regions interact strongly, whereas long-range anatomical connections or functional interactions connect very different modules).

The physical anatomical constraints of the human brain also constrain its function. Thus, two coherently active regions of the brain are often connected by a direct white matter pathway. Recently, researchers have attempted to map the wiring of the brain at different levels of spatial resolution (Section 1.3). Researchers have not yet clearly determined how structural connectivity might help predict function because a one-to-one relationship between structure and function is not plausible, and function appears to emerge from multiscale structures (a many-to-many mapping). Emergence occurs between multiple physical and functional levels. Causation seems to occur both upward and downward between multiple levels (located either in close proximity or distant regions) of the brain, creating a complementary or mutually constraining environment of mental and physical functions. The brain is nonreducible, and its organization is not a simple sum of its parts.

1.2   The Human Brain

The human brain has a similar structure to the brains of other mammals, but it is larger than any other species in relation to body size, namely, it has the largest encephalization quotient. Much of the expansion is derived from the part of the brain called the cerebral cortex, which is a thick layer of neural tissue that covers most of the brain. This layer is folded in a way that increases the surface area to fit into the available volume. The cerebral cortex is divided into four lobes, called the frontal lobe, parietal lobe, temporal lobe, and occipital lobe (see Figure 1.1). Numerous cortical areas exist within each lobe, each of which is associated with a particular function, including vision, motor control, language, etc. The left and right sides of the cortex are broadly similar in shape, and most critical areas are replicated on both sides. However, some areas, particularly areas that are involved in language, show strong lateralization. In most people, the left hemisphere is dominant for language, whereas the right hemisphere is usually responsible for spatiotemporal reasoning.

Some quantitative measures of this organ are described below. The brain weighs between 1,200 and 2,000 grams in adults (see Figure 1.2) and between 350 and 400 grams in newborns and accounts for only 2% of an adult's total body weight. The average brain is 140 mm wide, 167 mm long, and 93 mm high. With a thickness of 1.5 to 4.5 mm and a total surface area of 2,500 cm^2 (Peters and Jones, 1984), the cerebral cortex accounts for greater than 80% of the brain mass but contains only 19% of all brain neurons (similar to other mammals). The total cerebral cortical volume is divided across the four lobes as follows: frontal lobe (41%), temporal lobe (22%), parietal lobe (19%), and occipital lobe (18%). As estimated using a novel quantitative tool called isotopic fractionation (Herculano-Houzel and Lent, 2005), the cerebral cortex contains 86 billion neurons (greater than the

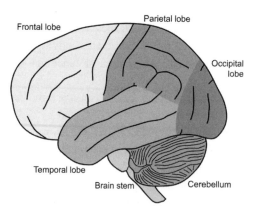

Figure 1.1 Lobes in the human cerebral cortex. Image taken from the Wikimedia Commons repository. For the color version, please refer to the plate section.

Figure 1.2 Name, age, occupation, nationality, and brain weight (grams) of different personalities. Taken from Spitzka (1907).

STUDY OF BRAINS OF SIX EMINENT SCIENTISTS AND SCHOLARS.

TABLE I.

Name	Age	Occupation	Nationality	Brain-weight
Turgenev.	65	Poet and novelist.	Russian.	2012
Bousy.		Jurist.	French.	1935
Cuvier.	63	Naturalist.	German descent.	1830
Knight, E. H.	59	Mechanician.	American.	1814
(Kraus, F. X.).	42	Theologian.	German.	1800
Abercrombie.	64	Physician.	English.	1786
Butler, Benj. F.	74	Statesman.	American.	1758
Olney, Edward.	59	Mathematician.	American.	1701
Levi, Herman.	60	Composer.	German.	1690
Winchell, A.	67	Geologist.	American.	1666
Thackeray.	52	Humorist.	English.	1658
Lenz, Rudolf.	53	Composer.	German.?	1636
Goodsir.	53	Anatomist.	English.	1629
Curtion.	68	Mathematician.	American.	1612
Atherton.	49	U. S. Senator.	American.	1602
Siemens.	68	Physicist.	German.	1600
Brown, George.	61	Journalist.	Canadian.	1596
Konstantinoff.	25	Author.	Bulgarian.	1595
Pepper, William.		Physician.	American.	1503
Harrison, R. A.	45	Jurist.	Canadian.	1590
Herman, F. R. W.	73	Economist.	German.	1590
Riebeck.	61	?	German.	1580
Büchner.	51	Hygienist.	German.	1560
Bittner.	57	Playwright.	German.	1556
Lavollay.		Merchant and publicist.	French.	1550
Cope.	57	Paleontologist.	American.	1545
McKnight.	57	Physician.	American.	1545
Allen, Harrison.	56	Anatomist.	American.	1531
Simpson.	59	Physician.	English.	1531
Train, G. F.	75	Promoter.	American.	1525
Taguchi.	66	Anatomist.	Japanese.	1520
Dirichlet.	54	Mathematician.	French.	1520
De Morny.	54	Statesman.	French.	1520
Webster.	70	Statesman.	American.	1518
Lord Campbell.	82	Statesman.	English.	1517
Wright, C.	45	Philosopher.	American.	1516
Schleich.	55	Author.	German.	1503
Chalmers.	67	Theologian.	English.	1503
Mallery.	63	Ethnologist.	American.	1503
Seguin, E. C.	56	Neurologist.	French descent.	1505
Napoleon III.	65	Sovereign.	French.	1500
Fuchs.	52	Pathologist.	German.	1499
Agassiz.	66	Naturalist.	French descent.	1495
Giacomini.	58	Anatomist.	Italian.	1495
De Morgan.	73	Mathematician.	English.	1494
Gauss.	78	Mathematician.	German.	1492
Letourneau.	71	Anthropologist.	French.	1492
(——.)	53	Statesman.	Swedish.	1489
Powell.	68	Anthropologist.	American.	1488
Pfenfer.	63	Physician.	German.	1488
Wuelfert.	63	Jurist.	German.	1485
Broca.	56	Anthropologist.	French.	1484
Mortillet.	77	Anthropologist.	French.	1480
Aylett.	58	Physician.	American.	1474

STUDY OF BRAINS OF SIX EMINENT SCIENTISTS AND SCHOLARS.

TABLE I.—Continued.

Name	Age	Occupation	Nationality	Brain-weight
Lord Jeffrey.	76	Jurist.	English.	1471
Asseline.	49	Journalist.	French.	1468
Skobeleff.	39	General.	Russian.	1457
Bischoff, C. H. E.	79	Physician.	German.	1452
Gylden.	55	Astronomer.	Swedish.	1452
Kobell.	79	Geologist.	German.	1445
Mihalkovics.	55	Biologist.	Hungarian.	1440
Dupuytren.	58	Surgeon.	French.	1437
Siljeström.	76	Physician.	Swedish.	1422
Rice, A. T.	35	Diplomat and editor.	American.	1418
Oliver.	65	Mathematician.	American.	1418
Meyr, M.	61	Philosopher.	German.	1415
Leidy, Philip.	53	Physician.	American.	1415
Nussbaum.	61	Surgeon.	German.	1410
Grote.	76	Historian.	English.	1410
Huber.		Author.	German.	1409
Pond, J. B.	65	Soldier and lecture-manager.	American.	1407
Babbage.	79	Mathematician.	English.	1403
Asselat.	45	Journalist.	French.	1493
Kupfer.	73	Anatomist.	French.	1400
Bertillon.	62	Anthropologist.	French.	1398
Goltz.	68	Physiologist.	German.	1395
Coudereau.	50	Physician.	French.	1390
Whewell.	72	Philosopher.	English.	1389
Wistar, Isaac J.	78	General.	American.	1389
Wilson.	61	U. S. Vice-president.	American.	1389
Szilagyi.	61	Statesman.	Hungarian.	1380
Büdinger.	64	Anatomist.	German.	1380
Schmid.	65	Author.	German.	1374
Hevelayque.	52	Statesman.	French.	1373
Bischoff, T. L. W.	76	Anatomist.	German.	1370
Cheva.		?	French.	1365
Gross, S. D.		Physician.	American.	1361
Hermann, C. F.	51	Philologist.	German.	1358
Liebig.	70	Chemist.	German.	1352
Schlagintweit.	31	Naturalist.	German.	1352
Pallmerayer.	71	Historian.	German.	1349
Bennett.	63	Physician.	English.	1332
Pettenkofer.	82	Pathologist.	German.	1320
Senzel.	50	Sculptor.	French.	1312
Zeyer.	56	Architect.	German.	1320
Kolar.	84	Dramatist.	Bohemian.	1300
Grant, R. E.	80	Astronomer.	English.	1290
Whitman.	72	Poet.	American.	1282
Cory.	55	Physician.	English.	1276
Guardia.	67	?	Spanish.	1272
Seguin, Edouard.	68	Psychiatrist.	French.	1257
Tiedemann.	79	Anatomist.	German.	1254
Lasaulx.	57	Philologist.	German.	1250
Laberde.	73	Physiologist.	French.	1234
Buhl.	64	Anatomist.	German.	1229
Hausmann.	71	Naturalist.	German.	1226
Ferris.	89	Jurist.	American.	1225
Gall.	70	Phrenologist and anatomist.	German.	1198

number of all known stars in the universe) and 240 trillion synapses (Koch, 1999). The relationship between the body and brain size that applies to other primates is not true for humans, where the brain size is five to seven times larger than expected according to the body size.

The appearance of the neocortex is a decisive event during the evolution of the mammalian telencephalon. Its activity is directly related to those capacities that distinguish humans from other mammals. By this reason, the neocortex can be considered as the most human part of the nervous system (DeFelipe, 2011).

1.2.1 Brain Sizes Variability for Different Species

Figure 1.3 shows the brain size for different mammalian species from human to mouse. The variability in brain weights is remarkable. For example, the insectivorous white-toothed pygmy brain weighs 0.060 g, while the heaviest brain corresponds to the sperm whale, with 9.200 kg on average. The brain of the Indian elephant weighs 6.900 kg, a similar quantity to the brain of the blue whale, the largest animal on Earth that has a body 20 times larger. By contrast, the gorilla and striped dolphin have similar body weights, although the gorilla's brain weight is less than half of the dolphin's.

The power law exponents that apply to the scaling of brain mass as a function of the number of neurons are 1,550, 1,016, and 1,056 for rodents, insectivores, and primates, respectively. The absolute number of neurons, in contrast to the body and brain size-centered view, has been proposed as the most relevant parameter for determining the cognitive abilities across species (Gazzaniga, 2008).

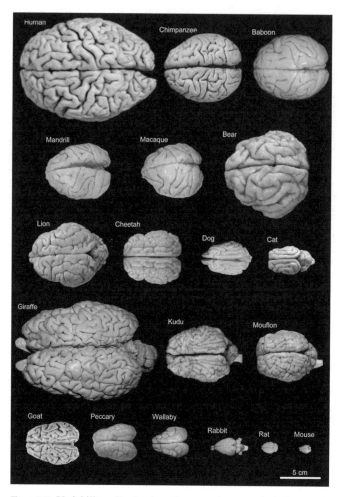

Figure 1.3 Variability of brain sizes for several mammals. Primates: human (1.176 kg), chimpanzee (273 g), baboon (151 g), mandrill (123 g), macaque (110 g). Carnivores: bear (289 g), lion (165 g), cheetah (119 g), dog (95 g), cat (32 g). Artiodactyls: giraffe (700 g), kudu (166 g), mouflon (118 g), goat (115 g), peccary (41 g). Marsupials: wallaby (28 g). Lagomorphs: rabbit (5.2 g). Rodents: rat (2.6 g), mouse (0.5 g). Image from DeFelipe (2011).

1.3   Brain Research Initiatives

In recent years, several brain-mapping initiatives have been initiated worldwide and are attempting to tackle one of the most fascinating challenges of the twenty-first century. Although these initiatives have different goals and areas of expertise, the common aim is to move closer to unlocking the elusive secrets of the human brain and to pursue myriad previously inaccessible scientific questions. This joint effort will require the merging of historically distinct scientific disciplines, such as engineering, chemistry, physics, and computer science, with neuroscience and psychology in so-called convergence science. This section describes the main goals of some of these initiatives developed by the European Commission, the United States, Japan, China, Canada, Korea, and Australia (see Figure 1.4).

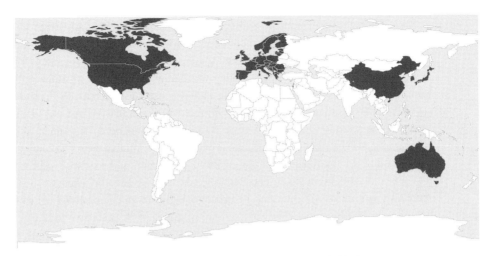

Figure 1.4 Regions around the world participating in brain research initiatives.

The **Human Brain Project** (HBP)[1] (Amunts et al., 2016), launched by the European Commission in 2013, is one of the first two Future and Emerging Technologies Flagship projects, a long-term (10 years) multinational research project. This project is based on the hypothesis that decoding the multiscale questions about the human brain requires deeper insights into structure and function of the brain at all levels of organization – from genes to the whole brain – with interdisciplinary experts, including neuroscientists, physicists, and mathematicians, as well as modern information and communication technologies (ICTs). More than 100 partner institutions in 19 countries in Europe collaborate by sharing data and tools. Four neuroscience subprojects, six research platforms, and two subprojects – ethics and society – and coordination and central services that cross-link all platforms and subprojects, as well as an education and training program that incorporates a multidisciplinary outlook, constitute the main elements of the HBP. The neuroscience subprojects aim to identify the organizational principles of spatial and temporal brain architecture and consist of (a) the organization of the mouse brain, (b) the organization of the human brain, (c) systems and cognitive neuroscience, and (d) theoretical neuroscience. The six research platforms are (a) the neuroinformatics platform, an effective ecosystem for software and data sharing; (b) the brain simulation platform, which aims to develop data-driven models and brain simulations at all scales; (c) the high-performance analytics and computing platform, which helps the neuroscience community compete using high-end supercomputers and systems for large-scale data analytics; (d) the medical informatics platform, which provides new diagnostic categories and new treatments for brain diseases as a result of the convergence between ICT, biology, and medicine; (e) the neuromorphic computing platform, which implements brain-like principles in machine learning and cognitive computing; and (f) the neurorobotics platform, which is developing simulating robots controlled by spiking neural networks.

The **Brain Research through Advancing Innovative Neurotechnologies Initiative** (BRAIN)[2] (Martin and Chun, 2016) was launched by President Obama in April 2013

---

[1] www.humanbrainproject.eu/en/.
[2] www.braininitiative.org.

to "accelerate the development and application of new technologies that will enable researchers to produce dynamic pictures of the brain that show how individual brain cells and complex neural circuits interact at the speed of thought." The BRAIN Initiative is a public–private partnership including the National Institutes of Health (NIH), the National Science Foundation (NSF), the Defense Advanced Research Projects Agency (DARPA), the Intelligence Advanced Research Projects Activity (IARPA), the Food and Drug Administration (FDA), and over 20 private foundations, institutes, universities, companies, and international partners. The BRAIN Initiative seeks to obtain a better understanding of the inner workings of the human mind and to improve how we treat, prevent, and cure brain disorders. These goals will be accomplished by pursuing the following activities: (a) advancing neurotechnologies to enable scientists to monitor and modulate brain circuit activity; (b) facilitating dynamic imaging to produce a dynamic picture of brain function in real time; (c) exploring brain functionality to investigate how the brain records, processes, uses, scores, and retrieves vast quantities of information; (d) linking function and behavior by incorporating new theories and computational models; and (e) advancing consumer applications by developing safe and effective products for patients and consumers. In addition, the BRAIN Initiative provides a monthly report aimed at a general audience describing the potential applications of these tools in research or in clinical settings, with the objective of creating an environment that sustains the enthusiasm of scientists, the general public, and even policy-makers.

The **Brain Mapping by Integrated Neurotechnologies for Disease Studies** (Brain/MINDS)[3] (Okano et al., 2016) is a national brain project started by Japan in 2014 with a 10-year roadmap. Brain/MINDS has adopted a fundamentally different approach compared to BRAIN and HBP by focusing on accelerating the development of the common marmoset as a model for the exploration and discovery of knowledge-based strategies for the eradication of major brain diseases. The achievement of this goal requires (a) the development of a multiscale marmoset brain atlas and integrated data platform to support functional studies, (b) the generation of a genetically modified marmoset for experimental and preclinical studies, and (c) the creation of a clinical data center using translational biomarkers for the diagnosis and treatment of human brain diseases. Currently, 65 laboratories and 47 institutions in Japan and several partner countries collaborate on this project. The research is organized into four major groups: (a) structural and functional mapping of the marmoset brain, (b) development of innovative neurotechnologies for brain mapping, (c) human brain mapping and clinical research, and (d) advanced technology and application development. The marmoset was chosen as the experimental model because it maintains a unique phylogenetic position and because the analysis of certain higher cognitive behaviors is, in some cases, easier in a nonhuman primate than in rodents or other simple vertebrate models.

The **China Brain Project** (Poo et al., 2016) is a 15-year project (2016–2030) that focuses on macaques and whose central pillar is understanding the neural basis of human cognition to develop new preventive, diagnostic, and therapeutic approaches, as well as brain-inspired computing methods and systems that are considered essential to achieving more robust artificial intelligence. This approach is known as the "one body-two wings" scheme. Research investigating the neural circuits underlying the mechanisms of cognition

---

[3] www.brainminds.jp.

will aim to understand human cognitive processes at different levels: from behavior to neural systems and circuits, to cells and molecules to the brain at the macroscopic and mesoscopic levels. One of the "wings" is the study of the pathogenic mechanisms and the development of effective and early diagnostic – at presymptomatic and prodromal stages – and therapeutic approaches for brain disorders with a developmental (e.g., autism and mental retardation), neuropsychiatric (e.g., depression and addiction), and neurodegenerative (e.g., Alzheimer's disease [AD] and PD) origin. This "wing" also refers to the efforts to provide a scientific basis for Chinese medicine, whose underlying mechanisms are largely unknown. The other "wing," brain-inspired computation, assumes that the human brain is currently the only truly generally intelligent system in nature that is capable of coping with different cognitive functions with extremely low energy consumption. Consequently, learning from the information processing mechanisms of the brain is clearly a promising method for building stronger and more general machine intelligence. One of the challenges of the China Brain Project is to make a general artificial intelligence that is capable of multitasking, learning, and self-adapting.

Brain Canada (Jabalpurwala, 2016)[4] is a project that was established by the Government of Canada in 2011 and expected to be completed in 6 years, but has been extended annually since 2016. Its vision is to understand the function of the brain in both healthy and disease states, improve lives, and achieve societal impacts. Brain Canada is achieving its goal by (a) increasing the scale and scope of funding to accelerate the pace of Canadian brain research; (b) creating a collective commitment to brain research across the public, private, and voluntary sectors; and (c) delivering transformative, original, and outstanding research programs. The approach is based on three main ideas: (a) one brain that considers this organ as a single complex system in which brain diseases and disorders often share common underlying mechanisms, such as cell loss, abnormal functioning of nerve cells, or chemical and molecular imbalances; (b) collaborative research encouraging high-risk, high-reward investigations that enable and support multidisciplinary teams; and (c) one community that includes governments, voluntary health organizations, philanthropists, business leaders, patients, caregivers, health administrators, clinicians, and, of course, researchers and their host institutions.

The **Korea Brain Initiative** (Jeong et al., 2016) was announced in May 2016, and the project was launched in 2018. The overall plan includes the development of novel neurotechnologies and the reinforcement of the neuroindustry with a vision to advance brain science by establishing and facilitating local, national, and global collaborative networks. The primary goal of the initiative is to foster neuroscience that improves the scientific understanding of the principles of higher brain functions to produce a new dynamic picture of healthy and diseased brains. Additional goals are to develop personalized treatments for mental and neurological disorders by extrapolating the concept of precision medicine and to stimulate collaboration among scientific institutes, academia and industry. The scope of the research project includes (a) constructing brain maps at multiple scales, (b) developing innovative neurotechnologies for brain mapping, (c) strengthening artificial intelligence-related research and development, and (d) developing personalized medicine for neurological disorders.

---

[4] www.braincanada.ca.

A proposed **Australian Brain Initiative** is being developed by members of the Australian Brain Alliance.[5] This initiative was presented and discussed with the scientific community, government, and public in 2017. Its mission is to create an innovative and healthy nation by cracking the brain's code through an understanding of the mechanisms underlying the development of the neural circuitry, how the brain encodes and retrieves information, complex behaviors, and the adaptations to external and internal changes. The initiative is designed to address the following four challenges: (a) optimizing and restoring healthy brain function throughout life, (b) developing neural interfaces to record and control brain activity to restore its function, (c) understanding the neural basis of learning across the lifespan, and (d) delivering new insights into brain-inspired computing.

The **International Brain Initiative** was launched on September 19, 2016 in the United Nations' General Assembly in New York City with the United States, Argentina, Japan, and Germany as partners. One of the several goals for the initiative is to create universal brain-mapping tools. Two interesting ideas proposed at the meeting were the creation of (a) an International Brain Observatory, with tools such as powerful microscopes and supercomputing resources that scientists around the world could access, and (b) an International Brain Station that would automatically convert data from studies of the human brain or animal gene expression into standardized formats that would allow more people to analyze them (Reardon, 2016a). At the same time, the World Health Organization (WHO) wishes to ensure that the early discoveries and technological advances of the different brain initiatives are translated into tests and treatments for brain disorders, avoiding health disparities between developed and underdeveloped countries (Reardon, 2016b).

1.4   Neurotechnologies

Neurotechnology is the area of technology that includes every advance that helps researchers understand the brain. The field has only reached maturity in the last 20 years, particularly due to the advent of various brain imaging techniques. However, extensive research is still needed. In addition to visualizing the brain both for clinical and research purposes, which is the focus of this section, technologies are available that are designed to improve and repair brain functions. Drugs are available to control depression or sleep; improve motor coordination in patients with PD, Huntington's disease (HD), amyotrophic lateral sclerosis (ALS), and stroke; reduce epileptic episodes; and alleviate phantom pain perception, among others.

1.4.1   Visualizing a Single Neuron

Currently, fine-scale recordings of the electrical activity of a *single* neuron or a small group of neurons (even in living humans) is relatively easy. Needle-like electrodes are inserted into the brains of laboratory animals to stimulate neurons. In addition to being an invasive technique, this approach provides an incomplete picture of the whole brain and samples brain activity very sparsely. The probable multineuronal level of organization (system,

---

[5] www.brainalliance.org.au/.

network, cellular, subcellular, and molecular levels) is not visualized using single-neuron recordings. New properties appear at each level of complexity.

The use of advanced microscopes is critical to examine neurons and their structures. **Confocal microscopy** (or confocal laser scanning microscopy), whose principle was patented in 1957 by Minsky (1988), one of the fathers of artificial intelligence, overcomes some limitations of traditional wide-field fluorescence microscopes. Confocal microscopes can examine thick samples, particularly samples with dense fluorescent staining of complex structures, where the relevant information may be hidden by out-of-focus haze. By adding a spatial pinhole placed at the confocal plane of the lens to eliminate out-of-focus light, the optical resolution and contrast are increased. Unlike a conventional microscope that can just view structures in the sample at the depth that the light penetrates, a confocal microscope only captures images at one depth level at a time. The depth of focus is controlled and limited. The surface of the sample is then scanned by moving either the sample or the light beam (horizontally), thereby reconstructing a 2D image at a specified depth. Next, vertical movements allow researchers to capture sets of images at different depths (optical sectioning), and 3D images of the sample are created using appropriate software.

The amount of magnification achieved by an optical microscope is limited by the wavelength of light. The shorter the wavelength of the light waves, the smaller the objects the microscope can see. The photons of visible light have a relatively large wavelength. However, electrons form waves with a much shorter length. This principle is the basis of **electron microscopy**, which uses a beam of accelerated electrons as a source of illumination instead of light. This technique allows researchers to examine tissues in greater detail – their ultrastructure – with magnifications of up to 10 million times, whereas most light microscopes achieve magnifications of less than 2,000x. At higher magnifications, the light waves start interfering with one another, and the images become blurry. The two most common types are the **transmission electron microscope** and the **scanning electron microscope** (SEM). Advances in microscopy for neuroscience are reviewed in Wilt et al. (2009).

Figure 1.5 shows (a) a confocal microscopy image of an intracellular injected layer III pyramidal neuron in the human cingulate cortex, and (b) an electron microscopy image of synapses in the rat cerebral cortex.

1.4.2 Tracking Circuits of Neuronal Activity

However, we need to record neural activity across complete neural circuits. A map of the anatomical connections, or synapses, among neurons (the so-called **connectome**) is only a starting point that is unable to depict the constantly varying electrical activity underlying specific cognitive processes. The interesting issue is how a collection of neurons interact intricately and give rise to an emergent property (Yuste and Church, 2014). Moreover, due to their plasticity, neurons are continuously subjected to dynamic rearrangements.

Large-scale recordings can be accomplished with the aid of nanotechnology; prototype arrays with more than 100,000 electrodes on a silicon base are able to track thousands of neurons in the retina. Stacking these arrays into 3D structures would multiply their scalability.

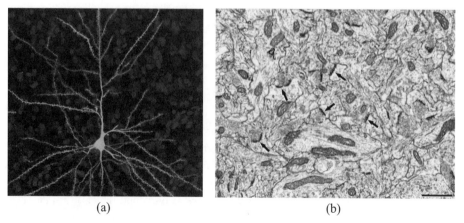

(a)   (b)

Figure 1.5 (a) An intracellular injected layer III pyramidal neuron of the human cingulate cortex imaged with a Leica TCS 4D confocal scanning laser attached to a Leitz DMIRB fluorescence microscope. DAPI staining is presented in blue. Image kindly supplied by Javier DeFelipe (Benavides-Piccione et al., 2013). (b) SEM image of the rat cerebral cortex. Arrows indicate some asymmetric synapses. Scale bar: 1 μm. Image kindly supplied by Javier DeFelipe (Morales et al., 2011). For the color version, please refer to the plate section.

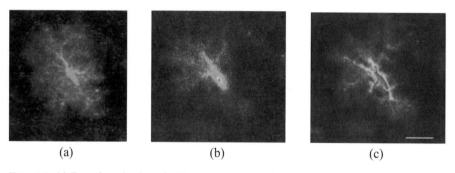

(a)   (b)   (c)

Figure 1.6 (a) Z-stack projection of a hippocampal astrocyte expressing the genetically encoded calcium indicator GCaMP6f. (b) Pseudocolor calcium images of the astrocyte depicted in (a) before electrical stimulation of the Schaffer collaterals. (c) The same image after stimulation. Scale bar: 20 μm. Images provided by Ana Covelo from the Alfonso Araque laboratory at the University of Minnesota. For the color version, please refer to the plate section.

In addition to electrical sensors (electrodes), new techniques for imaging neuronal activity are based on physics, chemistry, genetics, and engineering. Thus, in **calcium imaging**, cells are genetically engineered to fluoresce when calcium ions enter the neuron after it fires. The firing patterns of more than 1,000 neurons can be partially reconstructed in vitro or in vivo. This technique operates too slowly (limited time resolution compared to electrical recordings) to track the rapid firing of neurons. Additionally, new types of microscopes that show the simultaneous activity of neuronal populations in 3D are needed. Figure 1.6 shows a calcium image of a hippocampal astrocyte.

In **voltage imaging**, specific dyes alter the optical properties as the voltage of the neuronal membrane changes. The dyes are deposited on the neuron or across the cell membrane through genetic engineering. Although this technique is still in its infancy, the activity of every neuron in an entire circuit could be potentially recorded. Voltage sensors may be composed of organic dyes, genetic indicators, or even nonbiological materials borrowed from nanotechnology (i.e., nanoparticle quantum dots or nanodiamonds), which are sensitive to neuronal activity.

The delivery and collection of light from neural circuits located deep below the surface of the brain is difficult. **Computational optics** may help control the fluorescence emitted from dyes when subsurface neurons fire in a similar manner to the method used by astronomers to correct image distortions due to atmospheric effects on starlight. New optical hardware includes two-photon imaging, high-numerical aperture objectives, and light-field cameras, to name a few. Techniques such as **microendoscopy** are used by neuroradiologists to penetrate further into the tissue and image deeper structures. In this case, a flexible tube with light guides is inserted into the femoral artery and moved to many parts of the body (including the brain). Based on **synthetic biology**, lab animals have been genetically engineered to synthesize a molecule ("molecular ticker tape") that changes when a neuron is activated, or artificial cells function as sentinels that patrol the body or are placed near a neuron to detect its firing through a nanosized circuit implanted in the artificial cells that wirelessly transmits the data to a nearby computer.

In addition to monitoring circuits of neuronal activity, the ability to freely activate and inactivate these circuits will help researchers determine the functions of the selected cells and control some forms of brain activity (e.g., epileptic seizures, Parkinsonian tremors, reward responses). Recent technologies for this application rely on optical signals, such as **optogenetics** and **optochemistry**. In the former approach, genetically engineered neurons produce light-sensitive proteins (bacteria- or algae-derived), causing them to either become activated or inactivated upon exposure to light of a particular wavelength through an optical fiber. In the latter approach, neurotransmitters are attached to light-sensitive chemicals that are activated upon exposure to light. These techniques are minimally invasive, provide great spatial and temporal single-cell resolution, and have been applied to living tissues.

1.4.3   Imaging Large Brain Regions

Methods have been developed to track the activity of neurons across the *whole* brain within the field called cognitive neuroscience. Thus, in **electroencephalography** (EEG), electrodes placed on the skull measure the coordinated activity of more than 100,000 neurons. The brainwave activity associated with neuronal depolarization is registered over a few milliseconds, but without identifying whether a specific neuron is active. Thus, EEG offers high temporal (real-time) resolution but poor spatial resolution because the precise origin of the signal is difficult to locate (Burle et al., 2015). Other electrical techniques include **magnetoencephalography** (MEG), which measures the magnetic fields produced by electrical activity in the brain and is less sensitive to the head geometry compared to EEG, and **electrocorticography** (ECoG), an invasive procedure requiring a surgical incision into the skull to implant the electrode grid.

Other techniques are based on metabolism and indirectly measure neuronal activity. Metabolic techniques are classically considered as having very good spatial resolution but rather poor temporal resolution, while the opposite trends are observed for electrophysiological techniques. The most widely used technique is **functional magnetic resonance imaging** (fMRI). This technique illuminates active brain areas in 3D maps, where each

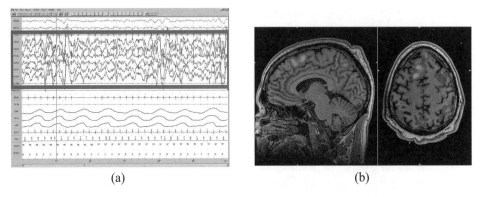

(a)   (b)

Figure 1.7 (a) EEG image. Screen shot of a patient during slow wave sleep when he or she is snoring (stage 3); the image represents 30 seconds. The high amplitude EEG is highlighted in red. Public domain from the English Wikipedia. (b) An fMRI image obtained during working memory tasks. Freely available at `ideas.ted.com`. For the color version, please refer to the plate section.

(cerebral cortical) voxel is composed of more than 600,000 neurons. The high spatial resolution and low temporal resolution (seconds and minutes) of fMRI allow researchers to record changes in blood flow within voxels, see Glover (2011) for a review. **Positron emission tomography** (PET) analyzes changes in blood flow and the consumption of oxygen and glucose. **Single-photon emission computed tomography** (SPECT) also monitors blood flow. PET and SPECT have a high detection sensitivity, see Lu and Yuan (2015) for a review of both. **Near infrared spectroscopy** (NIRS) is an optical technique used to measure blood oxygenation in the brain. Light in the near infrared part of the spectrum is transmitted through the skull, and the extent to which the remerging light is attenuated is measured, which depends on blood oxygenation.

Figure 1.7(a) shows an EEG image from a patient during slow wave sleep; Figure 1.7(b) shows an fMRI image obtained during working memory tasks.

The previous techniques are functional and are predominantly used in cognitive neuroscience because they enable researchers to determine the location and timing of neural activity associated with performance on a cognitive task in patients with a disease and in healthy subjects. However, anatomical techniques are used differently, e.g., to localize neuropathies or to compare the size of specific brain structures between subjects through a volumetric analysis. A powerful technique is **magnetic resonance imaging** (MRI), which allows researchers to distinguish gray matter (neuronal cell bodies) from white matter (myelinated tracts). MRI visualizes anatomical structures based on the behavior of atoms in water (their protons) in a magnetic field. New anatomical techniques, such as **diffusion tensor imaging** (DTI), are designed to specifically visualize myelinated tracts. Figure 1.8 shows MRI and DTI.

Even when these techniques are used in combination in multimodal neuroimaging, e.g., EEG and MEG or EEG and fMRI (Uludağ and Roebroeck, 2014), their applications are limited. Using images of large brain regions, researchers can coarsely examine neuronal activity because they are unable to identify whether circuits are activated or inactivated.

Figure 1.9 presents the approximate temporal (x-axis) and spatial (y-axis) resolution achieved using the main neurotechnologies. Approaches and techniques span from the nanoscale to the macroscale in terms of spatial and temporal resolution.

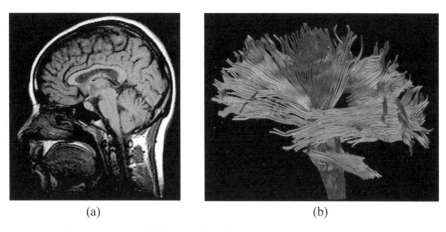

(a)   (b)

Figure 1.8 (a) MRI. Image available at Wikimedia Commons. (b) DTI of the lateral brain tractogram. Anonymous clinical image provided by Aaron G. Filler in Wikipedia. For the color version, please refer to the plate section.

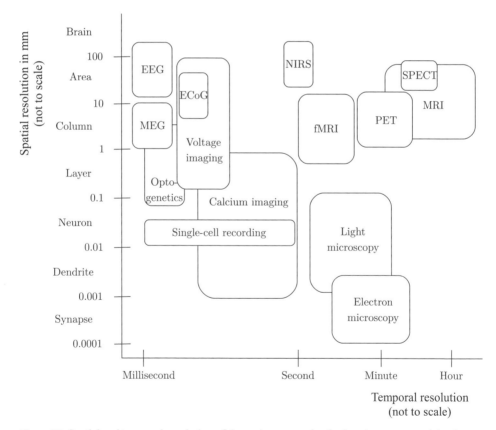

Figure 1.9 Spatial and temporal resolution of the main neurotechnologies. Acronyms explained within the text.

Nevertheless, new technologies that allow researchers to monitor, interpret, and alter the collective activity of vast neuronal populations (thousands or even millions of neurons) distributed across brain regions are required to improve our understanding of how the whole brain functions to drive thinking, behavior, cognition (perception, emotion, decision making, consciousness, etc.), and the consequences of circuit malfunctions in patients with neurological disorders (schizophrenia, autism, AD, and PD). Large initiatives being conducted worldwide (Section 1.3) are attempting to advance the development of these technologies.

1.5   Data-Driven Computational Neuroscience

Hypothesis-driven research has been (and even still is) the standard approach used in the great majority of neuroscience projects. The null hypothesis must be clearly stated, data must be collected in a repeatable manner with a clear sampling design, and conclusions must be based on p-values (see Section 4.2). In a high percentage of cases, neuroscience research practices are still based on pre-Internet methods and employ the following steps: (a) experimental design, (b) data collection, (c) local storage of data, (d) inaccessible metadata, (e) data analysis using software installed on local computers, and (f) publication of a summary of the results.

The daily practice of brain science is only beginning to benefit from cloudification, a **"software as a service"** framework in which locally installed programs are replaced by web apps. **Cloud neuroscience** proposes that the data, code, and analytical results all live in the cloud together as a set of programs that run in a scalable manner and are accessible anywhere. Benefits of this approach include the simplification of global collaborations, the facilitation of open science, and the testing of a variety of models using the same data set, allowing neuroscientists to accelerate the discovery process. A crucial factor in this new view of neuroscience research is the so-called **data-driven** paradigm that amasses vast quantities of data for the automatic modeling of complex interactions between the brain and behavior, for example, and informs about the diagnosis and prevention of neurological disorders and psychiatric diseases. The access to anatomical, biochemical, connectivity, developmental, and gene expression (**ABCDE**) data will allow researchers to view the scientific process as a virtuous cycle, namely, a collective effort where each new experiment yields data, and after their analysis, new or refined models are created that suggest novel experiments and allow the cycle to be repeated if necessary (Neuro Cloud Consortium, 2016).

Neuroscience is becoming more data-centric, as increasing numbers of brain atlases, connectomes, and imaging data sets are being published. The number of projects that provide large data sets for testing a specific hypothesis and enabling data-intensive discovery is increasing (Akil et al., 2011). Three examples are described next. The first example is the Human Connectome Project[6] that takes advantage of high-throughput anatomical methods, such as resting-state functional magnetic resonance imaging (R-fMRI) for macroconnectome, or serial section electron microscopy for microconnectome. In the functional connectome, R-fMRI studies the brain at rest and reveals large-amplitude spontaneous low-frequency fluctuations in the fMRI signal that are temporally connected across functionally related areas and appear to show a universal architecture of positive and negative functional connections and interindividual variability (Biswal et al., 2010). The **1,000 Functional Connectomes Project** data set provides researchers

---

[6] www.humanconnectomeproject.org.

Table 1.1 Multiples of the unit byte for digital information

Unit of digital information	Previous unit	Bytes
1 kilobyte	1,024 bytes	10^3
1 megabyte	1,024 kilobytes	10^6
1 gigabyte	1,024 megabytes	10^9
1 terabyte	1,024 gigabytes	10^{12}
1 petabyte	1,024 terabytes	10^{15}
1 exabyte	1,024 petabytes	10^{18}
1 zettabyte	1,024 exabytes	10^{21}

the opportunity to simultaneously interrogate multiple functional circuits without the requirement for an a priori hypothesis. For the anatomical connectome (Lichtman et al., 2014), electron microscopy images at the nanometre level provide sufficient resolution to visualize the finest details of synaptic connections, showing all cells and all organelles. A substantial amount of data are generated from electron microscopy images. A single cubic millimeter of the rat cortex generates approximately 2 petabytes of data. See Table 1.1 for an idea of the amount of data that this number represents.

A complete visualization of the rat cortex requires an exabyte, which far exceeds the storage capability of any system that is currently available. A complete visualization of the human cortex, which is approximately 1,000 larger than the rodent cortex, will require a zettabyte to depict the anatomical features of 86 billion neurons communicating with each other via more than 250 trillion synapses. In terms of the time required to generate the data, electron microscopes can currently process several terabytes of data per hour, allowing a researcher to process a cubic millimeter of rodent brain in approximately 800 hours. A complete visualization of the mouse cortex will require at least a decade. In Yuste and Church (2014), the ability to monitor and optically control a large percentage of the 100,000 neurons in a fruit fly brain was predicted to be achieved in 2019, whereas these data will not be recorded in the mouse before 2024.

The second example is the **Neuroscience Information Framework** (NIF)[7] that provides access to more than 3,500 resources (data sets, tools, and materials), where some domains, such as electrophysiology and behavior, are underrepresented compared to genomics and neuroanatomy. The third example is the **Allen Institute for Brain Science**,[8] which maintains and curates more than 3,000 terabytes of data. However, the vast majority of data and metadata in neuroscience continue to remain inaccessible.

Akil et al. (2011) provide several recommendations for best practices in mining neuroscience data. (a) First, powerful tools must be developed to study the temporal and spatial changes in brain anatomy and activity. (b) The informatics infrastructure must be sufficiently flexible to incorporate new types of data. (c) Best practices for producing new neuroscience data must be defined. (d) A cultural shift in the field of neuroscience to allow data sharing is needed. (e) Community ontologies and identifiers are needed. (f) Data must be published in standardized table formats to facilitate data science. (g) Interdisciplinary research in fields such as computer science, machine learning, and visualization should

---

[7] neuinfo.org/.
[8] www.alleninstitute.org/.

be fostered. (h) Educational strategies for the next generation of neuroscientists must be improved to ensure proficiency in data mining. These good practices will allow researchers to take advantage of the heterogeneity of neuroscience data with multiple spatial and temporal scales (Section 1.4) in all levels of neuronal organization: molecules (genotypes, protein interactions), cells (morphology and electrophysiology), cellular compartments (protein localization), brain regions, whole brain (functional and anatomical imaging), and organism (behavior) (French and Pavlidis, 2007) and to produce reproducible, collaborative, and large-scale neuroscience data needed for the twenty-first century. Ethical and legal issues must also be addressed (similar to the genome project).

1.5.1   Collecting Neuroscience Data

In addition to the obstacle of technology, the different ways laboratories work is another issue. Laboratories record different neurons in different brain regions from different animals performing different tasks. These disparate data are difficult to compare and combine. Modern neuroscience has shown a trend toward complementing the traditional, small laboratory culture by rewarding individual investigators with large, multidisciplinary teams using highly reproducible standards who are making all their methods, data, metadata, and software publicly available (Bouchard et al., 2016).

A survey by Tenopir et al. (2011) investigating **data-sharing** practices among scientists showed that approximately 50% of the respondents do not share data. However, 85% indicated an interest in having access to other researchers' data sets. In neuroscience, the culture of small laboratories that do not share data, metadata, or software is one of the causes of the **replication crisis**. The scandal highlighting bad scientific practices (Eklund et al., 2016) after the reanalysis of R-fMRI data from the public 1,000 Functional Connectomes Project may affect more than 3,000 published studies, almost all of which were funded by several national agencies. On the other hand, Wicherts et al. (2011) found that studies with accessible data tended to have fewer errors and more robust statistical and machine learning modeling approaches than studies where data sets were not available.

The culture shift in sharing data across laboratories is transforming "vertical" efforts, namely, applying single techniques to single problems in single species, into "horizontal" efforts, where the emphasis is placed on integrating data collected using a wide range of techniques (Sejnowski et al., 2014). These "horizontal" efforts will transform the current situation with many small models that encompass limited data sets and are more descriptive than explanatory. Sharing the **long-tail data** (Fergurson et al., 2014) is a way of obtaining large-scale data in neuroscience by merging small, granular data sets collected by individual laboratories in the course of day-to-day research. In the neurotrauma field, the traumatic brain injury (Maas et al., 2011) and spinal cord injury (Nielson et al., 2014) communities provide examples of the potential benefits of sharing long-tail neuroscience data.

Benefits of data sharing include (a) increased transparency and reproducibility of the results, (b) improving the research approach to employ the most recently developed experiments incorporating various research strategies, and (c) reduced economic costs derived from the lack of transparency and data inaccessibility. However, several reasons for the lack of motivation to share data also exist: (a) the competition to be the first to analyze the data set and to be recognized for publishing novel findings, (b) concerns regarding the privacy of the human research participants, as the regulatory mechanisms for consent for use of data in the context of open access databases have not been completely established, (c) public–private partnerships involved in large-scale data projects can produce tensions derived from the different interests, and (d) problems derived from credit sharing in the academic community based on authorship status on publications. Leitner et al. (2016) provide a comparative study of citations of data published in neuroscience between papers sharing data sets and papers without this material, and the former achieve a significantly larger citation impact than the latter.

Examples of data-sharing initiatives in neuroscience include (a) **NeuroMorpho.Org** (Ascoli et al., 2017), which follows pragmatic recipes to ensure a win–win outcome for both researchers who are sharing and receiving data. The good practices for the roles of data curators are to (i) serve the end-users by developing a complement, rather than duplicating existing resources with a clear scientific need; (ii) adopt standard formats that maximize interoperability rather than proprietary formats; (iii) design intuitive ergonomics requiring only minimal instructions; (iv) solicit feedback from the users to improve functionality; (v) publish statistics on data access, downloads, and reuse; (vi) facilitate the contribution of data by assuming that conversion and standardization are the curators' job; (vii) use concise, consistent, and specific metadata annotation; (viii) publicly acknowledge the labs contributing data; and (ix) be patient and persistent in finding, requesting, and collating data, establish quality standards to maximize research utility, and diversify the experience of your team. (b) At the Allen Institute for Brain Science, large teams are generating complete, accurate and permanent resources for the mouse and human brain. The need for a highly specialized workforce that collaborates and submerges the ego to the needs of the group as a whole is a characteristic of team science at this institution, a condition for developing large-scale data and open science. Based on this philosophy, the scientific rewards are not in the promise of first or senior authorship, but in the participation in a historic mission at the frontier of science where new knowledge is generated to benefit all humans (Koch and Jones, 2016). (c) The national and international brain initiatives described in Section 1.3 are all also working within this data-sharing perspective.

The **people-powered research science** (PPRS) revolution is creating a global community of new "experts," proving that anyone with motivation and a computer is able to help scientists and accelerate scientific progress. PPRS is viewed as a kind of **citizen science** that is based on the Internet and has provided people who were previously excluded from academic science the opportunity to collect and generate data or to contribute as individuals or teams to analyze the data (Roskams and Popovic, 2016). Examples of PPRS in neuroscience include (a) **Eyewire** (Helmstaedter et al., 2013), where over 250,000 players from more than 140 different countries have been contributing to the first-ever 3D reconstructions of high-resolution networks of cells within the mouse retina since 2010; (b) **DREAM**, a crowd-sourcing approach in the form of challenges that have developed new models in the field of neuroscience based on machine learning to predict the future progression of ALS (Küffner et al., 2015); (c) **Mozak** (Roskams and Popovic, 2016), a gaming platform designed to rapidly accelerate our understanding of memory diversity by providing gradual training to become an expert neuron reconstructor; and (d) the **BigNeuron** project (Peng et al., 2015), a community effort that combines modern bioimaging informatics, recent improvements in labeling and microscopy, and the wide need for openness and standardization to provide a resource for the automated reconstruction of the dendritic and axonal morphology of single neurons. While science has always benefited from standing on the shoulders of giants, the PPRS revolution will enable neuroscientists to stand on the shoulders of everyone.

1.5.2   Statistics and Machine Learning: The Two Cultures

This section discusses the similarities and differences between two disciplines, statistics and machine learning, whose objective is to analyze data by transforming them into computational models from which new knowledge and predictions are obtained.

1.5.2.1 *Statistics*

During the second half of the twentieth century, the nature of statistical practice changed with the advent of the computer. The progress in computer technology led to changes in statistical methodology and statistical ideas. Examples include the inversion of large matrices, iterative methods for the estimation of parameters, and the introduction of various types of resampling methods, such as bootstrapping, dynamic interactive visualization of data sets, and Bayesian statistics, a field that would not have been developed without the assistance of computers. Statistics was regarded as a mathematical discipline; however, it is currently regarded as a computational discipline focused on understanding the scientific problem and providing a correct interpretation (Hand, 2015).

The advent of computers also led to dramatic changes in statistical practice. The very easy use of software packages, particularly by statistically uninformed people, created risks of its own. This easy use has also contributed to trying many possible analyses instead of previously determining the proper method. An effective statistical analysis depends critically on understanding the scientific question, and thus automatic or rote strategies impose high risks. With the move to electronic rather than manual data collection, the dangers of multiple testing and overfitting became even greater.

The dominant statistical paradigm used in neuroscience studies is the **null hypothesis significance testing** (NHST), a hypothesis-driven approach (Section 4.2), in contrast with the data-driven approach advocated in this book (Section 1.5). The use of NHST in neuroscience must solve problems derived from the use of extremely small sample sizes and the so-called **pseudo-replication** that appears when non-independent samples are analyzed.

Nature journals published a set of guidelines for the correct reporting of statistical analyses that was presented by the *Nature of Neuroscience* journal (Nature Neuroscience Editorial, 2005). These guidelines are listed below. (a) Consult statistical experts to help design experiments and analyses, preferably before the data are collected. (b) Summarize all data sets with descriptive statistics before further analyses are performed. (c) Ensure that the statistical evidence is clearly described, providing information about what tests were used, how many samples were analyzed, the types of comparisons that were performed, the significance level found, etc. (d) Justify the choice of the analysis and confirm that the data conform to the assumptions underlying the tests (for example, most parametric tests require the data to be normally distributed). (e) Avoid the risk of false-positive results by using multiple comparisons tests (this situation is typically used for functional imaging data when multiple voxels are compared). Six years after these guidelines were published, Nieuwenhuis et al. (2011) found that in 157 of 513 behavioral, systems, and cognitive neuroscience articles published in *Science*, *Nature*, *Nature Neuroscience*, *Neuron*, and *The*

Journal of Neuroscience during 2009 and 2010, the authors compared 2 experimental effects. In 79 papers, the authors used an incorrect procedure to compare the 2 effects. The most common error was to report the difference between their significance levels instead of the statistical significance (Section 4.2) of their differences. When the same study was performed on 120 cellular and molecular neuroscience articles published in *Nature Neuroscience* during the same 2 years, no single study used the correct statistical procedure to compare effect sizes.

These facts highlight the need for solid statistical training for neuroscience researchers, both in classical and novel statistical methods for data acquisition and analysis.[9] Each of the methods used to collect neural data from human and animal subjects, such as neuroimaging (radiography, fMRI, MEG, and PET), electrophysiology from multiples electrodes (EEG, ECoG, and spike trains), calcium imaging, optogenetics, and anatomical methods (diffusion imaging, electron microscopy, and fluorescent microscopy), produces data with its own set of statistical and analytical challenges.

Part II of this book contains three chapters devoted to the introduction of statistical methodology. Chapter 2 introduces several graphical and numerical representations of univariate, bivariate, or multivariate data, such as pie charts, barplots, histograms, summary statistics and principal component analysis. Chapter 3 presents probability theory and some of the most common univariate and multivariate distributions in both discrete and continuous domains. This chapter also describes methods for simulating random variables and basic concepts of information theory. Parameter estimation and hypothesis tests are presented in Chapter 4.

1.5.2.2 *Machine Learning*

We are living in an era of abundant data, and tools for searching, visualizing, modeling, and understanding large data sets are needed. These tools should be able to (a) faithfully capture the intrinsic uncertainty of the domain, (b) induce models from data in an automated and adaptive manner, (c) exhibit robustness against noisy and imprecise data, and (d) scale well to large data sets. Machine learning methods incorporate these characteristics by defining a space for possible models and developing learning-from-data procedures of model parameters and structures. Machine learning provides tools for extracting reliable and meaningful relationships and for generating accurate predictions and reliable decisions (Hinton, 2011); this approach is likely to be one of the most transformative technologies of the twenty-first century. Currently, humanity has a new way of deriving knowledge apart from evolution, experience, and culture, namely, from machines that are able to learn automatically.

Machine learning is the field in which researchers build computers that improve automatically through experience and is also viewed as systems that learn from data. Machine learning is considered an interdisciplinary field focusing on both the mathematical foundations and practical applications with connections to pattern recognition, data mining, adaptive control, statistical modeling, data analytics, data science, and artificial intelligence. Its applications cover a wide spectrum of topics, e.g., automatic speech recognition, computer vision (object, face, and handwriting recognition), information retrieval and web

---

[9] As far back as 1938, Wells (1938) wrote, "...a certain elementary training in statistical method is becoming as necessary for anyone living in this world of today as reading and writing ..."

searches, financial prediction and automated trading, Industry 4.0, sport analytics, medical diagnosis, personalized medicine, bioinformatics, neuroscience, etc.

Conceptually, machine learning algorithms are viewed as searching through a large space of candidate models of different types to identify the model that optimizes the previously established performance metric (Jordan and Mitchell, 2015). Machine learning algorithms vary (a) in the way they represent candidate models (naive Bayes, classification trees, logistic regression, finite-mixture models, etc.) and (b) in the way in which they search through this space of models (exact or heuristic optimization algorithms). A key scientific and practical goal is to theoretically characterize the capabilities of specific learning algorithms. First, obtain the shape of the decision boundary to discriminate between positive and negative instances (in a binary classification problem). Second, characterize the sample complexity (the amount of data required to learn accurately) and computational complexity (how much computation is required), and how both (sample and computational) depend on features of the learning algorithm.

The most widely used machine learning methods are **supervised learning** methods. Starting from a collection of $(\mathbf{x}, \mathbf{c})$ pairs, the goal is to produce a prediction $\mathbf{c}^*$ in response to a query $\mathbf{x}^*$. Different types of output $\mathbf{c}$ have been studied: (a) the simple **binary classification** problem, where $\mathbf{c}$ is a 1D vector, c, with two possible values; (b) **multi-class classification**, where c has R possible labels; (c) **multi-label classification**, where $\mathbf{c}$ is a d-dimensional vector that simultaneously adopts several of the d labels; and (d) general **structured prediction**, where $\mathbf{c}$ is a combinatorial object whose components may be required to satisfy some set of constraints. Supervised learning also includes cases in which $\mathbf{c}$ has real valued components (regression or multi-output regression problems) that are not covered in this book. Many forms of modeling (providing mappings from $\mathbf{x}^*$ to $\mathbf{c}^*$) exist: non-probabilistic classifiers (Chapter 7), such as k-nearest neighbors, classification trees, rule induction, artificial neural networks and support vector machines, and probabilistic classifiers (Chapter 8), such as discriminant analysis, logistic regression analyses, and Bayesian network classifiers.

Unsupervised learning or clustering is defined as the problem of determining the partitioning or grouping of similar data in the absence of explicit labels, as $\mathbf{c}$. Non-probabilistic clustering (Chapter 11) includes the topics of hierarchical and partitional clustering, whereas probabilistic clustering (Chapter 12) is mainly based on finite-mixture models and the expectation-maximization algorithm.

Domingos (2015) considers five groups of machine learning approaches with respect to how the machines should learn while extracting the maximum possible knowledge from the data: (a) the **symbolic approach** based on logic and philosophy, (b) the **connectionist approach**, with foundations in the way the brain functions using neuroscience as the basic theory and the backpropagation (of artificial neural networks) as the main algorithm, (c) the **evolutionist approach** based on evolutionary biology and using evolutionary computation (i.e., genetic algorithms) as its main algorithm, (d) the **Bayesian approach** that uses statistics and probabilistic inference as fundamentals and is based on the idea of adapting the world interpretation as new evidence arrives, and (e) the **analogist approach**, which searches in its memory for similar situations that worked properly in the past to solve the current problem, and k-nearest neighbors is its favorite algorithm.

Machine learning is a young, continuously expanding discipline in which new methods and algorithms are being developed daily, mainly within the new paradigm of

big data.[10] Large data sets require scalable algorithms whose time and space requirements are linearly or sublinearly correlated with the size of the problem (number of points or number of dimensions). Several opportunities and challenges in machine learning remain: (a) contrasting current machine learning approaches to naturally occurring systems (humans and animals) that in some situations can discover patterns from only one instance, something called one-shot learning in the jargon of artificial intelligence, (b) organizing different types of skills and types of knowledge (supervised and unsupervised) into a single-to-more-difficult sequence, (c) constructing lifelong or never-ending computer learners that continuously operate for years, (d) team-based learning inspired by people who often work on teams to collect and analyze data, and (e) mixed-initiative learning that provides new machine learning methods the ability to work collaboratively with humans.

Predictions made by machine learning systems (or artificial intelligence in general) must be accurate. In addition, humans should understand the whys of the recommended decisions. For example, if a system selects Miss Smith for a very risky neurological surgery, or if another system predicts that Mr. Jones's cognitive deterioration will be aggravated in the next 2 years, understanding what those decisions are based on is important.

Hence the need to develop transparent, reliable, trustable, and explainable models avoiding the black boxes implicit in some machine learning paradigms. Among the paradigms presented in this book, classification trees, rule induction, Bayesian classifiers, Bayesian networks, and Markov networks stand out for their transparency, whereas random forests, support vector machines, artificial neural networks, and deep learning excel for their opacity and difficult interpretation. **Explainable artificial intelligence** is a trend that tries to develop systems that are interpretable for humans (Rudin, 2019).

Ethics is another aspect to take into account when developing intelligent systems in order to prevent them from having associated prejudices. Such prejudices can come either from the individual who has developed the system (and has conscious or unconscious preferences) or from the biases (for example, gender, race, age) implicit in the data set on which the automatic learning algorithm is applied, with problems both in the gathering or usage of data. Eliminating harmful biases is essential.

1.5.2.3 *Statistics versus Machine Learning*

This book is primarily concerned with the use of statistical methods and machine learning algorithms for transforming neuroscience data into computational models that are able to provide appropriate solutions for supervised and unsupervised classification problems (also called classification and clustering, respectively), as well as for discovering associations among the variables describing a problem. Statistics and machine learning are viewed as two different cultures for drawing conclusions from data (Breiman, 2001b). In both cultures, the input variables, $\mathbf{X}$, also known as predictor (machine learning) or independent (statistics) variables, are mapped to the output or response variables, $\mathbf{C}$, as illustrated in Figure 1.10.

---

[10] Four v's define the main issues of big data: (i) volume of the data to be processed, requiring different storage and processing capabilities than traditionally; (ii) velocity, referring to the speed with which data is generated; (iii) variety of sources of the data to be processed, including structured, semi-structured, and unstructured data; and (iv) veracity, which refers to the good quality of the data being analyzed.

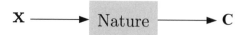

Figure 1.10 Transforming input variables, **X**, into output variables, **C**, through a process enacted by Nature.

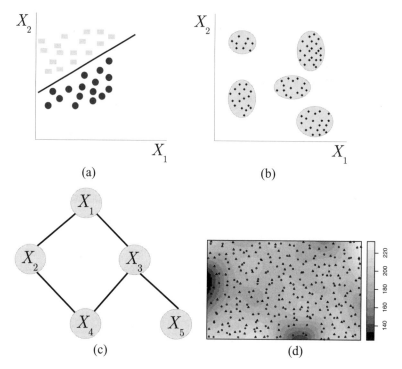

Figure 1.11 (a) Supervised classification (Part III). (b) Clustering (Part IV). (c) Discovery of associations (Part V). (d) Spatial statistics (Part VI).

In this book, we consider four main data analysis goals:

- **Prediction**: forecast the responses for future input variables. We consider discrete, both 1D and multidimensional, output variables.
- **Clustering**: merge similar inputs into groups.
- **Discovery of associations**: represent the relationships among the variables.
- **Spatial statistics**: study of the 2D/3D arrangement of points.

Figure 1.11 shows examples of each of these goals, which are developed throughout Parts III, IV, V, and VI of this book, respectively. All chapters in Part III assume that the output is unidimensional, c, except for Chapter 10, which considers a multidimensional output response, **c**. Chapters 11 and 12 in Part IV include situations where the output variable is hidden and should be determined by the model. Part V of the book, which is developed in Chapters 13 and 14, does not necessarily consider the distinction between input **x**, and output **c** and aims to discover the relationships among all variables. Chapter 15 in Part V includes exploratory data analysis and statistical modeling, as well as the simulation of spatial point processes.

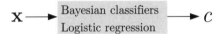

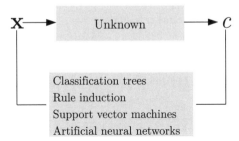

Figure 1.12 Examples of stochastic data models for prediction (supervised classification).

Figure 1.13 Examples of algorithm-based models for prediction (supervised classification).

The statistical methodology for modeling data is based on probability theory and assumes that a stochastic data model is responsible for mapping $\mathbf{x}$ to $\mathbf{c}$. In this approach, data analysis is based on the assumption of a stochastic data model for the inside of the box of Figure 1.10. A common assumption is that data are generated by independent draws from $\mathbf{c} = f(\mathbf{x}; \theta)$, where f is the mapping function specified by the model, and θ represents the parameters of the model (which are estimated from the data). Examples of stochastic data models for supervised classification are Bayesian classifiers and logistic regression, as illustrated in Figure 1.12.

Machine learning modeling considers the inside of the box to be complex and unknown. The approach is to find a mapping function $f(\mathbf{x})$, an algorithm that operates on $\mathbf{x}$ to predict the responses $\mathbf{c}$. Examples of algorithm-based models are classification trees, rules, support vector machines, and artificial neural networks, as shown in Figure 1.13.

Next we discuss the differences in some important issues between statistical and machine learning approaches. Table 1.2 presents some of these differences.

Model Assumptions. Statistical modeling requires a solid mathematical background and is based on its purest form on probability and measure theories, decision theory, Markov chains, asymptotic analysis, etc. The dependency of stochastic models on strong assumptions (e.g., multivariate Gaussian density, homoscedasticity, etc.) is justified by their mathematical malleability. In almost all real-world situations, however, these assumptions are not verified. In contrast, machine learning algorithms do not assume that conditions are met in the data set.

Model Selection. In statistics, the most appropriate model is selected as the model that best fits the data in terms of a measure related to the (penalized or marginal) likelihood. This process is usually enacted using a likelihood ratio-based hypothesis test comparing the fit between the current model and a candidate model. The candidate model will replace the current model only if the differences in likelihood are statistically significant. Search approaches include standard **forward selection** (starting from the empty model and incorporating the most informative variable at each step until there is no further improvement), **backward elimination** (starting from a model with all variables and deleting the worst variable at any time), and **stepwise selection** (where the inclusion and deletion stages are intermingled).

Table 1.2 Main differences between statistics and machine learning approaches to data modeling

Statistics	Machine learning
Stochastic data model	Algorithm modeling
Model selection	Structure and parameter learning
Fitting	Learning
Likelihood ratio	Predictive accuracy
Forward, backward, stepwise	Metaheuristic
Collinearity	Feature subset selection
Bayesian approaches	Ensembles
Probabilistic output	Deterministic output

Modeling in the machine learning field relies on two ideas: (a) using a score measuring the goodness of the proposed model that is more directly related to the final aim; for example, if the main goal is prediction, the estimated classification accuracy, the F_1-measure, or the area under the ROC curve (see Section 5.2 for details) are score candidates; and (b) searching in the space of possible models using more sophisticated and intelligent metaheuristics, such as simulated annealing, tabu search, and genetic algorithms (Section 6.3.1). The use of these metaheuristics that require intensive computational algorithms is justified by the usually large cardinality (sometimes more than exponential in the number of variables) of the space of models.

In any case, both cultures agree on the principle of **Occam's razor** (Thorburn, 1915) or law of parsimony, that is, simpler models are better.

Feature Subset Selection. The term "curse of dimensionality" introduced by Bellman (1957) is associated with the need to find a small number of input variables in prediction models that contain most of the information required for the output variables. In statistics, these variables are selected based on the concept of collinearity and assumes that a previously fixed number of variables k of the total number of predictor variables n, $k < n$, should be chosen. The machine learning approach for feature subset selection is more computational and tries to find the best combination of input variables (Section 6.3) for the output variable in terms of predictive accuracy. From this perspective, the search is conducted in a space whose cardinality is given by 2^n.

More than One Model. Breiman (2001b) referred to the situation where different models with approximately the same predictive accuracy are produced, which is known as the Rashomon effect.[11] This effect is typically when the initial number of input variables is very large. Instead of choosing one of the models and discarding the rest, one possible alternative is to merge or combine the outputs of the different models, particularly if the models belong to different families and the errors are committed in different cases. In machine learning, this approach is known as **ensemble learning** (Chapter 9) and is considered a practical implementation of the full (or selective) Bayesian approaches to models developed in statistics.

Validation. The honest estimation of the generalization power of the predictive models (see Section 5.3) is conducted in a similar way in both cultures. Both the statistics and machine learning communities partition the data set into training and test sets, or use

---

[11] This effect takes its name from Akira Kurosawa's film *Rashomon*, in which a crime witnessed by four individuals is described in four mutually contradictory ways.

Table 1.3 Statistical and machine learning methods described in this book

Statistics	Machine learning
Feature selection (filter)	Feature selection (wrapper)
k-nearest neighbors	k-nearest neighbors
Classification trees	Classification trees
Discriminant analysis	Rule induction
Logistic regression	Artificial neural networks
Bayesian network classifiers	Support vector machines
Multidimensional classification	Metaclassifiers
Hierarchical clustering	Multi-label classification
Partitional clustering	
Probabilistic clustering	
Spatial statistics	

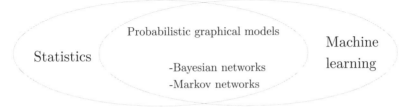

Figure 1.14 Probabilistic graphical models including Bayesian networks and Markov networks at the intersection between statistics and machine learning.

more sophisticated methods, including k-fold cross-validation, and bootstrapping. The probabilistic output provided by statistical models, which is richer than the deterministic response produced by almost all machine learning algorithms, indicates that statistical models can be validated with better measures, such as the Brier score.

Both the statistics and machine learning cultures are complementary rather than contradictory. Indeed, many machine learning algorithms incorporate statistics in their process, and some modern statistical modeling techniques have been developed by the machine learning community. An example is the probabilistic graphical models represented by Bayesian networks (Chapter 13) and Markov networks (Chapter 14) (Koller and Friedman, 2009), as illustrated in Figure 1.14.

Table 1.3 contains a list of other methods and algorithms covered in this book and organized as belonging to statistics or machine learning. Note that this organization is somewhat ambiguous, as k-nearest neighbors and classification trees were developed independently in both fields and constitutes an example of cooperation. k-nearest neighbor methods (Section 7.1) date back to the early 1950s (Fix and Hodges, 1951) and have been thoroughly investigated by the statistical community. Very similar algorithms, which are known as instance-based learning (Aha et al., 1991) and case-based reasoning (Kolodner, 1993), have been developed by the machine learning community. Classification trees (Section 7.2) were independently developed. They are designated as classification and regression trees (CART) in the statistics community (Breiman et al., 1984) and decision trees in the machine learning field (Quinlan, 1986). Seminal books comparing approaches from both cultures are Weiss and Kulikowski (1991) and Michie et al. (1994).

1.5.3   Brain-Inspired Machine Learning Methods and Hardware

The principles of the functions of the brain and the computer differ. The brain is able to work with novelty, complexity, and ambiguity, whereas computers are fast and very precise. However, the knowledge about the brain can serve as inspiration in the design of machines, both software and hardware, for example by applying the lessons learned from connectome graphs to making computers smarter.

In software, strategies used to unravel the algorithmic specializations of the sensory cerebral cortex are inspiring the next generation of high-performance machine learning. Brains exhibit a remarkable capacity for recognizing and learning about physical and abstract data that far exceeds the capabilities of the currently available state-of-the-art machine learning systems. A performance gap exists not only for high-level cognitive processes (e.g., understanding) but also for basic sensor information-processing tasks supporting these higher-level functions. Contemporary theories of cortical computing suggest that for sensory information-processing tasks, the brain employs algorithms with a limited set of computing primitives. These structural and/or functional motifs are used by one or more cortical area(s) to implement "core functions" of cortical algorithms that represent, transform data, and learn from data. A program of the American **IARPA** called **Machine Intelligence from Cortical Networks** (MICrONS) proposed in 2014 seeks to revolutionize machine learning by reverse-engineering the algorithms of the brain. MICrONS aims to design and implement novel machine learning algorithms that use the same "core functions" employed by the brain. Algorithms derived from the visual cortex will be tested on visual scenes, algorithms derived from olfactory cortex will be tested on olfactory cues, etc.

In hardware, **neuromorphic computing** takes its inspiration from observations of the complexity of the biological brain and considers brain knowledge as principles that can be applied to the design of hardware engineering systems. Seminal work on bio-inspired microelectronics culminated in the book published by Mead (1989). More recent examples of large-scale neuromorphic systems include (a) the **IBM TrueNorth** chip (Merolla et al., 2014), which is the outcome of a decade of work by the DARPA SYNAPSE program aimed at delivering a very dense, energy-efficient platform capable of supporting a range of cognitive applications, (b) **Neurogrid** (Benjamin et al., 2014), which is based on the heritage of Mead (1989), and uses subthreshold analogue circuits to model neuron and synapse dynamics in biological real time, (c) the **SpiNNAker** project (Furber et al., 2014), which has developed a massively parallel digital computer whose communication infrastructure is motivated by the objective of modeling large-scale spiking neural networks with connectivity similar to the brain in biological real time, and (d) the **BrainScaleS** neuromorphic system (Schemmel et al., 2010) developed at the University of Heidelberg with the aim of implementing physical models of neuronal processes.

1.6   Real Examples Discussed in This Book

The book is organized into the following six parts: I Introduction (Chapter 1), II Statistics (Chapters 2–4), III Supervised Classification (Chapters 5–10), IV Unsupervised Classifica-

Table 1.4 Book organization

Chapter	Title	Data Set
2	Exploratory data analysis	1. Interneurons vs. pyramidal neurons
3	Probability theory and random variables	1. Interneurons vs. pyramidal neurons
4	Probabilistic inference	1. Interneurons vs. pyramidal neurons
6	Feature subset selection	2. GABAergic interneuron nomenclature
7	Non-probabilistic classifiers	1. Interneurons vs. pyramidal neurons
8	Probabilistic classifiers	1. Interneurons vs. pyramidal neurons
9	Metaclassifiers	1. Interneurons vs. pyramidal neurons
10	Multidimensional classifiers	3. Quality of life in Parkinson's disease
11	Non-probabilistic clustering	4. Dendritic spines
12	Probabilistic clustering	4. Dendritic spines
13	Bayesian networks	5. Basal dendritic trees
14	Markov networks	6. Brain connectivity
15	Spatial statistics	7. Spatial location of synapses in the neocortex

tion (Chapters 11–12), V Probabilistic Graphical Models (Chapters 13–14), and VI Spatial Statistics (Chapter 15). Some real-world neuroscience examples are used to illustrate the methods described in each chapter in Parts III to VI. Seven data sets were used for these illustrations, and they are described below, see Table 1.4.

1.6.1   Data Set 1: Interneurons versus Pyramidal Neurons

Discerning different neuronal cell types is an essential first step toward understanding neural circuits. Classical classifications of neuronal cell types used qualitative descriptors (de Nó, 1922), with nomenclature varying among researchers. Quantitative classifications using both unsupervised and (less frequently) supervised classification methods are more recent. They are actually necessary to obtain an objective set of descriptors for each cell type that most investigators agree upon.

Neocortical GABAergic interneurons are particularly difficult to distinguish and will be the main issue analyzed in Data Set 2 below. First, we will try to solve an easier problem: automatically distinguishing pyramidal cells from interneurons in the mouse neocortex based solely on their morphological features. These cells are the two principal neuronal types in the cerebral cortex (Ramón y Cajal, 1899), see Figure 1.15.

Obviously, the "ground truth," given by the presence or absence of an apical dendrite, is used to reliably label each cell as a pyramidal neuron P or interneuron I, but it is not included in the morphological features.

The rows in the data set contain 327 cells composed of 199 interneurons (60.86%) and 128 pyramidal cells (39.14%) from the cortex of PND 14 C57/B6 mice. All pyramidal neurons had clear apical dendrites. Many different subtypes of interneurons were identified and collected from several different laboratory studies. A complete description of methods used to prepare the brain slices and the histological procedures is provided in Guerra et al. (2011). Neuronal morphologies were reconstructed using Neurolucida (MicroBrightField [Glaser and Glaser, 1990]). The columns in the data set show 64 morphological features of

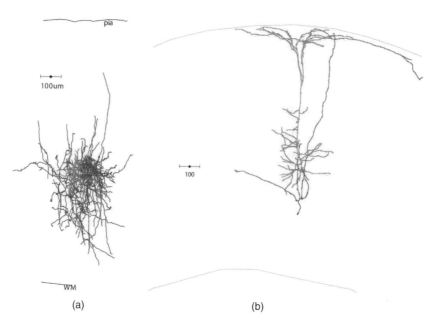

Figure 1.15 (a) Basket cell (interneuron). (b) Pyramidal cell. Both cells are located in the mouse neocortex, and their axonal arbor and their dendritic tree are shown in blue and red, respectively. Reprinted with permission from Guerra et al. (2011). For the color version, please refer to the plate section.

the reconstruction of each cell measured with the Neurolucida Explorer program, as well as the relative distance from the soma to the pia. Table 1.5 (somatic and axonal features) and Table 1.6 (dendritic features) list all 65 variables.

Some features, such as the somatic area and perimeter, number of axons and dendrites, axonal and dendritic length, axonal and dendritic branch angles, and number of axonal and dendritic nodes (branch points), are measured directly. Other features, such as the soma roundness, axonal and dendritic Sholl lengths (Sholl, 1953), convex hull analysis, and fractal analysis, are computed. Sholl length measures the radial distribution of the lengths of axonal or dendritic arbors around the soma. Concentric spheres centered on the soma are drawn at radius intervals of r μm. $r = 100$ μm for axons and $r = 50$ μm for dendrites. Then, the Sholl length at r μm is calculated as a fraction of the length of (axonal or dendritic) segments contained in the first Sholl ring divided by the total length of (axonal or dendritic) segments. The Sholl length at $2r$ μm is calculated as a fraction of the length of (axonal or dendritic) segments contained in the Sholl section from r to $2r$ (belonging to the second Sholl) divided by the total length of (axonal or dendritic) segments, and so forth. The convex hull analysis draws a 2D and 3D convex shape around the axons or dendrites. The area and perimeter of the 2D shape and the volume and surface area of the 3D shape are then calculated. The fractal analysis calculates the fractal dimension of the axon or dendrites using a linear regression analysis and therefore measures the extent to which the axonal or dendritic arbor fills the space. The relative distance from the soma to the pia is the ratio of the straight-line distance from the soma to the pia and the straight-line distance from the white matter to the pia. Thus, a value close to 0 (resp. 1) corresponds to a soma in a superficial (resp. deep) layer.

Table 1.5 Somatic and axonal features in Data Set 1

Feature	Description
Soma	
X_1	Somatic perimeter (μm)
X_2	Somatic area (μm^2)
X_3	Somatic aspect ratio
X_4	Somatic compactness
X_5	Somatic form factor
X_6	Somatic roundness
Axon	
X_7	Axonal node total (branching points)
X_8	Total axonal length (μm)
X_9	Total surface area of axon (μm^2)
X_{10}	Ratio of axonal length to surface area
X_{11}	Highest order axon segment
X_{12}	Axonal torsion ratio
X_{13}	Axonal planar angle ave
X_{14}	Axonal planar angle stdv
X_{15}	Axonal local angle ave
X_{16}	Axonal local angle stdv
X_{17}	Axonal spline angle ave
X_{18}	Axonal spline angle stdv
X_{19}	Ave tortuosity of axonal segments
X_{20}	Stdv of tortuosity of axonal segments
X_{21}	Axonal segment length ave
X_{22}	Axonal segment length stdv
X_{23}	Ave tortuosity of axonal nodes
X_{24}	Stdv of tortuosity of axonal nodes
X_{25}	Number axonal Sholl sections
X_{26}	Axonal Sholl length at 100 μm (fraction)
X_{27}	Axonal Sholl length at 200 μm (fraction)
X_{28}	Axonal Sholl length at 300 μm (fraction)
X_{29}	Axonal length density2
X_{30}	Axonal node density2
X_{31}	Convex hull axon area
X_{32}	Convex hull axon perimeter
X_{33}	Convex hull axon volume
X_{34}	Convex hull axon surface area
X_{35}	k-dim (fractal analysis)-axon

We are searching for a procedure that automatically distinguishes pyramidal cells from interneurons using this type of data, with cells characterized based on some morphological features and prior supervised information about the type of neuron (P or I).

An interesting issue is to identify which morphological features help distinguish the two neuron types i.e., to perform feature subset selection (Chapter 6).

Chapters 7 to 9 will show the performance of a battery of different supervised classification algorithms applied to this example. Note that procedures that omit this prior information aim to discover new or confirm some known hypotheses about subtypes of cells. This problem is tackled by unsupervised classification methods, which are described in

Table 1.6 Dendritic features in Data Set 1; the relative distance to the pia is included at the bottom

Feature	Description
Dendrites	
X_{36}	Number of dendrites
X_{37}	Dendritic node total (branching points)
X_{38}	Total dendritic length (μm)
X_{39}	Ave length of dendrites (μm)
X_{40}	Total surface area of dendrites (μm^2)
X_{41}	Ratio of dendritic length to surface area
X_{42}	Highest order dendritic segment
X_{43}	Dendritic torsion ratio
X_{44}	Dendritic planar angle ave
X_{45}	Dendritic planar angle stdv
X_{46}	Dendritic local angle ave
X_{47}	Dendritic local angle stdv
X_{48}	Dendritic spline angle ave
X_{49}	Dendritic spline angle stdv
X_{50}	Ave tortuosity of dendritic segments
X_{51}	Stdv of tortuosity of dendritic segments
X_{52}	Dendritic segment length ave
X_{53}	Dendritic segment length stdv
X_{54}	Ave tortuosity of dendritic nodes
X_{55}	Stdv of tortuosity of dendritic nodes
X_{56}	Number of dendritic Sholl sections
X_{57}	Dendritic Sholl length at 50 μm (fraction)
X_{58}	Dendritic Sholl length at 100 μm (fraction)
X_{59}	Dendritic Sholl length at 150 μm (fraction)
X_{60}	Convex hull dendrite area
X_{61}	Convex hull dendrite perimeter
X_{62}	Convex hull dendrite volume
X_{63}	Convex hull dendrite surface area
X_{64}	k-dim (fractal analysis)-dendrites
X_{65}	Relative distance to pia

Chapters 11 and 12. Surprisingly, this unsupervised approach is used by most researchers to classify cortical neurons based on morphological, physiological and/or molecular features (Cauli et al., 2000; Kozloski et al., 2001; Wong et al., 2002; Tsiola et al., 2003; Andjelic et al., 2009; Helmstaedter et al., 2009a, 2009b; Karagiannis et al., 2009; McGarry et al., 2010; Battaglia et al., 2013; Helm et al., 2013; Perrenoud et al., 2013).

In addition to morphology, Ascoli et al. (2008) and Yuste et al. (2020) suggested a multimodal neuronal type definition, including physiological, molecular, and morphological features.

1.6.2   Data Set 2: GABAergic Interneuron Nomenclature

The data for this example have been borrowed from a paper by DeFelipe et al. (2013) that develops a methodology based on a new community-based strategy (crowd sourcing)

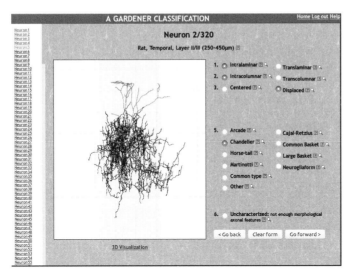

Figure 1.16 Screenshot of 1 of the 320 neurons included in the web-based interactive system. For each of the six class variables, the experts can select the most appropriate category describing the morphology of the neuron. For the color version, please refer to the plate section.

applied by a set of neuroanatomy experts with the objective of creating an accepted nomenclature for cortical GABAergic interneurons. The new methodology involves a web-based interactive system that enables experts to classify neurons with predetermined criteria (see Figure 1.16). Each expert has the option of classifying each neuron according to six class variables based on neuronal morphology. The first of these class variables refers to the geometric position of the neuron axonal arbor relative to cortical layers and includes the following categories: intralaminar, interneurons with axonal arbors that are mainly located in the layer of the parent soma, and translaminar, otherwise. The second class variable refers to the distribution of the axonal arbor relative to the size of cortical "columns" and covers two categories: intracolumnar, when the distance of the axonal arbors from the soma is not more than 300 μm in the horizontal dimension; and transcolumnar, if the neuron does not meet this constraint. The third class variable corresponds to the relative locations of the axonal and dendritic arbors and also includes two categories: centered, when the dendritic arbor is mainly located at the center of the axonal arborization, and displaced, otherwise. A fourth class is considered for interneurons categorized as translaminar and displaced. This variable has three possible categories: ascending, when the axonal arbor is mainly distributed toward the cortical surface; descending, when the distribution is mainly toward the white matter; and both, for neurons with axonal arbors distributed toward both the cortical surface and the white matter. The fifth class variable covers the common names of the cell types present in the literature (Jones and Peters, 1984): arcade, Cajal-Retzius, chandelier, common basket, common type, horse-tail, large basket, Martinotti, neurogliaform, and other. Finally, the sixth class variable examines whether a sufficient (or insufficient) number of morphological axonal characteristics is available to classify the interneuron and considers two categories: characterized and uncharacterized.

Table 1.7 Data set containing information for the 241 3D reconstructed interneurons. For each neuron, 2,886 morphological variables have been recorded, as well as the categorization provided by the 42 neuroanatomy experts into the 6 class variables, C_1 to C_6

Neuron	X_1	$\cdots$	$X_{2,886}$	C_1			$\cdots$	C_6		
				E1	$\cdots$	E42	$\cdots$	E1	$\cdots$	E42
1	10.8	$\cdots$	20.3	1	$\cdots$	1	$\cdots$	1	$\cdots$	1
$\cdots$	$\cdots$	$\cdots$	$\cdots$	$\cdots$	$\cdots$	$\cdots$	$\cdots$	$\cdots$	$\cdots$	$\cdots$
241	9.2	$\cdots$	18.9	2	$\cdots$	2	$\cdots$	1	$\cdots$	2

Forty-two neuroanatomy experts from different labs in Europe, the United States, Japan, and China participated in the experiment, providing their categorization for the 6 class variables. Branched structure, convex hull, Sholl, fractal, fan-in diagram, vertex, and branch angle morphological analyses were performed on each of the 241 neurons whose 3D reconstructions were available at NeuroMorpho.Org using the MicroBrightField Neurolucida package.

The initial data set (see Table 1.7) contains the 2,886 morphological variables described below, and the categorization provided by each of the 42 experts (E1,...,E42) according to the 6 class variables described in Figure 1.16 for each of the 241 interneurons.

In the original data set, in the Convex-Hull-2D block (see below), the number of intersections was measured in concentric spheres centered at the soma with increasing radii of 20 μm. Based on the advice of the neuroanatomists, this small radius was extended to 60 μm, resulting in a reduction of 300 variables. Thus, 2,586 final morphological variables were considered over which Chapter 6 will perform feature subset selection. The variables are organized into the following blocks:

- Box-Counting-Trees-Axons. The fractal dimension of the axon using the box-counting method (Mandelbrot, 1982). The fractal dimension is a quantity that indicates how completely the neuron fills the space. This value is measured by considering only the axonal arbor. The block contains a variable denoted as X_1.
- Box-Counting-Trees-Dendrites. The fractal dimension of the dendrites using the box-counting method. The block contains a variable denoted as X_2.
- Branch-Angle-Axon. We used planar, local, and spline angles that measure the direction of the branches at different levels. We computed the mean, standard deviation, and median of the three angles for the axonal arbor. Also, we measured these variables by dividing the data set according to the centrifugal order of the segments. The block contains variables from X_3 to X_{929}.
- Branch-Angle-Dendrite. Similarly, for the dendritic arbor, the result is variables from X_{930} to $X_{1,100}$.
- Cell-Bodies. The area, aspect ratio, compactness, convexity, contour size (maximum and minimum Feret), form factor, perimeter, roundness, and solidity of the soma. The block contains variables from $X_{1,101}$ to $X_{1,110}$.
- Convex-Hull-2D. This analysis measures the area and the perimeter of the 2D convex hull that includes the entire neuronal morphology. The block contains variables from $X_{1,111}$ to $X_{1,114}$.
- Convex-Hull-3D. This analysis measures the volume and the surface of the 3D convex hull that includes the entire neuronal morphology. The block contains variables from $X_{1,115}$ to $X_{1,118}$.

- Neuron-Summary-Axon. The number of axonal endings, the total length of the axon, the mean length of the axonal trees, and the number of nodes (branching points) in the axon. The block contains variables from $X_{1,119}$ to $X_{1,122}$.
- Neuron-Summary-Dendrites. The number of endings, the number of nodes (branching points), the total length, and the mean length of each dendritic arbor. The block contains variables from $X_{1,123}$ to $X_{1,126}$.
- Polar-Axon. The polar histogram is a $360°$ projection of data that accounts for the neurite length and direction. In the projection, the length of a wedge is equivalent to the total length of neurites in a specified direction. A fan-in diagram is generated to further study axon directionality. This diagram is divided into sectors. The numbers in the polar variables represent the sector in which the variable is measured. This approach only considers the axonal arbor. The block contains variables from $X_{1,127}$ to $X_{1,162}$.
- Polar-Dendrite. This analysis only considers the dendritic arbor. The block contains variables from $X_{1,163}$ to $X_{1,198}$.
- Segment-Axons. The total, mean, median, and standard deviation of the length of the segments belonging to the axonal arbor of the neuron. Also, we measured these variables by dividing the data set according to the centrifugal order of the segments. The block contains variables from $X_{1,199}$ to $X_{1,614}$.
- Segment-Dendrites. Similarly, for dendrites, the block contains variables from $X_{1,615}$ to X_{1694}.
- Sholl-Axon. The number of intersections in concentric spheres centered at the soma with increasing radii of 60 μm. The analysis also includes the number of endings, nodes, and the total length of the segments included in those spheres. Only the axonal arbor is analyzed. The block contains variables from $X_{1,695}$ to $X_{1,806}$.
- Sholl-Dendrite. Similarly, for dendrites, the block contains variables from $X_{1,807}$ to $X_{1,846}$.
- Tree-Totals-Axon. The number of endings and the number of segments of the axonal arborization. These variables were also measured according to the centrifugal order. The block contains variables from $X_{1,847}$ to $X_{2,052}$.
- Tree-Totals-Dendrite. Similarly, for dendrites, the block contains variables from $X_{2,053}$ to $X_{2,090}$.
- Vertex-Axon. Vertex analysis of the connectivity of the nodes in the branches is performed to describe the topological and metric properties of the axonal arbor. The block contains variables from $X_{2,091}$ to $X_{2,506}$.
- Vertex-Dendrite. Similarly, for dendrites, the block contains variables from $X_{2,507}$ to $X_{2,586}$.

The data set presented in Table 1.7 can be transformed in several alternative ways to reach a consensus among the responses of the 42 experts. After separately considering each of the 6 class variables, one possibility is to establish a consensus threshold, the simplest version of which would coincide with the majority vote. In this case, the category assigned to each neuron will be the one with highest frequency. Another possibility is to select those neurons with a given category frequency greater than 21 (half of the number of experts) from the data set. The last option is to use the information provided by the experts in terms of the relative frequency of each of the possible categories. This option is illustrated in Table 1.8 for the class variable C_5, representing the common usage of the interneuron names in the literature, encoded from 1 to 10.

Table 1.8 Data set containing information for the 241 3D reconstructed interneurons. For each neuron, 2,586 morphological variables have been recorded, as well as a probabilistic label for C_5, from the categories provided by the 42 neuroanatomists

Neuron	X_1	$\cdots$	$X_{2,586}$	C_5									
				1	2	3	4	5	6	7	8	9	10
1	10.8	$\cdots$	20.3	0.08	0.14	0.04	0.32	0.02	0.13	0.01	0.05	0.11	0.10
$\cdots$	$\cdots$	$\cdots$	$\cdots$	$\cdots$	$\cdots$	$\cdots$	$\cdots$	$\cdots$	$\cdots$	$\cdots$	$\cdots$	$\cdots$	$\cdots$
$\cdots$	$\cdots$	$\cdots$	$\cdots$	$\cdots$	$\cdots$	$\cdots$	$\cdots$	$\cdots$	$\cdots$	$\cdots$	$\cdots$	$\cdots$	$\cdots$
241	9.2	$\cdots$	18.9	0.07	0.10	0.05	0.23	0.08	0.21	0.03	0.06	0.12	0.05

1.6.3 Data Set 3: Quality of Life in Parkinson's Disease

The data for this example were derived from a study by Borchani et al. (2012) that attempted to predict the European Quality of Life-5 Dimensions (EQ-5D) from the 39-item Parkinson's Disease Questionnaire (PDQ-39). The EQ-5D is a generic health-related quality-of-life measure that is used in general populations and patients with any disorder. EQ-5D contains five items (Figure 1.17), namely Mobility, Self-care, Usual activities, Pain/Discomfort, and Anxiety/Depression. Each item has three possible responses: no problems, some problems, and severe problems. However, PDQ-39 (Figure 1.18) is a specific instrument that is widely used in individuals with PD to capture patients' perceptions of their illness. PDQ-39 measures the severity and degree of disability in patients with PD using 39 questions covering 8 dimensions (see Table 1.9): mobility, activities of daily living, emotional well-being, stigma, social support, cognitions, communication, and bodily discomfort. Each question is scored on a five-point scale: never, occasionally, sometimes, often, and always.

The analyzed data set includes 488 patients with PD, each of whom was characterized with 39 predictor variables (PDQ-39) and 5 variables to be predicted (EQ-5D). The objective is to learn a multidimensional classifier that is able to assign the 5 classes of the EQ-5D to each patient. As these 5 classes are believed to be interrelated, the solution of learning 5 unidimensional supervised classification models does not appear to be appropriate. Therefore, an approach based on multidimensional classification should be adopted. Chapter 10 will be devoted to this.

1.6.4 Data Set 4: Dendritic Spines

This example analyzes dendritic spines, which were first described by Cajal in 1888. Dendrites of a single neuron can contain hundreds or thousands of spines. Although their exact functions remain unclear (reviewed in Yuste [2010]), the morphology of dendritic spines appears to be critical for their functions. Pyramidal neuron spines are the targets of most excitatory synapses in the cerebral cortex. The shape of the dendritic spines may determine their synaptic strength and learning rules. Quantitative analyses have revealed strong correlations between spine morphological variables and the synaptic structure: (a) the spine head volume and total spine volume in the neocortex are positively correlated with the area of the post-synaptic density, with a remarkably small variance (Arellano et al., 2007). This area is correlated with the number of presynaptic vesicles, the number

By placing a tick in one box in each group below, please indicate which statements best describe your own health state today.

MOBILITY
I have no problems in walking about ☐
I have some problems in walking about ☐
I am confined to bed ☐

SELF-CARE
I have no problems with self-care ☐
I have some problems washing or dressing myself ☐
I am unable to wash or dress myself ☐

USUAL ACTIVITIES (e.g., work, study, housework, family or leisure activities)
I have no problems with performing my usual activities ☐
I have some problems with performing my usual activities ☐
I am unable to do my usual activities ☐

PAIN / DISCOMFORT
I have no pain or discomfort ☐
I have moderate pain or discomfort ☐
I have extreme pain or discomfort ☐

ANXIETY / DEPRESSION
I am not anxious or depressed ☐
I am moderately anxious or depressed ☐
I am extremely anxious or depressed ☐

Figure 1.17 Five classes of the EQ-5D quality-of-life measure.

Please complete the following

Due to having Parkinson's disease, how often during the last month have you....	Never	Occasionally	Sometimes	Often	Always or cannot do at all
1 Had difficulty doing the leisure activities which you would like to do?	☐	☐	☐	☐	☐
2 Had difficulty looking after your home, e.g., DIY, housework, cooking?	☐	☐	☐	☐	☐
3 Had difficulty carrying bags of shopping?	☐	☐	☐	☐	☐
4 Had problems walking half a mile?					
5 Had problems walking 100 yards?	☐	☐	☐	☐	☐
6 Had problems getting around the house as easily as you would like?	☐	☐	☐	☐	☐

⋮

Figure 1.18 Six questions of the PDQ-39 questionnaire.

of postsynaptic receptors, and the ready-releasable pool of transmitter, (b) the length of the spine neck is proportional to the extent of biochemical and electrical isolation of the spine from its parent dendrite (Harris and Stevens, 1989; Nusser et al., 1998; Yuste et al., 2000), (c) larger spines can generate larger synaptic currents than smaller spines (Matsuzaki et al.,

Table 1.9 The PDQ-39 items

Mobility:
pdq1	Had difficulty doing the leisure activities you would like to do
pdq2	Had difficulty looking after your home, e.g., DIY, housework, cooking
pdq3	Had difficulty carrying bags of shopping
pdq4	Had problems walking half a mile
pdq5	Had problems walking 100 yards
pdq6	Had problems getting around the house as easily as you would like
pdq7	Had problems getting around in public
pdq8	Needed someone else to accompany you when you went out
pdq9	Felt frightened or worried about falling over in public
pdq10	Been confined to the house more than you would like

Activities of daily living:
pdq11	Had difficulty washing yourself
pdq12	Had difficulty dressing yourself
pdq13	Had problems doing up buttons or shoe laces
pdq14	Had problems writing clearly
pdq15	Had difficulty cutting up your food
pdq16	Had difficulty holding a drink without spilling it

Emotional well-being:
pdq17	Felt depressed
pdq18	Felt isolated and lonely
pdq19	Felt weepy or tearful
pdq20	Felt angry or bitter
pdq21	Felt anxious
pdq22	Felt worried about your future

Stigma:
pdq23	Felt you had to conceal your Parkinson's from people
pdq24	Avoided situations which involve eating or drinking in public
pdq25	Felt embarrassed in public due to having PD
pdq26	Felt worried by other people's reaction to you

Social support:
pdq27	Had problems with your close personal relationships
pdq28	Lacked support in the ways you need from your spouse or partner
pdq29	Lacked support in the ways you need from your family or close friends

Cognitions:
pdq30	Unexpectedly fallen asleep during the day
pdq31	Had problems with your concentration, e.g., when reading or watching TV
pdq32	Felt your memory was bad
pdq33	Had distressing dreams or hallucinations

Communication:
pdq34	Had difficulty with your speech
pdq35	Felt unable to communicate with people properly
pdq36	Felt ignored by people

Bodily discomfort:
pdq37	Had painful muscle cramps or spasms
pdq38	Had aches and pains in your joints or body
pdq39	Felt unpleasantly hot or cold

2004), and (d) dendritic spines are dynamic structures with fluctuations in volume that appear to have important implications for cognition and memory (Dunaevsky et al., 1999; Matus, 2000; Kasai et al., 2010).

Dendritic spines present a wide variety of morphologies, particularly in the human cortex (Benavides-Piccione et al., 2013). Spines are highly motile and can undergo reshaping, even in the adult. In fact, the loss or alteration of these structures has been described in the pathogenesis of major neurological disorders. Thus, a statistical analysis of spine morphology is indispensable for providing formal support for these and other hypotheses.

Although different morphology-based classifications of spines have been proposed, the one that is still most widely used today categorizes spines into three essential types: thin, mushroom, and stubby (Peters and Kaiserman-Abramof, 1970). This classification relies solely on a visual inspection of microscopy images and focuses on the head-to-neck diameter ratio, length-to-head diameter ratio, and head diameter. However, researchers have also argued that the large diversity of spines portrays a continuum of morphologies rather than the existence of discrete classes (Arellano et al., 2007). Therefore, a detailed description of morphologies is needed to identify clusters of human spines that share similar characteristics. This approach will likely require a certain probability of cluster membership for a given spine, capturing that continuum.

The data set contains 2,000 individually 3D reconstructed dendritic spines from layer III pyramidal neurons located in the cingulate cortex of a human male age 40 years and constitutes a random sample extracted from the pool of more than 4,500 spines of this individual analyzed in Luengo-Sanchez et al. (2018). Eight hundred eighty-six spines (44.30%) were located on apical dendrites, whereas the remaining 1,114 spines (55.70%) were located on basal dendrites. The tissue was obtained at autopsy (2–3 h postmortem). Apical and basal dendrites were then scanned using confocal microscopy and completely reconstructed in 3D using a methodology detailed elsewhere (Benavides-Piccione et al., 2013). Then, for each spine, a particular threshold was selected to constitute a solid surface that exactly matched its contour, see Figure 1.19.

An important issue is to extract a set of variables describing the 3D spine shapes. These variables should be sufficiently representative to summarize the shape and sufficiently meaningful to be easily interpreted by domain experts. Graph-based techniques handle both global (coarser) and local (more detailed) features. The techniques extract a geometric meaning from a 3D shape using a graph showing the linkage of shape components. Of the many existing shape-matching methods (Tangelder and Veltkamp, 2008), we were partially inspired by the concept of the Reeb graph defined by a geodesic distance (length of the shortest path along the surface of the model) for this data set. A skeletal structure of the 3D model in the form of a graph (Figure 1.20) is built. This graph captures the global topology of the shape. Then, variables are attached to each graph node to consider local features.

Spines were approximated by a continuous surface composed of a sequence of seven sections S_i (coaxial tubular-shaped) with heights $h_i, i = 1, \ldots, 7$. In each section, curves defining top, T_i, and bottom, B_i, regions were assumed to be ellipses with major (T_i^R, B_i^R) and minor (T_i^r, B_i^r) radii or axes. Thus, B_i^R is the major radius of the ellipse separating sections S_{i-1} and S_i. The surface was required to be continuous, and therefore coherence constraints were imposed on adjacent sections: $B_i^R = T_{i-1}^R, B_i^r = T_{i-1}^r, \forall i = 1, \ldots, 7$. Ratios between sections S_i and S_j, denoted by $\varphi_{ij} = \frac{B_j^R B_j^r}{B_i^R B_i^r}$, provide information about the widening

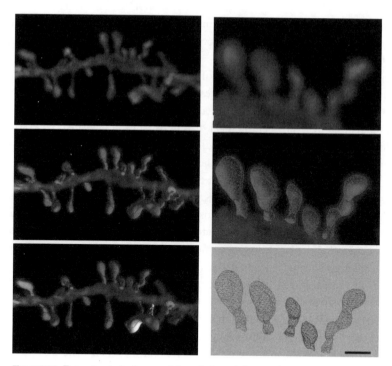

Figure 1.19 From top to bottom and from left to right: confocal microscopy z projection image of a dendritic segment from a horizontally projecting basal dendrite of an intracellular injected layer III pyramidal neuron of the human cingulate cortex (age 40 years). The complete morphology of each dendritic spine is reconstructed in 3D. Estimation of the spine volume values using color codes (blue-white: 0.0–0.8 μm^3). Ultimately, for each individual spine, 3D triangular meshes are output. Scales are: 2.5 μm (figures to the left) and 1 μm (figures to the right). Reprinted with permission from Luengo-Sanchez et al. (2018). For the color version, please refer to the plate section.

or narrowing along the spine. Three ratios, φ_{24}, φ_{26}, and φ_{46}, were considered. The growing direction of each ellipse of the spine is related to the mean direction of a region and is measured with the cosine of the azimuth angle, $cos(\phi_i)$, and by the polar angle θ_i for each ellipse, except the first one. The direction Φ of the perpendicular vector to the ith ellipse is called the instant direction and is determined with its azimuth angle and its polar angle, Θ_i, namely, the inclination of the vector perpendicular to the ellipse with respect to the z-axis. The volume of each region, V_i, is an approximation of the volume between two consecutive ellipses and computed from the convex hull of T_i and B_i. The volume of the spine, V, denotes the total volume of the spine and is computed as $V = \sum_{i=1}^{7} V_i$. In summary, the 54 features characterizing each spine (36 morphological features and 18 features necessary for their subsequent simulation) are shown in Table 1.10.

Figure 1.20 illustrates the meaning of the different morphological and simulation features presented in Table 1.10. Chapters 11 and 12 will find groups of these spines.

1.6.5   Data Set 5: Basal Dendritic Trees

This example concerns dendritic morphology, which is essential for understanding connectivity and the functional roles of neurons. Specifically, pyramidal neurons represent key

Table 1.10 The 54 features (36 morphological features and 18 features for simulation purposes) characterizing each spine in Data Set 4

Type	Feature	Description	Number
Morphological	h_1–h_7	Height of each section	7
Morphological	B_2^R–B_7^R	Major axis of the ellipse of each section	6
Morphological	B_2^r–B_7^r	Minor axis of the ellipse of each section	6
Morphological	φ_{24}, φ_{26}, φ_{46}	Ratio between sections	3
Morphological	$\cos(\phi_2)$–$\cos(\phi_7)$	Cosine of the azimuth angle of the growing direction	6
Simulation	θ_2–θ_7	Polar angle of the growing direction of each ellipse	6
Simulation	Φ_2–Φ_7	Direction of the perpendicular vector to the ellipse	6
Simulation	Θ_2–Θ_7	Inclination of the vector perpendicular to the ellipse	6
Morphological	V_1–V_7	Volume of each region	7
Morphological	V	Volume of the spine	1

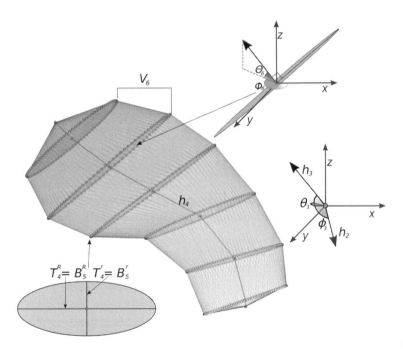

Figure 1.20 Illustration of the features used to characterize the spines. Observe the points at the centroids of the ellipses. They are connected by vectors whose lengths are denoted by h_i. Each ellipse is defined by its centroid, major axis ($T_{i-1}^R = B_i^R$), and minor axis ($T_{i-1}^r = B_i^r$). From the vectors connecting the centroids of the ellipses, angles ϕ_i, θ_i, and Φ_i, Θ_i are computed. The volumes of each section, V_i, are added for computing the volume V of the whole spine.

elements in the functional organization of the cerebral cortex, as they are the most frequent neuronal type (70–85%) and the main source of cortical excitatory synapses. The structure of the dendritic tree of pyramidal neurons affects the process of integration, and its size influences the topographic sampling map and the mixing of inputs (Wen et al., 2009). The branching patterns of the dendritic trees are related to synaptic input processing (Koch and Segev, 2000; Häusser and Mel, 2003) and affect the electrical behavior of the neurons (Mainen and Sejnowski, 1996; Vetter et al., 2001; Chen, 2009).

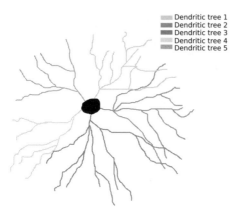

Dendritic tree 1
Dendritic tree 2
Dendritic tree 3
Dendritic tree 4
Dendritic tree 5

Figure 1.21 Basal dendritic arbor of a pyramidal neuron, where each dendritic tree is drawn in a different tone. Adapted from López-Cruz et al. (2011).

Researchers do not understand how and why vastly different arbor shapes form. In the last two decades, computational stochastic models have been used to measure relevant parameters of real neuronal arbors. These models and their subsequent use for simulating virtual neuron morphologies may help identify the basic structures and important features of neuronal classes.

Neuronal processes are not always easy to trace, and data on the complete dendritic tree of real neurons are rather scarce. However, in pyramidal neurons, the whole basal dendritic arbor – about 90% of the dendritic length in neurons from layers II/III and V (Larkman, 1991) – has been completely reconstructed in single horizontal sections (Elston and Rosa, 1997). This information is valuable for validating the simulated virtual neurons.

Thus, Data Set 5 includes a set of 3D reconstructions of 90 pyramidal neurons from the mouse neocortex (two BC57 black mice, 2 months old). The neurons were located in layer III of three different cortical regions: the secondary motor cortex (M2), secondary somatosensory cortex (S2), and lateral secondary visual cortex and association temporal cortex (V2L/TeA). The whole basal dendritic trees of the neurons were traced using the Neurolucida package (Glaser and Glaser, 1990). The tissue preparation and injection process are detailed in Benavides-Piccione et al. (2006). The reconstructions are publicly available at www.neuromorpho.org (Ascoli, 2007) as part of the DeFelipe laboratory archive.

Each basal dendritic arbor is composed of approximately 6 main trunks, which we will call dendritic trees, see Figure 1.21. One hundred four dendritic trees were observed in M2, 103 in S2, and 156 in V2L/TeA.

A segment is the straight line between two branching points. For each pair of sibling segments, a set of 41 morphological variables is measured from the 3D reconstructions of real dendrites, as described in López-Cruz et al. (2011). We distinguish two types of variables: first, construction variables that define the morphology of a segment (segment length, orientation, and bifurcation) and are necessary to incrementally build the virtual dendritic trees; and second, evidence variables that measure the part of the morphology of the dendritic tree located below a pair of sibling segments. Table 1.11 lists the 41 variables.

Table 1.11 Construction (C) and evidence (E) morphological variables for Data Set 5

No.	Type	Variable	No.	Type	Variable
1	E	Subtree degree (no. endings)	22	E	Neighbor distance
2	E	Subtree no. bifurcations (no. nodes)	23	E	Neighbor inclination
3	E	Subtree total length	24	E	Neighbor azimuth
4	E	Subtree width	25	E	Neighbor extension
5	E	Subtree height	26	E	Neighbor angle
6	E	Subtree depth	27	E	Parent segment length
7	E	Subtree box volume	28	E	Parent segment inclination
8	E	Subtree max distance between nodes	29	E	Parent segment azimuth
9	E	Subtree max distance to soma	30	E	Root segment length
10	E	Subtree max length	31	E	Root segment inclination
11	E	Subtree min length	32	E	Root segment azimuth
12	E	Subtree max order	33	E	Segment centrifugal order
13	E	Subtree min order	34	C	Left segment length
14	E	Subdendrite length	35	C	Left segment inclination
15	E	Subdendrite width	36	C	Left segment azimuth
16	E	Subdendrite height	37	C	Left segment bifurcates
17	E	Subdendrite depth	38	C	Right/root segment length
18	E	Subdendrite box volume	39	C	Right/root segment inclination
19	E	Subdendrite distance to soma	40	C	Right/root segment azimuth
20	E	Subdendrite inclination	41	C	Right/root segment bifurcates
21	E	Subdendrite azimuth			

More specifically, evidence variables describe the context of the segment and how the tree is constructed. These variables include information about the subtree (variables 1–13), subdendrite (variables 14–21) and nearest segment (variables 22–26). The centrifugal order (or branch order) of a segment is the number of bifurcations along the path to the soma. For a given pair of sibling segments with an order a, the subtree is the part of the dendritic tree including all the segments with an order less than a. Likewise, the subdendrite is the path from the soma to the sibling segments' branching point. Figure 1.22 shows a pair of sibling segments with a centrifugal order value of 5 (gray lines), its subtree (gray area), and subdendrite (dotted area). Finally, the nearest segment refers to the segment in the dendritic tree that does not belong to the subdendrite (neighboring segment in Figure 1.22).

Parent segment morphological variables (27–29) and root segment morphological variables (30–32), as well as the centrifugal order of the segment (variable 33), complete the set of evidence variables.

Construction variables specify the segment morphology (variables 34–41), whether the segments (left/right) branch, and the spherical coordinates of each segment end point.

Chapter 13 will deal with these variables and use their statistical distributions to automatically find their relationships in shaping the dendritic tree structure. Then, a simulation algorithm will sample the distributions to output virtual dendrites that should be indistinguishable from real dendrites.

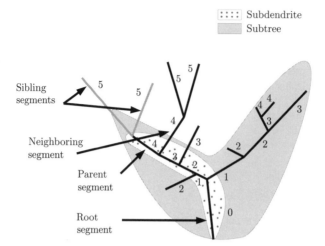

Figure 1.22 Subtree (gray area), subdendrite (dotted area), neighboring, parent and root segments for two sibling segments (gray lines). The numbers refer to the centrifugal order of the segments. Adapted from López-Cruz et al. (2011).

1.6.6   Data Set 6: Brain Connectivity

This data set, which was obtained from Huang et al. (2010), includes fluorodeoxyglucose PET images from 232 subjects: 49 with AD, 116 with mild cognitive impairment (MCI), and 67 normal controls (NCs). All images were downloaded from the Alzheimer's disease neuroimaging initiative (ADNI) database[12] to define the progression of AD. Image preprocessing, which is mainly performed with Statistical Parametric Mapping software (Wellcome Department of Cognitive Neurology[13]), ultimately yields average PET measurements for 42 anatomical volumes of interest, which are known to be most frequently affected by AD. These brain regions include the frontal, parietal, occipital, and temporal lobes. Table 1.12 lists the 42 variables.

In Chapter 14, we will use these data to identify functional brain connectivity networks for the three different types of subjects: patients with AD, patients with MCI, and NCs. Functional connectivity refers to the coherence of the activities among distinct brain regions (Horwitz, 2003). We search for statistical dependencies between different brain regions. Higher cognition is derived from the interactions between different brain regions rather than individual regions working independently. Thus, patients with AD, who are characterized by a global cognitive decline, may exhibit abnormal functional brain connectivity patterns. For example, the hippocampus and other regions in the brains of patients with AD exhibit reduced functional connectivity (Grady et al., 2001; Wang et al., 2007; Supekar et al., 2008), whereas increased connectivity has been observed between the frontal lobe and other regions in the brains of subjects with early AD and MCI, which is interpreted as a compensatory reallocation or recruitment of cognitive resources (Gould et al., 2006).

---

[12] adni.loni.usc.edu/.
[13] www.fil.ion.ucl.ac.uk/spm.

Table 1.12 Variables representing anatomical volumes of interest for Data Set 6 (L = left hemisphere, R = right hemisphere)

	Frontal lobe		Parietal lobe		Occipital lobe		Temporal lobe
Var.	Description	Var.	Description	Var.	Description	Var.	Description
X_1	Frontal_Sup_L	X_{13}	Parietal_Sup_L	X_{21}	Occipital_Sup_L	X_{27}	Temporal_Sup_L
X_2	Frontal_Sup_R	X_{14}	Parietal_Sup_R	X_{22}	Occipital_Sup_R	X_{28}	Temporal_Sup_R
X_3	Frontal_Mid_L	X_{15}	Parietal_Inf_L	X_{23}	Occipital_Mid_L	X_{29}	Temporal_Pole_Sup_L
X_4	Frontal_Mid_R	X_{16}	Parietal_Inf_R	X_{24}	Occipital_Mid_R	X_{30}	Temporal_Pole_Sup_R
X_5	Frontal_Sup_Medial_L	X_{17}	Precuneus_L	X_{25}	Occipital_Inf_L	X_{31}	Temporal_Mid_L
X_6	Frontal_Sup_Medial_R	X_{18}	Precuneus_R	X_{26}	Occipital_Inf_R	X_{32}	Temporal_Mid_R
X_7	Frontal_Mid_Orb_L	X_{19}	Cingulum_Post_L			X_{33}	Temporal_Pole_Mid_L
X_8	Frontal_Mid_Orb_R	X_{20}	Cingulum_Post_R			X_{34}	Temporal_Pole_Mid_R
X_9	Rectus_L					X_{35}	Temporal_Inf_L
X_{10}	Rectus_R					X_{36}	Temporal_Inf_R
X_{11}	Cingulum_Ant_L					X_{37}	Fusiform_L
X_{12}	Cingulum_Ant_R					X_{38}	Fusiform_R
						X_{39}	Hippocampus_L
						X_{40}	Hippocampus_R
						X_{41}	ParaHippocampal_L
						X_{42}	ParaHippocampal_R

1.6.7 Data Set 7: Spatial Location of Synapses in the Neocortex

One major issue in cortical circuitry is to determine the spatial distribution of synapses and whether synaptic connections are specific (DeFelipe et al., 2002). Two major morphological types of synapses have been identified: asymmetric and symmetric (Gray, 1959). The major sources of asymmetric synapses are spiny neurons (pyramidal and spiny non-pyramidal cells) and extrinsic cortical afferents, whereas the vast majority of symmetric synapses are formed by the population of aspiny or sparsely spiny interneurons.

The state-of-the-art methods for obtaining 3D data from which to estimate the spatial distribution, size, and number of synapses from ultrathin sections of brain tissue are based on serial reconstructions (Bock et al., 2011). The development of automated electron microscopy techniques has attempted to overcome the extremely time-consuming and difficult task of reconstructing large volumes of tissue (Briggman and Denk, 2006).

The tissues in this example (Merchán-Pérez et al., 2014) were obtained using a new dual-beam electron microscope that combines a focused ion beam (FIB) column and a SEM. The FIB column mills thin layers of material as a result of the collision of the gallium ion beam with the tissue. The SEM is then applied to the milled surface, obtaining a backscattered electron image. This milling/imaging process is automatically repeated to obtain a large series of images that represent a 3D sample of the tissue. Image resolution in the xy plane was 3.7 nm/pixel. The z-axis resolution (section thickness) was 20 nm.

Three male Wistar rats sacrificed on postnatal day 14 were used for this study. Animals were administered a lethal intraperitoneal injection of sodium pentobarbital (40 mg/kg) and were intracardially perfused with 2% paraformaldehyde and 2.5% glutaraldehyde in 0.1 M phosphate buffer. All animals were handled in accordance with the guidelines for animal research established in the European Union Directive 2010/63/EU, and all procedures were approved by the local ethics committee of the Spanish National Research Council.

Ten different samples of the neuropil in layer III of the somatosensory cortex were obtained from three different animals. All samples selected for FIB milling/SEM imaging were located at the mid-depth of layer III. After applying a 3D unbiased counting frame and correcting for tissue shrinkage (Merchán-Pérez et al., 2009), the volume of tissue

Table 1.13 Descriptive characteristics of the 10 samples of the neuropil in layer III

Sample no. and animal identification	Number of synapses per cubic micron	Mean distance to nearest neighbor (nm) $\pm$ sd	Mean Feret's diameter of synaptic junctions (nm) $\pm$ sd
1 (W31)	0.9857	519.55 $\pm$ 136.35	377.19 $\pm$ 159.63
2 (W31)	0.6936	594.07 $\pm$ 192.28	462.18 $\pm$ 177.52
3 (W33)	0.9279	537.43 $\pm$ 159.20	437.62 $\pm$ 168.04
4 (W33)	1.0088	537.39 $\pm$ 157.70	414.22 $\pm$ 169.04
5 (W33)	0.9474	597.30 $\pm$ 174.02	466.03 $\pm$ 215.91
6 (W33)	0.9399	533.21 $\pm$ 163.29	423.38 $\pm$ 169.83
7 (W33)	0.9881	487.17 $\pm$ 172.30	397.29 $\pm$ 168.22
8 (W35)	0.7997	568.21 $\pm$ 178.51	427.90 $\pm$ 168.15
9 (W35)	1.1267	501.38 $\pm$ 156.97	378.35 $\pm$ 166.60
10 (W35)	1.0178	523.74 $\pm$ 150.36	405.43 $\pm$ 175.62
All samples	0.9399	535.78 $\pm$ 166.81	417.06 $\pm$ 175.97

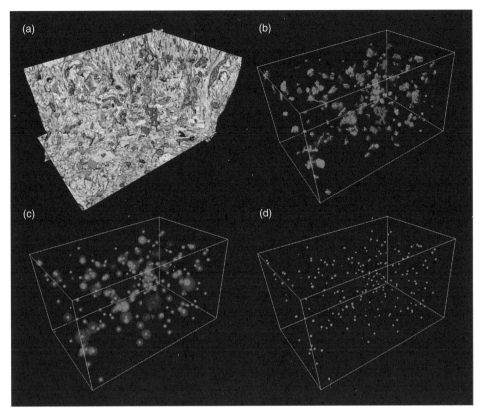

Figure 1.23 Example of a tissue volume whose dimensions are $7.16 \times 4.58 \times 3.98$ μm. (a) Asymmetric and symmetric synaptic junctions are shown in green and red, respectively. (b) Segmentation of the synaptic functions. (c) The smallest spheres circumscribing the synaptic junction used to calculate its Feret's diameter. (d) The centroids of the spheres. Image from Merchán-Pérez et al. (2014) reproduced with permission. For the color version, please refer to the plate section.

analyzed from each sample ranged from 149.13 to 247.58 μm³. Synaptic junctions within these volumes were visualized, automatically segmented, and reconstructed in three dimensions using Espina software (Morales et al., 2011). There were 1,695 synaptic junctions.

Table 1.13 contains the following information about the 10 samples: animal identification; densities of synapses, which were calculated by dividing the actual number of synaptic junctions by the volume of the counting frame; mean distance to the nearest neighboring synapses, which was calculated as the distance between the centroids of the synaptic junctions; and the mean Feret's diameter of synaptic junctions, which was computed as the diameter of the smallest sphere circumscribing the synaptic junction. Centroids that were located closer to the boundaries of the counting frame than to any other centroid were excluded from the calculations because their nearest neighbor might be outside the counting frame at an unknown distance.

Figure 1.23 displays the segmentation of the reconstructed synaptic functions, the smallest sphere containing each of the synapses, and the geometric centers, or centroids, of the spheres for 1 of the 10 tissues. These centroids were determined to indicate the spatial position of the synapses. The spatial statistical analysis of this data set is presented in Chapter 15.

Part II

Statistics

This Part II of the book describes statistical methods that are useful for the analysis of neuroscience data. Chapter 2 focuses on exploratory data analysis and includes techniques for visualizing and summarizing data of any nature: categorical, discrete numeric and continuous numeric (directional and non-directional). These techniques are valid for univariate, bivariate, and multivariate data. The chapter also covers preprocessing issues, namely, the imputation of missing data and several variable transformation methods. Chapter 3 introduces basic probability theory concepts and presents the most common univariate and multivariate, discrete and continuous (directional and nondirectional), probability distributions. Information theory elements and the basic methods for simulating random variates with a computer program are also explained, for their subsequent use in Part III and Parts V-VI of the book, respectively. Chapter 4 discusses the methods for parametric point estimation (frequentist and Bayesian) and parameter confidence intervals. Goodness-of-fit tests, paired and unpaired sample tests, multiple tests and permutation tests are some of the hypothesis tests also explained in the chapter.

2 Exploratory Data Analysis

Exploratory data analysis constitutes the first step in describing the data and becoming familiar with them. Hence, the researcher gathers some insights about the problem, which will be useful for establishing some hypothesis tests, e.g., on the shape of the distribution (and/or the values of some of its parameters) of the variables studied. The chapter is organized as follows. Section 2.1 introduces the three basic types of data covered in this book, which are categorical, discrete numeric, and continuous numeric (directional and nondirectional). Section 2.2 describes some popular graphs for visualizing data, such as pie charts, barplots, histograms, and boxplots, as well as measures of location, dispersion, and shape used as summary statistics. Section 2.3 explains some useful elements for describing bivariate data, such as two-way contingency tables, side-by-side barplots, stacked barplots, conditional histograms, data correlation coefficient, and data covariance. Section 2.4 covers exploratory data analysis methods for multivariate data, namely, panel displays, Chernoff faces, parallel coordinate plots, principal component analysis and t-SNE. Section 2.5 discusses the three types of missingness mechanisms (missing completely at random, missing not at random, and missing at random), as well as single and multiple imputation methods. Section 2.6 presents three useful variable transformation schemes, which are standardization, transformations toward Gaussianity, and discretization. The chapter closes with Section 2.7, which contains the bibliographic notes.

2.1 Data Types

Assume that we start working with a data set of N observations and n variables, denoted $X_1, \ldots, X_n$, gathering characteristics or features from the observations. Let $\mathcal{D} = \{\mathbf{x}^1, \ldots, \mathbf{x}^N\}$ denote the data set, where $\mathbf{x}^i = (x_1^i, \ldots, x_n^i)$, $i = 1, \ldots, N$. Think of $\mathcal{D}$ as a matrix, table, or spreadsheet of dimension $N \times n$, where the observations are arranged in N rows and the variables in n columns.

Exploratory data analysis (Tukey, 1977) is the first step in analyzing data sets. It gives an overview of the data, summarizing their main characteristics in an easy-to-understand way, often with visual graphs and simple measures, without using a statistical model. This analysis leads to the formulation of hypotheses, e.g., whether two variables are independent of each other or whether a variable has a higher mean than another variable.

There are three basic data types: categorical, discrete numeric, and continuous numeric. **Categorical data** record categories. **Discrete data** are numeric quantities usually reported as integers because they can take only a finite or countably infinite number of values. Finally, **continuous data** can take a continuously infinite range of values, typically an interval of $\mathbb{R}$.

In Data Set 1 (see Chapter 1), the Class variable encoding two labels, pyramidal neuron P and interneuron I, represents categorical data. The total number of axon nodes (X_7) and the number of dendrites (X_{36}) are discrete. Somatic compactness (X_4) and relative distance to the pia (X_{65}) are continuous (see Tables 1.5–1.6 for the full list of variables).

Numeric data are also called **linear data**, in contrast to directional data. Directional data deal with directions (unit vectors in $\mathbb{R}^n$), axes (lines through the origin in $\mathbb{R}^n$), or rotations in $\mathbb{R}^n$. Other data can be regarded as directional, such as temporal periods (e.g., time of day, week, month, year), compass directions, dihedral angles in molecules, and orientation. In Data Set 1, some variables include the angular information of axonal and dendritic branches. For example, to obtain the Axonal local angle ave (X_{15}), the (local) angles formed by lines passing through points adjacent to all axonal nodes are first computed and then averaged.

The methods for viewing and summarizing data depend on their type. We will start with univariate data (both linear and directional), which describe or measure a single variable, and then we will move on to bivariate and multivariate data with two and more than two variables, respectively.

2.2   Univariate Data

2.2.1   Pie Chart, Barplot, and Histogram

A **pie chart** is a popular graph for visualizing categorical or discrete data. A circle is divided into sectors, each one representing a category. The arc length of these sectors (and, consequently, their central angle and area) is proportional to the frequency with which the category has been observed in the data. The name of this chart comes from its resemblance to a pie that has been sliced.

Pie charts have been criticized because the human eye is a poor judge of relative areas. A **barplot** (also called a bar chart or a bar graph), represented by a set of rectangular bars with heights proportional to the frequency of each category, is preferable. The bars can be plotted vertically or horizontally. The human eye is a good judge of linear measures.

Figure 2.1 shows the distribution of interneurons (60.86%) and pyramidal neurons (39.14%) in Data Set 1 plotted using the two charts above.

The above charts are also useful for plotting discrete data without too many values. The most representative plot for continuous data is the **histogram**, a close relative of the barplot. A histogram represents the distribution of data as adjacent rectangles over a set of intervals (bins), with an area proportional to the absolute frequency of the data in the interval. Thus, the height of a rectangle is proportional to the absolute frequency divided by the width of the interval, and the total area of the histogram is proportional to N, the number of observations. When all the intervals are of equal width, as is usually the case, the height of a rectangle is also proportional to the frequency of the data in the interval. Density histograms display rectangular areas equal to relative frequencies. Thus, rectangle heights are relative frequencies divided by the width of the interval, with the total area of the histogram equaling 1. The only difference between the two histogram types is the scale on the y-axis. Obviously, how the data are binned is an important issue that influences the outcome.

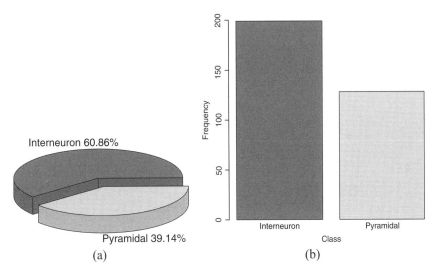

Figure 2.1 Plots for the categorical variable Class of Data Set 1. (a) Pie chart. (b) Barplot.

Example. The histograms of four variables from Data Set 1 are shown in Figure 2.2. We have also plotted the data points below each histogram, with tick marks added just above the *x*-axis. A little jitter has been introduced into the values of the discrete variable X_{56} to eliminate ties. A discrete variable taking many values, as X_{56}, can be treated as continuous. Note that all intervals are of equal width, and rectangle heights represent absolute frequencies of the data.

Note how the profiles differ. First, Somatic compactness has an asymmetric profile, with a long left tail (Figure 2.2(a)). This variable is defined as $\sqrt{(4/\pi)}\text{Area}/(\max$ diameter). Values closer to 1 represent a more compact soma. Second, there is a decay to the right in Axonal Sholl length at 100 μm (expressed as a fraction) (Figure 2.2(b)). Many neurons fall in the first interval, having a low portion of their axonal arbor in the sphere of radius 100 μm centered at the soma. A few neurons, located at the rightmost side of the histogram, have more branched axons in this first Sholl because their X_{26} values are close to 1. Third, the Number of dendritic Sholl sections appears to have 2 outstanding points, around 5 and 11 sections (Figure 2.2(c)). This variable is discrete and counts the number of Sholl sections containing dendritic processes. The sections are built as concentric spheres centered at the soma at intervals of 50 μ. Finally, the Relative distance to pia also exhibits a bimodal behavior – two maxima – (Figure 2.2(d)). These cells usually appear at a relative distance to the pia of either 0.25 or 0.55, but their profile is quite symmetric.   ■

2.2.2   Summary Statistics

Some of the above plots are useful for visualizing the frequency distribution, its shape, the most frequent value, and how other values spread away from it. These visual derivations can be more exactly quantified through summary statistics. These descriptive measures aim to summarize a data sample and should not be confused with the use of data to learn about the population that the sample of data represents. The latter are **inferential statistics**, whereas the former are **descriptive statistics**.

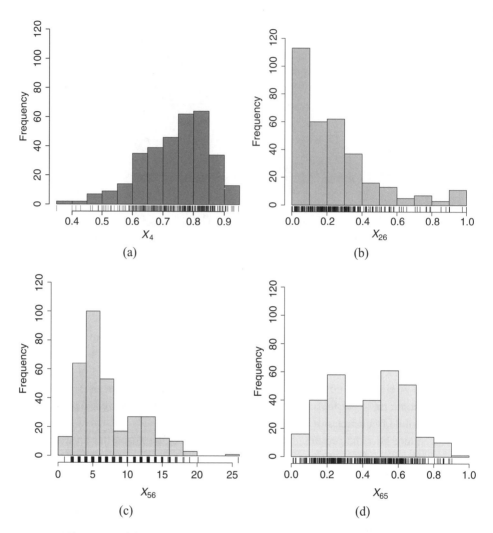

Figure 2.2 Histograms of four variables from Data Set 1. Data points are also plotted as tick marks just above the x-axis. (a) Somatic compactness (X_4). (b) Axonal Sholl length at 100 μm (X_{26}). (c) Number of dendritic Sholl sections (X_{56}). (d) Relative distance to pia (X_{65}).

Summary statistics can be grouped into the following:

- measures of location or central tendency, such as mean, median, and mode,
- measures of dispersion, such as standard deviation (or variance) and interquartile range, and
- measures of the shape of the distribution, such as skewness and kurtosis.

Location. Measures of location or central tendency indicate where the frequency distribution locates over $\mathbb{R}$ (for numeric data). We choose a central value as a summary of the data sample. This value will be between the minimum and the maximum value, around which the other data will be distributed.

Let X denote a generic variable of which we have a data sample $\{x_1, \ldots, x_N\}$ of size N. The main measure of location is the (arithmetic) **mean** $\bar{x}$ of the data, given by

$$\bar{x} = \frac{1}{N} \sum_{i=1}^{N} x_i.$$

As $\sum_{i=1}^{N}(x_i - \bar{x}) = 0$, the numbers that are lower than the mean are balanced by the numbers that are greater than the mean, which is the intuitive idea behind this measure, as a center of gravity. Furthermore, the mean is the minimum of function $h(a) = \sum_{i=1}^{N}(x_i - a)^2$, i.e., the mean is the locus of minimal sum-of-squared deviations. However, the mean is not a robust statistic, i.e., it is significantly influenced by outliers (abnormally extreme values) and is therefore not fully representative of the data when such outliers are present.

There are other means. The **geometric mean**, computed as $\bar{x}_G = \sqrt[N]{x_1 x_2 \cdots x_N}$, only applies to data of the same sign and is often used for values meant to be multiplied or which are exponential in nature. Tandrup (2004) computed the geometric mean of the volume of L5 dorsal root ganglion cells from rats.

The **harmonic mean** is the reciprocal of the arithmetic mean of the reciprocals of the data, i.e., $\bar{x}_H = \left(\sum_{i=1}^{N} \frac{x_i^{-1}}{N} \right)^{-1}$. It is appropriate for situations when the average of rates or ratios is sought. This mean cannot be made arbitrarily large by changing some data values into larger ones. For positive data containing at least two nonequal values, $\bar{x}_H \le \bar{x}_G \le \bar{x}$.

Unlike the mean, the median does not have the deficiency of being highly influenced by outliers. The **data median**, Me, is defined as the numerical value separating the top from the bottom half of the data sample, arranged in ascending order of values. Whereas the middle point is clear for an odd N, there is no single middle value for an even N, and the median is then usually defined as the mean of the two middle values. Note that the median, unlike the mean, considers the sample order rather than the value of each data point, and it is a better measure than the mean if the data contain many observations and extreme values. The median is an appropriate measure for ordinal variables. It is always advisable to compute both measures, the mean and the median. Both will differ in asymmetric distributions (see below under the measures of shape), suggesting data heterogeneity. Furthermore, the median is the minimum of function $h(a) = \sum_{i=1}^{N}|x_i - a|$, i.e., the median is the locus of minimal sum-of-absolute deviations.

The **data mode**, Mo, is the most frequent value in the data sample. It is not necessarily unique. Multiple modes appear as distinct peaks (local maxima) in the frequency distribution. Each peak is a mode of a portion of the distribution. The mode is the most representative measure for categorical data because we can neither order nor mathematically operate on these data. The mode is used especially when the values of the sample exhibit a high concentration around a certain value and when N is high. Otherwise, the mode is of limited use as a central tendency measure.

Dispersion. A location measure does not provide any idea about data dispersion. For instance, a sample of size 4 given by {0, 25, 75, 100} has $\bar{x} = Me = 50$, the same as the data {48, 49, 50, 51}, but the first data have much sparser observations than the second one. Spread measures complement location measures, computing their representativeness by measuring how far each point is from the respective measure. If all points are close to the location measure, this will be a good representative of the data points. If points are very far apart from the location measure, i.e., from what should be their synthesis, there is variability, and the location measure is less representative.

The most important dispersion measure of a data sample is the **data standard deviation**, s, which shows how much variation or dispersion there is from the mean $\bar{x}$. s is defined as

$$s = \sqrt{\frac{1}{N-1}\sum_{i=1}^{N}(x_i - \bar{x})^2},$$

which is always a nonnegative number. Low values indicate that the data points tend to be very close to the mean, whereas high values signify that points spread out over a large range of values. Deviations of each value x_i to the mean $\bar{x}$, $x_i - \bar{x}$, are squared to make them positive (remember that $\sum_{i=1}^{N}(x_i - \bar{x}) = 0$). The square of s is the **data variance**, s^2. This is measured in units that are the square of the units of the variable itself. For example, a variable measured in μm will have a variance measured in μm^2. This is why the use of s is usually preferred to s^2. Both s and s^2 are influenced by extreme values.

To reduce this influence, the absolute value is used instead of the square, as in the **mean absolute deviation** about the mean (mad), defined as

$$\text{mad} = \frac{1}{N}\sum_{i=1}^{N}|x_i - \bar{x}|.$$

As the median is more robust, the **median absolute deviation** about the median (MAD) is defined as the median of the absolute deviations from the data median, i.e., the median of the values $|x_i - Me|, i = 1, \ldots, N$.

To eliminate the dependency of the s measurement units, a relative dimensionless measure is the **coefficient of variation** (CV), the ratio of the standard deviation to the mean, often multiplied by 100 and only defined if $\bar{x} \neq 0$:

$$\text{CV} = \frac{s}{\bar{x}}100.$$

$s/\bar{x}$ is the inverse of the signal-to-noise ratio. The higher the CV is, the greater the dispersion in the variable is. Thanks to their unitless measurement scale, CVs can be compared with one another in a meaningful way to determine which variable has greater dispersion, even if the means are drastically different from one another, or the variables are measured in different units. Variables with a smaller CV are less dispersed than variables with a larger CV. CV is a reasonable measure if the variable contains only positive values.

The **data quartiles** are the three points that divide a sample arranged in increasing order into four groups, each containing a quarter of the points. Thus, the first or lower quartile, denoted Q_1, has the lowest 25% of data to its left and the highest 75% to its right, whereas for the third or upper quartile, denoted Q_3, the percentages are 75% to its left and 25% to its right. The second quartile is the median Me, with 50% – 50% on both sides. A sample with 10 divisions has 9 **data deciles**, whereas 100 divisions produce 99 **data percentiles**. Thus, the median is the 2nd quartile, 5th decile, and 50th percentile. In general, a **data quantile** of order $k \in (0,1)$ accumulates a proportion k of the data to its left and $1-k$ to its right. Quantiles are measures of location but not of centrality, as they account for the tendency of data to be grouped around some point, leaving a certain proportion of the data to their left and the rest to their right. They are also used to build some spread measures, as follows.

The difference between the upper and lower quartiles is called the **interquartile range**, IQR= $Q_3 - Q_1$, which is another measure of dispersion, with respect to its mean point, called a **midhinge** $(Q_1 + Q_3)/2$. The midhinge does not necessarily coincide with the median, especially for asymmetric distributions (see below). The **range** is the difference between the maximum and minimum values. If either of these two data sample values is extreme, the range will not be a realistic dispersion measure. IQR is then a better measure and is robust to outliers. It works well for skewed data.

Shape. To characterize the shape of a frequency distribution, we first need to define the rth central moments (or moments about the mean) of a data sample as

$$a_r = \frac{1}{N} \sum_{i=1}^{N} (x_i - \bar{x})^r.$$

A well-known measure of the asymmetry of a frequency distribution is **skewness**. Symmetric means that the distribution looks the same to the left and right of the center point. The most common statistic with respect to the mean point is

$$g_1 = \frac{a_3}{a_2^{3/2}},$$

where a_3 and a_2 are the third and second central moments, respectively. Note that g_1 is dimensionless. A negative value of g_1 indicates that the left tail of the distribution is longer than the right side, and the bulk of the values lie to the right of the mean. The distribution is said to be left skewed, left tailed, or skewed to the left. A positive value means the opposite. A zero value points out rather evenly distributed values on both sides of the mean, typically (but not always) implying a symmetric distribution.

If the distribution is symmetric, then $g_1 = 0$ and $\bar{x} = Me$. If, in addition, the distribution is unimodal, then $\bar{x} = Me = Mo$. The converse is not generally true, i.e., $g_1 = 0$ does not imply that the mean is equal to the median.

Generally speaking, left-skewed distributions have $\bar{x} < Mo$ and $Me < Mo$, and it often holds that $\bar{x} < Me < Mo$. For right-skewed distributions, $\bar{x} > Mo$ and $Me > Mo$, and it often holds that $\bar{x} > Me > Mo$. This rule can fail, e.g., in multimodal distributions (von Hippel, 2005). The median can be used as a measure of location when the distribution is skewed or when less importance is attached to outliers, e.g., because they may be measurement errors.

Another measure for the shape of the distribution is **kurtosis**, indicating whether the data are peaked or flat relative to a normal (Gaussian) distribution (Section 3.3.6). It is applied to bell-shaped (unimodal symmetric or slightly asymmetric) distributions. Kurtosis is given by the dimensionless statistic

$$g_2 = \frac{a_4}{a_2^2} - 3,$$

where a_4 and a_2 are the fourth and second central moments, respectively. Leptokurtic distributions $(g_2 > 0)$ are more peaked than normal, tend to have a distinct peak near the mean, decline rather rapidly, and have heavy tails. Platykurtic distributions $(g_2 < 0)$ are

Table 2.1 Summary statistics of four variables from Data Set 1: Somatic compactness (X_4), Axonal Sholl length at 100 μm (expressed as a fraction) (X_{26}), Number of dendritic Sholl sections (X_{56}), and Relative distance to pia (X_{65})

Measure	X_4	X_{26}	X_{56}	X_{65}
Location				
$\bar{x}$	0.74	0.23	7.57	0.42
Me	0.76	0.18	6	0.44
Mo	0.81	0	6	0.25, 0.57
Dispersion				
s	0.11	0.23	4.19	0.21
mad	0.09	0.17	3.35	0.18
MAD	0.12	0.21	2.96	0.25
CV	14.99	101.50	55.40	48.93
range	0.60	1	25	0.89
IQR	0.16	0.28	5	0.34
Shape				
g_1	−0.69	1.44	1.09	0.02
g_2	0.18	1.96	0.82	−0.93

less peaked (squashed normal) than normal. Mesokurtic distributions ($g_2 = 0$) have similar, or identical, kurtosis to a normal distribution. Their peak is neither high nor low, and it is considered a baseline for the two other categories.

Example. Table 2.1 shows all the measures described above for the four variables X_4, X_{26}, X_{56}, and X_{65} from Data Set 1, whose histograms were shown in Figure 2.2.

Somatic compactness (X_4) is left skewed ($g_1 < 0$), with $\bar{x} < Me < Mo$. Its s is almost 15% of its mean value (see the CV value), showing a rather homogeneous distribution. Its mad, MAD, and IQR measures are also small, showing a low spread. The Axonal Sholl length at 100 μm (expressed as a fraction) (X_{26}), however, has a very heterogeneous highly right-skewed and leptokurtic distribution, with CV = 101.5. The fact that both the median and the mode of X_{56} is 6 means that 6 dendritic Sholl sections are the middle value of the distribution and are also the most frequent value. Six sections are the global mode, and 13 sections could be considered the local mode corresponding to the right portion of the distribution (see the histogram in Figure 2.2(c)). X_{26} and X_{56} are right skewed ($g_1 > 0$), with $\bar{x} > Me \geq Mo$. Finally, the relative distance to the pia (X_{65}) is bimodal, with modes at 0.25 and 0.57. Its mean is almost equal to its median (slightly lower), showing that half the cells are at a relative distance to the pia of 0.44, with a rather symmetric profile ($g_1 = 0.02$). Because it is not bell shaped, g_2 should not be used. Multimodal distributions suggest that the data come from several populations. We could envisage two subgroups for X_{65} and report their mean and median. ∎

The final remark on summary statistics is that the most appropriate measure depends on the shape of the data distribution. The mean and mean-based measures (e.g., s, mad, MAD, CV) are highly affected by outliers and behave better for symmetric data. For skewed data and/or serious outliers, the median and median-based measures (e.g., IQR) are used. For categorical data, the mode is the most representative measure.

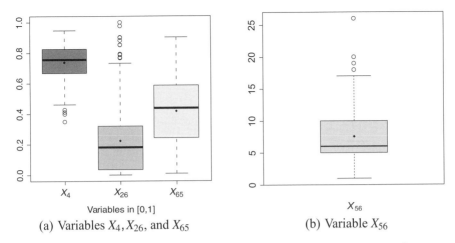

(a) Variables X_4, X_{26}, and X_{65} (b) Variable X_{56}

Figure 2.3 Boxplots of four variables from Data Set 1. (a) Somatic compactness (X_4), Axonal Sholl length at 100 µm (X_{26}), and Relative distance to pia (X_{65}). (b) Number of dendritic Sholl sections (X_{56}). The fillings for each variable are the same as those in Figure 2.2.

2.2.3 More Plots: Boxplot

A very useful graph is the box-and-whisker plot or the **boxplot** for short. It immediately shows whether the data are symmetric or have outliers. The spread is shown via the IQR, as a box is drawn with lines at Q_1 and Q_3. Another line is marked inside the box at the median. A whisker is drawn from Q_1 to the smallest data value greater than the lower fence, which is defined as $Q_1 - 1.5\,\text{IQR}$. Similarly, another whisker is drawn from Q_3 to the largest data value lower than the upper fence, defined as $Q_3 + 1.5\,\text{IQR}$. Any points beyond the whiskers are depicted by points and are, by convention, considered **outliers**. They may sometimes be marked differently if they are more than three box lengths away.

Example. Figure 2.3 shows the boxplots for the same variables from Data Set 1 as in Figure 2.2 for histograms. Variables X_4, X_{26}, and X_{65} are represented together in (a) because they have a common [0,1] domain, whereas X_{56} is shown in (b), taking discrete values in $\{1,\ldots,19,20,26\}$. The mean has been included inside the box as a black point to indicate its relative position with respect to the median. Note that asymmetry is apparent in X_4, X_{26}, and X_{56} because the shape looks unbalanced, whereas X_{65} is symmetric. Furthermore, the asymmetric distributions have outliers (points beyond the whiskers). The reader can identify information from Table 2.1 used in these plots, such as Me and IQR. Note that boxplots do not capture kurtosis. ∎

2.2.4 Directional Data: Plots and Summary Statistics

Directional information comes usually as **angular data** or **circular data**, measured in radians or compass degrees. A circular or angular variable Φ is defined in the unit circumference, i.e., its domain is $[-\pi, \pi)$ or $[0, 2\pi)$. If data come as a directional vector in an n-dimensional Euclidean space, this is a more general term referred to as **directional data**. Usually, the space is the $(n-1)$-dimensional unit sphere centered at the

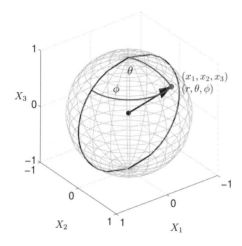

Figure 2.4 Equivalence between Cartesian (x_1, x_2, x_3) and polar (r, θ, ϕ) coordinates in the sphere.

origin: $\mathbb{S}^{n-1} = \{\mathbf{x} \in \mathbb{R}^n \mid \mathbf{x}^T \mathbf{x} = 1\}$. When $n = 2$, $\mathbb{S}^1$ is the unit circumference. When $n = 3$, we have the surface of the Euclidean solid known colloquially as a sphere. Note that a transformation from the Cartesian coordinates of a data point in the sphere to its **spherical polar coordinates** provides a way of moving equivalently between both representations (Figure 2.4). That is, for a unit vector $\mathbf{x} = (x_1, x_2, x_3)$ in sphere $\mathbb{S}^2$, we have the spherical polar coordinates (r, θ, ϕ):

$$r = \sqrt{x_1^2 + x_2^2 + x_3^2} = 1,$$

$$\theta = \cos^{-1}\left(\frac{x_3}{r}\right),$$

$$\phi = \tan^{-1}\left(\frac{x_2}{x_1}\right),$$

θ is the **polar angle** (also known as the **zenith angle** and **colatitude**) from the positive X_3-axis, with $0 \le \theta < \pi$, ϕ is the **azimuthal angle** in the $X_1 X_2$-plane from the X_1-axis, with $0 \le \phi < 2\pi$, and r is the distance (radius) from the point to the origin.

Conversely, from the spherical polar coordinates (r, θ, ϕ) we obtain the following Cartesian coordinates (x_1, x_2, x_3):

$$x_1 = r \sin \theta \cos \phi,$$

$$x_2 = r \sin \theta \sin \phi,$$

$$x_3 = r \cos \theta,$$

with $r = 1$.

Directional and angular data have some distinctive properties that make classical (linear) statistics unsuitable for analyzing and working with this kind of data. Directional statistics (Mardia and Jupp, 2000; Jammalamadaka and SenGupta, 2001) provides the theoretical background and tools necessary for correctly managing these data. The main property of a circular domain is its periodic behavior, e.g., the values 0 and 2π refer to the same point in the circle. Furthermore, the representation of directions by angles depends on the choice of initial direction and orientation. Thus, two researchers observing the same data but making different choices on where the circle is cut should arrive at the same inferences, and this requirement of coordinate-independent inference is important.

Circular Histogram and Rose Diagram. Special visualization tools are required to convey directional information. As with histograms on the real line, **circular histograms** represent grouped circular data. Each bar is centered at the midpoint of the corresponding group of angles, and its area is proportional to the frequency in that group. The usual convention is to measure angles anticlockwise and take the x-axis as the zero direction.

The **rose diagram** is a useful variant of the circular histogram, where each bar is replaced by a circular sector. Thus, the circle is divided into equal-width sectors (same arc length or central angle for all) with a radius proportional to the square root of the number of data in the bin. This ensures that the area of each sector is proportional to the frequency of data represented by the sector. The grouping used influences the visual impression given by the circular histogram or rose diagram.

Example: Branching Angles of Basal Dendrites in Pyramidal Cells (Rose Diagram and Circular Histogram). Complete basal dendritic arbors from a set of 288 3D pyramidal neurons from layers II, III, IV, Va, Vb, and VI of the P14 rat hind limb somatosensory (S1HL) neocortex are used here (Leguey et al., 2016). There were a total of 48 cells per layer: 6 cells per layer and 8 animals. The angles between two sibling segments originating from a bifurcation of the basal dendritic trees were measured. Angles were then grouped according to the order in which the bifurcation occurred: starting at the soma, bifurcations were progressively numbered 1, 2, ... and the corresponding angles were called order 1, order 2, ... angles. The maximum order was seven in this data set.

Figure 2.5 shows the rose diagram and the circular histogram of branching angles of order 1 in layer II ($N = 242$).[1] The circular histogram borders the circumference and seems more scattered than the rose diagram. Note that in the rose diagram, the frequency distribution appears to be unimodal and symmetric. ∎

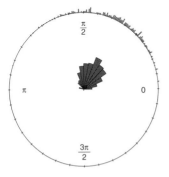

Figure 2.5 Rose diagram (inside the circumference) and circular histogram (outside) showing the distribution of branching angles (in radians) of order 1 (first bifurcation from the soma) found in dendritic arbors of layer II.

---

[1] All computations and plots in this section of directional data were obtained with the CircStats and circular R packages, as well as with an own implementation of the circular boxplot.

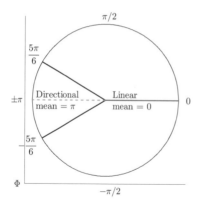

Figure 2.6 Classical linear mean (solid) and directional mean (dashed) of angles $5\pi/6$ and $-5\pi/6$.

Summary Statistics. Some summary statistics need to be redefined for circular data. For instance, the mean of angles $5\pi/6$ and $-5\pi/6$ is π and not 0, as the classical linear mean would yield, pointing in exactly the opposite direction, see Figure 2.6.

Given a set of N angular values $\{\phi_1, \ldots, \phi_N\}$ defined in the unit circle, $\phi_i \in [-\pi, \pi)$, $i = 1, \ldots, N$, and having vectors of Cartesian coordinates $\mathbf{x}_i = (\cos\phi_i, \sin\phi_i)$, the **mean angle** $\bar{\phi} \in [-\pi, \pi)$ is defined as the angle given by the center of mass $(\bar{C}, \bar{S})$:

$$\bar{\phi} = \arctan\frac{\bar{S}}{\bar{C}},$$

where

$$\bar{C} = \frac{1}{N}\sum_{i=1}^{N}\cos\phi_i,$$

$$\bar{S} = \frac{1}{N}\sum_{i=1}^{N}\sin\phi_i.$$

Therefore, $\bar{\phi}$ is the solution of the equations $\bar{C} = \bar{R}\cos\bar{\phi}$ and $\bar{S} = \bar{R}\sin\bar{\phi}$, where the **mean resultant length** $\bar{R}$ is the length of the center of the mass vector, i.e.,

$$\bar{R} = \sqrt{\bar{C}^2 + \bar{S}^2}. \tag{2.1}$$

$\bar{R}$ is defined in the interval $[0, 1]$ and can be used as a **concentration measure** of a data sample. Values of $\bar{R}$ close to one show tightly clustered values, whereas values close to zero show widely dispersed values. For a perfectly uniformly distributed variable, the center of mass is not defined: $(\bar{C}, \bar{S}) = (0, 0)$, so $\bar{R} = 0$ and $\bar{\phi}$ is not defined.

Under rotation, the mean angle is equivariant. That is, if a new initial direction is chosen, making angle α with the original initial direction, the data points in the new coordinate system are the angles $\phi_i' = \phi_i - \alpha, i = 1, \ldots, N$. Then, $\bar{\phi}' = \bar{\phi} - \alpha$ and $\bar{R}' = \bar{R}$. This equivariance is analogous to the equivariance under translation of the mean on the line: the mean of $x_1 - a, \ldots, x_N - a$ is $\bar{x} - a$. The importance of this property is that researchers using different coordinate systems will agree on where the mean is, although they use different numbers to describe its position.

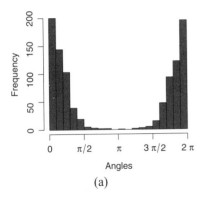
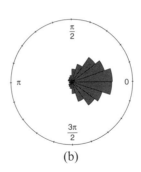

(a)   (b)

Figure 2.7 (a) Linear histogram of a sample of angles with a mean angle at $\bar{\phi} = 0$. (b) Rose diagram of the same sample.

Example. Figure 2.7 shows a classical histogram in (a) and a rose diagram in (b) of a sample of angles defined in $[0, 2\pi)$ with the mean angle at $\bar{\phi} = 0$. The classical histogram ignores the periodical nature of the domain and shows a U-shaped distribution with two modes. However, the rose diagram clearly portrays that the data set has only one mode. ∎

Given a data sample of n-dimensional unit vectors $\{\mathbf{x}^1, \ldots, \mathbf{x}^N\}$, $\mathbf{x}^i = \left(x_1^i, \ldots, x_n^i\right)$, $i = 1, \ldots, N$, defining points in the hypersphere $\mathbb{S}^{n-1}$, the **mean direction vector** $\bar{\mathbf{x}} \in \mathbb{S}^{n-1}$ is defined as

$$\bar{\mathbf{x}} = \frac{\sum_{i=1}^{N} \mathbf{x}^i}{\left\| \sum_{i=1}^{N} \mathbf{x}^i \right\|},$$

where $\|\cdot\|$ denotes its norm. The equation sums all the unit vectors and then normalizes the result so that $\|\bar{\mathbf{x}}\| = 1$. The mean direction is invariant under rotation. Similar to Equation (2.1), the mean resultant length $\bar{R}$ is the length of the mean vector computed over the set of unit vectors:

$$\bar{R} = \frac{\left\| \sum_{i=1}^{N} \mathbf{x}^i \right\|}{N}.$$

$\bar{R} \in [0, 1]$ is a bounded measure of the concentration of the sample of unit vectors. As before, an $\bar{R}$ close to one (zero) indicates tightly clustered (widely dispersed) values. When these vectors are uniformly distributed around the sphere, $\bar{R}$ becomes zero, and the mean direction $\bar{\mathbf{x}}$ is not defined. $\bar{R}$ is more important than any measure of dispersion. For purposes of comparison with linear data, sometimes, considering measures of dispersion is useful, and the simplest is **circular variance** defined as $1 - \bar{R}$ and lying in $[0, 1]$.

The **median direction** of circular data also requires special attention, as there is no natural ordering of circular observations, e.g., the concept of a first angle is not well defined when we have several angles. Fisher (1993) defined the median direction of circular data as the observation Me^c, which minimizes the sum of circular distances (length of the shorter arc joining a pair of observations, whether clockwise or anticlockwise) to each data.

To define the lower and upper **circular quartiles**, Q_1^c and Q_3^c, we divide the sample observations into two groups based on their locations with respect to the median direction.

Then, Q_1^c is the median of the first group, and Q_3^c is the median of the second. If the value of Q_1^c is larger than that of Q_3^c, their labels are simply interchanged. The **circular interquartile range** (CIQR) is analogous to the real line case: CIQR=$Q_3^c - Q_1^c$.

Circular Boxplot. A **circular boxplot** (Abuzaid et al., 2012) is the circular version of the boxplot. The same summary statistics, median, Q_3^c, Q_1^c, and CIQR, are shown but now as arcs inside a circle. Thus, thick lines (the box) extend from Q_1^c to Q_3^c of the data sample representing the CIQR. The median direction is shown with a marked black dot. Thin black lines (the whiskers) have a length dependent on the CIQR and the resistant constant v, which, in turn, depends on a concentration measure κ (a more general measure, in fact, a function of $\bar{R}$; see Section 4.1.2.2) of the sample. The lower fence is $Q_1^c - v \cdot$ CIQR, whereas the upper fence is $Q_3^c + v \cdot$ CIQR, where $v = 1.5$ if $2 \le \kappa \le 3$ and $v = 2.5$ if $\kappa > 3$.

In the linear boxplot, $v = 1.5$ always. However, this is not sensible here because of the bounded range of the circle, likely resulting in the overlapping of lower and upper fences for large values of v and small values of κ. For $\kappa < 2$, overlapping will be very likely, as the data are close to being uniform. Small dots outside the whiskers are considered outliers. Circular boxplots of different variables can be displayed in the same graph by plotting the corresponding arcs at different distances from the circle's center.

Example: Branching Angles of Basal Dendrites in Pyramidal Cells (Circular Boxplot). Figure 2.8 shows several circular boxplots. In (a), we compare branching angles of order 2 across the different layers, from the outermost (layer II) to the innermost (layer VI). The angle frequencies at each layer were 358 angles in layer II, 396 in layer III, 259 in layer IV, 366 in layer Va, 328 in layer Vb, and 365 in layer VI (a total of 2,072 angles). Apparently, the closer to the pia the layer is, the less concentrated the angular distribution is, although this effect is not very pronounced (no significant differences were found by Leguey et al. [2016], who have almost similar data).

In (b), we compare the angles of layer II across the different branch orders, from 1 (outermost) to 7 (innermost). The angle frequencies were 242 angles of order 1, 358 of

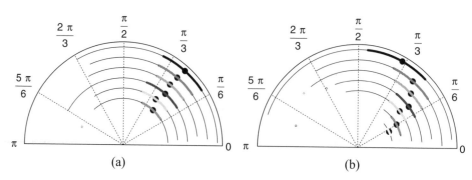

(a)   (b)

Figure 2.8 (a) Circular boxplots of angles of branch order 2 across the different layers (the outermost arc is layer II and the innermost arc is layer VI). (b) Circular boxplots of angles of layer II across the different branch orders (the outermost arc is order 1 and the innermost arc is order 7). The branching angles in basal dendrites do not take values wider than π. Therefore, the circular boxplots are displayed over a semicircle instead of a full circle.

order 2, 329 of order 3, 195 of order 4, 74 of order 5, 18 of order 6, and 2 of order 7 (a total of 1,218 angles). Note that the angles tend to have smaller values as the branching order increases. The widest CIQR is at order 1, and subsequent orders become narrowed. In fact, statistically significant differences were found in Leguey et al. (2016) for the angles of the first orders (orders 1 and 2). This suggests that the first orders determine to a large extent the space that the growing dendritic tree will fill. ∎

2.3 Bivariate Data

In this section, we focus on summarizing and plotting the relationships between two generic variables (bivariate data), X_1 and X_2. Thus, we only look at two variables from our data set $\mathcal{D}$ from which we have the subset $\{(x_{11}, x_{12}), \dots, (x_{N1}, x_{N2})\}$ of size N.

When both variables are categorical or discrete, a **two-way contingency table** will present the frequencies of each observed value (x_1, x_2). This information can be plotted in a **side-by-side barplot** or **grouped barplot**, where the bars of a variable of interest are grouped by a second variable, or in a **stacked barplot**, where the bars are divided into subparts to show the cumulative effect of the second variable.

Example. In Data Set 1, seeing how the Number of dendritic Sholl sections (X_{56}) varies for the different categories of neurons, i.e., according to the variable Class, would be interesting. Table 2.2 lists the number of interneurons (I) and pyramidal cells (P) for each possible number of dendritic Sholl sections. For example, there are 17 interneurons and 4 pyramidal neurons with 3 dendritic Sholl sections. Note that there are no interneurons with more than 15 dendritic Sholl sections.

This information is plotted in a side-by-side barplot in Figure 2.9. Within each number of dendritic Sholl sections, comparisons are shown side by side based on the neuron class. Observe that the distribution obtained for interneurons (in dark gray) and pyramidal cells (in light gray) differs; interneurons have fewer dendritic Sholl sections than pyramidal neurons (their distribution is further to the left). Interneurons exhibit a right-skewed distribution, whereas pyramidal cells show bimodality. ∎

When a variable is categorical or discrete and the other variable is continuous, histograms and boxplots of the continuous variable can be plotted for each subset given by a value of the other (categorical or discrete) variable.

Table 2.2 Two-way contingency table of the Number of dendritic Sholl sections (X_{56}) and the neuron class variable (Class) from Data Set 1. I and P denote interneuron and pyramidal neurons, respectively

Class	X_{56}																				
	1	2	3	4	5	6	7	8	9	10	11	12	13	14	15	16	17	18	19	20	26
I	1	11	17	38	39	39	26	12	5	3	2	1	4	0	1	0	0	0	0	0	0
P	0	1	4	5	10	12	10	5	5	4	11	13	12	11	6	5	7	3	2	1	1

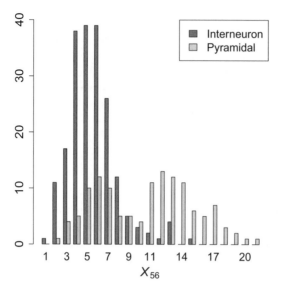

Figure 2.9 Side-by-side barplot for two variables from Data Set 1. The neuron class (Class) is grouped within the Number of dendritic Sholl sections (X_{56}).

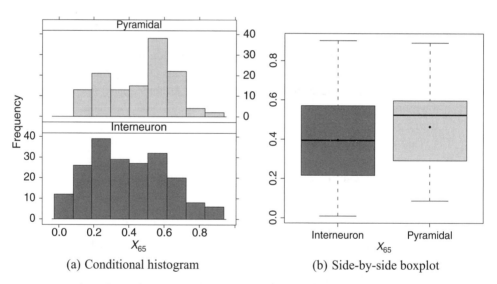

(a) Conditional histogram   (b) Side-by-side boxplot

Figure 2.10 Plots of a continuous variable given each category of a categorical variable. (a) Conditional histogram of Relative distance to pia (X_{65}) from Data Set 1 given the neuron class (Class); pyramidal cells (top) and interneurons (bottom). (b) Side-by-side boxplot for X_{65}, given Class; interneurons (left) and pyramidal cells (right).

Example. Figure 2.10 represents the Relative distance to pia (X_{65}) by conditioning on the neuron class (Class). Figure 2.10(a) shows a **conditional histogram**, which is again bimodal for pyramidal neurons (such as the whole histogram of X_{65} in Figure 2.2(d)) and is right skewed for interneurons. Small relative distances to the pia are more frequent for interneurons than for pyramidal cells. Another view is shown in the side-by-side boxplots illustrated in Figure 2.10(b). ∎

Finally, when both variables are continuous, a **scatterplot** gives an initial idea of their relationship. A scatterplot represents the Cartesian coordinates of points (x_1, x_2) on the plane.

An important measure of the strength and direction of the linear relationship between two continuous variables, X_1 and X_2, is the **data correlation coefficient** or the Pearson (product-moment) correlation coefficient, r_{12}, defined as the **data covariance** s_{12} of the two variables divided by the product of their data standard deviations:

$$r_{12} = \frac{s_{12}}{s_1 s_2} = \frac{\frac{1}{N}\sum_{i=1}^{N}(x_{i1} - \bar{x}_1)(x_{i2} - \bar{x}_2)}{s_1 s_2},$$

where $\bar{x}_i, s_i, i = 1, 2$, are the data mean and data standard deviation of the X_i data, respectively.

The numerator covariance involves a product moment, i.e., the mean of the product of the mean-adjusted data, hence the modifier product moment in the name. The value of r_{12} is always between -1 and 1. When r_{12} is close to 1, the data points lie close to a line with a positive slope, i.e., there is a strong positive linear relationship. Here, when one variable increases, so does the other one. A value close to -1 indicates points lying close to a line with a negative slope, i.e., a strong negative linear relationship. A variable decreases as the other increases. Finding that linear equation is a matter of linear regression via a best-fit procedure. Values of r_{12} close to zero indicate a weak linear relationship, i.e., variables are either not related, or they have another kind (nonlinear) of relationship. The correlation coefficient is invariant (up to a sign) to changes in location and scale, i.e., we can transform X_i into $a_i X_i + b_i, a_i, b_i \in \mathbb{R}, i = 1, 2$, without changing the correlation coefficient.

Example. Figure 2.11 shows three scatterplots and their respective correlation coefficients. All variables come from Data Set 1. In (a), Somatic compactness (X_4) and Relative distance to pia (X_{65}) do not appear to be related, as they have a correlation coefficient close to zero. In (b), Somatic compactness (X_4) and Somatic aspect ratio (X_3) exhibit a strong negative linear relationship, with $r = -0.89$. As mentioned above, somatic compactness is computed as $\sqrt{(4/\pi)\text{Area}}/(\text{max diameter})$, whereas the somatic aspect ratio is max diameter divided by min diameter. This explains why one variable decreases

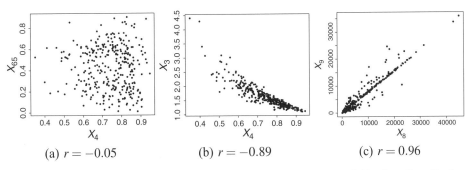

(a) $r = -0.05$ (b) $r = -0.89$ (c) $r = 0.96$

Figure 2.11 Scatterplots and correlation coefficients of some continuous variables from Data Set 1. (a) Somatic compactness (X_4) versus Relative distance to pia (X_{65}). (b) Somatic compactness (X_4) versus Somatic aspect ratio (X_3). (c) Total axonal length (X_8) versus Total surface area of axon (X_9).

as the other increases. In (c), there is a very strong positive linear relationship between Total axonal length (X_8) and Total surface area of axon (X_9). The total axonal length is calculated as the sum of all axon segment lengths, measured along the tracing (not as a straight line distance), and the total surface area of the axon is computed by modeling the axon as a cylinder, with the diameter defined as the thickness of the reconstructed segment. They have, as expected, a positive linear relationship.   ∎

2.4   Multivariate Data

This section generalizes Section 2.3, where we now have n-dimensional points, $\mathbf{x}^i = (x_1^i, \ldots, x_n^i)$, $i = 1, \ldots, N$, coming from $X_1, \ldots, X_n$ in our data set $\mathcal{D}$.

2.4.1   Panel Displays

A panel display arranges 2D graphs of pairs of variables from a multivariate data set in an array. A **scatterplot matrix** displays the scatterplots for all pairs of variables in an array.

Example. To illustrate this point, we will take four variables from Data Set 1. Figure 2.12 shows the scatterplot for all pairs of variables from $\{X_3, X_4, X_{26}, X_{65}\}$, all of which were used above. The two classes, interneurons (dark gray, circle) and pyramidal cells (light gray, triangle), are identified by their shading and symbols.

Observe that both neuron classes are rather intermingled for all pairs of variables. The scatterplot for variables X_4 and X_3 (bottom row, second column) is the same as that in Figure 2.11(b) and is the only pair with a clearly strong linear relationship. The data could, of course, have another structure, not revealed by these bivariate plots.   ∎

The mean n-dimensional vector $\bar{\mathbf{x}} = \frac{1}{N} \sum_{i=1}^{N} \mathbf{x}^i$ is the most important measure of location. An intuitive generalization of the notion of variance to multiple dimensions is the **data covariance matrix** (also called the data variance-covariance matrix), $\mathbf{S}$, whose elements are the covariances of each pair of variables, where the diagonal elements are therefore the variance of each variable. The inverse of this matrix, $\mathbf{S}^{-1}$, is known as the **concentration matrix** or **precision matrix**. Accordingly, the elements of the **correlation matrix R** are pairwise correlations (it has all ones on its diagonal).

3D scatterplots include three variables in 3D space. A categorical variable can be further added by using different colors/symbols for the points.

Example. Figure 2.13 shows a 3D scatterplot, where both neuron classes, interneurons and pyramidal cells (Data Set 1), are identified as different-shaded clouds in the 3D space spanned by variables X_8, X_9, and X_{56}. Some separation between each other is observed.   ∎

When there are many data points and a significant overlap exists, scatterplots become less useful. One solution to avoid overlapping is to produce a **2D** or **flat histogram**, where the density in each bin is represented by an appropriate color/shading rather than the actual points. Hexagonal binning is commonly used. Compare Figure 2.14 with Figure 2.11, both

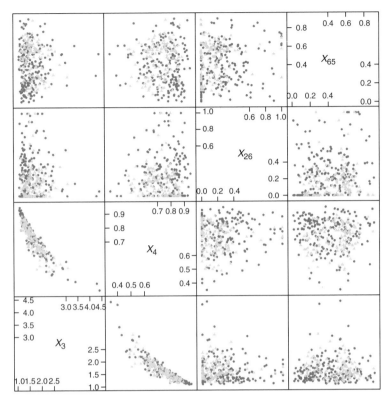

Figure 2.12 Scatterplot matrix comparing four continuous variables of Data Set 1: Somatic aspect ratio (X_3), Somatic compactness (X_4), Axonal Sholl length at 100 μm (expressed as a fraction) (X_{26}), and Relative distance to pia (X_{65}). Point fillings and symbols identify both classes of neurons: interneuron (dark, circle) and pyramidal (light, triangle).

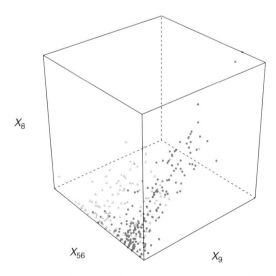

Figure 2.13 3D scatterplot of three variables from Data Set 1: Total axonal length (X_8), Total surface area of axon (X_9), and Number of dendritic Sholl sections (X_{56}). Point fillings and symbols identify both classes of neurons: interneuron (dark, circle) and pyramidal cells (light, triangle).

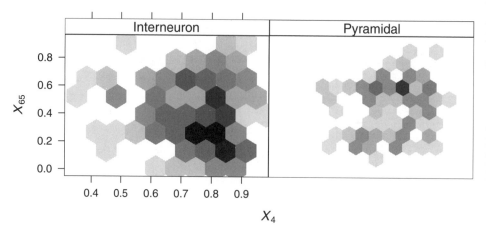

Figure 2.14 Multipanel plot of flat histograms with hexagonal binning for the variables Somatic compactness (X_4) and Relative distance to pia (X_{65}) from Data Set 1. Panels correspond with the interneuron subset (left) and the pyramidal cell subset (right).

in the $X_4 X_{65}$ space. The flat histogram in Figure 2.14 plots densities in hexagonal regions, whereas Figure 2.11 represents only the points. More populated regions are darker in 2D histograms.

Moreover, Figure 2.14 (referred to Data Set 1) is a multipanel plot, with the interneuron subset to the left and the pyramidal neuron subset to the right. Interneurons are seen to have a greater spread than pyramidal cells.

Rather than the use of colors/shading, the data frequencies could alternatively be represented on the z-axis of a 3D representation as the heights of a set of prisms, one for each bin. However, this **3D histogram** can conceal the rear prisms, and perspective is a relevant concern. In this case, the histogram should be viewed using interactive graphical tools so that it can be rotated through all angles.

We can use boxplots to visualize a continuous variable given a discrete and a categorical variable.

Example. The panels of Figure 2.15 show the data distribution of variable X_{26}, the Axonal Sholl length at 100 μm (expressed as a fraction) for each number of dendritic Sholl sections (X_{56}) given by each horizontal boxplot and for each neuron class given in each panel (the left panel for interneurons and the right panel for pyramidal cells).

Figure 2.9 above showed that compared with pyramidal neurons (light), interneurons (dark) had fewer dendritic Sholl sections. This is shown here in Figure 2.15 by the shortage of data at the top of the left panel compared with the right panel, which has data everywhere. We also find that interneurons and pyramidal cells differ considerably in the distribution of the Axonal Sholl length at 100 μm. This is very disperse within ranges 1–8 of the dendritic Sholl sections for interneurons and has a homogeneous spread across all ranges of the dendritic Sholl sections for pyramidal cells.   ■

Conditioning on more variables is also possible, although a moderate number of variables makes drawing conclusions easier.

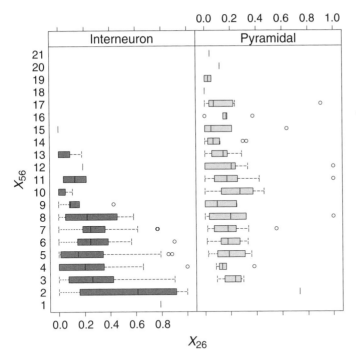

Figure 2.15 Panel display of the boxplots of a continuous variable given a discrete and a categorical variable. The boxplots are for the Axonal Sholl length at 100 μm (expressed as a fraction) (X_{26}), given each value of the Number of dendritic Sholl sections (X_{56}) and interneuron class (left) and given each value of the Number of dendritic Sholl sections (X_{56}) and pyramidal cell (right).

2.4.2   Plots of Multidimensional Observations

One approach to visualize multivariate data is to produce a plot of each observation in the data set.

Chernoff faces (Chernoff, 1973) display a cartoon human face choosing the size and shape of different facial features according to the values of the variables. For instance, the first three variable values can be used to define the face height, width, and shape, respectively. Mouth height and width may respectively represent the fourth and fifth variables, whereas the curve of the smile captures the sixth variable. Other features, such as the eyes, eyebrows, hair, and hat, can be added to cover up to 15–20 variables. Therefore, this kind of plot is useful for data sets with a moderate number of variables and observations. Ideally, more important variables should be mapped to more pre-attentive visual attributes of the face. In fact, some researchers, such as Tsurusawa et al. (2008), have investigated the differences in neural basis of the processing of facial expressions in adults and children in an event-related potential study using Chernoff faces as the visual stimuli. These simple line drawings contain much higher spatial frequency components than photographed faces, providing face shape information. Photographed faces also include components with low spatial frequency, which are important for processing holistic facial features. However, the spatial frequency components in each photograph can be different for the same facial expressions depicting the same emotion by two actors. This is not the case in Chernoff faces, making them a good instrument for evaluating facial expressions.

Other 2D icons or glyphs, such as stars or circle sectors, can be used instead of faces.

Example. For illustrative purposes, we have chosen 18 neurons from Data Set 1. Their Chernoff faces are shown in Figure 2.16. The above four variables, X_4, X_{26}, X_{56}, and X_{65}, are used to build different facial expressions. Note that the faces of neurons 200 to 205 could be grouped separately from the others. In fact, they are pyramidal cells, whereas the other cells are interneurons.   ■

The **parallel coordinate plot** was invented by d'Ocagne (1885) and independently rediscovered later by Inselberg (1985). In this diagram, parallel vertical equidistant lines are drawn, each representing a variable. Then, each coordinate of each observation point, $\mathbf{x}^i = (x_1^i, \ldots, x_n^i), i = 1, \ldots, N$, is plotted along its respective axis, and the points are joined together with line segments. This kind of plot is arrangement sensitive, i.e., the order of the axes is critical for visually discovering patterns within the data, as the plot is based on the linear interpolation of consecutive pairs of variables. The relationships among adjacent variables are easier to detect than the relationships among variables far from one another. Multiple reorderings can then be possible. Furthermore, a nonuniform spacing between two adjacent axes can be used to convey information about variables. Finally, removing some variables from the plot in high-dimensional data sets is crucial to avoid cluttering the plot while preserving the most important information on the data set. All these issues may have a major impact on the expressiveness of the visualization, and heuristics have been proposed in the literature (Yang et al., 2003; Boogaerts et al., 2012).

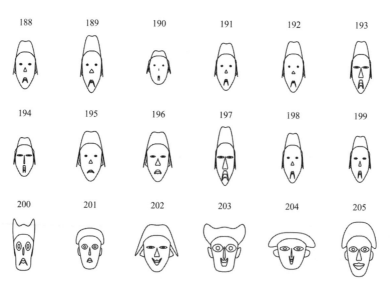

Figure 2.16 Chernoff faces of a subset of neurons in Data Set 1. The numbers match the ID numbers of neuron 188 to neuron 205 in the data file. Facial features have been built using Somatic compactness (X_4), Axonal Sholl length at 100 μm (expressed as a fraction) (X_{26}), Number of dendritic Sholl sections (X_{56}), and Relative distance to pia (X_{65}).

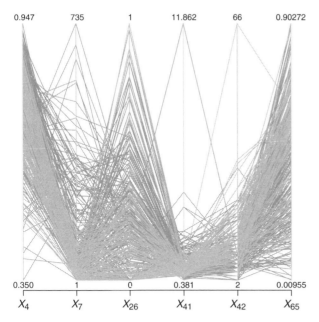

Figure 2.17 Parallel coordinate plot of all neurons from Data Set 1. The variables are Somatic compactness (X_4), Total axonal length (X_7), Axonal Sholl length at 100 μm (expressed as a fraction) (X_{26}), Ratio of dendritic length to surface area (X_{41}), Highest order dendritic segment (X_{42}), and Relative distance to pia (X_{65}). For the color version, please refer to the plate section.

Example. Figure 2.17 represents a parallel coordinate plot of all neurons from Data Set 1, showing only six variables, namely, $X_4, X_7, X_{26}, X_{41}, X_{42}$, and X_{65}. The polylines with vertices on the parallel axes have been drawn in a different color to distinguish interneurons (orange) from pyramidal cells (green). The minimum and maximum values are written over the axes.

Note that we see roughly 2 different profiles for both types of neurons. This is more remarkable for the Axonal Sholl length at 100 μm (X_{26}) and in the Total axonal length (X_7), where most pyramidal cells take lower values than interneurons do. The opposite behavior holds in the Highest order dendritic segment (X_{42}). The distinction is not so clear for the other variables. ∎

DeFelipe et al. (2013) used parallel coordinate plots to identify neurons on which neuroanatomists agreed, where these neurons were categorized according to some morphological features.

2.4.3   Principal Component Analysis

Principal component analysis (PCA) (Jolliffe, 1986) aims to describe the variation in a set of correlated variables in terms of another set of uncorrelated variables, each of which is a linear combination of the original variables. A linear transformation projects the high-dimensional data onto a lower-dimensional space. Thus, PCA is used not only for dimensionality reduction but also for data compression, feature extraction, and data visualization. PCA has other names, including discrete Karhunen–Loève transform.

PCA seeks a sequence of mutually uncorrelated projections of the data ordered by variance. Thus, the set of observations of possibly correlated variables is converted into a set of values of linearly uncorrelated variables called **principal components**. The first principal component is the linear combination of the original variables with the greatest data variance of all possible linear combinations, accounting for as much of the variability in the data as possible. The second principal component is defined as the linear combination of the original variables, accounting for a maximal proportion of the remaining variance subject to it being uncorrelated with the first principal component. Subsequent components are defined similarly. The question is how to find the coefficients specifying the linear combinations of the original variables defining each component.

Mathematically, suppose that again, we have a data set of N observations $\mathcal{D} = \{\mathbf{x}^1, \dots, \mathbf{x}^N\}$, where each one is an n-dimensional (column) vector $\mathbf{x}^i = (x_1^i, \dots, x_n^i)^T$, $i = 1, \dots, N$, corresponding with the values of n variables, $X_1, \dots, X_n$. Note that in this section we are looking at $\mathbf{x}^i$ columnwise for notation convenience. PCA seeks to project the data, $\mathcal{D}$, onto a space with dimensionality $m \leq n$, known as the principal subspace, while maximizing the variance of the projected data. Consider first projecting the data onto a 1D space whose direction is given by an n-dimensional vector $\mathbf{u}_1 = (u_{11}, \dots, u_{1n})^T$. The projection of each point $\mathbf{x}^i$ onto this 1D space is $y_1^i = \mathbf{u}_1^T \mathbf{x}^i$. As we are interested in the direction defined by $\mathbf{u}_1$ and not the magnitude, we decide, for convenience, that $\mathbf{u}_1$ is a unit vector, i.e., $\mathbf{u}_1^T \mathbf{u}_1 = 1$. This condition is used to fix the scale of the new variable $Y_1 = u_{11} X_1 + \cdots + u_{1n} X_n$ and is necessary because limitlessly increasing the Y_1 variance is possible by simply increasing the components $u_{11}, \dots, u_{1n}$ of $\mathbf{u}_1$.

The variance of the projected data is

$$\frac{1}{N} \sum_{i=1}^{N} \left(\mathbf{u}_1^T \mathbf{x}^i - \mathbf{u}_1^T \bar{\mathbf{x}} \right)^2 = \mathbf{u}_1^T \mathbf{S} \mathbf{u}_1,$$

where $\mathbf{u}_1^T \bar{\mathbf{x}}$ is the mean of the projected data, with $\bar{\mathbf{x}}$ being the data mean n-dimensional vector $\bar{\mathbf{x}} = \frac{1}{N} \sum_{i=1}^{N} \mathbf{x}^i$, and $\mathbf{S}$ is the data covariance matrix of $n \times n$ dimensions defined by

$$\mathbf{S} = \frac{1}{N} \sum_{i=1}^{N} (\mathbf{x}^i - \bar{\mathbf{x}})(\mathbf{x}^i - \bar{\mathbf{x}})^T. \tag{2.2}$$

Now, for Y_1 to be the first principal component, we need to solve

$$\max_{\mathbf{u}_1} \mathbf{u}_1^T \mathbf{S} \mathbf{u}_1 \quad \text{subject to} \quad \mathbf{u}_1^T \mathbf{u}_1 = 1,$$

which, by introducing a Lagrange multiplier λ_1, amounts to solving

$$\max_{\mathbf{u}_1} \mathbf{u}_1^T \mathbf{S} \mathbf{u}_1 + \lambda_1 \left(1 - \mathbf{u}_1^T \mathbf{u}_1 \right).$$

By setting the derivative with respect to $\mathbf{u}_1$ equal to zero, we have

$$\mathbf{S} \mathbf{u}_1 = \lambda_1 \mathbf{u}_1, \tag{2.3}$$

i.e., $\mathbf{u}_1$ must be an eigenvector[2] of $\mathbf{S}$. By left-multiplying by $\mathbf{u}_1$ and using the constraint $\mathbf{u}_1^T \mathbf{u}_1 = 1$, the resulting variance is

$$\mathbf{u}_1^T \mathbf{S} \mathbf{u}_1 = \lambda_1,$$

---

[2] The eigenvectors $\mathbf{u}$ corresponding to each eigenvalue can be found by solving $\mathbf{S}\mathbf{u} = \lambda\mathbf{u}$.

and then the variance is maximized when $\mathbf{u}_1$ is the eigenvector of $\mathbf{S}$ that has the largest eigenvalue λ_1.[3] This new axis, eigenvector $\mathbf{u}_1$, or the variable Y_1 itself, is known as the first principal component. The values of Y_1 are called the first principal component scores. We can replace the observations $\mathbf{x}^i$ in $y_1^i = \mathbf{u}_1^T \mathbf{x}^i$ by their centered versions, i.e., by $(\mathbf{x}^i - \bar{\mathbf{x}})$, to ensure that Y_1 will have a zero mean, which will not generally be the case.

The second principal component Y_2 is then defined by a new direction $\mathbf{u}_2$ such that the projected data $y_2^i = \mathbf{u}_2^T \mathbf{x}^i$ has the greatest (not yet accounted for) variance of all possible directions orthogonal to the first principal component, i.e., subject to $\mathbf{u}_2^T \mathbf{u}_2 = 1$ and $\mathbf{u}_2^T \mathbf{u}_1 = 0$. The second condition ensures that Y_1 and Y_2 are uncorrelated.

Additional principal components are added in the same way, each being uncorrelated to the previous principal components. Ordered by magnitude, eigenvalues λ_j give the variances of the new variables Y_j, and their respective eigenvectors $\mathbf{u}_j$ indicate how to form the new variables. After $\mathbf{u}_1, \ldots, \mathbf{u}_n$ are found, it holds that the total variance accounted for by all these components is the same as the total variance accounted for by the original data, $\sum_{j=1}^{n} \lambda_j = \sum_{j=1}^{n} s_j^2 = \mathrm{tr}(\mathbf{S})$, the trace of $\mathbf{S}$ (sum of the elements on its main diagonal). Consequently, the jth principal component accounts for a proportion of the total variation of the original data equal to $\lambda_j / \mathrm{tr}(\mathbf{S})$.

Note that the maximum number of principal components is equal to the number of variables, n. However, retaining n principal components does not reduce the dimensionality. It is simply a rotation of the coordinate axes for alignment with the principal components. The general assumption of PCA is that the first few components will account for a substantial proportion of the variation in the original variables and can then be used as a lower-dimensional summary of these variables. Therefore, $m \leq n$ principal components, corresponding to the m largest eigenvalues $\lambda_1, \ldots, \lambda_m$, are usually retained such that they account for a high percentage of the total variance of the original data.

Consider the plot of hypothetical observations given by two dimensions, X_1, X_2, in Figure 2.18. Suppose that we want to represent the data in only one dimension, given by the dotted less steep black axis representing the first principal component. The projected points onto this subspace are drawn as gray dots. This is better than the representation given by the dotted steeper gray axis, where many points project onto the same gray point and are indistinguishable. The data can be represented by one variable given by the black axis, with less loss of information than the variable given by the gray axis. The loss of information resulting from representing the data in a lower-dimensional space is typically measured as the sum of the variances of the new variables not used to represent the data, i.e., the amount of unexplained variance. Whether this loss is substantial depends on the objective of the study.

The (few) retained new variables will then be used by the researcher in further analyses, instead of the original variables. Note that data are reduced in terms of not how much data need to be collected, as all the original n variables are required to form the projected data, but in terms of how many new variables are retained for further analyses.

In geometrical terms, PCA can also be equivalently defined as the linear projection that minimizes the average projection cost, defined as the mean-square distance between the data and their projections (Bishop, 2006). Thus, the first principal component defines the line of best fit in the least squares sense to the n-dimensional observations in the

---

[3] Given a matrix $\mathbf{S}$, its eigenvalues are values λ that satisfy the equation $|\mathbf{S} - \lambda \mathbf{I}| = 0$.

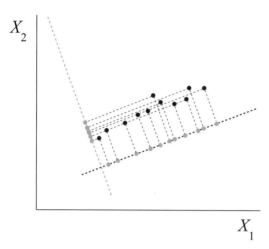

X_2

X_1

Figure 2.18 Principal component analysis. Representation of 2D observations (black dots) in two different 1D subspaces (dotted lines). The representation of points in the black 1D space is much better than that in the gray subspace, where some points cannot be distinguished from one another.

data. Similarly, the first two components give the best 2D fit subject to the orthonormality constraint and so on.

In summary, PCA involves computing the data covariance matrix $\mathbf{S}$ and then finding the m eigenvectors of $\mathbf{S}$ corresponding to the m largest eigenvalues. Many algorithms can be used to find the eigenvectors and eigenvalues of a matrix (see, e.g., Golub and van Loan [2012]).

The variances of the variables can have an effect on the PCA. When a variable has a very high variance compared with the other variables, it will tend to dominate the early components. Furthermore, with variables of different types, such as length, temperature, and blood pressure, the derived components will depend on the arbitrary choice of their measurement units (any change will alter the PCA). If we do not want the relative variance and the measurement units to have any effect, the data should be standardized before the PCA so that the variance of each variable is the same, i.e., one. A variable X is standardized by applying the transformation $(x - \bar{x})/s$, where the transformed variable has zero mean and unit variance (see Section 2.6). Calculating the principal components from the standardized data is equivalent to extracting the components as the eigenvectors of the correlation matrix $\mathbf{R}$ whose elements are the correlations between each pair of original variables. If there is any reason to believe that the variances of the variables indicate the importance of the variables, standardization should not be used.

Deciding how much information to omit is a question of judgment. There are, however, some heuristic rules to help decide how many principal components should be extracted. The first simple rule is called the eigenvalue-one criterion and states that for standardized data, we can retain only those components whose eigenvalues are greater than one. The rationale is as follows: for standardized data, each observed variable contributes one unit of variance to the total variance, so any component that displays an eigenvalue greater than one accounts for a greater amount of variance than any other variable. This is a meaningful amount of variance, and the component is worth retaining.

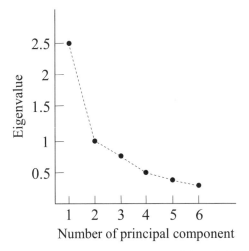

Figure 2.19 Scree plot from a PCA of six variables.

A second rule is called the **scree test** and is very popular. This test is applicable to any kind of data, standardized or otherwise. A (scree) plot of the eigenvalue (y-axis) associated with each principal component (x-axis) is examined for an "elbow," i.e., a "break" between the components with relatively large and small eigenvalues. The number of principal components to be retained is given by the elbow. Apart from the subjectivity involved in identifying the elbow, a scree plot can display several large breaks. In this case of multiple breaks, we should look for the last large break before the eigenvalues begin to level off. Only the components that appear before this last large break should be retained.

Figure 2.19 shows a fictitious scree plot from a PCA of six variables. It suggests that two principal components should be extracted, as the elbow appears to be at the second component. Obviously, all these rules should be used judiciously, in conjunction with additional criteria, such as the variance accounted for and the interpretability criterion.

Sometimes, only a few principal components may be unable to explain a substantial proportion of the variance. This usually happens when the variables are already uncorrelated with one another. Each principal component will account for the same amount of variance, and we do not really achieve any data reduction. On the contrary, for perfectly correlated variables, the first principal component will account for all the variance in the data. Therefore, the greater the correlation among the variables is, the greater the reduction we can achieve with the principal components, and vice versa. Moreover, some techniques (e.g., regression) do not work well with correlated variables. This multicollinearity problem is avoided if principal components are used. There are formal statistical tests to determine if the variables are significantly correlated with one another (we will look at statistical tests later in Section 4.2). At this point, we can gain a preliminary idea from covariances s_{ij} between variables X_i and X_j or, equivalently, from their correlation r_{ij}.

Finally, note that PCA does not account for groups within the data. So, if separate groups exist, they may be hidden. The space spanned by the vectors associated with the first few principal components will not necessarily be the best for discriminating groups. A visual example is shown in Figure 2.20. The separate groups of crosses and dots are removed when projecting the data onto the first principal component, whereas the second

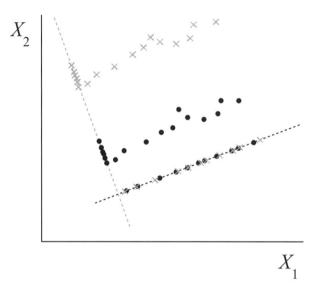

Figure 2.20 PCA is not necessarily the best option for discriminating separate groups.

component retains the group separation. This is also applied in the below example with interneuron and pyramidal cells. In this sense, PCA is an *unsupervised* feature extraction technique. If we picture the data as forming an n-dimensional hyperellipsoid-like cloud, then the eigenvectors of **S** are the principal axes of that hyperellipsoid. PCA reduces dimension n by looking at those directions along which the scatter of the cloud is greatest.

Example: Interneurons versus Pyramidal Neurons. To illustrate PCA on Data Set 1, we will only take 12 variables out of the whole set of 65. These variables have been chosen at random, although they attempt to cover all parts of a neuron: there are variables related to the soma (X_1, X_2), the axon (X_7, X_8, X_9, X_{10}), and dendrites $(X_{36}, X_{37}, X_{38}, X_{39}, X_{40}, X_{41})$. Table 2.3 lists the resulting output. The first principal component accounts for 84% of the variance of the original variables. The first two components together account for more than 97% of the variance. With 3 components, we account for almost all of the variance (the results for components 5 to 12 are not shown because their contributions to the variance are negligible). The corresponding scree plot in Figure 2.21(a) shows that the values fall sharply at component 2 before leveling off at small values. Therefore, we could decide to retain $m = 2$ principal components. Geometrically, we have rotated the axes of the original coordinate system to a new set of orthogonal axes ordered in terms of the proportion of variance of the original data that they account for.

From the eigenvectors in Table 2.3, a possible interpretation of the principal components follows. The first component might be regarded as some index of axonal length and area, with high coefficients for the Total axonal length (X_8) and the Total surface area of axon (X_9). A possible explanation of the fact that the first component accounts for such a high proportion of variance (84%) is the high correlation (0.96) between X_8 and X_9. The second component, however, is concerned with dendritic features, with high coefficients for the Total dendritic length (X_{38}) and the Total surface area of dendrites (X_{40}). Attempting to interpret components in this way is not without criticism. Note also that the sign of an eigenvector is basically arbitrary; the relative signs, however, could be meaningful.

Table 2.3 Results from the PCA of 12 variables from Data Set 1: X_1, X_2 (soma), X_7, X_8, X_9, X_{10} (axon), and $X_{36}, X_{37}, X_{38}, X_{39}, X_{40}, X_{41}$ (dendrites); blanks indicate near-zero values

Importance of components	Comp. 1	Comp. 2	Comp. 3	Comp. 4
Standard deviation $\left(\sqrt{\lambda_j}\right)$	9,619.2736	3,860.2368	1,429.3	840.8249
Proportion of variance	0.8393	0.1352	0.0185	0.0064
Cumulative proportion	0.8393	0.9745	0.9930	0.9994
Eigenvectors $\left(\mathbf{u}_j, j = 1, \ldots, 4\right)$	Comp. 1	Comp. 2	Comp. 3	Comp. 4
X_1				
X_2				
X_7				
X_8	0.769	−0.105	−0.541	0.324
X_9	0.637		0.641	−0.427
X_{10}				
X_{36}				
X_{37}				
X_{38}		0.561	−0.477	−0.644
X_{39}			−0.103	−0.174
X_{40}		0.817	0.239	0.518
X_{41}				

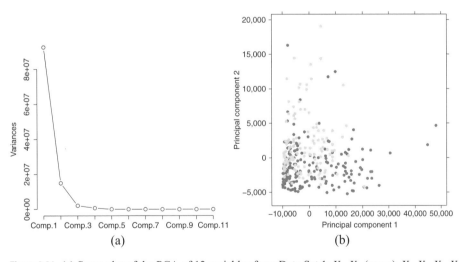

Figure 2.21 (a) Scree plot of the PCA of 12 variables from Data Set 1: X_1, X_2 (soma), X_7, X_8, X_9, X_{10} (axon), and $X_{36}, X_{37}, X_{38}, X_{39}, X_{40}, X_{41}$ (dendrites). (b) Scores of the first two principal components: interneurons are in dark gray and pyramidal cells are in light gray.

A more useful aspect of PCA is to plot the original multivariate data $\mathbf{x}^i, i = 1, \ldots, 327$ in the new space given by the principal components. Each original point (neuron) in the 12-dimensional space is projected onto the 2D space, $Y_1 Y_2$, by performing simple linear combinations: $y_1^i = \mathbf{u}_1^T (\mathbf{x}^i - \bar{\mathbf{x}})$ and $y_2^i = \mathbf{u}_2^T (\mathbf{x}^i - \bar{\mathbf{x}})$. For instance, vectors $\mathbf{u}_1, \mathbf{u}_2$ from Table 2.3 give for the 12 coordinates of the first neuron the 2 first principal component scores ($y_1^1 = -7,194.55, y_2^1 = 2,655.80$), of this neuron. All these points are jointly plotted in the scatterplot shown in Figure 2.21(b), where pyramidal cells and interneurons are distinguished by their shading. Observe how a few neurons are outliers.

Note that these 12 variables are on very different scales, e.g., X_{10} takes values in [0.39, 8.41], and X_9 has outcomes in [17,35900]. This is why the first principal component lies in the direction of X_8 and X_9, the variables with ranges that far exceed the others. Therefore, extracting the principal components from the correlation matrix **R** rather than **S** would have been a better choice in this case in real practice. ■

PCA has been used often in neuroscience, mostly to select variables (Chapter 6). Those variables highly correlated with the selected principal components are retained for further analyses. The other variables are removed from the data set. An outstanding example is the classification of neurons: projection cells (Marin et al., 2002), pyramidal cells (Benavides-Piccione et al., 2006), interneurons (Dumitriu et al., 2007), and pyramidal cells versus interneurons (Guerra et al., 2011). In the work of Laubach et al. (1999), however, PCA and independent component analysis (see Section 2.7) are compared to find the number of interacting groups in neuronal ensemble data, i.e., groupings of neurons that emerge from correlated firing. The data come from rats that are trained to perform a simple reaction-time task.

PCA for Data Sets with $N \ll n$ ("Large n, Small N" Problem). A special case involves data sets in which the number of observations N is much smaller than the number of variables n. This often occurs in genomic (DNA microarrays) or proteomic (mass spectrometry) data, in which there are tens of thousands of variables (gene/transcript expressions and mass-to-charge ratios reflecting the abundance of peptides of a set mass) and less than 100 cases (samples of patients). This is the so-called large n, small N problem, as it is an obstacle to proper parameter estimation (we shall deal with this later in this book, see Section 8.2.4 and Section 8.3.2.2).

A data set with N points in an n-dimensional space, where $N \leq n$, defines a linear subspace of dimensionality that is $N - 1$ at most. Hence, applying PCA for values $m > N - 1$ makes no sense. At least $n - N + 1$ eigenvalues will, in fact be zero, corresponding to eigenvectors in whose directions the data have zero variance. This is aggravated by the computational infeasibility of the algorithm that would calculate the eigenvectors of an $n \times n$ matrix.

A solution involves a small trick that will allow us to work in a lower-dimensional space. If **D** denotes the $N \times n$ dimensional centered data matrix, whose ith row is $(\mathbf{x}^i - \bar{\mathbf{x}})^T$, then the covariance matrix, defined in Equation (2.2), is $\mathbf{S} = \frac{1}{N}\mathbf{D}^T\mathbf{D}$. Equation (2.3) becomes

$$\frac{1}{N}\mathbf{D}^T\mathbf{D}\mathbf{u}_1 = \lambda_1\mathbf{u}_1.$$

If we pre-multiply by **D**, we have $\frac{1}{N}\mathbf{D}\mathbf{D}^T(\mathbf{D}\mathbf{u}_1) = \lambda_1(\mathbf{D}\mathbf{u}_1)$, which, by defining $\mathbf{v}_1 = \mathbf{D}\mathbf{u}_1$, is equivalent to

$$\frac{1}{N}\mathbf{D}\mathbf{D}^T\mathbf{v}_1 = \lambda_1\mathbf{v}_1.$$

This last equation states that vector $\mathbf{v}_1$ is an eigenvector of the $N \times N$ (a much lower dimensionality) matrix $\frac{1}{N}\mathbf{D}\mathbf{D}^T$. We see that this new matrix has the same $N-1$ eigenvalues λ_j as the original covariance matrix $\mathbf{S}$ (the additional $n-N+1$ eigenvalues of $\mathbf{S}$ are zero).

Now, to obtain the eigenvectors in the original data space, we should look for those corresponding to matrix $\mathbf{S}$, not to matrix $\frac{1}{N}\mathbf{D}\mathbf{D}^T = \mathbf{S}^T$. Therefore, we pre-multiply the last equation by $\mathbf{D}^T$:

$$\left(\frac{1}{N}\mathbf{D}^T\mathbf{D}\right)(\mathbf{D}^T\mathbf{v}_1) = \lambda_1(\mathbf{D}^T\mathbf{v}_1),$$

and we find that $(\mathbf{D}^T\mathbf{v}_1)$ is an eigenvector of matrix $\mathbf{S}$ with eigenvalue λ_1. As this eigenvector is not necessarily normalized, we finally rescale it as $\mathbf{u}_1 \propto \mathbf{D}^T\mathbf{v}_1$ by a constant such that $||\mathbf{u}_1|| = 1$.

To summarize, under $N \leq n$ settings with a large n, we first calculate the eigenvectors $\mathbf{v}_j$ and eigenvalues λ_j of $\mathbf{D}\mathbf{D}^T$, and then we compute the eigenvectors in the original data space as $\mathbf{u}_j \propto \mathbf{D}^T\mathbf{v}_j$.

2.4.4   *t*-SNE

PCA is a linear algorithm and will not be able to interpret complex polynomial relationships between variables. Linear dimensionality reduction algorithms focus on placing dissimilar data points far apart in a lower-dimension representation. However, they do not place similar data points close together, which is important to represent high-dimensional data on a low-dimensional nonlinear manifold.

t-**distributed stochastic neighbor embedding** (*t*-SNE) (van der Maaten and Hinton, 2008) is a more advanced and effective nonlinear dimensionality reduction method than PCA. It maps n-dimensional data $\mathcal{D} = \{\mathbf{x}^1, \dots, \mathbf{x}^N\}$ into 2D or 3D data $\{\mathbf{y}^1, \dots, \mathbf{y}^N\}$ that can be displayed in a scatterplot. Local approaches aim to map nearby points on the manifold to nearby points in the low-dimensional representation. Global approaches attempt to preserve geometry at all scales, i.e., mapping nearby points to nearby points and faraway points to faraway points. *t*-SNE can retain both the local and global structures of the original data at the same time.

t-SNE starts by converting Euclidean distances between points $\mathbf{x}^i$ into probabilities that represent similarities. Thus, the similarity of $\mathbf{x}^j$ to $\mathbf{x}^i$ is the conditional probability, $p_{j|i}$, that $\mathbf{x}^i$ would pick $\mathbf{x}^j$ as its neighbor if neighbors were picked in proportion to their probability density under an n-dimensional Gaussian centered at $\mathbf{x}^i$ (Section 3.4.4). That is,

$$p_{j|i} = \frac{\exp\left(-||\mathbf{x}^i - \mathbf{x}^j||^2/2\sigma_i^2\right)}{\sum_{k \neq i}\exp\left(-||\mathbf{x}^i - \mathbf{x}^k||^2/2\sigma_i^2\right)},$$

where σ_i is the (equal) variance of any component of that Gaussian, tuned by the user. $p_{j|i}$ is high for nearby points and almost zero for faraway points. Then, we define $p_{ij} = \frac{p_{j|i}+p_{i|j}}{2N}$ to symmetrize those probabilities, i.e., to have $p_{ij} = p_{ji}$, for all i, j. This makes the optimization problem to be solved easier.

For the low-dimensional counterparts $\mathbf{y}^i$ and $\mathbf{y}^j$, computing a similar conditional probability $q_{i|j}$ and $q_{j|i}$ is possible, this time using a Student's *t* distribution (Section 3.3.9) with one degree of freedom, having heavier tails than a Gaussian. This allows the "crowding problem" to be solved: the area of the 2D map that is available to accommodate moderately distant points is not large enough compared with the available area for nearby points (there is a tendency to crowd points together in the center of the map). Moderately distant points will have to be placed too far away in the 2D map if we want to model the small distances accurately in the new space. Symmetrized probabilities q_{ij} in the low-dimensional space are then

$$q_{ij} = \frac{(1 + ||\mathbf{y}^i - \mathbf{y}^j||^2)^{-1}}{\sum_{k \neq l}(1 + ||\mathbf{y}^k - \mathbf{y}^l||^2)^{-1}}.$$

Note that $q_{ij} = q_{ji}$, for all i, j. This makes probabilities almost invariant to changes in the scale of the map for map points that are far apart. Note that $p_{ii} = q_{ii} = 0, \forall i = 1, \dots, N$, as only pairwise similarities are modeled.

Now, for a perfect representation of the similarity of the data points in the different dimensional spaces, i.e., for the perfect replication of the plot in high and low dimensions, probabilities p_{ij} and q_{ij} should be equal. t-SNE minimizes the mismatch between both, which is given by

$$\sum_i \sum_j p_{ij} \log_2 \frac{p_{ij}}{q_{ij}}. \tag{2.4}$$

The minimization problem is easily solved with a gradient descent method. Equation (2.4) is, in fact, a Kullback–Leibler divergence (Section 3.6.5). This technique involves many computations (t-SNE has a quadratic time and space complexity in N). Therefore, t-SNE has a modified version to be able to cope with large data sets (say with $N > 10,000$); it displays a random subset of the data points (called landmark points) in a way that uses information from the entire data set.

Oliveira et al. (2018) applied t-SNE for discriminating neurologically healthy individuals from those suffering from PD treated with levodopa and those treated with deep brain stimulation. Inertial and electromyographic data were collected while the subjects executed a sequence of four motor tasks. The possibility of discriminating between these individuals highlights the fact that each treatment method produces distinct motor behavior. t-SNE was applied by Ridgway et al. (2012) to visualize the distribution of control subjects and groups of patients with three different variants of early-onset AD based on more than 300,000 cortical thickness values. The t-SNE visualization separated well controls from the three AD types, although no natural distinction emerged among patient groups. Mahfouz et al. (2015) used BH-SNE (Barnes and Hut, 1986), a variant of t-SNE, in gene expression data from the Allen Brain Atlases, mouse and human. BH-SNE maps were superior separating neuroanatomical regions to PCA and another dimensionality reduction technique called multidimensional scaling (see Section 2.7 for details).

2.4.5   Summary of Univariate, Bivariate, and Multivariate Plots

Tables 2.4–2.6 gather all visualization methods for univariate, bivariate, and multivariate data.

Table 2.4 Plots for univariate data representation

Name	Example	Data type	Section
Pie chart		Categorical, discrete	2.2.1
Barplot		Categorical, discrete	2.2.1
Histogram		Continuous	2.2.1
Boxplot		Continuous, discrete (ordinal)	2.2.3
Rose diagram and circular histogram		Directional	2.2.4
Circular boxplot		Directional	2.2.4

Table 2.5 Plots for bivariate data representation, all shown in Section 2.3

Name	Example	Variable 1	Variable 2
Side-by-side barplot		Categorical, discrete	Categorical, discrete
Conditional histogram		Continuous	Categorical, discrete
Side-by-side boxplot		Continuous	Categorical, discrete (ordinal)
Scatterplot		Continuous	Continuous

Table 2.6 Multivariate data representation; for multipanels, discrete or categorical variables are allowed for panels

Name	Example	Main variable type	Section
Scatterplot matrix		Continuous	2.4.1
3D scatterplot		Continuous	2.4.1
Multipanel 2D or flat histogram		Continuous	2.4.1
Multipanel 2D boxplot		Continuous conditioned on discrete	2.4.1
Chernoff faces		Continuous	2.4.2
Parallel coordinates		Continuous, discrete	2.4.2
PCA		Continuous	2.4.3

2.5   Imputation of Missing Data

Missing data are a common problem in all types of neuroscience data sets. Examples include the lack of information derived from imperfect digital reconstructions in confocal or electronic microscopies, as well as the absence of some diagnostic tests in clinical neurodegenerative data sets. Key concepts about missing data mechanisms were formalized by Rubin (1976), who distinguished the following three types of missingness mechanisms: (a) missing completely at random, (b) missing not at random, and (c) missing at random.

Missing completely at random (**MCAR**) refers to the situation in which cases (observations) having missing data are a random subset of the whole data of cases. A typical example is when a questionnaire of an AD study is accidentally lost. In MCAR, the reason for missingness is completely random, i.e., the probability that an observation is missing is not related to any other case characteristic. For the MCAR mechanism, the majority of simple techniques for handling missing data, including the available case analysis (see below), give unbiased results.

The **missing not at random** (**MNAR**) mechanism assumes that the probability of the information on some variables in a case being missing depends on the information that is not observed, such as the value of the case itself. For example, in AD studies, it might well be that missing data cases in cognitive tests are more likely to occur when a patient is in advanced disease stages. Here, the reason for missingness is not completely random but is related to unobserved patient variables. If missing data are MNAR, valuable information is lost from the data and there are no universal methods for handling missing data properly.

Mostly, missing data are neither MCAR nor MNAR. Instead, the probability that some information in a case is missing commonly depends on information for that case that is present, i.e., the reason for missingness is based on other observed patient characteristics. This type of missing data is called **missing at random** (**MAR**) because missing data can indeed be considered random, conditional on these other patient variables that determined their missingness and that are available at the time of analysis. For example, suppose we want to evaluate the predictive value of a particular pronostic test for AD patients, and the test results are known for all patients in the advanced disease stage but are unknown for a random sample of nondiseased subjects and for patients in early disease stages. In this example, the missing data would be MAR: conditional on a patient characteristic that is observable (here, the stage of the disease), missing data are random. For MAR, an available case analysis provides biased estimation, as it cannot be considered a random sample of the whole population of samples. However, more sophisticated techniques, such as single and multiple imputations (see below), provide unbiased results.

A way to deal with missing data is to discard from the analysis those cases with incomplete data and to work only with complete data cases. This strategy, called **complete-case analysis** (also known as **listwise deletion**), leads to inefficient and biased estimates. Alternatively, imputation of missing data on a variable replaces missing information by a value that is drawn from the probability distribution of this variable.

2.5.1   Single Imputation

Single imputation refers to imputing one value for each missing datum. Several methods have been proposed under this idea. **Unconditional mean** (median) **imputation** replaces each missing value with the mean (or median) of the observed values of that variable. A more sophisticated approach is **regression imputation**, in which the missing values for each variable are replaced with the values predicted from a regression of that variable on other variables. **Hot deck imputation** replaces each missing value with a random draw from a donor pool consisting of observed values of that variable in cases with complete data with observed values that are similar to those in the case with missing data. The concept of being similar can refer to exact matching on the categorical variables observed for all cases, or by using a distance observed for all cases or a distance measure on fully observed continuous variables. More sophisticated is imputation based on the expectation-maximization algorithm, a model-based imputation approach (see Section 12.1 for details).

2.5.2   Multiple Imputation

Multiple imputation creates not a single imputed data set but several or multiple imputed data sets in which different imputations are based on a random draw from different estimated underlying distributions. Each of the completed data sets is analyzed as if there were no missing data. The results of the analyses are combined, for example, by computing their arithmetic mean, to produce the final point estimate used as imputation.

The imputation of missing values has drawn the attention of the neuroscience community. Multiple imputation methods have been used by Lawton et al. (2015) when discovering PD subtypes and also, by van den Kommer et al. (2014) in identifying at-risk groups for incident memory complaints studies. Studies comparing the performance of several imputation methods include those of Coley et al. (2011), in which a complete case and multiple imputation were used in clinical trials involving AD; van Eeden et al. (2015), in which different strategies for post-stroke depressive patients with mean substitution and multiple imputation approaches were evaluated; and Rubin et al. (2007), in which a complete case, unconditional mean, regression, and expectation-maximization algorithm-based imputations in behavioral neuroscience were compared.

2.6   Variable Transformation

Data transformation in statistics refers to the application of a mathematical function to each point in a data set. After the transformation is performed, each data point x_i is transformed into z_i, where $z_i = t(x_i)$, with t denoting the mathematical function. The main reasons for transforming data are as follows: (a) the variable measurement units affect the statistical or machine learning procedure to be applied, (b) the transformed data more closely meet the assumptions of the procedure to be applied (e.g., Gaussianity), and (c) the procedure only works for discrete variables.

2.6.1   Standardization

Different variables can have different measurement units, such as X_{56} and X_{65} in Figure 2.2. X_{56} measures the number of dendritic Sholl sections and takes values in the range $[0, 25]$, whereas X_{65} refers to the relative distance to the pia and has all its values in $[0, 1]$. This discrepancy can be a drawback for some modeling methods (as we saw in PCA, Section 2.4.3). A common practice is to transform the original data such that the transformed variables share the same mean and standard deviation for all variables. This transformation is called **standardization** and is a linear transformation in which the mean of the original variable is subtracted from each data, and the result is divided by the standard deviation. More formally, let $x_1, \dots, x_N$ denote the original data, $\bar{x}$ and s_X, their mean and standard deviation, respectively. Then, the standardized data, $z_1, \dots, z_N$ are obtained as $z_i = \frac{x_i - \bar{x}}{s_X}$. The mean, $\bar{z}$, and the standard deviation, s_Z, of the transformed data verify $\bar{z} = 0$ and $s_Z = 1$, respectively.

2.6.2 Transformations toward Gaussianity

Some hypothesis tests that are useful for univariate filter feature selection (see Section 6.2.1) assume that the density of the predictor variable follows, for each value of the class variable, a normal distribution. The same assumption is made for the continuous predictor variables of a Gaussian naive Bayes classifier (see Section 8.4.2.1) or even for the joint density of predictor variables for each value of the class variable in linear discriminant analysis (see Section 8.2). Looking at the histogram of the variable, however, we may find that it is far away from Gaussianity, especially in situations in which the variable is substantially skewed.

The **power transform** is a member of a family of transformations parameterized by a nonnegative value λ that includes the square root, as well as a multiplicative inverse as a special case. The general expression is given by $z = x^\lambda, \lambda > 0$. According to Tukey's ladder of powers (Tukey, 1977), values of parameter λ greater than 1 will extend the right tail of the histogram, removing left skewness. Values $\lambda < 1$ have been shown to have the opposite effect.

Figure 2.22(a) and (c) show the frequency histograms of variables X_4 and X_{26}, respectively. In Figure 2.22(b) and (d), power transformations of the above variables with λ values of 3 and 0.5, respectively, result in symmetric histograms with skewness values of 0.0014 for X_4^3 and 0.07 for $\sqrt{X_{26}}$. Notice the skewness reduction for both variables. Before the transformation, the values of skewness were -0.69 and 1.44, respectively (see Table 2.1).

2.6.3 Discretization

Statistical and machine learning methods often involve continuous data. However, modeling from continuous data can be less effective and less efficient than that from categorical data. The assumptions (e.g., Gaussian density) on which the modeling method is based may not always hold. Discretization aims to transform continuous data into categorical data. Discretization can be seen as a data reduction method, as it maps data from a huge spectrum of numeric values to a reduced subset of discrete values.

Given a data set containing N values, $x_1, \dots, x_i, \dots, x_N$, extracted from a continuous random variable, X, we denote by X^d a discretization of X based on the cut points $d_0 < d_1 < \cdots < d_k$, which are called the **discretization scheme**, such that $x_i^d = j$ if and only if $x_i \in (d_{j-1}, d_j]$, with $d_0 = x_{(1)}$ and $d_k = x_{(N)}$, where $x_{(1)}$ $(x_{(N)})$ denotes the smallest (highest) value of the original N values, and k represents the number of intervals, i.e.,

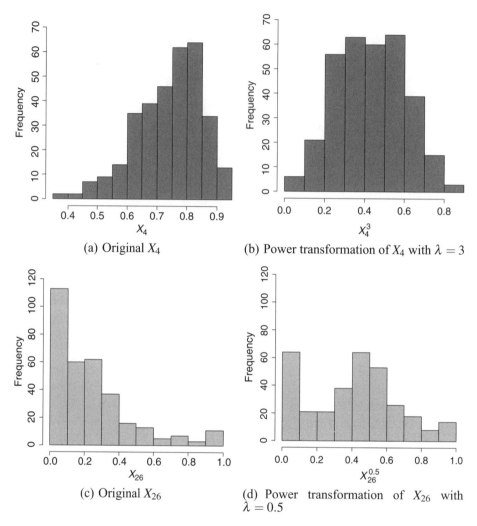

(a) Original X_4

(b) Power transformation of X_4 with $\lambda = 3$

(c) Original X_{26}

(d) Power transformation of X_{26} with $\lambda = 0.5$

Figure 2.22 Frequency histograms of Somatic compactness (X_4) and Axonal Sholl length at 100 μm (expressed as a fraction) (X_{26}) before (in (a) and (c)) and after (in (b) and (d)) power transformations.

the number of possible values of the discretized variable X^d. Figure 2.23 illustrates the notation.

Some reviews of discretization techniques can be found in the literature (Liu et al., 2002; Yang et al., 2010b; García et al., 2013). The different discretization methods can be organized according to, at least, the following concepts:

(a) *Parametric* versus *nonparametric*. This characteristic refers to whether a user input, for example, the number of intervals, is required. When this information exists, the method is parametric; otherwise, it is considered nonparametric.

(b) *Supervised* versus *unsupervised*. Discretization methods that use class labels (Section 1.5.2) to select the discretization cut points are supervised. Methods that do not use class information are unsupervised.

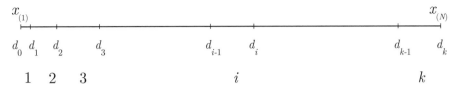

Figure 2.23 Diagram of the discretization transformation.

(c) *Hierarchical* versus *nonhierarchical*. Hierarchical discretization determines the cut points in an incremental process, forming an implicit hierarchy over the value range. The two main types of hierarchical discretization are *split* and *merge*. Split discretization starts with the whole value range as an interval, which it splits into subintervals until some criterion is met. Merge discretization initially places each value into an interval and then continues merging adjacent intervals until some threshold is met. Some discretization methods utilize both split and merge strategies. Nonhierarchical discretization does not form any hierarchy during discretization.

(d) *Univariate* versus *multivariate*. Methods that discretize each variable separately are univariate. Methods that consider relationships among variables during discretization are multivariate.

(e) *Global* versus *local*. Global methods discretize with respect to the whole data set. For each variable, there is a unique discretization. Local methods provide discretization of each variable, depending on the value of other previously discretized variables.

Two simple discretization methods are equal width and equal frequency. Both are parametric, unsupervised, nonhierarchical, univariate, and global methods. Other discretization methods include proportional k-interval discretization, class-attribute interdependence scheme maximization, and the minimum description length principle-based discretization.

Equal-width discretization (Catlett, 1991) predefines the value of k, the number of intervals. It then divides the line between $x_{(1)}$ and $x_{(N)}$ into k intervals of equal width, i.e., the size of each interval is given by $d_i - d_{i-1} = \frac{x_{(N)} - x_{(1)}}{k}$ for all $i = 1, \ldots, k$. The upper bound of the ith interval can be computed as $d_i = x_{(1)} + i \frac{x_{(N)} - x_{(1)}}{k}$.

Equal-frequency discretization (Catlett, 1991) predefines k, the number of intervals. It divides the sorted values into k intervals so that each interval contains approximately the same number of values. If the total number of values, N, is a multiple of the number of intervals, k, each interval should contain $\frac{N}{k}$ values. Denoting by $x_{(1)}, x_{(2)}, \ldots, x_{(l)}, \ldots, x_{(N)}$ the ordered sequence of values extracted from X, i.e., $x_{(1)} \leq x_{(2)} \leq \cdots \leq x_{(l)} \leq \cdots \leq x_{(N)}$, we have $d_i = x_{\left(\frac{iN}{k}\right)}$ for all $i = 1, \ldots, k$.

Proportional k-interval discretization (Yang and Webb, 2009) is a nonparametric, unsupervised, nonhierarchical, univariate, and global discretization method. In this method, the number of intervals is chosen in a data-dependent fashion and set to the largest integer not greater than the square root of the number of observations, i.e., $k = \lceil \sqrt{N} \rceil$. If N is a perfect square number, the number of values in each interval will be equal to k; otherwise, each interval will contain at least $\frac{N}{k}$ values.

Table 2.7 Contingency table for the class variable C and the discretized variable X^d; this variable has been obtained from X applying the discretization scheme $d_0 < d_1 < \cdots < d_k$

Class C	X^d					Marginal of C
	$[d_0, d_1]$	$\cdots$	$(d_{i-1}, d_i]$	$\cdots$	$(d_{k-1}, d_k]$	
c_1	N_{11}	$\cdots$	N_{1i}	$\cdots$	N_{1k}	$N_{1\bullet}$
$\cdots$	$\cdots$	$\cdots$	$\cdots$	$\cdots$	$\cdots$	$\cdots$
c_j	N_{j1}	$\cdots$	N_{ji}	$\cdots$	N_{jk}	$N_{j\bullet}$
$\cdots$	$\cdots$	$\cdots$	$\cdots$	$\cdots$	$\cdots$	$\cdots$
c_R	N_{R1}	$\cdots$	N_{Ri}	$\cdots$	N_{Rk}	$N_{R\bullet}$
Marginal of X^d	$N_{\bullet 1}$	$\cdots$	$N_{\bullet i}$	$\cdots$	$N_{\bullet k}$	N

Class-attribute interdependence scheme maximization (CAIM) (Kurgan and Cios, 2004) is based on the computation of the interdependence between the class variable, C, and the discretized variable X^d obtained from the continuous variable X following the discretization scheme $d_0 < d_1 < \cdots < d_k$. It is computed by combining the numbers in the contingency table of variables C and X^d, shown in Table 2.7. In the contingency table, N_{ji} with $j = 1, \ldots, R, i = 1, \ldots, k$, denotes the total number of cases belonging to the jth class that are within interval $(d_{i-1}, d_i]$, R is the number of possible values of the class variable, k is the number of intervals, $N_{j\bullet} = \sum_{i=1}^{k} N_{ji}$ is the total number of cases belonging to the jth class value, $N_{\bullet i} = \sum_{j=1}^{R} N_{ji}$ is the total number of cases within the interval $(d_{i-1}, d_i]$, and N is the sample size.

CAIM defines the interdependence between the class variable and the discretization scheme of X as $\frac{\sum_{i=1}^{k} \frac{(max_j \{N_{ji}\})^2}{N_{\bullet i}}}{k}$. The larger the value of this expression is, the better the generated discretization scheme will be. For a continuous variable, CAIM will test all possible cut points and then generate its associated discretization scheme in each loop. The corresponding interdependence measure is computed for each discretization scheme, and the discretization scheme with the highest value is chosen. CAIM usually generates a simple discretization scheme in which the number of intervals is close to the number of class values. One drawback of CAIM is that for each interval, it considers only the most frequent class value. CAIM is a nonparametric, supervised, nonhierarchical, univariate, and global discretization method.

The **minimum description length principle-based discretization** (MDLP) algorithm (Fayyad and Irani, 1993) uses information theory-based measures (Section 3.6) to recursively find the best bins. The main idea of the method is to look for the purest possible discretization in the sense that each interval should contain only one type of label, i.e., the method tries to minimize the entropy of the class variable in each interval. This objective leads to a high number of intervals. The number of intervals is then controlled by the MDLP principle, as explained below.

Given a discretization scheme, the decision of whether to add a new cut point (i.e., it is a split discretization) between consecutive bins of the current scheme is made according

Table 2.8 Characteristics of the discretization methods

	Parametric	Supervised	Hierarchical	Univariate	Global
Equal-width	✓			✓	✓
Equal-frequency	✓			✓	✓
Proportional k-interval				✓	✓
CAIM		✓		✓	✓
MDLP		✓	✓	✓	✓

to the MDLP criterion. This criterion establishes that the partition induced by a new cut point, t, for a subset S of N_S cases is accepted iff

$$Gain(X,t;S) > \frac{\log_2(N_S-1)}{N_S} + \frac{\triangle(X,t;S)}{N_S},$$

and is rejected otherwise. In the above inequation, $Gain(X,t;S)$ represents the information gain of the cut point t and is computed as

$$Gain(X,t;S) = \mathbb{H}_S(C) - \frac{N_{S<t}}{N_S}\mathbb{H}_{S<t}(C) - \frac{N_{S\geq t}}{N_S}\mathbb{H}_{S\geq t}(C),$$

where $\mathbb{H}_S(C)$ denotes the entropy (see Section 3.6.1) of class variable C over the set S, and $\mathbb{H}_{S<t}(C)$ (respectively $\mathbb{H}_{S\geq t}(C)$) denotes the entropy of class variable C over the subset of cases with values smaller than t (respectively $\geq t$) of size $N_{S<t}$ (respectively $N_{S\geq t}$). The term $\triangle(X,t;S)$ is calculated as

$$\triangle(X,t;S) = \log_2(3^k-2) - [-R_s\mathbb{H}_S(C) - R_{s_1}\mathbb{H}_{S<t}(C) - R_{s_2}\mathbb{H}_{S\geq t}(C)],$$

where R_{s_1} (respectively R_{s_2}) represents the number of different class values in the subset of cases $S < t$ (respectively $S \geq t$). The MDLP discretization scheme is a nonparametric, supervised, hierarchical (following a split strategy), univariate, and global discretization method.

Table 2.8 summarizes the characteristics of the five discretization methods introduced.

Example. Figure 2.24 shows the density histograms of six different discretizations of variable X_{26}. Figure 2.24(a) shows the default discretization provided by the R statistical package corresponding to an equal-width discretization by $k = 10$. Figure 2.24(b) represents the density histogram for an equal-width discretization by $k = 5$. Comparison of the two density histograms above shows that both are similar in shape, although the density of (b) is lower because its intervals sizes are double. Figure 2.24(c) displays the result of an equal-frequency discretization with $k = 5$. Note the difference in size of the first and last intervals. Figure 2.24(d) represents the density histogram of a proportional k-interval discretization, where the interval sizes are very short for small values of X_{26}, and they increase in size as the values of the variable move away from zero. The two supervised discretization methods, CAIM and MDLP, shown in Figure 2.24(e) and Figure 2.24(f), respectively, provide the same density histogram with $k = 2$. ∎

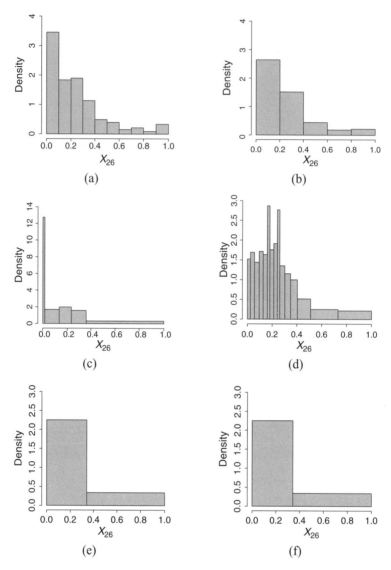

Figure 2.24 Density histograms of X_{26} for different discretizations. (a) Equal-width discretization of X_{26} with $k = 10$. (b) Equal-width discretization of X_{26} with $k = 5$. (c) Equal-frequency discretization of X_{26} with $k = 5$. (d) Proportional k-interval discretization. (e) CAIM. (f) MDLP.

2.7   Bibliographic Notes

Tukey (1977) promoted exploratory data analysis. The rose diagram was first used in 1858 by the nurse and statistician Florence Nightingale (1820–1910) to show the poor sanitary conditions of hospitals under which the British army was exposed during the Crimean War (1853–1856).

PCA is one of the oldest multivariate techniques originally introduced by Pearson (1901) from the average projection cost minimization perspective. PCA was independently developed (and named) later by Hotelling (1933) from the perspective of projected data variance maximization. It remains one the most widely used methods of multivariate analysis to display data in a lower-dimensional space and to possibly simplify other data analyses. Probabilistic PCA, Bayesian PCA, kernel PCA, and nonlinear PCA are not discussed here (Bishop, 2006). **Probabilistic PCA** is formulated with marginal and conditional Gaussian distributions and by introducing a latent variable corresponding to the principal component subspace. The model parameters are determined using maximum likelihood. **Bayesian PCA** uses probabilistic PCA to automatically estimate the number of principal components from the data. The analytically intractable marginalizations are approximated by using a variational framework. **Kernel PCA** extends PCA by using kernel method techniques. Unlike the originally linear operations of PCA, the data are nonlinearly mapped to an N-dimensional space by using a function that is never calculated explicitly (via the so-called kernel trick, see Section 7.5.3). This is useful for clustering (Part IV of this book) because while N points cannot, in general, be linearly separated in $n < N$ dimensions, they can almost always be linearly separated in $n \geq N$ dimensions. **Nonlinear PCA** (see, e.g., Gifi [1990]) is devised for any kind of variable, categorical, discrete and continuous, nominal and ordinal, and it can discover the nonlinear relationships between variables. The categories of such variables are assigned numeric values through a process called optimal quantification (also referred to as optimal scaling or optimal scoring). The variance in the quantified variables is accounted for as much as possible.

Similar to PCA, **multi-dimensional scaling** (Torgerson, 1952; Cox and Cox, 2000) projects the data set onto a lower-dimensional space. However, this technique finds a projection, such as to preserve as closely as possible the pairwise distances between data points. If the distance is Euclidean, it gives results that are equivalent to those of PCA. A modern competitor to PCA is independent component analysis, a technique for unveiling the hidden factors that underlie sets of random variables, measurements, or signals. For instance, EEG signals are a mixture of signals from many sources (not only from the brain but also from artifacts, such as eye blinks, breathing, and heartbeat). This technique cleans the EEG signal from artifacts. The multivariate signal is separated into additive subcomponents by assuming that the subcomponents are non-Gaussian signals and that they are all statistically independent from one another.

The seminal paper on imputation, in which MCAR, MNAR, and MAR were introduced, was presented by Rubin (1976). Classical books on this topic are those of Little and Rubin (1987), Schafer (1997), and van Buuren (2012), whereas surveys on methods for missing data can be found in the studies of Pigott (2001), Schafer and Graham (2002), Donders et al. (2006), and Rässler et al. (2013). Multiple imputation methods were reviewed by Rubin (1987) and Harel and Zhou (2007).

3 Probability Theory and Random Variables

This chapter reviews fundamental notions of probability theory (Section 3.1) and some of the most used probability distributions, including both discrete (Section 3.2) and continuous (Section 3.3) univariate and multivariate (Section 3.4) distributions. Section 3.5 explains how to generate random variates from a desired probability distribution for use in running simulation models. Section 3.6 reports key information theory concepts necessary in many learning methods set out later in the book. The chapter closes with some bibliographic notes (Section 3.7).

3.1 Probability Theory

3.1.1 Sample Space and Events

A **random experiment** is any activity that generates observations in a known set whose outcome is unknown beforehand. It may have a different result if repeated under similar conditions. The **sample space** of a random experiment, denoted by Ω, is the set of all possible outcomes of the experiment. This sample space can be finite or infinite. For example, the experiment may involve selecting one neuron at random and then determining whether it is a pyramidal cell or interneuron. In this case, the sample space is finite with only two possible outcomes. We can also measure the total axonal length of the neuron. In this case, the sample space is infinite, as the length can take any positive real number from a finite interval.

An **event**, denoted by E, is any subset of the sample space. Events are said to be **simple events** when they contain only one outcome; otherwise, they are called **compound**. Consider an experiment to identify the type (pyramidal P or interneuron I) of two neurons selected at random. The sample space is written as $\Omega = \{(P,P),(P,I),(I,P),(I,I)\}$. The event consisting of "both neurons are pyramidal," $E_1 = \{(P,P)\}$, is simple, whereas the event consisting of "at least one neuron is pyramidal," $E_2 = \{(P,I),(I,P),(P,P)\}$, is a compound event consisting of the union of three simple events.

3.1.2 Axiomatic Approach to Probability

Consider an experiment with a sample space Ω. For each event E of the sample space Ω, assume that a function $p(E)$, called **probability function**, is defined on $\mathbb{R}$. This function satisfies the following three axioms of probability, known as the **Kolmogorov axioms**:

1. $p(E) \geq 0$ for all E [**axiom of nonnegativity**].
2. $p(\Omega) = 1$ [**axiom of certainty**].
3. For any mutually exclusive events $E_1, E_2, \ldots, E_n$ (that is, $E_i \cap E_j = \varnothing$ for all $i \neq j$),

$$p\left(\bigcup_{i=1}^{n} E_i\right) = \sum_{i=1}^{n} p(E_i) \text{ [\textbf{axiom of additivity}]}.$$

Several results are easily derived using some algebra in conjunction with the above three probability axioms:

- $p(E) \leq 1$ for all E.
- Probability of the **complementary event**: $p(\bar{E}) = 1 - p(E)$.
- Probability of the **empty set**: $p(\varnothing) = 0$.
- Probability of the **event being included in another event**: If $E \subset F$, then $p(E) \leq p(F)$.
- Probability of the union of two events: $p(E \cup F) = p(E) + p(F) - p(E \cap F)$.
- Probability of the **union of n events**: $p\left(\bigcup_{i=1}^{n} E_i\right) = \sum_{i=1}^{n} p(E_i) - \sum_{i<j}^{n} p(E_i \cap E_j) + \cdots +$
  $(-1)^{n+1} p(E_1 \cap \cdots \cap E_n)$.
- **Subadditivity property**: $p\left(\bigcup_{i=1}^{n} E_i\right) \leq \sum_{i=1}^{n} p(E_i)$.

3.1.3   Probability Interpretations

Apart from the mathematical axiomatization of probability theory given above, complementarily, probability interpretations are useful for driving its application in real-world situations.

Suppose we have an experiment performed N times under the same conditions with sample space Ω. Let $N(E)$ denote the number of times that event E occurs in the N experiments. The **frequentist interpretation of probability** defines the probability of an event E, $p(E)$, as its relative frequency of occurrence if the experiment is repeated a large number of trials under similar conditions, i.e., $p(E) \approx \frac{N(E)}{N}$.

Example. Consider a hypothetical example where N synapses from a mouse brain have been chosen randomly, and we count how many of these synapses are asymmetric (event E) in different trials. Table 3.1 shows that, according to the frequentist interpretation of probability, $p(E) = 0.8929$.[1]   ■

This interpretation demands a repeatable objective process, which is not always available or clearly defined.

In other circumstances, for example when throwing a fair die, the probability of getting one of the six possible numbers can be calculated as the ratio of the number of favorable and equally possible outcomes, that is, $\frac{1}{6}$. This is called the **classical interpretation** of probability. This was historically the first dominant viewpoint and was based on the **principle of indifference** (or **principle of insufficient reason**) that assigns equal chances to mutually exclusive and indistinguishable (except for their names) collectively exhaustive events, a symmetry that, in many situations, does not hold.

---

[1] Example adapted from DeFelipe (2011).

Table 3.1 Frequencies $N(E)$ of asymmetric synapses output when sampling N synpases in a mouse brain

N	$N(E)$	$N(E)/N$
100	87	0.8700
500	460	0.9200
1,000	945	0.9450
5,000	4,445	0.8890
10,000	8,501	0.8501
50,000	41,350	0.8270
100,000	83,340	0.8334

Classical and frequentist interpretations do not support all needs, especially for events that occur only once. **Subjectivists**, also known as Bayesians, regard probability as a measure of the "degree of belief" of the individual assessing the uncertainty of a particular situation, thus rendering it subjective. For example, two neurologists may have different degrees of belief in the event that a cure for AD will be found before 2030. These subjective beliefs must adhere to the laws of probability if they are to be coherent. Heuristics and derived biases must be carefully monitored.

3.1.4   Conditional Probability

We define the conditional probability of event E, given that event F is true, as follows:

$$p(E|F) = \frac{p(E \cap F)}{p(F)} \quad \text{if } p(F) > 0.$$

In other words, the conditional probability is the probability that an event E will occur, when another event F is known to occur or to have occurred.

Example. According to DeFelipe (2011), layer I contains 7% of the synapses in mouse brains. In addition 5.95% of the synapses are asymmetric (as) and belong to layer I. If we select a synapse from layer I at random, the probability of it being asymmetric is given by

$$p(\text{as}|\text{layer I}) = \frac{p(\text{as} \cap \text{layer I})}{p(\text{layer I})} = \frac{0.0595}{0.07} = 0.85. \qquad \blacksquare$$

3.1.5   Independent Events

Conditional probability provides for a change in the probability of an event when additional information is discovered, that is, once we know that event F is true, the probability of event E can be altered.

Event E is independent of event F when the knowledge about event F does not alter the probability of event E, that is, $p(E|F) = p(E)$. Otherwise E is dependent on F. If E is independent of F, F is also independent of E.

Following on with the two previous examples, $p(\text{as}) = 0.8334$ is not equal to $p(\text{as}|\text{layer I}) = 0.85$. Hence we have that both events, "be an asymmetric synapse" and "belong to layer I," are dependent.

An equivalent definition is that event E and event F are **independent events** if and only if

$$p(E \cap F) = p(E) \cdot p(F).$$

Independence between two events is a special case of independence among n events. Events $E_1, \ldots, E_n$ are **mutually independent** if, for any k, with $2 \leq k \leq n$ and any subset of indices $\{i_1, i_2, \ldots, i_k\}$,

$$p(E_{i_1} \cap \cdots \cap E_{i_k}) = p(E_{i_1}) \cdots p(E_{i_k}).$$

3.1.6 Law of Total Probability

Let $F_1, \ldots, F_n$ be events such that $\cup_{i=1}^{n} F_i = \Omega$ and $F_i \cap F_j = \varnothing$ for all $i \neq j$, with $p(F_i) > 0$ for all i. Then for any event E,

$$p(E) = \sum_{i=1}^{n} p(E \cap F_i) = \sum_{i=1}^{n} p(E|F_i)p(F_i).$$

Example. Following DeFelipe (2011) for a mouse brain, the probability of synapses being asymmetric in layer I is 0.85, whereas this probability increases to 0.89 in layer II–III, and it is 0.77 in layer IV, increasing to 0.84 in layer V and layer VI. The distribution of synapses over the different layers is 0.07 for layer I, 0.19 for layer II–III, 0.24 for layer IV, 0.17 for layer V, and 0.33 for layer VI. The probability of a synapse being asymmetric in the whole brain mouse is calculated as

$$p(\mathsf{as}) = \sum_{i=1}^{VI} p(\mathsf{as}|\text{layer } i)p(\text{layer } i)$$

$$= 0.85 \cdot 0.07 + 0.89 \cdot 0.19 + 0.77 \cdot 0.24 + 0.84 \cdot 0.17 + 0.84 \cdot 0.33 = 0.8334. \quad \blacksquare$$

3.1.7 Bayes' Rule

If we combine the definition of conditional probability and the law of total probability, we get **Bayes' rule**, also called **Bayes' theorem**:

$$p(F_j|E) = \frac{p(F_j \cap E)}{p(E)} = \frac{p(E|F_j)p(F_j)}{\sum_{i=1}^{n} p(E|F_i)p(F_i)}.$$

Example. Given an asymmetric synapse, the probability that it comes from layer IV is

$$p(\text{layer IV}|\mathsf{as}) = \frac{p(\mathsf{as}|\text{layer IV})p(\text{layer IV})}{p(\mathsf{as})} = \frac{0.77 \cdot 0.24}{0.8334} = 0.2217. \quad \blacksquare$$

Bayes' rule is seen as a tool for belief revision from a Bayesian viewpoint. An initial **prior probability** is mixed using Bayes' rule with the likelihood of the observations resulting in a **posterior probability**. The posterior probability is the updated prior probability.

Example. A neurologist believes that a patient has a prior subjective probability of suffering from AD (A). Her initial belief after checking the medical history and performing a physical and neurological exam is $p(A) = 0.70$. Then the neurologist orders a mental status test (e.g., mini-mental state examination [MMSE] or mini-cog test) to reduce her uncertainty about the patient's state of health. Assume the sensitivity of this test (Section 5.2.1) is 85% (85% of sick people test positive: $p(T|A) = 0.85$) and its specificity is 90% (90% of healthy people test negative: $p(\bar{T}|\bar{A}) = 0.90$). If the patient tests positive, we can use Bayes' rule to calculate the chances that the patient is sick:

$$p(A|T) = \frac{p(T|A)p(A)}{p(T|A)p(A) + p(T|\bar{A})p(\bar{A})} = \frac{0.85 \cdot 0.70}{0.85 \cdot 0.70 + 0.10 \cdot 0.30} = 0.952.$$

Given a positive test, the prior probability (0.70) is updated to the posterior probability (0.952). This posterior can be used as the prior in subsequent learning phases, e.g., if more information is received later from new tests, like structural MRI or a genetic test. ∎

3.2   Univariate Discrete Distributions

We can extend the notion of events by defining a **random variable** X as a function from the sample space to $\mathbb{R}$. Random variables may be either discrete or continuous. X is said to be a **discrete random variable** if it can take a finite or at most countable number of possible values. If the random variable can take values on a continuum, it is a continuous random variable. Ω_X will denote the set of possible values of X.

3.2.1   Discrete Random Variables

We denote the probability of the event that $X = x$ by $p(X = x)$, or simply $p(x)$ for short.

For a discrete random variable, the **probability mass function (pmf)**, satisfies the properties:

1. $0 \leq p(x) \leq 1$.
2. $\sum_{x \in \Omega_X} p(x) = 1$.

The **(cumulative) distribution function (cdf)**, represents the probability for ordinal variables of values being less than or equal to a given value and is defined as $F(x) = p(X \leq x) = \sum_{k \leq x} p(k)$.

Below we define some theoretical characteristic measures associated with any random variable.

The **mode of a discrete probability distribution**, x_{mode}, is the value that is most likely to occur, that is, $x_{\text{mode}} = \arg\max_x p(x)$. The **median of a discrete probability distribution** is the value x_{median} such that $p(X < x_{\text{median}}) \leq 1/2$ and $p(X \leq x_{\text{median}}) \geq 1/2$. The jth **percentile of a distribution** is the value x_j such that $p(X < x_j) \leq \frac{j}{100}$ and $p(X \leq x_j) \geq \frac{j}{100}$. The 25th percentile is known as the 1st **quartile**, the mode corresponds to the 2nd quartile, and the 75th percentile is the 3rd quartile.

Given a discrete random variable X with pmf $p(x)$, the **expected value** or **expectation** of X is

$$\mathbb{E}[X] = \sum_x x \cdot p(x).$$

Table 3.2 Probability mass function of variable X denoting the number of dendrites of a neuron

x	0	1	2	3	4	5	6	7	8	9	10
$p(x)$	0	0	0.02	0.10	0.20	0.20	0.20	0.15	0.10	0.02	0.01

The expected value of a random discrete variable is the mean of its distribution and satisfies, for any real constants a and b, the property $\mathbb{E}[a+bX] = a+b\mathbb{E}[X]$. Given any function $h(X)$ of the random variable X, its expected value verifies $\mathbb{E}[h(X)] = \sum_x h(x) \cdot p(x)$. The expected value of a random variable X can be different from any of the variable values x. It can be regarded as the fulcrum on a balance beam, where the weight for each possible value of the variable is given by its probability.

Example. To illustrate this concept, let us consider a random variable X denoting the number of dendrites of a neuron. Let us assume that the pmf of X is given in Table 3.2. The expected value for X is calculated as

$$\mathbb{E}[X] = \sum_x x \cdot p(x)$$
$$= 2 \cdot 0.02 + 3 \cdot 0.10 + 4 \cdot 0.20 + 5 \cdot 0.20 + 6 \cdot 0.20 + 7 \cdot 0.15 + 8 \cdot 0.10$$
$$+ 9 \cdot 0.02 + 10 \cdot 0.01$$
$$= 6.37 \text{ dendrites.} \qquad \blacksquare$$

The **variance** of X measures the dispersion of the variable around its expected value and is defined as

$$Var[X] = \mathbb{E}[(X - \mathbb{E}[X])^2] = \mathbb{E}[X^2] - (\mathbb{E}[X])^2 = \sum_x (x - \mathbb{E}[X])^2 p(x).$$

The variance of a discrete random variable satisfies, for any real constants a and b, the property $Var[a+bX] = b^2 Var[X]$. The positive square root of the variance is called the **standard deviation**. The units of measurement for the standard deviation are the same as for the random variable X.

In the following, we review some commonly used discrete parametric distributions, giving their expected value and variance as a summary.

3.2.2 Uniform Distribution

The random variable X is said to follow a **discrete uniform distribution** with parameter n ($n \in \mathbb{N}$), written as $X \sim \text{Unif}(x|n)$, if there is an equal probability of the value of X being x for all $x \in \Omega_X = \{x_1, \dots, x_n\}$, that is, $p(X = x_i) = \frac{1}{n}$ for $i = 1, \dots, n$. When $x_i = i$ for $i = 1, \dots, n$, the expected value and variance are $\mathbb{E}[X] = \frac{n+1}{2}$ and $Var[X] = \frac{n^2-1}{12}$, respectively.

3.2.3 Bernoulli and Binomial Distributions

A Bernoulli trial is an experiment with only two possible mutually exclusive outcomes, for example, success or failure, true or false, pyramidal or interneuron. A **Bernoulli random variable** represents the uncertainty of a Bernoulli trial, assigning a probability to each of the two possible outcomes, usually denoted as 0 and 1. The Bernoulli distribution $X \sim \text{Ber}(x|\theta)$ is parameterized with θ that denotes the probability of value 1. The pmf of $X \sim \text{Ber}(x|\theta)$ is defined as

$$p(x|\theta) = \begin{cases} \theta & \text{if } x = 1 \\ 1 - \theta & \text{if } x = 0. \end{cases}$$

A compact way of representing this distribution is $p(x|\theta) = \theta^x(1-\theta)^{1-x}$ for $x = 0, 1$. The expected value and variance are $\mathbb{E}[X] = \theta$ and $Var[X] = \theta(1-\theta)$, respectively.

A binomial trial is a sequence of Bernoulli trials verifying the following requirements: (a) the experiment consists of a fixed number, n, of Bernoulli trials; (b) the probability of success for each trial, θ, is constant from trial to trial; (c) the trials are independent. The random variable X measuring the number of observed successes in a binomial trial with parameters n and θ is called **Binomial**, denoted as $X \sim \text{Bin}(x|n, \theta)$. Its pmf is given by

$$p(x|n, \theta) = \binom{n}{x}\theta^x(1-\theta)^{n-x} \quad \text{for } x = 0, 1, \dots, n,$$

where $\binom{n}{x} = \frac{n!}{x!(n-x)!}$ is known as the binomial coefficient. The expected value of a $X \sim \text{Bin}(x|n, \theta)$ is $\mathbb{E}[X] = n\theta$. Its variance is $Var[X] = n\theta(1-\theta)$.

Example. Let us assume that the probability of pyramidal cells in layer II of the primate cerebral cortex is 0.75. If 10 cells of layer II are selected at random, the probability of 9 of them being pyramidal would be $p(9|10, 0.75)$ from $\text{Bin}(x|10, 0.75)$. This is computed as $\binom{10}{9}0.75^9 0.25^1 \simeq 0.1877$. The expected number of pyramidal cells in this binomial experiment is given by $\mathbb{E}[X] = 10 \cdot 0.75 = 7.5$. ∎

See Figure 3.1 for some examples of the binomial distribution with different values of θ.

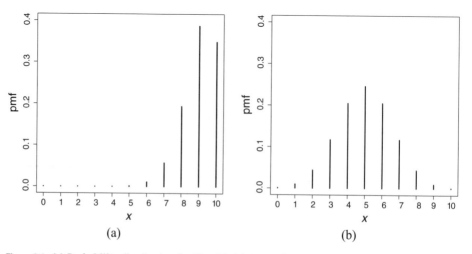

(a)   (b)

Figure 3.1 (a) Probability distribution for $X \sim \text{Bin}(x|10, 0.90)$. (b) Probability distribution for $X \sim \text{Bin}(x|10, 0.50)$.

3.2.4 Categorical Distribution

A **categorical distribution** generalizes the discrete uniform distribution, assigning different probabilities to each of the possible values of the variable, that is, $X \sim \text{Cat}(x|p_1, \ldots, p_n)$ if $p(X = x_i) = p_i$ for $i = 1, \ldots, n$, with $\sum_{i=1}^{n} p_i = 1, p_i \in [0,1]$. If X is numerical, then its expected value is $\mathbb{E}[X] = \sum_{i=1}^{n} x_i p_i$ and the variance is $Var[X] = \sum_{i=1}^{n} x_i^2 p_i - (\sum_{i=1}^{n} x_i p_i)^2$. If X is not numerical, the expectation does not make sense. This is the case for a variable accounting for three interneuron cell types: $x_1 = \texttt{chandelier}$, $x_2 = \texttt{common basket}$, and $x_3 = \texttt{Martinotti}$, and associated probabilities $p_1 = 0.30$, $p_2 = 0.25$, and $p_3 = 0.45$.

The categorical distribution is also the generalization of the Bernoulli distribution for a discrete variable with more than two possible outcomes. Moreover, it is a special case of the multinomial distribution (Section 3.4.3) insofar as it gives the probabilities of potential outcomes of a single trial rather than the multiple identical independent trials of the multinomial distribution.

3.2.5 Poisson Distribution

The Poisson distribution is used to model the number of times particular events occur in given continuous intervals (periods of time or spatial regions). It is particularly well suited for situations where there are "rare" phenomena or outcomes and the probability of success is small, like the number of sporadic AD cases with early onset in their 40s. The result of counting the number of outcomes in a given continuous interval will be a **Poisson process** with parameter λ if the following conditions are satisfied: (a) the number of outcomes in nonoverlapping intervals are independent; (b) the probability of two or more outcomes in a sufficiently short interval is virtually zero; and (c) the probability of exactly one outcome in a sufficiently short interval is proportional to the length of the interval.

The random variable X, representing the number of outcomes in a Poisson process, follows a **Poisson distribution** with parameter λ, $X \sim \text{Pois}(x|\lambda)$, if its pmf is

$$p(x|\lambda) = \frac{\lambda^x e^{-\lambda}}{x!}, \quad \text{for } x = 0, 1, 2, \ldots, \text{ and } \lambda > 0.$$

The expected value and variance of $X \sim \text{Pois}(x|\lambda)$ are $\mathbb{E}[X] = \lambda$ and $Var[X] = \lambda$, respectively. The parameter λ refers to the intensity of the Poisson process.

Poisson-distributed dendritic synaptic inputs were used by Proddutur et al. (2013) to activate the gamma frequency of fast-spiking basket cell network simulations.

3.2.6 Geometric Distribution

The **geometric distribution**, based on Bernoulli trials, computes the probability of the first success occurring after x failures. Denoting by θ the probability of success in each of the Bernoulli trials, the pmf of a geometric random variable, $X \sim \text{Geo}(x|\theta)$, is given by

$$p(x|\theta) = (1 - \theta)^x \theta, \quad \text{for } x = 0, 1, 2, \ldots$$

The expected value and variance of $X \sim \text{Geo}(x|\theta)$ are $\mathbb{E}[X] = \frac{1}{\theta}$ and $Var[X] = \frac{1-\theta}{\theta^2}$, respectively.

Example. Let us assume that the probability of an interneuron in layer II of a primate is $\theta = 0.25$. In a Bernoulli trial, where neurons from layer II are chosen at random, the probability of the first interneuron appearing after five pyramidal cells is $p(5|0.25)$ from $\text{Geo}(x|0.25)$. It is computed as $(1 - 0.25)^5 \cdot 0.25 \simeq 0.0593$. The expected number of trials until the first interneuron appears is the expected value of $X \sim \text{Geo}(x|0.25)$, that is, $\mathbb{E}[X] = \frac{1}{0.25} = 4$. ∎

3.2.7 Negative Binomial Distribution

The random variable X, defined as the number of failures in Bernoulli trials with parameter θ prior to the rth success, has a **negative binomial distribution** written $X \sim \text{NegB}(x|r, \theta)$. To find $p(x|r, \theta)$, first compute the probability of $r - 1$ successes in the first $x + r - 1$ trials and x failures and then multiply by the probability of success in the $(x + r)$-th trial. Thus, the pmf of a negative binomial distribution is given by

$$p(x|r, \theta) = \binom{x + r - 1}{r - 1} \theta^r (1 - \theta)^x, \quad \text{for } x = 0, 1, 2, \ldots$$

The expected value and variance of $X \sim \text{NegB}(x|r, \theta)$ are $\mathbb{E}[X] = r\frac{1-\theta}{\theta}$ and $Var[X] = r\frac{1-\theta}{\theta^2}$, respectively.

Example. Following on with the previous example, the probability of having 10 failures prior to the second success corresponds to $\text{NegB}(10|2, 0.25)$ and is calculated as $\binom{10+2-1}{2-1} 0.25^2 (1 - 0.25)^{10} \simeq 0.03871$. The expected number of failures prior to the second success is $\mathbb{E}[X] = 2\frac{1-0.25}{0.25} = 6$. ∎

3.2.8 Hypergeometric Distribution

The **hypergeometric distribution** applies to sampling n draws without replacement from a finite population of size N whose elements can be classified into two mutually exclusive categories of sizes K and $N - K$, respectively, like success/failure, pass/fail, interneuron/pyramidal. As random selections are made without replacement from the population, each subsequent draw decreases the population causing the probability of success to change with each draw. The hypergeometric distribution is written as $X \sim \text{Hyper}(x|K, N - K, n)$ and counts the number of draws from the category of size K when the sample size is n. Its pmf is given by

$$p(x|K, N - K, n) = \frac{\binom{K}{x}\binom{N-K}{n-x}}{\binom{N}{n}}, \quad \text{for } \max\{0, n + K - N\} \leq x \leq \min\{K, n\}.$$

The expected value and variance of $X \sim \text{Hyper}(x|K, N - K, n)$ are $\mathbb{E}[X] = \frac{Kn}{N}$ and $Var[X] = \frac{Kn(N-K)(N-n)}{N^2(N-1)}$, respectively.

The hypergeometric distribution was used to enrich functional categories in the identification of gene expression patterns in human dopamine neurons in the substantia nigra of PD patients (Cantuti-Castelvetri et al., 2007).

Table 3.3 Parameters, pmf, domain, expectation, and variance of the most commonly used discrete distributions: uniform Uni$(x|n)$, Bernoulli Ber$(x|\theta)$, binomial Bin$(x|n, \theta)$, categorical Cat$(x|p_1, \ldots, p_n)$, geometric Geo$(x|\theta)$, Poisson Pois$(x|\lambda)$, negative binomial NegB$(x|r, \theta)$, and hypergeometric Hyper$(x|K, N-K, n)$.

Distribution	Parameters	pmf	Domain	$\mathbb{E}[X]$	$Var[X]$
Uni$(x|n)$	n	$\dfrac{1}{n}$	$\{x_1, \ldots, x_n\}$	$\dfrac{n+1}{2}$	$\dfrac{n^2-1}{12}$
Ber$(x|\theta)$	$\theta \in [0,1]$	$\theta^x(1-\theta)^{1-x}$	$\{0,1\}$	θ	$\theta(1-\theta)$
Bin$(x|n, \theta)$	$\theta \in [0,1]$	$\binom{n}{x}\theta^x(1-\theta)^{n-x}$	$\{0,1,\ldots,n\}$	$n\theta$	$n\theta(1-\theta)$
Cat$(x|p_1, \ldots, p_n)$	$p_1, \ldots, p_n > 0$	p_i	$\{x_1, \ldots, x_n\}$	$\sum_{i=1}^{n} x_i p_i$	$\sum_{i=1}^{n} x_i^2 p_i - \left(\sum_{i=1}^{n} x_i p_i\right)^2$
Pois$(x|\lambda)$	$\lambda > 0$	$\dfrac{\lambda^x e^{-\lambda}}{x!}$	$\{0,1,\ldots\}$	λ	λ
Geo$(x|\theta)$	$\theta \in [0,1]$	$(1-\theta)^x \theta$	$\{0,1,\ldots\}$	$\dfrac{1}{\theta}$	$\dfrac{1-\theta}{\theta^2}$
NegB$(x|r, \theta)$	$\theta \in [0,1]$	$\binom{x+r-1}{r-1}\theta^r(1-\theta)^x$	$\{0,1,\ldots\}$	$r\dfrac{1-\theta}{\theta}$	$r\dfrac{1-\theta}{\theta^2}$
Hyper$(x|K, N-K, n)$	$K, N, n \in \mathbb{N}$	$\dfrac{\binom{K}{x}\binom{N-K}{n-x}}{\binom{N}{n}}$	$\max\{0, n+K-N\}r,$ $\ldots, \min\{K, n\}$	$\dfrac{Kn}{N}$	$\dfrac{Kn(N-K)(N-n)}{N^2(N-1)}$

Example. In a finite population of 12 neurons, 2 of which are interneurons and the other 10 are pyramidal cells, the probability of selecting 1 interneuron and 2 pyramidal cells when sampling three draws without replacement is calculated as $p(1|2,10,3) = \frac{\binom{2}{1}\binom{10}{2}}{\binom{12}{3}} \simeq$ 0.41. The expected number of interneurons is given by $\mathbb{E}[X] = \frac{2 \cdot 3}{12} = 0.50$. ∎
Table 3.3 outlines the main characteristics of the above discrete distributions.

3.3   Univariate Continuous Distributions

The number of outcomes of a discrete random variable is countable. A random variable X with values in a real interval is called a **continuous random variable**. For example, the total dendritic length, measured in μm, is a continuous random variable with values in a positive interval.

3.3.1   Continuous Random Variables

Each continuous random variable has an associated **probability density function (pdf)**, denoted by $f(x)$ verifying:

1. $f(x) \geq 0, \quad x \in \mathbb{R}$.

2. $\int_{-\infty}^{+\infty} f(x)\,dx = 1$.

3. $p(a < X \leq b) = \int_a^b f(x)\,dx$.

The cdf, $F(x)$, of a continuous random variable X with pdf $f(x)$ is defined as $F(x) = p(X \leq x) = \int_{-\infty}^{x} f(t)\,dt$. The probability in a given interval can now be expressed as $p(a < X \leq b) = \int_{-\infty}^{b} f(x)\,dx - \int_{-\infty}^{a} f(x)\,dx = F(b) - F(a) = \int_a^b f(x)\,dx$.

The **mode of a continuous probability distribution**, x_{mode}, is the x-value that is most likely to occur, that is, $x_{\text{mode}} = \arg\max_x f(x)$.

Let us denote by $F^{-1}(\cdot)$ the inverse of the cdf. This exists because $F(x)$ is a monotonically increasing function. If $F(x)$ is the cdf of variable X, then $F^{-1}(\alpha)$ is the value x_α such that $p(X \leq x_\alpha) = F(x_\alpha) = \alpha$, and it is called the **quantile** of order α, with $\alpha \in [0,1]$. The jth **percentile**, x_j, is a special case of quantile such that $F(x_j) = \frac{j}{100}$. The value $F^{-1}(0.5)$ is the **median of the continuous distribution**, whereas $F^{-1}(0.25)$ and $F^{-1}(0.75)$ are the lower and upper **quartiles**.

The **expected value of a continuous random variable** X, with pdf given by $f(x)$, is defined as $\mathbb{E}[X] = \int_{-\infty}^{+\infty} xf(x)\,dx$. The **variance** of X is a measure of the spread of a distribution and is defined as $Var[X] = \mathbb{E}[(X - \mathbb{E}[X])^2] = \int_{-\infty}^{+\infty} (x - \mathbb{E}[X])^2 f(x)\,dx$. The properties to be satisfied by the expected value and variance of a continuous random variable are the same as for discrete random variables. Thus, for any real constants a and b, $\mathbb{E}[a + bX] = a + b\mathbb{E}[X]$ and $Var[a + bX] = b^2 Var[X]$.

3.3.2   Uniform Distribution

X is a **uniform** random variable defined in the interval $[a, b]$, $X \sim \text{Unif}(x|a, b)$, if its pdf is given by

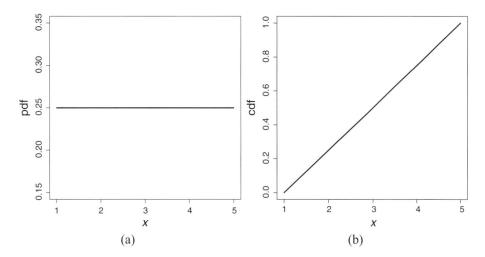

Figure 3.2 The pdf (a) and cdf (b) for the random variable $X \sim \text{Unif}(x|1,5)$.

$$f(x|\theta) = \begin{cases} \frac{1}{b-a} & \text{if } a \le x \le b \\ 0 & \text{otherwise.} \end{cases}$$

The expected value of $X \sim \text{Unif}(x|a,b)$ is $\mathbb{E}[X] = \frac{b+a}{2}$. Its variance is $Var[X] = \frac{(b-a)^2}{12}$. Any value x can be considered as mode because $f(x)$ is a constant.

Figure 3.2 shows the density and cumulative distribution functions of $X \sim \text{Unif}(x|1,5)$.

3.3.3 Exponential Distribution

The **exponential random variable** with parameter $\lambda > 0$, $X \sim \text{Exp}(x|\lambda)$, measures the waiting time between successive outcomes in a Poisson process with the same parameter λ. Its pdf is

$$f(x|\lambda) = \begin{cases} \lambda e^{-\lambda x} & \text{if } x \ge 0 \\ 0 & \text{otherwise.} \end{cases}$$

The expected value and variance of $X \sim \text{Exp}(x|\lambda)$ are $\mathbb{E}[X] = \frac{1}{\lambda}$ and $Var[X] = \frac{1}{\lambda^2}$, respectively. The exponential distribution is characterized by the **memoryless property**: $p(X > t_2 + t_1 | X > t_1) = p(X > t_2)$. This memorylessness is also known as the property of no aftereffect, meaning that if the variable values are greater than t_1, the conditional probability for values greater than $t_1 + t_2$ is the same as the probability of the variable being greater than t_2.

Figure 3.3 displays the density and cumulative distribution functions of $X \sim \text{Exp}(x|1)$.

3.3.4 Gamma Distribution

The **gamma distribution** is a two-parameter family of continuous probability distributions defined for positive real values. The two parameters, α, a shape parameter, and λ, an inverse scale parameter, called a rate parameter, are both positive and provide a flexible adaptation of the gamma distribution to very different empirical distributions.

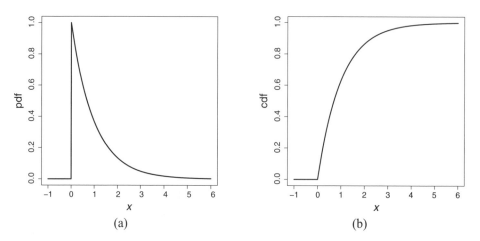

Figure 3.3 The pdf (a) and cdf (b) for the random variable $X \sim \text{Exp}(x|1)$.

The gamma distribution, $X \sim \text{Gamma}(x|\alpha, \lambda)$, measures the waiting time until the αth outcome in a Poisson process with parameter $\lambda > 0$ occurs. The pdf of $X \sim \text{Gamma}(x|\alpha, \lambda)$ is

$$f(x|\alpha, \beta) = \begin{cases} \frac{\lambda^\alpha x^{\alpha-1} e^{-\lambda x}}{\Gamma(\alpha)} & \text{if } x \geq 0 \\ 0 & \text{otherwise,} \end{cases}$$

where $\Gamma(\alpha)$ is the **gamma function** defined, for $\alpha > 0$, by $\Gamma(\alpha) = \int_0^\infty x^{\alpha-1} e^{-x}\, dx$. The gamma function verifies the following properties: (a) $\Gamma(\alpha + 1) = \alpha \Gamma(\alpha)$, (b) for $n \in \mathbb{N}, \Gamma(n) = (n-1)!$, and (c) $\Gamma(\frac{1}{2}) = \sqrt{\pi}$. The expected value and variance of $X \sim \text{Gamma}(x|\alpha, \lambda)$ are $\mathbb{E}[X] = \frac{\alpha}{\lambda}$ and $Var[X] = \frac{\alpha}{\lambda^2}$, respectively. The mode of the distribution is $x_{\text{mode}} = \frac{\alpha-1}{\beta}$.

The gamma distribution results in a generalization of an exponential distribution when $\alpha = 1$, that is, $\text{Gamma}(x|1, \lambda) \equiv \text{Exp}(x|\lambda)$. It also generalizes the chi-squared distribution $X \sim \chi^2(x|n)$ (see Section 3.3.8) when $\alpha = \frac{n}{2}$ and $\lambda = \frac{1}{2}$.

Figure 3.4 illustrates the density and cumulative distribution functions of some members of the family $X \sim \text{Gamma}(x|\alpha, 2)$ for different values of parameter α.

The gamma distribution was used by Suh et al. (2012) to study treatment patterns in PD levodopa-induced dyskinesia. The same probability distribution was applied by Torres (2013) to model stochastic trajectories of accelerometer data from mobile smartphones in patients with PD.

3.3.5   Beta Distribution

The standard **beta distribution** $\text{Beta}(x|a, b)$ is defined over the interval $[0, 1]$ with parameters $a > 0$ and $b > 0$ as follows:

$$f(x|a, b) = \frac{\Gamma(a+b)}{\Gamma(a)\Gamma(b)} x^{a-1}(1-x)^{b-1}.$$

It is often used to model proportions, especially in Bayesian analysis, where parameters are treated as random variables. The distribution can adopt a wide variety of shapes, as

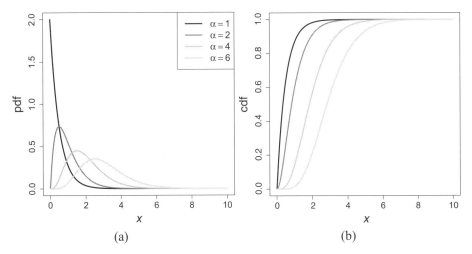

Figure 3.4 The pdf (a) and cdf (b) for the random variable $X \sim \text{Gamma}(x|\alpha, 2)$. Different values of parameter α are used.

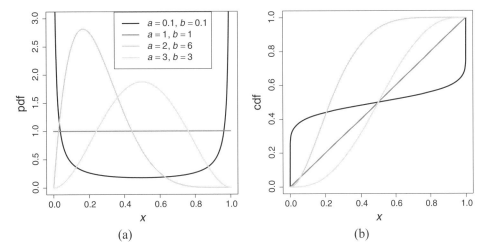

Figure 3.5 The pdf (a) and cdf (b) for some beta distributions.

illustrated in Figure 3.5. If a and b are both less than 1, the distribution is bimodal with modes at 0 and 1; if a and b are both greater than 1, the distribution is unimodal; if a and b are both equal to 1, the beta distribution is a uniform distribution.

The expected value and variance of $X \sim \text{Beta}(x|a, b)$ are $\mathbb{E}[X] = \frac{a}{a+b}$ and $Var[X] = \frac{ab}{(a+b)^2(a+b+1)}$, respectively. The mode of the distribution is located at $x_{\text{mode}} = \frac{a-1}{a+b-2}$.

3.3.6 Gaussian Distribution

The pdf of a **Gaussian distribution**, also called **normal distribution**, $X \sim \mathcal{N}(x|\mu, \sigma)$, or simply $\mathcal{N}(\mu, \sigma)$, is defined as

$$f(x|\mu, \sigma) = \frac{1}{\sqrt{2\pi\sigma^2}} e^{-\frac{1}{2\sigma^2}(x-\mu)^2},$$

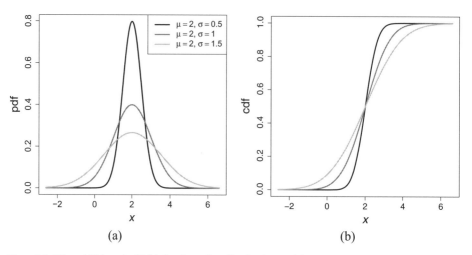

Figure 3.6 The pdf (a) and cdf (b) for Gaussian distributions with the same $\mu = 2$ and different $\sigma = 0.5, 1, 1.5$.

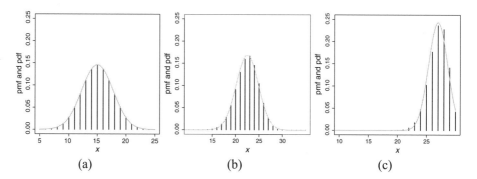

Figure 3.7 Fitting a Gaussian density to a: (a) $X \sim \text{Bin}(x|30, 0.50)$; (b) $X \sim \text{Bin}(x|30, 0.75)$; (c) $X \sim \text{Bin}(x|30, 0.90)$.

for $x, \mu \in \mathbb{R}$ and $\sigma \in \mathbb{R}^+$. The distribution is symmetric around μ and μ corresponds to its expected value and mode. The variance is given by σ^2. The standard deviation is the horizontal distance from the expected value μ to the point where the density curve changes from concave down to concave up. Figure 3.6 illustrates three different Gaussian densities with the same μ and increasing σ.

The (particular case) **standard Gaussian distribution** $X \sim \mathcal{N}(x|0, 1)$ is yielded by a transformation of the general Gaussian density, that is, if $X \sim \mathcal{N}(x|\mu, \sigma)$, then the distribution of $Z = \frac{X - \mu}{\sigma}$ is $Z \sim \mathcal{N}(z|0, 1)$.

The Gaussian distribution is the most widely used distribution in statistics and machine learning. There are several reasons for its popularity: (a) many real-world random variables follow, or can be approximated by, a Gaussian density (see, for example, Figure 3.7), (b) both parameters μ and σ are easy to interpret, (c) its mathematical ductility provides a great number of theoretical properties, and (d) some other parametric distributions, like the lognormal, chi-squared, Student's t, and Snedecor's F distributions, are defined based on the Gaussian distribution.

3.3.7   Lognormal Distribution

$X > 0$ follows a **lognormal distribution** with parameters $\mu > 0$ (scale) and $\sigma > 0$ (shape), $X \sim \text{Lognormal}(x|\mu,\sigma)$, if $Y = \ln X$ follows a Gaussian distribution $\mathcal{N}(y|\mu,\sigma)$. The pdf is

$$f(x|\mu,\sigma) = \frac{1}{\sqrt{2\pi\sigma^2}\,x}e^{-\frac{1}{2\sigma^2}(\ln x - \mu)^2},$$

for $x > 0$. The expectation is $e^{\mu + \frac{\sigma^2}{2}}$, and the variance is $e^{2\mu + \sigma^2}(e^{\sigma^2} - 1)$.

3.3.8   Chi-squared Distribution

The **chi-squared distribution** is one of the sampling distributions (Section 4.1) associated with the Gaussian distribution. This distribution is used in the popular chi-squared tests for goodness-of-fit of an observed sample to a theoretical distribution (Section 4.2.2) and in the independence test for two qualitative variables (Section 4.2.8). The chi-squared distribution with n degrees of freedom $X \sim \chi^2(x|n)$, or simply χ_n^2, is the distribution of a sum of the squares of n independent standard Gaussian random variables. Its pdf is defined as follows:

$$f(x|n) = \begin{cases} \frac{1}{\Gamma(\frac{n}{2})2^{\frac{n}{2}}}x^{\frac{n}{2}-1}e^{-\frac{x}{2}} & \text{if } x \geq 0 \\ 0 & \text{otherwise.} \end{cases}$$

The chi-squared distribution with n degrees of freedom is equivalent to a gamma distribution with parameters $\alpha = \frac{n}{2}$ and $\lambda = \frac{1}{2}$. The expected value and variance are $\mathbb{E}[X] = n$ and $Var[X] = 2n$, respectively. Its mode is located at point $x_{\text{mode}} = \max\{0, n-2\}$.

Figure 3.8 illustrates the pdf and cdf of some chi-squared distributions with different degrees of freedom.

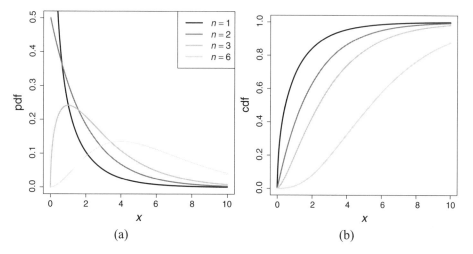

(a)   (b)

Figure 3.8 The pdf (a) and cdf (b) for the random variable $X \sim \chi^2(x|n)$ with different degrees of freedom.

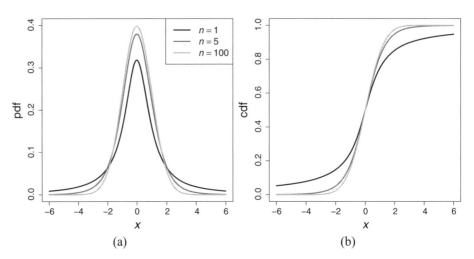

Figure 3.9 The pdf (a) and cdf (b) for the random variable $X \sim t_n$ with different degrees of freedom.

3.3.9 Student's t Distribution

Like the chi-squared distribution, **Student's t distribution** is another sampling distribution (Section 4.1) related to the Gaussian distribution. It is defined as the ratio of a standard Gaussian distribution divided by the square root of a chi-squared distribution divided by its degrees of freedom. Additionally, the Gaussian and the chi-squared distribution should be independent random variables (see Section 3.4.1).

Thus, given two independent random variables, $Z \sim \mathcal{N}(x|0,1)$ and $Y \sim \chi_n^2$, the random variable $X = \frac{Z}{\sqrt{\frac{Y}{n}}}$ follows a Student's t distribution with n degrees of freedom. It is denoted as $t_{x|n}$ or simply t_n.

The pdf is given by

$$f(x|n) = \frac{\Gamma(\frac{n+1}{2})}{\sqrt{\pi n}\ \Gamma(\frac{n}{2})} \left(1 + \frac{x^2}{n}\right)^{-\frac{n+1}{2}}, \quad \text{for } x \in \mathbb{R}.$$

The expected value of a $X \sim t_n$ is given by $\mathbb{E}[X] = 0$. Its variance, defined for $n > 2$ only, is $Var[X] = \frac{n}{n-2}$. The mode coincides with the expected value.

The shape of the t_n distribution is symmetric and similar to that of the standard Gaussian distribution. For smaller values of n, it has heavier tails than $\mathcal{N}(x|0,1)$. For large values of n, the pdf of t_n converges to the pdf of $\mathcal{N}(x|0,1)$, as illustrated in Figure 3.9. The main use of Student's t distribution is for assessing the statistical significance of the difference between two sample means (Sections 4.2.4 and 4.2.5).

3.3.10 Snedecor's F Distribution

Snedecor's F distribution (also known as the Fisher–Snedecor distribution or simply as the F distribution) is defined as the ratio of two independent chi-squared distributions, each divided by its associated degrees of freedom.

In mathematical notation, given two independent random variables, $Z \sim \chi^2_{n_1}$ and $Y \sim \chi^2_{n_2}$, the random variable $X = \frac{Z/n_1}{Y/n_2}$ follows a Snedecor's F distribution with n_1 and n_2 degrees of freedom. It is denoted as $F(x|n_1, n_2)$ or simply F_{n_1, n_2}.

Its pdf is given by

$$f(x|n_1, n_2) = \frac{\Gamma(\frac{n_1+n_2}{2})}{\Gamma(\frac{n_1}{2})} \frac{(\frac{n_1}{n_2})^{n_1/2}}{\Gamma(\frac{n_2}{2})} x^{\frac{n_1}{2}-1} \left(1 + \frac{n_1}{n_2} x\right)^{-\frac{n_1+n_2}{2}}, \qquad \text{for } x \in \mathbb{R}^+.$$

The expected value of $X \sim F_{n_1, n_2}$ is given by $\mathbb{E}[X] = \frac{n_2}{n_2-2}$ for $n_2 > 2$. Its variance, only defined for $n_2 > 4$, is $Var[X] = \frac{2n_2^2(n_1+n_2-2)}{n_1(n_2-2)^2(n_2-4)}$.

The F distribution arises frequently as the null distribution of a test statistic, most notably in the analysis of variance (see Sections 4.2.6 and 4.2.7).

3.3.11 Univariate von Mises Distribution

The **univariate von Mises distribution** (von Mises, 1918) is the circular analogue of the Gaussian distribution. A circular variable Φ that follows the von Mises distribution on the unit circle is denoted by $\Phi \sim v\mathcal{M}(\phi|\mu, \kappa)$, and its pdf is defined in the interval $[0, 2\pi)$ as

$$f(\phi|\mu, \kappa) = \frac{e^{\kappa \cos(\phi-\mu)}}{2\pi I_0(\kappa)},$$

where μ is the **mean direction angle**, $\kappa \geq 0$ is the **concentration** of the values around μ, and $I_\nu(\kappa)$ is the **modified Bessel function** (Abramowitz and Stegun, 1972) of the first kind of order $\nu \in \mathbb{R}$ defined as $I_\nu(z) = \left(\frac{1}{2}z\right)^\nu \sum_{k=0}^{\infty} \frac{(\frac{1}{4}z^2)^k}{k!\Gamma(\nu+k+1)}$.

The distribution of the points in the circle is uniform when $\kappa = 0$, whereas high values of κ yield points tightly clustered around μ. The von Mises distribution is unimodal and symmetrical around the mean direction. The mean direction is also the mode. The variance is given by $1 - \frac{I_1(\kappa)}{I_0(\kappa)}$.

Buzás et al. (2006) predicted the connection patterns of populations of nearby neurons as a function of cortical orientation that is modeled as a von Mises distribution. Morteza-pouraghdam et al. (2016) modeled the phase modulation of the auditory event-related potentials at four distinct stimuli levels with the same distribution. Bielza et al. (2014) used a von Mises distribution to analyze and model the branching angles in 3D reconstructed basal dendritic arbors of hundreds of intracellularly injected cortical pyramidal cells in seven different cortical regions of the frontal, parietal, and occipital cortex of the mouse. The same distribution was applied by Leguey et al. (2016) in a study of dendritic branching angles of pyramidal cells across layers of the juvenile rat somatosensory cortex.

Table 3.4 shows the main characteristics of the above continuous distributions.

3.4 Multivariate Probability Distributions

In real-world applications, the characterization of each observation may involve many variables. In Data Set 1 introduced in Section 1.6.1, pyramidal neurons versus inter-neurons, we store information about 65 variables for each neuron. The determination of

Table 3.4 Parameters, pdf, domain, expectation, and variance of the most commonly used continuous distributions: uniform $\text{Unif}(x|a,b)$, exponential $\text{Exp}(x|\lambda)$, gamma $\text{Gamma}(x|\alpha,\lambda)$, beta $\text{Beta}(x|a,b)$, Gaussian $\mathcal{N}(x|\mu,\sigma)$, lognormal $\text{Lognormal}(x|\mu,\sigma)$, Student's t t_n, Snedecor's F F_{n_1,n_2}, and univariate von Mises $v\mathcal{M}(\phi|\mu,\kappa)$

Distribution	Parameters	pdf	Domain	$\mathbb{E}[X]$	$Var[X]$
$\text{Unif}(x|a,b)$	$a,b \in \mathbb{R}$	$\frac{1}{b-a}$	$[a,b]$	$\frac{b+a}{2}$	$\frac{(b-a)^2}{12}$
$\text{Exp}(x|\lambda)$	$\lambda > 0$	$\lambda e^{-\lambda x}$	$\mathbb{R}^+$	$\frac{1}{\lambda}$	$\frac{1}{\lambda^2}$
$\text{Gamma}(x|\alpha,\lambda)$	$\alpha > 0, \lambda > 0$	$\frac{\lambda^\alpha x^{\alpha-1} e^{-\lambda x}}{\Gamma(\alpha)}$	$\mathbb{R}^+$	$\frac{\alpha}{\lambda}$	$\frac{\alpha}{\lambda^2}$
$\text{Beta}(x|a,b)$	$a > 0, b > 0$	$\frac{\Gamma(a+b)}{\Gamma(a)\Gamma(b)} x^{a-1}(1-x)^{b-1}$	$[0,1]$	$\frac{a}{a+b}$	$\frac{ab}{(a+b)^2(a+b+1)}$
$\mathcal{N}(x|\mu,\sigma)$	$\mu \in \mathbb{R}, \sigma \in \mathbb{R}^+$	$\frac{1}{\sqrt{2\pi\sigma^2}} e^{-\frac{1}{2\sigma^2}(x-\mu)^2}$	$\mathbb{R}$	μ	σ^2
$\text{Lognormal}(x|\mu,\sigma)$	$\mu \in \mathbb{R}^+, \sigma \in \mathbb{R}^+$	$\frac{1}{\sqrt{2\pi\sigma^2}x} e^{-\frac{1}{2\sigma^2}(\ln x - \mu)^2}$	$\mathbb{R}^+$	$e^{\mu+\frac{\sigma^2}{2}}$	$e^{2\mu+\sigma^2}(e^{\sigma^2}-1)$
$\chi^2(x|n)$	$n \in \mathbb{N}$	$\frac{1}{\Gamma\left(\frac{n}{2}\right)2^{\frac{n}{2}}} x^{\frac{n}{2}-1} e^{-\frac{x}{2}}$	$\mathbb{R}^+$	n	$2n$
t_n	$n \in \mathbb{N}$	$\frac{\Gamma\left(\frac{n+1}{2}\right)}{\sqrt{\pi n}\ \Gamma\left(\frac{n}{2}\right)} \left(1+\frac{x^2}{n}\right)^{-\frac{n+1}{2}}$	$\mathbb{R}$	0	$\frac{n}{n-2}$
F_{n_1,n_2}	$n_1, n_2 \in \mathbb{N}$	$\frac{\Gamma\left(\frac{n_1+n_2}{2}\right)}{\Gamma\left(\frac{n_1}{2}\right)}\frac{\left(\frac{n_1}{n_2}\right)^{n_1/2}}{\Gamma\left(\frac{n_2}{2}\right)} x^{\frac{n_1}{2}-1}\left(1+\frac{n_1}{n_2}x\right)^{-\frac{n_1+n_2}{2}}$	$\mathbb{R}^+$	$\frac{n_2}{n_2-2}$	$\frac{2n_2^2(n_1+n_2-2)}{n_1(n_2-2)^2(n_2-4)}$
$v\mathcal{M}(\phi|\mu,\kappa)$	$\mu \in [0,2\pi), \kappa \geq 0$	$\frac{e^{\kappa\cos(\phi-\mu)}}{2\pi I_0(\kappa)}$	$[0,2\pi)$	μ	$1-\frac{I_1(\kappa)}{I_0(\kappa)}$

the joint probability distribution of all (or a subset of) these variables could help to better understand the relationships between the different variables.

3.4.1 Joint Distribution of Two Random Variables

Joint, Marginal, and Conditional Distributions of Two Discrete Random Variables. Given X and Y, two discrete random variables defined in the sample spaces Ω_X and Ω_Y, respectively, the probability of the event $(X = x, Y = y)$ is denoted by $p(X = x, Y = y)$ or simply by $p_{(X,Y)}(x,y)$. A **bivariate probability mass function**, that is, a bivariate pmf, is any function that assigns a value $p_{(X,Y)}(x,y)$ to each pair of values (x,y) verifying the following two properties: (1) $p_{(X,Y)}(x,y) \geq 0$, and (2) $\sum_x \sum_y p_{(X,Y)}(x,y) = 1$.

Thus, for any event $A \subseteq \Omega_X \times \Omega_Y$, its probability is given by $p_{(X,Y)}[(X,Y) \in A] = \sum_{(x,y) \in A} p_{(X,Y)}(x,y)$.

The **cumulative distribution function**, $F_{(X,Y)}(x,y)$, associated with the bivariate random variable (X,Y), where both marginal variables are ordinal, computes, for each value (x,y), the probability of simultaneously taking values smaller than x for the first component and smaller than y for the second component. It is calculated as

$$F_{(X,Y)}(x,y) = p(X \leq x, Y \leq y) = \sum_{a \leq x} \sum_{b \leq y} p_{(X,Y)}(a,b).$$

The **marginal probability distribution** of X, $p(X = x)$, is calculated by summing the bivariate probability mass function over all possible values of Y. Thus, $p(X = x) = \sum_y p(X = x, Y = y)$. Analogously, for the marginal probability distribution of Y, $p(Y = y) = \sum_x p(X = x, Y = y)$.

The **conditional probability distribution** of X given that $Y = y$, provided that $p(Y = y) > 0$, is defined as

$$p_{X|Y}(x|y) = p(X = x | Y = y) = \frac{p(X = x, Y = y)}{p(Y = y)} = \frac{p_{(X,Y)}(x,y)}{p_Y(y)}.$$

Example. Table 3.5 shows the joint probability distribution of (X,Y), where X represents the random variable associated with mouse brain layers, and Y is the type of synapse (asymmetric (as) or symmetric (ss)).

From Table 3.5, we have:

$$p(Y = \text{ss}) = \sum_{x=\text{I}}^{\text{VI}} p(X = x, Y = \text{ss})$$

$$= 0.0105 + 0.0209 + 0.0552 + 0.0272 + 0.0528 = 0.1666.$$

Table 3.5 Joint probability distribution of Layer, X, and Synapse type, Y

Synapse type	Layer				
	I	II–III	IV	V	VI
as	0.0595	0.1691	0.1848	0.1428	0.2772
ss	0.0105	0.0209	0.0552	0.0272	0.0528

Table 3.6 Conditional probability distribution of $X = x$ given that $Y = \text{ss}$

		$p(X = x\|Y = \text{ss})$		
I	II–III	IV	V	VI
0.0630	0.1255	0.3313	0.1633	0.3169

Similarly, we get

$$p(X = \text{I}) = p(X = \text{I}, Y = \text{ss}) + p(X = \text{I}, Y = \text{as}) = 0.0595 + 0.0105 = 0.07.$$

From Table 3.5, the conditional probability of $X = \text{I}$ given that $Y = \text{ss}$ is calculated as

$$p(X = \text{I}|Y = \text{ss}) = \frac{p(X = \text{I}, Y = \text{ss})}{p(Y = \text{ss})} = \frac{0.0105}{0.1666} = 0.0630.$$

Table 3.6 contains the conditional probability of $X = x$ given that $Y = \text{ss}$, for all values of X (layer I to layer VI). ∎

Joint, Marginal, and Conditional Probability Densities of Two Continuous Random Variables. The probability of the bivariate continuous variable (X, Y) falling in a 2D region, A, is calculated by integrating the **bivariate probability density function**, or joint pdf, over A. The joint pdf of two continuous random variables (X, Y) is any function $f_{(X,Y)}(x, y)$ verifying:

1. $f_{(X,Y)}(x, y) \geq 0$ for all (x, y).
2. $\int_{-\infty}^{+\infty} \int_{-\infty}^{+\infty} f_{(X,Y)}(x, y)\, dx\, dy = 1$.
3. $p[(X, Y) \in A] = \iint\limits_{(x,y) \in A} f_{(X,Y)}(x, y)\, dx\, dy$.

The **cumulative distribution function**, $F_{(X,Y)}(x, y)$, is calculated by integrating the joint pdf $f_{(X,Y)}(x, y)$. Thus,

$$F_{(X,Y)}(x, y) = p(X \leq x, Y \leq y) = \int_{-\infty}^{x} \int_{-\infty}^{y} f_{(X,Y)}(r, s)\, dr\, ds.$$

The **marginal density function**, $f_X(x)$, is defined as the integral of the joint pdf for all possible values of random variable Y, that is, $f_X(x) = \int_{-\infty}^{+\infty} f_{(X,Y)}(x, y)\, dy$. Similarly, $f_Y(y) = \int_{-\infty}^{+\infty} f_{(X,Y)}(x, y)\, dx$.

The **conditional density function** of X given that $Y = y$, provided that $f_Y(y) > 0$, is defined as $f_{X|Y}(x|y) = \frac{f_{(X,Y)}(x,y)}{f_Y(y)}$. Analogously, $f_{Y|X}(y|x) = \frac{f_{(X,Y)}(x,y)}{f_X(x)}$.

Covariance and Correlation. The **covariance** between two random variables, X and Y, is defined as

$$\text{Cov}[X, Y] = \mathbb{E}[(X - \mathbb{E}[X])(Y - \mathbb{E}[Y])] = \mathbb{E}[XY] - \mathbb{E}[X]\mathbb{E}[Y],$$

and measures the degree to which X and Y are (linearly) related. The covariance is positive when the greater values of one variable mainly correspond with the greater values of the other variable, and the same holds for the lesser values. In the opposite case, when the greater values of one variable mainly correspond to the lesser values of the other, the covariance is negative. Therefore, the sign of the covariance denotes the tendency in the linear relationship between the variables. The value of the covariance can be between $-\infty$ and $+\infty$, and its magnitude is hard to interpret.

The normalized dimensionless version of the covariance, the **correlation coefficient**, is defined as

$$\rho[X,Y] = \frac{Cov[X,Y]}{\sqrt{Var[X]Var[Y]}},$$

and represents the strength of the linear relationship. It verifies $-1 \leq \rho[X,Y] \leq 1$. It can be proven that $\rho[X,Y] = -1$ if and only if $Y = aX + b$ with $a < 0$. Also $\rho[X,Y] = 1$ if and only if $Y = aX + b$ with $a > 0$.

Data covariance and data correlation coefficient were introduced in Section 2.3.

Independent Variables. The discrete random variable X **is independent of** Y if, for all possible values y of Y, the conditional probability distribution of X given $Y = y$ coincides with the marginal probability distribution of X. Thus, $p(X = x|Y = y) = p(X = x)$ for all x, y. It can be proven that when X is independent of Y, Y is also independent of X, and the previous condition can be reformulated as follows: two discrete random variables X and Y are independent if and only if $p(X = x, Y = y) = p(X = x)p(Y = y)$ for all x and y, that is, two discrete variables are independent if and only if the bivariate probability distribution factorizes as the product of both marginal probability distributions.

The two variables in Table 3.5 are not independent because $p(X = \text{I}, Y = \text{ss}) = 0.0105 \neq p(X = \text{I})p(Y = \text{ss}) = 0.07 \cdot 0.1666 = 0.0117$.

For two continuous random variables, X and Y are independent if and only if, $f(X = x, Y = y) = f(X = x)f(Y = y)$ for all x and y. The condition can also be expressed in terms of the conditional and marginal density functions: $f(X = x|Y = y) = f(X = x)$ or $f(Y = y|X = x) = f(Y = y)$ for all x and y.

If X and Y are independent then, $\mathbb{E}[XY] = \mathbb{E}[X]\mathbb{E}[Y]$, and therefore $Cov[X,Y] = 0$. Thus, they are uncorrelated. However, the converse is not true: uncorrelated does not imply independent. However, for Gaussian distributions both concepts are equivalent.

Bivariate Normal Density. An example of a bivariate random variable (X,Y) is the **bivariate normal distribution**. Its joint density is

$$f_{(X,Y)}(x,y) = \frac{1}{2\pi\sigma_X\sigma_Y\sqrt{1-\rho^2}}$$

$$\cdot \exp\left\{ -\frac{1}{2(1-\rho^2)} \left[\left(\frac{x-\mu_X}{\sigma_X}\right)^2 - 2\rho\left(\frac{x-\mu_X}{\sigma_X}\right)\left(\frac{y-\mu_Y}{\sigma_Y}\right) + \left(\frac{y-\mu_Y}{\sigma_Y}\right)^2 \right] \right\},$$

where $\mu_X = \mathbb{E}[X]$, $\mu_Y = \mathbb{E}[Y]$, $\sigma_X^2 = Var[X]$, $\sigma_Y^2 = Var[Y]$, and ρ denotes the correlation coefficient between X and Y. The marginal density of X is $X \sim \mathcal{N}(x|\mu_X, \sigma_X)$. Similarly, $Y \sim \mathcal{N}(y|\mu_Y, \sigma_Y)$. The conditional density of X given that $Y = y$ is $X|Y = y \sim \mathcal{N}(x|\mu_X + \rho\frac{\sigma_X}{\sigma_Y}(y - \mu_Y), \sigma_X\sqrt{1-\rho^2})$.

Figure 3.10 shows some examples of bivariate normal distributions with different values of ρ.

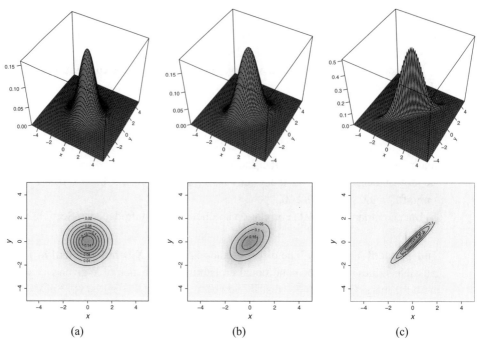

Figure 3.10 Probability density functions (top) and contour plots (bottom) for bivariate normal distributions. Contours are constant z slices on 2D. (a) $\rho = 0$. (b) $\rho = 0.5$. (c) $\rho = 0.95$.

3.4.2   Joint Distribution of n Random Variables

The above definitions concerning two random variables can be generalized for n random variables.

The **joint probability mass function of an n-dimensional discrete random variable $\mathbf{X} = (X_1, X_2, \ldots, X_n)$**, is any function $p(X_1 = x_1, X_2 = x_2, \ldots, X_n = x_n)$ satisfying the following two properties:

1. $p_{(X_1, X_2, \ldots, X_n)}(x_1, x_2, \ldots, x_n) \geq 0.$
2. $\sum_{x_1} \sum_{x_2} \cdots \sum_{x_n} p_{(X_1, X_2, \ldots, X_n)}(x_1, x_2, \ldots, x_n) = 1.$

Thus, for any event $A \subseteq \Omega_{X_1} \times \Omega_{X_2} \cdots \times \Omega_{X_n}$, its probability is given by

$$p_{(X_1, X_2, \ldots, X_n)}[(X_1, X_2, \ldots, X_n) \in A] = \sum_{(x_1, x_2, \ldots, x_n) \in A} p_{(X_1, X_2, \ldots, X_n)}(x_1, x_2, \ldots, x_n).$$

The concepts of cumulative distribution function, marginal probability distribution, and conditional probability distribution introduced for the joint distribution of two random variables can be easily generalized for n random variables.

The **joint pdf of an n-dimensional continuous random variable $\mathbf{X} = (X_1, X_2, \ldots, X_n)$**, is any integrable function $f_{(X_1, X_2, \ldots, X_n)}(x_1, x_2, \ldots, x_n)$ that satisfies:

1. $f_{(X_1, X_2, \ldots, X_n)}(x_1, x_2, \ldots, x_n) \geq 0$ for all $(x_1, x_2, \ldots, x_n)$.
2. $\int_{-\infty}^{+\infty} \int_{-\infty}^{+\infty} \cdots \int_{-\infty}^{+\infty} f_{(X_1, X_2, \ldots, X_n)}(x_1, x_2, \ldots, x_n)\, dx_1\, dx_2 \cdots dx_n = 1.$

3. $p_{(X_1,X_2,\ldots,X_n)}[(X_1,X_2,\ldots,X_n) \in A]$

$$= \int \cdots \int_{(x_1,x_2,\ldots,x_n) \in A} f_{(X_1,X_2,\ldots,X_n)}(x_1,x_2,\ldots,x_n)\,dx_1\,dx_2 \cdots dx_n.$$

The **covariance matrix** for $\mathbf{X}$, $\mathbf{Cov}[\mathbf{X}]$, is defined as the following symmetric, positive-definite matrix:

$$\mathbf{Cov}[\mathbf{X}] = \mathbb{E}\left[(\mathbf{X} - \mathbb{E}[\mathbf{X}])(\mathbf{X} - \mathbb{E}[\mathbf{X}])^T\right]$$

$$= \begin{pmatrix} Var[X_1] & Cov[X_1,X_2] & \cdots & Cov[X_1,X_n] \\ Cov[X_2,X_1] & Var[X_2] & \cdots & Cov[X_2,X_n] \\ \vdots & \vdots & \ddots & \vdots \\ Cov[X_n,X_1] & Cov[X_n,X_2] & \cdots & Var[X_n] \end{pmatrix}.$$

Note that the **mean vector** of $\mathbf{X}$, $\mathbb{E}[\mathbf{X}]$, consists of the means $\mathbb{E}[X_i]$ of each random variable X_i. The elements of the **correlation matrix** for $\mathbf{X}$, $\mathbf{Cor}[\mathbf{X}]$, are the values of the correlation coefficient $\rho[X_i, X_j]$ between any pair of variables X_i and X_j. Thus,

$$\mathbf{Cor}[\mathbf{X}] = \begin{pmatrix} 1 & \rho[X_1,X_2] & \cdots & \rho[X_1,X_n] \\ \rho[X_2,X_1] & 1 & \cdots & \rho[X_2,X_n] \\ \vdots & \vdots & \ddots & \vdots \\ \rho[X_n,X_1] & \rho[X_n,X_2] & \cdots & 1 \end{pmatrix}.$$

Mutually Independent Random Variables. The set of discrete variables $X_1, X_2, \ldots, X_n$ are said to be mutually independent if, for any finite subset of any size $m \leq n$, its joint probability distribution factorizes as a product of its marginal distributions, that is,

$$p_{(X_{i_1}, X_{i_2}, \ldots, X_{i_m})}(x_{i_1}, x_{i_2}, \ldots, x_{i_m}) = \prod_{j=1}^{m} p_{X_{i_j}}(x_{i_j}).$$

The definition for mutually independent continuous random variables is analogous. In this case, the joint density function factorizes as a product of univariate densities.

3.4.3 Multinomial Distribution

The **multinomial distribution** is an example of a discrete n-dimensional random variable and constitutes a generalization of the binomial distribution. Experiments where each trial can result in any one of the n possible mutually exclusive outcomes, $A_1, \ldots, A_n$, with associated probabilities $p(A_i) = p_i$, $0 < p_i < 1$, for $i = 1, \ldots, n$, such that $\sum_{i=1}^{n} p_i = 1$ can be modeled with a multinomial distribution. This multinomial distribution computes the probability that A_1 occurs x_1 times, A_2 occurs x_2 times,..., and A_n occurs x_n times in M independent trials, where $x_1 + x_2 + \cdots + x_n = M$. The multinomial distribution is denoted as $\mathbf{X} \sim \mathrm{MN}(\mathbf{x} \mid M; p_1, \ldots, p_n)$, and its joint probability mass function is given by the following formula:

$$p\left(\mathbf{X} = (x_1, x_2, \ldots, x_n) \mid M; p_1, \ldots, p_n\right) = \frac{M!}{x_1!x_2! \cdots x_n!} p_1^{x_1} p_2^{x_2} \cdots p_n^{x_n}.$$

The expected value of each X_i ($i = 1, \ldots, n$) is $\mathbb{E}[X_i] = Mp_i$, which shapes the mean vector. Likewise, $Var[X_i] = Mp_i(1 - p_i)$ and $Cov[X_i, X_j] = -Mp_ip_j$ constitute the covariance matrix.

The categorical distribution (Section 3.2.4) is a special case of the multinomial distribution, where $n = 1$ (a unidimensional distribution), $M = 1$ (a single trial), and x_1 is any possible value of X and not a frequency.

Considering the random variable X from Table 3.5, whose marginal distribution is given by $p_I = 0.07, p_{II-III} = 0.19, p_{IV} = 0.24, p_V = 0.17$ and $p_{VI} = 0.33$, and a 5-dimensional discrete variable $\mathbf{X}$ containing the number of times each possible value of $\mathbf{X}$ occurs when selecting 16 neurons from any of the 5 layers at random, the probability of 2 neurons being from layers I and VI, and 4 being from layers II–III, IV, and V is given by:

$$p(\mathbf{X} = (2,4,4,4,2) \mid 16; 0.07, 0.19, 0.24, 0.17, 0.33)$$
$$= \frac{16!}{2!4!4!4!2!}(0.07)^2(0.19)^4(0.24)^4(0.17)^4(0.33)^2.$$

3.4.4   Multivariate Normal Distribution

The **multivariate normal distribution** is denoted by $\mathbf{X} \sim \mathcal{N}(\mathbf{x}|\boldsymbol{\mu}, \boldsymbol{\Sigma})$, and its joint density function is

$$f_{\mathbf{X}}(\mathbf{x}|\boldsymbol{\mu}, \boldsymbol{\Sigma}) = \frac{1}{(2\pi)^{n/2}|\boldsymbol{\Sigma}|^{1/2}}\exp\left(-\frac{1}{2}(\mathbf{x} - \boldsymbol{\mu})^T\boldsymbol{\Sigma}^{-1}(\mathbf{x} - \boldsymbol{\mu})\right),$$

where $\boldsymbol{\mu}^T = \mathbb{E}[\mathbf{X}] = (\mu_1, \mu_2, \ldots, \mu_n) = (\mathbb{E}[X_1], \mathbb{E}[X_2], \ldots, \mathbb{E}[X_n])$ is the mean vector, and $|\boldsymbol{\Sigma}|$ represents the determinant of the covariance matrix of $\mathbf{X}$.

All marginal and conditional distributions of a multivariate normal distribution are also normal. Specifically, consider that the n-dimensional random variable $\mathbf{X}$ is partitioned arbitrarily as $\mathbf{X} = \begin{pmatrix} \mathbf{X}_1 \\ \mathbf{X}_2 \end{pmatrix}$, with dimension q and $n - q$ for $\mathbf{X}_1$ and $\mathbf{X}_2$, respectively. Similarly, $\boldsymbol{\mu}$ is partitioned as $\boldsymbol{\mu} = \begin{pmatrix} \boldsymbol{\mu}_1 \\ \boldsymbol{\mu}_2 \end{pmatrix}$ with dimension q and $n - q$ for $\boldsymbol{\mu}_1$ and $\boldsymbol{\mu}_2$, and $\boldsymbol{\Sigma}$ as $\boldsymbol{\Sigma} = \begin{pmatrix} \boldsymbol{\Sigma}_{11} & \boldsymbol{\Sigma}_{12} \\ \boldsymbol{\Sigma}_{21} & \boldsymbol{\Sigma}_{22} \end{pmatrix}$, where $\boldsymbol{\Sigma}_{11}$ has dimension $q \times q$ and $\boldsymbol{\Sigma}_{22}$ has dimension $(n - q) \times (n - q)$, and they denote the covariance matrix of $\mathbf{X}_1$ and $\mathbf{X}_2$, respectively. $\boldsymbol{\Sigma}_{12}$ represents the covariance matrix of $\mathbf{X}_1$ and $\mathbf{X}_2$ and is a $q \times (n - q)$-dimensional matrix, and $\boldsymbol{\Sigma}_{21} = \boldsymbol{\Sigma}_{12}^T$.

Then the marginal distribution of $\mathbf{X}_i$ is $\mathcal{N}(\mathbf{x}|\boldsymbol{\mu}_i, \boldsymbol{\Sigma}_i)$, $i = 1, 2$. The distribution of $\mathbf{X}_1$ conditioned on $\mathbf{X}_2 = \mathbf{x}_2$ is also a multivariate normal: $\mathbf{X}_1|\mathbf{X}_2 = \mathbf{x}_2 \sim \mathcal{N}(\mathbf{x}_1|\boldsymbol{\mu}_1 + \boldsymbol{\Sigma}_{12}\boldsymbol{\Sigma}_{22}^{-1}(\mathbf{x}_2 - \boldsymbol{\mu}_2), \boldsymbol{\Sigma}_{11} - \boldsymbol{\Sigma}_{12}\boldsymbol{\Sigma}_{22}^{-1}\boldsymbol{\Sigma}_{21})$.

These properties will be useful in exact inference on Gaussian Bayesian networks (Section 13.2.2.4), for example.

3.4.5   Dirichlet Distribution

The **Dirichlet distribution** is denoted by $\mathbf{X} = (X_1, \ldots, X_n) \sim \text{Dir}(\mathbf{x}|\alpha_1, \ldots, \alpha_n)$, and its joint density function is

$$f_{\mathbf{X}}(\mathbf{x}|\alpha_1, \ldots, \alpha_n) = \frac{\Gamma(\alpha_1 + \cdots + \alpha_n)}{\Gamma(\alpha_1) \cdots \Gamma(\alpha_n)}x_1^{\alpha_1 - 1} \cdots x_n^{\alpha_n - 1},$$

where all $x_i \in (0,1)$ and $x_1 + \cdots + x_n = 1$. $\alpha_1, \ldots, \alpha_n$ are positive real numbers called concentration parameters, and $\Gamma(\cdot)$ is the gamma function defined in Section 3.3.4.

Define $\alpha_0 = \sum_{i=1}^{n} \alpha_i$. The Dirichlet distribution is a multivariate generalization of the beta distribution. Thus, the marginal distributions are beta distributions, that is, $X_i \sim \text{Beta}(x_i | \alpha_i, \alpha_0 - \alpha_i)$. Hence, $\mathbb{E}[X_i] = \frac{\alpha_i}{\alpha_0}$ and $Var[X_i] = \frac{\alpha_i(\alpha_0 - \alpha_i)}{\alpha_0^2(\alpha_0+1)}$. Also, $Cov[X_i, X_j] = \frac{-\alpha_i \alpha_j}{\alpha_0^2(\alpha_0+1)}$.

The Dirichlet distribution is the conjugate prior of the categorical and multinomial distributions (see Table 4.1). Therefore, it is very often used as prior distribution in Bayesian statistics (Section 4.1.4). In Chapter 13 related to Bayesian networks, the Dirichlet distribution plays a key role in Bayesian parameter estimation (Section 13.3.1.2). It discusses interesting applications of special cases of this distribution.

3.4.6 Wishart Distribution

The Wishart distribution is a multidimensional generalization of the chi-squared distribution, or, in the case of non-integer degrees of freedom, of the gamma distribution. It is a distribution defined over $\mathbf{X}$, an $n \times n$ dimensional symmetric positive-definite matrix-valued random variable (also called "random matrix"). There are several possible parameterizations, of which we define the most common. The **Wishart distribution** is denoted by $\mathbf{X} \sim \mathcal{W}(\mathbf{x} | \alpha, \mathbf{T})$, with $\alpha > n - 1$ degrees of freedom (a real number) and $\mathbf{T}$, the $n \times n$ dimensional positive-definite scale matrix. Its density function is

$$f_{\mathbf{X}}(\mathbf{x} | \alpha, \mathbf{T}) = \frac{1}{2^{\alpha n/2} |\mathbf{T}|^{\alpha/2} \Gamma_n(\alpha/2)} |\mathbf{X}|^{(\alpha-n-1)/2} e^{-\frac{1}{2} \text{tr}(\mathbf{T}^{-1}\mathbf{X})},$$

where $\text{tr}(\cdot)$ is the trace function (sum of the elements on the main diagonal), $|\mathbf{X}|$ is the determinant of $\mathbf{X}$, and $\Gamma_n(\cdot)$ is the **multivariate gamma function**, given by:

$$\Gamma_n(\alpha) = \pi^{n(n-1)/4} \prod_{i=1}^{n} \Gamma\left(\frac{2\alpha + 1 - i}{2}\right).$$

This function is defined for any real $\alpha > n - 1$. If $\alpha \leq n - 1$, then the Wishart no longer has a density.

If $n = T = 1$, then this distribution is a chi-squared distribution with α degrees of freedom. Recall that the chi-squared distribution with α degrees of freedom is the distribution of a sum of squares of α independent standard Gaussian random variables, that is, if $Y_1, \ldots, Y_\alpha$ are independent $\mathcal{N}(y|0,1)$ random variables, then $X = \sum_{i=1}^{\alpha} Y_i^2 \sim \chi^2(x|\alpha)$. As an extended version, if $\mathbf{Y}_1, \ldots, \mathbf{Y}_\alpha$ are independent $\mathcal{N}(\mathbf{y}|\mathbf{0},\mathbf{T})$ random (column) vectors, then $\mathbf{X} = \sum_{i=1}^{\alpha} \mathbf{Y}_i \mathbf{Y}_i^T \sim \mathcal{W}(\mathbf{x}|\alpha, \mathbf{T})$. Also recall that the chi-squared distribution is a special case of the gamma distribution, from which we can infer that the Wishart distribution generalizes the gamma distribution for non-integer degrees of freedom.

The Wishart distribution plays a key role in the estimation of covariance matrices, because it is a conjugate prior for the precision parameter of the multivariate normal distribution (the inverse of the covariance matrix), provided the mean parameter is known (Section 13.3.1.2).

3.4.7 Normal-Wishart Distribution

A different type of generalization is the normal-Wishart distribution, essentially the product of a multivariate normal distribution and a Wishart distribution. Assume $\mu \in \mathbb{R}^n$ (a vector) and $\mathbf{W} \in \mathbb{R}^{n \times n}$ (a symmetric positive-definite random matrix), such that

$$f(\mu | \mathbf{W}) \sim \mathcal{N}(\mu_0, (\nu \mathbf{W})^{-1}),$$
$$f(\mathbf{W}) \sim \mathcal{W}(\alpha, \mathbf{T}_0),$$

where $\mu_0 \in \mathbb{R}^n$ is the location parameter, $\nu > 0$, $\mathbf{T}_0 \in \mathbb{R}^{n \times n}$ is the scale matrix (positive-definite), and $\alpha > n-1$ is the degrees of freedom. Then $(\mu, \mathbf{W})$ is said to follow a **normal-Wishart distribution**, denoted as $\mathcal{NW}((\mu, \mathbf{W}) | \mu_0, \nu, \mathbf{T}_0, \alpha)$, which depends on the four parameters, with a density:

$$f((\mu, \mathbf{W}) | \mu_0, \nu, \mathbf{T}_0, \alpha) = \frac{1}{(2\pi)^{n/2} |(\nu \mathbf{W})^{-1}|^{1/2}} \exp\left(-\frac{1}{2\nu} (\mu - \mu_0)^T \mathbf{W} (\mu - \mu_0) \right)$$
$$\cdot \frac{1}{2^{\alpha n/2} |\mathbf{T}_0|^{\alpha/2} \Gamma_n(\alpha/2)} |\mathbf{W}|^{(\alpha-n-1)/2} e^{-\frac{1}{2} \mathrm{tr}(\mathbf{T}_0^{-1} \mathbf{W})}.$$

The normal-Wishart distribution is the conjugate prior of a multivariate normal distribution with unknown mean and precision matrix (Section 13.3.1.2).

3.4.8 Multivariate von Mises Distribution

The **multivariate von Mises distribution** (Mardia et al., 2008), $\Theta \sim \nu \mathcal{M}_n(\theta | \mu, \kappa, \Lambda)$, is defined by the following joint density function

$$f_\Theta(\theta | \mu, \kappa, \Lambda) = \frac{1}{T(\kappa, \Lambda)} \exp\left(\kappa^T c(\theta, \mu) + \frac{1}{2} s(\theta, \mu)^T \Lambda s(\theta, \mu) \right), \qquad (3.1)$$

where

$$c(\theta, \mu)^T = (\cos(\theta_1 - \mu_1), \cos(\theta_2 - \mu_2), \ldots, \cos(\theta_n - \mu_n)),$$
$$s(\theta, \mu)^T = (\sin(\theta_1 - \mu_1), \sin(\theta_2 - \mu_2), \ldots, \sin(\theta_n - \mu_n)),$$

κ and μ are n-dimensional parameters $\kappa = (\kappa_1, \kappa_2, \ldots, \kappa_n)^T$, $\mu = (\mu_1, \mu_2, \ldots, \mu_n)^T$, and $-\pi < \theta_i \leq \pi, -\pi < \mu_i \leq \pi, \kappa_i \geq 0, \lambda_{ij} \in \mathbb{R}$, and $(\Lambda)_{ij} = \lambda_{ij} = \lambda_{ji}$, for $i \neq j$, $\lambda_{ii} = 0$. Also, $\frac{1}{T(\kappa, \Lambda)}$ is a normalizing constant such that Equation (3.1) is a probability density function. For $n = 1$, the multivariate von Mises distribution is a univariate von Mises density.

For large concentrations in the circular variables, the multivariate normal density provides a good approximation of the multivariate von Mises distribution. More specifically and without loss of generality, if $\mu = 0$, we have

$$\Theta = (\Theta_1, \Theta_2, \ldots, \Theta_n) \simeq \mathcal{N}(\mathbf{x} | \mathbf{0}, \Sigma), \quad \text{where} \quad (\Sigma^{-1})_{ii} = \kappa_i, \quad (\Sigma^{-1})_{ij} = -\lambda_{ij}, i \neq j.$$

A multivariate von Mises distribution to model the angles between basal dendrites of pyramidal cells was proposed in Rodriguez-Lujan et al. (2017).

Table 3.7 Parameters, pmf/pdf, and domain of the most commonly used multivariate distributions; the discrete multinomial distribution: $MN(\mathbf{x}|M; p_1,\ldots,p_n)$ and the continuous distributions: multivariate normal distribution $\mathcal{N}(\mathbf{x}|\boldsymbol{\mu}, \boldsymbol{\Sigma})$, Dirichlet distribution $Dir(\mathbf{x}|\alpha_1,\ldots,\alpha_n)$, Wishart distribution $\mathcal{W}(\mathbf{x}|\alpha, \mathbf{T})$, normal-Wishart distribution $\mathcal{NW}((\boldsymbol{\mu}, \mathbf{W})|\boldsymbol{\mu}_0, \nu, \mathbf{T}_0, \alpha)$, multivariate von Mises distribution $v\mathcal{M}_n(\boldsymbol{\theta}|\boldsymbol{\mu}, \boldsymbol{\kappa}, \boldsymbol{\Lambda})$, and multivariate von Mises–Fisher distribution $v\mathcal{MF}(\mathbf{x}|\boldsymbol{\mu}, \boldsymbol{\kappa})$

Distribution	Parameters	pmf/pdf	Domain
$MN(\mathbf{x}|M; p_1,\ldots,p_n)$	$M\in\mathbb{N}, p_1,\ldots,p_n\in\mathbb{R}^+$	$\frac{M!}{x_1!x_2!\cdots x_n!} p_1^{x_1} p_2^{x_2}\cdots p_n^{x_n}$	$\{0,\ldots,M\}^n$
$\mathcal{N}(\mathbf{x}|\boldsymbol{\mu},\boldsymbol{\Sigma})$	$\boldsymbol{\mu}\in\mathbb{R}^n, \boldsymbol{\Sigma}\in\mathbb{R}^{n\times n}$	$\frac{1}{(2\pi)^{n/2}|\boldsymbol{\Sigma}|^{1/2}}\exp\left(-\frac{1}{2}(\mathbf{x}-\boldsymbol{\mu})^T\boldsymbol{\Sigma}^{-1}(\mathbf{x}-\boldsymbol{\mu})\right)$	$\mathbb{R}^n$
$Dir(\mathbf{x}|\alpha_1,\ldots,\alpha_n)$	$\alpha_1,\ldots,\alpha_n\in\mathbb{R}^+$	$\frac{\Gamma(\alpha_1+\cdots+\alpha_n)}{\Gamma(\alpha_1)\cdots\Gamma(\alpha_n)}x_1^{\alpha_1-1}\cdots x_n^{\alpha_n-1}$	$(0,1)^n$
$\mathcal{W}(\mathbf{x}|\alpha,\mathbf{T})$	$\alpha\in\mathbb{R}^+, \mathbf{T}\in\mathbb{R}^{n\times n}$	$\frac{1}{2^{\alpha n/2}|\mathbf{T}|^{\alpha/2}\Gamma_n(\alpha/2)}|\mathbf{X}|^{(\alpha-n-1)/2}e^{-\frac{1}{2}\mathrm{tr}(\mathbf{T}^{-1}\mathbf{X})}$	$\mathbb{R}^{n\times n}$
$\mathcal{NW}((\boldsymbol{\mu},\mathbf{W})|\boldsymbol{\mu}_0,\nu,\mathbf{T}_0,\alpha)$	$\boldsymbol{\mu}_0\in\mathbb{R}^n, \nu\in\mathbb{R}^+$ $\mathbf{T}_0\in\mathbb{R}^{n\times n}, \alpha\in\mathbb{R}^+$	$\frac{1}{(2\pi)^{n/2}|(\nu\mathbf{W})^{-1}|^{1/2}}\exp\left(-\frac{1}{2\nu}(\boldsymbol{\mu}-\boldsymbol{\mu}_0)^T\mathbf{W}(\boldsymbol{\mu}-\boldsymbol{\mu}_0)\right)$ $\cdot\frac{1}{2^{\alpha n/2}|\mathbf{T}_0|^{\alpha/2}\Gamma_n(\alpha/2)}|\mathbf{W}|^{(\alpha-n-1)/2}e^{-\frac{1}{2}\mathrm{tr}(\mathbf{T}_0^{-1}\mathbf{W})}$	$\mathbb{R}^n\times\mathbb{R}^{n\times n}$
$v\mathcal{M}_n(\boldsymbol{\theta}|\boldsymbol{\mu},\boldsymbol{\kappa},\boldsymbol{\Lambda})$	$\boldsymbol{\mu}\in(-\pi,\pi)^n, \boldsymbol{\kappa}\in\mathbb{R}^n, \boldsymbol{\Lambda}\in\mathbb{R}^{n\times n}$	$\frac{1}{T(\boldsymbol{\kappa},\boldsymbol{\Lambda})}\exp\left(\boldsymbol{\kappa}^T c(\boldsymbol{\theta},\boldsymbol{\mu})+\frac{1}{2}s(\boldsymbol{\theta},\boldsymbol{\mu})^T\boldsymbol{\Lambda}s(\boldsymbol{\theta},\boldsymbol{\mu})\right)$	$(-\pi,\pi)^n$
$v\mathcal{MF}(\mathbf{x}|\boldsymbol{\mu},\boldsymbol{\kappa})$	$\boldsymbol{\mu}\in\mathbb{R}^n$ such that $\boldsymbol{\mu}^T\boldsymbol{\mu}=1, \kappa\in\mathbb{R}^+$	$C_n(\kappa)\exp\left(\kappa\boldsymbol{\mu}^T\mathbf{x}\right)$	$\mathbf{x}\in\mathbb{R}^n$ such that $\mathbf{x}^T\mathbf{x}=1$

3.4.9   Multivariate von Mises–Fisher Distribution

A directional variable $\mathbf{X} = (X_1, X_2, \ldots, X_n)$ follows a **multivariate von Mises–Fisher distribution** (Jupp and Mardia, 1979), $\mathbf{X} \sim \nu\mathcal{MF}(\mathbf{x}|\boldsymbol{\mu}, \kappa)$, on the $(n-1)$-dimensional unit sphere[2] if its joint density function is

$$f_{\mathbf{X}}(\mathbf{x}|\boldsymbol{\mu}, \kappa) = C_n(\kappa)\exp(\kappa\boldsymbol{\mu}^T\mathbf{x}),$$

where $\boldsymbol{\mu}$ is the population mean direction vector satisfying $\boldsymbol{\mu}^T\boldsymbol{\mu} = 1$, $\kappa \geq 0$ is the concentration parameter around $\boldsymbol{\mu}$, and the normalization constant $C_n(\kappa)$ is equal to

$$C_n(\kappa) = \frac{\kappa^{\frac{n}{2}-1}}{(2\pi)^{\frac{n}{2}}I_{\frac{n}{2}-1}(\kappa)},$$

where $I_\nu(\kappa)$ is the modified Bessel function of the first kind of order $\nu \in \mathbb{R}$ defined in Section 3.3.11.

The von Mises–Fisher distribution reduces to the von Mises distribution when $n = 2$ (Section 3.3.11) and is called the **Fisher distribution** (Fisher, 1953) when $n = 3$. The normalization constant for the Fisher distribution is $C_3(\kappa) = \frac{\kappa}{2\pi(e^\kappa - e^{-\kappa})}$. Like the von Mises distribution, the von Mises–Fisher distribution is also unimodal and symmetric around $\boldsymbol{\mu}$, the mode being located at $\boldsymbol{\mu}$.

Table 3.7 shows the parameters, the pmf (or pdf), and the domain of the above multivariate distributions in both the discrete and continuous domains.

3.5   Simulating Random Variates

Simulating a system or process where there are inherent random components requires a method to generate or output numbers that are somehow random. For instance, to model how 3D neuronal dendritic trees are grown (Section 13.5), we may require information about nearest segments, centrifugal orders, subtrees and subdendrites (see Section 1.6.5) that are "drawn" from a specified distribution. Therefore, it is important to know how random values can be generated from a desired probability distribution in order to run simulation models. In the strict sense, it is more precise to speak of generating or simulating random variates rather than random variables because random variables are mathematical probability functions.

There is more to simulation than just generating random variates. First, realizations of complex random processes can be got. For instance, if the spatial distribution of some cell locations in a specified region follows a homogeneous Poisson process, we can first simulate the number of cells by generating a Poisson random variate. The positions of the cells are then determined by simulating a binomial point process with the number of points found before (Section 15.2.2). Second, summary characteristics of complex processes for which there are no explicit analytical formulas can be estimated based on simulated points derived from processes. Third, simulations are employed to estimate the null hypothesis model in statistical tests, which does not have an easily derived distribution. Also,

---

[2] The $(n-1)$-dimensional unit sphere centered at the origin is defined by the set of n-dimensional points $\mathbb{S}^{n-1} = \{\mathbf{x} \in \mathbb{R}^n | \mathbf{x}^T\mathbf{x} = 1\}$, see Section 2.2.4.

the critical values for a test can be estimated by simulation. Sections 13.2.3, 15.3, 15.5, and 15.6 include many examples.

3.5.1 Random and Pseudo-Random Numbers

A key issue is to be able to generate random variates from the uniform distribution on the interval $(0, 1)$, i.e., U from $\text{Unif}(u|0, 1)$, which are known as **random numbers** (Kendall and Smith, 1938; Hull and Dobell, 1962). By first outputting independent random numbers, they can be transformed to get random variates from all other distributions (Gaussian, binomial,...) or realizations of various random processes (e.g., a homogeneous Poisson point process, see Chapter 15).

Mechanical and time-consuming random number generators include dice rolling, coin flipping, wheel spinning, and playing card shuffling. Faster, new, and sophisticated methods measure some physical phenomenon that is expected to be random and then corrects for possible biases in the measurement process. Examples include measuring atmospheric noise, thermal noise, radio noise, radioactive decay, cosmic background radiation, gamma rays, clock drift, timing of actual movements of a hard disk read/write head, etc.

Other methods use computational algorithms that can automatically produce long sequences of apparently random results, which are in fact completely determined by an initial value, known as a seed value or key. As a result, the entire sequence can be reproduced if the seed value is known. Reproducibility is important because it means that identical random numbers can be used to simulate and compare different systems and to make it easier to debug and verify a computer program. This type of random number generator is often called a **pseudo-random number** generator (not a "true" random number source in the purest sense of the word). The linear congruential generator is the most widely used method. In practice, they are generally sufficient, even for demanding security-critical cryptographic purposes. There are several tests to ascertain how well the generated numbers resemble values of true independent and identically distributed $\text{Unif}(u|0, 1)$ random variates.

The rest of this section concerns how to generate a random variate, that is, how to output an observation on a random variable from the desired distribution. This distribution is often the result of fitting (Chapter 4) some distributional form to observed data. Thus, we assume that we have a specified distribution, from which we want to generate random variates in order to run a simulation model. For example, if the numbers of synaptic junctions in a tissue volume of the somatosensory cortex in an animal (as observed by FIB milling/SEM imaging) fit a Poisson distribution with mean λ, then we require the generation of $\text{Pois}(\lambda)$ realizations to drive the simulation of "virtual" synaptic junctions.

3.5.2 Inverse-Transform

3.5.2.1 *Continuous Random Variables*

Suppose we wish to generate a continuous random variable X with cdf F that is strictly increasing when $0 < F(x) < 1$. Let F^{-1} denote the inverse function of F (also called **quantile function**), i.e., $F^{-1}(u)$ is defined as the value of x such that $F(x) = u$. A general method to generate such a random variable, called the **inverse-transform method**, is shown in Algorithm 3.1.

Algorithm 3.1: Inverse-transform method for continuous random variables

Input : A random number generator, the cdf F of the continuous random variable X that we want to generate

Output: A continuous random variable X with cdf F

1 Generate $U \sim \text{Unif}(u|0,1)$.
2 Return $X = F^{-1}(U)$.

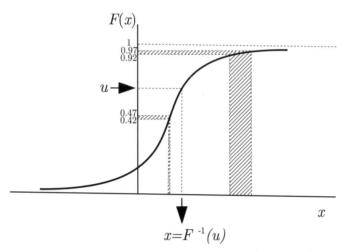

$$x = F^{-1}(u)$$

Figure 3.11 Inverse-transform method for continuous random variables. The random number u results in the random variate x. The Us on the vertical axis are always fairly evenly spread. However, the Xs on the horizontal axis are more closely packed if the density function f is high (and the cdf F climbs more steeply), and more widely spread if f is low (F is relatively flat). This is shown in the two intervals $[0.42, 0.47]$ and $[0.92, 0.97]$ on the vertical axis, which both contain about 5% of the Us but respectively lead to Xs in a narrow interval and Xs in a large interval on the horizontal axis. These intervals will also contain about 5% of the Xs, which will, however, be either compactly or sparsely packed.

X has cdf F since for any x, $p(X \leq x) = p(F^{-1}(U) \leq x) = p(U \leq F(x)) = \int_0^{F(x)} 1\, dt = F(x)$ because $U \sim \text{Unif}(u|0,1)$ and $0 \leq F(x) \leq 1$. Thus, we can generate a random variate X from the continuous cdf F by generating a random number U and then setting $X = F^{-1}(U)$. Figure 3.11 illustrates this point. Note that the inverse-transform method deforms the uniform distribution of the Us, leading to a distribution on the Xs that conforms to the desired distribution.

Example: Exponential. If $X \sim \text{Exp}(x|\lambda)$, then its cdf is $F(x) = \int_0^x \lambda e^{-\lambda t}\, dt = 1 - e^{-\lambda x}$ if $x \geq 0$. Thus, we set $u = F(x) = 1 - e^{-\lambda x}$ and solve for x to output the inverse function $F^{-1}(u) = x = -\frac{\ln(1-u)}{\lambda}$. Because $1 - U$ is also uniform in (0,1), we can generate an exponential with parameter λ by generating a random number U and then setting $X = -\frac{\ln U}{\lambda}$. Figure 3.12 shows this algorithm in action for $\text{Exp}(x|1)$. Note that the resemblance between the true and simulated cdfs is stronger with more draws (Figure 3.12(b)). ■

Example: Uniform in (a, b). If $X \sim \text{Unif}(x|a, b)$, then its cdf is $F(x) = \int_a^x \frac{1}{b-a}\, dt = \frac{x-a}{b-a}$ if $a < x < b$. Thus, we get $F^{-1}(U) = X = a + (b-a)U$, which is simply a linear transformation of U. ■

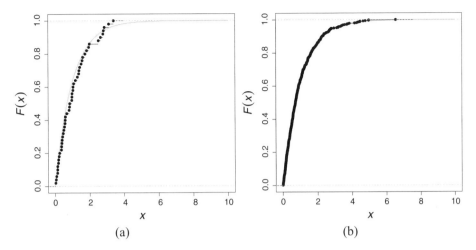

Figure 3.12 Inverse-transform method for $\text{Exp}(x|1)$ for (a) 50 random variates, and (b) 500 random variates. The empirical cdf (black) is compared against the true cdf (gray).

Example: Truncated Distribution. Suppose we have a density function f truncated to the interval $[a,b]$, that is, we have the truncated density

$$f^*(x) = \begin{cases} \frac{f(x)}{\int_a^b f(x)dx} & \text{if } a \le x \le b \\ 0 & \text{otherwise.} \end{cases}$$

For instance, a circular von Mises distribution (Section 3.3.11) can model the branching angles in 3D reconstructed basal arbors of pyramidal neurons in mice (Bielza et al., 2014) and rats (Leguey et al., 2016), but its truncated version to say, $[20, 97]$ and $[17, 92]$ degrees, respectively, gathered by empirical observation, may be more accurate, as reported by Fernández-González et al. (2017).

We know that $\int_a^b f(x)dx = F(b) - F(a)$, where F is the cdf. Because the truncated cdf F^* is

$$F^*(x) = \begin{cases} 0 & \text{if } x < a \\ \frac{F(x)-F(a)}{F(b)-F(a)} & \text{if } a \le x < b \\ 1 & \text{if } x \ge b, \end{cases}$$

then the inverse-transform method is

1. Generate $U \sim \text{Unif}(u|0,1)$.
2. Return $X = F^{-1}(F(a) + (F(b) - F(a))U)$.

If generating from f is easy, an alternative is to simulate from f^* by taking draws from f and only accepting those in $[a,b]$. ∎

3.5.2.2 *Discrete Random Variables*

Suppose that we now wish to generate a discrete random variable X with cdf F, i.e., $F(x) = p(X \le x) = \sum_{x_i \le x} p(x_i)$, where $p(x_i) = p(X = x_i) = p_i$ is the pmf, for $i = 1, 2, \ldots$ and $x_1 < x_2 < \cdots$. Then the inverse-transform method is listed in Algorithm 3.2.

Algorithm 3.2: Inverse-transform method for discrete random variables

Input : A random number generator, the pmf $p_1, p_2, \ldots$ of the discrete random variable X that we want to generate

Output: A discrete random variable X with pmf $p_1, p_2, \ldots$

1 Generate $U \sim \text{Unif}(u|0,1)$.

2 Return

$$X = \begin{cases} x_1 & \text{if } U < p_1 \\ x_2 & \text{if } p_1 \leq U < p_1 + p_2 \\ \vdots \\ x_j & \text{if } \sum_{i=1}^{j-1} p_i \leq U < \sum_{i=1}^{j} p_i \\ \vdots \end{cases}$$

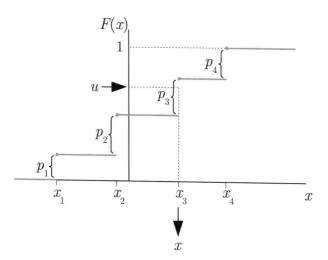

Figure 3.13 Inverse-transform method for discrete random variables. The random number u results in $X = x_3$ because $p_1 + p_2 \leq u < p_1 + p_2 + p_3$.

Thus

$$p(X = x_j) = p\left(\sum_{i=1}^{j-1} p_i \leq U < \sum_{i=1}^{j} p_i\right) = \sum_{i=1}^{j} p_i - \sum_{i=1}^{j-1} p_i = p_j,$$

and, therefore, X has the desired distribution. Thus, we can generate a random variable X from the discrete distribution F by generating a random number U and finding the interval $[\sum_{i=1}^{j-1} p_i, \sum_{i=1}^{j} p_i)$ containing U. Figure 3.13 illustrates this idea.

Example. Categorical Distribution. Let X denote interneuron cell types whose values are $x_1 = $ chandelier, $x_2 = $ common basket, and $x_3 = $ Martinotti, with probabilities $p_1 = 0.30$, $p_2 = 0.25$, and $p_3 = 0.45$, respectively, in a particular cell population. To generate a random variate from this categorical distribution, we first generate a random number U. We then set X to x_1 if $U < 0.30$, $X = x_2$ if $0.30 \leq U < 0.55$, and $X = x_3$ if $0.55 \leq U < 1$. Note that the same previous procedure applies although the x_i values are not ordered. ∎

In Chapter 13, the inverse-transform method is intensively employed to simulate virtual 3D morphologies of basal dendritic trees (López-Cruz et al., 2011). A number of morphological variables (Table 1.11) were measured on real reconstructions of pyramidal neurons from the mouse neocortex, layer III of three cortical regions, and simulations were drawn from the fitted distributions to build virtual dendritic trees.

3.5.3   Composition

The **composition method** applies when the baseline cdf F used for simulation can be expressed as a mixture (Section 12.2) or a composition, that is, as a convex combination (i.e., a weighted sum with nonnegative weights that sum 1) of other cdfs $F_1, F_2, \ldots, F_K$. Thus, $F(x) = \sum_{i=1}^{K} \pi_i F_i(x)$. We assume that it is easier to simulate from F_i than from the original F.

One way to simulate from F is first to simulate a discrete random variable Y, equal to i with probability π_i, $i = 1, 2, \ldots, K$, and then to simulate from cdf F_Y. Thus, if the simulated value of Y is $Y = j$, then the second simulation is from F_j.

Example. In probabilistic clustering, each data point or object $\mathbf{x}$ is assumed to come from a mixture $F(\mathbf{x}) = \sum_{i=1}^{K} \pi_i F_i(\mathbf{x})$ of K cdfs F_i, one for each cluster (Chapter 12). Each cdf $F_i(\mathbf{x})$ denotes the cumulative distribution, provided we know that the object belongs to the ith cluster, of the object taking value $\mathbf{x}$, and π_i is the prior probability of picking the ith cluster or mixture component.

After clustering dendritic spines into a number of groups with a probabilistic clustering method, then we can carry on simulating virtual spines according to these groups and their mixing coefficients π_i. The composition method applies here because we would first simulate which cluster (e.g., j) and then use cdf F_j for simulation to yield a virtual spine $\mathbf{x}$ from cluster j. This is detailed in Section 12.4, where $K = 8$, data point $\mathbf{x}$ is $n = 54$-dimensional, and F_is are Gaussian distributions. ∎

3.5.4   Use of Transformations

When the target random variable X is given in terms of other random variables that are more easily generated, the transformation relating them can be used for the purpose of simulation. For example, X follows a lognormal distribution with parameters μ and σ if $Y = \ln X \sim \mathcal{N}(y|\mu, \sigma)$ (Section 3.3.7). Then a simulation procedure for the lognormal distribution is

1. Generate $Y \sim \mathcal{N}(y|\mu, \sigma)$.
2. Return $X = \exp(Y)$.

Thus, a procedure to simulate from a normal distribution is sufficient here. Likewise we can take draws from χ_n^2 by summing the squares of n independent standard Gaussian random variates, and from $\text{Bin}(n, \theta)$ by summing n independent $\text{Ber}(\theta)$ random variates. To simulate from t_n, we can use $X = \frac{Z}{\sqrt{\frac{Y}{n}}} \sim t_n$, for $Z \sim \mathcal{N}(0, 1)$ and $Y \sim \chi_n^2$, both of which are independent. Generation from F_{n_1, n_2} can be accomplished by simulating independent $Z \sim \chi_{n_1}^2$ and $Y \sim \chi_{n_2}^2$ and returning $X = \frac{Z/n_1}{Y/n_2}$.

Note that the composition method can be considered as an example of the use of transformations.

Example. Data Set 7 includes 10 different samples of the neuropil in layer III of the somatosensory cortex from 3 different 14-day-old male Wistar rats (Table 1.13). These samples contained 1,695 synaptic junctions. Feret's diameters of synaptic junctions, as an estimate of their sizes, fitted a lognormal distribution, see Chapter 15. We can simulate Feret's diameters of synaptic junctions using the procedure described above. ■

3.5.5   Acceptance-Rejection

The **acceptance-rejection method** is less direct than the above techniques and can be useful when more direct techniques fail or are inefficient. The idea dates back to von Neumann (1951) at least.

Assume that we want to generate X from cdf F and a density function f. The method requires the specification of a function t that majorizes f, that is, $f(x) \le t(x)$ for all x. t will not, generally, be a density function because $\int_{-\infty}^{\infty} t(x)dx = a \ge \int_{-\infty}^{\infty} f(x)dx = 1$. But $g(x) = t(x)/a$ is a density function. Note that, because $f(x) \le ag(x)$ for all x, then we can take $a = \max_x \frac{f(x)}{g(x)}$. Assume that generation from g (usually taken as the uniform distribution) is straightforward. Algorithm 3.3 is the general statement of this method.

Algorithm 3.3: Acceptance-rejection method for continuous random variables

Input : A random number generator, an easy-to-generate density function g, and
a constant $a \ge 1$ such that $f(x) \le ag(x), \forall x$

Output: A continuous random variable X with density f

1 Generate $X \sim g$.
2 Generate $U \sim \text{Unif}(u|0, 1)$, independent of X.
3 If $U\,ag(X) \le f(X)$, return X. Otherwise reject X, go back to step 1 and try again.

Rather than proving that the method works, we provide some intuitive insights. Figure 3.14 shows hypothetical $f(x)$ and $t(x) = ag(x)$ curves. In step 3, $Y = 0 + t(X)U$ is a linear transformation of U. Hence, given a fixed $X = x$ generated from g in step 1 (see the vertical line in Figure 3.14), the method generates values $Y \sim \text{Unif}(y|0, t(x))$, which are accepted if $Y \le f(x)$. In geometric terms, this means that $Y = t(x)U$ will be accepted as an X if the point (x, Y) falls under the curve for density f (points in black in Figure 3.14). This way more Xs will be accepted if f is high because uniformly distributed dots are more likely to be under $f(x)$ there. Thus, the algorithm "thins out" the Xs from the g density function if t is much greater than f, but retains most of the Xs if t is only slightly greater than f. As a result, the concentration of the Xs from g is altered to match the desired density function f.

In order to avoid many rejections and increase the efficiency of the procedure, t should be chosen so that a is small (recall that $a \ge 1$). Therefore, a good t is a function that fits just above f, bringing a close to 1. Intuitively, this kind of t leads to a density g that will be close to f (the closer a is to 1, the more alike the two densities f and g will be). Thus, the X

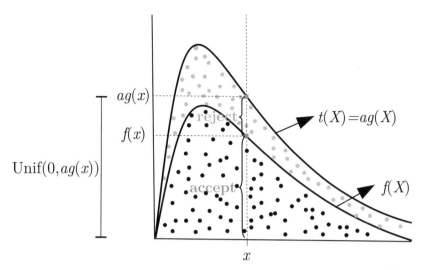

Figure 3.14 Illustration of the acceptance-rejection method. $X \sim g$ is accepted if $t(X)U \leq f(X)$. Therefore the probability of accepting a value x generated from g as generated from f is $\frac{f(x)}{t(x)}$. In regions where both f and t agree, points will probably be accepted; in regions where f is much smaller than t, most points will be rejected.

values generated from g in Step 1 are from a distribution that is almost correct. Therefore, we should accept most values.

Also, the method can lead to a lot of unwanted samples being taken if the sampled function f is highly concentrated in a certain region; for example, a function that has a spike at some location. For many distributions, this problem can be solved using an adaptive extension (Gilks and Wild, 1992) or modifying the proposal distribution g at each step (Casella et al., 2004).

Example: Beta. Consider the Beta$(2,2)$ distribution, whose density function is $f(x) = 6x(1-x)$ if $0 \leq x \leq 1$ and 0 otherwise. Its cdf $F(x)$ is a third-degree polynomial, and the inverse-transform approach would not be simple to apply, as numerical methods would be required to find polynomial roots. However, the acceptance-rejection method is easier. Let us take g as Unif$(0,1)$, that is, $g(x) = 1$ if $0 \leq x \leq 1$ and 0 otherwise. Now we determine a such that $f(x) \leq ag(x) = a$ for all x. By standard differential calculus, i.e., setting the derivative of f to 0, we find that the maximum value of $f(x)$ occurs at $x = 1/2$, with $f(1/2) = 3/2$. Thus, $f(x) \leq 3/2 = a = t(x)$. Functions f, t, and g are shown in Figure 3.15. Then the procedure for generation from the Beta$(2,2)$ distribution is

1. Generate $U_1 \sim$ Unif$(u|0,1)$.
2. Generate $U_2 \sim$ Unif$(u|0,1)$, independent of U_1.
3. If $\frac{3}{2}U_2 \leq 6U_1(1-U_1)$, return U_1. Otherwise reject U_1, go back to step 1 and try again.

The inequality in step 3 can be simplified as "If $U_2 \leq 4U_1(1-U_1)$." Note that the acceptance probability in step 3 is only $1/a = 2/3$, and $t(x)$ does not closely fit above f (Figure 3.15). More elaborate majorizing functions, like a piecewise linear density function, could be designed. ∎

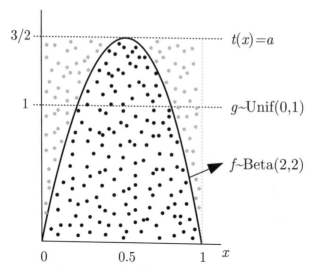

Figure 3.15 Functions $f(x), t(x)$, and $g(x)$ for the acceptance-rejection method applied to the Beta$(2, 2)$ distribution. All points have been generated from $g \sim$ Unif$(0, 1)$, but the gray points will be rejected. Note how the accepted (black) points will be concentrated according to the desired density f.

The acceptance-rejection method is the same for discrete random variables, where pmfs replace densities, that is, we first simulate a random variable X having pmf $\{q_j\}_j$, and we then accept this simulated value as coming from a random variable with pmf $\{p_j\}_j$ with a probability $p_X / a q_X$, where $p_j \leq a q_j$, for all j. Moreover, the method can also be extended to higher-dimensional spaces.

This method relates to the general field of Monte Carlo techniques, including **Markov chain Monte Carlo** (MCMC) algorithms that also use a proxy distribution to simulate from the target distribution f. MCMC methods construct a Markov chain whose stationary distribution is the desired distribution (even multivariate). The state of the chain after a number of steps is then used as a sample of the target distribution (Section 13.2.3).

3.5.6 Importance Sampling

Simulation can be a very useful tool for computing integrals because most integrals can be written as an expectation. This is called **Monte Carlo integration**, where the expectation is approximated as a sample average supported by the law of large numbers (Section 4.1.2.1). Thus, if $x^1, \ldots, x^N$ are independent draws from some distribution with density f, then

$$\mathbb{E}[X] = \int x f(x) dx \approx \frac{1}{N} \sum_{i=1}^{N} x^i. \tag{3.2}$$

As in the acceptance-rejection method, draws in **importance sampling** are taken from an alternative distribution defined in the target region. The principle of importance sampling is

$$\int x f(x) dx = \int x \frac{f(x)}{g(x)} g(x) dx,$$

where g is a density function defined in the same domain as f (in fact, it is enough to have $g(x) > 0$ whenever $xf(x) \neq 0$). Therefore, simulating x from f and approximating the expectation as in Equation (3.2) is equivalent to simulating $xw(x)$ from g, with importance sampling weights $w(x) = \frac{f(x)}{g(x)}$. Now

$$\mathbb{E}[X] = \int xf(x)dx \approx \frac{1}{N}\sum_{i=1}^{N} x^i w(x^i),$$

where $x^1, \ldots, x^N$ are independent draws from g. By making the multiplicative adjustment $\frac{f(x)}{g(x)}$ to x, we compensate for simulating from g instead of f. g is called the **importance distribution**. A good g is proportional to $xf(x)$, with spikes in the same places. This requires some educated guessing and numerical search. If f is a Gaussian, a common g is a Student's t distribution.

Example: Mean of Truncated Standard Normal Distribution. Suppose we wish to simulate the mean of a standard normal distribution, truncated to the unit interval $[0, 1]$. The density is $f^*(x) = \frac{f(x)}{\int_0^1 f(x)dx}$ if $0 \leq x \leq 1$ and 0 otherwise, where f is $\mathcal{N}(0, 1)$. The brute force simulation takes draws $x^i, i = 1, \ldots, N$, from $\mathcal{N}(0, 1)$ and only accepts those in $[0, 1]$. The simulated mean is approximated as $\frac{1}{N'}\sum_{i=1}^{N} x^i \mathbb{I}(x^i \in [0, 1])$, where $N' = \sum_{i=1}^{N} \mathbb{I}(x^i \in [0, 1])$, i.e., the number of accepted points, and $\mathbb{I}(t)$ is the indicator function, that is,

$$\mathbb{I}(t) = \begin{cases} 1 & \text{if } t \text{ is true} \\ 0 & \text{if } t \text{ is false.} \end{cases} \tag{3.3}$$

If $N' \ll N$, the procedure is inefficient, with a lot of unwanted samples being generated.

However, with importance sampling, we can draw from a g that is $\text{Unif}(0, 1)$. For each draw, the importance weight is $w(x^i) = f^*(x^i) = \frac{f(x^i)}{\int_0^1 f(x)dx}$, and the simulated mean is approximated as $\frac{1}{N}\sum_{i=1}^{N} x^i w(x^i)$, without rejecting any draw. ∎

Importance sampling is easier to implement than acceptance-rejection. In acceptance-rejection, the value of a, the upper bound of $\frac{f(x)}{g(x)}$, must be computed. This is not necessary in importance sampling. Furthermore, when $\sup_x \frac{f(x)}{g(x)} = \infty$, then acceptance-rejection is impossible, whereas importance sampling is still an option.

3.5.7 Specific Methods

There are particular methods for generating random variates from some widely used distributions. Simulation should be efficient, which is why many alternative algorithms are found in the literature. Here we first provide simple simulation methods for the Poisson and Gaussian distributions and then for some multivariate distributions.

Poisson Distribution. The Poisson distribution with parameter λ can be simulated with the inverse-transform method. Recall that $p_i = \frac{\lambda^i e^{-\lambda}}{i!}, i = 0, 1, \ldots$, and then we have $p_{i+1} = \frac{\lambda}{i+1}p_i$, a recursive formula amenable to compute the cdf. We have $p_0 = e^{-\lambda}$ for the initialization. The procedure is

1. Generate $U \sim \text{Unif}(u|0, 1)$.
2. Set $i = 0, p = e^{-\lambda}, F = p$.

3. If $U < F$, set $X = i$ and stop.
4. $p = \frac{\lambda}{i+1}p, F = F + p, i = i+1$.
5. Go to step 3.

F stores the probability that X is less than or equal to i, that is, the cdf. The algorithm first generates a random number U and then checks whether or not $U < e^{-\lambda} = p_0$. If so, it sets $X = 0$, else it computes (step 4) p_1 using recursion. It then checks whether $U < p_0 + p_1$, where this sum is the new value of F and, if so, it sets $X = 1$; and so on.

Gaussian Distribution. Note that given $X \sim \mathcal{N}(0,1)$, we can get $X' \sim \mathcal{N}(\mu,\sigma)$ via the transformation $X' = \mu + \sigma X$. Therefore, it suffices to find an algorithm for generating standard normal random variates. For the inverse-transform method, because neither the normal cdf F nor its inverse F^{-1} has a simple closed-form expression, we must use an approximation. A fast formula that is sometimes accurate enough is $X = \frac{U^{0.135} - (1-U)^{0.135}}{0.1975}$, with $U \sim \text{Unif}(u|0,1)$. Also, an approximation based on the central limit theorem (Section 4.1.2.1), considered as a transformation is

$$ X = \frac{\sum_{i=1}^{N} U_i - \frac{N}{2}}{\sqrt{N/12}} \approx \mathcal{N}(0,1), $$

for a large enough N and $U_1, \ldots, U_N$ independent draws from $\text{Unif}(u|0,1)$. With $N = 12$, the approximation is good, and the procedure is

1. Generate independent $U_1, \ldots, U_{12} \sim \text{Unif}(u|0,1)$.
2. Set $X = \sum_{i=1}^{12} U_i - 6$.
3. Return X.

An exact method based on the acceptance-rejection method can be devised to generate from the absolute value $|X|$, for $X \sim \mathcal{N}(x|0,1)$. By symmetry, we can then get our X by independently generating a discrete random variable S (for sign) that is $+1$ or -1 with a probability $1/2$ and setting $X = S|X|$. Thus, to generate from $|X|$, whose density is

$$ f(x) = \frac{2}{\sqrt{2\pi}} e^{-x^2/2}, \, x \geq 0, $$

we apply the acceptance-rejection method with $g(x) = e^{-x}, x \geq 0$ (exponential with parameter $\lambda = 1$), to which we apply the inverse-transform method (Section 3.5.2) for the purpose of simulation. We can prove that $\lambda = 1$ minimizes the value of a, and it is therefore the best choice for λ. We compute $a = \max_x \frac{f(x)}{g(x)} = \sqrt{2/\pi} e^{x-x^2/2}$, which is attained at the point maximizing the exponent $x - x^2/2$, namely, at $x = 1$. Hence, $a = \sqrt{2e/\pi} \approx 1.32$. Therefore, the complete algorithm for generating $X \sim \mathcal{N}(x|0,1)$ is

1. Generate $X \sim \text{Exp}(x|1)$.
2. Generate $U_1 \sim \text{Unif}(u|0,1)$.
3. If $U_1 \leq e^{-(X-1)^2/2}$, set $|X| = X$. Otherwise reject X, go back to Step 1 and try again.
4. Generate $U_2 \sim \text{Unif}(u|0,1)$. Return $|X|$ if $U_2 \leq 0.5$, otherwise return $-|X|$.

Multivariate Distributions. Consider that we want to simulate a random vector $\mathbf{X} = (X_1, \ldots, X_n)$ from a specified multivariate distribution $F_{\mathbf{X}}$. If the individual components X_i of the vector are independent random variables, then we can simply apply one of the previous algorithms to simulate from each univariate marginal distribution using independent sets of random numbers to produce a simulation from the desired distribution.

The general case is when variables X_i are not independent. Assume that, if $X_k = x_k$ for $k = 1, \ldots, i-1$, we can get the conditional cdfs of X_i, denoted as $F_{X_i}(x_i|x_1, \ldots, x_{i-1})$. Then Algorithm 3.4 can generate a random vector $\mathbf{X}$ with joint distribution $F_{\mathbf{X}}$.

Algorithm 3.4: General method for simulating a random vector

    Input : Easy-to-generate conditional distributions $F_{X_i}(x_i|x_1, \ldots, x_{i-1})$,
           $i = 1, \ldots, n$
    Output: A random vector $\mathbf{X}$ with joint distribution $F_{\mathbf{X}}$

1 Generate $X_1 \sim F_{X_1}$.
2 Generate $X_2 \sim F_{X_2}(\cdot|X_1)$.
3 Generate $X_3 \sim F_{X_3}(\cdot|X_1, X_2)$.

   $\vdots$

n Generate $X_n \sim F_{X_n}(\cdot|X_1, X_2, \ldots, X_{n-1})$.
n+1 Return $\mathbf{X} = (X_1, \ldots, X_n)$.

Note that the conditional cdfs used in line 2 through n are distributions with previously generated X_is. Thus, if x_1 was the value generated in line 1, the conditional cdf used in line 2 is $F_{X_2}(\cdot|x_1)$, etc. The algorithm validity relies on the chain rule (Equation (13.1)). It is often impossible to specify these conditional distributions. Bayesian networks (Chapter 13) exploit the conditional independencies leading to simpler conditional cdfs. Thus, this algorithm is used in the probabilistic logic sampling method for approximate inference in Bayesian networks (Section 13.2.3), where the probability of any variable (at any node), given some observed evidence (fixed values) for other variables, is approximately computed from the samples of the joint distribution, generated according to the above procedure.

Multivariate Gaussian Distribution. The previous method is straightforward in the case of the multivariate Gaussian distribution because all marginal and conditional distributions are still Gaussian (Section 3.4.4). Nevertheless, we can use a special property of this distribution to yield a simpler method than the above general method. We aim to simulate $\mathbf{X} = (X_1, \ldots, X_n) \sim \mathcal{N}(\mathbf{x}|\boldsymbol{\mu}, \boldsymbol{\Sigma})$. Matrix $\boldsymbol{\Sigma}$ is symmetric and positive-definite. Therefore, it can be factorized uniquely as $\boldsymbol{\Sigma} = \mathbf{LL}^T$, where $\mathbf{L} = \{l_{ij}\}_{i,j}$ is a lower triangular $n \times n$ matrix. $\mathbf{L}$ always exists (e.g., the Cholesky decomposition of $\boldsymbol{\Sigma}$ is a choice). The algorithm is

1.   Generate $Z_1, Z_2, \ldots, Z_n$ as independent random variates from $\mathcal{N}(0,1)$.
2.   Set $X_i = \mu_i + \sum_{j=1}^{i} l_{ij}Z_j, i = 1, \ldots, n$.
3.   Return $\mathbf{X} = (X_1, \ldots, X_n)$.

In Gaussian Bayesian networks of Chapter 13, this algorithm is useful for approximate inference (Section 13.2.3).

3.6   Information Theory

Information theory involves the quantification of information. Data compression and reliable data storage and communication are two of its main objectives. The underlying ideas in information theory can be explained considering human language as a tool for communication. Looking at the length of sentences, the most common words (e.g., "a," "the," "in," "and") should be shorter than the less common words (e.g., "pneumonoultramicroscopicsilicovolcanoconiosis," "pseudopseudohypoparathyroidism," "floccinaucinihilipilification"). Also, when part of a sentence is unheard or misheard due to noise, the listener should be able to infer this part of the message. This robustness in language is also a characteristic of communication systems developed according to information theory.

Some basic concepts of information theory, like entropy, mutual information, and Kullback–Leibler divergence, will be introduced in this section. They are all fundamental for the development of learning methods like classification trees (Section 7.2), Bayesian classifiers (Section 8.4), and Bayesian networks (Chapter 13).

3.6.1   Entropy

A key concept in information theory is **Shannon entropy** (Shannon, 1948). Entropy quantifies the uncertainty when predicting the value of a random variable. For example, the uncertainty in predicting the outcome of a fair coin flip is higher than when predicting the type of neuron (pyramidal or interneuron) for a randomly selected cell in layer II.

The Shannon entropy was used in Cao et al. (2013) as a postural parameter in an estimation of expanded disability status scale in multiple sclerosis (MS) from posturographic data. The entropy was computed from the kinematic measurements of the arms in Ruonala et al. (2014) to study essential tremor in PD patients. Entropy was also used by Pelykh et al. (2015) to analyze postural sway time series data in PD patients with and without symptoms of gait freezing. The Shannon entropy was applied in Huang et al. (2014) to compute the amount of information contained in a spike train in Golgi and Purkinje cells. Entropy-based methods were applied by Viggiano et al. (2015) to determine the spatial distribution of dendritic spines by computing the entropy of the distribution of spines along the dendrite.

The entropy of a discrete random variable X, with sample space $\Omega_X = \{x_1, \ldots, x_n\}$ and pdf given by $p(x)$, is denoted $\mathbb{H}(X)$ and defined as

$$\mathbb{H}(X) = - \sum_{i=1}^{n} p(X = x_i) \log_2 p(X = x_i).$$

The choice of logarithmic base in the above formula determines the unit of information entropy. The most common unit is the **bit**, which is based on binary logarithms. If e is the base, the unit is called **nat**. For decimal logarithms, that is, base 10, the unit is called **Hartley**.

The entropy of a discrete random variable, X, verifies $0 \le \mathbb{H}(X) \le \log_2 n$. The upper bound is calculated from the uniform distribution. For a Bernoulli distribution, the entropy is $\mathbb{H}(X) = -\theta \log_2 \theta - (1-\theta)\log_2(1-\theta)$, as a function of $\theta = p(X=1)$. The maximum

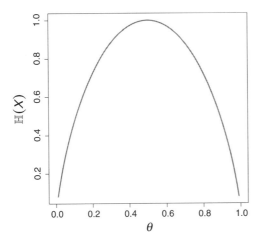

Figure 3.16 Entropy function $\mathbb{H}$ of a Bernoulli distribution with parameter θ.

value of this expression is $\log_2 2 = 1$ and is achieved at point $\theta = 0.5$, as illustrated in Figure 3.16.

The entropy of a continuous random variable X, with pdf given by $f(x)$, is called **differential entropy** and is defined as

$$h(X) = -\int_{\Omega_X} f(x)\ln f(x)\,dx.$$

For a Gaussian variable $X \sim \mathcal{N}(x|\mu,\sigma)$, the differential entropy is $h(X) = \ln(\sigma\sqrt{2\pi e})$. This verifies that it has the largest entropy of all random variables of equal variance (Cover and Thomas, 1991).

3.6.2 Joint Entropy

Given a bidimensional discrete random variable (X,Y), with a bivariate pmf $p(x,y)$, where $x \in \{x_1, \ldots, x_n\}$ and $y \in \{y_1, \ldots, y_m\}$, the **joint entropy** is defined by

$$\mathbb{H}(X,Y) = -\sum_{i=1}^{n}\sum_{j=1}^{m} p(x_i,y_j)\log_2 p(x_i,y_j).$$

Example. Given the joint probability distribution of (X,Y) shown in Table 3.5, where X represents the random variable associated with mouse brain layers, and Y is the class of synapse (asymmetric or symmetric), the joint entropy $\mathbb{H}(X,Y)$ is calculated as

$$\begin{aligned}
\mathbb{H}(X,Y) = -(&0.0595\log_2 0.0595 + 0.1691\log_2 0.1691 + 0.1848\log_2 0.1848\\
&+0.1428\log_2 0.1428 + 0.2772\log_2 0.2772 + 0.0105\log_2 0.0105\\
&+0.0209\log_2 0.0209 + 0.0552\log_2 0.0552\\
&+0.0272\log_2 0.0272 + 0.0528\log_2 0.0528)\\
\simeq\; & 2.8219.
\end{aligned}$$
■

3.6.3 Conditional Entropy

The **conditional entropy** of X given Y is defined as $\mathbb{H}(X|Y) = \sum_{j=1}^{m} p(y_j)\mathbb{H}(X|Y=y_j)$, where $\mathbb{H}(X|Y=y_j) = -\sum_{i=1}^{n} p(x_i|y_j)\log_2 p(x_i|y_j)$ is the entropy of X given that $Y = y_j$. After some algebraic manipulation, we get

$$\mathbb{H}(X|Y) = -\sum_{i=1}^{n}\sum_{j=1}^{m} p(x_i,y_j)\log_2 p(x_i|y_j).$$

The **total entropies law** expresses the joint entropy of two variables in terms of the entropy of one of the variables and the conditional entropy of the other variable given the first variable. The formula is as follows:

$$\mathbb{H}(X,Y) = \mathbb{H}(X) + \mathbb{H}(Y|X) = \mathbb{H}(Y) + \mathbb{H}(X|Y).$$

If X and Y are independent variables, the following equations are satisfied: (i) $\mathbb{H}(X|Y) = \mathbb{H}(X)$, (ii) $\mathbb{H}(Y|X) = \mathbb{H}(Y)$, and (iii) $\mathbb{H}(X,Y) = \mathbb{H}(X) + \mathbb{H}(Y)$.

3.6.4 Mutual Information

The **mutual information** $\mathbb{I}(X,Y)$ between two variables X and Y is defined as

$$\mathbb{I}(X,Y) = \mathbb{H}(X) - \mathbb{H}(X|Y) = \mathbb{H}(Y) - \mathbb{H}(Y|X).$$

Mutual information is interpreted as the reduction in uncertainty about X after observing Y, or, by symmetry, the reduction in uncertainty about Y after observing X. If X and Y are independent, the knowledge of one of the variables does not produce any reduction in the uncertainty about the other, thus mutual information is zero. It holds that $\mathbb{I}(X,Y) \geq 0$.

Replacing entropy and conditional entropy by their respective expressions, we can rewrite $\mathbb{I}(X,Y)$ as follows:

$$\mathbb{I}(X,Y) = \sum_{i=1}^{n}\sum_{j=1}^{m} p(x_i,y_j)\log_2 \frac{p(x_i,y_j)}{p(x_i)p(y_j)}.$$

Given three random variables, X, Y, and Z with $x \in \{x_1,\dots,x_n\}$, $y \in \{y_1,\dots,y_m\}$, and $z \in \{z_1,\dots,z_r\}$, the **conditional mutual information** of X and Y given Z, $\mathbb{I}(X,Y|Z)$, is defined as

$$\mathbb{I}(X,Y|Z) = \sum_{k=1}^{r} p(z_k)\mathbb{I}(X,Y|Z=z_k).$$

After some algebraic manipulations, $\mathbb{I}(X,Y|Z)$ can be rewritten as

$$\mathbb{I}(X,Y|Z) = \sum_{i=1}^{n}\sum_{j=1}^{m}\sum_{k=1}^{r} p(x_i,y_j,z_k)\log_2 \frac{p(x_i,y_j|z_k)}{p(x_i|z_k)p(y_j|z_k)}.$$

The conditional mutual information can be expressed in terms of conditional entropies, as

$$\mathbb{I}(X,Y|Z) = \mathbb{H}(X|Z) + \mathbb{H}(Y|Z) - \mathbb{H}(X,Y|Z).$$

Dendritic processing was characterized using the concept of mutual information by Gurney (2001). The impact of synaptic input on spike output was measured using mutual information in London et al. (2002). Studying the modulation of dendritic information processing in a Purkinje cell model, Coop et al. (2010) computed the mutual information between the total excitatory input current and the calcium and calcium-activated potassium currents. Lenne et al. (2013) showed that interhemispheric and right-hemisphere mutual information is significantly lower in patients with MS than in control subjects. Mutual information was also used to analyze electroencephalograms during intermittent photic stimulation in patients that may or may not suffer from AD (Chan et al., 2013). Co-expression networks for AD were built after computing the mutual information between pairs of genes in Dua et al. (2013). Sakar and Kursun (2010) established the relevance of dysphonia measurements in the telediagnosis of PD (yes/no) by means of mutual information.

3.6.5   Kullback–Leibler Divergence

The **Kullback–Leibler divergence** (Kullback and Leibler, 1951) is a way of comparing two probability distributions, $p(X)$ and $q(X)$, defined over the same sample space, $\{x_1, \dots, x_n\}$. One of the two distributions, $p(X)$, plays the role of a "true" distribution, whereas the other distribution, $q(X)$, is an arbitrary probability distribution. It is defined as

$$\mathbb{KL}(p||q) = \sum_{i=1}^{n} p(x_i) \log_2 \frac{p(x_i)}{q(x_i)}.$$

The Kullback–Leibler divergence is interpreted as the average number of extra bits needed to encode the data, when using the distribution $q(X)$ instead of the true distribution $p(X)$. The Kullback–Leibler divergence is not a true distance (in the mathematical sense of the term) because it is not symmetric and does not verify the triangle inequality.

$\mathbb{KL}(p||q)$ satisfies: $\mathbb{KL}(p||q) \geq 0$, and $\mathbb{I}(X,Y) = \mathbb{KL}(p(X,Y)||p(X)p(Y))$.

The Kullback–Leibler divergence was used by López-Cruz et al. (2011) for confirming that virtual dendrites simulated from a Bayesian network model were similar to real dendrites. Pokrajac et al. (2005) used the Kullback–Leibler divergence to compute the difference between spatial probability distributions of regions of interest in a 3D image of a new subject and each of the considered classes represented by historical data in a functional MRI activation data with AD patients.

3.6.6   Cross-Entropy

The **cross-entropy** between two probability distributions, $p(X)$ and $q(X)$, defined over the same sample space, $\{x_1, \dots, x_n\}$, measures the average number of bits needed to identify an event from a set of possibilities, if the coding scheme used is based on a "wrong" probability distribution, $q(X)$, rather than the "true" distribution $p(X)$. In mathematical notation,

$$\mathbb{H}(p,q) = \mathbb{E}_p[-\log_2 q(X)] = \mathbb{H}(p) + \mathbb{KL}(p||q) = -\sum_{i=1}^{n} p(x_i) \log_2 q(x_i).$$

This concept will be useful in some feature selection methods (Section 6.4).

3.7   Bibliographic Notes

Bayes' rule is named after Thomas Bayes (1763). The mathematical principle of the expected value was first published by Huygens (1657). The foundations of modern probability were established by Kolmogorov (1933b).

The Bernoulli trials take their name from the Swiss mathematician Jakob Bernoulli (1713a). Poisson (1837) published the distribution that bears his name by considering the limits of the binomial distribution. Pascal (1679) was the first to deal with the negative binomial distribution. The gamma distribution was originated by Laplace (1836). The first to publish the normal distribution as an approximation of the binomial distribution was de Moivre (1733). Laplace (1774) published a more formal and general result than de Moivre's approximation. Gauss (1809) established techniques based on the normal distribution. We owe the lognormal distribution to Galton (1879). Abbe (1836) discovered the chi-squared distribution. Student's t distribution was conceived by Gosset (1908) under the pseudonym of "Student" to avoid difficulties with other staff, when he was working at Guinness brewery.

4 Probabilistic Inference

In neuroscience, as in other experimental sciences, it is very common that access to all elements of a given objective population is limited. For example, if this population concerns all the neurons of a human brain, we must resign ourselves with collecting information from a reduced number of neurons. From the characteristics of this sample, we must generalize the results to the entire brain. This generalization, or inference process in statistical jargon, enables us to estimate parameters from a given probability distribution and also test hypotheses regarding the values of these parameters or even regarding the distributions themselves.

This chapter is organized as follows. Section 4.1 introduces the concept of random sampling. Two methods based on random sampling – the method of moments and maximum likelihood estimation method – for parameter point estimation are presented. Thereafter, properties that must be satisfied by a good point estimator – such as unbiasedness, efficiency or consistency – are discussed. Confidence intervals for the parameters (population mean and variance) of normal distributions and for parameter p in Bernoulli distributions are derived. Bayesian estimation is another perspective, where the parameter is considered to be a random variable following a prior distribution that is revised with the observed sample, via the Bayes' theorem, that yields a posterior distribution. Section 4.2 analyzes hypotheses testing. Different types of null hypotheses are considered: goodness-of-fit to a given distribution as well as paired and unpaired sample tests, both in parametric and nonparametric settings. Other hypothesis tests include those for measuring the degree of relationship between two random variables, multiple comparison tests, and permutation tests. The chapter concludes with Section 4.3 presenting bibliographic notes.

4.1 Parameter Estimation

4.1.1 Random Sampling

The primary objective of a statistical analysis is to gain knowledge regarding certain characteristics in a population of interest. When the population is small, it is possible to inspect all its elements. However, in real-word applications, this exhaustive approach is not feasible, mainly due to monetary and time constraints. In such situations, and under certain conditions, a random selection of certain elements of the population provides a means to generalize the sampled information to the entire population – a process that is known as **inferential statistics**.

As an illustrative example, let us assume that we are interested in ascertaining the proportion of pyramidal and interneuron cells in a given human brain. As it is not possible to study the $M = 86$ billion neurons (Herculano-Houzal, 2009), we can decide to study some of the cells taken at random from this brain. A simple random sampling assumes that each particular sample of size N has the same probability of occurrence. In finite populations, each of the $\binom{M}{N}$ samples of size N is taken without replacement and has the same probability of occurrence. If the population to be sampled is infinite, the distinction between sampling with replacement and sampling without replacement becomes insignificant. In an infinite population, the probability of selecting a given element is the same regardless of the sampling being done with or without replacement. Although the number of cells in a human brain is finite, considering this population as infinite, the inference process can provide sufficiently good approximations.

With the two standard ways of reconstructing human neurons, that is, with the help of confocal or electron microscopy, a stack of images contains a number of cells that are labeled by an expert as pyramidal or interneuron. Usually, some cubes of tissue are selected at random, and then all the neurons within each cube are reconstructed. This procedure constitutes an example of **cluster sampling**. Each cube of tissue is a cluster, and each cluster is treated as the sampling unit, as it is assumed that each cluster represents the entire population, and the analysis is conducted in a sample of clusters. Cluster sampling assumes that the different clusters are homogeneous between them. The previous example refers to **one-step cluster sampling**, where all elements are selected in the chosen clusters.

Stratified sampling is most commonly used when the population of interest can be easily partitioned into subpopulations or strata. Then, strata are selected to divide the population into nonoverlapping and homogeneous regions, in the sense that elements belonging to a given strata are expected to be similar. Stratified sampling assumes great heterogeneity between the different strata. Then simple random samples from each strata are taken in this type of sampling. For example, in a study on the year of debut in AD, the strata can correspond to female and male, particularly if we have the intuition that the debut year in both genders is different.

Systematic sampling is used when there is a list containing all M members of a given population and one decides to select every kth value in the sample. In this type of sampling, one only needs to select the initial starting point at random. After the starting point is selected, the remaining values to be sampled are automatically specified. For example, suppose we have an alphabetically ordered list of 50,000 AD patients, from which we plan to use systematic sampling to select a sample of size 200. We can proceed by selecting an initial starting point at random between 1 and 250 $\left(\text{as } \frac{50,000}{250} = 200\right)$. Thus, if the generated random number is 113, then the units in the sample of size 200 are the ones numbered $113, 363 \, (= 113 + 250), 613 \, (= 113 + 2 \cdot 250), \ldots, 49{,}863 \, (= 113 + 199 \cdot 250)$.

4.1.2   Parameter Point Estimation

Once a sample from a population is taken, the first objective is to estimate the **parameters** of the random variable that models the population under study.

Considering the first example introduced in the previous section, the random variable X denoting the type of neuron (interneuron (1) versus pyramidal (0)) follows a Bernoulli distribution, where parameter θ represents the probability that X is an interneuron cell. That is, $\theta = p(X = 1)$. For the second example, and assuming a Gaussian density for the variable measuring the onset year of AD, parameter θ becomes a vector with two components $\boldsymbol{\theta} = (\mu, \sigma)$ that refer to the expectation and the standard deviation of the population density, respectively.

The observed random sample of size N, that is, the values $x_1, x_2, \dots, x_N$ of the N **independent and identically distributed** (i.i.d.) $X_1, X_2, \dots, X_N$ random variables, are combined into a function (or statistic) $\hat{\theta} = t(X_1, X_2, \dots, X_N)$, known as **estimator** of θ. This estimator is also a random variable. The specific value of an estimator can only be known after a sample has been taken whose result is called an **estimate** of θ.

For example, the arithmetic mean of a sample or **sample mean**

$$\hat{\theta} = t(X_1, \dots, X_n) = \bar{X} = \frac{\sum_{i=1}^{N} X_i}{N}$$

is an estimator of the population mean. Sometimes $\bar{X}$ will be denoted $\bar{X}_N$ to highlight the sample size.

This estimator can be useful for examples such as the type of neuron and onset year of AD. In the first case, with a random sample of size $N = 10$, and after observing the following random sample:

$$x_1 = 0, x_2 = 1, x_3 = 0, x_4 = 0, x_5 = 1, x_6 = 0, x_7 = 0, x_8 = 0, x_9 = 1, x_{10} = 0,$$

the estimate for $\theta = p(X = 1) = p$ is given by

$$\hat{\theta} = \hat{p} = \bar{x} = \frac{0+1+0+0+1+0+0+0+1+0}{10} = 0.30.$$

In the second case, the estimate of μ from the random sample of size $N = 5$,

$$x_1 = 61, x_2 = 74, x_3 = 69, x_4 = 84, x_5 = 79,$$

is computed as the sample mean

$$\hat{\mu} = \bar{x} = \frac{61+74+69+84+79}{5} = 73.40 \text{ years old,}$$

whereas the **sample variance**,

$$\hat{\sigma}^2 = \frac{\sum_{i=1}^{N}(X_i - \bar{X})^2}{N},$$

can be an estimator for σ^2, the variance of the population. The estimate will be

$$\hat{\sigma}^2 = \frac{1}{5}\left[(61 - 73.40)^2 + (74 - 73.40)^2 + (69 - 73.40)^2 + (84 - 73.40)^2 + (79 - 73.40)^2\right]$$
$$= 67.88 \text{ years}^2 \text{ of age.}$$

The **sample quasi-variance** is the most commonly used estimator for σ^2 owing to its good properties (Section 4.1.2.1). It is defined as

$$\hat{\sigma}^2 = S^2 = \frac{\sum_{i=1}^{N}(X_i - \bar{X})^2}{N - 1}.$$

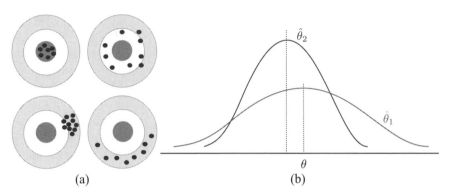

Figure 4.1 (a) Graphical representation of the concepts of bias and variance: low bias and low variance (top left), low bias and high variance (top right), high bias and low variance (bottom left), and high bias and high variance (bottom right). (b) $\hat{\theta}_1$ is an unbiased estimator of θ, and $\hat{\theta}_2$ is a biased estimator of θ. However, $\hat{\theta}_2$ has a smaller variance than $\hat{\theta}_1$.

4.1.2.1 *Properties*

The goodness of an estimator $\hat{\theta}$ can be measured by computing how close its estimates are to the true parameter θ. Because θ is unknown, this is approximated under the expectation operator. The estimates can be greater or smaller than θ, making their differences positive or negative with respect to θ, respectively. The squared values of these differences are always positive. Thus, the **mean square error** of an estimator $\hat{\theta}$ of θ, defined as $MSE(\hat{\theta}) = \mathbb{E}[(\hat{\theta} - \theta)^2]$, is used for measuring its goodness and also for comparing various estimators $\hat{\theta}_1, \hat{\theta}_2, \ldots$ of θ.

Estimators with small mean square errors are preferred. The MSE is decomposed into two nonnegative components, the variance of the estimator $Var[\hat{\theta}]$ and its squared bias, where **bias** is defined as $\mathbb{E}[\hat{\theta}] - \theta$. This decomposition is easily derived, as

$$MSE(\hat{\theta}) = \mathbb{E}\left[\left(\hat{\theta} - \mathbb{E}[\hat{\theta}] + \mathbb{E}[\hat{\theta}] - \theta\right)^2\right]$$

$$= \mathbb{E}\left[(\hat{\theta} - \mathbb{E}[\hat{\theta}])^2\right] + \mathbb{E}\left[(\mathbb{E}[\hat{\theta}] - \theta)^2\right] + 2\mathbb{E}\left[(\hat{\theta} - \mathbb{E}[\hat{\theta}])(\mathbb{E}[\hat{\theta}] - \theta)\right]$$

$$= Var[\hat{\theta}] + (\mathbb{E}[\hat{\theta}] - \theta)^2 + 2(\mathbb{E}[\hat{\theta}] - \mathbb{E}[\hat{\theta}])(\mathbb{E}[\hat{\theta}] - \theta)$$

$$= Var[\hat{\theta}] + (Bias(\hat{\theta}))^2.$$

Figure 4.1 illustrates the concepts of variance and bias of an estimator.

The bias measures the error of the estimator in expectation, that is, how closely its average estimate is able to approximate the target. The variance measures how much the estimate fluctuates for different samples (of the same size). A good estimator should have a small bias (property A below) and small variance (property B below).

A. Unbiased Estimators. We have seen that estimators are random variables, and consequently, the point estimation they provide will vary from sample to sample. An interesting property of an estimator is that its expected value be equal to the true value of the parameter it is estimating. An estimator $\hat{\theta}$ with this property, that is, such that $\mathbb{E}[\hat{\theta}] = \theta$ is an **unbiased**

estimator of θ. When $\mathbb{E}[\hat{\theta}] \neq \theta$, the estimator is biased. For unbiased estimators, the mean squared error is equal to its variance, that is, $MSE(\hat{\theta}) = Var[\hat{\theta}]$.

For a Bernoulli population, the empirical proportion of successes is an unbiased estimator of parameter p. The proof is based on the properties of the expectation (Section 3.2.1) and the binomial distribution (Section 3.2.3): $\mathbb{E}\left[\frac{1}{N}\sum_{i=1}^{N}X_i\right] = \frac{1}{N}\mathbb{E}\left[\text{Bin}(x|N,\theta)\right] = \theta$. In a Poisson distribution, the sample mean is also an unbiased estimator of parameter λ. In a Gaussian distribution, the sample mean $\hat{\mu} = \bar{X}$ and the sample quasi-variance $\hat{\sigma}^2 = S^2 = \frac{1}{N-1}\sum_{i=1}^{N}(X_i - \bar{X})^2$ are unbiased estimators of parameters μ and σ^2, respectively.

B. Efficiency. In addition to being unbiased (or having a small bias), a good estimator should also have a small variance, hence a small *MSE* value. The **efficiency of estimator** $\hat{\theta}_1$ relative to $\hat{\theta}_2$ is defined as

$$eff(\hat{\theta}_1, \hat{\theta}_2) = \frac{MSE(\hat{\theta}_2)}{MSE(\hat{\theta}_1)}$$

and provides a means to compare the *MSE* of two estimators. Estimator $\hat{\theta}_1$ is more efficient than estimator $\hat{\theta}_2$ if $MSE(\hat{\theta}_1) \leq MSE(\hat{\theta}_2)$, that is, when $eff(\hat{\theta}_1, \hat{\theta}_2) \geq 1$. When both estimators are unbiased, $Var[\hat{\theta}_1] \leq Var[\hat{\theta}_2]$ is equivalent to $eff(\hat{\theta}_1, \hat{\theta}_2) \geq 1$.

We are often interested in the estimator that has the smallest variance among all (infinite) possible unbiased estimators. However, to compute an infinite number of variances is not a viable solution.

Fortunately, it can be shown that if $\hat{\theta}$ is an unbiased estimator of θ defined on a random sample of size N, $X_1, X_2, \ldots, X_N$ with $f(x|\theta)$ as pdf, and under some regularity conditions, then the variance of $\hat{\theta}$ must satisfy the following inequality

$$Var[\hat{\theta}] \geq \frac{1}{N\mathbb{E}\left[\left(\frac{\partial \ln f(x|\theta)}{\partial \theta}\right)^2\right]}. \tag{4.1}$$

The expression in Equation (4.1) is known as the **Cramér–Rao inequality**, and the right-hand side of this expression is known as the Cramér–Rao lower bound. When the variance of an unbiased estimator equals the Cramér–Rao lower bound (this does not always exist), the estimator $\hat{\theta}$ is a **minimum variance unbiased** estimator of θ. In short, the variance of an **efficient estimator** is the minimum among the set of unbiased estimators. The quantity in the denominator of Equation (4.1) is known as the **Fisher information** on θ provided by the sample. The greater the Fisher information is, the smaller the variance of the estimator is. Equation (4.1) also holds for discrete distributions.

The sample mean is an efficient estimator of the λ parameter for a Poisson population. The same result is true for the λ parameter of an exponential population.

C. Consistency. Consistency is a property of a sequence of estimators rather than of a single estimator. The sequence of estimators $\hat{\theta}_1, \hat{\theta}_2, \ldots, \hat{\theta}_N$ can be obtained by using the same estimation procedure for samples of sizes $1, 2, \ldots, N$. The sequence is

$$\hat{\theta}_1 = t(X_1), \hat{\theta}_2 = t(X_1, X_2), \ldots, \hat{\theta}_N = t(X_1, X_2, \ldots, X_N).$$

A sequence of estimators $\hat{\theta}_1, \hat{\theta}_2, \ldots, \hat{\theta}_N$ is said to be a **consistent estimator** of parameter θ if

$$\lim_{N \to \infty} p(|\hat{\theta}_N - \theta| < \varepsilon) = 1 \quad \text{for all } \varepsilon > 0.$$

In other words, a consistent sequence of estimators converges in probability[1] to θ, the parameter that is being estimated by the sequence of estimators.

It can be proved that the sample (arithmetic) mean $\hat{\theta}_N = \bar{X}_N$ is a consistent estimator of the population mean $\mathbb{E}[X]$.

D. The Law of Large Numbers. The **law of large numbers** describes the result of conducting the same experiment a large number of times. According to the law, the average of the results obtained from a large number of trials should be close to the (theoretical) expected value and will tend to become closer as more trials are conducted. There are two different versions of this law: the weak and the strong law of large numbers. Both provide sufficient conditions for the convergence of the sample mean to the population mean (its expected value).

Mathematically, given an infinite sequence of i.i.d. random variables, $X_1, X_2, X_3, \ldots$, with population mean $\mathbb{E}[X]$, the sequence of sample means $\{\bar{X}_N = \frac{\sum_{i=1}^{N} X_i}{N}\}_{N=1,2,3,\ldots}$

(a) converges in probability to $\mathbb{E}[X]$ (**weak law of large numbers**), i.e.,

$$\lim_{N \to \infty} p(|\bar{X}_N - \mathbb{E}[X]| < \varepsilon) = 1 \quad \text{for all } \varepsilon > 0,$$

(b) converges almost surely to $\mathbb{E}[X]$ (**strong law of large numbers**), i.e.,

$$p(\lim_{N \to \infty} \bar{X}_N = \mathbb{E}[X]) = 1.$$

The **almost sure convergence** implies the convergence in probability.

E. Central Limit Theorem. The **central limit theorem** states that when i.i.d. random variables are added together, their normalized sum tends to follow a normal distribution even if the original variables are not normally distributed. The theorem is a key concept in probabilistic and statistical methods on account of its applicability to many problems that involve other types of distributions, not necessarily Gaussians.

Formally, consider $X_1, \ldots, X_N, \ldots$ a sequence of i.i.d. random variables drawn from a population X with expected value $\mathbb{E}[X]$ and variance $Var[X]$. Then, as N approaches infinity, the random variables $\sqrt{N}(\bar{X}_N - \mathbb{E}[X])$ converge in distribution to a normal distribution $\mathcal{N}(x|0, \sqrt{Var[X]})$. **Convergence in distribution** means that the cdf of $\sqrt{N}(\bar{X}_N - \mathbb{E}[X])$ converges pointwise to the cdf of a $\mathcal{N}(x|0, \sqrt{Var[X]})$. That is, for every real number z,

---

[1] A sequence of random variables $X_1, X_2, X_3, \ldots$ converges in probability to a random variable X, if $\lim_{N \to \infty} p(|X_N - X| < \varepsilon) = 1$, for all $\varepsilon > 0$. For the case of a consistent sequence of estimators, random variable X becomes a fixed value θ.

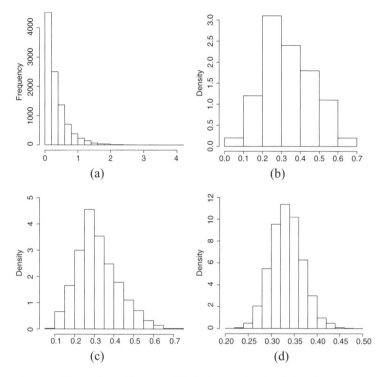

Figure 4.2 Illustration of the central limit theorem by simulating from an exponential (very skewed) distribution of parameter $\lambda = 3$. (a) Histogram of 10,000 samples generated from $\text{Exp}(x|3)$ (Section 3.5). (b) Histogram of $\bar{X}_5$ obtained from those samples. (c) Histogram of $\bar{X}_{10}$. (d) Histogram of $\bar{X}_{100}$.

$$\lim_{N \to \infty} p \left(\frac{\bar{X}_N - \mathbb{E}[X]}{\sqrt{\frac{Var[X]}{N}}} \le z \right) = F_{\mathcal{N}(z|0,1)}(z),$$

where $F_{\mathcal{N}(z|0,1)}$ is the cdf of a standard normal distribution evaluated at z.

By the law of large numbers, the sample averages converge in probability and almost surely to the expected value $\mathbb{E}[X]$, as N tends to infinity. The central limit theorem describes the size and the distributional form of the stochastic fluctuations around $\mathbb{E}[X]$ during this convergence. More precisely, it states that as N gets larger, the distribution of the difference between the sample average $\bar{X}_N$ and its limit $\mathbb{E}[X]$, when multiplied by the factor $\sqrt{N}$, approximates the normal distribution with mean 0 and variance $Var[X]$. The usefulness of the theorem is that the distribution of $\sqrt{N}(\bar{X}_N - \mathbb{E}[X])$ approaches normality regardless of the shape of the distribution of the random variables $X_1, X_2, \ldots$.

Figure 4.2 illustrates the central limit theorem with an exponential distribution.

4.1.2.2 Point Estimation Methods

This section presents two methods for deriving estimators from a given random sample of size N, $X_1, \ldots, X_N$, extracted from the population. The properties of the estimators provided with each of the methods are also given.

A. Method of Moments. The underlying idea in the **method of moments** is to equate **population moments** about the origin, $\alpha_r = \mathbb{E}[X]^r$, with their corresponding **sample moments** about the origin, $m_r = \frac{1}{N}\sum_{i=1}^{N} X_i^r$. The number of equations in the resulting system to be solved equals the number of parameters to be estimated. For a pdf, $f(x|\theta_1, \ldots, \theta_K)$, that depends on K parameters, the system to be solved is

$$\begin{cases} \alpha_1(\theta_1, \ldots, \theta_K) = m_1 \\ \alpha_2(\theta_1, \ldots, \theta_K) = m_2 \\ \quad \ldots \\ \alpha_K(\theta_1, \ldots, \theta_K) = m_K. \end{cases}$$

The method of moments is interesting due to its simplicity and also because of the consistency property it verifies.

For parameter $\theta_1 = p$ of a Bernoulli distribution, the estimator derived from the method of moments is the empirical proportion, that is, $\alpha_1(p) = p = \bar{X} = m_1$. A similar result is obtained for the $\theta_1 = \lambda$ parameter of a Poisson distribution. The resulting equation is $\alpha_1(\lambda) = \lambda = \bar{X} = m_1$. The method in a normal density $\mathcal{N}(\mu, \sigma)$ is implemented with the following system of two equations:

$$\begin{cases} \alpha_1(\mu, \sigma^2) = \mu = \bar{X} = m_1 \\ \alpha_2(\mu, \sigma^2) = \sigma^2 + \mu^2 = \frac{1}{N}\sum_{i=1}^{N} X_i^2 = m_2. \end{cases}$$

The solution of the previous system yields $\hat{\mu} = \bar{X}$ and $\hat{\sigma}^2 = \frac{1}{N}\sum_{i=1}^{N}(X_i - \bar{X})^2$.

Leguey et al. (2019) used the method of moments to estimate the parameters of a special circular distribution called wrapped Cauchy. The aim was to model the bifurcation angles of basal dendritic trees of 3D pyramidal neurons in several layers of the 14-day-old rat hind limb somatosensory neocortex.

B. Method of Maximum Likelihood. Maximum likelihood estimation assigns to θ the value that makes the observed sample most likely under the assumed probability model. Let $x_1, \ldots, x_N$ denote the observed values of i.i.d. random variables $X_1, X_2, \ldots, X_N$ from a population whose probability distribution depends on θ. The notation $\mathcal{L}(\theta|\mathbf{x}) = f(\mathbf{x}|\theta)$ (or $\mathcal{L}(\theta|\mathbf{x}) = f(\mathbf{x}; \theta)$ as in fact it is not a conditional probability) represents the **likelihood function** of θ, given $x_1, \ldots, x_N$, and can be computed as

$$\mathcal{L}(\theta|\mathbf{x}) = f(\mathbf{x}|\theta) = f(x_1|\theta) \cdot f(x_2|\theta) \cdots f(x_N|\theta). \tag{4.2}$$

The value of θ that maximizes $\mathcal{L}(\theta|\mathbf{x})$ is called the **maximum likelihood estimate (mle)** of θ. The mle is denoted as $\hat{\theta}(x_1, x_2, \ldots, x_N)$, and the **maximum likelihood estimator (MLE)**, a statistic, as $\hat{\theta}(X_1, X_2, \ldots, X_N)$. In general, it is usually more convenient and easy to work with the natural logarithm of $\mathcal{L}(\theta|\mathbf{x})$, called the **log-likelihood function**, $\ln \mathcal{L}(\theta|\mathbf{x})$. Thus, the expression of products of Equation (4.2) is converted into sums. The value of θ that maximizes the log-likelihood function $\ln \mathcal{L}(\theta|\mathbf{x})$ is the same value of θ that maximizes the likelihood function $\mathcal{L}(\theta|\mathbf{x})$, because the natural logarithm is a monotonically increasing function. If $\mathcal{L}(\theta|\mathbf{x})$ is differentiable with respect to θ, the mle must verify

$$\frac{\partial \ln \mathcal{L}(\theta|\mathbf{x})}{\partial \theta} = 0. \tag{4.3}$$

This is a necessary, but not sufficient, condition for the solution to be a maximum. An estimate of θ verifying Equation (4.3) and this other condition

$$\frac{\partial^2 \ln \mathcal{L}(\theta|\mathbf{x})}{\partial \theta^2}\bigg|_{\theta=\hat{\theta}(\mathbf{x})} < 0 \tag{4.4}$$

is an mle. MLEs have interesting properties. First, MLEs are not necessarily unbiased estimators. However, although they can be biased, they are always asymptotically unbiased and consistent estimators, that is, when the sample size is increasingly large, the probability that MLE differs from the true value of the parameter larger than a fixed small value tends to zero. Second, MLEs are not necessarily efficient estimators. However, if an efficient estimator of a parameter exists, this efficient estimator is also an MLE.

Example. MLE for Parameter p of a Bernoulli Distribution. Given a random sample $x_1, x_2, \ldots, x_N$ taken from a Bernoulli distribution with unknown parameter p, the likelihood function of p given $\mathbf{x}$, $\mathcal{L}(p|\mathbf{x})$, is computed as

$$\mathcal{L}(p|\mathbf{x}) = \prod_{i=1}^{N} p^{x_i}(1-p)^{1-x_i} \quad \text{with} \quad x_i = 0, 1.$$

Then, the log-likelihood function is

$$\ln \mathcal{L}(p|\mathbf{x}) = \sum_{i=1}^{N} \ln \left[p^{x_i}(1-p)^{1-x_i} \right] = \sum_{i=1}^{N} [x_i \ln p + (1-x_i) \ln(1-p)].$$

Equaling the first derivative of the log-likelihood function to zero yields

$$\frac{\partial \ln \mathcal{L}(p|\mathbf{x})}{\partial p} = \frac{\sum_{i=1}^{N} x_i}{p} - \frac{N - \sum_{i=1}^{N} x_i}{1-p} = 0,$$

and we obtain that $\hat{p}(X_1, \ldots, X_N) = \bar{X}$.

To check the condition of Equation (4.4), we compute the second-order partial derivative of the log-likelihood function

$$\frac{\partial^2 \ln \mathcal{L}(p|\mathbf{x})}{\partial p^2} = \frac{-\sum_{i=1}^{N} x_i}{p^2} - \frac{N - \sum_{i=1}^{N} x_i}{(1-p)^2}.$$

Further, evaluating the second-order partial derivative at $p = \bar{x}$ yields

$$\frac{\partial^2 \ln \mathcal{L}(p|\mathbf{x})}{\partial p^2}\bigg|_{p=\hat{p}(\mathbf{x})} = \frac{-N\bar{x}}{\bar{x}^2} - \frac{N - N\bar{x}}{(1-\bar{x})^2} = -\frac{N}{\bar{x}} - \frac{N}{1-\bar{x}},$$

which is less than zero, because $0 \leq \bar{x} \leq 1$ and $N > 0$.

The estimator presented in Section 4.1.2 for the probability p of an interneuron cell is, in fact, an MLE, and the value $\hat{p} = 0.30$ corresponds to its mle, given the random sample of size $N = 10$: $x_1 = 0, x_2 = 1, x_3 = 0, x_4 = 0, x_5 = 1, x_6 = 0, x_7 = 0, x_8 = 0, x_9 = 1, x_{10} = 0$. The method of moments provides the same result. ∎

Example. MLE for Parameter $\theta = (\mu, \sigma^2)$ of a Normal Density. The likelihood function of a sample $x_1, \ldots, x_N$ taken from a $\mathcal{N}(\mu, \sigma)$ is

$$\mathcal{L}(\mu, \sigma^2 | \mathbf{x}) = \prod_{i=1}^{N} \frac{1}{\sqrt{2\pi\sigma^2}} e^{-\frac{1}{2}\left(\frac{x_i - \mu}{\sigma}\right)^2} = \frac{1}{(\sqrt{2\pi})^N \sigma^N} e^{-\frac{1}{2}\sum_{i=1}^{N}\left(\frac{x_i - \mu}{\sigma}\right)^2},$$

and the log-likelihood function is

$$\ln \mathcal{L}\left(\mu, \sigma^2 | \mathbf{x}\right) = -\frac{N}{2}\ln(2\pi) - \frac{N}{2}\ln\left(\sigma^2\right) - \frac{\sum_{i=1}^{N}(x_i - \mu)^2}{2\sigma^2}.$$

The MLE $\left(\hat{\mu}, \hat{\sigma}^2\right)$ is the solution of the following system of equations

$$\begin{cases} \frac{\partial \ln \mathcal{L}(\mu, \sigma^2 | \mathbf{x})}{\partial \mu} = \frac{\sum_{i=1}^{N}(x_i - \mu)}{\sigma^2} = 0 \\ \frac{\partial \ln \mathcal{L}(\mu, \sigma^2 | \mathbf{x})}{\partial \sigma^2} = -\frac{N}{2\sigma^2} + \frac{\sum_{i=1}^{N}(x_i - \mu)^2}{2\sigma^4} = 0. \end{cases}$$

Solving the system yields easily

$$\hat{\mu}(X_1, \ldots, X_N) = \frac{\sum_{i=1}^{N} X_i}{N} = \bar{X}, \qquad \hat{\sigma}^2(X_1, \ldots, X_N) = \frac{\sum_{i=1}^{N}(X_i - \bar{X})^2}{N} = \frac{N-1}{N}S^2.$$

The estimator $(\hat{\mu}(X_1, \ldots, X_N), \hat{\sigma}^2(X_1, \ldots, X_N))$ is an MLE as it also verifies the condition of Equation (4.4) for the second-order derivative of the log-likelihood function.

Assuming Gaussianity in the sample of size 5 for the onset year of AD introduced in Section 4.1.2, the estimators used for μ and σ^2 in that example were MLEs. The method of moments provides the same result in this case. ∎

Example. MLE for Parameter $\theta = (\mu, \Sigma)$ of a Multivariate Normal Density. Given N vector values $\mathbf{x}^1, \ldots, \mathbf{x}^N$ of N i.i.d. random variables following a multivariate normal distribution $\mathcal{N}(\mathbf{x} | \mu, \Sigma)$, the mle of parameter μ is $\bar{\mathbf{x}} = \frac{1}{N}\sum_{i=1}^{N} x^i$, i.e., the sample mean vector. This follows a multivariate normal distribution as well. The mle of parameter Σ is $\mathbf{S} = \frac{1}{N}\sum_{i=1}^{N}(\mathbf{x}^i - \bar{\mathbf{x}})(\mathbf{x}^i - \bar{\mathbf{x}})^T$, i.e., the sample covariance matrix. Moreover, $N\mathbf{S} \sim \mathcal{W}(N-1, \Sigma)$. ∎

Example. MLE for Parameters μ and κ of a Univariate von Mises Distribution. Given a set of N values $\phi_1, \ldots, \phi_N$ randomly sampled from $\Phi \sim v\mathcal{M}(\phi | \mu, \kappa)$, the mle of parameters μ and κ of the distribution are the sample mean direction for μ,

$$\hat{\mu} = \arctan\frac{\bar{S}}{\bar{C}},$$

where

$$\bar{C} = \frac{1}{N}\sum_{i=1}^{N}\cos\phi_i \quad \text{and} \quad \bar{S} = \frac{1}{N}\sum_{i=1}^{N}\sin\phi_i,$$

and $\hat{\kappa} = A^{-1}(\bar{R})$ for κ, where

$$A(\hat{\kappa}) = \frac{I_1(\hat{\kappa})}{I_0(\hat{\kappa})} = \bar{R} = \sqrt{\bar{C}^2 + \bar{S}^2},$$

and $I_0(\hat{\kappa})$ and $I_1(\hat{\kappa})$ are the modified Bessel function of the first kind of orders 0 and 1, respectively, as defined in Section 3.3.11.

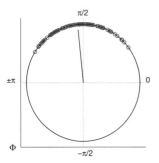

Figure 4.3 Sample of 100 points from a von Mises distribution $v\mathcal{M}(\phi|\pi/2,5)$. The black line indicates the sample mean direction $\hat{\mu}$, and its length is the mean resultant length $\bar{R}$.

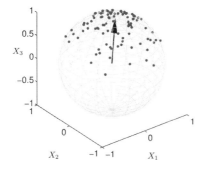

Figure 4.4 Sample of 100 points from a von Mises–Fisher distribution $v\mathcal{MF}(\mathbf{x}|(0,0,1)^T,5)$. The black arrow indicates the sample mean direction $\hat{\mu}$, and the value of $\bar{R}$ is given by the length of the arrow.

For example,[2] Figure 4.3 shows a random sample of 100 points from a von Mises distribution and the mle of μ and R. ∎

Example. MLE for Parameters μ and κ of a Multivariate von Mises–Fisher Distribution. The mles for the parameters of the n-dimensional distribution $v\mathcal{MF}(\mathbf{x}|\mu,\kappa)$ (see Section 3.4.9) given a sample of unit vectors $\mathbf{x}^1,\ldots,\mathbf{x}^N$, are the sample mean direction for μ

$$\hat{\mu} = \frac{\sum_{i=1}^N \mathbf{x}^i}{\left\|\sum_{i=1}^N \mathbf{x}^i\right\|},$$

and $\hat{\kappa} = A_n^{-1}(\bar{R})$ for the concentration parameter κ, where

$$A_n(\hat{\kappa}) = \frac{I_{\frac{n}{2}}(\hat{\kappa})}{I_{\frac{n}{2}-1}(\hat{\kappa})} = \bar{R} = \frac{\left\|\sum_{i=1}^N \mathbf{x}^i\right\|}{N}.$$

Unfortunately, $\hat{\kappa}$ cannot be found analytically. For numerical approximations, see Sra (2012).

---

[2] The functions provided in the Circular Statistics toolbox for MATLAB (Berens, 2009) have been used to sample the set of angles from the von Mises distribution.

Figure 4.4 shows a set of 100 points from the distribution $v\mathcal{MF}(\mathbf{x}|(0,0,1)^T,5)$ defined in a 3D space and the mle of μ and R. The sample has been generated from the algorithm proposed in Wood (1994).   ∎

4.1.3 Parameter Confidence Intervals

The point estimation of parameters does not provide information regarding the precision and reliability of the estimate. Expressing the results of the estimation process in terms of a **confidence interval** (CI), where its width (precision) as well as the reliability (confidence) that the true value of the parameter will be found, constitutes a more complete method for implementing the estimation.

A $(1-\alpha)$ CI for a parameter θ, denoted by $\text{CI}_{1-\alpha}(\theta)$, is built by first selecting a confidence level, denoted by $(1-\alpha)$, usually expressed as a percentage $(1-\alpha)\cdot 100\%$, where $\alpha \in (0,1]$. The **confidence level** is a measure of the degree of reliability in the procedure used to build the CI. For example, a CI of 95% implies that 95% of the samples would provide confidence intervals that would contain the true θ.

Although it is desirable to have a high degree of reliability, increasing this reliability causes an increase in the width of the CI. The CI has two limits, a lower limit, $L(\mathbf{X})$, and an upper limit, $U(\mathbf{X})$. That is, the CI should verify that

$$p(L(\mathbf{X}) \le \theta \le U(\mathbf{X})) = 1 - \alpha. \tag{4.5}$$

The interpretation of Equation (4.5) is that the probability that the random interval $[L(\mathbf{X}),U(\mathbf{X})]$ contains the true θ is $(1-\alpha)$. However, once the values of the random variables $X_1, \dots, X_N$ are observed, Equation (4.5) can be written as

$$\text{CI}_{1-\alpha}(\theta) = [L(\mathbf{x}),U(\mathbf{x})],$$

which is called the $(1-\alpha)$ CI.

CIs of the form $[L(\mathbf{X}),U(\mathbf{X})]$ are called **two-sided CIs**. **One-sided CIs** assume the form

$$p(L(\mathbf{X}) \le \theta) = 1 - \alpha \quad \text{or} \quad p(\theta \le U(\mathbf{X})) = 1 - \alpha,$$

depending on whether the CI is a lower CI $[L(\mathbf{X}),\infty)$, or an upper CI $(-\infty, U(\mathbf{X})]$, respectively.

4.1.3.1 Confidence Intervals for Population Means of a Normal Distribution

A. Population Mean with Known Population Variance. Given a sample of size N taken from a normal density with unknown mean μ and known variance σ^2, the statistic $\bar{x} \sim \mathcal{N}\left(x|\mu, \frac{\sigma}{\sqrt{N}}\right)$, or equivalently $\frac{\bar{x}-\mu}{\sigma/\sqrt{N}} \sim \mathcal{N}(x|0,1)$. These results are based on the properties of the expectation and variance operators (Section 3.2.1) and because a linear combination of Gaussians is also Gaussian.

A symmetric (with respect to $\bar{X}$) two-sided CI with a $(1-\alpha)$ CI can be built considering a region such that the area between $z_{\alpha/2}$ and $z_{1-\alpha/2}$ is $(1-\alpha)$ (see Figure 4.5).

In probability notation

$$p\left(z_{\alpha/2} \le \frac{\bar{X}-\mu}{\sigma/\sqrt{N}} \le z_{1-\alpha/2}\right) = 1 - \alpha. \tag{4.6}$$

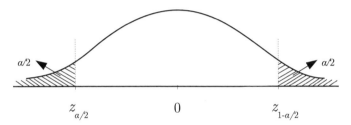

Figure 4.5 z_α value verifies that $p(\mathcal{N}(x|0,1) < z_\alpha) = \alpha$, i.e., it is the quantile of order α (Section 3.3.1).

After multiplying both sides of Equation (4.6) by $\sigma/\sqrt{N}$, and subtracting $\bar{X}$ from both sides, and multiplying both sides by -1, we obtain the symmetric two-sided CI with a $(1-\alpha)$ confidence level for μ, as

$$p\left(\bar{X} - z_{1-\alpha/2}\frac{\sigma}{\sqrt{N}} \le \mu \le \bar{X} - z_{\alpha/2}\frac{\sigma}{\sqrt{N}}\right) = 1 - \alpha.$$

Taking into account that in a $\mathcal{N}(x|0,1)$ density, $-z_{\frac{\alpha}{2}} = z_{1-\frac{\alpha}{2}}$, the CI is

$$\mathrm{CI}_{1-\alpha}(\mu) = \left[\bar{X} - z_{1-\alpha/2}\frac{\sigma}{\sqrt{N}}, \bar{X} + z_{1-\alpha/2}\frac{\sigma}{\sqrt{N}}\right].$$

Example. For a sample of size $N = 5$, for the onset year of AD from Section 4.1.2, assuming that $\sigma^2 = 67.88$, the CI for μ with a confidence level of $1 - \alpha = 0.95$ is given by

$$\mathrm{CI}_{0.95}(\mu) \simeq \left[73.40 - 1.96\frac{8.24}{2.24}, 73.40 + 1.96\frac{8.24}{2.24}\right] = [66.19, 80.61].$$

If the mean $\bar{X} = 73.40$ years corresponds to a sample size of $N = 500$ (instead of $N = 5$), the new CI with the same confidence level of 0.95 would be $[72.67, 74.13]$. As expected, increasing the sample size reduces the width of the CI because the variance of $\bar{X}$ reduces. ∎

B. Population Mean with Unknown Population Variance. The statistic used in this situation is $\frac{\sqrt{N}(\bar{X}-\mu)}{S} \sim t_{N-1}$ that follows a Student's t distribution. Operating in a similar manner, the derivation of the CI is

$$\mathrm{CI}_{1-\alpha}(\mu) = \left[\bar{X} - t_{N-1;1-\alpha/2}\frac{S}{\sqrt{N}}, \bar{X} + t_{N-1;1-\alpha/2}\frac{S}{\sqrt{N}}\right],$$

where $t_{N;\alpha}$ is the quantile of order α of a Student's t distribution with N degrees of freedom and S is the sample quasi-variance.

Example. Considering the same data as in the previous example, now with unknown variance estimated with $S^2 = 67.88$, the CI with a 0.95 confidence level is given by

$$\mathrm{CI}_{0.95}(\mu) \simeq \left[73.40 - 2.78\frac{8.24}{2.24}, 73.40 + 2.78\frac{8.24}{2.24}\right] = [63.17, 83.63],$$

as $t_{0.975;4} = 2.78$. Comparing this CI with that obtained when the value of the variance was assumed to be known, we observe that its width is enlarged, that is, it has less precision. ∎

C. Difference in the Means of Two Independent Populations with Known Unequal Variances. Assume two random samples of sizes N_X and N_Y, respectively, taken from two normal densities $\mathcal{N}(x|\mu_X,\sigma_X)$ and $\mathcal{N}(y|\mu_Y,\sigma_Y)$. For this situation the CI is given by

$$\text{CI}_{1-\alpha}(\mu_X - \mu_Y) = \left[(\bar{X} - \bar{Y}) - z_{1-\alpha/2}\sqrt{\frac{\sigma_X^2}{N_X} + \frac{\sigma_Y^2}{N_Y}}, (\bar{X} - \bar{Y}) + z_{1-\alpha/2}\sqrt{\frac{\sigma_X^2}{N_X} + \frac{\sigma_Y^2}{N_Y}} \right].$$

D. Difference in the Means of Two Independent Populations with Variances That Are Unknown but Assumed Equal. Now $\sigma_X = \sigma_Y = \sigma$ is unknown. The CI for $\mu_X - \mu_Y$ is based on the statistic

$$\frac{(\bar{X} - \bar{Y}) - (\mu_X - \mu_Y)}{\sqrt{S_p^2 \left(\frac{1}{N_X} + \frac{1}{N_Y} \right)}} \sim t_{N_X + N_Y - 2}.$$

The expression inside the square root is an estimator for the variance of $\bar{X} - \bar{Y}$, where

$$S_p^2 = \frac{(N_X - 1)S_X^2 + (N_Y - 1)S_Y^2}{N_X + N_Y - 2}$$

represents the pooled estimator of the variance σ^2. This estimator weighs the contributions of S_X^2 and S_Y^2, taking their respective samples sizes, N_X and N_Y, into account. The CI is

$$\text{CI}_{1-\alpha}(\mu_X - \mu_Y) = \left[(\bar{X} - \bar{Y}) - t_{N_X + N_Y - 2; 1 - \alpha/2} S_p \sqrt{\frac{1}{N_X} + \frac{1}{N_Y}}, \right.$$

$$\left. (\bar{X} - \bar{Y}) + t_{N_X + N_Y - 2; 1 - \alpha/2} S_p \sqrt{\frac{1}{N_X} + \frac{1}{N_Y}} \right].$$

E. Difference in the Means of Two Independent Populations with Unknown and Unequal Variances. Under these assumptions, the CI with a $1 - \alpha$ confidence level is

$$\text{CI}_{1-\alpha}(\mu_X - \mu_Y) = \left[(\bar{X} - \bar{Y}) - t_{N_X + N_Y - 2; 1 - \alpha/2} \sqrt{\frac{S_X^2}{N_X} + \frac{S_Y^2}{N_Y}}, \right.$$

$$\left. (\bar{X} - \bar{Y}) + t_{N_X + N_Y - 2; 1 - \alpha/2} \sqrt{\frac{S_X^2}{N_X} + \frac{S_Y^2}{N_Y}} \right].$$

4.1.3.2 Confidence Intervals for Population Variances of a Normal Distribution

A. Population Variance. Having a sample of size N of a $\mathcal{N}(x|\mu,\sigma)$ density, it holds that the statistic $\frac{(N-1)S^2}{\sigma^2} \sim \chi_{N-1}^2$. The χ_N^2 density is not symmetric, and its shape depends on its degrees of freedom N (see Figure 3.8(a)).

Based on the quantiles of orders $\frac{\alpha}{2}$ and $\left(1 - \frac{\alpha}{2}\right)$ of the χ_{N-1}^2 density, we obtain

$$P\left(\chi_{N-1;\alpha/2}^2 \le \frac{(N-1)S^2}{\sigma^2} \le \chi_{N-1;1-\alpha/2}^2 \right) = 1 - \alpha.$$

After algebraic manipulations, we have that the CI for σ^2 is

$$CI_{1-\alpha}(\sigma^2) = \left[\frac{(N-1)S^2}{\chi^2_{N-1;1-\alpha/2}}, \frac{(N-1)S^2}{\chi^2_{N-1;\alpha/2}} \right].$$

Example. The sample of size $N = 5$ introduced in Section 4.1.2 provides the following 0.95 confidence level CI for σ^2

$$CI_{0.95}(\sigma^2) = \left[\frac{4 \cdot 67.88}{11.14}, \frac{4 \cdot 67.88}{0.48} \right] = [24.37, 565.67].$$

The large width of this CI is motivated by the small sample size from which it has been calculated. ∎

B. Ratio of Population Variances. Given samples of sizes N_X and N_Y, respectively, taken from two normal and independent populations, $\mathcal{N}(x|\mu_X, \sigma_X)$ and $\mathcal{N}(y|\mu_Y, \sigma_Y)$, the CI for the ratio $\frac{\sigma_X^2}{\sigma_Y^2}$ is built on the basis of the statistic

$$\frac{S_Y^2/\sigma_Y^2}{S_X^2/\sigma_X^2} \sim F_{N_Y-1,N_X-1}.$$

The $(1-\alpha)$ CI is

$$CI_{1-\alpha}\left(\frac{\sigma_X^2}{\sigma_Y^2}\right) = \left[F_{N_Y-1,N_X-1;\alpha/2} \frac{S_X^2}{S_Y^2}, F_{N_Y-1,N_X-1;1-\alpha/2} \frac{S_X^2}{S_Y^2} \right],$$

where $F_{N_Y-1,N_X-1;\alpha/2}$ and $F_{N_Y-1,N_X-1;1-\alpha/2}$ are the quantiles of orders $\frac{\alpha}{2}$ and $\left(1-\frac{\alpha}{2}\right)$ of a F_{N_Y-1,N_X-1} density, respectively. Similarly to the difference in means, the variances are compared by their ratio. Thus, if the CI only includes values greater than 1, then $\sigma_X^2 > \sigma_Y^2$; if the values are smaller than 1, then $\sigma_X^2 < \sigma_Y^2$.

4.1.3.3 Confidence Interval for the Population Proportion

Given a sample of size N taken from a Bernoulli distribution with unknown parameter p, and assuming that N is sufficiently large to construct an asymptotic CI, it is given by

$$CI_{1-\alpha}(p) = \left[\hat{p} - z_{1-\alpha/2}\sqrt{\frac{\hat{p}(1-\hat{p})}{N}}, \hat{p} + z_{1-\alpha/2}\sqrt{\frac{\hat{p}(1-\hat{p})}{N}} \right],$$

where $\hat{p} = \bar{X}$.

Example. Consider that the estimate $\hat{p} = 0.30$ has been obtained in Section 4.1.2 from a sample of size $N = 500$ rather than with $N = 10$. The corresponding 0.95 CI is

$$CI_{0.95}(p) \simeq \left[0.30 - 1.96\sqrt{\frac{0.30 \cdot 0.70}{500}}, 0.30 + 1.96\sqrt{\frac{0.30 \cdot 0.70}{500}} \right] \simeq [0.26, 0.34].$$

∎

4.1.3.4 Determining Required Sample Size

Neuroscientists often wish to know how to determine the minimum required sample size for providing probabilistic guarantees that the value of the estimator $\hat{\theta}$ is within a given distance of the true value of parameter θ. Mathematically, the question can be written as the determination of the minimum sample size N such that

$$p\left(|\hat{\theta} - \theta| < \varepsilon\right) \geq 1 - \alpha,$$

where $\varepsilon > 0$ and $\alpha \in (0, 1)$ are given by the neuroscientist and $\hat{\theta}$ is a function of the sample $X_1, \ldots, X_N$.

The value of α determines the quantile of order $(1 - \alpha)$ of the distribution of estimator $\hat{\theta}$. Thus, we solve for N the equation where ε is equal to a function of N.

Example. This general approach can be particularized for the case of a population mean (i.e., $\theta = \mu$) in a normal distribution with known population variance (Section 4.1.3.1). Our question is what is the minimum sample size N for which the sample mean $\bar{X}$ differs from the expectation μ less than 0.1 units with a probability higher than 0.95 (i.e., $\alpha = 0.05$), assuming that $\sigma = \sqrt{67.88}$ units. According to the CI for μ (Section 4.1.3.1),

$$p\left(|\bar{X} - \mu| < z_{1-\alpha/2} \frac{\sigma}{\sqrt{N}}\right) \geq 1 - \alpha.$$

Therefore, $\varepsilon = 0.1 = z_{1-\alpha/2} \frac{\sigma}{\sqrt{N}}$, with $\alpha = 0.05$. After solving for N, we have

$$N = \frac{\left(z_{1-\alpha/2}\right)^2 \sigma^2}{\varepsilon^2} = \frac{1.96^2 \cdot 67.88}{0.1^2} = 26{,}076.78.$$

Therefore, the required sample size is $N = 26{,}077$.   ∎

4.1.4 Bayesian Estimation

The maximum likelihood method aims at identifying the parameter value that is best supported by the data, that is, maximizing the probability of obtaining the samples actually observed. The true parameter we seek, θ, is viewed to be fixed. In **Bayesian parameter estimation**, θ is considered to be a random variable with a known prior distribution. With the observed sample, this distribution is converted, through the Bayes' theorem, to a posterior distribution. This is the distribution used to perform inferences on θ.

As with MLE, we denote by $\mathbf{x} = \{x_1, \ldots, x_N\}$ the observed values of a random variable X from a population whose probability distribution depends on θ. The following are the basic assumptions here:

- The form of the conditional density $f(\mathbf{x}|\theta)$ is assumed to be known, although the value of θ is unknown. This is the likelihood function.
- Our initial knowledge regarding θ before observing the sample is assumed to be contained in a known prior density $f(\theta)$.

4.1.4.1 Prior and Posterior Distributions

After observing the sample, the basic problem is to compute the posterior density $f(\theta|\mathbf{x})$, which we hope is sharply peaked about the true value of θ. This is known as **Bayesian**

Table 4.1 Main conjugate distribution families. In the row displaying the Dirichlet and categorical distributions, $\boldsymbol{\theta} = (\theta_1, \ldots, \theta_n)$ with $\theta_1 + \cdots + \theta_n = 1$, X in the categorical distribution takes on values or categories $1, 2, \ldots, n$ with respective probabilities $\theta_1, \ldots, \theta_n$. The sample $\mathbf{x} = \{x_1, \ldots, x_N\}$ contains N_i occurrences (out of N) of category i, $i = 1, \ldots, n$ and $N_1 + \cdots + N_n = N$. In the row displaying the Dirichlet and multinomial distributions, $\boldsymbol{\theta} = (\theta_1, \ldots, \theta_n)$; $\mathbf{x} = (x_1, \ldots, x_n)$ in the multinomial distribution is such that $x_1 + \cdots + x_n = M$. The sample is $\mathbf{x}' = \{\mathbf{x}'_1, \ldots, \mathbf{x}'_N\}$, with $\mathbf{x}'_j = (x'_{j1}, \ldots, x'_{jn})$, for $j = 1, \ldots, N$. The sample is also $\mathbf{x}' = \{\mathbf{x}'_1, \ldots, \mathbf{x}'_N\}$ for the row including the Wishart and Gaussian distributions, where $\boldsymbol{\theta}$ is the precision matrix, that is, $\boldsymbol{\theta} = \mathbf{W} = \boldsymbol{\Sigma}^{-1}$, and the mean vector $\boldsymbol{\mu}$ is known. Finally, for the normal-Wishart distribution, $\boldsymbol{\theta} = (\boldsymbol{\mu}, \mathbf{W})$. The formulas of $\boldsymbol{\mu}_1$ and $\mathbf{T}_1$ are given in Table 13.3

Prior $f(\boldsymbol{\theta})$	Population $f(x\|\boldsymbol{\theta})$	Posterior $f(\boldsymbol{\theta}\|\mathbf{x})$
$\text{Beta}(\theta\|a_0, b_0)$	$\text{Bin}(x\|m, \theta)$	$\text{Beta}\left(\theta\|a_0 + \sum_{i=1}^{N} x_i, b_0 + mN - \sum_{i=1}^{N} x_i\right)$
$\text{Gamma}(\theta\|\alpha_0, \lambda_0)$	$\text{Pois}(x\|\theta)$	$\text{Gamma}\left(\theta\|\alpha_0 + \sum_{i=1}^{N} x_i, \lambda_0 + N\right)$
$\text{Gamma}(\theta\|\alpha_0, \lambda_0)$	$\text{Exp}(x\|\theta)$	$\text{Gamma}\left(\theta\|\alpha_0 + N, \lambda_0 + \sum_{i=1}^{N} x_i\right)$
$\mathcal{N}(\theta\|\mu_0, \sigma_0)$	$\mathcal{N}(x\|\theta, \sigma)$	$\mathcal{N}\left(\theta\|\frac{\sigma^2 \mu_0 + N\sigma_0^2 \bar{x}}{\sigma^2 + N\sigma_0^2}, \frac{\sigma\sigma_0}{\sqrt{\sigma^2 + N\sigma_0^2}}\right)$
$\text{Dir}(\boldsymbol{\theta}\|\alpha_{10}, \ldots, \alpha_{n0})$	$\text{Cat}(x\|\theta_1, \ldots, \theta_n)$	$\text{Dir}(\boldsymbol{\theta}\|\alpha_{10} + N_1, \ldots, \alpha_{n0} + N_n)$
$\text{Dir}(\boldsymbol{\theta}\|\alpha_{10}, \ldots, \alpha_{n0})$	$\text{MN}(\mathbf{x}\|M; \theta_1, \ldots, \theta_n)$	$\text{Dir}\left(\boldsymbol{\theta}\|\alpha_{10} + \sum_{i=1}^{N} x'_{i1}, \ldots, \alpha_{n0} + \sum_{i=1}^{N} x'_{in}\right)$
$\mathcal{W}(\boldsymbol{\theta}\|\alpha, \mathbf{T}_0)$	$\mathcal{N}(\mathbf{x}\|\boldsymbol{\mu}, \boldsymbol{\theta}^{-1})$	$\mathcal{W}\left(\boldsymbol{\theta}\|\alpha + N, \mathbf{T}_0 + \sum_{i=1}^{N} (\mathbf{x}'_i - \boldsymbol{\mu})(\mathbf{x}'_i - \boldsymbol{\mu})^T\right)$
$\mathcal{NW}(\boldsymbol{\theta}\|\boldsymbol{\mu}_0, \nu, \mathbf{T}_0, \alpha)$	$\mathcal{N}(\mathbf{x}\|\boldsymbol{\mu}, \mathbf{W}^{-1})$	$\mathcal{NW}(\boldsymbol{\theta}\|\boldsymbol{\mu}_1, \nu + N, \mathbf{T}_1, \alpha + N)$

learning. Using Bayes' theorem, the posterior density is given by

$$f(\boldsymbol{\theta}|\mathbf{x}) = \frac{f(\mathbf{x}|\boldsymbol{\theta})f(\boldsymbol{\theta})}{\int f(\mathbf{x}|\boldsymbol{\theta})f(\boldsymbol{\theta})d\boldsymbol{\theta}}, \tag{4.7}$$

where the integration extends over the entire parameter space. Because $x_1, \ldots, x_N$ come from i.i.d. $X_1, \ldots, X_N$ random variables, respectively, then $f(\mathbf{x}|\boldsymbol{\theta}) = \prod_{i=1}^{N} f(x_i|\boldsymbol{\theta})$.

When the prior and posterior belong to the same family of distributions, the prior is said to be a **conjugate prior**, which simplifies the calculation of the posterior distribution. $f(\boldsymbol{\theta}|\mathbf{x})$ is said to be a **reproducing density**. Examples of conjugate distributions are listed in Table 4.1.

Parameters of prior distributions are called **hyperparameters**. For example, parameters a and b of the beta prior distribution that models how parameter p of a binomial distributes (see Table 4.1) are hyperparameters. Hyperparameters themselves may have hyperprior distributions expressing beliefs regarding their values. A Bayesian model with more than one level of priors is called a **hierarchical Bayes** model.

The **predictive distribution** is the distribution of unobserved observations conditional on the observed data, that is, the distribution that a new data point x^* would have, given the observed values $\mathbf{x}$. It is computed by marginalizing over the parameters, using the following posterior distribution:

$$f(x^*|\mathbf{x}) = \int f(x^*|\mathbf{x}, \boldsymbol{\theta})f(\boldsymbol{\theta}|\mathbf{x})d\boldsymbol{\theta}, \tag{4.8}$$

where $f(x^*|\mathbf{x}, \boldsymbol{\theta}) = f(x^*|\boldsymbol{\theta})$ in many cases.

If another sample $\mathbf{x}'$ is subsequently received, we can use Equation (4.7) again to obtain

$$f(\boldsymbol{\theta}|\mathbf{x},\mathbf{x}') = \frac{f(\mathbf{x}'|\boldsymbol{\theta})f(\boldsymbol{\theta}|\mathbf{x})}{\int f(\mathbf{x}'|\boldsymbol{\theta})f(\boldsymbol{\theta}|\mathbf{x})d\boldsymbol{\theta}},$$

where now the old posterior $f(\boldsymbol{\theta}|\mathbf{x})$ is the prior. With more samples, the procedure would be similar. This is called the **recursive Bayes approach** to parameter estimation and is an example of an incremental or online learning method, where learning continues as the samples are collected. Here, the use of a conjugate prior is recommended because the posterior distribution typically becomes more complex with each added sample. Rather than preserving all samples to calculate the new distribution, for some distributions, just a few estimates of parameters associated with it – the **sufficient statistics** – suffice because they contain all the required information.

Performing these computations is an added difficulty of Bayesian estimation with respect to maximum likelihood methods, where the complex multidimensional integral is often computed numerically or by Monte Carlo techniques. Moreover, in many cases, the MLE is easier to interpret because it yields a single best model, unlike Bayesian methods that provide a weighted average of models and many parameter values, thereby leading to more complicated solutions. However, the posterior includes all the available information and the uncertainty in the possible models and the Bayesian estimation tells us how to use it. If the prior information is reliable, Bayesian methods are expected to yield better results.

The choice of the prior distribution lies in domain expert knowledge. It can be determined from past information, such as previous experiments, or elicited from the purely subjective assessment of an expert. These are informative priors that express specific and definite information regarding $\boldsymbol{\theta}$. However, if we think that the prior has no structure, we can create priors that are called noninformative. **Noninformative priors** can be created to reflect a balance among outcomes when no information is available. For example, we can assume each of the categories of a discrete random variable are equally likely in the absence of other information.

Priors can also be selected according to a certain principle. For example, to select a prior over a certain position parameter (as the mean μ of a Gaussian), we can assume that the prior should not depend on our arbitrary selected origin. This implies that translation invariance is required. The only prior with this property is the uniform over the entire set of real numbers. Such a prior is an **improper distribution**, that is, it does not integrate to 1. Similarly, for a noninformative prior over a scale parameter (as the standard deviation σ of a Gaussian), the spatial measurement units (meters, inches...) should be assumed to be irrelevant to the functional form of the prior. This implies that scale invariance is required. A prior with this property is $f(\sigma) = 1/\sigma$, which becomes "less likely" in inverse proportion to its value. This is also an improper distribution. Usual noninformative priors on continuous, unbounded variables are improper. Note that there is a danger of overinterpreting these priors because they are not probability densities.

4.1.4.2 *The Brain as a Bayesian Machine*

Bayesian theories have been applied to the study of perception, learning, memory, reasoning, language, decision making, and many other domains. They raise many foundational questions (like "Does the brain actually use Bayesian rules?"). The answers have been controversial. General textbooks on this are Knill and Richards (1996), Rao et al. (2002), and Doya et al. (2007).

A growing trend in theoretical neuroscience is that the brain (particularly the human perceptual system) can be considered a **Bayesian machine** (see, e.g., Friston [2012]), which infers the causes of sensory inputs in an optimal manner (but see Colombo and Seriès [2012]). The nervous system would encode a probabilistic model because sensory inputs are often noisy and uncertain. The models would be updated by neural processing of sensory information using Bayesian inference. Thus, the beliefs regarding the state of the world given sensory inputs would be computed using Bayes' theorem. For example, if Θ is the random variable representing the values of a certain physical property of an object (e.g., its shape), and X a sensory measurement (like vision) of the property, typically corrupted by noise, then perception can be modeled as Bayesian inference: the aim is to compute $f(\theta|x) \propto f(x|\theta)f(\theta)$, the probability of the state of the object at a certain time with respect to its shape at that time, which is proportional to the likelihood of the sensory measurement for different values of Θ and the prior probability of Θ. If we have another type of sensory measurement (e.g., haptic) Y, and both modalities are assumed to be independent given Θ (perhaps because neurons processing visual information are far apart from cortical neurons processing haptic information), then we have $f(\theta|x,y) \propto f(x|\theta)f(y|\theta)f(\theta)$, as the means to integrate sensory information. This is constantly done over time by the nervous system. With the posterior distribution, we can make judgments and decisions in the world (Körding, 2007) by using a Bayesian estimation (with a loss function, see below).

Generating decisions regarding sensory stimuli is also considered hypothesis testing (Section 4.2). If a stimulus is noisy, the nervous system needs to integrate information over a long time to make a good decision. A decision with regard to which hypothesis is more probable is reached when the sensory evidence to support or refute a hypothesis surpasses a threshold value. The threshold may be controlled by neural circuits that calculate the rate of the underlying reward. In fact, in the early 1940s, it is with such accumulation of evidence that Alan Turing and his colleagues broke the Enigma code used by the German navy during World War II – a process called "Banburismus" (Good, 1979; Gold and Shadlen, 2002; Larrañaga and Bielza, 2012).

It is difficult to infer which priors, likelihoods, and loss functions are used by people to make their decisions; this is called the inverse decision theory (Körding, 2007). Pellicano and Burr (2012) even speculated that perceptual abnormalities in autism can be explained by differences in how beliefs regarding the world are formed (the prior), or how they are combined with sensory information (how prior and likelihood are combined, differently from Bayes' rule). However, this is subject to criticism (Teufel et al., 2013). Further, it is possible that illusory percept is caused by applying a wrong prior (Weiss et al., 2002).

4.1.4.3 *Point Estimation*

Inferences with respect to θ are derived from the posterior distribution $f(\theta|\mathbf{x})$. In particular, to derive a point estimation is often convenient as a summary of the entire distribution. Assume that we have a loss function $L(\theta,\hat{\theta})$ that measures the extent of the difference between the estimate $\hat{\theta} = t(X_1, \ldots X_n)$ and the unknown parameter θ. The **Bayes estimator** is an estimator or decision rule that minimizes the Bayes risk among all estimators. The **Bayes risk** of $\hat{\theta}$ is the expected loss, where the expectation is taken with respect to the prior distribution of θ. In other words, the Bayes estimator is $\arg\min_{\hat{\theta}} \int L(\theta, \hat{\theta}) f(\theta) d\theta$, and it is specific to the prior $f(\theta)$ being used. The estimator that minimizes the posterior expected loss (or posterior risk), that is, the solution of $\min_{\hat{\theta}} \int L(\theta, \hat{\theta}) f(\theta|\mathbf{x}) d\theta$, for each $\mathbf{x}$, also minimizes the Bayes risk and, therefore, is a Bayes estimator. Typically, the converse is also true, that is, all Bayes estimators are minimizers of the posterior risk and for this reason some authors define the Bayes estimator as the minimizer of the posterior risk instead of as the minimizer of the Bayes risk.

The most common loss function is the squared error: $L(\theta, \hat{\theta}) = (\hat{\theta} - \theta)^2$. Using this loss function, the Bayes estimator is simply the mean of the posterior distribution because

$$\arg\min_{\hat{\theta}} \int (\hat{\theta} - \theta)^2 f(\theta|\mathbf{x}) d\theta = \mathbb{E}[\theta|\mathbf{x}] = \int \theta f(\theta|\mathbf{x}) d\theta.$$

Similarly, if the loss function is the absolute error, $L(\theta, \hat{\theta}) = |\hat{\theta} - \theta|$, then the Bayes estimator is the median of the posterior distribution, $Me_{\theta|\mathbf{x}}$, because

$$\arg\min_{\hat{\theta}} \int |\hat{\theta} - \theta| f(\theta|\mathbf{x}) d\theta = Me_{\theta|\mathbf{x}}.$$

Recall that in Section 2.2.2, we stated that the mean (median) is the locus of the minimal sum-of-squared (sum-of-absolute) deviations from which these two previous results are derived.

Having improper distributions does not need to be a problem whenever the posterior distribution is proper. If the prior is improper, an estimator that minimizes the posterior expected loss is called the **generalized Bayes estimator**. Bayes theorem can only be applied when all distributions are proper. However, with improper priors, one can define the posterior distribution using the same expression as that of Equation (4.7), and it is not uncommon that the resulting posterior be a valid distribution. Then, the posterior expected loss is typically well defined and finite.

An alternative method for formulating a point estimation from a Bayesian viewpoint is to select the value of θ that maximizes the posterior distribution, that is, the mode of this distribution. This is called **maximum a posteriori** (MAP) estimation. When the prior has no effect on the posterior (e.g., it is constant), then the posterior is similar to the likelihood and both estimation methods, maximum likelihood and Bayesian (computed as a MAP), yield similar estimates. If the likelihood function $f(\mathbf{x}|\theta)$ reaches a sharp peak at $\theta = \hat{\theta}$ (the MLE) and the prior density $f(\theta)$ is not zero at $\theta = \hat{\theta}$ and does not change much in its neighborhood, then the posterior density $f(\theta|\mathbf{x})$ also peaks at that point. Then, the influence of prior information on the uncertainty in the true value of θ can be ignored. In general, the prior will have an effect, and this is why we average $f(\mathbf{x}|\theta)$ over the possible values of θ in the integral.

In general, both (MLE and Bayesian) are asymptotically equivalent and consistent estimators.

Example. Bayesian Estimation. Consider that $f(x|\theta) = f(x|\mu) \sim \mathcal{N}(x|\mu, \sigma)$, where the only unknown parameter is the mean μ. Assume the prior knowledge regarding μ is expressed by $f(\mu) \sim \mathcal{N}(\mu|\mu_0, \sigma_0)$, where μ_0 and σ_0 are known. Thus, μ_0 is our best prior guess for μ, and σ_0^2 represents our uncertainty regarding this guess.

Hence, if a value is drawn from $f(\mu)$, it becomes the true value of μ and completely determines the density for x, $f(x|\mu)$. Suppose now that a sample $\mathbf{x} = \{x_1, \ldots, x_N\}$ is drawn from that population. Using Equation (4.7), we can derive the following posterior distribution $f(\mu|\mathbf{x})$:

$$f(\mu|\mathbf{x}) \propto \prod_{i=1}^{N} f(x_i|\mu) f(\mu)$$

$$\propto \prod_{i=1}^{N} \exp\left[-\frac{1}{2}\left(\frac{x_i-\mu}{\sigma}\right)^2\right] \exp\left[-\frac{1}{2}\left(\frac{\mu-\mu_0}{\sigma_0}\right)^2\right]$$

$$\propto \exp\left[-\frac{1}{2}\left(\sum_{i=1}^{N}\left(\frac{x_i-\mu}{\sigma}\right)^2 + \left(\frac{\mu-\mu_0}{\sigma_0}\right)^2\right)\right]$$

$$\propto \exp\left[-\frac{1}{2}\left[\left(\frac{N}{\sigma^2}+\frac{1}{\sigma_0^2}\right)\mu^2 - 2\left(\frac{1}{\sigma^2}\sum_{i=1}^{N}x_i + \frac{\mu_0}{\sigma_0^2}\right)\mu\right]\right],$$

where factors that do not depend on μ have been absorbed into the proportionality constant. Therefore, $f(\mu|\mathbf{x})$ again has normal density because its expression is an exponential function of the quadratic function of μ. Denoting by μ_N and σ_N the parameters of the posterior Gaussian distribution $f(\mu|\mathbf{x})$, they can be found by equating the coefficients in the previous equation and those in the generic Gaussian:

$$\frac{1}{\sigma_N^2} = \frac{N}{\sigma^2} + \frac{1}{\sigma_0^2}$$

$$\frac{\mu_N}{\sigma_N^2} = \frac{1}{\sigma^2}\sum_{i=1}^{N}x_i + \frac{\mu_0}{\sigma_0^2}.$$

Solving for μ_N and σ_N, we obtain

$$\mu_N = \frac{\sigma^2\mu_0 + N\sigma_0^2\bar{x}}{\sigma^2 + N\sigma_0^2} \tag{4.9}$$

$$\sigma_N = \frac{\sigma\sigma_0}{\sqrt{\sigma^2 + N\sigma_0^2}}, \tag{4.10}$$

where $\bar{x} = \frac{1}{N}\sum_{i=1}^{N}x_i$ is the sample mean. These equations are presented in Table 4.1. μ_N is our best guess after observing the sample, and it is a weighted combination of the sample mean $\bar{x}$ and the prior mean μ_0, and μ_N will always lie between them (see Equation (4.9)). If $\sigma_0 \neq 0$, $\mu_N \to \bar{x}$ as $N \to \infty$, where the prior knowledge has no effect. If $\sigma_0 = 0$, the prior distribution is degenerate, and we have a strong certainty that $\mu = \mu_0$ and the empirical data cannot change our opinion ($\mu_N = \mu_0$). σ_N^2 is the uncertainty regarding our best guess after observing the sample, and it decreases with N (see Equation (4.10)). That is, each observation decreases our uncertainty regarding the true value of μ. The posterior distribution becomes increasingly sharply peaked as N increases.

With a squared loss function, the Bayes estimator of μ is given by the posterior mean, that is, μ_N. Using a MAP approach, the point estimate is also μ_N because the Gaussian distribution is symmetric and its mean and mode coincide.

The predictive distribution is computed by using Equation (4.8), where $f(x^*|\mu) \sim \mathcal{N}(x|\mu,\sigma)$ and $f(\mu|\mathbf{x}) \sim \mathcal{N}(\mu|\mu_N,\sigma_N)$. With similar computations to those for the posterior, we obtain that $f(x^*|\mathbf{x}) \sim \mathcal{N}\left(x|\mu_N, \sqrt{\sigma^2 + \sigma_N^2}\right)$. Thus, the mean μ_N is treated as if it were the true mean, and the variance σ_N^2 is increased to account for the additional uncertainty in x^*, σ^2; this is due to our lack of knowledge about μ.   ∎

Bayesian estimation will be frequently used in Bayesian networks (Chapter 13), both for finding the graph structure and for estimating its parameters. Bayesian estimation will be also used in Markov networks (Section 14.8) and probabilistic clustering (Section 12.3.2).

4.2   Hypothesis Tests

A **statistical hypothesis test** is a method of making decisions scientifically by using the information within a data set containing values from a random variable. The term **statistically significant** refers to the situation where, according to a predetermined probability threshold, called significance level, the observed values are unlikely to have occurred by chance alone. Hypothesis tests, also known as **tests of significance** (Fisher, 1925), are used for determining what outcomes of a study would lead to a rejection of the **null hypothesis** for a prespecified level of significance. The **critical region** or **rejection region** of a hypothesis test is the set of all outcomes that cause the null hypothesis to be rejected when contrasted against the **alternative hypothesis**. Statistical hypothesis testing is classed as **confirmatory data analysis**, as opposed to exploratory data analysis (Chapter 2).

Example. Figure 2.10(b) shows that, in our sample (Data Set 1) of 128 pyramidal and 199 interneuron cells, the average values for the relative distance to the pia (X_{65}) are smaller for interneurons. It may be of interest to know whether or not these differences are due to randomness, according to the assumption (null hypothesis) that the values of the relative distance to the pia for pyramidal and interneurons cells have been generated from the same probability distribution.

The side-by-side barplot depicted in Figure 2.9 raises the question of whether the distributions of the number of dendritic Sholl sections are different (whether these differences are statistically significant, that is, do not happen by chance) for interneuron and pyramidal cells.   ∎

4.2.1   Basic Concepts

Null Hypothesis versus Alternative Hypothesis. The first step in a test of significance is to define the null hypothesis, H_0, which is assumed to be true prior to conducting the hypothesis test. The null hypothesis is compared to another hypothesis, called the alternative hypothesis, denoted by H_1. Both hypotheses are concerned with nonoverlapping subsets of the parameter space Θ in terms of θ values. When a hypothesis uniquely specifies the distribution of the population from which the sample is taken, the hypothesis is said to be a **simple hypothesis**. Any hypothesis that is not a simple hypothesis is called a **compound hypothesis**. A simple hypothesis completely specifies the population distribution, whereas an alternative hypothesis does not. Table 4.2 presents a few examples of a simple (a) or compound (b)–(d) alternative hypothesis. In all four situations, the null hypothesis is simple.

Table 4.2 Different types of alternative
hypotheses for a simple null hypothesis

Null hypothesis	Alternative hypothesis
(a) $H_0 : \theta = \theta_0$	$H_1 : \theta = \theta_1$
(b) $H_0 : \theta = \theta_0$	$H_1 : \theta < \theta_0$
(c) $H_0 : \theta = \theta_0$	$H_1 : \theta > \theta_0$
(d) $H_0 : \theta = \theta_0$	$H_1 : \theta \neq \theta_0$

The goal in hypothesis testing is to decide whether the evidence provided by the sample is sufficiently clear to reject the null hypothesis, H_0, compared to the alternative hypothesis H_1. To this end, based on a distribution of a test statistic under the null hypothesis, that is, assuming H_0 is true, its domain is partitioned into regions, the rejection region and the **acceptance region**. The splitting point(s) is computed according to the acceptable risk. This risk refers to the possibility of making the wrong decisions regarding H_0 and H_1 because the sample size is limited.

Example. Following on with the example illustrated in Figure 2.2(d) and assuming that the variable measuring the difference in relative distance to the pia between pyramidal and interneurons cells follows a Gaussian density with a population mean denoted by θ, we can attempt to confirm our exploratory findings by means of the following hypothesis test: $H_0 : \theta = 0$ versus $H_1 : \theta < 0$. This alternative hypothesis is suggested by the fact that the average distance is smaller for pyramidal cells in our sample of 327 neuronal cells. Taking the difference between the average relative distances to the pia for pyramidal and interneuron cells as a statistic for the test, a positive value, or even a value close to zero, will, intuitively, support H_0; on the contrary, a high negative value will refute H_0. The rejection region (and, alternatively, the acceptance region) is determined from the theoretical distribution of this test statistic under H_0, once the probability of making wrong decisions is fixed. Next, we compute the value of the test statistic in our sample of 327 neurons and decide whether to accept or reject H_0. ∎

Type I and Type II Errors. The decision made using a hypothesis test is always subject to error, that is, the null hypothesis may be rejected even though it is true. On the other hand, the null hypothesis may be accepted when H_1 is true. Simply put, we can never be sure that the decision is correct because it is made on a limited sample size.

This is rather like the hypothetical legal situation of an individual who is on trial for a capital offense. The law courts of most countries consider an individual to be innocent until proven guilty of an offense. Based on the presented evidence (which plays the role of the sample), the jury (the test statistic) can convict or not convict the defendant. As in a hypothesis test, there are four possibilities (see Table 4.3), depending on the decisions of the jury and whether or not the individual is innocent.

The four situations presented in Table 4.3 are discussed below:

(a) The null hypothesis is true, and based on the sample, the null hypothesis is rejected; thus, the decision is incorrect. This is called a **type I error**. The probability of committing a type I error is termed **level of significance** of the test and denoted by α, that

Table 4.3 Four possible situations when comparing the nature of H_0 with the decision based on a sample

		Decision	
		Reject H_0	Fail to reject H_0
H_0	True	(a) Type I error $p(\text{Reject } H_0\|H_0 \text{ is true}) = \alpha$	(b) Correct decision $p(\text{Accept } H_0\|H_0 \text{ is true}) = 1 - \alpha$
	False	(c) Correct decision $p(\text{Reject } H_0\|H_1 \text{ is true}) = 1 - \beta$	(d) Type II error $p(\text{Accept } H_0\|H_1 \text{ is true}) = \beta$

is, $\alpha = p(\text{Reject } H_0|H_0 \text{ is true})$. In the legal example, a type I error would be to convict an innocent defendant.

(b) The null hypothesis is true, and based on the sample, there is not sufficient evidence against it; thus, it is not rejected and the decision is correct. In the legal example, this is equivalent to a situation where the defendant is innocent and the jury decides that the defendant is not guilty of the charge, thereby making the jury's decision correct.

(c) The null hypothesis is false, and it is rejected based on the sample, thereby making the decision being correct. In the legal example, this translates into a jury convicting a guilty defendant.

(d) The null hypothesis is false, and sufficient evidence has not been collected from the sample to reject it. This error is called a **type II error**. The probability of committing a type II error is denoted by β, that is, $\beta = p(\text{Accept } H_0|H_1 \text{ is true})$. In the legal example, a type II error is made when a guilty person is not convicted.

The **statistical power** of a hypothesis test is the probability that the test correctly rejects the null hypothesis when the alternative hypothesis is true. If H_1 is simple (as in case (a) of Table 4.2), then the power is $p(\text{Reject } H_0|H_1 \text{ is true}) = 1 - \beta$, which is the complementary of type II error. Then, as the power increases, chances of a type II error decrease. In general, the power is a function of the possible distributions, often determined by a parameter, under compound hypotheses H_1 (as those in cases (b)–(d) in Table 4.2). Power analysis is appropriate when the correct rejection of a false null hypothesis is a concern. The power is used to compare different statistical testing procedures of the same hypothesis, as in Chapter 15.

The **p-value**. As explained above, the acceptance (and rejection) region is determined once the distribution of the test statistic is known under H_0 and after establishing, a priori, the level of significance α. Another possibility is to decide whether or not to reject the null hypothesis based on p-values. The p-value is defined as the probability of obtaining results in the statistic at least as extreme as the observed values, assuming that the null hypothesis is true.

Table 4.4 shows some examples of how to compute the p-value for different scenarios of the simple null hypothesis versus simple (top two) and composite (bottom three) alternative hypotheses. In all scenarios, the sample mean $\bar{x}$ plays the role of the test statistic, whose distribution under H_0 is assumed to be known. The value observed in the sample for this test statistic is denoted by $\bar{x}_{obs}$.

Table 4.4 Computing p-values for different null and alternative hypotheses based on the test statistic $\bar{X}$

Hypotheses	p-value
$H_0 : \mu = \mu_0, H_1 : \mu = \mu_1 \ (\mu_1 > \mu_0)$	$p(\bar{X} \geq \bar{x}_{obs}\|H_0)$
$H_0 : \mu = \mu_0, H_1 : \mu = \mu_1 \ (\mu_1 < \mu_0)$	$p(\bar{X} \leq \bar{x}_{obs}\|H_0)$
$H_0 : \mu = \mu_0, H_1 : \mu < \mu_0$	$p(\bar{X} \leq \bar{x}_{obs}\|H_0)$
$H_0 : \mu = \mu_0, H_1 : \mu > \mu_0$	$p(\bar{X} \geq \bar{x}_{obs}\|H_0)$
$H_0 : \mu = \mu_0, H_1 : \mu \neq \mu_0$	$2\min\{p(\bar{X} \leq \bar{x}_{obs}\|H_0), p(\bar{X} \geq \bar{x}_{obs}\|H_0)\}$

For an initial research hypothesis whose truth is unknown, we can summarize the usual testing process in the following manner:

1. State the relevant null hypothesis, H_0, and alternative hypothesis, H_1.
2. Consider the statistical assumptions made about the sample. If the data violate these assumptions, change the parametric test to a nonparametric one (see below).
3. Decide which test is appropriate, and state the relevant test statistic, T.
4. Derive the distribution of the test statistic under the null hypothesis. In standard cases, this will be a well-known result.
5. Select a significance level, α, a probability threshold below which the null hypothesis will be rejected. $\alpha = 0.05$ or $\alpha = 0.01$ are common values.
6. The distribution of the test statistic under the null hypothesis partitions the possible values of T into those for which the null hypothesis is rejected (rejection or critical region), and those for which the null hypothesis is not rejected (acceptance region).
7. Compute t_{obs}, the value of the test statistic T from the observed data values.
8. Decide whether or not to reject the null hypothesis in favor of the alternative hypothesis. The decision rule is to reject the null hypothesis H_0 if the observed value t_{obs} is in the rejection region and to accept (or "fail to reject") the null hypothesis otherwise.

An alternative process using the p-value, rather than determining the critical and acceptance regions, is described below:

1. Calculate the probability of obtaining a test statistic value at least as extreme as that actually observed t_{obs}, assuming that the null hypothesis is true, the so called p-value.
2. Decide whether or not to reject the null hypothesis in favor of the alternative hypothesis. The decision rule is to reject H_0 if and only if the p-value is lower than the significance level α.

Table 4.5 presents a list of the tests explained below in this section, organized according to the aim of the test and stating the test name and whether or not it is parametric or non-parametric. A **parametric test** is based on certain assumptions made over the distribution of the sample data, like, for example, Gaussian density. If the test statistic is not based on such an assumption, the test is said to be **nonparametric** (Siegel, 1956). The handbook by Sheskin (2000) provides in-depth coverage of parametric and nonparametric statistical procedures.

Table 4.5 Statistical tests classified according to the goal of the test and the parametric versus nonparametric issue

Goal of the test	Parametric/ nonparametric	Name
Goodness-of-fit	Parametric	Shapiro–Wilk test
	Parametric	Univariate Gaussianity test
	Parametric	Multivariate Gaussianity test
	Parametric	Watson test
	Nonparametric	Chi-squared test
	Nonparametric	Kolmogorov–Smirnov test
Mean from one Gaussian sample	Parametric	t-test (unknown variance)
Proportion	Parametric	Binomial test
From two paired samples		
-Comparison of means	Parametric	t-test
-Comparison of medians	Nonparametric	Wilcoxon signed-rank test
From two unpaired samples		
-Comparison of means	Parametric	t-test
-Comparison of distributions	Nonparametric	Mann–Whitney test
-Comparison of distributions	Nonparametric	Watson test for two samples
From three or more paired samples		
-Comparison of means	Parametric	One-way repeated-measures ANOVA
-Comparison of medians	Nonparametric	Friedman test
From three or more unpaired samples		
-Comparison of means	Parametric	One-way ANOVA
-Comparison of distributions	Nonparametric	Kruskal–Wallis test
Degree of relationship	Parametric	Pearson correlation test
	Nonparametric	Spearman rank correlation test
	Nonparametric	Chi-squared test of independence
Multiple comparisons	Nonparametric	Bonferroni correction
	Nonparametric	Šidák correction
	Nonparametric	Holm–Bonferroni method
General purpose	Nonparametric	Permutation test

4.2.2   Goodness-of-Fit Tests

Many statistical procedures require knowledge of the population from which the sample is taken. For example, Student's t test for testing a hypothesis assumes that the population is Gaussian. In supervised classification (Part III), some methods assume a Gaussian distribution of the predictor variables for each class value. Similar assumptions are made in clustering and regression. Goodness-of-fit tests will help to identify the distribution of the population from which the sample is drawn. The null hypothesis in a goodness-of-fit test is a statement regarding the entire probability distribution. We present a specific test for accepting that the sample comes from a normal or von Mises distribution (Shapiro–Wilk and Watson, respectively) and two general approaches, one designed primarily for discrete distributions (chi-squared goodness-of-fit) and the other designed for continuous distributions (Kolmogorov–Smirnov). Goodness-of-fit tests for univariate and multivariate Gaussian distributions based on asymmetry and kurtosis coefficients are also presented.

Shapiro–Wilk Normality Test. The Shapiro–Wilk test (Shapiro and Wilk, 1965) is appropriate for testing normality and is very useful with small samples ($N < 30$). The parameters of the normal distribution do not need to be specified in the null hypothesis of the test. The test statistic is based on the ordered sample. The null hypothesis and the alternative hypothesis of the Shapiro–Wilk test are

$$\begin{cases} H_0 : X \sim \mathcal{N}(\mu, \sigma) \\ H_1 : X \nsim \mathcal{N}(\mu, \sigma). \end{cases}$$

Given a random sample of size N, $x_1, x_2, \ldots, x_N$, extracted from a random variable X, the sample must be sorted: $x_{(1)} \leq x_{(2)} \leq \cdots \leq x_{(N)}$. The Shapiro–Wilk test statistic takes the following form:

$$W = \frac{\left(\sum_{i=1}^{N} a_i X_{(i)} \right)^2}{\sum_{i=1}^{N} (X_i - \bar{X})^2}.$$

The vector of weights $\mathbf{a}^T = (a_1, \ldots, a_N)$ is computed in the following manner:

$$\mathbf{a} = \frac{\mathbf{w}^T \mathbf{V}^{-1}}{(\mathbf{w}^T \mathbf{V}^{-1} \mathbf{V}^{-1} \mathbf{w})^{\frac{1}{2}}},$$

where the elements of the vector $\mathbf{w}$ are $w_i = \mathbb{E}[X_{(i)}]$, and $\mathbf{V}$ is the covariance matrix of the order statistics $X_{(1)}, \ldots, X_{(N)}$. Small values of W lead to the rejection of the null hypothesis. The p-values are obtained from a table computed by the test authors.

The parametric Shapiro–Wilk test was used for testing normality of encephalographic time series (Kipinski et al., 2011) and of several scales for depression in dementia in patients with AD (Vital et al., 2012).

Example. The Shapiro–Wilk test of normality has been applied to each continuous variable in our example of pyramidal and interneuron cells (Data Set 1). The null hypothesis of normality has been rejected in all of the variables. For the power transformation of X_4, X_4^3, depicted in Figure 2.22 (b), the R implementation of the Shapiro–Wilk test produced the following output: `W = 0.9887, p-value = 0.0123`, that is, the null hypothesis that the sample, with $N = 327$, of variable X_4^3 follows a normal distribution is not rejected at a significance level $\alpha = 0.01$. ∎

Univariate Gaussianity Test. There are several tests of the univariate normal density. The test below (Duda et al., 2001) is based on the sample moments of orders three (asymmetry) and four (kurtosis) around the mean. It admits a direct extension for the case of multivariate normal densities (see below). The null and alternative hypotheses are

$$\begin{cases} H_0 : X \sim N(x|\mu, \sigma) \\ H_1 : X \nsim N(x|\mu, \sigma). \end{cases}$$

Given a sample of size N, $x_1, \ldots, x_N$, extracted from a population X, recall (Section 2.2.2) that its sample moment of order r around the mean is defined as $a_r = \frac{1}{N} \sum_{i=1}^{N} (X_i - \bar{X})^r$. The skewness or sample asymmetry is defined from the sample moments of orders 3 and 2 as $g_1 = \frac{a_3}{a_2^{3/2}}$, and the sample kurtosis coefficient is based on the sample moments of orders 4 and 2: $g_2 = \frac{a_4}{a_2^2} - 3$.

The test is based on the asymptotic distributions of g_1 and g_2 under the null hypothesis H_0. It is verified that $g_1 \simeq \mathcal{N}\left(0, \sqrt{\frac{6}{N}}\right)$ and $g_2 \simeq \mathcal{N}\left(0, \sqrt{\frac{24}{N}}\right)$. The standardized statistic, $Z = \frac{Ng_1^2}{6} + \frac{Ng_2^2}{24}$, asymptotically follows a chi-squared distribution under H_0, with two degrees of freedom. H_0 is rejected with a significance level of α if $z_{obs} > \chi^2_{2;1-\alpha}$, where $\chi^2_{2;1-\alpha}$ denotes the quantile of order $1 - \alpha$ of a chi-squared distribution with two degrees of freedom.

Multivariate Gaussianity Test. This test is a generalization of the univariate normal test explained above. Given a sample of size N, $\mathbf{x}^1, \ldots, \mathbf{x}^N$, extracted from a multivariate distribution, the test must be able to discover whether or not this multivariate distribution is Gaussian of dimension n. The null and alternative hypotheses are

$$\begin{cases} H_0 : \mathbf{X} \sim \mathcal{N}(\mathbf{x}|\boldsymbol{\mu}, \boldsymbol{\Sigma}) \\ H_1 : \mathbf{X} \nsim \mathcal{N}(\mathbf{x}|\boldsymbol{\mu}, \boldsymbol{\Sigma}). \end{cases}$$

The test is based on $G_1 = \frac{1}{N^2} \sum_{i=1}^N \sum_{j=1}^N D_{ij}^3$ and $G_2 = \frac{1}{N} \sum_{i=1}^N D_{ii}^2$ statistics, where $D_{ij} = (\mathbf{X}_i - \bar{\mathbf{X}})^T \hat{\boldsymbol{\Sigma}}^{-1}(\mathbf{X}_j - \bar{\mathbf{X}})$ and $\hat{\boldsymbol{\Sigma}}^{-1}$ denotes the inverse of the sample covariance matrix $\hat{\boldsymbol{\Sigma}}$.

Assuming that H_0 is true, the asymptotic distribution of $N \frac{G_1}{6}$ is a chi-squared density with $f = \frac{1}{6}n(n+1)(n+2)$ degrees of freedom. For the G_2 statistic, we have $G_2 \sim \mathcal{N}(n(n+2), \sqrt{\frac{8n(n+2)}{N}})$. As G_1 and G_2 statistics are independent under H_0, we know that $Z = \frac{NG_1}{6} + \frac{N(G_2 - n(n+2))^2}{8n(n+2)}$ follows a chi-squared density with $f + 1$ degrees of freedom. The null hypothesis H_0 will be rejected with a significance level α if $z_{obs} > \chi^2_{f+1;1-\alpha}$, where $\chi^2_{f+1;1-\alpha}$ denotes the quantile of order $1 - \alpha$ of a chi-squared distribution with $f + 1$ degrees of freedom.

Watson Test for von Mises Distribution. Given a sample of angular values $\phi_1, \ldots, \phi_N$, defined in the unit circle $\phi_i \in [0, 2\pi), i = 1, \ldots, N$, taken from a population Φ, the following are the null and alternative hypotheses of Watson's U^2 test:

$$\begin{cases} H_0 : \Phi \sim v\mathcal{M}(\phi|\mu, \kappa) \\ H_1 : \Phi \nsim v\mathcal{M}(\phi|\mu, \kappa), \end{cases}$$

where the parameters μ and κ are estimated by maximum likelihood if they are unknown.

The definition of U^2 (Watson, 1961) is independent of the choice of origin for ϕ around the circle and measures the discrepancy between the empirical distribution function $\hat{F}_N(\phi)$ of N values ϕ (that is, $\hat{F}_N(\phi)$ is the proportion of $\phi_i \leq \phi$, for $0 \leq \phi \leq 2\pi$) and the distribution function $F_0(\phi)$ under the null hypothesis, that is, the von Mises $v\mathcal{M}(\phi|\mu, \kappa)$ distribution function:

$$U^2 = N \int_0^{2\pi} \left[\hat{F}_N(\phi) - F_0(\phi) - \int_0^{2\pi} (\hat{F}_N(\phi) - F_0(\phi))dF_0(\phi) \right]^2 dF_0(\phi). \tag{4.11}$$

The test procedure begins by calculating $y_i = F_0(\phi_i)$, for each i, from the von Mises $v\mathcal{M}(\phi|\mu,\kappa)$ distribution function and then putting y_i in ascending order: $y_{(1)}, \ldots, y_{(N)}$. Finally, U^2 is calculated as

$$U^2 = \sum_{i=1}^{N}\left(Y_{(i)} - \frac{2i-1}{2N}\right)^2 - N\left(\frac{\Sigma_i Y_{(i)}}{N} - \frac{1}{2}\right)^2 + \frac{1}{12N}.$$

If μ and κ are known, then the statistic is $U^* = (U^2 - 0.1/N + 0.1/N^2)(1 + 0.8/N)$. Critical points have been calculated and tabulated by Lockhart and Stephens (1985). H_0 is rejected at the approximate significance level α if U^2 or U^* exceeds the point given in the table. When μ and κ are known, the test is exact. For other cases the levels for U^2 are approximate because there are only approximate points, although they will be accurate for practical purposes for $N \geq 20$.

The Watson U^2 parametric test in Equation (4.11) can be used for other distributions, changing F_0 in H_0 accordingly.

In Bielza et al. (2014), von Misesness appeared to be suitable, via the Watson parametric test, for modeling the branching angles of the same order in basal dendrites of pyramidal neurons from seven different cortical areas of the frontal, parietal, and occipital cortex of adult mice. In Leguey et al. (2016), the von Mises distribution resulted in a good fit for modeling branching angles in pyramidal neurons from different layers when grouped according to their maximum tree order (a method to measure neuron complexity). When the angles were grouped just by their branch order, the Jones–Pewsey distribution (a generic circular distribution of which the von Mises distribution is one instance) was a more appropriate distribution according to certain tests, as the Watson U^2 parametric test, particularly for this distribution.

Chi-Squared Goodness-of-Fit Test. Given a random sample $x_1, \ldots, x_N$ from an unknown population $F(x)$, we may wish to test the null hypothesis that $F(x)$ has some known distribution $F_0(x)$ for all x, that is,

$$\begin{cases} H_0 : F \equiv F_0 \\ H_1 : F \not\equiv F_0. \end{cases}$$

For example, using the data of variable X_{36}, measuring the number of dendrites in a neuron, shown in Table 4.6, we may want to test whether the underlying population follows a Poisson distribution with a λ parameter (that coincides with the expectation) given by the mean of the number of dendrites in the 327 neurons, that is, $\hat{\lambda} = 5.716$.

The chi-squared goodness-of-fit is based on a normalized statistic that accounts for the deviations between what is observed and what is expected when H_0 is true in K mutually exclusive categories. In certain situations (particularly for continuous distributions), the data must be grouped according to a certain scheme to form the K mutually exclusive

Table 4.6 Observed frequencies in the sample of 327 cells for each of the possible values of X_{36} measuring the number of dendrites in a neuron

Number of dendrites	0	1	2	3	4	5	6	7	8	9	10	11	12	13	14	15
Observed frequencies	0	0	7	35	59	64	50	53	32	17	6	1	0	1	0	2

categories. When H_0 completely specifies the population, we can compute the probability that a random observation will fall into each of the selected categories. The expected counts for each category under H_0 are calculated by multiplying each of these probabilities by N. If H_0 is true, the differences between the observed counts and the expected counts for each of the K categories are likely to be small. The test statistic measuring these differences is given by

$$W = \sum_{i=1}^{K} \frac{(O_i - E_i)^2}{E_i}, \tag{4.12}$$

where W is the sum of the squared differences between what is observed in the sample, O_i, and what is expected under H_0, $E_i = N p_i$, in each of the K categories, divided by what is expected in each of the K categories. p_i refers to the probability of the ith category under H_0. The observed frequencies verify $\sum_{i=1}^{K} O_i = N$. The values of W are likely to be large when the observed data are inconsistent with the null hypothesis. On the contrary, small values of W can be interpreted as consistent with H_0. The exact distribution of W is complicated. However, for a large N, provided all expected count categories are at least 5, the test statistic distribution is approximated by a χ^2 density with $K - r - 1$ degrees of freedom, where r denotes the number of parameters estimated by maximum likelihood.

Example. Following on with the application of the chi-squared goodness-of-fit test to fit a Poisson distribution with $\hat{\lambda} = 5.716$ to the count data of Table 4.6, we noticed that the condition that all expected count categories are at least 5 is not verified by some values of X_{36}. Thus, we decided that $K = 9$ by grouping values 0, 1, and 2 into one category, and 10–15 in another category, as shown in Table 4.7. The result of the test is `X-squared = 26.1465, df = 8, p-value = 0.0010`, so the null hypothesis is rejected for $\alpha = 0.01$. ∎

Kolmogorov–Smirnov Test. The null and alternative hypotheses of the Kolmogorov–Smirnov goodness-of-fit test are the same as those in the chi-squared test:

$$\begin{cases} H_0 : F \equiv F_0 \\ H_1 : F \not\equiv F_0, \end{cases}$$

where F_0 denotes the distribution function under the null hypothesis, provided all parameters have been specified. This test only applies to continuous distributions. The test statistic measures the vertical deviations between the distribution function under H_0, that is, $F_0(x)$, and the empirical distribution function, $\hat{F}_N(x)$, for all x, where $\hat{F}_N(x)$ denotes

Table 4.7 Observed frequencies, O_i, and expected frequencies, E_i, under H_0: Poisson distribution, with $\hat{\lambda} = 5.716$, in the sample of 327 cells; the value of $K = 9$ has been selected as providing $E_i \geq 5$ for all i

	$\{0,1,2\}$	3	4	5	6	7	8	9	≥ 10
O_i	7	35	59	64	50	53	32	17	10
E_i	24.82	33.51	47.89	54.75	52.16	42.59	30.43	19.32	21.50

(as in the Watson test) the percentage of observations in the sample that are smaller than, or equal to, x, and is computed as

$$\hat{F}_N(x) = \begin{cases} 0 & x < x_{(1)} \\ \frac{i}{N} & x_{(i)} \leq x < x_{(i+1)} \\ 1 & x \geq x_{(N)}. \end{cases}$$

The test statistic D_N is defined as $\max_i D_N(x_{(i)})$, where:

$$D_N(x_{(i)}) = \max \left\{ \left| \hat{F}_N(x_{(i-1)}) - F_0(x_{(i)}) \right|, \left| \hat{F}_N(x_{(i)}) - F_0(x_{(i)}) \right| \right\}.$$

The statistic D_N does not depend on $F_0(x)$ as long as $F(x)$ is continuous. Given a significance level of α, the null hypothesis is rejected when $d_{N,\text{obs}} > D_{N;1-\alpha}$, where $D_{N;1-\alpha}$ denotes the quantile of order $1 - \alpha$ of distribution D_N, that is,

$$p(D_N > D_{N;1-\alpha}|H_0) = \alpha.$$

In terms of the p-value, if it is less than the largest acceptable α value, the null hypothesis is rejected as well.

If the null hypothesis is not completely specified, D_N can still be used by estimating the unknown parameters of $F_0(x)$ using their mles. However, in this case, the previous distribution of D_N only serves as an approximation to the true distribution of the statistic. The test becomes more conservative, that is, it tends not to reject H_0.

The nonparametric Kolmogorov–Smirnov test was applied to fit normal distributions to latencies and amplitudes in the use of vestibular-evoked myogenic potential for diagnosis of MS (Harirchian et al., 2013).

Example. As for the Shapiro–Wilk test, the Kolmogorov–Smirnov test for normality is applied to the data of variable X_4^3 (see Figure 2.22(b)). In this case, the R package provides the following results: D = 0.0512, p-value = 0.3580, thereby implying

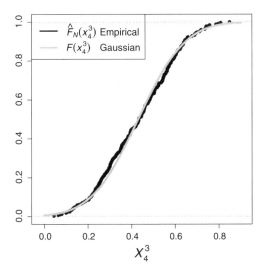

Figure 4.6 Empirical distribution function $\hat{F}_N(x)$ for X_4^3 (black) and distribution function for the normal density (gray).

that there is not sufficient evidence in the sample to reject H_0. Figure 4.6 illustrates the two main functions of the test: the empirical distribution function for X_4^3 according to the 327 cells (in black) and the distribution function for the normal density assumed in H_0 (in gray). ∎

4.2.3 One-Sample Tests

t-**Test for One Gaussian Sample (Unknown Variance).** The null and a two-sided alternative hypotheses for testing a value of the mean when sampling from a normal distribution with unknown variance are, respectively,

$$\begin{cases} H_0 : \mu - \mu_0 & (\sigma \text{ unknown}) \\ H_1 : \mu \neq \mu_0 & (\sigma \text{ unknown}). \end{cases}$$

The test statistic (already used in the CIs of Section 4.1.3.1) is

$$T = \frac{\bar{X} - \mu_0}{S/\sqrt{N}}.$$

If the null hypothesis is true, the distribution of this test statistic is a Student's t with $N-1$ degrees of freedom, that is, under H_0, $T \sim t_{N-1}$. Consequently, small (absolute) values of the test statistic support H_0, whereas large (absolute) values of T will be used to reject H_0.

Table 4.8 illustrates the rejection regions for different alternative hypotheses, as well as how to determine the cut points between acceptance and rejection regions. The significance level for all three tests is equal to α.

Example. Following on again with variable X_4^3 (see Figure 2.22(b)) that has passed the normality test, and considering the null hypothesis $H_0 : \mu = 0.43$ (a very close value to its sample mean) against the alternative hypothesis $H_1 : \mu \neq 0.43$, the result of the test statistic and its respective p-value provided by the R package is t = 0.0048, df = 326, p-value = 0.9961, that is, H_0 cannot be rejected. With the same sample, if we change the null and alternative hypotheses to $H_0 : \mu = 0.80$ and $H_1 : \mu < 0.80$ we get t = -39.2147, df = 326, p-value < 2.2e-16, thereby implying that the null hypothesis is rejected. However, if the null and alternative hypotheses are $H_0 : \mu = 0.80$ and $H_1 : \mu > 0.80$, the output is t = -39.2147, df = 326, p-value = 1, that is, according to the evidence provided by the sample, the null hypothesis cannot be rejected. ∎

Table 4.8 Rejection regions for testing the population mean from normal densities with unknown variance against different alternatives

	Null hypothesis $H_0 : \mu = \mu_0$	(with σ unknown)	
H_1	$\mu < \mu_0$	$\mu > \mu_0$	$\mu \neq \mu_0$
Rejection region	$t_{\text{obs}} < t_{N-1;\alpha}$	$t_{\text{obs}} > t_{N-1;1-\alpha}$	$|t_{\text{obs}}| > t_{N-1;1-\alpha/2}$
p-value	$p(t_{N-1} < t_{\text{obs}}|H_0)$	$p(t_{N-1} > t_{\text{obs}}|H_0)$	$p(|t_{N-1}| > t_{\text{obs}}|H_0)$

Table 4.9 p-value formulas for testing the proportion of successes in Bernoulli experiments for three different alternative hypotheses; $\mathbb{I}(\cdot)$ is the indicator function (Equation (3.3))

	Null hypothesis $H_0 : \theta = \theta_0$
Alternative hypothesis	p-value formula
$H_1 : \theta < \theta_0$	$p(E \leq e_{\text{obs}}|H_0) = \sum_{i=0}^{e_{\text{obs}}} \binom{N}{i} \theta_0^i (1 - \theta_0)^{N-i}$
$H_1 : \theta > \theta_0$	$p(E \geq e_{\text{obs}}|H_0) = \sum_{i=e_{\text{obs}}}^{N} \binom{N}{i} \theta_0^i (1 - \theta_0)^{N-i}$
$H_1 : \theta \neq \theta_0$	$\sum_{i=0}^{N} \mathbb{I}(p(E = i) \leq p(E = e_{\text{obs}})) \binom{N}{i} \theta_0^i (1 - \theta_0)^{N-i}$

Binomial Test for a Population Proportion. A null hypothesis where the proportion of successes in a number of independent Bernoulli experiments, θ, is equal to a certain value, θ_0, is tested with the statistic corresponding to the number of successes. In other words, given a sample $x_1, \ldots, x_N$ extracted from a Bernoulli distribution with parameter θ and considering the null hypothesis $H_0 : \theta = \theta_0$, the test statistic $E = \sum_{i=1}^{N} X_i$ follows a binomial distribution with parameters N and θ_0 under H_0. From an intuitive point of view, if the value of the test statistic is close to $N\theta_0$, H_0 is likely to be true. More specifically, the p-value formulas associated with each of the three possible alternative hypotheses are given in Table 4.9. Note the use of the indicator function to compute the p-value formula for the two-sided alternative hypothesis.

Example. The 327 neurons of Data Set 1 contains 128 pyramidal and 199 interneuron cells. Considering a pyramidal cell as a success in a Bernoulli distribution from which a sample of size 327 has been extracted, we can contrast the null hypothesis $H_0 : \theta = 0.50$ against $H_1 : \theta \neq 0.50$. In this case, the number of pyramidal cells is less than likely under H_0, as indicated by number of successes = 128, number of trials = 327, p-value =0.0001, and the null hypothesis is rejected. However, a value of θ closer under the null hypothesis than the observed proportion of success in the sample, $\hat{\theta} = 0.3914$, for example, $H_0 : \theta = 0.40$ against $H_1 : \theta \neq 0.40$, provides the following output: number of successes = 128, number of trials = 327, p-value = 0.7780. In this case, the null hypothesis is not rejected. ∎

The exact distribution of the test statistic $E = \sum_{i=1}^{N} X_i$ under H_0 is binomial with parameters N and θ_0. However, when $N\theta_0$ and $N(1 - \theta_0)$ are both greater than or equal to 10, the statistic $\frac{\sum_{i=1}^{N} X_i}{N}$, measuring the percentage of successes in the sample, can be asymptotically approximated by a normal distribution, that is, under H_0,

$$\frac{\sum_{i=1}^{N} X_i}{N} \sim \mathcal{N}\left(\theta_0, \sqrt{\frac{\theta_0(1 - \theta_0)}{N}}\right) \text{ as } N \to \infty.$$

The standardized test statistic under the assumption that $H_0 : \theta = \theta_0$ is true is

$$Z = \frac{\frac{\sum_{i=1}^{N} X_i}{N} - \theta_0}{\sqrt{\frac{\theta_0(1-\theta_0)}{N}}} \sim \mathcal{N}(0, 1).$$

Table 4.10 Rejection regions for testing the success rate in Bernoulli experiments for three different alternative hypotheses using the normal approximation

	Null hypothesis $H_0 : \theta = \theta_0$
Alternative hypothesis	Rejection region
$H_1 : \theta < \theta_0$	$z_{obs} < z_\alpha$
$H_1 : \theta > \theta_0$	$z_{obs} > z_{1-\alpha}$
$H_1 : \theta \neq \theta_0$	$|z_{obs}| > z_{1-\alpha/2}$

Table 4.10 illustrates the rejection region associated with different alternative hypotheses for testing the value of the success rate in a Bernoulli population using a normal approximation.

Example. Repeating the above two hypothesis tests with a test statistic Z based on the normal approximation, we find that the null hypothesis $H_0 : \theta = 0.50$ is rejected (p-value $=$ 8.626e-05), whereas there is not enough evidence to reject $H_0 : \theta = 0.40$ (p-value $=$ 0.7520), always with two-sided alternative hypotheses.   ∎

4.2.4   Two-Paired Sample Tests

Typically, paired samples comprise a sample of matched pairs of similar units, or one group of units that has been tested twice (also known as "repeated measures"). Paired samples are also called "dependent samples."

In neuroscience, a typical example of matched pairs is the length of the left and right branches of the bifurcation of a dendritic tree. An example of the "repeated measures" concept is the two measures (before and after a prescribed treatment) of the Hoehn and Yahr scale (Hoehn and Yahr, 1967), which describes how PD symptoms progress.

t-**Test for Two Paired Gaussian Samples.** Given a paired sample of size N extracted from two random Gaussian variables X and Y, their difference $D = X - Y$ is a normal density with parameters μ_D and σ_D, both of which are unknown. The test statistic is

$$T = \frac{\bar{D} - \mu_D}{S_D/\sqrt{N}} \sim t_{N-1}.$$

The null hypothesis for testing a difference of means with dependent samples is $H_0 : \mu_D = \mu_X - \mu_Y = \delta_0$. Table 4.11 illustrates the three alternative hypotheses and their respective rejection regions for H_0.

Example. For illustrative purposes, we consider variables X_{26} and X_{27} (Table 1.5) measuring the axonal Sholl length at 100 μm and between 100 μm and 200 μm, respectively, divided by the total length of axonal segments. Figure 4.7 illustrates the frequency histograms for both variables, as well as for the difference, $X_{26} - X_{27}$.

Table 4.11 Rejection regions for three different alternative hypotheses when testing the mean difference in paired samples with a normal distribution

	Null hypothesis $H_0 : \mu_D = \delta_0$
Alternative hypothesis	Rejection region
$H_1 : \mu_D < \delta_0$	$t_{obs} < t_{N-1;\alpha}$
$H_1 : \mu_D > \delta_0$	$t_{obs} > t_{N-1;1-\alpha}$
$H_1 : \mu_D \neq \delta_0$	$|t_{obs}| > t_{N-1;1-\alpha/2}$

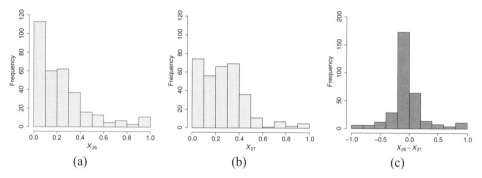

(a)   (b)   (c)

Figure 4.7 Frequency histograms for (a) X_{26}, (b) X_{27}, and (c) $X_{26} - X_{27}$.

Although the histogram of variable $X_{26} - X_{27}$ in Figure 4.7(c) appears symmetric and normally shaped, we obtain a `p-value < 2.2e-16` for the Shapiro–Wilk test, and `p-value = 2.901e-09` for the Kolmogorov–Smirnov test for normality. This implies that we should reject that the density of the sample from $X_{26} - X_{27}$ is normal, and the t-test for paired samples should not be used because the normality assumption is not verified. However, and for illustrative purposes only, we apply this test with a parameter value of $\delta_0 = 0$. With a general, nonspecific two-sided alternative hypothesis, $H_1 : \mu_D \neq 0$, we obtain a `p-value = 0.0764`, which is not sufficient evidence to reject H_0 against H_1. Taking into account the value of $\bar{d}_{obs} = -0.03003$, a more realistic alternative hypothesis is $H_1 : \mu_D < 0$. In this case, `p-value = 0.0382` is sufficient to reject H_0 at a significance level $\alpha = 0.05$. ∎

Yang et al. (2011) examined the formation and elimination of dendritic spines in the developing mouse cortex during and after (paired observations) anesthetics exposure with the application of the parametric t-test. This test was also applied by Mori et al. (2015) to study the long-term efficacy and safety of donepezil in patients with dementia with Levy bodies. They tested equality (H_0) in their responses, before and after treatment, to the MMSE for cognitive function and to the Neuropsychiatric Inventory for behavioral symptoms. A study with the objective of examining the effectiveness of rehabilitation in MS patients using three scales (functional, muscle strength, and disability) was conducted by Miller (2009) using also this test.

Wilcoxon Signed-Rank Test. An alternative to the paired t-test, when the population cannot be assumed to be normally distributed, is the **Wilcoxon signed-rank test** (Wilcoxon, 1945). We consider a sample size N_w for both random variables, X and Y. Thus, there is a total of $2N_w$ values, organized by pairs: $\{(x_1, y_1), \ldots, (x_{N_w}, y_{N_w})\}$. The null and alternative hypotheses are

$$\begin{cases} H_0 : \text{median difference between pairs is zero} \\ H_1 : \text{median difference between pairs is not zero.} \end{cases}$$

The test procedure can be summarized in the following manner:

1. Calculate $d_i = x_i - y_i$ for all $i = 1, \ldots, N_w$, and consider only the $N \leq N_w$ differences with $d_i \neq 0$.
2. Order these N pairs in ascending order of absolute difference. Denote their associated rank by r_i. Thus, $r_i = \text{rank}|d_i|$.
3. Sum the ranks for the positive differences. Denote the test statistic by T^+ and the value in the sample by t^+.
4. If $N \leq 15$, t^+ is compared to a percentile value from a reference table for the Wilcoxon signed-rank test. For $N > 15$, the sampling distribution of T^+, under H_0, can be reasonably approximated with the normal distribution. In this case, the standardized test statistic, Z, is used:

$$Z = \frac{T^+ - \frac{N(N+1)}{4}}{\sqrt{\frac{N(N+1)(2N+1)}{24}}} \sim \mathcal{N}(0, 1).$$

The rejection region is given by: $|z_{\text{obs}}| > z_{1 - \frac{\alpha}{2}}$.

Note that under the null hypothesis establishing that the median difference between pairs is zero, a value for t^+ close to $\frac{N(N+1)}{4}$ is expected. Significant discrepancies of t^+ from its expected value under H_0 would justify a rejection of the null hypothesis.

Example. The application of this test to the samples of variables X_{26} and X_{27}, considered as paired samples, provides a very high value of the test statistic, $t^+ = 15887$, as expressed by its `p-value = 3.589e-05`. Thus, the null hypothesis of equal median of axonal Sholl length at 100 μm and between 100 μm and 200 μm, respectively, divided by the total length of axonal segments is rejected. ∎

The Wilcoxon signed-rank test was used to compare the connectivity of right and left optic radiations by means of advanced MRI approaches, noninvasively in vivo, in healthy human brains by Arrigo et al. (2016). The results of a prospective trial of the impact of intraoperative cesium-131 on neurocognitive function and quality of life in patients with resected brain metastases were analyzed with the previous test in Pham et al. (2015). The test was also applied by Conijn et al. (2011) in the comparison of the visualization of microbleeds with 3D T2*-weighted imaging at 1.5T with respect to 3D dual-echo T2*-weighted imaging at 7T. Further, the effect of exercise therapy on cognitive functions in patients with MS was studied using the previous test by Sangelaji et al. (2015). The efficacy and tolerability of tetrabenazine, a monoamine depleter and dopamine receptor blocker for chorea associated with HD, was tested with a Wilcoxon signed-rank test in Ondo et al. (2002). The question regarding whether or not noninvasive brain stimulation of the right inferior frontal gyrus may improve attention in early AD was answered in Eliasova et al. (2014) with this nonparametric test for two paired samples. Sobstyl et al. (2014) used the same test in a 2-year follow-up study, to evaluate the quality of life among people with advanced PD after bilateral subthalamic stimulation.

4.2.5   Two Unpaired Sample Tests

Two samples are called unpaired when there is no relationship between any element from the first sample with any element from the second sample. The samples are also called independent, thereby emphasizing the fact that the elements of both samples are unrelated. Moreover, the sizes of both samples can be different. The null hypothesis will establish the value of a location measure, like, for example, the mean difference equal to zero. As in the previous section, we consider two situations: (a) both samples are normally distributed, and a parametric t-test can be applied, and (b) the normality assumption is not verified and a nonparametric test, the Mann–Whitney test, is the best option.

t-**Test for Two Unpaired Gaussian Samples.** Assume we have two unpaired (independent) samples of sizes N_X and N_Y, respectively, taken from two normal distributions, $\mathcal{N}(\mu_X, \sigma_X)$ and $\mathcal{N}(\mu_Y, \sigma_Y)$, where the population variances are unknown. An intuitive standardized test statistic for testing the null hypothesis, $H_0 : \mu_X = \mu_Y$, is

$$T = \frac{(\bar{X} - \bar{Y}) - (\mu_X - \mu_Y)}{\sqrt{\frac{S_X^2}{N_X} + \frac{S_Y^2}{N_Y}}}.$$

Although under H_0 the distribution of the T statistic is unknown, it can be approximated using a t-distribution with v degrees of freedom, where v is computed as the integer part of

$$\frac{\left(\frac{s_X^2}{N_X} + \frac{s_Y^2}{N_Y}\right)^2}{\frac{\left(s_X^2/N_X\right)^2}{N_X - 1} + \frac{\left(s_Y^2/N_Y\right)^2}{N_Y - 1}}.$$

The test based on this approximation is known as the **Welch two sample t-test**. Table 4.12 illustrates the three alternative hypotheses and their respective rejection regions for H_0.

Table 4.12 Rejection regions for three different alternative hypotheses when testing the mean difference in unpaired samples with a normal distribution

	Null hypothesis $H_0 : \mu_X - \mu_Y = 0$
Alternative hypothesis	Rejection region
$H_1 : \mu_X - \mu_Y < 0$	$t_{obs} < t_{v;\alpha}$
$H_1 : \mu_X - \mu_Y > 0$	$t_{obs} > t_{v;1-\alpha}$
$H_1 : \mu_X - \mu_Y \neq 0$	$|t_{obs}| > t_{v;1-\frac{\alpha}{2}}$

Example. The side-by-side boxplot in Figure 2.10(b) shows the Relative distance to pia (X_{65}) for each possible value of the variable Class, that is, for both pyramidal cells and interneurons. The relative distance to the pia for pyramidal cells appears to be higher on average than the respective average distance for interneurons. The question is whether the null hypothesis of equal means (or medians) can be accepted or, alternatively, whether there is sufficient evidence (randomness is not the cause of the difference between the relative distance of pyramidal cells and interneurons to the pia) to refute the null hypothesis.

Applying the t-test test to the two unpaired samples for the relative distance to the pia, X_{65}, according to the two types of cells, we obtain $N_X = 128$, $N_Y = 199$, $\bar{x} = 0.4641$, and $\bar{y} = 0.3960$. For $H_0 : \mu_X - \mu_Y = 0$ against $H_1 : \mu_X - \mu_Y \neq 0$, the R package provides t = 3.0452, df = 300, p-value = 0.002532. Thus, H_0 is rejected against this two-sided alternative hypothesis. According to the sample means, a more realistic alternative hypothesis is $H_1 : \mu_X - \mu_Y > 0$. In this case, again, the p-value is very small (p-value = 0.001266), and H_0 is rejected. Note that variable X_{65} does not follow a normal distribution, which is a necessary assumption for this test, and these results are presented only to illustrate the test. ∎

Olude et al. (2015) statistically compared the number of cells in different anatomical regions of the brain of juvenile and adult African giant rats by means of the parametric t-test for unpaired samples, thereby showing that in the first group, the counts were significantly higher in the cerebral cortex, pia, corpus callosum, rostral migratory stream, dentate gyrus, and cerebellum. Garg et al. (2015) used the same test for comparing the brainstem auditory-evoked potentials in drug abusers and control people. A study comparing MS patients with types A and B behavior patterns in terms of stress, nervousness, and anxiety based on t-tests was reported by Shaygannejad et al. (2013). Spisak et al. (2014) studied the importance of antioxidant defense system gene single nucleotide polymorphisms as risk factors of AD comparing the response in patients and healthy controls. Among PD patients, Stella et al. (2008) conducted a comparison between those diagnosed as clinically depressed and those who are nondepressed in terms of functional capacities measured by the Hoehn and Yahr staging, the united PD rating scale, and the Schwab and England evaluation.

Mann–Whitney Test. The Mann–Whitney U test (Mann and Whitney, 1947) is the non-parametric version of the t-test for two unpaired samples. It is also known as the Wilcoxon rank-sum test. It is assumed that all observations from both groups, $X_1, \ldots, X_{N_X}$ and $Y_1, \ldots, Y_{N_Y}$, are independent of each other, the responses are ordinal or continuous, and the underlying distributions of X and Y are identical in the null hypothesis. A usual representation of the null and alternative hypotheses is based on the distribution functions, that is,

$$\begin{cases} H_0 : F_X \equiv F_Y \\ H_1 : F_X \not\equiv F_Y. \end{cases}$$

The test procedure can be summarized in the following manner:

1. Arrange all the $N_X + N_Y$ observations into a single ranked series. Rank all the observations without taking into account the sample to which they belong.

2. Add up the ranks for values originating from population X. Denoting this rank addition as R_X, compute $U_X = R_X - \frac{N_X(N_X+1)}{2}$. Analogously, $U_Y = R_Y - \frac{N_Y(N_Y+1)}{2}$. Note that R_Y can be computed using the following equality: $R_X + R_Y = \frac{(N_X+N_Y)(N_X+N_Y+1)}{2}$.
3. Compute the statistic $U = \min\{U_X, U_Y\}$.
4. For small samples, $N_X + N_Y \leq 20$, the distribution of U is tabulated. For $N_X + N_Y > 20$, the approximation using the normal distribution is fairly good. In this case, the standardized test statistic, Z, is used:

$$Z = \frac{U - \frac{N_X N_Y}{2}}{\sqrt{\frac{N_X N_Y (N_X+N_Y+1)}{12}}} \sim \mathcal{N}(0,1).$$

The rejection region is given by $|z_{\text{obs}}| > z_{1-\frac{\alpha}{2}}$.

Example. The application of the Mann–Whitney test to the relative distance to the pia, X_{65}, according to the two types of cells, pyramidal and interneuron, provides a p-value = 0.0023. The conclusion is that the null hypothesis, according to which both samples of sizes $N_X = 128$ and $N_Y = 199$ are extracted from a common population, is rejected. ∎

The Mann–Whitney nonparametric test was used by Yuan et al. (2016) to show that there was a significant difference in the amount of lactate dehydrogenase release between hemoglobin plus saline and hemoglobin plus propofol in mouse cortical neurons. Resource-utilization measures were statistically compared in patients suffering nontraumatic intracerebral hemorrhage receiving and not receiving palliative care with the previous test in Murthy et al. (2016). Apparent diffusion coefficient values calculated in the entire normal-appearing white matter were compared between glioma and meningioma patients by Horváth et al. (2016). The Mann–Whitney test was also used by Cosottini et al. (2005) to statistically test several diffusion-tensor MRI indexes (mean diffusivity, fractional anisotropy, and eigenvalues) of corticospinal tract impairment in patients with progressive muscular atrophy and patients with ALS. In addition, Uszynski et al. (2015) applied the same test to show that foot vibration threshold scores differed between people with MS, with and without walking limitations. Teramoto et al. (2014) used the Mann–Whitney test to compare the behavioral assessment of the dysexecutive syndrome battery, which evaluates frontal function, in patients with PD with and without freezing of gait. A significant loss of pyramidal neurons in the angular gyrus of patients with HD compared with controls was demonstrated by MacDonald et al. (1997) using the previous test. Statistically significant differences in cerebrospinal fluid (CSF) biomarkers (concentrations of amyloid-β, total tau phospho-tau181, and an Aβ42-tau index) were found in Tsai et al. (2014) between clinically diagnosed idiopathic normal pressure hydrocephalus and AD patients.

Watson Two Sample Test for Comparing Two Circular Distributions. Watson two sample U^2 test (Watson, 1983) is for checking the equality of two circular distributions

$$\begin{cases} H_0 : F_{\Phi_1} \equiv F_{\Phi_2} \\ H_1 : F_{\Phi_1} \neq F_{\Phi_2} \end{cases}$$

on the basis of two independent random samples of angular values $\phi_{11}, \dots, \phi_{1N_1}$ from the first distribution and $\phi_{21}, \dots, \phi_{2N_2}$ from the second distribution. We denote the combined sample size by N, that is, $N = N_1 + N_2$. All sample values are defined in the unit circle and all $\phi_{ij} \in [0, 2\pi)$.

The definition of the statistic is

$$U^2_{N_1, N_2} = \frac{N_1 N_2}{N} \int_0^{2\pi} \left[\hat{F}_{N_1}(\phi) - \hat{F}_{N_2}(\phi) - \int_0^{2\pi} (\hat{F}_{N_1}(\phi) - \hat{F}_{N_2}(\phi)) d\hat{F}_N(\phi) \right]^2 d\hat{F}_N(\phi),$$

where $\hat{F}_{N_1}, \hat{F}_{N_2}$ are the empirical distribution functions of each sample and $\hat{F}_N$ is the distribution function of the combined sample, given by

$$\hat{F}_N(\phi) = \frac{N_1}{N} \hat{F}_{N_1}(\phi) + \frac{N_2}{N} \hat{F}_{N_2}(\phi).$$

Large values of $U^2_{N_1, N_2}$ lead to rejecting H_0. This test is invariant under rotation and reflection.

A more explicit form of $U^2_{N_1, N_2}$ (Burr, 1964), more useful for calculations, is expressed in terms of the linear ranks $r_1, \dots, r_{N_1}$ of the first sample in the ordered combined sample as in the Mann–Whitney test:

$$U^2_{N_1, N_2} = \frac{1}{N_1 N_2} \sum_{i=1}^{N_1} \left[(r_i - \bar{r}) - \frac{N(2i-1) - N_1}{2N_1} \right]^2 + \frac{N + N_1}{12 N N_1},$$

whose quantiles have been approximated and tabulated. $\bar{r}$ denotes the mean of $r_1, \dots, r_{N_1}$.

Another expression is due to Persson (1979):

$$U^2_{N_1, N_2} = \frac{1}{N N_1 N_2} \left(\frac{N_1 N_2 (N_1 N_2 + 2)}{12} - \sum_{i<j} \sum_{k<l} I_{ijkl} \right), \tag{4.13}$$

with

$$I_{ijkl} = \begin{cases} 1 & \text{if } \phi_{1i} \text{ and } \phi_{1j} \text{ lie on opposite sides of the chord from } \phi_{2k} \text{ to } \phi_{2l} \\ 0 & \text{otherwise.} \end{cases}$$

In the circle, the concept of order is not as easy as on the real line because not even three distinct points can be said to be in some particular order unless the circle is believed to be oriented. However, in the two sets of points ϕ_1 and ϕ_2, assuming all are distinct, two configurations are possible: $\phi_1 \phi_1 \phi_2 \phi_2$ or $\phi_1 \phi_2 \phi_1 \phi_2$. Equation (4.13) uses this concept of order, where in the last double sum, we count the number of pairs ($\{\phi_{1i}, \phi_{1j}\}, \{\phi_{2k}, \phi_{2l}\}$) of subsamples of size two for which the configuration is $\phi_1 \phi_2 \phi_1 \phi_2$. That is, $I_{ijkl} = 1$ if the configuration is $\phi_1 \phi_2 \phi_1 \phi_2$ (the two subsamples overlap) and $I_{ijkl} = 0$ if the configuration is $\phi_1 \phi_1 \phi_2 \phi_2$ (they do not overlap). If both samples come from the same distribution, a higher value of $\sum_{i<j} \sum_{k<l} I_{ijkl}$ is to be expected than if they come from different distributions. This shows that Watson's two sample U^2 test can be regarded as an analogue on the circle of the Mann–Whitney test on the line.

The Watson nonparametric test was used in Bielza et al. (2014) to identify differences between two data sets of branching angles in the basal dendrites of pyramidal neurons from seven different cortical areas of adult mice: (a) comparison of angles of branch order 1 originating from dendritic trees with a fixed maximum branch order and area, and (b) comparison of angles of the seven different areas when the branch order is fixed. Further,

Table 4.13 Measurements, conditions, and subjects in a one-way repeated-measurement test

		Conditions				
		X_1	$\cdots$	X_j	$\cdots$	X_k	Marginal
	1	x_{11}	$\cdots$	x_{1j}	$\cdots$	x_{1k}	$x_{1\bullet}$
	$\cdots$	$\cdots$	$\cdots$	$\cdots$	$\cdots$	$\cdots$	$\cdots$
Subjects	i	x_{i1}	$\cdots$	x_{ij}	$\cdots$	x_{ik}	$x_{i\bullet}$
	$\cdots$	$\cdots$	$\cdots$	$\cdots$	$\cdots$	$\cdots$	$\cdots$
	N	x_{N1}	$\cdots$	x_{Nj}	$\cdots$	x_{Nk}	$x_{N\bullet}$
Marginal		$x_{\bullet 1}$	$\cdots$	$x_{\bullet j}$	$\cdots$	$x_{\bullet k}$	$x_{\bullet\bullet}$

in Leguey et al. (2016), dendritic branching angles of pyramidal cells from layers II–VI of the juvenile rat somatosensory cortex were compared using the Watson nonparametric test. Finally, Fernández-González et al. (2017) performed similar distribution comparisons using this test, with branching angles in layers III and V in humans and also compared angles among species (humans, rats, and mice).

4.2.6   Three or More Paired Sample Tests

In this section, we present two hypothesis tests for comparing three or more paired samples. This is a generalization of the problem addressed in Section 4.2.4. The first test assumes normality of the different samples to be compared and is known as a one-way repeated-measures **ANOVA**.[3] The second test can be seen as a nonparametric version of the first one. In this Friedman test, the normality assumption is not a necessary condition.

One-Way Repeated-Measures ANOVA. We consider a measure that is repeated k times for each of the N subjects in the sample. We represent the variables as X_i (conditions), with $i = 1, \ldots, k$, and the values (measurements) for each of the subjects by means of x_{ij}, with $i = 1, \ldots, k$ and $j = 1, \ldots, N$. In addition, the normality is assumed over the k variables. Moreover, $x_{i\bullet} = \sum_{j=1}^{N} x_{ij}$, $x_{\bullet j} = \sum_{i=1}^{k} x_{ij}$, and $x_{\bullet\bullet} = \sum_{i=1}^{k} x_{i\bullet} = \sum_{j=1}^{N} x_{\bullet j}$ denote the marginal on conditions, the marginal on subjects, and the addition of all measurements, respectively. Table 4.13 presents this situation.

The one-way repeated-measures ANOVA is used for testing a single-factor within-subjects analysis of variance. The null and alternative hypotheses refer to the expectations of the conditions and can be fixed as

$$\begin{cases} H_0 : \mu_1 = \mu_2 = \cdots = \mu_k \\ H_1 : \mu_i \neq \mu_j \text{ for at least one pair } (i, j). \end{cases}$$

The following are the different steps involved in the test procedure:

1. Compute the total variability in the data, as expressed by a number of different components:

---

[3] ANOVA stands for analysis of variance.

a) The total sum of squares, SS_T:

$$SS_T = \sum_{i=1}^{k} \sum_{j=1}^{N} X_{ij}^2 - \frac{\left(\sum_{i=1}^{k} \sum_{j=1}^{N} X_{ij}\right)^2}{kN}.$$

b) The between-conditions sum of squares, SS_{BC}:

$$SS_{BC} = \sum_{i=1}^{k} \frac{\left(\sum_{j=1}^{N} X_{ij}\right)^2}{N} - \frac{\left(\sum_{i=1}^{k} \sum_{j=1}^{N} X_{ij}\right)^2}{kN}.$$

c) The between-subjects sum of squares, SS_{BS}:

$$SS_{BS} = \sum_{j=1}^{N} \left(\frac{\left(\sum_{i=1}^{k} X_{ij}\right)^2}{k}\right) - \frac{\left(\sum_{i=1}^{k} \sum_{j=1}^{N} X_{ij}\right)^2}{kN}.$$

d) The residual sum of squares, SS_{res}, that can be computed from the following equality:

$$SS_T = SS_{BC} + SS_{BS} + SS_{res}.$$

2. Compute the mean square variability of the different components:
   a) Mean square between conditions, MS_{BC}:

$$MS_{BC} = \frac{SS_{BC}}{df_{BC}} \text{ with } df_{BC} = k - 1.$$

   b) Mean square between subjects, MS_{BS}:

$$MS_{BS} = \frac{SS_{BS}}{df_{BS}} \text{ with } df_{BS} = N - 1.$$

   c) Mean square residual, MS_{res}:

$$MS_{res} = \frac{SS_{res}}{df_{res}} \text{ with } df_{res} = (N-1)(k-1).$$

3. Compute the standardized test statistic, F, which, under the null hypothesis, follows a Snedecor's F distribution:

$$F = \frac{MS_{BC}}{MS_{res}} \sim F_{k-1,(N-1)(k-1)}.$$

For a significance level of α, H_0 will be rejected if and only if $f_{obs} > F_{k-1,(N-1)(k-1);1-\alpha}$.

Friedman Test. The nonparametric test associated with the one-way repeated-measures ANOVA is the Friedman test. From a general viewpoint, the test has a design structure known as the randomized complete block design. In this design, there are b blocks[4] corresponding to the observations, and $k \geq 2$ treatments are applied to each observation. The aim of the test is to detect differences among the k treatments.

---

[4] The name "block" comes from the earliest experimental designs in agriculture, where fields used to be divided into "blocks."

Table 4.14 Blocks, treatments and ranked data in a randomized complete block design

		1	2	$\cdots$	k	Row totals
				Treatments		
Blocks	1	r_{11}	r_{12}	$\cdots$	r_{1k}	$k(k+1)/2$
	2	r_{21}	r_{22}	$\cdots$	r_{2k}	$k(k+1)/2$
	$\cdots$	$\cdots$	$\cdots$	$\cdots$	$\cdots$	$\cdots$
	b	r_{b1}	r_{b2}	$\cdots$	r_{bk}	$k(k+1)/2$
	Column totals	R_1	R_2	$\cdots$	R_k	$bk(k+1)/2$

Denoting the measurement for the ith block in the jth treatment by x_{ij}, with $i = 1, \ldots, b$ and $j = 1, \ldots, k$, we compute the rank value, r_{ij}, for each measurement according to the treatment k, obtaining an arrangement such as that shown in Table 4.14.

The Friedman test assumptions are that all sample populations are continuous and identical, except possibly for location. The null hypothesis is that all populations have the same location. Typically, the null hypothesis of no difference among the k treatments is written in terms of the medians, ψ_i. Both hypotheses, H_0 and H_1, can be written as

$$\begin{cases} H_0 : \psi_1 = \psi_2 = \cdots = \psi_k \\ H_1 : \psi_i \neq \psi_j \text{ for at least one pair } (i, j). \end{cases}$$

The standardized test statistic S, defined as

$$S = \left[\frac{12}{bk(k+1)} \sum_{j=1}^{k} R_j^2 \right] - 3b(k+1), \tag{4.14}$$

is used to evaluate the null hypothesis. Under the assumption that H_0 is true, S is well approximated by a χ_{k-1}^2 distribution. The rejection region, for a fixed significance level α, is $s_{\text{obs}} > \chi_{k-1;1-\alpha}^2$.

The Friedman test was used by Feys et al. (2009) to examine the effects of 6 weeks of oral levetiracetam administration on tremor severity and functionality in patients with MS. The same test was applied by Basaglia-Pappas et al. (2013) for the study of deficit in episodic memory in AD using several types of popular songs (melodic, chorus, autobiographical,...). In addition, the effects of an Ai Chi fall prevention program for patients diagnosed with PD (Hoehn and Yahr stages 1–3) were studied at baseline, at posttreatment, and after one month of follow-up by Pérez de la Cruz et al. (2016) using the Friedman test.

Example. The two tests will be illustrated with a sample of size 327 (Data Set 1), containing both, pyramidal and interneuron cells, of variables X_{26}, X_{27}, and X_{28} (described in detail in Table 1.5) measuring the axonal Sholl length at 100 μm, between 100 μm and 200 μm, and between 200 μm and 300 μm, respectively, divided by the total length of axonal segments. Figure 4.8 shows the frequency histograms for these 3 variables.

Table 4.15 shows the mean, standard deviation, and p-values for the Shapiro–Wilk and Kolmogorov–Smirnov tests applied to variables X_{26}, X_{27}, and X_{28}. As the null hypothesis of normality is rejected for all three variables in both tests and the normality assumption is

Table 4.15 Sample mean, sample standard deviation, and p-values of the Shapiro–Wilk and Kolmogorov–Smirnov tests for variables X_{26}, X_{27}, and X_{28}

Variable	Sample mean	Sample standard deviation	p-value Shapiro–Wilk	p-value Kolmogorov–Smirnov
X_{26}	0.2315	0.2349	<2.20e−16	6.76e−08
X_{27}	0.2615	0.1997	1.28e−12	0.0053
X_{28}	0.1738	0.1751	<2.20e−16	2.46e−08

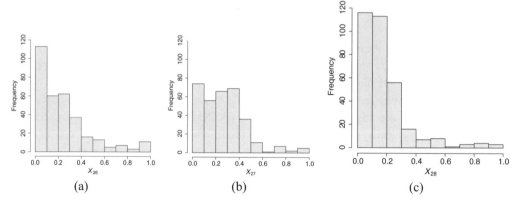

Figure 4.8 Frequency histograms for (a) X_{26}, (b) X_{27}, and (c) X_{28}, considered as three paired samples.

not met, we will not present, for this example, the result of the one-way repeated-measures ANOVA based on Snedecor's F.

The application of the Friedman test to the 3 treatments ($k = 3$) of variables X_{26}, X_{27}, and X_{28} – corresponding to the axonal Sholl length at 100μm, between 100 μm and 200 μm, and between 200 μm and 300 μm respectively – on 327 cells (blocks) ($b = 327$), as implemented in the R package, yields `Friedman chi-squared = 85.3306, df = 2, p-value < 2.2e-16`. Thus, the null hypothesis of equal medians is rejected. ∎

4.2.7   Three or More Unpaired Sample Tests

This section discusses two hypothesis tests for the comparison of three or more unpaired samples. This is a generalization of the problem addressed in Section 4.2.5. The first test assumes normality of the different samples to be compared and is known as one-way ANOVA. The second is a nonparametric version of the first one, where the normality assumption is not a necessary condition and is called the Kruskal–Wallis test.

One-Way ANOVA. We will consider a sample of size N extracted from a random variable X. These N values are organized into a different treatments, each of which has size N_i, where $i = 1, \ldots, a$. x_{ij} denotes the value of the jth observation, $j = 1, \ldots, N_i$, in the ith treatment. X_i denotes the random variable associated with the ith treatment. Normality is assumed over the a variables. Table 4.16 illustrates the situation.

Table 4.16 Observations, treatment means, and grand mean in a one-way ANOVA test

Treatment					Means
1	x_{11}	x_{12}	$\cdots$	x_{1N_1}	$\bar{x}_{1\bullet} = \sum\limits_{j=1}^{N_1} x_{1j}/N_1$
2	x_{21}	x_{22}	$\cdots$	x_{2N_2}	$\bar{x}_{2\bullet} = \sum\limits_{j=1}^{N_2} x_{2j}/N_2$
$\cdots$	$\cdots$	$\cdots$	$\cdots$	$\cdots$	$\cdots$
a	x_{a1}	x_{a2}	$\cdots$	x_{aN_a}	$\bar{x}_{a\bullet} = \sum\limits_{j=1}^{N_a} x_{aj}/N_a$
					$\bar{x}_{\bullet\bullet}$

The null and alternative hypotheses are

$$\begin{cases} H_0 : \mu_1 = \mu_2 = \cdots = \mu_a \\ H_1 : \mu_i \neq \mu_j \text{ for at least one pair } (i, j). \end{cases}$$

The test statistic is based on the identity

$$x_{ij} - \bar{x}_{\bullet\bullet} = (\bar{x}_{i\bullet} - \bar{x}_{\bullet\bullet}) + (x_{ij} - \bar{x}_{i\bullet}), \tag{4.15}$$

which partitions the deviation of any observation, x_{ij}, from the grand mean, $\bar{x}_{\bullet\bullet}$, into two parts. The first part, $(\bar{x}_{i\bullet} - \bar{x}_{\bullet\bullet})$, is the deviation of the ith treatment mean from the grand mean. The second part, $(x_{ij} - \bar{x}_{i\bullet})$, is the deviation of the observation from the ith treatment mean. By squaring and summing the overall observations on both sides of Equation (4.15) and after some algebraic manipulations, we obtain:

$$\sum_{i=1}^{a}\sum_{j=1}^{N_i}(x_{ij} - \bar{x}_{\bullet\bullet})^2 = \sum_{i=1}^{a} N_i(\bar{x}_{i\bullet} - \bar{x}_{\bullet\bullet})^2 + \sum_{i=1}^{a}\sum_{j=1}^{N_i}(x_{ij} - \bar{x}_{i\bullet})^2. \tag{4.16}$$

The left-hand side of Equation (4.16) represents the value of the statistic $\sum_{i=1}^{a}\sum_{j=1}^{N_i}(X_{ij} - \bar{X}_{\bullet\bullet})^2$, which is the total sum of squares corrected for the grand mean, and is denoted as SS_{Total}. Further, $\sum_{i=1}^{a} N_i(\bar{X}_{i\bullet} - \bar{X}_{\bullet\bullet})^2$ measures the difference between the observed treatment means and the grand mean. It can be interpreted as a measure of the variability due to the treatments and is denoted by $SS_{\text{Treatment}}$, that is, the sum of squares due to treatments. Finally, $\sum_{i=1}^{a}\sum_{j=1}^{N_i}(X_{ij} - \bar{X}_{i\bullet})^2$ measures the differences of observations within a treatment from the treatment mean and is denoted as SS_{Error}, that is, the sum of squares due to error.

The symbolic representation of Equation (4.16) is

$$SS_{\text{Total}} = SS_{\text{Treatment}} + SS_{\text{Error}}.$$

Because there are a total of N observations, SS_{Total} has $N - 1$ degrees of freedom. Analogously, $SS_{\text{Treatment}}$ and SS_{Error} have $a - 1$ and $N - a$ degrees of freedom, respectively. The mean square treatment is defined as $MS_{\text{Treatment}} = \frac{SS_{\text{Treatment}}}{a-1}$ and measures the error variance between treatments. Similarly, the mean square error is defined as $MS_{\text{Error}} = \frac{SS_{\text{Error}}}{N-a}$ and represents the within-treatments error variance.

$MS_{\text{Treatment}}$ and MS_{Error} will be used for defining the test statistics, because if there are no differences among the a treatment means, the ratio $\frac{MS_{\text{Treatment}}}{MS_{\text{Error}}}$ will be close to 1. If there are differences among the a treatment means, then the ratio $\frac{MS_{\text{Treatment}}}{MS_{\text{Error}}}$ should be greater than 1.

The test statistic $\frac{MS_{\text{Treatment}}}{MS_{\text{Error}}}$ follows, under H_0, a Snedecor's F distribution. Thus, if H_0 is true,

$$F = \frac{MS_{\text{Treatment}}}{MS_{\text{Error}}} \sim F_{a-1,N-a}.$$

Thus, H_0 is rejected with a significance level α if $f_{\text{obs}} > F_{a-1,N-a;1-\alpha}$.

Table 4.17 summarizes the above concepts.

Sepehri and Ganji (2016) used one-way ANOVA to compare results among treatment groups (one control group and three groups according to different doses) to examine if ascorbic acid protects neuronal morphology on hippocampal CA1 pyramidal neurons in a rat model. Assis et al. (2015) used the same test and found statistically significant differences in the apparent diffusion coefficient and in the radial diffusivity for several histopathological posterior fossa tumor types in children with diffusion tensor imaging on a 3T MRI scanner. Further, the effect of valproate on the sleep microstructure of juveline myoclonic epilepsy patients was compared in Nayak et al. (2016) with a group of drug-naive juveline myoclonic epilepsy patients and with a third group of healthy controls applying the same previous test. Malek et al. (2016) studied olfaction results in PD patients according to Parkin mutation status. Three groups were considered: Parkin compound heterozygotes, Parkin single heterozygotes, and noncarriers. Olfaction was tested with one-way ANOVA using the 40-item British version of the University of Pennsylvania smell identification test. Sturrock et al. (2015) studied HD biomarkers based on magnetic resonance (MR) spectroscopy and compared them among three groups (controls, pre-manifest HD, and early HD) using a one-way ANOVA test. AD patients were compared by Kester et al. (2015) with cognitively normal and MCI groups in two CSF proteins with the same previous test. Also with the ANOVA test, Varga et al. (2015) studied the tissue optical properties and texture descriptors of the retina in three groups: patients with MS with optic neuritis in their history, without optic neuritis, and healthy subjects used as controls. The differences in several optical layer indexes and total reflectance were statistically compared.

Table 4.17 One-way ANOVA table

Source of variation	Degrees of freedom	Sum of squares	Mean square	Test statistic
Treatment	$a-1$	$SS_{\text{Treatment}} = \sum_{i=1}^{a} N_i(\bar{x}_{i\bullet} - \bar{x}_{\bullet\bullet})^2$	$MS_{\text{Treatment}} = \dfrac{SS_{\text{Treatment}}}{a-1}$	$\dfrac{MS_{\text{Treatment}}}{MS_{\text{Error}}}$
Error	$N-a$	$SS_{\text{Error}} = \sum_{i=1}^{a}\sum_{j=1}^{N_i} (x_{ij} - \bar{x}_{i\bullet})^2$	$MS_{\text{Error}} = \dfrac{SS_{\text{Error}}}{N-a}$	
Total	$N-1$	$SS_{\text{Total}} = \sum_{i=1}^{a}\sum_{j=1}^{N_i} (x_{ij} - \bar{x}_{\bullet\bullet})^2$		

Kruskal–Wallis Test. The Kruskal–Wallis test (Kruskal and Wallis, 1952) is an extension of the Mann–Whitney test to the situation with a mutually independent samples of size $N_i, i = 1, \ldots, a$. It is the nonparametric version of the one-way ANOVA. The null hypothesis is that the a populations are identical. Then, the null and alternative hypotheses are written as

$$\begin{cases} H_0 : F_1(x) = F_2(x) = \cdots = F_a(x) \text{ for all } x \\ H_1 : F_i(x) \neq F_j(x) \text{ for at least one pair } (i, j) \text{ and some } x. \end{cases}$$

Due to the fact that the underlying distributions of the a populations are identical under H_0, the Kruskal–Wallis test can be applied to means, medians, or any other quantile. Usually H_0 and H_1 are expressed in terms of the population medians, ψ_i, as

$$\begin{cases} H_0 : \psi_1 = \psi_2 = \cdots = \psi_a \\ H_1 : \psi_i \neq \psi_j \text{ for at least one pair } (i, j). \end{cases}$$

To test H_0, all $N_1 + N_2 + \cdots + N_a$ observations are pooled into a single column and ranked from 1 to $N = \sum_{i=1}^{a} N_i$. The standardized test statistic is

$$H = \frac{12 \sum_{i=1}^{a} N_i (\bar{R}_i - \bar{R}_\bullet)^2}{N(N+1)},$$

where N_i is the number of observations in the ith treatment, $\bar{R}_i$ is the average of the ranks in the ith treatment, and $\bar{R}_\bullet$ is the average of all the ranks. Provided each $N_i \geq 5$, the distribution of H is, under H_0, approximately χ_{a-1}^2. In addition, small values of H correspond to situations where the differences between the average ranks in the a treatments are tiny, and the null hypothesis cannot be rejected, that is, H_0 is rejected with an acceptance level α if $h_{\text{obs}} > \chi_{a-1;1-\alpha}^2$, where h_{obs} denotes the value of the test statistic in the sample of size N.

The Kruskal–Wallis test was used in Salza et al. (2015) to compare the endostatin level in CSF of four groups of patients: with AD, with behavioral frontotemporal dementia, without any of them, and without neurodegenerative diseases. Šabanagić-Hajrić and Alajbegović (2015) studied MS patients in different patient groups categorized according to their education level and employment status using this test.

Example. The two methods will be illustrated with a sample of size 327 of variable X_4, measuring the somatic compactness organized according to a recodification of variable X_{56} that measures the number of dendritic Sholl sections. This variable X_{56} assumes values in the range of 1 to 26, and has been discretized into X_{56}^d, which can take four possible values as shown below:

$$X_{56}^d = \begin{cases} 1 & \text{if } X_{56} \in \{1,2,3,4\} \\ 2 & \text{if } X_{56} \in \{5,6\} \\ 3 & \text{if } X_{56} \in \{7,8,9,10\} \\ 4 & \text{if } X_{56} \in \{11, \ldots, 20, 26\}. \end{cases}$$

Figure 4.9 shows the side-by-side boxplot for X_4 given X_{56}^d. From this figure, we can confirm that the highest average value for X_4 is for $X_{56}^d = 1$, whereas the smallest average is for $X_{56}^d = 2$. The question is whether or not the different distributions of X_4 according to the values of X_{56}^d are statistically significantly different.

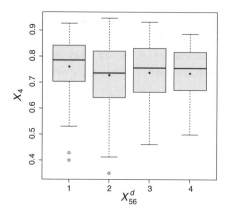

Figure 4.9 Side-by-side boxplot for X_4 given X_{56}^d, a discretization of X_{56}. The means (black points) are also represented within the box.

The output provided by the R package for the one-way ANOVA test when testing for equal means in X_4 according to the four different treatments, each of which corresponds to a value of variable X_{56}^d, is

	Df	SumSq	MeanSq	F value	p-value
X56d	3	0.050	0.0166	1.359	0.255
Residuals	323	3.956	0.0122		

We conclude that the differences among the four treatments are not statistically significant, that is, there is not sufficient evidence for rejecting H_0.

The application of the Kruskal–Wallis test to variable X_4, when the treatments are given by X_{56}^d, produces a value for the test statistic of $h_{obs} = 4.8127$ that for a χ_3^2 distribution corresponds to a p-value of 0.186. Thus, the null hypothesis is not rejected either. ∎

4.2.8   Degree of Relationship Tests

In this section, we present hypothesis tests that aim to answer questions related to the degree of relationship between two variables from which we have extracted a paired sample. For the case where both variables are continuous, we show two different tests: one based on the Pearson correlation coefficient and the other using Spearman rank correlation. If both variables are discrete, a test of independence based on the chi-squared distribution is introduced.

Testing Linear Dependency with the Pearson Correlation Coefficient. Given a paired sample of size N extracted from two random continuous variables X and Y, that is, $\{(x_1, y_1), \ldots, (x_N, y_N)\}$, we test if the Pearson product-moment correlation coefficient is zero. This coefficient is defined in the population as the covariance of the two variables divided by the product of their standard deviations (Section 3.4.1),

$$\rho[X,Y] = \frac{Cov[X,Y]}{\sqrt{Var[X]Var[Y]}} = \frac{\mathbb{E}[(X - \mathbb{E}[X])(Y - \mathbb{E}[Y])]}{\sqrt{Var[X]Var[Y]}} = \frac{\mathbb{E}[XY] - \mathbb{E}[X]\mathbb{E}[Y]}{\sqrt{Var[X]Var[Y]}}.$$

An estimator of the Pearson product-moment correlation coefficient based on the sample is the sample Pearson coefficient

$$r_P = \frac{N\sum\limits_{i=1}^{N} X_i Y_i - \sum\limits_{i=1}^{N} X_i \sum\limits_{i=1}^{N} Y_i}{\sqrt{N\sum\limits_{i=1}^{N} X_i^2 - \left(\sum\limits_{i=1}^{N} X_i\right)^2}\sqrt{N\sum\limits_{i=1}^{N} Y_i^2 - \left(\sum\limits_{i=1}^{N} Y_i\right)^2}}.$$

The sample Pearson coefficient, like $\rho[X,Y]$, also ranges from -1 to $+1$. Note that $(x_i - \bar{x})(y_i - \bar{y})$ is positive if and only if x_i and y_i lie on the same side of their respective means. Thus, the sample Pearson coefficient is positive if x_i and y_i tend to be simultaneously greater than, or simultaneously less than, their respective means. The sample Pearson coefficient is negative if x_i and y_i tend to lie on opposite sides of their respective means. A value of -1 or $+1$ indicates that a linear equation describes the relationship between the values of X and the values of Y perfectly, with all data points lying on a single line. In addition, a value of $+1$ implies that Y increases as X increases. Alternatively, a value of -1 implies that Y decreases as X increases. Finally, a value of 0 implies that there is no linear correlation between X and Y.

To test the null hypothesis that the population coefficient ρ is equal to 0, against the alternative hypothesis that is not equal to zero, that is,

$$\begin{cases} H_0 : \rho = 0 \\ H_1 : \rho \neq 0, \end{cases}$$

the standardized test statistic is $T = r_P\sqrt{\frac{N-2}{1-r_P^2}}$. Under the null hypothesis, and assuming that the sample has been obtained from a bivariate normal distribution, T follows a Student's t distribution with $N-2$ degrees of freedom. Namely, H_0 is rejected with a significance level α if $|t_{obs}| > t_{N-2;1-\frac{\alpha}{2}}$, where t_{obs} denotes the value of the test statistic in the sample of size N.

Example. In the example illustrated in Figure 2.11, we showed that variables X_4, Somatic compactness, and X_{65}, Relative distance to pia, have a very small correlation coefficient, whereas this coefficient is very high for variables, X_8, Total axonal length, and X_9, Total surface area of axon. We now want to check in which of the two situations the null hypothesis of lack of correlation between variables is true.

The application of this test to check whether the Pearson correlation coefficient is equal to zero for variables X_8 and X_9 provides a p-value < 2.2e-16, thereby implying that there is sufficient evidence in the sample to reject the lack of correlation.

However, when testing the same null hypothesis for variables X_{65} and X_4, the null hypothesis cannot be rejected (p-value = 0.3803). ∎

Spearman Rank Correlation Test. A nonparametric version of the Pearson correlation coefficient is Spearman's rank correlation coefficient, r_S. It is defined as the Pearson correlation coefficient between the ranked variables, that is, each value x_i is converted to its rank, r_{x_i}, computed as its position in ascending order in the sample of size N. Similarly, y_i is transformed into r_{y_i}. From r_{x_i} and r_{y_i} Spearman's rank correlation coefficient, r_S, is defined as

$$r_S = \frac{N \sum_{i=1}^{N} r_{x_i} r_{y_i} - \sum_{i=1}^{N} r_{x_i} \sum_{i=1}^{N} r_{y_i}}{\sqrt{N \sum_{i=1}^{N} r_{x_i}^2 - \left(\sum_{i=1}^{N} r_{x_i}\right)^2} \sqrt{N \sum_{i=1}^{N} r_{y_i}^2 - \left(\sum_{i=1}^{N} r_{y_i}\right)^2}}.$$

In samples where there are no duplicate values (ties), r_S can be computed more easily in the following manner:

$$r_S = 1 - \frac{6 \sum_{i=1}^{N} d_i^2}{N(N^2 - 1)},$$

where d_i denotes the difference between the two rank values, r_{x_i} and r_{y_i}, that is, $d_i = r_{x_i} - r_{y_i}$.

r_S is interpreted in terms of how well the relationship between X and Y can be described using a monotonic function. If there are no repeated data values, a perfect Spearman's rank correlation of $+1$ or -1 occurs when one variable is a perfect monotone function of the other. This concept can be compared with Pearson's correlation, which only yields a perfect value of $+1$ or -1 when the values of one of the variables can be obtained by a linear function of the values of the other variable.

As in the case of Pearson's correlation coefficient, the normalized test statistic for Spearman's rank correlation for

$$\begin{cases} H_0 : \rho = 0 \\ H_1 : \rho \neq 0 \end{cases}$$

is $T = r_S \sqrt{\frac{N-2}{1-r_S^2}}$. Under the null hypothesis, it follows a Student's t distribution with $N-2$ degrees of freedom.

The Spearman nonparametric correlation test was used in Freeman et al. (2009) to identify correlations between the expression of maturation molecules in dendrite cells and chronic obstructive pulmonary disease severity. The same test was used by Wang et al. (2013) to study the correlations between neurite densities measured by MRI and functional variables in an animal model of traumatic brain injury. Eriksson et al. (2007) studied the correlation of quantitative MRI with histopathology in patients with epilepsy. Spearman's rank correlations were also used by Inglese et al. (2010) to determine the association of regional tissue sodium concentration levels with measures of normalized whole brain and gray and white matter volumes. Spearman's rank correlations were analyzed by Painold et al. (2011) for HD patients using 3-min vigilance-controlled electroencephalography and psychometric data. In AD, Giil et al. (2015) showed that antibodies to the angioteusin 2 type 1 receptor levels correlated with CSF total tau and phosphorylated levels and inversely with blood pressure. Spearman's rank correlation coefficient was also used by Kosa et al. (2015) to show that a novel composite MRI scale correlates highly with disability in MS patients. Sako et al. (2016) showed that fractional anisotropy values derived from diffusion weighted images are correlated with both disease severity and duration in ALS patients.

Example. The output provided by the implementation in the R package of this test to variables X_8 and X_9 provides a p-value smaller than 2.2e$-$16, thereby rejecting H_0. For

Table 4.18 Contingency table

		y_1	y_2	$\cdots$	y_J	Marginal
				Y		
	x_1	N_{11}	N_{12}	$\cdots$	N_{1J}	$N_{1\bullet}$
	x_2	N_{21}	N_{22}	$\cdots$	N_{2J}	$N_{2\bullet}$
	.	.	.		.	.
X	.	.	.		.	.
	.	.	.		.	.
	x_I	N_{I1}	N_{I2}	$\cdots$	N_{IJ}	$N_{I\bullet}$
	Marginal	$N_{\bullet 1}$	$N_{\bullet 2}$	$\cdots$	$N_{\bullet J}$	N

variables X_{65} and X_4, the p-value was 0.2685, that is, H_0 cannot be rejected. In both cases, the decisions are the same as those for Pearson's correlation coefficient. ∎

Chi-Squared Test of Independence. Given two categorical variables X and Y with, respectively, I and J possible values, and a sample of size N with elements that can be categorized according to both categorical variables, the question is whether X and Y can be considered independent.

Table 4.18 contains the number of observations, N_{ij}, in the sample, taking the ith value in X and, simultaneously, the jth value in Y. The total number of observations in the ith row ($1 \leq i \leq I$) is $N_{i\bullet} = \sum_{j=1}^{J} N_{ij}$, whereas the total number of observations in the jth column ($1 \leq j \leq J$) is $N_{\bullet j} = \sum_{i=1}^{I} N_{ij}$.

The true population probability of an individual in cell (i, j) is denoted by θ_{ij}. Under the assumption of independence between variables X and Y, $\theta_{ij} = \theta_{i\bullet}\theta_{\bullet j}$, where $\theta_{i\bullet} = \sum_{j=1}^{J} \theta_{ij}$ and $\theta_{\bullet j} = \sum_{i=1}^{I} \theta_{ij}$, that is, $\theta_{i\bullet}$ is the probability of an individual being classified in category i of the row variable, and $\theta_{\bullet j}$ is the probability of an individual being classified in category j of the column variable. Estimations (mle) of $\theta_{i\bullet}$ and $\theta_{\bullet j}$ are given by $\hat{\theta}_{i\bullet} = \frac{N_{i\bullet}}{N}$ and $\hat{\theta}_{\bullet j} = \frac{N_{\bullet j}}{N}$, respectively. The expected number of observations in cell (i, j) is computed as $N\hat{\theta}_{ij}$. Under the assumption of independence, this expected number becomes $N\hat{\theta}_{ij} = N\hat{\theta}_{i\bullet}\hat{\theta}_{\bullet j} = \frac{N_{i\bullet}N_{\bullet j}}{N}$.

The null and alternative hypotheses for testing independence between X and Y is written as

$$\begin{cases} H_0 : \theta_{ij} = \theta_{i\bullet}\theta_{\bullet j} \\ H_1 : \theta_{ij} \neq \theta_{i\bullet}\theta_{\bullet j}. \end{cases}$$

An intuitive manner of going about this test is to compare the observed number of cases in the sample in each of the cells of the contingency table, denoted by O_{ij}, with the expected number under the null hypothesis, E_{ij}. The test statistic

$$W = \sum_{i=1}^{I} \sum_{j=1}^{J} \frac{(O_{ij} - E_{ij})^2}{E_{ij}}$$

is used for making the comparison, where $O_{ij} = N_{ij}$ and $E_{ij} = \frac{N_{i\bullet}N_{\bullet j}}{N}$. Thus, the test statistic becomes

Table 4.19 Contingency table for the example

		Class	
		I	P
	1	67	10
	2	78	22
X_{56}^d	3	46	24
	4	8	72

$$W = \sum_{i=1}^{I} \sum_{j=1}^{J} \frac{\left(N_{ij} - \frac{N_{i\bullet}N_{\bullet j}}{N}\right)^2}{\frac{N_{i\bullet}N_{\bullet j}}{N}}$$

and approximately follows a chi-squared density with $(I-1)(J-1)$ degrees of freedom. Therefore, the null hypothesis of independence is rejected with a significance level α when $w_{\text{obs}} > \chi^2_{(I-1)(J-1);1-\alpha}$. The chi-squared approximation is usually satisfactory if all E_{ij} are not too small. A conservative rule is to require all E_{ij} to be 5 or more, as explained in Section 4.2.2.

The chi-squared test was applied by Liao et al. (2013) to determine the association between sporadic PD patients and the single nucleotide polymorphism rs150689919 in the Tet methyl cytosine dioxygenase 1 gene. The same test was used by Léon et al. (2015) to quantify statistically significant differences in the changes in the French population perception of AD between 2008 and 2013. A study to investigate several food items concerning the etiology of MS was conducted by Bagheri et al. (2014) with the help of the chi-squared test for independence. The same test was applied to study the relationship between insomnia and disability in workers with mild traumatic brain injury in Mollayeva et al. (2015). The chi-squared test was also applied to explore the benefits of using palliative care in spontaneous intracerebral hemorrhage patients by Murthy et al. (2016). Skirton et al. (2010) used the same test to study the perceptions of family caregivers regarding the availability and adequacy of health and social care services for their family members with HD.

Example. In the side-by-side barplot shown in Figure 2.9, we observe a very different distribution of variable X_{56}, Number of dendritic Sholl sections, for the two values of the variable Class, interneuron, or pyramidal cells. Now, we test if the two variables are independent, after discretizing X_{56} as X_{56}^d, as used in the one-way ANOVA and Kruskal-Wallis tests above. Table 4.19 presents the contingency table output by R software used to apply the test to variable X_{56}^d and Class. The value of the test statistic for this table is $w_{\text{obs}} = 122.0049$, which, for a chi-squared density with three degrees of freedom, corresponds to a p-value smaller than 2.2e−16. The null hypothesis of independence is rejected. ∎

4.2.9   Multiple Comparison Tests

The multiple testing or multiple comparisons problem arises when one considers a set of statistical tests simultaneously. Type I errors, where the null hypothesis is incorrectly rejected, are more likely to occur when the set is considered as a whole. Several statistical procedures have been developed to avoid such mistakes. These procedures generally require a stronger level of evidence to be observed in order for an individual test to be considered "significant," as a way to compensate for the number of comparisons being made.

For example, in Small et al. (2005), microarray data corresponding to patients with AD were compared against control brains. A total of 7,610 gene expression levels were obtained from the entorhinal cortex of these individuals, as it is considered to be the brain site that is most likely to maximize the expression level differences between AD and control brains. The relevance of each gene was tested by means of a hypothesis test, where the null hypothesis consisted of equality in means between both groups (AD patients and control group). As the number of tests increases (7,610 hypothesis tests in this example), the groups to be compared are more likely to differ in terms of at least one gene.

Let $H_1, \ldots, H_m$ be a family of hypothesis tests and $p_1, \ldots, p_m$ the corresponding p-values. The **familywise error rate** (FWER) is defined as the probability of rejecting at least one of the hypothesis tests when they are true. The **Bonferroni correction** (Dunn, 1961) states that rejecting all p_i smaller than $\frac{\alpha}{m}$ will control FWER smaller or equal to α. By applying the Bonferroni correction to the microarray data of AD patients, we can ensure that adjusted p-values, $\tilde{p}_i = \frac{0.05}{7610} = 6.57 \cdot 10^{-6}$ for all $i = 1, \ldots, 7,610$ will yield an FWER of $\alpha = 0.05$.

The Bonferroni correction for multiple comparisons was applied in neuroscience in: (a) the assessment of CSF β-site amyloid precursor protein cleaving enzyme 1 activity in four different groups: NC, stable MCI, progressive MCI, and AD dementia cases (Perneczky et al., 2014), (b) a study, based on DTI, on white matter changes in healthy control subjects, traumatic brain injury patients, and cardiac arrest patients (van der Eerden et al., 2014), (c) a case-control autopsy study on the concentrations of glutamatergic synaptic markers in vascular dementia in four groups: patients with cerebrovascular disease with and without dementia, patients with AD, and controls (Kirvell et al., 2010), and (d) the information provided by cognitive endophenotypes on genome-wide expression profiling in schizophrenia, to find significant relations between expression levels for probes and California Verbal Learning Test performance (Zheutlin et al., 2016).

Further, a related correction, called the **Šidák correction** (Šidák, 1967), is often used. This correction is derived by assuming that all individual tests are independent, an assumption that is not required by the Bonferroni correction. Let α' denote the significance level for each test. The probability of rejecting at least one of the m hypothesis tests – that is, the FWER – is equal to one minus the probability that none of them are significant. Assuming that all tests are independent, the probability that all of them are not significant is the product of the probabilities that each of them is not significant, that is, $(1 - \alpha')^m$. Thus, FWER is equal to $1 - (1 - \alpha')^m$. Since this quantity should be equal to α, we obtain $\alpha' = 1 - (1 - \alpha)^{\frac{1}{m}}$. The Šidák correction provides a stronger bound than the Bonferroni correction because, for $m \geq 1$, we have $\frac{\alpha}{m} \leq 1 - (1 - \alpha)^{\frac{1}{m}}$. For the previous example with microarray data, we find that, with a significance level for each of the 7,610 tests of $1 - (1 - \alpha)^{\frac{1}{7,610}}$, the FWER is $\alpha = 0.05$.

The **Holm–Bonferroni correction** method (Holm, 1979) conducts more than one hypothesis test simultaneously by applying a sequential procedure. Let us assume that we have m hypothesis tests and we would like to obtain an FWER of α. The Holm–Bonferroni method begins by ordering the p-values and comparing the smallest p-value to $\frac{\alpha}{m}$. If that p-value is less than $\frac{\alpha}{m}$, the corresponding hypothesis test will be rejected and the process will begin with the same α and will test the remaining $m - 1$ hypotheses, that is, order the

Table 4.20 Critical values for the two-tailed Nemenyi test

k	2	3	4	5	6	7	8	9	10
$q_{0.05}$	1.960	2.343	2.569	2.728	2.850	2.949	3.031	3.102	3.164
$q_{0.10}$	1.645	2.052	2.291	2.459	2.589	2.693	2.780	2.855	2.920

$m-1$ remaining p-values and compare the smallest one to $\frac{\alpha}{m-1}$. The method will continue comparing the smallest p-value of the $m-s$ hypothesis tests to $\frac{\alpha}{m-s}$, until this smallest p-value is greater than $\frac{\alpha}{m-s}$. At this point, the method stops, and all hypothesis tests that have not been tested in previous steps are accepted.

Holm–Bonferroni correction for multiple testing was applied in the study of the correlation between fluid-attenuated inversion recovery and Pittsburgh compound-B positron emission tomography intensities in 29 regions of interest (Schreiner et al., 2014). Also, in testing the interactions between vascular factors (stroke, atrial fibrillation, angina, myocardial infarction,...), the APOEε4 allele and time as predictors of clinical progression of AD, measured by the MMSE and Clinical Dementia Rating-Sum of Boxes (Mielke et al., 2011).

Example. To illustrate the use of the Holm–Bonferroni correction, let us consider four hypothesis tests, H_1, H_2, H_3, and H_4 with unadjusted p-values of $p_1 = 0.01$, $p_2 = 0.015$, $p_3 = 0.03$, and $p_4 = 0.035$, respectively. The four hypotheses are tested with an FWER of $\alpha = 0.05$. The smallest is $p_1 = 0.01$, that is, less than $\frac{0.05}{4}$; thus H_1 is rejected. The next smallest p-value is $p_2 = 0.015$, that is, smaller than $\frac{0.05}{3}$; thus H_2 is also rejected. The next smallest p-value is $p_3 = 0.03$. This is not smaller than $\frac{0.05}{2}$. Therefore, H_3 and H_4 are not rejected. ∎

The Friedman test (Section 4.2.6) is used for multiple comparisons, where the null hypothesis establishes equality in all populations. If the null hypothesis is rejected, we can proceed with a post-hoc test.

The **Nemenyi post-hoc test** (Nemenyi, 1963) declares the performance of two samples as significantly different if the corresponding average rankings differ by at least $q_\alpha\sqrt{\frac{k(k+1)}{6b}}$, where critical values q_α are based on the Studentized range statistic divided by $\sqrt{2}$ (see Table 4.20).

The Nemenyi post-hoc test reports a p-value of a single comparison, but it does not take into account the remaining comparisons in the family. Therefore, the p-values have to be adjusted for making $k(k-1)/2$ comparisons. Thus, the adjusted p-value to be compared against any selected significance level α is the unadjusted p-value multiplied by $k(k-1)/2$. Equivalently, the unadjusted p-value should be compared with $\alpha/(k(k-1)/2)$. This procedure is known as **Nemenyi test with correction**.

4.2.10   Permutation Tests

A permutation test is a type of statistical significance test where the distribution of the test statistic under the null hypothesis is obtained by computing all (or a sampling of) possible values of the test statistic by rearranging the observed data cases according to specified groups (e.g., interneurons and pyramidal neurons).

Permutation tests are a subset of nonparametric tests, where it is not necessary to know the theoretical probability distribution of the test statistic. The only assumption is that, under the null hypothesis, the distribution of the different groups is the same. In fact, there is a permutation test for all parametric tests that is built by using the same test statistic as the parametric test, taking the p-value from the sample-specific permutation of that statistic rather than from the theoretical distribution derived from the parametric assumption.

A general procedure for a permutation test is described below:

1. Compute the value for the test statistic based on the sample data set. Let us denote this value as t_{obs}.
2. Pool the observations of the different groups to be compared under the null hypothesis.
3. Compute the value of the test statistic for every possible method of rearranging the pooled data set, maintaining the sizes of the different groups in the initial data set. If the possible rearrangements of the pooled data set are huge, a sampling should be sufficient to obtain an approximate permutation test.
4. Compute the one-sided p-value as the proportion of sampled permutations, where the value of the test statistic is greater than or equal to t_{obs}. Similarly, compute the two-sided p-value as the proportion of sampled permutations, where the value of the test statistic is greater than or equal to $|t_{obs}|$.

Permutation resamples must be drawn consistently with the null hypothesis. In an unpaired sample design, the null hypothesis establishes that the two populations are identical. In this setting, resampling randomly reassigns observations to the two groups. A paired-sample design randomly permutes the two observations within each pair, separately. In hypothesis tests for measuring the relationship between two variables, the resampling should randomly reassign values of one of the two variables.

Permutation tests have a number of advantages over parametric tests. First, they do not require specification of the theoretical distribution of populations from which the sample is drawn. Second, they are applicable across a range of situations, even if the test statistic does not have a simple distribution under the null hypothesis. Finally, if sufficient permutations are used, they can provide very accurate p-values, regardless of the shape of the population.

Permutation tests were used in several works. For example in: (a) a study of the effects of anti-Parkinsonian treatment on motor sequence learning in humans (Mure et al., 2012), (b) autism spectrum disorders, showing that deleterious mutations in the synaptic gene Eighty-Five Requiring 3A (EFR3A) were significantly associated with autism spectrum disorders (Gupta et al., 2014), (c) a haplotype association study in MS (Foote et al., 2005), (d) a HD transgenic model to estimate the number of false-positives (Xu et al., 2002), and (e) a prosodic analysis of neutral, stress-modified, and rhymed speech in patients with PD (Galaz et al., 2016).

4.3   Bibliographic Notes

The principle of sampling with or without replacement appeared for the first time in Huygens (1657). Nordin (1944) introduced the concept of the calculation of the sample size that guaranteed some properties of the estimation, whereas Cochran (1963) was the first book describing and analyzing sampling techniques. Robust estimation, that is, estimations that are not sensitive to outliers and small departures from model assumptions, was introduced by Box (1953). The concept of an unbiased estimator comes from Gauss (1821) when working on the least squares method. The concept of CI and how to calculate it was presented by Bowley (1906).

A special form of the law of large numbers valid for binary variables was first published by Bernoulli (1713b). Poisson (1837) further described it under the name *la loi des grands nombres*. The first version of the central limit theorem was postulated by de Moivre (1733). In 1901 Lyapunov defined it in general terms and proved precisely how it worked mathematically. The actual term *central limit theorem* was first used by Pólya (1920). He referred to the theorem as "central" due to its importance in probability theory. However, according to Le Cam (1986), the French school of probability interprets the word *central* in the sense that it describes the behavior of the center of the distribution as opposed to its tails.

Sir Harold Jeffreys was the initiator of the objective Bayes school, and his book (Jeffreys, 1961), originally published in 1939, has had a unique impact on the Bayesian community (Robert et al., 2009). Bayesian and frequentist statisticians have been in conflict with each other for a long time (see, e.g., Gelman [2008]), although the debates have shifted from theory to practice. A fundamental landmark to alleviate the computational problems in Bayesian estimation (integrations over many unknown parameters) were Markov chain Monte Carlo techniques.

An interesting account on how the adjective "Bayesian" was adopted relatively recently by the statistical community is Fienberg (2006). The author mentions that although Bayes' theorem has a 250-year history, Bayesian inference methods were referred to as the method of "inverse probability" until the middle of the twentieth century. Stigler (1983) called into question who was the first to discover Bayes' theorem (perhaps not Bayes himself). Classical textbooks on Bayesian statistics are Berger (1985), Robert (1994), Gelman et al. (1995), and Bernardo and Smith (2007), in which posterior credible regions (analogue of frequentist confidence intervals) and hypothesis testing (not shown here) are detailed.

Noninformative priors may be considered "objective" in the sense of being the logically correct choice to represent a particular state of knowledge, but they may also be considered the opposite because they depend on the observer and that person's knowledge. In fact, this is a philosophical controversy that divides Bayesians into two schools: "objective Bayesians," who believe that such priors exist in many useful situations, and "subjective Bayesians," who believe that priors usually represent subjective judgments of opinion that cannot be rigorously justified. Other principles have been introduced to create noninformative priors, for example, the Bernardo's **reference prior** (Bernardo, 1979). The idea is to maximize the expected Kullback–Leibler divergence of the posterior distribution relative to the prior. This maximizes the expected posterior information regarding parameter θ, and in a certain sense, this prior is the "least informative" prior about θ. Reference priors are often selected as objective priors in multivariate problems because other priors (e.g., Jeffreys') may yield problematic behaviors.

In **probability sensitivity analysis**, one considers a variety of prior distributions and checks whether the posterior probabilities vary slightly. In this case, the conclusion is not sensitive to the prior.

In **empirical Bayes methods** (Casella, 1985), also known as maximum marginal likelihood, the prior distribution is estimated from the data rather than being fixed before any data is observed. Thus, it represents one approach for setting hyperparameters.

The concepts of type I and II errors of a hypothesis test were presented in the seminal works by Neyman and Pearson (1928a, 1928b), whereas the term "null hypothesis" was coined by Fisher (1935). The goodness-of-fit test for a sample was invented by Kolmogorov (1933a), and the Kolmogorov two-sample test was introduced by Smirnov (1939). The chi-squared test was proposed by Bartlett (1937). The analysis of variance dates back to Fisher (1925).

Part III

Supervised Classification

Part III addressing supervised classification contains methods and algorithms for transforming a data set of labelled instances into a computational model able to make predictions about the class of new instances characterized merely by their predictor variable values. Part III is divided into six chapters.

Chapter 5 and Chapter 6 refer to two useful issues for any supervised classification method. Chapter 5 reviews a number of performance measures to assess learning algorithm behavior and their honest estimation. Chapter 5 also deals with statistical significance tests for comparing the performance of different supervised classification learning algorithms. Chapter 6 describes methods for detecting and removing variables that are, as far as the class variable is concerned, irrelevant or redundant. We account for three types of feature subset selection methods: filter (univariate and multivariate), wrapper, and embedded methods. Heuristic optimization strategies enabling intelligent searches for good subsets of features are also explained.

Chapters 7-9 present supervised classification methods for predicting the value of a 1D class variable. Chapter 7 elaborates on non-probabilistic classification models in which the prediction of the class variable is crisp. It covers k-nearest neighbors, classification trees, rule induction, artificial neural networks and support vector machines. Chapter 8 refers to probabilistic classifiers, where the prediction of the class variable is soft, i.e., a probability distribution over all class labels is output. This chapter explains discriminant analysis, logistic regression and Bayesian network classifiers. Chapter 9 accounts for ensemble learning of classifiers including several metaclassifiers, such as stacked generalization, cascading, bagging, randomization and random forests, boosting and hybridizations.

Finally, Chapter 10 introduces methods for learning multidimensional classifiers where the goal is to simultaneously predict the value of several class variables. Some examples of problem transformation methods and algorithm adaptation methods are included focusing especially on multidimensional Bayesian network classifiers.

5 Performance Evaluation

Supervised classification methods aim to learn models from labeled cases, that is, cases containing information about predictor variables and the class to which they each belong. The induced model will be used to predict (infer) the class value (label) of new instances, which are each characterized by their predictor variables only. The goal in Data Set 1 described in Chapter 1 is to learn a supervised classification model from the data set containing the following information for each of the 327 cells: morphological features of the cell represented by a vector with 65 predictor variables, and the class variable taking two possible values (interneuron or pyramidal). The learning process can be enacted applying different supervised classification algorithms (nearest neighbors, classification trees, rule induction, artificial neural networks, support vector machines, linear discriminant analysis, logistic regression, Bayesian classifiers, or metaclassifiers) that will be introduced in Chapters 7–9. The aim of this chapter is to present evaluation strategies of supervised classification learning algorithms.

One aspect of an evaluation strategy concerns the selection of a performance measure for quantifying learning algorithm assessments. This performance measure is usually a scalar that encapsulates the properties of the model as a unique number. A vector of measures, where each component of the vector refers to one characteristic of the evaluation, is sometimes a better choice. Performance measures are described in Section 5.2. Note that this book does not discuss qualitative measures like the transparency, simplicity, or comprehensibility of the learned model, which are, however, an important factor in decision making on model use (see Section 1.5.2).

Another issue is how to properly estimate the selected performance measures. Continuing with the above example, we might want to estimate the probability of the learned model outputting correct classifications or classifying a cell as pyramidal when it is really an interneuron. Estimates cannot be calculated on the same data set used for learning the classification model because the aim is to estimate the goodness of the model on new instances. Different honest performance estimation schemes will be introduced in Section 5.3.

The third issue discussed in this chapter refers to the comparison of several supervised classification learning algorithms. The aim is to clarify whether or not the empirical differences observed in the estimated performance measures of two or more supervised classification algorithms in one or more domains are statistically significant. Statistical hypothesis testing is used to answer this question. Section 5.4 contains material on this.

Finally, Section 5.5. is devoted to the current problem of dealing with imbalanced data sets and detecting anomalies, whereas Section 5.6 closes with some bibliographic notes.

5.1   The Learning Problem

The general scheme of a supervised classification learning method can be described using the following three components:

1. An **instance space**, Ω_X, from which random vectors $\mathbf{x} = (x_1, \ldots, x_n) \in \mathbb{R}^n$ are drawn independently according to some fixed but unknown probability distribution, $p(\mathbf{x})$. The ith component of $\mathbf{x}$, x_i, has been drawn from the subspace Ω_{X_i} for all $i = 1, \ldots, n$, and contains the value of the ith predictor variable, X_i, for one specific instance. The instance space Ω_X can be written in terms of the subspaces as $\Omega_X = \Omega_{X_1} \times \cdots \times \Omega_{X_n}$.
2. A **label space**, Ω_C, containing for each vector $\mathbf{x} = (x_1, \ldots, x_n)$ the value, c, of its label. The labels are obtained from a random variable, C. The conditional distribution of labels for a given vector of the instance space, $p(c|\mathbf{x})$, and the joint distribution, $p(\mathbf{x}, c)$, of cases (instances + labels) are also unknown.
3. A **learning algorithm** that implements a set of functions over the instance space, whose outputs are in the label space. The set of functions refers to a type of supervised classification method, like, for example, logistic regression or artificial neural networks. The application of the learning algorithm to a data set of labeled instances, $\mathcal{D} = \{(\mathbf{x}^1, c^1), \ldots, (\mathbf{x}^N, c^N)\}$, will provide a supervised classification model.

The **supervised classification model** (or simply the classifier), denoted by ϕ, transforms points from the instance space into points in the label space, that is,

$$
\begin{array}{ccc}
\Omega_X & \overset{\phi}{\to} & \Omega_C \\
\mathbf{x} & \to & \phi(\mathbf{x}).
\end{array}
$$

The supervised classification model partitions the instance space into **decision regions**, one per class label. $\mathbf{x}$ is in the decision region associated with c if $\phi(\mathbf{x}) = c$. These regions are separated by **decision boundaries**, surfaces in the instance space corresponding to pairs of class labels reaching the same ϕ value.

The supervised classification problem entails the choice of the best (or a good enough) supervised classification model for a given set of functions. The goodness of the classification model is determined by a performance measure (Section 5.2) and is estimated using an honest performance estimation method (Section 5.3) applied over a sample of cases (instances + labels) that are assumed to be drawn from the unknown distribution $p(\mathbf{x}, c)$.

5.1.1   Loss and Risk Functions

The **loss function**, $L(c, \phi(\mathbf{x}))$, is a quantitative measure of the loss when the true label c of the vector $\mathbf{x}$ is different from the label assigned by the classifier, $\phi(\mathbf{x})$, that is,

$$
\begin{array}{ccc}
\Omega_C \times \Omega_C & \overset{L}{\to} & \mathbb{R} \\
(c, \phi(\mathbf{x})) & \to & L(c, \phi(\mathbf{x})).
\end{array}
$$

An example of a loss function is the so-called **0-1 loss function**, i.e., $L(c, \phi(\mathbf{x})) = 1$ when $c \neq \phi(\mathbf{x})$ and 0 otherwise. Recall that the loss function was introduced in Section 4.1.4.3 within a Bayesian estimation setting instead of the supervised classification framework, where its arguments were the unknown parameter and its estimate.

The **expected risk** of classifier ϕ, $R(\phi)$, is defined as

$$R(\phi) = \int L(c, \phi(\mathbf{x})) \mathrm{d}p(\mathbf{x}, c).$$

The expected risk computes the expectation of the risk function over the unknown distribution, $p(\mathbf{x}, c)$, of cases (instances + labels). For the 0-1 loss function, the expected risk associated with a classifier ϕ is calculated as

$$R_{0-1}(\phi) = p(C \neq \phi(\mathbf{X})),$$

with cases drawn according to $p(\mathbf{x}, c)$.

As mentioned above, the true underlying distribution of the cases, $p(\mathbf{x}, c)$, is unknown, and this prevents the computation of the expected risk. As a result, the expected risk should be estimated using the information in the data set of labeled instances, $\mathcal{D} = \{(\mathbf{x}^1, c^1), \dots, (\mathbf{x}^N, c^N)\}$, by the **empirical risk function**, $R_{\mathcal{D}}(\phi)$, according to

$$R_{\mathcal{D}}(\phi) = \frac{1}{N} \sum_{i=1}^{N} L(c^i, \phi(\mathbf{x}^i)).$$

Example. Table 5.1 shows the output of a classifier for a binary supervised classification problem. The output of the classifier is incorrect for Cases 1 and 5. For Case 1, the true class is P, and the classifier output is I. For Case 5, the true class is I, and the classifier output is P. If each class is equally important, the loss associated with both types of mistakes is the same, and we have $L(c^i, \phi(\mathbf{x}^i)) = 1$ for $i \in \{1, 5\}$ and $L(c^j, \phi(\mathbf{x}^j)) = 0$ for $j \in \{2, 3, 4, 6, 7, 8, 9, 10\}$. The empirical risk for this 0-1 loss function would then be $R_{\mathcal{D}}(\phi) = \frac{1}{10} \cdot 2 = 0.20$. This empirical risk represents an estimation of the probability of the classifier being wrong.

Table 5.1 Output of a classifier, $\phi(\mathbf{x})$, for a hypothetical data set with 10 cases and two classes, P and I

	X_1	$\dots$	X_n	C	$\phi(\mathbf{x})$
$(\mathbf{x}^1, c^1)$	7.2	$\dots$	10.4	P	I
$(\mathbf{x}^2, c^2)$	7.1	$\dots$	11.7	P	P
$(\mathbf{x}^3, c^3)$	6.4	$\dots$	13.2	P	P
$(\mathbf{x}^4, c^4)$	6.7	$\dots$	10.1	P	P
$(\mathbf{x}^5, c^5)$	8.9	$\dots$	8.4	I	P
$(\mathbf{x}^6, c^6)$	9.2	$\dots$	7.9	I	I
$(\mathbf{x}^7, c^7)$	10.7	$\dots$	5.9	I	I
$(\mathbf{x}^8, c^8)$	8.1	$\dots$	8.8	I	I
$(\mathbf{x}^9, c^9)$	9.9	$\dots$	7.2	I	I
$(\mathbf{x}^{10}, c^{10})$	11.5	$\dots$	6.9	I	I

5.2   Performance Measures

Performance measures are used as figures of merit of supervised classifiers. From this perspective, the aim is to find the supervised classification model with the optimum (near optimum) value of a given performance measure. The algorithm that induces the model from the data set of cases is responsible for searching for this optimum model. In any case, an appropriate performance evaluation measure should be chosen beforehand, and this choice depends on the objective and characteristics of the supervised classification problem, as well as on the type of classifier used to carry out the classification.

A classifier can be broadly categorized according to whether or not its output is probabilistic. **Non-probabilistic classifiers** (Chapter 7) output a fixed class label for each instance. **Probabilistic classifiers** (Chapter 8) yield an estimation of the conditional probability of the class given a set of values for the predictor variables. A class assignment can then be typically obtained from the maximum a posteriori class. Some performance measures are only valid for probabilistic classifiers. However, they can be adapted to cope with the non-probabilistic classifier outputs (see Section 9.2).

One element that is important for defining performance measures is the **confusion matrix**. The (i, j)th element of the confusion matrix denotes the number of cases that actually have a class i label and that classifier ϕ assigns to class j. Standard performance measures are defined as a function of the confusion matrix entries, implicitly using a zero-one loss function. Cost-specific performance measures are defined based on the confusion matrix and a cost matrix. A cost matrix contains the cost associated with each possible error type made by the classification model.

Supervised classification models can be evaluated using a single performance measure or, alternatively, by a **vector of performance measures**. Using the latter, we pursue a multi-objective approach, where each component of the vector corresponds to a characteristic to be considered in the evaluation of the classification model.

All performance measures will be computed from a data set of N labeled instances: $\mathcal{D} = \{(\mathbf{x}^1, c^1), \ldots, (\mathbf{x}^N, c^N)\}$.

5.2.1   Numerical Performance Measures for Binary Classification

5.2.1.1   *Measures Defined from the Confusion Matrix*

The simplest supervised classification problem is when there are only two possible values for the class variable, C, represented, for example, as positive, +, and negative, -. In this setting, we have $|\Omega_C| = 2$ and also assume that $|\Omega_{\phi(\mathbf{X})}| = 2$, even if the classifier output only provides positive (or only negative) labels.

The four counters for the confusion matrix of a binary classification problem are the numbers of **true positives** (TP), **false positives** (FP), **false negatives** (FN), and **true negatives** (TN), that is,

$$
\phi(\mathbf{x})
$$

$$
C \begin{array}{c} + \\ - \end{array} \begin{pmatrix} \begin{array}{cc} + & - \\ \text{TP} & \text{FN} \\ \text{FP} & \text{TN} \end{array} \end{pmatrix}.
$$

Table 5.2 The main performance measures defined from the confusion matrix elements for binary classification

Name	Notation	Formula
Accuracy	$\text{Acc}(\phi)$	$\frac{\text{TP}+\text{TN}}{\text{TP}+\text{FN}+\text{FP}+\text{TN}}$
Sensitivity or Recall	$\text{Sensitivity}(\phi) = \text{Rec}(\phi)$	$\frac{\text{TP}}{\text{TP}+\text{FN}}$
Specificity	$\text{Specificity}(\phi)$	$\frac{\text{TN}}{\text{FP}+\text{TN}}$
Positive predictive value or Precision	$\text{PPV}(\phi) = \text{Prec}(\phi)$	$\frac{\text{TP}}{\text{TP}+\text{FP}}$
Negative predictive value	$\text{NPV}(\phi)$	$\frac{\text{TN}}{\text{TN}+\text{FN}}$
F_1-measure	$F_1(\phi)$	$\frac{2\text{Prec}(\phi)\text{Rec}(\phi)}{\text{Prec}(\phi)+\text{Rec}(\phi)}$
Cohen's kappa statistic	$\kappa(\phi)$	$\frac{\left(\frac{\text{TP}}{N}+\frac{\text{TN}}{N}\right)-\left[\left(\frac{\text{FN}+\text{TP}}{N}\right)\left(\frac{\text{FP}+\text{TP}}{N}\right)+\left(\frac{\text{FP}+\text{TN}}{N}\right)\left(\frac{\text{FN}+\text{TN}}{N}\right)\right]}{1-\left[\left(\frac{\text{FN}+\text{TP}}{N}\right)\left(\frac{\text{FP}+\text{TP}}{N}\right)+\left(\frac{\text{FP}+\text{TN}}{N}\right)\left(\frac{\text{FN}+\text{TN}}{N}\right)\right]}$

TP and TN thus stand for the number of cases that were correctly classified as positive and negative, respectively. Conversely, FN and FP stand for the number of positive and negative cases that were wrongly classified as negative and positive, respectively.

From the confusion matrix, it is possible to define the following seven performance measures, see Table 5.2. All measure values fall within the interval $[0,1]$, where values close to 1 are preferred.

The **accuracy** measures the fraction of cases that are correctly classified by the classification model. Its complementary is the **error rate**, denoted $\text{Err}(\phi)$, that measures the fraction of cases that are misclassified by the classification model. Thus, $\text{Acc}(\phi) + \text{Err}(\phi) = 1$. **Sensitivity** represents the proportion of true-positive cases successfully detected by the classifier. In the information retrieval domain, it is known as **recall**. **Specificity** denotes the proportion of true-negative cases successfully detected by the classifier. **Positive predictive value** measures the proportion of correctly assigned positive cases. In the information retrieval domain, it is known as **precision**. **Negative predictive value** measures the proportion of correctly assigned negative cases. The F_1-**measure** (Van Rijsbergen, 1979) is the harmonic mean of the precision and recall measures. **Cohen's kappa statistic** (Cohen, 1960) corrects the accuracy measure considering the result of a mere chance match between the classifier, $\phi(\mathbf{x})$, and the label generation process, C. This is the numerator, where the expected proportion of matched cases under the null hypothesis of independence (mere chance) is subtracted from the classification accuracy. The measure is then normalized with the denominator.

Example. Let us consider the following hypothetical confusion matrix for classifying the 327 cells into pyramidal (+), and interneuron (-)

$$\phi(\mathbf{x})$$

$$C \begin{array}{c} \\ + \\ - \end{array} \begin{pmatrix} + & \quad - \\ 120 & 8 \\ 60 & 139 \end{pmatrix}.$$

The values for the seven performance measures defined above are: $\text{Acc}(\phi) = 0.79$, $\text{Sensitivity}(\phi) = \text{Rec}(\phi) = 0.94, \text{Specificity}(\phi) = 0.74, \text{PPV}(\phi) = \text{Prec}(\phi) = 0.67$, $\text{NPV}(\phi) = 0.95, F_1(\phi) = 0.78$, and $\kappa(\phi) = 0.59$.

∎

5.2.1.2 Cost Matrix in Binary Classification Problems

In some domains, the costs associated with a false positive and with a false negative are not necessarily the same. The values of these costs constitute the entries of a **cost matrix**. For correct predictions, the cost is assumed to be zero. False-negative and false-positive cases will be penalized with $L(+, -)$ and $L(-, +)$, respectively. Both penalizations, $L(+, -)$ and $L(-, +)$, are usually positive.

The cost matrix can be represented as

$$\phi(\mathbf{x})$$

$$C \begin{array}{c} + \\ - \end{array} \begin{pmatrix} 0 & L(+, -) \\ L(-, +) & 0 \end{pmatrix}.$$

A performance measure used in these cost-sensitive domains is the **total cost error**, defined as

$$\text{TCE}(\phi) = \text{FN} \cdot L(+, -) + \text{FP} \cdot L(-, +).$$

It can be expressed in terms of the empirical risk function as $\text{TCE}(\phi) = N \cdot R_{\mathcal{D}}(\phi)$. The total cost error verifies $0 \le \text{TCE}(\phi) \le N \cdot \max\{L(+, -), L(-, +)\}$. Information for establishing cost matrix values in real-world applications is often difficult to gather. If the domain expert is not able to provide this information, costs are assumed to be symmetric, that is, $L(+, -) = L(-, +)$.

Example. Assuming $L(+, -) = 100$ and $L(-, +) = 5$, the classifier $\phi(\mathbf{x})$ shown in the example illustrated in Section 5.2.1.1 provides a total cost error of $\text{TCE}(\phi) = 8 \cdot 100 + 60 \cdot 5 = 1,100$. The upper bound for the total cost error is $327 \cdot 100 = 32,700$. This refers to a classifier where all 327 cases are false negatives.

∎

5.2.1.3 Brier Score

The **Brier score** (Brier, 1950) measures the accuracy of probabilistic classifications over cases. It can be interpreted as either a measure of the calibration of a set of probabilistic predictions or as a quadratic cost function. More precisely, the Brier score measures the mean square difference between the predicted probability assigned to the possible outcomes for each instance and its actual label. It is defined as

$$\text{Brier}(\phi) = \frac{1}{N} \sum_{i=1}^{N} d^2 \left(p_\phi(\mathbf{c}|\mathbf{x}^i), \mathbf{c}^i \right),$$

where N denotes the number of cases in $\mathcal{D}$, $p_\phi(\mathbf{c}|\mathbf{x}^i)$ is the vector $(p_\phi(+|\mathbf{x}^i), p_\phi(-|\mathbf{x}^i))$ containing the output of the probabilistic classifier, and $\mathbf{c}^i = (1,0)$ or $\mathbf{c}^i = (0,1)$ when the label of the ith instance is $+$ or $-$, respectively. The difference between the predicted probability assigned to the possible outcomes for each instance and its actual label is measured with the squared Euclidean distance, $d^2(p_\phi(\mathbf{c}|\mathbf{x}^i), \mathbf{c}^i)$. The Brier score for a binary classification problem verifies $0 \le \text{Brier}(\phi) \le 2$.

Table 5.3 Output of a probabilistic classifier, $p_\phi(c|\mathbf{x})$, for a hypothetical data set with 10 cases and two classes, P and I, considered as + and -, respectively

	X_1	$\cdots$	X_n	C	$p_\phi(c|\mathbf{x})$
$(\mathbf{x}^1, c^1)$	7.2	$\cdots$	10.4	P	(0.20, 0.80)
$(\mathbf{x}^2, c^2)$	7.1	$\cdots$	11.7	P	(0.65, 0.35)
$(\mathbf{x}^3, c^3)$	6.4	$\cdots$	13.2	P	(0.70, 0.30)
$(\mathbf{x}^4, c^4)$	6.7	$\cdots$	10.1	P	(0.87, 0.13)
$(\mathbf{x}^5, c^5)$	8.9	$\cdots$	8.4	I	(0.55, 0.45)
$(\mathbf{x}^6, c^6)$	9.2	$\cdots$	7.9	I	(0.25, 0.75)
$(\mathbf{x}^7, c^7)$	10.7	$\cdots$	5.9	I	(0.12, 0.88)
$(\mathbf{x}^8, c^8)$	8.1	$\cdots$	8.8	I	(0.07, 0.93)
$(\mathbf{x}^9, c^9)$	9.9	$\cdots$	7.2	I	(0.37, 0.63)
$(\mathbf{x}^{10}, c^{10})$	11.5	$\cdots$	6.9	I	(0.18, 0.82)

Example. Table 5.3 contains the predictions given by a probabilistic classifier ϕ on 10 cases. The Brier score of this probabilistic supervised classification model is computed as

$$\text{Brier}(\phi) = \frac{1}{10}\left[(0.20-1)^2 + (0.80-0)^2 + \cdots + (0.18-0)^2 + (0.82-1)^2\right] = 0.2971.$$

■

5.2.2 Numerical Performance Measures for Multi-class Classification

5.2.2.1 Measures Defined from the Confusion Matrix

In a general setting, we have $\Omega_C = \Omega_{\phi(\mathbf{X})} = \{c_1, \ldots, c_R\}$. In this case, the confusion matrix is an $R \times R$ matrix with entries N_{ij} denoting the number of cases where the true label is c_i and the classifier output is c_j. A general confusion matrix is as follows:

$$C \begin{array}{c} \\ c_1 \\ \cdots \\ c_j \\ \cdots \\ c_R \end{array} \begin{pmatrix} N_{11} & \cdots & N_{1j} & \cdots & N_{1R} \\ \cdots & \cdots & \cdots & \cdots & \cdots \\ N_{j1} & \cdots & N_{jj} & \cdots & N_{jR} \\ \cdots & \cdots & \cdots & \cdots & \cdots \\ N_{R1} & \cdots & N_{Rj} & \cdots & N_{RR} \end{pmatrix}$$

Obviously, $\sum_{i=1}^{R}\sum_{j=1}^{R} N_{ij} = N$.

The performance measures defined for the binary setting can be easily generalized, see Table 5.4.

The **total cost error** computes the cost of all the classifier errors, where $L(c_i, c_j)$ denotes the loss when the true label is c_i and the classifier output is c_j. In the Brier score, $p_\phi(c|\mathbf{x}^i)$ is the vector $(p(c_1|\mathbf{x}^i), \ldots, p(c_R|\mathbf{x}^i))$ containing the conditional probability distribution of C given $\mathbf{x}^i$, and $\mathbf{c}^i$ is a binary vector of length R with a one at the location of the true label for the ith case and zeros elsewhere.

Table 5.4 The main performance measures defined from the confusion matrix elements for multi-class classification

Name	Notation	Formula
Accuracy	$\mathrm{Acc}(\phi)$	$\dfrac{\sum\limits_{i=1}^{R} N_{ii}}{N}$
PPV or Prec for class c_j	$\mathrm{PPV}_j(\phi) = \mathrm{Prec}_j(\phi)$	$\dfrac{N_{jj}}{\sum\limits_{i=1}^{R} N_{ij}}$
Total cost error	$\mathrm{TCE}(\phi)$	$\sum\limits_{i=1}^{R}\sum\limits_{j>i}^{R} N_{ij} \cdot L(c_i, c_j)$
Brier score	$\mathrm{Brier}(\phi)$	$\dfrac{1}{N}\sum\limits_{i=1}^{N} d^2\left(p_\phi(\mathbf{c}|\mathbf{x}^i), \mathbf{c}^i\right)$

5.2.3   Receiver Operating Characteristic (ROC) Analysis

5.2.3.1 ROC Analysis in Binary Classification Problems

A receiver operating characteristic (ROC), or simply **ROC curve** (Lusted, 1960; Green and Swets, 1966), is a graphical plot that illustrates the performance of a binary classifier system as its discrimination threshold is varied. The discrimination threshold is a cutoff value for the posterior probability $p_\phi(c|\mathbf{x})$ for which the predicted label is +. A given discrimination threshold returns a point of the plot. The ROC curve is created by plotting (on the y-axis) the true-positive rate (TPR), fraction of true positives out of the positives, versus (on the x-axis) the false-positive rate (FPR), the fraction of false positives out of the negatives at various threshold settings. FPR is one minus specificity, and TPR coincides with sensitivity. The ROC curve is sometimes called the $(1 - \text{specificity})$ versus sensitivity plot and depicts the relative trade-offs between true positives and false positives.

The **ROC space** is a unit square because $0 \leq \text{FPR} \leq 1$ and $0 \leq \text{TPR} \leq 1$. The output of a non-probabilistic classifier results in a single point in this ROC space. However, a probabilistic classifier can generate as many points as threshold values. The ROC curve is the polygonal curve plotted by connecting all pairs of consecutive points. Point $(0,0)$, with both FPR and TPR equal to zero, denotes the model that classifies all instances as negative. Point $(1,1)$, with both FPR and TPR equal to one, represents the classifier labeling all instances as positive. The diagonal of the ROC space, that is, the line connecting points $(0,0)$ and $(1,1)$, verifies FPR = TPR at all points. The classifiers represented with points along this diagonal are regarded as **random classifiers**. The random classifier at point (a,a) means that, for a positive labeled case, $C = +$, the probability that the classifier, ϕ, classifies it as positive, $\phi = +$, equals a. In mathematical notation, $p(\phi = +|C = +) = a$. For a negative labeled case, $p(\phi = +|C = -) = a$. The classifiers represented by points above (or below) the diagonal perform better (or worse) than random. As a rule of thumb, for two points $(\text{FPR}_1, \text{TPR}_1)$ and $(\text{FPR}_2, \text{TPR}_2)$ in the ROC space, $(\text{FPR}_1, \text{TPR}_1)$ represents a better classifier than $(\text{FPR}_2, \text{TPR}_2)$ if $(\text{FPR}_1, \text{TPR}_1)$ is on the left and higher up than $(\text{FPR}_2, \text{TPR}_2)$ because these positions signify that $\text{FPR}_1 < \text{FPR}_2$ and $\text{TPR}_1 > \text{TPR}_2$.

Points $(1,0)$ and $(0,1)$ denote the other two endpoints of the ROC space. For point $(1,0)$, FPR = 1 and TPR = 0. It denotes a classifier that gets all its predictions wrong. At the opposite end of the scale, point $(0,1)$ represents the best classifier, which gets all the positive cases right and none the negative ones wrong.

A simple algorithm for the generation of a ROC curve is described in Fawcett (2006). Its pseudocode is presented in Algorithm 5.1. Let $\mathcal{D}$ be the set of cases, $\phi(\mathbf{x}^i)$ be the continuous output of the classifier for instance $\mathbf{x}^i$, *min* and *max* be the smallest and largest values returned by $\phi(\mathbf{x})$, respectively, and let *incr* be the smallest difference between any two output values. Finally, let N_+ and N_- be the number of real positive and negative cases, respectively.

The range of the threshold values t is $min, min + incr, min + 2 \cdot incr, \ldots, max$. TP and FP are initialized as 0 (lines 2 and 3). Then for each case whose classification output exceeds threshold t (line 5), the TP counter is incremented by one if the case is positive (lines 6–7); for negative cases (lines 8–9) the FP counter is incremented by one. TPR and FPR are respectively computed (lines 12 and 13) and the associated (FPR, TPR) is added to the ROC curve (line 14).

Algorithm 5.1: A simple algorithm for building an ROC curve

Input : A classifier ϕ, and constants $min, max, incr, N_+, N_-$

Output: An ROC curve

```
1  for t = min to max by incr do
2      TP = 0
3      FP = 0
4      for xⁱ ∈ D do
5          if φ(xⁱ) ≥ t then
6              if xⁱ is a positive case then
7                  TP = TP +1
8              else
9                  FP = FP +1
10         endif
11     endfor
12     TPR = TP/N₊
13     FPR = FP/N₋
14     Add point (FPR, TPR) to ROC curve
15 endfor
```

Example. Table 5.5 shows the hypothetical outputs assigned by a probabilistic classifier to 10 instances, along with their true class labels.

According to Algorithm 5.1, the first threshold will be set at 0.46. At this threshold, the five positive instances are well classified, whereas the five negative instances, all of which have outputs greater than or equal to 0.46, are misclassified. As a result, we get FPR = TPR = 1, which matches point $(1,1)$ in Figure 5.1. All the thresholds output by

Table 5.5 Cases used to generate an ROC curve

Instances	$\mathbf{x}^i$	1	2	3	4	5	6	7	8	9	10
Output	$p(+|\mathbf{x}^i)$	0.97	0.91	0.84	0.80	0.68	0.67	0.66	0.61	0.49	0.46
True class	c^i	+	−	+	+	−	+	−	+	−	−

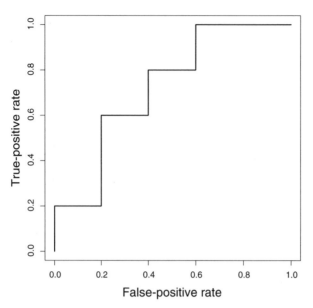

Figure 5.1 ROC graph for the data of Table 5.5 plotted with the ROCR R package (Sing et al., 2005).

increments of 0.01 (value of incr) up to 0.49 yield the same results. At the threshold of 0.49, the instance $\mathbf{x}^{10}$ is correctly classified as -, and we get FPR = 0.80, and TPR = 1. This point $(0.80, 1)$ represents the second point in Figure 5.1. The next significant threshold is 0.61, where we get the third point, $(0.60, 1)$, on the curve. The other points are output in a similar fashion. Plotting a polygonal to connect these points, we get the ROC curve in Figure 5.1. ∎

The **area under the ROC curve** (AUC) is the most popular summary statistic for the ROC curve. As the ROC space is a unit square, the AUC of any classifier verifies $\mathrm{AUC}(\phi) \in [0, 1]$. The upper bound is equivalent to a perfect classifier (FPR = 0, TPR = 1), whereas $\mathrm{AUC}(\phi_{\mathrm{random}}) = 0.5$ represents a random classifier. For a reasonable classifier, we expect the AUC to be greater than 0.5. AUC can be interpreted as a measurement indicator of whether a classifier is able to rank a randomly chosen positive instance higher than a negative one. According to this interpretation, the AUC is equivalent to Wilcoxon's rank sum test (Section 4.2.5) and can be easily calculated. A rank is assigned to the output provided by the classifier to each case in order of decreasing outputs. The AUC is computed as

$$\mathrm{AUC}(\phi) = 1 - \frac{\sum_{i=1}^{N_+}(i - \mathrm{rank}_i)}{N_+ \cdot N_-}, \tag{5.1}$$

where rank_i is the rank of the ith case in the subset of positive labels given by classifier ϕ, and N_+ and N_- denote the number of real positive and negative cases in $\mathcal{D}$, respectively.

Example. The application of the above formula to the instances in Table 5.5 results in

$$\mathrm{AUC}(\phi) = 1 - \frac{(1-1) + (3-2) + (4-3) + (6-4) + (8-5)}{5 \cdot 5} = 0.72.$$

Calculating the AUC directly from Figure 5.1 yields

$$\text{AUC}(\phi) = 0.20 \cdot 0.20 + 0.20 \cdot 0.60 + 0.20 \cdot 0.80 + 0.40 \cdot 1 = 0.72.$$

∎

5.2.3.2 ROC Analysis in Multi-class Problems

ROC analysis is much more complex for multi-class problems than in the binary classification setting. The AUC can be generalized as the **volume under the ROC surface** as introduced by Ferri et al. (2003) or, alternatively, as an average AUC of all possible two-class ROC curves that can be generated from the multi-class problem, as suggested by Hand and Till (2001). According to the latter approach, the AUC would be computed as

$$\text{AUC}_{\text{multi-class}}(\phi) = \frac{2}{R(R-1)} \sum_{\substack{c_i, c_j \in \Omega_C \\ c_i \neq c_j}} \text{AUC}_{c_i, c_j}(\phi),$$

where $\text{AUC}_{\text{multi-class}}(\phi)$ is the total AUC of the multi-class ROC for classifier ϕ, and $\text{AUC}_{c_i, c_j}(\phi)$ is the AUC of the two-class ROC curve of ϕ for classes c_i and c_j.

5.3 Performance Estimation

The main objective of a supervised classification problem is to induce a classification model capable of describing the training data, as well as generalizing well to unseen data taken from the same distribution as the training data. As already mentioned, this joint probability distribution, $p(\mathbf{x}, c)$, is unknown, and therefore the different performance evaluation metrics used to predict the behavior of the classifier over unseen instances have to be estimated from the current data set of cases $\mathcal{D} = \{(\mathbf{x}^1, c^1), \ldots, (\mathbf{x}^N, c^N)\}$. This section describes different methods for making an honest estimation. These **honest performance estimation methods** estimate the performance measure based on instances that have not previously been seen in the learning phase by the classifier. This contrasts with the **resubstitution method** that learns the classifier on a training set that is subsequently used as testing set. The resubstitution method usually overfits the data that it was trained on, and its error estimate is optimistically biased.

The honest performance estimation methods introduced in this section are organized according to their resampling characteristics: single versus multiple. By contrast with single sampling methods, the data set of cases, $\mathcal{D}$, is sampled several times in a multiple setting. Figure 5.2, adapted from Japkowicz and Mohak (2011), shows the respective methods: hold-out and k-fold cross-validation as representative of single resampling methods, and repeated hold-out, repeated k-fold cross-validation, and bootstrap as examples of multiple resampling.

Each performance measure estimated using the different honest methods presented below can be regarded as a random variable θ with a probability distribution and expectation $\mathbb{E}[\theta]$. The different honest methods, especially techniques belonging to the multiple resampling category, will provide a battery of estimation values that allow to build an empirical distribution. We are interested in methods providing estimators $\hat{\theta}$ of θ with

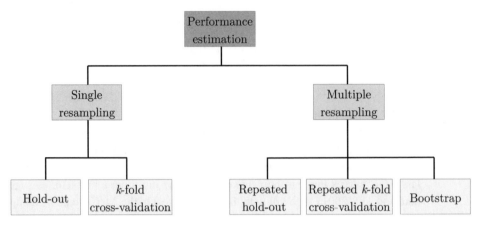

Figure 5.2 Honest estimation methods organized according to their sampling characteristics.

expected values close to $\mathbb{E}[\theta]$ (i.e., unbiased), whose variance is small (Section 4.1.2.1). We choose classification accuracy as the performance measure to illustrate the honest estimation methods in this section.

5.3.1   Single Resampling-Based Estimation Methods

5.3.1.1 *Hold-Out Estimation Method*

The **hold-out method** partitions the data set of cases, $\mathcal{D} = \{(\mathbf{x}^1, c^1), \ldots, (\mathbf{x}^N, c^N)\}$ into two disjoint data subsets, the **training data set**, $\mathcal{D}_{\text{training}} = \{(\mathbf{x}^1, c^1), \ldots, (\mathbf{x}^{N_1}, c^{N_1})\}$ with N_1 cases and the **test data set**, $\mathcal{D}_{\text{test}} = \mathcal{D} \setminus \mathcal{D}_{\text{training}} = \{(\mathbf{x}^{N_1+1}, c^{N_1+1}), \ldots, (\mathbf{x}^N, c^N)\}$ with $N - N_1$ cases. The supervised classification learning algorithm induces a classification model, denoted as ϕ_{training}, from the input of labeled cases in $\mathcal{D}_{\text{training}}$. This model is applied to the unlabeled set of instances of $\mathcal{D}_{\text{test}}$ and honestly estimates the chosen performance measure by comparing the true class labels with the predictions given by the model on each of the cases, $\phi_{\text{training}}(\mathbf{x})$, or $\hat{c}$. A general empirical risk function is estimated as follows:

$$R_{\mathcal{D}_{\text{test}}}(\phi_{\text{training}}) = \frac{1}{N - N_1} \sum_{(\mathbf{x}^i, c^i) \in \mathcal{D}_{\text{test}}} L(c^i, \phi_{\text{training}}(\mathbf{x}^i)).$$

The hold-out estimation of classification accuracy (as the performance measure) will be calculated as

$$\text{Acc}_h(\phi) = \text{Acc}_{\mathcal{D}_{\text{test}}}(\phi_{\text{training}}) = \frac{1}{N - N_1} \sum_{(\mathbf{x}^i, c^i) \in \mathcal{D}_{\text{test}}} \mathbb{I}(c^i = \phi_{\text{training}}(\mathbf{x}^i)),$$

where $\mathbb{I}(a)$ is the indicator function (Equation (3.3)).

The hold-out estimation process is shown in Figure 5.3. It is the simplest honest method but has several drawbacks: (i) the final model is learned from a subset of, rather than the whole, data set, namely, the training data set; (ii) the ratio between the training and test data sets is a method parameter, which should be fixed (the standard choice is a ratio of 2).

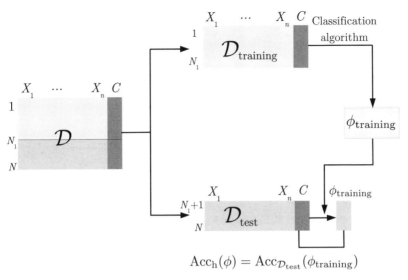

$$\mathrm{Acc_h}(\phi) = \mathrm{Acc}_{\mathcal{D}_{\text{test}}}(\phi_{\text{training}})$$

Figure 5.3 Diagram of the hold-out estimation method.

5.3.1.2 *k-Fold Cross-Validation*

k-**fold cross-validation** (Kurtz, 1948) randomly partitions the original labeled data set into k subsets of roughly equal sizes, called folds. Of the k folds, a single fold is retained as the test data set for testing the model, and the remaining $k-1$ folds are used as training data. The cross-validation process is then repeated k times, with each of the k folds used exactly $k-1$ times as training data and only once as testing data. The k results of the performance measure yielded for the test data can be averaged (or otherwise combined) to produce an estimation of the performance of the model induced from the whole original data set.

Formally, the original labeled data set, $\mathcal{D} = \{(\mathbf{x}^1, c^1), \dots, (\mathbf{x}^N, c^N)\}$, is partitioned into k folds, denoted as $\mathcal{D}_1, \dots, \mathcal{D}_k$, verifying $\mathcal{D} = \bigcup_{l=1}^{k} \mathcal{D}_l$ with $\mathcal{D}_w \cap \mathcal{D}_t = \varnothing$ for $w, t \in \{1, \dots, k\}, w \neq t$. The lth fold, $\mathcal{D}_l$, is used as test data for the model learned from a training data set formed by the other folds, $\mathcal{D} \setminus \mathcal{D}_l$. This model is denoted as ϕ_l. Its accuracy, Acc_l, is computed as

$$\mathrm{Acc}_l = \frac{1}{|\mathcal{D}_l|} \sum_{(\mathbf{x}^i, c^i) \in \mathcal{D}_l} \mathbb{I}\left(c^i = \phi_l(\mathbf{x}^i)\right).$$

The model, ϕ, used for classifying new instances is learned from the original labeled data set, $\mathcal{D}$, and its accuracy is estimated as follows:

$$\mathrm{Acc}_{\mathrm{cv}}(\phi) = \frac{1}{k} \sum_{l=1}^{k} \mathrm{Acc}_l.$$

The k-fold cross-validation estimator is very nearly unbiased, but its variance can be large (Stone, 1977). Figure 5.4 shows a diagram of a fourfold cross-validation method.

The advantage of this method over hold-out is that it induces the final model from the whole data set. The number of times each case is used for training and for testing is fixed in k-fold cross-validation, which is not the case in repeated hold-out. A drawback of the

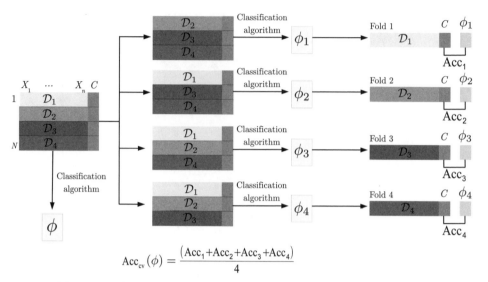

$$\text{Acc}_{cv}(\phi) = \frac{\left(\text{Acc}_1 + \text{Acc}_2 + \text{Acc}_3 + \text{Acc}_4\right)}{4}$$

Figure 5.4 Diagram of a fourfold cross-validation method.

method is that the parameter k is generally unfixed, although $k = 10$ is the most common value used. Another drawback is that the models ϕ_l learned on $k-1$ folds in each iteration are very similar because each one is trained on an overlapping set of cases, particularly $k-2$ folds. For this reason, these k models cannot be considered as independent.

Two special cases of k-fold cross-validation that are in widespread use are: leave-one-out cross-validation and stratified k-fold cross-validation. **Leave-one-out cross-validation** involves using a single case from the original sample as the test data, and the remaining cases as the training data. This is repeated such that each case in the original data set is used once as the test data. The scheme is equivalent to the number of folds being equal to the number of cases and is not a good choice when working with large data sets due to its computational burden. In **stratified k-fold cross-validation**, the folds are selected such that the probability distribution of the class variable is approximately equal in all folds and similar to the original class distribution in $\mathcal{D}$. Stratification is recommended for imbalanced data sets, where the class variable is far from being distributed ass uniform.

In neuroscience, some researchers have used honest estimation methods for the neuron classification problem that we have chosen to illustrate Part II of this book. For example, Guerra et al. (2011) adopted 10-fold cross-validation, and DeFelipe et al. (2013) employed a leave-one-out procedure.

5.3.2   Multiple Resampling-Based Estimation Methods

5.3.2.1 Repeated Hold-Out

Repeated hold-out extends the main idea of the hold-out scheme to a multiple resampling scenario. The partition in the hold-out scheme is repeated several times, each with a random assignment of training and test cases. This resampling scenario has the advantage of estimates being stable (variance is low), resulting from a large number of sampling repetitions. A drawback of the approach is that there is no control of how many times each case is used in the training data sets or in the test data sets.

Formally, the original labeled data set, $\mathcal{D} = \{(\mathbf{x}^1, c^1), \ldots, (\mathbf{x}^N, c^N)\}$, is randomly partitioned B times as training data sets, $\mathcal{D}^l_{\text{training}}$, and test data sets, $\mathcal{D}^l_{\text{test}}$. For each partition $l \in \{1, \ldots, B\}$, $\mathcal{D} = \mathcal{D}^l_{\text{training}} \cup \mathcal{D}^l_{\text{test}}$ and $\mathcal{D}^l_{\text{training}} \cap \mathcal{D}^l_{\text{test}} = \varnothing$ is verified for all l. The final model, ϕ, is learned from $\mathcal{D}$, and its accuracy is estimated as

$$\text{Acc}_{\text{rh}}(\phi) = \frac{1}{B} \sum_{l=1}^{B} \text{Acc}^l,$$

where Acc^l denotes the estimation of the accuracy of model ϕ^l_{training}, learned from $\mathcal{D}^l_{\text{training}}$, and tested over $\mathcal{D}^l_{\text{test}}$, that is,

$$\text{Acc}^l = \frac{1}{|\mathcal{D}^l_{\text{test}}|} \sum_{(\mathbf{x}^i, c^i) \in \mathcal{D}^l_{\text{test}}} \mathbb{I}(c^i = \phi^l_{\text{training}}(\mathbf{x}^i)).$$

5.3.2.2 Repeated k-Fold Cross-Validation

Repeated k-fold cross-validation reduces the variability of the estimator by multiple rounds of k-fold cross-validation performed using different partitions. The 5×2 cross-validation (Dietterich, 1998) and the 10×10 cross-validation (Bouckaert, 2003), performing 5 repetitions of 2-fold cross-validation and 10 repetitions of 10-fold cross-validation, respectively, are its most popular instantiations. In the neuron classification problem we can find that Marin et al. (2002) proposed a 40×5-fold cross-validation scheme, and Druckmann et al. (2013) used 10×10-fold cross-validation.

5.3.2.3 Bootstrap

Bootstrapping, introduced by Efron (1979), is a statistical method that aims to output estimator properties measured when sampling from an approximate distribution. One standard choice for this approximate distribution is the empirical distribution of the observed data. If a set of cases can be assumed to be i.i.d., bootstrapping can be implemented by using random sampling with replacement from the original data set to produce several resamples of equal size to the original data set.

Thus, the bootstrap sampling method consists of sampling with replacement N cases from the original labeled data set $\mathcal{D} = \{(\mathbf{x}^1, c^1), \ldots, (\mathbf{x}^N, c^N)\}$. This bootstrap sampling process is repeated B times, yielding the data sets $\mathcal{D}^l_b$, with $l \in \{1, \ldots, B\}$, all of size N. As the probability of selection is always the same for each of the N cases, the probability of a case not being chosen after N selections is $\left(1 - \frac{1}{N}\right)^N \approx \frac{1}{e} \approx 0.368$. Hence the expected number of distinct cases in each of the B data sets $\mathcal{D}^l_b$ used for training the classifier is $0.632N$. The lth test set, $\mathcal{D}^l_{b\text{-test}}$, with $l \in \{1, \ldots, B\}$, is then formed by all the cases from $\mathcal{D}$ not present in $\mathcal{D}^l_b$, that is, $\mathcal{D}^l_{b\text{-test}} = \mathcal{D} \setminus \mathcal{D}^l_b$. At each time, a classifier ϕ^l_b is induced from $\mathcal{D}^l_b$, and its accuracy, $\text{Acc}(\phi^l_b)$, is computed as $\text{Acc}(\phi^l_b) = \frac{1}{|\mathcal{D}^l_{b\text{-test}}|} \sum_{(\mathbf{x}^i, c^i) \in \mathcal{D}^l_{b\text{-test}}} \mathbb{I}(c^i = \phi^l_b(\mathbf{x}^i))$.

The **e0 bootstrap** estimate, $\text{Acc}_{\text{e0}}(\phi)$, of model ϕ, output when the learning algorithm is applied to the original data set $\mathcal{D}$, is calculated as

$$\text{Acc}_{\text{e0}}(\phi) = \frac{1}{B} \sum_{l=1}^{B} \text{Acc}\left(\phi^l_b\right).$$

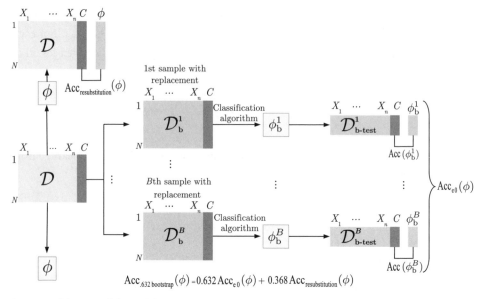

Figure 5.5 Diagram of the .632 bootstrap method.

The e0 bootstrap estimate can be pessimistic because the classifier is trained only over an expected number of $0.632N$ different cases at any time. Thus, the **.632 bootstrap** estimate, $\text{Acc}_{.632 \text{ bootstrap}}(\phi)$, aims to avoid this pessimistic estimation by introducing the optimistic bias of the resubstitution estimation in the following weighted expression:

$$\text{Acc}_{.632 \text{ bootstrap}}(\phi) = 0.632\text{Acc}_{e0}(\phi) + 0.368\text{Acc}_{\text{resubstitution}}(\phi),$$

where the resubstitution estimation corresponds to a classifier, ϕ, that is learned on a training set that is subsequently used as a testing set. It is calculated as

$$\text{Acc}_{\text{resubstitution}}(\phi) = \frac{1}{N} \sum_{(\mathbf{x}^i, c^i) \in \mathcal{D}} \mathbb{I}\left(c^i = \phi\left(\mathbf{x}^i\right)\right).$$

Figure 5.5 shows a diagram of the .632 bootstrap method. Bootstrap estimation is asymptotically (large values of B) unbiased, and its variance is small. These are interesting properties when working with small data sets.

5.4   Statistical Significance Testing

Machine learning aims to develop new supervised classification algorithms that perform well for a specific data set or even, more generally, for a battery of data sets. A new classification algorithm can be compared with the state-of-the-art algorithms from a theoretical point of view considering their memory and/or time complexity resources in both the learning and classification phases. However, the comparison of the prediction results of the new and the state-of-the-art algorithms is an inductive issue. Therefore, it can only be approached by means of statistical significance tests. Accordingly, hypothesis testing

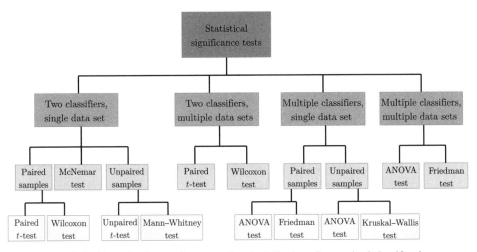

Figure 5.6 Statistical hypothesis tests for comparing the behavior of supervised classification algorithms.

addresses the question of whether or not the differences in performance between the new and the state-of-the-art algorithms are statistically significant. It is assumed that the null hypothesis represents the same behavior for both algorithms.

In this section, we present suitable hypothesis tests for four different comparisons: (a) two classifiers in a single data set, (b) two classifiers in multiple data sets; (c) multiple classifiers in a single data set; and (d) multiple classifiers in multiple data sets. Figure 5.6 illustrates the different tests for each of the four situations. For comparisons in a single data set, the performance values used for hypothesis testing are taken from k-fold cross-validation or repeated hold-out schemes. Because the data sets from which these values are taken in these two schemes are usually dependent, a lot of care needs to be taken with the design of the statistical tests in order to avoid problems with biased variance estimation. However, the result of running two or more algorithms on multiple data sets is, of course, a sample of independent numbers, and comparison is even simpler than for a single data set. Moreover, in a multiple data set scenario, the null hypothesis represents the same behavior of all the algorithms under comparison. For scenarios (b) and (d), the choice of multiple data sets on which the algorithms are run is a sensitive matter. For all scenarios, the determination of the performance measure to be considered is of great importance because the null hypothesis can be rejected for some but not for other measures.

The notation is as follows. We denote by J the number of supervised classification algorithms to be compared, where $J = 2$ in scenarios (a) and (b) or $J > 2$ in scenarios (c) and (d). The number of data sets will be represented by M with values $M = 1$ for (a) and (c) and $M > 1$ for (b) and (d). Notice that the term "multiple" has a different meaning when it refers to data sets or to algorithms. The performance value of classifier j in data set i is given by m_i^j. We assume that the performance measures are monotone increasing in the sense that if $m_i^j > m_i^k$, classifier j is said to behave better than classifier k. This interpretation is valid for performance measures that are monotone increasing, like accuracy. For decreasing performance measures, like error rate, the opposite holds.

5.4.1 Comparing Two Classifiers on a Single Data Set

5.4.1.1 Paired t-Test

Let us assume a paired sample representing the values of two supervised classification algorithms applied to a specific data set using a given performance measure. The sample is paired because the folds provided by the k-fold cross-validation scheme are the same across both algorithms. The **paired t-test for a k-fold cross-validation** scheme works with the k paired values of the performance measure, (m_i^A, m_i^B), containing the measure output by the pair of algorithms (A, B) at fold i. For each pair of values, its difference, $d_i^{A-B} = m_i^A - m_i^B$, is assumed to follow a normal distribution, $D \sim \mathcal{N}(d|\mu_D, \sigma_D)$, both parameters being unknown. The equality of behavior between both algorithms, A and B, can be tested using the following null and alternative hypotheses:

$$\begin{cases} H_0: & \mu_D = 0 \\ H_1: & \mu_D \neq 0. \end{cases}$$

The determination of the acceptance and rejection regions is based on the $t = \frac{\bar{d}}{S/\sqrt{k}}$ statistic, where $\bar{d}$ represents the sample mean of the k differences, $\bar{d} = \frac{\sum_{i=1}^{k} d_i^{A-B}}{k}$, and S^2 is its sample quasi-variance, $S^2 = \frac{\sum_{i=1}^{k} (d_i^{A-B} - \bar{d})^2}{k-1}$. Under the null hypothesis, the $t = \frac{\bar{d}}{S/\sqrt{k}}$ statistic follows a Student's t distribution with $k - 1$ degrees of freedom.

Example. Let us consider the (percentage) accuracies of algorithms A and B represented in Table 5.6 by classifying a data set based on a 10-fold cross-validation scheme (same folds for both).

Looking at these 10 pairs of accuracies, we find that A has outperformed B in 9 of the folds. The result of applying the t-test described above is conclusive: the null hypothesis of equal behavior is rejected with a p-value of 0.0009 corresponding to a value of 4.8587 for a Student's t statistic with 9 degrees of freedom. ∎

The above test is based on the assumption that the values d_i^{A-B}, for $i = 1, \ldots k$, are independent. However, as these values correspond to the performance measures output by each of the k models induced from the folds in the training data sets, and there is an overlap of $k - 2$ folds in any pair of training data sets, the independence assumption does not hold. This assumption does not hold for the repeated hold-out scheme of validation either.

The **corrected resampled t-test** (Nadeau and Bengio, 2003) solves this problem for the repeated hold-out scheme. The variance estimation in this method is corrected with the term $\frac{1}{B} + \frac{N_1}{N-N_1}$, where B denotes the number of repetitions of the hold-out partition, and N_1

Table 5.6 Percentage accuracy of algorithms A and B on a single data set with a 10-fold cross-validation scheme

						Fold i					
		1	2	3	4	5	6	7	8	9	10
A	m_i^A	80.06	80.11	81.12	81.86	81.25	79.98	80.54	81.13	78.89	80.77
B	m_i^B	80.02	79.98	81.05	81.88	80.09	79.94	80.45	81.03	78.82	80.65
D	d_i^{A-B}	0.04	0.13	0.07	−0.02	0.16	0.04	0.09	0.10	0.07	0.12

represents the sample size of the training data. The statistic used for the test is now given by $t = \dfrac{\bar{d}}{S\sqrt{\left(\frac{1}{B} + \frac{N_1}{N - N_1}\right)}}$ and follows a Student's t distribution with $B - 1$ degrees of freedom.

A **corrected repeated k-fold cross-validation** has also been proposed (Bouckaert and Frank, 2004) for the repeated k-fold cross-validation. Denoting by B, the number of times the k-fold cross-validation scheme is repeated, the sample variance is corrected with the term $\frac{1}{k \cdot B} + \frac{1}{k-1}$. The statistic for the hypothesis test, $t = \dfrac{\bar{d}}{S\sqrt{\left(\frac{1}{k \cdot B} + \frac{1}{k-1}\right)}}$, follows, under the null hypothesis, a Student's t distribution with $(k \cdot B) - 1$ degrees of freedom, and the sample mean, $\bar{d}$, and quasi-variance, S, are now computed from the $k \cdot B$ paired differences in behavior between the two algorithms.

When the performance values in the sample cannot be assumed to be normally distributed, an alternative to the paired t-test is the Wilcoxon signed-rank test (see Section 4.2.4).

5.4.1.2 Unpaired t-Test

The performance values for the two compared algorithms, A and B, cannot always be considered as a paired sample. In a k-fold cross-validation, for example, the two algorithms may not have the same number of folds, and even if they do, the folds will not necessarily be the same in all algorithms. Similarly, under a repeated hold-out scheme, the number of repetitions may not be the same, and even if they are, the same training and test sets do not necessarily have to be used in each of the repetitions of both algorithms.

The Welch two sample t-test (see Section 4.2.5) is applicable for this unpaired sample, assuming a normal distribution for the performance values of algorithms A and B. The test statistic is now

$$t = \frac{\bar{m}^A - \bar{m}^B}{\sqrt{\dfrac{S_A^2}{N_A} + \dfrac{S_B^2}{N_B}}},$$

where $\bar{m}^A$, S_A^2, and N_A ($\bar{m}^B$, S_B^2, and N_B) refer to the average, quasi-variance, and sample size of the set of values for the performance of algorithm A (B).

If the normality assumption does not hold, an alternative test is the Mann–Whitney test, as explained in Section 4.2.5.

5.4.1.3 McNemar Test

The behavior of two supervised classification algorithms, A and B, can also be compared based on the matching outputs of both classifiers for each instance. This is the approach taken by the **McNemar test** (McNemar, 1947).

The test is applied to a 2×2 contingency table, which contains the matching outcomes of two supervised classification algorithms, ϕ_A and ϕ_B, on a data set of N instances, as shown in Table 5.7.

The null hypothesis of the McNemar test is marginal homogeneity, which can be interpreted as both algorithms behaving in the same manner. Accordingly, the two marginal probabilities for each outcome are the same, i.e., $p(\phi_A = +) = p(\phi_B = +)$ and $p(\phi_A = -) = p(\phi_B = -)$. From the first equality, we get:

$$p(\phi_A = +, \phi_B = +) + p(\phi_A = +, \phi_B = -) = p(\phi_A = +, \phi_B = +) + p(\phi_A = -, \phi_B = +),$$

Table 5.7 Contingency table for the McNemar test

		ϕ_B		
		+	-	
ϕ_A	+	N_{++}	N_{+-}	$N_{+\bullet}$
	-	N_{-+}	N_{--}	$N_{-\bullet}$
		$N_{\bullet+}$	$N_{\bullet-}$	N

Table 5.8 Contingency table example for applying the McNemar test

		ϕ_B		
		+	-	
ϕ_A	+	183	45	228
	-	18	81	99
		201	126	327

or, equivalently, $p(\phi_A = +, \phi_B = -) = p(\phi_A = -, \phi_B = +)$. The same result holds when developing the second equality. Thus, the null and alternative hypotheses are:

$$\begin{cases} H_0: & p(\phi_A = +, \phi_B = -) = p(\phi_A = -, \phi_B = +) \\ H_1: & p(\phi_A = +, \phi_B = -) \neq p(\phi_A = -, \phi_B = +). \end{cases}$$

The McNemar test statistic is

$$\frac{(N_{+-} - N_{-+})^2}{N_{+-} + N_{-+}}.$$

Applying Yates's correction (Yates, 1934), the statistic is $\frac{(|N_{+-} - N_{-+}| - 0.5)^2}{N_{+-} + N_{-+}}$. An alternative correction of 1 instead of 0.5 was proposed by Edwards (1948), resulting in $\frac{(|N_{+-} - N_{-+}| - 1)^2}{N_{+-} + N_{-+}}$.

Under H_0, with a rather large number of mismatches ($N_{+-} + N_{-+} > 25$), a good approximation of above three statistics is a chi-squared distribution with one degree of freedom. If the number of mismatches is not large ($N_{+-} + N_{-+} \leq 25$), the binomial distribution can be used to get the exact distribution of the statistics. In this formulation, N_{+-} is compared to a binomial distribution with a number of Bernoulli trials equal to $N_{+-} + N_{-+}$ and a success rate of 0.5.

Example. Table 5.8 contains an imaginary contingency table with the number of matches and mismatches of two supervised classification algorithms applied to discriminate between pyramidal (+) and interneuron (-) cells using morphological features as predictors. The total number of cells was 327.

The value of the correction proposed by Edwards (1948) to the McNemar test is computed as $\frac{(|45-18|-1)^2}{45+18} = 10.73$. In a chi-squared distribution with one degree of freedom, this value has a p-value of 0.0011. The null hypothesis is rejected, meaning that there is enough evidence for not accepting an equal behavior of both algorithms in this data set. ∎

Table 5.9 Wilcoxon signed-rank test applied to 12 data sets on the hypothetical percentage accuracy of 2 classifiers A and B

Data set i	m_i^A	m_i^B	$m_i^A - m_i^B$	$\|m_i^A - m_i^B\|$	Ranks of $\|m_i^A - m_i^B\|$	Ranks with signs
1	78.34	76.59	1.75	1.75	7	+7
2	88.95	83.39	5.56	5.56	11	+11
3	63.78	64.91	−1.13	1.13	6	−6
4	90.12	87.24	2.88	2.88	9	+9
5	82.36	81.99	0.37	0.37	3	+3
6	93.75	93.56	0.19	0.19	1	+1
7	81.45	77.21	4.24	4.24	10	+10
8	66.19	66.19	0	0	−	−
9	73.47	75.28	−1.81	1.81	8	−8
10	91.26	90.61	0.65	0.65	5	+5
11	78.02	77.78	0.24	0.24	2	+2
12	86.14	85.53	0.61	0.61	4	+4

5.4.2 Comparing Two Classifiers on Multiple Data Sets

The behavior of two classifiers on multiple data sets is usually compared using the values provided by the estimation of the selected performance measure in each of the data sets. Thus, only one value is taken into account for the classifier and data set. This contrasts with the generation of values to be compared in a single data set scenario, where k-fold cross-validation or repeated hold-out schemes were required and compromised the independence of the values. Now the values to be compared, one per algorithm, can be regarded as paired, and we have the same number of pairs as data sets.

The hypothesis tests most often applied under these circumstances are the paired t-test and the Wilcoxon signed-rank test, both introduced in Section 4.2.4.

Example. Table 5.9 lists the accuracy for two supervised classification algorithms, A and B, on 12 data sets. These values, denoted as m_i^A and m_i^B with $i = 1, \ldots, 12$ for A and B, are located in the second and third columns, respectively. The next two columns show the differences and the absolute value of the differences for the two algorithms in each data set. The ranks of these absolute values and the ranks with the corresponding signs are listed in the last two columns. The value of the Wilcoxon statistic can be calculated from the last column, as the sum of all positive ranks. Thus, $t^+ = 7+11+9+3+1+10+5+2+4 = 52$, and the respective p-value is 0.1016. Therefore, the null hypothesis that the two algorithms behave equally cannot be rejected. ■

5.4.3 Comparing Multiple Classifiers on a Single Data Set

Multiple classifiers can only be compared on a single data set if there is more than one performance measure value for each classifier. As explained in Section 5.4.1, these values can be the result of a k-fold cross-validation or a repeated hold-out scheme and can form paired or unpaired samples. For paired samples, the one-way repeated-measures ANOVA test is applicable if the samples follow normal distributions, otherwise the Friedman test is the best option. The one-way ANOVA test can be used for unpaired and normal distributed samples, whereas the Kruskal–Wallis test should be chosen for non-normal samples. These four tests were introduced in Section 4.2. The ANOVA and Friedman tests were used for the first time to compare multiple models on a single data set in Pizarro et al. (2002).

Guerra et al. (2011) and DeFelipe et al. (2013) used hypothesis testing to compare multiple classifiers on a single data set. Pyramidal neurons versus interneurons were discriminated in Guerra et al. (2011), whereas different interneuron types had to be distinguished in DeFelipe et al. (2013).

Example. Table 5.10 shows the hypothetical accuracies output by 6 supervised classification algorithms, A–F, in each of the 10 folds of a cross-validation scheme. The elements from which the Friedman statistics are computed are shown in Table 5.11.

The terms "treatment" and "blocks" introduced in Section 4.2.6 explaining the Friedman test are now replaced by "algorithm" and "folds," respectively. The standardized Friedman statistic, S, is computed as $S = \left[\frac{12}{kJ(J+1)} \sum_{j=1}^{J} R_j^2 \right] - 3k(J+1)$, where k denotes the number of folds, J the number of algorithms, and R_j the sum of the ranks for the jth algorithm. Substituting the figures in Table 5.11 into the above formula, we get

Table 5.10 Hypothetical percentage accuracy of 6 classifiers in a 10-fold cross-validation scheme

Fold	A	B	C	D	E	F
1	79.55	80.22	78.55	81.15	79.74	80.11
2	79.87	80.34	78.49	81.67	79.89	80.23
3	78.90	80.05	78.91	81.03	79.92	80.17
4	79.99	80.23	78.33	81.22	79.45	80.19
5	79.24	81.27	78.25	81.74	79.21	80.45
6	79.46	79.86	79.49	81.16	80.45	80.07
7	79.59	80.27	79.55	80.12	80.11	80.17
8	79.81	78.84	79.84	81.52	79.88	80.20
9	80.15	79.96	78.02	81.79	79.93	80.16
10	80.01	80.25	78.26	81.28	80.03	80.11

Table 5.11 Ranks of the accuracy for each of the 6 classifiers in the 10 folds

Fold	A	B	C	D	E	F
1	5	2	6	1	4	3
2	5	2	6	1	4	3
3	6	3	5	1	4	2
4	4	2	6	1	5	3
5	4	2	6	1	5	3
6	6	4	5	1	2	3
7	5	1	6	3	4	2
8	5	6	4	1	3	2
9	3	4	6	1	5	2
10	5	2	6	1	4	3
R_j	48	28	56	12	40	26

$S = \left[\frac{12}{10 \cdot 6 \cdot 7}(48^2 + 28^2 + 56^2 + 12^2 + 40^2 + 26^2)\right] - 3 \cdot 10 \cdot 7 = 36.9714$. This figure corresponds to a p-value of 6.069e-07 for a chi-squared distribution with five degrees of freedom. Thus, the null hypothesis that the six algorithms behave equally is rejected.

The Nemenyi test (Section 4.2.9) provides statistically significant differences with $\alpha = 0.05$ for the following pairs of algorithms: $A - D$, $B - C$, $C - D$, $C - F$, and $D - E$. This result has been achieved after comparing the respective average rankings with $q_\alpha \sqrt{\frac{k(k+1)}{6b}} = 2.850\sqrt{\frac{6 \cdot 7}{6 \cdot 10}} = 2.38$. However, the Nemenyi test with correction only classes pairs $C - D$ and $A - D$ as statistically different.   ∎

5.4.4 Comparing Multiple Classifiers on Multiple Data Sets

The behavior of multiple classifiers on multiple data sets is compared by considering a value for each of the classifiers in each of the data sets. These values are paired, and the applicable tests are the one-way repeated-measures ANOVA test if the samples are Gaussian or the Friedman test otherwise. One special characteristic in this setting is the issue of multiple hypothesis testing, where some of the null hypotheses are rejected due to random chance. Several procedures to control the familywise error, that is, the probability of making at least one type I error in any of the comparisons, like the Bonferroni correction, the Šidák correction, and the Holm–Bonferroni correction, were discussed in Section 4.2.9. Demšar (2006) proposed the use of the nonparametric Friedman test in combination with Nemenyi test, as a way of controlling the familywise error.

5.5 Imbalanced Data Sets and Anomaly Detection

Many neuroscience applications deal with imbalanced data sets. For example, in the ADNI data set, the MCI cases eligible for the study are nearly twice as many AD patients for MRI modality and six times as numerous as the control cases for proteomics modality (Dubey et al., 2014). Class imbalance was approached using neuropsychological data, with the aim of differentiating AD from MCI and predicting the conversion from MCI to AD by Nunes et al. (2013). Khoury et al. (2019) used an imbalanced data set collected from gait cycles of healthy, PD, ALS, and HD subjects.

Constructing an accurate classifier from **imbalanced data** is a challenging task. Traditional classifiers tend to classify all data into the majority class. To avoid this naive behavior of the classifier, several methods have been proposed in the literature (Japkowicz, 2000; Chawla, 2009; Yanmin et al., 2009). The proposals can be divided into data-level strategies and cost-sensitive strategies. Data-level strategies, also called resampling strategies, alter the class distribution of the training data to balance it. This can be done undersampling the majority class or alternatively oversampling the minority one. However, random resampling presents some drawbacks. Random undersampling can potentially discard useful data, and random oversampling can increase the time necessary to learn the classifier and also increase the risk of overfitting if the oversampling consists of generating exact copies of existing instances. To overcome this situation the synthetic minority oversampling technique (SMOTE) (Chawla et al., 2002) has been developed, with more than 85 variants. SMOTE has, however, hardly any effect on most classifiers trained on high-dimensional data (Blagus and Lusa, 2013). Cost-sensitive strategies draw the attention of the classifiers to the minority class by using misclassification costs. Given the costs for correct and incorrect predictions, an instance is predicted to have the label that leads to the lowest expected cost, where the expectation is computed using the conditional probability of each class given the instance. This approach is based on the equivalence between varying the class prior probabilities and the misclassification costs (Elkan, 2001).

Anomaly detection (Chandola et al., 2009) refers to the problem of finding anomalies in data. Anomalies are the unusual, unexpected, surprising patterns in the observed world. While anomaly is a generally accepted term, other synonyms, such as outliers, discordant observations, exceptions, aberrations, surprises, peculiarities, or contaminants, are often used in different application domains. In neuroscience an anomalous MRI image may indicate early signs of AD or the presence of malignant tumors. The underlying principle of any statistical anomaly detection method is: "An anomaly is an observation which is suspected of being partially or wholly irrelevant because it is not generated by the stochastic model assumed" (Anscombe and Guttman, 1960). Statistical methods for anomaly detection fit a statistical model (usually for normal behavior) to the training data and then apply a statistical hypothesis test (also referred to as **discordancy test** in statistical outliers detection literature [Barnett and Lewis, 1994]) to determine if an unseen instance belongs to this model or not. The null hypothesis, H_0, for such tests is that the data instance $\mathbf{x}$ has been generated using the estimated distribution. If the discordancy test rejects H_0, $\mathbf{x}$ is declared to be an anomaly. The corresponding p-value can be used as a probabilistic anomaly score for $\mathbf{x}$.

Freezing of gait (FoG) is common in Parkinsonian gait and strongly relates to falls. Pham et al. (2017) developed an automated and objective detector with adaptive thresholding to identify FoG events based on anomaly detection techniques. For each patient, three walking tasks were conducted: walking a straight line, with numerous turns, and a daily living activity. Three tri-axial accelerometers were attached at the shank, thigh, and lower back using elasticized straps. Annotation and simultaneous videotaping were used by physiotherapists to determine the start/end times of FoG episodes. Jansson et al. (2015) carried out stochastic anomaly detection in eye-tracking data for the quantification of motor symptoms in PD. The two approaches were based on the discordancy test to detect anomalies.

5.6   Bibliographic Notes

A textbook on the topic of this chapter is Japkowicz and Mohak (2011). The book by Pepe (2003) provides a thorough discussion of ROC curves and performance measures for binary classifiers. The first application of ROC in machine learning was by Spackman (1989), who demonstrated the value of ROC curves in comparing and evaluating different classification algorithms. For a discussion of the use of the AUC in the evaluation of classifiers, see also Bradley (1997). Precision-recall curves have been suggested to be better than ROC curves in highly imbalanced data sets (Davis and Goadrich, 2006). Sokolova and Lapalme (2009) presented a systematic analysis of 24 performance measures used in classification tasks, and Ferri et al. (2008) showed an experimental comparison of 18 measures.

Some variants of the bootstrap estimation methods, like the double bootstrap, the randomized bootstrap, and the randomized double bootstrap, were introduced by Efron (1983). Chernick (2007) offered a comprehensive and practical guide of bootstrap methods. For a review of the bootstrap variants, see also Jain et al. (1987) and Hinkley (1988). Kim (2009) empirically compared bootstrap and repeated cross-validation. Apart from the bootstrap method, the bolstered estimation method (Braga-Neto and Dougherty, 2004), where more confidence is attributed to points far from than near to the decision boundary, has also provided satisfactory results for small sample sizes. An alternative way of studying classifier performance is to use permutation tests (Ojala and Garriga, 2010).

Dietterich (1998) proposed the statistical comparison of the behavior of two algorithms on the same data set in a 5×2 cross-validation scheme based on a t-test, resulting in a smaller type I error than the traditional paired t-test over the usual k-fold cross-validation. The 5×2 cross-validation t-test was improved by Alpaydın (1999), who constructed a more robust 5×2 cross-validation F test with a lower type I error and higher probability of rejecting the alternative hypothesis when it is false. Bengio and Grandvalet (2004) and Markatou et al. (2005) addressed the problem of approximating the variance of the estimator provided by a k-fold cross-validation in a general framework. For classifier comparison over multiple data sets, Hull (1994) was the first to use nonparametric tests for comparing classifiers in information retrieval, whereas Brazdil and Soares (2000) used average ranks to compare classification algorithms. Salzberg (1997) mentioned the Bonferroni correction for the problem of multiple comparison of algorithms for the first time in the machine learning community. García and Herrera (2008) extended the work of Demšar (2006) by proposing the use of adjusted p-values for several post-hoc tests.

6 Feature Subset Selection

Nowadays large volumes of data are accessible to researchers in almost all branches of science. Examples of this accessibility are the volume of data generated from microarray or mass spectrometry in bioinformatics, data streams from stock market prices in finance, characteristics of stars and galaxies in astronomy, etc. Neuroscience is another field where the volume of available data is growing exponentially (Section 1.5). This is especially true of neuroimaging (Mwangi et al., 2014), where techniques like fMRI, MRI, MEG or SPECT are able to generate terabytes of data. The review of Haynes and Rees (2006) about the problem of classifying the cognitive state of a human subject with the objective of "brain reading" has highlighted the benefits of feature selection methods in neuroimaging. The dimensionality of the data needs to be reduced because classification performance drops sharply if the number of voxels exceeds the number of data points. The new technologies being developed in the fields of neuroanatomy, electrophysiology, or neurogenomics produce huge quantities of data that should be modeled following Occam's razor or the law of parsimony (Section 1.5.2). In all the above examples, it is usual to store variables that are irrelevant or redundant for the class or target variable. The main objective of the methods described in this chapter is to detect and remove these variables from the data set, eliminating information that is not necessary for modeling supervised classifiers.

This chapter is organized as follows. Section 6.1 introduces the concepts of relevance and redundancy and explains why it is necessary to search for the best subset of features. We also present the four issues affecting this search, that is, the starting point, the search organization, the evaluation strategy, and the stopping criterion. The benefits of the feature subset selection scheme are listed. Filter approaches select the subset without considering the supervised classification model to be used later on. They are explained and analyzed in Section 6.2. Wrapper methods, where the selection of a feature subset is carried out considering the classifier model, are the focus of Section 6.3. This section points out the different search strategies (mainly heuristics) for intelligently searching the feature space. Heuristics are divided into deterministic and nondeterministic methods. Nondeterministic heuristics are categorized as single-solution methods, i.e., when the current solution considers only one point of the variable space, and population-based methods, where a set of solutions evolves toward the optimal feature subset. Apart from filter and wrapper approaches, other types of methods consider variable selection as part of the training process. These embedded methods are explained in Section 6.4. Section 6.5 introduces hybrid feature selection methods where a wrapper approach is applied to the output of a filter method. Ensemble feature selection is designed to avoid the instability of some of the above methods, which are sensitive to small perturbations in the data set, and is shown in Section 6.6. Section 6.7 reports the results of a running example of some of the methods introduced in this chapter applied to the GABAergic interneuron nomenclature data set (Data Set 2 in Section 1.6.2). Section 6.8 concludes with some pointers to the literature on feature subset selection methods.

6.1   Overview of Feature Subset Selection

Feature subset selection (FSS) or **variable selection** (Lewis, 1962; Sebestyen, 1962) is the process of identifying and removing as many irrelevant and redundant variables as possible. This reduces the dimensionality of the data and may help learning algorithms to operate faster and more effectively. In some cases, it may improve the accuracy of future classification; in others, the result is a more compact, easily interpreted representation of the target concept. The price to be paid is an additional layer of complexity in the modeling task, as this feature selection process can entail a large computational burden if there are a large number of predictor variables.

A discrete feature X_i is said to be a **relevant feature** for the class variable C iff there exists some x_i and c for which $p(X_i = x_i) > 0$ such that $p(C = c|X_i = x_i) \neq p(C = c)$. A feature is said to be a **redundant feature** if it is highly correlated with one or more of the other features. While irrelevant variables are pure noise and introduce bias in the prediction, redundant variables provide no extra information about the class.

Supervised classification algorithms can be adversely affected by irrelevant and redundant features. The nearest neighbor algorithm (Section 7.1) is sensitive to irrelevant variables (Aha et al., 1991). The naive Bayes classifier (Section 8.4.1.1) can be negatively affected by redundant variables (Langley and Sage, 1994b) due to its assumption that features are conditionally independent given the class.

FSS methods operate in a different way from **dimensionality reduction** based on multivariate statistics, like principal component analysis (Section 2.4.3), factor analysis, or multidimensional scaling (Section 2.7). These methods create new features, usually as linear combinations of the original ones and can be considered as **feature extraction** methods. On the contrary, FSS methods do not alter the original representation of the variables and preserve their original semantics.

All FSS methods require a criterion to measure the goodness of the selected variables. For filter approaches (Section 6.2), this criterion is based on the intrinsic properties of the variables expressed in terms of correlation, mutual information, likelihood, etc. For wrapper methods (Section 6.3), the criterion takes into account the performance of the classification model. This model is induced from a labeled subset of the original data set with only the selected features as predictors. This criterion can refer to e.g., the classification accuracy, the sensitivity, the specificity or the area under the ROC curve (Chapter 5). In embedded methods (Section 6.4), the FSS is built into the classifier construction with a filter-type criterion guiding this building process.

Statistical approaches to FSS have been mainly characterized by filter and embedded approaches, while wrapper methods have been proposed by the machine learning community. Other differences between these two cultures (Section 1.5.2) refer to the sophistication of the search method used to find the optimal subset of variables. Simpler search methods like forward selection, backward elimination or stepwise selection have been common in statistics. However, machine learning-oriented FSS strategies rely on more intelligent search procedures based on metaheuristics, like simulated annealing, genetic algorithms, or scatter search. All these procedures can conduct a faster and deeper exploration of the huge space of possible feature subsets. Both types of search methods are discussed in Section 6.3.1.

Computing optimal solutions is intractable for many optimization problems. In practice, we are usually satisfied with "good" solutions, which are obtained by heuristic or metaheuristic algorithms. **Metaheuristics** are a family of approximate optimization techniques that provide "acceptable" solutions in a reasonable time in order to solve hard and complex optimization problems. Unlike exact optimization algorithms, metaheuristics do not guarantee the optimality of the resulting solutions.

The word **heuristic** has its origin in the old Greek word *heuriskein*, meaning the art of discovering new strategies (rules) to solve problems. The suffix *meta*, another Greek word, means "upper-level methodology." Metaheuristic search methods (Glover, 1986) can be defined as upper-level general methodologies (templates) that can be used as guiding principles for designing underlying heuristics to solve specific optimization problems.

FSS based on multivariate filtering or on wrapper approaches can be seen as a combinatorial optimization problem as displayed in the example of Figure 6.1. Given a set of predictor variables $\mathcal{X} = \{X_1, \ldots, X_n\}$, the FSS problem consists of selecting the optimal subset $\mathcal{S}^* \subseteq \mathcal{X}$ with respect to an objective score that, without loss of generality, should be maximized. Examples of objective scores are the score used in the correlation-based feature selection (for a multivariate filter approach) or the area under the ROC curve (for a wrapper approach).

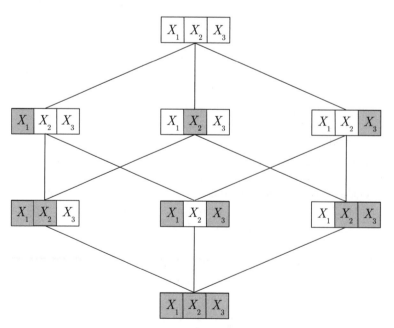

Figure 6.1 Search space for an FSS problem with three predictor variables. Each of the eight blocks represents one possible FSS. The filled rectangles in each block indicate the variables included in the selected subset. Edges connect two blocks accessible by the deletion or inclusion of one feature.

More formally, denoting this objective score by function f, we have:

$$f: \quad \begin{aligned} \mathcal{P}(\mathcal{X}) &\longrightarrow \mathbb{R} \\ \mathcal{S} \subseteq \mathcal{X} &\longmapsto f(\mathcal{S}), \end{aligned} \qquad (6.1)$$

where $\mathcal{P}(\mathcal{X})$ denotes the set of all possible subsets of $\mathcal{X}$, whose cardinality is given by 2^n. Each possible FSS $\mathcal{S}$ can be represented by a binary vector $\mathbf{s} = (s_1, \dots, s_n)$, with

$$s_i = \begin{cases} 1 & \text{if variable } X_i \text{ belongs to } \mathcal{S} \\ 0 & \text{otherwise} \end{cases}$$

for $i = 1, 2, \dots, n$. Using this bijection between subsets of $\mathcal{X}$ and binary vectors of dimension n, Equation (6.1) can be reformulated as

$$f: \quad \begin{aligned} \{0,1\}^n &\longrightarrow \mathbb{R} \\ \mathbf{s} = (s_1, \dots, s_n) &\longmapsto f(\mathbf{s}). \end{aligned}$$

With this notation, the optimal feature subset that $\mathbf{s}^*$ encodes, verifies $\mathbf{s}^* = \arg\max_{\mathbf{s} \in \{0,1\}^n} f(\mathbf{s})$.

Feature selection algorithms search the space of feature subsets. Four basic issues determine the nature of the search (Figure 6.2):

(a) *Starting point*. The selected point in the feature subset space from which to begin the search can affect the direction and the result of the search. One option is to begin with no features and successively add attributes. In this case, the search is said to move forward through the search space. Conversely, the search can begin with all features and successively remove attributes. In this case, the search moves backward through

(a) *Starting point*
   - No features
   - All features
   - A subset of features

(b) *Search organization*
   - Exhaustive
   - Forward
   - Backward
   - Stepwise
   - Based on metaheuristics

(c) *Evaluation strategy*
   - Filter
   - Wrapper

(d) *Stopping criterion*
   - Until no improvement of the objective function

Figure 6.2 Four characteristics affecting the nature of the search in the space of possible feature subsets.

the search space. Another alternative is to begin somewhere in the middle and move outward from this point.

(b) *Search organization*. An exhaustive search of the feature subspace is prohibitive for all but a small original number of features. Heuristic search strategies can yield good results, although they do not guarantee that the optimal subset will be found.

(c) *Evaluation strategy*. The manner in which feature subsets are evaluated is the largest differentiating factor of feature selection algorithms for classification. The filter approach operates independent of any learning algorithm, while the wrapper approach argues that a particular induction algorithm should be taken into account when selecting features.

(d) *Stopping criterion*. A feature selector must decide when to stop searching through the space of feature subsets. Depending on the evaluation strategy, a feature selector might stop adding or removing features when none of the evaluated alternatives improves upon the merit of the current feature subset. Alternatively, the algorithm might continue to revise the feature subset as long as the merit does not degrade.

6.2   Filter Approaches

Filter feature subset selection methods assess the relevance of a feature, or a subset of features, by looking only at intrinsic properties of the data. An example of these properties is the mutual information (Section 3.6) of each predictor variable and the class variable. Features with high mutual information are preferred over others that have small values for this objective score. Filter methods act as a preprocessing or screening step, which is independent of any supervised classification algorithm. They are designed to estimate the discriminatory power of predictor features based on scores founded on relevance (and sometimes redundancy).

In **univariate filtering**, a feature relevance score is calculated, and low-scoring features are removed. Afterwards, the subset of selected features is used as input variables for the classification algorithm. A clear disadvantage of univariate filter methods is that they ignore feature dependencies. For instance, they do not take into account redundancy among features. This redundancy can damage the behavior of the classification model. In order to overcome this problem, a number of **multivariate filter** techniques have been introduced. Figure 6.3 displays the main characteristics of both univariate and multivariate filter approaches.

Advantages of filter techniques are that they easily scale to very high-dimensional data sets, they are computationally simple and fast, they avoid overfitting problems, and they are independent of the classification algorithm. As a result, filter feature selection needs to be performed only once. This selection is evaluated later with different classification models.

One important aspect of FSS, using both filter and wrapper approaches is the correct evaluation of the classifiers (their performance estimation) which are built on the resulting data set (Smialowski et al., 2010). Figure 6.4 illustrates how to evaluate a filter subset selection method with a hold-out scheme (Figure 5.3). In the preprocessing step, filter

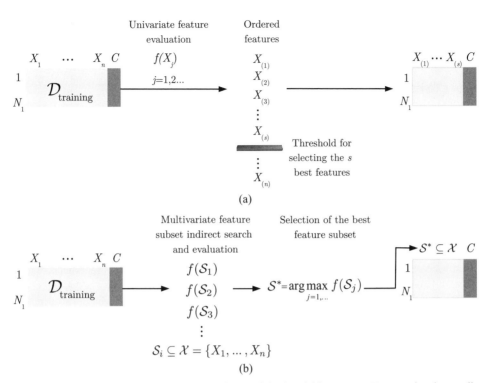

(a)

(b)

Figure 6.3 Filter approaches. (a) Univariate filter: original variables $X_1, \ldots, X_n$ are ordered according to $f(X_1), \ldots, f(X_n)$ resulting in the ordered variables $X_{(1)}, \ldots, X_{(n)}$. A threshold chooses the s best variables of that ranking, which is the final feature subset on which to start the classifier learning. (b) Multivariate filter: a subset of features S is searched and evaluated according to $f(S)$. The best subset S^* is found as an optimization problem, and this is the final feature subset on which to start the classifier learning.

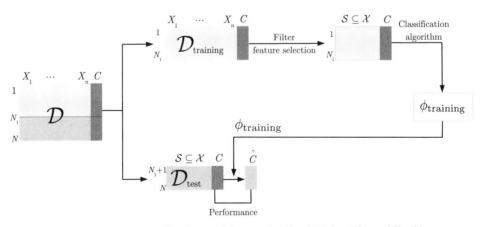

Figure 6.4 Evaluation of the classification model output by filter FSS (see Figure 6.3) with a hold-out scheme.

feature selection reduces the set of features $\mathcal{X} = \{X_1, \ldots, X_n\}$ to $S \subseteq \mathcal{X}$. Subsequently, the reduced training set is used to learn a classifier ϕ_{training}. During the testing phase, the trained classifier ϕ_{training} is evaluated using an independent test $\mathcal{D}_{\text{test}}$ with the feature space reduced to S according to the filter feature selection derived in the previous step. The classifier predicts $\hat{c}$ for each instance in $\mathcal{D}_{\text{test}}$. Various performance measures can then be computed by comparing c versus $\hat{c}$ values.

6.2.1   Univariate Filters

The operations carried out by univariate filter methods, that is, the computation of the score for each predictor variable and their posterior ranking, can be mathematically expressed by:

$$
\begin{array}{rcl}
f: & \mathcal{X} & \longrightarrow & \mathbb{R} \\
& X_j & \longmapsto & f(X_j),
\end{array}
$$

where the input space of the objective score f corresponds to the set of predictor variables $\mathcal{X}$. Note that this input space was for multivariate filtering or wrapper approaches (Equation (6.1)) equal to $\mathcal{P}(\mathcal{X})$, the set of all possible subsets of $\mathcal{X}$. After computing the objective function for each predictor variable, these variables are ordered according to their objective values. Finally, a threshold is used to remove variables whose objective values are below the specified limit.

Table 6.1 shows a list containing the different types of univariate filter methods introduced in this section.

6.2.1.1 Parametric Methods

These filter methods assume a parametric distribution on the marginal distribution of the features or even on the conditional distribution of the features given a value of the class variable. For discrete variables, these distributions are assumed to be categorical. For

Table 6.1 Univariate filter methods with their seminal paper

Univariate filter method	Seminal paper
Parametric methods:	
Discrete predictors:	
Mutual information	Blanco et al. (2005)
Gain ratio	Hall and Smith (1998)
Symmetrical uncertainty	Hall (1999)
Chi-squared	Forman (2003)
Odds ratio	Mladenic and Grobelnik (1999)
Probability ratio	Mladenic and Grobelnik (1999)
Bi-normal separation	Forman (2003)
Continuous predictors:	
t-test family	Jafari and Azuaje (2006)
ANOVA	Jafari and Azuaje (2006)
Model-free methods:	
Threshold number of misclassification	Ben-Dor et al. (2000)
P-metric	Slonim et al. (2000)
Mann–Whitney test	Thomas et al. (2001)
Kruskal–Wallis test	Lan and Vucetic (2011)
Between-groups to within-groups sum of squares	Dudoit et al. (2002)
Scores based on estimating probability density functions	Inza et al. (2004)
Random permutations	Pan (2003)

continuous variables, Gaussian assumptions have dominated the field, although other types of parametric approaches, like gamma distribution models (Newton et al., 2001), can be found in the literature. Parametric distributions are capable of outputting the density of the score used to rank the features. This density is used to establish the threshold, thereby transforming the decision of selecting or removing a feature into a hypothesis test.

A. Discrete Predictors. For discrete predictors, several univariate feature selection methods can be found in the literature. The **mutual information** (Section 3.6.4) between two variables X_j and C:

$$f(X_j) = \mathbb{I}(X_j, C) = - \sum_{i=1}^{R_j} \sum_{c=1}^{R} p(X_j = i, C = c) \log_2 p(X_j = i, C = c),$$

where R_j and R denote the cardinalities of X_j and C, respectively, measures the reduction in the uncertainty of one variable (variable C, for example) when the value of the other variable (X_j, for example) is known. Under the null hypothesis of independence between X_j and C, the statistic $2N\mathbb{I}(X_j, C) \sim \chi^2_{(R_j-1)(R-1)}$, with N denoting the sample size. This property was used in Blanco et al. (2005) to select the predictor variables with the s highest mutual information values, where s was fixed according to the p-values. Variables with small p-values (where the null hypothesis of independence is rejected) are selected as relevant for the class variable. The mutual information measure favors variables with many different values over others with few different values. A fairer selection is to use **gain ratio** (Hall and Smith, 1998) defined as $\frac{\mathbb{I}(X_j, C)}{\mathbb{H}(X_j)}$ (see Section 7.2 for details) or the **symmetrical uncertainty coefficient** (Hall, 1999) defined as $2\frac{\mathbb{I}(X_i, C)}{\mathbb{H}(X_i) + \mathbb{H}(C)}$.

Chi-squared based feature selection uses the common statistical test that measures the divergence from the distribution expected if one assumes that feature occurrence is actually independent of the class value.

In the example in Table 6.2, with binary predictor variable X_j and class variable C, the chi-squared score (Section 4.2.8) is computed as:

$$f(X_j) = \frac{\left(N_{11} - \frac{N_{1\bullet}N_{\bullet1}}{N}\right)^2}{\frac{N_{1\bullet}N_{\bullet1}}{N}} + \frac{\left(N_{12} - \frac{N_{1\bullet}N_{\bullet2}}{N}\right)^2}{\frac{N_{1\bullet}N_{\bullet2}}{N}} + \frac{\left(N_{21} - \frac{N_{2\bullet}N_{\bullet1}}{N}\right)^2}{\frac{N_{2\bullet}N_{\bullet1}}{N}} + \frac{\left(N_{22} - \frac{N_{2\bullet}N_{\bullet2}}{N}\right)^2}{\frac{N_{2\bullet}N_{\bullet2}}{N}}.$$

Features are ranked in ascending order according to their p-value for the null hypothesis of independence. For instance, the variables most dependent on the class (smallest p-values) rank first. After fixing a threshold for the p-value, the classifier will only take into account variables with p-values smaller than the threshold (Forman, 2003).

Table 6.2 Contingency table for binary feature X_j and a binary class variable C

		C		
		1	2	Marginal
X_j	1	N_{11}	N_{12}	$N_{1\bullet}$
	2	N_{21}	N_{22}	$N_{2\bullet}$
	Marginal	$N_{\bullet1}$	$N_{\bullet2}$	N

For binary feature X_j and binary class C, the **odds ratio** of X_j is its odds occurring in the positive class value normalized by that of the negative class value. With the notation introduced in Section 5.2.1.1 for the number of TP, FP, FN, and TN, all given in the matrix

$$X_j$$

$$C \begin{array}{c} + \\ - \end{array} \begin{pmatrix} \begin{array}{cc} + & - \end{array} \\ \begin{array}{cc} \text{TP} & \text{FN} \\ \text{FP} & \text{TN} \end{array} \end{pmatrix},$$

the odds ratio score for variable X_j is computed as

$$f(X_j) = \frac{\left(\frac{\text{TP}}{\text{TP+FN}}\right) \cdot \left(\frac{\text{FN}}{\text{FP+TN}}\right)}{\left(\frac{\text{FN}}{\text{TP+FN}}\right) \cdot \left(\frac{\text{FP}}{\text{FP+TN}}\right)}.$$

The features with the highest odds ratio scores will be selected (Mladenic and Grobelnik, 1999).

For binary feature X_j and binary class C, the **probability ratio** of X_j is the sample estimate of the probability of X_j occurring in the positive class divided by the sample estimate of the probability of X_j occurring in the negative class, that is,

$$f(X_j) = \frac{\frac{\text{TP}}{\text{TP+FN}}}{\frac{\text{FP}}{\text{FP+TN}}}.$$

As in the odds ratio score, features with the highest probability ratio scores will be selected (Mladenic and Grobelnik, 1999).

The **bi-normal separation** for a feature X_j (Forman, 2003) is defined as

$$f(X_j) = F_Z^{-1}\left(\frac{\text{TP}}{\text{TP + FN}}\right) - F_Z^{-1}\left(\frac{\text{FP}}{\text{FP + TN}}\right),$$

where F_Z^{-1} is the standard normal distribution's inverse cumulative probability function. The features with the highest bi-normal separation scores will be selected.

Plant et al. (2010) detected brain atrophy patterns for the prediction of AD applying a univariate filter based on mutual information with Bayesian classifiers and support vector machines.

B. Continuous Predictors. The two univariate filter methods described in this paragraph assume Gaussianity for the conditional density of each predictor variable given any value of the class variable. In binary classification problems, Welch t-test (Section 4.2.5) for the unpaired two-sample test was proposed as a member of univariate filter methods based on the t**-test family** (Jafari and Azuaje, 2006). For nonbinary classification problems, Jafari and Azuaje (2006) proposed the one-way repeated-measures ANOVA test (Section 4.2.7).

Chaves et al. (2009) chose a t-test based filter feature selection approach in combination with a support vector machine for the early detection of the AD with SPECT data.

6.2.1.2 *Model-Free Methods*

The filter methods within this category do not assume any probability distribution for the predictor variables. For this reason, the threshold for selecting features is determined based on a p-value, that can be derived from nonparametric tests (Table 4.5).

The **threshold number of misclassification** (TNoM) score (Ben-Dor et al., 2000) of a variable X_j is a measure of its relevance for classification purposes. The intuition is that an informative variable X_j has quite different values in the two classes (for binary problems). Therefore, we should be able to separate these by a threshold value t. TNoM seeks the best decision stump for each predictor variable X_j. A **decision stump** is a machine learning model consisting of a one-level classification tree (Section 7.2). They are sometimes also called 1-rule (Section 7.3).

More formally, in a binary classification problem with $\Omega_C = \{+, -\}$, the decision stump $\phi_{ds}(X_j, t)$ for variable X_j by a threshold value t is

$$\phi_{ds}(X_j, t) = \begin{cases} + & \text{if } X_j > t \\ - & \text{otherwise.} \end{cases}$$

The TNoM score of a variable is simply defined as the number of errors made by its best decision stump, that is,

$$f(X_j) = \min_t \text{Err}(\phi_{ds}(X_j, t)),$$

where $\text{Err}(\phi_{ds}(X_j, t))$ denotes the number of instances misclassified by the decision stump with a threshold value t. Small values of TNoM correspond to relevant variables.

The *P*-**metric** filter (Slonim et al., 2000) ranks the features according to the *P*-metric of a variable X_j and the binary class variable C (with $\Omega_C = \{c_1, c_2\}$), defined as $f(X_j) = P(X_j, C) = \frac{\bar{x}_{j_1} - \bar{x}_{j_2}}{s_{X_{j_1}} + s_{X_{j_2}}}$, where $\bar{x}_{j_1}$ and $\bar{x}_{j_2}$ denote the sample means of variable X_i for $C = c_1$ and $C = c_2$, respectively, and $s_{X_{j_1}}$ and $s_{X_{j_2}}$ represent the corresponding sampling standard deviations. Predictor variables are ranked in descending order according to their corresponding *P*-metric. The top ranked variables are selected.

The Mann–Whitney test based method for testing the equality of two population means in two unpaired samples (Section 4.2.5) was applied by Thomas et al. (2001) for a binary class. Variables are sorted according to their p-values. Small p-values are ranked highest.

The Kruskal–Wallis test based method (Section 4.2.7) for testing the equality of more than two population means from unpaired samples was applied in Lan and Vucetic (2011) for a multi-class problem.

The ranking of variables can also be carried out by the ratio of their **between-groups** ($BSS(X_j)$) to **within-groups sum of squares** ($WSS(X_j)$) (Dudoit et al., 2002). For variable X_j, this ratio is

$$f(X_j) = \frac{BSS(X_j)}{WSS(X_j)} = \frac{\sum_{i=1}^{N} \sum_{k=1}^{R} \mathbb{I}(C_i = c_k)(\bar{x}_{j_k} - \bar{x}_j)^2}{\sum_{i=1}^{N} \sum_{k=1}^{R} \mathbb{I}(C_i = c_k)(x_{ij} - \bar{x}_{j_k})^2},$$

where $\bar{x}_j$ denotes the sample mean of variable X_j across all samples, $\bar{x}_{j_k}$ denotes the sample mean of variable X_j across samples belonging to class c_k, x_{ij} is the value of variable X_j in sample i and $\mathbb{I}(\cdot)$ is the indicator function (Equation (3.3)). The variables with largest $\frac{BSS(X_j)}{WSS(X_j)}$ ratios are selected. The rationale of this selection is that variables whose sample means for the different class values are highly variable are good candidates for discriminating the class variable.

Scores based on estimating probability density functions were proposed in Inza et al. (2004). Examples include a variant of the Kullback–Leibler divergence (Section 3.6.5) for each variable X_j

$$f(X_j) = \sum_{i=1}^{R_j} p(X_j = i|C = c_1) \log_2 \frac{p(X_j = i|C = c_1)}{p(X_j = i)}$$
$$+ \sum_{i=1}^{R_j} p(X_j = i|C = c_2) \log_2 \frac{p(X_j = i|C = c_2)}{p(X_j = i)},$$

as well as the **Kolmogorov dependence**

$$f(X_j) = \sum_{i=1}^{R_j} |p(X_j = i|C = c_1) - p(X_j = i|C = c_2)| p(X_j = i).$$

Other measures based on probability density functions can be found in Cha (2007).

The use of random permutations of the data for estimating the reference distribution of the statistic and comparing the behavior of a variable among the different class values was used by Pan (2003).

6.2.2 Multivariate Filters

Multivariate filter methods choose the subset of features according to their relevance (with respect to the class) and redundancy. Table 6.3 contains a list of some representative methods of this approach.

The **FOCUS algorithm** was introduced by Almuallim and Dietterich (1992). FOCUS evaluates subset S of binary features in a binary classification problem, with the following information theoretic formula:

$$f(S) = -\sum_{i=1}^{2^{|S|}} \frac{N_i^+ + N_i^-}{N} \left(\frac{N_i^+}{N_i^+ + N_i^-} \log_2 \frac{N_i^+}{N_i^+ + N_i^-} + \frac{N_i^-}{N_i^+ + N_i^-} \log_2 \frac{N_i^-}{N_i^+ + N_i^-} \right), \quad (6.2)$$

where $2^{|S|}$ represents the number of possible value assignments of feature subset S, and N_i^+ and N_i^- denote the number of positive and negative cases, respectively, in the ith possible assignment of S. N denotes the total number of instances. Each of these possible assignments is added to the FOCUS score according to its purity with respect to the class variable. The FOCUS score measures the overall entropy of the class values in these different assignments. S is output by means of a forward search starting from scratch. At each stage, the feature that minimizes Equation (6.2) is added to the current feature subset.

Kira and Rendell (1992) introduced the **RELIEF algorithm**. Instead of generating feature subsets, RELIEF focuses on sampling instances without explicitly searching for feature subsets. The underlying idea is that features whose values can distinguish between

Table 6.3 Multivariate filter methods with their seminal paper

Multivariate filter method	Seminal paper
FOCUS algorithm	Almuallim and Dietterich (1992)
RELIEF algorithm	Kira and Rendell (1992)
Las Vegas algorithm for filter feature selection	Liu and Setiono (1996)
Correlation-based feature selection	Hall (1999)
Conditional mutual information	Fleuret (2004)

instances that are close to each other are relevant. Therefore, two nearest neighbors are sought for each instance $\mathbf{x} \in \mathcal{D}$, one is near-hit $\mathbf{x}^h$, the other is near-miss $\mathbf{x}^m$. Ideally, a feature is relevant if its values are the same in $\mathbf{x}$ and $\mathbf{x}^h$ and different in $\mathbf{x}$ and $\mathbf{x}^m$. This check can be implemented in terms of a distance between the feature values: the distance should be minimum for $\mathbf{x}$ and $\mathbf{x}^h$ and maximum for $\mathbf{x}$ and $\mathbf{x}^m$. The distance of each feature for each randomly picked instance is accumulated in a weight vector $\mathbf{w} = (w_1, \ldots, w_n)$ of the same dimension as the number of features. The features whose weights exceed a relevance threshold are relevant.

Algorithm 6.1: The RELIEF algorithm

Input : A data set $\mathcal{D}$ of N labeled instances, a vector $\mathbf{w} = (w_1, \ldots, w_n)$
   initialized as $(0, \ldots, 0)$
Output: The vector $\mathbf{w}$ of the relevance estimates of the n predictor variables

1 **for** $i = 1$ **to** N **do**
2   Randomly select an instance $\mathbf{x} \in \mathcal{D}$
3   Find near-hit $\mathbf{x}^h \in \mathcal{D}$, and near-miss $\mathbf{x}^m \in \mathcal{D}$
4   **for** $j = 1$ **to** n **do**
5          $w_j = w_j - \frac{1}{N} d_j(\mathbf{x}, \mathbf{x}^h) + \frac{1}{N} d_j(\mathbf{x}, \mathbf{x}^m)$
6   **endfor**
7 **endfor**

The pseudocode of RELIEF is presented in Algorithm 6.1. Expression $d_j(\mathbf{x}, \mathbf{x}^h)$ denotes the distance between the jth components of instances $\mathbf{x}$ and $\mathbf{x}^h$. The interpretation is analogous for $d_j(\mathbf{x}, \mathbf{x}^m)$. Notice that the random selection of N instances from $\mathcal{D}$ (line 2) is done with replacement.

Liu and Setiono (1996) described **Las Vegas algorithm for filter feature selection**. This algorithm generates a random subset $\mathcal{S}$ of random size from the feature subset space during each round of execution. If $\mathcal{S}$ contains fewer features than the current best subset, its **inconsistency rate** is compared with the inconsistency rate of the best subset. If $\mathcal{S}$ is at least as consistent as the current best subset, this subset is replaced by $\mathcal{S}$. The inconsistency rate of the labeled data set prescribed by a given feature subset $\mathcal{S}$ is defined based on all its possible value assignments. For an assignment of the variables in $\mathcal{S}$, the inconsistency count is the number of instances with this assignment minus instances with the most frequent class value for the same assignment. The overall inconsistency rate is the sum of the inconsistency counts of all possible value assignments divided by the total number of instances.

Correlation-based feature selection (CFS) was introduced by Hall (1999). CFS seeks for a feature subset that contains variables that are highly correlated with the class, yet uncorrelated with each other. More formally, denoting a subset of the predictive features $\mathcal{X}$ by $\mathcal{S}$, CFS looks for $\mathcal{S}^* = \arg\max_{\mathcal{S} \subseteq \mathcal{X}} f(\mathcal{S})$, where

$$f(\mathcal{S}) = \frac{\displaystyle\sum_{X_i \in \mathcal{S}} r(X_i, C)}{\sqrt{s + (s-1) \displaystyle\sum_{X_i, X_j \in \mathcal{S}} r(X_i, X_j)}},$$

s is the number of selected features, $r(X_i,C)$ is the correlation between feature X_i and class variable C, and $r(X_i,X_j)$ is the correlation between features X_i and X_j. The correlation $r(X_i,C)$ between one selected feature and the class variable (and also the correlation between features) is given by the symmetrical uncertainty coefficient defined in Section 6.2.1.1.

Because an exhaustive enumeration of all possible features subsets is prohibitive even for moderate values of n, Hall (1999) searched for the best subset using three heuristic search strategies: forward selection, backward elimination, and best-first search. Other metaheuristics like tabu search, variable neighbor search, genetic algorithms, and estimation of distribution algorithms, among others, have been applied for CFS. See Section 6.3.1 for details on these search procedures.

Fleuret (2004) proposed a **feature ranking criterion based on conditional mutual information** (Section 3.6.4) for binary data. The idea is that feature X_i is good only if $\mathbb{I}(X_i,C|X_j)$ is large for every already selected X_j. At each step, the feature X^* such that

$$X^* = \arg \max_{X_i \notin \mathcal{S}_c} \left\{ \min_{X_j \in \mathcal{S}_c} \mathbb{I}(X_i,C|X_j) \right\}$$

is added to the current subset $\mathcal{S}_c$ containing the selected features.

DeFelipe et al. (2013) used univariate filtering (gain ratio measure) and multivariate filtering (CFS) to classify cortical GABAergic interneurons. Based on a set of 2,886 morphological variables from the 3D reconstructions of 241 neurons, including information about dendrites, axons, and soma, the above two filter methods were applied to k-nearest neighbors, classification trees, support vector machines and artificial neural networks (Chapter 7), naive Bayes (Chapter 8), and metaclassifiers (Chapter 9). Morales et al. (2013) applied univariate and multivariate filter feature selection methods over MRI data in combination with Bayesian classifiers and support vector machines to predict dementia in PD patients.

6.3 Wrapper Methods

Wrapper methods (John et al., 1994; Langley and Sage, 1994a) evaluate each possible subset of features with a criterion consisting of the estimated performance of the classifier built with this subset of features. Any of the criteria introduced in Chapter 5, i.e., accuracy, error rate, sensitivity, specificity, precision, negative predictive value, F_1-measure, Cohen's kappa, or the area under the ROC curve, are possible objective functions for guiding the search for the best subset of features. Figure 6.5 illustrates the main characteristics of wrapper approaches for FSS.

Wrapper methods are dependent on the classifier as they perform a search over the space of all possible subsets of features, repeatedly calling the induction algorithm as a subroutine to evaluate various subsets of features. For large-scale problems, however, wrapper methods are often impractical, and instead filter feature scoring metrics are commonly used.

Wrapper methods provide interaction between the subset search and the model selection algorithm. Accordingly, they take into account feature dependencies. On the other hand, wrapper approaches have a high associated computational cost when n is large, and there is risk of overfitting if the estimation of the performance criteria is not properly designed.

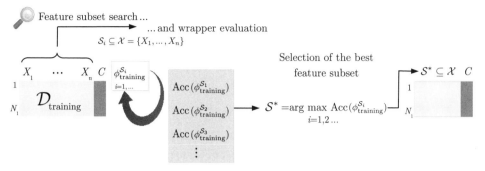

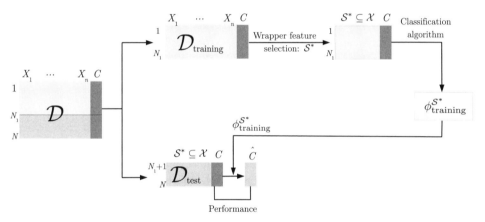

Figure 6.5 The wrapper approach for FSS. Each feature subset $\mathcal{S}_i \subseteq \mathcal{X} = \{X_1, \ldots, X_n\}$ is here evaluated with the (estimated) classification accuracy (Acc) of the classifier $\phi_{\text{training}}^{\mathcal{S}_i}$, built from $\mathcal{S}_i$ in the training set $\mathcal{D}_{\text{training}}$.

Figure 6.6 Evaluation of the classification model output by a wrapper FSS (see Figure 6.5) with a hold-out scheme.

Figure 6.6 illustrates how a wrapper FSS method is evaluated with a hold-out scheme. The only difference with the scheme for the filter feature subset evaluation shown in Figure 6.4 is how each candidate subset of features is evaluated. In a wrapper FSS, the algorithm interacts with the search process (see Figure 6.5).

Armañanzas et al. (2013) selected PD nonmotor severity symptoms applying a wrapper approach based on estimation of distribution algorithms for five different classification paradigms (naive Bayes, k-nearest neighbors, linear discriminant analysis, classification trees, and artificial neural networks) in a data set containing information on 410 patients and 87 predictor variables. These features came from a wide range of PD symptoms, such as cognitive impairment, psychiatric complications, autonomic dysfunctions, or sleep disturbance. Guerra et al. (2011) compared supervised and unsupervised classification to distinguish pyramidal neurons from interneurons. Classification trees, k-nearest neighbors, multi-layer perceptron, naive Bayes, and logistic regression were the selected supervised classification algorithms, whereas hierarchical clustering (Chapter 11) was the chosen clustering method for the comparison. They compared multivariate filter and wrapper FSS using, in both cases, forward selection, backward elimination and genetic algorithms as search strategies. Mitchell et al. (2004) presented different case studies to distinguish cognitive states, like looking at a picture or a sentence, reading an ambiguous or nonambiguous sentence. Filter and wrapper FSS methods were successfully applied to Bayesian classifiers, support vector machines and k-nearest neighbors. To solve the deception detection problem, Jin et al. (2009) used support vector machines in combination with two filter, two wrapper and one ensemble feature selection method[1] able to select only 124 features out of an original set of 65,166 features.

6.3.1   Search Strategies

An exhaustive search for the best subset of features can become computationally intensive and even prohibitive when the number n of features is large. Several heuristics have been proposed for intelligently exploring the space of features of cardinality 2^n. These heuristics are categorized as either deterministic or nondeterministic. The solution provided by a given deterministic heuristic for a fixed FSS problem is always the same. However, a non-deterministic heuristic incorporates stochasticity into the search process. Consequently the results can vary under its different executions. The nondeterministic heuristics presented in this section are organized (see Table 6.4) according to the number of solutions retained in each iteration: single-solution and population-based methods.

Notice that all the search strategies can be applied not only for wrapper approaches but also for multivariate filter procedures.

6.3.1.1 Deterministic Heuristics

Sequential feature selection algorithms (Fu, 1968) start with an empty (full set) and add features (remove features) until they reach the maximum or a local maximum objective function. **Sequential forward feature selection** (Fu, 1968) starts with an empty set of features and adds the feature yielding the highest value for the objective function at the first step. From the second step onward, the remaining features are added one by one to the current subset, and the new subset is evaluated. The feature whose selection most improves the objective is selected and added to the current subset. The process is repeated until the required number of features is added or there is no further improvement in the objective function. **Sequential backward feature elimination** algorithm (Marill and Green, 1963) starts from the complete set of variables and successively removes the feature whose removal yields the highest increase in the objective function. It has similar stopping criteria to the sequential forward feature selection algorithm. An alternative approach, called **stepwise bi-directional feature selection**, uses both addition and deletion of features. After adding each new variable, it removes any variables that no longer provide an improvement in the objective function. Sequential forward, sequential backward, and stepwise feature selection can be seen as instantiations of a general **greedy hill climbing** procedure (John et al. [1994] for feature selection). This procedure considers local changes to the current feature subset that are repeated until there is no further improvement. A local change is simply the addition or deletion of a single feature from the subset. **Best-first search** (see Xu et al. [1988] in the context of feature selection) is a search strategy that can backtrack along the search path. Like greedy hill climbing, best-first search moves through the search space by making local changes to the current feature subset. However, unlike hill climbing,

---

[1] Ensemble feature selection aims to combine the outputs of multiple feature selectors, thereby producing a more robust result for the subsequent classifier learning tasks.

Table 6.4 Heuristic strategies for FSS

Heuristic	Seminal paper in FSS
Deterministic heuristics:	
Sequential feature selection	Fu (1968)
Sequential forward feature selection	Fu (1968)
Sequential backward feature elimination	Marill and Green (1963)
Greedy hill climbing	John et al. (1994)
Best-first	Xu et al. (1988)
Plus-L-Minus-r algorithm	Stearns (1976)
Floating search selection	Pudil et al. (1994)
Tabu search	Zhang and Sun (2002)
Branch and bound	Narendra and Fukunaga (1977)
Nondeterministic heuristics:	
Single-solution metaheuristics:	
Simulated annealing	Doak (1992)
Las Vegas algorithm	Liu and Motoda (1998)
Greedy randomized adaptive search procedure	Bermejo et al. (2011)
Variable neighborhood search	García-Torres et al. (2005)
Population-based metaheuristics:	
Scatter search	García-López et al. (2006)
Ant colony optimization	Al-Am (2005)
Particle swarm optimization	Lin et al. (2008)
Evolutionary algorithms:	
Genetic algorithms	Siedlecki and Sklansky (1989)
Estimation of distribution algorithms	Inza et al. (2000)
Differential evolution	Khushaba et al. (2009)
Genetic programming	Muni et al. (2004)
Evolution strategies	Valtokin et al. (2009)

if the path being explored begins to look less promising, the best-first search can backtrack to a more promising previous subset and continue the search from there.

The **Plus-L-Minus-r algorithm** (Stearns, 1976) is a procedure allowing some back-tracking during the feature selection process. If $L > r$, it is a bottom-up (forward) procedure. L features are added to the current subset using sequential forward feature selection, and the worst r features are removed using sequential backward feature elimination. If $L < r$, then the procedure is top-down (backward), starting from the complete set of features, removing r, then adding L successively until the stopping criterion is met. **Floating search selection** methods (Pudil et al., 1994), with sequential forward floating selection and sequential backward floating selection, may be seen as a variant of the above Plus-L-Minus-r algorithm, in which the values of L and r are allowed to "float," that is, they may change at different stages of the selection process.

Tabu search was proposed by Glover (1989). The use of memory, which stores information on the search process, is the particular characteristic of tabu search. Tabu search works like a local search algorithm. However, it accepts worse solutions to escape from local optima when all neighbors are non-improving solutions. Usually, the whole neighborhood is explored. The best solution in the neighborhood is selected as the new current solution, even if it does not improve the best found solution.

Tabu search dynamically transforms the neighborhood generating cycles, whereby previously visited solutions could possibly be visited again. To avoid this drawback, tabu search manages a memory of the recently applied solutions or movements. This is called the tabu list and can be seen as a short-term memory. It is updated at each iteration of tabu search and usually contains a constant number of tabu movements. A seminal paper on tabu search for FSS was presented by Zhang and Sun (2002).

Branch and bound (Lawler and Wood, 1966) is a very efficient algorithm that avoids exhaustive enumeration by rejecting suboptimal subsets without direct evaluation and guarantees that the selected subset yields the global maximum of any criterion satisfying monotonicity. The FSS problem solved by branch and bound is to select a subset of m features from a larger set of n features. In this formulation of the FSS problem, the cardinality of the search space is given by $\binom{n}{m}$, a smaller quantity than the cardinality of the standard formulation, that is, 2^n.

An objective score f verifies the monotonicity property if for all pairs of subsets, $\mathcal{S}_1$ and $\mathcal{S}_2$ such that $\mathcal{S}_2 \subseteq \mathcal{S}_1$, then $f(\mathcal{S}_1) \geq f(\mathcal{S}_2)$ is satisfied. In other words, a subset of features should not be better than any larger set that contains that subset.

The branch and bound algorithm uses a representation of the search space in the form of a tree. This tree represents the variables to be discarded at each step of the algorithm at different levels. The algorithm applies the monotonicity criterion to this enumeration tree by determining a lower bound, B, for the value of the criterion (objective score). This means that whenever the criterion evaluated for any node in the tree is less than B, the subsets represented by all nodes that are successors of that node also have criterion values less than B (according to the monotonicity property). Therefore they cannot be the optimal solution.

The branch and bound algorithm successively generates portions of the solution tree and computes the criterion. Whenever a suboptimal partial sequence or node is found with a criterion value smaller than B, the subtree under the node is implicitly rejected, and enumeration begins on partial sequences that have not yet been explored (Figure 6.7).

The algorithm is independent of the ordering of the features in the solution tree. No sequence is enumerated more than once, and all possible sequences are considered, either explicitly or implicitly, guaranteeing the optimality of the target subset. Narendra and Fukunaga (1977) and Kohavi and John (1997) applied branch and bound for FSS.

6.3.1.2 Nondeterministic Heuristics

A. Single-Solution Metaheuristics. Simulated annealing (Kirkpatrick et al., 1983) is based on the principles of statistical mechanics, whereby a metal is heated and then slowly cooled to produce a strong crystalline structure. The strength of the structure produced by the annealing process depends on the cooling rate of the metals. If the initial temperature is not high enough or the cooling rate is too fast, imperfections occur. In this case, the cooling solid will not attain thermal equilibrium at each temperature. Strong crystals are grown from careful and slow cooling. The simulated annealing algorithm simulates the energy changes in a system subject to a cooling process until it converges to an equilibrium state.

Simulated annealing is a stochastic algorithm that enables, under some conditions, the degradation of a solution. The objective is to avoid trapping in local optima and thus to delay convergence. From an initial solution, **s**, simulated annealing proceeds in several

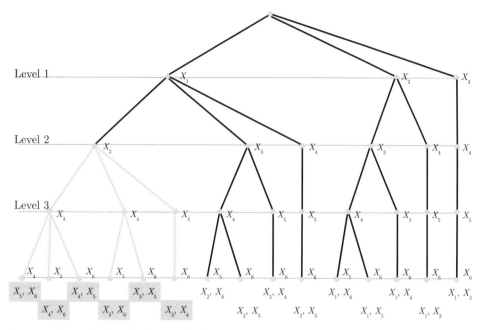

Figure 6.7 Example of a solution tree for the branch and bound algorithm, with $n = 6$ and $m = 2$. We are searching for the best subset of two features from the initial set of six. The nodes at a given level do not have the same number of terminal nodes. Branch (X_1, X_2) has three successors, while branch (X_1, X_4) has only one. If the suboptimality condition is not satisfied for branch (X_1, X_2) (i.e., $f(\mathcal{X} \setminus \{X_1, X_2\}) = f(\{X_3, X_4, X_5, X_6\}) < B$), six feature subsets of size two ($\{X_5, X_6\}$, $\{X_4, X_6\}$, $\{X_4, X_5\}$, $\{X_3, X_6\}$, $\{X_3, X_5\}$, and $\{X_3, X_4\}$), are rejected (without any evaluation) as being suboptimal (in gray). For branch (X_1, X_4), only one single subset $\{X_2, X_3, X_5, X_6\}$ could be rejected. In this example, the subtree in gray is the only rejected part. This would be pruned and not actually shown in a branch and bound tree. Thus, the nine subsets (with two features each) shown in black are the selected subsets.

iterations. At each iteration, a random neighbor is generated. Movements that improve the objective function are always accepted. Otherwise, the neighbor $\mathbf{s'}$ is selected with a given probability that depends on the current temperature, T, and the amount of degradation, $f(\mathbf{s}) - f(\mathbf{s'}) > 0$, of the objective function. This probability usually follows the **Boltzmann distribution**:

$$p(\mathbf{s'}|\mathbf{s}, T) = e^{-\frac{f(\mathbf{s}) - f(\mathbf{s'})}{T}}.$$

Temperature $T > 0$ acts as a control parameter. In the first iterations, there is a high probability of worse solutions that the current one being accepted with high values of T. At a particular value of T, many trials are explored. Once some sort of equilibrium is reached,[2] the temperature is gradually reduced according to a cooling schedule, expressed by a function $g(T)$, verifying that the probability of accepting non-improving solutions is almost zero at the end of the search. An example of a cooling scheme is an exponential schedule, $g(T) = T_0 \alpha^T$, where T_0 denotes the initial temperature and α is a constant factor $(0 < \alpha < 1)$.

---

[2] This might be a certain number of iterations or it could be until there has been no change in the solution for a certain number of iterations.

Algorithm 6.2 describes the simulated annealing algorithm template. The use of simulated annealing for FSS was first proposed by Doak (1992).

Algorithm 6.2: The simulated annealing algorithm

Input : Cooling schedule $g(T)$; $\mathbf{s} = \mathbf{s}_0$; $T = T_0$
Output: Best solution found

1 **repeat**
2 | **repeat**
3 | | Generate a random neighbor $\mathbf{s}'$
4 | | $\triangle f = f(\mathbf{s}) - f(\mathbf{s}')$
5 | | **if** $\triangle f \leq 0$ **then** $\mathbf{s} = \mathbf{s}'$
6 | | **else** Accept $\mathbf{s}'$ with a probability $e^{\frac{-\triangle f}{T}}$
7 | **until** Equilibrium condition is met
8 | $T = g(T)$
9 **until** Stopping criterion is satisfied

Las Vegas algorithm (Babai, 1979) consists of a procedure that generates subsets of features at random and an evaluation procedure that checks if each subset satisfies a chosen measure. The evaluation measure used in filter versions of the Las Vegas algorithm for feature selection (Liu and Motoda, 1998) is inconsistency rate as defined in Section 6.2.2. One of the two required parameters is an allowed inconsistency rate that can be estimated from the inconsistency rate of the data set when all features are used. The other parameter is the maximum number of randomly generated subsets. The output of the algorithm is the subset with the minimum inconsistency rate. The wrapper version of the Las Vegas algorithm (Liu and Motoda, 1998) considers the classifier's estimated accuracy as the first parameter.

Greedy randomized adaptive search procedure (GRASP) (Feo and Resende, 1995) is a metaheuristic algorithm with two clear stages:

(a) *Construction phase*. In this stage a specific heuristic is taken as a basis for constructing a solution. Thus, starting from the empty set, the algorithm adds elements from all the possible candidates until a solution is found. However, some randomness is introduced at this stage in GRASP in order to build a greedy randomized construction method. Thus, instead of picking the best element at each step of the construction, the algorithm chooses at random from a list of promising elements. This list of promising features depends on the heuristic applied. For example, if a greedy forward approach is implemented, the list can be output by all variables whose inclusion improves the current objective function.

(b) *Improving phase*. The constructed solution is taken as the starting point for a local search in order to get an improved solution. GRASP algorithms run the above two stages a number of times, thus operating like a multi-start method. Bermejo et al. (2011) show the application of GRASP to the FSS problem.

Variable neighborhood search (VNS) was proposed by Mladenovic and Hansen (1997). VNS is a stochastic algorithm first defining a set of neighborhood structures

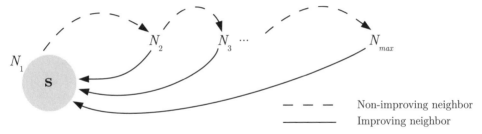

Figure 6.8 The principle of the variable neighborhood search algorithm.

$\mathfrak{N} = \{N_1, N_2, \ldots, N_{max}\}$. For example, N_k can contain all possible solutions at a k distance from the current solution. Then, each iteration of VNS is composed of three steps, called shaking, local search, and move. At each iteration, an initial solution is shaken from the current neighborhood N_k with $1 \leq k \leq max$. For instance, a solution $\mathbf{s}'$ is generated randomly in the current neighborhood $N_k(\mathbf{s})$ of the current solution $\mathbf{s}$. A local search procedure is applied to the initial solution $\mathbf{s}'$ to generate solution $\mathbf{s}''$. The current solution is moved to the new local optimum $\mathbf{s}''$ if and only if it is a better solution (i.e., if $f(\mathbf{s}'') > f(\mathbf{s})$). The same procedure is thus restarted from solution $\mathbf{s}''$ (playing the role of $\mathbf{s}$) in its first neighborhood $N_1(\mathbf{s}'')$, that is, it randomly generates a new solution in this neighborhood (shaking), and attempts to improve it (local search).

Figure 6.8 is a diagram of the successive neighborhoods used by the VNS algorithm. Algorithm 6.3 lists the pseudocode of the VNS algorithm. The first application of VNS in FSS was developed by García-Torres et al. (2005).

Algorithm 6.3: The variable neighborhood search algorithm

Input : A set of neighborhood structures $\mathfrak{N} = \{N_1, N_2, \ldots, N_{max}\}$ for shaking
Output: Best solution found

1 **repeat**
2     $k = 1$
3   **repeat**
4   Shaking: pick a random solution $\mathbf{s}'$ from the kth neighborhood $N_k(\mathbf{s})$ of $\mathbf{s}$
5   Local search: apply local search to $\mathbf{s}'$ to get $\mathbf{s}''$
6   **if** $f(\mathbf{s}'') > f(\mathbf{s})$ **then** $\mathbf{s} = \mathbf{s}''$
7   Continue to search with N_1; $k = 1$
8   **else** $k = k + 1$
9   **until** $k = max$
10 **until** Stopping criterion is satisfied

B. Population-Based Metaheuristics. Scatter search (Glover, 1977) (SS) is an evolutionary and population-based metaheuristic that recombines solutions selected from a reference set to build other solutions. SS starts by generating an initial population satisfying some criterion of diversity and quality. Generally, greedy procedures are applied to diversify the search while selecting high-quality solutions. This initial population is

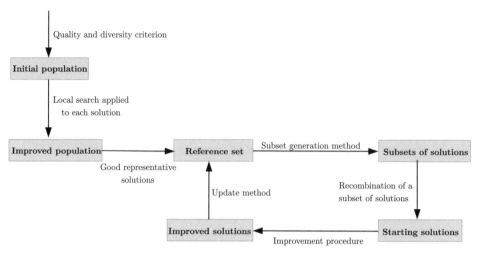

Figure 6.9 Steps in a scatter search algorithm.

improved by transforming each of its trial solutions into one or more enhanced trial solu-tions using a local search algorithm. The reference set of moderate size is then constructed by selecting good representative solutions from the improved population. A subset gen-eration method is then applied to this reference set to produce a subset of solutions as a basis for creating combined solutions. This subset generation method usually selects all the subsets of fixed size r (in general, $r = 2$). A given subset of solutions produced by the subset generation method are recombined[3] to provide input solutions for an improvement procedure, commonly based on local search. According to the result of this procedure, the reference set, and possibly even the population of solutions, is updated to include both high-quality and diversified solutions. The process is iterated until a stopping criterion is satisfied.

Figure 6.9 shows the steps of a scatter search algorithm. García-López et al. (2006) applied SS to the FSS problem.

Optimization algorithms inspired by the collective behavior of species such as ants, bees, wasps, termites, fish, and birds are referred to as **swarm intelligence** algorithms. The most successful swarm intelligence inspired optimization algorithms include ant colony and particle swarm optimization, explained below.

Ant colony optimization. Ant colony optimization (Dorigo et al., 1996) (ACO) is inspired by the pheromone-depositing behavior of ants. Ants communicate mainly by using pheromones, which are chemical substances that they excrete. When ants travel along a path to a food source and bring it back to their colony, they leave a trail of pheromones. Other ants smell the pheromones with their antennae, follow the path, and bring back more food to the colony. In the process, ants continue to lay down pheromones, which other ants continue to smell, and the path to the food source is reinforced. The shortest path to the food thus becomes more attractive over time as it is strengthened by positive feedback. This general process is illustrated in Figure 6.10. Al-Am (2005) introduced an FSS procedure based on ACO.

---

[3] This operator can be seen as a generalization of the crossover operator in evolutionary algorithms (see below) where more than two individuals are recombined.

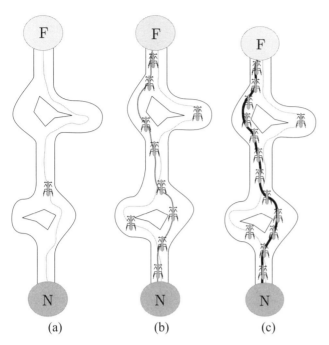

(a)   (b)   (c)

Figure 6.10 (a) The first ant moves from the nest (N) and finds a food source (F); it then returns to the nest, laying a pheromone trial. (b) The ants follow one of the four possible paths. Reinforcement of the trail makes the shortest path more appealing as more pheromones are laid on it. (c) Many more ants choose the shortest path, increasing its pheromone concentration while the pheromone on the other paths evaporates.

Particle swarm optimization. Particle swarm optimization (Kennedy and Eberhart, 1995) mimics the social behavior of natural organisms such as bird flocking and fish schooling to find a place with enough food. Indeed, coordinated behavior based on local movements emerges without any central control in such swarms. In the basic model, a swarm consists of N particles flying around in an n-dimensional search space. Each particle is a candidate solution for the optimization problem and is represented by a vector **s**. A particle has its own position, flying direction, and velocity. Optimization takes advantage of the cooperation between particles. The success of some particles will influence the behavior of their peers. Each particle successively adjusts its position **s** toward the global optimum according to the best position it and the whole swarm have visited (see Figure 6.11). Lin et al. (2008) applied particle swarm optimization to the FSS problem.

Evolutionary algorithms. Darwin (1859) introduced the theory of evolution in his famous book *On the Origin of Species*. In the 1980s, these theories of creation of new species and their evolution inspired computer scientists to design evolutionary algorithms (Goldberg, 1989).

Evolutionary algorithms (Simon, 2013) are stochastic population-based metaheuristics relying on the notion of competition. They represent a class of iterative optimization algorithms that simulate the evolution of species. They are based on the evolution of a population of individuals. Initially, this population is usually generated randomly. Every individual in the population is the encoded version of a tentative solution. At each step, individuals are selected to form the parents, according to which the individuals with a

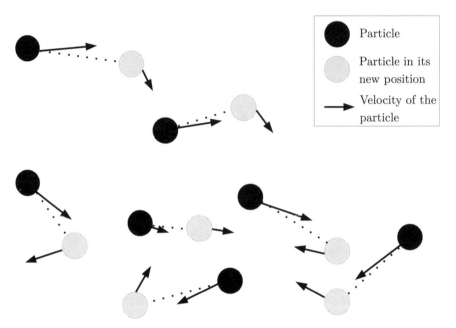

Figure 6.11 Particle swarm optimization with the associated positions and velocities of some particles. At each iteration a particle moves from one position to another in the decision space, adjusting its position and velocity according to the best position that it and other particles have visited.

better objective function are more likely to be selected. Then, selected individuals are reproduced using variation operators (e.g., crossover, mutation) to generate new offspring. Finally, a replacement scheme is applied to determine which in the population of the offspring and parents will survive. This iteration represents one generation in the evolution of the algorithm. This process is iterated until a stopping criterion is met.

Algorithm 6.4 illustrates the evolutionary algorithm template.

Algorithm 6.4: An evolutionary algorithm

> **Input** : Generate the initial population, $Pop(0)$
> **Output:** Best individual found

1 **while** Stopping criterion$(Pop(t))$ is not met **do**
2   Evaluate$(Pop(t))$
3      $Pop'(t) = \text{Selection}(Pop(t))$
4      $Pop'(t) = \text{Reproduction}(Pop'(t))$; Evaluate$(Pop'(t))$
5      $Pop(t+1) = \text{Replace}(Pop(t), Pop'(t))$
6      $t = t+1$
7 **endwhile**

Genetic algorithms (GAs) (Holland, 1975) are traditionally associated with the use of binary representations. A GA usually applies a crossover operator to two solutions that play the role of parents, plus a mutation operator that randomly modifies the results of

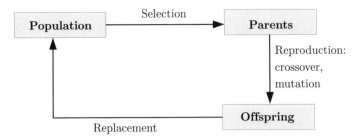

Figure 6.12 Basic scheme of a generation in a genetic algorithm.

the crossover operator. The crossover operator is usually based on the uniform crossover,[4] while the mutation operator is usually bit flipping. A fixed probability p_c (p_m) is applied to the crossover (mutation) operator. Each individual in the population has a probability of becoming a parent that is proportional to its objective value. The replacement of individuals is generational, that is, the previous generation is systematically replaced by the offspring.

Figure 6.12 illustrates the main steps (selection, reproduction, and replacement) in a generation of a genetic algorithm. Siedlecki and Sklansky (1989) applied GAs for the first time to the FSS problem.

Estimation of distribution algorithms (EDAs) (Larrañaga and Lozano, 2002) are an adaptation of GAs. In EDAs, there are neither crossover nor mutation operators. At each generation, the new population of individuals is sampled from a probability distribution that is estimated from the pool of selected individuals. The probabilistic model learned at each generation can be as simple as assuming independence among the variables used for representing the individuals. Alternatively, the model can consider all types of (multivariate dependence) relationships among these variables.

Algorithm 6.5 illustrates the EDA template. Inza et al. (2000) published the seminal paper on the use of EDAs in FSS.

Algorithm 6.5: An estimation of distribution algorithm

    Input : Initial population $Pop(0)$ with A randomly generated individuals
    Output: Best individual found

1 **repeat**
3 | Select $B \leq A$ individuals from $Pop(t)$ to yield $Pop^{Se}(t)$
4 | Estimate the probability distribution of selected individuals:
       | $p_t(\mathbf{x}) = p_t(\mathbf{x}|Pop^{Se}(t))$
5 | Output the new population $Pop(t+1)$ of A individuals by sampling from
       | $p_t(\mathbf{x})$
6 **until** The stopping criterion is met

Differential evolution (Storn and Price, 1997) was designed to optimize functions in an n-dimensional continuous domain. Differential evolution is based on the idea of taking the difference vector between two individuals, $\mathbf{s}_1$ and $\mathbf{s}_2$, in the current population, and adding

---

[4] Each encoding position has the same probability of becoming a cut point in uniform crossover.

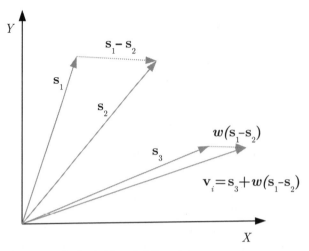

Figure 6.13 The basic idea of differential evolution, illustrated in a 2D optimization problem. A mutant vector $\mathbf{v}_i$, which is a new candidate solution, is created from the addition to an individual solution $\mathbf{s}_3$ of a scaled version of the difference between individuals $\mathbf{s}_1$ and $\mathbf{s}_2$.

a scaled version of the difference vector, $\mathbf{s}_1 - \mathbf{s}_2$, to a third individual, $\mathbf{s}_3$, to create a new candidate solution, $\mathbf{u}_i$, by means of a mutant, $\mathbf{v}_i$, as explained below.

Figure 6.13 illustrates the creation of a mutant $\mathbf{v}_i$ for a differential evolution in a 2D space. Two individuals, $\mathbf{s}_1$ and $\mathbf{s}_2$, are randomly chosen from the current population. A scaled version of the difference between these two individuals, $w(\mathbf{s}_1 - \mathbf{s}_2)$, is added to a third randomly selected individual, $\mathbf{s}_3$, yielding the mutant $\mathbf{v}_i$. This mutant vector $\mathbf{v}_i$ is combined (crossover) with a randomly selected individual $\mathbf{s}_i$ (different from $\mathbf{s}_1, \mathbf{s}_2, \mathbf{s}_3$) from the current population. The trial vector $\mathbf{u}_i$ is a component-by-component combination of $\mathbf{v}_i$ and $\mathbf{s}_i$. After as many trial vectors as the population size have been created, the $\mathbf{u}_i$ and $\mathbf{s}_i$ solutions are compared for all i. The fittest solution in each pair $(\mathbf{u}_i, \mathbf{s}_i)$ is kept for the next generation of the differential evolution, while the worst is discarded. Khushaba et al. (2009) applied an adapted version of differential evolution for discrete optimization to the FSS problem.

Genetic programming (Koza, 1992) considers evolving individuals as programs (represented as trees) instead of fixed length strings from a limited alphabet of symbols. Genetic programming can automatically generate programs that solve a given task. Generally, parents are selected according to an objective proportional scheme, replacement is generational, the crossover operator is based on subtree exchange, and the mutation operator is applied as a random change in the tree. Muni et al. (2004) was the first to develop a genetic programming-based FSS.

Evolution strategies (Rechenberg, 1973) are mostly applied to continuous optimization, where representations are based on real-valued vectors. Evolution strategies usually implement elitist replacement and a specified normally (Gaussian) distributed mutation. Crossover is rarely used. Evolution strategies distinguish between the population of parents with μ individuals and the populations of offspring of size $\lambda \geq \mu$. The selection operator is deterministic and is based on the objective function. Valtokin et al. (2009) adapted evolution strategies for the FSS problem.

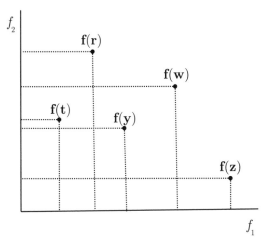

Figure 6.14 Example of a Pareto front in a two-objective maximization problem, $\mathbf{f}(\mathbf{s}) = (f_1(\mathbf{s}), f_2(\mathbf{s}))$. Points $\mathbf{w}$ and $\mathbf{r}$ dominate $\mathbf{t}$, while $\mathbf{y}$ is dominated by $\mathbf{w}$. Points $\mathbf{r}$, $\mathbf{w}$, and $\mathbf{z}$ are non-dominated and constitute the Pareto set. The Pareto front of this example is the set $\{\mathbf{f}(\mathbf{r}), \mathbf{f}(\mathbf{w}), \mathbf{f}(\mathbf{z})\}$.

6.3.1.3 Multi-objective Approaches

Some supervised classification problems may aim to simultaneously maximize two or more objectives. For example, we may want to develop a classifier able to distinguish between the interneuron and pyramidal neurons of Data Set 1 with high sensitivity and specificity values. These two objectives may be conflicting making impossible their simultaneous maximization.

A generic **multi-objective optimization problem** can be stated as follows:

$$\text{maximize} \quad \mathbf{f}(\mathbf{s}) = (f_1(\mathbf{s}), \dots, f_m(\mathbf{s}))$$

$$\text{subject to} \quad \mathbf{s} \in \Omega.$$

In this formulation, m denotes the number of objectives (two for the above interneuron and pyramidal neuron example). As mentioned above, the binary vector of dimension n, $\mathbf{s} = (s_1, \dots, s_n)$, represents a possible FSS. The domain for these n-dimensional binary vectors is $\Omega = \{0,1\}^n$. Thus, $\mathbf{s} = (1,0,\dots,0,1)$ means that only the first and the last features have been selected. $\mathbf{f}(\mathbf{s})$ denotes the vector of m objective components associated with $\mathbf{s}$. Following on with the above example, $\mathbf{f}(1,0,\dots,0,1) = (0.78, 0.64)$ means that the sensitivity and specificity of the classifier built with the subset $\{X_1, X_n\}$ is 0.78 and 0.64, respectively.

A point $\mathbf{y}$ evaluated as $\mathbf{f}(\mathbf{y})$ is said to dominate $\mathbf{z}$ evaluated as $\mathbf{f}(\mathbf{z})$ if $f_i(\mathbf{y}) \geq f_i(\mathbf{z})$ for every $i = 1, \dots, m$ and $f_j(\mathbf{y}) > f_j(\mathbf{z})$ for at least one $j = 1, \dots, m$. A point is said to be **non-dominated** if it is not dominated by any other point. A point $\mathbf{s} \in \Omega$ is **Pareto-optimal** if $\mathbf{s}$ is non-dominated. The set of all Pareto-optimal points is called the **Pareto set**, and the set of all the Pareto-optimal objective vectors is the **Pareto front**.

Figure 6.14 illustrates the above concepts. A comparative study of multi-objective FSS methods using metaheuristic techniques was carried out by Khan et al. (2013).

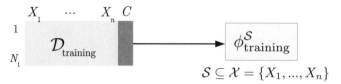

Figure 6.15 The embedded approach for FSS. While building the classifier, the subset of features $\mathcal{S}$ is found. The classification algorithm has its own variable selection process and performs feature selection and classification simultaneously.

6.4   Embedded Methods

Embedded methods include variable selection (a built-in mechanism) as part of the model training process. The search for an optimal subset of features is built into the classifier construction. This can be seen as a search in the combined space of feature subsets and models. Just like wrapper approaches, embedded approaches are specific to a given learning algorithm. Embedded methods can interact with the learning algorithm and are, at the same time, far less computationally intensive than wrapper methods. Figure 6.15 outlines the main characteristics of embedded approaches for FSS.

Particular instantiations of a general method for producing sparse and robust models known as **regularization** (Tikhonov, 1943) can be considered as an embedded feature selection approach. Regularization refers to a process of introducing additional information in order to solve an ill-posed optimization problem or to avoid overfitting. This information usually takes the form of a penalty on an objective function (usually the likelihood) to reduce the model complexity. Consequently, the regularized solutions are less complex and, hence, more stable. Regularization avoids model overfitting by trading off bias against variance as a consequence of imposing some restrictions (parameter shrinkage) on the optimization problem.

The **lasso** regularization method (Tibshirani, 1996) is based on an L_1 norm penalty and is in widespread use for FSS because it converts the parameters associated with some variables to zero. Consequently, these variables should be omitted from the classification model. Regularization is applied to discriminant analysis in Section 8.2.4, whereas its application to logistic regression and naive Bayes can be consulted in Sections 8.3.2.2 and 8.4.1.2, respectively.

Van Gerven et al. (2009) classified multisensor EEG signals recorded for a motor imagery task using groupwise regularized logistic regression. Regularization based on L_2 and L_1 was applied by Rasmussen et al. (2012) to support vector machines, logistic regression, and Fisher's discriminant analysis on two fMRI data sets, one in a finger tapping experiment and the other in a trail-making test. Santana et al. (2012) selected channels for classifying the direction in which a subject is covertly focusing her attention from MEG data using regularized logistic regression in combination with a wrapper FSS strategy.

Each of the other embedded methods in this section refer to one specific classification paradigm. Classification tree induction algorithms (Section 7.2), like **C4.5** (Quinlan, 1993), are embedded feature selection methods. Classification trees are recursively built by splitting the data depending on the value of a specific variable. The "splitting" variable is chosen according to its importance for the class variable, usually with some criterion based on mutual information between a predictor variable and the class variable. Thus, trees (implicitly) select important features along their paths.

Incremental reduced error pruning (IREP) is a rule induction algorithm proposed by Fürnkranz and Widmer (1994) that greedily searches for the best rule set (Section 7.3). A rule set is formed as a conjunction of literals (each literal is associated with a variable). The search for the best rule set is a two-stage process. The first stage involves growing a rule process from scratch. The second stage is a pruning process that sequentially deletes literals, hence also deleting variables.

Feature weighting in multi-layer perceptron networks was proposed in Setiono and Liu (1997) for a three-layer feedforward neural network (Section 7.4). The algorithm considers the complete set of features as input and trains the weight of the connections by means of the backpropagation algorithm. The embedded feature selection method works in a greedy backward manner. An augmented error function is computed for each feature in the input layer, in which all the weights of the connections associated with this feature are set to zero. This augmented error consists of two components. The first component is a measure of artificial neural network fitting, and the second component is a measure of the artificial neural network complexity. The fitting component is measured using the cross-entropy error function (Section 3.6.6), while the complexity of the network is measured by a penalty term. The feature that yields the smallest decrease in this augmented error function is removed. The artificial neural network is retrained after removal of a feature, and the selection process is repeated until no feature meets the criterion for exclusion.

Recursive feature elimination (Guyon et al., 2002) was proposed for support vector machines (Section 7.5). It attempts to find the best subset of size $m < n$ applying a kind of greedy backward selection. Recursive feature elimination should choose the m features that lead to the largest margin of class separation, using a support vector machine classifier. This combinatorial optimization problem is approached in a greedy fashion at each iteration of the training process by removing the variable that decreases the margin the least. This removal is repeated until only m variables remain.

Linear discriminant analysis (Section 8.2) assumes that samples conditional upon the class value have a multivariate normal distribution, where each conditional has its own mean vector. One version assumes that the covariance matrix is the same for all class values. Model selection is essentially a choice of a structure for the covariance matrix. Thus, a simple method would perform feature selection for both diagonal (Section 8.2.1) and full covariance matrix (Section 8.2.2) structures and pick the best of both. Pique-Regi and Ortega (2006) presented an embedded approach that considers both the classifier design and FSS. The method is a **sequential greedy algorithm for block diagonal linear discriminant analysis** designed to find both a feature subset and a block diagonal structure. The method sequentially adds to the model one feature at a time. The process starts by selecting the best feature measured with the score given in Equation (8.13). Then, there are two possible options at each stage: (i) add another feature that is independent of all previously selected features for consideration, thus leading to a new block in the block-diagonal structure, and (ii) grow the current block in the matrix structure by adding one more feature. Both options are evaluated with a score based on Equation (8.13), and the best is selected.

Logistic regression modeling (Section 8.3) usually selects features based on a backward elimination strategy (Hosmer and Lemeshow, 2000) that deletes variables from the current model according to the results of a hypothesis test. The difference in the deviance (see Equation (8.20)) of both models is the statistic for the test. When this difference is small, the complex model is rejected. The model including the variable deletion specified by the test is now the reference model. This elimination process is repeated until the deletion of any of the variables in the current model leads to a significant difference in the deviance.

The **selective tree-augmented naive Bayes** (Section 8.4.1.4) proposed by Blanco et al. (2005) is an example of embedded feature selection for Bayesian classifiers. The idea is to first filter, with a χ^2 test of independence, the weights (and hence the associated variables) of the undirected tree based on conditional mutual information.

6.5   Hybrid Feature Selection

Hybrid feature selection methods combine filter and wrapper approaches, especially when the initial number of features is so large that wrapper methods cannot be used on computational grounds. In the first stage, the filter method drastically reduces the number of features. In the second stage, the wrapper approach is applied on the output of the filter method.

An example of hybridization was proposed by Peng et al. (2005) and consists of the combination of the **minimal-redundancy-maximal-relevance** based criterion (mrMR) and a wrapper approach. mrMR is based on a criterion, $\Phi_{(r,R)}(\mathcal{S},C)$, which combines the redundancy r and the relevance R of a subset of features $\mathcal{S} \subseteq \mathcal{X}$. Both concepts are defined in terms of the mutual information quantities between individual features X_i and the class C. The **maximal relevance criterion** tries to find the subset $\mathcal{S}^*$ verifying

$$\mathcal{S}^* = \arg\max_{\mathcal{S}\subseteq\mathcal{X}} R(\mathcal{S},C) = \arg\max_{\mathcal{S}\subseteq\mathcal{X}} \frac{1}{|\mathcal{S}|} \sum_{X_i\in\mathcal{S}} \mathbb{I}(X_i,C).$$

Relevance could have rich redundancy, i.e., the dependency among these features could be strong. The following **minimal redundancy criterion** can be added to select subsets of features

$$\mathcal{S}^* = \arg\min_{\mathcal{S}\subseteq\mathcal{X}} r(\mathcal{S},C) = \arg\min_{\mathcal{S}\subseteq\mathcal{X}} \frac{1}{|\mathcal{S}|^2} \sum_{X_i,X_j\in\mathcal{S}} \mathbb{I}(X_i,X_j).$$

The criterion combining the above two constraints is called minimal-redundancy-maximal-relevance, that is,

$$\mathcal{S}^* = \arg\max_{\mathcal{S}\subseteq\mathcal{X}} \Phi_{(r,R)}(\mathcal{S},C) = \arg\max_{\mathcal{S}\subseteq\mathcal{X}} (R(\mathcal{S},C) - r(\mathcal{S},C)).$$

The hybrid approach proposed by Peng et al. (2005) is a two-stage feature selection algorithm. The first stage outputs a candidate feature subset using an mrMR incremental selection method. The second stage further reduces this subset by applying a wrapper approach.

During the first stage, the mrMR criterion is used to incrementally select k sequential features from $\mathcal{X}$. This leads to k sequential feature sets $\mathcal{S}_1 \subset \mathcal{S}_2 \subset \cdots \subset \mathcal{S}_{k-1} \subset \mathcal{S}_k$ where each $\mathcal{S}_i$ includes i features. These sequential feature sets are compared to find the range q between 1 and k within which the respective error (estimated by cross-validation) is small. The objective of this first stage is to find a small set of candidate features on which the wrapper approaches can be applied at a much lower cost in the second stage. This second stage considers the feature set $\mathcal{S}_q$ as the initial solution. Starting from $\mathcal{S}_q$, two wrapper selection schemes, i.e., backward and forward selections, are implemented, taking the feature set $\mathcal{S}_k$ as the reference set, that is, the possible maximal subset to be selected, for the forward approach.

6.6   Feature Selection Stability

Stability measures quantify how different training sets affect FSS. They try to determine the sensitivity of feature selection algorithms to variations in the training set. The motivation for investigating the stability of feature selection algorithms stems from the need to provide domain experts with quantified evidence that the selected features are relatively robust to variations in the training data. Domain experts tend to have less confidence in feature sets that change radically with slight variations in the training data.

Feature selection algorithm stability (Haury et al., 2011) can be viewed as the capability of an algorithm to consistently produce similar feature subsets when new training samples are added or when some training samples are removed. If the algorithm produces very different subsets in response to small perturbations in the training data, then that algorithm is unreliable for the purposes of feature selection.

Consider a data set of N labeled instances: $\mathcal{D} = \{(\mathbf{x}^1, c^1), \dots, (\mathbf{x}^N, c^N)\}$. k subsamplings are drawn randomly from data set $\mathcal{D}$. If replacement is allowed, the subsampling data sets can be of size N, otherwise their size should be smaller than N. Let $\{\mathcal{S}_1, \dots, \mathcal{S}_k\}$ be a set of k selected feature subsets, where each subset of features is associated with subsampling data with k associated binary vectors of dimension n, $\mathbf{s}_j = (s_{j1}, \dots, s_{ji}, \dots, s_{jn})$, whose components are defined as in Section 6.1

$$s_{jr} = \begin{cases} 1 & \text{if variable } X_r \text{ belongs to } \mathcal{S}_j \\ 0 & \text{otherwise} \end{cases}$$

for $r = 1, 2, \dots, n$ and $j = 1, 2, \dots, k$.

Measures for feature stability (Somol and Novovicová, 2010) are defined by comparing the features selected for each of the k subsamplings. The more similar all selections are, the higher the stability measure will be. The overall stability, Sta_{overall}, can then be defined as the average over all pairwise similarity comparisons between all selections from the k subsamplings:

$$Sta_{\text{overall}} = \frac{2 \sum_{i=1}^{k} \sum_{j=i+1}^{k} Sta_{\text{pair}}(\mathbf{s}_i, \mathbf{s}_j)}{k(k-1)}.$$

Different options for pairwise stability (Sta_{pair}) can be found in the literature. Dunne et al. (2002) suggested measuring this pairwise stability using the **Hamming distance** between the two associated binary vectors. For instance, $Sta_{\text{pair}}^{\text{Hamming}}(\mathbf{s}_i, \mathbf{s}_j) = \frac{1}{n} \sum_{r=1}^{n} |s_{ir} - s_{jr}|$. Kalousis et al. (2007) proposed the **Tanimoto index coefficient** defined as the size of the intersection of the two selected subsets divided by the size of the union. In terms of the selected subsets, $\mathcal{S}_i$ and $\mathcal{S}_j$, the pairwise stability based on the Tanimoto index coefficient is expressed as $Sta_{\text{pair}}^{\text{Tanimoto}}(\mathbf{s}_i, \mathbf{s}_j) = \frac{|S_i \cap S_j|}{|S_i \cup S_j|}$. For a pair of selected subsets with fixed subset size (i.e., $\sum_{r=1}^{n} s_{i,r} = \sum_{r=1}^{n} s_{jr} = d$), Kuncheva (2007) introduced the **Kuncheva index** as the pairwise stability coefficient, $Sta_{\text{pair}}^{\text{Kuncheva}}(\mathbf{s}_i, \mathbf{s}_j) = \frac{n|S_i \cap S_j| - d^2}{d(n-d)}$.

6.7   Example: GABAergic Interneuron Nomenclature

This section contains the results of the application of some filter, wrapper, and embedded FSS methods described above to the GABAergic interneuron nomenclature introduced in Data Set 2 of Section 1.6.2. The fifth class variable containing GABAergic interneurons cell types as values is considered as a target for supervised classification models. In particular, we will build different supervised classification models with the aim of distinguishing between common type, Martinotti, common basket, and large basket interneuron types. The 75 common type, 37 Martinotti, 71 common basket, and 35 large basket cells are characterized by 2,586 morphological variables extracted from the 3D reconstructions built using the MicroBrightField Neurolucida package.

These morphological variables refer to different parts of the neuron (dendrites, axon, and soma) and cover different types of information (length of segments, number of nodes and segments, convex hull analysis, Sholl analysis, fractal analysis, vertex analysis, and branch angle analysis).

The 2,586 variables are divided into the following blocks as explained in the description of Data Set 2 (Chapter 1): Box-Counting-Trees-Axons with variable X_1 only; Box-Counting-Trees-Dendrites containing variable X_2; Branch-Angle-Axon with variables from X_3 to X_{929}; Branch-Angle-Dendrite, X_{930} to $X_{1,100}$; Cell-Bodies, $X_{1,101}$ to $X_{1,110}$; Convex-Hull-2D, $X_{1,111}$ to $X_{1,114}$; Convex-Hull-3D, $X_{1,115}$ to $X_{1,118}$; Neuron-Summary-Axon, $X_{1,119}$ to $X_{1,122}$; Neuron-Summary-Dendrites, $X_{1,123}$ to $X_{1,126}$; Polar-Axon, $X_{1,127}$ to $X_{1,162}$; Polar-Dendrite, $X_{1,163}$ to $X_{1,198}$; Segment-Axons, $X_{1,199}$ to $X_{1,614}$; Segment-Dendrites, $X_{1,615}$ to $X_{1,694}$; Sholl-Axon, $X_{1,695}$ to $X_{1,806}$; Sholl-Dendrite, $X_{1,807}$ to $X_{1,846}$; Tree-Totals-Axon, $X_{1,847}$ to $X_{2,052}$; Tree-Totals-Dendrite, $X_{2,053}$ to $X_{2,090}$; Vertex-Axon, $X_{2,091}$ to $X_{2,506}$; and Vertex-Dendrite, $X_{2,507}$ to $X_{2,586}$.

6.7.1   Results with Univariate and Multivariate Filter FSS Methods

In a first analysis, we compared the results provided by filter FSS methods against outcomes using the full set of predicted variables. The continuous original 2,586 predictor variables were discretized into three bins using the equal frequency method (Section 2.6.3). This discretized version of the data set was used in the two univariate filter methods (gain ratio and symmetric uncertainty) and the four multivariate filter approaches (RELIEF and CFS, in the latter applying three different search heuristics including best-first search, greedy backward search, and genetic algorithms). All models in this and the next section, were induced running WEKA (The Waikato Environment for Knowledge Analysis) (Hall et al., 2009) software with the default parameter values.

Table 6.5 shows the results in terms of accuracy and number of selected features for each combination of seven supervised classification models (Chapters 7 and 8) and FSSs

Table 6.5 Percentage accuracy of the following seven supervised classification models: 1-nearest neighbor (1-NN), classification tree (C4.5), rule induction (RIPPER), artificial neural network (ANN), support vector machine (SVM), explained in Chapter 7, and logistic regression (Logistic), and naive Bayes (NB), described in Chapter 8. The accuracies correspond to different situations regarding their predictor variables: all initial variables (continuous and three-interval discrete variables), two univariate filter methods (gain ratio and symmetric uncertainty), and four multivariate filter methods (RELIEF and CFS using best-first search, greedy backward search, and genetic algorithms as heuristics)

| | All variables | | Filter | | | | | |
| | | | Univariate | | Multivariate | | | |
	Continuous	Discrete	Gain ratio	Symmetric uncertainty	RELIEF	CFS best-first	CFS greedy	CFS GAs
1-NN	26.61	27.98	30.73	38.07	36.70	38.07	39.45	27.06
C4.5	24.77	32.57	33.03	44.50	35.78	32.11	33.94	27.52
RIPPER	31.19	30.28	34.40	41.74	43.58	36.70	30.73	34.86
ANN	33.94	34.40	34.86	37.61	38.53	38.99	40.37	33.94
SVM	31.65	31.19	35.32	45.87	41.74	51.38	50.92	34.40
Logistic	28.44	33.03	34.86	44.04	37.61	44.50	44.95	31.19
NB	19.72	26.15	35.78	42.20	39.45	53.67	57.34	28.90
No. of features	2,586	2,586	93	14	24	82	85	1,031

(two with all variables, plus six with filter subsets). The discretized classifiers outperform almost all classifiers with the original continuous features (except RIPPER and SVM) in terms of accuracy. Artificial neural networks provide the best results in both situations with estimated accuracies of 33.94 and 34.40, respectively.

The features were selected for the two filter approaches following the principles of the elbow method. For instance, after ordering the features according to the gain ratio (or symmetric uncertainty), the feature selection threshold was determined as the first time that a score was significantly reduced. This criterion resulted in 93 and 14 selected features for gain ratio and symmetric uncertainty, respectively. The accuracies of each of the 7 classifiers with the 93 features selected by gain ratio were better than the equivalent results when all original features are discretized and used as predictors. However, when comparing the accuracies for the gain ratio and symmetric uncertainty univariate filters, symmetric uncertainty outperforms gain ratio for each of the 7 classifiers. SVM achieves the best accuracy with a percentage of 45.87.

The 4 multivariate filter methods differ with respect to the number of selected features, with RELIEF (24), CFS + best-first search (82), and CFS + greedy backward search (85) selecting very few and CFS + genetic algorithms (1,031) selecting many more. Multivariate filters are best in 23 out of the possible 28 (= 7 × 4) comparisons against all original discrete features. The only exceptions are 1-NN with CFS + genetic algorithms, C4.5 with CFS + best-first, C4.5 with CFS + genetic algorithms, ANN with CFS + genetic algorithms, and logistic regression with CFS + genetic algorithms. It is also noteworthy that the best accuracies (exceeding 50.00) were achieved with combinations of SVM and naive Bayes with CFS + best-first search and CFS + greedy backward search.

Table 6.6 Number of variables containing anatomical features within each block, as well as number of selected features in each block broken down by the different univariate filters (gain ratio and symmetrical uncertainty) and multivariate filters (RELIEF, correlation feature selection with best-first, greedy, or genetic algorithms as search methods); zeros are omitted

Block of variables	All	Gain ratio	Symm. uncert.	RELIEF	CFS best-first	CFS greedy	CFS GAs
Box-Counting-Trees-Axons	1						1
Box-Counting-Trees-Dendrites	1						
Branch-Angle-Axon	927		6	8	29	30	452
Branch-Angle-Dendrite	171	36			5	9	69
Cell-Bodies	10		1	1	3		3
Convex-Hull-2D	4						2
Convex-Hull-3D	4						1
Neuron-Summary-Axon	4						1
Neuron-Summary-Dendrites	4						3
Polar-Axon	36				2	2	21
Polar-Dendrite	36			1	7	7	13
Segment-Axons	416		2	3	7	9	171
Segment-Dendrites	80	16		2	5	5	25
Sholl-Axon	112	10	2	1	4	4	42
Sholl-Dendrite	40		1		3	3	16
Tree-Totals-Axon	206			2	3	2	72
Tree-Totals-Dendrite	38	8			2	2	9
Vertex-Axon	416	5	2	5	8	8	114
Vertex-Dendrite	80	18		1	4	4	16
Number of selected features	2,586	93	14	24	82	85	1,031

Analyzing the best FSS strategy for each classifier, CFS + greedy backward won for 1-nearest neighbor, artificial neural networks, logistic regression, and naive Bayes. Alternatively, CFS + best-first, RELIEF, and symmetric uncertainty provided the best results for SVM, RIPPER, and C4.5, respectively.

Table 6.6 shows the number of selected variables according to the blocks of variables described above. A characteristic of gain ratio based selection is that no features were selected in 3 of the largest blocks (Branch-Angle-Axon, Segment-Axons, Tree-Totals-Axon), all of which are related to axon measures. This behavior contrasts with the selection using symmetric uncertainty, where 10 out of the 14 selected features belong to Branch-Angle-Axon, Segment-Axons and Vertex-Axon. The behavior of RELIEF is similar where more than half of the selected features are in the above 3 blocks. CFS + best-first search and CFS + greedy backward search also selected more than half of the features from Branch-Angle-Axon, Segment-Axons, and Vertex-Axon. In addition, blocks like Branch-Angle-Dendrite, Polar-Dendrite, and Segment-Dendrites are well represented in both approaches. Finally, the large number of features selected by CFS + genetic algorithms mainly belong to the 3 blocks with most components, although Branch-Angle-Dendrite, Sholl-Axon and Tree-Total-Axons are also well represented.

There is a big difference in the behavior of the different blocks according to their selection rate, where blocks like Box-Counting-Trees-Axons, Box-Counting-Trees-Dendrites, Convex-Hull-2D, Convex-Hull-3D, Neuron-Summary-Axon, Neuron-Summary-Dendrites,

Table 6.7 Percentage accuracy of seven supervised classification models in different scenarios regarding their predictor variables: all initial variables (continuous and three-interval discretized variables) and two wrapper approaches with different search heuristics (best-first search, and genetic algorithms)

	All variables		Wrapper	
	Continuous	Discrete	Best-first	Genetic algorithms
1-NN	26.61	27.98	36.70	34.86
C4.5	24.77	32.57	50.00	30.28
RIPPER	31.19	30.28	44.04	35.32
SVM	31.65	31.19	49.08	37.61
ANN	33.94	34.40	47.25	34.40
Logistic	28.44	33.03	52.75	32.57
NB	19.72	26.15	49.08	30.73

Polar-Axon, Sholl-Dendrite and Tree-Totals-Axon account for a small percentage of selected features for almost all the filter methods.

6.7.2   Results with Wrapper FSS Methods

This section reports the results for accuracy (Table 6.7) and number of selected variables per block (Table 6.8) for two wrapper strategies using best-first search and genetic algorithms, respectively, as search heuristics.

The best-first heuristic provided very competitive results in terms of accuracy (with very high values for all classifiers except 1-NN) and number of variables (in the range of 4–15, with a minimum number of selected features for RIPPER and a maximum for SVM). The low number of features selected from some of the most populated blocks like Branch-Angle-Axon, Tree-Totals-Axon, and Vertex-Axon is noteworthy. Also, notice that some blocks of variables were not selected by any of the seven classifiers. The accuracies of two classifiers (C4.5 and logistic regression) were equal to or greater than the 50.00% mark.

The wrapper classifiers based on genetic algorithms were very poor in terms of accuracy (none of the 7 classifiers achieved more than 40.00% accuracy) and the number of selected features (in the range of 579–1,416). This poor performance may be due to the decision to set the genetic algorithm parameters (population size, number of generations, crossover and mutation probabilities) to their default values. Finer tuning may significantly improve the results in terms of accuracy.

As a general conclusion, filter and wrapper approaches to FSS built classifiers that dramatically reduced the number of predictor variables while at the same time provided very competitive results in terms of accuracy.

6.8   Bibliographic Notes

Liu and Motoda (1998, 2008) are good books about FSS methods. Journal review papers include general surveys by Dash and Liu (1997) and Chandrashekar and Sahin (2013);

Table 6.8 Number of variables containing anatomical features within each block, and number of features selected by the wrapper strategies (with best-first and genetic algorithms search methods) in each block for each of the seven classifiers (A = 1-NN; B = C4.5; C = RIPPER; D = SVM; E = ANN; F = Logistic; G = NB); zeros are omitted

Block of variables	All	Best-first search							Wrapper Genetic algorithms						
		A	B	C	D	E	F	G	A	B	C	D	E	F	G
Box-Counting-Trees-Axons	1											1	1	1	1
Box-Counting-Trees-Dendrites	1									1					1
Branch-Angle-Axon	927	2	3	1	1	1			249	538	147	411	503	451	468
Branch-Angle-Dendrite	171	1	2	1	2	1	2		43	104	31	72	84	80	52
Cell-Bodies	10							1		7	3	4	5	5	4
Convex-Hull-2D	4								1	4		3	2	1	1
Convex-Hull-3D	4	1								1	1	2	3	2	3
Neuron-Summary-Axon	4									3	1	2	3	1	1
Neuron-Summary-Dendrites	4								2	3		2		1	1
Polar-Axon	36		1						9	17	7	12	15	13	10
Polar-Dendrite	36		1				2		8	23	3	14	24	17	12
Segment-Axons	416	1	2		3	1		1	115	241	88	192	221	198	124
Segment-Dendrites	80			1	1				19	44	10	32	34	43	22
Sholl-Axon	112	2							35	65	21	50	62	50	40
Sholl-Dendrite	40	1		1	2	1	1	2	12	25	16	17	83	15	9
Tree-Totals-Axon	206								82	120	68	86	109	97	50
Tree-Totals-Dendrite	38								18	9	8	21	22	13	18
Vertex-Axon	416	2			2	1	3		164	95	139	192	200	136	129
Vertex-Dendrite	80	2			2				42	17	36	20	45	28	26
Number of selected features	2,586	11	10	4	15	7	9	5	799	1,317	579	1,133	1,416	1,152	969

bioinformatics applications by Saeys et al. (2007); filter techniques in gene expression microarray analysis by Lazar et al. (2012); FSS methods based on mutual information by Vergara and Estévez (2013); and variable selection in high dimensional feature spaces by Fan and Lv (2010).

The wrapper approach has been applied in: (a) non-probabilistic classifiers, like nearest neighbors (Langley and Sage, 1994a), classification trees (John et al., 1994), rule induction (Vafaie and Jong, 1991), support vector machines (Weston et al., 2001), neural networks (Sietsma and Dow, 1991); and (b) probabilistic classifiers, like discriminant analysis (Habbema and Hermans, 1977), logistic regression (Lee and Koval, 1997), and Bayesian network classifiers (Langley and Sage, 1994b).

Lasso-based regularization has been adapted as an embedded FSS method for support vector machines (Bradley and Mangasarian, 1988), neural networks (Costa and Braga, 2006), linear discriminant analysis (Witten and Tibshirani, 2011), logistic regression (Tibshirani, 1996), and Bayesian classifiers (Vidaurre et al., 2013a).

7 Non-probabilistic Classifiers

In this chapter, we focus on non-probabilistic classification models, i.e., their output is the predicted class of each configuration of values for the features. Chapter 8 deals with probabilistic classifiers, where the output is the posterior distribution of the class variable conditioned on a given set of values for the features.

We explain many models more or less in order of complexity. Specifically, the classifiers are k-nearest neighbor algorithm (Section 7.1), classification trees (Section 7.2), rule induction (Section 7.3), artificial neural networks (Section 7.4), and support vector machines (Section 7.5). All classifiers are applied to the interneurons versus pyramidal neurons problem of Data Set 1. Section 7.6 provides some bibliographic notes. Figure 7.1 shows a temporal representation of the seminal works for each model.

We are given a labeled data set of n variables forming the vector $\mathbf{X} = (X_1, \dots, X_n)$, including features from N observations. Let $\mathcal{D} = \{(\mathbf{x}^1, c^1), \dots, (\mathbf{x}^N, c^N)\}$ denote the data set, where $\mathbf{x}^i = (x_1^i, \dots, x_n^i)$, $i = 1, \dots, N$, and c^i denotes its label from a class variable C with domain $\Omega_C = \{c_1, \dots, c_R\}$ (or sometimes simply $\Omega_C = \{1, \dots, R\}$). Accordingly, the domain of each X_i is denoted $\Omega_{X_i} = \{x_1, \dots, x_{R_i}\}$, $i = 1, \dots, n$, where i is not used (unless it is necessary) for the values for simplicity, and only for the number of values.

7.1 Nearest Neighbors

The k-**nearest neighbor** (k-NN) classifier (Fix and Hodges, 1951) is one of the best-known and most widely used nonparametric classifiers. Despite its simplicity, it has been empirically proven to be one of the most useful and effective algorithms for supervised classification. Its theoretical properties and its ease of implementation are what makes this lazy learner so popular. Table 7.1 shows some illustrative neuroscience examples using this classifier.

7.1.1 The Basic k-NN Algorithm

The basic idea of using nearest neighbors for classification was first introduced in two technical reports (Fix and Hodges, 1951, 1952) and was published again formally as

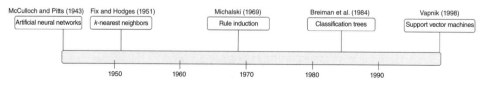

Figure 7.1 Timeline of the seminal papers for non-probabilistic classifiers.

Table 7.1 Neuroscience problems solved with the k-nearest neighbor classifier

Reference	Aim	Predictor variables
Chang et al. (2010)	PD vs. control	Auto- and cross-correlations between hand, wrist, elbow, and shoulder movements
Benvenuto et al. (2002)	AD vs. control	Evoked response potentials time segments across different electrodes
Firpi et al. (2006)	Predict epileptic seizures	Intracranial EEG data (baseline and preictal epochs)
Borujeny et al. (2013)	Detect epileptic seizures	Accelerometer sensors
Acharya et al. (2011)	Normal vs. ictal vs. pre-ictal (epilepsy)	EGG signals in recurrence plots
Wu et al. (2006)	MS lesion subtypes	T1, T2-weighted, proton density MRI
Gokgoz and Subasi (2014)	ALS vs. myopathic vs. normal	Electromyography signals
Höller et al. (2013)	Consciousness disorder types	EEG signals from a motor imagery task
Mohamed et al. (2001)	White matter intracranial lesion	T1, T2-weighted, proton density MRI
de Boer et al. (2009)	CSF vs. gray matter vs. white matter	Multimodal MRI

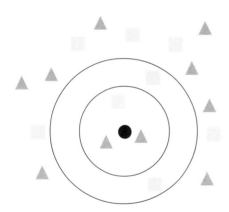

Figure 7.2 Example of a k-NN classifier.

a review by Silverman and Jones (1989). k-NN is a local method without an explicit associated model. Moreover, it does not impose any assumptions on data distribution.

To classify a query instance $\mathbf{x}$, the method of k-nearest neighbors predicts the unknown class based on the classes associated with the k instances of the training set that are closer to $\mathbf{x}$, using a simple majority decision rule.

For example, consider the task of classifying the test instance (black circle) in Figure 7.2 that should be classified either as the first class (squares) or as the second class (triangles). If $k = 3$ (inner circle), the instance is assigned to the second class because there are two triangles and only one square inside the inner circle. If $k = 5$ (outer circle), it is assigned to the first class (three squares versus two triangles inside the outer circle).

Algorithm 7.1 illustrates the above ideas. Given a new query instance to be classified, **x**, a subset $\mathcal{D}_\mathbf{x}^k$ of the original training data $\mathcal{D}$ is selected. This subset contains the k labeled instances closest to **x**. The k-NN classifier will assign to **x** the class most frequently represented in $\mathcal{D}_\mathbf{x}^k$. A special case of k-NN is when $k = 1$. In 1-NN, the class of the nearest neighbor will be assigned to **x**.

Algorithm 7.1: The basic k-nearest neighbor classifier

    Input : A data set $\mathcal{D} = \{(\mathbf{x}^1, c^1), \ldots, (\mathbf{x}^N, c^N)\}$ of labeled instances, a new
                instance $\mathbf{x} = (x_1, \ldots, x_n)$ to be classified
    Output: The class label for instance $\mathbf{x} = (x_1, \ldots, x_n)$

1 **for** each labeled instance $(\mathbf{x}^i, c^i)$ $i = 1$ **to** N **do**
2 | Calculate $d(\mathbf{x}^i, \mathbf{x})$
3 **endfor**
4 Order $d(\mathbf{x}^i, \mathbf{x})$ from lowest to highest, $i = 1$ **to** N
5 Select the k nearest instances to **x** obtaining the subset $\mathcal{D}_\mathbf{x}^k \subseteq \mathcal{D}$
6 Assign to **x** the most frequent class in $\mathcal{D}_\mathbf{x}^k$

This rule can be used to partition the predictor variable space into cells consisting of all points closest to a given training instance $\mathbf{x}^i$ than to any other training points. If a 1-NN classifier is used, all points in a cell are thus labeled by the class of the training instance. This results in the so-called **Voronoi tessellation** of the space (Figure 7.3).

Unlike the other supervised classification paradigms discussed in this book, the k-NN algorithm does not really have a training phase. It is the only method that does not induce a model as an abstraction of the labeled training data set. Before the testing phase, training

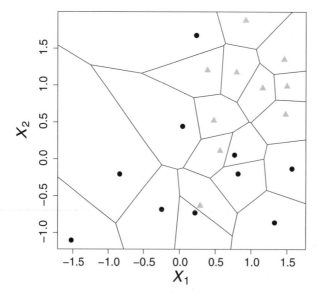

Figure 7.3 Example of a Voronoi tessellation useful for a 1-NN classifier. It includes 20 training instances in a 2D space with their respective influence regions.

instances are stored. Storage may involve some sort of indexing to reduce the time taken to find neighbors. In the testing phase, k nearest neighbors of each instance are found. This algorithm behavior explains why it is described as a *lazy learner*.

The advantages of the k-NN algorithm include: (i) it is able to learn complex decision boundaries, (ii) there is no loss of information because there is no modeling (abstraction) phase, (iii) it is a local method, (iv) it uses few assumptions about the data, (v) it can be easily adapted as an incremental algorithm and also works when the input is a data stream of instances, and (vi) it can be more or less directly adapted to regression problems (with a continuous response variable to be predicted).

The main disadvantage is its high storage requirements and slow classification speed. Prototype selection methods (Section 7.1.6) can reduce storage requirements, whereas data indexing is helpful for speeding up times. In addition, the algorithm is sensitive to the value of k, the distance metric choice, the existence of irrelevant variables, and noisy data sets. Many of these issues will be detailed below. Another disadvantage, derived from the fact that there is no explicit model, is that it does not provide any information about the data structure.

7.1.2 Theoretical Results

For unlimited quantities of data, the k-NN algorithm is guaranteed to yield an error rate no worse than twice the Bayes error rate (the minimum achievable error rate given the data distribution, see Section 8.1), when k increases as a function of the number of data points (Covert and Hart, 1967). Devijver and Kittler (1982) proved a more powerful result by showing that the repeated application of Wilson's editing, a prototype selection method explained in Section 7.1.6, will lead to the Bayes error rate. In practical applications, these consistency results require a lot of training data, which are not always available. Bremmer et al. (2005) specified explicit decision boundaries for k-NN algorithms.

7.1.3 Variants of the Basic k-NN

Several variants of the basic formulation of the k-NN have been developed.

7.1.3.1 Weighting Neighbors

The main idea behind k-**NN with weighted neighbors** is that the contribution of each neighbor depends on its distance to the query instance, with more weight being attached to nearer neighbors. To implement this idea, the weight w_j of the jth neighbor can be defined as a decreasing function h of its distance to the instance to be classified, $\mathbf{x}$, that is, $w_j = h(d(\mathbf{x}^j, \mathbf{x}))$. After computing these weights, the query instance will be assigned to the label with the largest total weight.

7.1.3.2 Weighting Predictor Variables

k-NN is easily misled by the existence of irrelevant variables, especially in high-dimensional problems. For example, consider a training data set with instances characterized by a large number of predictor variables, where only two are relevant for the class variable. In this scenario, identical instances of these two relevant variables may be distant from one another in the other $n - 2$ dimensions, distorting the computation of the neighbors and, consequently, the label assignment. **k-NN with weighted predictor variables** deals with this problem by assigning a weight to each predictor variable. This weight can be proportional to its relevance with respect to the class variable. The distance between the instance query, $\mathbf{x}$, and any of the training instances, $\mathbf{x}^i$, is now computed as $d(\mathbf{x}, \mathbf{x}^i) = \sum_{j=1}^{n} w_j \delta(x_j, x_j^i)$, where w_j is the weight assigned to variable X_j, and $\delta(x_j, x_j^i)$ measures the distance between the jth components of $\mathbf{x}$ and $\mathbf{x}^i$. For example, the weight w_j may be proportional to the mutual information between X_j and C. This distance based on weighted variables is used to determine the neighbors.

This approach can be transformed into a feature selection method by simply establishing a threshold to the weights.

7.1.3.3 Average Distance

Unlike the basic k-NN, the decision rule of **k-NN with average distance** is not based on the frequency of each class among the k neighbors. Now, distances of the neighbors to the query instance are averaged for each class label, and the label associated with the minimum average distance is assigned to the query.

7.1.3.4 Rejection

k-NN with rejection demands some guarantees before an instance is classified. If the guarantees are not met, the instance remains unclassified until processed by another supervised classification algorithm according to a cascading procedure (see Section 9.3.2 for details). A usual guarantee refers to the threshold for the most frequent class for the neighbors of the instance to be classified. For example, given $k = 13$ and considering a binary classification problem, this variant of the k-NN can establish the threshold for predicting the above label at 10 instead of fixing the minimum number of neighbors with the same class label at 7. The query instances equal to or below this threshold of 10 will be set aside as a subset of testing instances to be classified by another method later.

7.1.4   Distance Selection

Most implementations of k-NN compute simple Euclidean distances. Unfortunately, the Euclidean distance attaches the same importance to any variable and is not informative enough for multidimensional sparse data. Ideally, the distance metric should be adaptable to the application at hand. On these grounds, a number of empirical works have demonstrated that k-NN classification can be greatly improved by learning an appropriate distance metric from the training data. This is the so-called **metric learning problem**.

The term *metric* refers to any distance function between two instances. The term has a formal meaning in mathematics. Denoting by $d(\mathbf{x}, \mathbf{y})$ the distance between two instances $\mathbf{x}$ and $\mathbf{y}$, a **metric** must conform to the following four conditions:

1. $d(\mathbf{x}, \mathbf{y}) \geq 0$ (nonnegativity)
2. $d(\mathbf{x}, \mathbf{y}) = 0$ if and only if $\mathbf{x} = \mathbf{y}$ (identity of indiscernibles)
3. $d(\mathbf{x}, \mathbf{y}) = d(\mathbf{y}, \mathbf{x})$ (symmetry)
4. $d(\mathbf{x}, \mathbf{z}) \leq d(\mathbf{x}, \mathbf{y}) + d(\mathbf{y}, \mathbf{z})$ (triangle inequality or subadditivity)

Although it is possible to build a k-NN classifier based on an affinity measure that is not a metric, the basic k-NN algorithm can avoid the computation of all distances between the instance to be classified, $\mathbf{x}$, and the labeled instances in $\mathcal{D}$ when using a metric, thanks to the triangle inequality.

A general expression for a metric between $\mathbf{x} = (x_1, \ldots, x_n)$ and $\mathbf{x}^i = (x_1^i, \ldots, x_n^i)$ for all $i = 1, \ldots, N$ (like the k-NN with weighted predictor variables discussed in Section 7.1.3.2) is given by:

$$d\left(\mathbf{x}, \mathbf{x}^i\right) = \sum_{j=1}^{n} w_j \delta\left(x_j, x_j^i\right),$$

where w_j is the weight assigned to variable X_j, and $\delta(x_j, x_j^i)$ measures the distance between the jth components of $\mathbf{x}$ and $\mathbf{x}^i$.

Discrete Predictors. For discrete predictors an intuitive expression for the δ function will count the *number of non-matching* variables, as follows:

$$\delta_{\text{non-matching}} = \begin{cases} 1 & \text{if } x_j \neq x_j^i \\ 0 & \text{if } x_j = x_j^i. \end{cases}$$

A more sophisticated distance is the **value difference metric** that uses class conditional probabilities to refine the contribution of each discrete variable to the distance calculation. It is defined as:

$$d_{\text{VDM}}(\mathbf{x}, \mathbf{x}^i) = \sum_{j=1}^{n} w(x_j) \delta\left(x_j, x_j^i\right),$$

with $\delta\left(x_j, x_j^i\right) = \sum_{c \in \Omega_C} \left(p(c|x_j) - p\left(c|x_j^i\right) \right)^2$, where $p(c|x_j)$ is the conditional probability of class label c given that $\mathbf{x}$ has value x_j in variable X_j (analogously for $p(c|x_j^i)$). The weight $w(x_j)$ is calculated as $w(x_j) = \sqrt{\sum_{c \in \Omega_C} p(c|x_j)^2}$. The weight will be high for variable values that discriminate well between the class labels.

Continuous Predictors. For continuous variables, the most used metrics are special cases of the **Minkowski distance**, whose general formula is

$$d_{\text{Minkowski}}(\mathbf{x}, \mathbf{x}^i) = \left(\sum_{j=1}^{n} |x_j - x_j^i|^p \right)^{\frac{1}{p}} \quad \text{for } p \geq 1.$$

The L_1 distance ($p = 1$) is also known as the **Manhattan distance**, and the L_2 distance is the Euclidean distance. Larger values of p have the effect of attaching greater weight to the variables on which the instances differ most. Another important Minkowski distance is the L_∞ or **Chebyshev distance** defined as:

$$d_{\text{Chebyshev}}(\mathbf{x}, \mathbf{x}^i) = \max_j |x_j - x_j^i|.$$

7.1.5   Determining the Optimal Value of k

The neighborhood parameter k, which controls the volume of the neighborhood and consequently the smoothness of the decision boundaries, plays an important role in the performance of a nearest neighbors classifier. Increasing k is supposed to increase the bias and reduce the variance of classification error. Existing theoretical results (Loftsgaarden and Quesenberry, 1965; Covert and Hart, 1967) suggest that if the Euclidean distance is used for classification, k should vary with N in such a way that $k \to \infty$ and $k/N \to 0$ as $N \to \infty$. However, for small or moderately large sample sizes, there is no theoretical guideline for choosing the optimum value of k. This optimum value depends on the specific data set, and it is to be estimated using the available training sample observations. In this context, likelihood cross-validation (Silverman, 1986) is an applicable idea, searching for the optimum value of k by maximizing the cross-validated log-likelihood (Section 4.1.2.2) score. In practice, cross-validation methods (Lachenbruch and Mickey, 1968; Stone, 1977) are used to estimate the misclassification rate for different values of k, and the value that leads to the lowest estimate of the misclassification rate is selected. This approach often fails to provide sound guidance for selecting k mainly because there are multiple values of k minimizing the estimated misclassification rate. Ghosh (2006) proposed a Bayesian method that solves the problem of multiple optimizers.

7.1.6   Prototype Selection

The selection of proper prototypes is one of the most promising solutions for avoiding the drawbacks of k-NN when working with big data sets. These techniques aim to output a representative smaller-sized training set than the original one that has a similar or even higher classification accuracy for new incoming data. Prototype selection aims to choose the best subset of the original training set (each subset assessed according to its corresponding accuracy), then it classifies a new pattern using the k-NN rule applied to the subset instead of the original training set. Ideally prototype selection methods try to find subsets that are both decision boundary consistent (the decision boundary found with the subset is identical to the boundary for the entire training set) and minimum consistent (the smallest subset of the training data where the majority label in the k nearest neighbors is the same as in the entire training data).

A standard categorization of prototype selection methods (García et al., 2012) considers three technique types: condensation methods, edition methods, and hybrid methods. Condensation methods aim to remove superfluous instances. Edition methods try to remove noisy instances in order to increase classifier accuracy. Finally, hybrid methods search for a subset of the training set that simultaneously eliminates both noisy and superfluous instances.

The **condensed nearest neighbors algorithm** (Hart, 1968) is iterative and starts by initializing the subset with a single training instance. In a second step, it classifies all remaining instances based on the subset, transferring any incorrectly classified samples to the subset. The last step repeatedly goes back to the second step until no transfers occur or the subset is full. The algorithm is incremental, order dependent, and neither minimal nor decision boundary consistent. The output subset will retain points that are closer to the decision boundaries, also called border points. At the same time, it will remove internal points. Gates (1972) proposed a variant of the condensed nearest neighbors algorithm, called **reduced nearest neighbors** based on removing an instance provided that this does not cause any incorrect classifications.

Edition methods (Wilson, 1972) produce smooth decision boundaries by removing points that do not agree with most of their k nearest neighbors (noisy instances), often retaining points far from the decision boundaries. This strategy results in homogeneous groups of points. Devijver and Kittler (1982) showed that the repeated application of Wilson's editing, called multi-edit, will lead to the Bayes error rate.

Hybrid methods combine edition and condensation strategies, for example, by first editing the training set to remove noise and smooth the decision boundary and then condensing the output of the edition to yield a smaller subset.

7.1.7   Instance-Based Learning

Instance-based learning (Aha et al., 1991) (IBL) extends k-NN by providing incremental facilities, significantly reducing the storage requirements and introducing a hypothesis test to detect noisy instances. Normalization of predictor variable ranges (avoiding, or reducing, the differences in scale for the Euclidean distance between two instances) and incremental instance processing are the main characteristics of the first member of this algorithm family: IB1. Thanks to this incrementality, decision boundaries can be changed over time as new data arrives.

IB2 was designed to reduce storage requirements. Its underlying idea is that only instances near the decision boundaries are needed to produce an accurate approximation of the classification. Instances not close to the boundaries do not really matter for classification purposes. IB2 saves space by storing only informative instances. The set of informative instances is approximated as the training instances misclassified by IB1.

IB3 is a noise-tolerant extension of IB2 that decides, using a simple test, which of the saved instances should be used to make classifications. Thus, IB3 maintains a classification record of each saved instance. This classification record contains the performance of each instance that is used to classify new ones. Finally, IB3 uses a significance test to determine which instances are good classifiers and which are believed to be noisy. The good classifiers are used to classify the new instances. The noisy instances are discarded.

7.1.8   Example: Interneurons versus Pyramidal Neurons

Data Set 1 described in Chapter 1 was designed to discriminate between interneurons (I) and pyramidal neurons (P). The IB1 and IB3 classifiers were run with the following FSS strategies: (a) considering all original variables as predictors, (b) using a univariate filter based on the gain ratio of a variable with respect to the class (Section 6.2.1), where variables falling below a cutoff point were discarded, (c) using the CFS multivariate filter (Section 6.2.2), using as the search method greedy forward hill-climbing with a backtracking facility, that is, specifying how many consecutive non-improved variables (fixed in our case at 5) must be found before the search backtracks, and (d) using a wrapper approach with the same search method. The experiments were conducted in WEKA (Hall et al., 2009) using classifiers IB1, and IBk with $k = 3$, and `GainRatioAttributeEval`, `CfsSubsetEval`, and `WrapperSubsetEval` as variable evaluators for strategies (b), (c), and (d), respectively, and `BestFirst` as the search method for strategies (c) and (d).

Table 7.2 Main performance measures of an IB3 classification algorithm for Data Set 1. A wrapper approach selected these 18 variables out of 65: Somatic aspect ratio (X_3), Somatic roundness (X_6), Axonal node total (X_7), Axonal local angle ave (X_{15}), Stdv of tortuosity of axonal segments (X_{20}), Axonal segment length stdv (X_{22}), Number axonal Sholl sections (X_{25}), Axonal node density2 (X_{30}), Convex hull axon surface area (X_{34}), Ave length of dendrites (µm) (X_{39}), Ratio of dendritic length to surface area (X_{41}), Highest order dendritic segment (X_{42}), Ave tortuosity of dendritic segments (X_{50}), Stdv of tortuosity of dendritic segments (X_{51}), Dendritic segment length ave (X_{52}), Stdv of tortuosity of dendritic nodes (X_{55}), Number dendritic Sholl sections (X_{56}), and Convex hull dendrite volume (X_{62})

Measure	Value
Accuracy	0.8928
Sensitivity	0.9146
Specificity	0.8594
F_1-measure	0.9123
Cohen's kappa	0.7750
Brier score	0.1949
AUC	0.9235

The univariate filter selected 15 variables, using 0.1178 as a threshold for the gain ratio (variables ordered by the gain ratio):

$$X_{56}, X_{22}, X_{42}, X_{21}, X_{60}, X_{63}, X_{30}, X_{61}, X_{35}, X_7, X_4, X_6, X_{47}, X_{53}, \text{ and } X_{38}.$$

The CFS multivariate filter selected the following 17 variables:

$$X_4, X_5, X_{10}, X_{14}, X_{21}, X_{22}, X_{25}, X_{30}, X_{35}, X_{37}, X_{40}, X_{42}, X_{51}, X_{53}, X_{56}, X_{59}, \text{ and } X_{63}.$$

The accuracy of IB1 and IB3 improved as they move from strategy (a), with no feature selection, toward strategy (d) using a wrapper approach. Also IB3 provided better performance than IB1 in all four strategies. The IB3 algorithm achieved the best accuracy, 0.8928, using a wrapper FSS strategy. Table 7.2 includes that accuracy and other performance measures, all of which were estimated with 10-fold stratified cross-validation. Additionally, the list of 18 selected variables is shown.

The confusion matrix, with real labels in rows and predicted labels in columns, is

$$\begin{matrix} & \text{I} & \text{P} \\ \text{I} & \begin{pmatrix} 182 & 17 \\ \text{P} & 18 & 110 \end{pmatrix} \end{matrix}.$$

Approximately the same number of pyramidal neurons were wrongly classified as interneurons (18) as interneurons that were wrongly classified as pyramidal neurons (17), where there are more real interneurons (199) than real pyramidal cells (128). Of the 65 variables, the 18 selected by the wrapper IB3 to predict the class of neuron include 2 soma (X_3 and X_6), 7 axonal (X_7, X_{15}, X_{20}, X_{22}, X_{25}, X_{30}, X_{34}), and 9 dendritic features (X_{39}, X_{41}, X_{42}, X_{50}, X_{51}, X_{52}, X_{55}, X_{56}, X_{62}).

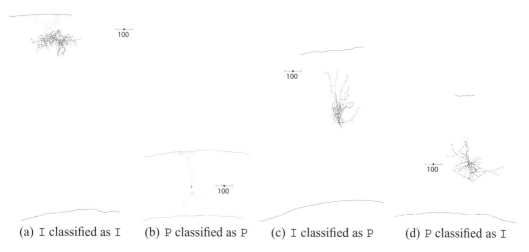

(a) I classified as I   (b) P classified as P   (c) I classified as P   (d) P classified as I

Figure 7.4 Some neurons and their classification by IB3. (a) Correctly classified interneuron $\mathbf{x}^{145}$. (b) Correctly classified pyramidal neuron $\mathbf{x}^{241}$. (c) Misclassified interneuron $\mathbf{x}^{64}$. (d) Misclassified pyramidal cell $\mathbf{x}^{207}$. Axonal arbor in blue and dendritic tree in red. For the color version, please refer to the plate section.

Figure 7.4 illustrates four examples of neurons with different classification results. In (a), interneuron $\mathbf{x}^{145}$ was correctly classified by IB3; in (b), pyramidal cell $\mathbf{x}^{241}$ was correctly classified; in (c), interneuron $\mathbf{x}^{64}$ was misclassified as a pyramidal cell; and in (d), pyramidal neuron $\mathbf{x}^{207}$ was misclassified as an interneuron.

7.2   Classification Trees

Classification trees, also called **decision trees**, are classifiers expressed as a recursive partition of the instance space. They are very popular due to their comprehensibility. The tree has three kinds of nodes. First is a root node with no incoming edges and several outgoing edges. Second is internal nodes or test nodes, with one incoming edge and several outgoing edges. Third is terminal nodes or decision nodes, also known as leaves, with one incoming edge and no outgoing edges.

Each non-leaf node splits the instance space into two or more subspaces according to a function of the variable values. This function is normally simply a value (for a discrete variable) or a range of values (for a continuous variable). Nodes are labeled with the variable(s) that they test, and their branches are labeled with their respective values. Each leaf node is assigned to one class value. Leaves are represented by rectangles as opposed to the circles representing all other nodes. The root node contains the training sample from which the tree is grown. The partition at offspring nodes is finer than at the preceding nodes. Therefore, offspring nodes contain subsets of the training sample.

Unseen instances are classified by sorting down the tree from the root to a leaf node according to the outcome of the tests along the path. The leaf contains the predicted class. Each path from the root of a classification tree to one of its leaves can be transformed into a rule (Section 7.3) simply by conjoining the tests along the path to form the antecedent part of the rule and taking the leaf class prediction to form the consequent of the rule. Thus, the tree represents a disjunction of conjunctions on the instance variable values. Nodes of continuous variables X are commonly tested for $X \geq x$ or $X < x$. Hence, classification trees can be geometrically interpreted as a set of hyperplanes, each orthogonal to one of the axes.

Example. To understand the main features of a classification tree, let us take a subset of Data Set 1 to be classified as interneurons or pyramidal cells, including 20 neurons handpicked to better illustrate the ideas. Both selected variables are discrete: Number of dendritic Sholl sections (X_{56}) and Number of axonal Sholl sections (X_{25}), see Table 7.3. The reduced data set is further simplified by grouping the values of both variables into two categories: "2 to 5" and "more than 5."

Figure 7.5(a) shows the data set as a scatterplot of points (X_{56}, X_{25}), where the dot color distinguishes interneurons (dark gray) from pyramidal cells (light gray). Figure 7.5(b) shows the resulting classification tree. It contains one root node, one internal node, and three leaves. The three paths from the root node to a leaf can be transformed into three IF-THEN rules as follows:

$\mathcal{R}_1$: IF $(X_{25} \in \{2,3,4,5\}$ AND $X_{56} \in \{2,3,4,5\})$ THEN $C = $I
$\mathcal{R}_2$: IF $(X_{25} \in \{2,3,4,5\}$ AND $X_{56} > 5)$ THEN $C = $P
$\mathcal{R}_3$: IF $X_{25} > 5$ THEN $C = $P

Thus the instance space is split into two subspaces: one corresponding to the values of X_{25} and X_{56} from 2 to 5, labeled as interneuron, and the remaining space (union of two partitions), labeled as pyramidal cell.

Table 7.3 Subset of Data Set 1 with 20 neurons and 2 variables: Number of dendritic Sholl sections (X_{56}) and Number of axonal Sholl sections (X_{25})

Obs.	X_{56}	X_{25}	Class
x^{11}	2	4	I
x^{23}	4	3	I
x^{45}	7	14	I
x^{51}	4	5	I
x^{79}	3	5	I
x^{122}	7	9	I
x^{126}	4	4	I
x^{185}	2	2	I
x^{211}	5	7	P
x^{219}	3	7	P
x^{221}	14	14	P
x^{234}	13	11	P
x^{239}	13	13	P
x^{241}	11	2	P
x^{242}	5	9	P
x^{244}	6	8	P
x^{246}	14	10	P
x^{249}	12	5	P
x^{251}	3	6	P
x^{321}	14	5	P

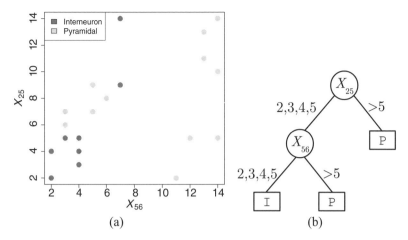

Figure 7.5 (a) Scatterplot of Number of dendritic Sholl sections (X_{56}) versus Number of axonal Sholl sections (X_{25}) for the subset of Data Set 1 listed in Table 7.3. (b) Classification tree learned from this data set.

Given this classifier, the neuroscientist can predict whether a cell is pyramidal or interneuron by sorting the cell down the tree. For instance, a neuron with 4 axonal sections ($X_{25} = 4$) and 10 dendritic Scholl sections ($X_{56} = 10$) will be classified as pyramidal. This instance will navigate from the root node X_{25} down to the internal node X_{56} to finally reach the leaf where label P is found (second path or rule $\mathcal{R}_2$).

The tree was output using WEKA software (Hall et al., 2009) and achieves 90% accuracy, estimated by means of 10-fold stratified cross-validation. All pyramidal neurons (12) are correctly classified. Only 2 ($\mathbf{x}^{45}$ and $\mathbf{x}^{122}$) out of 8 interneurons are misclassified as pyramidal cells (see the 2 dark gray points closest to the legend in Figure 7.5(a)).

Note that the third path involves just one variable implying that the instances with $X_{25} > 5$ only require X_{25} to be classified and X_{56} is not used. ∎

Thus, classification trees perform FSS by using an embedded approach (see Section 6.4). In Sampat et al. (2009), a decision tree discriminated clinical subtypes of MS: relapsing-remitting MS, secondary-progressive MS, and primary-progressive MS. Of the 10 features considered, only 2 were retained by the tree: the medulla oblongata volume and the central corpus callosum segment area.

The algorithms that automatically construct a classification tree from a given data set may have different goals: minimizing the generalization error, number of nodes, leaves, variables used, average depth, etc. Less complex classification trees are preferred (parsimonious principle or Occam's razor, Section 1.5.2). The simplest decision trees with only one level are called decision stumps (see also Section 6.2.1.2).

Finding an optimal decision tree is considered to be a hard task (in fact, constructing a minimal binary decision tree with the fewest tests required to classify an unseen instance is an NP-complete problem [Hyafil and Rivest 1976]) and is only feasible for small problems. Therefore, efficient heuristics are required, where top-down methods are usually preferred to bottom-up methods. These algorithms are greedy and recursively partition the training set using the outcome of a splitting function of the input variables. Each node further subdivides the training set into smaller subsets until a stopping criterion is satisfied. This will output only local – not necessarily global – optimal solutions.

7.2.1 The Basic ID3 Algorithm

Most algorithms for learning classification trees are variations on a core algorithm called **ID3** (Quinlan, 1986). ID3 stands for *iterative dichotomiser* and is based on the Concept Learning Systems algorithm that used only binary variables. The algorithm has to determine which tests (questions) best divide the instances into separate classes, forming a tree. Each split partitions the instances into two or more parts. If there is only one class label in a part, then this subset of instances is pure, else it is impure. The purer the partition is, the better it is.

The key issue then is to find the best split. ID3 chooses to maximize the mutual information, or **information gain** achieved when using a variable X_i, to branch the tree, that is, to select the root node of the tree ID3 solves

$$\max_i \mathbb{I}(C, X_i) = \mathbb{H}(C) - \mathbb{H}(C|X_i) = -\sum_c p(c)\log_2 p(c) + \sum_c \sum_{x_i} p(c, x_i)\log_2 p(c|x_i), \quad (7.1)$$

where $\mathbb{I}$ is the mutual information and $\mathbb{H}$ the entropy (Section 3.6). Thus, the difference in Equation (7.1) between the two entropy terms reflects the decrease in the entropy (uncertainty) of C or the information gained from partitioning the examples according to X_i. After selecting the variable to be used as the test at the root node, a descendant is created for each value of this variable, and the training examples are sorted to the appropriate descendant node. Recall that $\mathbb{H}(C|X_i) = \sum_{x_i} p(x_i)\mathbb{H}(C|X_i = x_i) = -\sum_{x_i} p(x_i)\sum_c p(c|x_i)\log_2 p(c|x_i)$. Then the second term in Equation (7.1) is simply the sum of the entropies of C in the subset for which $X_i = x_i$, weighted by $p(x_i)$, i.e., this second term is the weighted entropy of the descendant nodes after splitting. Hence ID3 attempts to solve

$$\min_i \mathbb{H}(C|X_i) = \sum_{x_i} p(x_i)\mathbb{H}(C|X_i = x_i). \quad (7.2)$$

The process is repeated using the examples associated with each descendant node to select the best variable to be tested at that point in the tree. The algorithm never backtracks to reconsider earlier choices. Variables not yet used in each path are node candidates. ID3 stops at a node when the tree correctly classifies all its examples (all the instances in a node are of the same class, called pure node) or when all variables have been used.

Example. To illustrate the operation of ID3, consider again the reduced data set of Table 7.3. The entropy of the class is $\mathbb{H}(C) = -\frac{8}{20}\log_2\frac{8}{20} - \frac{12}{20}\log_2\frac{12}{20} = 0.9709$. To decide which variable is to be tested first in the tree, ID3 computes the information gain of each variable: $\mathbb{I}(C, X'_{56}) = 0.9709 - 0.8464 = 0.1245, \mathbb{I}(C, X'_{25}) = 0.9709 - 0.7895 = 0.1814$. Primed variables denote the binary variable X' resulting from grouping the X values into 2 categories (0 for "2 to 5" X values and 1 for "more than 5" X values). Then X'_{25} is selected as the root node, and 2 branches are created below it for each of its possible values (0 and 1).

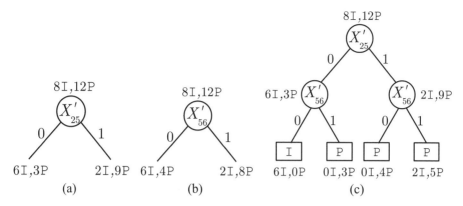

Figure 7.6 (a) Result of choosing X'_{25} as the root node for the classification tree learned from the subset of Data Set 1 listed in Table 7.3. (b) Result of the choice of X'_{56} as the root node. (c) Whole partitioning process during classification tree learning from this data set.

The resulting partial classification tree is shown in Figure 7.6(a), along with the training examples sorted to each new descendant node. Figure 7.6(b) shows the equivalent situation if X'_{56} is selected. Thus, sorting the initial collection of 8 interneurons and 12 pyramidal cells by their number of axonal Sholl sections produces collections of 6 interneurons and 3 pyramidal cells (2–5 axonal Sholl sections) and 2 interneurons and 9 pyramidal cells (>5 axonal Sholl sections). More information is gained from this partitioning than is produced by the number of dendritic Sholl sections.

The process of selecting a variable and partitioning the training instances is repeated for each nonterminal descendant node, this time using only the instances associated with the respective node. Considering branch $X'_{25} = 0$ with 9 instances (6 interneurons and 3 pyramidal cells), the entropy of the class is now $\mathbb{H}\left(C_{X'_{25}=0}\right) = -\frac{6}{9}\log_2\frac{6}{9} - \frac{3}{9}\log_2\frac{3}{9} = 0.9182$. $C_{X'_{25}=0}$ denotes the class variable restricted to instances with $X'_{25} = 0$. Because there is only one variable left, X'_{56} is chosen. All the instances have the same class value along the two branches of X'_{56} and $\mathbb{H}\left(C_{X'_{25}=0}|X'_{56}\right) = 0$ (hence $\mathbb{I}\left(C_{X'_{25}=0},X'_{56}\right) = 0.9182$). Therefore, both descendants become leaves with classification $C =$ I for the left branch and $C =$ P for the right branch, see Figure 7.6(c).

Finally, considering branch $X'_{25} = 1$ with 11 instances (2 interneurons and 9 pyramidal cells), the entropy of the class is now $\mathbb{H}\left(C_{X'_{25}=1}\right) = -\frac{2}{11}\log_2\frac{2}{11} - \frac{9}{11}\log_2\frac{9}{11} = 0.6840$. When X'_{56} is chosen, $\mathbb{H}\left(C_{X'_{25}=1}|X'_{56}\right) = 0.5493$, and hence $\mathbb{I}\left(C_{X'_{25}=1},X'_{56}\right) = 0.1347$. Instances with $X'_{56} = 0$ (left branch) are perfectly classified, and the descendant becomes a leaf with the classification $C =$ P. However, 2 interneurons out of 7 instances with $X'_{56} = 1$ (right branch) are misclassified. If there are no further variables, the algorithm must stop with above two errors in the right branch, and the descendant becomes a leaf also with the classification $C =$ P, the majority label. The final classification tree is shown in Figure 7.6(c), which is equivalent to Figure 7.5(b). ∎

7.2.2 Splitting Criteria

A change to the splitting criterion leads to ID3 variants. In most cases, the splitting functions are univariate, i.e., the node is split according to the value of a single variable. In multivariate splitting criteria, several, usually linearly combined, variables may be tested

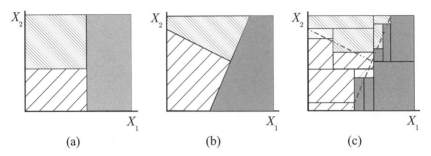

Figure 7.7 (a) Typical hyperrectangle partitioning of a classification tree in the feature space. (b) Polygonal partitioning produced by an oblique classification tree. (c) An axis-parallel tree designed to approximate the polygonal space partitioning of (b). Colors/filling refer to different class labels.

at a node. These are **oblique classification trees** because the splits are not necessarily axis-parallel.

Figure 7.7(a) shows a typical feature space partitioning of an axis-parallel classification tree that uses two continuous variables X_1 and X_2, where the tests at the internal nodes have the form $X_i \leq a$ and $X_i > a, i = 1, 2$. In Figure 7.7(b), the tests are linear combinations of the variables, i.e., they have the form $a_0 + a_1X_1 + a_2X_2 > 0$ $(a_0, a_1, a_2 \in \mathbb{R})$. These tests are equivalent to hyperplanes at an oblique angle to the axes (producing a polygonal partitioning), as opposed to the axis-parallel hyperplanes (hyperrectangle partitioning) in Figure 7.7(a). If the underlying separation of class labels were as shown in Figure 7.7(b), an oblique tree would be a simple and accurate model defined by two oblique hyperplanes. However, axis-parallel methods would have to approximate the correct model in this domain using a staircase-like structure as is shown in Figure 7.7(c).

Oblique trees select the best linear combination rather than the best variable, i.e., which features to use and their weights in the linear combination. Others like Yildiz and Alpaydın (2001) use nonlinear models (e.g., a multi-layer perceptron) for nodes close to the root, where the decision complexity is greater, and linear models as we move down the tree, where the decisions are simpler. Greedy search, linear programming, and others can find the best multivariate criteria. This more complex setting renders these criteria less popular.

Interestingly, the choice of the splitting criteria does not make much difference to tree performance, as pointed out by many researchers. There does not appear to be one particular node splitting that performs best in all cases, as the no free lunch theorem (Section 9.1) suggests. Nevertheless, common univariate splitting criteria are explained below and summarized in Table 7.4.

Many splitting criteria are (im)purity functions. They emphasize the purity of the split subsets. This group is divided into three measures: the information gain (used in ID3), the gain ratio, and the Gini index.

The information gain criterion tends to favor variables with many outcomes. An extreme case of a key variable (an identifier like the neuron ID in the above example) would yield the optimum tree regarding its information gain (with only this variable), but this tree would be useless for classifying unseen data. This led to the introduction of "normalized" information gain. This is the **gain ratio** criterion, which solves

$$\max_i \frac{\mathbb{I}(C, X_i)}{\mathbb{H}(X_i)}. \tag{7.3}$$

Table 7.4 Most common univariate splitting criteria for building classification trees

Criterion	Equation #
(Im)Purity measures:	
Information gain	(7.1) or (7.2)
Gain ratio	(7.3)
Gini index	(7.4)
Disparity measures:	
Distance measure	(7.4)
Degree of orthogonality measure	(7.5)
Statistical measures:	
Chi-squared statistic	(7.6)
Likelihood-ratio chi-squared statistic	(7.7)
Other measures:	
AUC	(5.1)

Note that gain ratio was also used as a univariate filter method in FSS (Section 6.2.1). Note that this ratio is not defined when the denominator is zero. The ratio tends to favor variables whose denominator is very small and may choose variables with very low $\mathbb{H}(X_i)$ rather than high gain. Consequently, the recommendation is to choose the variable with the maximum gain ratio from among the variables whose initial (non-modified) information gain is at least as high as the average information gain of all the variables. Both the information gain and gain ratio criteria tend to build quite unbalanced trees because the entropy measures on which they are based favor uneven partitions when the purity of one partition is high. The gain ratio has been shown to outperform information gain in terms of both accuracy and classifier complexity. This is the splitting criterion used in the C4.5 algorithm explained below (Section 7.2.5).

The **Gini index** of diversity aims at minimizing the impurity contained in the training subsets yielded after branching the decision tree. Modeled on the decrease of entropy (or information gain) used in Equation (7.2), the decrease in this case is of impurity:

$$\min_i \text{Gini}(X_i) = \sum_{x_i} p(x_i)\text{Gini}(C|X_i = x_i)$$

$$= \sum_{x_i} p(x_i) \sum_c p(C = c|x_i)p(C \neq c|x_i)$$

$$= \sum_{x_i} p(x_i)(1 - \sum_c p^2(c|x_i)).$$

$\text{Gini}(C|X_i = x_i)$ is just the expected error rate at branch $X_i = x_i$ if the class labels are selected according to the class distribution present in that branch, that is, the probability of a random sample being misclassified if we classified instances into class c with probability $p(C = c|x_i)$. Alternatively, if we code each instance as 1 for class c and 0 otherwise, the variance over the branch is $p(C = c|x_i)p(C \neq c|x_i)$. The summation of these products over all c values yields $\text{Gini}(C|X_i = x_i)$. Note how similar this expression and Equations (7.1)–(7.2) are because we have just replaced $-\log_2 p(c|x_i)$ by $p(\neg c|x_i)$. In fact, both are alternative impurity measures. Breiman (1996b) showed a theoretical comparison between the Gini index and information gain for binary trees. The conclusion was that, with many classes (R is large), the Gini index prefers splits that put the largest class into one pure node and all others into the other node, whereas information gain balances the sizes at the two descendant nodes. For small R, both should produce similar results. Like entropy, $\text{Gini}(C|X_i = x_i)$ is maximal if the classes are perfectly mixed. The Gini index is the splitting criterion used in CART (Breiman et al., 1984), see Section 7.2.5.

The Gini index can also be seen as a divergence measure between the probability distributions of the C values. This somewhat resembles another group of splitting measures that compute the difference between the split subsets using distances or angles, thereby emphasizing their disparity. This group is again divided into two measures. One is an alternative to the gain ratio normalization using a **distance measure** (López de Mántaras, 1991):

$$\max_i \frac{\mathbb{I}(C, X_i)}{-\sum_c \sum_{x_i} p(c, x_i) \log_2 p(c, x_i)}. \tag{7.4}$$

The second is for binary variables ($\Omega_{X_i} = \{x_{i1}, x_{i2}\}$) and proposes a **degree of orthogonality measure** (angular disparity) (Fayyad and Irani, 1992):

$$\max_i \left(1 - \frac{\sum_c p(c, x_{i1}) p(c, x_{i2})}{\sqrt{(\sum_c p^2(c, x_{i1}))(\sum_c p^2(c, x_{i2}))}}\right). \tag{7.5}$$

Note that the fraction is the cosine of the angle between the two vectors of the probability distribution of C in the partitions given by X_i, i.e., the vectors $(p(c_1|x_{i1}), \ldots, p(c_R|x_{i1}))$ and $(p(c_1|x_{i2}), \ldots, p(c_R|x_{i2}))$, which should be uneven (cosine close to zero).

A third group of splitting functions is derived from statistical measures of independence between the class proportions and the split subsets, emphasizing the reliability of class predictions. We present the two most important functions, the chi-squared statistic and the likelihood-ratio chi-squared statistic. Both start from the contingency table of N instances in the parent node arranging the splits of C ($\Omega_C = \{1, 2, \ldots, R\}$) and variable X_i ($\Omega_{X_i} = \{1, 2, \ldots, R_i\}$) (Table 7.5).

The null hypothesis of the chi-squared test of independence (Section 4.2.8) is that the class frequencies are independent of the split, that is, the a priori class frequencies (before choosing the split node) and the class frequencies because of the split are very similar. Under this hypothesis, the chi-squared statistic

Table 7.5 Contingency table of the splits of C and X_i. The parent node has N instances, and N_{jk} is the number of instances where $C = j$ and $X_i = k$. This is the same notation as for selecting the root node of the tree; for any other node this should be changed accordingly (because the node will include a subset of the original N instances)

		X_i				
		1	2	$\ldots$	R_i	
	1	N_{11}	N_{12}	$\ldots$	N_{1R_i}	$N_{1\bullet}$
	2	N_{21}	N_{22}	$\ldots$	N_{2R_i}	$N_{2\bullet}$
	.	.	.		.	.
C	.	.	.		.	.
	.	.	.		.	.
	R	N_{R1}	N_{R2}	$\ldots$	N_{RR_i}	$N_{R\bullet}$
		$N_{\bullet 1}$	$N_{\bullet 2}$	$\ldots$	$N_{\bullet R_i}$	N

$$W = \sum_{j=1}^{R} \sum_{k=1}^{R_i} \frac{(O_{jk} - E_{jk})^2}{E_{jk}}, \tag{7.6}$$

where $O_{jk} = N_{jk}$ are the observed frequencies (because of the split) and $E_{jk} = \frac{N_{j\bullet}N_{\bullet k}}{N}$ are the expected frequencies (a priori class frequencies), is distributed approximately as $\chi^2_{(R-1)(R_i-1)}$. Thus, for any variables rejecting the null hypothesis, the splitting criterion will choose X_i with the smallest p-value.

The **likelihood-ratio chi-squared statistic** is

$$G^2 = 2 \sum_{j=1}^{R} \sum_{k=1}^{R_i} N_{jk} \ln \left(\frac{O_{jk}}{E_{jk}} \right) = 2N \, (\ln 2) \, \mathbb{I}(C, X_i). \tag{7.7}$$

G^2 also approximately follows a $\chi^2_{(R-1)(R_i-1)}$ distribution (its convergence is slower than W) under the null hypothesis that the class frequencies are independent of the split. Note that, thanks to the above equality, we can use G^2 to measure the statistical significance of the information gain criterion.

Other splitting criteria can be found in the literature (Berzal et al., 2003). Ferri et al. (2002) proposed selecting the variable that yields the maximal area under the ROC curve (Section 5.2.3). This outperforms other criteria with respect to both AUC and classification accuracy. Most of the prolific comparisons of univariate splitting criteria (Buntine and Niblett, 1992; Fayyad and Irani, 1992; Shih, 1999; Rokach and Maimon, 2005b; Osei-Bryson and Giles, 2006) are based on empirical results.

7.2.3   Stopping Criteria and Pruning

The depth of the tree in the above example is two. Tree complexity has a crucial effect on its accuracy and is controlled by the stopping criteria and the pruning method. Heavily pruned trees are expected to have smaller variance and larger bias than fully grown trees.

The tree-growing phase continues until a stopping criterion is triggered. Apart from having pure nodes like ID3, there are other stopping rules. We can halt the algorithm when (a) the maximum tree depth has been reached, (b) the best splitting criterion is not greater than a certain threshold, or (c) the number of instances in a descendant node is fewer than some threshold, etc.

Tight stopping criteria will create small and underfitted decision trees, whereas loose stopping criteria will produce large and overfitted trees. For instance, ID3 loosely creates leaves when the instances at a node are pure. If there is noise in the data, we can learn the noise. If we have a few examples associated with a leaf, then it is hard to produce a representative sample of the true target function. Therefore, the resulting trees are likely to be **overfitted** to the training set, i.e., they perform well on training data but poorly on unseen data. The model is then unable to generalize. An overfitted decision tree can be indirectly simplified by means of data preprocessing, that is, by performing FSS to build a simpler tree.

However, the overfitting problem has been traditionally tackled using pruning methods. In **prepruning**, a termination condition determines when to stop growing some branches while the decision tree is generated. This is usually performed by means of a statistical hypothesis test. In **postpruning**, the tree is grown in full and is then pruned, replacing some

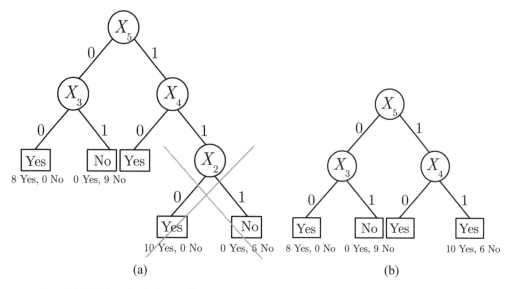

Figure 7.8 (a) Hypothetical tree where the bottommost subtree is to be pruned. (b) Resulting tree after pruning.

subtrees by a leaf. Postpruning is more successful in practice, although computationally more costly.

A node is pruned if this improves a specified criterion. Many splitting criterion options have been proposed. A simple procedure is known as **reduced error pruning** (Quinlan, 1987). It performs a bottom-up traversal of the nodes. Thus, it moves from the bottom to the top, checking that replacing a node with the most frequent class label of the training instances affiliated with the respective node does not reduce tree accuracy. If accuracy is not reduced, the node is pruned, i.e., the subtree rooted by the node is removed and converted into a leaf node. When many nodes are marked for pruning, the node whose removal most increases accuracy is selected. The procedure continues until any further pruning would lower accuracy. Accuracy is estimated by a pruning set.

Figure 7.8(a) shows a hypothetical tree with two potential subtrees for pruning: subtrees rooted at X_3 and X_2. The instances sorted to each new descendant node are also shown. If tree accuracy increases most after pruning node X_2, a leaf node replaces the subtree rooted at X_2 in the resulting tree, shown in Figure 7.8(b). The label is "Yes," which is the most frequent class label in the 16 respective instances.

Other pruning criteria are cost-complexity pruning (implemented in the well-known CART algorithm), minimum error pruning, pessimistic pruning, error-based pruning (used in the C4.5 algorithm), optimal pruning, minimum description length pruning, and the critical value method. Muata and Bryson (2007) proposed pruning as a multi-objective problem (e.g., accounting for accuracy, simplicity, interpretability...). Some studies (Quinlan, 1987; Esposito et al., 1997) empirically compared their performance concluding that some are biased toward overpruning (smaller but less accurate trees) and others toward underpruning. Indeed, the no free lunch theorem (Section 9.1) once again applies, and there is no pruning method that outperforms other pruning methods across the board. Most pruning algorithms have poor time complexities. Based on a greedy strategy, they cannot guarantee solution optimality. However, they often improve the generalization accuracy.

7.2.4 Other Issues

The first issue is how to handle continuous variables. Such variables X_i can be prediscretized. However, a more powerful solution is to extend the above ideas. We will restrict the options to a simple binary split, i.e., $X_i < a$ and $X_i \geq a$ ($a \in \mathbb{R}$), although testing against several constants is also possible. To find the breakpoint a, we first sort the instances according to the X_i values. Candidate breakpoints are for instances from different classes and are commonly taken as the average between the two values with different labels. For example, if the X_i values, already sorted, with their corresponding class values are

X_i	20	22.6	34	45	62	65
C	No	No	Yes	Yes	Yes	No

then we have two a candidates: $a_1 = (22.6+34)/2 = 28.3$ and $a_2 = (62+65)/2 = 63.5$. The splitting criterion would be computed for each candidate $X_i < 28.3$ and $X_i \geq 28.3$ versus $X_i < 63.5$ and $X_i \geq 63.5$, both competing with the other discrete variables to become a splitting node.

Note that whereas a discrete variable can only be tested once on any path from the root of a tree to the leaf, a continuous variable can be tested many times. This yields trees that are harder to understand because the tests on any single continuous variable are scattered along the path.

The second issue is how to deal with missing values in the predictor variables. There are several options. The most drastic solution is to eliminate all instances with some unknown value. This will lead to the loss of a lot of information if the data set is not large because instances with missing values often provide a good deal of information. A less drastic alternative is to simply ignore instances with unknown X_i, forming the set $\mathcal{D}_{X_i=?}$, when calculating the splitting criterion over X_i. The criterion should be reduced proportionally, i.e., by multiplying it by $\frac{|\mathcal{D} \backslash \mathcal{D}_{X_i=?}|}{|\mathcal{D}|}$, as nothing will have been learned from such instances. If the criterion value is normalized (like the gain ratio), the denominator should be calculated as if the missing values represent an additional value in the variable domain.

Alternatively, missing values can be estimated based on other instances, i.e., by imputation (Section 2.5). A missing value for discrete X_i can be imputed by its mode, i.e., the most common value for X_i within the instances associated with the node. More refinedly, we can impute the missing value as the mode of X_i among the instances with the same label as the instance with the missing value. Furthermore, we can even split the instance into pieces, one piece per branch. The pieces are passed down at the same rate as the known instances move down the branches. These pieces are weighted accordingly in the splitting criterion computation. Instead of having integer counts, the weights are used to compute gain figures, for example.

Missing values in a new instance to be classified can be handled similarly. When the instance arrives at a node at which it cannot be tested because of a missing value, it is split into pieces and passed down all its branches, as mentioned above. Each branch outputs a class distribution. Eventually, the various pieces of the instance will each reach a leaf node, and the predicted class will be the class with the highest probability in the weighted union of all leaf nodes reached by this instance. Alternatively, when the value of a variable in a split is missing, another approach is to find a surrogate split (a mimic, clone, or substitute for the primary splitter), which uses a different variable and which most resembles the original split. This is used in the CART algorithm (see Section 7.2.5).

Another issue is how to include costs. Misclassification costs can be included in an algorithm by penalizing the different errors. Also, the splitting criterion can account for predictor variable measurements that have different costs (e.g., conducting a biopsy is more expensive than taking a temperature). The idea is to try to favor lower-cost variables for the starting nodes (closer to the root) because they are tested on more instances. Thus, if the cost of X_i is $\text{Cost}(X_i)$, the information gain would turn into $\mathbb{I}(C, X_i)/\text{Cost}(X_i)$. Finally, some decision tree algorithms treat instances differently by weighting their contribution to the analysis according to a specified weight between 0 and 1.

7.2.5   Popular Classification Tree Algorithms

Some popular classification tree algorithms are briefly explained below.

Recall that ID3 does not apply any pruning method and does not handle continuous variables or missing values. **C4.5** (Quinlan, 1993) is an evolution of ID3. It uses gain ratio as a splitting criterion and can handle continuous variables and missing values. After the growing phase, error-based pruning is performed. C4.5 is stopped when the number of instances to be split is below a specified threshold. A special feature of C4.5 is that postpruning is performed over the set of rules generated from the decision tree. Pruning consists of eliminating antecedents from a rule whenever accuracy increases. The rule is completely deleted if it has no antecedents. Using rules instead of the tree, contexts or (sub)paths rather than subtrees can be pruned.

The C4.5 tree of Tripoliti et al. (2013) was built to detect freezing of gait events in patients suffering from PD using signals received from wearable sensors (accelerometers and gyroscopes) placed on the patient's body. Other classifiers were also tested: naive Bayes (Section 8.4.1.1), random forests and random trees (Section 9.3.4). The severity staging of a PD patient (the Hoehn & Yahr index and the clinical impression of severity index) was predicted with a C4.5 classification tree in Armañanzas et al. (2013) using scores of non-motor symptoms. Other classifiers were also tested: k-NN, artificial neural networks (Section 7.4), linear discriminant analysis, and selective (discrete) naive Bayes (Section 8.4.1.2).

The C4.5 classification tree algorithm was also used in Frantzidis et al. (2010). The aim was to robustly discriminate emotional physiological signals evoked upon viewing pictures, i.e., signals taken as multichannel recordings (electrodermal activity measured by a pair of electrodes placed on digit middle phalanges and EEG) of both the central and the autonomic nervous system. The tree distinguished between the affective conditions of pleasant and unpleasant. A wrapper FSS process based on the best-first search method (Section 6.3.1.1) was performed before applying C4.5.

Classification and Regression Trees or CART (Breiman et al., 1984) constructs binary trees (two outgoing edges per node). CART offers many splitting criteria, mainly the Gini index (univariate) and a linear combination of continuous predictor variables (multivariate). It applies cost-complexity pruning. CART can consider misclassification costs and prior probability distributions provided by users. It has the ability to generate regression trees, where a real number prediction of a continuous variable C rather than a class is found at the leaves.

Handley et al. (2014) used CART to determine specific risk profiles to predict suicidal ideation at the five-year follow-up in older adults. Profiles were determined from psychological, physical, and social factors, including psychological distress, physical functioning, and social support. Lipkovich et al. (2006) used CART to help predict substantial weight gain (5 kg or 7% of initial weight in 30 ± 2 weeks) during treatment of bipolar disorder with olanzapine. Predictor variables included ethnicity, age, lower body mass index, nonrapid cycling, and psychotic features. Boykin et al. (2012) investigated the ability to correctly infer effective connectivity (the direct causal influence of one neuron over the other) from neural time series recordings. Bivariate time series data were generated from a simple network of two coupled Morris Lecar neuron models under different coupling scenarios. A CART algorithm used three predictor variables from the observed neural time series data: phase coherence, coefficient of variation of interspike intervals, and difference in intrinsic firing frequencies. The class labels indicated the correctness or incorrectness of interaction directionality detection by the technique. The investigated techniques were Granger causality, partial directed coherence, and phase dynamic modeling.

Chi-square Automatic Interaction Detection or CHAID (Kass, 1980) finds for each X_i the pair of values that is least significantly different with respect to C. Both values are merged if the p-value for a pair is greater than a specified merge threshold. The search for pairs to be merged is repeated until no significant pairs are found. Like CART, CHAID can be used for discrete C (classification) and continuous C (regression). The statistical significance is tested with an F test (ANOVA) for a continuous C, a Pearson's chi-squared test for a nominal C, and a likelihood ratio test for an ordinal C. The best variable for splitting the current node is then selected such that the descendant nodes are made up of a group of homogeneous values of the selected variable. CHAID handles missing values by treating them as a single valid category. It does not employ pruning and stops when it reaches a maximum tree depth or a minimum number of instances for a node to be a parent/child.

Slaets et al. (2013) presented a classification tree built with the CHAID algorithm. The aim was to test whether the accuracy of the differential dementia diagnosis improved by adding the concentration of amyloid-β_{1-40} (Aβ_{1-40}) to the existing CSF biomarker panel of Aβ_{1-42}, total tau (T-tau), and phosphorylated tau (P-tau$_1$81P). The tree tried to differentiate AD from non-AD patients according to their CSF samples. The tree had a significantly better diagnostic accuracy with than without Aβ_{1-40} and the Aβ_{1-42}/Aβ_{1-40} ratio, especially for patients with intermediate CSF P-tau$_1$81P values. In accordance with a logistic regression model (Section 8.3), T-tau was entered but not retained in the model (Engelborghs et al., 2008). A possible explanation is that T-tau is a general marker for neurodegeneration and is not a specific marker for AD.

The QUEST (**Quick, Unbiased, Efficient, Statistical Tree**) algorithm (Loh and Shih, 1997) can use univariate or linear combination splits. Quadratic discriminant analysis (Section 8.2.3) finds the optimal splitting point for the continuous variables. The variable with the highest association with C is selected for splitting. This is measured with the ANOVA F test possibly after a Levene's test for unequal variances (for ordinal and continuous variables) and Pearson's chi-squared test (for nominal variables). QUEST yields binary trees, uses imputation to deal with missing values and prunes the trees.

More flexible than linear models, the regression function at the split is approximated using products of linear splines (Section 8.4.2.2) in MARS (**Multivariate Adaptive Regression Splines**) (Friedman, 1991).

7.2.6   Example: Interneurons versus Pyramidal Neurons

Data Set 1 in Chapter 1 is meant to discriminate between interneurons (I) and pyramidal neurons (P). We apply different classification tree algorithms across the whole data set. First, we include all the variables, and then we apply feature selection as mentioned in Section 7.1.8. The best FSS techniques here are filter approaches. Thus, as for k-NN, we use a univariate filter based on the gain ratio of a variable with respect to the class (Section 6.2.1) and the CFS multivariate filter (Section 6.2.2). All the algorithms were run using WEKA (Hall et al., 2009) software. The variable evaluators were `GainRatioAttributeEval` and `CfsSubsetEval` using `BestFirst` as the search method. The selected variables were listed in Section 7.1.8.

Three classifiers were employed: `DecisionStump` (only one node), `Id3`, and `J48` (algorithm C4.5 with reduced error pruning). J48 stands for C4.5 revision 8, the last public version of this family of algorithms before the commercial implementation C5.0. Because the ID3 algorithm can only deal with discrete feature variables, simple binning in 10 equal-width intervals (Section 2.6.3) was used for the purpose of discretization. Table 7.6 lists the classification accuracy of all these models, estimated with 10-fold stratified cross-validation.

The simplest model, decision stump, chose variable X_{56} as its unique node based on entropy. Missing values of X_{56} were treated as yet another value. The tree states that if $X_{56} \leq 10.5$, the neuron is classified as I; otherwise as P. If the X_{56} value is missing, it is classified as I. Algorithm ID3 with 10 equal-width intervals for the continuous features performed worse than the decision stump, although it raised the accuracy from 0.6147 to 0.7370 for a discretization into five equal-width intervals. However, this tree was very complex, with 137 leaves, of which 50 were null or unclassified (empty leaves). We tried using supervised discretization, taking into account the class variable (e.g., according to the MDLP algorithm [Fayyad and Irani, 1993] explained in Section 2.6.3), but many variables resulted in a single interval, and a tree made no sense. C4.5 performed best (above 83% accuracy), and feature preselection with gain ratio or CFS had little effect (about 1% improvement). Moreover, due to pruning, the C4.5 algorithm yielded simple trees of size 13 (7 leaves, 5 internal nodes and the root node), see Figure 7.9. Gray tones in that figure refer to features related to dendrites (light gray), axon (gray), and soma (black). They were defined in Tables 1.5 and 1.6.

Note that the selected variables are Number of dendritic Sholl sections (X_{56}), with the breakpoint at 9 sections; Number of axonal Sholl sections (X_{25}), with the break-

Table 7.6 Classification accuracy of different classification tree algorithms for Data Set 1

Algorithm	Accuracy
Decision stump	0.7951
ID3	0.6147
C4.5	0.8318
C4.5-gain ratio	0.8471
C4.5-CFS	0.8348

Table 7.7 Main performance measures
of the C4.5 algorithm for Data Set 1

Measure	Value
Accuracy	0.8318
Sensitivity	0.8945
Specificity	0.7343
F_1-measure	0.8662
Cohen's kappa	0.6405
Brier score	0.2947
AUC	0.8025

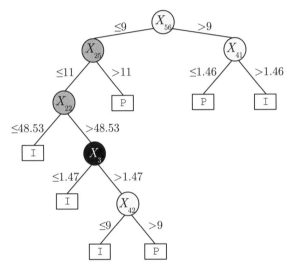

Figure 7.9 Classification tree yielded by the C4.5 algorithm with reduced error pruning. Its accuracy is 0.8318. Node colors identify features related to dendrites (light gray), axon (gray), and soma (black).

point at 11 sections; Axonal segment length stdv (X_{22}); with the split at 48.53 μm; Somatic aspect ratio (X_3), with the breakpoint at 1.47; Highest order dendritic segment (X_{42}), with the split at order 9; and Ratio of dendritic length to surface area (X_{41}), with the breakpoint at 1.46.

Besides classification accuracy, some performance measures of this tree, all estimated with 10-fold stratified cross-validation, are shown in Table 7.7.

The confusion matrix, with real labels in rows and predicted labels in columns, is

$$
\begin{array}{cc}
 & \begin{array}{cc} \text{I} & \text{P} \end{array} \\
\begin{array}{c} \text{I} \\ \text{P} \end{array} & \left(\begin{array}{cc} 178 & 21 \\ 34 & 94 \end{array} \right)
\end{array}.
$$

Figure 7.10 shows neurons where the C4.5 algorithm succeeded or failed. In (a) and (b), the algorithm successfully classified interneuron $\mathbf{x}^{43}$ and pyramidal neuron $\mathbf{x}^{299}$. In (c), interneuron $\mathbf{x}^{18}$ was misclassified as pyramidal neuron, whereas in (d), pyramidal neuron $\mathbf{x}^{327}$ was misclassified as interneuron.

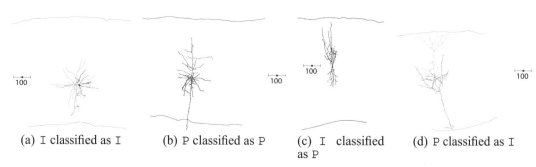

(a) I classified as I | (b) P classified as P | (c) I classified as P | (d) P classified as I

Figure 7.10 Some neurons and their classification by the C4.5 algorithm. (a) Correctly classified interneuron $\mathbf{x}^{43}$. (b) Correctly classified pyramidal neuron $\mathbf{x}^{299}$. (c) Misclassified interneuron $\mathbf{x}^{18}$. (d) Misclassified pyramidal neuron $\mathbf{x}^{327}$. Axonal arbor in blue and dendritic tree in red. For the color version, please refer to the plate section.

7.3 Rule Induction

Rule induction is one of the most transparent supervised classification methods. The first artificial intelligence tools were based on expert systems. Computer scientists codified the rules elicited from an expert in a given domain. Rule induction aims to extract these rules by, instead, applying an algorithm to a set of instances. Usually rules are expressions of the form

$$\text{IF } (X_j = x_j \text{ AND } X_i = x_i \text{ AND } \cdots \text{ AND } X_k = x_k) \text{ THEN } C = c,$$

where $(X_j = x_j \text{ AND } X_i = x_i \text{ AND } \cdots \text{ AND } X_k = x_k)$ is called the antecedent of the rule, and $C = c$ is the consequent of the rule. Some rule induction systems induce more complex rules, in which variable values may be expressed by the negation of some values or by a subset of values in the variable domain.

Rule induction models are easy to understand and apply. They are more general than classification trees because each classification tree can be transformed into a rule induction model; however, the opposite is not always true.

7.3.1 1R Algorithm

Weiss et al. (1990) provided the most compelling initial indication that very simple rules often perform well. Motivated by this result, Holte (1993) developed a specific kind of rules called "**1-rules**" or **1R**. These are rules that classify an instance on the basis of a single variable.

For continuous variables, 1R discretizes the range of possible values into several disjoint intervals using a straightforward method, the only constraint being that all intervals should contain more than a predefined number of instances with the same class value. Missing values are considered as new values for both discrete and continuous variables. For each possible value x_i of variable X_i, 1R constructs a rule selecting its optimal class value as the consequent. A class value is optimal for a given antecedent if it is the most frequent class value for the antecedent. If several class values are optimal for $X_i = x_i$, 1R chooses one randomly. Then 1R selects only one rule per variable to be added to a set of possible hypotheses. Finally, 1R selects the rule having the highest accuracy for the training set from the set of hypotheses (if there are several best rules, one is chosen at random).

7.3.2 AQR Algorithm

The **AQ rule-generation algorithm** (AQR) (Michalski and Chilausky, 1980) is an induction system that uses the basic AQ algorithm (Michalski, 1969), regarded as the precursor of rule induction. AQR generates a set of classification rules, one for each class. Each rule is of the form IF "*cover*" THEN "*class*," where *cover* is a combination of variable tests. These variable tests are combined by means of disjunctions or conjunctions. The basic test for a variable is called a **selector**. Consider the following variables of Data Set 1 (Section 1.6.1): X_{36} measuring the Number of dendrites in a neuron, X_{56} for the Number of dendritic Sholl sections, X_{26} containing the Axonal Sholl length at 100 µm, divided by the total length of axonal segments, and X_4 that refers to the Somatic compactness. Then $X_{36} = 5$, $X_{56} = 6, 7$, $X_{26} < 0.5$, and $X_4 > 0.9$ are all selectors. A conjunction of selectors is called a complex, like $X_{36} = 5$ AND $X_4 > 0.9$. A disjunct of complexes is called a cover, like, for example, $(X_{36} = 5$ AND $X_4 > 0.9)$ OR $(X_{56} = 6$ AND $X_{26} < 0.5)$. An expression (a selector, complex, or cover) is said to cover an instance of the data set if the expression is true for the instance. A cover is stored along with an associated class value, which is the most common class label of the training instances that it covers.

AQR induces a classification rule for each class value in turn. Having chosen a class value on which to focus, it forms a disjunct of complexes (the cover) to serve as the antecedent of the rule for that class label. This process is a stagewise process, where each stage generates a single complex and then removes the instances it covers from the training data set. This step is repeated until enough complexes have been found to cover all the instances of the chosen class. The entire process is repeated for each class in turn. The heuristic used by AQR to trim the antecedent during the generation of a complex is the maximization of the positive instances covered and negative instances excluded. In the case of a tie for either heuristic, AQR prefers complexes with fewer selectors.

In AQR, a new instance is classified by finding which of the conditions of the induced rules are satisfied by the instance. If the instance satisfies only one rule, this assigns its predicted class to the instance. If the instance satisfies more than one rule, the prediction is the most common class in the training instances that were covered by the above rules. If the instance is not covered by any rule, then it is assigned by default to the class that occurred most frequently in the training instances.

7.3.3 CN2 Algorithm

CN2 algorithm (Clark and Niblett, 1989) combines aspects of AQR and ID3. It produces an ordered list of IF-THEN rules, a version of what Rivest (1987) termed **decision lists**, rather than the unordered set of rules like that generated by AQ-based systems. For the search of complexes, it applies a cutoff method similar to decision-tree pruning (Section 7.2.3) to halt specialization when no further specializations are statistically significant.

CN2 works iteratively, where each iteration searches for a complex that covers a large number of instances of a single class and few instances of other classes. The complex must be both predictive and reliable, as determined by CN2 evaluation functions. Having found a good complex, the algorithm removes the instances that it covers from the training data set, and the corresponding rule is added to the end of the rule list. This process iterates until no more satisfactory complexes can be found.

CN2 searches for complexes by carrying out a pruned general-to-specific search. At each stage of the search, CN2 retains a size-limited set of best complexes found so far. The system only considers specializations of this set. A complex is specialized by either adding a new conjunctive term or removing a disjunctive element in one of its selectors. CN2 generates and evaluates all possible specializations of each complex. The size-limited set containing the best complexes found so far is trimmed after completion of this step by removing its lowest-ranking elements as measured by an evaluation function. CN2 deals with missing data in an instance variable using the simple method of imputing data with the variable mean or mode for continuous or discrete variables, respectively.

The quality of a complex is heuristically assessed by computing the entropy of the class variable estimated from the instances covered by this complex. The heuristic prefers complexes covering a large number of examples of a single class and few examples of other classes. Therefore, a complex with a lower entropy is better.

The significance of a complex is determined by comparing the observed distribution among the labels of the instances satisfying the complex with the expected distribution of the complex selecting instances randomly. To test the significance of a complex, CN2 uses the likelihood ratio statistic (Equation (7.7)). This is given by $2\sum_{i=1}^{R} O_i \ln \frac{O_i}{E_i}$, where the distribution $(O_1, \ldots, O_R)$ is the observed frequency distribution of instances among class labels of instances satisfying a given complex, and $(E_1, \ldots, E_R)$ is the expected frequency distribution of the same number of instances under the assumption that the complex selects instances randomly. The likelihood ratio statistic is under H_0 approximately distributed as χ^2_{R-1}.

New instances are classified by CN2 in order (from first to last) until one rule is found whose conditions are satisfied by the instance to be classified. The class prediction of this rule is then assigned as the instance label. If no induced rules are satisfied, the final default rule assigns the most common class (in the whole training set) to the new instance.

7.3.4   REP, IREP, RIPPER Algorithms

Pagallo and Hausler (1990) managed noise in the data sets with an adaptation of the reduced error pruning (REP) (see also Section 7.2.3) approach to rule learning systems. In REP for rules, the training data is split into a growing set and a pruning set. First, an initial rule set is formed that overfits the growing set, using some heuristic method. This overlarge rule set is then repeatedly simplified by applying one of a set of pruning operators. Typical pruning operators would be to delete any **single literal** (see below) or any single rule. The preferred pruning operator yields the greatest error reduction on the pruning set. Simplification ends when applying any pruning operator that would increase the error on the pruning set.

Cohen (1995) developed **repeated incremental pruning to produce error reduction** (RIPPER) to achieve efficiency on large noisy data sets. RIPPER proposed a number of modifications of the algorithm called **incremental reduced error pruning** (IREP) introduced by Fürnkranz and Widmer (1994). IREP tightly integrates REP with a divide-and-conquer rule learning algorithm.

Algorithm 7.2 illustrates a two-class version of IREP. In the Boolean case, an antecedent of a rule is simply a conjunction of literals (e.g., $X_{36} = 5$ AND $X_{56} = 6$ AND $X_{26} < 0.5$ AND $X_4 > 0.9$), and a rule set is a disjunction of rules. Like a standard divide-and-conquer algorithm, IREP greedily builds up a rule set in, one rule at a time. After a rule is found, all instances covered by the rule (both positive and negative) are deleted from the growing set (line 8). This process is repeated until there are no positive instances (line 1) or until the rule found by IREP has an unacceptably large error rate (line 5).

Algorithm 7.2: The IREP algorithm

    Input : A split of the data set on Pos and Neg, an empty Ruleset
    Output: A Ruleset

1 **while** Pos $\neq \varnothing$ **do**
      /* *grow and prune a new rule* */
2   Split (Pos, Neg) into (GrowPos, GrowNeg) and (PrunePos, PruneNeg)
3   Rule = GrowRule(GrowPos, GrowNeg)
4   Rule = PruneRule(Rule, PrunePos, PruneNeg)
5   **if** The error rate of Rule on (PrunePos, PruneNeg) exceeds 50% **then return**
        Ruleset
6   **else if then**
7   Add Rule to Ruleset
8   Remove instances covered by Rule from (Pos, Neg)
9   **endif**
10 **endwhile**

In order to build a rule, IREP uses the following strategy. First, the positive (Pos) and negative (Neg) uncovered instances are randomly partitioned into two subsets: a growing set and a pruning set (line 2). The four disjoint subsets are denoted by: GrowPos (positive instances used for growing the rules), GrowNeg (negative instances used for growing the rules), PrunePos (positive instances used for pruning the rules), and PruneNeg (negative instances used for pruning the rules). Next, a rule is "grown" (line 3). GrowRule begins with an empty conjunction of literals and considers adding any literal of the form $X_i = x_i$, $X_i < x_i$, $X_i > x_i$ depending on whether X_i is a discrete (first literal) or a continuous (second and third literal) variable. GrowRule repeatedly adds the literal that maximizes an information gain criterion introduced in the **first-order inductive learner** (FOIL) algorithm (Quinlan, 1990). This FOIL criterion is improved until the rule covers no negative instances from the growing data set. Given a rule $\mathcal{R}$ and a more specific rule $\mathcal{R}'$ obtained from $\mathcal{R}$ after adding a literal, the FOIL criterion is defined as:

$$\text{FOIL}\left(\mathcal{R}, \mathcal{R}', \text{GrowPos}, \text{GrowNeg}\right) = co\left[-\log_2\left(\frac{pos}{pos + neg}\right) + \log_2\left(\frac{pos'}{pos' + neg'}\right)\right],$$

where co denotes the percentage of positive instances covered by $\mathcal{R}$ and also covered by $\mathcal{R}'$ in GrowPos, pos is the number of positive instances covered by $\mathcal{R}$ in GrowPos (similarly for pos' and $\mathcal{R}'$), and neg is the number of negative instances covered by $\mathcal{R}$ in GrowNeg (similarly for neg' and $\mathcal{R}'$).

After growing a rule, the rule is immediately pruned (line 4) by considering deleting any final sequence of literals from the rule output by the growing phase, choosing the deletion that maximizes the function

$$v(\mathcal{R}, \text{PrunePos}, \text{PruneNeg}) = \frac{pos_R + (|\text{PruneNeg}| - neg_R)}{|\text{PrunePos}| + |\text{PruneNeg}|},$$

where $|\cdot|$ denotes cardinality and pos_R (neg_R) is the number of instances in PrunePos (PruneNeg) covered by rule $\mathcal{R}$. This is repeated until no deletion improves the value of v.

RIPPER differs from the original IREP in (i) an alternative metric to v for assessing the value of rules in the pruning phase, (ii) a new heuristic for determining when to stop adding rules to a rule set, and (iii) a postpass that improves a rule set.

DeFelipe et al. (2013) reported an application of the RIPPER algorithm to discriminate between different interneuron cell types characterized by a large number of morphological variables.

7.3.5   Example: Interneurons versus Pyramidal Neurons

The WEKA implementation of the RIPPER algorithm, known as JRip, was run on Data Set 1 of Section 1.6.1 with the same four FSS strategies as in Section 7.1.8. Similarly, RIPPER improved its accuracy as the complexity of the feature selection strategy grew, starting with 0.8165 accuracy for the model including all predictor variables and rising to 0.8415 using the wrapper strategy. Table 7.8 illustrates accuracy, as well as other standard performance measures, estimated with 10-fold stratified cross-validation, together with the list of 7 selected variables for the wrapper approach. This list includes 1 soma (X_5), 3 axonal (X_{17}, X_{22}, and X_{25}), and 3 dendritic (X_{42}, X_{52}, and X_{56}) variables. The last 5 were also selected by the wrapper IB3.

Table 7.8 Main performance measures of the RIPPER classification algorithm for Data Set 1. A wrapper approach selected these 7 variables out of 65: Somatic form factor (X_5), Axonal spline angle ave (X_{17}), Axonal segment length stdv (X_{22}), Number axonal Sholl sections (X_{25}), Highest order dendritic segment (X_{42}), Dendritic segment length ave (X_{52}), and Number dendritic Sholl sections (X_{56})

Measure	Value
Accuracy	0.8415
Sensitivity	0.8894
Specificity	0.7656
F_1-measure	0.8719
Cohen's kappa	0.6625
Brier score	0.2744
AUC	0.8336

The confusion matrix, with real labels in rows and predicted labels in columns,

$$
\begin{array}{cc}
 & \text{I} \quad\text{P} \\
\begin{array}{c}\text{I}\\\text{P}\end{array} & \begin{pmatrix} 177 & 22 \\ 30 & 98 \end{pmatrix},
\end{array}
$$

shows a large number of mistakes when classifying pyramidal neurons. This is also reflected in the specificity (0.7656) and sensitivity (0.8894) estimations.

The RIPPER model consists of the following set of four ordered rules:

$\mathcal{R}_1$: IF $X_{56} \geq 9$ THEN C=P
$\mathcal{R}_2$: IF ($X_{22} \geq 48.10$ AND $X_5 \leq 0.77$ AND $X_{42} \geq 9$) THEN C=P
$\mathcal{R}_3$: IF ($X_{22} \geq 52.02$ AND $X_5 \leq 0.79$ AND $X_{52} \leq 58.62$ AND $X_{25} \geq 7$) THEN C=P
$\mathcal{R}_4$: C=I

Rule $\mathcal{R}_1$ refers to the Number of dendritic Sholl sections (X_{56}). If this number is greater than or equal to 9, the neuron is classified as a pyramidal cell. The mean value for X_{56} in the whole sample of 327 neurons is 7.57 sections. For neurons not verifying $\mathcal{R}_1$, $\mathcal{R}_2$ considers neurons whose Axonal segment length stdv (X_{22}) is greater than or equal to 48.10 (the mean for this variable is 74.91), whose Somatic form factor (X_5) is less than or equal to 0.77 (mean is 0.71), and whose Highest order dendritic segment (X_{42}) is greater than or equal to 9 (mean is 9.78) as the antecedent. Rule $\mathcal{R}_3$ applies to neurons whose characteristics match neither $\mathcal{R}_1$ nor $\mathcal{R}_2$. It considers the intersection of four conditions as antecedents. The first two are similar to conditions in $\mathcal{R}_2$. The third condition, Dendritic segment length ave (X_{52}) that is less than or equal to 58.62 (mean of 49.78), refers to neurons (in dendrites) that are not very large, while the fourth, Number axonal Sholl sections (X_{25}) that are greater than or equal to 7 (mean of 5.95), identifies neurons with a large number of axonal Sholl sections.

Figure 7.11 shows four examples of neurons with different classification results. In (a), RIPPER correctly classified interneuron $\mathbf{x}^1$, in (b), it correctly classified pyramidal cell $\mathbf{x}^{202}$, in (c), interneuron $\mathbf{x}^{144}$ was misclassified as a pyramidal cell, and in (d), pyramidal neuron $\mathbf{x}^{218}$ was misclassified as an interneuron.

7.4 Artificial Neural Networks

Artificial neural networks (ANNs) are computational models for information processing that attempt to mimic the learning of biological neural networks. They are inspired by an animal's central nervous system (in particular the brain) and are used to estimate or approximate functions that can depend on a large number of inputs. ANNs are represented as systems of interconnected "neurons" that are able to solve supervised and unsupervised (Section 11.3.5) problems thanks to their adaptive nature.

For example, an ANN for discriminating between pyramidal and interneuron cells is defined as a set of input neurons, each of which contains a morphological variable. After weighting and transforming the inputs using a function, which depends on the ANN type and topology, the neuron activations are then passed on to other neurons. This process is repeated until an output neuron is activated. This determines the type of the cell: pyramidal or interneuron.

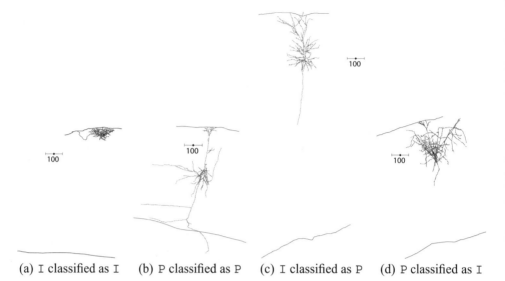

(a) I classified as I   (b) P classified as P   (c) I classified as P   (d) P classified as I

Figure 7.11 Classification of four neurons by RIPPER. (a) Correctly classified interneuron x^1. (b) Correctly classified pyramidal neuron x^{202}. (c) Misclassified interneuron x^{144}. (d) Misclassified pyramidal neuron x^{218}. Axonal arbor in blue and dendritic tree in red. For the color version, please refer to the plate section.

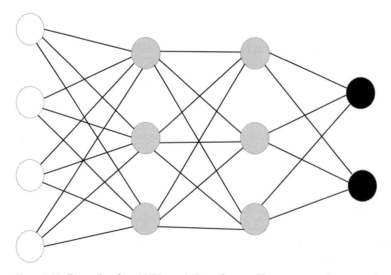

Figure 7.12 Example of an ANN consisting of a set of interconnected groups of nodes (input, hidden, and output nodes). Each node represents an artificial neuron. Edges represent connections from the output of a neuron to the input of another.

Figure 7.12 shows a graphical representation of an ANN arranged as four layers with four input, six hidden, and two output neurons (white, gray and black, respectively). The edges connect nodes from one layer to the next one. These connections consist of a set of adaptive weights, that is, numerical parameters that are tuned by the learning algorithm. The inclusion of hidden nodes means that ANNs can approximate nonlinear functions.

Table 7.9 Neuroscience problems solved with ANNs (OCT means optical coherence tomography)

Reference	Aim	Predictor variables
Ryzhikova et al. (2015)	AD vs. other dementias vs. control	Near-infrared Raman microspectroscopy of blood serum
Hossen (2013)	Essential vs. Parkinson's tremors	Accelerometers and EMG signals
de Tommaso et al. (2003)	HD vs. subjects at HD risk vs. control	EEG signals
Garcia-Martin et al. (2013)	MS vs. control	Retinal nerve fiber layers damage with OCT
Guerra et al. (2011)	Pyramidal cells vs. interneurons	Morphological features
DeFelipe et al. (2013)	Interneuron cell types	Morphological features

ANNs are extremely simple abstractions of biological systems. Although, compared to biological neural networks, they are very limited in size, ability, and power, they do share two very important characteristics: parallel processing of information and learning and generalization from experience. Some advantages of ANNs are (a) they do not require a priori assumptions about the underlying data generating process, (b) the modeling process is highly adaptive, (c) they fulfill well-established mathematical properties for accurately approximating functions,[1] (d) ANNs are nonlinear and nonparametric models, and (e) they are fault tolerant, able to model incomplete and noisy information. The main disadvantage of ANNs is the difficulty of interpreting the weights of the incoming and outgoing arcs at the hidden nodes. Characteristics to be taken into account when using ANNs in real-world applications are that they are **black box** systems, have a high computational burden, and are prone to overfitting.

Azimi et al. (2015) includes an interesting revision on applications of ANNs in neurosurgery. It includes (a) diagnosis and assessment of disease progression in low back pain, brain tumors, and primary epilepsy; (b) enhancement of clinically relevant information extraction from radiographic images, intracranial pressure processing, low back pain, and real-time tumor tracking; (c) outcome prediction in epilepsy, brain metastases, lumbar spinal stenosis, lumbar disc herniation, childhood hydrocephalus, trauma mortality, and the occurrence of symptomatic cerebral vasospasm in patients with aneurysmal subarachnoid hemorrhage; and (d) use in the biomechanical assessments of spinal disease. The revision concluded that ANNs can be effectively employed for diagnosis, prognosis, and outcome prediction in neurosurgery. Other neuroscience areas where ANNs have been used are listed in Table 7.9.

Many types of ANNs have been proposed. We focus on the most commonly used ANNs for supervised classification: the multi-layer perceptron.

---

[1] Standard multi-layer feedforward networks (Section 7.4.1) with a single hidden layer containing a finite number of neurons can approximate any continuous function to any desired degree of accuracy under mild assumptions on the activation function (**universal approximation theorem**, Hornik et al. [1989]). In particular, arbitrary decision regions can be well approximated by a multi-layer feedforward ANN with a single hidden layer and continuous input and output units (Cybenko, 1989). This universal approximation capability suggests that ANNs are a very general and flexible modeling paradigm.

7.4.1   Multi-layer Perceptron

The **multi-layer feedforward neural network**, also called **multi-layer perceptron** (MLP), is the most widely studied and used ANN model. An MLP consists of a number of interconnected simple computing units called neurons, nodes, or cells, which are organized in layers. Each neuron performs simple information processing tasks by converting the received inputs into processed outputs. The edges linking these neurons are stored as edge weights representing the strength of the relationship between different nodes. Although each neuron implements very simple functions, collectively an MLP is able to efficiently and accurately perform a variety of (hard) tasks. MLPs are suitable for modeling relationships between a set of predictor (input) variables and one or more response (output) variables. When there is a unique continuous response variable, MLPs can provide solutions to regression problems. Furthermore, MLPs can solve a **multi-output regression** problem to predict several continuous response variables. MLPs are also suitable models for the simultaneous prediction of several discrete variables, as in multi-label or multidimensional classification (Chapter 10). In this section, we discuss how to accommodate MLPs for standard supervised classification problems with a single class variable.

Figure 7.13 shows the architecture of a three-layer MLP for supervised classification. The architecture consists of neurons (represented by circles) organized in three layers: input layer (white circles), hidden layer (gray circles), and output layer (one black circle). The neurons in the input layer correspond to the predictor variables, $X_1, \ldots, X_n$, useful for predicting the class variable, C, which is represented as the output neuron. Neurons in the hidden layer have no clear semantic meaning; they are connected to both input and output neurons and are key to learning the data pattern and mapping the relationship from input variables to the output variable. The strength of these connecting links is codified by a vector of weights, denoted by $\mathbf{w}$. The MLP is characterized by its architecture determined by the number of layers, the number of nodes in each layer, the transfer function (see

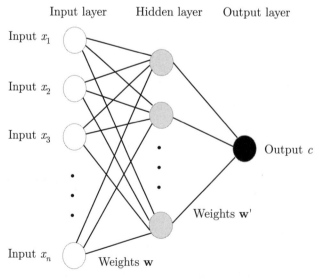

Figure 7.13 Multi-layer perceptron neural network for supervised classification.

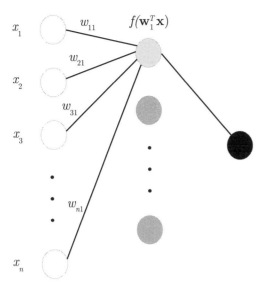

Figure 7.14 Information processing in a single neuron.

below) used in each layer, as well as how the nodes in each layer connect to nodes in adjacent layers. The most commonly used MLP contains only one hidden layer, and it is fully connected, that is, each node in one layer is fully connected to all nodes in the adjacent layers. An example of this common MLP for supervised classification is shown in Figure 7.13.

Figure 7.14 shows how each neuron processes information from several inputs and then transforms it into an output. This is a two-step process. In the first step, the inputs, $\mathbf{x}^T = (x_1, x_2, x_3, \ldots, x_n)$, are combined with the weights of the connecting links, for example, $\mathbf{w}_1^T = (w_{11}, w_{21}, w_{31}, \ldots, w_{n1})$ for the first hidden neuron, to form a weighted sum of inputs and weights, that is, $\sum_{i=1}^n w_{i1} x_i$. In the second step, the neuron transforms this weighted sum of inputs to an output via a **transfer function**, $f(\sum_{i=1}^n w_{i1} x_i)$, or, alternatively, $f(\mathbf{w}_1^T \mathbf{x})$ in vectorial notation. Generally, the transfer function is often a bounded, nondecreasing, and differentiable function. Although there are many possible choices of transfer functions, only a few are used in practice. These include the sigmoid or logistic function, $f(r) = (1 + e^{-r})^{-1}$; the hyperbolic tangent function, $f(r) = \frac{e^r - e^{-r}}{e^r + e^{-r}}$; the sine function, $f(r) = \sin(r)$; the cosine function, $f(r) = \cos(r)$; and the linear or identity function, $f(r) = r$. Expansions of basis functions that are **kernel functions**,[2] that is, $f(r) = \sum_{j=1}^M \beta_j \kappa_{\lambda_j}(r)$, are special transfer functions, where M denotes the number of kernels, β_j is the importance of each kernel, and $\kappa_{\lambda_j}(r)$ is the jth kernel function with a bandwidth (a smoothing parameter) given by $\lambda_j > 0$. These models are called **radial basis function ANNs**, where Gaussian densities are a popular choice as the kernel function. We omit bias terms associated with each transfer function for the sake of simplifying the notation.

For a three-layer MLP for supervised classification, with n input neurons, $X_1, \ldots, X_n$, h hidden neurons, $H_1, \ldots, H_h$, and one output neuron, C, there are h vectors of weights connecting input and hidden neurons, $\mathbf{w}_j^T = (w_{1j}, w_{2j}, w_{3j}, \ldots, w_{nj})$ for the jth hidden

---

[2] A kernel is a nonnegative real-valued integrable function verifying: (1) $\int_{-\infty}^{\infty} \kappa(r) dr = 1$, and (2) $\kappa(r) = \kappa(-r)$ for all r. The term *kernel* has a different meaning in support vector machines, see Section 7.5.3.2.

neuron, $j = 1, \ldots, h$. Let us denote $\mathbf{w}^T = (w_{11}, \ldots, w_{nh})$ the vector of all w_{ij} weights. The result of applying the transfer function to this jth hidden unit is denoted as $f(\mathbf{w}_j^T \mathbf{x}) = f(\Sigma_{i=1}^n w_{ij} x_i)$. The h outputs, $f(\mathbf{w}_1^T \mathbf{x}), \ldots, f(\mathbf{w}_h^T \mathbf{x})$, provided by the h hidden units should be also weighted with the vector $\mathbf{w}'^T = (w_1', \ldots, w_h')$, resulting in the output of the MLP for a generic instance $\mathbf{x}$, that is, $\hat{c} = \Sigma_{j=1}^h w_j' f(\mathbf{w}_j^T \mathbf{x}) = \Sigma_{j=1}^h w_j' f(\Sigma_{i=1}^n w_{ij} x_i)$. This output $\hat{c}$ is compared with the real label c that is known. All MLP weights should be established such that the N predictions provided by the ANN model, $\hat{c}^1, \ldots, \hat{c}^N$, are as close as possible to the true labels, $c^1, \ldots, c^N$.

The MLP training process consists of three main steps. First, the MLP is fed with training instances. Second, the input values for each training instance are weighted and summed at each hidden layer neuron, and the transfer function converts the weighted sum into the input of the output node layer. At this point, the MLP output values are calculated and compared to known labels to determine how closely the actual MLP matches the desired labels. Finally, the weights $(\mathbf{w}, \mathbf{w}')$ of the connections are changed so that the MLP can provide a better approximation of the desired labels. This process repeats many times until differences between MLP output values and the known labels for all training instances are as small as possible.

MLP training can be regarded as the minimization of some weight-dependent error measure, $E(\mathbf{w}, \mathbf{w}')$. The mean squared error, $E(\mathbf{w}, \mathbf{w}') = \frac{1}{N} \Sigma_{k=1}^N (c^k - \hat{c}^k)^2$, is an example of an error measure often used as the objective function to be minimized. The most important method to solve this unconstrained nonlinear optimization problem is the **backpropagation algorithm**. This algorithm is a **gradient descent method** or method of steepest descent that finds the direction in which it is best to change the weights in the error space to reduce the error measure most (see Figure 7.15). This requires partial derivatives of the error function E with respect to the weights to be calculated because the partial derivative

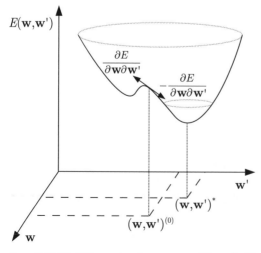

Figure 7.15 Multidimensional error space $E(\mathbf{w}, \mathbf{w}')$. The gradient descent method or method of steepest descent starts with the initialization of weights at $(\mathbf{w}, \mathbf{w}')^{(0)}$ and tries to find their optimum configuration at point $(\mathbf{w}, \mathbf{w}')^*$. Weights are updated according to the partial derivative of the error function with respect to the weights.

represents the error function change rate. Accordingly, the weight updating from w_{ij}^{old} to w_{ij}^{new} therefore adheres to the following rule:

$$w_{ij}^{new} = w_{ij}^{old} - \eta \frac{\partial E}{\partial w_{ij}},$$

where $\frac{\partial E}{\partial w_{ij}}$ is the gradient of the error function E with respect to w_{ij} and η is called the learning rate and controls the size of the gradient descent step. A similar procedure is accomplished with the w'_j weights. The backpropagation algorithm requires an iterative process, and there are two versions of weight updating schemes: batch mode and on-line mode. In the batch mode, weights are updated after all training instances are evaluated, while in the on-line mode, the weights are updated after each instance evaluation. Each pass of all instances is called an *epoch*. Generally, each weight update reduces the total error by only a small amount. Therefore, many epochs are often required to minimize the error.

ANN training is quite an art. The most important issues are explained next. First, initial weight values are chosen as near-zero random values, resulting in an initial model that starts out as nearly linear and becomes nonlinear as the weights increase. Second, over-fitting was avoided in the early implementations of ANNs using an early stopping rule. However, **weight decay** is a better option, as it is an explicit method for regularization that is able to shrink some of the weights toward zero. Third, input scaling determines the effective scaling of the weights, and it can have a large effect on the final solution quality, where it is preferable to standardize all inputs to mean zero and standard deviation one. Fourth, the number of hidden neurons and layers has an impact on how flexible the model is at capturing data nonlinearities, where more hidden units are generally preferred. The number of hidden units increases with the number of input variables and number of training instances, and a common practice is to put down a reasonably large number of units and train them with weight decay or another regularization method. The choice of the number of hidden layers is guided by background knowledge and experimentation. Fifth, a multi-start strategy is used to minimize the nonconvex $E(\mathbf{w}, \mathbf{w}')$ error function based on trying a number of random initial configurations of the weights and choosing the solution that yields the lowest error.

MLPs utilize a highly simplified mathematical abstraction of a neuron where it is not clear to what extent real biophysical neurons with morphologically extended nonlinear dendritic trees and conductance-based synapses could realize perceptron-like learning. Some attempts to develop models of ANNs closer to the biological principles on which the real neural networks are based have been made. A biophysical perceptron based on a realistic model of a layer V cortical pyramidal cell has been proposed by Moldwin and Segev (2020).

7.4.2 Example: Interneurons versus Pyramidal Neurons

As in previous sections containing the running example of Data Set 1 outlined in Chapter 1, four FSS strategies were applied in combination with the WEKA implementation of a multi-layer perceptron neural network classifier using its default parameter configuration. The MLP model to be fitted contains 65 input units (1 input unit for every predictor variable), 1 hidden layer consisting of 3 units, and 1 output unit (the class variable). For this

Table 7.10 Main performance measures of multi-layer perceptron neural network classification algorithm for Data Set 1. A multivariate filter approach selected the following 17 out of the possible 65 variables: Somatic compactness (X_4), Somatic form factor (X_5), Ratio of axonal length to surface area (X_{10}), Axonal planar angle stdv (X_{14}), Axonal segment length ave (X_{21}), Axonal segment length stdv (X_{22}), Number axonal Sholl sections (X_{25}), Axonal node density2 (X_{30}), k-dim (fractal analysis)-axon (X_{35}), Dendritic node total (branching points) (X_{37}), Total surface area of dendrites (μm^2) (X_{40}), Highest order dendritic segment (X_{42}), Stdv of tortuosity of dendritic segments (X_{51}), Dendritic segment length stdv (X_{53}), Number dendritic Sholl sections (X_{56}), Dendritic Sholl length at 150 μm (fraction) (X_{59}), and Convex hull dendrite surface area (X_{63})

Measure	Value
Accuracy	0.8661
Sensitivity	0.8894
Specificity	0.8281
F_1-measure	0.8894
Cohen's kappa	0.7176
Brier score	0.2343
AUC	0.9189

MLP structure, the multivariate filter strategy provided the best accuracy of 0.8661, estimated using a 10-fold stratified cross-validation scheme. Table 7.10 shows this accuracy, as well as other standard figures of merit, together with the list of 17 selected variables for the multivariate filter approach. Two soma variables (X_4 and X_5), 7 axonal ($X_{10}, X_{14}, X_{21}, X_{22}, X_{25}, X_{30}$, and X_{35}), and 8 dendritic ($X_{37}, X_{40}, X_{42}, X_{51}, X_{53}, X_{56}, X_{59}$, and X_{63}) variables form this list. The wrapper IB3 (RIPPER) also selected 6 (4) of these 17 variables.

The confusion matrix, with real labels in rows and predicted labels in columns,

$$\begin{array}{c} \\ I \\ P \end{array}\begin{array}{cc} I & P \\ \begin{pmatrix} 177 & 22 \\ 22 & 106 \end{pmatrix} \end{array},$$

shows that the number of mistakes when classifying pyramidal neurons and interneurons is the same, although there is a larger population of interneurons. Specificity and sensitivity performance estimations are 0.8281 and 0.8894, respectively.

Figure 7.16 shows four examples of neurons with different classification results. An interneuron $\mathbf{x}^{103}$ was correctly classified by MLP in (a), a pyramidal cell $\mathbf{x}^{246}$ was correctly classified in (b), an interneuron $\mathbf{x}^{93}$ was misclassified as a pyramidal cell in (c), and a pyramidal neuron $\mathbf{x}^{244}$ was misclassified as an interneuron in (d).

7.4.3   Deep Neural Networks

Deep neural networks, defined as ANNs with multiple hidden layers of units between the input and output layers, have attracted the attention of many researchers because their learning process relates to a class of theories of brain development proposed by cognitive neuroscientists and summarized by Quartz and Sejnowski (1997). Deep learning is based

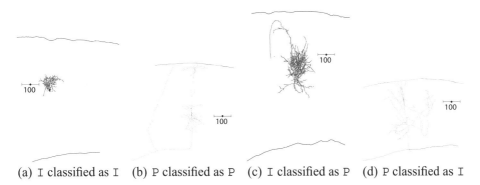

(a) I classified as I   (b) P classified as P   (c) I classified as P   (d) P classified as I

Figure 7.16 Classification of four neurons provided by the multi-layer perceptron neural network. (a) Correctly classified interneuron $\mathbf{x}^{103}$. (b) Correctly classified pyramidal cell $\mathbf{x}^{246}$. (c) Misclassified interneuron $\mathbf{x}^{93}$. (d) Misclassified pyramidal cell $\mathbf{x}^{244}$. Axonal arbor in blue and dendritic tree in red. For the color version, please refer to the plate section.

on the fact that each level learns to transform its input data into a slightly more abstract and composite representation. By varying the numbers of hidden layers and layer sizes, the deep learning process can provide different degrees of abstraction. However, a hand-tuning step becomes necessary in practical applications. The **credit assignment problem** (Minsky, 1961) is about finding the optimal neural network architecture and associated weights that make the model exhibit a desired behavior. Deep learning architectures are often constructed with a greedy layer-wise training method that considers a layer at a time.

The empirical good results of deep neural networks are justified by an adaptation of the universal approximation theorem for multi-layer feedforward networks (see the first footnote in Section 7.4) concerning the capacity of an ANN with bounded width but where its depth is allowed to grow. Lu et al. (2017) have proved that width-bounded ANNs with rectified linear activation units,[3] where the width exceeds at least in four units the input dimension, are universal approximators.

The search for a good solution of the credit assignment problem is computationally intensive and requires large training data sets. In addition, the interpretability of the ANN architecture and its parameters is difficult. The work by Rohekar et al. (2018) tries to alleviate both difficulties by proposing a new interpretation for depth and inter-layer connectivity, where conditional independencies in the probability distribution of the inputs are encoded hierarchically in the network structure. Thus, the depth of the ANN is determined inherently. The proposed method is based on transforming the problem of neural network structure learning into a problem of Bayesian network structure learning (see Section 13.3.2).

Zhang (2017) developed a deep neural network telediagnosis PD system using a smartphone. The predictor variables include personal information, as gender, age, and a brief health history, and also time frequency variables, which are extracted from the voice samples of the patients. One of the main characteristics of the method is that it is based on the study of vocal impairment symptoms including loudness, decrease, breathiness, roughness, and exaggerated vocal tremor in voice. Grover et al. (2018) proposed a deep

---

[3] The rectified linear activation function is a piecewise linear function that will output the input directly if it is positive; otherwise, it will output zero.

neural network for the prediction of PD severity using the UCI's Parkinson's telemonitoring voice data set of patients. This data set contains 16 biomedical voice measurements of 42 patients. The architecture of the neural network consists of 3 hidden layers with 10, 20, and 10 units, respectively. Lee et al. (2019) predicted the conversion from MCI to AD with a multimodal deep neural network that combines not only cross-sectional neuroimaging biomarkers at baseline but also longitudinal CSF and cognitive performance biomarkers obtained from the ADNI cohort. Successful surgical resection in epilepsy patients depends on preserving functionally critical brain regions while removing pathological issues. Electro-cortical stimulation mapping (ESM) is the gold standard method for localizing the function of eloquent cortex through electrical stimulation of the electrodes placed on the cortical brain surface of the patient. However, ESM can increase the risk of provoked seizures, and electrocorticography based functional mapping (ECoG-FM) has been established as a safe alternative method but with a low success rate in localization of eloquent language cortex. RaviPrakash et al. (2020) developed a new deep learning algorithm for ECoG-FM with an accuracy comparable to that of ESM.

7.4.4   Spiking Neural Networks

Spiking neural networks (SNNs) (Maas, 1997) are ANNs with closer imitation of real neural networks. The two main differences between both models are that SNNs incorporate the concept of time, and they do not fire (or spike) at each propagation cycle (as with MLPs). Instead, they only fire when a membrane potential (an intrinsic quality of the neuron related to its electric charge) exceeds a certain threshold. When a neuron is activated in an SNN, it produces a signal that is passed on to other neurons, raising or lowering their membrane potential. SNNs are able to process spatiotemporal data. Space refers to the fact that neurons are only connected to nearby neurons so that they can process input blocks separately. Time refers to the fact that pulse training occurs over time.

SNNs are able to carry out probabilistic inference in Bayesian networks (see Section 13.2) with discrete variables (Pecevski et al., 2011). This result constitutes a theoretical framework for the functional role of structured motifs of cortical microcircuits, as probabilistic inference in Bayesian networks are abstract descriptions of a large class of computational tasks that the brain has to solve: The formation of coherent interpretation of incomplete and ambiguous sensory stimuli, the integration of previously acquired knowledge with new information, movement planning, and reasoning and decision making in the presence of uncertainty.

SNNs have been used to model the central nervous system of a virtual insect when seeking food (Zhang et al., 2013a). They are also able to study biological neural circuits by comparing the electrophysiological recordings of a specific circuit to the output of the corresponding SNNs simulated on a computer. SNNs have been applied to supervised classification problems of real-world data with comparable performance to state-of-the-art methods, as shown in Bako (2010).

7.5   Support Vector Machines

Support vector machines (SVMs) originated from statistical learning theory research (Vapnik, 1998), which models classification as a function estimation problem.

The resulting learning algorithm is an optimization algorithm. Classification trees and ANNs can efficiently learn nonlinear decision surfaces. However, they do not have a sound theoretical basis and are at risk of getting trapped in local minima. SVMs belong to a family of generalized linear classifiers and can be regarded as an extension of the multi-layer perceptron. They are not affected by local minima, do not suffer from the curse of dimensionality, and have empirically good performance.

SVMs apply a simple linear method to the data, albeit in a high-dimensional feature space that is nonlinearly related to the original input space. The data, represented as points in space, are mapped such that there is a clear and as wide as possible gap or margin dividing separate categories. New instances are then mapped into the new space and predicted to belong to a category depending on which side of the gap they fall on.

As in Sections 2.4.3 and 7.4, we look at each observation $\mathbf{x}$ columnwise for notation convenience. Thus, we have a data set of N observations $\mathcal{D} = \{(\mathbf{x}^1, c^1), \ldots, (\mathbf{x}^N, c^N)\}$, where $\mathbf{x}^i = (x_1^i, \ldots, x_n^i)^T, i = 1, \ldots, N$, is an n-dimensional (column) vector corresponding with the values of n variables, $X_1, \ldots, X_n$. Also we initially assume that the class variable C is binary, and hence $c^i \in \Omega_C = \{-1, +1\}$. Using label -1 rather than 0 simplifies subsequent formulas.

Assume a hypothetical $\mathcal{D}$ with only two predictor variables ($n = 2$), which contains cells from two classes of neurons, denoted -1 and $+1$. They are represented geometrically in Figure 7.17(a) as points in the feature space spanned by X_1 and X_2. The points can be also considered vectors in $\mathbb{R}^2$ whose tail is at the point with 0 coordinates and whose head is at the point with the feature values. Here the data are linearly separable, i.e., we can draw a line (a hyperplane for $n > 2$) separating the two classes, that is, the **decision rule** $\phi(\mathbf{x})$ defining how to assign a (predicted) label for every observation $\mathbf{x}$ is a line: the label differs depending on which side of the line the observation falls on.

In fact, there are infinite possible separating lines in this example. If the margin is the width by which the line can be increased before hitting a data point (Figure 7.17(b)), the simplest SVM (linear SVM) is the linear classifier with the maximum margin (Figure 7.17(c)), that is, the linear SVM aims at choosing the furthest separating line from the closest points of both classes. These closest points to the separating line are called support vectors. This simple model is explained in Section 7.5.1.

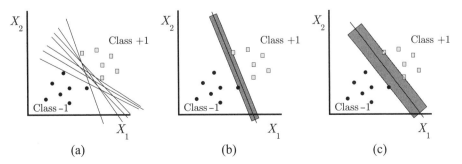

Figure 7.17 (a) Many possible separating lines through two linearly separable classes. (b) Margin (gray box) for a separating line. (c) Linear SVM classifier maximizing the margin around the separating hyperplane.

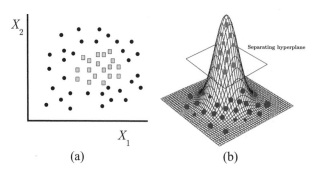

Figure 7.18 (a) Example with two nonlinearly separable classes. (b) Both classes are linearly separable in a high-dimensional space to which the original data are mapped.

If this linear decision boundary does not exist (Figure 7.18(a)), there are two solutions. One is to use slack variables to allow a few points to be on the wrong side (see Section 7.5.2). Another solution is to map the data to a much higher dimensional space where there is a linear decision rule (Figure 7.18(b)). This new space is constructed by means of a very clever mathematical projection known as a "**kernel trick**," see Section 7.5.3.

In line with Section 7.4.4, Le Mouel et al. (2014) described an adaptation of SVMs to spiking neurons, whose margin allows for the training of more general firing rate modulations than 0/1 spike. They found that a moderate training margin increases the learning speed of single neurons in linearly separable tasks and increases their performance in nonlinearly separable tasks.

7.5.1   Linearly Separable Data: Hard-Margin Linear SVM

Here we assume the simplest case: linear SVMs trained on linearly separable data or **hard-margin linear SVM**. This means that there is a hyperplane $\mathcal{H}$ that separates the positive from the negative instances. This hyperplane can be mathematically described by $\mathbf{w}^T \mathbf{x} + b = 0$, where vector $\mathbf{w}$ is normal (perpendicular) to the hyperplane, $|b|/||\mathbf{w}||$ is the (perpendicular) distance from the hyperplane to the origin, and $||\mathbf{w}||$ is the Euclidean norm (length) of $\mathbf{w}$.

Recall that the distance d between two parallel hyperplanes, $\mathbf{w}^T \mathbf{x} + b_1 = 0$ and $\mathbf{w}^T \mathbf{x} + b_2 = 0$, is $d = |b_1 - b_2|/||\mathbf{w}||$. The derivation is easy. First, the distance is $d = |t| \cdot ||\mathbf{w}||$ (Figure 7.19(a)). Second, take $\mathbf{x}_1$ and $\mathbf{x}_2$, a point on each hyperplane, respectively. We have that $\mathbf{x}_2 = \mathbf{x}_1 + t\mathbf{w}, t \in \mathbb{R}$, and then

$$0 = \mathbf{w}^T \mathbf{x}_2 + b_2 = \mathbf{w}^T (\mathbf{x}_1 + t\mathbf{w}) + b_2 = \mathbf{w}^T \mathbf{x}_1 + t||\mathbf{w}||^2 + b_2 = -b_1 + t||\mathbf{w}||^2 + b_2$$

because $\mathbf{w}^T \mathbf{x}_1 = -b_1$. Hence $t = (b_1 - b_2)/||\mathbf{w}||^2$ and the distance is derived.

Points $\mathbf{x}$ that lie on $\mathcal{H}$ satisfy $\mathbf{w}^T \mathbf{x} + b = 0$. Let d_1 (d_2) be the distance from the separating hyperplane $\mathcal{H}$ to the closest negative (positive) instance. The **margin** of $\mathcal{H}$ is defined to be $d_1 + d_2$. The linear SVM looks for the separating hyperplane with the **largest margin**. Therefore, we find that $\mathcal{H}$ is formulated as an optimization problem.

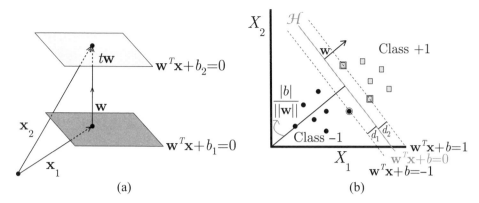

Figure 7.19 (a) Derivation of the distance between two parallel hyperplanes. (b) Linear SVM: hyperplane $\mathbf{w}^T\mathbf{x}+b=0$ for linearly separable data. Its margin is d_1+d_2. The support vectors have double lines.

Because data are linearly separable, we assume that they satisfy the constraints $\mathbf{w}^T\mathbf{x}^i+b\geq 1$ for $c^i=+1$ and $\mathbf{w}^T\mathbf{x}^i+b\leq -1$ for $c^i=-1$, which can be combined into

$$c^i\left(\mathbf{w}^T\mathbf{x}^i+b\right)\geq 1, \quad i=1,\ldots,N. \tag{7.8}$$

Notice that we now have some space between the decision boundary and the nearest data points of either class. Because $\mathbf{w}^T\mathbf{x}+b=0$ is a separating hyperplane, points above (below) $\mathcal{H}$ should have label $+1$ (-1), that is, the decision rule is $\phi(\mathbf{x})=\text{sign}\left(\mathbf{w}^T\mathbf{x}+b\right)$. Consider the points for which the equality in Equation (7.8) holds (the points can be found by choosing an appropriate scale for $\mathbf{w}$ and b); they are the points that lie closest to the separating hyperplane $\mathcal{H}$ (points shown with double lines in Figure 7.19(b)). These points are the **support vectors**: (a) the points that lie on the support hyperplane $\mathbf{w}^T\mathbf{x}+b=-1$, with normal $\mathbf{w}$ and distance $d_1=1/||\mathbf{w}||$ to $\mathcal{H}$, and (b) the points that lie on the support hyperplane $\mathbf{w}^T\mathbf{x}+b=1$, again with normal $\mathbf{w}$ and distance $d_2=1/||\mathbf{w}||$ to $\mathcal{H}$. Both support hyperplanes are equidistant from $\mathcal{H}$. The margin is $2/||\mathbf{w}||$. The three hyperplanes are parallel (they have the same normal) and no training points from $\mathcal{D}$ fall between them. $\mathcal{H}$ must be as far as possible from the support vectors (the hardest points to classify). This is intuitive because we want to avoid misclassifications and thus we want the points from the two classes to lie as far away from each other as possible. Note that the support vectors have a direct bearing on the optimum location of the decision boundary, and their removal changes the solution found.

7.5.1.1 *Primal and Dual Forms*

Maximizing the margin $2/||\mathbf{w}||$ is equivalent to minimizing $\frac{1}{2}||\mathbf{w}||^2$, making it possible to perform (easier to solve) **quadratic programming optimization**. Therefore, finding the separating hyperplane $\mathcal{H}$ that maximizes the margin is tantamount to solving

$$\text{Primal: } \min_{\mathbf{w},b} \frac{1}{2}||\mathbf{w}||^2$$

subject to

$$1-c^i\left(\mathbf{w}^T\mathbf{x}^i+b\right)\leq 0, \quad \forall i=1,\ldots,N. \tag{7.9}$$

We have expressed the constraints as being non-positive because this is a common format in optimization. We refer to this problem as the **primal problem**, with primal variables $\mathbf{w}$ and b. This constrained optimization problem is solved by allocating a **Lagrange multiplier** or **dual variables** $\lambda_i \geq 0$ to each constraint ($\boldsymbol{\lambda}$ denotes the N-vector of all λ_i), resulting in a new objective function, the **primal Lagrangian** L_P of this problem:

$$L_P(\mathbf{w}, b, \boldsymbol{\lambda}) = \frac{1}{2}||\mathbf{w}||^2 + \sum_{i=1}^{N} \lambda_i \left(1 - c^i \left(\mathbf{w}^T \mathbf{x}^i + b\right)\right). \tag{7.10}$$

Based on the primal Lagrangian, we can now build a new function (of the dual variables only), the **dual Lagrangian**

$$L_D(\boldsymbol{\lambda}) = \min_{\mathbf{w}, b} L_P(\mathbf{w}, b, \boldsymbol{\lambda}). \tag{7.11}$$

This always provides a lower bound for the primal problem because the summation in Equation (7.10) is obviously non-positive for a primal feasible point. It appears to be easier to compute $L_D(\boldsymbol{\lambda})$ in Equation (7.11) with constant $\boldsymbol{\lambda}$ than the original problem because there are no constraints. In our case, the objective function (L_P as a function of $\mathbf{w}$ and b) is convex, hence global optima are characterized by setting the derivatives to zero:

$$\frac{\partial L_P}{\partial \mathbf{w}} = 0 = \mathbf{w} - \sum_{i=1}^{N} \lambda_i c^i \mathbf{x}^i \Rightarrow \mathbf{w} = \sum_{i=1}^{N} \lambda_i c^i \mathbf{x}^i, \tag{7.12}$$

$$\frac{\partial L_P}{\partial b} = 0 \Rightarrow \sum_{i=1}^{N} \lambda_i c^i = 0. \tag{7.13}$$

By substituting Equation (7.12) back into L_D, we have the explicit expression of L_D:

$$
\begin{aligned}
L_D(\boldsymbol{\lambda}) &= \frac{1}{2} \left(\sum_{i=1}^{N} \lambda_i c^i (\mathbf{x}^i)^T\right) \left(\sum_{j=1}^{N} \lambda_j c^j \mathbf{x}^j\right) + \sum_{i=1}^{N} \lambda_i \\
&\quad - \sum_{i=1}^{N} \lambda_i c^i \left(\sum_{j=1}^{N} \lambda_j c^j (\mathbf{x}^j)^T\right) \mathbf{x}^i - b \sum_{i=1}^{N} \lambda_i c^i \\
&= -\frac{1}{2} \sum_{i=1}^{N} \sum_{j=1}^{N} \lambda_i \lambda_j c^i c^j (\mathbf{x}^i)^T \mathbf{x}^j + \sum_{i=1}^{N} \lambda_i,
\end{aligned}
\tag{7.14}
$$

where we have used Equation (7.13) in the second equality.

We know that the lower bound for the primal problem is valid for every $\lambda_i \geq 0$. Therefore, the best lower bound will be the largest, that is, we have to solve

$$\text{Dual: } \max_{\boldsymbol{\lambda}} L_D(\boldsymbol{\lambda}) = -\frac{1}{2} \sum_{i=1}^{N} \sum_{j=1}^{N} \lambda_i \lambda_j c^i c^j (\mathbf{x}^i)^T \mathbf{x}^j + \sum_{i=1}^{N} \lambda_i$$

subject to

$$\lambda_i \geq 0, \quad \forall i = 1, \dots, N$$

$$\sum_{i=1}^{N} \lambda_i c^i = 0. \tag{7.15}$$

This is the dual problem with dual variables λ_i, which is often easier to solve. Its optimal value is also a lower bound for the primal problem. In some cases, both values coincide (strong duality holds), and then solving dual and primal problems is equivalent, i.e., the solution of the problems posed in (7.9) and (7.15) is the same.[4] This holds in our case because the objective function in (7.9) is convex (it is quadratic), and the equality constraints are linear. Note that the dual problem only requires the dot or scalar product (also called inner product in more general spaces than the Euclidean) of input vectors $\mathbf{x}^i$. This is important for the kernel trick described below.

The problem posed in (7.15) is a convex quadratic optimization problem.[5] A global maximum can always be found (every local solution is also global in convex programming problems, although uniqueness may not hold when the Hessian is not positive-definite). Many optimization methods (Fletcher, 2000) can be employed (projection methods, interior point methods, active set methods...), most of which are numerical in real-world cases. The most popular method is **sequential minimal optimization** (SMO) (Platt, 1999a). SMO is iterative and breaks down the problem into a series of smaller subproblems involving two variables (λ_i, λ_j). The subproblems can be solved analytically because it is a matter of finding an optimum of a 1D quadratic function.

Note that the primal problem has n variables (number of variables in the original problem), whereas the dual problem has N variables (number of observations in the original problem), which could be beneficial for high-dimensional problems with $N \ll n$. We thus compute one Lagrange multiplier per training instance instead of one weight per variable.

Any method will return all $\lambda_i, i = 1, \ldots, N$. Any points $\mathbf{x}^i$ for which $\lambda_i > 0$ are called support vectors. All other points have $\lambda_i = 0$. With the optimal solution, $\lambda_i \left(1 - c^i \left(\mathbf{w}^T \mathbf{x}^i + b \right) \right) = 0$ holds for all i (λ_i is always nonnegative and $1 - c^i \left(\mathbf{w}^T \mathbf{x}^i + b \right)$ must be non-positive). This is called the **complementary slackness condition**, one of the **Karush–Kuhn–Tucker conditions**. These are necessary conditions for a solution in nonlinear programming to be optimal, provided that some regularity conditions are satisfied (Fletcher, 2000). The condition states that the product of any Lagrange multiplier and the primal constraint is zero. Hence points $\mathbf{x}^i$ for which $\lambda_i > 0$ are support vectors because they satisfy $c^i \left(\mathbf{w}^T \mathbf{x}^i + b \right) = 1$ (i.e., they lie on a support hyperplane), and $\lambda_i > 0$ is due to the complementary slackness condition.

With the λ_i values from Equation (7.12), we can then recover $\mathbf{w}$, which can be rewritten as $\mathbf{w} = \sum_{i \in S} \lambda_i c^i \mathbf{x}^i$, where S denotes the set of indices of the support vectors. This "sparse" representation can be viewed as data compression, similar to the construction of the prototype selection in the k-NN classifier (Section 7.1.6). Again we can see just how critical these boundary instances are, because the solution (the separating hyperplane) changes if they change. The support vectors completely determine the SVM classifier. The other data points can be discarded once training is complete.

Let us now discuss the procedure to obtain offset b. Any support vector $\mathbf{x}^s$ will satisfy $c^s \left(\mathbf{w}^T \mathbf{x}^s + b \right) = 1$. Multiplying both sides by c^s and using the above expression for $\mathbf{w}$, we have

$$(c^s)^2 \left(\sum_{i \in S} \lambda_i c^i (\mathbf{x}^i)^T \mathbf{x}^s + b \right) = c^s.$$

---

[4] For a feasible point $(\mathbf{w}, b, \boldsymbol{\lambda})$, we have that $\min_{\mathbf{w}, b} \max_{\boldsymbol{\lambda}} L_P(\mathbf{w}, b, \boldsymbol{\lambda}) = \max_{\boldsymbol{\lambda}} \min_{\mathbf{w}, b} L_P(\mathbf{w}, b, \boldsymbol{\lambda}) = \max_{\boldsymbol{\lambda}} L_D(\boldsymbol{\lambda})$.

[5] A useful quadratic programming page is www.numerical.rl.ac.uk/people/nimg/qp/qp.html.

Because $(c^s)^2 = 1$, then $b = c^s - \sum_{i \in S} \lambda_i c^i (\mathbf{x}^i)^T \mathbf{x}^s$. In practice, instead of using an arbitrary support vector $\mathbf{x}^s$, it is better (or numerically safer) to take an average over all the support vectors in S and

$$b = \frac{1}{|S|} \sum_{s \in S} \left(c^s - \sum_{i \in S} \lambda_i c^i (\mathbf{x}^i)^T \mathbf{x}^s \right). \tag{7.16}$$

Algorithm 7.3 summarizes the procedure for classifying with a linear SVM.

Algorithm 7.3: Classification with hard margin linear SVMs: Linearly separable data

Input : A data set $\mathcal{D} = \{ (\mathbf{x}^1, c^1), \dots, (\mathbf{x}^N, c^N) \}$ with $c^i \in \{-1, +1\}$
Output: Classification c^* of each new observation $\mathbf{x}$

1 Solve problem in (7.9) by solving problem in (7.15) to yield $\lambda_i, i = 1, \dots, N$
2 Find set S, the indices i of support vectors such that $\lambda_i > 0$
3 Calculate $\mathbf{w} = \sum_{i \in S} \lambda_i c^i \mathbf{x}^i$
4 Calculate $b = \frac{1}{|S|} \sum_{s \in S} \left(c^s - \sum_{i \in S} \lambda_i c^i (\mathbf{x}^i)^T \mathbf{x}^s \right)$ (Equation (7.16))
5 Classify each new point $\mathbf{x}$ as $c^* = \phi(\mathbf{x}) = \text{sign}(\mathbf{w}^T \mathbf{x} + b)$

In Kloppel et al. (2009) a linear SVM separated presymptomatic HD gene mutation carriers from controls on the basis of the gray matter segment of MRI scans.

7.5.2 Nonlinearly Separable Data: Soft-Margin Linear SVM

In this section, we consider nonlinearly separable data, e.g., data containing outliers, noisy data, or data that are slightly nonlinear. The aim is to deal with such data without changing the family of decision functions. The above algorithm will not find a feasible solution when applied to nonlinearly separable data, evidenced by the fact that the dual Lagrangian grows arbitrarily large.

The first solution is to relax the constraints in (7.8) slightly to allow for misclassified points. This, however, comes at a cost. The second solution is explained in Section 7.5.3. Constraints can be relaxed by introducing nonnegative slack variables ξ_i (Cortes and Vapnik, 1995):

$$c^i (\mathbf{w}^T \mathbf{x}^i + b) \geq 1 - \xi_i,$$
$$\xi_i \geq 0, \quad \forall i = 1, \dots, N.$$

In this **soft-margin linear SVM**, points on the wrong side of $\mathcal{H}$ have a penalty that increases with the distance from $\mathcal{H}$. ξ_i can be thought of as the distance from the support hyperplane for misclassified instances and 0, for correct classifications (Figure 7.20). ξ_i thereby measures the degree of misclassification of $\mathbf{x}^i$.

7.5.2.1 Primal and Dual Forms

For a misclassification to occur, it must be $\xi_i > 1$, and then $\sum_{i=1}^N \xi_i$ is an upper bound on the number of training errors. Let $\boldsymbol{\xi}$ denote the N-vector of all ξ_i. Hence the objective function in (7.9) is changed to reduce the number of errors as

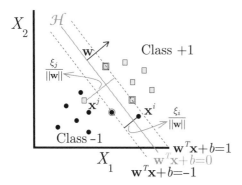

Figure 7.20 Soft-margin linear SVM. $\xi_i/||\mathbf{w}||$ is the distance from $\mathbf{x}^i$ to its support hyperplane.

$$\text{Primal:} \min_{\mathbf{w},b,\boldsymbol{\xi}} \left[\frac{1}{2}||\mathbf{w}||^2 + M \sum_{i=1}^{N} \xi_i \right]$$

subject to   (7.17)

$$1 - c^i \left(\mathbf{w}^T \mathbf{x}^i + b \right) - \xi_i \leq 0$$

$$- \xi_i \leq 0, \quad \forall i = 1, \dots, N.$$

$M > 0$ is a parameter to be fixed by the user. A larger M assigns a higher penalty to errors. M controls the trade-off between the slack variable penalty or errors and the size of the margin. Thus, if $M \to \infty$, we recover the penalty-free SVM, whereas if M is small, we admit misclassifications at the expense of having a small $||\mathbf{w}||$, i.e., a large margin.

Again, this new problem is a convex quadratic problem. For the primal Lagrangian L_P, we need to allocate Lagrange multipliers $\lambda_i \geq 0$ for the first set of constraints and $\mu_i \geq 0$ for the second set of constraints ($\boldsymbol{\mu}$ denotes the N-vector of this second set of constraints):

$$L_P(\mathbf{w},b,\boldsymbol{\xi},\boldsymbol{\lambda},\boldsymbol{\mu}) = \frac{1}{2}||\mathbf{w}||^2 + M \sum_{i=1}^{N} \xi_i + \sum_{i=1}^{N} \lambda_i \left(1 - c^i \left(\mathbf{w}^T \mathbf{x}^i + b \right) - \xi_i \right) - \sum_{i=1}^{N} \mu_i \xi_i.$$

When computing the derivatives of L_P to yield the dual Lagrangian,

$$L_D(\boldsymbol{\lambda},\boldsymbol{\mu}) = \min_{\mathbf{w},b,\boldsymbol{\xi}} L_P(\mathbf{w},b,\boldsymbol{\xi},\boldsymbol{\lambda},\boldsymbol{\mu}),$$

the derivatives with respect to $\mathbf{w}$ and b are the same as for the hard margin, i.e., Equations (7.12)–(7.13), whereas

$$\frac{\partial L_P}{\partial \xi_i} = 0 \Rightarrow M = \lambda_i + \mu_i. \tag{7.18}$$

Substituting these back into L_D, we get exactly the same expression (7.14) because, thanks to Equation (7.18), $\boldsymbol{\xi}$ and $\boldsymbol{\mu}$ vanish, and L_D is a function of just $\boldsymbol{\lambda}$. The equality in (7.18), together with $\mu_i \geq 0, \forall i$, implies that $\lambda_i \leq M$. Therefore, the dual problem is

$$\text{Dual: } \max_{\boldsymbol{\lambda}} L_D(\boldsymbol{\lambda}) = -\frac{1}{2}\sum_{i=1}^{N}\sum_{j=1}^{N}\lambda_i\lambda_j c^i c^j (\mathbf{x}^i)^T \mathbf{x}^j + \sum_{i=1}^{N}\lambda_i$$

subject to

$$0 \le \lambda_i \le M, \quad \forall i = 1,\dots,N$$

$$\sum_{i=1}^{N}\lambda_i c^i = 0.$$

(7.19)

Again a quadratic programming solver can be applied. The complementary slackness conditions are now

$$\lambda_i\left(1 - c^i\left(\mathbf{w}^T\mathbf{x}^i + b\right) - \xi_i\right) = 0 \tag{7.20}$$

$$\mu_i\xi_i = 0, \quad \forall i = 1,\dots,N. \tag{7.21}$$

With the optimal solution, points $\mathbf{x}^i$ for which $\lambda_i < M$ verify $\mu_i > 0$ (due to Equation (7.18)). Condition (7.21) leads then to $\xi_i = 0$. If, additionally, $\lambda_i > 0$, then condition (7.20) yields $c^i\left(\mathbf{w}^T\mathbf{x}^i + b\right) = 1$, that is, points for which $0 < \lambda_i < M$ lie on a support hyperplane and are the support vectors. Hence the intercept b is calculated as above, though S is now determined by finding the indices where $0 < \lambda_i < M$. The complete procedure is shown in Algorithm 7.4.

Algorithm 7.4: Classification with soft-margin linear SVMs: Nonlinearly separable data

---

Input : A data set $\mathcal{D} = \{(\mathbf{x}^1,c^1),\dots,(\mathbf{x}^N,c^N)\}$ with $c^i \in \{-1,+1\}$, a constant $M > 0$

Output: Classification c^* of each new observation $\mathbf{x}$

1 Solve problem in (7.17) by solving problem in (7.19) to yield $\lambda_i, i = 1,\dots,N$
2 Find set S, the indices i of support vectors such that $0 < \lambda_i < M$
3 Calculate $\mathbf{w} = \sum_{i \in S}\lambda_i c^i \mathbf{x}^i$
4 Calculate $b = \frac{1}{|S|}\sum_{s \in S}\left(c^s - \sum_{i \in S}\lambda_i c^i (\mathbf{x}^i)^T\mathbf{x}^s\right)$ (Equation (7.16))
5 Classify each new point $\mathbf{x}$ as $c^* = \phi(\mathbf{x}) = \text{sign}\left(\mathbf{w}^T\mathbf{x} + b\right)$

If needed, we can also derive ξ_i when it is positive as follows. $\xi_i > 0$ means $\mu_i = 0$ (due to Equation (7.21)), which in turn yields $\lambda_i = M$ (due to Equation (7.18)). Then, from Equation (7.20), we can derive ξ_i as $\xi_i = 1 - c^i\left(\mathbf{w}^T\mathbf{x}^i + b\right)$.

7.5.3   Nonlinearly Separable Data: Nonlinear SVM

Introducing slack variables still yields linear SVMs. However, many real cases will not be linearly solvable classification problems. **Cover's theorem** (Cover, 1965) states that a set of training data that are nonlinearly separable is highly likely to be able to be transformed into a linearly separable data set by projecting it into a higher-dimensional space via some nonlinear transformation.

This is a theoretical motivation for the following idea. Suppose we map the data to some other (possibly infinite dimensional) feature (Hilbert) space $\mathcal{F}$ by means of a nonlinear mapping

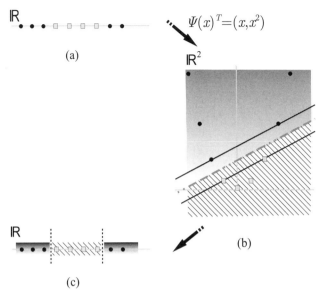

Figure 7.21 (a) Nine points in $\mathbb{R}$. Colors/shape indicate the class. (b) The points are mapped into $\mathbb{R}^2$ by means of $\psi(x) = (x, x^2)^T$ and are rendered linearly separable. The dashed line is the separating hyperplane, and the background colors and shapes indicate the corresponding assigned class label. (c) Original space with the classification and the associated boundaries.

$$\psi : \mathbb{R}^n \mapsto \mathcal{F}$$
$$\mathbf{x} \mapsto \psi(\mathbf{x}).$$

Although the data are nonlinearly separable in the input space, they can be linearly separable in the new feature space. Viewed from the original input space, the classifier is nonlinear.

A simpler example than that shown in Figure 7.18 is illustrated below.

Example. Suppose that, in a 1D space ($n = 1$), we have the data set

$$\mathcal{D} = \{(-4, \text{black}), (-3, \text{black}), (-2, \text{black}), (-1, \text{gray}), (0, \text{gray}), (1, \text{gray}),$$
$$(2, \text{gray}), (3, \text{black}), (4, \text{black})\},$$

where $\Omega_C = \{\text{black}, \text{gray}\}$, see Figure 7.21(a). This is a nonlinear 1D problem. We could use slack variables as in the previous section. However, the approach is now different. We can map data x from $\mathbb{R}$ to $\mathbb{R}^2$ using $\psi(x) = (x, x^2)^T$, outputting the points in Figure 7.21(b).

Now the data are linearly separable in the new (2D) space, and we can build a linear SVM in this new space. The linear decision boundary in the new space corresponds to a nonlinear boundary in the original space, see Figure 7.21(c). ∎

7.5.3.1 *Primal and Dual Forms*

To build an SVM in the new space, the formulation of the quadratic programming problem is as above, save that all occurrences of $\mathbf{x}$ are replaced by their mapped versions $\psi(\mathbf{x})$ in problems posed in (7.17) and (7.19). Note that $\mathbf{w}$ lives now in feature space $\mathcal{F}$. A new instance is assigned the label

$$c^* = \phi(\mathbf{x}) = \text{sign}\left(\mathbf{w}^T \boldsymbol{\psi}(\mathbf{x}) + b\right), \tag{7.22}$$

with

$$\mathbf{w} = \sum_{i \in S} \lambda_i c^i \boldsymbol{\psi}(\mathbf{x}^i), \tag{7.23}$$

$$b = \frac{1}{|S|} \sum_{s \in S} \left(c^s - \sum_{i \in S} \lambda_i c^i \boldsymbol{\psi}(\mathbf{x}^i)^T \boldsymbol{\psi}(\mathbf{x}^s) \right), \tag{7.24}$$

where S contains the indices i such that $0 < \lambda_i < M$.

Although this solves the problem of expressing complex functions, it raises other problems due to multidimensionality. First, a large memory may be required to compute and store each large vector $\boldsymbol{\psi}(\mathbf{x})$. Second, $\mathcal{F}$ might have to be a very high dimensional space to achieve linear separability (i.e., $\mathcal{F} = \mathbb{R}^{n'}, n' \gg n$). Third, $\boldsymbol{\psi}$ might be a complicated function and costly to evaluate. Fourth, it is not known which mapping $\boldsymbol{\psi}$ produces a linearly separable problem for a given nonlinear problem. This is where the kernel trick comes into play. Using this trick, we can recast the problem efficiently without using $\mathbf{w}$ or even just $\boldsymbol{\psi}(\mathbf{x})$.

7.5.3.2 The Kernel Mapping

Note first that the dual problem in (7.19), where $\mathbf{x}$ is replaced by $\boldsymbol{\psi}(\mathbf{x})$, only requires the inner product of mapped points $\boldsymbol{\psi}(\mathbf{x}^i)$. Moreover, substituting Equation (7.23) into Equation (7.22), we find that the solution is also achieved through inner products as

$$c^* = \phi(\mathbf{x}) = \text{sign}\left(\sum_{i \in S} \lambda_i c^i \boldsymbol{\psi}(\mathbf{x}^i)^T \boldsymbol{\psi}(\mathbf{x}) + b\right),$$

and b is also expressed in terms of inner products in Equation (7.24). Therefore, it is the inner products $\boldsymbol{\psi}(\mathbf{x}^i)^T \boldsymbol{\psi}(\mathbf{x}^j)$ instead of the function $\boldsymbol{\psi}$ that have to be explicitly known or computed. It would still appear to be infeasible if the dimension of $\mathcal{F}$ is high (infinite). However, a smart way to compute such inner product is via a kernel.

A **kernel function** or simply a **kernel** κ is defined as a symmetric function of two arguments (i.e., $\kappa(\mathbf{x}, \mathbf{x}') = \kappa(\mathbf{x}', \mathbf{x})$) that returns in $\mathbb{R}$ the value of the inner product of both mapped arguments, that is,

$$\kappa(\mathbf{x}, \mathbf{x}') = \boldsymbol{\psi}(\mathbf{x})^T \boldsymbol{\psi}(\mathbf{x}'). \tag{7.25}$$

Thus, kernel functions are based on calculating inner products of two vectors.

The kernelized dual problem is then

$$\text{Dual:} \max_{\lambda} L_D(\lambda) = -\frac{1}{2} \sum_{i=1}^{N} \sum_{j=1}^{N} \lambda_i \lambda_j c^i c^j \kappa(\mathbf{x}^i, \mathbf{x}^j) + \sum_{i=1}^{N} \lambda_i$$

subject to

$$0 \leq \lambda_i \leq M, \quad \forall i = 1, \ldots, N \tag{7.26}$$

$$\sum_{i=1}^{N} \lambda_i c^i = 0.$$

It can be less costly to compute $\kappa(\mathbf{x}^i, \mathbf{x}^j)$ directly than $\boldsymbol{\psi}(\mathbf{x}^i)^T \boldsymbol{\psi}(\mathbf{x}^j)$, and this avoids having to compute $\boldsymbol{\psi}$ explicitly. Also, because there are not usually too many support vectors, the classification decisions can be calculated reasonably quickly.

Example. For $\mathbf{x} = (x_1, x_2)^T \in \mathbb{R}^2$, if $\boldsymbol{\psi}$ is defined in a 6D space as

$$\boldsymbol{\psi}(\mathbf{x}) = \left(1, \sqrt{2}x_1, \sqrt{2}x_2, \sqrt{2}x_1x_2, x_1^2, x_2^2\right)^T,$$

the dot product in the expanded feature space for two points $\mathbf{x}, \mathbf{x}'$ is

$$\boldsymbol{\psi}(\mathbf{x})^T \boldsymbol{\psi}(\mathbf{x}') = 1 + 2x_1x_1' + 2x_2x_2' + 2x_1x_1'x_2x_2' + x_1^2x_1'^2 + x_2^2x_2'^2.$$

Hence if we define the kernel function as in Equation (7.25), we have

$$\kappa(\mathbf{x}, \mathbf{x}') = \boldsymbol{\psi}(\mathbf{x})^T \boldsymbol{\psi}(\mathbf{x}') = (1 + x_1x_1' + x_2x_2')^2 = \left(1 + \mathbf{x}^T\mathbf{x}'\right)^2.$$

The last expression operates on the lower-dimensional vectors $\mathbf{x}$ and $\mathbf{x}'$ to produce a value equivalent to the inner product of the higher-dimensional vectors.

Note that neither the mapping $\boldsymbol{\psi}$ nor the space $\mathcal{F}$ are unique for a given kernel. We might just as well have chosen a 7D space and the function

$$\boldsymbol{\psi}(\mathbf{x}) = \left(1, \sqrt{2}x_1, \sqrt{2}x_2, x_1x_2, x_1x_2, x_1^2, x_2^2\right)^T,$$

because again $\boldsymbol{\psi}(\mathbf{x})^T \boldsymbol{\psi}(\mathbf{x}') = \left(1 + \mathbf{x}^T\mathbf{x}'\right)^2.$ ∎

The implicit mapping to a kernel-induced feature space saves computations, and there is no need to know $\boldsymbol{\psi}$ explicitly, i.e., there is no need to specify which data features are being used. In fact, it can be shown that, for kernels of this polynomial form, $\kappa(\mathbf{x}, \mathbf{x}') = (\mathbf{x}^T\mathbf{x}')^p, p \in \mathbb{N}$, inner products in $\mathcal{F}$ would require a number of operations proportional to $\binom{n+p-1}{p}$, whereas the number is only linear in n to compute $\kappa(\mathbf{x}, \mathbf{x}')$.

Algorithm 7.5 shows the complete procedure for classifying nonlinearly separable data in the input space using a kernel to render the data as linearly separable in a new feature space.

Algorithm 7.5: Classification with nonlinear SVMs

Input : A data set $\mathcal{D} = \{(\mathbf{x}^1, c^1), \dots, (\mathbf{x}^N, c^N)\}$ with $c^i \in \{-1, +1\}$, a constant $M > 0$

Output: Classification c^* of each new observation $\mathbf{x}$

1 Solve problem in (7.26) and yield $\lambda_i, i = 1, \dots, N$
2 Find set S, the indices i of support vectors such that $0 < \lambda_i < M$
3 Calculate $b = \frac{1}{|S|} \sum_{s \in S} \left(c^s - \sum_{i \in S} \lambda_i c^i \kappa(\mathbf{x}^i, \mathbf{x}^s)\right)$
4 Classify each new point $\mathbf{x}$ as $c^* = \phi(\mathbf{x}) = \text{sign}\left(\sum_{i \in S} \lambda_i c^i \kappa(\mathbf{x}^i, \mathbf{x}) + b\right)$

If we start by defining $\kappa(\mathbf{x}, \mathbf{x}') = \left(1 + \mathbf{x}^T\mathbf{x}'\right)^2$ in the above example, it is easy to find $\mathcal{F}$ and $\boldsymbol{\psi}$ such that $\left(1 + \mathbf{x}^T\mathbf{x}'\right)^2 = \boldsymbol{\psi}(\mathbf{x})^T \boldsymbol{\psi}(\mathbf{x}')$. In practical SVM use, the user specifies the kernel function, whereas transformation $\boldsymbol{\psi}$ is not explicitly stated. See Figure 7.22 for a summary of both options, that is, direct or indirect use of the mapping function $\boldsymbol{\psi}$ with SVMs.

Table 7.11 Typical kernel functions

Name	$\kappa(\mathbf{x}, \mathbf{x}')$	Parameters
Homogeneous polynomial	$(\mathbf{x}^T \mathbf{x}')^p$	degree $p \in \mathbb{N}$
Inhomogeneous polynomial	$(1 + \mathbf{x}^T \mathbf{x}')^p$	degree $p \in \mathbb{N}$
Gaussian radial basis function	$e^{-\frac{1}{2\sigma^2} \lVert \mathbf{x} - \mathbf{x}' \rVert^2}$	width $\sigma > 0$
Sigmoidal	$\tanh\left(\alpha \mathbf{x}^T \mathbf{x}' - \theta \right)$	α, θ

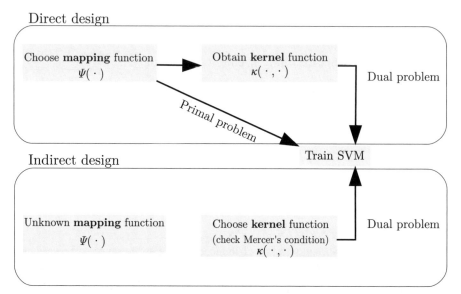

Figure 7.22 The direct design (top) explicitly uses ψ and then constructs the kernel function. The indirect design (bottom) selects the kernel function without requiring explicit knowledge of ψ.

The kernel function is actually a similarity measure between the input data. The decision boundary for any new point $\mathbf{x}$ (line 4 in Algorithm 7.5) is essentially a weighted sum of the similarity between $\mathbf{x}$ and a preselected set of objects (the support vectors). However, not all similarity measures can be used as kernel functions. For a function $\kappa(\cdot, \cdot)$ to be a valid kernel, that is, to be decomposed as an inner product (Equation (7.25)), it needs to satisfy **Mercer's condition** (Mercer, 1909). If the condition is satisfied, it guarantees the existence of an underlying mapping ψ such that Equation (7.25) holds. Mercer's condition means that the $N \times N$ **kernel matrix** (also called the **Gram matrix**) $\mathbf{K}$ in which the (i, j) entry is $\kappa\left(\mathbf{x}^i, \mathbf{x}^j\right)$ is always positive-semidefinite, i.e., $\mathbf{x}^T \mathbf{K} \mathbf{x} \geq 0, \forall \mathbf{x} \neq 0$ in the training set. The specific mapping ψ may be unknown, though the SVM can be learned with knowledge of $\kappa(\cdot, \cdot)$. This also means that the associated quadratic programming problem is convex and can be solved in polynomial time.

7.5.3.3 *Model Selection*

In practice, SVMs have a limitation, namely, the choice of the kernel (and its parameters). Popular kernels are shown in Table 7.11.

Homogeneous polynomial kernels are equivalent to an implicit ψ with all terms of order p. Inhomogeneous polynomial kernels are equivalent to an implicit ψ with all terms of all

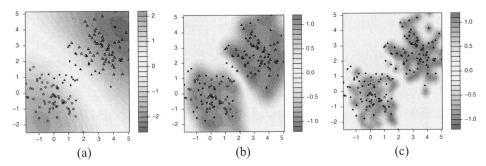

Figure 7.23 Effect of parameter σ of the Gaussian RBF kernel over the decision boundary. The data points are 2D. There are two class labels represented by different shapes (circles and triangles). The color gradient shows the change in decision rule values for making classifications. The dark blue areas should be considered as the highest-confidence regions for positive classification, and the dark red areas as the highest-confidence regions for negative classification. For large values of σ (a), the decision boundary is nearly linear. As σ decreases ((b) and (c)), the flexibility of the decision boundary increases and can lead to overfitting. Points in solid black are the support vectors. Note that a smaller σ calls for more support vectors. For the color version, please refer to the plate section.

orders less than or equal to p. Both produce a classifier that is a polynomial of degree p in the data. With $p = 1$, the kernel is linear.

The expression of a Gaussian radial basis function (RBF) kernel corresponds to an infinite dimensional feature space. It is essentially zero if the distance between $\mathbf{x}$ and $\mathbf{x}'$ is much greater than $\sqrt{2}\sigma$, i.e., it is localized to a region around $\mathbf{x}'$ for a specified $\mathbf{x}'$. The expression for the decision rule (line 4 in Algorithm 7.5) is thus a sum of Gaussian "bumps" centered around each support vector $\mathbf{x}^i$. Given a data point $\mathbf{x}$, all support vectors for large σ affect the decision boundary (all $\kappa(\mathbf{x}^i, \mathbf{x}) \neq 0$), and this becomes smooth. When σ is smaller, the curvature of the decision boundary increases because the locality increases. With very small σ, the decision boundary is essentially constant outside the close proximity of the region where the data are concentrated, and the classifier overfits the data. Therefore, hyperparameter σ plays a similar role as the degree of the polynomial kernel in controlling the flexibility of the resulting classifier. Figure 7.23 shows an example with three different values for σ, which decreases to the right.

The SVM with a Gaussian RBF kernel is closely related to radial basis function ANNs (Section 7.4.1). Finally, the sigmoidal kernel satisfies Mercer's condition only for some values of α, θ and gives a particular kind of two-layer sigmoidal ANN.

For kernel selection, a low-degree polynomial kernel, starting from the linear kernel, or a Gaussian RBF kernel with a reasonable width, are sensible initial options.

Another hyperparameter to be tuned is the soft-margin parameter M. Remember that M balances the effect of minimizing errors in the training set and the size of the margin. A large M does not admit misclassifications, implying a more complex model with perhaps overfitting. A small M is laxer with regard to misclassifications, providing a much larger margin perhaps leading to underfitting.

It is essential to choose appropriate values for M and the kernel to achieve good performance. The best combination of M and kernel parameters (Table 7.11) are often selected by a grid search with exponentially growing sequences of them. A validation data set can be helpful for estimating the accuracy for each point on the grid. Ben-Hur and Weston (2010) published an SVM user guide, discussing all these topics.

The area of clinical diagnosis is full of SVM applications. In Zhang et al. (2013b), RBF kernel SVMs were used to classify a given MR brain image as either normal or abnormal. The abnormal images consisted of many different diseases, like glioma, metastatic adeno-carcinoma, meningioma, sarcoma, AD, HD, motor neuron disease, cerebral calcinosis, Pick's disease, MS, Lyme encephalopathy, herpes encephalitis, and Creutzfeldt–Jakob disease, among others.

In AD, Patil and Ramakrishnan (2014) built an SVM with a polynomial kernel of degree 5 to discriminate AD patients from healthy controls. Features were DTI indices of white matter regions. Labels came from the MMSE score. Decision stumps and logistic regression classifiers were also used. Scheubert et al. (2012) aimed at identifying the genes involved in AD from microarray data. An SVM (linear and Gaussian RBF kernel) was used to compute the fitness function of a genetic algorithm designed to find gene set combinations that are good biomarkers.

The SVM developed by Khan et al. (2014) used a universal kernel based on the Pearson VII function (well-known in the field of spectroscopy). The aim was the objective assessment of rapid-finger-tapping test, a method for clinical evaluation of movement disorders, including PD. With videos tracking the index-finger motion, different features were collected from tapping time series. The SVM was able to classify by symptom severity levels and by PD patients and healthy controls.

Other diseases include schizophrenia (Su et al., 2013), where a linear kernel was used to differentiate patients with schizophrenia from healthy controls using the whole brain functional connectivity extracted by the Pearson correlation and mutual information coefficients; or attention-deficit/hyperactivity disorder (ADHD) (Poil et al., 2014), where an RBF kernel SVM based on resting electroencephalogram (eyes closed) biomarkers differentiated ADHD adults from controls.

Ambert et al. (2013) used SVMs with a linear kernel in a text mining task. The resulting system *Virk* identifies documents containing information of interest for a knowledge base. The input features were derived from neuroscience-related publications in the primary literature. In just 3 months, it greatly increased the size of the Neuron Registry, a knowledge base of neuron-related information. This task would have taken up to 2 years using standard biocuration methods.

7.5.3.4 *Flexibility of SVMs: The Vapnik–Chervonenkis Dimension*

An intriguing question is why SVMs usually do so well if mapping the data to a feature space with an enormous number of dimensions may detract from the generalization performance, i.e., may cause overfitting. It is common to think that a classifier in a high-dimensional space has many parameters and is hard to estimate. We have seen that SVMs use kernels to achieve tractable computation. Also, Vapnik (1998) argues that the fundamental problem is not the number of parameters to be estimated but the flexibility of the classifier. Flexibility is not always equivalent to having many parameters. For instance, the data set $\mathcal{D} = \{x^i = 10^{-i} : i = 1, \ldots, n\}$ can be correctly separated by the classifier $\phi(x) = \text{sign}(\sin(\alpha x))$ for all possible combinations of class labels on x^i. This classifier is very flexible and has only one parameter. Flexibility (also called capacity) is formalized by the **Vapnik–Chervonenkis (VC) dimension** of a classification algorithm. The VC

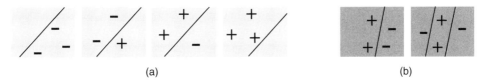

(a)   (b)

Figure 7.24 Illustration of the Vapnik–Chervonenkis dimension of a linear classifier in 2D. (a) Three points are always perfectly classified with a linear model. (b) This is not always possible for four points: the four points can be perfectly classified in the left figure, whereas in the right figure they cannot. Thus, the VC dimension of a linear classifier in 2D is three.

dimension is the cardinality of the largest set of points that the algorithm can shatter. A classifier with any parameter vector θ is said to shatter a set of data points if, for all possible label assignments to those points, there is a θ such that the model makes no errors when evaluating that set of data points.

The VC dimension of a constant (parameterless) classifier is zero because it cannot even shatter a single point. The VC dimension of a linear classifier in a 2D space is three because, if we have three points in the training set, perfect classification is always possible irrespective of the labeling, whereas perfect classification may not be possible for four points (see Figure 7.24). The VC dimension of the 1-NN classifier is infinity because training data classification is perfect no matter how many points you have.

The expected test error of a classifier (or expected risk, see Section 5.1.1) is, with high probability, upper bounded by the sum of its empirical risk and a term depending on the VC dimension. **Structural risk minimization** is a principled method for choosing a classifier designed to minimize the expected error by trading off both the empirical risk and the VC dimension, that is, training data errors and classifier flexibility. SVMs can be regarded as implementing structural risk minimization because $\sum \xi_i$ approximates the training error, and $||\mathbf{w}||^2$ has been shown to be related to the VC dimension of the resulting classifier.

7.5.4   Example: Interneurons versus Pyramidal Neurons

Once again Data Set 1 described in Chapter 1 is used to illustrate the performance of SVMs when discriminating between interneurons (I) and pyramidal neurons (P). We applied different kernel functions: polynomial of degrees 1 and 2 and Gaussian RFB with $\sigma = 0.41$. The value of M was the default value ($M = 1$). As in the remainder of this chapter, we built the SVMs taking into account all variables and feature selection using a univariate filter based on the gain ratio and the CFS multivariate filter in WEKA (Hall et al., 2009) (see Section 7.1.8 for the list of selected variables), as well as a wrapper approach. The SVM implementation in WEKA is SMO (Platt, 1999a). SVMs are known to be sensitive to how variables are scaled, and either the original data or the kernelized data can be normalized. WEKA normalizes all variables by default. Table 7.12 shows how good these models are as regards their classification accuracy, also specifying the number of selected variables.

The most accurate SVMs were the most complex, i.e., SVMs with a polynomial kernel of degree 2 and SVMs with a Gaussian RBF kernel, both as part of a wrapper approach yielding a classification accuracy above 90%.

Table 7.12 Classification accuracy of SVM classifiers for Data Set 1 (# means the number of variables included in the model)

	Kernel function					
	Polynomial $p = 1$		Polynomial $p = 2$		Gaussian RBF $\sigma = 0.41$	
FSS	Accuracy	#	Accuracy	#	Accuracy	#
None	0.8471	65	0.8776	65	0.7798	65
Gain ratio	0.8226	15	0.8349	15	0.8471	15
CFS	0.8379	17	0.8624	17	0.8563	17
Wrapper	0.8563	10	**0.9052**	28	**0.9052**	17

Table 7.13 Main performance measures of the Gaussian RBF kernel-based SVM for Data Set 1 with $\sigma = 0.41$; a wrapper approach selected 17 variables out of 65

Measure	Value
Accuracy	0.9052
Sensitivity	0.9598
Specificity	0.8203
F_1-measure	0.9250
Cohen's kappa	0.7968
Brier score	0.1896
AUC	0.8901

We take the second model, with 17 selected variables, for further analysis. These variables were X_3 (related to somata); X_{10}, X_{25}, and X_{30} (related to axons); and $X_{39}, X_{42}, X_{46}, X_{50}, X_{51}, X_{52}, X_{53}, X_{55}, X_{56}, X_{57}, X_{58}, X_{59}$, and X_{61} (related to dendrites). Tortuosity and Sholl-related variables seem to be relevant in this model (see the meaning of all variables in Tables 1.5 and 1.6). The main performance measures, all estimated with 10-fold cross-validation, are shown in Table 7.13. There were 177 support vectors.

The confusion matrix, with real labels in rows and predicted labels in columns, is

$$\begin{array}{cc} & \begin{array}{cc} \text{I} & \text{P} \end{array} \\ \begin{array}{c} \text{I} \\ \text{P} \end{array} & \left(\begin{array}{cc} 191 & 8 \\ 23 & 105 \end{array} \right). \end{array}$$

Figure 7.25 shows neurons and their correct or incorrect classification by the SVM model. In (a) and (b), the algorithm successfully classified interneuron $\mathbf{x}^{18}$ and pyramidal neuron $\mathbf{x}^{252}$, respectively. In (c), interneuron $\mathbf{x}^{64}$ was misclassified as a pyramidal neuron, whereas in (d), pyramidal neuron $\mathbf{x}^{225}$ was misclassified as an interneuron.

7.5.5 Multi-class SVMs

Binary or two-class SVMs can be extended to a class variable with more than two categories, $\Omega_C = \{1, \dots, R\}, R > 2$. This is referred to as a **multi-class SVM**. One possibility

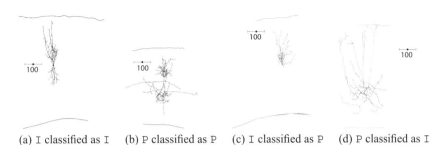

(a) I classified as I   (b) P classified as P   (c) I classified as P   (d) P classified as I

Figure 7.25 Some neurons and their classification by the SVM. (a) Correctly classified interneuron $\mathbf{x}^{18}$, however misclassified by the C4.5 algorithm, see Figure 7.10(c). (b) Correctly classified pyramidal neuron $\mathbf{x}^{252}$. (c) Misclassified interneuron $\mathbf{x}^{64}$. (d) Misclassified pyramidal neuron $\mathbf{x}^{225}$. Axonal arbor in blue and dendritic tree in red. For the color version, please refer to the plate section.

is to change the primal-dual formulation into a multi-class expression. However, the most used option is to build and then combine many binary SVMs (Hsu and Lin, 2002). Thus, in the **one-category-versus-rest** method, R SVM classifiers are built to separate one class from the rest (say, +1 for training instances with that category and -1 for instances with a different category). In the classification phase of a new instance, we pick the label that puts this instance furthest into the positive region, that is, we label the instance according to the classifier with the highest decision rule value. In the **one-versus-one** method (called pairwise classification), each of the $\binom{R}{2}$ classifiers are trained on data from two classes. A new instance is classified by voting, i.e., by selecting the most frequently predicted label by these classifiers.

To summarize the SVMs, we must emphasize that they are a useful alternative to ANNs. Training SVMs is relatively easy. Unlike ANNs, where there are usually many local minima, SVMs always find a global solution. By using slack variables, SVMs are robust to outliers and noise. The two core concepts are to maximize the margin and the kernel trick. The choice of the kernel is a key point. The soft-margin parameter can control the trade-off between classifier complexity and error. SVMs scale relatively well to high-dimensional data. The number of free parameters is bounded by the number of support vectors and not by the number of variables. SVMs do not require direct access to data because they work only with inner products of data points.

Classification trees sequentially combine several linear classifiers, whereas SVMs take a rather different approach because they use a suitable nonlinear mapping to render the problem linear. Compared to ANNs, SVMs can be seen as an advanced multi-layer perceptron. The support vectors alone determine the weights and thus the boundary in SVMs. Multilayer perceptrons apply a final linear model after nonlinear input processing. SVMs adopt a similar idea, but it is harder to put into practice as margin maximization is a tricky issue.

7.6   Bibliographic Notes

k-**NN.** The choice of the appropriate distance function among instances influences the quality of the figures of merit associated with the k-NN classifiers as shown by Dasarathy (1991) and in the overview by Cunningham (2009). Flexible or adaptive metrics have been developed by Friedman (1994) and Hastie and Tibshirani (1996).

Classification Trees. Lim et al. (2000) compared 22 classification tree induction algorithms on many data sets (and also algorithms from other paradigms, like k-NN, rule induction, ANNs, linear discriminant analysis and logistic regression) and found that QUEST with linear splits was the most accurate algorithm. Other classification tree algorithms not explained here are THAID, FACT, LMDT, PUBLIC, CRUISE, CTree, and GUIDE. Safavian and Landgrebe (1991), Loh (2014), and Kotsiantis (2013) provide good classification tree overviews. Kotsiantis (2013) reviewed special problems, i.e., the management of very large data sets, cost-sensitive problems, concept drift, uncertain labels, ordinal class variable and multi-instance learning. Li and Belford (2002) showed the instability inherent in decision trees, i.e., small changes in the training set can cause dramatic changes in the tree topology. Some metaclassifiers like bagging (Section 9.3.3) exploit this feature by ensembling the results produced from several trees learned on slightly different training sets.

Rule Induction. In addition to the different rule inductors introduced in Section 7.3, there is an approach that uses evolutionary computation to evolve a set of rules. It is known as genetics-based machine learning algorithms for rule induction. There are two different families of algorithms: the Michigan approach (Holland, 1976), where each rule is coded as a single chromosome in the genetic algorithm, and the Pittsburgh approach (Smith, 1980), which considers a set of rules as a chromosome (see Fernández et al. [2010] for a review). Advances in the rule induction methodology can be consulted in the edited book by Triantaphyllou and Felici (2006).

ANNs. The field of ANNs has benefited from research in diverse areas such as biology, cognitive science, computer science, mathematics, neuroscience, physics, and psychology. The field has passed through periods of enthusiasm and skepticism, with the resulting ups and downs with regard to progress. Bishop (1995) and Ripley (1996) authored the classic books on ANNs.

McCulloch and Pitts (1943) are considered to have made the first attempt to mathematically model neuron operation. In their simple neuron model, a weighted sum of input signals is compared to a threshold to determine the neuron output. Hebb (1949) introduced the idea that behavior can be explained by the action of neurons, proposing one of the first learning mechanisms. Rosenblatt (1958) introduced the perceptron and its associated learning rule. At about the same time, Widrow and Hoff (1960) developed a learning algorithm for their **ADALINE** (ADAptive LInear NEuron). ADALINE is similar to a perceptron but has a linear transfer function instead of the hard-limiting function typically used in perceptrons. However, both perceptrons and ADALINE networks can only solve linearly separable problems. Minsky and Papert (1969) proposed multi-layer networks with hidden units to overcome that limitation, but they were not able to find an algorithm to learn such networks from data. This was at the root of much of the pessimism reigning in the field of ANNs during the 1970s when it was essentially dormant with very little research activity. The most important milestone in the field was the development of an efficient training algorithm for multi-layer perceptrons: the backpropagation algorithm. This algorithm was capable of overcoming the linear separability limitation of the simple perceptron. The backpropagation algorithm originated from the **Widrow–Hoff learning rule** (also known as least mean square rule) was created by Werbos (1974) and popularized by Rumelhartand et al. (1986) and is the basis of today's popular ANN learning methods.

Hopfield (1982) used statistical mechanics to develop a class of **recurrent networks** trained as an associative memory. Kohonen (1982) proposed an ANN based on self-organization, where similar model inputs are topologically close in 2D maps. Kohonen's self-organizing maps are used for clustering (see Section 11.3.5 for details).

For a historical overview of deep neural networks see Schmidhuber (2015). Goodfellow et al. (2016) is a good introductory book on the subject.

ANNs are used in a recent successful model called **generative adversarial network** (GAN) (Goodfellow et al., 2014). GANs are used in unsupervised learning to automatically discover patterns in the input data, and then they can generate new instances that plausibly could have been drawn from the original data set. GANs can learn to mimic any distribution of data. Training GANs is posed as a supervised learning problem with two networks: a discriminator network D, and a generator network G. G is trained to generate new instances, and then D tries to classify instances as either real (from the domain) or synthetic (generated). The two models are trained together in a minimax game until D is fooled about half the time, meaning that G is generating plausible examples.

Creswell et al. (2018) review GANs methodology including networks different from multi-layer perceptrons. More recent applications of GANs in neuroscience are Seeliger et al. (2018) to reconstruct natural images from brain activity, Pan et al. (2018) for the missing PET data imputation in a multimodal (MRI and PET) neuroimage application of the ADNI data set, and Bowles et al. (2018) to model the progression of AD in MRI.

SVMs. Boser et al. (1992) reported the most important milestone for the development of modern SVMs, after which SVMs developed enormously and have been active ever since. Burges (1998) offered a good tutorial on SVMs. As a curiosity, the Karush–Kuhn–Tucker conditions were originally named after Harold W. Kuhn and Albert W. Tucker, who first published the conditions in 1951 (Kuhn and Tucker, 1951). Later it was discovered (Kjeldsen, 2000) that they had been stated by William Karush in his master's thesis (Karush, 1939).

Further details on the VC dimension of SVMs are of interest. For instance, it can be shown that the VC dimension of an SVM is $1 + \dim(\mathcal{F})$. Thus, for SVMs with a homogeneous polynomial kernel, $\dim(\mathcal{F}) = \binom{n+p-1}{p}$, and with a Gaussian RBF kernel, the VC dimension is infinite.

SVMs are a particular instance of **kernel machines** (Cristianini and Shawe-Taylor, 2000). Kernel classifiers were first described back in the 1960s, when the kernel perceptron was invented (Aizerman et al., 1964). Their use grew in the 1990s when SVMs became popular because it was found that they were able to compete with ANNs with respect to tasks such as handwriting recognition. The implicit mapping trick described for SVMs works for any algorithm in which the data appear as inner products, e.g., the k-NN algorithm, linear regression, logistic regression and PCA. Thus, nonlinear versions of these algorithms can be derived. Extensions of SVMs to real-valued outputs are called **support vector regression** (Drucker et al., 1997). Also, extensions of the basic SVM algorithm can be applied to solve other machine learning tasks, like clustering (Ben-Hur et al., 2002; Hardin et al., 2004), FSS (Weston et al., 2001), and outlier detection (Tax and Duin, 1999).

8 Probabilistic Classifiers

Supervised classification aims at assigning labels or categories to instances described by a set of predictor variables or features. The classification model that assigns labels to instances is automatically induced from a data set containing labeled instances. In this chapter we focus on classification models that are probabilistic, that is, their output is the posterior distribution of the class variable conditioned on a given set of values for the features. Three important models will be covered: discriminant analysis (Section 8.2), logistic regression (Section 8.3), and Bayesian network classifiers (Section 8.4). Discriminant analysis and Bayesian network classifiers are generative approaches because they model the joint probability distribution of the class and feature variables. Logistic regression, however, is a discriminative model, designed to directly find the conditional probability of the class variable given the features. All models are applied to the interneurons versus pyramidal neurons problem of Data Set 1. Section 8.5 includes bibliographic notes of these models. Figure 8.1 shows the year when the seminal paper of each model was published.

We start with a data set of n variables, $\mathbf{X} = (X_1, \dots, X_n)$, including characteristics or features from N labeled instances. Let $\mathcal{D} = \{(\mathbf{x}^1, c^1), \dots, (\mathbf{x}^N, c^N)\}$ denote the data set, where for each $\mathbf{x}^i = (x_1^i, \dots, x_n^i)$, $i = 1, \dots, N$, we have the respective value c^i of a class variable denoted by C with labels in the domain $\Omega_C = \{c_1, \dots, c_R\}$ (or sometimes simply $\Omega_C = \{1, \dots, R\}$). The domain of each X_i is accordingly denoted $\Omega_{X_i} = \{x_1, \dots, x_{R_i}\}$ (or sometimes simply $\Omega_i = \{1, \dots, R_i\}$), $i = 1, \dots, n$, where i is not used (unless it is necessary) for the values for simplicity, and only for the number of values.

The output of a probabilistic classifier is the posterior distribution of the class variable conditioned on $\mathbf{x}$, i.e., $p(C = c_r | \mathbf{x})$. A common further step is to use these probabilities to classify future instances into one of the class labels $c_1, \dots, c_R$. There are several ways to convert probabilities into predicted labels. Typically a criterion to be optimized is defined, and then a **decision rule** $\phi(\mathbf{x})$ defining how to assign a (predicted) label for every possible instance $\mathbf{x}$ is derived. The next section describes the Bayes decision rule, the most natural rule in this probabilistic setting.

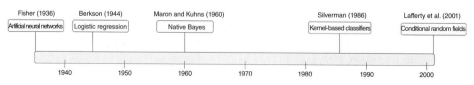

Figure 8.1 Timeline of the seminal papers for probabilistic classifiers.

8.1   Bayes Decision Rule

Suppose first that we have a binary class $\Omega_C = \{c_1, c_2\}$. When working with probabilistic classifiers, we have the **prior probability** (or a priori probability) over the class variable $p(C = c_r), r = 1, 2$. This reflects our prior knowledge and could be used in a naive way to build a decision rule to separate the two labels:

$$\text{Decide } c_1 \text{ if } p(C = c_1) > p(C = c_2); \text{ otherwise decide } c_2. \qquad (8.1)$$

This does not appear to be a meaningful rule for repeated use. We would always make the same decision, although we know that both labels can appear. Of course, the values of these priors affect the performance of this rule. If $p(C = c_1) = 0.9$, our decision in favor of c_1 will be right most of the time, whereas if $p(C = c_1) = 0.5$, we will have a 50% chance of being right.

We also have the conditional probabilities of $\mathbf{X}$ given each value of the class, $p_{\mathbf{X}|C=c_r}(\mathbf{x}|c_r)$, or simply $p(\mathbf{x}|c_r)$,[1] called the **class-conditional probability** (mass or density) function, giving information about the variability of $\mathbf{x}$ for each class label. Figure 8.2 shows the difference in the distribution of the Number of dendritic Sholl sections (X_{56}) between populations of interneurons and pyramidal neurons. The densities have been fitted[2] using Data Set 1.

Suppose further that we measure $\mathbf{X}$ for an instance (i.e., the number of dendritic Sholl sections of a neuron) and see that it is $\mathbf{x}$. This new information influences our belief about the true label of the instance (i.e., interneuron or pyramidal). With the Bayes formula, we convert the prior probability $p(C = c_r), r = 1, 2$, to the **posterior probability** (or a

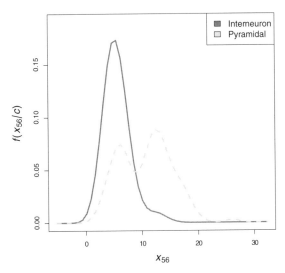

Figure 8.2 Class-conditional probability density functions of X_{56} (Number dendritic Sholl sections) given a neuron in category $c = \text{I}$ (interneuron, in solid black line) or category $c = \text{P}$ (pyramidal, in dashed gray line).

---

[1] Subscripted notation will only be used when there is a possibility of misinterpretation.
[2] We have used a normal kernel density estimate; see Section 8.4.2.2.

posteriori probability), that is, the probability of the class being c_r given that feature value $\mathbf{x}$ has been observed,

$$p(C = c_r | \mathbf{x}) = \frac{p(\mathbf{x} | c_r) p(C = c_r)}{\sum_{i=1}^{2} p(\mathbf{x} | c_i) p(C = c_i)}.$$

The denominator is equal to $p(\mathbf{x})$, called the **evidence**, which is simply a scale factor to guarantee that the posterior probabilities add up to 1. $p(\mathbf{x} | c_r)$ is usually called the **likelihood** of c_r with respect to $\mathbf{x}$, indicating that the category c_r for which $p(\mathbf{x} | c_r)$ is large is more "likely" to be the true category. Then, the posterior computation can be informally summarized as

$$\text{posterior} = \frac{\text{likelihood} \times \text{prior}}{\text{evidence}}.$$

With this more complete piece of information, we can build a more meaningful (Bayes) decision rule:

$$\text{Decide } c_1 \text{ if } p(C = c_1 | \mathbf{x}) > p(C = c_2 | \mathbf{x}); \text{ otherwise decide } c_2. \tag{8.2}$$

The term *Bayes* emphasizes the role of the posterior probabilities and will be more formally derived later. Because the evidence does not affect the decision, an equivalent decision rule is

$$\text{Decide } c_1 \text{ if } p(\mathbf{x} | c_1) p(C = c_1) > p(\mathbf{x} | c_2) p(C = c_2); \text{ otherwise decide } c_2. \tag{8.3}$$

Bayes' formula combines both factors, the likelihood and the prior, in making the decision. Two exceptions are (a) if $p(C = c_1) = p(C = c_2)$, that is, both labels are equally probable, then the decision is based only on the likelihood; and (b) if an instance $\mathbf{x}$ is such that $p(\mathbf{x} | c_1) = p(\mathbf{x} | c_2)$, that is, $\mathbf{x}$ gives no information about the class, then the decision is entirely based on the prior probabilities.

Example. Figure 8.3(a) illustrates two Gaussian distributions as class-conditional density functions. First, we have $X | c_1 \sim \mathcal{N}(x | 5, 2)$ in solid line. Second, there is $X | c_2 \sim \mathcal{N}(x | 10, 5)$ in dashed lines, shifted to the right of $f(x | c_1)$ and with a greater variance. This shows how different X is, depending on the class label. Figure 8.3(b) shows the respective posterior probabilities $p(C = c_i | x), i = 1, 2$, for the priors $p(C = c_1) = 0.7$ and $p(C = c_2) = 0.3$. Thus, given an instance with $x = 7$ for its X value, the probability of it being in category c_1 is $p(c_1 | x) = 0.8$, and of it being in c_2 is $p(c_2 | x) = 0.2$. The posteriors add up to 1 at any given value of X. Then, the classification rule based on posterior probabilities would decide to classify this instance as c_1. Note that near $x = 5$ (the mean of the first Gaussian), c_1 will be preferred over c_2 because $p(C = c_1 | x) > p(C = c_2 | x)$. However, c_2 is preferred near $x = 9$ and further away. For $x < 0$, c_2 is also preferred.

The effect of changing the priors is observed in Figure 8.4, where $p(C = c_1) = 0.2$ and $p(C = c_2) = 0.8$ in (a). Now c_2 is given more weight. This is captured by the posterior because $p(C = c_2 | x) > p(C = c_1 | x)$ most of the time, resulting in c_2 decisions. In (b), the posterior $p(C = c_1 | x)$ is plotted when X is fixed at $x = 7$, and the prior $p(C = c_1)$ varies on the x-axis. The points at $p(C = c_1) = 0.7$ and 0.2 are also shown in Figure 8.3(b) and Figure 8.4(a), respectively. The posterior increases as long as $p(C = c_1)$ increases. The posterior $p(C = c_2 | x)$ is $1 - p(C = c_1 | x)$. ∎

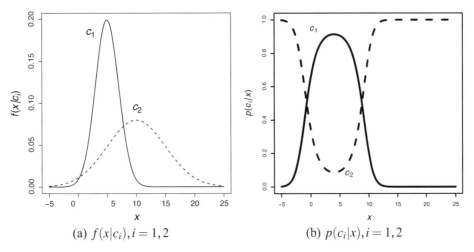

(a) $f(x|c_i), i = 1, 2$ (b) $p(c_i|x), i = 1, 2$

Figure 8.3 (a) Class-conditional probability density functions of two Gaussian distributions of X given category c_i. $X|c_1 \sim \mathcal{N}(x|5, 2)$ in solid curve and $X|c_2 \sim \mathcal{N}(x|10, 5)$ in dashed curve. (b) Their respective posterior probabilities $p(C = c_i|x), i = 1, 2$, for the priors $p(C = c_1) = 0.7$ and $p(C = c_2) = 0.3$.

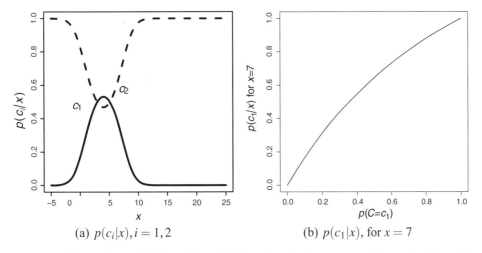

(a) $p(c_i|x), i = 1, 2$ (b) $p(c_1|x)$, for $x = 7$

Figure 8.4 (a) Posterior probabilities $p(C = c_i|x), i = 1, 2$, under the same conditions as in Figure 8.3, except that the priors are $p(C = c_1) = 0.2$ and $p(C = c_2) = 0.8$. (b) Posterior $p(C = c_1|x)$ when $x = 7$ and the prior $p(C = c_1)$ ranges from 0 to 1 on the x-axis.

For error prevention, it makes sense to look for a rule that minimizes the **probability of error**, also called the error rate. The above decision rule minimizes the probability of error of a particular $\mathbf{x}$, $p(\text{error}|\mathbf{x})$, that is, whenever we make a decision

$$p(\text{error}|\mathbf{x}) = \begin{cases} p(C = c_1|\mathbf{x}) & \text{if we decide } c_2 \\ p(C = c_2|\mathbf{x}) & \text{if we decide } c_1, \end{cases}$$

and this is clearly minimized by using the rule in Equation (8.2). The (most interesting) *average* probability of error is given by

$$p(\text{error}) = \int p(\text{error}, \mathbf{x}) d\mathbf{x} = \int p(\text{error}|\mathbf{x}) p(\mathbf{x}) d\mathbf{x},$$

which is also minimized by the same rule because it minimizes the integrand. We are assuming that $\mathbf{x}$ lies in an n-dimensional Euclidean space $\mathbb{R}^n$ and hence the integral symbol. In discrete cases it would be replaced by a sum symbol.

These ideas can be stated in a more general setting. Again, let $\Omega_C = \{c_1, \ldots, c_R\}$. We can define a more general loss function (see Section 5.1.1) than the probability of error. The loss function $L(c_i, \phi(\mathbf{x}))$ quantifies the cost of a decision, that is, of an $\mathbf{x}$-assignment $\phi(\mathbf{x})$ (one label from Ω_C) when the true label is c_i. This can capture situations where some classification mistakes are more costly than others. Depending on the objective of the study, the cost of misclassifying c_1 as c_2 may be not the same as misclassifying c_2 as c_1. The corresponding classification problems are called **cost-sensitive**. We will now see that the loss function can be used to convert the probability output of a probabilistic classifier into a decision rule.

If we observe a particular $\mathbf{x}$, and the classifier assigns $\phi(\mathbf{x}) = c_r$ to $\mathbf{x}$, the **expected loss**, also called **conditional risk** in decision-theoretic terminology, of this action c_r is

$$R(c_r|\mathbf{x}) = \sum_{i=1}^{R} L(c_i, c_r) p(C = c_i|\mathbf{x}). \tag{8.4}$$

Given $\mathbf{x}$, we can minimize the expected loss by selecting the c_r that minimizes the conditional risk. This is the **Bayes decision rule**. Table 8.1 shows the ingredients for computing this rule. For $\mathbf{x}$, the Bayes decision rule will decide the label c_r achieving the lowest of the numbers in the bottom row of the table.

As with the probability of error, the best option is to have a general decision rule telling us which label to assign for *every* possible instance $\mathbf{x}$. Then our problem is to find a decision rule that minimizes the **overall risk** R, that is, the expected loss associated with a given decision rule:

$$R = \int R(\phi(\mathbf{x})|\mathbf{x}) p(\mathbf{x}) d\mathbf{x}.$$

Again, a decision rule $\phi(\mathbf{x})$ that minimizes $R(\phi(\mathbf{x})|\mathbf{x})$ for every $\mathbf{x}$ also minimizes the overall risk. Note that this is the Bayes decision rule. Therefore, to minimize the overall risk, we compute the expected loss in Equation (8.4) for $r = 1, \ldots, R$ and then we select the c_r for which $R(c_r|\mathbf{x})$ is minimum. The Bayes risk R^* is the resulting minimum overall risk, the best performance that can be achieved. The Bayes decision rule provides that best performance and hence is a minimum-risk decision rule.

Table 8.1 Elements for calculating the conditional risk for a given $\mathbf{x}$ and a probabilistic classifier producing the posterior $p(C = c_r|\mathbf{x})$; the Bayes decision rule is computed from these elements

	Assigned by $\phi(\mathbf{x})$			
True	c_1	$\cdots$	c_R	Posterior
c_1	$L(c_1, c_1)$	$\cdots$	$L(c_1, c_R)$	$p(C = c_1|\mathbf{x})$
$\vdots$	$\vdots$		$\vdots$	$\vdots$
c_R	$L(c_R, c_1)$	$\cdots$	$L(c_R, c_R)$	$p(C = c_R|\mathbf{x})$
Conditional risk	$R(c_1|\mathbf{x})$	$\cdots$	$R(c_R|\mathbf{x})$	

Let us consider the particular case of a 0-1 loss function (also called symmetric), i.e., $L(c_i, c_r) = 1$ if $i = r$ and $L(c_i, c_r) = 0$ if $i \neq r$. This function quantifies all errors equally. The conditional risk is

$$R(c_r|\mathbf{x}) = \sum_{i=1}^{R} L(c_i, c_r)p(C = c_i|\mathbf{x}) = \sum_{i \neq r} p(C = c_i|\mathbf{x}) = 1 - p(C = c_r|\mathbf{x}).$$

Therefore the Bayes decision rule minimizing $R(c_r|\mathbf{x})$, with a 0-1 loss, is equivalent to minimizing the probability of error $1 - p(C = c_r|\mathbf{x})$ or equivalent to maximizing the posterior probability $p(C = c_r|\mathbf{x})$. Thus, the Bayes decision rule is a minimum-error rate decision rule or MAP decision rule. Thus, with a 0-1 loss, we should

$$\text{Decide } c_r \text{ if } p(C = c_r|\mathbf{x}) > p(C = c_i|\mathbf{x}); \text{for all } i \neq r,$$

and for $\Omega_C = \{c_1, c_2\}$, we should

$$\text{Decide } c_1 \text{ if } p(C = c_1|\mathbf{x}) > p(C = c_2|\mathbf{x}); \text{ otherwise decide } c_2,$$

which is the same rule as in Equation (8.2). This is, in fact, why we referred to it as the Bayes decision rule too.

In summary, for a probabilistic classifier to convert its outputs into predicted labels, we can let

$$\phi(\mathbf{x}) = \arg\max_r [-R(c_r|\mathbf{x})]$$

for the general minimum-risk case, and we can let

$$\phi(\mathbf{x}) = \arg\max_r p(C = c_r|\mathbf{x}) = c^* \tag{8.5}$$

for the particular case of minimum error-rate. Both functions, the conditional risk and the posterior distribution, are then **discriminant functions**, computed for each c_r. The classifier will select the c_r corresponding to the largest discriminant. In the minimum error-rate case, we can use the following computationally simpler equivalent function, which yields the same classification results:

$$\phi(\mathbf{x}) = \arg\max_r [\ln p(\mathbf{x}|c_r) + \ln p(C = c_r)]. \tag{8.6}$$

This is the same rule as in Equation (8.3) after applying the log function, a monotonically increasing function that leaves the classification results unchanged.

When applying a decision rule, the feature space is divided into R decision regions, $\mathcal{R}_1, \ldots, \mathcal{R}_R$. $\mathbf{x}$ is in $\mathcal{R}_r$ if $\phi(\mathbf{x}) = c_r$. These regions are separated by decision boundaries, surfaces in the feature space corresponding to pairs of class labels reaching the (same) optimum in the max function of ϕ.

8.2   Discriminant Analysis

In this section we assume that the instances $\mathbf{x}$ are any point (columnwise) in an n-dimensional Euclidean space $\mathbb{R}^n$. Then variable $\mathbf{X} = (X_1, \ldots, X_n)$ conditioned on a class value $C = c_r$ is assumed to have a class-conditional density function $f(\mathbf{x}|c_r)$.

In **(Gaussian) discriminant analysis** the class-conditional densities are assumed to follow a multivariate Gaussian, $\mathbf{X}|c_r \sim \mathcal{N}(\mathbf{x}|\boldsymbol{\mu}_r, \boldsymbol{\Sigma}_r)$ (see Section 3.4.4), i.e.,

$$f(\mathbf{x}|c_r, \boldsymbol{\mu}_r, \boldsymbol{\Sigma}_r) = \frac{1}{(2\pi)^{n/2}|\boldsymbol{\Sigma}_r|^{1/2}} \exp\left(-\frac{1}{2}(\mathbf{x}-\boldsymbol{\mu}_r)^T \boldsymbol{\Sigma}_r^{-1}(\mathbf{x}-\boldsymbol{\mu}_r)\right),$$

where $\boldsymbol{\mu}_r$ is the n-dimensional mean vector, $\boldsymbol{\Sigma}_r$ is the $n \times n$ covariance matrix, and $|\boldsymbol{\Sigma}_r|$ is its determinant, for any $r = 1, \dots, R$.

The function to be maximized in Equation (8.6), which we denote by $g_r(\mathbf{x})$ henceforth, is now

$$g_r(\mathbf{x}) = \ln f(\mathbf{x}|c_r) + \ln p(C = c_r) \tag{8.7}$$

$$= -\frac{1}{2}(\mathbf{x}-\boldsymbol{\mu}_r)^T \boldsymbol{\Sigma}_r^{-1}(\mathbf{x}-\boldsymbol{\mu}_r) - \frac{n}{2}\ln 2\pi - \frac{1}{2}\ln|\boldsymbol{\Sigma}_r| + \ln p(C = c_r). \tag{8.8}$$

The parameters $\boldsymbol{\mu}_r$ and $\boldsymbol{\Sigma}_r$ are generally unknown and will be estimated from the data using their maximum likelihood estimates: the sample mean for $\boldsymbol{\mu}_r$, the sample covariance for $\boldsymbol{\Sigma}_r$, and the relative frequency of class-c_r cases for $p(C = c_r)$ (see Section 4.1.2), that is,

$$\hat{\boldsymbol{\mu}}_r = \frac{1}{N_r} \sum_{i:c^i=c_r} \mathbf{x}^i, \tag{8.9}$$

$$\hat{\boldsymbol{\Sigma}}_r = \frac{1}{N_r} \sum_{i:c^i=c_r} (\mathbf{x}^i - \hat{\boldsymbol{\mu}}_r)(\mathbf{x}^i - \hat{\boldsymbol{\mu}}_r)^T, \tag{8.10}$$

$$\hat{p}(C = c_r) = \frac{N_r}{N}, \tag{8.11}$$

where N_r is the number of class-c_r cases in the data set, that is, the cases whose class label is $c^i = c_r$. Further, the application of a multivariate Gaussian goodness-of-fit test will be necessary (Section 4.2.2).

Discriminant analysis has been used in neuroscience, for example, to classify projection cells (Marin et al., 2002), to distinguish depressed from nondepressed people with HD (Rickards et al., 2011), to discriminate female schizophrenia patients from healthy women (Ota et al., 2012), or to account for temporally localized events in neuronal spike train data from the motor cortex (Laubach, 2004). A regularized linear discriminant analysis (Section 8.2.4) is used in Matell et al. (2011) to compare the firing patterns produced in two situations: one signal indicated availability of reward for a rat nosepoke response after a short duration, and a different signal indicated the same reward after a long duration.

Let us analyze this discriminant function and the resulting decision rule for three cases, from the most particular to the most general. We mostly follow the presentation of Duda et al. (2001). The first two cases are **linear discriminant analysis** (LDA), whereas the last case is a **quadratic discriminant analysis** (QDA).

8.2.1   Linear Discriminant Analysis. Equal Spherical Covariance Matrices

This is the simplest case with a spherical covariance matrix, $\boldsymbol{\Sigma}_r = \sigma^2\mathbf{I}$, that is, σ^2 times the identity matrix $\mathbf{I}$ for all r. Variables $X_1, \dots, X_n$ are independent (because their covariances are zero and they are Gaussians, see Section 3.4.1), and they all have the same variance σ^2. We can easily compute: $|\boldsymbol{\Sigma}_r| = \sigma^{2n}$ and $\boldsymbol{\Sigma}_r^{-1} = (1/\sigma^2)\mathbf{I}$. The second and third addends in Equation (8.8) can be ignored because they do not depend on r. The discriminant function is

$$g_r(\mathbf{x}) = -\frac{1}{2\sigma^2}(\mathbf{x} - \boldsymbol{\mu}_r)^T(\mathbf{x} - \boldsymbol{\mu}_r) + \ln p(C = c_r).$$

Because the quadratic term $\mathbf{x}^T\mathbf{x}$ does not depend on r, we obtain the equivalent *linear* discriminant function

$$g_r(\mathbf{x}) = \mathbf{w}_r^T\mathbf{x} + w_{r0},$$

where

$$\mathbf{w}_r = \frac{1}{2\sigma^2}\boldsymbol{\mu}_r,$$

$$w_{r0} = -\frac{1}{2\sigma^2}\boldsymbol{\mu}_r^T\boldsymbol{\mu}_r + \ln p(C = c_r).$$

The decision boundary for the corresponding classifier is defined by $g_r(\mathbf{x}) = g_k(\mathbf{x})$ for the two categories with the highest posterior probabilities. This surface is

$$\mathbf{w}^T(\mathbf{x} - \mathbf{x}_0) = 0,$$

where

$$\mathbf{w} = \boldsymbol{\mu}_r - \boldsymbol{\mu}_k,$$

$$\mathbf{x}_0 = \frac{1}{2}(\boldsymbol{\mu}_r + \boldsymbol{\mu}_k) - \frac{\sigma^2}{(\boldsymbol{\mu}_r - \boldsymbol{\mu}_k)^T(\boldsymbol{\mu}_r - \boldsymbol{\mu}_k)}\ln\frac{p(c_r)}{p(c_k)}(\boldsymbol{\mu}_r - \boldsymbol{\mu}_k).$$

Therefore all decision boundaries are linear in $\mathbf{x}$, and the decision regions $\mathcal{R}_1, \ldots, \mathcal{R}_R$ in $\mathbb{R}^n$ classified as classes $c_1, \ldots, c_R$, respectively, are separated by hyperplanes. The equations define a hyperplane orthogonal to the vector $\mathbf{w}$ (the line linking the means) and passing through point $\mathbf{x}_0$. If $p(c_r) = p(c_k)$, then $\mathbf{x}_0 = \frac{1}{2}(\boldsymbol{\mu}_r + \boldsymbol{\mu}_k)$, i.e., it is halfway between the means, see Figure 8.5(a). If $p(c_r) \neq p(c_k)$, then $\mathbf{x}_0$ shifts away from the mean $\boldsymbol{\mu}_r$ if $p(c_r) > p(c_k)$ and biases the decision in favor of c_r or approaches $\boldsymbol{\mu}_r$ if $p(c_r) < p(c_k)$ in favor of c_k. The shift will also depend on the magnitude of $\frac{\sigma^2}{(\boldsymbol{\mu}_r - \boldsymbol{\mu}_k)^T(\boldsymbol{\mu}_r - \boldsymbol{\mu}_k)}$, the ratio of the variance, and the squared Euclidean distance between the means. In Figure 8.5(b) with a binary class, $p(c_1) = 0.99 > p(c_2) = 0.01$.

If the prior probabilities $p(C = c_r)$ are the same for all r, then maximizing g_r is the same as minimizing $(\mathbf{x} - \boldsymbol{\mu}_r)^T(\mathbf{x} - \boldsymbol{\mu}_r)$, i.e., the squared Euclidean distance from $\mathbf{x}$ to each of the R mean vectors $\boldsymbol{\mu}_r$. Therefore, the decision rule $\phi(\mathbf{x})$ assigns to $\mathbf{x}$ the class label of the nearest mean. This idea is closely related to the nearest-neighbor classifier (Section 7.1.6).

8.2.2 Linear Discriminant Analysis. Equal Covariance Matrices

In this case $\boldsymbol{\Sigma}_r = \boldsymbol{\Sigma}$, that is, all the covariance matrices are equal, although arbitrary, for all classes. This is referred to as the **homoscedasticity** assumption. The shared covariance matrix $\boldsymbol{\Sigma}$ is estimated using the entire data set as the **pooled sample covariance** matrix

$$\hat{\boldsymbol{\Sigma}} = \frac{1}{N-R}\sum_{r=1}^{R}\sum_{i:c^i=c_r}(\mathbf{x}^i - \hat{\boldsymbol{\mu}}_r)(\mathbf{x}^i - \hat{\boldsymbol{\mu}}_r)^T.$$

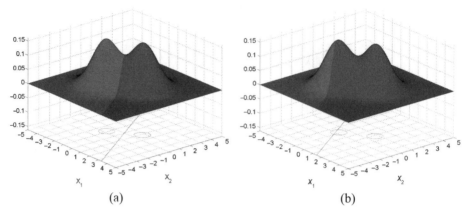

Figure 8.5 Linear discriminant analysis. Equal spherical covariance matrices. 2D case ($n = 2$), $\mathbf{X} = (X_1, X_2)$, and binary class ($R = 2$). The class-conditional densities, $f(\mathbf{x}|c_1)$ (right) and $f(\mathbf{x}|c_2)$ (left), are spherical in 3D, that is, $\mathbf{X}|c_r \sim \mathcal{N}\left(\mathbf{x}|\boldsymbol{\mu}_r, \left(\begin{smallmatrix} 1 & 0 \\ 0 & 1 \end{smallmatrix}\right)\right), r = 1, 2$, where $\boldsymbol{\mu}_1 = (1.2, 0.8)^T, \boldsymbol{\mu}_2 = (-1.2, -0.8)^T$. The decision boundary is a hyperplane in 2D, perpendicular to the line separating the means. Regions $\mathcal{R}_1, \mathcal{R}_2$ in $\mathbb{R}^2$ are separated by the hyperplane. (a) $p(c_1) = p(c_2) = 0.5$, and the hyperplane passes through the halfway point between the means. (b) $p(c_1) = 0.99 > p(c_2) = 0.01$, and the decision is biased in favor of c_1.

The second and third addends in Equation (8.8) can be ignored again to get the discriminant function

$$g_r(\mathbf{x}) = -\frac{1}{2}(\mathbf{x} - \boldsymbol{\mu}_r)^T \boldsymbol{\Sigma}^{-1}(\mathbf{x} - \boldsymbol{\mu}_r) + \ln p(C = c_r).$$

The term $\mathbf{x}^T \boldsymbol{\Sigma}^{-1}\mathbf{x}$ in the expansion of the first addend of g_r does not depend on r either, and the resulting equivalent *linear* discriminant function is

$$g_r(\mathbf{x}) = \mathbf{w}_r^T \mathbf{x} + w_{r0}, \tag{8.12}$$

where

$$\mathbf{w}_r = \boldsymbol{\Sigma}^{-1} \boldsymbol{\mu}_r, \tag{8.13}$$

$$w_{r0} = -\frac{1}{2}\boldsymbol{\mu}_r^T \boldsymbol{\Sigma}^{-1} \boldsymbol{\mu}_r + \ln p(C = c_r). \tag{8.14}$$

The decision boundary between $\mathcal{R}_r$ and $\mathcal{R}_k$ is again a hyperplane

$$\mathbf{w}^T (\mathbf{x} - \mathbf{x}_0) = 0,$$

where

$$\mathbf{w} = \boldsymbol{\Sigma}^{-1}(\boldsymbol{\mu}_r - \boldsymbol{\mu}_k),$$

$$\mathbf{x}_0 = \frac{1}{2}(\boldsymbol{\mu}_r + \boldsymbol{\mu}_k) - \frac{1}{(\boldsymbol{\mu}_r - \boldsymbol{\mu}_k)^T \boldsymbol{\Sigma}^{-1}(\boldsymbol{\mu}_r - \boldsymbol{\mu}_k)} \ln \frac{p(c_r)}{p(c_k)}(\boldsymbol{\mu}_r - \boldsymbol{\mu}_k).$$

The hyperplane will not necessarily be orthogonal to the line linking the means because $\mathbf{w}$ is not generally in the direction of $\boldsymbol{\mu}_r - \boldsymbol{\mu}_k$, see Figure 8.6. However, the assertions given for $\mathbf{x}_0$ in the above case of a diagonal covariance matrix are still valid.

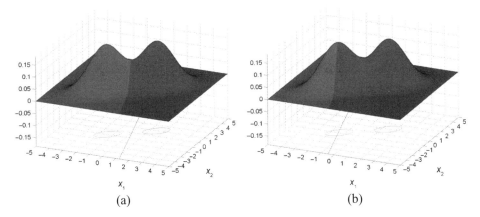

Figure 8.6 Linear discriminant analysis. Equal covariance matrices. 2D case $(n = 2)$, $\mathbf{X} = (X_1, X_2)$, and binary class $(R = 2)$. The class-conditional densities $f(\mathbf{x}|c_1)$ (right) and $f(\mathbf{x}|c_2)$ (left) are $\mathbf{X}|c_r \sim \mathcal{N}\left(\mathbf{x}|\boldsymbol{\mu}_r, \left(\begin{smallmatrix} 1 & 0.5 \\ 0.5 & 1 \end{smallmatrix}\right)\right)$, $r = 1, 2$, where $\boldsymbol{\mu}_1 = (1.5, 1)^T$, $\boldsymbol{\mu}_2 = (-1.5, -1)^T$. The decision boundary is a hyperplane in 2D, not necessarily perpendicular to the line separating the means. Regions $\mathcal{R}_1, \mathcal{R}_2$ in $\mathbb{R}^2$ are separated by the hyperplane. (a) $p(c_1) = 0.5 = p(c_2)$. (b) $p(c_1) = 0.99 > p(c_2) = 0.01$.

If the prior probabilities $p(C = c_r)$ are the same for all r (Figure 8.6(a)), then maximizing g_r is the same as minimizing $(\mathbf{x} - \boldsymbol{\mu}_r)^T \boldsymbol{\Sigma}^{-1}(\mathbf{x} - \boldsymbol{\mu}_r)$, i.e., the squared **Mahalanobis distance** from $\mathbf{x}$ to each of the R mean vectors $\boldsymbol{\mu}_r$. Therefore, the decision rule $\phi(\mathbf{x})$ assigns to $\mathbf{x}$ the class label of the nearest mean (measured by this distance).

8.2.3 Quadratic Discriminant Analysis. Arbitrary Covariance Matrices

This is the general case with different covariance matrices for each class label $\boldsymbol{\Sigma}_r$. The second addend in Equation (8.8) can be ignored. The discriminant function is now quadratic:

$$g_r(\mathbf{x}) = \mathbf{x}^T \mathbf{W}_r \mathbf{x} + \mathbf{w}_r^T \mathbf{x} + w_{r0},$$

where

$$\mathbf{W}_r = -\frac{1}{2} \boldsymbol{\Sigma}_r^{-1},$$

$$\mathbf{w}_r = \boldsymbol{\Sigma}_r^{-1} \boldsymbol{\mu}_r,$$

$$w_{r0} = -\frac{1}{2} \boldsymbol{\mu}_r^T \boldsymbol{\Sigma}_r^{-1} \boldsymbol{\mu}_r - \frac{1}{2} \ln |\boldsymbol{\Sigma}_r| + \ln p(C = c_r).$$

For a binary class, the decision boundaries are *hyperquadrics* with any general form: hyperplanes, pairs of hyperplanes, hyperspheres, hyperellipsoids, hyperparaboloids, etc. (see Figure 8.7). For more than two classes, the extension is straightforward and may result in many different and complicated regions.

8.2.4 High Dimensions: Regularized Discriminant Analysis

We may encounter problems of overfitting of the MLE in high dimensions. The MLE for a full covariance matrix, $\hat{\boldsymbol{\Sigma}}_r$, is singular if $N_r < n$ and even ill-conditional (close to singular)

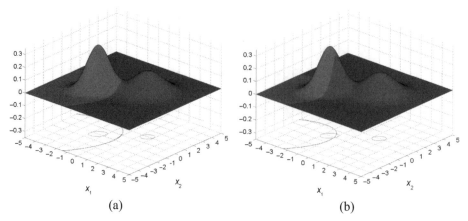

Figure 8.7 Quadratic discriminant analysis. Arbitrary covariance matrices. 2D case ($n = 2$), $\mathbf{X} = (X_1, X_2)$, and binary class ($R = 2$). The class-conditional densities $f(\mathbf{x}|c_1)$ (right) and $f(\mathbf{x}|c_2)$ (left) are $\mathbf{X}|c_1 \sim \mathcal{N}\left(\mathbf{x}|(1.5\ 1)^T, \left(\begin{smallmatrix} 1 & 0.3 \\ 0.3 & 1 \end{smallmatrix}\right)\right)$ and $\mathbf{X}|c_2 \sim \mathcal{N}\left(\mathbf{x}|(-1.5\ -1)^T, \left(\begin{smallmatrix} 0.5 & 0.2 \\ 0.2 & 0.5 \end{smallmatrix}\right)\right)$. The decision boundary here is a hyperbola in 2D. Regions $\mathcal{R}_1, \mathcal{R}_2$ in $\mathbb{R}^2$ are separated by the hyperbola. (a) $p(c_1) = 0.5 = p(c_2)$. (b) $p(c_1) = 0.99 > p(c_2) = 0.01$.

if $N_r > n$. Possible solutions include (a) using a diagonal covariance matrix for each class (which assumes the variables are conditionally independent given the class), (b) using a full covariance matrix but forcing it to be shared by all classes, and (c) using regularized discriminant analysis. The first two options are LDA. The third option is explained below.

The separate covariances $\boldsymbol{\Sigma}_r$ of QDA (Section 8.2.3) can be shrunk toward a common covariance as in LDA (Sections 8.2.1 and 8.2.2), as a way of compromise between linear and quadratic discriminant analysis. This is known as **regularized discriminant analysis** (Friedman, 1989), where the covariance matrices are

$$\hat{\boldsymbol{\Sigma}}_r(\alpha) = \alpha\hat{\boldsymbol{\Sigma}}_r + (1-\alpha)\hat{\boldsymbol{\Sigma}}, \tag{8.15}$$

$\hat{\boldsymbol{\Sigma}}$ being the covariance matrix as used in LDA with equal covariance matrices and $\alpha \in [0, 1]$ putting more weight on LDA ($\alpha \approx 0$) or on QDA ($\alpha \approx 1$). α is chosen based on the performance of the model with validation data or by cross-validation.

Moreover, a similar idea can be applied to $\hat{\boldsymbol{\Sigma}}$ to shrink it toward the scalar or spherical covariance (Section 8.2.1):

$$\hat{\boldsymbol{\Sigma}}(\gamma) = \gamma\hat{\boldsymbol{\Sigma}} + (1-\gamma)\hat{\sigma}^2\mathbf{I},$$

for $\gamma \in [0, 1]$. Substituting $\hat{\boldsymbol{\Sigma}}$ in Equation (8.15) by $\hat{\boldsymbol{\Sigma}}(\gamma)$ leads to a very general family of covariances, $\hat{\boldsymbol{\Sigma}}(\alpha, \gamma)$, with two parameters.

There have been a few attempts to regularize the LDA coefficients to get sparsity. Sparsity is assumed for high-dimensional and correlated features or under the so-called "large n, small N" problem ($N \ll n$). Rather than merely performing an FSS step – a filter approach – before building the LDA model, these attempts combine regularization with discriminant analysis. The idea is to cast LDA into a regression problem via **optimal scoring** (Hastie et al., 1994). The categorical response of the class variable is turned into a quantitative response, and we look for the minimum of a least squared error. Regularization is then easily plugged in. Thus, the most relevant proposals are penalized linear discriminant analysis (Hastie et al., 1995), which uses an L_2-penalty, and sparse linear discriminant analysis (Clemmensen et al., 2011), which uses an L_1-penalty.

8.2.5 Example: Interneurons versus Pyramidal Neurons

Data Set 1 in Chapter 1 motivates one to discriminate between interneurons (I) and pyramidal neurons (P). We apply an LDA with equal covariance matrix over the entire data set, disregarding the nature (Gaussian, continuous) of all the predictor variables given the class. Some performance measures, estimated with 10-fold cross-validation, are shown in Table 8.2.[3]

The confusion matrix, with real labels in rows and predicted labels in columns, is

$$\begin{array}{cc} & \begin{array}{cc} \text{I} & \text{P} \end{array} \\ \begin{array}{c} \text{I} \\ \text{P} \end{array} & \begin{pmatrix} 175 & 24 \\ 30 & 98 \end{pmatrix} \end{array}.$$

The prior probabilities are $p(C = \text{I}) = 0.6086, p(C = \text{P}) = 0.3914$. The means are 65D vectors: $\mu_I = (55.3070, 174.0737, 1.6308, 0.7525, 0.7261, \ldots, 0.3960)^T$ and $\mu_P = (59.0797, 186.5890, 1.6694, 0.7187, 0.6760, \ldots, 0.4641)^T$, for $(X_1, \ldots, X_{65})^T$. For some instances $\mathbf{x}^i$, the real c^i, and predicted $\hat{c}_\mathbf{x}$ labels (from a probability threshold of 0.5), together with the posterior probabilities $p(C = \text{I}|\mathbf{x})$, are shown in Table 8.3.

The decision boundary is a hyperplane orthogonal to the 65D vector $\mathbf{w} = (0.0224, -0.0053, 0.2556, 2.8321, -0.9220, \ldots, -0.1527)^T$.

Figure 8.8 represents as (conditional) histograms the predicted probabilities for the subsample defined by each class value: interneurons in dark gray (histogram on the left) or pyramidal cells in light gray (histogram on the right).

Figure 8.9 illustrates two examples of neurons. In Figure 8.9(a), interneuron $\mathbf{x}^3$ was correctly classified by the LDA, whereas the pyramidal neuron $\mathbf{x}^{327}$ in Figure 8.9(b) was misclassified, see also Table 8.3 for their respective posterior predicted probabilities.

Table 8.2 Main performance measures of an LDA for Data Set 1

Measure	Value
Accuracy	0.8349
Sensitivity	0.8794
Specificity	0.7656
F_1-measure	0.8663
Cohen's kappa	0.6504
Brier score	0.2273
AUC	0.9196

---

[3] All obtained with the `caret` and `MASS` R packages using the "`lda`" method.

Table 8.3 Observation, real class c^i, predicted class $\hat{c}_{\mathbf{x}}$, and predicted posterior probability $p(C = \text{I}|\mathbf{x})$ output from an LDA on Data Set 1

Obs.	c^i	$\hat{c}_{\mathbf{x}}$	$p(C = \text{I}|\mathbf{x})$
$\mathbf{x}^1$	I	I	0.9449
$\mathbf{x}^2$	I	I	0.9971
$\mathbf{x}^3$	I	I	0.9965
$\mathbf{x}^4$	I	I	0.9400
$\mathbf{x}^5$	I	I	0.9977
...			...
$\mathbf{x}^{326}$	P	P	0.3423
$\mathbf{x}^{327}$	P	I	0.6454

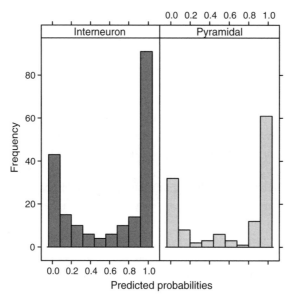

Figure 8.8 Histograms of predicted posterior probabilities $p(C = \text{I}|\mathbf{x})$ produced by the LDA model for Data Set 1.

8.3   Logistic Regression

When the predictor variables are a mixture of categorical and continuous variables, the multivariate normality assumption of discriminant analysis will not hold. Logistic regression is more general, as it does not make any assumptions about the distribution of the predictor variables, also called independent or explanatory variables in this context. It can include continuous and categorical predictor variables. We start with the classical binary logistic regression, which we extend to the multi-class case.

Logistic regression was the tool used in Langleben et al. (2005) to distinguish lie and truth from fMRI data and a carefully controlled query procedure. Two non-semantic variants of primary progressive aphasia (PPA), nonfluent/agrammatic PPA and logopenic PPA, may be difficult to distinguish for nonlanguage experts because they share language

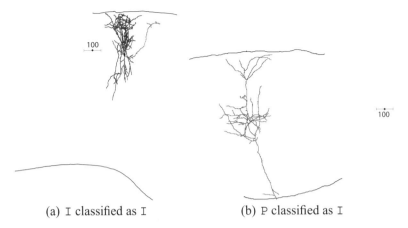

(a) I classified as I   (b) P classified as I

Figure 8.9 Some neurons and their classification by LDA. (a) Correctly classified interneuron $\mathbf{x}^3$. (b) Misclassified pyramidal neuron $\mathbf{x}^{327}$. Axonal arbor is shown in blue and dendritic tree in red. For the color version, please refer to the plate section.

features despite their different underlying pathology. Piguet et al. (2014) took PPA dementia patients (from the two syndromes) and controls who underwent a comprehensive assessment of cognition and emotion processing, as well as a high-resolution structural MRI and a Pittsburgh compound-B PET scan. Logistic regression and decision trees (Section 7.2) were used. They found nonlanguage distinguishing features (episodic memory and emotion processing scores together with visuospatial ability).

8.3.1   Model Specification

Binary logistic regression can be seen as a generalization of linear regression to binary classification. Because the response C is binary, its conditional distribution is modeled as a Bernoulli distribution, and it is more convenient to denote $\Omega_C = \{0,1\}$, that is,

$$C|\mathbf{x} \sim \text{Ber}(c|\theta_\mathbf{x}),$$

where $\theta_\mathbf{x} = \mathbb{E}[C|\mathbf{x}] = p(C=1|\mathbf{x})$ and $\mathbf{x} = (x_1, x_2, \ldots, x_n)^T$ is the vector of instances. This is more appropriate than the Gaussian distribution assumed for C in linear regression. As in linear regression, we compute a linear combination of the inputs. However, because if $\theta_\mathbf{x}$ is to be interpreted as a probability it should lie in $[0,1]$, we pass this linear combination through a function that maps the real line to $[0,1]$. We define

$$\theta_\mathbf{x} = \text{sigm}(\beta_0 + \beta_1 x_1 + \cdots + \beta_n x_n) = \frac{e^{\beta_0 + \beta_1 x_1 + \cdots + \beta_n x_n}}{1 + e^{\beta_0 + \beta_1 x_1 + \cdots + \beta_n x_n}},$$

where sigm refers to the **sigmoid function**, $\text{sigm}(y) = \frac{e^y}{1+e^y}$. Sigmoid means S-shaped, see Figure 8.10.

Hence, the **logistic regression** model is formulated as

$$p(C=1|\mathbf{x}, \boldsymbol{\beta}) = \theta_\mathbf{x} = \frac{e^{\beta_0 + \beta_1 x_1 + \cdots + \beta_n x_n}}{1 + e^{\beta_0 + \beta_1 x_1 + \cdots + \beta_n x_n}} = \frac{1}{1 + e^{-(\beta_0 + \beta_1 x_1 + \cdots + \beta_n x_n)}}, \tag{8.16}$$

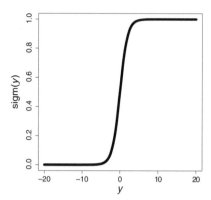

Figure 8.10 The sigmoid or logistic function.

implying that

$$p(C = 0|\mathbf{x}, \boldsymbol{\beta}) = 1 - \theta_{\mathbf{x}} = \frac{1}{1 + e^{\beta_0 + \beta_1 x_1 + \cdots + \beta_n x_n}}, \qquad (8.17)$$

where $\boldsymbol{\beta} = (\beta_0, \beta_1, \ldots, \beta_n)^T$ are the parameters that have to be estimated from the data.

It is termed *regression* because of its similarity to linear regression induced by the linear combination, although it is a classification and not a regression model. Logistic comes from the sigmoid function, also known as the logistic distribution function.

Unlike linear regression, we cannot expect to find a relationship between the explanatory variables $X_1, \ldots, X_n$ and the response variable C. Our data only have two possible values, 0 and 1, and scatterplots are not useful. Rather, we look for a relationship between the explanatory variables and the response mean $\theta_{\mathbf{x}}$ as given by Equation (8.16).

Example. Assume the prediction of the class variable in Data Set 1 encoding interneuron I (1) or pyramidal cell P (0) is made from a continuous variable Somatic compactness (X_4). Thus, $n = 1$. We expect to have $\theta_{\mathbf{x}} \approx 1$ for large X_4 values, i.e., a neuron to have a high probability of being an interneuron if its soma is very compact. Conversely, we expect $\theta_{\mathbf{x}} \approx 0$ for low X_4 values, with a higher probability for pyramidal neurons. We also expect $\theta_{\mathbf{x}}$ to increase nonlinearly for many values of X_4, to increase more linearly for medium values of X_4, whereas $\theta_{\mathbf{x}}$ will asymptotically approximate 0 and 1 for extreme X_4 values. After fitting a logistic regression model (Section 8.3.2), we obtain the estimates $\hat{\beta}_0 = -1.5911$ and $\hat{\beta}_1 = 2.7608$, giving the model

$$p(C = 1|\mathbf{x}, \boldsymbol{\beta}) = \hat{\theta}_{\mathbf{x}} = \frac{1}{1 + e^{-(-1.5911 + 2.7608 x_4)}}.$$

Figure 8.11 plots this function for a general range $[-0.5, 1.5]$ (black). The X_4 domain is, in fact, $[0,1]$, marked with two vertical lines. We also plot the resulting predictions of each X_4 value from Data Set 1 (blue circles) and their real class values, 1 or 0, for interneurons (orange) and pyramidal (green) neurons, respectively.

Note that there are many neurons with the same X_4 value but with different values for the class, 1 and 0, i.e., some are pyramidal and others are interneurons. Hence the data are not perfectly linearly separable, i.e., there is no straight line separating the 1s from the 0s using just X_4. If we threshold the output probability at (the usually assumed) 0.5, we can

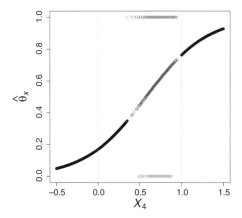

Figure 8.11 The logistic regression fitted using Somatic compactness (X_4) to explain the binary class interneuron/pyramidal cell in Data Set 1. For the color version, please refer to the plate section.

derive a decision rule $\phi(\mathbf{x})$ to classify a future instance $\mathbf{x}$ as a 1:

$$\phi(\mathbf{x}) = \hat{c}_{\mathbf{x}} = 1 \iff \hat{\theta}_{\mathbf{x}} > 0.5 \iff -1.5911 + 2.7608x_4 > 0 \iff x_4 > 0.5763.$$

Imagine a vertical line at $x_4 = 0.5763$. This would be a decision boundary, which, in this case, is linear. Any neuron whose X_4 value is to the left of this line is classified as pyramidal, and any neuron with a value to the right of the line, i.e., with a somatic compactness greater than 0.5763, is classified as an interneuron. Observe the nonzero error rate even on the training data. In fact, the accuracy of this model is only 0.5841 (10-fold cross-validated). Thus, we can try to improve the model by including more explanatory variables. ■

In linear regression it is easy to interpret the β_j coefficients. For instance, in a linear regression with three explanatory variables, $y = \beta_0 + \beta_1 x_1 + \beta_2 x_2 + \beta_3 x_3$, if we compute $y' = \beta_0 + \beta_1 x_1 + \beta_2 (x_2 + 1) + \beta_3 x_3$, then $y' - y = \beta_2$, i.e., if X_1 and X_3 are fixed, then for each increase of one unit in X_2, the average change in the (conditional) mean of Y is about β_2 units. Although we write y, recall that the linear equation estimates its conditional mean when β_js are replaced by their estimates. Thus, for any $j = 1, \ldots, n$, β_j is a rate of change of a conditional mean. In logistic regression, the β_j interpretation is not so straightforward due to the quotient and the exponential function.

We first try to eliminate the effect of the quotient by switching from probabilities to odds:

$$Odds(\mathbf{x}) = \frac{p(C = 1 | \mathbf{x}, \boldsymbol{\beta})}{1 - p(C = 1 | \mathbf{x}, \boldsymbol{\beta})} = e^{\beta_0 + \beta_1 x_1 + \cdots + \beta_n x_n}.$$

We often hear about the odds of a given sports team winning some competition or the odds of winning a state lottery (e.g., "odds are 3 to 1 in favor of some event," sometimes written as 3:1). Then,

$$\frac{p(C = 1 | (x_1, \ldots, x_j + 1, \ldots, x_n), \boldsymbol{\beta}) / p(C = 0 | (x_1, \ldots, x_j + 1, \ldots, x_n), \boldsymbol{\beta})}{p(C = 1 | (x_1, \ldots, x_j, \ldots, x_n), \boldsymbol{\beta}) / p(C = 0 | (x_1, \ldots, x_j, \ldots, x_n), \boldsymbol{\beta})} = e^{\beta_j},$$

which is still not very interpretable. This is usually called the **odds ratio** because each exponentiated coefficient is the ratio of two odds, or the change in odds on the multiplicative scale for 1-unit increase in the corresponding predictor variable if the values of other variables are held constant.

A related concept is the **risk ratio**,

$$\frac{p(C = 1|(x_1, \ldots, x_j + 1, \ldots, x_n), \boldsymbol{\beta})}{p(C = 1|(x_1, \ldots, x_j, \ldots, x_n), \boldsymbol{\beta})},$$

where only the probabilities of the event in question ($C = 1$) are compared. The name *risk* comes from the medical domain, where C typically encodes suffering from some disease. Thus, if this ratio is 1.82, then the risk for an instance (patient) is 82% higher (almost double) when moving from $X_j = x_j$ to $X_j = x_j + 1$.

For better interpretability, we then eliminate the effect of the exponential by taking the natural log of the odds, obtaining the **logit**[4] **form** of the logistic regression model:

$$logit\ (p(C = 1|\mathbf{x}, \boldsymbol{\beta})) = \ln\ Odds(\mathbf{x}) = \ln \frac{p(C = 1|\mathbf{x}, \boldsymbol{\beta})}{1 - p(C = 1|\mathbf{x}, \boldsymbol{\beta})} = \beta_0 + \beta_1 x_1 + \cdots + \beta_n x_n.$$

$$(8.18)$$

Therefore, the logit is the inverse of the logistic distribution function.[5] The odds can vary on a scale of $(0, \infty)$, whereas the log of the odds can vary on $(-\infty, \infty)$.

On this new logarithmic scale, we finally obtain a linear function of the predictor variables, and consequently their coefficients can be interpreted as in linear regression, except that the log of the odds is the dependent variable. Let $\mathbf{x}$ and $\mathbf{x}'$ be vectors such that $x_l = x'_l$ for all $l \neq j$ and $x'_j = x_j + 1$. Then, $logit\ p(C = 1|\mathbf{x}', \boldsymbol{\beta}) - logit\ p(C = 1|\mathbf{x}, \boldsymbol{\beta}) = \beta_0 + \sum_{l=1}^{n} \beta_l x'_l - (\beta_0 + \sum_{l=1}^{n} \beta_l x_l) = \beta_j x'_j - \beta_j x_j = \beta_j(x_j + 1 - x_j) = \beta_j$. Therefore, in a logistic regression model, coefficient β_j represents the logit change when the jth variable $X_j\ (j = 1, \ldots, n)$ increases by 1 unit, if the other variables are fixed. The logistic regression coefficients should then be interpreted with respect to their effects on the log of the odds and not on the probability $p(C = 1|\mathbf{x}, \boldsymbol{\beta})$.

Note that a positive sign of β_j, for example, means that the log of the odds increases as X_j increases, that is, the log of the odds of an instance with a greater X_j having $C = 1$ is greater than that of an instance with a smaller X_j.

8.3.2   Model Fitting

8.3.2.1 *Parameter Estimation*

Maximum likelihood estimation is the most popular procedure for obtaining the parameter estimates of the logistic regression model.

Because each instance is a Bernoulli trial, for the ith instance $\mathbf{x}^i$, the probability function is $p(C = c^i|\mathbf{x}^i, \theta_{\mathbf{x}^i}) = \theta_i^{c^i} (1 - \theta_i)^{1 - c^i}, c^i = 0, 1$, where, for simplicity, we write θ_i instead of $\theta_{\mathbf{x}^i}$. Assuming that all the N instances are i.i.d., the (conditional) likelihood function is

---

[4] *logit* stands for logistic probability unit.
[5] There are, apart from the logit, other not so popular functions to link the probability and the linear combination of the predictors, such as the *normit* or *probit* (inverse of the standard normal distribution function) and the complementary log-log or *gompit* (inverse of the Gompertz distribution function). They each have their respective model.

$$\mathcal{L}\left(\boldsymbol{\beta}|\mathbf{x}^1,\dots,\mathbf{x}^N\right) = p\left(c^1,\dots,c^N|\mathbf{x},\boldsymbol{\theta}_{\mathbf{x}}\right) = \prod_{i=1}^{N}\theta_i^{c^i}(1-\theta_i)^{1-c^i},$$

and the (conditional) log-likelihood (Section 4.1.2.1) function is given by

$$
\begin{aligned}
\ln\mathcal{L}\left(\boldsymbol{\beta}|\mathbf{x}^1,\dots,\mathbf{x}^N\right) &= \ln p\left(c^1,\dots,c^N|\mathbf{x},\boldsymbol{\theta}_{\mathbf{x}}\right) \\
&= \sum_{i=1}^{N}[c^i\ln\theta_i + (1-c^i)\ln(1-\theta_i)] \\
&= \sum_{i=1}^{N}c^i\ln\frac{\theta_i}{1-\theta_i} + \sum_{i=1}^{N}\ln(1-\theta_i) \\
&= \sum_{i=1}^{N}c^i(\beta_0 + \beta_1 x_{i1} + \dots + \beta_n x_{in}) - \sum_{i=1}^{N}\ln(1 + e^{\beta_0 + \beta_1 x_{i1} + \dots + \beta_n x_{in}}),
\end{aligned}
$$

$$(8.19)$$

where Equation (8.18) and Equation (8.17) have been used, respectively, in each addend of the above equality. For simplicity, we will write $\mathcal{L}(\boldsymbol{\beta})$ rather than $\mathcal{L}\left(\boldsymbol{\beta}|\mathbf{x}^1,\dots,\mathbf{x}^N\right)$.

The estimate for the parameter vector $\boldsymbol{\beta}$ is obtained by maximizing Equation (8.19). We first take the first-order derivatives of the equation with respect to each coefficient, setting each equation to zero, and then we solve the resulting equation system. The likelihood equations are

$$\frac{\partial \ln\mathcal{L}(\boldsymbol{\beta})}{\partial\beta_0} = \sum_{i=1}^{N}c^i - \sum_{i=1}^{N}\frac{e^{\beta_0 + \beta_1 x_{i1} + \dots + \beta_n x_{in}}}{1 + e^{\beta_0 + \beta_1 x_{i1} + \dots + \beta_n x_{in}}} = 0,$$

$$\frac{\partial \ln\mathcal{L}(\boldsymbol{\beta})}{\partial\beta_1} = \sum_{i=1}^{N}c^i x_{i1} - \sum_{i=1}^{N}x_{i1}\frac{e^{\beta_0 + \beta_1 x_{i1} + \dots + \beta_n x_{in}}}{1 + e^{\beta_0 + \beta_1 x_{i1} + \dots + \beta_n x_{in}}} = 0,$$

$$\vdots$$

$$\frac{\partial \ln\mathcal{L}(\boldsymbol{\beta})}{\partial\beta_n} = \sum_{i=1}^{N}c^i x_{in} - \sum_{i=1}^{N}x_{in}\frac{e^{\beta_0 + \beta_1 x_{i1} + \dots + \beta_n x_{in}}}{1 + e^{\beta_0 + \beta_1 x_{i1} + \dots + \beta_n x_{in}}} = 0.$$

Notice that the first equation states $\sum_{i=1}^{N}c^i = \sum_{i=1}^{N}\theta_i$; the expected number of class 1s matches the observed number (and the same applies for class 0).

Unfortunately, the system does not have an analytical solution because there are non-linear functions of the β_js. Consequently, the MLE of $\boldsymbol{\beta}$, $\hat{\boldsymbol{\beta}}$, is approximated using efficient iterative techniques such as the Newton–Raphson method. Now it is convenient to use matrix notation.

The **Newton–Raphson method** requires the first and second derivatives (Hessian matrix), where the update to obtain a new estimate is

$$\hat{\boldsymbol{\beta}}^{\text{new}} = \hat{\boldsymbol{\beta}}^{\text{old}} - \left(\frac{\partial^2 \ln\mathcal{L}(\boldsymbol{\beta})}{\partial\boldsymbol{\beta}\partial\boldsymbol{\beta}^T}\right)^{-1}\frac{\partial \ln\mathcal{L}(\boldsymbol{\beta})}{\partial\boldsymbol{\beta}},$$

and where the derivatives are evaluated at $\hat{\boldsymbol{\beta}}^{\text{old}}$, the estimate in the last iteration. Let $\mathbf{c} = \left(c^1,\dots,c^N\right)^T$ denote the N-vector of class values, $\mathbf{Z}$ the design matrix (an $N \times n$ matrix with the data) augmented with an N-vector of 1s added as its first column $\hat{\boldsymbol{\theta}}^{\text{old}}$ the N-vector of fitted probabilities, i.e., its ith component is $\hat{\theta}_i^{\text{old}} = \left[1 + e^{-\left(\hat{\beta}_0^{\text{old}} + \hat{\beta}_1^{\text{old}}x_{i1} + \dots + \hat{\beta}_n^{\text{old}}x_{in}\right)}\right]^{-1},$

and finally $\mathbf{W}$ an $N \times N$ diagonal matrix with elements $\hat{\theta}_i^{\text{old}} \left(1 - \hat{\theta}_i^{\text{old}}\right)$ on the diagonal and zero everywhere else. Then it holds that $\frac{\partial \ln \mathcal{L}(\boldsymbol{\beta})}{\partial \boldsymbol{\beta}} = \mathbf{Z}^T \left(\mathbf{c} - \hat{\boldsymbol{\theta}}^{\text{old}}\right)$ and $\frac{\partial^2 \ln \mathcal{L}(\boldsymbol{\beta})}{\partial \boldsymbol{\beta} \partial \boldsymbol{\beta}^T} = -\mathbf{Z}^T \mathbf{W}^{\text{old}} \mathbf{Z}$.

Therefore, the Newton–Raphson step is

$$\hat{\boldsymbol{\beta}}^{\text{new}} = \hat{\boldsymbol{\beta}}^{\text{old}} + \left(\mathbf{Z}^T \mathbf{W}^{\text{old}} \mathbf{Z}\right)^{-1} \mathbf{Z}^T \left(\mathbf{c} - \hat{\boldsymbol{\theta}}^{\text{old}}\right).$$

We can easily rewrite the above equation as

$$\hat{\boldsymbol{\beta}}^{\text{new}} = \left(\mathbf{Z}^T \mathbf{W}^{\text{old}} \mathbf{Z}\right)^{-1} \mathbf{Z}^T \mathbf{W}^{\text{old}} \left[\mathbf{Z}\hat{\boldsymbol{\beta}}^{\text{old}} + \left(\mathbf{W}^{\text{old}}\right)^{-1} \left(\mathbf{c} - \hat{\boldsymbol{\theta}}^{\text{old}}\right)\right]$$

$$= \left(\mathbf{Z}^T \mathbf{W}^{\text{old}} \mathbf{Z}\right)^{-1} \mathbf{Z}^T \mathbf{W}^{\text{old}} \mathbf{a},$$

where $\mathbf{a} = [\mathbf{Z}\hat{\boldsymbol{\beta}}^{\text{old}} + (\mathbf{W}^{\text{old}})^{-1} (\mathbf{c} - \hat{\boldsymbol{\theta}}^{\text{old}})]$, or, in component form,

$$a_i = \left(\hat{\beta}_0^{\text{old}} + \hat{\beta}_1^{\text{old}} x_{i1} + \cdots + \hat{\beta}_n^{\text{old}} x_{in}\right) + \frac{c_i - \hat{\theta}_i^{\text{old}}}{\hat{\theta}_i^{\text{old}} \left(1 - \hat{\theta}_i^{\text{old}}\right)}, \quad \text{for } i = 1, \ldots, N,$$

can be seen as the (adjusted) response useful for expressing the Newton–Raphson step as a weighted least squares step as follows. At each iteration $\hat{\boldsymbol{\theta}}^{\text{old}}$ changes, and hence $\mathbf{W}^{\text{old}}$ and $\mathbf{a}$ also change. This algorithm is referred to as the **iteratively reweighted least squares algorithm** (IRLS) because each iteration solves the weighted least squares problem

$$\min_{\boldsymbol{\beta}} (\mathbf{a} - \mathbf{Z}\boldsymbol{\beta})^T \mathbf{W} (\mathbf{a} - \mathbf{Z}\boldsymbol{\beta}),$$

or equivalently, in component form,

$$\min_{\boldsymbol{\beta}} \sum_{i=1}^{N} \hat{\theta}_i (1 - \hat{\theta}_i)(a_i - (\beta_0 + \beta_1 x_{i1} + \cdots + \beta_n x_{in}))^2.$$

If the model is correct, then the asymptotic likelihood theory states that $\hat{\boldsymbol{\beta}}$ is consistent (Section 4.1.2.1) (i.e., it converges to the true $\boldsymbol{\beta}$), and its distribution converges to $\mathcal{N}(\hat{\boldsymbol{\beta}}|\boldsymbol{\beta}, (\mathbf{Z}^T \mathbf{W} \mathbf{Z})^{-1})$.

The Newton–Raphson formula is initialized using an arbitrary $\hat{\boldsymbol{\beta}}^{\text{old}}$ value such as $\hat{\boldsymbol{\beta}}^{\text{old}} = \mathbf{0}$. Its choice is not relevant. The procedure is stopped when it is deemed to have converged: when the parameter estimates converge or the log-likelihood function converges (the change between successive steps is negligible) or after a specified maximum number of iterations have been performed. No single convergence criterion appears to be better than the others. Although convergence is never guaranteed, the algorithm typically converges because the log-likelihood is concave.

There are three cautionary facts to consider during the iterative process. First, a parameter estimate can tend to infinity and will, obviously, never converge. This is usually due to a poorly specified model caused by data sparseness in one class label. Detection of an infinite parameter can be done by comparing its estimate against a threshold above which it is considered to be infinite. Sometimes it is useful to allow the model to converge even with infinite parameters, continuing the iterations while keeping the detected infinite parameters constant (ignoring their new subsequent values) and outputting a message of non-convergence. Second, under some conditions, an estimate may overshoot the true solution of the likelihood equations, with subsequent iterations entering a repeating non-converging cycle. This is detected when there is a log-likelihood decrease at some point. To address this, halving step size will guarantee convergence: find half the distance between the current and previous estimates; if the log-likelihood at that point is still lower than that of the last iteration then halve the distance again; continue this for a reasonable number of "sub-iterations" until the log-likelihood increases. Third, the maximum likelihood approach will generally perform well for large sample sizes. However, the MLEs do not exist when the data are quasi-completely separated (Albert and Anderson, 1984). This means that there are constants $\alpha_0, \dots, \alpha_n$, with at least one $\alpha_j \neq 0$, $j = 1, \dots, n$, such that $\alpha_0 + \alpha_1 x_{i1} + \cdots + \alpha_n x_{in} \geq 0$ when its respective class value is $c^i = 1$, and $\alpha_0 + \alpha_1 x_{i1} + \cdots + \alpha_n x_{in} \leq 0$ when $c^i = 0$. In other words, there is a plane such that all $\mathbf{x}$s corresponding to $c^i = 1$ ($c^i = 0$) are placed on one side (opposite side) of this plane. This results in undefined expressions in the log-likelihood but is not a major problem because prediction might be expected to be perfect when the data are separated.

A typical model output includes data on: (a) the final MLEs $\hat{\beta}_j$ of the β_j parameters; (b) their estimated standard errors SE_j, computed as the square root of the corresponding diagonal element of the estimated covariance matrix $Cov[\hat{\boldsymbol{\beta}}] = (\mathbf{Z}^T \mathbf{W} \mathbf{Z})^{-1}$; and (c) the Z-score for each predictor variable, computed as the parameter estimate divided by its standard error estimate, $\hat{\beta}_j / SE_j$, sometimes called the **Wald statistic**. A nonsignificant Z-score, commonly encountered in any logistic regression package, suggests that the coefficient can be dropped from the model. This formally corresponds to a test for exclusion of the term, i.e., with a null hypothesis that the β_j coefficient is 0, whereas all the others are not. A Z-score greater than approximately 2 in absolute value is significant at the 5% level. It is *asymptotically* normally distributed, requiring a large sample size, and some authors have questioned its use (see, e.g., Hosmer and Lemeshow [2000]). In Section 8.3.2.2, other, sounder tests will be detailed.

Finally, the predicted responses $\hat{\theta}_i$ for each instance i, together with (approximate) confidence intervals for the probabilities θ_i, are also commonly output. The 95% confidence intervals for θ_i are obtained from the formula $\left(\frac{1}{1+e^{-a}}, \frac{1}{1+e^{-b}} \right)$, where

$$a = \hat{\beta}_0 + \hat{\beta}_1 x_{i1} + \cdots \hat{\beta}_n x_{in} - 1.96 \cdot ASE$$

$$b = \hat{\beta}_0 + \hat{\beta}_1 x_{i1} + \cdots \hat{\beta}_n x_{in} + 1.96 \cdot ASE$$

$$ASE = \sqrt{Var[\hat{\beta}_0 + \hat{\beta}_1 x_{i1} + \cdots \hat{\beta}_n x_{in}]} = \sqrt{\left(\frac{1}{\mathbf{x}^i} \right)^T Cov[\hat{\boldsymbol{\beta}}] \left(\frac{1}{\mathbf{x}^i} \right)},$$

with *Var* and ASE standing for variance and asymptotic standard error, respectively.

8.3.2.2 *Feature Subset Selection*

As in linear regression, the very first action is to remove multicollinearity among the predictor variables. Strong correlations among these variables, implying that some are redundant, produce unstable β_j estimates with high standard errors. Thus, very different coefficients could be induced from new similar data sets, which is unreliable. Although treated extensively in the linear regression literature, multicollinearity has received very little attention in the logistic regression literature (Ryan, 1997). Scatter plots, and especially the correlation matrix, help to detect this issue. Once detected, the corresponding predictor variables should be removed. The experimenter chooses which variable in a pair of correlated variables to remove, at random, or according to some target criterion.

If there are many variables, not all possible models can be explored, and general FSS strategies such as sequential approaches (forward selection, backward elimination, stepwise) can be used (Section 6.3.1.1).

Specifically for logistic regression, there are hypothesis tests on the β_j coefficients to assess the statistical significance of the terms. The idea is to assess the model goodness compared to another model when they are nested, that is, when all terms of the simpler model occur in the complex model. Thus, as part of the sequential approaches, we can test the hypothesis that a simpler model M_0 holds against a more complex alternative M_1.

Suppose first that M_0 contains the same terms as M_1, except variable X_r. This would be a typical situation faced in a backward elimination process. Testing the elimination of X_r amounts to testing the null hypothesis $H_0 : \beta_r = 0$ against the alternative hypothesis $H_1 : \beta_r \neq 0$. The two models can be compared by comparing their deviances. The **deviance** in logistic regression corresponds to the residual sum of squares of linear regression. Given a model M with expected values $\hat{\theta}_i$, its deviance D_M is defined as

$$D_M = -2 \sum_{i=1}^{N} \left[c^i \ln \left(\frac{\hat{\theta}_i}{c^i} \right) + (1 - c^i) \ln \left(\frac{1 - \hat{\theta}_i}{1 - c^i} \right) \right]. \tag{8.20}$$

Note that the first (second) term is considered 0 when $c^i = 0$ ($c^i = 1$). The statistic for testing that M_0 holds against M_1 is $D_{M_0} - D_{M_1}$, which follows an approximate chi-squared distribution χ_1^2. If H_0 is rejected, then we select M_1, the complex model, over M_0.

Example. As an artificial example, imagine that in a backward elimination process the current model is M_1, with three variables X_1, X_2, X_3. Now we consider eliminating X_1 to obtain model M_0^a with X_2, X_3, eliminating X_2 to obtain model M_0^b with X_1, X_3, or eliminating X_3 to obtain model M_0^c with X_1, X_2. The test results are shown in Table 8.4.

Now we should remove the least significant variable that does not meet the threshold to be retained in the model. The term in the model that yields the largest p-value when we test whether its coefficient equals zero is X_2, which is then excluded, and M_0^b is chosen as the current model. This model will play the role of M_1 in the next stage, where it is decided whether to remove X_1 or X_3. The process is repeated until no other variable in the current model meets the specified level for removal, that is, until all possible models M_0 have a p-value lower than a pre-fixed value. ∎

In general, the procedure for eliminating several terms from M_1 to yield M_0 is analogous to the above, the only change being in the degrees of freedom of the chi-squared

Table 8.4 Results from an artificial example where a backward elimination process is carried out, starting from model M_1

Model	Eliminated	$D_{M_0} - D_{M_1}$	p-value
$M_1(X_1, X_2, X_3)$			
$M_0^a(X_2, X_3)$	X_1	Large	0
$M_0^b(X_1, X_3)$	X_2	Small	0.7
$M_0^c(X_1, X_2)$	X_3	Medium	0.4

distribution, which is equal to the number of additional parameters that are in M_1 but not in M_0 (Agresti, 2013). For instance, if M_1 contains X_1, X_2, X_3, X_4 and M_0 only contains X_1, X_2, then $D_{M_0} - D_{M_1}$ follows a χ_2^2. The null hypothesis here is $H_0 : \beta_3 = \beta_4 = 0$.

Regularization (Section 6.4) can also be used in logistic regression, especially when $N \ll n$ (i.e., the so-called "large n, small N" problem, see Section 2.4.3). Regularization that drives the coefficients exactly to 0 is quite convenient for FSS. This is the case of L_1-regularization introduced in Tibshirani (1996) for linear regression via the so-called lasso, where the L_1-penalty for logistic regression was first mentioned. Rather than computing the MLE, a MAP estimation is proposed:

$$\max_{\boldsymbol{\beta}} \left[\ln \mathcal{L}(\boldsymbol{\beta}) - \lambda \sum_{j=1}^{n} |\beta_j| \right],$$

where $\ln \mathcal{L}(\boldsymbol{\beta})$ is the (conditional) log-likelihood function given in Equation (8.19), and $\lambda \geq 0$ is the penalization parameter that controls the amount of shrinkage (the larger the λ, the greater the shrinkage and the smaller the β_js). By imposing restrictions on the optimization problem, regularization trades a little bias in exchange for a larger reduction in variance and hence avoids overfitting. The above optimization problem is solved in different ways: by adapting the algorithm proposed by Osborne et al. (2000) for the lasso (Roth, 2004) or directly (Shevade and Keerthi, 2003). For a comprehensive list of state-of-the-art algorithms for the sparse logistic regression problem, see Shi et al. (2010).

L_1-penalty for logistic regression was used in Zhao et al. (2012) to detect short-term neuronal interactions in multielectrode recordings of neuronal spike train data. The regularization in van Gerven et al. (2010) imposed over a Bayesian logistic regression spatiotemporal constraints that couple parameters located closely together in space and/or time. The goal was to examine whether the class to which handwritten characters (sixes or nines) belong can be predicted from fMRI data acquired while subjects were shown the digits.

The variables are sometimes grouped beforehand, and we may want to include only entire groups in the model, that is, perform variable selection at group level. The **group lasso** was introduced in linear regression for this setting (Yuan and Lin, 2006), where a trivial application is the presence of categorical variables, each codified as a group of indicator dummy variables (e.g., a factor with four levels has three dummy variables). The lasso solution is not satisfactory as it only selects individual dummy variables instead of whole factors and depends on how the dummy variables are encoded. The so-called **logistic group lasso** (Meier et al., 2008) adapts the group lasso to binary logistic regression, aiming to maximize the group L_1-penalized log-likelihood function, i.e.,

$$\max_{\boldsymbol{\beta}} \left[\ln \mathcal{L}(\boldsymbol{\beta}) - \lambda \sum_{g=1}^{G} w_g ||\boldsymbol{\beta}_g|| \right],$$

where G is the number of groups and $||\boldsymbol{\beta}_g||$ is the L_2-norm. For groups based on the dummy variables of a factor, if a predictor is categorical, then $\boldsymbol{\beta}_g$ are the parameters for the set of dummy variables, whereas if a predictor is continuous, $\boldsymbol{\beta}_g$ has only one component. The weights w_g rescale the penalty term with respect to the dimensionality of $\boldsymbol{\beta}_g$ (e.g., take w_g as the square root of the dimension of vector $\boldsymbol{\beta}_g$) to ensure that the penalty is of the order of the number of parameters.

Finally, it is worth mentioning that despite the parsimony principle (Section 1.5.2), it is very common in logistic regression to consider both the linear and quadratic effects, that is, the X_j and X_jX_k terms, respectively. Quadratic terms are useful for assessing interactions between two predictor variables. To include these nonlinear terms, the respective variable $X_j \cdot X_k$ have to be first obtained from the original variables X_j and X_k. However, the interpretation of the regression coefficients becomes more involved. Although the treatment is the same, the **hierarchy principle** is usually applied to reduce the number of terms. According to this principle, a high-order component should not be included without its main (component) effects (Kleinbaum, 1994). For example, in a model with three variables X_1, X_2, and X_3, if X_1 and X_2 are highly correlated and it is decided to remove X_2 from the model, then the linear and quadratic effects to be considered will be X_1, X_3 and X_1X_3, and neither X_1X_2 nor X_2X_3 will be included because variable X_2 is not included either.

Moreover, we can move further from linearity by replacing the linear expression of Equation (8.18) by a nonlinear additive expression (a sum of n smooth functions $\sum_{j=1}^{n} h_j(x_j)$). This is the **additive logistic model**, which can also be regularized, as the sparse additive logistic regression with an L_1-penalty of Ravikumar et al. (2009).

8.3.3 Decision Boundary for Logistic Regression

As in discriminant analysis, logistic regression outputs the posterior probabilities of the class variable, $p(C = 1|\mathbf{x}, \boldsymbol{\beta}) = \hat{\theta}_{\mathbf{x}}$. For classification purposes, we can convert these probabilities into predicted labels by fixing a cutoff value θ^*. Thus, for an instance $\mathbf{x}$, we assign $\hat{c}_{\mathbf{x}} = 1$ iff $\hat{\theta}_{\mathbf{x}} \geq \theta^*$, otherwise, $\hat{c}_{\mathbf{x}} = 0$. Any model performance measure can be computed (accuracy, sensitivity, specificity, ROC curve, etc.) from these predictions.

For the standard cutoff value $\theta^* = 0.5$ (i.e., decide $c^* = \arg\max_c p(c|\mathbf{x})$, see Equation (8.5)), where $p(C = 1|\mathbf{x}, \boldsymbol{\beta}) = p(C = 0|\mathbf{x}, \boldsymbol{\beta})$, the decision boundary will be given by the solution of

$$p(C = 1|\mathbf{x}, \boldsymbol{\beta}) = \frac{1}{1 + e^{-(\beta_0 + \beta_1 x_1 + \cdots + \beta_n x_n)}} = 0.5.$$

This occurs when

$$\beta_0 + \beta_1 x_1 + \cdots + \beta_n x_n = 0.$$

Because this is a linear equality in the predictor variables, the boundary is a linear plane or hyperplane in the instance space, whose normal (perpendicular) is given by $\boldsymbol{\beta}$. For the nonlinear expressions mentioned above (quadratic terms and additive logistic model), the boundary will be more complex.

8.3.4 Multi-class Logistic Regression

Binary or two-class logistic regression can be extended to the case of a class variable with more than two categories, $\Omega_C = \{1, \ldots, R\}, R > 2$. This is referred to as **multiclass, multinomial logistic regression** or **polytomous logistic regression**. The distribution of $C|\mathbf{x}$ is now modeled as a categorical distribution. One possibility is to perform a binary logistic regression independently for each category, making the output equal to one for training cases with that category and zero for those with a different category.

Unfortunately, this will not necessarily produce probability estimates that add up to one. The individual models for each category have to be coupled to obtain proper probabilities. Another option follows. Equation (8.18) is now the set of $R - 1$ equations

$$\ln \frac{p(C = 1|\mathbf{x}, \boldsymbol{\beta})}{p(C = R|\mathbf{x}, \boldsymbol{\beta})} = \beta_{10} + \beta_{11}x_1 + \cdots + \beta_{1n}x_n, \tag{8.21}$$

$$\ln \frac{p(C = 2|\mathbf{x}, \boldsymbol{\beta})}{p(C = R|\mathbf{x}, \boldsymbol{\beta})} = \beta_{20} + \beta_{21}x_1 + \cdots + \beta_{2n}x_n, \tag{8.22}$$

$$\vdots$$

$$\ln \frac{p(C = R - 1|\mathbf{x}, \boldsymbol{\beta})}{p(C = R|\mathbf{x}, \boldsymbol{\beta})} = \beta_{(R-1)0} + \beta_{(R-1)1}x_1 + \cdots + \beta_{(R-1)n}x_n. \tag{8.23}$$

The model is specified in terms of $R - 1$ logit transformations, reflecting the constraints of the probabilities summing to 1. Using the last category R as the denominator is a convention, and the estimates do not vary under any other arbitrary choice. We can derive the formulas for the probabilities

$$p(C = r|\mathbf{x}, \boldsymbol{\beta}) = \frac{e^{\beta_{r0} + \beta_{r1}x_1 + \cdots + \beta_{rn}x_n}}{1 + \sum_{l=1}^{R-1} e^{\beta_{l0} + \beta_{l1}x_1 + \cdots + \beta_{ln}x_n}}, \quad r = 1, \ldots, R - 1 \tag{8.24}$$

$$p(C = R|\mathbf{x}, \boldsymbol{\beta}) = \frac{1}{1 + \sum_{l=1}^{R-1} e^{\beta_{l0} + \beta_{l1}x_1 + \cdots + \beta_{ln}x_n}},$$

which add up to 1. Note that the entire parameter set now includes $(n + 1)(R - 1)$ parameters, $\{\beta_{10}, \beta_{11}, \ldots, \beta_{1n}, \ldots, \beta_{(R-1)0}, \beta_{(R-1)1}, \ldots, \beta_{(R-1)n}\}$. The maximum likelihood estimates can also be found by the IRLS algorithm derived from the Newton–Raphson method.

In Jammalamadaka et al. (2013) the logistic regression classified spine types (mushroom, thin, and stubby) from the day in vitro on which the spine was imaged and the first, second, and third nearest neighbor spine type along the dendrite.

Regularization is also used here. Park and Hastie (2008) include quadratic terms and regularize with an L_2-penalty (**ridge logistic regression**). In Tian et al. (2008) a quadratic lower-bound algorithm to solve the L_1-regularized logistic regression is proposed for situations where the log-likelihood function is not well-behaved and the IRLS algorithm is not guaranteed to converge.

Logistic regression was used in Santana et al. (2012) for classifying task-related mental activity from MEG data, with elastic net (a combination of lasso and ridge penalties) regularization for an automatic MEG channel selection.

From the posterior probabilities of the class variable, we predict the class label of a general instance $\mathbf{x}$ by obtaining the highest posterior probability, that is, $\phi(\mathbf{x}) = \hat{c}_{\mathbf{x}} = \arg\max_r p(C = r|\mathbf{x}, \boldsymbol{\beta})$. Likewise, the decision boundary between each pair of categories is again a hyperplane, as in the binary case. For instance, the decision boundary between categories 1 and 2 will be computed by solving $p(C = 1|\mathbf{x}, \boldsymbol{\beta}) = p(C = 2|\mathbf{x}, \boldsymbol{\beta})$. The solution, using Equation (8.24), is

$$e^{\beta_{10} + \beta_{11}x_1 + \cdots + \beta_{1n}x_n} = e^{\beta_{20} + \beta_{21}x_1 + \cdots + \beta_{2n}x_n},$$

or equivalently

$$(\beta_{10} - \beta_{20}) + (\beta_{11} - \beta_{21})x_1 + \cdots + (\beta_{1n} - \beta_{2n})x_n = 0.$$

Note that the boundary between two categories is governed by parameters related to those categories only and is not affected by the other categories.

8.3.5   Linear Discriminant Analysis versus Logistic Regression

The linear functions obtained in logistic regression for the log-posterior odds between classes r and R (Equations (8.21)–(8.23)) are also linear functions in LDA. From Equations (8.12)–(8.14) in Section 8.2.2 we have

$$g_r(\mathbf{x}) - g_R(\mathbf{x}) = (\boldsymbol{\Sigma}^{-1}(\boldsymbol{\mu}_r - \boldsymbol{\mu}_R))^T \mathbf{x} - \frac{1}{2}(\boldsymbol{\mu}_r + \boldsymbol{\mu}_R)^T \boldsymbol{\Sigma}^{-1}(\boldsymbol{\mu}_r - \boldsymbol{\mu}_R) + \ln \frac{p(c_r)}{p(c_R)}$$

$$= \beta_{r0}' + \beta_{r1}' x_1 + \cdots + \beta_{rn}' x_n.$$

Obviously,

$$g_r(\mathbf{x}) - g_R(\mathbf{x}) = \ln \frac{p(C = r, \mathbf{X} = \mathbf{x} | \boldsymbol{\beta}')}{p(C = R, \mathbf{X} = \mathbf{x} | \boldsymbol{\beta}')} = \ln \frac{p(C = r | \mathbf{x}, \boldsymbol{\beta}')}{p(C = R | \mathbf{x}, \boldsymbol{\beta}')},$$

see Equation (8.7). Therefore, both models, logistic regression and LDA, have the same form: the log-posterior odds for a pair of classes is a linear function of $\mathbf{x}$.

The difference between these models lies in how the parameters are estimated. For continuous variables, the joint distribution of $\mathbf{X}$ and C is $f(\mathbf{x}, c) = f(\mathbf{x})p(c|\mathbf{x})$. Both LDA and logistic regression model the second factor $p(c|\mathbf{x})$ in a logit-linear form as explained in the previous paragraph. Logistic regression fits the parameters of this distribution by maximizing the *conditional* log-likelihood – it is a **discriminative classifier** – while totally ignoring $f(\mathbf{x})$. We can think of this marginal as being estimated using the empirical distribution function, giving a mass of $1/N$ to each case. However, LDA fits the parameters by maximizing the full log-likelihood – it is a **generative classifier**[6] – based on the joint density $f(\mathbf{x}, c) = f(\mathbf{x}|c)p(c)$, where the conditional f is a Gaussian density. The LDA parameters $\boldsymbol{\beta}'$ are functions of the Gaussian parameters $\boldsymbol{\Sigma}$ and $\boldsymbol{\mu}_r$, and their MLEs are calculated by plugging in the MLE of these Gaussian parameters, see Equations (8.9)–(8.11). The marginal density is a Gaussian mixture density, $f(\mathbf{x}) = \sum_{c=1}^{R} f(\mathbf{x}|c)p(c)$, which is not ignored.

Thus, LDA is less flexible and makes some assumptions. They can be relied upon to provide more information about the parameters, and the parameters can be estimated more efficiently (with lower variance). In LDA we are then using $f(\mathbf{x})$ without class labels, and this is giving us information about the parameters. It is sometimes expensive to get labels, whereas unlabeled data are cheaper. Logistic regression makes no assumptions and is able to include categorical and discrete predictor variables.

Hernández et al. (2014) aimed to evaluate whether a number of clinically diagnosed frontotemporal dementia patients were actually "frontal variants" of AD. Logistic regression and LDA (and classification trees, see Section 7.2) were used to discriminate between clinical AD and clinical frontotemporal dementia patients. Predictor variables included neuropathological data, genetic association studies of Apolipoprotein E (APOE), and phenotype-APOE genotype correlations.

---

[6] Despite the fact that it has *discriminative* in its name.

Table 8.5 Main performance measures of a logistic regression for Data Set 1. A wrapper approach selected 7 variables out of 65: Ratio of axonal length to surface area (X_{10}), Axonal planar angle stdv (X_{14}), Stdv of tortuosity of axonal nodes (X_{25}), Highest order dendritic segment (X_{42}), Dendritic segment length ave (X_{52}), Number dendritic Sholl sections (X_{56}), and Convex hull dendrite perimeter (X_{61})

Measure	Value
Accuracy	0.8868
Sensitivity	0.9447
Specificity	0.7968
F_1-measure	0.9104
Cohen's kappa	0.7574
Brier score	0.1916
AUC	0.9297

8.3.6 Example: Interneurons versus Pyramidal Neurons

Let us take again Data Set 1 where the binary class contains labels for interneurons (I) and pyramidal neurons (P). We obtained a poor model, with an accuracy of only 0.5841, when the Somatic compactness variable (X_4) was the only predictor included. With all the variables, however, we cross the 80% threshold (0.8104). As with the previous classifiers, we tested two filter FSS techniques: (a) the gain ratio univariate filter (Section 6.2.1) using variable evaluator `GainRatioAttributeEval` of WEKA (Hall et al., 2009), and (b) the CFS multivariate filter (Section 6.2.2), searching with greedy forward hill-climbing using `CfsSubsetEval` and `BestFirst` of WEKA. The selected variables were listed in Section 7.1.8.

With the same search method, we also tested a wrapper approach (`WrapperSubset Eval` and `logistic` as classifier), yielding the best accuracy result: 0.8868. Table 8.5 includes this result and other standard performance measures, estimated with 10-fold stratified cross-validation. Note that the results (quite similar to Guerra et al. [2011]) are acceptable.

The confusion matrix, with real labels in rows and predicted labels in columns, is

$$\begin{array}{c} \quad\quad\ \text{I} \quad\ \text{P} \\ \begin{array}{c} \text{I} \\ \text{P} \end{array} \left(\begin{array}{cc} 188 & 11 \\ 26 & 102 \end{array} \right). \end{array}$$

Here we have used the standard cutoff value $\theta^* = 0.5$. Note than there are more pyramidal neurons wrongly classified as interneurons (26) than interneurons wrongly classified as pyramidal neurons (11). This is also observed in the value of specificity (0.7968), which is lower than that of sensitivity (0.9447). Depending on the purpose of the study, these two errors could be measured differently. For example, a researcher studying interneurons could be more interested in correctly classifying interneurons than pyramidal cells.

Of the 65 variables, the 7 that help to predict the class of a neuron include 3 axonal and 4 dendritic features: Ratio of axonal length to surface area (X_{10}), Axonal planar angle stdv (X_{14}), Stdv of tortuosity of axonal nodes (X_{25}), Highest order dendritic segment (X_{42}),

Table 8.6 Coefficients of a logistic regression fitted to Data Set 1. Model obtained using a wrapper approach. See Table 8.5 for a description of the seven selected variables

Variable	Coefficient	Value	SE	Z-score
Intercept	$\hat{\beta}_0$	8.0443	1.6504	4.8741
X_{10}	$\hat{\beta}_1$	1.9622	0.4828	4.0642
X_{14}	$\hat{\beta}_2$	−0.0879	0.0292	−3.0103
X_{25}	$\hat{\beta}_3$	−0.3094	0.0652	−4.7454
X_{42}	$\hat{\beta}_4$	−0.2646	0.0528	−5.0114
X_{52}	$\hat{\beta}_5$	−0.0198	0.0147	−1.3469
X_{56}	$\hat{\beta}_6$	−0.6985	0.0995	−7.0201
X_{61}	$\hat{\beta}_7$	0.0035	0.0007	5.0000

Dendritic segment length ave (X_{52}), Number dendritic Sholl sections (X_{56}), and Convex hull dendrite perimeter (X_{61}). The estimated logistic regression coefficients are shown in Table 8.6.[7]

From the coefficient column, we can build the formula (Equation (8.16)) to predict the posterior probability of any neuron defined by its 65 morphological features being classified as an interneuron. Its complementary probability, given by Equation (8.17), would give the posterior probability for pyramidal neurons. Looking at the coefficients, $\hat{\beta}_7 = 0.0035$ means that the logit (in Equation (8.18)) increases by 0.0035 when the Convex hull dendrite perimeter (X_{61}) increases by 1 unit, if the other 6 variables are fixed. Equivalently, for a 1-unit increase in the Number of dendritic Sholl sections (X_{56}), the odds of a given neuron being an interneuron is multiplied by a factor of $e^{-0.6985} = 0.4973$, the odds ratio. This says that if the other 6 variables are unchanged, we will see a 51% decrease in the odds of the cell being an interneuron for a 1-unit increase in the number of dendritic Sholl sections.

The Z-score (Wald statistic) column suggests the statistical significance of each predictor variable, except for that of X_{52}. Remember, however, that this statistic should be used cautiously.

The predicted posterior probabilities for each instance $p(C = \mathtt{I}|\mathbf{x}, \boldsymbol{\beta}) = \hat{\theta}_\mathbf{x}$ are obtained in a cross-validated fashion, that is, if $\mathbf{x}$ falls into the first fold, $\hat{\theta}_\mathbf{x}$ will be computed from the model built with folds 2 to 10 ($\mathbf{x}$ will never be in the training set). The (conditional) histograms of Figure 8.12 represent all these predicted probabilities for each subsample given by the class value: interneurons in dark gray (left histogram) or pyramidal cells in light gray (right histogram). Observe that there are many more interneurons than pyramidal neurons that are given high probabilities of being interneurons. This contrasts with the corresponding graph for LDA, Figure 8.8.

Figure 8.13 illustrates three examples of neurons. In (a), interneuron $\mathbf{x}^{34}$ was correctly classified by logistic regression; in (b), interneuron $\mathbf{x}^{144}$ was misclassified as a pyramidal cell, with $p(C = \mathtt{I}|\mathbf{x}) = 0.183$; in (c), pyramidal neuron $\mathbf{x}^{220}$ was misclassified as an interneuron, with $p(C = \mathtt{I}|\mathbf{x}) = 0.834$. Neurons $\mathbf{x}^3$ and $\mathbf{x}^{327}$, which LDA misclassified (see Figure 8.9), were correctly classified by this logistic regression model.

---

[7] WEKA does not provide the standard errors of the coefficients, and they were obtained with R, using the `caret` package and the `glm` method.

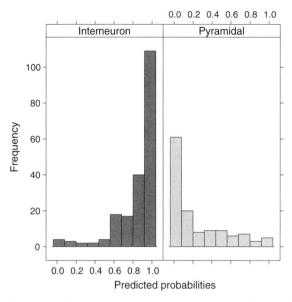

Figure 8.12 Histograms of predicted posterior probabilities $p(C = \text{I}|\mathbf{x}, \boldsymbol{\beta}) = \hat{\theta}_{\mathbf{x}}$ yielded by the logistic regression model for Data Set 1.

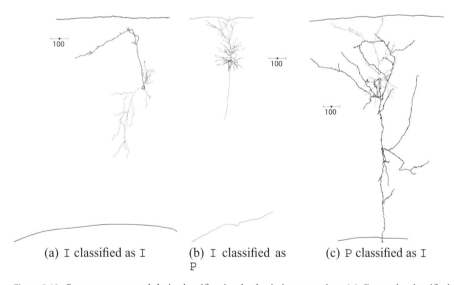

(a) I classified as I   (b) I classified as P   (c) P classified as I

Figure 8.13 Some neurons and their classification by logistic regression. (a) Correctly classified interneuron $\mathbf{x}^{34}$. (b) Misclassified interneuron $\mathbf{x}^{144}$. (c) Misclassified pyramidal neuron $\mathbf{x}^{220}$. Axonal arbor in blue and dendritic tree in red. For the color version, please refer to the plate section.

8.4   Bayesian Network Classifiers

Bayesian network classifiers, like LDA, create a joint model $p(\mathbf{x}, c)$, that is, they are generative approaches. This joint model then is used to obtain $p(c|\mathbf{x})$ and hence a classification rule. Bayesian network classifiers have many advantages over other classification techniques. They offer an explicit, graphical, and interpretable representation of uncertain knowledge. Their semantics is based on the sound concept of conditional independence because they are special types of Bayesian networks, designed for classification problems. Research into these models is an active field, with a plethora of learning from data algorithms being developed. Such algorithms are computationally efficient, with a learning time complexity that is linear in the number of cases N, and linear, quadratic, or cubic (depending on model complexity) in the number of variables n, and whose classification time is linear in the number of variables n.

This section will distinguish between discrete and continuous (linear and directional) Ω_{X_i} domains, resulting in **discrete Bayesian network classifiers** (Section 8.4.1), and **continuous Bayesian network classifiers** (Section 8.4.2), respectively. Section 8.4.2 will also account for directional predictors and the mixed case, with both discrete and continuous predictor variables. Bayesian network classifiers can be organized hierarchically according to their structural complexity, and we will follow this organization throughout this section. Much of the material is based on the detailed review reported in Bielza and Larrañaga (2014a).

Bielza and Larrañaga (2014b) thoroughly surveyed Bayesian networks in neuroscience, finding more than 30 applications with Bayesian network classifiers, although only in general their simplest versions (naive Bayes and Gaussian naive Bayes) were present. The problems consisted of categorizing interneurons, decoding cognitive states, or discriminating control subjects from neuropathological patients (PD, AD, schizophrenia, depression, glioma, epilepsy, bipolar disorder, dementia, brain metastasis, glioblastomas). Few works performed FSS, a salient issue in modern neuroscience where data volume is growing exponentially.

8.4.1   Discrete Bayesian Network Classifiers

Discrete Bayesian network classifiers (Friedman et al., 1997) approximate $p(\mathbf{x}, c)$ with a factorization according to a Bayesian network (Pearl, 1988) (see Chapter 13). The structure of a Bayesian network on the random discrete variables $X_1, \ldots, X_n$, and the class C is a directed acyclic graph (DAG), whose vertices correspond to the random variables and whose arcs encode the probabilistic (in)dependencies among triplets of variables, that is, each variable has a categorical distribution $p(x_i|\mathbf{pa}(x_i))$ or $p(c|\mathbf{pa}(c))$, where $\mathbf{pa}(x_i)$ is a value of the set of variables $\mathbf{Pa}(X_i)$, which are parents of variable X_i in the graphical structure, i.e., the nodes pointing at X_i. An analogous statement applies for $\mathbf{pa}(c)$. Thus,

$$p(\mathbf{x}, c) = p(c|\mathbf{pa}(c)) \prod_{i=1}^{n} p(x_i|\mathbf{pa}(x_i)).$$

When the sets $\mathbf{Pa}(X_i)$ are sparse, it is not necessary – thanks to this factorization – to estimate an exponential number of parameters, which would otherwise be the case.

With a 0–1 loss, we saw in Section 8.1 (see Equation (8.5)) that the Bayes decision rule consists of finding c^* such that

$$c^* = \arg\max_c p(c|\mathbf{x}) = \arg\max_c p(\mathbf{x}, c). \tag{8.25}$$

For the special case of $\mathbf{Pa}(C) = \varnothing$, the problem is to maximize on c the following probability:

$$p(\mathbf{x}, c) = p(c)p(\mathbf{x}|c).$$

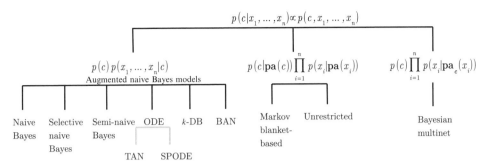

Figure 8.14 Categorization of discrete Bayesian network classifiers according to the factorization of $p(\mathbf{x}, c)$.

The different Bayesian network classifiers explained below match up with different factorizations of $p(\mathbf{x}|c)$. The simplest model is the naive Bayes, where C is the parent of all predictor variables and there are no dependence relationships among them, see Section 8.4.1.1. A progressive increase of the level of dependence in these relationships (one-dependence, k-dependence, etc.) gives rise to a family of **augmented naive Bayes models**, explained in Sections 8.4.1.3–8.4.1.6, see Figure 8.14, left.

If $\mathbf{Pa}(C) \neq \varnothing$, $p(\mathbf{x}, c)$ is factorized in different ways, and we have to search the Markov blanket of C to solve Equation (8.25) (Section 8.4.1.7). The **Markov blanket** (see Pearl [1988], p. 97) of C is the set of variables $\mathbf{MB}(C)$, which make C conditionally independent of the other variables in the network, given $\mathbf{MB}(C)$, i.e.,

$$p(c|\mathbf{x}) = p(c|\mathbf{x}_{\mathbf{MB}(C)}), \tag{8.26}$$

where $\mathbf{x}_{\mathbf{MB}(C)}$ denotes the projection of $\mathbf{x}$ onto the variables in $\mathbf{MB}(C)$. Therefore, the Markov blanket of C is the only knowledge needed to predict its behavior. A probability distribution p is **faithful** to a DAG representing a Bayesian network if, all triplets of variables are conditionally independent (Section 13.1.1) with respect to p if they are d-separated in the DAG (d-separation is a graph criterion explained in Section 13.1.2). For such a faithful p, $\mathbf{MB}(C)$ is unique and is composed of C's parents, children, and the children's other parents (spouses) (Pearl, 1988). A more general approach is to learn an unrestricted Bayesian network classifier. This can be induced with any existing Bayesian network structure learning algorithm considering all variables, C included, equally. The Markov blanket of C can be used later for classification purposes (Section 8.4.1.8), see Figure 8.14, middle.

Finally, specific conditional independence relationships can be modeled for different c values, giving rise to specific Bayesian networks, which are then joined in the more complex Bayesian multinet (Section 8.4.1.9). The parents of X_i, $\mathbf{Pa}_c(X_i)$, may be different depending on c, see Figure 8.14, right.

Apart from learning the network structure, the probabilities $p(x_i|\mathbf{pa}(x_i))$ are estimated from $\mathcal{D}$ by standard methods like maximum likelihood or Bayesian estimation. The mle is given by

$$\frac{N_{ijk}}{N_{ij}},$$

where N_{ijk} is the frequency in $\mathcal{D}$ of cases with $X_i = k$ and $\mathbf{Pa}(X_i) = j$, and N_{ij} is the frequency in $\mathcal{D}$ of cases with $\mathbf{Pa}(X_i) = j$ (i.e., $N_{ij} = \sum_{k=1}^{R_i} N_{ijk}$).

In Bayesian estimation (Section 4.1.4), assuming a Dirichlet prior distribution over $(p(X_i = 1|\mathbf{Pa}(X_i) = j), \dots, p(X_i = R_i|\mathbf{Pa}(X_i) = j))$ with all hyperparameters equal to α, the posterior distribution is Dirichlet with hyperparameters equal to $N_{ijk} + \alpha, k = 1, \dots, R_i$. Hence, $p(X_i = k|\mathbf{Pa}(X_i) = j)$ is estimated by

$$\frac{N_{ijk} + \alpha}{N_{ij} + R_i\alpha}. \tag{8.27}$$

This is called the **Lindstone rule**. Special cases are the **Laplace estimation** and the **Schurmann–Grassberger rule**, with $\alpha = 1$ and $\alpha = \frac{1}{R_i}$ in Equation (8.27), respectively (see more rules in Section 13.3.1.2).

8.4.1.1 *Naive Bayes*

Naive Bayes (Maron and Kuhns, 1960; Minsky, 1961) is the simplest Bayesian network classifier. The predictive variables are assumed to be conditionally independent given the class. This assumption is useful when n is high and/or N is small, making $p(\mathbf{x}|c)$ difficult to estimate. Equation (8.25) is simplified as

$$p(c|\mathbf{x}) \propto p(c)\prod_{i=1}^{n} p(x_i|c). \tag{8.28}$$

Figure 8.15 shows an example of naive Bayes structure with five predictor variables. From a theoretical point of view, if all variables (predictors and class) are binary, the decision boundary has been shown to be a hyperplane (Minsky, 1961). The proof is easy. We first write

$$p(x_i|c) = p(X_i = 0|C = c)\left[\frac{p(X_i = 1|C = c)}{p(X_i = 0|C = c)}\right]^{x_i},$$

with $x_i = 0, 1$. Then, substituting this in Equation (8.28) and taking the natural log, we have

$$\ln p(c|\mathbf{x}) \propto \ln p(c) + \ln\prod_{i=1}^{n} p(X_i = 0|C = c) + \sum_{i=1}^{n} x_i \ln\left[\frac{p(X_i = 1|C = c)}{p(X_i = 0|C = c)}\right].$$

If we denote

$$w_{c0} = \ln p(c) + \ln\prod_{i=1}^{n} p(X_i = 0|C = c)$$

$$w_{ci} = \ln\left[\frac{p(X_i = 1|C = c)}{p(X_i = 0|C = c)}\right],$$

then

$$\ln p(c|\mathbf{x}) \propto w_{c0} + \mathbf{w}_c^T\mathbf{x},$$

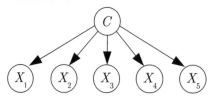

Figure 8.15 A naive Bayes structure from which $p(c|\mathbf{x}) \propto p(c)p(x_1|c)p(x_2|c)p(x_3|c)p(x_4|c)p(x_5|c)$.

with $\mathbf{w}_c^T = (w_{c1}, \ldots, w_{cn})$. The decision boundary is

$$\ln p(C = 0|\mathbf{x}) - \ln p(C = 1|\mathbf{x}) = (w_{00} - w_{10}) + (\mathbf{w}_0 - \mathbf{w}_1)^T \mathbf{x} = 0,$$

which defines a hyperplane.

For ordinal nonbinary predictor variables, the decision boundary is a sum of n polynomials, one for each variable X_i, with a degree equal to $R_i - 1$ (Duda et al., 2001).

From a practical point of view, the model classification performance may still be good even if the assumption of conditional independence does not hold, although the probabilities are not well calibrated (Domingos and Pazzani, 1997). A possible explanation is that naive Bayes requires few parameters (conditional probabilities). This reduces the variance of the estimates, and their biases may not matter because the aim is classification rather than accurate posterior class probability estimation (Hand and Yu, 2001). Thus, the decision boundaries become insensitive to the specificities of the class-conditional probabilities $p(x_i|c)$. A bound for the degradation of the probability of correct classification when naive Bayes is used as an approximation of the Bayes decision rule is given in Ekdahl and Koski (2006).

The inclusion of variables irrelevant to the class does not worsen the performance of a naive Bayes classifier. However, the presence of redundant variables does have a harmful effect (Langley and Sage, 1994b). Hence it is important to remove irrelevant, and especially redundant variables, as the so-called selective naive Bayes should ideally do (see Section 8.4.1.2).

An important variant of naive Bayes is the **weighted naive Bayes**. It adjusts the naive Bayesian probabilities *during classification* to improve predictive accuracy. A general formula is

$$p(c|\mathbf{x}) \propto w_c p(c) \prod_{i=1}^{n} [p(x_i|c)]^{w_i}$$

for some weights $w_c, w_i, i = 1, \ldots, n$. Some particular examples follow. First, $w_c = 1$ and $w_i = w \in (0,1), \forall i$, are used in Hilden and Bjerregaard (1976), attaching more importance to the prior probability of the class variable. w is fixed by looking for a good performance after some trials. Second, in Hall (2007), $w_c = 1$ and w_i are set to $1/\sqrt{d_i}$, where d_i is the minimum depth at which variable X_i is tested in the unpruned decision tree (Section 7.2) constructed from the data. Fixing the root node to depth 1, d_i weighs X_i according to the degree to which it depends on the values of other variables. Finally, in Webb and Pazzani (1998), the linear adjustment w_c is found by employing a hill-climbing search maximizing the resubstitution accuracy and $w_i = 1, \forall i$.

The violation of the conditional independence assumption in naive Bayes can be interpreted as an indication of the presence of hidden or latent variables. The hidden variables are introduced in different ways. The simplest option is when there is a hidden variable as a child of the class variable and parent of all predictor variables (Kwoh and Gillies, 1996), see Figure 8.16(a). The usual setup is to have many hidden variables arranged in a tree-shaped Bayesian network called **hierarchical naive Bayes** (Zhang et al., 2004; Langseth and Nielsen, 2006). The root is the class variable, the leaves are the predictor variables, and the internal nodes are the hidden variables. An example is given in Figure 8.16(b).

There are other options for relaxing the conditional independence assumption. The finite mixture model (Section 12.2) introduced in Kontkanen et al. (1996) leaves the class

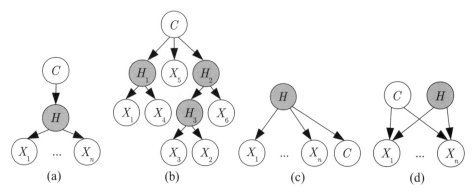

Figure 8.16 (a) Naive Bayes with a hidden variable H (Kwoh and Gillies, 1996). (b) Hierarchical naive Bayes (Zhang et al., 2004; Langseth and Nielsen, 2006). (c) Finite mixture model, with a hidden variable as a parent of the predictor variables and the class (Kontkanen et al., 1996). (d) Finite-mixture augmented naive Bayes (Monti and Cooper, 1999).

variable as a child node, whereas the common parent for both the discrete or continuous predictors and the class variable is a hidden variable, see Figure 8.16(c). This unmeasured discrete variable is learned using the expectation-maximization algorithm (Section 12.1) and models the interaction between the predictor variables and between the predictor variables and the class variable. Thus, the class and the predictor variables are conditionally independent given the hidden variable. The **finite-mixture augmented naive Bayes** (Monti and Cooper, 1999) is a combination of this model and naive Bayes. The standard naive Bayes is augmented with another naive Bayes, with a hidden variable acting as parent of the predictor variables, see Figure 8.16(d). The hidden variable models the dependencies among the predictor variables that are not captured by the class variable. Therefore it is expected to have fewer states in its domain (i.e., the mixture will have fewer components) than the finite mixture model.

8.4.1.2 *Selective Naive Bayes*

As mentioned above, the classification performance of naive Bayes will improve if only relevant, and especially nonredundant, variables are selected to be in the model. The **selective naive Bayes** (Figure 8.17) is stated as an FSS problem where Equation (8.28) is now

$$p(c|\mathbf{x}) \propto p(c|\mathbf{x}_F) = p(c) \prod_{i \in F} p(x_i|c).$$

$\mathbf{X}_F$ denotes the projection of $\mathbf{X}$ onto the indices $F \subseteq \{1, 2, \ldots, n\}$ of the selected features.

Despite the short times for learning and classifying new instances with naive Bayes, the exhaustive search in the space of all possible selective naive Bayes requires the computation of 2^n structures, and this can be prohibitive. This justifies the use of heuristic approaches for this search.

The most used scoring measure in univariate filter approaches is the mutual information (Section 3.6.4) of each feature and the class variable $\mathbb{I}(X_i, C)$ (Pazzani and Billsus, 1997). Other scoring measures for a feature can be used, like the odds ratio, weight of evidence, or symmetric uncertainty coefficient, some of which are empirically compared in Mladenic and Grobelnik (1999). A standard and appropriate scoring measure in multivariate filter

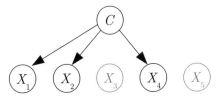

Figure 8.17 A selective naive Bayes structure for which $p(c|\mathbf{x}) \propto p(c)p(x_1|c)p(x_2|c)p(x_4|c)$. The variables in the shaded nodes have not been selected.

methods is CFS (Section 6.2.2), which promotes the inclusion of variables that are relevant for classification and, at the same time, avoids including redundant variables. Any kind of heuristic (forward selection, backward elimination, best-first, etc.) can be used to search for this optimal subset. Another possibility is to simply select those features that the C4.5 algorithm would use in its classification tree, as in Ratanamahatana and Gunopulos (2003).

Morales et al. (2013) used naive Bayes and selective naive Bayes to discriminate between cognitively intact patients with PD, with MCI, and with dementia, based on (discretized) magnetic-resonance volume measurements of subcortical structures and cortical thickness. Mutual information and CFS were the scoring measures to filter variables in the selective naive Bayes.

The more computationally costly wrapper approaches use strategies ranging from simple heuristics, like greedy forward (Langley and Sage, 1994b) and floating search (Pernkopf and O'Leary, 2003), to more sophisticated population-based heuristics, like genetic algorithms (Liu et al., 2001) and estimation of distribution algorithms (Inza et al., 2000). If n is large, a wrapper approach may be impracticable even with the simplest heuristics. In this case a wrapper strategy can be applied over a reduced filtered subset, thereby adopting a hybrid filter-wrapper option (Inza et al., 2004) (Section 6.5).

Finally, as with LDA and logistic regression, regularization techniques can be used to select features in an embedded way. A penalty term on the size of the model parameters is added to the log-likelihood function of the data given the model. An L_1/L_2-**regularized naive Bayes** for continuous and discrete predictor variables is the natural choice for applying regularization to the naive Bayes model (Vidaurre et al., 2012). Considering the discrete case, the parameters to be estimated can be denoted as $\theta_{ijk} = p(X_i = k|C = j)$. The entire set of parameters is $\Theta = \{\theta_{ijk} : i = 1, \ldots, n; j = 1, \ldots, R; k = 1, \ldots, R_i\}$. Then the L_1/L_2-regularized discrete naive Bayes solves the (convex) optimization problem

$$\max_{\Theta} \left[\ln \mathcal{L}(\Theta) - \lambda \sum_{i=1}^{n} \sqrt{\sum_{j=1}^{R} \sum_{k=1}^{R_i} \left(\theta_{ijk} - \hat{\theta}_{ijk}^{(0)} \right)^2} \right]$$

subject to

$$0 < \theta_{ijk} < 1, \forall i, j, k$$

$$\sum_{k=1}^{R_i} \theta_{ijk} = 1, \forall i, j,$$

(8.29)

where $\mathcal{L}(\Theta) = \prod_{l=1}^{N} p(C = c^l) \prod_{i=1}^{n} p(X_i = x_i^l|C = c^l)$ is the likelihood function, and $\theta_{ijk}^{(0)}$ are the parameters of X_i so that they are equal for all class values $j = 1, \ldots, R$. This equality is equivalent to removing predictor X_i from the model because it means that

X_i and C are independent. The regularization term in Equation (8.29) is hence a group lasso-type penalty (Section 8.3.2.2), which is able to discard entire groups. Therefore, all the parameters θ_{ijk} of some predictors will be prompted to be equal to $\hat{\theta}_{ijk}^{(0)}$, so that such predictors will be effectively excluded. This model discards irrelevant but not redundant predictors.

A more cautious version is the **forward stagewise naive Bayes** (Vidaurre et al., 2012). The selective naive Bayes decides between the MLEs, denoted as $\hat{\theta}_{ijk}^{(1)}$, and $\hat{\theta}_{ijk}^{(0)}$, that is, between including or excluding, respectively, predictor X_i. However, the forward stagewise naive Bayes uses a point of compromise between $\hat{\theta}_{ijk}^{(1)}$ and $\hat{\theta}_{ijk}^{(0)}$, that is, $\hat{\theta}_{ijk}^{(\alpha_i)} = \alpha_i \hat{\theta}_{ijk}^{(1)} + (1 - \alpha_i)\hat{\theta}_{ijk}^{(0)}$, where $\alpha_i \in [0,1]$ refers to predictor X_i. Starting from $\hat{\theta}_{ijk}^{(0)}$ (no predictors included in the model), it checks the classification accuracy for $\hat{\theta}_{ijk}^{(\alpha_i+\varepsilon)}, \hat{\theta}_{ijk}^{(\alpha_i+2\varepsilon)}, \ldots, \hat{\theta}_{ijk}^{(\alpha_i+t\varepsilon)}, \ldots, \hat{\theta}_{ijk}^{(\alpha_i+v\varepsilon)}$, where $\varepsilon > 0$ is some small constant. At each iteration, the optimal values α_i and t are selected, and the parameters are updated accordingly. Parameters ε and v define how detailed the search is at each step. This model can discard both irrelevant and redundant predictors. More sophisticated ideas have also been devised (Vidaurre et al., 2013a).

8.4.1.3 Semi-naive Bayes

The **semi-naive Bayes** model (Figure 8.18) relaxes the conditional independence assumption of naive Bayes by introducing new features obtained as the Cartesian product of two or more original predictor variables. This way, the model is able to represent dependencies between original predictor variables. These new predictor variables are still conditionally independent given the class variable. Thus, Equation (8.28) is now

$$p(c|\mathbf{x}) \propto p(c)\prod_{j=1}^{K} p(\mathbf{x}_{S_j}|c),$$

where $S_j \subseteq \{1, 2, \ldots, n\}$ denotes the indices in the jth feature (original or Cartesian product), $j = 1, \ldots, K$, $S_j \cap S_l = \varnothing$, for $j \neq l$.

The standard algorithm for learning a semi-naive Bayes model (Pazzani, 1996) is guided wrapper-wise (the objective function is the classification accuracy). This avoids including redundant variables because these degrade accuracy, as mentioned in Section 8.4.1.1. The **forward sequential selection and joining** algorithm starts from an empty structure. The accuracy is obtained by using the simple decision rule of Equation (8.1), where the most likely label is assigned to all instances. Then the algorithm considers the best option between (a) adding a variable not used by the current classifier as conditionally independent of the features (original or Cartesian products) used in the classifier, and

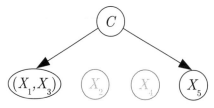

Figure 8.18 A semi-naive Bayes structure for which $p(c|\mathbf{x}) \propto p(c)p(x_1,x_3|c)p(x_5|c)$.

(b) joining a variable not used by the current classifier with each feature (original or Cartesian products) present in the classifier. An alternative backward version starting from a naive Bayes, called **backward sequential elimination and joining** is also proposed in Pazzani (1996). Both are greedy search algorithms, which stop when there is no accuracy improvement. Alternatively, evolutionary computation can be used to guide the search for the best semi-naive Bayes model, as in Robles et al. (2003), with estimation of distribution algorithms.

Example. Figure 8.19 illustrates how to build a semi-naive Bayes structure using the forward sequential selection and joining algorithm. Initially the graph is empty and all instances are classified in the most frequent label; this gives the initial accuracy. After checking all selective naive Bayes models that include one variable, variable X_2 has been selected because its respective model (Figure 8.19(a)) improves the accuracy the most. Figure 8.19(b) shows the winner model among those with the following subsets of predictor variables: $\{X_2,X_1\}, \{X_2,X_3\}, \{X_2,X_4\}, \{(X_2,X_1)\}, \{(X_2,X_3)\}$, and $\{(X_2,X_4)\}$. Finally, Figure 8.19(c) shows the winner model after checking all the possibilities at this point: $\{X_1,(X_2,X_4)\}, \{X_3,(X_2,X_4)\}, \{(X_1,X_2,X_4)\}, \{(X_3,X_2,X_4)\}$. The process stops because the accuracy does not improve with models with the following subsets of predictor variables:

$$\{X_1,X_3,(X_2,X_4)\}, \{(X_1,X_3),(X_2,X_4)\}, \{X_3,(X_1,X_2,X_4)\}.$$

■

A filter adaptation of the forward sequential selection and joining algorithm (Blanco et al., 2005) uses independence tests. Options (a) and (b) above are evaluated with a χ^2 test of independence based on the mutual information $\mathbb{I}(C,X_i)$ of the class and each variable not in the current model (for (a)) and on the mutual information of the class and a joint variable formed by a variable not in the current model and a feature present in the model (for (b)). The variable with the smallest p-value is selected until no more new variables can be added to the model (because they do not reject the null hypothesis of independence). Other filter approaches to choose the variables to join use alternative metrics like the

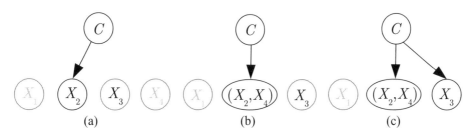

(a)   (b)   (c)

Figure 8.19 An example of semi-naive Bayes structure construction using the forward sequential selection and joining algorithm. (a) The selective naive Bayes with X_2 has yielded the best accuracy. (b) After building the models with these sets of predictor variables: $\{X_2,X_1\}, \{X_2,X_3\}, \{X_2,X_4\}$, $\{(X_2,X_1)\}, \{(X_2,X_3)\}$, and $\{(X_2,X_4)\}$, the last option is selected according to its accuracy. (c) The winner model out of $\{X_1,(X_2,X_4)\}, \{X_3,(X_2,X_4)\}, \{(X_1,X_2,X_4)\}$, and $\{(X_3,X_2,X_4)\}$. The accuracy does not improve with $\{X_1,X_3,(X_2,X_4)\}, \{(X_1,X_3),(X_2,X_4)\}$, and $\{X_3,(X_1,X_2,X_4)\}$, and the process stops.

likelihood-equivalent Bayesian Dirichlet score (see Section 13.3.2.2), the expected log-likelihood estimated with a leave-one-out procedure (Section 5.3.1.2) and a log-likelihood ratio test, as in Abellán et al. (2007), including an additional step aimed at merging values of the new joint variable to reduce its cardinality and computation time.

8.4.1.4 One-Dependence Bayesian Classifiers

One-dependence estimators (ODEs) are more general naive Bayes where each predictor variable is allowed to depend on at most one other predictor in addition to the class. They can improve the naive Bayes' accuracy when its conditional independence assumption is violated.

Tree-Augmented Naive Bayes. The predictor subgraph of a **tree-augmented naive Bayes** (TAN) (Friedman et al., 1997) is necessarily a tree. Thus, all predictor variables contain exactly one parent, except for one variable that has no parents, called the *root* (Figure 8.20). The posterior distribution in Equation (8.25) is then

$$p(c|\mathbf{x}) \propto p(c)p(x_r|c) \prod_{i=1, i \neq r}^{n} p(x_i|c, x_{j(i)}), \qquad (8.30)$$

where X_r denotes the root node and $\{X_{j(i)}\} = \mathbf{Pa}(X_i) \setminus \{C\}$, for any $i \neq r$.

Algorithm 8.1 shows the pseudocode for learning a TAN structure (Friedman et al., 1997). The mutual information of any pair of predictor variables conditioned on C is computed (line 2). This measures the information that one variable provides about the other variable when the value of C is known. Then, in line 4, the edges of a complete undirected graph with nodes $X_1, \dots, X_n$ are annotated by the $n(n-1)/2$ conditional mutual information numbers computed in line 2. In line 5, Kruskal's algorithm (Kruskal, 1956) is used to find a maximum weighted spanning tree (MWST) in that graph, containing $n-1$ edges. This procedure selects a subset of edges from the graph such that they form a tree and the sum of their weights is maximized. The resulting solution is unique if the edge weights are all different. If some weights are equal, there are multiple solutions but they all have the same maximum weight. The undirected tree is then converted into a directed tree by selecting a variable at random to be the root node and replacing the edges by arcs (line 11). This is the tree shaping the predictor subgraph. Finally, a naive Bayes structure is superimposed to form the TAN structure (line 12). This procedure has been proven to build a TAN that maximizes the likelihood given the data.

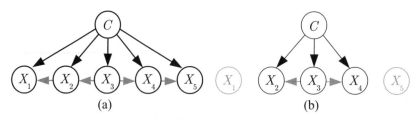

Figure 8.20 (a) A TAN structure, whose root node is X_3, for which $p(c|\mathbf{x}) \propto p(c)p(x_1|c,x_2)$ $p(x_2|c,x_3)p(x_3|c)p(x_4|c,x_3)p(x_5|c,x_4)$. (b) Selective TAN (Blanco et al., 2005), for which $p(c|\mathbf{x}) \propto p(c)p(x_2|c,x_3)p(x_3|c)p(x_4|c,x_3)$.

Algorithm 8.1: Learning a TAN structure

Input : A data set $\mathcal{D} = \{(\mathbf{x}^1, c^1), \dots, (\mathbf{x}^N, c^N)\}$ with $\mathbf{X} = (X_1, \dots, X_n)$
Output: A TAN structure

1 **for** $i < j, i, j = 1, \dots, n$ **do**
2 $\quad$ Compute $\mathbb{I}(X_i, X_j | C) = \sum_{i,j,r} p(x_i, x_j, c_r) \log_2 \frac{p(x_i, x_j | c_r)}{p(x_i | c_r) p(x_j | c_r)}$
3 **endfor**
4 Build a complete undirected graph where the nodes are $X_1, \dots, X_n$. Annotate the
$\quad$ weight of an edge connecting X_i and X_j by $\mathbb{I}(X_i, X_j | C)$
5 Build a MWST:
6 $\quad$ Select the two edges with the heaviest weights
7 $\quad$ **while** The tree contains fewer than $n - 1$ edges **do**
8 $\quad\quad$ **if** They do not form a cycle with the previous edges **then** Select the next
$\quad\quad\quad$ heaviest edge
9 $\quad\quad$ **else** Reject the edge and continue
10 $\quad$ **endwhile**
11 Transform the resulting undirected tree into a directed one by choosing a root
$\quad$ node and setting the direction of all edges to be outward from this node
12 Construct a TAN structure by adding a node C and an arc from C to each X_i

---

These ideas are adapted from Chow and Liu (1968), where several trees, one for each value c of the class, were constructed rather than a single tree for the entire domain. This works like TAN, but only uses the cases from $\mathcal{D}$ satisfying $C = c$ to construct each tree. This collection of trees is a special case of a Bayesian multinet, a term first introduced by Geiger and Heckerman (1996) (see Section 8.4.1.9).

Example. Figure 8.21 illustrates an example of TAN structure learning. If the conditional mutual information quantities are ordered as

$$\mathbb{I}(X_1, X_3 | C) > \mathbb{I}(X_2, X_4 | C) > \mathbb{I}(X_1, X_2 | C) > \mathbb{I}(X_3, X_4 | C) > \mathbb{I}(X_1, X_4 | C) > \mathbb{I}(X_3, X_5 | C)$$
$$> \mathbb{I}(X_1, X_5 | C) > \mathbb{I}(X_2, X_3 | C) > \mathbb{I}(X_2, X_5 | C) > \mathbb{I}(X_4, X_5 | C),$$

then the MWST starts with the edge $X_1 - X_3$ (Figure 8.21(a)). Next, edges $X_2 - X_4$ (Figure 8.21(b)) and $X_1 - X_2$ are added (Figure 8.21(c)). When the next edge, $X_3 - X_4$, is added, a cycle is formed making the tree structure invalid (Figure 8.21(d)), and this edge is discarded. This also happens in the case of the $X_1 - X_4$ edge (Figure 8.21(e)). Edge $X_3 - X_5$ can be added (Figure 8.21(f)), and we obtain the MWST, with four edges and five nodes. By choosing X_1 as the root node, the undirected tree becomes a directed tree (Figure 8.21(g)). By superimposing a naive Bayes structure, the final TAN structure shows up (Figure 8.21(h)). ■

If the weights of the undirected tree based on conditional mutual information are first filtered with a χ^2 test of independence, the resulting structure is the **selective TAN** (Blanco et al., 2005) (Figure 8.20(b)). The predictor subgraph could be a forest (i.e., a disjoint union of trees) rather than a tree because it may result in many root nodes.

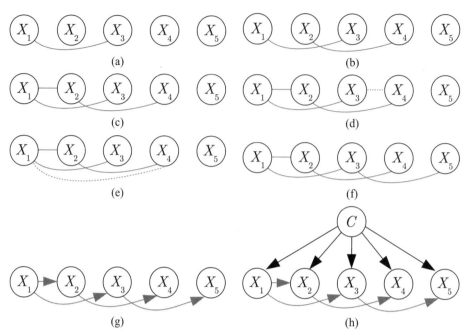

Figure 8.21 An example of a TAN structure construction. (a–c) Edges are added according to conditional mutual information quantities arranged in ascending order. (d–e) Edges $X_3 - X_4$ and $X_1 - X_4$ (dashed lines) cannot be added because they form a cycle. (f) Maximum weighted spanning tree. (g) The directed tree obtained by choosing X_1 as the root node. (h) Final TAN structure.

Other authors propose the use of a wrapper rather than a filter approach. Thus, initializing the network to a naive Bayes, we can consider adding possible arcs from X_i to X_j, with X_j without any predictor variable as parent, and selecting the arc giving the highest accuracy improvement. This hill-climbing search algorithm is described in Keogh and Pazzani (2002). Also starting from a naive Bayes, a sequential floating search heuristic is used in Pernkopf and O'Leary (2003). The approach described in Blanco et al. (2005) starts from an empty predictor subgraph. Then an algorithm greedily decides whether to add a new predictor or to create an arc between two predictors already in the model. Unlike the last two wrapper techniques, it actually performs an FSS. The three ideas described in this paragraph lead to forest predictor structures.

Forest Augmented Naive Bayes. The **forest augmented naive Bayes** (FAN) was first defined in Lucas (2004), with a forest – i.e., a disjoint union of trees – in the predictor subgraph, augmented with a naive Bayes (Figure 8.22(a)). The forest is obtained using a maximum weighted spanning forest algorithm (e.g., Fredman and Tarjan [1987]).

The **selective FAN** introduced in Ziebart et al. (2007) allows the predictor variables to be optionally dependent on the class variable, that is, missing arcs from C to some X_i can be found (Figure 8.22(b)). Moreover, the learning approach is based on maximizing the likelihood of the data but penalized for avoiding the class variable as a parent.

Superparent-One-Dependence Estimators. **Superparent-one-dependence estimators** (SPODEs) are an ODE where all predictors depend on the same predictor, called the superparent, in addition to the class (Keogh and Pazzani, 2002) (Figure 8.23). Note that

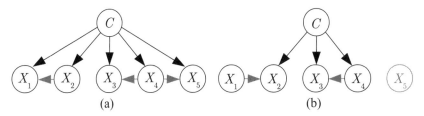

Figure 8.22 (a) FAN (Lucas, 2004) with two root nodes X_2 and X_4: $p(c|\mathbf{x}) \propto p(c)p(x_1|c,x_2)p(x_2|c)$ $p(x_3|c,x_4)p(x_4|c)p(x_5|c,x_4)$. (b) Selective FAN (Ziebart et al., 2007): $p(c|\mathbf{x}) \propto p(c)p(x_2|c,x_1)$ $p(x_3|c,x_4)p(x_4|c)$.

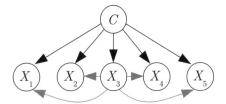

Figure 8.23 A SPODE structure, with X_3 as superparent, for which $p(c|\mathbf{x}) \propto p(c)p(x_1|c,x_3)$ $p(x_2|c,x_3)p(x_3|c)p(x_4|c,x_3)p(x_5|c,x_3)$.

this is a particular case of a TAN model. The posterior distribution in Equation (8.25) is

$$p(c|\mathbf{x}) \propto p(c)p(x_{sp}|c) \prod_{i=1,i\neq sp}^{n} p(x_i|c,x_{sp}),$$

where X_{sp} denotes the superparent node. This equation is similar to Equation (8.30), particularized as $X_r = X_{j(i)} = X_{sp}$, for any $i \neq sp$.

One of the most used variants of SPODE is the **averaged one-dependence estimator** (AODE) (Webb et al., 2005). This model averages the predictions of all qualified SPODEs, where "qualified" means including, for each instance $\mathbf{x} = (x_1, \ldots, x_{sp}, \ldots, x_n)$, only the SPODEs for which the probability estimates are accurate, that is, where the training data contain more than m cases satisfying $X_{sp} = x_{sp}$. The authors suggest fixing $m = 30$. The average prediction is given by

$$p(c|\mathbf{x}) \propto p(c,\mathbf{x}) = \frac{1}{|\mathcal{SP}_{\mathbf{x}}^m|} \sum_{X_{sp} \in \mathcal{SP}_{\mathbf{x}}^m} p(c)p(x_{sp}|c) \prod_{i=1,i\neq sp}^{n} p(x_i|c,x_{sp}), \qquad (8.31)$$

where $\mathcal{SP}_{\mathbf{x}}^m$ denotes for each $\mathbf{x}$ the set of predictor variables qualified as superparents, and $|\cdot|$ is its cardinality. AODE avoids model selection, thereby decreasing the variance component of the classifier. It is, in fact, a metaclassifier, a collection of classifiers, see Chapter 9.

AODE can be improved with the **lazy AODE** (Jiang and Zhang, 2006), which builds an AODE for each test case. The training data are expanded by adding a number of copies (clones) of each training case equal to its similarity to the test case. This similarity is the number of identical predictor variables.

The AODE proposed in Yang et al. (2005) employs a wrapper strategy. Different metrics (like minimum description length, minimum message length, leave-one-out classification accuracy, and accuracy from backward sequential elimination or forward sequential addition processes) may be used to order the n possible SPODEs for selection. The stopping criterion is based on the classification accuracy.

The idea of Yang et al. (2007) is to compute the final predictions as a *weighted* average in Equation (8.31) rather than as an average. Four different weighting schemes are then proposed.

Finally, the **hidden one-dependence estimator** classifier (Flores et al., 2009) obviates any SPODE use. It introduces, via the expectation-maximization algorithm (Section 12.1), a new variable (the hidden variable H with values h), with the aim of representing the links existing in the n SPODE models. Node C in the naive Bayes structure is replaced by the Cartesian product of C and H. Then we have to estimate the probability of c conditioned on $\mathbf{x}$, by searching for $\arg\max_c \sum_h p(c,h) \prod_{i=1}^n p(x_i|c,h)$.

8.4.1.5 k-Dependence Bayesian Classifiers

The **k-dependence Bayesian classifier** (k-DB) (Sahami, 1996) allows each predictor variable to have a maximum of k parent variables apart from the class variable (Figure 8.24). Naive Bayes and TAN are particular cases of k-DBs, with $k=0$ and $k=1$, respectively. The posterior distribution in Equation (8.25) is

$$p(c|\mathbf{x}) \propto p(c) \prod_{i=1}^n p(x_i|c,x_{i_1},\dots,x_{i_k}),$$

where $X_{i_1},\dots,X_{i_k}$ are the parents of X_i in the structure.

According to Sahami (1996), the inclusion order of the predictor variables X_i in the model is given by $\mathbb{I}(X_i,C)$, starting with the highest. Once X_i enters the model, its parents are selected by choosing the k variables X_j in the model with the highest values of $\mathbb{I}(X_i,X_j|C)$.

Example. Figure 8.25 illustrates an example of k-DB structure learning, with $k=2$. We first obtain that:

$$\mathbb{I}(X_3,C) > \mathbb{I}(X_1,C) > \mathbb{I}(X_4,C) > \mathbb{I}(X_5,C) > \mathbb{I}(X_2,C).$$

Further,

$$\mathbb{I}(X_3,X_4|C) > \mathbb{I}(X_2,X_5|C) > \mathbb{I}(X_1,X_3|C) > \mathbb{I}(X_1,X_2|C) > \mathbb{I}(X_2,X_4|C) > \mathbb{I}(X_2,X_3|C)$$
$$> \mathbb{I}(X_1,X_4|C) > \mathbb{I}(X_4,X_5|C) > \mathbb{I}(X_1,X_5|C) > \mathbb{I}(X_3,X_5|C).$$

X_3 is the first variable to enter the model because $\mathbb{I}(X_3,C)$ is the largest $\mathbb{I}(X_i,C), i = 1,\dots,5$ (Figure 8.25(a)). Then X_1 enters the model. Because two predictor parents are

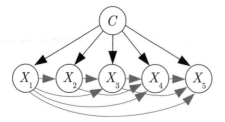

Figure 8.24 An example of a 3-DB structure for which $p(c|\mathbf{x}) \propto p(c)p(x_1|c)p(x_2|c,x_1)p(x_3|c,x_1,x_2)$ $p(x_4|c,x_1,x_2,x_3)p(x_5|c,x_1,x_3,x_4)$.

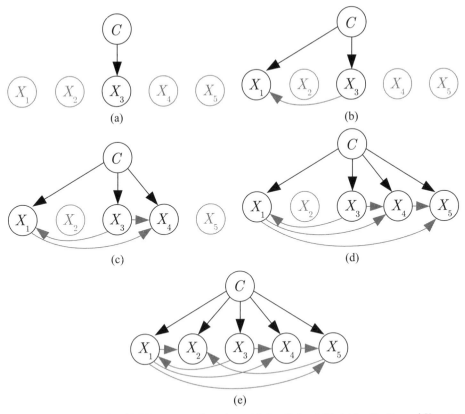

Figure 8.25 An example of k-DB structure learning with $k = 2$. (a–c) Variables X_3, X_1, and X_4 enter the model one by one, taking as parents the current predictor variables. (d) X_5 enters the model with parents X_1 and X_4. (e) X_2 enters the model with parents X_1 and X_5. This is the final k-DB structure.

allowed, X_3 becomes X_1's parent (Figure 8.25(b)). The same holds for the next variable X_4, having X_1 and X_3 as its parents (Figure 8.25(c)). When X_5 enters the model, its parents are X_1 and X_4 (Figure 8.25(d)) because $\mathbb{I}(X_4, X_5|C) > \mathbb{I}(X_1, X_5|C) > \mathbb{I}(X_3, X_5|C)$. Finally, X_2 enters the model, and $\mathbf{Pa}(X_2) \setminus \{C\} = \{X_5, X_1\}$ (Figure 8.25(e)). ∎

The main disadvantages of the standard k-DB are that it does not include feature selection (all the original predictor variables are included in the final model), and it is necessary to determine the optimal value for k. In addition, once k has been fixed, the number of parents of each predictor variable is inflexible. Note that the first k variables entering the model will have fewer than k parents (the first variable entering the model has no parents, the second variable has one parent, and so on), and the remaining $n - k$ variables have exactly k parents.

To compensate for the missing feature selection, filter and wrapper approaches to k-DB are followed in Blanco et al. (2005). In the filter approach, an initial step selects the predictor variables for which a χ^2 test of independence based on the mutual information $\mathbb{I}(C, X_i)$ is rejected. Then the standard k-DB algorithm is applied on this reduced subset, considering only those arcs that pass an analogous independence test based on the conditional mutual information $\mathbb{I}(X_i, X_j|C)$. In the wrapper approach, as in the wrapper TAN approach discussed above, the decision whether to add a new predictor or to create an arc between two predictors already in the model is guided by accuracy, provided that the added arc does not violate the k-DB restrictions. Consequently, all the predictors in the structures output by this wrapper approach have at most k parents, but there are not necessarily $n - k$ variables with exactly k parents. In general, graphs where each node has at most k parents are called k-**graphs**. Some relevant references for learning k-graphs are Carvalho et al. (2007), Xiao et al. (2009), and Pernkopf and Bilmes (2010).

8.4.1.6 *Bayesian Network Augmented Naive bayes*

The **Bayesian network augmented naive Bayes** (BAN), a term first coined by Friedman et al. (1997), has any Bayesian network structure as the predictor subgraph (Figure 8.26). Thus, the number of parents, k, which we have in a k-DB, is relaxed. The factorization is

$$p(c|\mathbf{x}) \propto p(c) \prod_{i=1}^{n} p(x_i|\mathbf{pa}(x_i)).$$

Varando et al. (2015) derived theoretically the decision boundaries of BAN classifiers. The first reference to a learning algorithm for this model is Ezawa and Norton (1996). First, the n predictor variables are ranked based on $\mathbb{I}(X_i, C)$, and then we select the minimum number of predictor variables k satisfying $\sum_{j=1}^{k} \mathbb{I}(X_j, C) \geq t_{CX} \sum_{j=1}^{n} \mathbb{I}(X_j, C)$, where $0 < t_{CX} < 1$ is the threshold. Second, $\mathbb{I}(X_i, X_j|C)$ is computed for all pairs of the selected variables. The edges corresponding to the highest values are selected until a percentage t_{XX} of the overall conditional mutual information $\sum_{i<j}^{k} \mathbb{I}(X_i, X_j|C)$ is surpassed. Edge directionality is based on the variable ranking of the first step: higher-ranked variables point toward lower-ranked variables. Note that this algorithm resembles the initial proposal for learning a k-DB model (Sahami, 1996), see Section 8.4.1.5.

Because the predictor graph is a Bayesian network, we can use any existing Bayesian network structure learning algorithm to learn that graph. The learning strategies fall into two categories: testing conditional independencies (constraint-based techniques [Spirtes et al., 1993]) and searching the space of models guided by a score to be optimized (score + search techniques [Cooper and Herskovits, 1992]). They can also be combined in hybrid techniques. These are detailed in Section 13.3.2. An example of the first approach based on conditional independence tests is Cheng and Greiner (1999), whereas Friedman et al. (1997), van Gerven and Lucas (2004), and Pernkopf and O'Leary (2003) use a score + search technique.

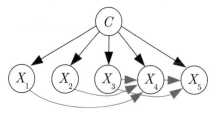

Figure 8.26 A Bayesian network augmented naive Bayes structure for which $p(c|\mathbf{x}) \propto p(c)p(x_1|c)$ $p(x_2|c)p(x_3|c)p(x_4|c,x_1,x_2,x_3)p(x_5|c,x_3,x_4)$.

8.4.1.7 Markov Blanket-Based Bayesian Classifier

If C can have parents, we do not have an augmented naive Bayes model. Equation (8.25) is

$$p(c|\mathbf{x}) \propto p(c|\mathbf{pa}(c)) \prod_{i=1}^{n} p(x_i|\mathbf{pa}(x_i)).$$

The Markov blanket of C is the only knowledge needed to predict its behavior (see Equation (8.26)), and some classifiers have been designed to search for this blanket, that is, Bayesian classifiers based on identifying the Markov blanket of the class variable. Again, we can use constraint-based or score + search techniques.

We start with constraint-based techniques. Finding the Markov blanket of C (Figure 8.27), $\mathbf{MB}(C)$, can be stated as a feature selection problem, where we start from the set of all the predictor variables and eliminate a variable at each step (backward greedy strategy) until we have approximated $\mathbf{MB}(C)$. A feature is eliminated if it gives little or no additional information about C beyond what is subsumed by the remaining features. This is the idea in Koller and Sahami (1996), which eliminates feature by feature trying to keep $p(C|\mathbf{MB}^{(t)}(C))$, the conditional probability of C given the current estimation of the Markov blanket at step t, as close to $p(C|\mathbf{X})$ as possible. Closeness is defined by the expected Kullback–Leibler divergence (Section 3.6.5).

Alternatively, starting from an empty Markov blanket, we can add variable by variable using forward selection. A variable X_i is added as long as the Markov blanket property of C is violated, i.e., when X_i and C are conditionally dependent given the current Markov blanket of C, $\mathbf{CMB}(C)$, denoted as $\neg I_p(C, X_i|\mathbf{CMB}(C))$, until there are no more such variables. This is based on the observation that if $X_i \notin \mathbf{MB}(C)$ then $I_p(C, X_i|\mathbf{MB}(C))$ holds, that is, C and X_i are conditionally independent under p given $\mathbf{MB}(C)$. This addition step is the growing phase of the **grow-shrink (GS) Markov blanket algorithm** (Margaritis and Thrun, 2000). Many false positives may have entered the $\mathbf{MB}(C)$ during the growing phase. Thus, the second phase identifies and removes the variables that are independent of C given the other variables in the $\mathbf{MB}(C)$ one by one (shrinking phase). Orientation rules are then applied to this Markov blanket to get its directed version. GS is the first correct Markov blanket induction algorithm under the faithfulness assumption, i.e., it returns the true $\mathbf{MB}(C)$. GS is scalable because it outputs the Markov blanket of C without learning a Bayesian network for all variables $\mathbf{X}$ and C. GS has to condition on at least as many variables simultaneously as the Markov blanket size, and it is therefore impractical, because it requires a sample that grows exponentially to this size if the conditional independence tests are to be reliable. This means that GS is not data efficient. A randomized version of the GS algorithm with members of the conditioning set chosen randomly from $\mathbf{CMB}(C)$ is also proposed as a faster and more reliable variant.

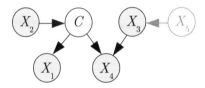

Figure 8.27 A Markov blanket structure for C for which $p(c|\mathbf{x}) \propto p(c|x_2)p(x_1|c)p(x_2)p(x_3)$ $p(x_4|c,x_3)$. The Markov blanket of C is $\mathbf{MB}(C) = \{X_1, X_2, X_3, X_4\}$.

Modified versions of this algorithm are the incremental association Markov boundary (IAMB) algorithm (Tsamardinos and Aliferis, 2003), the InterIAMBnPC algorithm (Tsamardinos et al., 2003a), the fast-IAMB (Yaramakala and Margaritis, 2005), the HITON algorithm (Aliferis et al., 2003), the max-min Markov blanket algorithm (Tsamardinos et al., 2003b), and the **parents and children based Markov boundary** (PCMB) algorithm (Peña et al., 2007). The PCMB incorporates the so-called symmetry correction. The parents-children relationship is symmetric in the sense that X_i belongs to the set of parents and children of C, and C should also belong to the set of parents and children of X_i. A breach of this symmetry is a sign of a false positive member in the Markov blanket. This leads to the first algorithm that is correct, scalable, and data efficient.

A common assumption in all these algorithms is that $\mathcal{D}$ is a sample from a probability distribution p faithful to a DAG representing a Bayesian network. Few algorithms have tried to relax this assumption, proposing weaker conditions that do not guarantee the Markov blanket being unique.

As far as using score + search techniques is concerned, the search can be guided wrapper-wise using classification accuracy as the score. An example is given in Sierra and Larrañaga (1998), where the search is performed by means of a genetic algorithm. Each individual in the population represents a Markov blanket structure for C. For small samples, a bootstrap procedure for determining membership in the Markov blanket is proposed in Friedman et al. (1999a).

8.4.1.8 Unrestricted Bayesian Classifiers

General **unrestricted Bayesian classifiers** do not consider C as a special variable in the induction process (Figure 8.28), where any existing Bayesian network structure learning algorithm can be used. The corresponding Markov blanket of C can be used later for classification purposes. Equation (8.25) is the same as for the Markov blanket-based Bayesian classifier.

The complexity of algorithms that learn Bayesian networks from data identifying high-scoring structures in which each node has at most k parents, for all $k \geq 3$, has been shown to be NP-hard (Chickering et al., 2004). This holds whenever the learning algorithm uses a consistent scoring criterion and is applied to a sufficiently large data set. This justifies the use of search heuristics.

The **K2-attribute selection** (K2-AS) algorithm (Provan and Singh, 1995) consists of two main steps. The node selection phase chooses the set of nodes from which the final network is built. In the network construction phase, the network is built with those nodes. Nodes are selected incrementally by adding the variable whose inclusion results in the maximum increase in accuracy (of the resulting network). Using these selected variables

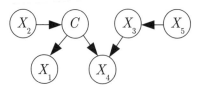

Figure 8.28 An unrestricted Bayesian network classifier structure for which $p(c|\mathbf{x}) \propto p(c|x_2)p(x_1|c)$ $p(x_2)p(x_3|x_5)p(x_4|c,x_3)p(x_5)$.

the final network is built using the **CB algorithm** (Singh and Valtorta, 1995). This algorithm uses conditional independence tests to generate a "good" node ordering and then uses the K2 algorithm (see Section 13.3.2) on that ordering to induce the Bayesian network. A variant of K2-AS is **Info-AS** (Singh and Provan, 1996). The two algorithms differ only as to node selection being guided by a conditional information-theoretic metric (conditional information gain, conditional gain ratio, or complement of conditional distance). A simpler approach is to use a node ordering for the K2 algorithm given by the ranking of variables yielded with a score (like information gain or chi-squared score) as in Hruschka and Ebecken (2007).

8.4.1.9 *Bayesian Multinets*

Bayesian networks are unable to encode *asymmetric* independence assertions in their topology, that is, conditional independence relationships only hold for some but not all the values of the variables involved. **Bayesian multinets** (Geiger and Heckerman, 1996) offer a solution. They consist of several (local) Bayesian networks associated with a subset of a partition of the domain of a variable H, called the hypothesis or distinguished variable, that is, each local network represents a joint probability of all variables (but H) conditioned on a specific subset of H values. As a result of this conditioning, asymmetric independence assertions are represented in each local network topology. Consequently, structures are expected to be simpler, with computational and memory requirement savings. Although the typical setting is when H is a root node, other situations are addressed in Geiger and Heckerman (1996): H is a non-root node, and there is more than one variable representing hypotheses.

For classification problems, the distinguished variable is naturally the class variable C. All subsets of the C domain partition are commonly singletons. Thus, conditioned on each c, the predictors can form different local networks with different structures. Therefore, the relations among variables do not have to be the same for all c. Equation (8.25) is, for Bayesian multinets, given by

$$p(c|\mathbf{x}) \propto p(c) \prod_{i=1}^{n} p(x_i|\mathbf{pa}_c(x_i)),$$

where $\mathbf{Pa}_c(X_i)$ is the parent set of X_i in the local Bayesian network associated with $C = c$, see Figure 8.14, right. Therefore, a Bayesian multinet is defined via its local Bayesian networks and the prior distribution on C.

Bayesian multinets whose local Bayesian networks are trees or forests are the most common. We mentioned a multinet with trees (Chow and Liu, 1968) in the TAN section (Section 8.4.1.4). It uses only the cases from $\mathcal{D}$ satisfying $C = c$ to build each tree. Rather than trees, a collection of forests, one for each value c of the class, is built in Pham et al. (2002). Figure 8.29 shows an example of these two types of Bayesian multinets.

Trees are also used in Kłopotek (2005), although their learning is based on a new algorithm designed for very large data sets rather than Kruskal's algorithm. The trees in Huang et al. (2003) are learned by optimizing a function that includes a penalty term representing the divergence between the different joint distributions defined at each local network. Finally, the trees in Gurwicz and Lerner (2006) are learned from all cases, instead of learning the local structures from only those cases with $C = c$. The process is guided by a score that simultaneously detects class patterns and rejects patterns of the other classes.

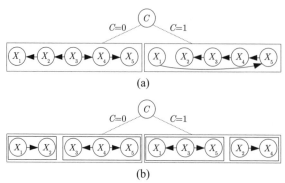

Figure 8.29 (a) Bayesian multinet as a collection of trees (Chow and Liu, 1968):
$p(C = 0|\mathbf{x}) \propto p(C = 0)p(x_1|C = 0,x_2)p(x_2|C = 0,x_3)p(x_3|C = 0)p(x_4|C = 0,x_3)p(x_5|C = 0,x_4)$
and $p(C = 1|\mathbf{x}) \propto p(C = 1)p(x_1|C = 1)p(x_2|C = 1,x_3)p(x_3|C = 1,x_4)p(x_4|C = 1,x_5)p(x_5|C = 1,x_1)$. (b) Bayesian multinet as a collection of forests (Pham et al., 2002):
$p(C = 0|\mathbf{x}) \propto p(C = 0)p(x_1|C = 0)p(x_2|C = 0,x_1)p(x_3|C = 0,x_4)p(x_4|C = 0)p(x_5|C = 0,x_4)$ and
$p(C = 1|\mathbf{x}) \propto p(C = 1)p(x_1|C = 1,x_3)p(x_2|C = 1)p(x_3|C = 1)p(x_4|C = 1,x_2)p(x_5|C = 1,x_3)$.

Thus, for the local network for $C = c$, the score of $\mathbf{x}$ with true class value c is higher when $p(C = c|\mathbf{x}) \geq p(C = c'|\mathbf{x}), \forall c' \neq c$, and the score of $\mathbf{x}$ with true class value $c' \neq c$ is higher when $p(C = c'|\mathbf{x}) \geq p(C = c|\mathbf{x})$. The search is based on the hill-climbing algorithm described in Keogh and Pazzani (2002), mentioned in the TAN section.

Other researchers use general unrestricted Bayesian networks for the local structures (Friedman et al., 1997). The approach taken in Hussein and Santos (2004) is different because the data are not partitioned according to $C = c$. The training data are first partitioned into clusters, from which a set of rules characterizing their cases are derived. Then a local Bayesian network is learned from the cases satisfying the rules. This is why the resulting models are called **case-based Bayesian network classifiers**, capturing case-dependent relationships, a generalization of hypothesis-specific relationships.

Some relevant papers (Friedman et al., 1997; Cheng and Greiner, 1999, 2001; Pernkopf, 2005; Madden, 2009) do include empirical comparisons of the algorithms for learning naive Bayes, TAN, BAN, unrestricted Bayesian classifiers, and Bayesian multinets. They all use data sets from the UCI machine learning repository (Bache and Lichman, 2013). The general findings are that more complex structures perform better whenever the sample size is large enough to guarantee reliable probability estimates. Additionally, smoothing parameter estimation (as Equation (8.27)) can significantly improve the classification rate.

8.4.1.10 Summary of Discrete Bayesian Network Classifiers
Table 8.7 shows the discrete Bayesian network classifiers hierarchized by rows, whereas the columns give an example of their graphical structure and the associated seminal paper.

8.4.1.11 Example: Interneurons versus Pyramidal Neurons
As with previous non-probabilistic (Chapter 7) and probabilistic (this chapter) classifiers, we employ Bayesian network classifiers to distinguish between interneurons and pyramidal neurons. Naive Bayes, TAN, and BAN models were used. These classifiers assume all variables are discrete and therefore, a previous discretization by simple binning in 10 equal-width intervals was performed on the continuous variables.

Table 8.7 Summary of discrete Bayesian network classifiers and their most relevant references

Name	Structure	Seminal paper
Naive Bayes		Maron and Kuhns (1960)
Selective naive Bayes		Langley and Sage (1994b)
Semi-naive Bayes		Pazzani (1996)
Tree-augmented naive Bayes		Friedman et al. (1997)
Forest augmented naive Bayes		Lucas (2004)
Superparent-one-dependence estimator		Keogh and Pazzani (2002)
k-dependence Bayesian classifier		Sahami (1996)
Bayesian network augmented naive Bayes		Ezawa and Norton (1996)
Markov blanket-based classifiers Bayesian		Koller and Sahami (1996)
Unrestricted Bayesian classifier		Provan and Singh (1995)
Bayesian multinet		Geiger and Heckerman (1996)

Table 8.8 Classification accuracy of different Bayesian network classifiers for Data Set 1 (# means the number of variables included in the model)

FSS	Naive Bayes		TAN		BAN	
	Accuracy	#	Accuracy	#	Accuracy	#
None	0.8196	65	0.8287	65	0.8379	65
Gain ratio	0.8043	15	0.8257	15	0.8257	15
CFS	0.8318	17	0.8593	17	0.8563	17
Wrapper	0.8287	8	**0.9144**	25	0.9052	13

Table 8.9 Main performance measures of a selective TAN for Data Set 1; a wrapper approach selected 25 variables out of 65

Measure	Value
Accuracy	0.9144
Sensitivity	0.9447
Specificity	0.8672
F_1-measure	0.9307
Cohen's kappa	0.8188
Brier score	0.1485
AUC	0.9499

As usually, we tried models including all the variables and reduced models selecting features. The latter give rise to the corresponding selective models. The FSS techniques were the same again: two filter approaches (univariate based on the gain ratio of a variable with respect to the class and the CFS multivariate filter) and a wrapper approach. All of them were run with WEKA (Hall et al., 2009) software, with the classifiers NaiveBayesSimple, TAN and BayesNet. Table 8.8 lists the classification accuracy of all these combinations of models.

Selecting variables seems to improve accuracy, especially using CFS and the wrapper approach. The best performing classifier is the selective TAN with 25 variables obtained with a wrapper approach (similar to Keogh and Pazzani [2002]), with 91.44% accuracy. Let us analyze this model in further detail. Table 8.9 shows the main performance measures, estimated with 10-fold stratified cross-validation.

The confusion matrix, with real labels in rows and predicted labels in columns, is

$$\begin{array}{cc} & \begin{array}{cc} \text{I} & \text{P} \end{array} \\ \begin{array}{c} \text{I} \\ \text{P} \end{array} & \begin{pmatrix} 188 & 11 \\ 17 & 111 \end{pmatrix} \end{array}.$$

A standard cutoff value of 0.5 has been used. In logistic regression we also obtained the same numbers for the interneuron classification (the same first row and the same sensitivity). This does not mean that both models make the same mistakes. However, pyramidal neurons are more correctly classified with this TAN model, with only 17 errors.

Neurons $\mathbf{x}^3$ and $\mathbf{x}^{327}$, which LDA misclassified (see Figure 8.9), were correctly classified by this TAN model (and by logistic regression). TAN classified neurons $\mathbf{x}^{34}$, $\mathbf{x}^{144}$, and

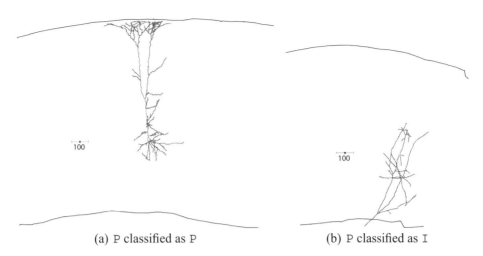

(a) P classified as P   (b) P classified as I

Figure 8.30 Some neurons and their classification by TAN. (a) Pyramidal neuron $\mathbf{x}^{216}$ correctly classified by TAN, but misclassified by logistic regression. (b) Pyramidal neuron $\mathbf{x}^{214}$ incorrectly classified by TAN, but correctly classified by logistic regression. Axonal arbor in blue and dendritic tree in red. For the color version, please refer to the plate section.

$\mathbf{x}^{220}$, shown in Figure 8.13, the same as logistic regression. In contrast, in Figure 8.30 we have two examples where classifications made by TAN and logistic regression differ. In (a), the pyramidal neuron $\mathbf{x}^{216}$ was correctly classified by the TAN model with $p(C = \text{I}|\mathbf{x}) = 0.162$, whereas it was misclassified as an interneuron by the logistic regression, with $p(C = \text{I}|\mathbf{x}) = 0.891$. The opposite situation arises in (b). The pyramidal neuron $\mathbf{x}^{214}$ was correctly classified by logistic regression (although with $p(C = \text{I}|\mathbf{x}) = 0.497$) and misclassified as an interneuron by the TAN model with $p(C = \text{I}|\mathbf{x}) = 0.697$.

Figure 8.31 shows the structure of this TAN model. Although variables should be named as X_i^d because they have been discretized, for the sake of simplicity the figure maintains the X_i notation. Colors refer to features related to dendrites (light gray), axon (gray), and soma (black). Their meaning can be found in Tables 1.5 and 1.6. The tree, rooted at X_{40} (Total surface area of dendrites) is easily observed through the gray arrows.

Some relationships are worth mentioning. Total surface area of dendrites (X_{40}) is related to the Highest order dendritic segment (X_{42}) and to the Convex hull dendrite surface area (X_{63}). Average tortuosity of dendritic segments (X_{50}) is related to Dendritic torsion ratio (X_{43}, its child) and to Average tortuosity of dendritic nodes (X_{54}, its parent). Total axonal length (X_8) is related to the Axonal node total (X_7). Somatic aspect ratio (X_3) and Somatic compactness (X_4) are also related. All these relationships are between variables from the same part of the neuron (soma, dendrite, or axon). Note that there are other relationships of variables from two different parts, for example, Ratio of dendritic length to surface area (X_{41}) and Ratio of axonal length to surface area (X_{10}).

The probabilistic part of the model allows further inspection of these relationships. As an example, Table 8.10 shows the probabilities attached to the root node of the tree, i.e., $p(X_{40}^d = i|C = \text{I})$ and $p(X_{40}^d = i|C = \text{P}), i = 1, \ldots, 10$, where X_{40}^d is the discretized variable obtained from X_{40} using 10 equal-width intervals. Note how the distribution of the total surface area of dendrites varies from interneurons to pyramidal neurons,

Table 8.10 Conditional probability table of X_{40}^d (discretized Total surface area of dendrites) given C. The discretization was 10 equal-width intervals (first column); X_{40} is measured in μm^2

Intervals for X_{40}	i	$p(X_{40}^d = i \mid C = \text{I})$	$p(X_{40}^d = i \mid C = \text{P})$
≤ 2236	1	0.3996	0.1391
(2236,4334]	2	0.3603	0.3421
(4334,6432]	3	0.1348	0.2368
(6432,8530]	4	0.0564	0.0940
(8530,10627]	5	0.0123	0.0714
(10627,12725]	6	0.0123	0.0263
(12725,14823]	7	0.0024	0.0639
(14823,16921]	8	0.0171	0.0113
(16921,19019]	9	0.0024	0.0038
>19019	10	0.0024	0.0113

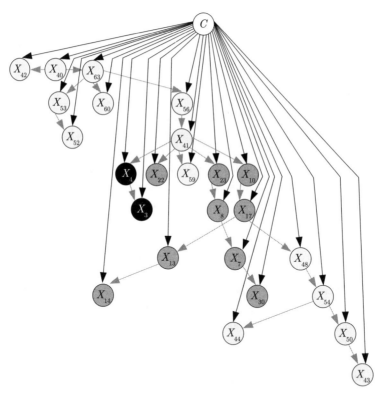

Figure 8.31 The selective TAN model structure obtained with a wrapper approach. Colors identify features related to dendrites (light gray), axon (gray), and soma (black).

especially in regard to the smallest areas (less than 2,236 μm^2), which are more frequent for interneurons.

Finally, Figure 8.32 represents in (conditional) histograms the predicted probabilities for each subsample given by the class value: interneurons in dark gray (left histogram) or pyramidal cells in light gray (right histogram). Compared to Figures 8.8 and 8.12, these histograms are clearer, with very high predicted probabilities of being an interneuron for

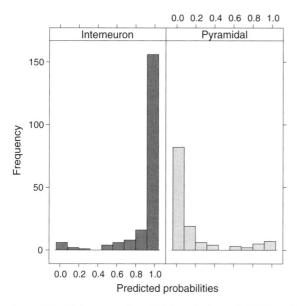

Figure 8.32 Histograms of predicted posterior probabilities $p(C = \mathrm{I}|\mathbf{x})$ yielded by the TAN model for Data Set 1.

the real interneurons and very low predicted probabilities of being an interneuron for the real pyramidal neurons.

8.4.2 Continuous Bayesian Network Classifiers

This section covers Bayesian classifiers for continuous predictor variables. Some of these classifiers assume conditional Gaussian densities for the predictors, but other approaches do not.

8.4.2.1 Gaussian Predictors

The classifiers discussed in this section are adaptations of discrete predictor classifiers and were introduced in Pérez et al. (2006).

Gaussian Naive Bayes Classifier. This model (Friedman et al., 1998a) assumes that the class-conditional density function of each predictor variable X_i, given a value of the class variable, c, is Gaussian, that is, $X_i|C = c \sim \mathcal{N}(x_i|\mu_{c,i}, \sigma_{c,i})$ for all $i = 1, \ldots, n; c = 1, \ldots, R$. The Gaussian naive Bayes classifier assigns to each instance $\mathbf{x}$ the value c^* satisfying:

$$c^* = \arg\max_c p(c) \prod_{i=1}^{n} \left[\frac{1}{\sqrt{2\pi}\sigma_{c,i}} e^{-\frac{1}{2}\left(\frac{x_i-\mu_{c,i}}{\sigma_{c,i}}\right)^2} \right].$$

The total number of parameters to be estimated is given by $(R-1)+2nR$, and they refer to the a priori probabilities of the class variable in addition to the mean and standard deviation of each predictor variable for each value of the class variable. Maximum likelihood is usually used for estimations.

This model is equivalent to a particular case of a quadratic discriminant analysis (Section 8.2.3) with a diagonal covariance matrix $\boldsymbol{\Sigma}_c$ for each class c.

The **filter selective Gaussian naive Bayes classifier** version induces the classifier with the subset of variables $\{X_{(1)}, \ldots, X_{(h)}\}$, where h is the last order for which $\mathbb{I}(X, C) > t$, and t denotes the a priori fixed threshold for the selection of variables.

Gaussian naive Bayes was used to classify the cognitive state of a human subject based on fRMI data (Mitchell et al., 2004), whereas Gaussian and discrete naive Bayes classified interneurons based on morphological measures from 3D reconstructions (DeFelipe et al., 2013).

A **filter-wrapper selective Gaussian naive Bayes classifier** can be developed based on the mutual information between a normal density variable, X_i, and a categorical variable, C, computed as

$$\mathbb{I}(X_i, C) = \frac{1}{2} \left[\log_2 \left(\sigma_i^2 - \sum_{c=1}^{R} p(c) \log_2 (\sigma_{c,i})^2 \right) \right],$$

where σ_i^2 is the variance of variable X_i. First, $\mathbb{I}(X_i, C)$ is computed for each predictor variable, and this information is used to sort the predictor variables in descending order of mutual information. In this step, the set of predictor variables is initialized to the empty set, and all instances are classified in the most frequent class. In a second step, variables are added one by one in order of mutual information to the set of predictor variables, and the accuracy of the model is estimated. The final step outputs the selective classifier associated with the feature subset that has achieved the best estimated accuracy in the search process.

Gaussian Semi-Naive Bayes Classifier. This classifier directly applies the semi-naive Bayes classifiers outlined above. The conditional density for each joint variable $\mathbf{Y}$ with m components is given by $f(\mathbf{y}|c) = (2\pi)^{-\frac{1}{2}m} |\boldsymbol{\Sigma}_c|^{-\frac{1}{2}} e^{-\frac{1}{2}(\mathbf{y}-\boldsymbol{\mu}_c)^T (\boldsymbol{\Sigma}_c)^{-1}(\mathbf{y}-\boldsymbol{\mu}_c)}$, where $\boldsymbol{\Sigma}_c$ and $\boldsymbol{\mu}_c$ are the covariance matrix and mean vector of $\mathbf{Y}$ conditioned on a class value c, respectively. The forward sequential selection and joining and the backward sequential elimination and joining algorithms are applicable in this setting.

A novel model proposed in Pérez et al. (2006) is the **wrapper condensed backward semi-naive Bayes**, which is a wrapper greedy backward algorithm using a selection of the predictor variables as a multidimensional joint Gaussian at each step. At the beginning, all predictor variables belong to the multidimensional joint Gaussian. At each step of the algorithm, one variable is chosen for exclusion. This process is repeated until further removals fail to improve accuracy.

Gaussian Tree-Augmented Naive Bayes Classifier. A filter version was proposed in Pérez et al. (2006) by simply adapting the TAN classifier put forward in Friedman et al. (1997) to the situation where X_i and X_j, conditioned on each value c of variable C, follow a bivariate normal density. Under this assumption, the conditional mutual information between X_i and X_j given C is computed as

$$\mathbb{I}(X_i, X_j | C) = -\frac{1}{2} \sum_{c=1}^{R} p(c) \log_2 (1 - \rho_c^2(X_i, X_j)),$$

where $\rho_c^2(X_i, X_j)$ denotes the correlation coefficient of X_i and X_j when $C = c$.

A wrapper version can be obtained by adapting the algorithm in Keogh and Pazzani (2002).

Gaussian k-Dependence Bayesian Classifier. The adaptation of the algorithm by Sahami (1996) is called **Gaussian filter k-dependence Bayesian classifier** in Pérez et al. (2006). The **Gaussian wrapper k-dependence Bayesian classifier** is a greedy forward approach guided by accuracy. In each step it chooses the best option between: (a) considering each variable that should be but is not included in the model as a new predictor conditionally independent of the other predictor variables given the class; and (b) including an arc between predictor variables already included in the model as long as its inclusion fulfills the k-dependence Bayesian classifier structure. The inclusion of the arcs continues until neither option further improves accuracy.

Gaussian Mixture Model Classifier. A **Gaussian mixture model** (Day, 1969) is an example of a finite mixture model (Section 12.2) (McLachlan and Peel, 2000), where a mixture of several Gaussian distributions is used to fit the density of the sample data when the fitting provided by a single density is not good enough. The probability density function in a Gaussian mixture model is defined as a weighted sum of Gaussians:

$$g(\mathbf{x}|\boldsymbol{\theta}) = \sum_{k=1}^{K} \pi_k f(\mathbf{x}|\theta_k),$$

where π_k is the weight of component k, $0 < \pi_k < 1$ for all components, $\sum_{k=1}^{K} \pi_k = 1$, and $f(\mathbf{x}|\theta_k)$ denotes a $\mathcal{N}(\mathbf{x}|\boldsymbol{\mu}_k, \boldsymbol{\Sigma}_k)$ density. The parameter vector $\boldsymbol{\theta} = (\pi_1, \boldsymbol{\mu}_1, \boldsymbol{\Sigma}_1, \ldots, \pi_K, \boldsymbol{\mu}_K, \boldsymbol{\Sigma}_K)$ defines a particular Gaussian mixture model and is usually estimated with the expectation-maximization algorithm (Dempster et al., 1977), see Section 12.2.

Example: Fitting a Univariate and Bivariate Mixture of Gaussian Densities. Figure 8.33(a) shows the graphical representation of a two-component Gaussian mixture model fitted to the Relative distance to pia variable (X_{65}). This mixture density, $g(x_{65})$, has the following expression:

$$g(x_{65}) = 0.3943\mathcal{N}(x_{65}|0.2125, 0.0931) + 0.6057\mathcal{N}(x_{65}|0.5594, 0.1316).$$

The bivariate Gaussian mixture density fitted for Relative distance to pia (X_{65}) and Somatic compactness (X_4), $g(x_{65}, x_4)$, is shown in Figure 8.33(b)–(c) and has the following three components:

$$g(x_{65}, x_4) = 0.3325\mathcal{N}((x_{65}, x_4)|\boldsymbol{\mu}_1, \boldsymbol{\Sigma}_1) + 0.3543\mathcal{N}((x_{65}, x_4)|\boldsymbol{\mu}_2, \boldsymbol{\Sigma}_2)$$
$$+ 0.3132\mathcal{N}((x_{65}, x_4)|\boldsymbol{\mu}_3, \boldsymbol{\Sigma}_3),$$

where the mean and covariance parameters for each of the components are $\boldsymbol{\mu}_1 = (0.2366, 0.7114)^T$, $\boldsymbol{\mu}_2 = (0.5802, 0.6869)^T$, $\boldsymbol{\mu}_3 = (0.4420, 0.8282)^T$, and $\boldsymbol{\Sigma}_1 = \left(\begin{smallmatrix} 0.0098 & 0 \\ 0 & 0.0109 \end{smallmatrix}\right)$, $\boldsymbol{\Sigma}_2 = \left(\begin{smallmatrix} 0.0089 & 0 \\ 0 & 0.0120 \end{smallmatrix}\right)$, and $\boldsymbol{\Sigma}_3 = \left(\begin{smallmatrix} 0.0503 & 0 \\ 0 & 0.0021 \end{smallmatrix}\right)$. ∎

A Gaussian mixture model for the entire data set can be used for clustering the data (Part IV of this book), assigning each point $\mathbf{x}$ to the component that provides it with the highest posterior probability. This partition can be used for supervised classification, especially if

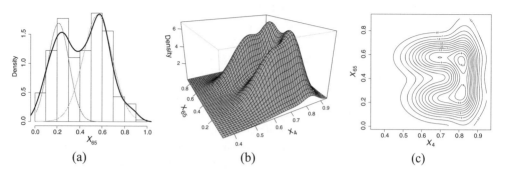

Figure 8.33 (a) Gaussian mixture model (black line) with two components (gray lines) of variable X_{65} (Relative distance to pia). (b) Joint density of variables X_{65} (Relative distance to pia) and X_4 (Somatic compactness) as a Gaussian mixture model with three components. (c) Contour plot corresponding to the density in (b).

the number of components coincides with the number of class values. In this case, any point will be assigned to the class value representing that component.

For supervised classification purposes, a more direct strategy is to fit one Gaussian mixture model for each class value (Fraley and Raftery, 2002). The posterior probability of the class variable is now computed as

$$p(c|\mathbf{x}) \propto p(c) \sum_{k=1}^{K_c} \pi_{c,k} f(\mathbf{x}|\boldsymbol{\theta}_{c,k}),$$

where $\pi_{c,k}$ is the weight of component k in class c, $0 < \pi_{c,k} < 1$, for all components in all class values, and $\sum_{k=1}^{K_c} \pi_{c,k} = 1$ for each fixed value c. $f(\mathbf{x}|\boldsymbol{\theta}_{c,k})$ follows a $\mathcal{N}(\mathbf{x}|\boldsymbol{\mu}_{c,k}, \boldsymbol{\Sigma}_{c,k})$ density. The parameters $\boldsymbol{\mu}_{c,k}$ and $\boldsymbol{\Sigma}_{c,k}$ denote the mean vector and covariance matrix, respectively, of component k in class c.

A Gaussian mixture model classifier was used in Chubb et al. (2006) to classify senile plaques and neurofibrillary tangles in several test cases of Alzheimer's brain immunostained for beta-amyloid and PHF-tau.

8.4.2.2 Non-Gaussian Predictors

A simple solution for non-Gaussian predictor variables is discretization (Section 2.6.3). Some works have studied the effect of discretization procedures in Bayesian network classifiers (Dougherty et al., 1995; Hsu et al., 2000, 2003; Yang and Webb, 2003; Flores et al., 2011b). The methods described in Section 8.4.1 can then be applied to the discretized variables. More sophisticated solutions require the approximation of the class-conditional density functions through nonparametric methods. First, we review kernel density estimation methods. Then we present a family of functions (exponentials or polynomials) defined piecewise, thereby being referred to as mixtures of truncated exponentials or mixtures of polynomials.

Finally, if the variables are angular or directional, the class-conditional densities can be fitted by von Mises or von Mises–Fisher distributions.

Kernel-Based Bayesian Classifiers. Kernel-based Bayesian classifiers use nonparametric **kernel density estimation** (Silverman, 1986) for modeling the conditional density of multidimensional continuous variables given a specific value of their parents. The general form[8] of a kernel-based n-dimensional estimator is

$$f_{\text{Kernel}}(\mathbf{x}) = \frac{1}{N} \sum_{i=1}^{N} \kappa_{\mathbf{H}}(\mathbf{x} - \mathbf{x}^i), \tag{8.32}$$

where $\mathbf{H}$ is an $n \times n$ bandwidth matrix, and $\kappa_{\mathbf{H}}$ is the kernel function. The kernel-based density estimator $f_{\text{Kernel}}(\mathbf{x})$ is determined by averaging N kernel functions $\kappa_{\mathbf{H}}(\mathbf{x} - \mathbf{x}^i)$ placed at each observation $\mathbf{x}^i$. The **kernel function** $\kappa_{\mathbf{H}}$ is defined as

$$\kappa_{\mathbf{H}}(\mathbf{x}) = |\mathbf{H}|^{\frac{1}{2}} K\left(\mathbf{H}^{\frac{1}{2}}\mathbf{x}\right),$$

where K is an n-dimensional density function. The kernel density estimate is built by centering a scaled kernel at each instance of the data set and can be seen as a sum of bumps placed at these instances. The value of the kernel estimate at point $\mathbf{x}$ is computed as the average of the N kernels at that point. An example of a kernel function is an n-dimensional Gaussian density centered at $(0, 0, \dots, 0)$ with the identity as variance-covariance matrix, that is, $K(\mathbf{x}) = (2\pi)^{-n/2} \exp\left(-\frac{1}{2}\mathbf{x}^T\mathbf{x}\right)$.

The kernel function $\kappa_{\mathbf{H}}(\mathbf{x})$ determines the shape of the aforementioned bumps. The **bandwidth matrix** $\mathbf{H}$ establishes the degree of smoothing of the kernel-based n-dimensional estimator. A good selection of $\mathbf{H}$ is crucial. For n-dimensional kernel-based estimators, the number of parameters required to specify a full bandwidth matrix is $n(n+1)/2$. As this number becomes unmanageable very quickly as n increases, a simple way to estimate $\mathbf{H}$ is using the **differential scaled** approach (Simonoff, 1996), which depends on a unique smoothing parameter h. The differential scaled method considers $\mathbf{H}$ as a diagonal matrix, whose jth element is computed as $h^2 s_j^2$, with s_j^2 being the sample standard deviation of X_j, $j = 1, \dots, n$. The **normal rule** (Silverman, 1986) is often used for determining the h value, which is fixed as

$$h = \left(\frac{4}{(m+2)N}\right)^{\frac{1}{m+4}},$$

where m is the number of continuous variables to be estimated by the kernel density. This number can differ from the total number of continuous variables in the domain, n. Figure 8.34 shows the effect of parameter h in the smoothing degree of the density function for a 1D density function based on 10 instances. For h near 0 an undersmooth effect is observed (Figure 8.34 (a)). As h increases, the kernel density estimator begins to approximate the true density (Figure 8.34 (b)). Higher values of h produce oversmooth effects (Figure 8.34 (c)).

To transform standard Bayesian classifiers (naive Bayes, tree-augmented naive Bayes, k-dependence Bayesian classifiers) into kernel-based Bayesian classifiers, it is enough to be able to compute the conditional (given the class variable) mutual information of the pairs of continuous variables ($\mathbf{X}$ and $\mathbf{Y}$) of any dimensionality. As shown by Pérez et al. (2009), this can be done with the following expression

$$\mathbb{I}(\mathbf{X}, \mathbf{Y}|C) = \sum_{c=1}^{R} p(c) \sum_{i=1}^{N_c} \log_2 \frac{f_{\text{Kernel}}(\mathbf{x}^i, \mathbf{y}^i | C = c)}{f_{\text{Kernel}}(\mathbf{x}^i | C = c) f_{\text{Kernel}}(\mathbf{y}^i | C = c)},$$

---

[8] Without considering the value of the class variable and the rest of the parents for simplicity.

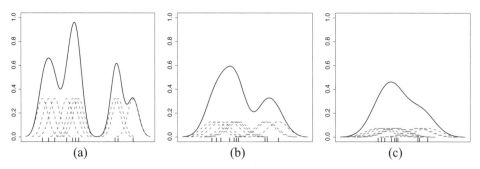

Figure 8.34 Effects in the kernel density estimator of the smoothing degree controlled by parameter h. (a) h under the optimum. (b) Close to optimum value of h. (c) h value over the optimum.

where N_c is the number of instances satisfying $C = c$, and superindex i refers to the ith instance in the partition induced by the value c of the class variable.

The adaptation to naive Bayes, which was done by John and Langley (1995), is known as **flexible naive Bayes**, whereas Pérez et al. (2009) presented the **flexible tree-augmented naive Bayes** and **flexible k-dependence Bayesian classifiers**. The **Parzen window classifier** (Parzen, 1962) can also be seen as an example of a kernel-based Bayesian classifier with a complete graph representing the relationships between continuous variables.

Mixtures of Truncated Exponentials. Given a variable X defined on Ω_X, the approximation of its density, $f(x)$, based on a **mixture of truncated exponential** (MTE) density, $f_{MTE}(x)$, is defined as an L-piece and d-term function

$$f_{MTE}(x) = \begin{cases} a_{0j} + \sum_{m=1}^{d} a_{mj}\, e^{b_{mj}x} & \text{if } x \in A_j, \quad j = 1, \dots, L \\ 0 & \text{otherwise,} \end{cases}$$

with $A_1, \dots, A_L$ being a partition of Ω_X. The parameters $a_{0j}, a_{mj}, b_{mj} \in \mathbb{R}$ for $m = 1, \dots, d; j = 1, \dots, L$. L and d represent the number of pieces (intervals), and the number of terms of the MTE, respectively.

The process of fitting an MTE density to a sample involves (a) determining the number of pieces, L, into which Ω_X will be partitioned; (b) determining the lower and upper ends for each interval, A_j; (c) determining the number of terms (number of exponential terms), d, in the function of each interval; and (d) estimating the parameters, a_{0j}, a_{mj}, b_{mj}. Options (a), (b), and (c) require a trial-and-error approach. Least squares (Rumí et al., 2006) and maximum likelihood methods (Langseth et al., 2010) have been proposed for estimation purposes.

Example: Fitting a Standardized Normal Density with an MTE. In Rumí et al. (2006) a sample of size 1,000, simulated from $\mathcal{N}(x|0,1)$, was fitted with the following 4-piece and 2-term MTE, shown in Figure 8.35:

$$f_{MTE}(x) = \begin{cases} 0.0013 + 2.6763e^{2.0995x} - 0.0004e^{0.0022x} & \text{if } x \in (-4,-1] \\ 0.4201 - 0.0253e^{-1.9593x} & \text{if } x \in (-1,0] \\ 0.4087 - 0.0138e^{2.6184x} & \text{if } x \in (0,1] \\ 0.0076 + 2.2257e^{-2.0417x} + 0.0049e^{0.0076x} & \text{if } x \in (1,4]. \end{cases}$$

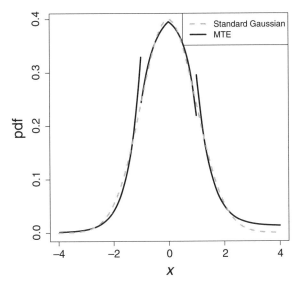

Figure 8.35 Simulation of a standard Gaussian density and the fitted MTE model from a sample of size 1,000, adapted from Rumí et al. (2006).

The use of MTEs for supervised classification has been proposed for naive Bayes (Rumí et al., 2006) and AODEs (Flores et al., 2011a). Thus, the **MTE-naive Bayes classifier** needs to fit for each predictor variable, X_i, a conditional MTE density model for each value c of the class variable. The posterior probability of the class variable is

$$p_{\text{MTE-naiveBayes}}(c|\mathbf{x}) \propto p(c) \prod_{i=1}^{n} f_{\text{MTE}}(x_i|c),$$

where $f_{\text{MTE}}(x_i|c)$ is $a_{0j,c,i} + \sum_{m=1}^{d} a_{mj,c,i} e^{b_{mj,c,i} x}$ in partition j of X_i, given a value c of the class variable. $a_{0j,c,i}, a_{mj,c,i}$, and $b_{mj,c,i}$ represent its parameters.

The **MTE-AODE classifier** is based on an MTE approximation of $f(x_i|x_j,c)$ for every pair of predictor variables, X_i and X_j. The variables in the conditioning part are discretized. Denoting by X_j^d the discretization of variable X_j, for each of the MTE-SPODE classifiers, from which the MTE-AODE classifier is derived (see Section 8.4.1.4), it is necessary to fit a conditional MTE for X_i given each possible combination of x_j^d and c.

Mixtures of Polynomials. Let X be a 1D continuous random variable with probability density $f(x)$. Shenoy and West (2011) defined a 1D **mixture of polynomial** (MoP) approximation of $f(x)$ over a closed domain $\Omega_X = [\varepsilon, \xi] \subset \mathbb{R}$ as an L-piece d-degree piecewise function of the form

$$\varphi(x) = \begin{cases} \text{pol}_j(x) & \text{if } x \in A_j, \, j = 1, \dots, L \\ 0 & \text{otherwise,} \end{cases} \tag{8.33}$$

where $\text{pol}_j(x) = b_{0j} + b_{1j}x + b_{2j}x^2 + \cdots + b_{dj}x^d$ is a polynomial function of degree d (and order $r = d + 1$), $b_{0j}, \dots, b_{dj} \in \mathbb{R}$ are constants, and $A_1, \dots, A_L$ constitute a partition of Ω_X.

The MoP approximation can be learned from data using **B-spline interpolation**. As opposed to previously proposed methods, like Taylor series (Shenoy and West, 2011) or Lagrange interpolation (Shenoy, 2012), the use of B-splines does not assume any prior knowledge about the true density underlying the data. Additionally, it ensures that the resulting MoP approximation is continuous, is nonnegative, and integrates to one.

B-splines or basis splines (Schoenberg, 1946) are polynomial curves that form a basis for the space of piecewise polynomial functions over a closed domain $\Omega_X = [\varepsilon, \xi] \subset \mathbb{R}$. Therefore, any piecewise polynomial function can be written as a linear combination of B-splines. A method for finding B-spline approximations of 1D and 2D probability density functions from data was proposed in Zong (2006).

Thus, given a nondecreasing knot sequence of $L+1$ real numbers $\varepsilon = a_0 \leq a_1 \leq \cdots \leq a_L = \xi$ in the approximation domain $\Omega_X = [\varepsilon, \xi]$, one can define $M = L+r-1$ different B-splines with order r spanning the entire domain Ω_X. The jth B-spline with order r, $B_j^r(x), j = 1, \ldots, M$ is written as

$$B_j^r(x) = (a_j - a_{j-r})H(x - a_{j-r}) \sum_{t=0}^{r} \frac{(a_{j-r+t} - x)^{r-1} H(a_{j-r+t} - x)}{w'_{j-r}(a_{j-r+t})}, \quad x \in \Omega_X, \quad (8.34)$$

where $w'_{j-r}(x)$ is the first derivative of $w_{j-r}(x) = \prod_{t=0}^{r}(x - a_{j-r+t})$, and $H(x)$ is the **Heaviside function**

$$H(x) = \begin{cases} 1 & x \geq 0 \\ 0 & x < 0. \end{cases}$$

B-splines have a number of interesting properties for learning MoP approximations of probability densities: (a) each B-spline, $B_j^r(x)$, is right-side continuous, differentiable, positive in and zero outside the interval (a_j, a_{j-r}) (Prautzsch et al., 2002); (b) B-splines form a basis in the space of piecewise polynomials, and MoPs are piecewise polynomials; and (c) every MoP can be written as a linear combination of B-splines.

When the points in the knot sequence are equally spaced, the B-splines are called uniform. A B-spline $B_j^r(x)$ can be written as an MoP function (Equation (8.33)) with L pieces, where each piece $\text{pol}_j(x)$ is defined as the expansion of Equation (8.34) in the interval $A_j = [a_{j-1}, a_j), j = 1, \ldots, L$. Figure 8.36 shows 10 uniform B-splines defined in $\Omega_X = [0, 10]$ for orders (a) $r = 3$ and (b) $r = 4$. With the exception of the B-splines on the limits of Ω_X, we find that each B-spline is nonzero in r intervals and zero in the rest. Further, for each interval A_j, we find r nonzero B-splines.

Zong (2006) suggested using B-spline interpolation to find an approximation of the density $f(x)$ as a linear combination of $M = L+r-1$ B-splines,

$$\varphi(x; \boldsymbol{\alpha}) = \sum_{j=1}^{M} \alpha_j B_j^r(x), \quad x \in \Omega_X, \quad (8.35)$$

where $\boldsymbol{\alpha} = (\alpha_1, \ldots, \alpha_M)$ are the mixing coefficients, and $B_j^r(x), j = 1, \ldots, M$, are B-splines with order r (degree $d = r - 1$) as defined in Equation (8.34). MoPs are closed under multiplication and addition. Thus, the linear combination of M B-splines with order r (Equation (8.35)) yields an MoP function with L pieces, where each piece $\text{pol}_j(x)$ is a polynomial with order r defined in the interval A_j.

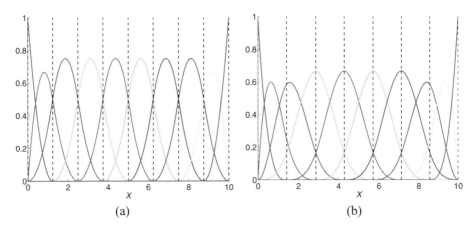

Figure 8.36 Ten uniform B-splines defined in the domain $\Omega_X = [0,10]$. Each B-spline is shown in a different color. The vertical dashed lines show the knot sequence $\{a_0, \ldots, a_L\}$, where $L = M - r + 1$ and $M = 10$ B-splines. (a) B-splines with $r = 3$. (b) B-splines with $r = 4$. Figures reproduced from López-Cruz et al. (2014a) with permission. For the color version, please refer to the plate section.

Four elements need to be specified to define an MoP using B-spline interpolation: the order, r; the number of pieces, L; the knot sequence, $\varepsilon = a_0 \le a_1 \le \cdots \le a_L = \xi$; and the mixing coefficients, $\boldsymbol{\alpha}$. The use of uniform B-splines, where the pieces, A_j, have an equal width of $a_j - a_{j-1} = \frac{\xi - \varepsilon}{L}$ facilitates the determination of the knot sequence. The values of the order, r, and the number of pieces, L, of the MoP can be found by testing different values and selecting the ones with the highest BIC score (Section 13.3.2.2), as proposed in López-Cruz et al. (2014a). The maximum likelihood estimates of the mixing coefficients, $\hat{\boldsymbol{\alpha}}$, can be computed with an iterative procedure derived by Zong (2006).

Thus, given a data set $\mathcal{D}_X = \{x_1, \ldots, x_N\}$ with N instances of variable X, the maximum likelihood estimates of the mixing coefficients are computed using the formula:

$$\hat{\alpha}_j^{(q)} = \frac{1}{N e_j} \sum_{x \in \mathcal{D}_X} \frac{\hat{\alpha}_j^{(q-1)} B_j^r(x)}{\varphi\left(x; \hat{\boldsymbol{\alpha}}^{(q-1)}\right)}, \quad j = 1, \ldots, M, \tag{8.36}$$

where q is the iteration number in the optimization process. The term e_j is defined as $e_j = \frac{a_j - a_{j-r}}{r}, j = 1, \ldots, M$. Zong (2006) showed that Equation (8.36) yields the only maximum of the log-likelihood of $\mathcal{D}_X$ given the approximation $\varphi(x; \hat{\boldsymbol{\alpha}})$. The initial values $\hat{\alpha}_j^{(0)}$ are set to $1/\sum_{j=1}^M e_j$. The relative change in the log-likelihood of $\mathcal{D}_X$ given $\varphi\left(x; \hat{\boldsymbol{\alpha}}^{(q)}\right)$ is used as a stopping criterion.

Figure 8.37 shows the MoP approximations, following the method described above, for simulations of size 1,000 from 5 theoretical probability densities.

A **naive Bayes classifier with a B-spline MoP approximation** to the conditional density of each predictor variable given each class value was presented in López-Cruz et al. (2014a). There, an extension of the maximum likelihood estimation method for the mixing coefficients to several dimensions is also introduced, allowing the development of a **tree-augmented naive Bayes classifier with a B-spline MoP approximation**.

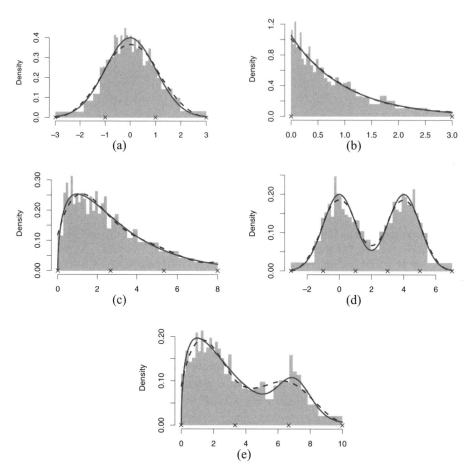

Figure 8.37 B-spline-based MoP approximations learned from a training data set of $N = 1,000$ instances. The MoP approximations are represented with dashed lines. Crosses along the horizontal axis mark the limits of the pieces for the learned MoPs. A thick solid line represents the true density used to generate the training data sets. (a) $\mathcal{N}(0,1)$. (b) $\mathrm{Exp}(1)$. (c) χ_3^2. (d) $0.5\mathcal{N}(0,1) + 0.5\mathcal{N}(4,1)$. (e) $0.8\chi_3^2 + 0.2\mathcal{N}(7,1)$. Reprinted with permission from López-Cruz et al. (2014a).

8.4.2.3 *Directional Predictors*

The consideration of linear continuous, that is, nondirectional, predictor variables is not appropriate in supervised classification problems with directional continuous predictor variables, like, for example, the angles between two segments of a dendritic tree. In this section we explain two proposals introducing directional continuous predictors that are assumed to be conditionally independent given any value of the class variable.

The von Mises Naive Bayes. A simple classification model can be obtained assuming that the class-conditional density of each directional variable follows a univariate von Mises distribution (López-Cruz et al., 2015), that is, for each of the n directional predictor variables, $\Phi_1, \Phi_2, \ldots, \Phi_n$, we have $\Phi_i | C = c \sim v\mathcal{M}(\phi_i | \mu_{c,i}, \kappa_{c,i})$.

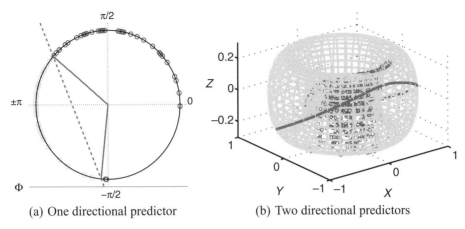

(a) One directional predictor   (b) Two directional predictors

Figure 8.38 Dark blue circles represent points for class $C = 1$, and light blue circles represent points for class $C = 2$. The solid lines in (a) show the angles defining the bounds of each class region. The dashed line is the decision line induced by the von Mises naive Bayes classifier. The quadratic decision surface for the two directional predictor variables is drawn in green in (b). Reprinted with permission from López-Cruz et al. (2015). For the color version, please refer to the plate section.

In this **von Mises naive Bayes** model, the posterior most probable class value is computed as

$$c^* = \arg\max_c p(c) \prod_{i=1}^{n} \frac{\exp(\kappa_{c,i} \cos(\phi_i - \mu_{c,i}))}{2\pi I_0(\kappa_{c,i})},$$

where $I_0(\cdot)$ is the modified Bessel function of the first kind of order 0. See Section 3.3.11 for its definition.

The von Mises naive Bayes classifier with a binary class ($c \in \{1,2\}$) and one predictive directional variable Φ is a linear classifier with the following decision line:

$$(\kappa_1 \cos \mu_1 - \kappa_2 \cos \mu_2)x + (\kappa_2 \sin \mu_1 - \kappa_2 \sin \mu_2)y + \ln \frac{p(C = 1)I_0(\kappa_2)}{p(C = 2)I_0(\kappa_1)} = 0,$$

where $(x,y) = (\cos \phi, \sin \phi)$ are the Cartesian coordinates in $\mathbb{R}^2$ of the point defined by the angle ϕ on the unit circle. The proof is given in López-Cruz et al. (2015). An illustration of this result is shown in Figure 8.38(a).

The decision surfaces for a von Mises naive Bayes classifier with two directional predictor variables and a binary class are quadratic as proven in López-Cruz et al. (2015). Figure 8.38(b) illustrates this scenario. This result contrasts with the behavior of the naive Bayes classifier for nondirectional predictors, where the decision surfaces are always linear no matter how many predictor variables there are (Section 8.4.1.1).

A **filter-wrapper selective von Mises naive Bayes** classifier, similar to the one introduced in Section 8.4.2.1, was proposed in López-Cruz et al. (2015). In this case, the mutual information between a directional and a discrete variable is estimated from the data set of cases.

The Multivariate von Mises–Fisher Naive Bayes. Predictive data points that form directional unit vectors in $\mathbb{R}^n$ can be modeled with the multidimensional von Mises–Fisher density (Section 3.4.9). We assume a different conditional von Mises–Fisher density for

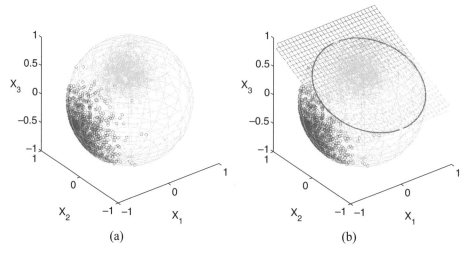

Figure 8.39 True class and class predicted using the multivariate von Mises–Fisher naive Bayes for a sample of 1,000 points. Class $C = 1$ points are shown in dark blue, whereas class $C = 2$ data are drawn in light blue. (a) True classification. (b) Class predicted by the multivariate von Mises–Fisher naive Bayes. Reprinted with permission from López-Cruz et al. (2015). For the color version, please refer to the plate section.

each value of the class variable. Thus, for a binary class ($c \in \{1, 2\}$), the classifier has only one n-dimensional predictor variable $\mathbf{X}$, and that the conditional densities $\mathbf{X}|C = c$ are assumed to follow a von Mises–Fisher distribution $v\mathcal{MF}(\mathbf{x}|\boldsymbol{\mu}_c, \kappa_c)$. The **multivariate von Mises–Fisher naive Bayes** is a linear classifier (López-Cruz et al., 2015) yielding the decision hyperplane

$$(\kappa_1 \boldsymbol{\mu}_1 - \kappa_2 \boldsymbol{\mu}_2)^T \mathbf{x} + \ln \frac{p(C = 1)(\kappa_1)^{\frac{n}{2}-1} I_{\frac{n}{2}-1}(\kappa_2)}{p(C = 2)(\kappa_2)^{\frac{n}{2}-1} I_{\frac{n}{2}-1}(\kappa_1)} = 0.$$

Figure 8.39(a) shows a set with 1,000 simulated points from $\mathbf{X}|C = 1 \sim v\mathcal{MF}(\mathbf{x}|(-1, 0, -0.2)^T, 10)$ (dark blue) and $\mathbf{X}|C = 2 \sim v\mathcal{MF}(\mathbf{x}|(-0.5, -0.5, 1)^T, 20)$ (light blue). The classes are considered equiprobable a priori. Figure 8.39(b) shows the classification, the decision hyperplane, and the circumference that bounds the class regions given by a multivariate von Mises–Fisher naive Bayes classifier.

8.4.2.4 *Mixed Predictors*

Interesting scenarios for classification arise when combining directional and nondirectional (discrete and continuous) predictor variables.

A frequent case of these hybrid approaches is when nondirectional discrete and continuous predictors are involved. Assuming that there is conditionally independence among discrete and among continuous predictor variables given the class, as well as between discrete and continuous predictors, a **naive Bayes classifier with discrete and continuous predictors** can be used.

Given a value of the class variable, the class-conditional densities of the continuous predictor variables can be modeled by means of univariate Gaussians, kernels, MTEs, or

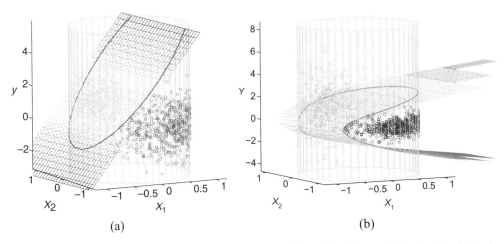

Figure 8.40 Decision surfaces for naive Bayes with conditional bivariate von Mises–Fisher, (X_1, X_2), and conditional univariate Gaussian, Y, with (a) equal variances, and (b) nonequal variances, based on a sample of 1,000 points. Class $C = 1$ points are plotted in dark blue, whereas class $C = 2$ data are plotted in light blue. Reprinted with permission from López-Cruz et al. (2015). For the color version, please refer to the plate section.

MoPs. For the case of univariate Gaussians, the class value c^* is computed as the maximum a posteriori

$$c^* = \arg\max_c p(c|\mathbf{x}, \mathbf{y}) = \arg\max_c p(c) \prod_{i=1}^{n_1} p(x_i|c) \prod_{j=1}^{n_2} \left[\frac{1}{\sqrt{2\pi}\sigma_{c,j}} e^{-\frac{1}{2}\left(\frac{y_j - \mu_{c,j}}{\sigma_{c,j}}\right)^2} \right],$$

where $\{X_1, \ldots, X_{n_1}\}$ and $\{Y_1, \ldots, Y_{n_2}\}$ denote the subsets of discrete and continuous predictor variables, respectively.

A hybrid **naive Bayes with conditional multivariate von Mises–Fisher and conditional multivariate Gaussians** for directional and continuous predictors, respectively, was introduced in López-Cruz et al. (2015). The vector of directional predictors, $\mathbf{X} = (X_1, \ldots, X_{n_1})$, is assumed to follow a multivariate von Mises–Fisher density for each value of the class variable, $\mathbf{X}|C = c \sim v\mathcal{MF}(\mathbf{x}|\boldsymbol{\mu}_{c,\mathbf{X}}, \kappa_{c,\mathbf{X}})$ whereas the nondirectional continuous predictors, $\mathbf{Y} = (Y_1, \ldots, Y_{n_2})$, have a class-conditional multivariate Gaussian density, that is, $\mathbf{Y}|C = c \sim \mathcal{N}(\mathbf{y}|\boldsymbol{\mu}_{c,\mathbf{Y}}, \boldsymbol{\Sigma}_{c,\mathbf{Y}})$. The maximum a posteriori class value, c^*, is obtained as

$$c^* = \arg\max_c p(c|\mathbf{x}, \mathbf{y})$$

$$= \arg\max_c p(c) C_{n_1}(\kappa_{c,\mathbf{X}}) \exp(\kappa_{c,\mathbf{X}} \boldsymbol{\mu}_{c,\mathbf{X}}^T \mathbf{x}) \frac{1}{(2\pi)^{n_2/2} |\boldsymbol{\Sigma}_{c,\mathbf{Y}}|^{1/2}}$$

$$\exp\left(-\frac{1}{2}(\mathbf{y} - \boldsymbol{\mu}_{c,\mathbf{Y}}) \boldsymbol{\Sigma}_{c,\mathbf{Y}}^{-1} (\mathbf{y} - \boldsymbol{\mu}_{c,\mathbf{Y}})^T\right).$$

The definition of function $C_n(\kappa)$ was given in Section 3.4.9.

A simple example of this hybrid naive Bayes includes one circular bidimensional variable $\mathbf{X} = (X_1, X_2)$ and one continuous nondirectional variable Y. A theoretical study of the decision surfaces when (a) the variance of Y is the same for each value of a binary class variable C or (b) the variances are different is shown in López-Cruz et al. (2015). The

Table 8.11 Summary of continuous Bayesian network classifiers and their most relevant references

Name	Seminal paper
Gaussian naive Bayes	Friedman et al. (1998a)
Gaussian semi-naive Bayes	Pérez et al. (2006)
Gaussian tree-augmented naive Bayes	Pérez et al. (2006)
Gaussian k-dependence Bayesian classifier	Pérez et al. (2006)
Gaussian mixture model classifier	Day (1969)
Kernel based classifiers	John and Langley (1995)
MTE-naive Bayes	Rumí et al. (2006)
MTE-AODE	Flores et al. (2011a)
MoP-naive Bayes with B-splines	López-Cruz et al. (2014a)
MoP-tree-augmented naive Bayes with B-splines	López-Cruz et al. (2014a)
von Mises naive Bayes	López-Cruz et al. (2015)
Multivariate von Mises–Fisher naive Bayes	López-Cruz et al. (2015)

decision surface is a hyperplane for (a) and a hyperquadratic curve for (b). Figure 8.40 shows the decision surfaces for a set of 1,000 simulated points in each case.

An example of a hybrid with one discrete and one class-conditional bivariate von Mises–Fisher distribution is given in López-Cruz et al. (2015).

8.4.2.5 *Summary of Continuous Bayesian Network Classifiers*

Table 8.11 shows the continuous Bayesian network classifiers and their associated seminal papers.

8.5   Bibliographic Notes

LDA. Fisher's LDA (Fisher, 1936) is slightly different from the LDA described above. Gaussianity or equal class covariances are not assumed. The method looks for the linear combination of the predictor variables, $\mathbf{w}^T\mathbf{x}$, such that the between-class scatter matrix is maximized relative to the within-class scatter matrix. The between-class scatter matrix is $\mathbf{S}_B = \sum_{r=1}^{R}(\hat{\boldsymbol{\mu}}_r - \hat{\boldsymbol{\mu}})(\hat{\boldsymbol{\mu}}_r - \hat{\boldsymbol{\mu}})^T$, where $\hat{\boldsymbol{\mu}}$ is the estimated mean vector of all data. The within-class scatter matrix is $\mathbf{S}_W = \sum_{r=1}^{R}\sum_{i:c^i=c_r}(\mathbf{x}^i - \hat{\boldsymbol{\mu}}_r)(\mathbf{x}^i - \hat{\boldsymbol{\mu}}_r)^T$. Fisher's LDA maximizes $\frac{\mathbf{w}^T\mathbf{S}_B\mathbf{w}}{\mathbf{w}^T\mathbf{S}_W\mathbf{w}}$ in $\mathbf{w}$. To classify an instance $\mathbf{x}$, we first obtain the linear combination $\mathbf{w}^T\mathbf{x}$ and then check whether this value surpasses a threshold, which is easily found for two classes, as in the one-category-versus-rest and one-versus-one methods, commonly used to solve the general multi-class setting (Section 7.5.5).

Logistic Regression. Berkson (1944) can be considered as the seminal paper. Good textbooks on logistic regression are Sharma (1996), Ryan (1997), Hosmer and Lemeshow (2000), Hastie et al. (2008), Murphy (2012), and Agresti (2013). Different methods of its parameterization, like dummy coding or full-rank center-point, are not discussed here. Also omitted is **Bayesian logistic regression**, where the parameters β_j are random variables, and one of the main tasks is to compute the posterior distribution over these variables, $p(\boldsymbol{\beta}|\mathcal{D})$. Because there is no conjugate prior, the only option is to approximate this posterior using, for example, MCMC, variational inference, or expectation propagation.

An interesting viewpoint in logistic regression is not only to maximize the likelihood, but also the area under the ROC curve (Robles et al., 2008). An original way of regularizing logistic regression without a penalty term is presented in Bielza et al. (2011c) by using evolutionary computation. A special simulation process during the evolution accounts intrinsically for the regularization. Reviews on L_1-regularization including logistic regression are Hesterberg et al. (2008) and Vidaurre et al. (2013b). Logistic regression is part of the larger family of **generalized linear models** (McCullagh and Nelder, 1989).

Bayesian Network Classifiers. Bayesian network classifiers have been viewed as generative models, creating a joint model $p(\mathbf{x}, c)$ that is then used with Bayes' rule to obtain $p(c|\mathbf{x})$ for classification. Bayesian network classifiers can also be designed as discriminative classifiers, directly modeling the posterior probability of the class variable. Generative models maximize the log-likelihood or a related function, whereas discriminative models maximize the **conditional log-likelihood** (CLL), $\sum_{i=1}^{N} \ln p\left(c^i|\mathbf{x}^i\right)$. Unfortunately, the CLL function does not decompose into a separate term for each variable, and there is no known closed-form solution for this maximization problem. This is why most works (at least in the discrete domain) use a modified or approximated CLL function (Grossman and Domingos, 2004; Burge and Lane, 2005; Guo and Greiner, 2005; Narasimhan and Bilmes, 2005; Drugan and Wiering, 2010; Carvalho et al., 2011).

Besides the structure, the parameters can also be learned discriminatively. For a fixed Bayesian network structure, the problem is to find the values for the conditional probabilities that maximize the CLL. In fact, logistic regression can be viewed as a discriminatively trained naive Bayes classifier (Agresti, 2013). See also Ng and Jordan (2002) for an empirical and theoretical comparison of the two models, where generative naive Bayes can outperform the discriminatively trained naive Bayes models for small sample sizes. In general, discriminatively trained classifiers are usually more accurate when N is high. Relevant references for discrete classifiers are Roos et al. (2005), Greiner et al. (2005), Guo et al. (2005), Feelders and Ivanovs (2006), Su et al. (2008), Pernkopf and Wohlmayr (2009), and Zaidi et al. (2013). Generative-discriminative learning, through hybrid parameter learning (partly generative and partly discriminative) and generative modeling (Raina et al., 2004; Kang and Tian, 2006; Fujino et al., 2007; Xue and Titterington, 2010), is also an option.

MTE distributions were introduced in the context of hybrid Bayesian networks (containing discrete and continuous variables) in Moral et al. (2001). Shenoy and West (2011) found MoP approximations of parametric probability density functions by computing the Taylor series expansion around the middle point of each subinterval A_j in the MoP. However, the mathematical expression of the probability density $f(x)$ needs to be known for computing the Taylor series expansion, preventing its use when the MoP should be learned from data. Later, Shenoy (2012) proposed estimating $\text{pol}_j(x)$ as Lagrange interpolating polynomials over the Chebyshev points defined in A_j. However, the true probability densities of the Chebyshev points in each A_j need to be known or estimated beforehand (e.g., using empirical histograms or kernel density estimation techniques). Lagrange interpolation can ensure nonnegativity by increasing the order of the polynomials, and continuity by putting interpolation points at the limits of the intervals. However, it cannot ensure that the resulting MoP integrates to 1.

Dynamic versions of Bayesian network classifiers have been introduced: with time discretization (van der Heijden et al., 2014) or with continuous time (Stella and Amer, 2012; Codecasa and Stella, 2014).

Bayesian network classifiers are based on Bayesian networks, and hence other related models can inspire new approaches, for example, models with cycles like dependency networks (Gámez et al., 2008) or undirected models like Markov networks (Chapter 14). Classification in data streaming situations (Castillo and Gama, 2009), with multi-labels (Chapter 10), with probabilistic labels (López-Cruz et al., 2013) or even semisupervised classification (Cohen et al., 2004), are also important issues.

9 Metaclassifiers

In Chapters 7 and 8, we discussed many different classification algorithms none of which, however, is universally the most accurate. This chapter deals with methods that train and then combine a set (or ensemble) of classifiers to solve the same classification problem. The classifiers complement each other with the aim of achieving a higher accuracy, at the expense, of course, of increased complexity. Metaclassifiers are less sensitive to noise and redundant variables than single classifiers, thereby being more unlikely to suffer from overfitting. One disadvantage of ensembles is that the combined model is not interpretable. The decision to use a metaclassifier inevitably involves a trade-off between (increased) complexity and (better) accuracy.

The main ideas for building metaclassifiers and their motivation are introduced in Section 9.1. Then Section 9.2 covers basic methods for combining the outputs of different classifiers (fusion of labels and continuous-valued outputs) to generate the final model. Section 9.3 presents the most popular metaclassifiers, namely, stacking, cascading, bagging, randomization (including random forests), boosting, and hybridizations. Section 9.4 builds a number of representative metaclassifiers learned from Data Set 1 to discriminate between interneurons and pyramidal neurons. Section 9.5 compares the accuracies given by all the best classifiers from Chapter 7, Chapter 8, and this chapter addressing the same classification problem. Finally, Section 9.6 adds some bibliographic notes. Figure 9.1 shows a temporal representation of the seminal works for the main metaclassifiers.

As in previous chapters, $\mathcal{D} = \{(\mathbf{x}^1, c^1), \ldots, (\mathbf{x}^N, c^N)\}$ denotes the (supervised) data set, where, for each $\mathbf{x}^i = (x_1^i, \ldots, x_n^i)$, $i = 1, \ldots, N$, we have its respective value c^i of a class variable denoted by C with labels in the domain $\Omega_C = \{c_1, \ldots, c_R\}$. A classifier is denoted ϕ.

9.1 Main Ideas on Metaclassifiers

It is hard to pinpoint the groundbreaking work in this field because the use of multiple models dates back a long time. In fact, we combine expert opinions (models) in our daily lives, e.g., when we seek a second medical opinion before making a final health or treatment-related decision.

Metaclassifiers, also called **multiple classifier systems**, have been a hot topic in machine learning since the 1990s and have been successful in many real-world problems. These models have won many data mining competitions many times. The most famous

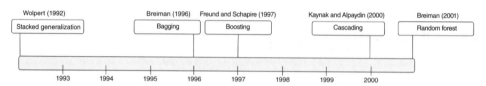

Figure 9.1 Timeline of the seminal papers for metaclassifiers.

competitions are the *KDD-Cup*[1] running annually since 1997, and the *Netflix Prize*,[2] launched in 2006, to substantially improve the accuracy of predictions about how much someone is going to enjoy a movie based on how much he liked or disliked other movies ($1,000,000 was the grand prize for the team capable of achieving a 10% accuracy improvement upon Netflix's own algorithm).

Learning is an ill-posed problem, and, with finite data, each algorithm converges to a different solution and fails under different circumstances. Learning "for free" by just looking at training instances is not possible. To solve a given classification problem, it is common practice to try several algorithms and fine-tune their hyperparameters to get the best possible performance. Still there will be instances for which even the best classifier is not accurate enough. Moreover, each algorithm relies on a set of assumptions that should hold for the data.

The **no free lunch theorem** (Wolpert and Macready, 1997) has shown that learning algorithms cannot be universally good, i.e., "any two algorithms are equivalent when their performance is averaged across all possible problems." This means that different search algorithms may yield different results for a particular problem and, nevertheless, be equivalent across all problems. Although a general-purpose universal classification algorithm is theoretically impossible, it is worthwhile in practice to make the effort to specialize the algorithm in the specific problem under consideration. The idea is that there is perhaps another algorithm that performs well for instances where the best current algorithm fails. The combination of multiple algorithms, which is not computationally expensive nowadays, can improve overall performance. The theorem name suggests that it is impossible to get something for nothing.

Example. Figure 9.2 illustrates how, by combining two classifiers, ϕ_1 (black) and ϕ_2 (gray), the resulting metaclassifier improves the overall classification accuracy. The aim is to separate crosses and dots in a feature space given by X_1 and X_2. We use two nonlinear classifiers. ϕ_1 classifies all points falling below its defining curve as a dot; otherwise the cross label is assigned. ϕ_2 classifies all points to the right of its defining curve as a dot; otherwise the cross label is assigned. ϕ_1 performs well with 70% accuracy (it hits 8 dots and 6 crosses out of 20 points), whereas ϕ_2 performs better with 80% accuracy (it hits 9 dots and 7 crosses). Observe how both classifiers differ in their decisions: e.g., the leftmost crosses are correctly classified by ϕ_2 and misclassified by ϕ_1, whereas the opposite is true for the rightmost crosses.

We now build a metaclassifier that decides to assign the dot label only when ϕ_1 and ϕ_2 predict a dot; otherwise a cross is assigned. This new classifier outperforms ϕ_1 and ϕ_2, with 90% accuracy (it hits 8 dots and all 10 crosses).   ∎

---

[1] www.kdd.org.
[2] www.netflixprize.com/.

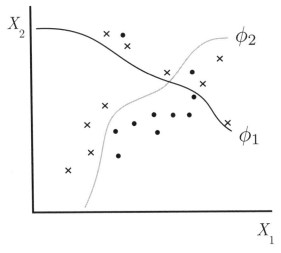

Figure 9.2 Two nonlinear classifiers ϕ_1 (black) and ϕ_2 (gray) to separate crosses from dots. ϕ_1 classifies all points falling below its curve as a dot and ϕ_2 all points to the right of its curve; otherwise the label is predicted as a cross.

Dietterich (2000) explained the benefits of combining many models rather than using a single classifier from three different viewpoints. First, with the usual limited available training data, it is hard to explore the whole space of classifiers and properly predict future data. This effect may be reduced by combining different models. The risk of picking an inadequate single classifier will be mitigated. This is sometimes called the **statistical issue**. Second, many classification algorithms perform a local search and can get trapped in local optima. A local search starting from many different points in the metaclassifier may lead to a better approximation of the best classifier for the problem – this is called **computational issue**. Third, the classifier space considered might not contain the best classifier. For example, the optimal classifier for the data in Figure 9.2 is nonlinear. The best classifier will not be found if only the space of linear classifiers is considered. However, a set of linear classifiers can approximate any decision boundary with any predefined accuracy. A metaclassifier is useful for expanding the space of representable functions because it defines a new classifier space. Hence it can more accurately approximate the best classifier, which would otherwise be unattainable with only a single model – called **representational issue**.

A classification algorithm that suffers from the statistical problem is generally said to have a high "variance"; if it suffers from the computational problem the algorithm has a high "computational variance"; finally, for the representational issue, it has a high "bias." Note the decomposition of the expected error of an estimator into variance and bias (Section 4.1.2.1). With metaclassifiers, the variance of learning algorithms is reduced without increasing the bias. In some situations, a metaclassifier can also reduce the bias, as shown by the theory of support vector machines. This has been confirmed by many empirical studies (Bauer and Kohavi, 1999; Opitz and Maclin, 1999).

A metaclassifier contains a number of models called **base classifier** (or **base learner**, or **individual classifier**). Therefore, the construction of a metaclassifier is a two-step process: first, the base learners are generated, and second, they are combined. Several taxonomies

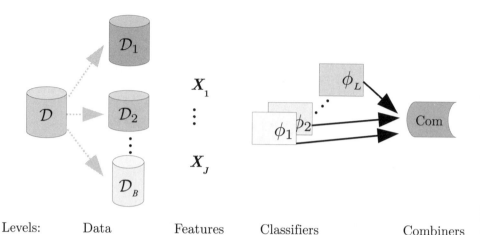

Levels: Data   Features   Classifiers   Combiners

Figure 9.3 Four layers for building classifier ensembles. Data sets may or may not be derived from the original data set $\mathcal{D}$ (dashed arrows). If they are not, they may be different from $\mathcal{D}$. Feature selection from $\mathbf{X} = (X_1, \ldots, X_n)$ is denoted as $\mathbf{X}_1, \ldots, \mathbf{X}_J$. L classifiers are at the end combined.

have been proposed in the literature to categorize the huge variety of metaclassifiers from the algorithm designer point of view. According to Kuncheva (2004), there are four layers representing the different building blocks (see Figure 9.3):

- Data level – indicates which data set is used to train each base classifier.
- Feature level – indicates which feature subsets are used for the different classifiers.
- Classifier level – indicates which classifiers will shape the metaclassifier.
- Combination level – indicates how the classifier predictions are combined.

Hence there are many alternatives to conduct the first step of base learner generation:

1. Use the same classification algorithm (homogeneous metaclassifiers) but with *different hyperparameters*. Examples for a multi-layer perceptron are the number of hidden units, the initial state, and the initial weights in the associated optimization problem. For logistic regression, we can vary the Newton–Raphson initialization parameters, the penalization parameter λ (if a regularization is applied), the FSS strategy, or the significance level in the hypothesis test for removing predictor variables.
2. Use *different classification algorithms* to train the different base learners. For example, models like naive Bayes, ANNs, logistic regression, etc.
3. Use different base classifiers each built from *different representations of the same input object*, i.e., using different feature spaces. Examples include sensor fusion, where different sensors produce data that are then integrated (e.g., acoustic voice signals or video images of the movements for PD diagnosis).
4. Use different base learners each built from *different training sets*. These sets can be built randomly, by drawing random training sets from the original data set, for example. An example is bagging (Section 9.3.3). Alternatively, we can prioritize cases for which the preceding (in a serially arranged metaclassifier) base learners are not accurate, thereby trying to actively generate complementary models. Examples are cascading (Section 9.3.2) and boosting (Section 9.3.5).

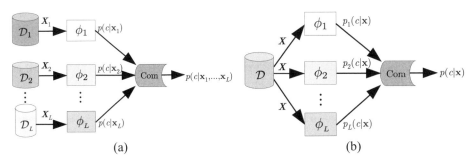

Figure 9.4 Two parallel structures of L probabilistic classifiers ϕ_i. (a) Each classifier ϕ_i is learned from a specific data set $\mathcal{D}_i$ with features $\mathbf{X}_i$. (b) All classifiers are learned from the same data set $\mathcal{D}$ and features $\mathbf{X}$.

As mentioned above, the base classifiers can be arranged in different ways. In a parallel structure, all the classifiers can be trained simultaneously and then output their decision for a given instance. The final decision is built upon some combination rule. Examples are voting (Section 9.2.1) and stacked generalization (Section 9.3.1). In a serial topology, each classifier is invoked sequentially, and the instances to be used will depend on the results output by the preceding classifiers. Examples are cascading and boosting. We can also devise other classifier arrangements, for instance, in a hierarchy, with parent node outputs being passed on as inputs to child nodes.

Figure 9.4 shows two examples of metaclassifiers. In (a), L different base classifiers ϕ_i are learned from different data sets $\mathcal{D}_i$, each containing different features $\mathbf{X}_i$, as in sensor fusion. The classifiers are probabilistic, each outputting $p(c|\mathbf{x}_i)$. The combiner finally yields $p(c|\mathbf{x}_1, \dots, \mathbf{x}_L)$. In (b), the same data set $\mathcal{D}$ and features $\mathbf{X}$ are the inputs for the base classifiers. These can be the same classification algorithm with different hyperparameters, different algorithms, or trained irrespectively with different subsamples from $\mathcal{D}$. Both examples are parallel structures.

Another grouping of ensemble methods is decision optimization versus coverage optimization. **Decision optimization** includes methods that choose and optimize the combiner for a fixed set of base classifiers. In **coverage optimization**, the methods try to generate diverse base classifiers for a fixed combiner.

In this process of generating the base learners, they should be reasonably, albeit not necessarily very, accurate individually. They should be chosen for simplicity, without putting a big effort into optimizing each one separately. The aim is no longer to optimize an individual classifier but to use all available classifiers intelligently. Unnecessary classifiers should not be added. Two poor classifiers that agree do not necessarily yield more correct decisions. It is generally believed that the base classifiers must be as diverse as possible to form a good ensemble. They should be accurate for different instances, specializing in problem subdomains.

How to combine the base learners to generate the final output will be explained in Section 9.2. This step is not coupled with a specific base classifier. The simplest combiner works by voting. A possible rationale for seeking diversity is easily found for a meta-classifier given by a combination of learners with equal weights. Its squared error can be decomposed in terms of the averaged bias and averaged variance of the base learners, but it also depends on their averaged covariance. Covariance models the correlation between the individual classifiers. The smaller the covariance, the smaller the error and the better the metaclassifier. This is called the **bias-variance-covariance decomposition** (Geman et al., 1992). Therefore, if all classifiers make the same errors, the covariance will be large, whereas if they make different errors, i.e., they are diverse, the covariance will be smaller, and overall accuracy will be better. Thus, although diversity is still an ill-defined concept in the classification field, it is believed to be related to the statistical concept of correlation.

A number of measures have been proposed in the literature to quantify **metaclassifier diversity**. A classic approach is to measure the pairwise similarity/dissimilarity between two classifiers and then average all the pairwise measurements. Examples of well-known pairwise measures are the proportion of cases in which two classifiers make different predictions or Cohen's kappa statistic (Section 5.2.1.1). There are also non-pairwise measures that assess metaclassifier diversity directly. For instance, a tie in the votes of individual classifiers signals maximum disagreement, and hence we can measure diversity by computing Shannon entropy of C given each specific $\mathbf{x}^i$ (Section 3.6.1) and then averaging over $\mathcal{D}$, that is,

$$-\frac{1}{N}\sum_{i=1}^{N}\sum_{j=1}^{R}p(c_j|\mathbf{x}^i)\log_2 p(c_j|\mathbf{x}^i).$$

The larger this measurement is, the larger the diversity will be. The probability $p(c_j|\mathbf{x}^i)$ can be estimated as the proportion of classifiers that predict c_j as the label of $\mathbf{x}^i$, i.e., $p(c_j|\mathbf{x}^i) = \frac{1}{L}\sum_{k=1}^{L}\mathbb{I}(\phi_k(\mathbf{x}^i) = c_j)$, where $\mathbb{I}(\cdot)$ is the indicator function (Equation (3.3)).

Another example of non-pairwise diversity measure is "difficulty." Let A be a random variable denoting the proportion of classifiers that correctly classify a randomly selected instance $\mathbf{x}$. A takes values in $\{0, \frac{1}{L}, \frac{2}{L}, \dots, 1\}$. The pmf of A can be estimated by running L classifiers on $\mathcal{D}$. If the same instances are difficult for all classifiers and the other instances are easy for all classifiers, A distribution will have two extreme and separated peaks (no diversity in the ensemble; all classifiers are identical); if the instances that are difficult for some classifiers are easy for others, the shape will have a peak (negatively dependent classifiers); if all instances are equally difficult for all classifiers (independent classifiers), there will be no clear peak. The variance of A used to capture its distribution shape will be a diversity measure. Diversity is larger with a smaller variance.

The utility of diversity measures is limited. There does not appear to be any clear relation between diversity measures and metaclassifier performance (the measures are related to average individual accuracies). Trying to optimize such measures does not explicitly guarantee stronger ensembles. An accepted formal formulation and measures for diversity are open issues. The basic idea for generating diversity is to inject some randomness into the learning process. As mentioned above, common mechanisms include the manipulation of data samples, input variables, algorithm hyperparameters... all detailed in the remainder of this chapter.

9.2   Combining the Outputs of Different Classifiers

The possible ways of combining the outputs of L classifiers $\phi_1, \dots, \phi_L$ in a metaclassifier depend on the type of information produced by the individual classifiers. The classifier output of an instance $\mathbf{x}$ can be a class label $\phi(\mathbf{x}) = \hat{c}$ from the domain $\Omega_C = \{c_1, \ldots, c_R\}$ of the class variable C, see Chapter 7. Alternatively, the classifier output can be probabilistic, producing for each $\mathbf{x}$ a distribution $(p(c_1|\mathbf{x}), \ldots, p(c_R|\mathbf{x}))$ with the estimated posterior probabilities of the class variable conditioned on $\mathbf{x}$, see Chapter 8. Both output types lead, respectively, to methods of fusion of label outputs (Section 9.2.1) and methods of fusion of continuous-valued outputs (Section 9.2.2).

Note that the value $p(c_j|\mathbf{x})$ represents the support for the hypothesis that instance $\mathbf{x}$ belongs to class c_j, and this can be converted into a predicted label by using the maximum a posteriori or any other threshold. Note that although the non-probabilistic classifiers produce label outputs, we can still devise ways to get estimates of the posterior probabilities $p(c_j|\mathbf{x})$ and then apply the fusion of continuous-valued outputs. For example, for any point $\mathbf{x}$ that reaches the leaf of a classification tree (Section 7.2), we can estimate $p(c_j|\mathbf{x})$ as the c_j-class proportions of the training data set that reached that leaf (maximum likelihood estimates). The tree-growing strategies that promote deep structures (e.g., the ID3 algorithm, see Section 7.2.1) cause few points to reach the leaves, on which ground these estimates are unreliable. Also, most of the above points belong to the same class and make the estimates close to 0 and 1. This is then addressed using other kinds of estimates: Laplace correction, m-estimation, etc.

Another example are SVMs (Section 7.5), which can yield probabilistic outputs by first obtaining the signed distance of each testing instance $\mathbf{x}$ from the separating hyperplane (negative distance for class $+1$ and positive distance for class -1) and then applying them a sigmoid filter (that is, $p(C = +1|\mathbf{x}) = 1/(1 + e^{\alpha_1 d + \alpha_2})$, where d is that distance). Parameters α_i can be determined by maximizing the likelihood of the data from a validation set (a small part of the original labeled data set). This is the Platt's method (Platt, 1999b), which in fact fits a logistic regression model to the distances. Rather than distances, the estimated decision rule values can also be used. Alternatively, one can create a histogram using the distances of points of a validation set to the separating hyperplane. Then a testing instance $\mathbf{x}$ is placed in its corresponding bin of the histogram, and the posterior probability $p(C = +1|\mathbf{x})$ is estimated as the fraction of positives in this bin.

Likewise, posterior probabilities can be intuitively calculated using distances in the k-NN classifier (Section 7.1). Thus, $p(c_j|\mathbf{x})$ would average the similarities (inverse of the distance) between $\mathbf{x}$ and its nearest neighbors from class c_j: If $\{\mathbf{x}^{n_1}, \ldots, \mathbf{x}^{n_k}\}$ denote the k nearest neighbors of $\mathbf{x}$ with respective labels $\{c^{n_1}, \ldots, c^{n_k}\}$, and d is a distance,

$$p(c_j|\mathbf{x}) = \frac{\displaystyle\sum_{l:c^{n_l} = c_j} \frac{1}{d(\mathbf{x}, \mathbf{x}^{n_l})}}{\displaystyle\sum_{l=1}^{k} \frac{1}{d(\mathbf{x}, \mathbf{x}^{n_l})}}.$$

These formulas are not necessarily good approximations of the probabilities. Note, however, that accurate estimates are a sufficient but not a necessary condition for high classification accuracy. A poor estimate could lead to a good classification as long as the label with the highest true probability is ranked top by the classifier. It is worth refining the probability estimates when R is large.

9.2.1   Fusion of Label Outputs

Let us introduce the following notation for the label outputs of the classifiers:

$$d_{i,j}(\mathbf{x}) = \begin{cases} 1 & \text{if } \phi_i \text{ classifies } \mathbf{x} \text{ as } c_j \\ 0 & \text{otherwise.} \end{cases}$$

There are many voting strategies for decision making. Some can be traced back to ancient Greece and Rome. Different voting rules result in the following metaclassifier decisions.

- **Dictatorship**: The decision is c_j if the authoritarian dictator classifier (if any) says it is c_j. This rule is not good if we are looking for some sort of consensus among all classifiers.
- **Unanimity vote**: The decision is c_j if all L classifiers agree on c_j.
- **Majority vote** or **plurality vote**: The decision is c_j if this is the label with most votes, i.e., $\mathbf{x}$ is assigned the label $\arg_{k=1,\dots,R} \max \sum_{i=1}^{L} d_{i,k}(\mathbf{x})$, or equivalently, $\sum_{i=1}^{L} d_{i,j}(\mathbf{x}) = \max_{k=1,\dots,R} \sum_{i=1}^{L} d_{i,k}(\mathbf{x})$. Ties are resolved arbitrarily. Majority vote is the most often used rule (see Kuncheva [2004] for some properties).
- **Simple majority vote**: The decision is c_j if this label receives more than half of the votes. If the number of classifiers L is even, c_j needs $\frac{L}{2} + 1$ votes; if L is odd, c_j needs $\frac{L+1}{2}$ votes. For $R = 2$, majority and simple majority vote are equivalent.
- **Thresholded majority vote**: $\mathbf{x}$ is assigned the label

$$\begin{cases} c_j & \text{if } \sum_{i=1}^{L} d_{i,j}(\mathbf{x}) \geq \alpha L \\ c_{R+1} & \text{otherwise,} \end{cases}$$

where $0 < \alpha \leq 1$. The votes of a fraction α of the L classifiers at least are required. The new label c_{R+1} is introduced for all instances for which the metaclassifier fails to determine a class label with sufficient confidence or produces a tie. When $\alpha = 1$, this is the unanimity vote rule (in the absence of a complete agreement, the metaclassifier refuses to decide and assigns label c_{R+1}). When $\alpha = \frac{1}{2} + \varepsilon$, with $0 < \varepsilon < 1/L$, we have a simple majority.

- **Weighted majority vote**: Each classifier ϕ_i is given a weight or coefficient of importance w_i, e.g., in accordance with its goodness. This is reasonable if we want more competent classifiers to have more influence on the final decision. Then $\mathbf{x}$ is assigned the label $\arg_{k=1,\dots,R} \max \sum_{i=1}^{L} w_i d_{i,k}(\mathbf{x})$. Coefficients are usually normalized so that $\sum_{i=1}^{L} w_i = 1, w_i \in [0,1]$.

Example. Assume that we have $L = 7$ classifiers $\phi_1, \dots, \phi_7$ and $R = 3$ possible class labels $\Omega_C = \{c_1, c_2, c_3\}$. For a particular input $\mathbf{x}$, each classifier ϕ_i ($i = 1, \dots, 7$) produces an output $\phi_i(\mathbf{x}) = \hat{c}$, then recoded by the $d_{i,j}(\mathbf{x})$-notation, $j = 1, 2, 3$. Table 9.1 contains the details.

In this example, there is no unanimity. Label c_1 has four votes, i.e., $\sum_{i=1}^{7} d_{i,1}(\mathbf{x}) = 4$. Label c_2 has two votes, i.e., $\sum_{i=1}^{7} d_{i,2}(\mathbf{x}) = 2$. Label c_3 has only one vote given by the last classifier ϕ_7, i.e., $\sum_{i=1}^{7} d_{i,3}(\mathbf{x}) = 1$. Therefore, the final decision is c_1 if we use majority vote, simple majority vote, and thresholded majority vote for $\alpha \leq 4/7$. For $\alpha > 4/7$, none

Table 9.1 Seven classifiers ϕ_i with their prediction for a given $\mathbf{x}$, their equivalent $d_{i,j}(\mathbf{x}), j = 1, 2, 3$, notation, their classification accuracy $\text{Acc}(\phi_i)$, and their weights w_i after normalizing the accuracies over the seven classifiers

Classifier i	$\phi_i(\mathbf{x})$	$d_{i,1}(\mathbf{x})$	$d_{i,2}(\mathbf{x})$	$d_{i,3}(\mathbf{x})$	$\text{Acc}(\phi_i)$	w_i
ϕ_1	$\hat{c}_1$	1	0	0	.6	.12
ϕ_2	$\hat{c}_1$	1	0	0	.6	.12
ϕ_3	$\hat{c}_1$	1	0	0	.6	.12
ϕ_4	$\hat{c}_1$	1	0	0	.6	.12
ϕ_5	$\hat{c}_2$	0	1	0	.9	.18
ϕ_6	$\hat{c}_2$	0	1	0	.9	.18
ϕ_7	$\hat{c}_3$	0	0	1	.8	.16

of the classifiers surpass the threshold, and the metaclassifier opts for an artificial label c_4 (no decision).

For a weighted majority vote rule, the use of weights w_i proportional to classifier accuracies $\text{Acc}(\phi_i)$ results (in this case) in the same final decision, labeling $\mathbf{x}$ as c_1, because $\sum_{i=1}^{7} w_i d_{i,1}(\mathbf{x}) = .48$, $\sum_{i=1}^{7} w_i d_{i,2}(\mathbf{x}) = .36$, and $\sum_{i=1}^{7} w_i d_{i,3}(\mathbf{x}) = .16$. ∎

9.2.2 Fusion of Continuous-Valued Outputs

In this section, the notation $d_{i,j}(\mathbf{x})$ means the estimated posterior probabilities of value c_j conditioned on a given input $\mathbf{x}$ for classifier ϕ_i, i.e., $p_i(c_j|\mathbf{x})$. Sometimes it can also be interpreted as the confidence in label c_j. In general, $d_{i,j}(\mathbf{x})$ indicates how much support classifier ϕ_i lends to the possibility of $\mathbf{x}$ belonging to class c_j, which, without loss of generality, always lies in $[0, 1]$, although it does not necessarily sum one for a fixed i.

The methods described below use $d_{i,j}(\mathbf{x})$ to find the overall degree of support for each class given by the metaclassifier. Then the final label for $\mathbf{x}$ will be the class with most support. Let $\mu_j(\mathbf{x}) = f(d_{1,j}(\mathbf{x}), \ldots, d_{L,j}(\mathbf{x}))$ denote that overall degree of support for class c_j, which is a function f of $d_{i,j}(\mathbf{x}), i = 1, \ldots, L$. As with the label outputs, there are multiple options for f, which should summarize all the continuous-valued outputs given by the L classifiers. Combiners f can use the L supports $\{d_{i,j}(\mathbf{x}) : i = 1, \ldots, L\}$ for each class c_j separately, or alternatively, they can use the whole set $\{d_{i,j}(\mathbf{x}) : i = 1, \ldots, L, j = 1, \ldots, R\}$. The first group of combiners is called **class-conscious**, whereas the second is **class-indifferent**.

The most widely used class-conscious combiners f are as follows:

- Simple mean (average or arithmetic mean): $\mu_j(\mathbf{x}) = \frac{1}{L} \sum_{i=1}^{L} d_{i,j}(\mathbf{x})$.
- Minimum: $\mu_j(\mathbf{x}) = \min_{i=1,\ldots,L} \{d_{i,j}(\mathbf{x})\}$.
- Maximum: $\mu_j(\mathbf{x}) = \max_{i=1,\ldots,L} \{d_{i,j}(\mathbf{x})\}$.
- Median: $\mu_j(\mathbf{x}) = Me\{d_{1,j}(\mathbf{x}), \ldots, d_{L,j}(\mathbf{x})\}$.
- **Trimmed mean**: The $K\%$ trimmed mean is the mean of the degrees of support after excluding $K\%$ of the sorted values on each side (the smallest and the largest). It is more resistant to outliers than the arithmetic mean. A particular case is the **competition jury** combiner. When assessing sports performance (e.g., in gymnastics), the jury often omits

the highest and the lowest marks to reduce subjective bias and averages the remaining $L - 2$ marks.

- Product: $\mu_j(\mathbf{x}) = \prod_{i=1}^{L} d_{i,j}(\mathbf{x})$. The geometric mean, $\left(\prod_{i=1}^{L} d_{i,j}(\mathbf{x})\right)^{\frac{1}{L}}$, is equivalent to the product combiner because the monotone transformation of raising to the power of $1/L$ does not depend on c_j and will produce the same "winning" label for both combiners.

- **Generalized mean**: $\mu_j^{\alpha}(\mathbf{x}) = \left(\frac{1}{L} \sum_{i=1}^{L} d_{i,j}(\mathbf{x})^{\alpha}\right)^{\frac{1}{\alpha}}$, where α is the "level of optimism" of the combiner. This is fixed beforehand or tuned taking into account the metaclassifier performance. The most pessimistic choice is for $\alpha \to -\infty$, where $\mu_j^{\alpha}(\mathbf{x})$ is the minimum combiner, i.e., $\mu_j(\mathbf{x}) = \min_{i=1,\dots,L}\{d_{i,j}(\mathbf{x})\}$, and c_j is supported by all classifiers at least as much as $\mu_j^{\alpha}(\mathbf{x})$. For $\alpha = -1, 1$, we respectively have the harmonic and arithmetic means. Finally, the most optimistic choice is for $\alpha \to \infty$, where $\mu_j^{\alpha}(\mathbf{x})$ is the maximum combiner, i.e., $\mu_j(\mathbf{x}) = \max_{i=1,\dots,L}\{d_{i,j}(\mathbf{x})\}$, and c_j is supported by at least one classifier as much as $\mu_j^{\alpha}(\mathbf{x})$. For $\alpha = 0$, the result is the geometric mean, which is the limit of means with exponents approaching zero (as can be proved).

- **Ordered weighted averaging**: For a fixed j, the outputs $d_{i,j}(\mathbf{x})$ are sorted in descending order, and then a weighted sum is computed using coefficients $b_1, \dots, b_L$, where $\sum_{l=1}^{L} b_l = 1, b_l \in [0,1]$, that is, if the sorting yields $d_{i_1,j}(\mathbf{x}) \geq \cdots \geq d_{i_L,j}(\mathbf{x})$, then the support for c_j is

$$\mu_j(\mathbf{x}) = \sum_{l=1}^{L} b_l\, d_{i_l,j}(\mathbf{x}).$$

Choices of vector $\mathbf{b} = (b_1, \dots, b_L)^T$ can model the above combiners. For instance, the simple mean is $\mathbf{b} = (1/L, \dots, 1/L)^T$, the minimum is $\mathbf{b} = (0, \dots, 0, 1)^T$, and the competition jury is $\mathbf{b} = (0, 1/(L-2), \dots, 1/(L-2), 0)^T$. Vector $\mathbf{b}$ can also be found from data.

- **Weighted average**: Weights w_{ij}, specific for each classifier ϕ_i and each label c_j, are given:

$$\mu_j(\mathbf{x}) = \sum_{i=1}^{L} w_{ij} d_{i,j}(\mathbf{x}). \tag{9.1}$$

For a fixed j, $d_{i,j}(\mathbf{x})$ are L estimates of $p(c_j|\mathbf{x})$. Suppose they are unbiased. Provided that $\sum_{i=1}^{L} w_{ij} = 1$ (w_{ij} could be negative) and w_{ij} is found by minimizing the variance of $\mu_j(\mathbf{x})$ in Equation (9.1), we have a minimum variance estimate $\mu_j(\mathbf{x})$ of $p(c_j|\mathbf{x})$. This will be a better estimate than any of the metaclassifier members. A simple case is when the classifier outputs for class c_j are independent. Here the derived weights are

$$w_{ij} = \frac{\frac{1}{\sigma_{ij}^2}}{\sum_{k=1}^{L} \frac{1}{\sigma_{kj}^2}}, \text{ where } \sigma_{ij}^2 \text{ is the sample variance of the values } c^l - d_{i,j}(\mathbf{x}^l), l = 1, \dots, N.$$

Because an estimate of the posterior probability does not in fact have to be unbiased for classification purposes, the weights do not necessarily sum one. A more natural strategy would be to directly minimize the classification error rather than the variance of an estimate of the posterior probability. However, this is a more complex problem without any analytical solution for the weights.

A simplified version of Equation (9.1) uses only L weights, one per classifier, instead of $L \cdot R$, i.e., $w_{ij} = w_i$. Weight w_i is usually based on ϕ_i performance.

Table 9.2 Seven classifiers ϕ_i with their degrees of support $d_{i,j}(\mathbf{x})$ to c_j ($j = 1, 2, 3$) for a given $\mathbf{x}$, their classification accuracy $\mathrm{Acc}(\phi_i)$, and their weights w_i after normalizing the accuracies over the seven classifiers

Classifier i	$d_{i,1}(\mathbf{x})$	$d_{i,2}(\mathbf{x})$	$d_{i,3}(\mathbf{x})$	$\mathrm{Acc}(\phi_i)$	w_i
ϕ_1	.1	.8	.1	.6	.12
ϕ_2	1	0	0	.6	.12
ϕ_3	.4	.3	.3	.6	.12
ϕ_4	.05	.9	.05	.6	.12
ϕ_5	.2	.7	.1	.9	.18
ϕ_6	.6	.4	0	.9	.18
ϕ_7	.3	.5	.2	.8	.16

Table 9.3 Combiners of the seven classifiers shown in Table 9.2. The columns list the overall degree of support $\mu_j(\mathbf{x})$ for class c_j, $j = 1, 2, 3$, and the metaclassifier decision given by the label with the largest support. The weighted average combiner employs weights w_i proportional to classifier accuracies

Combiner	$\mu_1(\mathbf{x})$	$\mu_2(\mathbf{x})$	$\mu_3(\mathbf{x})$	Decision
Simple mean	.38	.51	.11	c_2
Minimum	.05	0	0	c_1
Maximum	1	.9	.3	c_1
Median	.3	.5	.1	c_2
Competition jury	.32	.54	.09	c_2
Product	.00007	0	0	c_1
Weighted average	.38	.52	.10	c_2

Example. Suppose again that we have $L = 7$ probabilistic classifiers $\phi_1, \dots, \phi_7$ and $R = 3$ possible class labels $\Omega_C = \{c_1, c_2, c_3\}$. For a particular input $\mathbf{x}$, each classifier ϕ_i ($i = 1, \dots, 7$) lends a degree of support $d_{i,j}(\mathbf{x})$ to class c_j ($j = 1, 2, 3$) given by the posterior probability $p_i(c_j | \mathbf{x})$, see Table 9.2. The above combiners use the tabular data columnwise to achieve the results reported in Table 9.3.

Depending on the combination method, c_1 or c_2 is the final label assigned to $\mathbf{x}$. Observe that c_3 is never chosen by the metaclassifier. Thus, the choice of combiners is a major challenge for a practitioner. ∎

Consensus theory, well developed in social and management sciences, is a source of inspiration in the field of metaclassifiers. Expert opinions are under this theory combined, in particular, opinions given as probability distributions. The weighted average is the well-known rule called **linear opinion pool**, whereas the weighted product, $\mu_j(\mathbf{x}) = \prod_{i=1}^{L} d_{i,j}(\mathbf{x})^{w_i}$, is the **logarithmic opinion pool**.

In contrast to the above combiners, the decision template described next uses all $L \cdot R$ degrees of support, i.e., it is a class-indifferent combiner.

- **Decision template**: A decision template for class c_j, $\mathbf{DT}_j$, is the $L \cdot R$ matrix, where the (i, k)th entry is the mean of the degrees of support for c_k lent by classifier ϕ_i to each instance $\mathbf{x}^l$ from $\mathcal{D}$ with true class label $c^l = c_j$:

$$DT_j(i,k) = \frac{1}{N_j} \sum_{l:c^l = c_j} d_{i,k}\left(\mathbf{x}^l\right) \quad i = 1,\ldots,L, k = 1,\ldots,R,$$

where N_j is the number of instances of $\mathcal{D}$ with true label c_j. This plays the role of a typical profile for c_j because it contains, for each data subset with that label c_j, an average of the supports lent to each label. Then for a given input $\mathbf{x}$, the metaclassifier support for c_j will compare $d_{i,k}(\mathbf{x})$ and $DT_j(i,k)$ using a similarity measure. The closest match will yield the final label for $\mathbf{x}$. For instance, the squared Euclidean distance gives

$$\mu_j(\mathbf{x}) = 1 - \frac{1}{L \cdot R} \sum_{i=1}^{L} \sum_{k=1}^{R} (DT_j(i,k) - d_{i,k}(\mathbf{x}))^2.$$

Other distances could be used.

A number of theories (Bayesian, supra-Bayesian, Kullback–Leibler divergence, conditionally independent representations) are designed to underpin at least the simplest combiners assuming different hypotheses and criteria to be optimized. For the sake of brevity, we outline the theoretical framework for the simple mean and product combiners based on the Kullback–Leibler divergence (see Section 3.6.5).

First, we again consider $\mathbf{p}_i = (p_i(c_1|\mathbf{x}), \ldots, p_i(c_R|\mathbf{x}))$, with $p_i(c_j|\mathbf{x}) = d_{i,j}(\mathbf{x})$, $j = 1, \ldots, R$, the probability distribution on Ω_C provided by classifier ϕ_i, and $\mathbf{p}_{\text{meta}} = (\mu_1(\mathbf{x}), \ldots, \mu_R(\mathbf{x}))$ the distribution on Ω_C agreed upon by the ensemble $\{\phi_1, \ldots, \phi_L\}$. Then the averaged Kullback–Leibler divergence across the L members is

$$\mathbb{KL}_{\text{av}} = \frac{1}{L} \sum_{i=1}^{L} \mathbb{KL}(\mathbf{p}_{\text{meta}} || \mathbf{p}_i). \tag{9.2}$$

We now search for $\mathbf{p}_{\text{meta}}$ that minimizes Equation (9.2). To avoid a cumbersome notation, we drop $\mathbf{x}$. Take $\partial \mathbb{KL}_{\text{av}}/\partial \mu_j$, include the term with the Lagrangian multiplier λ ensuring that $\mathbf{p}_{\text{meta}}$ is a distribution, and set to zero

$$\frac{\partial}{\partial \mu_j}\left[\mathbb{KL}_{\text{av}} + \lambda\left(1 - \sum_{k=1}^{R} \mu_k\right)\right] = \frac{1}{L} \sum_{i=1}^{L} \frac{\partial}{\partial \mu_j}\left[\sum_{k=1}^{R} \mu_k \log_2\left(\frac{\mu_k}{d_{i,k}}\right)\right] - \lambda$$

$$= \frac{1}{L} \sum_{i=1}^{L}\left(\log_2\left(\frac{\mu_j}{d_{i,j}}\right) + \frac{1}{\ln 2}\right) - \lambda$$

$$= \log_2 \prod_{i=1}^{L}\left(\frac{\mu_j}{d_{i,j}}\right)^{1/L} + \frac{1}{\ln 2} - \lambda = 0.$$

Solving for μ_j

$$\mu_j = 2^{\lambda - \frac{1}{\ln 2}} \prod_{i=1}^{L} d_{i,j}^{1/L}. \tag{9.3}$$

Now we substitute Equation (9.3) in $\sum_{k=1}^{R} \mu_k = 1$ and solve for λ to yield

$$\lambda = \frac{1}{\ln 2} - \log_2\left(\sum_{k=1}^{R} \prod_{i=1}^{L} d_{i,k}^{1/L}\right).$$

Finally, this λ is inserted in Equation (9.3) to get an expression for the metaclassifier probability for c_j given $\mathbf{x}$ as the normalized geometric mean

$$\mu_j = \frac{\prod_{i=1}^{L} d_{i,j}^{1/L}}{\sum_{k=1}^{R} \prod_{i=1}^{L} d_{i,k}^{1/L}}.$$

Note that this is equivalent to the product combiner $\mu_j = \prod_{i=1}^{L} d_{i,j}$ because the denominator does not depend on j, and the power $1/L$ will not change the ordering of the supports.

Second, by swapping the positions of $\mathbf{p}_{\text{meta}}$ and $\mathbf{p}_i$ in Equation (9.2), i.e., by minimizing

$$\text{KL}_{\text{av}} = \frac{1}{L}\sum_{i=1}^{L} \text{KL}(\mathbf{p}_i\|\mathbf{p}_{\text{meta}}),$$

we likewise get

$$\frac{\partial}{\partial \mu_j}\left[\text{KL}_{\text{av}} + \lambda\left(1 - \sum_{k=1}^{R}\mu_k\right)\right] = \frac{1}{L}\sum_{i=1}^{L}\frac{\partial}{\partial \mu_j}\left[\sum_{k=1}^{R} d_{i,k}\log_2\left(\frac{d_{i,k}}{\mu_k}\right)\right] - \lambda$$

$$= -\frac{1}{L}\sum_{i=1}^{L}\left(\frac{d_{i,j}}{\mu_j}\cdot\frac{1}{\ln 2}\right) - \lambda = 0.$$

Solving for μ_j and then for λ,

$$\mu_j = -\frac{1}{\lambda L \ln 2}\sum_{i=1}^{L} d_{i,j} \quad \text{and} \quad \lambda = -\frac{1}{\ln 2}.$$

Finally,

$$\mu_j = \frac{1}{L}\sum_{i=1}^{L} d_{i,j},$$

which is the simple mean combiner. Therefore, the product and simple mean combiners are the result of minimizing an averaged Kullback–Leibler divergence between the posterior probabilities of the metaclassifier and each of its members. The only change in the combiners is whether the probability of the metaclassifier or of its members plays the role of "true" distribution in the Kullback–Leibler divergence.

The simple mean and the product are the most researched combiners. However, there is no guide as to which is better for a specific problem. Some results suggest that the simple mean combiner is much more resilient to estimation errors of the posterior probabilities than the product combiner. The product combiner is very sensitive to estimates close to zero: if $p_i(c_j|\mathbf{x}) \approx 0$ for some $i = 1, \ldots, L$, then the product combiner is unlikely to support c_j regardless of the estimates given by the other classifiers.

9.3   Popular Metaclassifiers

9.3.1   Stacked Generalization

Stacked generalization (Wolpert, 1992) is a generic methodology, where the outputs of the constituent classifiers, $\phi_1, \ldots, \phi_L$, are combined through another classifier ϕ^*. Thus, the method can be viewed as a specific combination method that combines by learning; the combiner tries to learn which classifiers are reliable, learn why they make errors, and discover how to best combine their outputs.

Like general metaclassifiers, the base classifiers should be diverse so that they complement each other. This is why they are commonly based on *different* classification algorithms. Also, outputs may be labels or continuous values. Figure 9.4(b) is an example of stacked generalization, where the combiner "Com" would be classifier ϕ^*.

Stacking is a means of estimating and correcting for the biases of the base classifiers. Therefore, the combiner ϕ^* should be learned on data not used to train the base classifiers to avoid overfitting. This can be achieved by using k-fold cross-validation. Thus, the output of each classifier for each instance $\mathbf{x}^l, l = 1, \ldots, N$, will be taken from the version of the classifiers that was tested on the fold where $\mathbf{x}^l$ is and built on the remaining folds. The combiner is trained on this data set, where these outputs along with the true class labels are used as inputs.

At classification time, when confronted with an unseen instance, each classifier predicts the class, and then these predictions are fed into the combiner ϕ^* to produce the final decision. Probabilistic predictions can be converted into labels or used directly because they provide information about the confidence of each classifier, if the combiner is capable of managing continuous-valued inputs, like, for example, a decision tree or a linear regression. In fact, we would have R classification problems, one per class label c_j. The input variables for predicting c_j are the probabilities of class c_j, output by the different classifiers ϕ_i, i.e., $p_i(c_j|\mathbf{x})$. The class labels or the response values for regressing c_j are one if c_j is the correct class label and zero otherwise. These predictions can be used to make a voting decision or a maximum a posteriori class value decision.

In the above explanation, two layers are stacked. The base classifiers form layer-0, and their predictions are the inputs for the combiner at layer-1. Stacking may have more layers of classifiers. The last layer always has one classifier that makes the final decision. Most of the work is done by layer-0 classifiers; the combiner is only a referee and should therefore be a simple method (e.g., a classification tree).

Stacked generalization is less widely used than other schemes like bagging (Section 9.3.3) and boosting (Section 9.3.5), partly because it is difficult to analyze theoretically and partly because there is no generally accepted way of setting up this metaclassifier (there are many variations).

9.3.2   Cascading

Cascading (Kaynak and Alpaydın, 2000) is a serial approach where the next classifier is only trained/tested with the instances about which the preceding classifiers are not sufficiently confident. The classifiers $\{\phi_1, \ldots, \phi_L\}$ are sorted in increasing order of complexity in terms of either space, time, or representation cost. A complex classifier is only used if the preceding classifiers are not sufficiently confident. The confidence associated with a classifier is related to its output. Thus, a probabilistic classifier that makes a decision based on the maximum a posteriori class value $c^* = \arg\max_c p(c|\mathbf{x})$ (see Equation (8.5)) could require a specific threshold (like the cutoff value θ^*; see Section 8.3.3) for the maximum posterior probability. If the threshold is not crossed (i.e., the probability is not high enough), then the classifier is not considered confident, and the next classifier is applied.

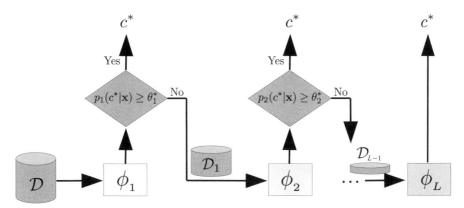

Figure 9.5 Cascading metaclassifier. The next classifier is used only when the preceding classifiers are not confident. The prediction of an instance $\mathbf{x}$ received by classifier ϕ_i is the maximum a posteriori class $c^* = \arg\max_c p_i(c|\mathbf{x})$ whenever $p_i(c^*|\mathbf{x}) \geq \theta_i^*$ (and $\mathbf{x}$ is a correct classification). The procedure for $\mathbf{x}$ stops here. Otherwise, if $\mathbf{x}$ is a misclassification or the threshold for θ_i^* is not exceeded, $\mathbf{x}$ is passed on to the next classifier ϕ_{i+1}, which will require another threshold θ_{i+1}^* for the maximum posterior probability. Classifiers could be, e.g., Bayesian classifiers of increasing complexity.

Given a data set $\mathcal{D}$, we first train ϕ_1. We then find all instances with respect to which ϕ_1 is not confident (predictions of ϕ_1 are calculated on a separate validation set or on $\mathcal{D}$ via cross-validation). These instances and their true class labels form the input data set $\mathcal{D}_1$ for ϕ_2, and so on. Needless to say, we choose both these instances and misclassifications. Figure 9.5 illustrates the learning process of the cascading metaclassifier.

The idea behind increasing classifier complexity is to try to handle most instances with the first simple classifiers and only use more complex classifiers for a few instances. In this manner, there is not a significant increase in overall complexity. Note that this contrasts with the metaclassifiers explained above, where all base classifiers generate their output for any instance.

To limit the number L of classifiers, the few instances not covered by any classifier are stored and treated by a nonparametric classifier, like the k-NN algorithm. In the end, a small number of "rules" of increasing complexity can explain the classes, and there are a few "exceptions" not covered by the rules, best handled by a nonparametric model.

9.3.3 Bagging

Bagging (Breiman, 1996a) stands for Bootstrap AGGregatING. Multiple versions of the *same* classification algorithm are generated, each built from bootstrap replicates of the original data set $\mathcal{D}$ of size N. According to Breiman (1996a), the bagging predictor variance is smaller than or equal to the variance of a simple predictor, leading to an increasing classification accuracy. Remember that bootstrapping (Section 5.3.2.3) consists of randomly sampling with replacement N labeled instances from $\mathcal{D}$. We repeat the bootstrapping L times to yield replicate data sets $\mathcal{D}_b^l$, $l = 1, \ldots, L$, all of size N. About 36.8% of the original examples are not chosen for each l.

Then a classifier ϕ_i is learned from $\mathcal{D}_b^l, l = 1, \ldots, L$. This learning can be parallelized, see Figure 9.6. This speeds up computation using multi-core processors or parallel

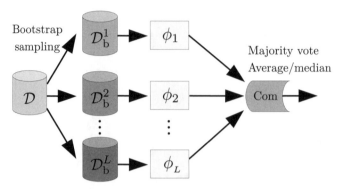

Figure 9.6 Bagging metaclassifier. The same type of classifier is trained from bootstrap replicates. Majority vote (label outputs) or average/median (continuous outputs) are the combiner rules.

computers. The goodness of each base classifier can be estimated using the non-selected cases (36.8% of N), known as **out-of-bag cases**. Thus, the out-of-bag prediction for an instance $\mathbf{x}$ will only involve classifiers that have not been trained on $\mathbf{x}$.

All predictions provided by the base classifiers are aggregated by the majority vote combiner for label outputs or by the average/median combiner for continuous-valued outputs. Note that, alternatively, probabilistic outputs can be converted into predicted labels (using the maximum a posteriori c^* or any threshold θ^*). The majority vote combiner is then applied to the above labels.

Nice bagging (Skurichina, 2001) only accepts classifiers whose training accuracy is greater than is achieved by an individual classifier built on the whole data set. The variant of bagging called **wagging** (Bauer and Kohavi, 1999) uses a weighting distribution over the instances rather than random bootstrap samples.

A key factor for improving bagging performance is the stability of the classification algorithm. Improvement will occur for unstable algorithms, where a small change in $\mathcal{D}$, i.e., a replicate $\mathcal{D}_b^l$, can cause large changes in the classifier output. This is why bagging works well for unstable classifiers, as they provide diversity in the ensemble due to be learned over slightly different training sets. Classification trees, rule induction, and artificial neural networks are unstable. Unpruned trees are more unstable than pruned trees. k-nearest neighbors, decision stumps, Bayesian classifiers, SVMs, logistic regression, and linear discriminant classifiers are considered stable.

It has been theoretically shown that the performance of bagging (its testing error) converges to a steady error rate as the metaclassifier size L grows.

Finally, for a large N, bootstrap replicates will be rather similar, ϕ_i will be highly correlated, and bagging is not worthwhile. Then we may want to generate smaller bootstrap replicates, i.e., of size $N' < N$. For data sets with $N \ll n$ ("large n, small N" problem), the linear discriminant analysis is no longer stable and can be used for bagging.

9.3.4   Randomization and Random Forest

Bagging introduces randomness into the learning algorithm input, often with excellent results. This serves as inspiration for other ways of creating diversity by introducing **randomization**. A simple idea is to train base classifiers on randomly selected feature subsets, rather than on the entire feature set. This is the **random subspace metaclassifier**

(Ho, 1998), which makes the final decision by majority vote. L feature subsets of size $M < n$ are drawn without replacement from a uniform distribution over $\mathbf{X} = (X_1, \ldots, X_n)$.

This is particularly suitable for data sets with $N \ll n$ ("large n, small N" problem), such as are typically found in fMRI data, because it reduces the number of variables while retaining the original number of instances for training. For example, in Plumpton et al. (2012), random subspaces were used with LDA classifiers to discriminate positive, negative, or neutral emotions from data acquired by fMRI. The novelty was the use of real-time classification from streaming fMRI data. An interesting application is neurofeedback, where the participant receives real-time activity-based feedback through the measurement of brain activity during task performance and can learn to exercise self-control of specific brain regions, e.g., related to pain perception.

Almost every learning method is open to some kind of randomization. In random split selection in classification trees, for instance, instead of picking a single winner, one of the best splits can be randomly selected at each node. Alternatively, a random subset of features can be selected at each node, then choosing the best split among them. This last option is called **random tree** and tends to be quite weak (poor performance). This is why it is usually used as "building block" in random forests, where several random trees are bagged.

A **random forest** (Breiman, 2001a) is a variant of bagging. The base classifiers are typically classification trees. The term "random" refers to the generation of independent identically distributed random vectors $\boldsymbol{\gamma}_i, i = 1, \ldots, L$. Each tree ϕ_i is grown using $\boldsymbol{\gamma}_i$. This means that besides randomizing the data set instances, we can use random feature selection, or even randomly vary some tree parameter. By combining these sources of diversity, we get different versions of random forests. If we sample from the data set and from the feature set, $\boldsymbol{\gamma}_i$ will include the bootstrap sample of data points (size N) and the random features selected (size $M < n$, to be fixed). Breiman (2001a) recommended using the first integer less than $\log_2 n + 1$ as M. His experimental study carried out random feature selection *at each node* of the tree, that is, he used random trees, choosing a random subset with M variables at each node of the tree and then picking the best variable to split the node. Note that further randomization could be introduced into the choice of split points for continuous (and selected) features. Finally, the bagged trees are combined by majority vote.

The importance of each variable in the final random forest model can be estimated in two different ways. One option is calculating the decrease in accuracy when that variable is excluded from the model (Breiman, 2001a). To do this, the classification accuracy on the out-of-bag sample is measured for each tree. Then, the values of the variable in this out-of-bag sample are randomly shuffled, keeping all other variables the same, and the decrease in accuracy on the shuffled data is measured. The importance of that variable is scored as the mean decrease in accuracy across all trees. Such measure is often called permutation importance index. Intuitively, if a variable has strong predictive power, shuffling would lead to a sharp decrease, whereas with little predictive power we can have a slight increase in accuracy due to random noise. The latter results in small negative importance scores, equivalent to zero importance. Permutation importance overestimates the variable importance of highly correlated variables, and some solutions have been proposed (Strobl et al., 2008). A second option is based on computing the decrease in the Gini index (Section 7.2.2) when the variable is chosen to split a node. Thus, given the variable, the sum of the Gini decrease across all trees accumulate each time that variable is selected for the split. The final accumulated value is divided by the number of trees in the forest to estimate the importance of the variable, which is more for higher values.

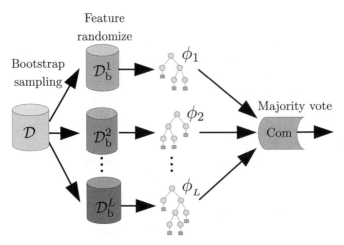

Figure 9.7 Random forest metaclassifier. The base classifiers are all trees. Each tree is trained from randomly selected bootstrap replicates and features, where this selection can be carried out at each node of the tree. Each test point is pushed through all trees starting at the root until it reaches the leaves containing an output. All outputs are combined by majority vote.

Figure 9.7 outlines the random forest metaclassifier. Note that unlike bagging, the width of each bootstrapped data set $\mathcal{D}_b^l, l = 1, \ldots, L$ is not drawn constant (equal to n in $\mathcal{D}$), due to the random feature selection.

Random forests perform similarly to boosting (Section 9.3.5), and they are simple and easy to build. Consequently, random forests are very popular and widely used.

Unlike bagging, which is not effective with stable base classifiers, the idea of random forests can be used with the k-nearest neighbor classifier. This model is heavily dependent on the variables used to compute distances between instances to get neighbors. Accordingly, although k-nearest neighbors is a stable model when learned from bootstrapped data, the addition of feature selection randomization to each model, as in random forest, can lead to a well-behaved metaclassifier.

Rotation forests (Rodriguez et al., 2006) combine random subspace and PCA (Section 2.4.3) to create an ensemble of (typically) decision trees. At each iteration, the n features are randomly divided into g disjoint subsets (a parameter of the algorithm). PCA is applied to each subset to form linear combinations of the original variables that are rotations of the original axes. All principal components are retained. The data are transformed according to these new variables and will be the input data for the trees to be learned. To prevent the use of the same coefficients if the same feature subset is chosen in different iterations, PCA is applied to training instances from a randomly chosen subset of the class values. Before applying PCA, bootstrap samples of the data can also be created at each iteration to further increase diversity. The final decision is fused using the sample mean rule. Experiments have shown that rotation forests perform similarly to random forests, with fewer trees. A classification scheme based on a linear SVM (Section 7.5) was used to select features (voice measurements) in (Ozcift, 2011), according to the absolute value of the weight in the decision function, i.e., those features with larger weights are better ranked. Then the selected features are used to train rotation forests with k-NN, ANNs and classification trees as base classifiers in PD diagnosis.

9.3.5   Boosting

Boosting (Freund and Schapire, 1997) builds the ensemble of classifiers incrementally, adding one classifier at a time. The classifier added at step i is selectively trained on a data set sampled from $\mathcal{D}$. The initial sampling distribution is uniform (as in bagging), and then shifts to increase the likelihood of "difficult" instances, i.e., instances where the preceding classifiers failed. Thus step i updates this distribution, increasing the likelihood of the instances misclassified at step $i-1$. The main algorithm is called **AdaBoost**, which stands for ADAptive BOOSTing, initially proposed for binary classes. Apart from base classifier selection, the algorithm is almost fully automated. Algorithm 9.1 shows the **AdaBoost.M1** pseudocode, which is the most straightforward extension of AdaBoost to the multi-class case, where "M" stands for multi-class.

Algorithm 9.1: AdaBoost.M1

Input : A data set $\mathcal{D} = \{ (\mathbf{x}^1, c^1), \ldots, (\mathbf{x}^N, c^N) \}$
Output: A metaclassifier $\{ \phi_1, \ldots, \phi_L \}$

1 Initialize the parameters: set the weight of each instance $w_j^1 = \frac{1}{N}, j = 1, \ldots, N$
   and the maximum number of classifiers L to learn
2 **for** $i = 1, \ldots, L$ **do**
3 $\quad$ Draw a sample $\mathcal{D}_i$ from $\mathcal{D}$ using distribution $(w_1^i, \ldots, w_N^i)$
4 $\quad$ Learn a classifier ϕ_i by using $\mathcal{D}_i$ as the training set
5 $\quad$ Compute the weighted error ε_i at step i by $\varepsilon_i = \sum_{j=1}^N w_j^i l_j^i$
   $\quad$ ($l_j^i = 1$ if ϕ_i misclassifies $\mathbf{x}^j$ and $l_j^i = 0$ otherwise)
6 $\quad$ **if** $\varepsilon_i = 0$ *or* $\varepsilon_i \geq 0.5$ **then** Ignore ϕ_i, set $L = i-1$, and stop
7 $\quad$ **else** Set $\beta_i = \frac{\varepsilon_i}{1-\varepsilon_i}$. Update weights: $w_j^{i+1} = \dfrac{w_j^i \beta_i^{1-l_j^i}}{\sum_{k=1}^N w_k^i \beta_i^{1-l_k^i}}$, for $j = 1, \ldots, N$
8 **endfor**
9 For an instance $\mathbf{x}$ to be classified, calculate the support for class c_k by
   $\quad \mu_k(\mathbf{x}) = \sum_{\phi_i(\mathbf{x})=c_k} \ln(1/\beta_i)$
10 Select the class with the maximum support as the label for $\mathbf{x}$

In line 3, all N instances are randomly sampled with replacement according to distribution $(w_1^i, \ldots, w_N^i)$, which is initially uniform (line 1) and then updated (line 7). The resulting data set $\mathcal{D}_i$ of size N is the input for learning classifier ϕ_i (line 4). The weighted error of ϕ_i is calculated as the sum of the weights of all its misclassifications (line 5). If this error is greater than 0.5 or zero, ϕ_i is ignored as part of the ensemble, the loop is aborted, and the number of classifiers is $i-1$ (line 6). Otherwise, the weights are updated in line 7 by multiplying the above weights by a function of the weighted errors, $\beta_i \in (0, 0.5)$. Instances correctly classified by ϕ_i have lower weights, whereas misclassifications have greater weights. The denominator is a normalization factor. Then, decisions are combined in the classification phase (lines 9 and 10) using a weighted majority vote scheme, where each classifier's vote is a function of its accuracy in the training set, given by $\ln(1/\beta_i)$. Note that a zero error ($\varepsilon_i = 0$ in line 6) is a potential overfitting. In this case, $\beta_i = 0$, and ϕ_i has an infinite voting-weight (because $\ln(1/\beta_i) = \infty$). Classifier ϕ_i then becomes despotic

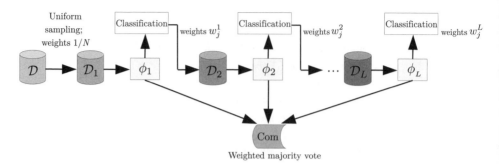

Figure 9.8 Boosting metaclassifier. The base classifiers are all of the same type. Each classifier ϕ_i is trained on data set $\mathcal{D}_i$ of size N sampled from $\mathcal{D}$, which focuses more on the mistakes of the previous classifier ϕ_{i-1}. All outputs are combined by weighted majority vote.

and is the sole decision-making power. This is why it should be avoided. Classifiers with $\varepsilon_i < 0.5$ are called weak classifiers, and are AdaBoost.M1 targets.

Figure 9.8 is a flowchart showing how AdaBoost.M1 works. Thus, a succession of weak classifiers ϕ_i can then be boosted to build a strong classifier, which is usually much more accurate than the best weak classifier for the training data (although there is no guarantee of better generalization performance for unseen instances).

This is the resampling implementation of AdaBoost. There is another implementation with reweighting. In the first few iterations, AdaBoost drives the ensemble training error to zero without overfitting. This is one reason for the success of this algorithm and is founded on a theory proving an upper bound on the training error (Freund and Schapire, 1997): if the ϕ_i classifiers consistently have weighted errors $\varepsilon_i < 0.5$, then the metaclassifier error drops to zero exponentially fast as more classifiers are added to the ensemble. Note that this is a weighted error (the error could be larger or smaller). Again the main disadvantage of AdaBoost.M1 is that it is unable to handle classifiers with weighted errors greater than 1/2, which is a stringent requirement for a multiple-class base classifier.

The **AdaBoost.M2** algorithm (Freund and Schapire, 1997) is another version of AdaBoost that does not require $\varepsilon_i < 0.5$. **Boosting with restart** does not include the classifier with $\varepsilon_i \geq 0.5$ that halts the AdaBoost.M1 algorithm, but a new sample can be generated on which a new classifier will be trained. This avoids early termination long before the L specified rounds. Other theoretical explanations for the success of AdaBoost have been sought in its relationship with logistic regression, i.e., its **LogitBoost** variant (Collins et al., 2002), and with SVMs and margin theory (Schapire et al., 1998).

Three applications of AdaBoost in neuroscience are described below. Martínez-Ramón et al. (2006) used AdaBoost with multi-class SVMs as base classifiers. t-maps of fMRI data were acquired during experiments of four interleaved tasks: visual (8 Hz checkerboard stimulation), motor (2 Hz right index finger tapping), auditory (syllable discrimination), and cognitive (mental calculation). In order to reduce the dimensionality of the data without reducing image resolution, the activation maps were split into smaller areas applying a base classifier to each one, that is, they used different feature spaces (voxels from different functional areas using a neuroanatomical atlas). The SVM classifiers were then aggregated through boosting. Yang et al. (2010a) combined genetic (single nucleotide polymorphisms, or SNPs for short) and fMRI data to classify schizophrenia patients and healthy controls.

The fMRI data were collected during the performance of an auditory oddball task: detecting an infrequent sound within a series of frequent sounds. An ensemble of SVMs with AdaBoost was first built from SNPs. An ensemble of SVMs with AdaBoost was then built from fMRI activation maps. Both cases previously performed an FSS. An SVM was also learned from using independent components extracted from fMRI data with independent component analysis. Finally, the three models were combined using majority vote. Finally, Polikar et al. (2008) used metaclassifiers for early diagnosis of AD. Each component classifier was trained on several data sources (data fusion) believed to contain complementary information. Specifically, they used the event-related potentials recorded from the Pz, Cz, and Fz electrodes of the EEG in response to different stimuli and decomposed into different frequency bands using multiresolution wavelet analysis. The ensemble was Learn^{++}, similar to AdaBoost. However, Learn^{++} generates an ensemble for each available data set and combines these ensembles to create an ensemble of ensembles or a meta-ensemble of classifiers. The base classifiers are multi-layer perceptrons, later combined using a weighted majority vote procedure.

The **arcing** family of algorithms (Breiman, 1998), which stands for Adaptive Resample and CombinING, includes AdaBoost and other variants because boosting is the most active subarea of classifier combination. AdaBoost is called **arc-fs** there, where "fs" stands for its inventors, Freund and Schapire. The **arc-x4** algorithm was designed to investigate whether the success of AdaBoost lay in its technical details or in its resampling scheme. Unlike AdaBoost, arc-x4 updates the weight of $\mathbf{x}^j$ at step i as the proportion m_j of times $\mathbf{x}^j$ has been misclassified by the classifiers built so far. For instance,

$$w_j^{i+1} = \frac{1 + m_j^4}{\sum_{k=1}^{N} \left(1 + m_k^4\right)}, \text{ for } j = 1, \dots, N,$$

where the exponent 4 in m_j for which the algorithm is named was derived empirically. Another difference between AdaBoost and arc-x4 is that the final decision (lines 9 and 10) is made by majority vote rather than weighted majority vote. Although AdaBoost is based on a theory and arc-x4 is an ad-hoc algorithm, both have been found to be comparable. Breiman (1998) found that AdaBoost made more abrupt moves and had larger standard deviations of weights for each data point than arc-x4.

The bias-variance decomposition of the classification error (Section 4.1.2.1) is sometimes used to analyze an algorithm. Experimental studies confirm that AdaBoost reduces both the bias (at early iterations) and variance (at later iterations) components of the expected classification error. Bagging has less effect on bias and more effect on variance. Note that the choice of bagging or boosting at best is an ill-posed problem because there is no best method for all problems. Boosting is sensitive to noise and outliers, especially for small data sets. Random forests tend to be comparable in performance to AdaBoost.

Example. To illustrate how the weights change in AdaBoost.M1, suppose we have a toy example with only five neurons from Data Set 1 to be classified as interneurons or pyramidal cells. Initially, $w_j^1 = 1/5, j = 1, \dots, 5$, which is a uniform distribution. This returns $\mathcal{D}_1$ of size five from which the first classifier ϕ_1 is learned. Suppose Neurons 2 and 3 are a miss, then $\varepsilon_1 = 2/5$ and $\beta_1 = 2/3$. The updated weights for the next iteration are

Table 9.4 Characteristics of the most popular metaclassifiers. Random forest randomly selects features. Stacking, cascading, and boosting could also perform feature selection, although this is not how they were originally described. Note that homogeneous metaclassifiers use the same base classifier

	Input data	FSS	Homogeneous	Combiner	Topology
Stacking	Original (layer-0), Predicted (layer-1)	No	No	Another classifier ϕ^*	Layered
Cascading	Non-confident instances	No	No	Confident prediction	Sequential
Bagging	Boostrap samples	No	Yes	Voting	Parallel
Random forest	Boostrap samples	Yes	Yes (trees)	Voting	Parallel
Boosting	Weighted samples	No	Yes	Weighted vote	Sequential

$$w_1^2 \propto w_1^1 \beta_1 = 2/15,$$
$$w_2^2 \propto w_2^1 = 1/5,$$
$$w_3^2 \propto w_3^1 = 1/5,$$
$$w_4^2 \propto w_4^1 \beta_1 = 2/15,$$
$$w_5^2 \propto w_5^1 \beta_1 = 2/15,$$

yielding, after normalization, $w_1^2 = w_4^2 = w_5^2 = 1/6$ and $w_2^2 = w_3^2 = 1/4$. Note that Neurons 2 and 3 are now more likely to be chosen as input data for the second classifier. The second iteration starts drawing a sample $\mathcal{D}_2$ of size five from the same five instances according to the weights w_j^2, and then ϕ_2 is learned. Suppose Neuron 3 is again a misclassification. The weighted error is $\varepsilon_2 = 1/4$ and $\beta_2 = 1/3$. The weights are updated as

$$w_1^3 \propto w_1^2 \beta_2 = 1/18,$$
$$w_2^3 \propto w_2^2 \beta_2 = 1/12,$$
$$w_3^3 \propto w_3^2 = 1/4,$$
$$w_4^3 \propto w_4^2 \beta_2 = 1/18,$$
$$w_5^3 \propto w_5^2 \beta_2 = 1/18,$$

yielding $w_1^3 = w_4^3 = w_5^3 = 1/9$ and $w_2^3 = 1/6, w_3^3 = 1/2$. Neuron 3 now has a 50% chance. The third iteration builds classifier ϕ_3, trained on $\mathcal{D}_3$, which is sampled from the data set of the five neurons with weights w_j^3. Suppose all neurons are correctly classified, then $\varepsilon_3 = 0$, and the process stops at $L = 2$ with two classifiers ϕ_1, ϕ_2. Suppose ϕ_1 assigns the pyramidal label to a new instance $\mathbf{x}$ for classification, whereas ϕ_2 classifies $\mathbf{x}$ as an interneuron. The final decision of the metaclassifier for $\mathbf{x}$ is "interneuron," because this label has a support of $\ln(1/\beta_2) = \ln 3 \approx 1.0986$, whereas the pyramidal label has only $\ln(1/\beta_1) = \ln 1.5 = 0.4055$. ∎

Table 9.4 lists the main features characterizing the most popular metaclassifiers.

9.3.6 Hybrid Classifiers

To round out the set of popular metaclassifiers, this section includes three well-known metaclassifiers that hybridize two classification algorithms.

Naive Bayes tree (NBTree) (Kohavi, 1996) combines classification trees and naive Bayes to leverage the strengths of both, i.e., the robustness of naive Bayes to irrelevant predictors and the segmentation produced by the recursive partitioning of the trees. Thus, the instance space is recursively split into subspaces, and a (local) naive Bayes classifier is generated in each subspace. Each leaf contains a local naive Bayes classifier that does not consider the features involved in the tests on the path leading to the leaf. It is the local naive Bayes classifier that predicts the class label of the instances that reach the leaf.

The data is first discretized. Then the utility of a node is calculated by estimating the accuracy of using naive Bayes at that node by means of five-fold cross-validation. The utility of a split is the weighted sum of the utility of the nodes, where the weight is proportional to the number of instances that go down to that node. The best split (with the highest utility) is chosen, say on X_i.

According to Kohavi (1996), a split is significant (and hence the data is partitioned) if the relative error reduction is greater than 5%, and there are at least 30 instances at that node. This avoids splits of low value. Partitioning the data on a discrete X_i is a usual multi-way split made for all its possible values. For a continuous (albeit discretized) X_i, a breakpoint is found as usual (Section 7.2.4) over the original data. This breakpoint is used to do the splitting. If the split is not significant, we create a naive Bayes classifier for the current node and stop.

The induction algorithm segments the data so that the conditional independence hypothesis required by naive Bayes is likely to be true. Note that when the assumption of strong independence required by the naive Bayes is violated, accuracy does not improve much as the data set size increases. This is why, by using the accuracy of naive Bayes to drive splitting, the NBTree identifies regions of the instance space in which the conditional independence is unlikely to be violated.

NBTree scales up well to large data sets, mainly due to the fast computation of the cross-validated accuracy of the naive Bayes over discrete data. Thus, it is a convenient model when there are many relevant attributes for classification and that are not necessarily independent given the class.

The main drawback of NBTree is the problem of small disjuncts. This means that leaves with few training cases are likely to produce poor predictions. This is what motivated the proposal of the **lazy Bayesian rule** (LBR) learning algorithm (Zheng and Webb, 2000). This algorithm combines naive Bayes and rules. In order to avoid the small disjunct problem, LBR retains all training cases until classification time (lazy learning). Before classifying a test instance, LBR generates a rule whose antecedent is a conjunction of predictor-value pairs (in the form of $X_i = x_i$) – continuous features are previously discretized – and whose consequent is a local naive Bayes classifier created from the training cases satisfying the antecedent. Like NBTree, the local model only uses the features that do not appear in the antecedent of the rule. Therefore, the selected training cases for a given test instance exclude any whose inclusion may harm the naive Bayes classifier. The values in the antecedent are always the same as the corresponding values of the test instance. This subset of selected instances defines a subspace to which the test instance belongs. The antecedent is grown such that the error of the local naive Bayes classifier in the consequent is decreased.

The idea of selecting a set of predictors for which the independence assumption holds, given other predictors besides the class is also behind **logistic model trees**

(Landwehr et al., 2003). These are classification trees with logistic regression models at the leaves, applied to instances that reach such leaves.

9.4   Example: Interneurons versus Pyramidal Neurons

Data Set 1 in Chapter 1 built with the aim of discriminating between interneurons (I) and pyramidal neurons (P) was managed by different non-probabilistic and probabilistic classifiers in Chapters 7 and 8, respectively. Here they are combined into a number of representative metaclassifiers.

Table 9.5 shows the stratified cross-validated accuracies (with a 10-fold scheme). All were output using WEKA software (Hall et al., 2009).

The first metaclassifier takes five classifiers and averages their probability estimates. In this particular case, the base classifiers were (1) 1-NN (classifier `IB1` in WEKA); (2) C4.5 decision tree (`J48`); (3) SVM (`SMO`); (4) logistic regression (`logistic`), and (5) TAN (`BayesNet` with TAN as search algorithm). The same five models were used in the second metaclassifier (stacking), where a naive Bayes (`NaiveBayesSimple`) acts as the combiner ϕ^*. The third metaclassifier is bagging, where the base classifiers are 10 pruned decision trees learned with the C4.5 algorithm, which outperformed other base classifiers.

The random subspace is the fourth metaclassifier. The number of features, M, randomly drawn from the n original variables was $n/2$. There were 10 base classifiers in this ensemble (all of which were logistic regressions) that were slightly better than the C4.5 algorithm. The next metaclassifier, the random tree, only achieves 77.68% accuracy. Random tree constructs a tree that considers $\log_2 n + 1$ randomly chosen variables at each node. It performs no pruning. The random forest included 10 bagged random trees. Its accuracy increased from 0.8318 with 10 trees to 0.8654 with 20 trees. The rotation forest used 10 iterations, where each had 2 decision trees (`J48`), learned from the data transformed via PCA. PCA was run using $n/2$ randomly selected features and 50% of instances. It is equally as accurate (0.8716) as the first metaclassifier. With 20 iterations, the accuracy grew to 0.8807. AdaBoost.M1 achieved 0.8654 accuracy with $L = 10$ classifiers, equal

Table 9.5 Accuracy results produced by the main metaclassifiers for Data Set 1

Metaclassifier	Accuracy
Vote	0.8716
Stacking	0.8623
Bagging	0.8685
Random subspace	0.8654
Random tree	0.7768
Random forest	0.8318
Rotation forest	0.8716
AdaBoost.M1	0.8654
NBTree	0.7768
LBR	0.8593
Logistic model tree	0.8685

to the random subspace metaclassifier. Like random tree, the accuracy of NBTree is only 77.68%. The continuous features have to be previously discretized for LBR. The MDLP method (Section 2.6.3) was applied for discretization. MDLP uses the class information. The resulting accuracy was 0.8593. Finally, the logistic model tree yields an accuracy of 0.8685, like bagging.

Except for random tree and NBTree, all metaclassifiers perform similarly. Note that they improve the results given by some single classifiers, e.g., 0.6147 accuracy for ID3 and 0.8318 for C4.5 (Table 7.6), 0.8561 accuracy for LDA (Table 8.2), 0.8104 for logistic regression (Section 8.3.6), 0.8196 for naive Bayes, 0.8287 for TAN, and 0.8379 for BAN (Table 8.8). However, after feature selection, some single classifiers outperform these metaclassifiers, e.g., an accuracy of 0.9052 for Gaussian RBF kernel-based SVM (Table 7.13) and of 0.9144 for TAN (Table 8.8), both applying a wrapper approach.

Therefore, for Data Set 1, feature selection has a substantial effect on performance, and metaclassifiers, which do not apply feature selection (except for some that select features at random), lag behind some single classifiers with feature selection. Feature selection could be built into the metaclassifiers, although this is not usually the case.

9.5   Example: Interneurons versus Pyramidal Neurons; Comparison of All Classifiers

In Chapter 7 many non-probabilistic classifiers were applied to Data Set 1 to discriminate between interneurons (I) and pyramidal neurons (P). In Chapter 8, probabilistic classifiers were tested on the same data set. This chapter also looked at a number of metaclassifiers in action to separate labels I and P. This section compares most of the above classifiers in terms of their accuracy.

In this case, multiple classifiers are compared on a single data set (see Section 5.4.3 and the example therein). Each measurement is the classification accuracy of each algorithm (the "treatment" introduced in Section 4.2.6) in each of the 10 folds in a cross-validation scheme (the "blocks" of Section 4.2.6). Because we used the same folds for all algorithms, the samples (accuracies) are paired, and the Friedman test must be applied because samples are not normally distributed.

We used 14 classifiers of all types. First, the following non-probabilistic classifiers: k-nearest neighbor algorithm (algorithm IB3, see Table 7.2), classification trees (algorithm C4.5, see Table 7.6), rule induction (algorithm RIPPER, see Table 7.8), ANNs (MLP model, see Table 7.10), and SVMs (with a Gaussian RBF kernel, see Table 7.13). Second, we consider the following probabilistic classifiers: logistic regression (Table 8.5) and Bayesian network classifiers (a TAN model, see Table 8.9). Third, we focus on the following metaclassifiers: bagging, random tree, random forest, rotation forest, boosting (algorithm AdaBoost.M1), LBR, and NBTree (see Table 9.5 above).

Thus, we had $k = 14$ classifiers and their classification accuracy over each of the $b = 10$ folds, i.e., a data matrix of 10 rows and 14 columns. The Friedman statistic S shown in Equation (4.14) is, under the null hypothesis of no difference among the 14 classifiers, approximately distributed according to χ^2_{13}. For this data matrix, the value of S was 46.9057, yielding a p-value of 1.0022e–05, thereby rejecting the null hypothesis. Table 9.6

Table 9.6 Average rankings of the classification accuracy results for each of the 14 classifiers applied to Data Set 1. Averages were computed over the 10 folds

Classifier	Ranking
IB3	5.85
Tree	9.20
Rules	9.45
ANN	7.10
SVM	4.00
Logistic	5.70
TAN	3.40
Bagging	6.70
Random tree	11.05
Random forest	9.70
Rotation forest	6.50
AdaBoost.M1	6.85
LBR	7.45
NBTree	12.05

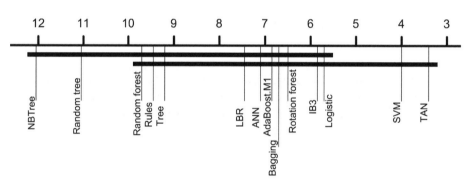

Figure 9.9 Critical difference diagram showing the results of all pairwise classifier comparisons according to the Nemenyi test.

lists the algorithm average rankings, i.e., R_j/b for algorithm j, $j = 1, \ldots, k$, with the notation of Equation (4.14). Note that, on average, TAN and SVM ranked best.

Because the null hypothesis was rejected, we conducted a post-hoc test to identify which pairs of algorithms were significantly different. The number of pairwise tests to be conducted was $k(k-1)/2 = 91$. We used the Nemenyi test with correction (Section 4.2.9). This test takes into account that multiple comparisons are performed, and the adjusted p-value is calculated as the unadjusted p-value multiplied by $k(k-1)/2$. In this case, TAN versus NBTree, SVM versus NBTree, TAN versus random tree and SVM versus random tree were the only pairs with adjusted p-values less than 0.05, and were thus considered as significantly different.

The results of the post-hoc test can be plotted using the **critical difference diagram** (Demšar, 2006), see Figure 9.9. The top line is an axis on which the average ranks of the classifiers are plotted; see their values in Table 9.6. Lowest ranks (the best) are positioned to the right because the right side is regarded as better. The algorithms that are not significantly different (p-value is greater than 0.05) are connected by the thick lines. Note that TAN and SVM are not connected to NBTree and random tree because they are significantly different.

9.6   Bibliographic Notes

Rokach (2009) cites Tukey's twicing (Tukey, 1977) as the first ensemble method, an ensemble of two linear regression models fitted to the original data and to the residuals, respectively. However, Kuncheva (2004) refers to a cascade machine as being the first metaclassifier (Sebestyen, 1962). Rokach (2009) and Wozniak et al. (2014) are surveys on metaclassifiers. This new (meta)level, where we look for the best set of classifiers and best combination method, could soon lead us to look for the best set of metaclassifiers causing a loop of more and more complex combination schemes, as criticized by Ho (2002). Further research is needed before resorting to new complicated designs because there is still a lot of discussion on how or why classifier combination works. Some researchers advocate the stochastic discrimination theory, a general method for separating points in multidimensional spaces through the use of stochastic processes (Kleinberg, 1990) as the only consistent theory of metaclassifier success.

We have not dealt with **ensemble pruning** or **ensemble thinning**, whose aim is to select only a subset of all the trained individual classifiers. This seeks to improve efficiency by reducing the computational resources and increasing overall accuracy. A category of ensemble pruning methods ranks the base classifiers according to some criterion and selects the top ranked options. Another category selects only representative individual classifiers in the ensemble, after they have been grouped in classifiers that behave similar to each other and different from the other groups. A third category poses the ensemble pruning problem as an optimization problem that finds the base classifiers optimizing a criterion related to metaclassifier accuracy.

Brown et al. (2005) published a survey on diversity generation approaches. There is yet another mechanism to generate diversity in the metaclassifier, not detailed in this chapter. This is the use of different output representations. For instance, we can randomly change the labels of some training instances or add artificial instances with labels that are very unlike the predictions of the current ensemble, as in the DECORATE (Diverse Ensemble Creation by Oppositional Relabeling of Artificial Training Examples) metaclassifier (Melville and Mooney, 2005).

Beyond diversity, other issues with respect to the behavior and relationships between the metaclassifier members warrant investigation. Inza et al. (1999) applied a set of different classifiers on a number of data sets. They then learned a Bayesian network (Chapter 13) from the results (predicted classes) of each classifier for the data sets. Because the network reflected the joint probability distribution of the class label predictions of the classifiers that were used, their dependence and (conditional) independence relations could be analyzed.

Zhou (2012) discussed other variants of boosting not covered here. An open question is which base classifiers are ideal for boosting. It is easy to underfit if they are too weak, yet easy to overfit if they are too strong. For binary classification, base classifiers should be better than random guess. For multi-class problems with R labels, the requirement of being better than random guess (expected error is $1 - 1/R$) or having an accuracy greater than 50% is too weak and too strong, respectively. Some approaches study this issue (Mukherjee and Schapire, 2013).

A challenge is to automatically choose the best model or ensemble technique. A tendency is **meta-learning** (Brazdil et al., 2009), which, rather than testing multiple algorithms to assess which is best for a given data set, tries to answer the question of what works well where. If one method outperforms others for a particular data set, then this method should be preferable when dealing with other problems with similar characteristics. Thus, meta-learning takes into account data set characteristics stored in a metadata set, together with the performance of all investigated methods on various data sets. The most appropriate model will be selected for a new unseen data set, with particular characteristics.

Other topics not covered here are metaclassifiers in semisupervised classification, active learning, cost-sensitive learning, and class-imbalance learning (Zhou, 2012). The ensemble methodology also extends to other tasks apart from classification, such as clustering (Smeraldi et al., 2011; Vega-Pons and Ruiz-Shulcloper, 2011) (see Section 11.6), regression (Gey and Poggi, 2006; Tutz and Binder, 2007), and density estimation (Ridgeway, 2002).

10 Multidimensional Classifiers

Chapters 7–9 introduced different types of supervised classification paradigms useful for predicting the class value of new instances characterized only by their predictor variables. The problem of discriminating between interneurons (I) and pyramidal neurons (P) from the morphological variables of the neurons is an example of the behavior of the models induced from data using each of these paradigms. In some situations, however, e.g., Data Set 3 in Chapter 1, we want to learn a mapping between the 39 responses to the Parkinson's Disease Questionnaire (PDQ-39) and the five answers of the European Quality of Life-5 Dimensions (EQ-5D) from data.

From the machine learning point of view, this mapping can be interpreted as a supervised classification problem where the aim is to simultaneously predict the five EQ-5D class variables. A naive approach to this problem is to develop five independent classifiers, each associated with one of the EQ-5D responses. However, this approach is far from being satisfactory as the class variables associated with the responses are usually dependent. The methods presented in this chapter consider different degrees of dependencies in different ways.

The chapter is organized as follows. Section 10.1 shows the differences and similarities between multi-label and multidimensional classification problems. Section 10.2 presents two equivalent notations for multi-label classification, one based on assigning the set of associated labels to each instance, and a second notation where a class variable is related to each of the possible labels. Section 10.3 introduces different performance evaluation measures for multi-label and multidimensional classifiers. The measures are organized from the point of view of both instances and labels. Methods for learning these types of classifiers from data are explained and analyzed in Section 10.4. Section 10.5 develops the example above about the application of multidimensional classification for predicting the quality of life of patients suffering from PD. The chapter closes with Section 10.6, which includes some bibliographic notes on the topic.

10.1 Multi-label and Multidimensional Classification

From a machine learning point of view, the task to be solved in Data Set 3 of Section 1.6.3 is to simultaneously predict the values of five discrete variables (Mobility, Self-care, Usual activities, Pain/Discomfort, and Anxiety/Depression) from the discrete values collected by the 39 PDQ-39 predictor variables. This task, called multidimensional classification, will be explained in this chapter.

Table 10.1 Example of a data set with information on the 39 predictor ordinal variables (PDQ_1 to PDQ_{39}) and the 5 output class variables (EQ_1 to EQ_5)

PDQ_1	PDQ_2	$\cdots$	$\cdots$	PDQ_{39}	EQ_1	EQ_2	EQ_3	EQ_4	EQ_5
3	1	$\cdots$	$\cdots$	3	1	3	3	2	1
2	3	$\cdots$	$\cdots$	2	1	1	2	3	2
5	2	$\cdots$	$\cdots$	4	1	3	3	1	2
$\cdots$	$\cdots$	$\cdots$	$\cdots$	$\cdots$	$\cdots$	$\cdots$	$\cdots$	$\cdots$	$\cdots$
4	4	$\cdots$	$\cdots$	3	3	1	2	3	2
4	4	$\cdots$	$\cdots$	3	3	1	2	3	2
5	5	$\cdots$	$\cdots$	4	2	3	2	3	3

Table 10.1 shows a hypothetical example of a data set, where each row of the table contains the information related to a PD patient in terms of the results of both the PDQ-39 and EQ-5D questionnaires. Multidimensional classification calls for PDQ-39 to be mapped to EQ-5D, that is, finding

$$\phi : (PDQ_1, \ldots, PDQ_{39}) \to (EQ_1, \ldots, EQ_5).$$

Suppose $\Omega_{\mathbf{X}}$ for $\mathbf{X} = (X_1, \ldots, X_n)$ denotes an n-dimensional input space for the predictor variables, with $\Omega_{\mathbf{X}} = \underset{i=1}{\overset{n}{\times}} \Omega_{X_i}$, where $\Omega_{X_i} \subseteq \mathbb{N}$ (for categorical and discrete features) or $\Omega_{X_i} \subseteq \mathbb{R}$ (for numeric continuous features), and $\mathbf{C} = (C_1, \ldots, C_d)$ refers to the d-dimensional output space for the class variables, with $\Omega_{\mathbf{C}} = \underset{i=1}{\overset{d}{\times}} \Omega_{C_i}$.

A **multidimensional data set** with N training examples is $\mathcal{D} = \{(\mathbf{x}^1, \mathbf{c}^1), \ldots, (\mathbf{x}^N, \mathbf{c}^N)\}$, where $\mathbf{x}^i = (x_1^i, \ldots, x_n^i) \in \Omega_{\mathbf{X}}$ and $\mathbf{c}^i = (c_1^i, \ldots, c_d^i) \in \Omega_{\mathbf{C}}$ for all $i = 1, \ldots, N$ (Section 1.5.2.2). $\mathcal{D}$ contains information about the values of n predictor variables and d class variables from a sample of size N. This information will be considered as training data for the multidimensional classifier.

With this notation, the learning task for a **multidimensional classification** paradigm is to output a function ϕ

$$\Omega_{X_1} \times \cdots \times \Omega_{X_n} \overset{\phi}{\to} \Omega_{C_1} \times \cdots \times \Omega_{C_d}$$
$$(x_1, \ldots, x_n) \quad \to (c_1, \ldots, c_d).$$

Multi-label classification refers to a particular case of multidimensional classification, where all class variables, $C_1, \ldots, C_d$, are binary. Early studies on multi-label classification focus on text categorization, whereas it has been widely applied to diverse problems from automatic annotation of multimedia contents to bioinformatics, web mining, information retrieval, tag recommendations, drug discovery, medical diagnosis, HIV drug resistance, weather forecast, music categorization, international patent classification, demographic classification of human faces from images, etc., over the last decade. The first overview of multi-label classification was written by Tsoumakas and Katakis (2007). Later reviews on the topic include Zhang and Zhou (2014), Gibaja and Ventura (2015), and Herrera et al. (2016).

Very few problems in neuroscience have been formulated as multidimensional (or multi-label) classification. In neuroanatomy, Fernández-González et al. (2015) predicted species, gender, cell type, development stage, and area of the neurocortex for a neuron based on a set of morphological features measured with Neurolucida software (Glaser and

Glaser, 1990) and taken from the NeuroMorpho repository (Ascoli et al., 2017). Also, Mihaljević et al. (2014) approached the problem of the simultaneous prediction of interneuronal types and four axonal features (intralaminar versus translaminar; intra-columnar versus transcolumnar; centered versus displaced; and ascending, descending, both, or none) using 18 morphological predictor variables. The novelty of the method was to deal with the different assignments of the five class variables provided by each of the 42 experts who labeled them. Finally, Turner et al. (2013) tried to replicate stimuli, cognitive paradigms, response types, and other relevant dimensions of functional imaging experiments when the predicted variables were output by text mining abstracts of published functional neuroimaging papers.

10.2 Equivalent Notations for Multi-label Classification

Multi-label classification normally represents the present labels as a subset from $\mathcal{Y} = \{\lambda_1, \dots, \lambda_d\}$, where $\mathcal{Y}$ refers to the set of d possible output labels. Table 10.2 shows an example of this representation, where $n = 5$, $d = 4$, and $N = 5$.

With this notation, the learning task is to output a function ϕ

$$\Omega_{X_1} \times \cdots \times \Omega_{X_n} \xrightarrow{\phi} Y \subseteq \mathcal{Y}$$
$$(x_1, \dots, x_n) \quad \to \{\lambda_r, \dots, \lambda_u\} \subseteq \mathcal{Y},$$

where $\{\lambda_r, \dots, \lambda_u\}$ denotes the labels that are present for instance $(x_1, \dots, x_n)$.

In line with multidimensional classification, the labels associated with each instance can also be represented by a binary vector of size d, $(C_1, \dots, C_d)$, where a value of 1 in its ith component, $C_i = 1$, means that this instance comes together to label λ_i (λ_i is present). Thus, a class variable is considered for each label, resulting in a d-dimensional class variable, $C = (C_1, \dots, C_d)$, where C_i is the binary class variable associated with label λ_i, with $i = 1, \dots, d$. The learning task consists of outputting a function ϕ

$$\Omega_{X_1} \times \cdots \times \Omega_{X_n} \xrightarrow{\phi} \Omega_{C_1} \times \cdots \times \Omega_{C_d}$$
$$(x_1, \dots, x_n) \quad \to (c_1, \dots, c_d).$$

As mentioned in the previous section, this representation can be used to address multi-dimensional classification problems, where some of the class variables are not binary (multi-class case).

Table 10.2 Example of a data set composed of five cases, each of which is characterized by five predictor variables and four possible labels; representation with associated labels

X_1	X_2	X_3	X_4	X_5	$Y \subseteq \mathcal{Y}$
3.2	1.4	4.7	7.5	3.7	$\{\lambda_1, \lambda_4\}$
2.8	6.3	1.6	4.7	2.7	$\{\lambda_3, \lambda_4\}$
7.7	6.2	4.1	3.3	7.7	$\{\lambda_1, \lambda_4\}$
9.2	0.4	2.8	0.5	3.9	$\{\lambda_2\}$
5.5	5.3	4.9	0.6	6.6	$\{\lambda_1, \lambda_2, \lambda_3\}$

Table 10.3 Example of a data set composed of five cases, each of which is characterized by five predictor variables and four class variables; representation with class variables

X_1	X_2	X_3	X_4	X_5	C_1	C_2	C_3	C_4
3.2	1.4	4.7	7.5	3.7	1	0	0	1
2.8	6.3	1.6	4.7	2.7	0	0	1	1
7.7	6.2	4.1	3.3	7.7	1	0	0	1
9.2	0.4	2.8	0.5	3.9	0	1	0	0
5.5	5.3	4.9	0.6	6.6	1	1	1	0

Table 10.3 illustrates the same example as in Table 10.2, now with the class variables-based representation.

Multi-label data sets tend to be characterized by several multi-label indicators. A natural way to measure the degree of multi-labeledness is **label cardinality**, label_{car}, defined as $\text{label}_{car} = \frac{1}{N}\sum_{i=1}^{N}\sum_{j=1}^{d} c_j^i$, i.e., the average number of labels per example. **Label density**, denoted by label_{den}, normalizes label cardinality by the number of possible labels in the label space and is defined as $\text{label}_{den} = \frac{\text{label}_{car}}{d}$. **Label diversity**, label_{div}, refers to the number of distinct label sets that there are in the data set. Its normalization by the number of examples in the data set indicates the **proportion of distinct label sets**, defined as $\text{label}_{prop} = \frac{\text{label}_{div}}{N}$. For Table 10.3, we obtain: $\text{label}_{car} = \frac{2+2+2+1+3}{5} = 2$; $\text{label}_{den} = \frac{2}{4} = 0.5$; $\text{label}_{div} = 4$ and $\text{label}_{prop} = \frac{4}{5} = 0.8$.

10.3   Performance Evaluation Measures

One-dimensional supervised classification algorithms (see Chapters 7–9) are usually evaluated with conventional performance measures such as classification accuracy, error rate, sensitivity, specificity, positive predictive value, negative predictive value, F_1-measure, Cohen's kappa statistic, Brier score, area under the ROC curve, etc. (see Section 5.2 for details). Performance evaluation in multi-label learning is much more complex, as each instance can be associated with multiple labels simultaneously. A number of evaluation measures specific to multi-label learning have been proposed. They are divided into two groups, i.e., **instance-based measures** and **label-based measures**.

Instance-based measures start evaluating the multi-label classification model performance on each test instance separately. They then return the mean or average value across the test set. Label-based measures need the evaluation of the multi-label classification model on each class label (class variable) separately. They then return a mean or average value across all class labels. Figure 10.1 shows a summary of multi-label evaluation measures. Both instance-based measures and label-based measure will be exemplified with the data set of Table 10.4.

10.3.1   Instance-Based Measures

- **Exact Match**. This measure computes the fraction of correctly classified instances. In a multi-label problem an instance is correctly classified when its predicted label set is identical to the ground-truth label set. In terms of class variables, the instance will be

Table 10.4 Toy data set for computing the different instance-based and label-based measures. C_1, C_2, C_3, C_4, and C_5 denote the five class variables, whereas Y^i represents the subset of selected labels for the ith instance. Their corresponding predictions are denoted by $\hat{C}_1, \hat{C}_2, \hat{C}_3, \hat{C}_4, \hat{C}_5$, and $\hat{Y}^i$

$\mathbf{x}^i$	C_1	C_2	C_3	C_4	C_5	Y^i	$\hat{C}_1$	$\hat{C}_2$	$\hat{C}_3$	$\hat{C}_4$	$\hat{C}_5$	$\hat{Y}^i$
$\mathbf{x}^1$	1	0	1	0	0	$\{\lambda_1, \lambda_3\}$	1	0	0	1	0	$\{\lambda_1, \lambda_4\}$
$\mathbf{x}^2$	0	1	0	1	0	$\{\lambda_2, \lambda_4\}$	0	1	0	1	0	$\{\lambda_2, \lambda_4\}$
$\mathbf{x}^3$	1	0	0	1	0	$\{\lambda_1, \lambda_4\}$	1	0	0	1	0	$\{\lambda_1, \lambda_4\}$
$\mathbf{x}^4$	0	1	1	0	0	$\{\lambda_2, \lambda_3\}$	0	1	0	0	0	$\{\lambda_2\}$
$\mathbf{x}^5$	1	0	0	0	0	$\{\lambda_1\}$	1	0	0	1	0	$\{\lambda_1, \lambda_4\}$

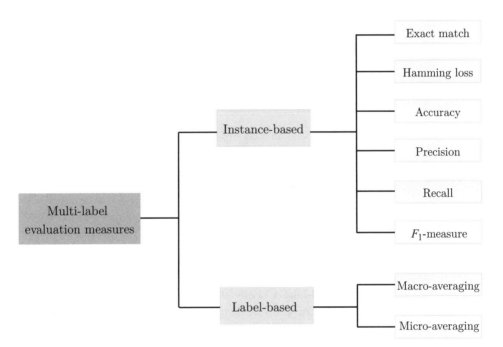

Figure 10.1 Instance-based and label-based multi-label evaluation measures.

correctly classified if the binary vector containing the values of each binary class variable coincides with the binary vector containing their predictions. Exact match tends to be overly strict, especially when the size of the label space or the number of class variables (d) is large. For a classifier ϕ, it is computed as

$$\text{Exact-match}(\phi) = \frac{1}{N}\sum_{i=1}^{N}\mathbb{I}(\hat{\mathbf{c}}^i = \mathbf{c}^i) = \frac{1}{N}\sum_{i=1}^{N}\mathbb{I}\left(\hat{y}^i = y^i\right),$$

where $\mathbb{I}(\text{true}) = 1$ and $\mathbb{I}(\text{false}) = 0$. The application of this equation to the data set of Table 10.4 provides a value of $\text{Exactmatch}(\phi) = \frac{1}{5}(0+1+1+0+0) = 0.4$.

- **Hamming Loss**. The measure is defined as

$$\text{Hamming-loss}(\phi) = \frac{1}{d}\cdot\frac{1}{N}\sum_{i=1}^{N}|\hat{\mathbf{c}}^i \,\Delta\, \mathbf{c}^i| = \frac{1}{d}\cdot\frac{1}{N}\sum_{i=1}^{N}|\hat{Y}^i \,\Delta\, Y^i|,$$

where Δ stands for the symmetric difference between two binary vectors (or two sets), i.e., the elements which are in either of the vectors (sets) and not in their intersection. The Hamming loss evaluates the fraction of misclassified instance-label pairs, i.e., a label that is present is missed or a label that is absent is predicted. With the data set of Table 10.4 we have Hamming-loss$(\phi) = \frac{1}{5} \cdot \frac{1}{5}(2+0+0+1+1) = 0.16$.

- **Accuracy for Multi-label Classification**. The accuracy is defined as the average of the individual instance accuracies. These are computed as the quotient between the number of labels correctly predicted over the union of the true and predicted labels. In terms of the class labels, it is evaluated as

$$\text{Accuracy}(\phi) = \frac{1}{N} \sum_{i=1}^{N} \frac{|\hat{Y}^i \cap Y^i|}{|\hat{Y}^i \cup Y^i|}.$$

The formula applied to Table 10.4 results in Accuracy$(\phi) = \frac{1}{5} \left(\frac{1}{3} + \frac{2}{2} + \frac{2}{2} + \frac{1}{2} + \frac{1}{2} \right) = 0.66$.

- **Precision for Multi-label Classification**. For multi-label classification, precision is computed as the average of the precisions of each instance. In mathematical terms,

$$\text{Precision}(\phi) = \frac{1}{N} \sum_{i=1}^{N} \frac{|\hat{Y}^i \cap Y^i|}{|\hat{Y}^i|}.$$

For the data set in Table 10.4, we have Precision$(\phi) = \frac{1}{5} \left(\frac{1}{2} + \frac{2}{2} + \frac{2}{2} + \frac{1}{1} + \frac{1}{2} \right) = 0.80$.

- **Recall for Multi-label Classification**. For multi-label classification, recall is computed as the average of the recalls of each instance. Formally,

$$\text{Recall}(\phi) = \frac{1}{N} \sum_{i=1}^{N} \frac{|\hat{Y}^i \cap Y^i|}{|Y^i|}.$$

For the data set of Table 10.4, we have Recall$(\phi) = \frac{1}{5} \left(\frac{1}{2} + \frac{2}{2} + \frac{2}{2} + \frac{1}{2} + \frac{1}{1} \right) = 0.80$.

- **F_1-Measure for Multi-label Classification**. The F_1-measure in multi-label classification is calculated as the average of the harmonic means between the precisions and recalls computed over the set of instances. Its equation is written as

$$F_1\text{-measure}(\phi) = \frac{1}{N} \sum_{i=1}^{N} \frac{2|\hat{Y}^i \cap Y^i|}{|\hat{Y}^i| + |Y^i|}.$$

For the data set of Table 10.4, the F_1-measure(ϕ) value is given by $\frac{1}{5} \cdot 2(\frac{1}{4} + \frac{2}{4} + \frac{2}{4} + \frac{1}{3} + \frac{1}{3}) = 0.71$.

10.3.2 Label-Based Measures

Label-based measures are defined in terms of the four basic quantities characterizing the binary classification performance on each label (or each class variable). These four quantities are: true positive, false positive, true negative, and false negative, denoted for the jth label (or variable) as TP_j, FP_j, TN_j, and FN_j, respectively.

Based on the above four quantities, most of the binary classification measures can be derived accordingly. For example, for the classification of the jth label, we have $\text{Accuracy}_j = \frac{\text{TP}_j + \text{TN}_j}{\text{TP}_j + \text{FP}_j + \text{TN}_j + \text{FN}_j}$. Let $B(\text{TP}_j + \text{FP}_j + \text{TN}_j + \text{FN}_j)$ represent some specific binary classification measure of the four quantities. The label-based classification measures can be computed in either of the following ways:

- **Macro-Averaging**. Macro-averaging measures are calculated as the mean across all possible labels (or class variables) of a given specific binary classification measure. Symbolically,

$$B_{\mathrm{macro}}(\phi) = \frac{1}{d} \sum_{j=1}^{d} B(\mathrm{TP}_j + \mathrm{FP}_j + \mathrm{TN}_j + \mathrm{FN}_j).$$

- **Micro-Averaging**. Micro-averaging measures are defined in terms of a specific binary classification measure applied to the addition of each of the four basic quantities associated with each label (class variable). Mathematically,

$$B_{\mathrm{micro}}(\phi) = B\left(\sum_{j=1}^{d} \mathrm{TP}_j, \sum_{j=1}^{d} \mathrm{FP}_j, \sum_{j=1}^{d} \mathrm{TN}_j, \sum_{j=1}^{d} \mathrm{FN}_j \right).$$

10.4   Learning Methods

This section introduces a simple categorization of multi-label learning algorithms. It comprises: (i) **problem transformation methods**, which transform the multi-label problem into one or more single-label problems, each of which is solved with a single-label classification algorithm, and (ii) **algorithm adaptation methods**, which adapt popular learning techniques to deal with multi-label data directly.

Briefly, the key idea of problem transformation methods is to fit data to algorithms, developing algorithm-independent proposals, whereas algorithm adaptation methods fit algorithms to data.

10.4.1   Problem Transformation Methods

The different approaches are categorized in Figure 10.2.

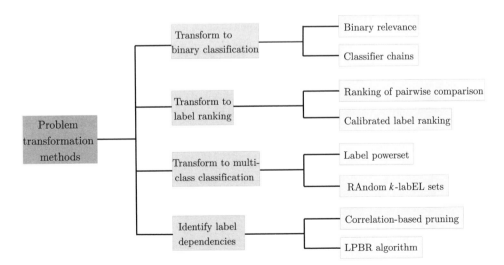

Figure 10.2 Categorization of problem transformation methods.

Table 10.5 Toy data set used for explaining the characteristics of binary relevance, ranking of pairwise comparison, calibrated label ranking, and label powerset

x^i	Y^i	C_1	C_2	C_3	C_4
x^1	$\{\lambda_1, \lambda_4\}$	1	0	0	1
x^2	$\{\lambda_3, \lambda_4\}$	0	0	1	1
x^3	$\{\lambda_1, \lambda_4\}$	1	0	0	1
x^4	$\{\lambda_2\}$	0	1	0	0
x^5	$\{\lambda_1, \lambda_2, \lambda_3\}$	1	1	1	0

Table 10.6 The four data sets resulting from Table 10.5, after considering the prediction of each class variable (label) as an independent task

x^i	C_1	x^i	C_2	x^i	C_3	x^i	C_4
x^1	1	x^1	0	x^1	0	x^1	1
x^2	0	x^2	0	x^2	1	x^2	1
x^3	1	x^3	0	x^3	0	x^3	1
x^4	0	x^4	1	x^4	0	x^4	0
x^5	1	x^5	1	x^5	1	x^5	0

10.4.1.1 Transformation to Binary Classification

Binary Relevance. The basic idea of this algorithm (Godbole and Sarawagi, 2004) is to decompose the multi-label learning problem with d possible labels or classes into d independent binary classification problems. Each binary classification problem is associated with each of the d class variables (labels in the label space). We then use any of the 1D (single-class or single-label) supervised classification algorithm for binary classes, explained in Chapters 7–9, to induce a classifier able to predict one of the d possible class variables, $C_1, \ldots, C_d$. These d classifiers are learned independent of each other, and this is one of the main drawbacks of the binary relevance approach. The multi-label prediction for a test instance is carried out as the concatenation of the predictions provided by the d independent 1D binary classifiers. Table 10.5 shows a toy data set containing five cases and their associated labels in both representations (based on sets of labels or in class variables). The four data sets in Table 10.6 are the result of approaching the multi-label classification problem as d independent 1D binary supervised problems.

In addition to ignoring dependencies among classes, binary relevance may suffer from the issue of class-imbalance (Section 5.5) when d is large and the label density is low. Its main advantage is the low computational complexity and the fact that it scales linearly with the number of class variables (labels). Because class variables are treated as independent, they can be added and removed without affecting the rest of the global model. In this manner, binary relevance is applicable to evolving or dynamic scenarios.

Classifier Chain. This approach aims to overcome the label independence assumption in the binary relevance method. Its basic idea is to transform the multi-label learning problem into a chain of binary classification problems, where each binary classifier in the chain is

Table 10.7 Data set for predicting C_3 using $X_1, \ldots, X_n$ and $\hat{C}_1$ and $\hat{C}_2$ as predictor variables in a classifier chain approach

Predictors					Class
X_1	$\ldots$	X_n	$\hat{C}_1$	$\hat{C}_2$	C_3
x_1^1	$\ldots$	x_n^1	1	0	0
x_1^2	$\ldots$	x_n^2	0	0	1
x_1^3	$\ldots$	x_n^3	1	0	0
x_1^4	$\ldots$	x_n^4	0	1	0
x_1^5	$\ldots$	x_n^5	1	1	1

built upon the predictions (probabilistic predictions in our notation) of preceding classifiers (Read et al., 2011).

In mathematical notation, the classifier chain method learns d functions ϕ_i on augmented input spaces, $\Omega_{\mathbf{X}} \times \{0,1\}^{i-1}$, respectively, taking $\hat{c}_1, \ldots, \hat{c}_{i-1}$ as additional features:

$$\Omega_{\mathbf{X}} \times \{0,1\}^{i-1} \xrightarrow{\phi} [0,1]$$
$$(\mathbf{x}, \hat{c}_1, \ldots, \hat{c}_{i-1}) \rightarrow p(c_i | \mathbf{x}, \hat{c}_1, \ldots, \hat{c}_{i-1}).$$

One-dimensional classifiers ϕ_i can be learned using $c_1, \ldots, c_{i-1}$ instead of $\hat{c}_1, \ldots, \hat{c}_{i-1}$. However, when applied to new instances, where the values of the class variables (labels) are unknown, the classifier chain method necessarily uses predictions $\hat{c}_1, \ldots, \hat{c}_{i-1}$. Note that a total order among the class variables should be defined beforehand, where the result of the classifier chains is dependent on that order.

An example of this method is shown in Table 10.7. This table contains the information needed to predict the values of C_3 using $X_1, \ldots, X_n$ and $\hat{C}_1$ and $\hat{C}_2$ as the predictor variables. C_4 should be predicted including $\hat{C}_3$ in the set of predictor variables. If C_3 is used last, two possible orders among the class variables are valid for predicting C_4: 1–2–3–4 or alternatively 2–1–3–4.

10.4.1.2 Transformation to Label Ranking

Ranking of Pairwise Comparisons. This method (Hüllermeier et al., 2008) transforms a data set with d binary class variables into $d(d-1)/2$ binary data sets, one per each pair of labels, and a binary classifier is built for each data set. Each of the $d(d-1)/2$ binary data sets, λ_i versus λ_j, contains the instances that are annotated by at least one, but not both, of the labels. Considering the data set of Table 10.5 where $d = 4$, the $4 \cdot \frac{3}{2} = 6$ data sets used for inducing the binary models are shown in Table 10.8.

Given a new instance, all models are invoked and ranked by counting the votes received by each label. Table 10.9 shows the results of applying each of the binary 1D classification models on a hypothetical new instance, $\mathbf{x}$. The corresponding ranking of labels, output by counting the number of times each label was predicted, is $r_{\mathbf{x}}(\lambda_3) < r_{\mathbf{x}}(\lambda_1) < r_{\mathbf{x}}(\lambda_4) < r_{\mathbf{x}}(\lambda_2)$. The assignment of labels that are consistent with the ranking is $\{\lambda_3\}$ or $\{\lambda_3, \lambda_1\}$ or $\{\lambda_3, \lambda_1, \lambda_4\}$ or $\{\lambda_3, \lambda_1, \lambda_4, \lambda_2\}$. Unfortunately, the method does not provide any criterion for selecting the best label set from the pool of consistent labels.

Table 10.8 The six data sets from where the binary models for discriminating between two labels, λ_i (true) versus λ_j (false), are learned

$\lambda_1-\lambda_2$		$\lambda_1-\lambda_3$		$\lambda_1-\lambda_4$		$\lambda_2-\lambda_3$		$\lambda_2-\lambda_4$		$\lambda_3-\lambda_4$	
$\mathbf{x}^1$	True	$\mathbf{x}^1$	True	$\mathbf{x}^2$	False	$\mathbf{x}^2$	False	$\mathbf{x}^1$	False	$\mathbf{x}^1$	False
$\mathbf{x}^3$	True	$\mathbf{x}^2$	False	$\mathbf{x}^5$	True	$\mathbf{x}^4$	True	$\mathbf{x}^2$	False	$\mathbf{x}^3$	False
$\mathbf{x}^4$	False	$\mathbf{x}^3$	True			$\mathbf{x}^3$	False	$\mathbf{x}^5$	True		
								$\mathbf{x}^4$	True		
								$\mathbf{x}^5$	True		

Table 10.9 Example of the prediction provided by each of the six models built from the data sets in Table 10.8 on a new example x

	$\lambda_1-\lambda_2$	$\lambda_1-\lambda_3$	$\lambda_1-\lambda_4$	$\lambda_2-\lambda_3$	$\lambda_2-\lambda_4$	$\lambda_3-\lambda_4$
x	λ_1	λ_3	λ_1	λ_3	λ_4	λ_3

Table 10.10 Another 4 data sets generated from Table 10.5 that are used in conjunction with the 6 data sets of Table 10.8, to induce the 10 (=6+4) binary classification models underlying the final calibrated label ranking.

$\lambda_1-\lambda_0$		$\lambda_2-\lambda_0$		$\lambda_3-\lambda_0$		$\lambda_4-\lambda_0$	
$\mathbf{x}^1$	True	$\mathbf{x}^1$	False	$\mathbf{x}^1$	False	$\mathbf{x}^1$	True
$\mathbf{x}^2$	False	$\mathbf{x}^2$	False	$\mathbf{x}^2$	True	$\mathbf{x}^2$	True
$\mathbf{x}^3$	True	$\mathbf{x}^3$	False	$\mathbf{x}^3$	False	$\mathbf{x}^3$	True
$\mathbf{x}^4$	False	$\mathbf{x}^4$	True	$\mathbf{x}^4$	False	$\mathbf{x}^4$	False
$\mathbf{x}^5$	True	$\mathbf{x}^5$	True	$\mathbf{x}^5$	True	$\mathbf{x}^5$	False

Table 10.11 Example of prediction with the calibrated label ranking method

	$\lambda_1-\lambda_2$	$\lambda_1-\lambda_3$	$\lambda_1-\lambda_4$	$\lambda_2-\lambda_3$	$\lambda_2-\lambda_4$	$\lambda_3-\lambda_4$	$\lambda_1-\lambda_0$	$\lambda_2-\lambda_0$	$\lambda_3-\lambda_0$	$\lambda_4-\lambda_0$
x	λ_1	λ_3	λ_1	λ_3	λ_4	λ_3	λ_1	λ_0	λ_3	λ_0

Calibrated Label Ranking. This proposal (Fürnkranz et al., 2008) extends the previous ranking by introducing an additional virtual label denoted as λ_0. The above $d(d-1)/2$ binary models are now accompanied by d models to discriminate between each label and λ_0. All data sets derived from Table 10.5 are shown in Table 10.10.

The final ranking includes the virtual label, which is used as a splitting point between labels. Table 10.11 contains the results of the $6 + 4 = 10$ binary classifiers over a new instance **x**. These results provide the ranking: $r_{\mathbf{x}}(\lambda_3) < r_{\mathbf{x}}(\lambda_1) < r_{\mathbf{x}}(\lambda_0) < r_{\mathbf{x}}(\lambda_4) < r_{\mathbf{x}}(\lambda_2)$. The two labels with a best ranking than λ_0 are λ_3 and λ_1, and hence the assignment of the calibrated label ranking method to **x** is $\{\lambda_3, \lambda_1\}$.

10.4.1.3 Transformation to Multi-class Classification

Label Powerset. The **label powerset** approach (Boutell et al., 2004) generates a new class value for each possible combination of d labels and then approaches the problem as

Table 10.12 Label powerset for the data set in Table 10.5. The class variable C refers to a new class with as many different values as are present in the four-dimensional class variable $\mathbf{C} = (C_1, C_2, C_3, C_4)$

$\mathbf{x}^i$	$Y^i \subseteq \mathcal{Y}$	C_1	C_2	C_3	C_4	C
$\mathbf{x}^1$	$\{\lambda_1, \lambda_4\}$	1	0	0	1	1
$\mathbf{x}^2$	$\{\lambda_3, \lambda_4\}$	0	0	1	1	2
$\mathbf{x}^3$	$\{\lambda_1, \lambda_4\}$	1	0	0	1	1
$\mathbf{x}^4$	$\{\lambda_2\}$	0	1	0	0	3
$\mathbf{x}^5$	$\{\lambda_1, \lambda_2, \lambda_3\}$	1	1	1	0	4

Table 10.13 Example of RAkEL application in an 8D classification problem. Predictions of $L = 6$ label powerset models, ϕ_1 to ϕ_6, with random subsets of size $k = 3$ (i.e., three-labelsets). The ratio of the predictions achieved for each label is compared with the fixed threshold. The RAkEL output is $\{\lambda_1, \lambda_3, \lambda_4, \lambda_5, \lambda_7, \lambda_8\}$

Model	3-labelsets	Predictions							
		λ_1	λ_2	λ_3	λ_4	λ_5	λ_6	λ_7	λ_8
ϕ_1	$\{\lambda_1, \lambda_2, \lambda_8\}$	1	0	–	–	–	–	–	1
ϕ_2	$\{\lambda_3, \lambda_4, \lambda_7\}$	–	–	0	1	–	–	1	–
ϕ_3	$\{\lambda_2, \lambda_5, \lambda_6\}$	–	1	–	–	1	0	–	–
ϕ_4	$\{\lambda_1, \lambda_7, \lambda_8\}$	1	–	–	–	–	–	1	0
ϕ_5	$\{\lambda_3, \lambda_4, \lambda_6\}$	–	–	1	1	–	0	–	–
ϕ_6	$\{\lambda_2, \lambda_6, \lambda_8\}$	–	0	–	–	–	0	–	1
Average votes		2/2	1/3	1/2	2/2	1/1	0/3	2/2	2/3
Prediction (threshold= 0.5)		1	0	1	1	1	0	1	1

a 1D classification one (see the last column in Table 10.12 for an example). For a new unknown instance to be classified, the label powerset outputs a class, which is actually a value of a class variable C that is output as the Cartesian product of the d class variables, $C_1, \ldots, C_d$. The rationale of working with the new variable C whose cardinality coincides with the Cartesian product of the whole class variables is the assumption of a complete dependence among these d class variables. Most implementations of label powerset classifiers essentially ignore label combinations that are not present in the training set, assuming that the classifier is not able to predict unseen label sets. After the transformation from $\mathbf{C} = (C_1, \ldots, C_d)$ to C, many values of C are expected to have a limited number of training examples, resulting in imbalance classification problems.

RAndom k-labEL Sets. RAndom k-labEL sets (RAkEL) (Tsoumakas et al., 2010) builds an ensemble of label powerset classifiers over subspaces of dimension $k < d$ of the original class space of dimension d. In a first step, RAkEL randomly (without replacement) breaks the large set of d class variables (labels) into a number, denoted by L, of small subsets with k labels (classes), called k-labelsets. In a second step, a multi-label classifier is trained for each of these k-labelsets using the label powerset method. Finally, given a new instance to be classified, the predictions carried out by the L label powerset models are averaged to output the multi-label assignment. Table 10.13 gives an example.

Table 10.14 Frequency counts of the co-occurrences of labels λ_i and λ_j

	λ_j	$\neg\lambda_j$	Total
λ_i	a	b	$a+b$
$\neg\lambda_i$	c	d	$c+d$
Total	$a+c$	$b+d$	$a+b+c+d$

10.4.1.4 Identifying Label Dependencies

Correlation-Based Pruning and Stacked Binary Models. Tsoumakas et al. (2009) proposed a stacking of binary relevance classifiers in the spirit of stacked generalization (Wolpert, 1992) (see Section 9.3.1) in their **correlation-based pruning and stacked binary models**. The idea is that binary relevance is used in two consecutive layers. In the first layer, binary relevance is applied to each label. Then label correlations are identified explicitly using the φ coefficient. Given two labels, λ_i and λ_j, and the frequency counts of their co-occurrences (see Table 10.14), the φ coefficient is computed as

$$\varphi(\lambda_i, \lambda_j) = \frac{a \cdot d - b \cdot c}{\sqrt{(a+b)(c+d)(a+c)(b+d)}}.$$

In the second layer, the predictions given by the base classifier models for labels whose $|\varphi|$ is greater than or equal to a certain threshold t, with $0 \leq t \leq 1$, will be the input variables of a second binary relevance model. For the other labels, the predictions given in the first layer will be the final output.

Label powerset binary relevance algorithm. Tenenboim et al. (2010) proposed the **label powerset binary relevance** algorithm to induce a model that strikes a balance between the simplicity of binary relevance and the complexity of label powerset approaches. This balance is achieved by modeling existing dependencies between labels by means of the computation of the χ^2 score (Section 4.2.8). The algorithm starts with the binary relevance model. In a second step, it clusters the pair of most dependent labels. Depending on whether the labels of this pair belong to other previous groups of labels, there are three options: a new group can be formed with these two labels, they can be added to a previous group, or two previous groups can be merged to include this pair of labels. In a third step, the new (label powerset) model is built and evaluated. The fourth step compares the accuracy of the current with the previous model. If there is improvement, the new model is accepted. Steps 2 to 4 are repeated until a stopping criterion is met.

10.4.2 Algorithm Adaptation Methods

Almost all 1D classification paradigms have been revisited for adaptation to multi-label data. In this section, we provide the main ideas underlying these adaptations, giving a more detailed description of the formalism of multidimensional Bayesian network classifiers as they are the basis for the neuroscience application developed in Section 10.5.

Classification Trees. Clare and King (2001) published a seminal work on this topic under the name of ML-C4.5. The basic idea is to adapt the C4.5 classification tree algorithm (Section 7.2) to deal with multi-label data, where an information gain criterion based on multi-label entropy is utilized to build the classification tree recursively. Multi-label entropy is computed in ML-C4.5 by adding the entropies associated with each label, assuming independence among the different class variables. Each unseen instance **x** will traverse the paths until reaching a leaf node affiliated with a number of training instances. Then the predicted label set corresponds to the labels whose frequency in the leaf exceeds a given threshold.

Artificial Neural Networks. Zhang and Zhou (2006) proposed an extension of the popular back propagation algorithm for learning ANNs (Section 7.4) able to deal with multi-label data. The network architecture consisted of three layers: (a) the input layer with as many units as dimensions in the input space, that is, n; (b) the output layer with as many units as labels, that is, d; and (c) the hidden layer that is fully connected to its adjacent layers. The network is trained with gradient descent and error back propagation with an error function capturing the characteristics of multi-label learning.

k-Nearest Neighbors. Multi-label k-nearest neighbor (Zhang and Zhou, 2007) is a binary relevance classifier that adapts the k-nearest neighbor technique (Section 7.1) to deal with multi-label data. For each of the labels, the frequency of instances in the neighborhood of the instance to be classified is obtained as a d-dimensional counting vector. Conditional upon this evidence, the method computes for each label the ratio of the posterior probabilities of whether or not, they are relevant for the instance given each count. If this ratio favors the relevancy, the label is assigned to the instance.

Support Vector Machines. Elisseeff and Weston (2002) proposed a maximum margin approach for multi-label learning implemented with the kernel trick (Section 7.5) to incorporate nonlinearity. Assuming one classifier for each individual label, the authors defined a multi-label margin on the whole training set, which is then minimized under the quadratic programming framework.

Ensembles. Read et al. (2011) proposed the **ensemble of classifiers chain** that takes into account different orders to construct the chain among class variables. In this approach, the final prediction is obtained by a voting scheme applied to the predictions provided by the multiple classifier chains resulting from the different random label orders considered. Schapire and Singer (1999) adapted the AdaBoost algorithm of boosting (Section 9.3.5) to the multi-label classification problem. Madjarov et al. (2012) introduced ensemble methods whose base classifiers are algorithms for solving multi-label tasks, in particular a random forest of ML-C4.5.

Bayesian Networks. The multi-label classification problem is formulated directly in terms of a probabilistic classifier by assigning the most likely combination of classes to each **x**. This is equivalent to searching for the most probable a posteriori combination of classes or the **most probable explanation** (MPE). The aim is to compute

$(c_1^*, \ldots, c_d^*) = \arg\max_{(c_1, \ldots, c_d)} p(C_1 = c_1, \ldots, C_d = c_d | X_1 = x_1, \ldots, X_n = x_n)$. It holds that $p(C_1 = c_1, \ldots, C_d = c_d | X_1 = x_1, \ldots, X_n = x_n) \propto p(C_1 = c_1, \ldots, C_d = c_d, X_1 = x_1, \ldots, X_n = x_n)$, whereby, in the simplest scenario (predictor and class variables are all binary), $2^d - 1 + 2^d(2^n - 1)$ parameters have to be assigned. Besides this high cardinality, it is also hard to estimate the required parameters from a (sometimes sparse) data set.

The factorization of this joint probability distribution when using a Bayesian network (Section 13.1.1) can somehow reduce the number of parameters required and alleviate the computational burden for the computation of the MPE. Bayesian networks provide exact and approximate inference methods (Section 13.2) that take advantage of the above factorization. In addition, the DAG representing the structure of the Bayesian network is able to explicitly show the structure of the multi-label classification problem (dependencies among class variables, among predictor variables, and also among class variables and predictor variables). Another advantage associated with the use of Bayesian networks is that multi-label classification problems can be naturally extended to multidimensional classification problems, where the class variables are not necessarily binary.

A **multidimensional Bayesian network classifier** (MBC) (van der Gaag and de Waal, 2006; Bielza et al., 2011b) is a Bayesian network with structure $\mathcal{G} = (V, A)$ designed to solve classification problems with multiple class variables. V denotes the set of vertices, partitioned into $V_C = \{C_1, \ldots, C_d\}$, that corresponds to the set of class variables and $V_{\mathcal{X}} = \{X_1, \ldots, X_n\}$ associated with the set of feature (predictor) variables. The set of arcs A in $\mathcal{G}$ is partitioned into three subsets: A_C, $A_{\mathcal{X}}$, $A_{C\mathcal{X}}$ such that $A_C \subseteq V_C \times V_C$ denotes the arcs between the class variables, and $\mathcal{G}_C = (V_C, A_C)$ is called the **class subgraph**; $A_{\mathcal{X}} \subseteq V_{\mathcal{X}} \times V_{\mathcal{X}}$ refers to the arcs between the feature variables, and $\mathcal{G}_{\mathcal{X}} = (V_{\mathcal{X}}, A_{\mathcal{X}})$ is the **feature subgraph**; and $A_{C\mathcal{X}} \subseteq V_C \times V_{\mathcal{X}}$ represents the arcs from the class variables to the feature variables, and $\mathcal{G}_{C\mathcal{X}} = (V, A_{C\mathcal{X}})$ is named the **bridge subgraph**. Figure 10.3 shows an example of an MBC structure.

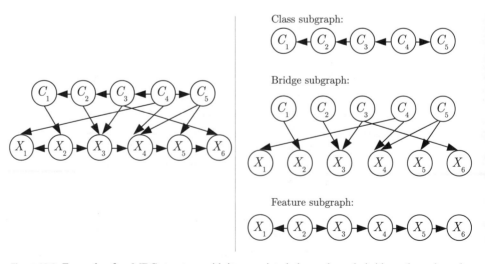

Figure 10.3 Example of an MBC structure with its associated class subgraph, bridge subgraph, and feature subgraph.

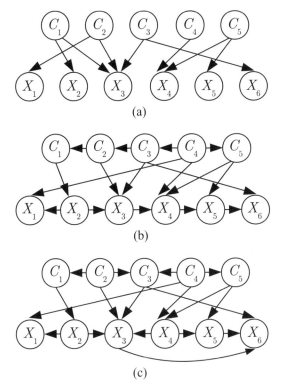

Figure 10.4 Three examples of MBCs varying the complexity of the class and feature subgraph structures. (a) Empty-empty MBC. (b)Tree-tree MBC. (c) Polytree-DAG MBC.

Depending on the degree of connectivity in the above three subgraphs, a variety of MBCs with different representational power can be reproduced to highlight the relationships among classes, features, and classes with features. **Empty-empty MBCs** (Figure 10.4(a)) have an empty class subgraph and feature subgraph. This is equivalent to a binary relevance approach where each class variable is predicted using a selective naive Bayes model (Zhang et al., 2009). The **tree-tree MBC** structure (Figure 10.4(b)) is output when both the class subgraph and the feature subgraph are tree shaped. Van der Gaag and de Waal (2006) proposed a learning algorithm for inducing tree-tree MBCs from data. The algorithm is a three-step procedure, each associated with one type of subgraph. The class subgraph is learned and fixed by searching for the maximum weighted undirected spanning tree (Algorithm 8.1) and transforming it into a directed tree using the algorithm proposed by Chow and Liu (1968). For a fixed bridge subgraph, the feature subgraph is then learned by building a maximum weighted directed spanning tree (Chu and Liu, 1965). Finally, the bridge subgraph is greedily changed in a wrapper-like way in an attempt to improve the multidimensional performance measure taken into account (exact match, for example).

The **polytree-DAG MBC** structure (Figure 10.4(c)) is an example of the general **DAG-DAG MBC** structure, that accounts for the situation where both class subgraph and feature subgraph have no restricted topologies. For this type of model, Bielza et al. (2011b) introduced the **class-bridge-decomposable MBC** concept to facilitate MPE computations.

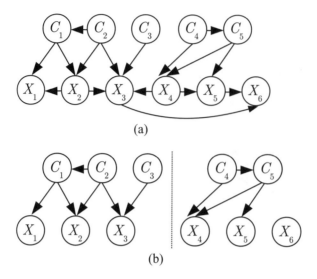

(a)

(b)

Figure 10.5 Class-bridge-decomposable MBC alleviating the MPE computations. (a) A class-bridge-decomposable MBC. (b) Its two maximal connected components.

An MBC is class-bridge-decomposable if two conditions are verified: (a) the union of the class subgraph and the bridge subgraph can be written as the union of some maximal connected components,[1] and (b) the class subgraphs associated with these maximal connected components do not share child nodes in the feature subgraph (non-shared child property). Figure 10.5 shows an example of a class-bridge-decomposable MBC (in (a)) with two maximal connected components (in (b)). The MPE of the class variables is configured by concatenating the MPEs computed in both maximal connected components. Benjumeda et al. (2018) proved that in MBCs an MPE can be computed in polynomial time if the number of class variables d and the number of parents of each feature variable are bounded. The same result is valid in class-bridge-decomposable MBCs, when the number of class variables per maximal connected component is bounded.

Bielza et al. (2011b) presented a learning algorithm for DAG-DAG MBCs that greedily searches for one arc to be added or removed in any position without altering the MBC structure, such that the micro-averaging measure, as defined in Section 10.3.2, is improved. The algorithm stops if no arcs can be added or deleted to or from the current structure to improve the micro-averaging measure.

Borchani et al. (2010) proposed the first algorithm for learning class-bridge-decomposable MBCs. This algorithm is based on a wrapper greedy forward selection approach. First, it builds the bridge subgraph by learning a selective naive Bayes for each class variable. The d resulting selective naive Bayes models represent d maximal connected components by which they may have common children (violating condition (b)). On this ground, the non-shared children property is checked to yield an initial class-bridge-decomposable MBC. This is carried out by, if necessary, removing all common children based on maximizing the micro-averaging accuracy measure. The result of this first phase is a simple class-bridge-decomposable MBC, where only the bridge subgraph

---

[1] A subgraph is a connected component if every pair of nodes in the subgraph is connected by a path. The subgraph is a maximal connected component if it is not properly contained in a connected subgraph.

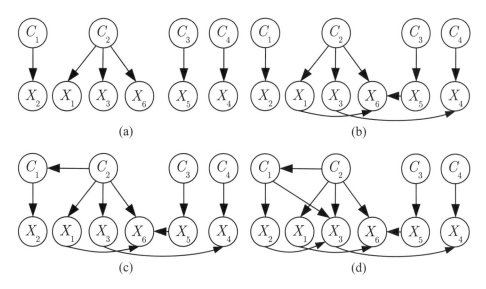

Figure 10.6 Illustration of the different phases of the wrapper greedy forward algorithm for learning class-bridge-decomposable MBCs (Borchani et al., 2010). (a) Phase I: Learning the bridge subgraph. (b) Phase II: Learning the feature subgraph (there are four components). (c) Phase III: Learning the class subgraph (now there are three components). (d) Phase IV: Updating the bridge and the feature subgraphs.

is defined and the class and feature subgraphs are still empty (Figure 10.6(a)). The second phase involves learning the feature subgraph by introducing dependencies among feature variables. An arc between a pair of features is selected at random in each iteration. The arc is added to the current structure if it provides an accuracy improvement; otherwise it is discarded. The number of iterations is bounded by a previously fixed parameter (Figure 10.6(b)). The third phase involves learning the class subgraph, in order to merge the maximal connected components of the current class-bridge-decomposable MBC (Figure 10.6(c)). Finally, the bridge and feature subgraphs are updated again until there is no further improvement in the accuracy (Figure 10.6(d)).

Borchani et al. (2012) proposed an alternative (filter) approach for learning MBCs based on detecting conditional independencies between triplets of variables, called **Markov blanket MBC** (MB-MBC). It starts by determining the Markov blanket (see Equation (8.26)) of each class variable using the **HITON algorithm** (Aliferis et al., 2003). HITON is a three-step algorithm for classifying a single variable C, very similar to the GS algorithm of Section 8.4.1.7. First, HITON-PC identifies the set of nodes containing the parents and children of C, denoted by **PC**. The recovery of this set from data is initialized from an empty set, and starts including the variable that has the highest mutual information with C in the current set of parents and children of C, denoted as **CPC**. In this recovery process, a variable belonging to **CPC** that is conditionally dependent on C given any subset of **CPC** is removed from **CPC** and is never considered again for admission. The process is repeated until no more variables are left. After outputting **PC**, HITON-PC is again applied to each variable in **PC** to output **PCPC**, the parents and children of **PC**, in the second step of HITON. Thus, the current Markov blanket of C is given by **CMB** = **PC** $\cup$ **PCPC**. In order to retain only the spouses of C, false positives are removed from **CMB**. A variable X_j will remain in **CMB** if there is not a subset of **CMB** $\setminus$ **PC** such that X_j and C are conditionally dependent given the subset. Finally, a greedy backward elimination approach is applied wrapper-like in a third step to the above Markov blanket, outputting the final Markov blanket of C, that is, $\mathbf{MB}(C)$.

Unlike the HITON algorithm that only recovers the Markov blanket of a single class variable, MB-MBC considers d class variables for the induction of the MBC structure. According to the MBC definition, the direct parents of any class variable C_i $(i = 1, \ldots, d)$ must be among the remaining class variables, whereas direct children or spouses of C_i can include either class or feature variables. Based on the results of the HITON algorithm applied to each of the d class variables, MB-MBC outputs the three subgraphs of the MBC model structure as follows:

(a) Class subgraph: first, insert an edge between each class variable C_i and any class variable belonging to its corresponding $\mathbf{PC}$ set; second, direct all these edges using the PC algorithm's edge orientation rules (Section 13.3.2.1);
(b) Bridge subgraph: insert an arc from each class variable to every feature variable belonging to its $\mathbf{PC}$ set;
(c) Feature subgraph: for every feature X_j in the set $\mathbf{MB}(C_i) \setminus \mathbf{PC}(C_i)$, i.e., for every spouse of X_j, MB-MBC inserts an arc from X_j to the corresponding common child, given by $\mathbf{PC}(X_j) \cap \mathbf{PC}(C_i)$.

Gil-Begue et al. (2018) presented a hybrid between MBCs and classification trees extending the NBTree model (Section 9.3.6) to multidimensional classification. The new model is called MBCTree, and it places general MBCs in the leaf nodes of a classification tree. Thus, MBCTrees have feature variables as internal nodes with as many children nodes as possible values of those internal nodes. To classify a new instance, it is enough to follow the branch of the tree whose values coincide with those of the instance until arriving at a leaf node. Then the corresponding MBC will be in charge of the multidimensional classification. An algorithm for learning MBCTrees from data was also proposed. A wrapper-like learning greedily adds an internal node from top to bottom of the tree as the feature variable that best splits the data (i.e., that improves the exact match as much as possible) until any splitting no longer achieves an accuracy improvement.

For a recent survey on MBCs, see Gil-Begue et al. (2020).

10.5   Example: Quality of Life in Parkinson's Disease

This section summarizes the work by Borchani et al. (2012) predicting the EQ-5D from the PDQ-39 as introduced in Data Set 3 in Chapter 1.

The PD data set was taken from an international multipurpose database collected by the National Center of Epidemiology, at the Carlos III Institute of Health, Madrid. The data set included patients diagnosed with all stages of PD. The analyzed data set contains a total of 488 patients. Information about the PDQ-39 items represented in Table 1.9 was collected for each patient, i.e., 39 feature variables for the MBC model organized in eight dimensions, each with five possible values: `never, occasionally, sometimes, often` and `always`, coded in the data set using numbers ranging from 1 (`never`) to 5 (`always`); and the corresponding EQ-5D (i.e., 5 class variables for the MBC model): Mobility, Self-care, Usual activities, Pain/Discomfort, and Anxiety/Depression coded with numbers ranging from 1 (no problems) to 3 (severe problems).

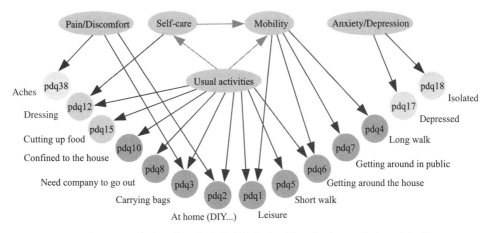

Figure 10.7 MBC structure induced by the MB-MBC algorithm for the prediction of the European quality of life-5 dimensions (EQ-5D) from the 39-item Parkinson's disease questionnaire (PDQ-39). The class subgraph (red arcs) shows probabilistic dependence relationships between classes (EQ-5D variables), the bridge subgraph (blue arcs) shows probabilistic dependence relationships from classes (EQ-5D) to features (PDQ-39), and the feature subgraph is empty due to an additional constraint imposed for this example on the algorithm. A name describing each feature has been added next to its corresponding node to facilitate the interpretation of dependencies. Node colors refer to groups shown in Table 1.9. Adapted from Borchani et al. (2012). For the color version, please refer to the plate section.

The application of the MB-MBC algorithm described in Section 10.4.2 to this data set resulted in the MBC structure illustrated in Figure 10.7. The feature subgraph is empty due to an additional restriction imposed on the MB-MBC algorithm in this problem to alleviate the inference process of computing the MPE of each instantiation of the features for assessment. The macro-averaging measure of this MBC model was 0.7119 ± 0.0338, whereas the micro-averaging measure scored 0.2030 ± 0.0718.

PD is characterized by motor manifestations (bradykinesia, rest tremor, and balance impairment) and nonmotor symptoms (depression, psychosis, and sleep disturbance) (Lees et al., 2009). For the huge majority of patients suffering from the earliest to the most advanced stages of PD, the commonly perceived health problems materialize as limitations to mobility and daily living activities, whereas the most prevalent nonmotor symptoms are associated with the impact on patients' health status perception (pain and depression, for example).

Analyzing the class subgraph in Figure 10.7, we find associations between the three class variables Mobility, Self-care, and Usual activities, related to physical aspects. Pain/Discomfort is not directly related to any other class variable, but its Markov blanket includes the class Usual activities. Anxiety/Depression has no connections with the remaining classes, probably because it is more related to emotional issues than to the physical health problems expressed by the other classes.

The bridge subgraph reveals direct dependence relationships between EQ-5D classes and the selected PDQ-39 features. Note that the detected associations are very fitting and clearly related to pain/discomfort, self-care, usual activities, and mobility. For Pain/Discomfort, the associations are, as a whole, well explained from the point of view of aches, not being able to go out alone, and not being able to carry shopping bags. The relationship between Self-care and difficulty with dressing was expected.

Usual activities appear to be related to difficulty with dressing, difficulty cutting up food, being confined to the house, not being able to go out alone, and difficulty with: carrying shopping bags, DIY, housework and cooking, leisure activities, short walks, and getting around the house. Mobility shows a probabilistic relationship with problems with leisure activities, difficulty getting around the house, and getting out, and for going long walks. For Anxiety/Depression, depression appears to be quite well represented by the detected PDQ-39 items (feelings of depression and isolation and loneliness), but not anxiety. In fact, there are PDQ-39 items related to anxiety (pdq21 with respect to feeling anxious and pdq22 with respect to feeling worried about the future), but they are not associated with the EQ-5D class variable Anxiety/Depression. This can be explained by the well-known close relationship between depression and anxiety.

Taking the previous arguments into account, the findings of this study make sense from a clinical point of view. Moreover, the content of EQ-5D is more restricted than for PDQ-39. This explains why several PDQ-39 components may converge in an EQ-5D domain. Therefore, we can conclude that the combination of the selected variables in the network properly represents the relationships between the generic (EQ-5D) and specific (PDQ-39) instruments and covers both the motor and nonmotor symptoms of PD.

10.6   Bibliographic Notes

A related field of multidimensional classification is the diagnosis of systems with multiple faults introduced in a probabilistic formalism by Peng and Reggia (1987a, 1987b). In engineering applications, these systems can be devices composed of components (class variables) that can be in either good or poor condition, and there are some input variables (features) related to the system function. The diagnosis of multiple neurodegenerative diseases on the same patient can be seen as an application of this **multiple fault diagnosis problem**.

The output space (class variables) can consist of structured objects, such as sequences, strings, trees, lattices, or graphs. In this case, the multi-label (or multidimensional) classification problem is known as **structured prediction** (Bakir et al., 2007). The different hierarchical levels used by NeuroMorpho.Org for cell types can be one example of a structured prediction problem in neuroscience.

Feature selection in the input space is, as in the 1D supervised classification problem, an interesting problem that has received a lot of attention in this field. See Lee and Kim (2013) for the extension of the mutual information-based filter selection method to multilabel classification.

The generalization of k-fold cross-validation method to multi-label problems was proposed by Sechidis et al. (2011).

Multi-instance multi-label learning is based on a bag of instances associated with a set of labels (Zhou et al., 2012). In neuroanatomy, each instance might correspond to a dendritic tree, whereas the bag would be the whole neuron morphology. For this example, the set of labels could be the species, gender, cell type, and layer of the neuron to be classified.

Part IV

Unsupervised Classification

Chapters 5-10 (Part III) developed some methods for supervised classification where each instance in the data set is characterized by predictive features and a class (scalar or vector) label. Chapters 11-12 of Part IV on unsupervised classification each explain two different approaches to clustering: non-probabilistic clustering and probabilistic clustering. Both approaches aim to group, or cluster, a set of similar instances, known as objects within this context, in the same group, different groups being very dissimilar. Each object belongs to only one cluster in non-probabilistic clustering (Chapter 11). Using probabilistic clustering (Chapter 12), however, an object can be a member of more than one cluster at the same time, each with a membership probability.

11 Non-probabilistic Clustering

The chapter is organized as follows. Section 11.1 introduces cluster analysis. Section 11.2 describes methods for grouping objects into a hierarchical structure from both the agglomerative and divisive perspectives. Eleven different algorithms for partitional clustering are presented in Section 11.3. The important issue of determining the optimal number of clusters is discussed in Section 11.4. Clustering methods able to characterize the clusters with subsets of the original set of features are explained in Section 11.5, whereas Section 11.6 introduces methods for combining the results of several clustering outputs, and Section 11.7 presents measures for assessing the goodness of a clustering solution. Section 11.8 describes the application of the K-means algorithm to the set of 2,000 human dendritic spines introduced in Chapter 1 (Data Set 4). Section 11.9 containing bibliographic notes concludes the chapter.

11.1 Similarity/Dissimilarity between Objects

Cluster analysis, also called **unsupervised classification**, has the main objective of grouping or segmenting a collection of objects into subsets, or clusters, such that the objects within each cluster are more closely related to one another than objects assigned to different clusters. An object can be described by a set of features or by its similarity (or dissimilarity) to other objects. In some problems, the goal is to organize the clusters into a natural hierarchy, successively grouping the clusters such that clusters within the same group at each level of the hierarchy are more similar to each other than others in different groups. Other problems do not require a cluster hierarchy, and it suffices to partition the objects into clusters, each of which groups similar objects.

In mathematical notation, we start with a data set of n variables, $\mathbf{X} = (X_1, \dots, X_n)$, including characteristics or features from N objects. Let $\mathcal{D} = \{\mathbf{x}^1, \dots, \mathbf{x}^N\}$ denote the data set, with $\mathbf{x}^i = (x_1^i, \dots, x_n^i)$, an n-dimensional vector, for $i = 1, \dots, N$.

Cluster analysis is used for a descriptive purpose in an attempt to answer the question of whether or not the objects in the data set consist of a set of distinct subgroups, where each subgroup represents objects with significantly different properties from other subgroups. This goal requires an assessment of the degree of difference between the objects belonging to each cluster.

Thus, a key element for all clustering methods is the notion of the degree of similarity (or dissimilarity) between the individual objects to be clustered. A clustering method tries to group objects based on the definition of (dis)similarity. Figure 11.1 shows the importance of the similarity measure chosen to compare the objects, resulting in two completely

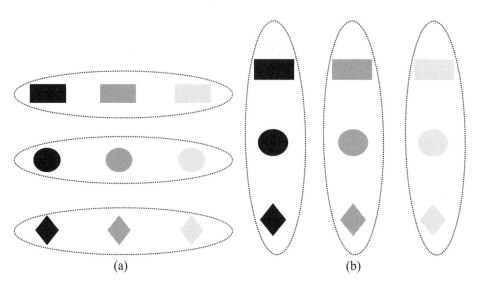

Figure 11.1 Influence of the similarity measure on the clustering results. (a) Shape-based similarity measure. (b) Color-based similarity measure. Dotted lines show the resulting clusters.

different cluster solutions, depending on whether the shape (in (a)) or the color (in (b)) of the objects is considered as the similarity criterion.

The data to be analyzed by hierarchical clustering and partitional clustering methods are commonly presented as a **dissimilarity matrix**. This dissimilarity matrix is the result of a transformation of the data set. The dissimilarity matrix is an $N \times N$ matrix $\mathbf{D} \equiv \{d(\mathbf{x}^i, \mathbf{x}^j)\}_{i,j}$, where $d(\mathbf{x}^i, \mathbf{x}^j)$ denotes the dissimilarity between the ith and jth objects. A **dissimilarity measure** satisfies the following properties: $d(\mathbf{x}^i, \mathbf{x}^j) \geq 0, d(\mathbf{x}^i, \mathbf{x}^i) = 0$, and $d(\mathbf{x}^i, \mathbf{x}^j) = d(\mathbf{x}^j, \mathbf{x}^i)$ for all $\mathbf{x}^i, \mathbf{x}^j$ objects. In the dendritic spines example (Section 11.8), the data set includes $N = 2{,}000$ objects, each containing the $n = 54$ values characterizing a given spine. Its dissimilarity matrix is a $2{,}000 \times 2{,}000$ symmetric matrix with diagonal elements equal to zero, where each entry measures the dissimilarity between two spines.

Standard dissimilarity measures $d(\mathbf{x}^i, \mathbf{x}^j)$ include the **Minkowski distance** for numeric features: $d_{\text{Minkowski}}(\mathbf{x}^i, \mathbf{x}^j) = \left(\sum_{h=1}^{n} |x_h^i - x_h^j|^g\right)^{1/g}$, with $g \geq 1$. As special cases, the Euclidean distance is achieved when $g = 2$, the **Manhattan distance** when $g = 1$ and the **Chebyshev distance** when $g \to \infty$ (see also Section 7.1.4). In the case of binary features, the dissimilarity between objects can be computed based on a contingency table. For symmetric binary features, where both states (0/1) are equally valuable, the dissimilarity can be defined as $d_{\text{binary}}(\mathbf{x}^i, \mathbf{x}^j) = \frac{r+s}{q+r+s+t}$, where q is the number of features equal to 1 for both objects, t is the number of features equal to 0 for both objects, and r and s are the number of features that are unequal for both objects. The **Jaccard coefficient**, $d(\mathbf{x}^i, \mathbf{x}^j) = \frac{r+s}{q+r+s}$, is used for asymmetric binary features, where the positive outcome (or 1) is considered more important than the negative outcome (or 0). Rokach and Maimon (2005a) adapted the above dissimilarity measures for nominal, ordinal, and mixed-type features.

In some applications, it is more natural or convenient to consider the **similarity** $s(\mathbf{x}^i, \mathbf{x}^j)$ between the ith and jth objects. Only minor changes are needed to transform from one representation to the other. Some of the most common similarity measures between two objects $\mathbf{x}^i$ and $\mathbf{x}^j$, $s\left(\mathbf{x}^i, \mathbf{x}^j\right)$, in continuous domains, used in clustering are the **cosine measure**, defined as the normalized inner product: $s(\mathbf{x}^i, \mathbf{x}^j) = \frac{\mathbf{x}^{iT} \cdot \mathbf{x}^j}{||\mathbf{x}^i|| \cdot ||\mathbf{x}^j||}$, where $||\mathbf{x}^i||$ denotes the norm of vector $\mathbf{x}^i$; the **normalized Pearson correlation measure**: $s\left(\mathbf{x}^i, \mathbf{x}^j\right) = \frac{(\mathbf{x}^i - \bar{\mathbf{x}})^T \cdot (\mathbf{x}^j - \bar{\mathbf{x}})}{||\mathbf{x}^i - \bar{\mathbf{x}}|| \cdot ||\mathbf{x}^j - \bar{\mathbf{x}}||}$, where $\bar{\mathbf{x}}$ is the mean over the N points; and the **extended Jaccard measure**: $s\left(\mathbf{x}^i, \mathbf{x}^j\right) = \frac{\mathbf{x}^{iT} \cdot \mathbf{x}^j}{||\mathbf{x}^i||^2 + ||\mathbf{x}^j||^2 - \mathbf{x}^{iT} \cdot \mathbf{x}^j}$. Note that $\mathbf{x}^i$ is a column vector in these formulas.

11.2 Hierarchical Clustering

Hierarchical clustering algorithms (Gordon, 1987; Murtagh and Contreras, 2012) organize data into a hierarchical structure depicted by a binary tree or **dendrogram** (Figure 11.2). *Déndron* is an ancient Greek word meaning *tree*. The root node of the dendrogram represents the whole data set, and each leaf node is regarded as a data object. The intermediate nodes describe how proximal the objects are to each other. The height of the dendrogram represents the dissimilarity between each pair of objects or clusters or between an object and a cluster. The clustering results can be output by cutting the dendrogram at different heights.

Hierarchical clustering algorithms can be classified as agglomerative and divisive methods. **Agglomerative clustering** starts with N clusters, each of which includes exactly one object. A series of merging operations follows designed to group all objects within the same cluster. The procedure for **divisive clustering** is the exact opposite. All objects originally belong to the same cluster, and an algorithm recursively divides this cluster until all clusters are singletons, where each singleton corresponds to an object.

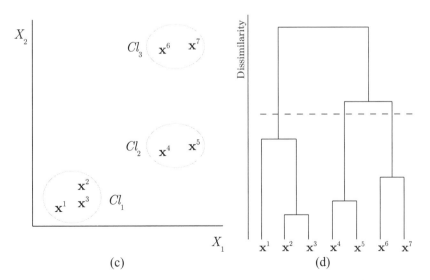

(c)   (d)

Figure 11.2 Example of hierarchical clustering. (a) Seven points represented in a 2D space with three clusters. (b) The dendrogram associated with the hierarchical clustering. The clustering yielded after cutting the dendrogram at the dotted line matches the clusters Cl_1, Cl_2 and Cl_3 in (a).

Hierarchical clustering was applied in neuroanatomy to solve a supervised classification problem consisting of discriminating between interneuron and pyramidal cells from the mouse neocortex (Guerra et al., 2011). It was also applied to current-clamp measurements of electrophysiological properties to characterize the postnatal development of the electrical phenotype of the substantia nigra dopaminergic neurons (Dufour et al., 2014). In genomics, Cameron et al. (2012) reported the identification, validation, and spatial grouping of genes selectively expressed within the Eomes + cortical excitatory neuron lineage during early cortical development. Neuroimage is another field where hierarchical clustering has been applied. Thus, Moreno-Dominguez et al. (2014) parcelled functional brain areas on the basis of diffusion MRI and tractography.

Several neurodegenerative diseases have benefited from the application of hierarchical clustering. Research on AD includes identification of cognitive subtypes based on neuropsychological findings (Cappa et al., 2014) and 14 differentially expressed transcripts (Uhring et al., 2009). Discriminant analysis and hierarchical clustering methods were used (although for solving a supervised classification problem) to explore the utility of the Wechsler Adult Intelligent Scale for discriminating patients with HD, persons at risk for the disease and controls (Strauss and Brandt, 1986). Hierarchical clustering was also used to characterize subgroups of hemiplegic patients based on temporal-distance parameters and joint kinematic measures (Manca et al., 2014). Grades II and IV glioma were distinguished by means of hierarchical clustering (again used as a supervised classification method) with MR spectroscopy data in Yang et al. (2015).

11.2.1 Agglomerative Hierarchical Clustering

Initially, there are N singleton clusters, each of which is associated with an object. At each stage of the algorithm, the most similar pair of clusters is merged until all the objects belong to one cluster (Figure 11.2).

There are different linkage strategies for cluster merging depending on the definition of the dissimilarity between two clusters of objects. **Single linkage** (Florek et al., 1951) computes the dissimilarity between two clusters as the minimum distance between all pairs of objects drawn from the two clusters (one object from the first cluster, the other from the second), that is,

$$d_{\text{singlelinkage}}(Cl_i, Cl_j) = \min_{\mathbf{x}^i \in Cl_i, \mathbf{x}^j \in Cl_j} d\left(\mathbf{x}^i, \mathbf{x}^j\right),$$

where Cl_i denotes cluster i. The single linkage is also known as **nearest neighbor clustering**.

Complete linkage (Sorensen, 1948) considers the maximum of all pairwise distances between objects in the two clusters. In mathematical notation,

$$d_{\text{completelinkage}}(Cl_i, Cl_j) = \max_{\mathbf{x}^i \in Cl_i, \mathbf{x}^j \in Cl_j} d\left(\mathbf{x}^i, \mathbf{x}^j\right).$$

Unlike single linkage, which tends to produce elongated clusters, this linkage algorithm produces compact clusters. However, the single linkage algorithm is more versatile than complete linkage, as it can extract concentric clusters, which is a feature not provided by complete linkage. It is also known as the **farthest neighbor** method.

Table 11.1 Hierarchical agglomerative clustering: Linkage strategies

Name	$d(Cl_i, Cl_j)$	Reference
Single linkage	$\min\limits_{\mathbf{x}^i \in Cl_i, \mathbf{x}^j \in Cl_j} d\left(\mathbf{x}^i, \mathbf{x}^j\right)$	Florek et al. (1951)
Complete linkage	$\max\limits_{\mathbf{x}^i \in Cl_i, \mathbf{x}^j \in Cl_j} d\left(\mathbf{x}^i, \mathbf{x}^j\right)$	Sorensen (1948)
Average linkage	$\dfrac{1}{\lvert Cl_i \rvert \cdot \lvert Cl_j \rvert} \sum\limits_{\mathbf{x}^i \in Cl_i} \sum\limits_{\mathbf{x}^j \in Cl_j} d\left(\mathbf{x}^i, \mathbf{x}^j\right)$	Sokal and Michener (1958)
Centroid linkage	$d(\mathbf{c}_i, \mathbf{c}_j)$	Sokal and Michener (1958)

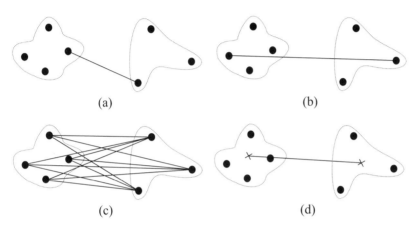

Figure 11.3 Examples of intercluster dissimilarities in hierarchical clustering. (a) Single linkage. (b) Complete linkage. (c) Average linkage. (d) Centroid linkage.

Average linkage (Sokal and Michener, 1958) calculates the dissimilarity between two clusters as the mean distance over all pairs of objects from each cluster. That is,

$$d_{\text{averagelinkage}}(Cl_i, Cl_j) = \frac{1}{\lvert Cl_i \rvert \cdot \lvert Cl_j \rvert} \sum_{\mathbf{x}^i \in Cl_i} \sum_{\mathbf{x}^j \in Cl_j} d\left(\mathbf{x}^i, \mathbf{x}^j\right),$$

where $\lvert Cl_i \rvert$ denotes the cardinality of Cl_i.

Centroid linkage (Sokal and Michener, 1958) computes the dissimilarity between two clusters as the distance between their respective centroids. In mathematical notation:

$$d_{\text{centroidlinkage}}(Cl_i, Cl_j) = d(\mathbf{c}_i, \mathbf{c}_j),$$

where $\mathbf{c}_i = (c_{i1}, \dots, c_{in})$, and $\mathbf{c}_j = (c_{j1}, \dots, c_{jn})$ denote the centroids of clusters Cl_i and Cl_j, respectively, computed as $c_{ir} = \frac{1}{\lvert Cl_i \rvert} \sum_{\mathbf{x}^i \in Cl_i} x_r^i, r = 1, \dots, n$.

Figure 11.3 illustrates these four different clustering linkage methods. Table 11.1 shows their respective formulas for computing dissimilarities between clusters.

Ward's method, or the **minimal increase of sum-of-squares** (Ward, 1963), computes the dissimilarity between two clusters, Cl_i and Cl_j, as the difference between the summed square distances to the centroid within cluster $Cl_i \cup Cl_j$ and the addition of the summed square distances to the centroid within cluster Cl_i and cluster Cl_j, that is,

$$d_{\text{Ward}}(Cl_i, Cl_j) = \sum_{\mathbf{x}^k \in Cl_i \cup Cl_j} d^2\left(\mathbf{x}^k, \mathbf{c}_{ij}\right) - \left[\sum_{\mathbf{x}^i \in Cl_i} d^2\left(\mathbf{x}^i, \mathbf{c}_i\right) + \sum_{\mathbf{x}^j \in Cl_j} d^2\left(\mathbf{x}^j, \mathbf{c}_j\right)\right],$$

where d^2 denotes the squared Euclidean distance, and $\mathbf{c}_{ij}$, $\mathbf{c}_i$, and $\mathbf{c}_j$ are the centroids of clusters $Cl_i \cup Cl_j$, Cl_i, and Cl_j, respectively.

Average linkage, complete linkage, and Ward's method are used when the clusters are expected to be more or less round clouds. Ward's method is the closest, in terms of its properties and efficiency, to K-means (Section 11.3.1). Unlike complete linkage and Ward's method, single linkage and centroid linkage tend to exhibit a chaining behavior with the objects.

From an optimization point of view, the usual agglomerative hierarchical clustering algorithms are greedy because the closest pair of clusters is merged at each stage. However, this does not guarantee any optimality properties either at any level of the constituent clusters or throughout the complete hierarchy.

11.2.2 Divisive Hierarchical Clustering

Initially, there is one cluster containing all N objects. At each stage of the algorithm, an existing cluster is divided into two until all objects are singleton clusters. Algorithms that find the globally optimal division (Edwards and Cavalli-Sforza, 1965) are computationally very demanding and only applicable when N is small, as there are $2^{N-1} - 1$ possible two-subset divisions of N objects (Everitt et al., 2001). Some algorithms for dividing a cluster into two successively remove objects from the cluster depending on their value in a binary variable (Macnaughton-Smith et al., 1964). Other algorithms select the pair of objects in the cluster with the largest pairwise dissimilarity as the seeds for the two subclusters (Hubert, 1973).

Only when the objects are described by a set of binary variables has the family of divisive algorithms been widely used in clustering. At each stage of the algorithm, the objects in one cluster are assigned to one of the two subclusters based on their values for a single variable. This variable is that which maximizes the difference between the two subclusters. This family contains the so-called **monothetic divisive algorithms** (Williams and Lambert, 1959).

11.3 Partitional Clustering

Partitional clustering aims to simultaneously partition the data set into clusters without forming a hierarchical structure of clusters. Like hierarchical clustering, each data set object will belong to one and only one cluster (with the exception of fuzzy C-means, see Section 11.3.4) with an empty set intersection between any two clusters.

Partitional clustering assumes that the data set can be represented by a set of **prototypes**, and therefore it is also called **prototype-based clustering**. The main goal is to summarize and compress the data set using the cluster prototypes, leading to a concise description and a meaningful partition of the original data set.

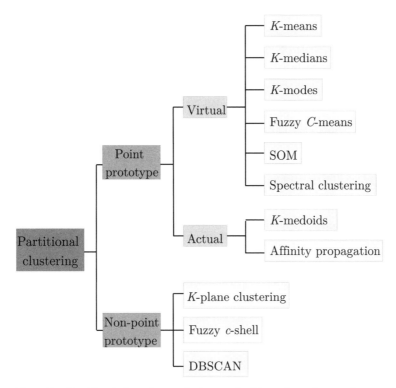

Figure 11.4 Partitional clustering methods organized by point and non-point prototypes.

The various partitional clustering algorithms differ mainly as to how the prototypes are defined and how to search for the optimal prototypes and clusters according to a specified criterion. Existing methods can be generally categorized into two groups: **point prototype-based clustering** and **non-point prototype-based clustering** (see Figure 11.4).

Point prototype-based clustering is the most commonly studied clustering method in the literature. It assumes that each cluster can be represented by a point in the feature space. This kind of clustering methods can be divided into **virtual point prototype clustering** and **actual point prototype clustering**. In virtual point prototype clustering, cluster prototypes are not guaranteed to be objects from the original data set, whereas objects in actual point prototype clustering are. K-means, K-medians, K-modes, fuzzy C-means, self-organizing maps, and spectral clustering are examples of virtual point prototype clustering, whereas K-medoids and affinity propagation are representative of actual data point prototype clustering methods.

Non-point prototype-based clustering builds the partition of the original data set based on non-point prototypes, such as lines, hyperplanes, or hyperspheres. Therefore, these methods are able to provide good solutions to data sets containing clusters with complex shapes. Examples are K-plane clustering, fuzzy c-shell algorithms, and density-based clustering.

Partitional clustering methods are based upon the idea of optimizing a function F, referred to as the **partitional clustering criterion**. This criterion should translate intuitive notions on clusters into a rational mathematical formula. The function value usually depends on the current partition $\{Cl_1, \ldots, Cl_K\}$ of the data set into K clusters, that is,

$$F : \mathcal{P}_K(\mathcal{D}) \to \mathbb{R},$$

where $\mathcal{P}_K(\mathcal{D})$ is the set of all partitions of the data set $\mathcal{D} = \{\mathbf{x}^1, \dots, \mathbf{x}^N\}$ in K nonempty clusters. The clusters verify $\mathcal{D} = \cup_{i=1}^{K} Cl_i$ with $Cl_i \cap Cl_j = \emptyset$ for all $i, j = 1, \dots, K$ and $i \neq j$.

The cardinality of $\mathcal{P}_K(\mathcal{D})$ is typically denoted by $S(N, K)$ and is known as the **Stirling number of the second kind**. It computes the number of possible groupings of a set of N objects into K nonempty subsets. Stirling numbers of the second kind obey the recurrence relation

$$S(N, K) = K \cdot S(N - 1, K) + S(N - 1, K - 1) \tag{11.1}$$

for $K > 0$, with initial conditions

$$S(0,0) = 1 \quad \text{and} \quad S(N,0) = S(0,N) = 0$$

for $N > 0$.

To understand this recurrence, notice that a partition of the N objects into K nonempty subsets either does or does not contain the Nth object as a singleton. $S(N - 1, K - 1)$ denotes how often the singleton is a subset because the remaining $N - 1$ objects must be partitioned into the available $K - 1$ subsets. Otherwise, the Nth object belongs to a subset containing other objects. The number of possibilities is given by $K \cdot S(N - 1, K)$. Obviously, $S(N, N) = 1$ and for $N \geq 1$, $S(N, 1) = 1$.

The solution of the recurrence in Equation (11.1) is given by the following explicit formula (Sharp, 1968):

$$S(N, K) = \frac{1}{K!} \sum_{i=0}^{K} (-1)^{K-i} \binom{K}{i} i^N.$$

This number is huge even for small values of N, making it infeasible to run an exhaustive search for the best clustering partition and justifying the use of heuristics to carry out this task.

11.3.1 K-Means

The **K-means algorithm** (MacQueen, 1967) finds a locally optimal solution for a clustering criterion based on the sum of the squared Euclidean distance between each object and its nearest cluster center (centroid), which plays the role of a prototype. This criterion is sometimes referred to as **square-error criterion**. In mathematical notation, the function to be minimized is given by

$$F_{\text{means}}(\{Cl_1, \dots, Cl_K\}) = \sum_{k=1}^{K} \sum_{\mathbf{x}^i \in Cl_k} ||\mathbf{x}^i - \mathbf{c}_k||^2, \tag{11.2}$$

where K is the number of clusters, $\mathbf{x}^i = (x_1^i, \dots, x_n^i)$ denotes the n components of the ith object in the original data set, Cl_k refers to the kth cluster, and $\mathbf{c}_k = (c_{k1}, \dots, c_{kn})$ is its corresponding centroid.

The main steps of the K-means algorithm are shown in Algorithm 11.1. The K-means algorithm is somehow fed with an initial partition of the data set, and the centroids of these initial clusters are calculated. Then, the objects of the data set are reallocated to the cluster represented by the nearest centroid in an attempt to reduce the square-error criterion. Objects are reallocated taking into account the storage ordering: when the cluster membership of an object changes, the respective cluster centroids and the square-error must be recomputed. This process is repeated until convergence, that is, until the square-error cannot be further reduced and the cluster membership of all the objects is unchanged.

Algorithm 11.1: The K-means algorithm (MacQueen, 1967)

Input : An initial partition of the data set into K clusters $\{Cl_1, \ldots, Cl_K\}$
Output: Final partition of the data set into K clusters minimizing the square-error
criterion

1 **repeat**
2   Calculate cluster centroids: $\mathbf{c}_k = (c_{k1}, \ldots, c_{kn})$ with $c_{kr} = \frac{1}{|Cl_k|} \sum_{\mathbf{x}^i \in Cl_k} x_r^i$,
     $r = 1, \ldots, n, k = 1, \ldots, K$
3   **for** $i = 1$ **to** N **do**
4   Reassign object $\mathbf{x}^i$ to its closest cluster centroid, that is, $\mathbf{x}^i \in Cl_s$ is moved
         from Cl_s to Cl_t if $||\mathbf{x}^i - \mathbf{c}_t||^2 < ||\mathbf{x}^i - \mathbf{c}_s||^2$ for all $t = 1, \ldots, K, s \neq t$
5   Recalculate centroids for clusters Cl_s and Cl_t
6   **endfor**
7 **until** Cluster membership is stabilized

K-means can be regarded as an iterative refinement process that greedily proposes object reallocations at each iteration to reduce the square-error criterion. These reallocations are constrained by the object storage ordering. The main drawbacks of the K-means algorithm are as follows: (a) initial partition, (b) storage ordering of the objects, and (c) greedy search in the space of possible partitions. They have a major impact on its output.

Forgy (1965) proposed a method that differs from the above K-means algorithm with respect to how the cluster prototypes are updated: while the new prototypes are computed after *each* object assignment in K-means, Forgy's method only calculates the new prototypes *once all* objects have been assigned to their respective clusters (see Figure 11.5). This avoids the influence of the object storage ordering.

The K-means algorithm was used to cluster morphologies of inner retinal neurons in mice (Badea and Nathans, 2004), where each neuron was characterized by features from arbor area, stratification level, and neurite branching patterns. An application in electrophysiology includes the identification of four parvalbumin-expressing interneurons in layers 2/3 of the visual cortex based on their firing patterns (Helm et al., 2013).

Neurodegenerative disease subtypes have also been determined by the K-means algorithm. Raamana et al. (2015) identified groups of AD patients from features extracted from the interregional covariation of cortical thickness by spatial K-means clustering. Subtypes of PD revealing the clinical heterogeneity of this disease were reported by Mu et al. (2017) from demographic features, disease progression, and motor and nonmotor symptoms. Zhu et al. (2015) used the K-means algorithm as a supervised classification algorithm for distinguishing epileptic EEG signals. Tardif et al. (2010) segmented cortical MS lesions from a high-resolution quantitative MR data set.

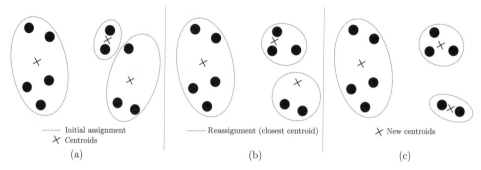

----- Initial assignment   ----- Reassignment (closest centroid)   ✗ New centroids
✗ Centroids

(a)   (b)   (c)

Figure 11.5 Forgy's method. (a) Ten objects are initially partitioned into three groups, and their corresponding centroids are then computed. (b) Each object is reallocated according to its nearest centroid. (c) The centroids of the three new groups are then computed. The process is over because the cluster membership of all objects is unchanged.

Hierarchical and K-means clustering were compared by Shahrbanian et al. (2015) to group patients suffering from MS based on different symptoms like fatigue, pain, sleep disturbance, depression, anxiety, irritability, cognitive impairment, spasticity, and poor balance.

11.3.2 *K*-Medians

The **K-medians algorithm** (Jain and Dubes, 1988) is a variation of K-means, where the median instead of the mean of a cluster is used to calculate its centroid. The aim in K-medians is to minimize the sum of the Manhattan distance between each object and its centroid. In mathematical notation, the kth centroid, $\mathbf{c}_k$, is computed as

$$\mathbf{c}_k = Me\left\{\mathbf{x}^i \in Cl_k\right\},$$

where $Me\{\mathbf{x}^i \in Cl_k\}$ denotes the median of the points in cluster k, computed component-wise, and the function to be minimized is now expressed as

$$F_{\text{medians}}(\{Cl_1, \ldots, Cl_K\}) = \sum_{k=1}^{K} \sum_{\mathbf{x}^i \in Cl_k} ||\mathbf{x}^i - \mathbf{c}_k||_1, \tag{11.3}$$

with $||\mathbf{x}^i - \mathbf{c}_k||_1 = \sum_{r=1}^{n} |x_r^i - c_{kr}|$.

Because the median is a better measure of location than the mean (Section 2.2.2), the K-medians algorithm provides more compact clusters than K-means in the presence of extreme values and outliers, and its use is also recommended when the variable distributions are not symmetric.

11.3.3 *K*-Modes

K-modes (Huang, 1998) is an adaptation of K-means for categorical variables. The K-modes algorithm uses a simple matching measure to deal with categorical objects and replaces the means of clusters with modes.

Let $\mathbf{x}^i$ and $\mathbf{x}^r$ be two categorical objects described by n categorical attributes. The dissimilarity measure, d, between $\mathbf{x}^i$ and $\mathbf{x}^r$ can be defined by the total mismatches of the corresponding attribute categories of the two objects. The smaller the number of mismatches is, the more alike the two objects are. This measure is based on **simple matching** (Kaufman and Rousseeuw, 1990). In mathematical notation,

$$d\left(\mathbf{x}^i, \mathbf{x}^j\right) = \sum_{r=1}^{n} \left(1 - \mathbb{I}(x_r^i = x_r^i)\right),$$

where $\mathbb{I}(\cdot)$ is the indicator function (Equation (3.3)). The kth centroid, $\mathbf{c}_k$, is computed as

$$\mathbf{c}_k = Mo\left\{\mathbf{x}^i \in Cl_k\right\},$$

where $Mo\{\mathbf{x}^i \in Cl_k\}$ denotes the mode of the points in cluster k, computed component-wise, and the function to be minimized is given by

$$F_{\text{modes}}\left(\{Cl_1, \ldots, Cl_K\}\right) = \sum_{k=1}^{K} \sum_{\mathbf{x}^i \in Cl_k} \sum_{j=1}^{n} \left(1 - \mathbb{I}\left(x_j^i = c_{kj}\right)\right). \tag{11.4}$$

For example, the mode of the following five categorical objects – $\{\mathbf{x}^1 = (a,b), \mathbf{x}^2 = (a,c), \mathbf{x}^3 = (a,b), \mathbf{x}^4 = (b,c), \mathbf{x}^5 = (b,a)\}$ – can be either (a,b) or (a,c). Each component of the mode contains the most frequent value in the set of objects in the specified component.

11.3.4 Fuzzy C-Means

Fuzzy C-means (Dunn, 1973; Bezdek, 1981) is a generalization of the K-means algorithm, where each object can be simultaneously assigned to multiple clusters with **fuzzy membership coefficients** between 0 and 1. This soft assignment is richer than the hard or crisp (Boolean) membership values provided by K-means and its variants and somewhat resembles probabilistic clustering developed in Chapter 12. Compared to K-means-like algorithms, fuzzy C-means captures the degree of membership of each object to each prototype, that is, it provides more information about the hidden structure of the data set.

The membership value of the ith object belonging to cluster k is denoted by m_{ki}. These membership values are subject to the following restrictions: $0 \leq m_{ki} \leq 1, \sum_{k=1}^{K} m_{ki} = 1$, for all $i = 1, \ldots, N$, and $0 < \sum_{i=1}^{N} m_{ki} < N$, for all $k = 1, \ldots, K$. The equality means that the total membership of each object across all clusters equals one, whereas the last two inequalities indicate that the total membership of each cluster is positive and smaller than the number of objects.

Fuzzy C-means aims to minimize the following partitional clustering criterion:

$$F_{\text{fuzzy-C-means}}\left(\{Cl_1, \ldots, Cl_K\}\right) = \sum_{k=1}^{K} \sum_{i=1}^{N} m_{ki}^{\alpha} ||\mathbf{x}^i - \mathbf{c}_k||^2, \tag{11.5}$$

where $\alpha \geq 1$ denotes the parameter that controls the fuzziness of the clustering. The smaller the α, the harder (less fuzzy) the membership value is. In the extreme case where $\alpha = 1$, the memberships m_{ki} converge to 0 or 1, which implies a crisp partitioning. For a discussion on how to choose an appropriate value for α, see Yu et al. (2004).

The main steps of fuzzy C-means and the K-means algorithm are similar. However, at each iteration of the algorithm, the adaptations of m_{ki}^{α} and $\mathbf{c}_k$ are given by

$$m_{ki}^{\alpha} = \frac{1}{\sum_{j=1}^{K} \left(\frac{||\mathbf{x}^i - \mathbf{c}_k||^2}{||\mathbf{x}^i - \mathbf{c}_j||^2} \right)^{\frac{2}{\alpha-1}}},$$

and

$$\mathbf{c}_k = \frac{\sum_{i=1}^{N} m_{ki}^{\alpha} \mathbf{x}^i}{\sum_{i=1}^{N} m_{ki}^{\alpha}}.$$

The fuzzy C-means algorithm was used to investigate differences in cerebral macro-molecular tissue composition in several regions (entorhinal cortex, hippocampal head and body, insula, and temporal neocortex) comparing patients with AD, MCI and healthy controls (Wiest et al., 2013). In this application, fuzzy C-means was used as a supervised classification technique. Abdullah et al. (2013) quantified changes in the CSF flow dynamics in the brain and spinal cord, volume and/or pressure gradient using MRI techniques as input for a spatial fuzzy C-means for the segmentation of CSF images.

Farzan et al. (2015) used the longitudinal percentage of brain volume changes in a 2-year follow-up as features for automatically discriminating patients with AD and normal controls running the K-means and fuzzy C-means algorithms.

11.3.5 Self-Organizing Map

A **self-organizing map** (SOM) (Kohonen, 1982, 1997) is a type of artificial neural network (Section 7.4) that produces a low-dimensional (typically 2D), discretized representation of the input data $\mathcal{D} = \{\mathbf{x}^1, \ldots, \mathbf{x}^N\}$, called a map. Like multidimensional scaling (Section 2.7), the mapping transforms input data into K discretized points in the low-dimensional space preserving the relative distance between the original points. This means that objects that are close to each other in the input space are mapped to nearby map units by a SOM. The K points, $\mathbf{c}_1, \ldots, \mathbf{c}_K$, in the low-dimensional space are the representative points of clusters $Cl_1, \ldots, Cl_K$, respectively.

The network architecture of a SOM (Figure 11.6) consists of two layers of units. The input layer contains n units, one per variable X_i, with $i = 1, \ldots, n$. The output layer has

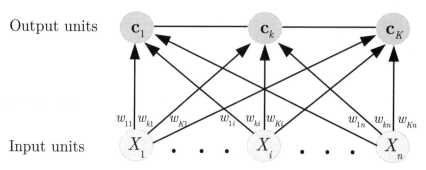

Figure 11.6 Network architecture of a SOM. $X_1, \ldots, X_n$ denote the input units (variables in the original space) and $\mathbf{c}_1, \ldots, \mathbf{c}_K$ the output units (cluster representatives). Weight w_{ki} is assigned to the connection between X_i and $\mathbf{c}_k$. A 1D arrangement has been selected for the output layer topology.

K units, one per cluster representative $\mathbf{c}_k$ with $k = 1, \ldots, K$. The input units are fully connected with weights w_{ki}, with $k = 1, \ldots, K$ and $i = 1, \ldots, n$, to output units. Weight w_{ki} is associated with the connection between input X_i and output $\mathbf{c}_k$. The output layer topology (Figure 11.7) defines which output layer units are neighbors of others and is given as input to the SOM procedure. These connections do not contain any weight between connected units and are represented by edges (undirected arcs). This topology is used by the SOM to update weights at each iteration.

Algorithm 11.2 illustrates the schema of the SOM with sequential training. The output layer network topology is used in conjunction with $D(t)$, a distance function of iteration t regarding neighborhood distance, to update the weights between input and output units. The SOM initializes these weights randomly to small values. As long as computational boundaries are not exceeded, the difference in weight values of two consecutive iterations is smaller than a given threshold, or any other stopping criterion is not met, the SOM repeats several steps at each iteration. First, an input object is randomly selected (line 2). Then, the input object is assigned to the output unit (cluster representative) whose weight vector is closest (lines 3–4). The weight vector of the kth output unit, $\mathbf{c}_k$, is given by $(w_{k1}, \ldots, w_{kn})$. Finally, weights are updated at all nodes whose topological distance is smaller than $D(t)$, that is, a distance restricted by the initially defined output layer network topology (line 5).

Algorithm 11.2: The SOM procedure

Input : Output layer network topology; neighborhood distance $D(1)$; weights from input to outputs are initialized to small random values; $t = 1$

Output: A low-dimensional projection of the input objects into $\mathbf{c}_1, \ldots, \mathbf{c}_K$

1 **repeat**
2   Select an input object $\mathbf{x}^i$
3   Compute the squared Euclidean distance of $\mathbf{x}^i$ from the weight vectors $\mathbf{w}_k(t) = (w_{k1}(t), \ldots, w_{kn}(t))$, with $k = 1, \ldots, K$, associated with each output point $\mathbf{c}_k$: $\sum_{j=1}^{n}(x_j^i - w_{kj}(t))^2$
4   Select the output point $\mathbf{c}_{k*}$ having the weight vector with minimum value at the previous step
5   Update weights to all points within a topological distance smaller than $D(t)$ from $\mathbf{c}_{k*}$, using the weight updating rule: $w_{kj}(t+1) = w_{kj}(t) + \eta(t)(x_j^i - w_{kj}(t))$ with a learning rate, $\eta(t)$, decreasing with time, that is, $0 < \eta(t+1) \le \eta(t) < 1$
6   Increment t
7 **until** The stopping criterion is met

Ortiz et al. (2014) employed a SOM to model the tissue distribution of normal and abnormal images generating a set of representative prototypes from the regions of interest (ROIs) in a set of images from the ADNI database. Singh and Samavedham (2015) applied SOM to extract features (ROIs) from preprocessed brain MRIs. These features were used as input for an SVM classifier to develop an intelligent system to aid in the diagnosis of neurodegenerative diseases.

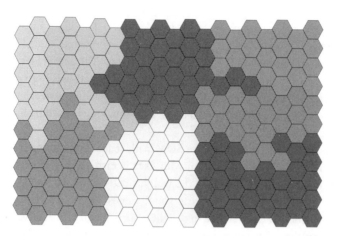

Figure 11.7 Illustration of the result of a SOM algorithm in a 2D map space. This hexagonal heatmap includes eight clusters, one per color. Each hexagon represents an object of data set $\mathcal{D}$. The output layer topology refers to the neighborhood scheme among the clusters. For example, the representative of the purple cluster is connected to two output units representing the yellow and green clusters. For the color version, please refer to the plate section.

11.3.6   Spectral Clustering

Spectral clustering (Donath and Hoffman, 1973; Luxburg, 2007) is based on the representation of the objects to be clustered as an undirected graph whose associated connectivity matrix is transformed in search of a sparse description that makes their posterior clustering task easier. This clustering technique makes use of the eigenvalues of a transformation of the data similarity matrix to perform dimensionality reduction in advance of the clustering process. This transformation provides better cluster solutions for data sets with arbitrary-shaped clusters than traditional hierarchical and partitional clustering methods.

Given any pair of objects, $\mathbf{x}^i$ and $\mathbf{x}^j$ with $i, j = 1, \ldots, N$, their similarity is denoted by $s\left(\mathbf{x}^i, \mathbf{x}^j\right)$ and is nonnegative. These similarities between pairs of objects are the elements of the similarity matrix denoted by $\mathbf{S} \in \mathbb{R}^{N \times N}$ and are used as the weights w_{ij} associated with the edges, connecting both objects in the similarity graph $\mathcal{G} = (V, E)$. $V = \{v_1, \ldots, v_N\}$ denotes the vertex set, with a vertex v_i associated with an object $\mathbf{x}^i$, where E is the set of edges between the objects.

Simple transformations of the similarity graph that look for a sparse representation of the data are: the ε-**neighborhood graph**, where only those vertices whose similarity is bigger than ε are connected; the k-**nearest neighbor graph** that connects v_i with v_j if v_j is one of the k-nearest neighbors of v_i;[1] and the **fully connected graph** where all pairs of objects (vertices) with positive similarity are connected.

The nonnegative weights, w_{ij} $(i, j = 1, ..., N)$, are the elements of a symmetric matrix $\mathbf{W}$, known as the **weighted adjacency matrix**. In this matrix, $w_{ij} = 0$ if vertices v_i and v_j are not connected. The **degree of a vertex** $v_i \in V$, denoted by d_i, is defined as the sum of the weights over all vertices that are adjacent to v_i, that is, $d_i = \sum_{j=1}^{N} w_{ij}$. The **degree matrix** $\mathbf{D}$ is defined as a diagonal matrix with degrees $d_1, \ldots, d_N$ on the diagonal. Given a

---

[1] As the neighborhood relationship is not symmetric, this definition leads to a directed graph. However, it is enough to use OR or AND operators to convert it into an undirected graph.

subset of vertices $A \subset V$, its size can be defined by either $|A|$ (the number of vertices in A) or $\text{vol}(A) = \sum_{i \in A} d_i$ (the sum of the degrees of its vertices). Both the weighted adjacency matrix and the degree matrix play an important role when defining graph Laplacians. Note that there is no one convention denoting a graph Laplacian in the literature. As far as we are concerned here, a **graph Laplacian** is a graph whose associated matrix is defined from weighted adjacency and degree matrices whose algebraic properties can transform the original objects into a sparse representation according to which they can be easily grouped.

The **unnormalized graph Laplacian matrix** is defined as $\mathbf{L} = \mathbf{D} - \mathbf{W}$. $\mathbf{L}$ is symmetric and positive semi-definite. The smallest eigenvalue of $\mathbf{L}$ is 0 with a corresponding eigenvector given by $(1, \dots, 1)$. $\mathbf{L}$ has N nonnegative real-valued eigenvalues $0 = \lambda_1 \leq \cdots \leq \lambda_N$.

The standard spectral clustering algorithm starts by computing the similarity matrix from the N objects, $\mathbf{x}^1, \dots, \mathbf{x}^N$, to be clustered. This similarity matrix is used to output the associated similarity graph, which can be transformed into an ε-neighborhood graph, a k-nearest neighbor graph, or a fully connected graph. The unnormalized graph Laplacian matrix $\mathbf{L}$ is then calculated, and the K eigenvectors corresponding to the smallest eigenvalues of $\mathbf{L}$ are output. These K vectors are organized into a matrix with N rows and K columns. Each row of this new matrix can be interpreted as the transformation of an original object $\mathbf{x}^i$, with $i = 1, \dots, N$, into a space where the objects can be grouped more easily than in the original space. In principle, these N transformed objects can be clustered using any clustering method. However, standard spectral clustering uses the K-means algorithm. Algorithm 11.3 illustrates the main steps of spectral clustering based on the unnormalized graph Laplacian matrix.

Algorithm 11.3: Standard spectral clustering

Input : Similarity matrix $\mathbf{S} \in \mathbb{R}^{N \times N}$, number of clusters K
Output: Clusters $Cl_1, \dots, Cl_K$

1 Construct a similarity graph from the original similarity matrix or from one of the three simple transformations. Let $\mathbf{W}$ be its weighted adjacency matrix and $\mathbf{D}$ its degree matrix
2 Compute the unnormalized graph Laplacian matrix $\mathbf{L} = \mathbf{D} - \mathbf{W}$
3 Compute the first K eigenvectors $\mathbf{v}_1, \dots, \mathbf{v}_K$ corresponding to the K smallest eigenvalues of $\mathbf{L}$
4 Compute $\mathbf{V} \in \mathbb{R}^{N \times K}$ the matrix containing the K vectors $\mathbf{v}_1, \dots, \mathbf{v}_K$ as columns
5 Let $\mathbf{y}^i \in \mathbb{R}^K$, with $i = 1, \dots, N$, be the vector corresponding to the ith row of $\mathbf{V}$
6 Cluster the points $\mathbf{y}^1, \dots, \mathbf{y}^N$ in $\mathbb{R}^K$ with the K-means algorithm into clusters $Cl_1, \dots, Cl_K$

The properties of graph Laplacians are also used for an approximated output to clustering formulated as a graph partitioning problem. This graph cut approach to clustering is based on the intuition that, given a similarity graph, we wish to find a partition of the graph such that the edges between different groups have a very low weight (objects in different clusters are dissimilar from each other), and the edges within a group have a high weight (objects within the same cluster are similar to each other).

More formally, given a graph $\mathcal{G} = (V, E)$ with associated $\mathbf{W}$, the most direct way to construct a partition of V is to solve the **mincut problem**:

$$\{A_1^*, \ldots, A_K^*\} = \arg\min_{A_1, \cdots, A_K} \sum_{l=1}^{K} \mathrm{cut}(A_l, \bar{A}_l),$$

where $A_1 \cup \cdots \cup A_K = V$ and $A_i \cap A_k = \varnothing$, for $i \neq k$, $\bar{A}_l = V \setminus A_l$ and $\mathrm{cut}(A_l, \bar{A}_l) = \sum_{i \in A_l, j \in \bar{A}_l} w_{ij}$. In many cases, the solution to the mincut problem contains several clusters with very few objects. The RatioCut (Hagen and Kahng, 1992) and the NCut (Shi and Malik, 2000) measures are minimized to yield balanced clusters with a reasonably large number of objects. They are defined as

$$\mathrm{RatioCut}(A_1, \ldots, A_K) = \sum_{l=1}^{K} \frac{\mathrm{cut}(A_l, \bar{A}_l)}{|A_l|} \tag{11.6}$$

and

$$\mathrm{NCut}(A_1, \ldots, A_K) = \sum_{l=1}^{K} \frac{\mathrm{cut}(A_l, \bar{A}_l)}{\mathrm{vol}(A_l)}. \tag{11.7}$$

The relaxed RatioCut minimization problem derived from Equation (11.6) is solved by the unnormalized spectral clustering algorithm (Algorithm 11.3). Similarly, the relaxed NCut minimization problem (Equation (11.7)) is output by the **normalized spectral clustering algorithm** that uses the **normalized graph Laplacian** given by $\mathbf{L}_{\mathrm{sym}} = \mathbf{D}^{-1/2}\mathbf{L}\mathbf{D}^{-1/2} = \mathbf{I} - \mathbf{D}^{-1/2}\mathbf{W}\mathbf{D}^{-1/2}$, used in line 2 of Algorithm 11.3 instead of $\mathbf{L}$.

Spectral clustering was applied by Craddock et al. (2012) to model human brain atlases for resting state functional connectivity. ROI size, and hence the number of ROIs in a parcellation, had the greatest impact on their suitability for functional connectivity analysis. With 200 or fewer ROIs, the resulting parcellations consist of ROIs with anatomic homology and thus offer increased interpretability. This interpretability was lost in parcellations containing higher numbers of ROIs (600 or 1,000). Lee et al. (2007a) used spectral clustering to identify active task-related regions in human brains affected by PD.

11.3.7 *K*-Medoids

The *K*-**medoids algorithm** (Kaufman and Rousseeuw, 1997) is an actual data point prototype clustering algorithm. The cluster representatives are objects, called **medoids**, belonging to the initial data set. *K*-medoids aims to find clusters minimizing a sum of pairwise dissimilarities instead of a sum of squared Euclidean distances like *K*-means.

A medoid $\mathbf{x}_{\mathrm{medoid}k}$ of a cluster Cl_k is defined as the object that is the least dissimilar to all the other objects in the cluster. It is identified as being the most centrally located object in the cluster. In mathematical notation,

$$\mathbf{x}_{\mathrm{medoid}k} = \arg\min_{\mathbf{x}^i \in Cl_k} \sum_{\mathbf{x}^i} d(\mathbf{x}^i, \mathbf{x}_{\mathrm{medoid}k}),$$

where $d(\mathbf{x}^i, \mathbf{x}_{\mathrm{medoid}k})$ denotes the dissimilarity between objects $\mathbf{x}^i$ and $\mathbf{x}_{\mathrm{medoid}k}$. The criterion to be minimized by *K*-medoids is

$$F_{\mathrm{medoids}}(\{Cl_1, \ldots, Cl_K\}) = \sum_{k=1}^{K} \sum_{\mathbf{x}^i \in Cl_k} d(\mathbf{x}^i, \mathbf{x}_{\mathrm{medoid}k}). \tag{11.8}$$

The most common implementation of the K-medoids clustering is the **partitioning around medoids** (PAM) algorithm (Kaufman and Rousseeuw, 1990). PAM first computes the dissimilarity matrix, whose (i, j)th element contains the dissimilarity between $\mathbf{x}^i$ and $\mathbf{x}^j$ objects, with $i, j = 1, \ldots, N$. In a second step, it randomly selects, without replacement, K of the N objects as the medoids. During the third step, each object is associated with its closest (most similar) medoid. Finally, PAM iterates the swapping of all non-medoid objects and medoids until there is no further improvement in $F_{\text{medoids}}(\{Cl_1, \ldots, Cl_K\})$.

Nikas and Low (2011) used hierarchical clustering, K-means, fuzzy C-means, and K-medoids for a supervised classification problem involving the diagnosis of HD in mice from nuclear MR spectroscopy features.

11.3.8   Affinity Propagation

Affinity propagation algorithm (Frey and Dueck, 2007) is based on the concept of message passing between objects. Its aim is to find a subset of representative objects as cluster prototypes, called **exemplars**. As in the K-medoids algorithm, the exemplars are members of the input data set. Unlike K-medoids, the affinity propagation algorithm simultaneously considers all objects as potential exemplars, avoiding the selection of initial cluster prototypes. The affinity propagation algorithm does not require the number of clusters to be determined or estimated before running the algorithm.

This algorithm takes a similarity matrix, with elements $s(\mathbf{x}^i, \mathbf{x}^j)$ for $i, j = 1, \ldots, N$, computing the similarity between objects $\mathbf{x}^i$ and $\mathbf{x}^j$ as input. These similarities verify that $s(\mathbf{x}^i, \mathbf{x}^j) > s(\mathbf{x}^i, \mathbf{x}^k)$ if and only if $\mathbf{x}^i$ is more similar to $\mathbf{x}^j$ than to $\mathbf{x}^k$. An example of similarity is the negative squared error (Euclidean distance): $s(\mathbf{x}^i, \mathbf{x}^j) = -||\mathbf{x}^i - \mathbf{x}^j||$.

The affinity propagation algorithm considers a graph where each object is represented as a node, and real-valued messages are sent recursively along the edges of the graph until a good set of exemplars and their corresponding clusters emerge. The algorithm proceeds by alternating two message-passing steps to update the following two matrices: the **responsibility matrix** and the **availability matrix**. The values $r(\mathbf{x}^i, \mathbf{x}^k)$ of the responsibility matrix quantify how much better suited $\mathbf{x}^k$ is to serve as the exemplar for $\mathbf{x}^i$ than other candidate exemplars for $\mathbf{x}^i$. The availability matrix contains elements $a(\mathbf{x}^i, \mathbf{x}^k)$ that represent how much better it would be for $\mathbf{x}^i$ to pick $\mathbf{x}^k$ as its exemplar, considering the preference of other objects for $\mathbf{x}^k$ as an exemplar.

Both matrices are zero initialized. The algorithm then performs the following updates iteratively:

1. First, responsibility updates are sent:

$$r\left(\mathbf{x}^i, \mathbf{x}^k\right) \leftarrow s\left(\mathbf{x}^i, \mathbf{x}^k\right) - \max_{k' \neq k}\left\{a(\mathbf{x}^i, \mathbf{x}^{k'}) + s\left(\mathbf{x}^i, \mathbf{x}^{k'}\right)\right\}.$$

2. Then, availabilities are updated:

$$a\left(\mathbf{x}^i, \mathbf{x}^k\right) \leftarrow \min\left\{0, r\left(\mathbf{x}^k, \mathbf{x}^k\right) + \sum_{i' \notin \{i,k\}} \max\left\{0, r\left(\mathbf{x}^{i'}, \mathbf{x}^k\right)\right\}\right\} \quad \text{for } i \neq k$$

$$a\left(\mathbf{x}^k, \mathbf{x}^k\right) \leftarrow \sum_{i' \neq k} \max\left\{0, r\left(\mathbf{x}^{i'}, \mathbf{x}^k\right)\right\}.$$

The iterations continue until the stopping condition is met. For object $\mathbf{x}^i$, the object $\mathbf{x}^j$ that maximizes $a\left(\mathbf{x}^i, \mathbf{x}^j\right) + r\left(\mathbf{x}^i, \mathbf{x}^j\right)$ identifies its exemplar. Objects with the same exemplar are grouped into the same cluster, and the selected exemplar is considered as the cluster prototype.

Ge et al. (2013) ran the affinity propagation algorithm to cluster corpus callosum fibers derived from DTI tractography into bundles. Niso et al. (2015) applied the same algorithm in functional epileptic brain network research to discriminate among healthy controls, frontal focus epileptic patients, and generalized epileptic patients. MEG data using two orthogonal planar gradiometers were analyzed in an interictal resting state with eyes closed. Also as a supervised classification task, Santana et al. (2013) applied the affinity propagation algorithm to classify interneurons into four previously identified subtypes based on morphological and physiological features.

11.3.9 *K*-Plane Clustering

The **K-plane clustering algorithm** (Bradley and Mangasarian, 2000) assumes that the objects are grouped around flat surfaces such as planes. These planes play the role of prototypes. The function to be minimized is the sum of squares of the distances of each point to its nearest plane. Representing the kth plane as $P_k = \{\mathbf{x} \mid \mathbf{x}^T \mathbf{w}_k = \gamma_k\}$, where $\mathbf{x} \in \mathbb{R}^n, \mathbf{w}_k \in \mathbb{R}^n$ (column vectors), and $\gamma_k \in \mathbb{R}$ for $k = 1, \dots, K$, the criterion to be minimized is

$$F_{\text{plane}}(\{Cl_1, \dots, Cl_K\}) = \sum_{k=1}^{K} \sum_{\mathbf{x}^i \in Cl_k} ||\mathbf{x}^{iT} \mathbf{w}_k - \gamma_k||^2.$$

The K-plane algorithm works in a similar way to K-means. It alternates between assigning objects to its nearest cluster plane and updating each cluster plane to minimize the sum of squares of distances to all points in the cluster.

11.3.10 Fuzzy *c*-Shell

The **fuzzy c-shell algorithms** were first proposed by Dave (1990) with the objective of detecting ring-shaped clusters (Dave, 1992) or hyperspherical shell-shaped clusters (Krishnapuraxa et al., 1992). Regarded as an extension of the fuzzy C-means algorithm, the fuzzy c-shell algorithms use a ring or a hyperspherical shell instead of a point as the cluster prototype.

11.3.11 DBSCAN

Density-based clustering (Kriegel et al., 2011) is a nonparametric approach,[2] and the clusters are considered to be high-density areas of objects. Intuitively, the output of a density-based cluster groups the objects in high-density regions separated from other density-based clusters by contiguous low-density regions of objects. Density-based clustering is capable of finding arbitrary-shaped clusters, can handle varying amounts of noise, and requires no prior knowledge about the number of clusters.

---

[2] This is their main difference from finite-mixture models for clustering purposes (Section 12.2), which assume a parametric model regarding the data distribution.

The **density-based spatial clustering of applications with noise algorithm** (DBSCAN) (Ester et al., 1996) is an example of density-based clustering methods. DBSCAN estimates the density around a point using the concept of ε-neighborhood. The **ε-neighborhood**, $N_\varepsilon(\mathbf{x}^i)$, of an object $\mathbf{x}^i$, is the set of objects within a specific radius ε around $\mathbf{x}^i$, that is, $N_\varepsilon(\mathbf{x}^i) = \{\mathbf{x}^j \in \mathcal{D} | d\left(\mathbf{x}^i, \mathbf{x}^j\right) < \varepsilon\}$, where d is some distance measure and $\varepsilon \in \mathbb{R}$. By convention, the object $\mathbf{x}^i$ is always in its own ε-neighborhood, i.e., $\mathbf{x}^i \in N_\varepsilon(\mathbf{x}^i)$ always holds.

DBSCAN classifies the objects of the data set $\mathcal{D}$ according to the cardinality of $N_\varepsilon(\mathbf{x}^i)$ into core, border, or noise points. An object $\mathbf{x}^i$ is a **core point** if $N_\varepsilon(\mathbf{x}^i)$ has high density, i.e., $|N_\varepsilon(\mathbf{x}^i)| \geq \text{minPts}$, where $\text{minPts} \in \mathbb{N}$ is a density threshold. An object is a **border point** if it is not a core point, but it is in the neighborhood of a core point. Finally, **noise points** are objects that are neither core nor border points. Figure 11.8 illustrates core, border, and noise points.

To form contiguous dense regions from individual points, DBSCAN uses the notions of reachability and connectedness. Given ε and minPts, an object $\mathbf{x}^j \in \mathcal{D}$ is **directly density-reachable** from $\mathbf{x}^i \in \mathcal{D}$ if and only if $|N_\varepsilon(\mathbf{x}^i)| \geq \text{minPts}$ and $\mathbf{x}^j \in N_\varepsilon(\mathbf{x}^i)$, that is, $\mathbf{x}^i$ is a core point and $\mathbf{x}^j$ is in its ε-neighborhood. An object $\mathbf{x}^j \in \mathcal{D}$ is **density-reachable** from $\mathbf{x}^i \in \mathcal{D}$ if there is a chain of objects $\mathbf{x}^{i(1)}, \ldots, \mathbf{x}^{i(q)} \in \mathcal{D}$ with $\mathbf{x}^{i(1)} = \mathbf{x}^i$ and $\mathbf{x}^{i(q)} = \mathbf{x}^j$ such that $\mathbf{x}^{i(r+1)}$ is directly density-reachable from $\mathbf{x}^{i(r)}$ for $r = 1, \ldots, q-1$. An object $\mathbf{x}^i \in \mathcal{D}$ is **density-connected** to an object $\mathbf{x}^j \in \mathcal{D}$ if there exists an object $\mathbf{x}^0 \in \mathcal{D}$ such that both $\mathbf{x}^i$ and $\mathbf{x}^j$ are density-reachable from $\mathbf{x}^0$. Figure 11.9 illustrates the concepts of density-reachability and density-connectivity.

DBSCAN uses the notion of density-connection to form clusters as contiguous dense regions. In DBSCAN, a cluster Cl is a nonempty subset of $\mathcal{D}$ satisfying the following conditions: (i) if $\mathbf{x}^i \in Cl$ and $\mathbf{x}^j$ is density-reachable from $\mathbf{x}^i$, then $\mathbf{x}^j \in Cl$ (maximality); and (ii) for all $\mathbf{x}^i, \mathbf{x}^j \in Cl$, $\mathbf{x}^i$ is density-connected to $\mathbf{x}^j$ (connectivity).

The DBSCAN algorithm outputs all such clusters by finding objects that act as core points and expanding each cluster to all density-reachable objects. The algorithm begins with an arbitrary object $\mathbf{x}^i \in \mathcal{D}$ and retrieves its ε-neighborhood. If $\mathbf{x}^i$ is a core point, then

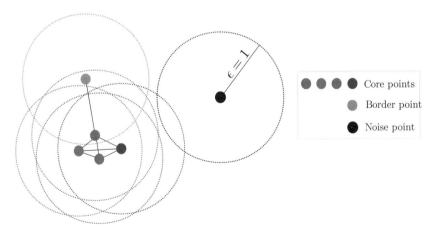

Figure 11.8 Illustration of the three types of points (core, border, and noise) in the DBSCAN algorithm with $\varepsilon = 1$, minPts $= 4$, and the Euclidean distance. For the color version, please refer to the plate section.

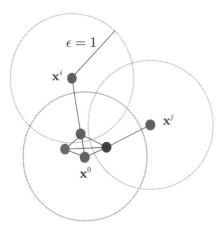

Figure 11.9 Given $\varepsilon = 1$, minPts $= 4$, and the Euclidean distance, $\mathbf{x}^i$ and $\mathbf{x}^j$ are density-reachable from $\mathbf{x}^0$. Therefore, $\mathbf{x}^i$ and $\mathbf{x}^j$ are density-connected. For the color version, please refer to the plate section.

it will start a new cluster that is expanded by assigning all points in its neighborhood to the cluster. If an additional core point is found in the neighborhood, then the search is expanded to also include all objects in its neighborhood. This expansion is repeated until no more core points are found. The cluster is then complete, and the remaining objects are searched to see if another core point can be found to start a new cluster. After processing all objects, any that were not assigned to a cluster are considered noise points.

In the DBSCAN algorithm, core points are always part of the same cluster regardless of the order in which the objects in $\mathcal{D}$ are processed. However, border points might be density-reachable from core points in several clusters. The algorithm assigns these points to the first of these processed clusters which depends on the order in which the data objects are stored in $\mathcal{D}$. To alleviate this problem, Campello et al. (2015) introduced HDBSCAN*, which considers all border points as noise and leaves them unassigned.

Sengupta et al. (2015) used the DBSCAN algorithm to cluster groups of variables (instead of objects) and then selected one variable from each cluster to build a supervised classification model to distinguish between PD patients and healthy individuals. Baselice et al. (2015) used an evolved version of DBSCAN to cluster human brain MR images.

11.4   Choice of the Number of Clusters

The problem of determining the "right" number of clusters (Mirkin, 2011) in a data set is an important problem in data clustering that has received a lot of attention in the specialized literature. All the partitional clustering algorithms described in Section 11.3, with the exception of the affinity propagation algorithm, require the specification of this parameter. The height at which the dendrogram is cut to yield the clusters is the analogous problem in hierarchical clustering.

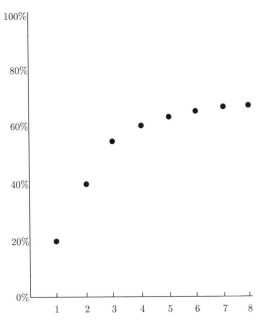

Figure 11.10 Illustration of the elbow method. Number of clusters on the *x*-axis and percentage of explained variance on the *y*-axis. The marginal gain in the percentage of explained variance starts dropping at four clusters. This is the number of selected clusters provided by the method.

The term "right number of clusters" is often ambiguous, as it depends on the clustering resolution desired by the user. Additionally, the clustering criteria will always improve if the number of clusters, K, is increased without penalization up to the extreme case where the number of clusters equals the number of objects (i.e., $K = N$). Intuitively, the optimal choice of K should provide a balance between a maximum compression of the data set using a single cluster (i.e., $K = 1$), and a maximum performance of the clustering criterion by assigning each object to its own cluster (i.e., $K = N$).

A simple rule of thumb sets the value of K to $K \approx \sqrt{\frac{N}{2}}$ (Mardia et al., 1979). The original **elbow method**, as proposed by Thorndike (1953), is based on representing the percentage of explained variance (ratio between the sum of within-cluster variances and the data variance) as a function of the number of clusters. The first clusters in this graph explain a lot of variance, but the marginal gain will drop at some point. The best number of clusters is chosen at this point; this is known as the elbow criterion. It is also common to find the clustering criterion F in the y-axis. Figure 11.10 shows an example. Notice that this graph somewhat resembles the scree plot in Section 2.4.3.

11.4.1 Hierarchical Clustering

Cutting the dendrogram at an appropriate height yields a partition of the objects into clusters. Two main types of methods have been proposed for searching for the optimal cutoff level.

(a) Moving the cutoff level by one level at a time (Duda and Hart, 1973). The idea is based on the computation of a ratio. First, the numerator provides the value of a given criterion (i.e., square-error criterion) when splitting a cluster into two to yield $L +$ 1 rather than L clusters. Then, the same criterion is computed in the denominator, using the original cluster solution (without splitting). If the ratio is extreme (very low for the square-error criterion), the splitting process stops, outputting the cutoff level. Alternatively, an inverse process of merging (two clusters into one) rather than splitting (one cluster into two) could be enacted.

(b) Choosing a cutoff level in a completed hierarchy. Mojena (1977) proposed calculating the optimization (maximization) criterion values, $f(k)$, for all k-cluster partitions by cutting the dendrogram ($k = 1, \ldots, N-1$). The final K is such that $f(K)$ is significantly greater than the average of all $f(k)$. Milligan (1981) included 30 different criteria for f in his seminal paper on rules for cutting cluster hierarchies.

11.4.2 Partitional Clustering

The different approaches for choosing the number of clusters in partitional clustering can be categorized as: (a) postprocessing multiple runs of the cluster algorithm with random initializations and different values of K, and (b) preanalyzing a set of potential centroids.

(a) Postprocessing. According to Chiang and Mirkin (2010), several approaches have been proposed: (i) variance-based approaches, which use a partitional clustering criterion, such as in Equations (11.2)–(11.5) or Equation (11.8) to search for "elbow" values at a correct K; (ii) structural approach, which compares within-cluster cohesion versus between-cluster separation at different K values; (iii) a combination of multiple clusterings, where the most stable value of K is selected for multiple clustering results at different K values; and (iv) a resampling approach, which selects K according to the similarity of clustering results (see Section 11.6) on randomly disturbed or sampled data.

(b) Preanalysis. This approach uses several cluster evaluation criteria for estimating the optimal value of K. For example, two heuristic measures have been proposed by Milligan and Cooper (1985) known as the Calinski and Harabasz criterion (Calinski and Harabasz, 1974) and Hartigan's statistic (Hartigan, 1975). Another popular heuristic involves the so-called **gap statistic** (Tibshirani et al., 2001). This statistic compares the value of $F(\{Cl_1, \ldots, Cl_K\})$ with its expectation according to the uniform distribution of the data set over the clusters. For the purpose of comparison, the gap statistic is computed as the logarithm of the average ratio of $F(\{Cl_1, \ldots, Cl_K\})$ values in the observed data set and in multiple-generated random data. The optimal value of K is estimated as the smallest K for which the difference between the above ratios at K and $K + 1$ is greater than its standard deviation.

11.5   Subspace Clustering

Subspace clustering (Parsons et al., 2004; Kriegel et al., 2009; Vidal, 2011) refers to the task of identifying clusters of similar objects where the similarity is defined with respect to a subset of variables (i.e., a subspace of the data space). This subspace is not necessarily the same for different clusters.

High-dimensional data pose new challenges to the clustering problem requiring special-ized solutions. The fact that some variables are irrelevant for characterizing the objects may interfere with the aim of finding the clusters. At the same time, the possible existence of strong correlations among subsets of variables can affect the result of the grouping pro-cess, especially when correlations in the different clusters differ. **Local feature relevance** accounts for the need for multiple subspaces because each cluster may exist in a different subspace. Unlike FSS in supervised classification (Chapter 6), where only one subspace is selected, local feature relevance picks several subspaces.

The existence of irrelevant features and correlated features originates two types of subspaces: (a) axis-parallel subspaces and (b) arbitrarily oriented subspaces.

(a) **Axis-parallel subspaces.** An axis-parallel subspace contains a subset of the original features that are preserved without any kind of transformation. The subspace should contain the features that are relevant for one (or more) clusters. A characteristic of a feature that is relevant for a cluster is that it has a smaller variance for the objects that are members of that cluster than for objects outside the cluster. Figure 11.11(a) shows an example.

An example of subspace clustering based on axis-parallel subspaces is **projected clustering** (PROCLUS) (Aggarwal et al., 1999). PROCLUS aims to find K pairs $(\mathcal{D}_1, \mathcal{X}_1), \ldots, (\mathcal{D}_K, \mathcal{X}_K)$, where $\mathcal{D}_i$ denotes the objects in the ith cluster and $\mathcal{X}_i$, the set of their relevant features, with $i = 1, \ldots, K$. PROCLUS is a K-medoids-like clustering algorithm that first randomly selects potential medoids denoted by $\mathcal{P}$. For each of the current K medoids (extracted from $\mathcal{P}$), the relevant subspace is determined by minimizing the standard deviation of the distances of the points in the neighborhood of the medoids to the corresponding medoid across each dimension. Points are then assigned to the closest medoid considering the relevant subspace of each medoid.

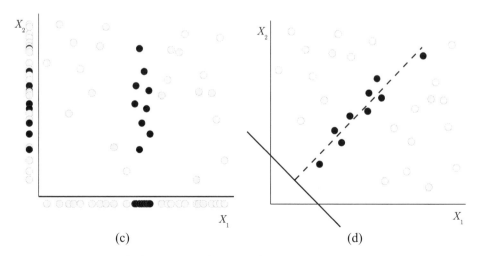

(c)   (d)

Figure 11.11 Examples of subspace clustering. (a) Axis-parallel subspace, where X_1 is the relevant subspace for the objects in black, whereas X_2 is an irrelevant variable. The projections of the 2D points onto each of the two axes are also displayed. (b) Arbitrary oriented subspace, where the relevant subspace (solid line) for the objects in black is perpendicular to the regression line (dashed line).

The clusters are refined by replacing bad medoids with new medoids selected from $\mathcal{P}$ as long as the resulting clustering quality increases.

(b) **Arbitrarily oriented subspaces**. Two attributes that are linearly correlated for a subset of objects will scatter the points along a hyperplane defined by the linear dependency between both attributes. The subspace orthogonal to this hyperplane is a subspace with densely clustered objects (see Figure 11.11(b) for an example). The orientation of this hyperplane is arbitrary, accounting for a more general case than axis-parallel subspaces.

PCA (Section 2.4.3) is a basic technique for accommodating arbitrarily oriented subspaces. The first approach was the ORCLUS algorithm (Aggarwal and Yu, 2000). ORCLUS is a K-means-like approach, which first selects $K' > K$ seeds. The objects are assigned to the above seeds according to a distance function based on an eigensystem (derived from the PCA) of the corresponding cluster. The distance is computed across the projected subspace, where the density of the cluster objects is high. The eigensystem is iteratively adapted to the current state of the updated cluster. The number K' of clusters is reduced iteratively by merging the closest pairs of clusters until the user-specified number K is reached.

11.6   Cluster Ensembles

Cluster ensembles (Day, 1986) combine multiple base clusterings of a set of objects into a single consolidated clustering, often referred to as **consensus clustering**. Alikhanian et al. (2013) showed how several clustering techniques cooperate to localize active brain regions from MEG brain signals, where agglomerative hierarchical clustering with the Ward's algorithm, and affinity propagation algorithm worked in tandem. Ryali et al. (2015) used a consensus clustering approach to combine the results of multiple clustering methods to segment brain regions using resting-state fMRI. Cluster ensemble is similar to the problem of combining different supervised classification models (Chapter 9). However, the combination of multiple clusterings poses additional challenges: (a) the number of clusters across the different base clusterings may differ, and the optimal number of clusters in the consensus is not known; (b) the cluster labels used by the different base clustering solutions are symbolic, and a tough correspondence problem has to be solved for the purposes of alignment; and (c) there is no access in some formulations of the problem to the original data yielding multiple base clustering solutions, which are the only available information.

The motivations for and benefits of using a cluster ensemble are wide ranging, including the following (Ghosh and Achraya, 2011): (a) a way to integrate and reuse already existent cluster solutions; (b) an improvement of the quality of the solution compared to each of the base clusterings; (c) a much more robust solution able to provide good results across a very wide range of data sets, (d) a novel approach to determine the final number of clusters; (e) an original proposal for the **multiview clustering** problem, where each base clustering corresponds to multiple aspects (or "views"), distinct views may involve nonidentical sets of variables or subsets of the original data set; and (f) a solution for clustering data sets that are inherently distributed when the entire data set cannot be assembled at a central site.

Consider r base clusterings of a data set of N objects, $\mathbf{x}^i$, $i = 1, \ldots, N$. The qth clustering denoted by $\lambda^{(q)} = \{Cl_1^{(q)}, \ldots, Cl_{K_q}^{(q)}\}$ partitions the data set into K_q clusters. Given the r base clusterings, denoted by $\lambda^{(1)}, \ldots, \lambda^{(q)}, \ldots, \lambda^{(r)}$, the cluster ensemble problem consists of finding a consensus cluster, $\hat{\lambda} = \{\hat{Cl}_1, \ldots, \hat{Cl}_K\}$, where the value of K as well as the objects in each of the clusters should be found. We review two groups of methods below.

11.6.1 Based on the Similarity between Two Cluster Partitions

An intuitive manner of defining $\hat{\lambda}$ is as the cluster partition whose average similarity with respect to the set of r base clusterings, $\Lambda = \{\lambda^{(1)}, \ldots, \lambda^{(q)}, \ldots, \lambda^{(r)}\}$, is maximum, that is,

$$\hat{\lambda} = \arg\max_{\lambda} \Phi(\Lambda, \lambda) = \frac{1}{r} \sum_{q=1}^{r} \phi(\lambda^{(q)}, \lambda), \qquad (11.9)$$

where $\Phi(\Lambda, \lambda)$ denotes the similarity between a set, Λ, of r cluster partitions and a given cluster, λ. This similarity is computed as the average of the similarities, $\phi(\lambda^{(q)}, \lambda)$, between each base clustering, $\lambda^{(q)}$, and λ.

Table 11.2 shows a contingency table from which some similarity functions ϕ between two base clusterings can be calculated.

The **adjusted Rand index** (Hubert and Arabie, 1985), ϕ^{ARI}, of the two base clusterings, $\lambda^{(a)}$ and $\lambda^{(b)}$, is defined as

$$\phi^{\text{ARI}}\left(\lambda^{(a)}, \lambda^{(b)}\right) = \frac{\sum_{fg} \binom{N_{fg}}{2} - S_a S_b / \binom{N}{2}}{\frac{1}{2}(S_a + S_b) - S_a S_b / \binom{N}{2}},$$

where $S_a = \sum_f \binom{N_{f\bullet}^{(a)}}{2}$ and $S_b = \sum_g \binom{N_{\bullet g}^{(b)}}{2}$. The second term in both numerator and denominator represents the expected number of overlaps under the hypothesis of no correlation between the cluster labels in $\lambda^{(a)}$ and $\lambda^{(b)}$. This is why $\phi^{\text{ARI}}\left(\lambda^{(a)}, \lambda^{(b)}\right)$ is said to adjust the Rand index (see Section 11.7).

Table 11.2 Contingency table for two base clusterings, $\lambda^{(a)}$ and $\lambda^{(b)}$, with K_a and K_b clusters respectively. The counter N_{fg} denotes the number of objects that are at the same time in clusters $Cl_f^{(a)}$ and $Cl_g^{(b)}$, whereas $N_{f\bullet}^{(a)}$ counts the number of objects in cluster $Cl_f^{(a)}$, and $N_{\bullet g}^{(b)}$ counts the number of objects in cluster $Cl_g^{(b)}$

		$\lambda^{(b)}$			
		$Cl_1^{(b)}$	$Cl_2^{(b)}$	$\ldots$	$Cl_{K_b}^{(b)}$	
	$Cl_1^{(a)}$	N_{11}	N_{12}	$\ldots$	N_{1K_b}	$N_{1\bullet}^{(a)}$
	$Cl_2^{(a)}$	N_{21}	N_{22}	$\ldots$	N_{2K_b}	$N_{2\bullet}^{(a)}$
$\lambda^{(a)}$	$\ldots$	$\ldots$	$\ldots$	$\ldots$	$\ldots$	$\ldots$
	$Cl_{K_a}^{(a)}$	$N_{K_a 1}$	$N_{K_a 2}$	$\ldots$	$N_{K_a K_b}$	$N_{K_a \bullet}^{(a)}$
		$N_{\bullet 1}^{(b)}$	$N_{\bullet 2}^{(b)}$	$\ldots$	$N_{\bullet K_b}^{(b)}$	N

The **normalized mutual information** (Strehl and Ghosh, 2002) computes the similarity between two base clusterings using the entropy (Section 3.6.1) associated with a clustering, $\mathbb{H}\left(\lambda^{(a)}\right) = -\sum_f \frac{N_{f\bullet}^{(a)}}{N} \log_2 \frac{N_{f\bullet}^{(a)}}{N}$, and the joint entropy (Section 3.6.2) of $\lambda^{(a)}$ and $\lambda^{(b)}$, $\mathbb{H}\left(\lambda^{(a)}, \lambda^{(b)}\right) = -\sum_{fg} \frac{N_{fg}}{N} \log_2 \frac{N_{fg}}{N}$. It is defined as

$$\phi^{\text{NMI}}\left(\lambda^{(a)}, \lambda^{(b)}\right) = \frac{\mathbb{H}\left(\lambda^{(a)}\right) + \mathbb{H}\left(\lambda^{(b)}\right) - \mathbb{H}\left(\lambda^{(a)}, \lambda^{(b)}\right)}{\sqrt{\mathbb{H}\left(\lambda^{(a)}\right) \mathbb{H}\left(\lambda^{(b)}\right)}}.$$

The numerator represents the mutual information (Section 3.6.4) between two base clusterings $\lambda^{(a)}$ and $\lambda^{(b)}$, whereas the geometric mean (Section 2.2.2) of $\mathbb{H}\left(\lambda^{(a)}\right)$ and $\mathbb{H}\left(\lambda^{(b)}\right)$ in the denominator is used for normalization. This makes interpretation and comparisons easier as the range of $\phi^{\text{NMI}}\left(\lambda^{(a)}, \lambda^{(b)}\right)$ goes from 0 (no agreement) to 1 (complete agreement).

The **variation of information** (Meilă, 2003) is another information theoretic measure proposed for cluster agreement and is defined as

$$\phi^{\text{VI}}\left(\lambda^{(a)}, \lambda^{(b)}\right) = \mathbb{H}\left(\lambda^{(a)}\right) + \mathbb{H}\left(\lambda^{(b)}\right) - 2\mathbb{I}\left(\lambda^{(a)}, \lambda^{(b)}\right),$$

where $\mathbb{I}\left(\lambda^{(a)}, \lambda^{(b)}\right)$ is the mutual information between two clusterings, i.e., $\mathbb{I}\left(\lambda^{(a)}, \lambda^{(b)}\right) = \mathbb{H}\left(\lambda^{(a)}\right) + \mathbb{H}\left(\lambda^{(b)}\right) - \mathbb{H}\left(\lambda^{(a)}, \lambda^{(b)}\right)$. A version of the variation of information that works with data sets of different sizes and clusterings with different number of clusters is the **normalized variation of information** (Wu et al., 2009), computed as

$$\phi^{\text{NVI}}\left(\lambda^{(a)}, \lambda^{(b)}\right) = \frac{\phi^{\text{VI}}\left(\lambda^{(a)}, \lambda^{(b)}\right)}{\mathbb{H}\left(\lambda^{(a)}\right) + \mathbb{H}\left(\lambda^{(b)}\right)}.$$

The range of $\phi^{\text{NVI}}\left(\lambda^{(a)}, \lambda^{(b)}\right)$ lies in $[0,1]$. A value of 1 means maximum agreement between $\lambda^{(a)}$ and $\lambda^{(b)}$.

The solution of Equation (11.9) when $\phi\left(\lambda^{(q)}, \lambda\right)$ refers to ϕ^{ARI}, ϕ^{NMI}, ϕ^{NVI}, or any other similarity measure is generally intractable, and heuristic approaches (Section 6.3.1) should be applied.

11.6.2   Based on the Ensemble Coassociation Matrix

The result of a base clustering $\lambda^{(q)}$ can be represented by a binary, symmetric $N \times N$ **coassociation matrix**, with elements, $c_{ij}^{(q)}$, which is 1 if objects $\mathbf{x}^i$ and $\mathbf{x}^j$ are in the same cluster and 0 otherwise. An **ensemble coassociation matrix** with entries given by $e_{ij} = \frac{1}{r}\sum_{q=1}^r w_q c_{ij}^{(q)}$ can be obtained from the r base clusterings, where the weights w_q specify the importance of $\lambda^{(q)}$. This can be interpreted as a similarity matrix to be used to create the consensus matrix. A single-linkage hierarchical clustering can be applied for this purpose.

Example. Table 11.3 displays three coassociation matrices associated with three base clusterings of seven objects.

Table 11.3 Three examples of coassociation matrices. The matrix on the left corresponds to $\lambda^{(1)} = \{Cl_1^{(1)}, Cl_2^{(1)}, Cl_3^{(1)}\}$, where $C_1^{(1)} = \{\mathbf{x}^1, \mathbf{x}^2\}$, $Cl_2^{(1)} = \{\mathbf{x}^3, \mathbf{x}^4, \mathbf{x}^5\}$, and $Cl_3^{(1)} = \{\mathbf{x}^6, \mathbf{x}^7\}$. In the middle, $\lambda^{(2)} = \{Cl_1^{(2)}, Cl_2^{(2)}, Cl_3^{(2)}\}$ where $Cl_1^{(2)} = \{\mathbf{x}^1, \mathbf{x}^2, \mathbf{x}^3\}$, $Cl_2^{(2)} = \{\mathbf{x}^4, \mathbf{x}^5, \mathbf{x}^6\}$, and $Cl_3^{(2)} = \{\mathbf{x}^7\}$. On the right, $\lambda^{(3)} = \{Cl_1^{(3)}, Cl_2^{(3)}, Cl_3^{(3)}\}$ where $Cl_1^{(3)} = \{\mathbf{x}^1, \mathbf{x}^2\}$, $Cl_2^{(3)} = \{\mathbf{x}^3, \mathbf{x}^4\}$, and $Cl_3^{(3)} = \{\mathbf{x}^5, \mathbf{x}^6, \mathbf{x}^7\}$

	$\lambda^{(1)}$								$\lambda^{(2)}$								$\lambda^{(3)}$						
	1	2	3	4	5	6	7		1	2	3	4	5	6	7		1	2	3	4	5	6	7
1	1	1	0	0	0	0	0	1	1	1	1	0	0	0	0	1	1	1	0	0	0	0	0
2	1	1	0	0	0	0	0	2	1	1	1	0	0	0	0	2	1	1	0	0	0	0	0
3	0	0	1	1	1	0	0	3	1	1	1	0	0	0	0	3	0	0	1	1	0	0	0
4	0	0	1	1	1	0	0	4	0	0	0	1	1	1	0	4	0	0	1	1	0	0	0
5	0	0	1	1	1	0	0	5	0	0	0	1	1	1	0	5	0	0	0	0	1	1	1
6	0	0	0	0	0	1	1	6	0	0	0	1	1	1	0	6	0	0	0	0	1	1	1
7	0	0	0	0	0	1	1	7	0	0	0	0	0	0	1	7	0	0	0	0	1	1	1

Table 11.4 Ensemble coassociation matrix resulting from the three association matrices shown in Table 11.3 considering that the weights for all center partitions are the same

	1	2	3	4	5	6	7
1	1	1	1/3	0	0	0	0
2	1	1	1/3	0	0	0	0
3	1/3	1/3	1	2/3	1/3	0	0
4	0	0	2/3	1	2/3	1/3	0
5	0	0	1/3	2/3	1	2/3	1/3
6	0	0	0	1/3	2/3	1	2/3
7	0	0	0	0	1/3	2/3	1

Table 11.4 shows the ensemble coassociation matrix yielded by the three coassociation matrices shown in Table 11.3, assuming that the weights for $\lambda^{(1)}$, $\lambda^{(2)}$, and $\lambda^{(3)}$ are equal, i.e., $w_1 = w_2 = w_3 = \frac{1}{3}$. Hierarchical clustering applied on a matrix whose elements are one minus the respective element in the coassociation matrix (in order to account for dissimilarities rather than associations) would provide the consensus clustering. ■

11.7 Evaluation Criteria

As suggested by Bonner (1964), the evaluation of the clustering result is a difficult and controversial issue. Although, for the most part, evaluation is in the eye of the beholder, several evaluation criteria have been used. They have been classed as internal and external quality criteria.

11.7.1 Internal Quality Criteria

Internal quality criteria are based on the compactness of the clusters measuring intracluster homogeneity, intercluster separability, or a combination of both. The different measures do not use any external information apart from the actual data. Some examples follow:

- **Sum of squared errors**. This is the simplest criterion for measuring the **intracluster homogeneity** as expressed by the K-means criterion:

$$F_{\text{SSE}}(\{Cl_1, \dots, Cl_K\}) = \sum_{k=1}^{K} \sum_{\mathbf{x}^i \in Cl_k} ||\mathbf{x}^i - \mathbf{c}_k||^2.$$

  The minimization of the sum of squared errors criterion results in compact and well-separated clusters.

- **Scatter criteria**. The scalar scatter criteria are derived from the scatter matrices. For the kth cluster, the **scatter matrix**, $\mathbf{S}_k$, is calculated as $\mathbf{S}_k = \sum_{\mathbf{x}^i \in Cl_k}(\mathbf{x}^i - \mathbf{c}_k)(\mathbf{x}^i - \mathbf{c}_k)^T$. Note that $\mathbf{x}^i$ is treated as a column vector. The **within-cluster scatter matrix**, $\mathbf{S}_W$, is computed as the summation of the scatter matrices over all clusters, i.e., $\mathbf{S}_W = \sum_{k=1}^{K} \mathbf{S}_k$. The **between-cluster scatter matrix** is output as $\mathbf{S}_B = \sum_{k=1}^{K} |Cl_k|(\mathbf{c}_k - \mathbf{c})(\mathbf{c}_k - \mathbf{c})^T$, where $\mathbf{c}$ is the mean vector of the data set, defined as $\mathbf{c} = \frac{1}{N}\sum_{k=1}^{K} |Cl_k|\mathbf{c}_k$, and $|Cl_k|$ denotes the number of objects in the kth cluster. The total scatter matrix is calculated as $\mathbf{S}_T = \sum_{k=1}^{K} \sum_{\mathbf{x}^i \in Cl_k}(\mathbf{x}^i - \mathbf{c})(\mathbf{x}^i - \mathbf{c})^T$. Three scalar criteria can be derived from $\mathbf{S}_W, \mathbf{S}_B$, and $\mathbf{S}_T$ as follows:

  - **The trace criterion** corresponds to the sum of the diagonal elements of a matrix. The minimization of the trace of $\mathbf{S}_W$ is equivalent to the sum of squared errors criterion, that is, $\text{tr}(\mathbf{S}_W) = \sum_{k=1}^{K} \sum_{\mathbf{x}^i \in Cl_k} ||\mathbf{x}^i - \mathbf{c}_k||^2$. Another alternative is to maximize the trace of $\mathbf{S}_B$, $\text{tr}(\mathbf{S}_B) = \sum_{k=1}^{K} |Cl_k| ||\mathbf{c}_k - \mathbf{c}||^2$.
  - **The determinant criterion** is based on the fact that the determinant of a scatter matrix roughly measures the square of the scattering volume. The criterion to be minimized is $|\mathbf{S}_W| = |\sum_{k=1}^{K} \mathbf{S}_k|$.
  - **The invariant criterion** considers the eigenvalues $\lambda_1, \dots, \lambda_N$ of $\mathbf{S}_W^{-1}\mathbf{S}_B$ as they are the linear invariants of the scatter matrices. Good cluster partitions are consistent with large eigenvalues. Three such criteria are (a) $\max \sum_{i=1}^{N} \lambda_i$, (b) $\min \sum_{i=1}^{N} \frac{1}{1+\lambda_i}$, and (c) $\min \prod_{i=1}^{N} \frac{1}{1+\lambda_i}$.

11.7.2 External Quality Criteria

External quality criteria are used to evaluate whether the clusters match a given classification of the objects that can be provided either by some experts or it is found in the state of the art.

- **Mutual information-based measure**. Given a previous classification of the N objects based on r possible classes, $\{c_1, \dots, c_r\}$, that has been clustered as $\{Cl_1, \dots, Cl_K\}$, the mutual information-based measure is defined as

$$F_{\text{MI}}(\{Cl_1, \dots, Cl_K\}) = \sum_{l=1}^{K} \sum_{h=1}^{r} \frac{N_{lh}}{N} \log_2 \frac{N_{lh}N}{N_{l\bullet}N_{\bullet h}},$$

  where N_{lh} denotes the number of objects that are in cluster Cl_l and also in the hth class, $N_{l\bullet}$ denotes the number of objects in cluster Cl_l, and $N_{\bullet h}$ the number of objects in the hth class. A high value for F_{MI} is interpreted as a good match between the provided classification and the clustering. This measure is easily interpretable when $r = K$, that is, when the number of clusters coincides with the number of possible classes.

- **Precision and recall-based measure**. Precision, recall, and F_1-measure (Section 5.2.1.1 and 5.2.2.1) have been used as external criteria for assessing the match between the partition of a data set provided by a clustering method and a given labeled version of this data set.

- **Rand index**. Given two clusterings of N objects, denoted by $\lambda^{(1)}$ and $\lambda^{(2)}$, the Rand index (Rand, 1971) is a criterion for comparing the match between the two, where one of them is assumed to be provided. Let a be the number of pairs of objects that are assigned to the same cluster in $\lambda^{(1)}$ and $\lambda^{(2)}$; b be the number of pairs of objects that are assigned to the same cluster in $\lambda^{(1)}$, but not in the same cluster in $\lambda^{(2)}$; c be the number of pairs of objects that are assigned to the same cluster in $\lambda^{(2)}$, but are not in the same cluster in $\lambda^{(1)}$; and d be the number of pairs of objects that are assigned to different clusters in $\lambda^{(1)}$ and $\lambda^{(2)}$. The numbers a and d are interpreted as matches, whereas b and c are mismatches. The Rand index is defined as

$$\text{Rand index} = \frac{a+d}{a+b+c+d},$$

and lies between 0 and 1. High Rand index values are associated with good matches between both clusterings.

11.8   Example: Dendritic Spines

This section contains the results of applying agglomerative hierarchical clustering and K-means to Data Set 4 (Section 1.6.4) that consists of 2,000 individually 3D reconstructed dendritic spines of layer III pyramidal neurons from the cingulate cortex of a human male age 40. This is a subset of the spines used in Luengo-Sanchez et al. (2018).

Agglomerative hierarchical clustering using the Euclidean distance to compute the dissimilarity between pairs of spines and the average linkage strategy output the dendrogram shown in Figure 11.12. Following the simple criterion proposed by Mojena (1977) (Section 11.4.1), three appears to be a good choice for the number of clusters considering dissimilarity as the optimization criterion.

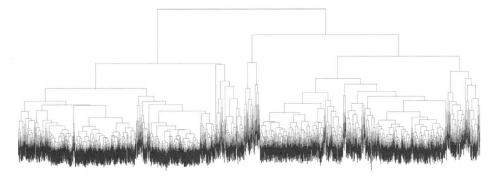

Figure 11.12 Dendrogram associated with the agglomerative hierarchical clustering (with average linkage) of the 2,000 spines in Data Set 4. Plot output using the `hclust` R package.

Cluster 1

Cluster 2

Cluster 3

Figure 11.13 Five examples of spines for each of the three clusters yielded by the agglomerative hierarchical clustering (with average linkage). For the color version, please refer to the plate section.

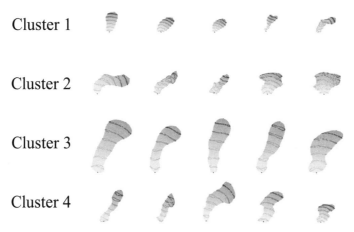

Cluster 1

Cluster 2

Cluster 3

Cluster 4

Figure 11.14 Five examples of spines for each of the four clusters yielded by the K-means partitional clustering method. For the color version, please refer to the plate section.

Figure 11.13 shows five examples of spines belonging to each of the three clusters. The first cluster contains 68 spines characterized by their large head volume. The second cluster contains 956 spines. They do not have extremely small heads, their total volumes are not particularly large, and their head-to-neck ratios are not big. The third cluster is the most populated, with 976 spines, which have the characteristic of being very small.

The elbow method (Thorndike, 1953) explained in Section 11.4 was used to determine the best number of clusters for applying the K-means method. This resulted in $K = 4$. We used the kmeans R package. Figure 11.14 shows 5 examples of spines for each of the 4 clusters. The 876 spines in the first cluster are extremely small. The second cluster contains 499 spines, which have a rather large central region (of a similar size to the head) and a small size, even though they are not as small as the ones in the first cluster. The third cluster includes only 150 spines. Compared with the other clusters, its spines are much bigger. Finally, the 475 spines of the fourth cluster have a longer neck than the others.

11.9   Bibliographic Notes

Early approaches found clusters of personality types (Stephenson, 1936; Cattell, 1944). Tryon (1939) was the first systematic research and proposed the average linkage strategy for hierarchical clustering, also focused on grouping personality types.

The so-called numerical taxonomy (Florek et al., 1951) established the principles of single-linkage agglomerative hierarchical clustering. Hierarchical clustering and applications grew fast in the 1950s and 1960s due to the availability of computer technologies for implementing the developed algorithms. Numerical taxonomy emerged in biology to classify animals (Sneath and Sokal, 1973). Also, Sonquist and Morgan (1964) applied these hierarchical clustering methods in social science to characterize typologies of individuals. Later several agglomerative hierarchical clustering algorithms with a linear (in N) computational complexity were proposed in response to the need for large-scale data set management (Zhang et al., 1996). Parallel techniques for hierarchical clustering were discussed by Olson (1995).

The term K-means was first introduced by MacQueen (1967), though the general idea dates back to Steinhaus (1956) and was first proposed as an algorithm by Lloyd in 1957. However, it was not published outside Bell Labs until 25 years later (Lloyd, 1982). An efficient version of K-means was proposed by Hartigan (1975). Jain (2010) provided an overview of the development and improvements of the K-means algorithm on the occasion of its 50th anniversary. The strong dependence of the K-means algorithm on the initial clustering has been widely investigated in the literature. The use of the output provided by hierarchical agglomerative clustering as the initial clusters for the K-means algorithm was suggested by Milligan (1980) and Fisher (1996). Peña et al. (1999a) reported an empirical comparison of several initialization methods. Extensions of the basic K-means algorithm include **attribute weighted K-means** (Huang et al., 2005), where a weight denoting its degree of importance is assigned to each variable. For domains with mixed numeric and categorical objects, Huang (1998) proposed the K**-prototypes algorithm**. This algorithm integrates the K-means and the K-modes algorithms by defining a combined dissimilarity measure.

A variant of the fuzzy C-means algorithm is possibilistic C-means (Krishnapuram and Keller, 1996), where the cluster membership of objects is based on possibility theory instead of fuzzy theory.

Spectral clustering goes back to Donath and Hoffman (1973), who first suggested the construction of graph partitions based on eigenvectors of the adjacency matrix. In the same year, Fiedler (1973) noticed the connections between the bi-partitions of a graph and the second eigenvector of the graph Laplacian. Luxburg (2007) provides a review on spectral clustering.

Kaufman and Rousseeuw (1990) proposed an adaptation of K-medoids for large data sets that combines sampling and PAM. The algorithm is called the **Clustering LARge Application** (CLARA). CLARA does not use all objects for the purpose of clustering; instead, it outputs multiple samples of the data set and then applies PAM to each sample, finally returning the optimal medoids.

A notable drawback of the DBSCAN algorithm is its inability to find clusters of varying density. The so-called **ordering points to identify clustering structure** (OPTICS) (Ankerst et al., 1999) algorithm was designed to overcome this shortcoming. OPTICS returns an ordering of the objects in $\mathcal{D}$ according to a distance. They can be postprocessed to extract a hierarchy of the objects that can be adapted to represent local densities within $\mathcal{D}$. This uses a special distance representing the density needed in a cluster to accept a pair of objects as its members. Hartigan (1975) contains an algorithm that can be regarded as a general formalization of a density-based cluster. This algorithm computes clusters as maximal connected sets of points having a density greater than a given threshold.

Conceptual clustering methods (Michalski and Stepp, 1983; Fisher, 1987) group objects characterized by categorical variables and also produce conceptual descriptions of clusters, helpful for interpreting clustering results. Unlike other clustering methods for categorical variables such as K-modes, these methods are based on a search for objects representing the same or similar concepts.

Biclustering is a special type of clustering whose aim is to yield a simultaneous grouping of objects and variables. This problem was originally introduced by Hartigan (1972) and is also known as **block clustering**, **co-clustering**, or **two-mode clustering**. Biclustering somewhat resembles the axis-parallel subspace approach in subspace clustering insofar as biclustering selects a different subspace of variables for each cluster. For a review of biclustering algorithms, see Madeira and Oliveira (2004).

Milligan and Cooper (1985) showed the empirical behavior of several quality criteria, many not explained here, such as the silhouette coefficient, and Dunn's and the Davis–Bouldin indices. Guerra et al. (2012) compared five internal and one external quality criteria in harder data sets, with outliers or noisy variables.

12 Probabilistic Clustering

Clustering algorithms discussed in Chapter 11, that is, hierarchical and partitional methods, are **crisp clustering** (also called **hard clustering**) procedures that assign each object to one and only one cluster. However, in some practical applications in neuroscience, for example, the anatomical diversity of spines, it has been suggested that there is a continuum of morphologies rather than crisp clusters (Arellano et al., 2007). For these scenarios, cluster solutions assigning to each object a degree of membership to each of the clusters can be helpful. This is known as **soft clustering**. A natural and intuitive manner of defining this degree of membership is using a probability distribution over the objects. Thus, each object will have a certain probability of belonging to each cluster. This is the main idea of **probabilistic clustering**.

Probabilistic clustering is a type of model-based clustering based on fitting the density of all the sample data with finite mixture models. This kind of model fits the density of the data with a weighted finite number of different component densities, usually assumed to be parametric. Figure 12.1 shows an example of a finite mixture model for fitting the head volume of the three standard clusters of spines ("stubby," "thin," and "mushroom") as introduced by Peters and Kaiserman-Abramof (1970). In this example, each of the three component densities of the mixture are Gaussian.

The fitting of these parametric finite mixture models requires the estimation of some parameters characterizing the component densities and some mixing proportions.

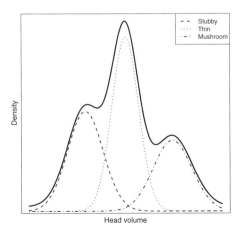

Figure 12.1 Example of a finite mixture model with three components for adjusting the density of the head volume of spines. The three components correspond to "stubby," "thin," and "mushroom" clusters of spines.

Estimations are based on maximizing the log-likelihood of the data. However, these estimations are not direct, as they have non-closed solutions, and ad hoc procedures, like the expectation-maximization algorithm, are widely applied.

Section 12.1 presents the expectation-maximization algorithm and some of its variants in detail. The application of this algorithm for finite mixture modeling is introduced in Section 12.2. Section 12.3 shows how Bayesian networks (Chapter 13) are used for probabilistic clustering. A probabilistic clustering based on morphological variables extracted from more than 2,000 3D reconstructed human dendritic spines (Data Set 4 of Section 1.6.4) is discussed in Section 12.4. Section 12.5 contains some bibliographic notes.

12.1   The Expectation-Maximization Algorithm

The **expectation-maximization** (EM) algorithm (Dempster et al., 1977) approximates the MLE of a parameter θ of a probability distribution.

12.1.1   An Example in Neuroanatomy

Imagine[1] you ask N neuroanatomists to assign labels representing four cell types – basket, chandelier, horsetail, and Martinotti – to a 3D reconstructed neuron. Let $\mathbf{Y} = (Y_1, Y_2, Y_3, Y_4)$ denote a multinomial distributed random vector, where Y_1, Y_2, Y_3, and Y_4 are random variables expressing the number of times (out of N) that the basket, chandelier, horsetail, and Martinotti cell types have been selected. This multinomial distribution depends on two parameters: N, the known number of experts, and $\mathbf{p} = (p_1, p_2, p_3, p_4)$, the probability vector for selecting each cell type, where $p_1 + p_2 + p_3 + p_4 = 1$, with $0 \le p_i \le 1$. Let us assume that $\mathbf{p}$ is parameterized by some $\theta \in (0, 1)$ such that

$$\mathbf{p}_\theta = \left(\frac{1}{2} + \frac{\theta}{4}, \frac{1-\theta}{4}, \frac{1-\theta}{4}, \frac{\theta}{4} \right).$$

The probability of observing $\mathbf{y} = (y_1, y_2, y_3, y_4)$, with $y_1 + y_2 + y_3 + y_4 = N$, can be written as (Section 3.4.3):

$$p(\mathbf{y}|\theta) = \frac{N!}{y_1! y_2! y_3! y_4!} \left(\frac{1}{2} + \frac{\theta}{4} \right)^{y_1} \left(\frac{1-\theta}{4} \right)^{y_2} \left(\frac{1-\theta}{4} \right)^{y_3} \left(\frac{\theta}{4} \right)^{y_4}.$$

Based on this information the log-likelihood, $\log p(\mathbf{y}|\theta)$, can be maximized directly after equaling its derivative with respect to θ to zero.

As regards the argument for the use of the EM algorithm, consider that we want to use another multinomial distribution that admits five (instead of four) cell types: large basket, common basket, chandelier, horsetail, and Martinotti. Our new variable $\mathbf{X} = (X_1, X_2, X_3, X_4, X_5)$ verifies $X_1 + X_2 = Y_1, X_3 = Y_2, X_4 = Y_3$, and $X_5 = Y_4$. In addition, the probability vector for $\mathbf{X}$ is now

$$\mathbf{q}_\theta = \left(\frac{1}{2}, \frac{\theta}{4}, \frac{1-\theta}{4}, \frac{1-\theta}{4}, \frac{\theta}{4} \right).$$

---

[1] Example adapted from the seminal paper by Dempster et al. (1977).

The vector $\mathbf{y} = (y_1, y_2, y_3, y_4)$ matches the observed data, which are incomplete data, whereas vector $\mathbf{x} = (x_1, x_2, x_3, x_4, x_5)$ includes the complete data. The complete-data likelihood is given by

$$
\begin{aligned}
p(\mathbf{x}|\theta) &= \frac{N!}{x_1!x_2!x_3!x_4!x_5!} \left(\frac{1}{2}\right)^{x_1} \left(\frac{\theta}{4}\right)^{x_2} \left(\frac{1-\theta}{4}\right)^{x_3} \left(\frac{1-\theta}{4}\right)^{x_4} \left(\frac{\theta}{4}\right)^{x_5} \\
&= \frac{N!}{x_1!x_2!x_3!x_4!x_5!} \left(\frac{1}{2}\right)^{x_1} \left(\frac{\theta}{4}\right)^{x_2+x_5} \left(\frac{1-\theta}{4}\right)^{x_3+x_4}.
\end{aligned}
\tag{12.1}
$$

Now, for the complete data, as opposed to the incomplete (observed) data situation, the maximum likelihood estimation of θ has not a closed form because the values of X_1 and X_2 are unknown, although we know that $X_1 + X_2 = Y_1$, and this number has been observed. We can guess that the value of X_1 should be proportional to $\frac{1}{2}y_1$, while X_2 should be proportional to $\frac{\theta}{4}y_1$. As the addition of both expected quantities is y_1, it is intuitive to impute the missing information of X_1 and X_2 with their expected values, yielding

$$
\mathbb{E}_{\mathbf{X}|\mathbf{y},\theta}[\mathbf{X}] = \left(\frac{2}{2+\theta}y_1, \frac{\theta}{2+\theta}y_1, y_2, y_3, y_4\right).
$$

These imputed values are now considered as real values. They offer a means of iteratively solving the maximization of the expected value of the log-likelihood function of Equation (12.1) with respect to the distribution of $\mathbf{X}$ given $\mathbf{y}$ and the current estimate, $\theta^{(t)}$, of the parameters. By ignoring the terms that do not depend on θ, the estimation of θ at iteration $t+1$ is given by:

$$
\begin{aligned}
\theta^{(t+1)} &= \arg\max_{\theta \in (0,1)} \mathbb{E}_{\mathbf{X}|\mathbf{y},\theta^{(t)}}\left[(X_2+X_5)\log\theta + (X_3+X_4)\log(1-\theta)\right] \\
&= \arg\max_{\theta \in (0,1)} \left[\log\theta\left(\mathbb{E}_{\mathbf{X}|\mathbf{y},\theta^{(t)}}[X_2] + \mathbb{E}_{\mathbf{X}|\mathbf{y},\theta^{(t)}}[X_5]\right) \right. \\
&\qquad\qquad\qquad \left. + \log(1-\theta)\left(\mathbb{E}_{\mathbf{X}|\mathbf{y},\theta^{(t)}}[X_3] + \mathbb{E}_{\mathbf{X}|\mathbf{y},\theta^{(t)}}[X_4]\right)\right] \\
&= \arg\max_{\theta \in (0,1)} \left[\log\theta\left(\frac{\theta^{(t)}y_1}{2+\theta^{(t)}} + y_4\right) + \log(1-\theta)(y_2+y_3)\right].
\end{aligned}
$$

Taking the derivative of the expected value of the log-likelihood with respect to θ, we have:

$$
\frac{\partial}{\partial\theta}\left[\log\theta\left(\frac{\theta^{(t)}y_1}{2+\theta^{(t)}} + y_4\right) + \log(1-\theta)(y_2+y_3)\right] = \frac{\frac{\theta^{(t)}y_1}{2+\theta^{(t)}} + y_4}{\theta} - \frac{y_2+y_3}{1-\theta}.
$$

After equaling to zero, we get the updated formula for the parameter:

$$
\theta^{(t+1)} = \frac{\frac{\theta^{(t)}}{2+\theta^{(t)}}y_1 + y_4}{\frac{\theta^{(t)}}{2+\theta^{(t)}}y_1 + y_2 + y_3 + y_4}.
$$

Reproducing the results of the seminal paper by Dempster et al. (1977), now adapted for our example in neuroanatomy, with $N = 197$ experts, and $y_1 = 125$ basket cells, $y_2 = 18$ chandelier cells, $y_3 = 20$ horsetail cells, and $y_4 = 34$ Martinotti cells as observed data, and $\theta^{(0)} = 0.5$ as the starting parameter value, the above iterative procedure estimates the values of θ shown in Table 12.1.

Table 12.1 Results of the iterative estimation of parameter θ provided by the EM algorithm in the seminal paper by Dempster et al. (1977), adapted to the first six decimals. After two consecutive iterations with the same value, the iteration process is assumed to have converged

Iteration	$\theta^{(t)}$
0	0.500000
1	0.608247
2	0.624321
3	0.626488
4	0.626777
5	0.626815
6	0.626820
7	0.626821
8	0.626821

In this example $Y_1 = T(X_1, X_2)$, that is, the observed data was a function of the complete data. In other situations, as in the clustering formulation with finite mixture models, the EM algorithm will be applied in the presence of a hidden variable.

12.1.2 General Formulation

The EM algorithm is an iterative procedure to approximate the mle in the presence of missing or hidden data. Each iteration of the EM algorithm consists of two steps: the expectation or **E-step** and the maximization or **M-step**. In the E-step, the missing data are estimated given the observed data and the current estimate of the model parameters. This is achieved using the conditional expectation of the missing data. The estimates of the missing data from the E-step are used to output a version of the complete data. In the M-step, the complete-data log-likelihood function is maximized under the assumption that the missing data are known. The EM algorithm is guaranteed to increase the likelihood at each iteration, ensuring its convergence.

In mathematical notation, given a model that generates a set of observed data $\mathbf{X}$, a set of unobserved hidden (latent) data or missing values $\mathbf{Z}$, and a vector of unknown parameters $\boldsymbol{\theta}$, where $\mathcal{L}(\boldsymbol{\theta}; \mathbf{X}, \mathbf{Z})$ denotes the likelihood function, the MLE of the unknown parameters is determined by maximizing the marginal likelihood of the observed data

$$\mathcal{L}(\boldsymbol{\theta}; \mathbf{X}) = p(\mathbf{X}|\boldsymbol{\theta}) = \sum_{\mathbf{Z}} p(\mathbf{X}, \mathbf{Z}|\boldsymbol{\theta}). \tag{12.2}$$

Maximizing Equation (12.2) is often intractable, and the EM algorithm tries to find the MLE by iteratively applying the following two steps:

E-step: Calculate the expected value of the log-likelihood function with respect to the conditional distribution of $\mathbf{Z}$ given $\mathbf{X}$ under the current estimate of the parameters

$\theta^{(t)}$. An auxiliary function[2] $Q\left(\theta|\theta^{(t)}\right)$ is defined for this computation as

$$Q\left(\theta|\theta^{(t)}\right) = \mathbb{E}_{\mathbf{Z}|\mathbf{X},\theta^{(t)}}[\log \mathcal{L}(\theta;\mathbf{X},\mathbf{Z})].$$

M-step: Find the parameter value

$$\theta^{(t+1)} = \arg\max_{\theta} Q\left(\theta|\theta^{(t)}\right).$$

The EM algorithm computes $Q\left(\theta|\theta^{(t)}\right)$ at each iteration, based on the expectations of the complete-data log-likelihood rather than directly improving $\log p(\mathbf{X}|\theta)$. However, improvements to the expectations lead to improvements in $\log p(\mathbf{X}|\theta)$. In addition, there is a monotonicity in the improvement of the marginal likelihood as the iterations progress, that is, the inequality $\log p\left(\mathbf{X}|\theta^{(t+1)}\right) \geq \log p\left(\mathbf{X}|\theta^{(t)}\right)$ can be proved (McLachlan and Krishnan, 1997) using Jensen's inequality.

The monotonicity of the EM algorithm guarantees that its associated likelihood will not get worse as it iterates. However, this monotonicity alone cannot guarantee the convergence of the sequence $\{\theta^{(t)}\}$ because the monotonicity implies the convergence of the sequence $\{p\left(\mathbf{X}|\theta^{(t)}\right)\}$ but not necessarily of the sequence $\{\theta^{(t)}\}$ if the observed data likelihood is bounded.

The convergence of the sequence $\{\theta^{(t)}\}$ depends on the characteristics of $p\left(\mathbf{X}|\theta^{(t)}\right)$, $Q\left(\theta|\theta^{(t)}\right)$, and also on the starting point $\theta^{(0)}$. Under certain regularity conditions, it can be proved (Wu, 1983) that $\{\theta^{(t)}\}$ converges to a stationary point (not necessarily a local maximum) of $p(\mathbf{X}|\theta)$.

The initialization of the EM algorithm is crucial, but no method uniformly outperforms the others (Figueiredo and Jain, 2002). The suggested proposals in clustering problems (see Section 12.2) include (a) the use of hierarchical clustering, (b) finding the most separated local modes, and (c) the so-called **emEM algorithm**, which consists of two EM stages. During the first stage, the "short em" starts from several random points and runs the EM algorithm until some lax convergence criterion is verified. The best solution in terms of log-likelihood is selected as the initial point for a "long EM," where the usual convergence criterion is met.

It is sometimes difficult to apply the trick used by the EM algorithm, which instead of directly maximizing $p(\mathbf{X}|\theta)$, repeatedly maximizes $Q\left(\theta|\theta^{(t)}\right)$. One way to deal with a hard or intractable M-step is to find a $\theta^{(t+1)}$, which is not necessarily the maximum, that satisfies $Q\left(\theta^{(t+1)}|\theta^{(t)}\right) > Q\left(\theta^{(t)}|\theta^{(t)}\right)$. This is called **generalized EM** (Neal and Hinton, 1999).

Other variants of the EM algorithm include

- **ECM algorithm** (Meng and Rubin, 1993), that stands for **expectation conditional maximization**, where the M-step optimizes θ component-wise.
- **CEM algorithm** (Celeux and Govaert, 1992), a classification version of the EM algorithm, which introduces a C-step between the E-step and M-step. This C-step updates

---

[2] Following the notation introduced in the original paper by Dempster et al. (1977), Q stands for *quixotic* because it is crazy and hopeful and beautiful to think that the MLE of θ can be found in this way.

the partition by assigning each **x** to the cluster that provides the maximum posterior probability.

- **Over-relaxed EM** (Salakhutdinov and Roweis, 2003), that tries to speed up convergence of the standard EM by updating the estimation of the parameters using the equation $\theta^{t+1} = \theta^{(t)} + \eta \left(\theta_M^{(t)} - \theta^{(t)} \right)$, where $\eta \geq 1$ is a step-size parameter, and $\theta_M^{(t)}$ is the usual update output during the M-step.
- **Monte Carlo EM** (Wei and Tanner, 1990), that draws samples from $p\left(\mathbf{Z}|\mathbf{X}, \theta^{(t)}\right)$ and, after computing the sufficient statistics for $(\mathbf{x}^i, \mathbf{z}^i)$, averages the results as an approximation to the expectation of the E-step. The so-called **stochastic EM** (Celeux and Diebolt, 1985) is a special case of Monte Carlo EM, where a single sample is drawn.
- **EM for MAP estimation** (Fraley and Raftery, 2007), that is an easy solution for the "collapsing variance problem," where, as a consequence of assigning one of the clusters (see Section 12.2) to a single data point, the likelihood goes to infinity. In this situation, a MAP estimation replaces the MLE in the M-step, that is,

$$\hat{\theta}_{MAP} = \arg\max_{\theta} \log p(\theta|\mathbf{X}) = \arg\max_{\theta} (\log p(\mathbf{X}|\theta) + \log p(\theta)),$$

where $p(\theta)$ is a prior distribution of θ. By modifying the M-step, the EM algorithm can be extended for MAP estimation.

12.2   Finite-Mixture Models for Clustering

As explained above, **finite mixture models** constitute a key element for probabilistic clustering. A hidden (latent) variable represents the clustering membership (in terms of probability), and the EM algorithm is used to estimate the vector of parameters associated with the model itself. **Z** plays the role of hidden variable to accommodate the clustering problem to the EM algorithm.

Mathematically, let $\mathbf{x}^1, \mathbf{x}^2, \ldots, \mathbf{x}^N$ be a sample of size N (independent and identically distributed values) of an n-dimensional random variable with a probability density function given by a finite mixture model

$$f(\mathbf{x}; \pi) = \sum_{k=1}^{K} \pi_k f_k(\mathbf{x}), \tag{12.3}$$

where π_k represents the kth mixing proportion (or component prior) and $f_k(\mathbf{x})$ denotes the probability density function on the kth mixture component. The number of components of the mixture is K, and the parameter vector $\pi = (\pi_1, \pi_2, \ldots, \pi_K)$ verifies $0 \leq \pi_k \leq 1$ for all $k = 1, 2, \ldots, K$ and $\sum_{k=1}^{K} \pi_k = 1$.

Equation (12.3) denotes the most general form of a finite mixture model. However, the probability density of the mixture components is usually assumed to be of some parametric form, i.e., $f_k(\mathbf{x}) \equiv f_k(\mathbf{x}; \boldsymbol{\theta}_k)$, where the functional form of $f_k(\mathbf{x}; \boldsymbol{\theta}_k)$ is known. Thus, the parametric finite mixture model has the form

$$f(\mathbf{x}; \boldsymbol{\theta}) = \sum_{k=1}^{K} \pi_k f_k(\mathbf{x}; \boldsymbol{\theta}_k),$$

where $\boldsymbol{\theta} = (\pi_1, \ldots, \pi_K, \boldsymbol{\theta}_1, \ldots, \boldsymbol{\theta}_K)$ denotes the parameter vector.

When the number of mixture components K is known, only parameter $\boldsymbol{\theta}$ has to be estimated. When K is not given, we have to additionally estimate the number of components in the mixture.

The most popular parametric finite mixture model consists of Gaussian components (Wolfe, 1967; Day, 1969; Fraley and Raftery, 2006), although others like the Poisson (Vardi et al., 2006), Student's t (McLachlan and Krishnan, 1997), or von Mises–Fisher (Banerjee et al., 2005) densities have also been used. Gaussian and categorical distributions are detailed below.

Finite mixture models provide a convenient and formal setting for **model-based clustering**, although they have distinct goals. Finite mixture modeling is typically related to inference on the model and its parameters, whereas the final goal of model-based clustering is to partition the data into groups of homogeneous points. To do this, model-based clustering requires an additional step (after fitting the mixture model and computing the probabilistic membership of each of the clusters for each data point) that assigns each point to a cluster according to some previously established rules.

Ratnarajah et al. (2011) proposed probabilistic clustering of white matter fiber pathways in a 3D curve space, where a set of fiber trajectories is considered as sequences of points generated from a finite mixture model. Digitally reconstructed GABAergic interneuron morphologies were automatically classified by probabilistic semi-supervised clustering leading to the formation of new subtypes of cells in Mihaljević et al. (2015). Luengo-Sanchez et al. (2018) used finite mixture modeling to morphologically cluster 3D reconstructed dendritic spines from human cortical pyramidal neurons. The discriminative characteristics of each group were identified as a set of rules induced using the RIPPER algorithm (Section 7.3.4). The mixture model was also useful for simulating accurate 3D virtual representations of spines. Ozenne et al. (2015) proposed an unsupervised multivariate segmentation approach based on finite mixture modeling that incorporates spatial information to differentiate lesioned from non-lesioned voxels in stroke patients.

12.2.1 Multivariate Gaussian Mixture Models

Multivariate Gaussian mixture models are the most popular choice in finite mixture models. The corresponding mixture density function is given by

$$f(\mathbf{x}; \boldsymbol{\theta}) = \sum_{k=1}^{K} \pi_k f_k(\mathbf{x}; \boldsymbol{\mu}_k, \boldsymbol{\Sigma}_k),$$

where $\boldsymbol{\mu}_k$ is the mean vector and $\boldsymbol{\Sigma}_k$ is the variance-covariance matrix for the kth component, and the multivariate normal density (Section 3.4.4) is given by

$$f_k(\mathbf{x}; \boldsymbol{\mu}_k, \boldsymbol{\Sigma}_k) = (2\pi)^{-\frac{n}{2}} |\boldsymbol{\Sigma}_k|^{-\frac{1}{2}} \exp\left(-\frac{1}{2}(\mathbf{x} - \boldsymbol{\mu}_k)^T \boldsymbol{\Sigma}_k^{-1}(\mathbf{x} - \boldsymbol{\mu}_k)\right).$$

The parameter vector $\boldsymbol{\theta}$ is composed of the weights of the different clusters, π_k, and the parameters, $\boldsymbol{\theta}_k = (\boldsymbol{\mu}_k, \boldsymbol{\Sigma}_k)$, of each component of the mixture, that is,

$$\boldsymbol{\theta} = (\pi_1, \ldots, \pi_K, \boldsymbol{\mu}_1, \boldsymbol{\Sigma}_1, \ldots, \boldsymbol{\mu}_K, \boldsymbol{\Sigma}_K).$$

The missing information $\mathbf{z} = (z_1, \ldots, z_N)$ relates to the assignment (yes/no) of each data point to each cluster. The auxiliary function representing the expected complete-data log-likelihood is given by

$$Q\left(\boldsymbol{\theta}|\boldsymbol{\theta}^{(t)}\right) = \sum_{i=1}^{N}\sum_{k=1}^{K} r_{ik}^{(t)} \log \pi_k + \sum_{i=1}^{N}\sum_{k=1}^{K} r_{ik}^{(t)} \log f_k(\mathbf{x};\boldsymbol{\theta}_k),$$

where $r_{ik}^{(t)} = p\left(Z_i = k|\mathbf{x}^i, \boldsymbol{\theta}^{(t)}\right)$ is the **responsibility** that cluster k takes for the ith data point. The responsibility is computed in the E-step.

E-step: The E-step has the following simple form:

$$r_{ik}^{(t)} = \frac{\pi_k^{(t)} f_k\left(\mathbf{x}^i; \boldsymbol{\mu}_k^{(t)}, \boldsymbol{\Sigma}_k^{(t)}\right)}{\sum_{r=1}^{K} \pi_r^{(t)} f_r\left(\mathbf{x}^i; \boldsymbol{\mu}_r^{(t)}, \boldsymbol{\Sigma}_r^{(t)}\right)}.$$

M-step: In the M-step we optimize $Q\left(\boldsymbol{\theta}|\boldsymbol{\theta}^{(t)}\right)$ with respect to $\boldsymbol{\theta} = (\pi_1, \ldots, \pi_K, \boldsymbol{\mu}_1, \boldsymbol{\Sigma}_1, \ldots, \boldsymbol{\mu}_K, \boldsymbol{\Sigma}_K)$.
For π_k, we have, for all $k = 1, \ldots, K$,

$$\pi_k^{(t+1)} = \frac{1}{N}\sum_{i=1}^{N} r_{ik}^{(t)}.$$

The new parameter estimates for $\boldsymbol{\mu}_k$ and $\boldsymbol{\Sigma}_k$ can be computed as

$$\boldsymbol{\mu}_k^{(t+1)} = \frac{\sum_{i=1}^{N} r_{ik}^{(t)} \mathbf{x}^i}{\sum_{i=1}^{N} r_{ik}^{(t)}}$$

and

$$\boldsymbol{\Sigma}_k^{(t+1)} = \frac{\sum_{i=1}^{N} r_{ik}^{(t)} \left(\mathbf{x}^i - \boldsymbol{\mu}_k^{(t+1)}\right)\left(\mathbf{x}^i - \boldsymbol{\mu}_k^{(t+1)}\right)^T}{\sum_{i=1}^{N} r_{ik}^{(t)}},$$

respectively. The intuition behind these equations is as follows: the weight $\pi_k^{(t+1)}$ of each mixture component is updated as the average responsibilities, the mean of cluster k, $\boldsymbol{\mu}_k^{(t+1)}$, is computed as the weighted average of all data points, where the weights involve responsibilities of cluster k, and, finally, the variance-covariance matrix, $\boldsymbol{\Sigma}_k^{(t+1)}$, is proportional to the weighted (using responsibilities again) empirical variance-covariance matrix.
The new estimates

$$\boldsymbol{\theta}^{(t+1)} = \left(\pi_1^{(t+1)}, \ldots, \pi_K^{(t+1)}, \boldsymbol{\mu}_1^{(t+1)}, \boldsymbol{\Sigma}_1^{(t+1)}, \ldots, \boldsymbol{\mu}_K^{(t+1)}, \boldsymbol{\Sigma}_K^{(t+1)}\right)$$

will be used by the E-step in a new iteration of the algorithm.

12.2.2　Mixtures of Products of Categorical Distributions

Clustering by mixtures of products of categorical distributions can be motivated by Data Set 2 in Chapter 1 (Section 1.6.2), where we are interested in clustering $N = 42$ neuroanatomy experts according to their responses to $n = 1,446$ variables (241 interneurons times 6 questions for each interneuron). The possible categories for each question vary from 2 (1st, 2nd, 3rd, and 6th questions) or three (fourth question) to 10 (5th question).

Assuming that the categorical random variables for the responses to each of the n variables are independent, the n responses of each neuroanatomist is an observation from the **finite product-of-categorical mixture model**

$$p(\mathbf{x}; \boldsymbol{\theta}) = \sum_{k=1}^{K} \pi_k \prod_{j=1}^{n} \prod_{r=1}^{r_j} \theta_{kjr}^{x_{jr}},$$

where the parameter vector is

$$\boldsymbol{\theta} = (\pi_1, \ldots, \pi_K, \theta_{111}, \ldots, \theta_{1nr_1}, \ldots, \theta_{K11}, \ldots, \theta_{Knr_n}),$$

with π_k denoting the weight of the kth cluster, and θ_{kjr} representing the probability that the rth value in the jth variable belongs to the kth cluster. The superindex x_{jr} is defined as $x_{jr} = \sum_{i=1}^{N} x_{ijr}$, with $x_{ijr} = 1$ if the ith expert selects the rth value for the jth variable, and 0 otherwise. For each combination of k and j, $\sum_{r=1}^{r_j} \theta_{kjr} = 1$ holds. The missing information encoded by $\mathbf{z} = (z_1, \ldots, z_N)$ corresponds to the assignment (yes/no) of each expert to a cluster.

The expected complete-data log-likelihood is expressed as follows:

$$Q\left(\boldsymbol{\theta}|\boldsymbol{\theta}^{(t)}\right) = \sum_{i=1}^{N} \sum_{k=1}^{K} r_{ik}^{(t)} \log \pi_k + \sum_{i=1}^{N} \sum_{k=1}^{K} r_{ik}^{(t)} \sum_{j=1}^{n} \sum_{r=1}^{r_j} x_{ijr} \log \theta_{kjr},$$

where $r_{ik}^{(t)} = p\left(Z_i = k|\mathbf{x}^i, \boldsymbol{\theta}^{(t)}\right)$ denotes the responsibility of cluster k for the ith data point and is updated during the E-step.

E-step:　The responsibilities are updated similarly to the Gaussian mixture models (Section 12.2.1), now given by

$$r_{ik}^{(t)} = \frac{\pi_k \prod_{j=1}^{n} \prod_{r=1}^{r_j} \left(\theta_{kjr}^{(t)}\right)^{x_{ijr}}}{\sum_{h=1}^{K} \pi_h \prod_{j=1}^{n} \prod_{r=1}^{r_j} \left(\theta_{hjr}^{(t)}\right)^{x_{ijr}}}.$$

M-step:　The optimization of $Q\left(\boldsymbol{\theta}|\boldsymbol{\theta}^{(t)}\right)$ with respect to $\boldsymbol{\theta} = (\pi_1, \ldots, \pi_K, \theta_{111}, \ldots, \theta_{1nr_1}, \ldots, \theta_{K11}, \ldots, \theta_{Knr_n})$ provides the following updates for any $k = 1, \ldots, K$:

$$\pi_k^{(t+1)} = \frac{1}{N} \sum_{i=1}^{N} r_{ik}^{(t)},$$

$$\theta_{kjr}^{(t+1)} = \frac{\sum_{i=1}^{N} r_{ik}^{(t)} x_{ijr}}{\sum_{i=1}^{N} r_{ik}^{(t)}}.$$

Once again, E-step and M-step alternate until convergence.

12.2.3   Model Selection

Two important aspects to be considered in finite mixture modeling are the problem of choosing the optimal number of components K and the identification of the more discriminative variables for clustering purposes.

12.2.3.1 Optimal Number of Components

Roughly speaking, there are two main groups of methods (Melnykov and Maitra, 2010) for choosing the appropriate number of components in a finite mixture model: parsimony-based methods and testing procedures.

Parsimony-based approaches choose the value of K, which minimizes the negative log-likelihood function augmented by some penalty expression that reflects the complexity of the model. The BIC criterion (Section 13.3.2.2) is the most used score, mainly due to its easy implementation and its consistency property. However, BIC tends to underestimate K with small sample sizes.

Testing-based approaches specify the evidence in favor of a complex as opposed to a simpler model in terms of the p-value associated with a likelihood ratio test or some derivation thereof.

12.2.3.2 Variable Selection

The subspace clustering problem (see Section 11.5) has been researched within the finite-mixture modeling paradigm from different perspectives.

A greedy variable selection algorithm based on approximate Bayes factors was introduced by Raftery and Dean (2006). The idea is to split the whole set of variables into three subsets: a first subset containing already selected variables, a second subset composed by the variables currently under consideration for inclusion into the first subset, and the last subset with the remaining variables. At each step of the greedy procedure, two competing models are compared according to their BIC differences, which is used as an approximation for the Bayes factor. The first model assumes that the second subset of variables is not relevant when the first subset is known, whereas, in the second model, the second subset of variables is assumed to be relevant. The greedy process starts from scratch, and at each step, it adds the variable that most improves the BIC differences to the subset of selected variables.

Different types of the log-likelihood function regularization have been used in the Gaussian mixture for variable selection (Pan and Shen, 2006; Wang and Zhu, 2008; Xie et al., 2008).

12.3   Clustering with Bayesian Networks

Bayesian networks (Chapter 13) provide an intuitive and natural way of performing model-based clustering. It is sufficient to introduce a hidden node representing the cluster variable, C, to yield models with a latent structure (Lazarsfeld and Henry, 1968) where data are systematically missing.

These Bayesian networks can express the probability distribution of the observed data $\mathbf{X}$ as a parametric finite mixture model (Figure 12.2). This has two main advantages: (a) the

Table 12.2 Example of data set $\mathcal{D}$ to be clustered using the structural EM algorithm

Obs.	X_1	X_2	X_3	C
1	0	0	0	?
2	0	1	1	?
3	0	1	1	?
...	...	...	...	...
...	...	...	...	...
...	...	...	...	...
$N-2$	1	1	1	?
$N-1$	1	0	0	?
N	1	0	1	?

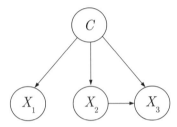

Figure 12.2 Structure of a Bayesian network with a hidden variable represented by C. The probability distribution of the observed data can be written as a parametric finite mixture model like $p(x_1,x_2,x_3;\boldsymbol{\theta}) = \sum_{c=1}^{K} p(c;\boldsymbol{\theta})p(x_1|c;\boldsymbol{\theta})p(x_2|c;\boldsymbol{\theta})p(x_3|x_2,c;\boldsymbol{\theta})$, where $\boldsymbol{\theta}$ denotes the parameter vector and K the number of clusters.

factorization of the distribution according to the structure of the probabilistic graphical model, and (b) the use of efficient methods for exact inference (Section 13.2.2) to provide a probability distribution over the values of the cluster variable.

12.3.1 The Structural EM Algorithm for Bayesian Networks

Lauritzen (1995) proposed the use of the EM algorithm exploiting the message passing procedure for inference (Lauritzen and Spiegelhalter [1988], Section 13.2.2.3) in order to efficiently perform the E-step in Bayesian networks. A more sophisticated method that can search for the appropriate structure at each iteration is known as the **structural EM algorithm** (Friedman, 1998). We use the hypothetical data set shown in Table 12.2 to illustrate its main ideas.

For iteration 0, let us initialize the parameters of the Bayesian network model for clustering, assuming a naive Bayes for simplicity. Let us consider $K = 2$ as the number of clusters and $p^{(0)}(C=0) = p^{(0)}(C=1) = 0.5$ as its initial parameters, assuming a complete lack of information on the distribution of the cluster variable. This distribution is used for weighting $\mathcal{D}^{(0)}$, the data set output as the duplication of observations included in $\mathcal{D}$ (see Table 12.2). The last column of $\mathcal{D}^{(0)}$, named w, contains these weights. In the M-step, we learn a Bayesian network classifier (Section 8.4.1) from $\mathcal{D}^{(0)}$. Let us assume that the structure $\mathcal{G}^{(1)}$ and parameters $\boldsymbol{\theta}^{(1)}$ are expressed in Figure 12.3 (right).

Iteration 0

E-step

Obs.	X_1	X_2	X_3	C	w
1	0	0	0	0	0.5
2	0	0	0	1	0.5
3	0	1	1	0	0.5
4	0	1	1	1	0.5
5	0	1	1	0	0.5
...	...	...	...	...	...
...	...	...	...	...	...
2N-5	1	1	1	0	0.5
2N-4	1	1	1	1	0.5
2N-3	1	0	0	0	0.5
2N-2	1	0	0	1	0.5
2N-1	1	0	1	0	0.5
2N	1	0	1	1	0.5

$$\mathcal{D}^{(0)}$$

M-step

Structure learning

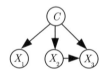

$$\mathcal{G}^{(1)}$$

Parameter learning

$$p^{(1)}(C{=}0) = 0.50$$

$$p^{(1)}(X_1{=}0|C{=}0) = 0.47$$
$$p^{(1)}(X_1{=}0|C{=}1) = 0.51$$

$$p^{(1)}(X_2{=}0|C{=}0) = 0.36$$
$$p^{(1)}(X_2{=}0|C{=}1) = 0.44$$

$$p^{(1)}(X_3{=}0|C{=}0, X_2{=}0) = 0.70$$
$$p^{(1)}(X_3{=}0|C{=}0, X_2{=}1) = 0.52$$
$$p^{(1)}(X_3{=}0|C{=}1, X_2{=}0) = 0.41$$
$$p^{(1)}(X_3{=}0|C{=}1, X_2{=}1) = 0.36$$

$$\boldsymbol{\theta}^{(1)}$$

Iteration 1

E-step

Obs.	X_1	X_2	X_3	C	w
1	0	0	0	0	0.5628
2	0	0	0	1	0.4372
3	0	1	1	0	0.4413
4	0	1	1	1	0.4487
5	0	1	1	0	0.4413
...	...	...	...	...	...
...	...	...	...	...	...
2N-5	1	1	1	0	0.4811
2N-4	1	1	1	1	0.5189
2N-3	1	0	0	0	0.6017
2N-2	1	0	0	1	0.3983
2N-1	1	0	1	0	0.3103
2N	1	0	1	1	0.6897

$$\mathcal{D}^{(1)}$$

M-step

Structure learning

$$\mathcal{G}^{(2)}$$

Parameter learning

$$p^{(1)}(C{=}0) = 0.54$$

$$p^{(1)}(X_1{=}0|C{=}0, X_2{=}0) = 0.51$$
$$p^{(1)}(X_1{=}0|C{=}0, X_2{=}1) = 0.33$$
$$p^{(1)}(X_1{=}0|C{=}1, X_2{=}0) = 0.66$$
$$p^{(1)}(X_1{=}0|C{=}1, X_2{=}1) = 0.57$$

$$p^{(1)}(X_2{=}0|C{=}0) = 0.39$$
$$p^{(1)}(X_2{=}0|C{=}1) = 0.47$$

$$p^{(1)}(X_3{=}0|C{=}0) = 0.69$$
$$p^{(1)}(X_3{=}0|C{=}1) = 0.47$$

$$\boldsymbol{\theta}^{(2)}$$

Figure 12.3 Example of the application of the structural EM algorithm (iterations 0 and 1) to the data set of Table 12.2.

This Bayesian network $(\mathcal{G}^1, \boldsymbol{\theta}^{(1)})$ is now used at the E-step of iteration 1 to compute the posterior probabilities of the two possible values of the cluster variable. In particular, for the first observation, we have

$$p^{(1)}(C = 0|X_1 = 0, X_2 = 0, X_3 = 0)$$
$$\propto p^{(1)}(C = 0)p^{(1)}(X_1 = 0|C = 0)p^{(1)}(X_2 = 0|C = 0)p^{(1)}(X_3 = 0|C = 0, X_2 = 0)$$
$$= 0.50 \cdot 0.47 \cdot 0.36 \cdot 0.70$$
$$= 0.05922$$

and

$$p^{(1)}(C = 1|X_1 = 0, X_2 = 0, X_3 = 0)$$
$$\propto p^{(1)}(C = 1)p^{(1)}(X_1 = 0|C = 1)p^{(1)}(X_2 = 0|C = 1)p^{(1)}(X_3 = 0|C = 1, X_2 = 0)$$
$$= 0.50 \cdot 0.51 \cdot 0.44 \cdot 0.41$$
$$= 0.046002.$$

Thus, $p^{(1)}(C = 0|X_1 = 0, X_2 = 0, X_3 = 0) = \frac{0.05922}{0.05922 + 0.046002} = 0.5628$, and $p^{(1)}(C = 1|X_1 = 0, X_2 = 0, X_3 = 0) = 0.4372$. These are the weights of the first observation.

The weights of the other observations are computed similarly, completing $\mathcal{D}^{(1)}$. Notice that, thanks to the simplicity of structure $\mathcal{G}^{(1)}$, there is no need to apply the message passing algorithm to make inference on the cluster variable. Once $\mathcal{D}^{(1)}$ has been completed, the structure and parameters $(\mathcal{G}^{(2)}, \boldsymbol{\theta}^{(2)})$ are updated in the M-step of iteration 1. Iterations are repeated until a previously fixed convergence criterion is met.

12.3.2   Clustering with Bayesian Networks in Discrete Domains

Several approaches to probabilistic clustering based on Bayesian networks have been proposed in the literature. They differ as to the complexity of the Bayesian network structures learned by the structural EM algorithm.

12.3.2.1 Naive Bayes

Assuming a (fixed) naive Bayes structure, the EM algorithm will be used only to iteratively estimate the marginal parameters (prior probabilities for C, and conditional probabilities of all observed variables X_i given C) and the mixture weights. Subspace clustering (Section 11.5) by means of FSS can be incorporated to the modeling process. In addition, this selection could be different at each iteration of the EM algorithm.

A Bayesian approach to clustering based on a naive Bayes structure, called **AutoClass**, was introduced by Cheeseman et al. (1988). The prior probabilities over the number of clusters prefer fewer clusters and offset the likelihood of the data that prefers more. In this way, AUTOCLASS is able to automatically determine the appropriate number of clusters.

Bayesian model averaging of naive Bayes for clustering aims to average over all selective naive Bayes structures, where, for each structure, the averaging over parameters is approximated by its MAP configuration. This results in a unique naive Bayes model as shown by Santafé et al. (2006a), where the Bayesian model averaging approach for supervised classification described by Dash and Cooper (2004) was extended to clustering. The M-step of the EM algorithm is replaced by a model averaging step (MA-step), yielding the unique naive Bayes model. This variant of the EM algorithm is known as the **expectation model averaging** (EMA) algorithm.

A Bayesian multinet (Section 8.4.1.9) for clustering, where each component corresponds to a context-specific selective naive Bayes, was proposed by Barash and Friedman (2002). This Bayesian approach assumes Dirichlet prior distributions (Section 3.4.5) over the parameters for categorical variables.

12.3.2.2 Semi-naive Bayes

Semi-naive Bayes is introduced in supervised classification (Section 8.4.1.3) as a model that respects the simplicity of naive Bayes and still improves its quality. Peña et al. (1999b) proposed the use of semi-naive Bayes structures for model clustering. The log-marginal likelihood score is used to evaluate the goodness of the candidate structures on complete data. The algorithm performs constructive induction, creating new variables (supernodes) from previous variables. As in supervised classification (Pazzani, 1996), the models can be selected using a forward or backward search. In the forward approach, the structure search step starts from the naive Bayes model. In addition to the hill-climbing search, Peña et al. (1999b) also introduced simulated annealing due to the limitations of a local search algorithm like hill-climbing.

12.3.2.3 Tree Augmented Naive bayes

Pham and Ruz (2009) suggested relaxing the conditional independence restrictions of the naive Bayes models for clustering by assuming a tree augmented naive Bayes model (Section 8.4.1.4). The proposal starts using the stochastic EM up to a certain number of iterations, and then it swaps the stochasticity for the assignment of the cluster with the maximum posterior probability during the final iterations. In these final iterations the M-step maximizes the **classification maximum likelihood** (CML) criterion (Celeux and Govaert, 1995)

$$\text{CML}\left(\mathbf{z}^1, \dots, \mathbf{z}^N, \boldsymbol{\theta}, \mathbf{x}^1, \dots, \mathbf{x}^N\right) = \sum_{k=1}^{K} \sum_{\mathbf{x}^r Cl_k} \log p_k(\mathbf{x}^r) + \sum_{k=1}^{K} N_k \log \pi_k,$$

where Cl_k is the kth crisp clustering, as a result of the C-step of the CEM algorithm (Section 12.1.2), and N_k denotes the number of observations belonging to the kth cluster. The joint probability distribution, $p_k(\mathbf{x})$, is learned from the complete data by means of the MWST algorithm, providing a tree-shape factorization. A different tree could be learned at each iteration using the structural EM algorithm.

Santafé et al. (2006b) presented a extension of the EMA algorithm for Bayesian model averaging of TAN models.

12.3.2.4 Bayesian Networks for Data Clustering

Peña et al. (2004) did not place constraints on the relationships among the variables in the DAG structure, apart from the fact that the cluster variable C cannot have any parent. In addition, the search strategy in the structural EM algorithm is based on the simplest version of the estimation of distribution algorithms (see Section 6.3.1.2).

12.3.2.5 Chow–Liu Multinets

Pham and Ruz (2009) introduced a Bayesian multinet with the cluster variable as distinguished variable and a tree structure learned with the Chow–Liu algorithm in each component of the multinet. The CML criterion is used, and a new S-step is introduced between E and M steps during the first iterations. This S-step assigns each object to a cluster that is simulated from the E-step output distribution. After these first iterations, S and C steps are swapped.

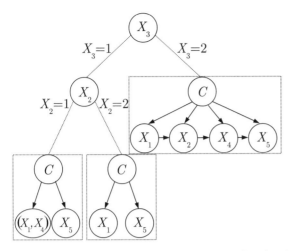

Figure 12.4 Structure of a recursive Bayesian multinet for clustering. C denotes the cluster variable. There are two distinguished variables: X_3 and X_2. The distinguished tree has three Bayesian networks involving the cluster variable in the leaves. The structures of these three Bayesian networks are, from left to right, a semi-naive Bayes, a selective naive Bayes and a tree augmented naive Bayes.

12.3.2.6 Recursive Bayesian Multinets

Recursive Bayesian multinets for clustering (Peña et al., 2002) are extensions of Bayesian multinets that can have more than one distinguished variable. The cluster variable in recursive Bayesian multinets cannot be the distinguished variable. Here we have a case of **distinguished decision trees**, as in Figure 12.4.

A decomposable extension of the log-marginal likelihood introduced by Thiesson et al. (1998) for Bayesian multinets that has closed form calculation is used to evaluate the different candidate models. The learning algorithm starts with an empty distinguished structure and, at each iteration, increases the depth of the structure by one. In each iteration, each leaf should be replaced by the Bayesian network that has the highest log-marginal likelihood for the variables that are not in the respective tree branch. This procedure should be iterated until either a specified structure depth is reached or there are no more Bayesian networks to replace a component of the Bayesian multinet such that it increases the log-marginal likelihood.

12.3.3 Clustering with Bayesian Networks in Continuous Domains

Conditional Gaussian networks for data clustering show an ideal trade-off between efficiency and effectiveness, i.e., a balance between the cost of the unsupervised model learning process and the quality of the learned models. Peña et al. (2001a) introduced two families of compromise conditional Gaussian networks: naive Bayes and semi-naive Bayes models. A constrained structural EM algorithm is used in both models to search the best model within the family.

Peña et al. (2001b) presented the dimensionality reduction of conditional Gaussian networks. The relevant variables for clustering are identified using a simple relevance measure to select a subset of the original variables. The main idea is to remove variables that are not very correlated with the other variables. A simple, and thus efficient, measure to assess the relevance of each variable X_i with $i = 1, \ldots, n$, is given by $\sum_{j=1, j \neq i}^{n} \frac{-N \log\left(1 - r_{ij|\text{rest}}^2\right)}{n-1}$, where n is the number of variables, N is the number of objects, and $r_{ij|\text{rest}}$ is the **sample partial correlation** of X_i and X_j adjusted for the remaining variables. The partial correlation between X_i and X_j given the rest of the variables measures the linear dependence of X_i and X_j when the influence of the remaining variables is eliminated, i.e., the correlation between the residuals resulting from the linear regressions of each of the two variables given the rest. The sample partial correlation can be expressed in terms of the maximum likelihood estimates of the elements of the inverse covariance matrix, $\mathbf{W}$, as $r_{ij|\text{rest}} = -\hat{w}_{ij}(\hat{w}_{ii}\hat{w}_{jj})^{-\frac{1}{2}}$ (Whittaker, 1990). Then, the relevance measure value for each variable X_i is defined as the average likelihood ratio test for excluding an edge between X_i and any other variable in a graphical Gaussian model (Smith and Whittaker, 1998).

After computing the relevance measure value for every variable, features can be ranked in order of decreasing relevance. A heuristic is used to determine the relevance threshold for retaining the most relevant variables. This approximates the distribution function, $F(x)$, of the likelihood ratio test statistic by means of

$$F(x) = G_{\chi}(x) - \frac{1}{2}(2n+1)x\frac{1}{\sqrt{2\pi}}x^{-\frac{1}{2}}e^{-\frac{x}{2}}N^{-1},$$

where $G_{\chi}(x)$ is the distribution function of a χ_1^2 random variable. Thus, for a significance level α, the rejection region boundary (considered as the relevance threshold) is given by solving the equation $1 - \alpha = F(x)$. The Newton–Raphson method is a technique for approximately solving the above equation.

There is hardly any clustering with Bayesian networks in neuroscience. Luengo-Sanchez et al. (2016) clustered 500 3D dendritic spines reconstructed from pyramidal neurons extracted from the cingular cortex of a human male age 40 (a subset of the whole set in Luengo-Sanchez et al. (2018)). Each spine was characterized by two kinds of morphological features, continuous (Gaussian) and directional (von Mises). A Bayesian network with a specific topology was learned for clustering using the structural EM: it assumes conditional independence of Gaussian and von Mises variables and of von Mises variables, given the cluster variable in both cases. Hence, Gaussian dependencies are freely learned, the structure of von Mises variables is naively fixed, and dependencies between Gaussian and von Mises variables are ruled out.

Luengo-Sanchez et al. (2019) generalized the previous model by allowing directional variables to be parents of Gaussian features. The joint directional-linear model follows an extension of the Mardia–Sutton distribution, from the bivariate to the multivariate case. This is applied to the clustering and simulation of human pyramidal somas characterized by 39 directional and linear morphological 3D features.

12.4   Example: Dendritic Spines

The mclust package in R has been used to model the 2,000 spines of Data Set 4 presented in Section 1.6.4 using a 54D multivariate Gaussian mixture model. Eight was fixed as the number of clusters, as this was the number that optimized the BIC criterion. Figure 12.5 shows five examples of spines of each of the eight clusters.

Cluster 1

Cluster 2

Cluster 3

Cluster 4

Cluster 5

Cluster 6

Cluster 7

Cluster 8

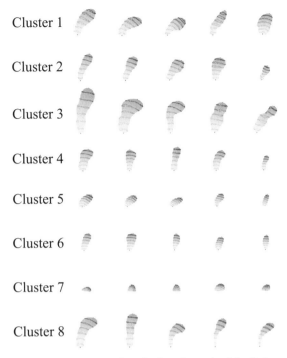

Figure 12.5 Five examples of spines for each of the 8 clusters provided by the multivariate Gaussian mixture model fitted to the 2,000 spines in Section 1.6.4. For the color version, please refer to the plate section.

The 286 spines in the first cluster characteristically have a large size in the middle of their body. The second cluster has spines with a relatively large volume head, not very long in the middle of the body and a neck smaller than their head. There are 237 spines in this cluster. The third is the smallest cluster in terms of number of spines with 180 objects. They have a very big head. The 217 spines belonging to the fourth cluster have twisted necks with similarly sized necks and middle of their bodies. The head of the 181 spines of the fifth cluster is very small, and they have twisted shapes in their central body part and neck. The sixth cluster has spines with very small heads and not very big necks. This cluster contains 269 spines. The neck of the 277 spines in the seventh cluster is extremely small. Finally the heads of the 353 spines in the eighth cluster emerge from the middle of the spine.

12.5 Bibliographic Notes

The seminal paper for the EM algorithm was introduced by Dempster et al. (1977), although the main idea behind the algorithm was previously published for exponential families[3] by Sundberg (1974), Sundberg (1976), and Martin-Lof (1974), and in a more

---

[3] An **exponential family** (Pitman and Wishart, 1936) is a set of probability distributions of a certain form, chosen for mathematical convenience. The exponential family includes many of the most common distributions. The family includes the following discrete distributions: Bernoulli, binomial, categorical, Poisson, negative binomial, and multinomial. The following continuous densities also belong to the exponential family: exponential, gamma, beta, Gaussian, chi-squared, Dirichlet, and Wishart. Examples of common distributions that are not exponential families are the uniform distribution and Student's t. A

general context, by Hartley (1958). For details on theory and extensions of the basic EM algorithm, see the book by McLachlan and Krishnan (1997) and the review by Gupta and Chen (2010).

Finite mixture models were proposed for the first time in the literature by Newcomb (1886) for a problem of outlier modeling. Pearson (1894) used a mixture of two univariate Gaussian densities. The books by Titterington et al. (1985) and McLachlan and Peel (2000) and the survey by Melnykov and Maitra (2010) offer good reviews of the topic.

Spatial clustering aims to find clusters of objects that are according to some measure similar and geographically close. Ambroise and Govaert (1998) introduced the **neighborhood EM** algorithm, which takes advantage of the spatial distributions of the observations, and proved its convergence.

Nonparametric mixture modeling assumes that the observations come from a mixture of nonparametric densities, i.e., $p(\mathbf{x}) = \sum_{k=1}^{K} \pi_k p_k(\mathbf{x})$. Li et al. (2007) proposed associating every point not with a particular mixture component but rather with a local maximum, or mode. The method uses kernel density functions (see Equation (8.32)) to estimate $p_k(\mathbf{x})$, and it employs a variant of the EM algorithm called **modal EM** that tries to find the "hill tops" of the given density.

Semi-supervised clustering refers to the situation where there is some, perhaps uncertain, information available on the labels or classes of some observations. In the standard adaptation of the EM algorithm for these scenarios (Inoue and Ueda, 2003) the M-step is unchanged, whereas the posterior probabilities for labeled data do not need to be updated in the E-step. In addition to this update, Mihaljević et al. (2015) assumed in a GABAergic interneuron cell types discovery problem that K_0 (out of $K \geq K_0$) classes are identified in the data set.

Two main approaches have been adopted with regard to the use of EM for **clustering big data**: (a) clustering a sample of the data set into K clusters and then classifying the other observations in the K classes provided by the cluster algorithm (Maitra, 2001), and (b) adapting the ideas of Hadoop, Map-Reduce, or SPARK technologies to this iterative procedure (Remington, 2011).

Data clustering using hybrid (discrete and continuous variables) Bayesian networks was introduced by Fernández et al. (2014), where continuous variables with non-Gaussian densities are represented as MTEs.

Continuous time Bayesian networks for clustering were proposed by Codecasa and Stella (2015) for multivariate discrete variables, where their values can change in continuous time and a homogeneous Markov process with time-independent transition intensities is assumed.

Multidimensional clustering refers to the situation where data is clustered simultaneously according to different criteria (by using several hidden variables). This contrasts with the standard clustering problem that can be seen as a unidimensional clustering. Model-based multidimensional clustering was proposed by Zhang (2004) and Chen et al. (2012). Multidimensional clustering based on Bayesian networks was proposed by Keivani and Peña (2016).

---

single-parameter exponential family is a set of probability distributions that can be expressed in the form:
$f_X(x|\theta) = h(x)\exp(\eta(\theta) \cdot T(x) - A(\theta))$ where $h(x), T(x), \eta(\theta)$, and $A(\theta)$ are known functions.

Part V

Probabilistic Graphical Models

Part V of this book addresses probabilistic graphical models. It covers two families: directed models (Bayesian networks) in Chapter 13 and undirected models (Markov networks) in Chapter 14. Directed models are easier to interpret and may sometimes be used to infer causal relationships. Part I of this book was related to computational neuroscience, Part II concerned statistics and Parts III and IV were closer to machine learning. Part V lies at the intersection between statistics and machine learning.

13 Bayesian Networks

This chapter reviews Bayesian networks, which are powerful tools for encoding dependence relationships among the variables of a domain under uncertainty. They have appealing advantages with respect to their representation and usability. Bayesian networks explicitly represent uncertain knowledge graphically and intuitively. They can accommodate both continuous and discrete variables, and even temporal variables. They are applicable even when some data are missing. Special emphasis will be placed on Gaussian continuous variables.

This representation can be learned with the aid of an expert in the domain, or automatically from data (or both). This chapter will mainly cover the data-driven approach (with the exception perhaps of Section 13.1.3). This is promising in the big data era, where data accessibility is very high, whereas the expert-driven approach can be time consuming and error prone. A user can take advantage of these networks for probabilistic reasoning and decision making, i.e., given evidence with respect to some variables, any query can be launched and a probabilistic answer retrieved. This process is founded on sound probability theory.

The great thing about Bayesian networks is that they can support all machine learning tasks (Section 1.5.2): association discovery, supervised classification and clustering. In **association discovery** (reviewed in Daly et al., 2011), we search for relationships among the variables of interest from data on those variables. No distinction is made between input and output (or target) variables, which are all treated as a whole. For instance, functional connectivity analysis with fMRI or the discovery of relationships among morphological variables in dendritic trees. This chapter will focus on association discovery with Bayesian networks. Supervised classification and clustering with Bayesian networks have already been dealt with in Section 8.4 (and even multidimensional classification in Section 10.4.2) and in Section 12.3, respectively.

Bielza and Larrañaga (2014b) surveyed Bayesian network learning from morphological, electrophysiological, -omics, and neuroimaging (fMRI, MRI, MEG, EEG, ECoG, PET, and multimodal mechanisms) data. In doing so, this work covered different scales of the brain: molecular, cellular, structural, functional, cognitive, and medical. The authors found more than 60 papers related to Bayesian networks in neuroscience, and half of them concerned the topic of this chapter, Bayesian networks to discover associations and perform inferences. For -omics data, Bayesian networks were used to conduct SNP studies in depression, epilepsy, AD, age-related macular degeneration, and autism; to analyze relationships between some proteins and their mRNA levels in cerebral ischemia; and to identify gene-gene interactions in genome-wide association study of late-onset AD. For temporal data, like electrophysiological data or data from fMRI and EEG experiments, dynamic Bayesian networks (especially hidden Markov models) were used in connectivity analyses, for both task-based and resting-state data and in healthy and diseased patients. Data were commonly discretized or assumed to be Gaussian.

This survey found that neuroscience applications using Bayesian networks for probabilistic reasoning are rare. The work on dendritic tree simulation models described below (Section 13.5) is one of the few applications. However, besides the Bayesian network graph being an expressive tool showing how the variables relate to each other, its conditional probability tables convey further knowledge, notably how these probabilities vary in the light of new observations, providing insights, predictions, and explanations. Inference facilities certainly have a role to play in neuroscience.

The chapter is organized as follows. Section 13.1 sets out the basics of Bayesian networks. Section 13.2 explains how to exploit the knowledge in the network through reasoning. Section 13.3 describes the learning algorithms used to construct a (Gaussian) Bayesian network, including all its elements, i.e., its structure and probabilities. Section 13.4 concerns Bayesian networks in domains that evolve over time. Section 13.5 illustrates the content of this chapter by modeling 3D neuronal dendritic trees with Bayesian networks learned from Data Set 5 (Section 1.6.5). Dependencies between morphological features describing the trees are captured, and the networks are then used to simulate new (virtual) trees. Finally, Section 13.6 wraps up the chapter with bibliographic nodes.

13.1   Basics of Bayesian Networks

Suppose that we start with a data set of N observations and n variables, denoted $X_1, \ldots, X_n$, which specify the characteristics or features of the observations. Let $\mathcal{D} = \{\mathbf{x}^1, \ldots, \mathbf{x}^N\}$ denote the data set, where $\mathbf{x}^h = (x_1^h, \ldots, x_n^h)$, $h = 1, \ldots, N$, $\mathbf{X} = (X_1, \ldots, X_n)$ and $x_i \in \Omega_{X_i} = \{1, 2, \ldots, R_i\}, i = 1, \ldots, n$.

13.1.1   Definition

A **Bayesian network** (BN) (Pearl, 1988; Koller and Friedman, 2009) is a compact representation of the joint probability distribution (JPD) $p(X_1, \ldots, X_n)$ over a set of discrete random variables $X_1, \ldots, X_n$.

The JPD over all the variables of a domain encompasses all the information and can be used to ask any probabilistic question. The problem is that the JPD requires a number of values that grow exponentially with the number n of variables (e.g., we need 2^n values if all variables are binary). Basic tools from probability theory can help factorize the JPD. The **chain rule** allows the JPD to be written as

$$p(X_1, \ldots, X_n) = p(X_1)p(X_2|X_1)p(X_3|X_1, X_2) \cdots p(X_n|X_1, \ldots, X_{n-1}). \qquad (13.1)$$

Note that this expression can employ any ordering of the set $\{X_1, \ldots, X_n\}$. The JPD (global model) is thus specified via marginal and conditional distributions (local models involving fewer variables). This locality needs to be greatly reduced, using small subsets of variables within each factor, beacause the number of parameters in Equation (13.1), which encodes **complete dependence** among $X_1, \ldots, X_n$, still blow up (see, e.g., the last factor).

Different degrees of independence can solve this problem of intractability. The most extreme (and unrealistic) case is **mutual independence**, where

$$p(X_1, \ldots, X_n) = p(X_1)p(X_2)p(X_3) \cdots p(X_n).$$

Note that only n values would be required if all variables are binary. Halfway between the complete dependence in Equation (13.1) and mutual independence is **conditional independence**. Two random variables X and Y are **conditionally independent** (c.i.) given another random variable Z if

$$p(x|y,z) = p(x|z) \quad \forall x,y,z \text{ values of } X,Y,Z,$$

that is, whenever $Z = z$, the information $Y = y$ does not influence the probability p of x. Let $I_p(X,Y|Z)$ denote this condition. X,Y,Z can even be disjoint random *vectors*. The definition can be written equivalently as

$$p(x,y|z) = p(x|z)p(y|z) \quad \forall x,y,z \text{ values of } X,Y,Z.$$

Conditional independence is central to BNs. By exploiting the conditional independence between variables, we can avoid intractability by using fewer parameters (probabilities) and a compact expression. Suppose that we find, for each X_i, a subset $\mathbf{Pa}(X_i) \subseteq \{X_1, \ldots, X_{i-1}\}$ such that given $\mathbf{Pa}(X_i)$, X_i is c.i. of all variables in $\{X_1, \ldots, X_{i-1}\} \setminus \mathbf{Pa}(X_i)$, i.e.,

$$p(X_i|X_1, \ldots, X_{i-1}) = p(X_i|\mathbf{Pa}(X_i)). \tag{13.2}$$

Then using Equation (13.2), the JPD in Equation (13.1) is

$$p(X_1, \ldots, X_n) = p(X_1|\mathbf{Pa}(X_1)) \cdots p(X_n|\mathbf{Pa}(X_n)), \tag{13.3}$$

with a (hopefully) substantially smaller number of parameters. This modularity permits an easy maintenance and efficient reasoning, as we will see below.

A BN represents this factorization of the JPD with a DAG, which is the structure of a BN. A graph $\mathcal{G}$ is given as a pair (V,E), where V is the set of nodes and E is the set of edges between the nodes in V. Nodes of a BN represent the domain random variables $X_1, \ldots, X_n$. *Variable* and *node* will be used as similar terms. The graph is directed when its edges are directed – called arcs – from one node to another. Arcs of a BN represent probabilistic dependencies among variables. They are quantified by conditional probability distributions shaping the interaction between the linked variables. The **parents** of a node X_i, $\mathbf{Pa}(X_i)$, are all the nodes pointing at X_i. Similarly, X_i is their **child**. The term **acyclic** means that the graph contains no cycles, that is, there is no sequence of nodes starting and ending at the same node following the direction of the arcs.

Thus, a BN has two components: a DAG and a collection of conditional probability distributions attached to each node X_i given its parents in the network, $p(X_i|\mathbf{Pa}(X_i))$, that determine a unique JPD shown in Equation (13.3). The JPD over all variables is computed as the product of all these conditional probabilities dictated by the arcs. The first qualitative component is called the **BN structure**, and the second quantitative component is called the **BN parameters**. When all the nodes are discrete variables, these parameters are tabulated in what is usually referred to as **conditional probability table** (CPT).

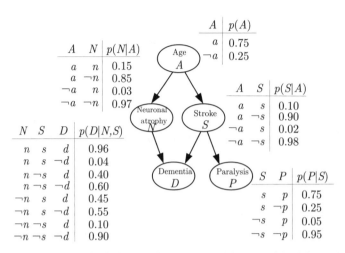

A	N	$p(N|A)$
a	n	0.15
a	$\neg n$	0.85
$\neg a$	n	0.03
$\neg a$	$\neg n$	0.97

A	$p(A)$
a	0.75
$\neg a$	0.25

A	S	$p(S|A)$
a	s	0.10
a	$\neg s$	0.90
$\neg a$	s	0.02
$\neg a$	$\neg s$	0.98

N	S	D	$p(D|N,S)$
n	s	d	0.96
n	s	$\neg d$	0.04
n	$\neg s$	d	0.40
n	$\neg s$	$\neg d$	0.60
$\neg n$	s	d	0.45
$\neg n$	s	$\neg d$	0.55
$\neg n$	$\neg s$	d	0.10
$\neg n$	$\neg s$	$\neg d$	0.90

S	P	$p(P|S)$
s	p	0.75
s	$\neg p$	0.25
$\neg s$	p	0.05
$\neg s$	$\neg p$	0.95

Figure 13.1 Hypothetical example of a BN modeling the risk of dementia.

Example. Risk of Dementia. Figure 13.1 shows a hypothetical example of a BN, inspired by Burge et al. (2009), modeling the risk of dementia. All variables are binary, with x denoting "presence" and $\neg x$ denoting "absence," for Dementia D, Neuronal atrophy N, Stroke S, and Paralysis P. For Age A, a means "age 65+" and otherwise the state is $\neg a$. Note from the BN structure that both Stroke and Neuronal atrophy are influenced by Age (their parent in the DAG). These two conditions influence Dementia (their child). Paralysis is directly associated with having a stroke. CPTs are the BN parameters and indicate the specific conditional probabilities attached to each node. For instance, if someone has neuronal atrophy and has had a stroke, there is a 0.96 probability that the person will have dementia: $p(d|n,s) = 0.96$. However, in the absence of neuronal atrophy and stroke, this probability is only 0.10, i.e., $p(d|\neg n, \neg s) = 0.10$.

Note that there are no cycles. The JPD is factorized as

$$p(A,N,S,D,P) = p(A)p(N|A)p(S|A)p(D|N,S)p(P|S).$$

Thus, the JPD $p(A,N,S,D,P)$ requires $2^5 = 32$ parameters to be fully specified. However, using this BN, which provides for JPD factorization, 22 input probabilities are needed, as shown in Figure 13.1 (there are, in fact, 11 because complementary probabilities can be derived). ∎

13.1.2 Properties

Using different properties, we can derive conditional independencies encoded by a BN.

The **descendants** of a node X_i are all the nodes reachable from X_i by repeatedly following the arcs. If the arcs are followed in the opposite direction, we find the **ancestors**. Let $\mathbf{ND}(X_i)$ denote the **non-descendants** of X_i. The conditional independencies encoded by a BN that can factorize the JPD as in Equation (13.3) are

$$X_i \text{ and } \mathbf{ND}(X_i) \text{ are c.i. given } \mathbf{Pa}(X_i), i = 1, \ldots, n,$$

Table 13.1 Some properties of the conditional independence relationship. Note that Y and W are not necessarily disjoint in the decomposition property.

Name	Property		
Symmetry	$I_p(X,Y\|Z)$	$\Leftrightarrow$	$I_p(Y,X\|Z)$
Decomposition	$I_p(X,\{Y,W\}\|Z)$	$\Rightarrow$	$I_p(X,Y\|Z)$ and $I_p(X,W\|Z)$
Weak union	$I_p(X,\{Y,W\}\|Z)$	$\Rightarrow$	$I_p(X,Y\|W,Z)$ and $I_p(X,W\|Y,Z)$
Contraction	$I_p(X,Y\|Z)$ and $I_p(X,W\|Y,Z)$	$\Rightarrow$	$I_p(X,\{Y,W\}\|Z)$

that is, each node is c.i. of its non-descendants, given its parents, or $I_p(X_i, \mathbf{ND}(X_i)| \mathbf{Pa}(X_i))$ for short. Then it is said that $\mathcal{G}$ satisfies the **Markov condition** or **local directed Markov property** with a probability distribution p and that $(\mathcal{G}, p)$ is a BN.

It is easy to prove that the Markov condition is equivalent to the factorization in Equation (13.3). Indeed, if the Markov condition holds, and we simply use the chain rule (13.1) with an ancestral (also called topological) node ordering, i.e., parents come before their children in the sequence, then the non-descendants and parents will be in the conditioning sets $\{X_1, \ldots, X_{i-1}\}$ of the chain rule. Thus the application of the Markov condition will give Equation (13.2) and hence Equation (13.3). Conversely and analogously, given a DAG $\mathcal{G}$ and the product in Equation (13.3), then the Markov condition holds.

Some other conditional independencies may be derived from the properties of the conditional independence relationship (Castillo et al., 1997), see Table 13.1. These properties are useful if we have a list of conditional independencies (e.g., given by the domain expert) because we can derive new independence relationships. Also, they can be used to find additional conditional independencies apart from those given by the Markov condition. Thanks to the decomposition property, for example, the statements given by the Markov condition can be broken into simpler statements, involving fewer variables.

An easier way to look for conditional independencies is to check a property called d-separation over the graph. This is always a sufficient condition for conditional independencies in p. There are three basic types of connections among three nodes A, T, B in a DAG: A **converging connection** (or **collider**) at T is $A \rightarrow T \leftarrow B$; a **serial connection** (or **chain connection**) is $A \rightarrow T \rightarrow B$ or $A \leftarrow T \leftarrow B$; a **diverging connection** (or **fork connection**) is $A \leftarrow T \rightarrow B$.

Let $\mathbf{X}$, $\mathbf{Y}$, and $\mathbf{Z}$ be disjoint random vectors (with several nodes in the DAG). $\mathbf{X}$ and $\mathbf{Y}$ are **d-separated** by a third set $\mathbf{Z}$ if and only if every undirected path[1] between $\mathbf{X}$ and $\mathbf{Y}$ is "blocked," i.e., there is an intermediate variable T (not belonging to $\mathbf{X}$ or $\mathbf{Y}$) for which either:

(a) The connection is converging at T, and neither T nor any of its descendants belong to $\mathbf{Z}$, or

(b) The connection is serial or diverging, and T belongs to $\mathbf{Z}$.

Therefore, given the local directed Markov property, if $\mathbf{X}$ is d-separated from $\mathbf{Y}$ given $\mathbf{Z}$, then $\mathbf{X}$ and $\mathbf{Y}$ are c.i. given $\mathbf{Z}$ (Verma and Pearl, 1990b). Then it is said that $\mathcal{G}$ satisfies the **global directed Markov property**. This property also implies the local directed Markov

---

[1] An undirected path is a set of nodes that are joined by edges sequentially. For example, P-S-A-N in Figure 13.1. Note that arc directions are irrelevant because we look at the undirected version of the BN.

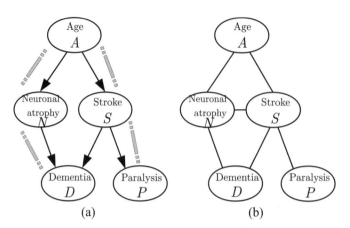

(a)   (b)

Figure 13.2 (a) A path, D-N-A-S-P, from D to P in the risk of dementia example. (b) Moralized ancestral graph to check whether D and P are u-separated by $\{N,S\}$ and whether P and A are u-separated by D.

property. BNs are said to be an **independence map** of p, or **I-map** for short. If the reverse also holds, i.e., conditional independence implies d-separation (which is not always the case for every distribution), then it is said that $\mathcal{G}$ is a **perfect map** (or **P-map** for short) of p or p is **faithful** to $\mathcal{G}$. In this case, all the independencies in the distribution are read directly from the DAG.

An alternative equivalent criterion to d-separation is known as **u-separation** (Lauritzen et al., 1990), where u refers to the fact that checks are run on an undirected graph. There are three steps for checking whether **X** and **Y** are u-separated by **Z**:

1. Get the smallest subgraph that contains **X**, **Y**, and **Z** and their ancestors (this is called **ancestral graph**).
2. **Moralize** the resulting subgraph, i.e., add an undirected link between parents having a common child and then drop directions on all directed links.
3. **Z** u-separates **X** and **Y** whenever every path from a variable in **X** to a variable in **Y** contains a variable in **Z**.

Example. Risk of Dementia (d- and u-Separation). Examples of ancestral orderings are A-N-S-D-P or A-S-P-N-D. All nodes are descendants of node A (A has no non-descendants). The descendants of S are D and P, and the Markov condition states that S and N are c.i. given A. All nodes are non-descendants of D, and hence D and $\{A,P\}$ are c.i. given $\{N,S\}$. By using the decomposition property, this last conditional independence implies: D and A are c.i. given $\{N,S\}$, and D and P are c.i. given $\{N,S\}$.

Let us check this last conditional independence with d-separation, that is, let us check whether D and P are d-separated by $\{N,S\}$. We find two paths from D to P. In the longest path, D-N-A-S-P (see Figure 13.2(a)), the intermediate variable T must be N or S because the connection is serial at any N or S, and they belong to $\{N,S\}$. Node A cannot be selected to be T because the connection is diverging at A and $A \notin \{N,S\}$. In the shortest path D-S-P, S qualifies as T because the connection diverges at S and $S \in \{N,S\}$. Therefore, D and P are d-separated by $\{N,S\}$. Hence D and P are c.i. given $\{N,S\}$.

We can also check whether D and P are u-separated by $\{N,S\}$. The ancestral subgraph is the whole DAG. This is moralized in Figure 13.2(b), where the undirected link N-S has been added because both nodes have D as a common child. The arc directions have also been dropped. Now it is easy to check that we always find N or S in every path from D to P. Therefore, D and P are u-separated by $\{N,S\}$. Hence D and P are c.i. given $\{N,S\}$.

However, A and P are not d- or u-separated by D. For the d-separation, the path P-S-A only contains S as an intermediate variable. There is a serial connection at S, but $S \notin \{D\}$. In fact, the reader can check that there is no valid T in the other path P-S-D-N-A either. Figure 13.2(b) is still valid for u-separation, and we find that we can go from P to A through S, without crossing D. ∎

With a perfect map of p, we would have a clear graphical representation of all conditional independent variables. Unfortunately, this requirement is often strong, and some distributions do not have perfect maps in graphs. We must therefore relax this requirement and omit some independencies from the representation.

Example. Model without a Perfect Map. This is a working example reported in Kjaerulff and Madsen (2008). Suppose that we have four variables X,Y,Z,W, and p given as a list of independence statements

1. $I_p(X,Y)$
2. $I_p(X,W|Y,Z)$
3. $I_p(Y,Z|X,W)$.

Next we find that it is only possible to represent a subset of these statements in a DAG. This means that the DAG language is not rich enough to capture all sets of independence statements.

Thus, if we try to build a DAG that is a perfect map of p, there must be links between each pair of nodes except $(X,Y),(X,W)$, and (Y,Z), for which an independence statement has been specified. A preliminary skeleton of the possible DAG is shown in Figure 13.3(a).

Recalling d-separation, there must be a converging connection at Z or W for the first independence statement to hold, e.g., at Z, see Figure 13.3(b). This implies that X and W are d-separated (given $\varnothing$), but they are not independent (otherwise this independence would be listed). Thus, this graph cannot be an I-map of p as this d-separation does not

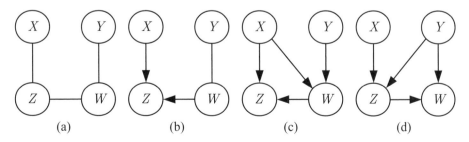

Figure 13.3 (a) Preliminary skeleton of the DAG for the example. (b) There must be a converging connection at Z for the first statement to hold true. (c) A perfect map of the first and third independence statements. (d) A perfect map of the first and second independence statements.

imply $I_p(X,W|\varnothing)$. To solve this problem, a link between X and W must be included. Now, there must be a converging connection at W to ensure that X and Y are d-separated, see Figure 13.3(c). This DAG in (c) is an I-map of p. It is not, however, perfect because $I_p(X,W|Y,Z)$ holds, but X and W are not d-separated by $\{Y,Z\}$. Similarly, with the converging connection at W, the DAG is as shown in Figure 13.3(d). This is an I-map of p but is not perfect because $I_p(Y,Z|X,W)$ holds, but Y and Z are not d-separated by $\{X,W\}$.

Therefore, we have to be content with the DAG in Figure 13.3(c) or (d), which are both I-maps of p but not perfect maps. ∎

Naturally, we wish a graph that displays only genuine independencies of p and maximizes the number of such displayed independencies. This is the same as requiring that the graph be a **minimal I-map** of p. A minimal I-map $\mathcal{G}$ is an I-map where if some arc is removed it is no longer an I-map (some independence external to p is added), that is, no arc can be deleted without destroying the I-mapness of $\mathcal{G}$.

With an I-map of p, the graph $\mathcal{G}$ of the BN does not make any false independence assumptions and is not misleading with respect to independencies in p, that is, any independence reported by d- or u-separation in $\mathcal{G}$ is satisfied by the underlying distribution p. Thus, $\mathcal{G}$ does not entail any independence that is not contained in p. $\mathcal{G}$ does not invent new independencies not present in p. However, p may have some independencies that are not reflected in $\mathcal{G}$ by d-separations.

Note that a complete graph (all pairs of nodes are connected) is always a trivial I-map of any p. Remember that there are $n!$ different factorizations in Equation (13.1). Each factorization has a unique DAG, but all these DAGs are equivalent in terms of dependence and independence properties, as they are all complete graphs and hence do not represent any independence statements.

The formal definition of a BN follows. Let p be a JPD over $V = \{X_1, \dots, X_n\}$. A BN is a tuple $(\mathcal{G}, p)$, where $\mathcal{G} = (V,A)$ is a DAG such that (A stands for arcs):

- Each node of $\mathcal{G}$ represents a variable of V.
- The Markov condition holds, or equivalently, each node has a local probability distribution $p(X_i|\mathbf{Pa}(X_i))$, such that $p(X_1, \dots, X_n) = \prod_{i=1}^{n} p(X_i|\mathbf{Pa}(X_i))$.
- $\mathcal{G}$ is a minimal I-map of p.

Finally, we mention another useful property of BNs. This property states that each node X_i is c.i. of all other nodes in the network given the set of variables called **Markov blanket**, $\mathbf{MB}(X_i)$, i.e.,

$$p(X_i|\mathbf{X} \setminus \{X_i\}) = p(X_i|\mathbf{MB}(X_i)). \tag{13.4}$$

If p is faithful to $\mathcal{G}$, the Markov blanket of a node is composed of its parents, its children, and the parents of its children (spouses). Therefore, the only knowledge required to predict the behavior of X_i is $\mathbf{MB}(X_i)$. This is relevant in supervised classification problems, where the main interest is to compute the posterior probability of the class variable C given the other variables $p(C|X_1, \dots, X_n)$. This then would be computed as just $p(C|\mathbf{MB}(C))$, see Section 8.4.1.7. In the risk of dementia example, $\mathbf{MB}(N) = \{A,D,S\}$. A is the parent of N, D is its child, and S is its spouse.

13.1.3 Building Bayesian Networks

A procedure for building a minimal I-map was introduced at the beginning of Section 13.1.2. From an ancestral ordering of nodes, say X_1-X_2-$\cdots$-X_n, we select the minimal subset of nodes in $\{X_1, \dots, X_{i-1}\}$ that renders X_i c.i. of $\{X_1, \dots, X_{i-1}\} \setminus \mathbf{Pa}(X_i)$ as parents of X_i, $\mathbf{Pa}(X_i)$. The ancestral ordering is unknown, and we take an arbitrary ordering in practice. The resulting DAG with its associated factorization will be an I-map (and also often a perfect map) of the independence statements entailed by the JPD.

This is, in fact, how a BN is almost always specified: a domain expert or a learning process from a data set (or both) provide a DAG $\mathcal{G}$ describing the dependence structure among the variables and their associated conditional probability distributions. Then the JPD p is derived from the factorization in Equation (13.3). This is equivalent to $\mathcal{G}$ being an I-map of p (Castillo et al., 1997).

Indeed, DAGs defined as recursive factorizations of JPDs will often be perfect maps, and it is not a big concern therefore if there is no perfect map of a probability distribution. In the rare cases, where a model is instead described in terms of a list of independence statements of some (unknown) JPD, there may be no such perfect map, in which case the best option is a DAG, which is a minimal I-map of the distribution.

Remember that arcs in a BN represent probabilistic dependencies, and variables at the tails of the arcs will not necessarily be **causally dependent** on variables at the head. Arc reversals in causal relationships would change their meaning. Also, causality cannot generally be inferred from observational data alone (the usual kind of data in machine learning). Data subjected to interventions are required (Ellis and Wong, 2008; Hauser and Bühlmann, 2015). Some prior knowledge (ruling out certain directions) or the application of external interventions that probe some arc direction using a hypothesis test are necessary in order to differentiate between arcs. For a BN to be a **causal Bayesian network** (Spirtes et al., 1993; Pearl, 2000; Pearl et al., 2016; Peters et al., 2017), there has to be an explicit requirement for the relationships to be causal. In these networks, the impact of external interventions can be predicted from data collected prior to intervention (we cannot predict the effect of manipulations in BNs). The causal Bayesian network is a formalism that we can use to model and reason with causality and define a *causal* Markov condition. We have $X \rightarrow Y$ causally if experimental interventions that change the value of X can affect the distribution of Y but not vice versa. Once the values of the causal parents of Y are fixed by intervention, the distribution of Y will not be affected by intervention on any other variables in the set of variables.

When building a BN manually with the aid of an expert in the domain, if causality exists, the BN structure should be built in the causal direction because it results in simpler and intuitive BNs with fewer unnecessarily added dependencies. Otherwise there are many arcs, and some conditional independencies cannot be represented (with separations in the DAG).

The expert will identify the problem variables and their outcomes. We usually look for three kinds of variables: hypothesis variables, information variables, and mediator variables. Hypothesis variables are unobservable, like diagnosis and classification variables. We want to discover their posterior probabilities. Information variables are observable, like sensor readings and test results, and provide relevant information for hypothesis variables. Mediator variables are unobservable and are introduced for a special purpose: properly

account for the independence properties in the domain, make it easier to acquire probabilities, reduce the number of distributions for elicitation, and so on (Jensen and Nielsen,
2007).

The estimation of probabilities from data will be explained in Section 13.3.1 via statistical methods. Expert subjective estimation may also be used, although psychological biases
should be taken into account (Tversky and Kahneman, 1974; Kahneman et al., 1982).

13.1.4   Equivalent Bayesian Networks

Two BNs with the same set of nodes are **Markov equivalent** if the set of distributions
that can be represented using one of the DAGs is identical to the set of distributions that
can be represented using the other (Chickering, 1995). Both DAGs induce the same set of
conditional independence statements among variables. Because equivalence is reflexive,
symmetric, and transitive, the relation partitions the space of DAGs into a set of equivalence classes. This will be useful for learning BNs (see Section 13.3).

Some researchers (Frydenberg, 1990; Verma and Pearl, 1990a) showed that two
DAGs are Markov equivalent if and only if they have the same skeleton and the same
immoralities, also called **v-structures**. An immorality is a structure $X \rightarrow Y \leftarrow Z$, where
X and Z are not connected. For instance, the three-node BN structures $X \rightarrow Y \rightarrow Z$,
$X \leftarrow Y \rightarrow Z$ and $X \leftarrow Y \leftarrow Z$, are (Markov) equivalent and shape the equivalence class for
three nodes.

A useful tool would be to have a representative of an equivalence class. The **completed
partially DAG** (CPDAG) or **essential graph** uniquely represents all members of an equivalence class. It has an arc $X \rightarrow Y$ if it appears in every DAG belonging to the same
equivalence class and otherwise has a link $X - Y$ (meaning that either direction $X \rightarrow Y$
or $X \leftarrow Y$ is possible in the DAGs within the equivalence class), see Figure 13.4(a)–(b).
The individual DAGs in the equivalence class can be derived from an essential graph by
assigning any direction to the undirected edges, provided that this does not introduce any
cycle or immorality into the graph, see Figure 13.4(c)–(e).

13.1.5   Gaussian Bayesian Networks

A common approach is to discretize (Section 2.6.3) any continuous variables $X_1, \ldots, X_n$,
i.e., transform them into intervals. For instance, the continuous blood-oxygen-level-
dependent (BOLD) responses measured by an fMRI scanner can be discretized into two

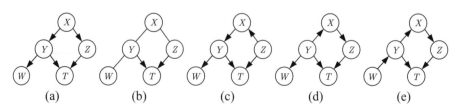

Figure 13.4 (a) A DAG with five variables. There is one immorality at T. (b) Its essential graph.
(c)–(e) The three DAGs equivalent to the DAG in (a). The five graphs have the same skeleton and
the same immorality. DAGs (a),(c)–(e) form the equivalence class, represented by the essential
graph (b).

categories: low and high. This is usually done by discretizing the continuous variables into discrete variables prior to and independent of the learning or inference algorithm for the BN. Once the variables have been discretized, the procedure is the same as for a regular discrete BN (Fu, 2005). More complex methods consider discretizing the continuous variables while learning the BN (Friedman and Goldszmidt, 1996; Monti and Cooper, 1998; Steck and Jaakkola, 2004) or adjusting discretization for each inference (Kozlov and Koller, 1997).

Discretization involves some loss of information and the assignment of many parameters. Therefore models with continuous variables following parametric densities are a good choice. The most popular density is the Gaussian density. Thus, **Gaussian BNs** (Shachter and Kenley, 1989; Geiger and Heckerman, 1994) assume that the associated JPD for $\mathbf{X} = (X_1, \ldots, X_n)$ is a multivariate (nonsingular) normal distribution $\mathcal{N}(\boldsymbol{\mu}, \boldsymbol{\Sigma})$, given by (Section 3.4.4)

$$f(\mathbf{x}) = \frac{1}{(2\pi)^{n/2}|\boldsymbol{\Sigma}|^{1/2}} \exp\left(-\frac{1}{2}(\mathbf{x}-\boldsymbol{\mu})^T\boldsymbol{\Sigma}^{-1}(\mathbf{x}-\boldsymbol{\mu})\right), \quad (13.5)$$

where $\boldsymbol{\mu} = (\mu_1, \ldots, \mu_n)^T$ is the vector of means, $\boldsymbol{\Sigma}$ is the $n \times n$ covariance matrix, and $|\boldsymbol{\Sigma}|$ is its determinant. Its inverse is called the precision or concentration matrix $\mathbf{W} = \boldsymbol{\Sigma}^{-1}$. The required parameters are then $\boldsymbol{\mu}$ and $\boldsymbol{\Sigma}$. An interesting property is that a variable X_i is c.i. of X_j given the other variables iff $w_{ij} = 0$, where w_{ij} is the (i, j)-element of $\mathbf{W}$ (Anderson, 1984). This will be useful in undirected probabilistic graphical models (Chapter 14).

The JPD in a Gaussian BN can be equivalently defined as in Equation (13.1) by the product of n univariate (linear) Gaussian conditional densities

$$f(\mathbf{x}) = f_1(x_1)f_2(x_2|x_1)\cdots f_n(x_n|x_1, \ldots, x_{n-1}), \quad (13.6)$$

each defined as

$$f_i(x_i|x_1, \ldots, x_{i-1}) \sim \mathcal{N}\left(\mu_i + \sum_{j=1}^{i-1}\beta_{ij}(x_j - \mu_j), v_i\right), \quad (13.7)$$

where μ_i is the unconditional mean of X_i (i.e., the ith component of $\boldsymbol{\mu}$), v_i is the conditional variance of X_i given values for $x_1, \ldots, x_{i-1}$, and β_{ij} is the linear regression coefficient of X_j in the regression of X_i on $X_1, \ldots, X_{i-1}$. It reflects the strength of the relationship between X_i and X_j: there is no arc from X_j to X_i whenever $\beta_{ij} = 0$. This formulation states that X_i is a linear function of $X_1, \ldots, X_{i-1}$, with the addition of Gaussian noise with mean 0 and variance v_i. Note that v_i does not depend on the conditioning values $x_1, \ldots, x_{i-1}$. Root nodes (without parents) follow unconditional Gaussians. Thus, the parameters that determine a Gaussian BN are $\boldsymbol{\mu} = (\mu_1, \ldots, \mu_n)^T$, $\mathbf{v} = (v_1, \ldots, v_n)^T$, and $\{\beta_{ij}, j = 1, \ldots, i-1; i = 1, \ldots, n\}$. Note that we are using the standard chain rule of Equation (13.1), but Equation (13.3) can be expressed more simply in terms of parents by taking an ancestral node ordering in the chain rule. This means that some β_{ij} will be zero.

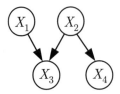

Figure 13.5 A Gaussian BN.

Example. Gaussian BN. In the Gaussian BN of Figure 13.5, distributions are

$$f_1(x_1) \sim \mathcal{N}(\mu_1, v_1)$$
$$f_2(x_2) \sim \mathcal{N}(\mu_2, v_2)$$
$$f_3(x_3|x_1, x_2) \sim \mathcal{N}(\mu_3 + \beta_{31}(x_1 - \mu_1) + \beta_{32}(x_2 - \mu_2), v_3)$$
$$f_4(x_4|x_2) \sim \mathcal{N}(\mu_4 + \beta_{42}(x_2 - \mu_2), v_4).$$

∎

The standard representation of the multivariate Gaussian density given by Equation (13.5) is in terms of its unconditional statistics, mean vector μ, and covariance matrix Σ. When assessing this multivariate density directly, the covariance matrix Σ must be guaranteed to be positive-definite. This is done by applying complex procedures to alter the user-provided correlations. Fortunately, it is simpler to assess a Gaussian BN using the product of normal densities given in Equations (13.6)–(13.7) than by directly assessing the covariance matrix. When there is conditional independence, the Gaussian BN has fewer parameters (unconditional means μ_i, conditional variances v_i, and linear coefficients β_{ij}), often with a natural physical meaning, and giving rise to a typically positive-definite covariance matrix. This is because Σ is positive-definite if and only if $v_i > 0$ for all $i = 1, \dots, n$ (Shachter and Kenley, 1989). It would be absurd to assess a negative variance v_i. Therefore, Σ will be always positive semi-definite (this means $v_i \geq 0$ for all $i = 1, \dots, n$). It will, in fact, be positive-definite unless any variable is a deterministic function of other variables in the model (its v_i is zero). The source of the zeros in Σ are pairs of marginally independent variables. Zeros in $\mathbf{W}$ are equivalent to the conditional independence of a variable given the other variables.

Furthermore, there are efficient and closed formulas to transform one representation, Equation (13.5), into the other, Equation (13.7), and vice versa (Wermuth, 1980; Shachter and Kenley, 1989; Geiger and Heckerman, 1994), using whichever is better suited for the task. The unconditional means μ_i are the same in both representations.

Thus, from v_i and β_{ij} of a given Gaussian BN, matrix $\mathbf{W}$ of the multivariate Gaussian density can be built recursively with

$$\mathbf{W}(i+1) = \begin{pmatrix} \mathbf{W}(i) + \dfrac{\beta_{i+1}\beta_{i+1}^T}{v_{i+1}} & \dfrac{-\beta_{i+1}}{v_{i+1}} \\[2ex] \dfrac{-\beta_{i+1}^T}{v_{i+1}} & \dfrac{1}{v_{i+1}} \end{pmatrix}, \tag{13.8}$$

where $\mathbf{W}(i)$ denotes the $i \times i$ upper-left submatrix of $\mathbf{W}$, β_i is the $(i-1)$-dimensional vector of coefficients $(\beta_{i1}, \dots, \beta_{ii-1})$, and $\mathbf{W}(1){=}1/v_1$. Note that vector β_i contains $\beta_{i1}, \dots, \beta_{ii-1}$, the coefficients in the regression of X_i on $X_1, \ldots, X_{i-1}$ and, accordingly, incoming arcs (from parents) to X_i in the graph.

Example. From Conditional Gaussian Densities to the Multivariate Gaussian. Suppose that we have a structure of a Gaussian BN with three nodes X_1, X_2, and X_3, with only two arcs: $X_1 \rightarrow X_3$ and $X_2 \rightarrow X_3$. The JPD factorization is given, as in Equation (13.6), by

$$f(\mathbf{x}) = f_1(x_1)f_2(x_2)f_3(x_3|x_1, x_2),$$

where

$$f_1(x_1) \sim \mathcal{N}(4, 3)$$
$$f_2(x_2) \sim \mathcal{N}(5, 1)$$
$$f_3(x_3|x_1, x_2) \sim \mathcal{N}(3 - 0.2(x_1 - 4) + 0.5(x_2 - 5), 2).$$

Hence, the unconditional means are $\mu_1 = 4, \mu_2 = 5$, and $\mu_3 = 3$; the conditional variances are $v_1 = 3, v_2 = 1$, and $v_3 = 2$; and the linear coefficients are $\beta_{31} = -0.2, \beta_{32} = 0.5$ (the other β_{ij} are zero).

In the other representation, $\mathbf{X} = (X_1, X_2, X_3)$ follows a multivariate Gaussian distribution $\mathcal{N}(\boldsymbol{\mu}, \boldsymbol{\Sigma})$, where $\boldsymbol{\mu} = (4, 5, 3)^T$, and $\boldsymbol{\Sigma}$ is computed using the recursive formula of Equation (13.8), which requires only v_i and β_{ij}. First, we have that $\mathbf{W}(1) = 1/3$, and then because $\boldsymbol{\beta}_2 = \beta_{21} = 0$,

$$\mathbf{W}(2) = \begin{pmatrix} 1/3 & 0 \\ 0 & 1 \end{pmatrix}.$$

Finally,

$$\mathbf{W}(3) = \begin{pmatrix} \dfrac{1}{v_1} + \dfrac{\beta_{31}^2}{v_3} & \dfrac{\beta_{31}\beta_{32}}{v_3} & \dfrac{-\beta_{31}}{v_3} \\[2ex] \dfrac{\beta_{31}\beta_{32}}{v_3} & \dfrac{1}{v_2} + \dfrac{\beta_{32}^2}{v_3} & \dfrac{-\beta_{32}}{v_3} \\[2ex] \dfrac{-\beta_{31}}{v_3} & \dfrac{-\beta_{32}}{v_3} & \dfrac{1}{v_3} \end{pmatrix} = \begin{pmatrix} 0.354 & -0.050 & 0.100 \\ -0.050 & 1.125 & -0.250 \\ 0.100 & -0.250 & 0.500 \end{pmatrix}.$$

Thus, $\mathbf{W}(3) = \mathbf{W} = \boldsymbol{\Sigma}^{-1}$, and hence

$$\boldsymbol{\Sigma} = \begin{pmatrix} 3 & 0 & -0.6 \\ 0 & 1 & 0.5 \\ -0.6 & 0.5 & 2.37 \end{pmatrix}.$$

∎

On the other hand, β_{ij} and v_i of the Gaussian BN can be derived from matrix $\boldsymbol{\Sigma}$ of the multivariate Gaussian density. In this case, it is useful to rewrite Equation (13.7) as

$f_i(x_i|x_1, \ldots, x_{i-1}) \sim \mathcal{N}\left(\beta_{i0} + \sum_{j=1}^{i-1} \beta_{ij} x_j, v_i\right)$, where $\beta_{i0} = \mu_i - \sum_{j=1}^{i-1} \beta_{ij} \mu_j$. The formulas are

$$\boldsymbol{\beta}_i = \boldsymbol{\Sigma}_{1:i-1}^{-1} \boldsymbol{\Sigma}_{1:i-1,i}$$
$$v_i = \Sigma_{ii} - \boldsymbol{\Sigma}_{1:i-1,i}^T \boldsymbol{\beta}_i,$$

where $\boldsymbol{\Sigma}_{1:i-1}$ is the covariance matrix between variables $X_1, \ldots, X_{i-1}$; $\boldsymbol{\Sigma}_{1:i-1,i}$ is the vector with the covariances of each variable $X_j, j = 1, \ldots, i-1$; and X_i and Σ_{ii} is the (i,i)-element of $\boldsymbol{\Sigma}$ (unconditional variance of X_i).

Importantly from a practical perspective, Gaussian BNs assume that the interactions between variables are modeled by linear relationships with Gaussian noise. Discrete BNs are more general and capable of modeling nonlinear relationships.

Gaussianity often does not hold in practice. However, this distribution is still very useful due to its compact representation and computational tractability. Thus we will sometimes assume Gaussianity even if it is only a rough approximation. Otherwise the assumption can be relaxed, mainly with non- and semi-parametric density estimation techniques: kernel-based densities (Hofmann and Tresp, 1996; Bach and Jordan, 2003), Gaussian process networks (Friedman and Nachman, 2000), nonparametric regression models (Imoto et al., 2002), copula density functions (Elidan, 2011), MTEs (Moral et al., 2001) and MoPs (Shenoy and West, 2011) (both in Section 8.4.2.2), and general mixtures of truncated basis functions (Langseth et al., 2012). The last three nonparametric densities are all expressed as piecewise (exponential, polynomials, truncated basis) functions defined in regions, and a trade-off must be made between the number of pieces (components) and the number of exponential terms or polynomial degrees. Fortunately, these families are closed under multiplication, addition, and integration, the operations required during inference. Nevertheless, the use of these kinds of models for learning and simulation is still in its infancy, and many problems have yet to be solved.

13.1.6 Hybrid Bayesian Networks

Hybrid BNs refer to BNs where discrete and continuous random variables coexist. **Conditional linear Gaussian networks** (CLGs) (Lauritzen and Wermuth, 1989; Olesen, 1993) are the most widely used BN model. A continuous variable X_i can have continuous $Y_1, \ldots, Y_k$ and discrete $U_1, \ldots, U_m$ parents. For each configuration $\mathbf{u} = (u_1, \ldots, u_m)$ of its discrete parents, its conditional probability distribution is the so-called conditional linear Gaussian on its continuous parents, i.e., Equation (13.7) is now

$$f_i(x_i|\mathbf{u}, y_1, \ldots, y_k) \sim \mathcal{N}\left(\mu_i^{\mathbf{u}} + \sum_{j=1}^{k} \beta_{ij}^{\mathbf{u}}(y_j - \mu_j), y_i^{\mathbf{u}}\right).$$

For every instantiation of the discrete network variables, the JPD of the continuous variables is, like the Gaussian BN, a multivariate Gaussian whose parameters can be derived from the parameters in the CLG representation and vice versa. Hence CLG networks induce a JPD, which takes the form of a mixture of multivariate Gaussians with one component for each configuration of the discrete network variables. The weight of the component is the probability of that configuration. CLG networks have been studied at length because they provide tractable inference (Lauritzen, 1992; Lauritzen and Jensen, 2001) and learning (Bøttcher, 2004).

CLG networks impose the restriction that discrete variables cannot have continuous parents. If we have a discrete variable with a continuous parent, then we do not have a mixture of multivariate Gaussians. To address the case of a discrete child X with a continuous parent Y, we can use a logistic model (or its multinomial extension if X is not binary) to model $p(X|Y)$, as in Lerner et al. (2001). Other options with no constraints on the structure of the networks are to use mixtures of Gaussians (Shenoy, 2006) or even nonparametric densities like MTEs (Moral et al., 2001), MoPs (Shenoy and West, 2011), and mixtures of truncated basis functions (Langseth et al., 2012) instead of conditional Gaussian distributions.

13.2   Inference in Bayesian Networks

13.2.1   What Is Inference?

Besides visualizing the relationships between variables in a BN and deriving their conditional independencies, these models are extremely useful for predictions, diagnoses, explanations, and the like. This mainly entails computing the conditional probability distribution of a variable (or a set of variables) of interest given the values of some other variables. The observed variables are called the **observed evidence $\mathbf{E} = \mathbf{e}$**. There are three kinds of variables in $\mathbf{X}$: a query variable X_i (typically a variable, although a vector is also possible), the evidence variables $\mathbf{E}$, and the other, unobserved variables $\mathbf{U}$.

Evidence is very important. The three types of connections – converging, serial, and diverging – among three nodes A, T, B in a DAG, signify different information transmission capabilities. The capabilities change in the presence of evidence. In the risk of dementia example, information may flow through the serial connection $A \to N \to D$ because Age (A) has an influence on Neuronal atrophy (N), which also has an influence on Dementia (D). However, if there is evidence of neuronal atrophy, then any information about age is irrelevant to our belief about dementia (and vice versa), and the information flow from A to D is blocked by N. A and D are dependent without any evidence about N; however, A and D are c.i. given N. Therefore, information may flow through a general serial connection $A \to T \to B$, unless the state of T is known.

Second, Stroke (S) has an influence on both Dementia (D) and Paralysis (P), and the information flows through this diverging connection $D \leftarrow S \to P$. However, if we know the state of S (say the patient has had a stroke), then any information about the state of dementia is irrelevant to our belief about paralysis (and vice versa), and the information flow is blocked by S. D and P are dependent without any evidence about S; however, D and P are c.i. given S. Therefore, information may flow through a general diverging connection $A \leftarrow T \to B$, unless the state of T is known.

Finally, information about Neuronal atrophy will not affect our belief about the state of Stroke (and vice versa); the information flow $N \to D \leftarrow S$ is blocked at (the converging connection) D because both variables S and N act independently. However, with evidence about Dementia, then any information about Neuronal atrophy will affect our belief that Stroke is the cause of dementia (and vice versa). N and S are independent without any evidence about D; however, N and S are c.i. given D. Therefore, information may flow through a general converging connection $A \to T \leftarrow B$ only when there is evidence of T (or one of its descendants).

Inference refers to finding the probability of any variable X_i (or vector of variables) conditioned on $\mathbf{e}$, i.e., $p(x_i|\mathbf{e})$, or more generally the conditional probability distribution $p(X_i|\mathbf{e})$. The realm of statistics offers exact and approximate inference tools to compute $p(X_i|\mathbf{e})$. This computation is called **probabilistic reasoning** under uncertainty, where the evidence is propagated through the graphical structure to update probabilities. If there is no evidence, probabilities of interest are prior distributions $p(X_i)$. Inference in BNs can combine evidence from all parts of the network and perform any kind of query. Under causality, we can predict the effect given the causes (**predictive reasoning**), diagnose the causes given the effects (**diagnostic reasoning**), explain away a cause as responsible for an effect (intercausal reasoning) or any other mixed reasoning. **Intercausal reasoning** is unique to BNs: for the v-structure $A \to X \leftarrow B$, A and B are independent, but once their shared child variable X is observed they become dependent. That is, when the effect X is known, the presence of one explanatory cause renders the alternative cause less likely (it is explained away).

Inference also refers to finding values of a set of variables that best explain the observed evidence. This is called **abductive inference**. In **total abduction**, we solve $\arg\max_{\mathbf{U}} p(\mathbf{U}|\mathbf{e})$, i.e., the aim is to find the **most probable explanation** (MPE), whereas the problem in **partial abduction** is the same but for a subset of variables in $\mathbf{u}$ (the explanation set), referred to as **partial maximum a posteriori**. This involves not only computing probabilities but also solving an optimization problem. Solving a supervised classification problem with probabilistic models (Chapter 8), i.e., $\max_r p(C = c_r|\mathbf{x})$ is a particular case of finding the MPE.

Example. Risk of Dementia (Different Types of Probabilistic Reasoning). Let us take the risk of dementia example in Figure 13.1 to see how a BN is actually used. The first probabilities that should be examined are the prior distributions $p(X_i)$, i.e., without any observed evidence. Figure 13.6(a) shows these probabilities as bar charts. For instance, note that the probability of suffering dementia is 0.17. All the inferences and figures were output using GeNIe.[2]

Now suppose that we have a patient who has had a stroke ($\mathbf{E} = S = s$). The updated probabilities given this evidence, i.e., $p(x_i|s)$ for any state x_i of nodes A, N, D or P, are shown in Figure 13.6(b). Note how the state s for Stroke is fixed as the full bar with 100% probability. The probability of suffering dementia has now increased to $p(d|s) = 0.52$. However, for the opposite state – not having a stroke – $p(d|\neg s) = 0.14$ (not shown). This is an example of predictive reasoning.

By querying the BN in this manner, we find other interesting probabilities. As an example of diagnostic reasoning, given the effect of paralysis ($P = p$), the probability of the cause being a stroke is high, $p(s|p) = 0.57$. To perform intercausal reasoning, we can take N, S, and D. Neuronal atrophy (N) and Stroke (S) are independent of each other and have $p(n) = 0.12, p(s) = 0.08$ (Figure 13.6(a)), but once Dementia (D) is observed, e.g., $D = d$, the probability of both possible causes, n and s, increases: $p(n|d) = 0.33$ and $p(s|d) = 0.25$.

---

[2] www.bayesfusion.com/.

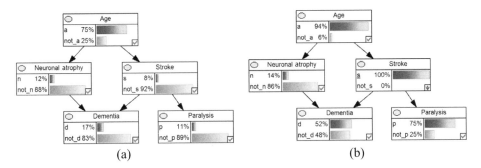

Figure 13.6 Exact inference on the risk of dementia example. (a) Prior distributions $p(X_i)$ are shown as bar charts, for each node X_i. (b) After observing someone who has had a stroke ($S = s$), the distributions are updated as $p(X_i|s)$. For the color version, please refer to the plate section.

The presence of neuronal atrophy ($N = n$), would explain the observed dementia d, which in turn lowers the probability of Stroke being the cause, i.e., $p(s|d,n) = 0.20 < p(s|d) = 0.25$. On the other hand, the presence of stroke makes neuronal atrophy less likely, and neuronal atrophy is explained away: $p(n|d,s) = 0.26 < p(n|d) = 0.33$.

Moreover, we can find the most probable explanation for a patient with paralysis, that is, we solve $\arg\max_{\{A,N,S,D\}} p(A, N, S, D|P = p)$ and get $(a, \neg n, s, \neg d)$, with probability 0.25. That is, paralysis is explained by: being age 65+, having had a stroke, and not having either neuronal atrophy or dementia. The other possible configurations are less likely. Finally, we perform a partial abduction, searching for the (reduced) explanation set (A, S) given the same evidence of paralysis. In other words, we solve $\arg\max_{\{A,S\}} p(A, S|P = p)$ and get the configuration (a, s), with probability 0.53. This tells us that paralysis is (partially) explained by being age 65+ and having had a stroke. ∎

13.2.2 Exact Inference

13.2.2.1 The Brute-Force Approach

Computing any probability is conceptually simple because by definition

$$p(X_i|\mathbf{E} = \mathbf{e}) = \frac{p(X_i, \mathbf{e})}{p(\mathbf{e})} \propto \sum_{\mathbf{U}} p(X_i, \mathbf{e}, \mathbf{U}). \qquad (13.9)$$

This is the **brute-force approach**. Each instantiation of $p(X_i, \mathbf{e})$ is a probability $p(x_i, \mathbf{e})$, which can be computed by summing out all entries $p(x_i, \mathbf{e}, \mathbf{u}) = p(\mathbf{x})$ in the JPD corresponding to assignments consistent with $(x_i, \mathbf{e})$. The JPD then is given by factorization (13.3) which uses the information provided by the BN, the conditional probabilities of each node given its parents. Using the JPD we can respond to all possible inference queries by marginalization (summing out over irrelevant variables $\mathbf{U}$). However, exhaustively summing out entries in the JPD is not the best way to proceed because it leads to the exponential blow up of the JPD that the BN aimed to avoid.

The problem of **exact inference** in graphical models is NP-hard (Cooper, 1990). This means that in the worst case, it probably takes exponential time. Fortunately, we are generally concerned with cases found in real practice and not with the worst case. Many cases can be tackled very efficiently using the algorithms shown below, which are designed to cut down the possibly exponential time taken. The key issue is how to exploit the factorization encoded by the BN without having to generate the full JPD.

A first idea is to use its factorization for efficient marginalization. When summing (marginalizing) out irrelevant terms, the distributive law can be used to try to "push sums in" as far as possible, performing summations over the product of only a subset of factors.

Example. Risk of Dementia (Inference with Brute Force). Suppose that we are interested in the probability distribution of Dementia, $p(D)$. We have

$$p(D) = \sum_{A,N,S,P} p(A,N,S,P,D)$$

$$= \sum_{A,N,S,P} p(A)p(N|A)p(S|A)p(D|N,S)p(P|S)$$

$$= \sum_A p(A) \sum_N p(N|A) \sum_S p(S|A)p(D|N,S) \sum_P p(P|S).$$

Note that with $p(D)$ notation, we compute sets of values rather than single values (the whole distribution, with $p(d)$ and $p(\neg d)$). The first line corresponds to the brute-force approach. This requires building a table with 32 entries, one for each configuration of (A,N,S,P,D). Each entry requires four multiplications. This amounts to computing $32 \cdot 4 = 128$ multiplications. Also 16 additions are required to yield $p(d)$ and 16 for $p(\neg d)$.

Note, however, that certain terms are repeated in the expression. Computations can then be arranged more efficiently, with common terms only computed once and used multiple times. This is the basis of the distributive law, shown in the second line. We define function $g_1(S) = \sum_P p(P|S)$, which requires 2 additions. Then we define $g_2(A,N,D) = \sum_S p(S|A)p(D|N,S)g_1(S)$, which requires 16 multiplications and 8 additions. Function $g_3(A,D) = \sum_N p(N|A)g_2(A,N,D)$ comes next, requiring 8 multiplications and 4 additions. Finally, $\sum_A p(A)g_3(A,D)$ yields the final result, requiring 4 multiplications and 2 additions. The biggest table has 16 entries (when computing $g_2(A,N,D)$). The total number is 28 multiplications and 16 additions, fewer than are required by the brute-force approach. Therefore,

$$p(D) = \sum_A p(A) \sum_N p(N|A) \sum_S p(S|A)p(D|N,S)g_1(S)$$

$$= \sum_A p(A) \sum_N p(N|A)g_2(A,N,D)$$

$$= \sum_A p(A)g_3(A,D).$$

Observe that $g_1(S) \equiv 1$, $g_2(a,n,d) = 0.456$, $g_2(a,\neg n,d) = 0.135$, $g_2(\neg a,n,d) = 0.411$, $g_2(\neg a, \neg n, d) = 0.107$, $g_3(a,d) = 0.183$, and $g_3(\neg a,d) = 0.116$. This yields $p(d) = 0.17$ and similarly $p(\neg d) = 0.83$ (Figure 13.6(a)).   ■

13.2.2.2 Variable Elimination Algorithm

Note that all the functions that contain an unobserved variable in the above expression are multiplied before marginalizing out the variable. The innermost sums create new terms that need to be summed over. These ideas are the basis of the **variable elimination algorithm** (Zhang and Poole, 1994), see Algorithm 13.1. The local distributions of the BN are viewed as functions, also called **potentials**, which are manipulated. Thus, $p(N|A)$ is a function $f_N(N,A)$, and, generally, $p(X_i|\mathbf{Pa}(X_i)) = f_i(X_i,\mathbf{Pa}(X_i))$. The key step is the sum-product g_k in line 5, where the summation on X_k is done after taking the product of all functions involving X_k. This generates a new function which is added to our list of functions to be dealt with (line 6). Because functions rather than probability distributions are used, a normalization may be required to get a distribution at the end (line 8).

Algorithm 13.1: Variable elimination algorithm

> **Input** : A BN over $\mathbf{X} = (X_1, \dots, X_n)$, one target variable X_i, evidence $\mathbf{e}$, and a list $\mathcal{T} = \{f_1, \dots, f_n\}$ containing all the probability functions in the BN
> **Output:** $p(X_i|\mathbf{e})$

1 Select an elimination ordering σ containing all the variables but X_i
2 **for** $k = 1$ *to* $n - 1$ *in* σ **do**
3   Let $\mathcal{F}_k$ be the set of functions in $\mathcal{T}$ that involve X_k
4   Delete $\mathcal{F}_k$ from $\mathcal{L}$
5   Compute $g_k = \sum_{X_k} \prod_{f \in \mathcal{F}_k} f$
6   Add g_k to $\mathcal{T}$
7 **endfor**
8 Multiply all the functions in $\mathcal{T}$ to get a single function and normalize this function

---

The summation ordering σ (line 1) in the dementia example was *P-S-N-A* and could have been any other, achieving the same result but possibly at a different computational cost. Finding the optimal (minimum cost) elimination ordering is an NP-hard problem (Bertelè and Brioschi, 1972), and many heuristics have been proposed to find good orderings. Note that it is the size of the factors created by algorithms that dominates the computational cost of the algorithm. This grows exponentially according to the number of factor variables. Thus, a good heuristic is to choose a variable that minimizes the size of the factor that will be added to the graph.

The above example does not contain any evidence. To deal with evidence and get $p(X_i|\mathbf{e})$, we can compute the non-normalized distribution $p(X_i,\mathbf{e})$ by applying the variable elimination algorithm to the list of functions instantiated by $\mathbf{E} = \mathbf{e}$ and eliminating the variables different from X_i and $\mathbf{E}$. Then we can compute the conditional probability as in Equation (13.9) by renormalizing by $p(\mathbf{e})$. Thus, if X_i is binary, $p(x_i|\mathbf{e}) = \frac{p(x_i,\mathbf{e})}{p(x_i,\mathbf{e}) + p(\neg x_i,\mathbf{e})}$, where these probabilities are all in $p(X_i,\mathbf{e})$, yielded by the variable elimination algorithm.

Example. Risk of Dementia (Inference with Variable Elimination). Suppose that we are interested in the probability of Stroke for a patient not suffering from dementia, $p(S|\neg d)$. Initially, $\mathcal{T}$ contains all local distributions given in the BN instantiated by $D = \neg d$:

$$\mathcal{T} = \{f_A(A), f_N(N,A), f_S(S,A), f_P(P,S), f_D(\neg d, S, N)\}.$$

Let us take the ordering P-A-N. First, we eliminate P by computing $\sum_P f_P(P,S) \equiv 1$. The new list does not contain $f_P(P,S)$. Second, we eliminate A by computing

$$\sum_A f_A(A) f_N(N,A) f_S(S,A) = g_1(N,S),$$

which yields $g_1(n,s) = 0.0114, g_1(\neg n,s) = 0.0686, g_1(n,\neg s) = 0.1086, g_1(\neg n,\neg s) = 0.8114$. Now the list is $\mathcal{T} = \{g_1(N,S), f_D(\neg d,S,N)\}$. Finally, we eliminate N by computing

$$\sum_N f_D(\neg d,S,N) g_1(N,S) = g_2(S),$$

with $g_2(s) = 0.0382, g_2(\neg s) = 0.7954$. Now $\mathcal{T} = \{g_2(S)\}$. $g_2(S)$ is $p(\neg d,S)$. To get $p(S|\neg d)$, a normalization is needed: $p(s|\neg d) = \frac{0.0382}{0.0382+0.7954} = 0.0458$ and $p(\neg s|\neg d) = \frac{0.7954}{0.0382+0.7954} = 0.9542$.

Written more compactly, the expression computed by the algorithm is

$$p(S|\neg d) \propto \sum_N p(\neg d|N,S) \sum_A p(N|A) p(S|A) p(A) \sum_P p(P|S).$$

■

13.2.2.3 Message Passing Algorithm

It is clear that the variable elimination algorithm can be computationally much more efficient than generating the entire JPD. The main idea is that by factorizing the JPD, we can perform local computations on the necessary factors. We now present an alternative implementation of this idea known as the **message passing algorithm**. The message passing algorithm has a more global data structure for scheduling factor manipulation that has major computational benefits.

Let us first consider the simplest case when the BN is a **polytree**, that is, a DAG with no loops (cycles in the undirected graph). These BNs are also called **singly connected BNs** because there is at most only one undirected path between any pair of nodes. Note that the dementia example is not singly connected because, e.g., nodes D and A are linked with two paths: D-N-A and D-S-A. In polytrees, we can select any node as a root node to orient the graph and follow the links down to the leaves. Any non-root node that is connected to only one other node is called a leaf. The message passing algorithm operates by passing messages among the nodes of the network. A node acts as an autonomous processor that collects the incoming messages (factors) from its neighboring nodes, performs some multiplications and additions, and sends results as an outgoing message to its neighboring nodes. Specifically, the query node is selected as the root node, and all messages flow "upward" from the leaves to the root along the (unique) path toward the root. The process terminates when the root has received messages from all its adjoining nodes.

If f_j with domain $\mathbf{dom}_j = \{X_j, \mathbf{Pa}(X_j)\}$ is the potential associated with X_j, that is, $p(X_j|\mathbf{Pa}(X_j)) = f_j(X_j, \mathbf{Pa}(X_j))$, a **message** $M^{j \rightarrow k}$ from node X_j to node X_k is defined over $\mathbf{dom}_j \cap \mathbf{dom}_k$ and is given by

$$M^{j \rightarrow k} = \sum_{\mathbf{dom}_j \backslash \mathbf{dom}_j \cap \mathbf{dom}_k} f_j \prod_{l \in (\mathrm{Nb}_j \backslash \{k\})} M^{l \rightarrow j},$$

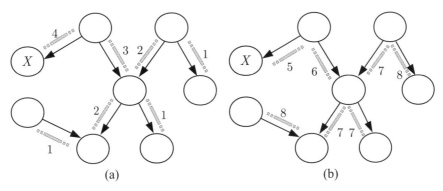

Figure 13.7 Two rounds of message passing, with X as root. (a) Collect evidence: first round where messages are passed upward from the leaves to the root. (b) Distribute evidence: second round where messages are passed downward from the root to the leaves. All posterior distributions at each node are output by the end of the second round. Note that some computations can start simultaneously and run parallely.

where Nb_j is the set of indexes of nodes that are neighbors (parents and children) of X_j. Any node gets all its incoming messages from its downstream neighbors before it sends its outgoing message toward its upstream neighbor. At the root we perform the final computation, multiplying all received messages by its own potential:

$$p(X_i|\mathbf{e}) = \text{normalize}\left(\sum_{\mathbf{X}\setminus\{X_i,\mathbf{E}\}} f_i \prod_{l\in\text{Nb}_i} M^{l\to i}\right). \qquad (13.10)$$

Computations (messages) can be stored and reused. Indeed, by scheduling variable elimination in this manner, we can compute the posterior distributions of all variables in twice the time it takes to compute the posterior distribution of a single variable. Thus, we can use two rounds of messages rather than repeating the message passing algorithm for each variable acting as a root node, to get $p(X_i|\mathbf{e})$ for all unobserved variables X_i at once as follows. Any node is designated as root to initialize the procedure. In the first round, messages are passed upward from the leaves to the root as explained above (Figure 13.7(a)). This step is called "collect evidence." Then a second round of messages are passed downward from the root to the leaves, a step called "distribute evidence" (Figure 13.7(b)). The process is completed when all leaves have received their messages. The posterior distribution at each node is then computed as in Equation (13.10), using the incoming messages. The complexity of this message passing algorithm is linear in the size of CPTs in the BN; so the cost of the algorithm grows exponentially with the number of parents of a node.

Polytrees received a lot of attention in the early days of BNs because the first widely known inference algorithm was Pearl's message passing algorithm for simple trees (Pearl, 1982), later extended to polytrees (Kim and Pearl, 1983). This procedure does not work for (the more general) **multiply-connected BNs**. Due to the presence of loops, messages cycle indefinitely. However, we can still use variable elimination implemented via message passing in an auxiliary structure other than the original BN. This structure is called **junction tree**, **clique tree**, or **join tree**, and the respective algorithm is the **junction tree algorithm** (Lauritzen and Spiegelhalter, 1988; Shafer and Shenoy, 1990; Shenoy and Shafer, 1990).

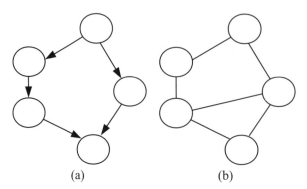

(a)   (b)

Figure 13.8 (a) A multiply-connected BN. (b) Its moral graph, where a new edge has been added to marry two parents with a common child, and the arc directions have been dropped.

A junction tree may have complex nodes formed by several merged or clustered variables avoiding the multiple paths between two nodes. A standard message passing algorithm is then run over the junction tree. Therefore, as a message passing algorithm, junction tree propagation is based on the same principle as the variable elimination algorithm but with a sophisticated strategy for caching computations, whereby multiple executions of variable elimination can be performed much more efficiently than simply performing each one separately.

The following three steps are necessary before running the message passing algorithm over multiply-connected BNs:

1. Moralize the BN and output the moral graph.
2. Triangulate the moral graph and output the cliques (nodes of the junction tree).
3. Create the junction tree and assign initial potentials to each clique.

In the first step we need to moralize the BN. Moralize the BN means connecting ("marrying") all parents with a common child. The undirected graph output after dropping arc directions is the **moral graph**, see Figure 13.8. Moralization was also used in the u-separation criterion (Section 13.1.2).

In the second step the moral graph must be triangulated. An undirected graph is a **triangulated graph** or **chordal graph** if all cycles of four or more vertices have a "shortcut" or chord, which is an edge that is not part of the cycle but connects two vertices of the cycle, that is, every minimal loop in the graph is of length three. Polytrees are always triangulated graphs. There are graph triangulation methods. The basic technique repeatedly eliminates nodes following an elimination ordering. Eliminating node X means: (1) adding edges so that all nodes adjacent to X become pairwise adjacent (if they are not), and (2) deleting node X and its adjacent edges. The added edges are called **fill-in edges**. If an elimination ordering does not lead to any fill-in edges, we say that this is a **perfect elimination ordering**. A graph is chordal if and only if it has a perfect elimination ordering. Figure 13.9 shows an example of the triangulation process applied to the graph of Figure 13.8(b). Only one fill-in edge has been added.

The addition of edges can lead to the loss of independence information implied by the graph structure, and hence an optimal triangulation should yield the fewest fill-in edges. This is an NP-hard problem (Arnborg et al., 1987). Lots of approaches, most of which are based on heuristics, have been proposed to find good triangulations (Tarjan

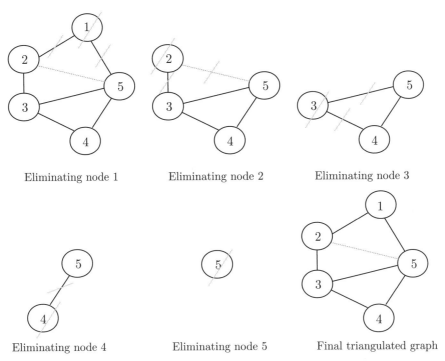

Figure 13.9 Steps to triangulate the graph illustrated in Figure 13.8(b). The triangulated graph using the illustrated elimination ordering required one fill-in edge (dashed gray line). Nodes and edges to be deleted are marked with gray lines.

and Yannakakis, 1984; Kjærulff, 1992; Larrañaga et al., 1997; Gámez and Puerta, 2002; Flores and Gámez, 2003; Romero and Larrañaga, 2009; Ottosen and Vomlel, 2012; Li and Ueno, 2017; see a review in Flores and Gámez, 2007). For example, each of the variables remaining in the network is greedily evaluated for elimination next based on some cost function: eliminate the node having the smallest number of neighbors, eliminate the node requiring the smallest number of fill-in edges to be added, etc. Figure 13.10 shows a worse triangulation than Figure 13.9 because three instead of one fill-in edges have been added.

Suppose that we have a subgraph over a set of vertices $\mathbf{C}$ that is complete (all nodes are pairwise linked) and maximal (it is not a subset of another complete set). Then $\mathbf{C}$ is called a **clique**. The term clique may also directly refer to the subgraph. A clique j is a node in the junction tree, associated with a subset of variables $\mathbf{C}_j \subseteq \{X_1, \ldots, X_n\}$. Cliques can be retrieved from the fill-in process because, when eliminating a node X, edges are added to make the subgraph given by X and its neighbors complete. For example, we derive from Figure 13.9 that the cliques are $\mathbf{C}_1 = \{X_1, X_2, X_5\}, \mathbf{C}_2 = \{X_2, X_3, X_5\}$, and $\mathbf{C}_3 = \{X_3, X_4, X_5\}$. The set $\{X_4, X_5\}$ is not a clique because it is not maximal; it is in fact part of $\{X_3, X_4, X_5\}$, a larger clique. Likewise, there are only two cliques in Figure 13.10: $\mathbf{C}_1 = \{X_1, X_2, X_4, X_5\}$ and $\mathbf{C}_2 = \{X_2, X_3, X_4, X_5\}$.

In the last step a (junction) tree satisfying the **running intersection property** is then built. This property states that given two nodes $\mathbf{C}_j$ and $\mathbf{C}_k$ then all nodes included in the path between $\mathbf{C}_j$ and $\mathbf{C}_k$ must contain $\mathbf{C}_j \cap \mathbf{C}_k$. A **separator** $\mathbf{S}_{jk}$ of two adjacent cliques $\mathbf{C}_j$ and $\mathbf{C}_k$ is its intersection, i.e., $\mathbf{C}_j \cap \mathbf{C}_k = \mathbf{S}_{jk}$. An MWST algorithm (Section 8.4.1.4), where the weight for the edge between cliques $\mathbf{C}_j$ and $\mathbf{C}_k$ is equal to the number of variables in $\mathbf{S}_{jk}$ (i.e., the cliques are tree-wise arranged trying to link them to create bigger separators),

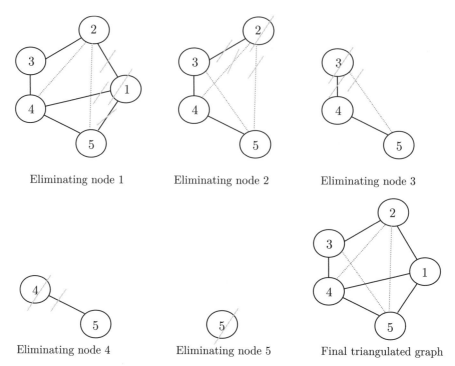

Figure 13.10 Steps to triangulate the graph shown in Figure 13.8(b) with different elimination ordering than in Figure 13.9, this time requiring three instead of one fill-in edges (dashed gray lines). Nodes and edges to be deleted are marked with gray lines.

is an efficient approach for building the junction tree. The junction trees formed with the cliques inferred from Figure 13.9 and Figure 13.10 are shown in Figure 13.11(a) and (b), respectively.

The potential ψ_j assigned to each clique $\mathbf{C}_j$ must be identified in the new structure. Each potential in the BN is attached to a clique that contains its domain. Whenever there is more than one potential attached to the same clique, the potential at this clique is the product of these potentials. If a clique has no attached potential, we attach the constant function 1. Consequently, the product of all the potentials in the junction tree is the product of all the potentials in the original BN (same information but different representation).

Again we can send all messages in the junction tree toward a root clique containing the query variable or perform a full propagation with two passes, upward and downward, to compute the posterior distributions of multiple (all) query variables at once.

A message $M^{j \to k}$ from clique $\mathbf{C}_j$ to clique $\mathbf{C}_k$ is defined over $\mathbf{S}_{jk}$ as

$$M^{j \to k} = \sum_{\mathbf{C}_j \setminus \mathbf{S}_{jk}} \psi_j \prod_{l \in (\mathrm{Nb}_j \setminus \{k\})} M^{l \to j},$$

and when the message passing ends each clique $\mathbf{C}_i$ contains

$$p(\mathbf{C}_i, \mathbf{e}) = \psi_i \prod_{l \in \mathrm{Nb}_i} M^{l \to i}. \tag{13.11}$$

Note that the junction tree is an alternative representation of the JPD that directly reveals the clique marginals. Then we can compute the marginal (unnormalized) distribution over a particular variable X by selecting a clique containing X and summing out the other

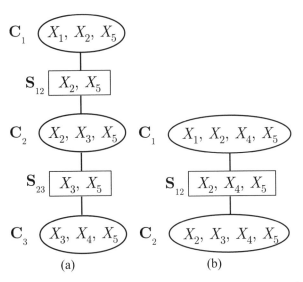

Figure 13.11 Two junction trees of the BN in Figure 13.8: (a) derived from the cliques yielded by the triangulation shown in Figure 13.9; (b) derived from the cliques yielded by the triangulation illustrated in Figure 13.10. Separators are shown as boxes.

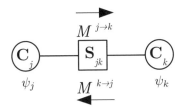

Figure 13.12 Schema of message passing between clique $\mathbf{C}_j$ and clique $\mathbf{C}_k$. As separators are shown as boxes at the junction tree, and messages are defined on separators, messages can be envisaged as being stored at these boxes.

variables in the clique. Figure 13.12 shows the main elements in message passing between two generic cliques.

The cost of this message passing algorithm is exponential in the size of the largest clique or equivalently in the **treewidth**[3] of the network, which then depends strongly on how the triangulation is performed. There is a misconception that inference is tractable in polytrees and NP-hard in other BNs. However, it depends on the treewidth of the polytree. In polytrees with bounded indegree, probabilistic inference can be done in polynomial time with e.g., the message passing algorithm because the polytree treewidth is determined by the maximum number of parents (maximum indegree). This is why many learning algorithms force all variables to have a limited number of parents.

Essentially variable elimination and junction tree algorithms have the same computational complexity. In practice, however, they offer different trade-offs. Junction trees provide answers to multiple queries, at the expense, however, of increasing the space required to store all intermediate messages, which variable elimination does away with.

---

[3] The treewidth of a graph is the size of the largest clique in the chordal graph that contains the graph with the smallest clique number, minus one.

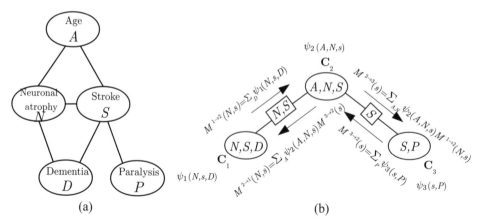

Figure 13.13 (a) Moral graph for the risk of dementia example. (b) Its junction tree and the message passing procedure. The evidence is $S = s$.

Example. Risk of Dementia (Inference with Message Passing). Let us illustrate the message passing algorithm for the risk of dementia example. Our patient has had a stroke, and the evidence is $\mathbf{E} = S = s$. To propagate this evidence and get $p(X_i|s)$ for any X_i different from the evidence (i.e., X_i is A, N, D or P), the first step is to output the moral graph because this BN is multiply connected. The moral graph is built by linking nodes N and S, which are both parents of D, and removing arc directions, see Figure 13.13(a).

The moral graph is already triangulated in this particular case. Three cliques are identified: $\mathbf{C}_1 = \{N, S, D\}, \mathbf{C}_2 = \{A, N, S\}$, and $\mathbf{C}_3 = \{S, P\}$. They will be the nodes of the junction tree. To assign a potential ψ_1 to $\mathbf{C}_1$, we set $\psi_1(N, s, D) = p(D|N, s)$ because this is the potential in the BN whose domain is included in $\mathbf{C}_1$. Similarly, $\psi_2(A, N, s) = p(N|A)p(s|A)p(A)$ and $\psi_3(s, P) = p(P|s)$ are attached to $\mathbf{C}_2$ and $\mathbf{C}_3$, respectively. Figure 13.13(b) shows a junction tree including separators and messages. Note that the running intersection property holds.

In Figure 13.13(b) the root node is set as $\mathbf{C}_1$. The upward pass includes messages $M^{1\to2}$ and $M^{2\to3}$. The downward pass includes messages $M^{3\to2}$ and $M^{2\to1}$. The application of Equation (13.11) then yields

$$p(\mathbf{C}_1, e) = p(N, s, D) = \psi_1(N, s, D)M^{2\to1}(N, s)$$
$$p(\mathbf{C}_2, e) = p(A, N, s) = \psi_2(A, N, s)M^{1\to2}(N, s)M^{3\to2}(s)$$
$$p(\mathbf{C}_3, e) = p(s, P) = \psi_3(s, P)M^{2\to3}(s).$$

Note that S is always instantiated as evidence s. Now we can compute $p(D|s)$ and $p(N|s)$ from $p(N, s, D)$ in the first clique, $p(A|s)$ from $p(A, N, s)$ in the second clique, and $p(P|s)$ from $p(s, P)$ in the third clique (in fact, $p(P|s)$ is already given in the BN). The results are shown in Figure 13.6(b).

For instance, the computation of $p(D|s)$ is

$$p(D|s) = \frac{\sum_N p(N, s, D)}{\sum_{N,D} p(N, s, D)},$$

which is 0.52 for d and 0.48 for $\neg d$.   ∎

13.2.2.4 Exact Inference in Gaussian Bayesian Networks

In Gaussian BNs, inference is easy because any conditional and marginal distribution is still Gaussian, and the updated parameters, mean and variance, have closed formulas (Lauritzen and Jensen, 2001; Cowell, 2005). Thus, the parameters of the density function $f(x_i|\mathbf{e})$ are all derived from Equation (13.5), as

$$\text{mean} = \mu_i + \mathbf{\Sigma}_{X_i\mathbf{E}} \mathbf{\Sigma}_{\mathbf{EE}}^{-1}(\mathbf{e} - \boldsymbol{\mu}_\mathbf{E})$$
$$\text{variance} = v_i - \mathbf{\Sigma}_{X_i\mathbf{E}} \mathbf{\Sigma}_{\mathbf{EE}}^{-1} \mathbf{\Sigma}_{X_i\mathbf{E}}^T,$$

where $\mathbf{\Sigma}_{X_i\mathbf{E}}$ is the vector with the covariances of X_i, and each variable in $\mathbf{E}$, $\mathbf{\Sigma}_{\mathbf{EE}}$ is the covariance matrix of $\mathbf{E}$, and $\boldsymbol{\mu}_\mathbf{E}$ is the unconditional mean of $\mathbf{E}$. These formulas are easily generalizable to a subset of variables rather than only one in X_i (see Section 3.4.4).

Note that we are generating the JPD (Equation (13.5)). Unlike the case of discrete distributions, the representation size of this JPD is quadratic rather than exponential with respect to the number of variables. For networks with thousands of variables, a quadratic cost might be not feasible. This is why message passing algorithms have been adapted within this context to perform more local computations. Inference in Gaussian BNs is linear with respect to the number of cliques and at most cubic with respect to the size of the largest clique (Koller and Friedman, 2009, p. 612).

Marginalization obviously requires integration rather than summation. This can cause problems (infinite, ill-defined, or non-closed-form integrals) for general continuous distributions. Unlike Gaussian distributions, choosing $p(X_i|\mathbf{Pa}(X_i))$ from the same parametric family will not necessarily lead to be still within that family when multiplying factors or marginalizing a factor. Thus it is not clear how to represent the intermediate results in the inference process. This is even more complex if $p(X_i|\mathbf{Pa}(X_i))$ is chosen from different parametric families. In some cases, most notably in hybrid networks with discrete and continuous variables, the intermediate factors cannot be represented using any fixed number of parameters; this number grows exponentially with the size of the network.

These limitations make it very hard to design variable elimination or message passing algorithms in such general models. Besides, structures that may be tractable in the discrete case (such as polytrees) become intractable (NP-hard inference problems) in general hybrid networks (Lerner and Parr, 2001). Lauritzen (1992) and Lauritzen and Jensen (2001) proposed the algorithm that is commonly used for CLG models. This is an extension of the standard clique tree algorithm. In general BNs with nonparametric density estimation techniques, inference has been performed on networks with a small number of nodes only (Cobb and Shenoy, 2006; Cobb et al., 2006; Rumí and Salmerón, 2007; Shenoy and West, 2011). Approximate inference methods (see next section) are the only available approach in such cases.

13.2.3 Approximate Inference

As mentioned above, exact inference is tractable for many real-world models. However, it is limited by its worst-case exponential performance, and many models are simply too complex for exact inference. In such cases approximate inference is the only alternative that will produce any result at all. Approximate inference methods trade off the accuracy of the results against the capability to deal with more complex models. Like exact inference, approximate inference is also NP-hard in general BNs (Dagum and Luby, 1993).

Many stochastic simulation techniques are based on Monte Carlo methods, where we use the network to generate a large number of cases (full instantiations) from the JPD, and then estimate the probability by counting observed frequencies in the samples. By the law of large numbers (Section 4.1.2.1), the estimate converges to the exact probability as more cases are generated.

Consider that our aim is to estimate the probability $p(\mathbf{Y} = \mathbf{y}|\mathbf{e})$ for any $\mathbf{Y}$, a random vector of variables in $\{X_1, \ldots, X_n\}$. A well-known method is **probabilistic logic sampling** (Henrion, 1988). Given an ancestral node ordering, we sample a node X after sampling from all its parents $\mathbf{Pa}(X)$ that results in a fixed value $\mathbf{pa}(X)$ (forward sampling scheme). Sampling from such a discrete distribution $p(X|\mathbf{pa}(X))$ is straightforward, whereas complex but efficient methods exist (Section 3.5) for continuous distributions $f(X|\mathbf{pa}(X))$. Yet, with Gaussian BNs, conditionals and marginals are still Gaussian, and the procedure is straightforward.

Having sampled from all nodes, we have a sample from $p(\mathbf{X})$, the joint probability distribution. Then we repeat the process a great many times M. Hence $p(\mathbf{y}|\mathbf{e})$ is estimated as the fraction of samples where we have seen $(\mathbf{y}, \mathbf{e})$, relative not to M but to the number of samples where we have seen $\mathbf{e}$. Equivalently, because $p(\mathbf{y}|\mathbf{e}) = \frac{p(\mathbf{y}, \mathbf{e})}{p(\mathbf{e})}$, the estimation of the numerator is the fraction of samples (out of M) where we have seen $(\mathbf{y}, \mathbf{e})$ and for the denominator the fraction of samples (out of M) where we have seen $\mathbf{e}$. Note that the samples can be reused to estimate any other probability.

In Gaussian BNs, sampling directly from the JPD is easy, using, e.g., a decomposition of $\boldsymbol{\Sigma}$, like Cholesky's (see a specific procedure in Section 3.5.7).

Samples not compatible with the evidence $\mathbf{e}$ are rejected and not considered. This simulation process is very wasteful if the number of unrejected samples is small. The expected number of unrejected samples is $Mp(\mathbf{e})$. Thus, if $\mathbf{e}$ is very unlikely, say $p(\mathbf{e}) = 0.001$, then we expect only 10 unrejected samples even for $M = 10,000$ samples. Evidence probability is very often low, for example, any set of symptoms in medical diagnosis. Generally, when $\mathbf{E}$ includes k variables, $p(\mathbf{e})$ decreases exponentially with k.

The **likelihood weighting** method addresses this problem (Shachter and Peot, 1989; Fung and Chang, 1990). This method forces the samples to take the observed values at variables in $\mathbf{E}$. That is, we do not sample from nodes in $\mathbf{E}$ and simply set them to their observed values. The other variables are generated according to probabilistic logic sampling. However this simple approach can fail. Thus, if we use this process to approximate $p(X_i|s)$ for the risk of dementia example, the expected number of samples where $A = a$ is 75%, as in the prior distribution (Figure 13.6(a)), whereas, $p(a|s) = 0.94$ (Figure 13.6(b)), that is, it is higher when we observe $S = s$.

The process has to account for the fact that 10% of the samples with $A = a$ would have generated $S = s$, whereas only 2% of the samples with $A = \neg a$ would have generated $S = s$. Therefore, in a single sample capturing this long-term behavior $A = a$ where $S = s$ should be worth 10% of the sample, whereas $A = \neg a$ where $S = s$ should be worth only 2% of the sample. In other words, for each sample, we have to consider the probability of each instantiated node, if used in standard forward sampling, resulting in its observed values. This probability is the likelihood of each piece of evidence given the sampled node values. It is used to increment (weigh) the count of each sample. If the evidence involves several nodes, the weight of each sample will be the product of the weights induced

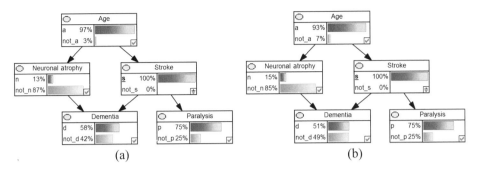

Figure 13.14 Approximate inference for the risk of dementia example. Updated approximate distributions $p(X_i|s)$ after observing someone who has had a stroke ($S = s$): (a) using probabilistic logic sampling with $M = 1,000$ samples; (b) using likelihood weighting with $M = 1,000$ samples. For the color version, please refer to the plate section.

by each evidence node separately because the samples for each node are independent in forward sampling. Formally, given the observed values $\mathbf{e} = (e_1, \ldots, e_l)$ at variables $\mathbf{E} = (E_1, \ldots, E_l)$, we assign to a sample a weight w given by

$$w = \prod_{j=1}^{l} p(E_j = e_j | \mathbf{pa}(E_j)),$$

where $\mathbf{pa}(E_j)$ is the assignment to $\mathbf{Pa}(E_j)$ in probabilistic logic sampling. The estimated probability distribution $p(X_i|\mathbf{e})$ is output by normalizing after all samples have been generated. Note that probabilistic logic sampling is a particular case of likelihood weighting where $w = 1$ for all samples consistent with $\mathbf{e}$, and $w = 0$ otherwise.

Example. Risk of Dementia (Approximate Inference with Probabilistic Logic Sampling and Likelihood Weighting). Once again we have evidence that the patient has had a stroke, i.e., $\mathbf{E} = S = s$. First we use probabilistic logic sampling with $M = 1,000$ samples to approximate distributions $p(X_i|s)$.

To generate a sample, we would first simulate from $p(A)$ (which has a 0.75 probability of taking the value a, see Figure 13.1). Suppose that this results in a. Now we simulate from $p(N|a)$ (which has a 0.15 probability of taking the value n, see Figure 13.1) and yields $\neg n$. Then we simulate from $p(S|a)$, and $\neg s$ is the result. Next we generate from $p(D|\neg n, \neg s)$, which has a 0.10 probability of taking the value d, producing d. Finally, by simulating from $p(P|\neg s)$, $\neg p$ is returned. Therefore, the generated sample is $(a, \neg n, \neg s, d, \neg p)$ for (A, N, S, D, P). By repeating the process 1,000 times, the probabilities $p(X_i|s)$ are estimated by their relative frequencies, see Figure 13.14(a). Compare the numbers with Figure 13.6(b), computed by means of exact inference.

The probability of the evidence is low because $p(s) = 0.08$ (Figure 13.6(a)). Therefore many samples will be rejected when computing frequencies for estimating $p(X_i|s)$.

The likelihood weighting algorithm aims to improve the efficiency of probabilistic logic sampling, and node S will not be sampled. To understand how a sample is generated by this method, we start by simulating from A and then N as before (suppose we get a and $\neg n$). Now S is fixed as s, and we record $w = p(s|a) = 0.10$ as the weight. We then simulate from $p(D|\neg n, s)$ and $p(P|s)$ (note that $\neg s$ is not possible any more), giving $\neg d$

and p, respectively. Then the sample is $(a, \neg n, s, \neg d, p)$ with weight 0.10. Let us repeat the process, supposing that the next two samples are $(\neg a, \neg n, s, \neg d, \neg p)$ and $(a, n, s, d, \neg p)$, with weights $w = p(s|\neg a) = 0.02$ and $w = p(s|a) = 0.10$, respectively. Hence from these three samples, $p(d|s) \approx \frac{0.10}{0.10+0.02+0.10} = 0.45$, and $p(a|s) \approx \frac{0.20}{0.22} = 0.91$, which are still far from the exact values of 0.52 and 0.94, respectively (Figure 13.6(a)). If the number of samples M is increased, the estimations should be more accurate.   ∎

Other techniques are **Gibbs sampling** (Pearl, 1987) and, more generally, MCMC methods. MCMC methods build a Markov chain, which generates samples from a distribution arbitrarily close to the posterior target distribution of the inference, $p(\mathbf{Y}|\mathbf{e})$, when it converges (to its stationary distribution). In Gibbs sampling, we generate samples from the distribution of each individual X_i conditioned on all our current values for all other variables at each step. This distribution of X_i conditioned on all other variables is available in BNs for efficient generation because it only involves the potentials that contain X_i. Thus, for each unobserved variable X_i, we will sample from the **full conditional** for variable X_i, where it holds that

$$p(X_i|\mathbf{X}_{-i}) \propto p(X_i|\mathbf{Pa}(X_i)) \prod_{X_j \in \mathrm{Ch}(X_i)} p(X_j|\mathbf{Pa}(X_j)), \tag{13.12}$$

where $\mathrm{Ch}(X_i)$ denotes X_i children and $\mathbf{X}_{-i}$ includes all variables different from X_i. We first use evidence variables $\mathbf{E}$ to instantiate all potentials for the observations $\mathbf{e}$. Therefore, these variables are not sampled.

Example. Risk of Dementia (Approximate Inference with Gibbs Sampling). Again our target distribution is $p(X_i|s)$. After instantiation, the potentials are

$$p(A), p(s|A), p(N|A), p(D|N,s), p(P|s).$$

We can sample efficiently if we start from A given all other variables because

$$p(A|N,D,P,s) = \frac{p(A)p(s|A)p(N|A)p(D|N,s)p(P|s)}{\sum_A p(A)p(s|A)p(N|A)p(D|N,s)p(P|s)}$$
$$= \frac{p(A)p(s|A)p(N|A)}{\sum_A p(A)p(s|A)p(N|A)},$$

which is Equation (13.12). Note that we only use the potentials involving A. To start simulating from this distribution, it needs to be initialized by fixing arbitrary values for N and D. Let $n^{(0)}, d^{(0)}$ denote these values. All other distributions $p(X_i|\mathbf{X}_{-i})$ can be output similarly. Then the complete Gibbs sampling procedure is

1. Fix arbitrary $N = n^{(0)}, D = d^{(0)}$. Do $j = 1$.
2. Until convergence is judged

   Generate $A = a^{(j)} \sim p(A|N,D,P,s) = \alpha_1 p(A)p(s|A)p\left(n^{(j-1)}|A\right)$

   Generate $N = n^{(j)} \sim p(N|A,D,P,s) = \alpha_2 p\left(N|a^{(j)}\right)p\left(d^{(j-1)}|N,s\right)$

   Generate $D = d^{(j)} \sim p(D|A,N,P,s) = \alpha_3 p\left(D|n^{(j)},s\right)$

   Generate $P = p^{(j)} \sim p(P|A,N,D,s) = \alpha_4 p(P|s)$

   $j = j+1$.

Suppose that $n^{(0)} = n, d^{(0)} = d$. Then $p(A = a|N, D, P, s) = \alpha_1 \cdot 0.75 \cdot 0.10 \cdot 0.15 = \alpha_1 \cdot 0.01125$ and, for $A = \neg a$, $\alpha_1 \cdot 0.00015$. Renormalizing, we have $p(A = a|N, D, P, s) = 0.98$. Once $a^{(1)} = \neg a$, we continue to sample from $p(N|A, D, P, s)$ and so on. Note that the distribution for N is conditioned on the new sample value $a^{(1)}$.

The first iteration produces the sample $\left(a^{(1)}, n^{(1)}, d^{(1)}, p^{(1)}\right)$. By repeating this iterative process and discarding the burn-in samples not corresponding to the stationary distribution, we will generate a sample of size M from the distribution $p(A, N, D, P|s)$. Hence $p(A = a|s)$ is approximated as the relative frequency of samples that match $A = a$. The other distributions $p(N|s), p(D|s), p(P|s)$ are likewise approximated. In fact, $p(P|s)$ is, in this case, given in the BN, and it would not need to be approximated. ∎

Note that the sampling step of the Gibbs sampler is easy for discrete graphical models. In continuous models, sampling from $f(X_i|\mathbf{X}_{-i})$ can, depending on the conditional distributions used, be troublesome.

The **MCMC** framework provides a general approach for generating samples from the posterior distribution whenever it is hard to sample directly from the posterior. MCMC sampling mirrors the dynamics of the Markov chain. We move from one state $\mathbf{x}$ to another $\mathbf{x}'$ with a probabilistic transition model. In the particular case of the Gibbs sampler, the chain moves from $\mathbf{x}$ to $\mathbf{x}'$ one coordinate at a time (in the above risk of dementia example, we follow the sequence A-N-D-P to achieve a complete state), and we transition from $(\mathbf{x}_{-i}, x_i)$ to $(\mathbf{x}_{-i}, x'_i)$ with $p(x'_i|\mathbf{x}_{-i})$.

Other chains also guarantee the desired stationary distribution. The **Metropolis–Hastings algorithm** (Metropolis et al., 1953; Madigan and York, 1995; Giudici and Castelo, 2003) generalizes Gibbs sampling. We sample from a proposal distribution. We then accept the proposed transition of X_i or stay at the old state with a probability that corrects for the discrepancy between the proposal and target distributions. If the target distribution is $p(\mathbf{x})$ and the proposal distribution is q with the transition model from $(\mathbf{x}_{-i}, x_i)$ to $(\mathbf{x}_{-i}, x'_i)$ given by $q((\mathbf{x}_{-i}, x'_i)|(\mathbf{x}_{-i}, x_i))$, then the acceptance probability of this movement is

$$\alpha((\mathbf{x}_{-i}, x_i) \rightarrow (\mathbf{x}_{-i}, x'_i)) = \min\left\{1, \frac{p(\mathbf{x}_{-i}, x'_i)\, q((\mathbf{x}_{-i}, x_i)|(\mathbf{x}_{-i}, x'_i))}{p(\mathbf{x}_{-i}, x_i)\, q((\mathbf{x}_{-i}, x'_i)|(\mathbf{x}_{-i}, x_i))}\right\}.$$

These ratios are easy to compute. The proposal distributions q are usually fairly simple. In continuous settings, a common choice is a Gaussian or Student's t distribution centered on the current value x_i, or even a uniform distribution over a finite interval centered on x_i. As for p, we can use the property of Equation (13.4) in BNs and eliminate any variables not in the Markov blanket of X_i from the p probabilities.

The Metropolis–Hastings algorithm is widely used for continuous networks because the products in Equation (13.12) might not have a closed form for sampling purposes.

When these processes converge to a limit, the probability of being in a state should be the same as the probability of transitioning to that state from a randomly sampled state. This equilibrium relative to the transition model characterizes the stationary distribution. In practice, the convergence of the Markov chain, whose stationary distribution is the posterior, must be judged. That is, we must find how many iterations should be performed – the burn-in time – before a sample can be assessed as being (almost) generated from the posterior.

Specifying the burn-in time is by no means straightforward. When it takes the chain a long time to "mix," i.e., to get close to the stationary distribution (as in multimodal posterior distributions), samples generated early in the process will not be representative of the desired stationary distribution. This may be the case with chains where the state space has several well connected regions, but the probability of transitions between regions is low. A common approach is to use heuristics to evaluate when a sample trajectory has mixed. They are used to compute some estimator, e.g., when mixed, the sample mean at different time windows should be similar. Because consecutive samples are correlated resulting in a higher variance of the estimator than for independent samples, the chain is run for many iterations between sample collections to reduce the variance. Another heuristic design idea is that if we use multiple chains starting out in different regions of the space, they should, upon convergence, yield similar estimates.

Unlike forward sampling methods, MCMC methods do not degrade when the probability of the evidence is low or when the posterior is very different from the prior. They are widely applicable to a very general class of networks (including undirected networks, see Chapter 14) and distributions. They are broader spectrum than any other currently available inference method, being applicable to virtually any model. With continuous variables (general nonparametric models) and hybrid networks, there are very few other choices. With these methods, however, parameters have to be manually tuned and many options specified: the proposal distribution, how many chains to run, how the mixing is evaluated, how long a delay there should be between samples to be considered independent, etc.

13.3   Learning Bayesian Networks from Data

As mentioned above, the learning task involves two subtasks: *parametric learning* (Section 13.3.1) and *structure learning* (Section 13.3.2). We start with parameter learning, although this might appear to be counterintuitive, given that it actually requires knowledge of the structure. Formally, a BN to be learned is given as a pair $\mathcal{B} = (\mathcal{G}, \boldsymbol{\theta})$, where $\mathcal{G}$ is its structure (DAG) and $\boldsymbol{\theta}$ are its parameters, i.e., the entries in the CPTs.

13.3.1   Learning Bayesian Network Parameters

Recall that R_i is the cardinality of Ω_{X_i}, the number of possible values of variable X_i. Let $q_i = |\Omega_{\mathbf{Pa}(X_i)}|$ be the number of possible combinations, each denoted $\mathbf{pa}_i^j$, of the values of X_i parents, i.e., $\Omega_{\mathbf{Pa}(X_i)} = \{\mathbf{pa}_i^1, \dots, \mathbf{pa}_i^{q_i}\}$. Then the CPT of X_i contains the parameters $\theta_{ijk} = p(X_i = k | \mathbf{Pa}(X_i) = \mathbf{pa}_i^j)$, the conditional probability that X_i takes its kth value given that its parents take their jth value. Therefore, the CPT of X_i requires the estimation of parameters $\boldsymbol{\theta}_i$, a vector of $R_i q_i$ components. $\boldsymbol{\theta} = (\boldsymbol{\theta}_1, \dots, \boldsymbol{\theta}_n)$ includes all the parameters in the BN, i.e., $\theta_{ijk}, \forall i = 1, \dots, n, j = 1, \dots, q_i, k = 1, \dots, R_i$, and hence it is a vector with $\sum_{i=1}^{n} R_i q_i$ components. Actually, only $\sum_{i=1}^{n} (R_i - 1) q_i$ parameters are required because complementary probabilities can be derived.

Once the BN structure $\mathcal{G}$ has been found (Section 13.3.2), parameters θ_{ijk} are estimated from data set $\mathcal{D}$, a classic problem in statistics. Let N_{ij} be the number of cases in $\mathcal{D}$ in which the configuration $\mathbf{Pa}(X_i) = \mathbf{pa}_i^j$ has been observed, and N_{ijk} be the number of cases in $\mathcal{D}$ where $X_i = k$ and $\mathbf{Pa}(X_i) = \mathbf{pa}_i^j$ have been observed at the same time $\left(N_{ij} = \sum_{k=1}^{R_i} N_{ijk}\right)$. There are two main approaches for the estimation: maximum likelihood and Bayesian estimation.

13.3.1.1 Maximum Likelihood Estimation

The **maximum likelihood estimation** looks for the values $\hat{\boldsymbol{\theta}}^{\text{ML}}$ of the parameters that maximize the likelihood of the data set given the model (Section 4.1.2.2):

$$\hat{\boldsymbol{\theta}}^{\text{ML}} = \arg\max_{\boldsymbol{\theta}} \mathcal{L}(\boldsymbol{\theta} \,|\, \mathcal{D}, \mathcal{G}) = \arg\max_{\boldsymbol{\theta}} p(\mathcal{D} \,|\, \mathcal{G}, \boldsymbol{\theta}) = \arg\max_{\boldsymbol{\theta}} \prod_{h=1}^{N} p\left(\mathbf{x}^h \,|\, \mathcal{G}, \boldsymbol{\theta}\right). \quad (13.13)$$

In BNs, probabilities $p\left(\mathbf{x}^h \,|\, \mathcal{G}, \boldsymbol{\theta}\right)$ in Equation (13.13) are factorized according to $\mathcal{G}$, that is, $p\left(\mathbf{x}^h \,|\, \mathcal{G}, \boldsymbol{\theta}\right) = \prod_{i=1}^{n} p\left(x_i^h \,|\, \mathbf{pa}_i^{h,\mathcal{G}}, \boldsymbol{\theta}\right)$. By using the assumption of **global parameter independence** (Spiegelhalter and Lauritzen, 1990), stating that the parameters associated with each variable in a network structure are independent, we have that the product in Equation (13.13) is

$$\prod_{h=1}^{N} \prod_{i=1}^{n} p\left(x_i^h \,|\, \mathbf{pa}_i^{h,\mathcal{G}}, \boldsymbol{\theta}\right) = \prod_{h=1}^{N} \prod_{i=1}^{n} p\left(x_i^h \,|\, \mathbf{pa}_i^{h,\mathcal{G}}, \boldsymbol{\theta}_i\right),$$

which means that it is possible to estimate the parameter $\boldsymbol{\theta}_i$ for each variable X_i independently of the other variables. Thus, in a BN where the only parent of X_2 is X_1, we can estimate $p(X_2|X_1)$ just by using the X_1 and X_2 columns of the data set. Moreover,

$$\prod_{h=1}^{N} \prod_{i=1}^{n} p\left(x_i^h \,|\, \mathbf{pa}_i^{h,\mathcal{G}}, \boldsymbol{\theta}_i\right) = \prod_{h=1}^{n} \prod_{j=1}^{q_i} \prod_{h_j=1}^{N_{ij}} p\left(x_i^{h_j} \,|\, \mathbf{pa}_i^{j,\mathcal{G}}, \boldsymbol{\theta}_i\right).$$

By using the **local parameter independence** assumption (Spiegelhalter and Lauritzen, 1990), stating that the parameters associated with each state of the parents of a variable, $\boldsymbol{\theta}_{ij}$, are independent, we have

$$\prod_{h=1}^{n} \prod_{j=1}^{q_i} \prod_{h_j=1}^{N_{ij}} p\left(x_i^{h_j} \,|\, \mathbf{pa}_i^{j,\mathcal{G}}, \boldsymbol{\theta}_i\right) = \prod_{h=1}^{n} \prod_{j=1}^{q_i} \prod_{h_j=1}^{N_{ij}} p\left(x_i^{h_j} \,|\, \mathbf{pa}_i^{j,\mathcal{G}}, \boldsymbol{\theta}_{ij}\right).$$

In the above example, this means that we can estimate $p(X_2|X_1 = 0)$ by using only the X_1 and X_2 columns of the data set and the rows containing $X_1 = 0$. Finally, because $\prod_{h_j=1}^{N_{ij}} p\left(x_i^{h_j} \,|\, \mathbf{pa}_i^{j,\mathcal{G}}, \boldsymbol{\theta}_{ij}\right) = \prod_{k=1}^{R_i} \theta_{ijk}^{N_{ijk}}$,

$$\mathcal{L}(\boldsymbol{\theta} \,|\, \mathcal{D}, \mathcal{G}) = \prod_{i=1}^{n} \prod_{j=1}^{q_i} \prod_{k=1}^{R_i} \theta_{ijk}^{N_{ijk}}. \quad (13.14)$$

Therefore, we can easily infer that the parameters maximizing the likelihood function of Equation (13.14) can be estimated via frequency counts in $\mathcal{D}$ (as in Section 4.1.2.2):

$$\hat{\theta}_{ijk}^{\text{ML}} = \frac{N_{ijk}}{N_{ij}}, \quad (13.15)$$

where $N_{ij} = \sum_{k=1}^{R_i} N_{ijk}$.

With sparse data sets, N_{ij} can be zero and $\hat{\theta}_{ijk}^{\text{ML}}$ undefined. Also, if $\mathbf{pa}_i^j$ or $X_i = k$ are unlikely, the estimation $\hat{\theta}_{ijk}^{\text{ML}}$ will be based on very few cases from $\mathcal{D}$ and therefore be unreliable. In practice, a smoothing technique is usually implemented to address this. For instance, the **Laplace estimator** provides

$$\hat{\theta}_{ijk}^{\text{Lap}} = \frac{N_{ijk} + 1}{N_{ij} + R_i}. \tag{13.16}$$

If $\mathcal{D}$ has incomplete instances (with missing values), the estimations can be calculated by ignoring these instances. Fortunately, when estimating θ_{ijk}, we can ignore just the instances with missing values in variables X_i or $\mathbf{Pa}(X_i)$, that prevent the computation of N_{ijk} or N_{ij}, and use instances with missing values in other variables. Rather than discarding instances that do not fully exploit all the available information, we can use imputation methods to fill in missing values (Section 2.5). Simple imputation techniques use statistics as the mode (or conditional mode) of the variable. More sophisticated techniques are the EM algorithm (Dempster et al., 1977), presented in Section 12.1 and first applied in BNs by Lauritzen (1995). A more elaborate version is the **structural EM** (Friedman, 1998), where both parameters and structures can be updated at each iteration of the EM (Section 12.3.1).

In Gaussian BNs represented as a multivariate Gaussian, see Equation (13.5), the parameters are $\boldsymbol{\theta} = (\boldsymbol{\mu}, \boldsymbol{\Sigma})$. Their maximum likelihood estimates are, respectively, the sample mean vector of the data $\mathcal{D} = \{\mathbf{x}^1, \ldots, \mathbf{x}^N\}$ and the sample covariance matrix $\mathbf{S} = \frac{1}{N} \sum_{i=1}^{N} (\mathbf{x}^i - \bar{\mathbf{x}})(\mathbf{x}^i - \bar{\mathbf{x}})^T$ (Section 4.1.2.2). When they are represented as the product of conditional Gaussian densities, see Equation (13.7), the parameters are $\boldsymbol{\mu} = (\mu_1, \ldots, \mu_n)^T$, $\mathbf{v} = (v_1, \ldots, v_n)^T$, and $\{\beta_{ij}, j = 1, \ldots, i-1; i = 1, \ldots, n\}$. The means are estimated as before. Parameters v_i and β_{ij} in $f_i(x_i|x_1, \ldots, x_{i-1})$ are estimated, respectively, with the sample conditional variance and with the coefficients of X_j in the regression of X_i on $X_1, \ldots, X_{i-1}$.

13.3.1.2 Bayesian Estimation

The **Bayesian estimation approach** (Section 4.1.4) adds prior knowledge to the parameter estimation problem. Thus, parameters $\boldsymbol{\theta}$ are modeled with a random variable $\boldsymbol{\Theta}$, and a probability distribution $f(\boldsymbol{\theta}|\mathcal{G})$ encodes the prior knowledge about the possible values of $\boldsymbol{\theta}$. The posterior distribution given the data $\mathcal{D}$, and the graph $\mathcal{G}$ is then computed by applying Bayes' rule: $f(\boldsymbol{\theta}|\mathcal{D}, \mathcal{G}) \propto p(\mathcal{D}|\mathcal{G}, \boldsymbol{\theta}) f(\boldsymbol{\theta}|\mathcal{G})$. This distribution can be then summarized using some central tendency measure, typically the posterior mean

$$\hat{\boldsymbol{\theta}}^{\text{Ba}} = \int \boldsymbol{\theta} f(\boldsymbol{\theta}|\mathcal{D}, \mathcal{G}) d\boldsymbol{\theta},$$

or the posterior mode (MAP estimate)

$$\hat{\boldsymbol{\theta}}^{\text{Ba}} = \arg\max_{\boldsymbol{\theta}} f(\boldsymbol{\theta}|\mathcal{D}, \mathcal{G}).$$

Recall that the Dirichlet distribution (Section 3.4.5) is a conjugate family (see Table 4.1) for categorical distributions (likes the ones present in BNs). Therefore, assuming a Dirichlet distribution for the prior (Spiegelhalter and Lauritzen, 1990), then the posterior will be easily derived because it is also Dirichlet distributed. Thus, the posterior distribution for parameters $\boldsymbol{\theta}_{ij} = (\theta_{ij1}, \ldots, \theta_{ijR_i})$ in the distribution of $X_i|\mathbf{pa}_i^j$, if

$(\boldsymbol{\theta}_{ij}|\mathcal{G}) \sim \text{Dir}(\alpha_{ij1}, \dots, \alpha_{ijR_i})$, is $(\boldsymbol{\theta}_{ij}|\mathcal{D}, \mathcal{G}) \sim \text{Dir}(\alpha_{ij1} + N_{ij1}, \dots, \alpha_{ijR_i} + N_{ijR_i})$, and hence the posterior mean of each θ_{ijk} $(k = 1, \dots, R_i)$ yields the Bayesian estimation

$$\hat{\theta}_{ijk}^{\text{Ba}} = \frac{N_{ijk} + \alpha_{ijk}}{N_{ij} + \alpha_{ij}}, \tag{13.17}$$

where $\alpha_{ij} = \sum_{k'=1}^{R_i} \alpha_{ijk'}$. The hyperparameters α_{ijk} can be thought of as "imaginary" counts or "pseudocounts" from our prior experience. α_{ij} is called **equivalent sample size**. The larger the equivalent sample size, the more confident we are in our prior. The interpretation of the Dirichlet distribution would be that we virtually observed a sample of size α_{ij}, with our event of interest, $X_i = k|\mathbf{pa}_i^j$, being observed α_{ijk} times before obtaining $\mathcal{D}$.

Note that Laplace estimates (Equation (13.16)) are a particular case of Bayesian estimation, with $\alpha_{ijk} = 1, \forall k$, in Equation (13.17). This Dirichlet with all hyperparameters equal to 1 is called **flat Dirichlet** and is equivalent to a uniform distribution. A generalization of Laplace estimate is the Lindstone rule:

$$\hat{\theta}_{ijk}^{\text{Ba}} = \frac{N_{ijk} + \alpha}{N_{ij} + \alpha R_i},$$

with $\alpha > 0$, which comes from a Dirichlet distribution picking $\alpha_{ijk} = \alpha, \forall k$. This Dirichlet is called **symmetric Dirichlet distribution** and does not favor any component of the vector over another. Particular cases are Laplace estimate ($\alpha = 1$), **Jeffreys–Perks rule** ($\alpha = 0.5$), and **Schurmann–Grassberger rule** ($\alpha = 1/R_i$). All these estimates take values between the empirical estimate (the relative frequence N_{ijk}/N_{ij}) and the uniform probability ($1/R_i$).

Example. Parameters θ_{ijk} in a BN and Their Estimates. Figure 13.15(a) shows a BN structure with four nodes and $\Omega_{X_i} = \{1, 2\}, i = 1, 3, 4, \Omega_{X_2} = \{1, 2, 3\}$. Hence $R_1 = R_3 = R_4 = 2, R_2 = 3$ and $q_1 = q_2 = 0, q_3 = 6, q_4 = 2$. All 21 parameters θ_{ijk} are shown in Table 13.2.

Suppose that we have a data set (Figure 13.15(b)) to estimate these parameters. To estimate $\theta_{1-1} = p(X_1 = 1)$, we look at the X_1 column (Figure 13.15(b)) and see three out of six instances (hence the probability is estimated as $\hat{\theta}_{1-1}^{\text{ML}} = 1/2$). To estimate $\theta_{322} = p(X_3 = 2|X_1 = 1, X_2 = 2)$, we find that neither of the two instances with $X_1 = 1, X_2 = 2$ include neither $X_3 = 2$, and thus $\hat{\theta}_{322}^{\text{ML}} = 0$ (i.e., $N_{ijk} = 0$). Besides, to estimate $\theta_{361} = p(X_3 = 1|X_1 = 2,$

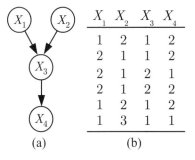

	X₁	X₂	X₃	X₄
	1	2	1	2
	2	1	1	2
	2	1	2	1
	2	1	2	2
	1	2	1	2
	1	3	1	1

(a)   (b)

Figure 13.15 (a) A BN structure with four nodes. X_1, X_3, and X_4 are binary, whereas X_2 has three possible values. (b) A data set with six instances for $\{X_1, \dots, X_4\}$ from which the BN in (a) has been learned.

Table 13.2 Parameters θ_{ijk} of the BN shown in Figure 13.15(a)

Parameters	Meaning
$\boldsymbol{\theta}_1 = (\theta_{1-1}, \theta_{1-2})$	$(p(X_1 = 1), p(X_1 = 2))$
$\boldsymbol{\theta}_2 = (\theta_{2-1}, \theta_{2-2}, \theta_{2-3})$	$(p(X_2 = 1), p(X_2 = 2), p(X_2 = 3))$
$\boldsymbol{\theta}_3 = (\theta_{311}, \theta_{312}, \ldots, \theta_{361}, \theta_{362})$	$(p(X_3 = 1\|X_1 = 1, X_2 = 1), p(X_3 = 2\|X_1 = 1, X_2 = 1), \ldots$
	$\ldots, p(X_3 = 1\|X_1 = 2, X_2 = 3), p(X_3 = 2\|X_1 = 2, X_2 = 3))$
$\boldsymbol{\theta}_4 = (\theta_{411}, \theta_{412}, \theta_{421}, \theta_{422})$	$(p(X_4 = 1\|X_3 = 1), p(X_4 = 2\|X_3 = 1), p(X_4 = 1\|X_3 = 2),$
	$p(X_4 = 2\|X_3 = 2))$

Table 13.3 Hyperparameters of a Gaussian BN for a normal-Wishart prior joint distribution of $\boldsymbol{\theta} = (\boldsymbol{\mu}, \mathbf{W})$

Prior	Posterior
$\boldsymbol{\mu}_0$	$\boldsymbol{\mu}_1 = \frac{\nu\boldsymbol{\mu}_0 + N\bar{\mathbf{x}}}{\nu+N}$
ν	$\nu + N$
α	$\alpha + N$
$\mathbf{T}_0$	$\mathbf{T}_1 = \mathbf{T}_0 + N\mathbf{S} + \frac{\nu N}{\nu+N}(\boldsymbol{\mu}_0 - \bar{\mathbf{x}})(\boldsymbol{\mu}_0 - \bar{\mathbf{x}})^T$

$X_2 = 3$), we find that $\hat{\theta}_{361}^{\mathrm{ML}}$ is undefined because there are no instances with $X_1 = 2, X_2 = 3$ (i.e., $N_{ij} = 0$). However, the Laplace estimates yield $\hat{\theta}_{322}^{\mathrm{Lap}} = 1/4$, $\hat{\theta}_{361}^{\mathrm{Lap}} = 1/2$. ∎

In Gaussian BNs, the parameters are $\boldsymbol{\theta} = (\boldsymbol{\mu}, \boldsymbol{\Sigma})$, although it is more common to take $\boldsymbol{\theta} = (\boldsymbol{\mu}, \mathbf{W})$, where $\mathbf{W} = \boldsymbol{\Sigma}^{-1}$ is the precision matrix. We assume that the prior joint distribution of $\boldsymbol{\theta}$, $f(\boldsymbol{\theta}|\mathcal{G})$, is normal-Wishart (Section 3.4.7), that is,

$$f(\boldsymbol{\mu}|\mathbf{W}) \sim \mathcal{N}\left(\boldsymbol{\mu}_0, (\nu\mathbf{W})^{-1}\right)$$
$$f(\mathbf{W}) \sim \mathcal{W}(\alpha, \mathbf{T}_0),$$

where $\nu > 0$, $\alpha > n - 1$ are the degrees of freedom and $\mathbf{T}_0$ is the scale matrix. The posterior distribution $f(\boldsymbol{\theta}|\mathcal{D}, \mathcal{G})$ is also normal-Wishart, with

$$f(\boldsymbol{\mu}|\mathcal{D}, \mathcal{G}, \mathbf{W}) \sim \mathcal{N}(\boldsymbol{\mu}_1, ((\nu+N)\mathbf{W})^{-1})$$
$$f(\mathbf{W}|\mathcal{D}, \mathcal{G}) \sim \mathcal{W}(\alpha + N, \mathbf{T}_1),$$

where

$$\boldsymbol{\mu}_1 = \frac{\nu\boldsymbol{\mu}_0 + N\bar{\mathbf{x}}}{\nu+N}, \quad \mathbf{T}_1 = \mathbf{T}_0 + N\mathbf{S} + \frac{\nu N}{\nu+N}(\boldsymbol{\mu}_0 - \bar{\mathbf{x}})(\boldsymbol{\mu}_0 - \bar{\mathbf{x}})^T, \tag{13.18}$$

and $\bar{\mathbf{x}}$ is the sample mean vector of the data $\mathcal{D} = \{\mathbf{x}^1, \ldots, \mathbf{x}^N\}$, and $\mathbf{S} = \frac{1}{N}\sum_{i=1}^{N}(\mathbf{x}^i - \bar{\mathbf{x}})(\mathbf{x}^i - \bar{\mathbf{x}})^T$ is the sample covariance matrix. Hence if we take the posterior means as estimates, then $\hat{\boldsymbol{\mu}}^{\mathrm{Ba}} = \boldsymbol{\mu}_1$ and $\hat{\mathbf{W}}^{\mathrm{Ba}} = (\alpha + N)\mathbf{T}_1$, where both $\boldsymbol{\mu}_1$ and $\mathbf{T}_1$ are given in Equation (13.18). Table 13.3 shows how hyperparameters are updated from the prior to the posterior distribution.

There are four hyperparameters to assess for the prior (Geiger and Heckerman, 1994): $\boldsymbol{\mu}_0, \nu, \alpha$, and $\mathbf{T}_0$. To assess $\boldsymbol{\mu}_0$ and $\mathbf{T}_0$, we can ask the expert to build a prior Gaussian BN for $\mathbf{X}$ and take the mean vector and covariance matrix (using Equation (13.8) to generate a covariance matrix) as μ_0 and $\mathbf{T}_0^{-1}$, respectively. To assess v and α, both can be considered as weights to measure the relative importance of the prior information with respect to the information provided by the data. For v, note that after examining N instances, the posterior mean μ_1 is updated as a weighted average of the prior mean computed based on v instances and the sample mean based on N instances (Equation (13.18)). For a larger v, the prior distribution has more influence on the posterior distribution for μ, as more prior observations are assumed to have been gathered. Thus, v can be thought of as being an equivalent sample size for μ, that is, the equivalent number of instances that the expert has seen since he or she was ignorant about μ. Finally, to assess $\alpha > n - 1$, recall (Section 3.4.6) that for $\mathbf{Y}_1, \dots, \mathbf{Y}_\alpha$, independent $\mathcal{N}(\mathbf{0}, \mathbf{T}_0)$ random (column) vectors, we have $\sum_{i=1}^{\alpha} \mathbf{Y}_i \mathbf{Y}_i^T \sim \mathcal{W}(\alpha, \mathbf{T}_0)$, and then α may be interpreted as the equivalent sample size for $\mathbf{T}_0$.

13.3.2 Learning Bayesian Network Structures

There are two separate ways of approaching structure learning. A first idea is to test the conditional independencies of the variables, the key concept behind BNs. The second idea is to score the goodness of each candidate structure and move toward the best-scoring candidate. We explain both ideas below.

13.3.2.1 Constraint-Based Methods

Constraint-based methods statistically test conditional independencies among triplets of variables from data. A DAG that represents a large percentage (and whenever possible all) of identified conditional independence constraints is drawn (the minimal I-map).

The most representative method is the **PC algorithm**[4] (Spirtes and Glymour, 1991; Spirtes et al., 1993). The data-generating distribution is assumed to be faithful to the DAG. PC starts from a complete undirected graph (all nodes are connected) and follows three stages. Stage 1 outputs the adjacencies in the graph (the skeleton of the learned structure) via edge elimination by hypothesis testing (like χ^2 tests, Section 4.2, or G^2 test, Equation (7.7)). Stage 2 identifies colliders. Stage 3 aims to orient the edges and output the CPDAG, the Markov equivalence class of DAGs (see Section 13.1.4).

Under faithfulness, both conditional independence and d-separation are equivalent. We could test whether each pair of variables X_i, X_j is independent, given all sorts of conditioning variable sets $\mathbf{S}$. Under faithfulness, when we find that $I_p(X_i, X_j | \mathbf{S})$, we know that $\mathbf{S}$, a separating set for X_i, X_j, blocks all paths linking X_i and X_j. Therefore, we learn something about the graph (edge $X_i - X_j$ can be removed). If $\neg I_p(X_i, X_j | \mathbf{S})$ for all $\mathbf{S}$, then we conclude that X_i and X_j are directly connected.

Note, however, that it is not necessary to apply the **SGS algorithm**[5] (Spirtes and Glymour, 1991; Spirtes et al., 1993) that checks *all* conditional dependencies. First, it is enough to find one $\mathbf{S}$ making X_i and X_j independent to remove the edge between them. Second, PC uses the following property of DAGs: X_i and X_j in a DAG are d-separated by some set $\mathbf{S}$ if and only if they are d-separated by $\mathbf{Pa}(X_i)$ or $\mathbf{Pa}(X_j)$. This means that we only need to condition on variables adjacent to X_i or X_j. Thus, PC yields the same result as SGS with fewer tests.

[4] PC stands for Peter and Clark, after the names of its inventors.
[5] SGS stands for Spirtes, Glymour, and Scheines after the surnames of its inventors.

Algorithm 13.2 shows a pseudocode of this stage of skeleton estimation. Adj_i denotes the adjacency set of node X_i.

Algorithm 13.2: Stage 1 of the PC algorithm: estimation of the skeleton

---

Input : A complete undirected graph and an ordering σ on the variables $\{X_1, \ldots, X_n\}$

Output: Skeleton $\mathcal{G}$ of the learned structure and separation sets $\mathbf{S}_{ij}$

1 Form the complete undirected graph $\mathcal{G}$ on nodes $\{X_1, \ldots, X_n\}$
2 $t = -1$
3 **repeat**
4 $\quad$ $t = t + 1$
5 $\quad$ **repeat**
6 $\quad\quad$ Select a pair of adjacent nodes $X_i - X_j$ in $\mathcal{G}$ using ordering σ
7 $\quad\quad$ Find $\mathbf{S} \subset Adj_i \setminus \{X_j\}$ in $\mathcal{G}$ with $|\mathbf{S}| = t$ (if any) using ordering σ
8 $\quad\quad$ Remove edge $X_i - X_j$ from $\mathcal{G}$ iff X_i and X_j are c.i. given $\mathbf{S}$ and set $\mathbf{S}_{ij} = \mathbf{S}_{ji} = \mathbf{S}$
9 $\quad$ **until** All ordered pairs of adjacent nodes have been tested
10 **until** All adjacent pairs $X_i - X_j$ in $\mathcal{G}$ satisfy $|Adj_i \setminus \{X_j\}| \leq t$

Thus, the first iteration of PC checks all pairs of nodes (X_i, X_j) for marginal independence, i.e., not conditioning on any other variables ($\mathbf{S} = \varnothing$). If they are independent, the connection is removed, and the empty set is saved as a separation set in $\mathbf{S}_{ij} = \mathbf{S}_{ji}$ (inner *repeat* in Algorithm 13.2, lines 6–8). At the next iteration (outer *repeat* in Algorithm 13.2), the size t of $\mathbf{S}$ increases by one unit. Thus, the algorithm checks whether for each ordered pair (X_i, X_j) still adjacent in $\mathcal{G}$, X_i, and X_j are c.i. given $\mathbf{S}$, for any $\mathbf{S}$ of size $t = 1$ of $Adj_i \setminus \{X_j\}$, i.e., the null hypothesis of independence $I_p(X, Y | \mathbf{S})$ is not rejected. All possible sets $\mathbf{S}$ are considered according to the ordering. The edge $X_i - X_j$ is removed if and only if we find a set $\mathbf{S}$ that renders X_i and X_j c.i. This $\mathbf{S}$ is saved as a separation set in $\mathbf{S}_{ij} = \mathbf{S}_{ji}$. If all ordered pairs of adjacent nodes have been considered for conditional independence given all subsets $\mathbf{S}$ of size t of their adjacency sets, the algorithm again increases t by one. Therefore the process is repeated for conditioning sets $\mathbf{S}$ with two nodes, then three nodes, etc., thinning out the graph until all possibilities (up to $n - 2$ variables) are exhausted, and there are no more adjacency sets to check. The number of conditional independence tests for a given pair (X_i, X_j) is reduced with this one-by-one increase of t, where the search for $\mathbf{S}$ with $t + 1$ variables starts only when the search of all sets of t variables fails. Note that as PC progresses, the reliability of the statistical tests checking conditional independencies drops because sets $\mathbf{S}$ include an increasing number of variables (thereby outputting smaller samples on which to apply the tests). Then there is a tendency to always decide independence. Some solutions for addressing this problem have been proposed elsewhere (e.g., Abellán et al., 2006).

Based on the skeleton and separation sets, Stage 2 of the PC algorithm identifies colliders to orient some edges. Remember that in all diverging $(X_i \leftarrow X_j \rightarrow X_k)$ and serial $(X_i \rightarrow X_j \rightarrow X_k)$ connections among three nodes, then X_i and X_k are independent given X_j. For a converging $(X_i \rightarrow X_j \leftarrow X_k)$ connection, X_i and X_k are dependent given X_j. Hence if we take $X_i - X_j - X_k$ (where X_i and X_k are not adjacent) in $\mathcal{G}$, we first identify a collider on

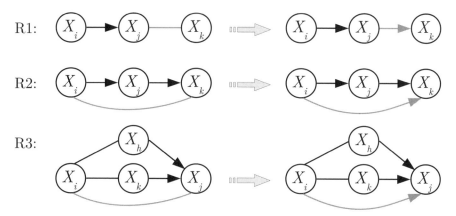

R1:

R2:

R3:

Figure 13.16 PC orientation rules for edges in gray. Undirected edges in the last graph would be $X_i \to X_h$ and $X_i \leftarrow X_k$ or $X_i \leftarrow X_h$ and $X_i \to X_k$.

X_j by testing whether X_i and X_k are dependent given X_j. If they are, we draw $X_i \to X_j \leftarrow X_k$. This can be inferred from the tests already performed to remove the edge between X_i and X_k and the separating sets saved. X_j is a collider if and only if $X_j \notin \mathbf{S}_{ik}$, i.e., X_j was not included in the conditioning set that rendered X_i and X_k c.i.

Finally, Stage 3 orients as many of the remaining undirected edges as possible. This process is induced by consistency with already oriented edges and such that no new colliders or cycles are formed. It is enacted recursively until no more edges can be oriented. The following three rules (Figure 13.16) are applied repeatedly:

R1: Orient $X_j - X_k$ as $X_j \to X_k$ whenever there is a directed edge $X_i \to X_j$ such that X_i and X_k are not adjacent (otherwise a new collider is created).

R2: Orient $X_i - X_k$ as $X_i \to X_k$ whenever there is a chain $X_i \to X_j \to X_k$ (otherwise a directed cycle is created).

R3: Orient $X_i - X_j$ as $X_i \to X_j$ whenever there are two chains $X_i - X_k \to X_j$ and $X_i - X_h \to X_j$ such that X_k and X_h are not adjacent (otherwise a new collider or a directed cycle is created).

The final graph is in general a CPDAG because there may be multiple (Markov equivalent) graphs implying the same independence relations, even under the faithfulness assumption. Observational data cannot distinguish between equivalent DAGs; that is, the BN structure is not **identifiable** from the data. We should have experimental data to distinguish between a fork (where a change in Y produces a change in both X and Z) and a chain (where a change in Y produces a change in only one variable X or Z).

Example. Steps of the PC Algorithm. Figure 13.17 shows a hypothetical example with four variables $X_1, \ldots, X_4$ drawn as nodes $1, \ldots, 4$. The ordering σ of the variables is the natural ordering $\{1, 2, 3, 4\}$, and all edges are arranged in rows accordingly. In the first iteration ($t = 0$), edges $1 - 4$ and $2 - 4$ are removed because the variables in the ordered pairs (X_1, X_4) and (X_2, X_4) are found to be independent ($\mathbf{S} = \varnothing$). We save $\mathbf{S}_{14} = \mathbf{S}_{24} = \varnothing$. Tests with symbol $-$ do not have to be checked; e.g., checking that nodes 1 and 2 are independent is the same as checking that nodes 2 and 1 are independent.

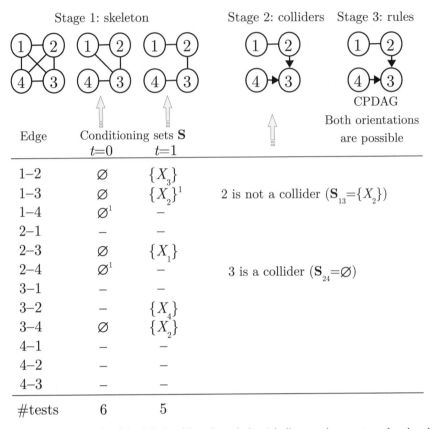

Stage 1: skeleton   Stage 2: colliders Stage 3: rules

Edge	Conditioning sets **S**		
	$t=0$	$t=1$	
1–2	∅	$\{X_3\}$	
1–3	∅	$\{X_2\}^1$	2 is not a collider ($\mathbf{S}_{13}=\{X_2\}$)
1–4	$∅^1$	–	
2–1	–	–	
2–3	∅	$\{X_1\}$	
2–4	$∅^1$	–	3 is a collider ($\mathbf{S}_{24}=∅$)
3–1	–	–	
3–2	–	$\{X_4\}$	
3–4	∅	$\{X_2\}$	
4–1	–	–	
4–2	–	–	
4–3	–	–	
#tests	6	5	

Figure 13.17 Example of the PC algorithm. Superindex 1 indicates when a set rendered nodes independent. Symbol – indicates a check that is unnecessary.

In the second iteration ($t = 1$), X_2 renders X_1 and X_3 c.i., and we save $\mathbf{S}_{13} = \{X_2\}$. Again, many tests are unnecessary. For instance, because node 1 is not adjacent to node 4 (detected when $t = 0$) and node 3 is not adjacent to node 1 (detected when $t = 1$), there are no checks for edges $1 - 4, 3 - 1$. On the other hand, for edge $3 - 2$, we should in principle check that $\mathbf{S} = \{X_1\}$ and $\mathbf{S} = \{X_4\}$; however, it suffices to check that $\mathbf{S} = \{X_4\}$ because nodes 1 and 3 were previously disconnected when checking edge $1 - 3$, and thus node 1 is not adjacent to node 3. It is not necessary to iterate for conditioning set $\mathbf{S}$ ($t = 2$) with two nodes because there are no adjacency sets of size 2. Stage 1 is over.

In Stage 2, nodes 2 and 3 are potential colliders. Node 2 is not a collider (in $1 - 2 - 3$) because $\{X_2\} = \mathbf{S}_{13}$, that is, when edge $1 - 3$ was removed, X_1 and X_3 were found to be independent given X_2. Therefore they are not dependent given X_2. However, node 3 is a collider (in $2 - 3 - 4$) because $\{X_3\} \notin \mathbf{S}_{24} = ∅$, that is, node 3 was not included in the conditioning set that rendered nodes 2 and 4 independent. Finally, no additional orientations could be determined in Stage 3 because both $1 \rightarrow 2$ and $1 \leftarrow 2$ are possible. ∎

The PC algorithm is statistically consistent, i.e., if variables that are c.i. are correctly identified, then the true CPDAG is found. In practice, conditional independence is checked using statistical tests based on limited finite data. We are seldom given the list of true conditional independencies or the true JPD. A possible consequence is that PC makes mistakes when keeping/removing edges. Because we only have limited finite data, the most we can say is that the probability of reaching a CPDAG different from the true one is zero in the limit (with $N \to \infty$). PC results can be used as the first step for some other improved approaches, like the fast causal inference algorithm (Spirtes et al., 1999) and the really fast causal inference algorithm (Colombo et al., 2012).

Note that PC is order-dependent, that is, its output depends on the order in which the variables are given. This has a major impact in high-dimensional settings, leading to highly variable results. Colombo and Maathuis (2014) proposed some modifications to PC to build an order-independent PC algorithm. For instance, to solve the order-dependence in the estimation of the skeleton, the algorithm stores the edges that should be removed for each size t of $\mathbf{S}$, but these edges are not removed until the algorithm goes to the next iteration with $t = t + 1$. This way, the adjacency sets are unchanged during an iteration and are not affected by edge removals. In high-dimensional settings, this can be parallelizable at each t. Other modifications can be pursued to make decisions about colliders, orientation rules, and separating sets again with an order-independence view. The statistical consistency property of the original PC is still valid.

Other variants and extensions of the PC algorithm include a reduction in the number of conditional independence tests by identifying each node's Markov blankets (Margaritis and Thrun, 2000) (this is the GS Markov blanket algorithm explained in Section 8.4.1.7), the control of the false positive rate (false edges found) (Li and Wang, 2009), and the case of Gaussian BNs with conditional independence tests based on sample partial correlations (Kalisch and Bühlmann, 2007). If everything is linear and multivariate Gaussian, $I_p(X_i, X_j | X_k)$ is equivalent to zero partial correlation, a property of the multivariate normal distribution (Lauritzen, 1996). The partial correlation between X_i and X_j given X_k is the correlation between X_i and X_j after linearly regressing each one on X_k separately, that is, it is the correlation of their residuals. This property of equivalence between conditional independence and zero partial correlation is the basis of **edge exclusion tests** (Smith and Whittaker, 1998), where the edge $X_i - X_j$ is excluded from the graph if the null hypothesis on zero partial correlation between X_i and X_j is not rejected (see Section 12.3.3 and 14.4.1). The preferred test is usually the likelihood ratio test.

13.3.2.2 Score and Search-Based Methods

These methods use a score function relative to data for measuring the goodness of each candidate BN. The goal is to find a network structure that maximizes the scoring function. The methods usually start from an initial structure (generated randomly or from domain knowledge). Then best scored BNs are proposed using a search method responsible for intelligent movements in the space of possible network structures. There are three possible spaces of structures: (a) the space of DAGs, (b) the space of Markov equivalent classes, and (c) the space of orderings of variables. There follow details on these spaces (A), common scores (B) and search methods (C), see Figure 13.18.

A. Spaces. The cardinality of the **space of DAGs** is, according to Robinson's formula (Robinson, 1977), super-exponential in the number of nodes: the number $f(n)$ of possible BN structures that contain n nodes is given by the recurrence

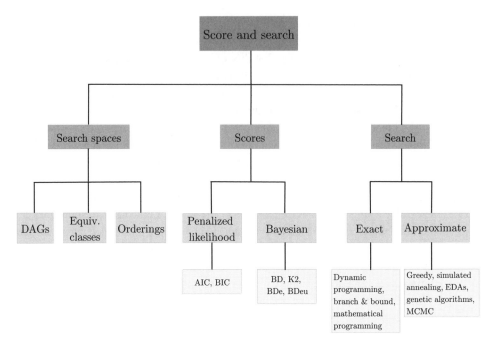

Figure 13.18 Methods for BN structure learning based on score and search.

$$f(n) = \sum_{i=1}^{n}(-1)^{i+1}\binom{n}{i}2^{i(n-i)}f(n-i), \quad \text{for } n > 2,$$

which is initialized with $f(0) = f(1) = 1$. For instance, $f(2) = 3, f(3) = 25, f(4) = 543, f(5) = 29,281$, and $f(10) \approx 4.2 \cdot 10^{18}$. The task of finding a network structure that optimizes the score is a combinatorial optimization problem and is known to be NP-hard (Chickering, 1996; Chickering et al., 2004), even if we restrict the number of parents of each node to at most two. It is then infeasible to evaluate all possible structures in most practical domains, where the number of variables is typically large. Therefore, a well-established approach uses heuristic search algorithms, see below and Figure 13.18, right.

The **space of Markov equivalence classes** is a reduced version of the space of DAGs where all Markov equivalent DAGs are represented by a unique structure, the CPDAG or essential graph (Section 13.1.4). See, e.g., Figure 13.4, where there are four DAGs in the same equivalence class (DAGs in (a), and (c)–(e)), all of which are, however, represented by only one CPDAG (in (b)). Working in this new space avoids the movements between DAGs within the same equivalence class, thereby reducing the cardinality of the search space. It is important to know the #DAGs/#CPDAGs ratio to decide which space to search. If this ratio is high, then it may be preferable to search the space of CPDAGs rather than the space of DAGs. While the number of DAGs can be computed with Robinson's formula without all having to be enumerated, enumeration is the only method for counting CPDAGs. Gillispie and Perlman (2002) found that the #DAGs/#CPDAGs ratio approaches an asymptote of about 3.7 for graphs with up to 10 nodes. Sonntag et al. (2015) used MCMC sampling to approximate the ratio for graphs with up to 31 nodes, with a similar result. Hence no more than moderate gain in efficiency is to be expected when searching the space of CPDAGs instead of the space of DAGs. Also, when working in the CPDAG space, it is time consuming to check whether or not a structure belongs to an equivalence class.

Chickering (2002a) authored a seminal paper on the use of equivalence classes, and the **greedy equivalence search** (GES) algorithm (Meek, 1997; Chickering, 2002b) is nowadays considered as a reference algorithm in BN learning because, under faithfulness, it asymptotically outputs a perfect map of the target distribution. In a first pass, GES starts with no edges and greedily adds dependencies by considering all possible single-edge additions that can be made to all DAGs in the current equivalence class. When the algorithm stops at a local maximum score (usually the BIC function, see below), a second pass is applied that greedily considers all possible single-edge deletions that can be made to all DAGs in the current equivalence class. The algorithm terminates with the local maximum identified in the second phase. Extensions of GES include its randomized version (Nielsen et al., 2003), an adaptation to Gaussian BNs (Vidaurre et al., 2010), and a scaling up version (Alonso-Barba et al., 2013). Theoretical issues are discussed by Chickering and Meek (2015).

The **space of orderings** of the variables is justified by the fact that some learning algorithms only work with a fixed order, assuming that only the variables previous to a given variable in the ordering can be its parents (e.g., the K2 algorithm explained below). The score of an ordering is defined as the score of the best network that is consistent with that ordering. Given an ordering, there are $2^{n(n-1)/2}$ possible BN structures. Also, $n!$ possibilities have to be searched to find a good ordering. The advantage of working in the space of orderings is that each step in the search makes more global modifications than in the space of DAGs, and it is therefore less susceptible to local optima. Moreover, there is no need to perform costly acyclicity checks because, given an ordering, acyclicity is not an issue. Although each step is more expensive, the algorithms are faster. Relevant works include Bouckaert (1992), who manipulates the ordering of the variables with operations similar to arc reversals; Singh and Valtorta (1995), who use conditional independence tests to generate an ordering on the nodes; Larrañaga et al. (1996a), who introduce a genetic algorithm-based search; Romero et al. (2004), who use estimation of distribution algorithms for the search; and Teyssier and Koller (2005), who preferred a greedy hill-climbing search with a tabu list and random restarts. See Section 6.3.1 for details on heuristic search strategies.

B. Scores. A score $Q(\mathcal{D}, \mathcal{G})$ measures the goodness of fit of a BN structure $\mathcal{G}$ to the data set $\mathcal{D}$ (the better the fit is, the higher the score is). The structure learning problem is to find $\arg\max_{\mathcal{G}} Q(\mathcal{D}, \mathcal{G})$. One simple criterion is the estimated **log-likelihood of the data given the BN**:

$$\log \mathcal{L}(\hat{\boldsymbol{\theta}} | \mathcal{D}, \mathcal{G}) = \log p(\mathcal{D} | \mathcal{G}, \hat{\boldsymbol{\theta}}) = \log \prod_{i=1}^{n} \prod_{j=1}^{q_i} \prod_{k=1}^{R_i} \hat{\theta}_{ijk}^{N_{ijk}} = \sum_{i=1}^{n} \sum_{j=1}^{q_i} \sum_{k=1}^{R_i} N_{ijk} \log \hat{\theta}_{ijk}, \quad (13.19)$$

whose notation was given in Section 13.3.1. $\hat{\theta}_{ijk}$ is usually taken as the maximum likelihood estimate (Section 4.1.2.1) shown in Equation (13.15), i.e., $\hat{\theta}_{ijk} = \hat{\theta}_{ijk}^{\text{ML}} = \frac{N_{ijk}}{N_{ij}}$, the relative frequency counts in $\mathcal{D}$.

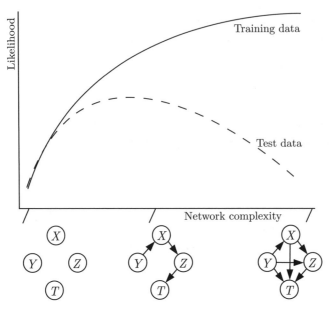

Figure 13.19 Structural overfitting: the denser the graph is, the higher the likelihood of the training data is, whereas performance degrades for the unseen test data.

A drawback of using likelihood as the score is that it increases monotonically with the complexity of the model – **structural overfitting** – see Figure 13.19. Arc addition never decreases the likelihood of the network. Consequently, the structure that maximizes the likelihood coincides with the complete graph. We can limit the number of parents per network variable to address the overfitting problem. Alternatively, a family of **penalized log-likelihood** scores has been proposed to penalize network complexity. Their general expression is

$$Q^{Pen}(\mathcal{D}, \mathcal{G}) = \sum_{i=1}^{n} \sum_{j=1}^{q_i} \sum_{k=1}^{R_i} N_{ijk} \log \frac{N_{ijk}}{N_{ij}} - dim(\mathcal{G}) pen(N), \qquad (13.20)$$

where $dim(\mathcal{G}) = \sum_{i=1}^{n}(R_i - 1)q_i$ denotes the model dimension (number of parameters needed in the BN), and $pen(N)$ is a nonnegative penalization function of N. The scores are different depending on $pen(N)$: if $pen(N) = 1$, the score is called **Akaike's information criterion** (AIC) (Akaike, 1974), and if $pen(N) = \frac{1}{2} \log N$, the score is the **Bayesian information criterion** (BIC) (Schwarz, 1978). BIC calculation is equivalent to the **minimum description length** (MDL) criterion (Lam and Bacchus, 1994). Whereas MDL is interpreted in terms of information theory, BIC is an asymptotic approximation of the Bayesian score (see below). The penalty for the BIC/MDL score is larger than for AIC. Therefore, optimal BIC/MDL networks tend to be sparser than optimal AIC networks.

We can alternatively adopt a Bayesian approach. The goal of a **Bayesian approach** is to find the structure with the maximum a posteriori probability given the data, that is, $\arg\max_{\mathcal{G}} p(\mathcal{G}|\mathcal{D})$. Using Bayes' formula, $p(\mathcal{G}|\mathcal{D}) \propto p(\mathcal{D}, \mathcal{G}) = p(\mathcal{D}|\mathcal{G})p(\mathcal{G})$. The second factor, $p(\mathcal{G})$, denotes the prior distribution over structures. The first factor, $p(\mathcal{D}|\mathcal{G})$, is the **marginal likelihood** of the data, defined as

$$p(\mathcal{D}|\mathcal{G}) = \int p(\mathcal{D}|\mathcal{G},\boldsymbol{\theta}) f(\boldsymbol{\theta}|\mathcal{G}) d\boldsymbol{\theta}, \tag{13.21}$$

where $p(\mathcal{D}|\mathcal{G},\boldsymbol{\theta})$ is the likelihood of the data given the BN (structure $\mathcal{G}$ and parameters $\boldsymbol{\theta}$), and $f(\boldsymbol{\theta}|\mathcal{G})$ is the prior distribution over the parameters (Section 13.3.1.2). Note that both the estimated likelihood (Equation (13.19)) and the marginal likelihood (Equation (13.21)) scores examine the likelihood function of the data given the structure. Estimated likelihood returns the maximum of this function, which it evaluates using the most likely parameter values given the data, $\hat{\boldsymbol{\theta}}^{\text{ML}}$. This can be overly "optimistic." Marginal likelihood averages this function based on the prior $f(\boldsymbol{\theta}|\mathcal{G})$ over the parameters, that is, it is averaged over several (not just the maximum) choices of parameter $\boldsymbol{\theta}$, along with the measure of how likely each parameter value is. Therefore, we measure the expected likelihood. In doing so, the model goodness estimate is more conservative, avoiding overfitting.

We now detail each component of the Bayesian approach, $p(\mathcal{G})$ and $f(\boldsymbol{\theta}|\mathcal{G})$. The prior over network structures $p(\mathcal{G})$ plays a minor role in asymptotic analysis because it is not affected by the number N of instances. This is why all structures are often assumed to be equally likely, that is, $p(\mathcal{G})$ follows a uniform distribution. Then the maximization of $p(\mathcal{G}|\mathcal{D})$ is equivalent to the maximization of the marginal likelihood. For small N, however, $p(\mathcal{G})$ will play a major role. To encode the penalization of arcs in the graph, for example, we can use $p(\mathcal{G}) \propto a^{|\mathcal{G}|}$, where $a < 1$ and $|\mathcal{G}|$ is the number of arcs in the graph.

Suppose that all network parameters have a Dirichlet distribution $(\boldsymbol{\theta}_{ij}|\mathcal{G}) \sim \text{Dir}(\alpha_{ij1}, \dots, \alpha_{ijR_i})$, as in Section 13.3.1.2. We simply say that $f(\boldsymbol{\theta}|\mathcal{G})$ is Dirichlet. Under other natural assumptions, Cooper and Herskovits (1992) and Heckerman et al. (1995) obtained the following expression for the marginal likelihood

$$p(\mathcal{D}|\mathcal{G}) = \prod_{i=1}^{n} \prod_{j=1}^{q_i} \frac{\Gamma(\alpha_{ij})}{\Gamma(\alpha_{ij}+N_{ij})} \prod_{k=1}^{R_i} \frac{\Gamma(\alpha_{ijk}+N_{ijk})}{\Gamma(\alpha_{ijk})},$$

where Γ denotes the gamma function (defined in Section 3.3.4), and $\alpha_{ij} = \sum_{k=1}^{R_i} \alpha_{ijk}$. As it is easier to work in the logarithmic space, the scoring functions (like the log-likelihood and its penalized versions) use the value $\log p(\mathcal{D},\mathcal{G})$ instead of $p(\mathcal{D},\mathcal{G})$. Thus, the **Bayesian Dirichlet** (BD) score (Bayesian metric with Dirichlet priors) is

$$Q^{BD}(\mathcal{D},\mathcal{G}) = \log p(\mathcal{G}) + \sum_{i=1}^{n} \sum_{j=1}^{q_i} \left(\log \frac{\Gamma(\alpha_{ij})}{\Gamma(\alpha_{ij}+N_{ij})} + \sum_{k=1}^{R_i} \log \frac{\Gamma(\alpha_{ijk}+N_{ijk})}{\Gamma(\alpha_{ijk})} \right). \tag{13.22}$$

It can be proved that when $N \to \infty$, $Q^{BD}(\mathcal{D},\mathcal{G})$ tends to the BIC score, which is then an asymptotic approximation of the Bayesian score, as mentioned above. Thus, the Bayesian score trades off likelihood (fit to data) against model complexity, and the larger N is, the more emphasis will be given to the fit to data.

The BD score is of little practical interest because it requires the specification of all hyperparameters α_{ijk} for all i, j, k. This is why some simpler particular cases have been proposed. Cooper and Herskovits (1992) proposed the **K2 score**[6] which uses the

---

[6] K2 refers to the name of the software system in which it was first used, Kutató, which means "explorer" or "investigator" in Hungarian.

uninformative assignment $\alpha_{ijk} = 1$, for all i, j, k (flat Dirichlet or uniform distribution), obviously resulting in

$$Q^{K2}(\mathcal{D}, \mathcal{G}) = \log p(\mathcal{G}) + \sum_{i=1}^{n} \sum_{j=1}^{q_i} \left(\log \frac{(R_i - 1)!}{(N_{ij} + R_i - 1)!} + \sum_{k=1}^{R_i} \log N_{ijk}! \right). \qquad (13.23)$$

The **K2 algorithm** (Cooper and Herskovits, 1992) uses a greedy-search method and the K2 score. It begins with a structure with no parents, an ordering on the nodes, and an upper bound t on the maximum number of parents that any node is permitted to have, as designated by the user. The algorithm incrementally adds, from the set of nodes that precede each node X_i in the node ordering, the parent whose addition most increases the function

$$g(X_i, \mathbf{Pa}(X_i)) = \prod_{j=1}^{q_i} \frac{(R_i - 1)!}{(N_{ij} + R_i - 1)!} \prod_{k=1}^{R_i} N_{ijk}!.$$

When the addition of no single parent further increases the score, no more parents are added to node X_i, and we move on to the next node in the ordering.

The **likelihood-equivalent Bayesian Dirichlet** (BDe) score (Heckerman et al., 1995) ("e" for likelihood equivalence) has the same expression as the BD score but constrains the hyperparameters as $\alpha_{ijk} = \alpha \, p(X_i = k, \mathbf{Pa}(X_i) = \mathbf{pa}_i^j | \mathcal{G})$. Instead of the Dirichlet distribution assumption, the same formula as the BD score is derived by using the likelihood equivalence assumption: if two structures $\mathcal{G}_1, \mathcal{G}_2$ are equivalent, their parameter JPD functions are identical, i.e., $f(\boldsymbol{\theta}|\mathcal{G}_1) = f(\boldsymbol{\theta}|\mathcal{G}_2)$. This implies the Dirichlet distribution assumption. The equivalent sample size α expresses the user's confidence in his prior network. Low α values favor structures that differ from his or her prior network. Low α values typically result in sparser networks than higher α values. The behavior of BDe is very sensitive to α (Silander et al., 2007). Although we only require one equivalent sample size for the entire domain (rather than for each i, j, k), BDe may sometimes be overly simple if the user has more knowledge about some variables than others. Also, the need for specifying $p(X_i = k, \mathbf{Pa}(X_i) = \mathbf{pa}_i^j | \mathcal{G})$ for *all* i, j, k, may not be easy.

Moreover, Buntine (1991) independently introduced the **BDeu score**, a particular case of the BDe score, where $p(X_i = k, \mathbf{Pa}(X_i) = \mathbf{pa}_i^j | \mathcal{G}) = \frac{1}{q_i R_i}$, i.e., the same value for each i regardless of j, k. The "u" then stands for uniform joint distribution (resulting in uniform parameter priors $f(\boldsymbol{\theta}|\mathcal{G})$). Because $\alpha_{ij} = \sum_{k=1}^{R_i} \alpha \frac{1}{q_i R_i} = \frac{\alpha}{q_i}$, the expression of the BDeu score is

$$Q^{BDeu}(\mathcal{D}, \mathcal{G}) = \log p(\mathcal{G}) + \sum_{i=1}^{n} \sum_{j=1}^{q_i} \left(\log \frac{\Gamma\left(\frac{\alpha}{q_i}\right)}{\Gamma\left(\frac{\alpha}{q_i} + N_{ij}\right)} + \sum_{k=1}^{R_i} \log \frac{\Gamma\left(\frac{\alpha}{q_i R_i} + N_{ijk}\right)}{\Gamma\left(\frac{\alpha}{q_i R_i}\right)} \right).$$

$$(13.24)$$

This score depends on only one parameter, α, the equivalent sample size. Because, as mentioned above, α has a big influence on the score, several values are tested.

A **decomposable score** (Heckerman et al., 1995) can be expressed as a sum of values that depend on only one node and its parents. Thus, when adding/removing single edges, typical movements in local search strategies (as in **Algorithm B** by Buntine [1991]), these additions/removals will only affect a limited number of terms in the sum, reducing the computational overhead. A desirable property of a scoring criterion for a search in

Table 13.4 Characteristics of the main scores

Score	Equation	Prior $f(\boldsymbol{\theta}\|\mathcal{G})$	Decomposable	Score equivalent
$Q^{Pen}(\mathcal{D},\mathcal{G})$	(13.20)		$\checkmark$	$\checkmark$
$Q^{BD}(\mathcal{D},\mathcal{G})$	(13.22)	Dirichlet	$\checkmark$	
$Q^{K2}(\mathcal{D},\mathcal{G})$	(13.23)	flat Dirichlet	$\checkmark$	
$Q^{BDeu}(\mathcal{D},\mathcal{G})$	(13.24)	$\alpha_{ij} = \frac{\alpha}{q_i}$	$\checkmark$	$\checkmark$

the space of Markov equivalence classes is the **score equivalence** (Heckerman et al., 1995), that is, all graphs within the same equivalence class are equally scored. All the above scores – estimated log-likelihood, AIC, BIC/MDL, BD, K2, BDe and BDeu – are decomposable. All but K2 and BD are also score equivalent. Table 13.4 summarizes the characteristics of the main scores.

Note that if a node ordering is specified, only one of the equivalent structures is possible. Therefore any learning algorithm requiring a node ordering, like the K2 algorithm, hardly benefits from the score equivalence property. Moreover, in causal networks, this property is not useful either because equivalent structures represent different causal relationships: if Y causes X and Z, i.e., the true network is $X \leftarrow Y \rightarrow Z$, then we need a score metric to distinguish this structure from its equivalent $X \rightarrow Y \rightarrow Z$ or $X \leftarrow Y \leftarrow Z$.

For Gaussian BNs, Geiger and Heckerman (1994) derived the **BGe score** (for Bayesian Gaussian likelihood equivalent), assuming a normal-Wishart prior joint distribution (Section 3.4.7). See also Kuipers et al. (2014), where some typos are corrected.

In neuroimaging, the specificities of fMRI (continuous) data have given rise to a bunch of structure learning methods (reviewed in Mumford and Ramsey, 2014). An fMRI experiment will produce a sequence of 3D images, where we have a time series of BOLD signals sampled according to the temporal resolution in each voxel (candidate features). These data are typically of the $N \ll n$ type ("large n, small N" problem), temporal, noisy, and with multiple participating subjects. With regard to their main use in functional connectivity analysis, the literature makes a distinction between the statistical dependencies between brain regions – functional connectivity – and the causal interactions between those regions – directional functional connectivity or effective connectivity. The BN nodes represent the activated brain regions, where an arc is a dependence/interaction between regions. In $X \rightarrow Y$, the activation of region Y is caused by the activation of region X.

The most common networks are Gaussian BNs. However some authors (Gudbjartsson and Patz, 1995) have mentioned that fMRI data follow a Rice distribution.[7] Generally, methods that rely on the Gaussian assumption can accurately locate connections in the graph but not their correct orientation (Smith et al., 2011). Some proposals address the problem by relaxing the Gaussian to a non-Gaussian assumption, e.g., linear non-Gaussian acyclic model (LiNGAM), pairwise LiNGAM, and linear non-Gaussian orientation fixed structure (LOFS).

The between-subject variability has to be considered if there are multiple subjects participating in the fMRI. If the whole group is assumed to have the same brain network, BOLD time series from each individual are concatenated and treated as sampled from a

---

[7] Named after S.O. Rice and also known as Rician or Ricean distribution. It is used to model scattered signals that reach a receiver by multiple paths.

single subject. This is appropriate for small and homogeneous samples. Unfortunately, it can result in statistical dependencies (arcs) in the estimated group network that do not exist in any of the single subject data sets – the **Yule–Simpson paradox** –. Alternatively, we can learn a different network for each individual and then perform group analysis on the individual networks. This is appropriate for large and heterogeneous samples. An intermediate approach considers the same brain network for a group (same BN structure) but different patterns of connectivity for each individual (different parameters).

This is the idea behind the **independent multiple-sample GES** (iMaGES) algorithm (Ramsey et al., 2010), an extension of GES. First, GES (with the BIC score) is applied to each single-subject data $\mathcal{D}_m$ to learn structure $\mathcal{G}_m, m = 1, ..., M$, where M is the number of subjects. Second, a group score is defined as

$$\frac{1}{M} \sum_{m=1}^{M} \log \mathcal{L}_m(\hat{\boldsymbol{\theta}} | \mathcal{D}_m, \mathcal{G}_m) - k \, dim(\mathcal{G}) \frac{1}{2} \log N,$$

where N is the whole sample size, $dim(\mathcal{G})$ is the number of arcs plus number of nodes, and $k > 0$ is a constant to increase the usual penalty of the BIC score to control spurious triangles, i.e., relationships of the form $X \rightarrow Y \rightarrow Z$ and $X \rightarrow Z$. Variables are measured indirectly (BOLD data are a surrogate of the underlying unmeasured neural activity), and if the real relationship is only the first chain $X \rightarrow Y \rightarrow Z$, the indirect measurement can lead to the formation of the false positive weak connection $X \rightarrow Z$ due to the indirect link between the real counterparts. When triangles are found, k is slowly increased until they disappear. The graph $\mathcal{G}$ that represents the group is updated by adding (or in the backwards phase, deleting) the arc whose group score obtained over the scores from the several data sets is best. However, the parameters of each $\mathcal{G}_m$ represent each subject.

C. Search. The huge search space has led to the use of mainly heuristics for structure learning. See Section 6.3.1 for details on search procedures. Almost all types of heuristics have been applied, including greedy search (Buntine, 1991; Cooper and Herskovits, 1992), simulated annealing (Heckerman et al., 1995), genetic algorithms (Larrañaga et al., 1996b), MCMC methods (Giudici and Green, 1999; Friedman and Koller, 2003; Grzegorczyk and Husmeier, 2008), and estimation of distribution algorithms (Larrañaga et al., 2000; Blanco et al., 2003). Also, there are other approaches based on restricting the search space, e.g., the parents of each variable must belong to a small subset of candidates (Friedman et al., 1999b).

For example, the **greedy thick thinning algorithm** (Heckerman, 1995), like GES, starts with an empty graph and repeatedly adds the arc (without creating a cycle) that maximizes the Bayesian score until no arc addition results in a positive increase (thickening). Then it repeatedly removes arcs until no arc deletion results in a positive increase in the score (thinning).

Exact methods to find optimal BN structures with several dozens of variables have been developed, including dynamic programming (Koivisto and Sood, 2004; Silander and Myllymäki, 2006; Malone et al., 2011), branch and bound (de Campos and Ji, 2011), and mathematical programming (Martínez-Rodríguez et al., 2008; Jaakkola et al., 2010). These methods guarantee that optimal solutions are found when they are able to finish successfully. However, their efficiency and scalability are still limited.

Finally, there are a few works on parametric and structure learning in non-Gaussian continuous BNs (Romero et al., 2006; Rumí et al., 2006; Langseth et al., 2010) although this is an open issue.

13.4   Dynamic Bayesian Networks

In domains that evolve over time (e.g., the sequential activation of brain areas during cognitive decision making), **dynamic BNs** (Dean and Kanazawa, 1989; Murphy, 2002) are appropriate models. A discrete time-stamp is introduced, and the same local model is repeated for each unit of time or time slice. The above local model represents a snapshot of the underlying evolving temporal process. Within time slice t, there can be arcs connecting nodes. Also, arcs between nodes of different time slices are known as temporal or transition arcs that specify how variables change from one time point to another. They only flow forward in time because the state of a variable at one time point is determined by the states of a set of variables at previous time points. Setting arc directions across time guarantees the acyclicity of the graph. A prior BN specifies the initial conditions.

In dynamic BNs, the structures of the time slices are identical, and the CPTs are also identical over time. Therefore, dynamic BNs are time-invariant models, and *dynamic* merely means that they can model dynamic systems.

In mathematical terms, a dynamic BN represents a discrete-time stochastic process with a vector of interest $\mathbf{X}[t] = (X_1[t], \ldots, X_n[t])$ at each time $t = 1, \ldots, T$, for example, the BOLD response of n ROIs at time t. Stationarity is commonly assumed, i.e., the probability does not depend on t. If the stochastic process is also assumed to be a **first-order Markovian transition model**, i.e., $p(\mathbf{X}[t] \mid \mathbf{X}[t-1], \ldots, \mathbf{X}[1]) = p(\mathbf{X}[t] \mid \mathbf{X}[t-1])$, then

$$p(\mathbf{X}[1], \ldots, \mathbf{X}[T]) = p(\mathbf{X}[1]) \prod_{t=2}^{T} p(\mathbf{X}[t] \mid \mathbf{X}[t-1]).$$

$p(\mathbf{X}[1])$ are the initial conditions, factorized according to the prior BN. $p(\mathbf{X}[t] \mid \mathbf{X}[t-1])$ is also factorized over each $X_i[t]$ as $\prod_{i=1}^{n} p(X_i[t] \mid \mathbf{Pa}[t](X_i))$, where $\mathbf{Pa}[t](X_i)$ may be in the same or previous time slice.

In continuous settings, a Gaussian distribution is mostly assumed for $p(X_i[t] \mid \mathbf{Pa}[t](X_i))$ (auto-regressive model). Although higher-order and non-stationary Markov models can account for more complex temporal processes, there are obvious challenges to structure and parameter estimation.

Example. Dynamic BN. The structure of a dynamic BN is shown in Figure 13.20. There are three variables, hence $\mathbf{X}[t] = (X_1[t], X_2[t], X_3[t])$. The prior network with the initial conditions is given in (a). The transition network in (b) represents conditional independencies between consecutive time slices and within the same time slice. In this case, it is a first-order Markovian transition model. With arcs from time t to $t+2$, the order would be two. This network conveys the template in a generic time from t to $t+1$ of probabilities for each variable conditioned on other variables of previous and current time slices.

For the purposes of inference with dynamic BNs, the transition network can be unfolded in time to constitute a single network, see Figure 13.20(c). For $T = 3$, the JPD factorizes as

$$p(\mathbf{X}[1], \mathbf{X}[2], \mathbf{X}[3]) = p(X_1[1])p(X_2[1] \mid X_1[1])p(X_3[1] \mid X_2[1], X_1[1])$$

$$\prod_{t=2}^{3} (p(X_1[t] \mid X_1[t-1])p(X_2[t] \mid X_1[t], X_1[t-1],$$

$$X_2[t-1], X_3[t-1])p(X_3[t] \mid X_2[t], X_2[t-1])).$$

∎

Note that dynamic BNs are able to model recurrent networks, with loops and feedback. This is important in neural systems as there are cyclic functional networks in the brain, such as cortico-subcortical loops.

The above methods (constraint-based or score and search) can be adapted to learn from data a first-order Markovian dynamic BN. The prior network can be learned from a data set containing instances at time $t = 1$, whereas the transition network can be learned from a data set including $2n$ variables, instances from times $t - 1$ and also from t ($t = 1, 2, \ldots, T$). Trabelsi (2013) proposed the **dynamic max-min hill-climbing**, an adaptation to dynamic settings of **max-min hill-climbing** (Tsamardinos et al., 2006), a constraint-based learning algorithm that learns an undirected graph that is then oriented with a Bayesian-scoring greedy hill-climbing search. Hence this is a hybridization of constrained-based and score-and-search methods. Friedman et al. (1998b) adapted score and search learning methods to dynamic scenarios. Thus, the **dynamic hill-climbing** algorithm is a hill-climbing search procedure that iteratively improves the BIC score of the prior and transition networks.

Dynamic BNs may assume full or partial observability of states at the nodes. For instance, as mentioned in Section 13.3.2.2, the real state of the neural activity of an ROI is unknown, and only indirect observations, like the BOLD response in fMRI experiments, are given. Another example is the target characters imagined mentally in brain-computer interfaces (like the virtual keyboard P300 Speller), which are indirectly observed via EEG signals. A hidden or latent variable can model this situation. **Hidden Markov models** (HMMs) (Rabiner and Juang, 1986; Ghahramani, 2001) are simple dynamic BNs used to model Markov processes that cannot be directly observed but can be indirectly

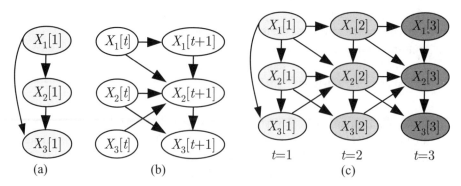

Figure 13.20 Example of dynamic BN structure with three variables, X_1, X_2, and X_3, and three time slices ($T = 3$). (a) Prior network. (b) Transition network, with a first-order Markov assumption. (c) Dynamic BN unfolded in time for three time slices.

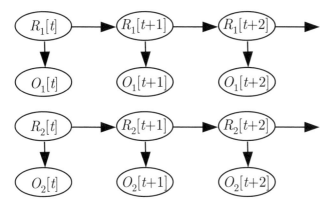

Figure 13.21 Example of HMM. The real state of two ROIs is unknown (state variables R_i), and this is indirectly observed with BOLD responses (observation variables O_i) in an fMRI experiment.

estimated by state-dependent output, that is, the state is not directly visible, but the state-dependent output is. The goal is to determine the optimal sequence of states that could have produced an observed output sequence. The popular Kalman filter (Kalman, 1960) is a continuous-state version of HMMs. Despite their simplicity, HMMs are an extremely useful architecture.

Example. Hidden Markov Model. The HMM in Figure 13.21 represents a simple functional connectivity analysis, identifying two ROIs. State variable R_i of region i ($i = 1, 2$) represents neural activity in ROI i, e.g., whether or not it is activated. This is unknown, and, therefore, nodes R_i are hidden variables. The observations are measures O_i, e.g., the BOLD response.

The model shown in Figure 13.21 is a parallel HMM, where the state space factorizes into multiple independent temporal processes (in this case two) without intermediate connections. That is, the activity in ROI 1 and ROI 2 is assumed to be independent. There are also more complex versions of HMMs. ∎

13.5   Example: Basal Dendritic Trees

Data Set 5 in Section 1.6.5 is used to illustrate how BNs can model 3D neuronal dendritic trees from real data. There are indeed dependencies between their morphological features, as complex interactions with extracellular elements and intrinsic factors have been widely reported for real neurons (Scott and Luo, 2001). Moreover, we can then simulate new (virtual) morphologies by sampling from the BN. These virtual trees should be visually and statistically indistinguishable from real ones. López-Cruz et al. (2011) reports the full study.

Recall that Data Set 5 includes 3D reconstructions of 90 pyramidal neurons from the mouse neocortex, layer III of three cortical regions: secondary motor cortex (M2), secondary somatosensory cortex (S2), and lateral secondary visual cortex and association temporal cortex (V2L/TeA). The 41 morphological variables measured from the 3D reconstructions of real traced dendrites were listed in Table 1.11. For a pair of sibling segments,

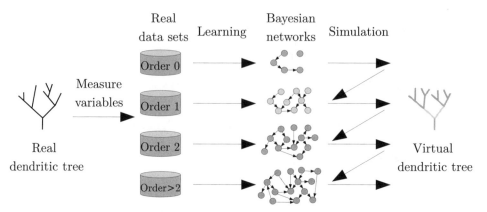

Figure 13.22 BN model and simulation approach of 3D neuronal dendritic trees. We measure key morphological variables in 3D reconstructions of real pyramidal neurons and learn BNs that estimate their joint probability distribution. We then simulate from the BNs to output virtual dendrites. For the color version, please refer to the plate section.

there are two types of variables: (a) construction variables, meant to incrementally build the virtual dendritic trees forwardly, and (b) evidence variables, meant to look back and measure the already grown part of the dendritic tree.

This has a number of advantages over other research (see, e.g., Ascoli and Krichmar, 2000; Donohue and Ascoli, 2008; Torben-Nielsen et al., 2008):

(1) Dependencies between morphological properties are automatically found from real data (data-driven approach) instead of using predefined relationships or assumed independencies; thus non-reported relationships can be discovered instead of relying on expert knowledge.
(2) The joint probability distribution of all variables is modeled, instead of having at most trivariate distributions.
(3) The model is reliably evaluated with statistical tests to compare both uni- and multivariate, original versus simulated distributions, instead of checking against new emergent 1D parameters (global variables not included in the model) or by just visual inspection.

The whole process is summarized in Figure 13.22.

A BN was defined for each part of the dendrite, that is, the original data set was split into four data sets according to the centrifugal order of segments: root segments (order 0), first-order segments (order 1), second-order segments (order 2), and segments with a higher order (order > 2). Accordingly, the relationships may change in the different sections, and heterogeneous developmental factors or spatial influences can be modeled, as reported in the literature. Also, continuous variables were cautiously discretized by mimicking their histograms. The parameters of the BNs were learned using maximum likelihood estimation (Equation (13.15)). The BN structures were learned using the K2 algorithm, albeit applying the BIC score, where a maximum of three parents per node were allowed, and the nodes were ordered such that evidence variables always come before the construction variables (because the construction variables rely on the evidence variables). The centrifugal order (variable 33) was always used as the first node.

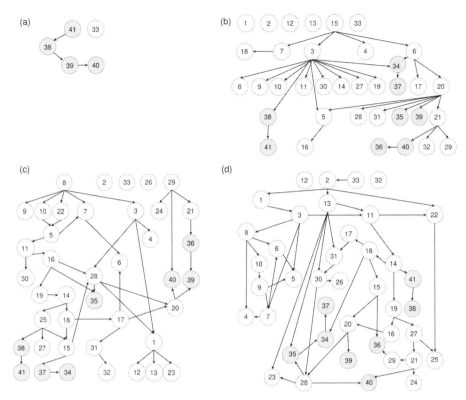

Figure 13.23 The four BNs of the M2 area. (a) Root segments. (b) First-order segments. (c) Second-order segments. (d) Segments with a higher centrifugal order. Numbers in the nodes refer to the variables in Table 1.11. Shaded nodes represent construction variables. Adapted from López-Cruz et al. (2011).

For illustrative purposes, we show the four BNs of the M2 area, whose basal trees have more complex branching patterns and dimensions (Benavides-Piccione et al., 2006), see Figure 13.23. The first BN (Figure 13.23(a)) was very simple because it only captured root segment morphology. In the second BN (Figure 13.23(b)), variables 22–26 were unavailable because the root segment was the only segment, and hence the neighboring segment could not be defined. The structures shown in Figure 13.23(c) and Figure 13.23(d) contain all variables.

The relationships in the BNs matched current neuroanatomical knowledge, which supports model correctness. Also, new relationships were discovered. A common arc in Figure 13.23(b)–(d) is the arc between segment length (variables 34 and 38) and bifurcation occurrence (variables 37 and 41). This means that terminal segments in basal dendrites were longer than intermediate segments. Inclination angles (variable 35) were more likely to be small when subdendrites were tall (variable 16), see Figure 13.23(c). This makes the dendrite grow straight in one direction and helps to model dendritic tropism. Also in Figure 13.23(c), subdendrite width (variable 15) was related to segment bifurcation (variable 37), preventing the segment from splitting for wide subdendrites as a way to constrain tree size and capture resource division and competition between branches. See López-Cruz et al. (2011) for further details.

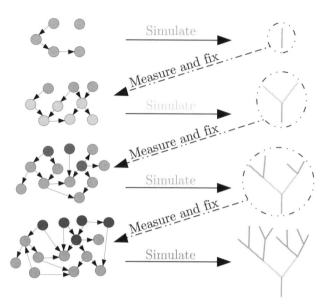

Bayesian networks   Virtual dendritic tree

Figure 13.24 Schematic view of the simulation process. After measuring the evidence variables in the current simulated tree, the corresponding nodes are instantiated in the next BN (dark-colored nodes), and then the virtual dendrite is built incrementally by simulating from the construction variables (light-colored nodes). For the color version, please refer to the plate section.

The simulation process uses the BNs to generate virtual dendritic trees. It starts by creating the root segment by sampling from the first BN. Then it measures evidence variables from the dendritic tree built so far. These measurements are introduced as fixed values in the second BN. Now the construction variables from this second BN are sampled. This scheme of measuring evidence variables in BN_{i-1} to set their values in BN_i followed by sampling from the construction variables in BN_i, is repeated for as long as there are incomplete dendrites, i.e., while the current segment bifurcates. Else, the dendrite ends.

Figure 13.24 illustrates the simulation process. Note that simulated values are discrete, and they have to be converted back to continuous values in order to build a virtual dendritic tree. This is done by building the histogram of the real continuous values in the data set corresponding to the simulated discrete values and then by selecting the median of a randomly selected bin.

The number of dendritic trees in the original data set were counted, and the same number of virtual dendritic trees were simulated from the model. The Wilcoxon rank-sum (or Mann–Whitney U test, see Section 4.2.5), Kolmogorov–Smirnov (Section 4.2.2), and Kullback–Leibler divergence-based (Section 3.6.5) tests were used to compare each variable independently, i.e., real versus simulated. Because BNs model the JPD over all variables, it is more interesting to perform a *multivariate* test (using a Kullback–Leibler divergence estimation in this case) to compare real and simulated JPDs. To consider statistical variability, the simulation was repeated 100 times. With the outputs of each of the four tests (rejections, non-rejections), a sign test was performed to check for the statistical significance of the number of rejections in the 100 repetitions. A sign test is used to decide whether a binomial distribution has an equal chance of success and failure. Having at least

61 rejections in the 100 repetitions is considered to be significant (p-value is smaller than 0.05). The results confirmed that virtual dendrites were similar to real ones.

13.6   Bibliographic Notes

Basics. Useful textbooks on BNs are Pearl (1988), Lauritzen (1996), Castillo et al. (1997), Cowell et al. (1999), Neapolitan (2003), Jensen and Nielsen (2007), Holmes and Jain (2008), Darwiche (2009), Koller and Friedman (2009), and Sucar (2015).

BNs are also useful for making decisions and retrieve optimal decisions. Optimality refers to searching for decisions of maximum expected utility. In this case, the graph is augmented with decision and value nodes that model, decisions and objectives, respectively. The best example is **influence diagrams** (Howard and Matheson, 1984; Shachter, 1986). Key issues are: (a) how to cope with decision problem asymmetries, continuous variables, and different types of decision-chance sequences (Bielza et al., 2011a), and (b) how, like probability models, to engineer or induce utility models from a domain expert or data (Bielza et al., 2010).

An interesting notion when modeling hierarchically structured physical systems is the **conditional BN** or **encapsulated BN** (Srinivas, 1994). Here a CPT within a BN may in turn define another BN and so on, continuing this hierarchy as necessary. The distribution of Y given $\mathbf{X}$ in the higher-level BN is defined as $p(Y|\mathbf{X}) = \sum_{\mathbf{Z}} p(Y, \mathbf{Z}|\mathbf{X})$, where $\mathbf{Z}$ are encapsulated variables, specified in the next-level BN. The conditional random field (Section 14.6) is its undirected counterpart. Encapsulation can simplify the model from a knowledge engineering viewpoint. In a complex system composed of lower-level subsystems, the general model can be decoupled from other detailed models. Encapsulated BNs were then generalized within the framework of **object-oriented BNs** (Koller and Pfeffer, 1997).

A more refined concept of independence is **context-specific independence** (Shimony, 1991; Boutilier et al., 1996). Let $\mathbf{X}, \mathbf{Y}, \mathbf{Z}$ be pairwise disjoint sets of variables, and let $\mathbf{W}$ be a set of variables (that might overlap with $\mathbf{X} \cup \mathbf{Y} \cup \mathbf{Z}$), and let $\mathbf{w} \in \Omega_{\mathbf{W}}$. $\mathbf{X}$ and $\mathbf{Y}$ are said to be **contextually independent** given $\mathbf{Z}$ and the context $\mathbf{w}$ if

$$p(\mathbf{X}|\mathbf{Y}, \mathbf{Z}, \mathbf{w}) = p(\mathbf{X}|\mathbf{Z}, \mathbf{w}).$$

These additional independencies are not visible at the level of the original graph and in the CPTs. However they provide more compact parameterization. Other data structures for representing conditional distributions (like probability trees) and specially designed inference and learning algorithms can exploit these independencies (Chickering et al., 1997; Cano et al., 2011). A generalization of context-specific independence is partial conditional independence (Pensar et al., 2016). **Probabilistic decision graphs** (Jaeger et al., 2006) can encode context-specific independence relations that cannot be captured in a BN structure, and can sometimes provide computationally more efficient representations than BNs. Extensions to the continuous domain also exist (Nielsen et al., 2012).

Interestingly, Reichenbach (1956), who introduced the notion of forks and colliders, thought that X and Z are c.i. given Y not only in forks but also in colliders, a mistake that delayed the development of causal inference by 30 years or more. Another curious point is that the term *clique* was coined by Luce and Perry (1949), who used complete subgraphs in social networks to model cliques of people, all of whom know each other.

Recently two GANs (Section 7.6) based on probability theory have been proposed. Li et al. (2018) introduced **graphical GANs** which use the power of Bayesian networks to compactly represent the dependency structures among random variables and the expressiveness of GANs to learn dependency functions. He et al. (2019) presented **probabilistic GANs**, a probabilistic framework for GANs with theoretical guarantees about the faithfulness of the generator distribution to the real data distribution.

Inference. We have seen that junction trees immediately compute the posterior probability of any set of variables present together in a single clique. An even broader range of queries, with, e.g., a set of query variables present in *different* cliques or with *incremental* evidence, is also possible. In Butz et al. (2016), **marginal tree inference** is introduced as middle ground between variable elimination and junction tree propagation to answer a sequence of queries and avoid unused and repeated computations. Also, we have seen a three-step procedure for building a junction tree. However, an execution of the variable elimination algorithm can be associated with a specific junction tree (Koller and Friedman, 2009), and hence we can use any variable elimination to find a junction tree and any junction tree to define an elimination ordering.

The **conditioning algorithm** (Pearl, 1986; Suermondt and Cooper, 1990; Díez, 1996) is an alternative approach to message passing in a clique tree for exact inference. Here some variables are instantiated to each of their values to simplify the variable elimination process. Then the results for the different values are aggregated. In terms of number of operations, this algorithm does not offer any benefit over the variable elimination algorithm. However, it does offer space savings, which are important if the factors created by the variable elimination algorithm are too big to be accommodated in the main memory.

Also, **network polynomials** (Darwiche, 2003; Park and Darwiche, 2004) provide an alternative view of variable elimination, and their derivatives can be used for several purposes, including retracting or modifying evidence in the network, and sensitivity analysis.

There is a class of approximate inference methods that focus on constructing an approximation to the target distribution. The inference is formulated as a constrained optimization problem. For instance, methods that use junction tree message passing schemes on structures other than trees (like the **loopy belief propagation** algorithm by Murphy et al. [1999]) or with approximate messages (like the **expectation propagation** algorithm by Minka [2001]). **Variational inference methods** are also important approximate methods, providing strategies for maximizing the energy functional or, equivalently, minimizing the relative entropy (Beal, 2003; Winn et al., 2005). Other methods are approximate versions of exact algorithms, like bounded conditioning (Horvitz et al., 1989), probabilistic partial evaluation (Poole, 1997), and mini-bucket elimination (Dechter and Rish, 2003). Alternatively, several approaches combine sampling with message passing, i.e., a hybrid propagation (Kjærulff, 1995; Hernández and Moral, 1997).

Likelihood weighting is a special case of a very general approach called importance sampling (Shachter and Peot, 1989; Cano et al., 1996; Yuan and Druzdzel, 2006; Fernández et al., 2012), see Section 3.5.6. In this case, samples are generated from a different distribution to the one used in the BN. Importance sampling can be applied to undirected graphical models, whereas likelihood weighting only applies to directed models.

An interesting issue is **real-time BN inference**, reviewed in Guo and Hsu (2002), where a real-time application requires a response within a shorter time than it usually takes to reach an exact solution.

MCMC methods were first proposed for models in statistical physics (Metropolis et al., 1953). Geman and Geman (1984) introduced Gibbs sampling for image restoration within computer vision and Pearl (1987) for BNs. Extensive research has been conducted since then, see, e.g., Gelman and Rubin (1992), Gilks et al. (1995), Liang et al. (2010), and Brooks et al. (2011). The BUGS system (Lunn et al., 2012) provides useful software for MCMC methods, supporting sampling for many continuous families, a core problem in statistics. Robert and Casella (2009) provided a practical overview of MCMC methods through a guided implementation in the R language.

MCMC methods require a careful analysis of many issues that are beyond the scope of this book. Concepts like ergodic, regular, and reversible Markov chains are central to guaranteeing that the Markov chain converges to a stationary distribution and that this is unique. Gibbs sampling is a special case of Metropolis–Hastings when choosing a particular proposal distribution. Also, the Gibbs sampler can be modified to iteratively sample blocks of variables, rather than individual variables, leading to much longer-range transitions in the state space (this is called **block Gibbs**).

The random sampling in approximate inference explores the state space of the distribution "uniformly" because each state is generated proportionately to its probability. **Deterministic search methods** (Poole, 1993) explicitly search for high-probability states.

The approximate inference methods described here can be extended to their **collapsed** versions, where a subset of the network variables $\mathbf{X}_a$ is instantiated, and the other $\mathbf{X}_b$ are associated with a closed-form distribution. Samples are "collapsed" – also called **Rao–Blackwellized samples** – because some variables are not instantiated but rather summarized using a distribution. We generate samples $\mathbf{x}_a$ from $\mathbf{X}_a$ and perform exact inference on $\mathbf{X}_b$ given $\mathbf{x}_a$ (Bidyuk and Dechter, 2007).

Learning. An interesting issue in BN learning is to study the number of samples needed in order to learn the correct network *structure* (correct equivalence class, as the specific structure within the equivalence class cannot be distinguished based on observational data alone). Zuk et al. (2006) reported asymptotic results (lower and upper bounds) for the probability of learning a wrong structure, valid in the large sample limit. Sample complexity results, which should approximate the original *distribution* in the **probably approximately correct** (PAC) **learning** sense, i.e., the minimum sample size guaranteeing that there is a high probability of the learned and the original distributions being close to each other, are a different matter. Researchers use the Kullback–Leibler distance between both distributions to measure the approximation quality (Friedman and Yakhini, 1996; Abbeel et al., 2006).

The PC algorithm is widely used in high-dimensional settings ($N \ll n$) because it is computationally feasible for sparse graphs with thousands of variables (Kalisch and Bühlmann, 2007) or with massive data (de Jongh, 2014). For edge orientation in the PC algorithm, we followed the steps of the **inductive causation algorithm**, as described in Pearl (2000). However, there are other orientation rules (Zhang, 2008). To address the identifiability problem mentioned with the PC algorithm (leaving some edges undirected), several proposals have focused on the continuous and causal domain (Peters et al., 2014). This constitutes an interesting alternative to the faithfulness assumption and the identification of only the Markov equivalence class of the graph.

Other scoring functions have been proposed besides those mentioned in this chapter. They include the global uniform metric (Kayaalp and Cooper, 2002), mutual information tests score (de Campos, 2006), factorized normalized maximum likelihood (fNML) (Silander et al., 2008), or SparsityBoost (Brenner and Sontag, 2013). There have been empirical comparisons of scores, see, e.g., Liu et al. (2012), where BIC outperformed AIC, BDeu, and fNML in recovering the underlying BN structure.

Also, hybridations of constraint-based and score-and-search methods have been suggested, like the max-min hill-climbing algorithm (Tsamardinos et al., 2006), mentioned in Section 13.4. The combination of expert knowledge and learning-from-data approaches has also been explored (Heckerman et al., 1995; Masegosa and Moral, 2013), as has the combination of different BNs elicited from various experts (Matzkevich and Abramson, 1992; Peña, 2011; López-Cruz et al., 2014b). Eliciting BNs from expert knowledge is, however, beyond the scope of this book.

In **Bayesian model averaging** (Hoeting et al., 1999), we try to average the prediction of all possible structures. This provides a measure of confidence in predictions relating to structural properties (for example, the probability of a certain arc). Because the number of structures is immense, this task is restricted to simple models (Dash and Cooper, 2004) or networks with few variables (Koivisto and Sood, 2004). Alternatively, the task is approximated with an MCMC approach (the superexponentially large summation is computed over only a subset of possible structures) (Madigan et al., 1996). Broom et al. (2012) reported research in this field.

Benjumeda et al. (2019) efficiently bounded the inference complexity of each BN during the learning process. This is accomplished in polynomial time with respect to the number of network variables and in linear time with respect to its treewidth.

Dynamic. The discrete temporal representation of dynamic BNs is computationally expensive when the absolute time of events is important and observations occur irregularly. This is because the granularity of each dynamic BN time slice must correspond to the smallest possible interval between observations. For instance, MEG and fMRI have different sampling frequencies. Therefore, the time slices in the dynamic BN must be (more detailed) MEG sampling time periods, also including nodes corresponding to (many) unobserved BOLD time points. **Continuous time Bayesian networks** (Nodelman et al., 2002, 2003) model discrete-state systems that evolve continuously in time, without resorting to time discretization. The time spent in a state is exponentially distributed. These networks are a factored representation of continuous-time Markov chains. The distribution over the state of the process at any future time can be computed from the intensity matrix of a homogeneous Markov process that defines the dynamics of the process.

Extensions include **hybrid time BNs** (Liu et al., 2015), which combine discrete-time and continuous-time BNs. They can model dynamic systems with regular and irregular periods for variable changes more naturally.

14 Markov Networks

Chapter 13 elaborated on BNs. BNs are probabilistic graphical models whose structures are directed acyclic graphs. However, the use of arcs (directed edges) may be unsuitable in some domains. For example, it is rather natural to assume that the intensity values of neighboring ROIs are correlated when modeling changes associated with MRI blood flow. Considering a DAG model as shown in Figure 14.1(a) and applying the conditional independence properties to node X_5, we find that its Markov blanket (see Section 13.1.2) contains the nodes in light gray rather than the four neighbors that one might expect.

Alternatively, using an undirected graphical model known as **Markov random field** (Kindermann and Snell, 1980) or **Markov network**, edge orientations do not have to be specified, and it is much more natural in domains where the spatial location of the elements under study is crucial, as in neuroimaging problems. The nodes in light gray in Figure 14.1(b) show the Markov blanket of node X_5, that is, its four neighbors, as we explain below.

Figure 14.2 shows an example of a Markov network structure representing functional brain connectivity of the temporal lobe (see Table 1.12 for the meaning of the different variables) induced from PET images of 49 AD patients (Huang et al., 2010). Each node in the graph corresponds to an anatomical volume of interest in the temporal lobe. The Markov network structure was estimated assuming a multivariate Gaussian distribution of all variables, using a regularization procedure explained in Section 14.7.

The main advantages of Markov networks with respect to their directed version, BNs, are: (a) they are a more intuitive and natural model for some situations with spatial characteristics, and (b) discriminative Markov networks, known as conditional random fields (Section 14.6), can provide better solutions than the discriminative learning of BN based-classifiers (Section 8.5). The disadvantages of Markov networks with respect to BNs include: (a) they are less modular, and (b) parameter and structure learning algorithms are more difficult to develop and computationally more expensive.

The most interesting Markov network applications in neuroscience are in the neuroimaging field, where these models take advantage of the spatial location of pixels and voxels. Some of these applications use spatial regularization to yield parsimonious models.

Some Markov network-based research has been developed on fMRI. Descombes et al. (1998) showed some results for three cognitive processes (visual, motor, and word recognition) with a Markov network as part of a Bayesian framework. Liu et al. (2010) presented spatial regularization of functional connectivity maps. Ryali et al. (2013) proposed a novel spatio-temporal probabilistic parcellation scheme modeling the fMRI time series of a voxel as a von Mises–Fisher distribution and the latent cluster labels as a Markov network in order to identify the functional subdivisions of the human brain. Woolrich et al. (2005)

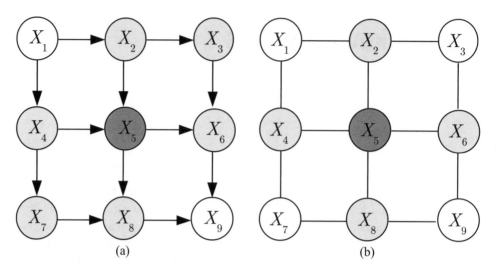

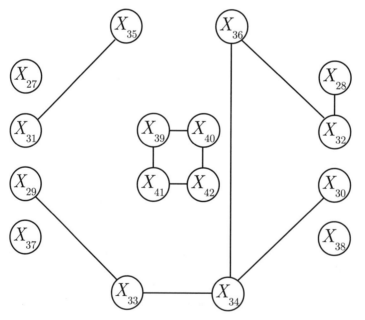

Figure 14.1 Directed and undirected graphical model structures. (a) DAG representing the structure of a BN. The gray node X_5 is independent of all other nodes given its Markov blanket (in light gray), that is, its parents (X_2 and X_4), children (X_6 and X_8), and the parents of its children (X_3 and X_7). (b) Undirected graphical model representing the structure of a Markov network. The gray node X_5 is independent of all other nodes given its neighbors (light gray nodes).

Figure 14.2 Markov network structure for the temporal lobe induced for AD subjects. Adapted from Huang et al. (2010). Table 1.12 has the meaning of the nodes.

proposed a mixture model of Markov networks with spatial regularization for the segmentation of fMRI images. The amount of regularization does not have to be tuned heuristically but is adaptively determined from the data. Tomson et al. (2013) represented with Markov networks direct relationships between regions from fMRI in humans suffering from colored sequence synesthesia, a neurological phenomenon in which stimulation of one sensory or cognitive pathway leads to automatic, involuntary experiences in a second sensory or cognitive pathway.

MRI is another medical imaging used in neuroscience where Markov networks have been useful for discovering new knowledge. Subtle focal cortical dysplasia (the most frequent malformation of cortical development in patients with intractable epilepsy) was identified by means of more accurate brain cortex MRI segmentation in Despotović et al. (2011) using Markov networks. MS was studied with the help of Markov networks by Harmouche et al. (2014), who developed a classifier for discriminating among healthy tissues and two types of lesions. Sharief et al. (2008) used Markov networks for the automatic segmentation of the actively stained mouse brain using multi-spectral MRI.

The chapter is organized as follows. The definition and basic properties of Markov networks are introduced in Section 14.1. Then Section 14.2 covers the factorization of the JPD provided by a Markov network. Section 14.3 presents exact and approximate methods for inference in Markov networks. Several algorithms for learning continuous and discrete Markov networks are explained in Section 14.4 and Section 14.5, respectively. Section 14.6 introduces conditional random fields. Section 14.7 discusses an application of functional brain connectivity in AD with Data Set 6 (Section 1.6.6). Finally, Section 14.8 adds some bibliographic notes.

14.1 Definition and Basic Properties

A Markov network structure, called a **Markov graph**, over a vector of random variables $\mathbf{X} = (X_1, \ldots, X_n)$ is defined by means of an undirected graph $\mathcal{G} = (V, E)$, where $V = \{X_1, \ldots, X_n\}$ denotes the set of nodes (variables) and E is the set of edges between pairs of nodes in V. Two nodes X_i and X_j are called adjacent if they are joined by an edge. This is denoted by $X_i - X_j$, as in Chapter 13. In the Markov graph of Figure 14.3, for example, X_2 and X_5 nodes are adjacent, but X_1 and X_6 are not adjacent. A path $X_{i_1}\text{-}X_{i_2}\text{-}\cdots\text{-}X_{i_r}$ is a set of nodes that are joined, that is, there is an edge $X_{i_{k-1}} - X_{i_k}$ for $k = 2, \ldots, r$. The graph of Figure 14.3 contains the path $X_1\text{-}X_3\text{-}X_5\text{-}X_4\text{-}X_7$. Every pair of nodes is joined by an edge in a complete graph. The Markov graph of the example is not complete. For instance, X_3 and X_4 are not joined by an edge. A Markov subgraph, $\mathcal{G}' = (V', E')$ of $\mathcal{G} = (V, E)$, consists of a subset of nodes V' of V and their corresponding edges E'. In the example, $V' = \{X_4, X_5, X_6, X_7\}$ is the set of nodes of a complete Markov subgraph. Recall that a

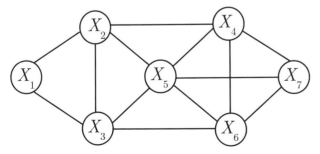

Figure 14.3 Example of a Markov graph or Markov network structure.

clique is a subset of nodes of an undirected graph that is complete and maximal (Section 13.2.2.3). In Figure 14.3, the subgraph of $\{X_4, X_5, X_6\}$ is complete, but not maximal. Considering also X_7, we now find that $\{X_4, X_5, X_6, X_7\}$ is a clique.

If $\mathbf{T}$, $\mathbf{Y}$, and $\mathbf{Z}$ are subsets of variables from a Markov graph $\mathcal{G}$ with no intersection, $\mathbf{Z}$ is said to **separate** $\mathbf{T}$ and $\mathbf{Y}$ (and $\mathbf{Z}$ is said to be a separator) if every path in $\mathcal{G}$ between $\mathbf{T}$ and $\mathbf{Y}$ intersects a node in $\mathbf{Z}$ (note that this is the main step to check in u-separation, Section 13.1.2). For example, $\{X_3, X_4, X_5\}$ separates $\{X_1, X_2\}$ and $\{X_6, X_7\}$ in Figure 14.3. Separators have the nice property that they break the Markov graph into conditionally independent pieces. Specifically, if $\mathbf{Z}$ separates $\mathbf{T}$ and $\mathbf{Y}$ in a Markov graph $\mathcal{G}$ then $\mathbf{T}$ and $\mathbf{Y}$ are c.i. given $\mathbf{Z}$, and this will be denoted as $I_P(\mathbf{T}, \mathbf{Y}|\mathbf{Z})$. This is known as the **global undirected Markov property** of $\mathcal{G}$.

As for BNs (Section 13.1), the set of nodes that renders a node X_i c.i. of all the other nodes in a Markov graph is called the **Markov blanket** of X_i. Mathematically, the Markov blanket of X_i, $\mathbf{MB}(X_i)$, satisfies the following property: $I_P(X_i, \mathbf{X} \setminus \{X_i, \mathbf{MB}(X_i)\}|\mathbf{MB}(X_i))$. In a Markov graph, a node's Markov blanket is the set of its neighbors. For example, in Figure 14.3, we have $\mathbf{MB}(X_5) = \{X_2, X_3, X_4, X_6, X_7\}$. This is called the **local undirected Markov property**.

A direct consequence of the local Markov property is that two nodes are c.i. given the others if they are not joined by a direct edge. This is called the **pairwise undirected Markov property**. Denoting by $e_{i,j}$ the edge between two nodes X_i and X_j in the Markov graph, the property can be written as: $e_{i,j} \notin E \Leftrightarrow I_P(X_i, X_j|\mathbf{X} \setminus \{X_i, X_j\})$. In Figure 14.3, for example, we have $I_P(X_1, X_6|X_2, X_3, X_4, X_5, X_7)$.

Figure 14.4 shows the implication relationships between the above three properties. The global Markov property implies the local Markov property, which implies the pairwise Markov property. This weakest property implies the strongest property when $p(\mathbf{x}) > 0$ for all $\mathbf{x}$, i.e., when p is a positive probability distribution (Koller and Friedman, 2009). From a practical point of view, this implication is useful, as it is easier to empirically assess pairwise conditional independence. The Markov graph can be constructed from these pairwise assessments supplied by an expert or learned from data, and it can be used to derive conditional independencies related to the global Markov property.

The expressive power of directed and undirected graphical models refers to the different conditional independence assessments that the two different types of graphs can express. A graph is said to be a **D-map** (for "dependency map") of a probability distribution if every conditional independence statement satisfied by the distribution is reproduced in the graph (via separations). As an extreme example, a completely disconnected graph (no links) will be a trivial D-map for any distribution.

Alternatively, if every separation between triplets of variables verified by a graph is satisfied by a specific probability distribution as conditional independencies, then the graph

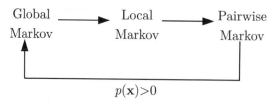

Figure 14.4 Relationships between global, local, and pairwise Markov properties in Markov networks.

Table 14.1 The necessary and sufficient properties of conditional independence relationships for a probability distribution to be graph isomorphic

Name	Property		
Symmetry	$I_P(\mathbf{T},\mathbf{Y}\vert\mathbf{Z})$	$\Leftrightarrow$	$I_P(\mathbf{Y},\mathbf{T}\vert\mathbf{Z})$
Decomposition	$I_P(\mathbf{T},\{\mathbf{Y},\mathbf{W}\}\vert\mathbf{Z})$	$\Leftrightarrow$	$I_P(\mathbf{T},\mathbf{Y}\vert\mathbf{Z})$ and $I_P(\mathbf{T},\mathbf{W}\vert\mathbf{Z})$
Intersection	$I_P(\mathbf{T},\mathbf{Y}\vert\{\mathbf{Z},\mathbf{W}\})$ and $I_P(\mathbf{T},\mathbf{W}\vert\{\mathbf{Z},\mathbf{Y}\})$	$\Rightarrow$	$I_P(\mathbf{T},\{\mathbf{Y},\mathbf{W}\}\vert\mathbf{Z})$
Strong union	$I_P(\mathbf{T},\mathbf{Y}\vert\mathbf{Z})$	$\Rightarrow$	$I_P(\mathbf{T},\mathbf{Y}\vert\{\mathbf{Z},\mathbf{W}\})$
Transitivity	$I_P(\mathbf{T},\mathbf{Y}\vert\mathbf{Z})$	$\Rightarrow$	$I_P(\mathbf{T},\mathbf{W}\vert\mathbf{Z})$ or $I_P(\mathbf{W},\mathbf{Y}\vert\mathbf{Z})$

is said to be an **I-map** (for "independence map") of that distribution. A fully connected graph will be a trivial example of an I-map for any probability distribution.

A graph is said to be a **P-map** (for "perfect map") of a probability distribution if the graph reflects every conditional independence assessment of the probability distribution, and vice versa, i.e., any separation in the graph implies a conditional independence assessment of the probability distribution. Therefore, a P-map is both an I-map and a D-map. These concepts are similar to their directed versions, for Bayesian networks (Section 13.1.2).

Structure learning algorithms that detect conditional independencies (Section 14.5), commonly assume the underlying probability distribution to be **graph isomorphic** (Pearl, 1988) or faithful (Spirtes et al., 1993). This means that the probability distribution has a faithful undirected graph. A probability distribution is said to be **faithful** to a graph if the graph connectivity exactly represents any conditional dependencies and independencies existing in the distribution, i.e., the graph is a P-map of the distribution. It has been proved (Pearl, 1988) that a necessary and sufficient condition for a distribution to be graph isomorphic is for its set of conditional independence relationships to satisfy the properties in Table 14.1 for all disjoint sets of variables **T, Y, Z, W**.

The set of probability distributions such that there is, for each distribution, a directed graph that is a P-map is not necessarily the same as the set of distributions for which there is an undirected graph that is a P-map. Additionally, there are distributions for which neither directed nor undirected graphs offer a P-map. Finally, some probability distributions can be modeled perfectly by either directed or undirected graphs. The resulting graphs are **chordal graphs** (Beeri et al., 1983).

Figure 14.5(a) shows an example of a DAG satisfying the conditional independence assessments $I_P(X_1,X_2\vert\varnothing)$ and $\neg I_P(X_1,X_2\vert X_3)$. There is no corresponding Markov graph over the same three variables that is a P-map for both assessments. Alternatively, the Markov graph in Figure 14.5(b) verifies the following conditional independence assertions: $\neg I_P(X_1,X_2\vert\varnothing)$, $I_P(X_3,X_4\vert\{X_1,X_2\})$, and $I_p(X_1,X_2\vert\{X_3,X_4\})$. There is no DAG over these four variables that is a P-map for the above three conditional independence assessments.

14.2   Factorization of the Joint Probability Distribution

The factorization of the JPD $p(\mathbf{x}\vert\boldsymbol{\theta})$ (or density if the variables are continuous) in a Markov network depends on parameter $\boldsymbol{\theta}$ and cannot use the topological ordering (with parents

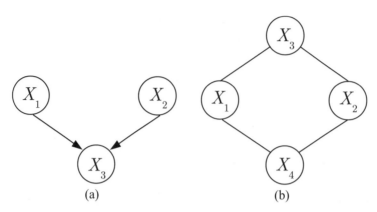

Figure 14.5 Examples of the expressive power of directed and undirected graphical models. (a) A DAG whose conditional independence assessments cannot be expressed with a Markov graph. (b) A Markov graph whose conditional independence assessments cannot be expressed with a DAG.

and children), as this does not exist as in BNs. Hence the chain rule is not applicable and instead of relating a conditional probability distribution with each node, potential functions or simply **potentials** (as in Section 13.2.2.3) are associated with each clique in the Markov graph. The potential function for clique $\mathbf{C}$ will be denoted by $\psi_{\mathbf{C}}(\mathbf{x}_{\mathbf{C}}|\boldsymbol{\theta}_{\mathbf{C}})$, where $\mathbf{C} \in \mathcal{C}$ (the set of cliques in the Markov graph), $\mathbf{x}_{\mathbf{C}}$ is the projection of the n-dimensional random variable to clique $\mathbf{C}$, and $\boldsymbol{\theta}_{\mathbf{C}}$ denotes the parameter vector for clique $\mathbf{C}$. A potential function can be any non-negative function of its arguments. The JPD, $p(\mathbf{x}|\boldsymbol{\theta})$, is then defined to be proportional to the product of the potential functions over the cliques. Additionally, any positive probability distribution whose conditional independence assessments can be represented by a Markov graph factorizes accordingly.

In mathematical notation, this type of factorization is established by the **Hammersley–Clifford theorem** (Hammersley and Clifford, 1971): a positive probability distribution $p(\mathbf{x}|\boldsymbol{\theta}) > 0$ satisfies the conditional independence assessments of a Markov graph, $\mathcal{G}$, if and only if $p(\mathbf{x}|\boldsymbol{\theta})$ can be represented as a product of factors, one per clique, i.e.,

$$p(\mathbf{x}|\boldsymbol{\theta}) = \frac{1}{Z(\boldsymbol{\theta})} \prod_{\mathbf{C} \in \mathcal{C}} \psi_{\mathbf{C}}(\mathbf{x}_{\mathbf{C}}|\boldsymbol{\theta}_{\mathbf{C}}),$$

where Z is the **partition function** given by

$$Z(\boldsymbol{\theta}) = \sum_{\mathbf{x}} \prod_{\mathbf{C} \in \mathcal{C}} \psi_{\mathbf{C}}(\mathbf{x}_{\mathbf{C}}|\boldsymbol{\theta}_{\mathbf{C}}),$$

which ensures that the JPD is well defined (it adds up to 1). The computation of $Z(\boldsymbol{\theta})$ is generally intractable, but a great deal of research has been conducted on how to approximate its calculation.

A **Markov network** over a specified Markov graph $\mathcal{G}$ is determined by the potential functions, $\psi_{\mathbf{C}}(\mathbf{x}_{\mathbf{C}}|\boldsymbol{\theta}_{\mathbf{C}})$, defined over cliques in $\mathcal{C}$, and this representation essentially gives the number of parameters necessary to determine the JPD. This number is exponential in the clique sizes, and therefore, they should be kept small.

Example. Consider the Markov graph in Figure 14.3. There are five cliques: $\mathbf{C}_1 = \{X_1, X_2, X_3\}$ $\mathbf{C}_2 = \{X_2, X_3, X_5\}$, $\mathbf{C}_3 = \{X_2, X_4, X_5\}$, $\mathbf{C}_4 = \{X_3, X_5, X_6\}$, and $\mathbf{C}_5 = $

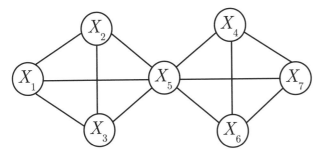

Figure 14.6 Example of a Markov graph with two cliques.

$\{X_4, X_5, X_6, X_7\}$. If $p(\mathbf{x}|\boldsymbol{\theta})$ is a probability distribution for which the graph is a P-map, then $p(\mathbf{x}|\boldsymbol{\theta})$ factorizes as follows:

$$p(\mathbf{x}|\boldsymbol{\theta}) = \frac{1}{Z(\boldsymbol{\theta})} \psi_1(x_1, x_2, x_3|\boldsymbol{\theta}_1) \psi_2(x_2, x_3, x_5|\boldsymbol{\theta}_2) \psi_3(x_2, x_4, x_5|\boldsymbol{\theta}_3) \psi_4(x_3, x_5, x_6|\boldsymbol{\theta}_4)$$
$$\psi_5(x_4, x_5, x_6, x_7|\boldsymbol{\theta}_5), \tag{14.1}$$

where

$$Z(\boldsymbol{\theta}) = \sum_{\mathbf{x}} \psi_1(x_1, x_2, x_3|\boldsymbol{\theta}_1) \psi_2(x_2, x_3, x_5|\boldsymbol{\theta}_2) \psi_3(x_2, x_4, x_5|\boldsymbol{\theta}_3) \psi_4(x_3, x_5, x_6|\boldsymbol{\theta}_4)$$
$$\psi_5(x_4, x_5, x_6, x_7|\boldsymbol{\theta}_5).$$

$\boldsymbol{\theta}_i$ ($i = 1, \ldots, 5$) denotes the local parameter vector associated with the ith clique. Assuming binary variables, the number of parameters needed in Equation (14.1) are $8 + 8 + 8 + 8 + 16 = 48$.

By removing edges $X_2 - X_4$ and $X_3 - X_6$ from Figure 14.3 and adding edge $X_1 - X_5$, we output the Markov graph of Figure 14.6. This graph has only two cliques: $\mathbf{C}_1 = \{X_1, X_2, X_3, X_5\}$, and $\mathbf{C}_2 = \{X_4, X_5, X_6, X_7\}$. The JPD $p(\mathbf{x}|\boldsymbol{\theta})$ is now factorized as:

$$p(\mathbf{x}|\boldsymbol{\theta}) = \frac{1}{Z(\boldsymbol{\theta})} \psi_1(x_1, x_2, x_3, x_5|\boldsymbol{\theta}_1) \psi_2(x_4, x_5, x_6, x_7|\boldsymbol{\theta}_2),$$

where

$$Z(\boldsymbol{\theta}) = \sum_{\mathbf{x}} \psi_1(x_1, x_2, x_3, x_5|\boldsymbol{\theta}_1) \psi_2(x_4, x_5, x_6, x_7|\boldsymbol{\theta}_2).$$

The number of parameters needed by this new factorization is reduced to $16 + 16 = 32$. ∎

The structure of a Markov graph can be represented by a **factor graph** (Kschischang et al., 2001). A factor graph is a bipartite graph $\mathcal{G} = (V, E, F)$, where V is the set of nodes, E the set of edges between pairs of nodes in V, and F the set of factor nodes. $X \in V$ is connected to a factor node $\psi_A \in F$, if X is an argument of ψ_A, with A a set of indices of nodes in V. An example of a factor graph is shown in Figure 14.7.

Some popular probability models are expressed as examples of Markov networks below.

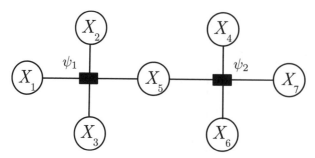

Figure 14.7 The Markov graph of Figure 14.6 as a factor graph with two factor nodes represented as black rectangles, with $\{X_1, X_2, X_3, X_5\}$ and with $\{X_4, X_5, X_6, X_7\}$ as arguments, respectively.

The **Gibbs distribution** (Gibbs, 1902) is a statistical physics model that factorizes the JPD according to cliques as follows:

$$p(\mathbf{x}|\boldsymbol{\theta}) = \frac{1}{Z(\boldsymbol{\theta})} \exp\left(-\sum_{\mathbf{C}} E(\mathbf{x}_{\mathbf{C}}|\boldsymbol{\theta}_{\mathbf{C}})\right),$$

where $E(\mathbf{x}_{\mathbf{C}}|\boldsymbol{\theta}_{\mathbf{C}})$ is the energy associated with the variables in clique $\mathbf{C}$. This model can be written as a Markov network by defining $\psi_{\mathbf{C}}(\mathbf{x}_{\mathbf{C}}|\boldsymbol{\theta}_{\mathbf{C}}) = \exp(-E(\mathbf{x}_{\mathbf{C}}|\boldsymbol{\theta}_{\mathbf{C}}))$. Low-energy configurations will correspond to high-probability states.

Pairwise Markov random fields restrict the parametrization to the edges of the Markov graph rather than to the cliques. This parametrization, in the form of $\psi_{i,j}(x_i, x_j|\boldsymbol{\theta}_{i,j})$ for pair (X_i, X_j), results in simple factorizations of the JPD, where each factor needs only two-order statistics. In Figure 14.6, we get

$$p(\mathbf{x}|\boldsymbol{\theta}) \propto \psi_{1,2}(x_1, x_2|\boldsymbol{\theta}_{1,2}) \psi_{1,3}(x_1, x_3|\boldsymbol{\theta}_{1,3}) \psi_{1,5}(x_1, x_5|\boldsymbol{\theta}_{1,5}) \psi_{2,3}(x_2, x_3|\boldsymbol{\theta}_{2,3}) \psi_{2,5}(x_2, x_5|\boldsymbol{\theta}_{2,5})$$
$$\psi_{3,5}(x_3, x_5|\boldsymbol{\theta}_{3,5}) \psi_{4,5}(x_4, x_5|\boldsymbol{\theta}_{4,5}) \psi_{5,6}(x_5, x_6|\boldsymbol{\theta}_{5,6}) \psi_{5,7}(x_5, x_7|\boldsymbol{\theta}_{5,7}) \psi_{4,6}(x_4, x_6|\boldsymbol{\theta}_{4,6})$$
$$\psi_{4,7}(x_4, x_7|\boldsymbol{\theta}_{4,7}) \psi_{6,7}(x_6, x_7|\boldsymbol{\theta}_{6,7}).$$

Log-linear models can be seen as examples of Markov networks for discrete variables when defining the log-potential functions, $\log \psi_{\mathbf{C}}(\mathbf{x}_{\mathbf{C}}|\boldsymbol{\theta}_{\mathbf{C}})$, as a linear function of parameters $\boldsymbol{\theta}_{\mathbf{C}}$, that is,

$$\log \psi_{\mathbf{C}}(\mathbf{x}_{\mathbf{C}}|\boldsymbol{\theta}_{\mathbf{C}}) = \boldsymbol{\phi}_{\mathbf{C}}(\mathbf{x}_{\mathbf{C}})^T \boldsymbol{\theta}_{\mathbf{C}}, \tag{14.2}$$

where $\boldsymbol{\phi}_{\mathbf{C}}(\mathbf{x}_{\mathbf{C}})$ is a vector with the same number of components as $\boldsymbol{\theta}_{\mathbf{C}}$. In log-linear models, the joint probability factorizes as follows:

$$p(\mathbf{x}|\boldsymbol{\theta}) = \frac{1}{Z(\boldsymbol{\theta})} \prod_{\mathbf{C} \in \mathcal{C}} e^{\boldsymbol{\phi}_{\mathbf{C}}(\mathbf{x}_{\mathbf{C}})^T \boldsymbol{\theta}_{\mathbf{C}}}. \tag{14.3}$$

The log-probability for the log-linear model is

$$\log p(\mathbf{x}|\boldsymbol{\theta}) = \sum_{\mathbf{C} \in \mathcal{C}} \boldsymbol{\phi}_{\mathbf{C}}(\mathbf{x}_{\mathbf{C}})^T \boldsymbol{\theta}_{\mathbf{C}} - \log Z(\boldsymbol{\theta}).$$

The **Ising model** (Ising, 1925) was originally used for modeling the behavior of magnets in statistical physics. Let us consider a random variable $X_s \in \{-1, +1\}$ representing the spin of an atom. In particular, -1 represents spin down and $+1$ spin up. In ferro-magnets, neighboring spins tend to line up in the same direction, whereas the spins of anti-ferro-magnets are usually different from their neighbors. A Markov graph similar to the 2D lattice shown in Figure 14.1(b) can be a graphical example. The JPD verifies

$$p(\mathbf{x}|\boldsymbol{\theta}) \propto \prod_{X_s - X_t} \psi_{s,t}(x_s, x_t | \boldsymbol{\theta}_{s,t}),$$

where the product is extended to any pairs of connected nodes in the Markov graph, and $\psi_{s,t}(x_s, x_t | \boldsymbol{\theta}_{s,t})$ denotes a pairwise clique potential that takes on values depending on weights $w_{s,t}$, the coupling strength between nodes X_s and X_t, according to

$$\psi_{s,t}(x_s, x_t | \boldsymbol{\theta}_{s,t}) = \begin{cases} e^{w_{s,t}} & \text{if } x_s = x_t \\ e^{-w_{s,t}} & \text{if } x_s \neq x_t. \end{cases}$$

For nodes that are not connected in the Markov graph, we set $w_{s,t} = 0$. It is often assumed that all edges have the same strength-associated values, $w_{s,t}$. If this quantity is positive, then neighboring spins are likely to be in the same state, as can be expected in ferro-magnets. A negative strength value will mean that the spins are likely to have different values from their neighbors, as in anti-ferro-magnets.

A **Hopfield network** (Hopfield, 1982) can be regarded as a fully connected Ising model with symmetric weights $w_{s,t}$ that can be learned using (approximate) maximum likelihood estimation. Exact inference is intractable in these models, and **iterative conditional modes** (a coordinate descent algorithm) is used as a standard approximation. The main idea is to assign to each node its most probable state given the values of all its neighbors.

The **Boltzmann machine** (Ackley et al., 1985) increases the representation power of Hopfield networks by introducing some hidden variables. Both hidden and visible variables are pairwise connected. Inference is now approximate using Gibbs sampling (as in Section 13.2.3), which is a stochastic version of the iterative conditional modes method. **Restricted Boltzmann machines** (Smolensky, 1986) have been proposed in order to reduce the complexity of these models and accommodate a number of edges that is quadratic in the total number of visible and hidden variables. In restricted Boltzmann machines, the only existing connections (dependencies) are between hidden and visible variables, and there are none between units of the same type (no hidden-hidden or visible-visible connections).

Figure 14.8 shows examples of graphs for (a) a Hopfield network, (b) a Boltzmann machine, and (c) a restricted Boltzmann machine.

14.3 Inference in Markov Networks

Inference methods in Markov networks are similar to the BN methods reported in Section 13.2 and can be also organized as exact and approximate approaches.

14.3.1 Exact Inference

The variable elimination algorithm described in Section 13.2.2 can be easily adapted for Markov networks. We explain the main ideas with the example of Figure 14.9, a transformation of the BN structure of Figure 13.1.

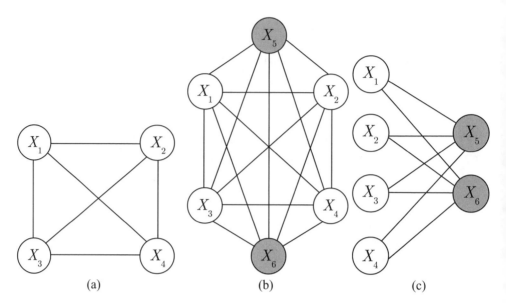

Figure 14.8 Examples of Markov graphs. (a) A Hopfield network with four variables. (b) A Boltzmann machine with four visible and two hidden variables. (c) Restricted Boltzmann machine with four visible and two hidden variables. Hidden variables are shaded.

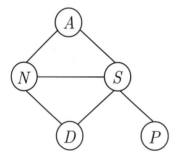

Figure 14.9 Markov network structure of a hypothetical model for the risk of dementia, where A = Age, N = Neuronal atrophy, S = Stroke, D = Dementia, and P = Paralysis.

The JPD factorizes according to the cliques of the Markov graph as follows:

$$p(A,N,S,D,P) = \frac{1}{Z}\psi_1(A,N,S)\psi_2(N,S,D)\psi_3(S,P).$$

Now suppose that we wish to compute $p(D=d)$, the marginal probability that a person has dementia. We could simply enumerate over all possible assignments of all the variables (except D), adding up the probability of each joint instantiation:

$$p(D) = \frac{1}{Z}\sum_{A,N,S,P}\psi_1(A,N,S)\psi_2(N,S,D)\psi_3(S,P). \tag{14.4}$$

Using the elimination order given by A-N-S-P, we get

$$p(D) = \frac{1}{Z}\sum_{P}\sum_{S}\psi_3(S,P)\sum_{N}\psi_2(N,S,D)\sum_{A}\psi_1(A,N,S).$$

We evaluate this expression by operating from right to left. First we marginalize out A to get a new factor $\psi_4(N,S)$. Equation (14.4) is now transformed into

$$p(D) = \frac{1}{Z} \sum_P \sum_S \psi_3(S,P) \sum_N \psi_2(N,S,D) \psi_4(N,S). \tag{14.5}$$

After computing $\sum_N \psi_2(N,S,D)\psi_4(N,S)$, we obtain a new factor, $\psi_5(S,D)$, and Equation (14.5) is now written as

$$p(D) = \frac{1}{Z} \sum_P \sum_S \psi_3(S,P) \psi_5(S,D).$$

Once we marginalize out S yielding a new factor $\psi_6(P,D)$, we have $p(D) = \frac{1}{Z} \sum_P \psi_6(P,D)$. Finally, $p(D)$ is calculated after summing up on P and normalizing the result to yield a probability distribution.

The application of the message passing or junction tree algorithm (Section 13.2.2) is more or less straightforward for Markov networks. The Markov graph should be transformed into a chordal graph, also called triangulated graph. This transformation is carried out by introducing edges such that every undirected cycle X_1-$X_2 \cdots X_K$-X_1 of length $K \geq 4$ has a chord, i.e., an edge that connects every pair of nonadjacent nodes in the cycle. As in the BN case, the cliques of the chordal graph, $\mathbf{C}_j$, are the nodes of the junction tree. Denoting the separators of this junction tree by $\mathbf{S}_{jk}$, the joint distribution can be expressed as

$$p(\mathbf{x}) = \frac{\prod_{\mathbf{C}_j} \psi_{\mathbf{C}_j}(\mathbf{x}_{\mathbf{C}_j})}{\prod_{\mathbf{S}_{jk}} \psi_{\mathbf{S}_{jk}}(\mathbf{x}_{\mathbf{S}_{jk}})},$$

where $\psi_{\mathbf{C}_j}$ and $\psi_{\mathbf{S}_{jk}}$ are potential functions over $\mathbf{x}_{\mathbf{C}_j}$ and $\mathbf{x}_{\mathbf{S}_{jk}}$, respectively.

The junction tree algorithm also works for **Gaussian Markov networks**, where the joint density function follows a multivariate Gaussian. It takes cubic time in the treewidth (Section 13.6) of the graph, smaller than the exponential time required for discrete Markov networks.

14.3.2 Approximate Inference

Approximate methods based on the idea of Monte Carlo simulation introduced in Section 3.5.5 are an alternative to exact methods. In this section, we discuss the application of Gibbs sampling (Section 13.2.3) to Markov networks. Gibbs sampling (Geman and Geman, 1984) produces dependent samples but works well in high dimensions. The main idea is that each variable is sampled in turn, conditioned on the values of all the other variables in the distribution. Given a sample $\mathbf{x}^{(s)}$ of all the n variables at iteration s, we generate a new sample $\mathbf{x}^{(s+1)}$ by sampling each variable in turn, based on the most recent values of the other variables, that is,

$$\text{Generate } X_1 = x_1^{(s+1)} \sim p\left(x_1 | x_2^{(s)}, \ldots, x_n^{(s)}\right),$$

$$\text{Generate } X_2 = x_2^{(s+1)} \sim p\left(x_2 | x_1^{(s+1)}, x_3^{(s)}, \ldots, x_n^{(s)}\right),$$

$$\cdots$$

$$\text{Generate } X_i = x_i^{(s+1)} \sim p\left(x_i | x_1^{(s+1)}, \ldots, x_{i-1}^{(s+1)}, x_{i+1}^{(s)}, \ldots, x_n^{(s)}\right),$$

$$\cdots$$

$$\text{Generate } X_n = x_n^{(s+1)} \sim p\left(x_n | x_1^{(s+1)}, \ldots, x_{n-1}^{(s+1)}\right).$$

Generally, variable X_i may only depend on some of the other variables. If the joint probability distribution $p(\mathbf{x})$ factorizes according to a Markov network, X_i will only depend on the variables in its Markov blanket, which are its neighbors in the graph, $\mathbf{MB}(X_i)$. For example, for pairwise Markov random fields, the **full conditional** for variable X_i can be expressed as

$$
\begin{aligned}
p(X_i = k|\mathbf{x}_{-i}) &= \frac{p(X_i = k, \mathbf{x}_{-i})}{\sum_r p(X_i = r, \mathbf{x}_{-i})} \\
&= \frac{\frac{1}{Z}\prod_{X_j \in \mathbf{MB}(X_i)} \psi_{i,j}(X_i = k, x_j) \prod_{X_j, X_k \notin \mathbf{MB}(X_i)} \psi_{j,k}(x_j, x_k)}{\frac{1}{Z}\sum_r \prod_{X_j \in \mathbf{MB}(X_i)} \psi_{i,j}(X_i = r, x_j) \prod_{X_j, X_k \notin \mathbf{MB}(X_i)} \psi_{j,k}(x_j, x_k)} \\
&= \frac{\prod_{X_j \in \mathbf{MB}(X_i)} \psi_{i,j}(X_i = k, x_j)}{\sum_r \prod_{X_j \in \mathbf{MB}(X_i)} \psi_{i,j}(X_i = r, x_j)}.
\end{aligned}
$$

14.4   Learning Continuous Markov Networks

Contrary to the approach applied with BNs, we start here with methods for learning continuous rather than discrete Markov networks. This is motivated by the extensive research that has been conducted on learning Gaussian Markov networks from data. This task is facilitated by the mathematical properties of multivariate Gaussian densities. Figure 14.10 shows the organization of this and the next section.

14.4.1   Edge Exclusion Approaches

One of the simplest algorithms for learning Gaussian Markov networks consists of assuming that an edge $X_i - X_j$ between nodes X_i and X_j, is in the Markov graph $\mathcal{G}$ if and only if X_i and X_j are conditionally dependent given the other variables, i.e., $\neg I_P(X_i, X_j | \mathbf{X} \setminus \{X_i, X_j\})$ (Speed and Kiiveri, 1986). This corresponds to the pairwise Markov property introduced

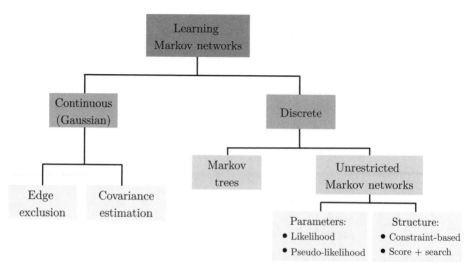

Figure 14.10 Organization of learning Markov network methods covered by Sections 14.4 and 14.5.

in Section 14.1. It is the basis for the **edge exclusion algorithm** (Smith and Whittaker, 1998). It starts from the complete undirected graph and excludes all the edges $X_i - X_j$ for which $I_P(X_i, X_j | \mathbf{X} \setminus \{X_i, X_j\})$ holds.

For multivariate Gaussian distributions, two variables are c.i. given the other variables if and only if the population partial correlation between both variables given the rest equals zero. In mathematical notation,

$$I_P(X_i, X_j | \mathbf{X} \setminus \{X_i, X_j\}) \Leftrightarrow \rho_{X_i X_j | \mathbf{X} \setminus \{X_i, X_j\}} = 0.$$

For a collection of variables, the **population partial correlation coefficient** is a measure of the linear dependence of a pair of variables when the influence of the remaining variables is eliminated. Specifically, suppose that variables $X_1, \dots, X_n$ have a JPD, and let $X_{1|3,\dots,n}^*$, $X_{2|3,\dots,n}^*$ be the best linear approximations to variables X_1 and X_2, respectively, based on $X_3, \dots, X_n$. Then the population partial correlation between X_1 and X_2 given $X_3, \dots, X_n$, denoted as $\rho_{12|3,\dots,n}$, is defined as the ordinary correlation coefficient between variables $Y_1 = X_1 - X_{1|3,\dots,n}^*$ and $Y_2 = X_2 - X_{2|3,\dots,n}^*$, i.e.,

$$\rho_{12|3,\dots,n} = \frac{\mathbb{E}\left[(Y_1 - \mathbb{E}[Y_1])(Y_2 - \mathbb{E}[Y_2])\right]}{\sqrt{Var[Y_1] Var[Y_2]}}.$$

In other words, the population partial correlation coefficient between two variables given the other variables is the correlation between the residuals resulting from the linear regressions of each of the two variables given the rest. From this definition, it follows that $-1 \le \rho_{12|3,\dots,n} \le 1$.

Assume that a sample of size N from a multivariate normal distribution, $\mathbf{X} \sim \mathcal{N}(\mathbf{x}|\boldsymbol{\mu}, \boldsymbol{\Sigma})$, is available. Let $r_{X_i, X_j | \mathbf{X} \setminus \{X_i, X_j\}}$ denote the sample partial correlation between X_i and X_j given the rest of variables (see also Section 12.3.3). The sample partial correlation can be computed from the precision matrix, $\mathbf{W} = \boldsymbol{\Sigma}^{-1}$. For example, $r_{12|3,\dots,n}$, the sample partial correlation of X_1 and X_2 given the other variables, $X_3, \dots, X_n$, can be expressed in terms of the MLEs of the elements of $\mathbf{W}$, as $r_{12|3,\dots,n} = -\hat{w}_{12}(\hat{w}_{11}\hat{w}_{22})^{-1/2}$ (Whittaker, 1990).

Under the null hypothesis that $\rho_{X_i, X_j | \mathbf{X} \setminus \{X_i, X_j\}} = 0$, the test statistic $\frac{1}{2} \ln \left(\frac{1 + r_{X_i, X_j | \mathbf{X} \setminus \{X_i, X_j\}}}{1 - r_{X_i, X_j | \mathbf{X} \setminus \{X_i, X_j\}}} \right)$, known as **Fisher's transform of the partial correlation**, has an asymptotic $\mathcal{N}(0, \frac{1}{\sqrt{N-n-1}})$ distribution (Fisher, 1925). Using this distribution, an approximate hypothesis test can be applied to check the removal of each edge in the Markov network.

The above edge exclusion-based algorithm can be seen as performing simultaneous hypothesis tests, i.e., one test per edge, giving a total of $\frac{n(n-1)}{2}$ tests. As this modeling is founded on the results of hypothesis tests and decisions based on samples are subject to errors, policies for controlling these errors should be applied.

The important thing in many problems is the expected percentage of false discoveries (edges included or removed from the Markov network) over all the discoveries made rather than whether a false discovery is made. The **false discovery rate** (FDR) (Benjamini and Yekutieli, 2001) is designed to control this proportion, conceptualizing the rate of type I errors in null hypothesis testing when conducting multiple comparisons. Suppose that we test m null hypotheses $H_0^1, \dots, H_0^m$. The FDR is formally defined as the expected proportion of rejected null hypotheses that are false, i.e., $\mathbb{E}\left[\frac{|F|}{|D|}\right]$, where $|F|$ is the number of rejected true null hypotheses (i.e., false discoveries), and $|D|$ is the number of rejected null hypotheses (i.e., discoveries). Let $p_1, \ldots, p_m$ denote the p-values corresponding to $H_0^1, \ldots, H_0^m$, respectively. Moreover, let $p_{(i)}$ denote the ith smallest p-value and $H_0^{(i)}$ its corresponding hypothesis. The following procedure controls the FDR at level α (i.e., $\mathbb{E}\left[\frac{|F|}{|D|}\right] \leq \alpha$): reject $H_0^1, \ldots, H_0^j$, where j is the largest i for which $p_{(i)} \frac{m}{i} \sum_{k=1}^m \frac{1}{k} \leq \alpha$.

Peña (2008) proposed an extension of the edge exclusion algorithm. The algorithm called **IAMB-FDR** is a modification of the IAMB proposed by Tsamardinos and Aliferis (2003) (Section 8.4.1.7), which incorporates a mechanism for controlling FDR. The algorithm can be applied under the sparsity assumption when $N \ll n$ ("large n, small N" problem).

IAMB-FDR is based on a characterization, where an edge $X_i - X_j$ is in the Markov graph if and only if X_j belongs to the Markov boundary of X_i, denoted as $\mathbf{MBo}(X_i)$. A **Markov boundary** of $X_i \in \mathbf{X}$ is any subset $\mathbf{MBo}(X_i)$ of $\mathbf{X} \setminus X_i$, such that (i) it is a Markov blanket of X_i, i.e., $I_P(X_i, \mathbf{X} \setminus \{\mathbf{MBo}(X_i), X_i\} | \mathbf{MBo}(X_i))$; and (ii) no proper subset of $\mathbf{MBo}(X_i)$ satisfies (i). A Markov boundary of X_i is its minimal Markov blanket.

IAMB-FDR starts estimating its Markov boundary, $\mathbf{MBo}(X_i)$ of each variable X_i. To do this, IAMB-FDR computes p-values for the null hypotheses $I_P(X_i, X_j | \mathbf{MBo}(X_i) \setminus X_j)$ for all X_j variables. It iteratively adds the variable with the smallest p-value to $\mathbf{MBo}(X_i)$, changing the configuration of the current Markov boundary for X_i at each step. This forward (admission) phase finishes when the smallest p-value is greater than a prefixed threshold. At this point, a backward phase starts with the objective of eliminating false positives. At each step of this backward phase, the variable whose p-value is the highest is considered for removal. This variable is removed if its value is greater than the threshold. Note that the Markov boundary for X_i is updated at each step in both forward and backward phases. Once the Markov boundary of each variable X_i is estimated, a Markov network structure can be derived from these n Markov boundaries. The Markov graph will contain the edge between X_i and X_j if and only if $X_i \in \mathbf{MBo}(X_j)$ or, alternatively, $X_j \in \mathbf{MBo}(X_i)$.

Unfortunately, this method of constructing the Markov graph cannot be construed as performing simultaneous hypothesis tests, and it cannot embed the procedure proposed by Benjamini and Yekutieli (2001) for controlling FDR. IAMB-FDR (Peña, 2008) modifies the Markov graph induction process so that the resulting nodes in the output Markov boundary includes precisely the nodes X_j whose corresponding null hypotheses, $I_P(X_i, X_j | \mathbf{MBo}(X_i) \setminus \{X_j\})$, are rejected when running the procedure proposed by Benjamini and Yekutieli (2001) at level α.

14.4.2 Covariance Estimation Approaches

A popular approach for outputting an estimator of a sparse Markov network precision matrix, $\boldsymbol{\Sigma}^{-1}$, is given by the L_1-norm regularized maximum likelihood estimation, also known as the **graphical lasso** (Friedman et al., 2007). The negative Gaussian log-likelihood of $\boldsymbol{\Sigma}^{-1}$ for a sample $\mathbf{x}^1, \ldots, \mathbf{x}^N$ of i.i.d. values from $\mathbf{X} \sim \mathcal{N}(\mathbf{x}|\boldsymbol{\mu}, \boldsymbol{\Sigma})$ after plugging $\boldsymbol{\mu}$ into its MLE, $\hat{\boldsymbol{\mu}} = N^{-1} \sum_{i=1}^N \mathbf{x}^i$, is

$$-\frac{N}{2} \log |\boldsymbol{\Sigma}^{-1}| + \frac{N}{2} \mathrm{tr}(\mathbf{S}\boldsymbol{\Sigma}^{-1}) + D,$$

where $|\boldsymbol{\Sigma}^{-1}|$ is the determinant of $\boldsymbol{\Sigma}^{-1}$, $\mathbf{S} = \frac{1}{N} \sum_{i=1}^N (\mathbf{x}^i - \hat{\boldsymbol{\mu}})(\mathbf{x}^i - \hat{\boldsymbol{\mu}})^T$ is the sample covariance matrix, and D is a constant with respect to $\boldsymbol{\Sigma}^{-1}$. As for the lasso, we add an L_1 norm penalty and consider the estimator:

$$\hat{\boldsymbol{\Sigma}}^{-1}(\lambda) = \arg\min_{\boldsymbol{\Sigma}^{-1}\succ 0}\left(-\log|\boldsymbol{\Sigma}^{-1}| + \mathrm{tr}(\mathbf{S}\boldsymbol{\Sigma}^{-1}) + \lambda\,||\boldsymbol{\Sigma}^{-1}||_1\right), \tag{14.6}$$

where the minimization is over positive-definite matrices and $||\boldsymbol{\Sigma}^{-1}||_1 = \sum_{j,k}|\boldsymbol{\Sigma}_{jk}^{-1}|$. Because $\hat{\boldsymbol{\Sigma}}^{-1}(\lambda)$ is positive-definite, its inverse $\hat{\boldsymbol{\Sigma}}(\lambda)$ exists and is an estimate of the covariance matrix $\boldsymbol{\Sigma}$. The minimization in Equation (14.6) amounts to a convex optimization problem, and fast algorithms have been proposed (Banerjee et al., 2008). This type of algorithms shrink some of the non-diagonal elements to exactly zero, i.e., $\boldsymbol{\Sigma}_{jk}^{-1} = 0$ for some (j,k) (depending on the size of λ). The regularization parameter λ can be selected using cross-validation for the previous negative Gaussian log-likelihood loss.

14.5 Learning Discrete Markov Networks

14.5.1 Markov Trees

Maximum likelihood Markov trees are distributions in which the dependencies follow a tree structure, with only pairwise direct dependencies and no loops. This class of Markov networks ensures that reasoning with the model via evidence propagation will be tractable. Chow and Liu (1968) provided an algorithm for learning maximum likelihood Markov trees from data, showing that the associated distribution minimizes the Kullback–Leibler divergence (Section 3.6.5) between the empirical distribution and the distribution associated with the Markov tree. The structure of the tree corresponds to a MWST (Section 8.4.1.4), where the weight on the edge $X_i - X_j$ is defined by the mutual information measure $\mathbb{I}(X_i, X_j)$, i.e.,

$$\mathbb{I}(X_i, X_j) = \sum_{i,j} p(x_i, x_j) \log_2 \frac{p(x_i, x_j)}{p(x_i)p(x_j)},$$

and probabilities are estimated using a maximum likelihood approach. The MWST solution can be found in a number of steps that is quadratic in n and requires only bivariate distributions. The Chow and Liu MWST algorithm for learning maximum likelihood Markov trees from data is summarized in the following steps (adapted from Pearl [1988]):

1. From the observed sample, $\mathbf{x}^1, \dots, \mathbf{x}^N$, estimate the bivariate distributions $p(x_i, x_j)$ for all pairs of variables.
2. Using the pairwise distributions (step 1), compute all $n(n-1)/2$ branch weights and order them by magnitude.
3. Assign the heaviest two branches to the tree to be constructed.
4. Examine the next-heaviest branch, and add it to the tree unless it forms a loop, in which case it is discarded and the next-heaviest branch is examined.
5. Repeat step 4 until $n-1$ branches have been selected (and a spanning tree has been constructed).
6. The maximum likelihood Markov tree can be computed by selecting an arbitrary root node X_r and forming the product:

$$p(x_1, \dots, x_n) = p(x_r) \prod_{i=1, i\neq r}^{n} p(x_i|x_{j(i)}),$$

where the distribution of X_i depends on $X_{j(i)}$ for $i = 1, \dots, n, i \neq r$.

Note the similarity between this procedure and step 5 of Algorithm 8.1 where a TAN classifier was induced from data, which both use Kruskal's algorithm (Kruskal, 1956), albeit with different weights.

The factorization provided by the maximum likelihood Markov tree is

$$p(x_1, \ldots, x_n | \boldsymbol{\theta}) = \frac{1}{Z(\boldsymbol{\theta})} \prod_{i=1}^{n} \psi_{i,j(i)}(x_i, x_{j(i)} | \boldsymbol{\theta}_{i,j(i)}),$$

where each of the $n - 1$ potential functions verify: $\psi_{i,j(i)}(x_i, x_{j(i)} | \boldsymbol{\theta}_{i,j(i)}) \propto p(x_i | x_{j(i)})$ for $i = 1, \ldots, n, i \neq r$ and ψ is proportional to $p(x_r)$ for $i = r$.

14.5.2 Unrestricted Markov Networks

Beyond Markov trees, this section presents some approaches for recovering general Markov networks. As in BNs, the task of learning discrete Markov networks from data can be decomposed into two subtasks: parameter estimation and structure learning.

14.5.2.1 Parameter Estimation

The task of estimating parameters from data in Markov networks has proved to be an NP-hard problem (Barahona, 1982). Maximum likelihood is the most common method for estimating the parameters of a Markov network. Any Markov network can be re-parametrized as a log-linear model (Koller and Friedman, 2009), thus having a log-likelihood similar to Equation (14.2).

Given a set of i.i.d. training instances, $\mathbf{x}^1, \ldots, \mathbf{x}^N$, from $p(\mathbf{x}|\boldsymbol{\theta})$, its **scaled log-likelihood** is

$$\ell_s(\boldsymbol{\theta}) = \frac{1}{N} \sum_{i=1}^{N} \log p(\mathbf{x}^i | \boldsymbol{\theta}) = \frac{1}{N} \sum_{i=1}^{N} \left[\sum_{C \in \mathcal{C}} \boldsymbol{\theta}_C^T \boldsymbol{\phi}_C(\mathbf{x}_C^i) - \log Z(\boldsymbol{\theta}) \right]. \tag{14.7}$$

Although it is not possible to output a closed-form expression for the MLE, the scaled log-likelihood function is convex in $\boldsymbol{\theta}$. Therefore, it has a unique global maximum. Iterative methods such as simple gradient ascent yield this global maximum.

The derivative of the scaled log-likelihood for the parameters of a particular clique, $\mathbf{C}$, is

$$\frac{\partial \ell_s}{\partial \boldsymbol{\theta}_C} = \frac{1}{N} \sum_{i=1}^{N} \left[\boldsymbol{\phi}_C(\mathbf{x}_C^i) - \frac{\partial}{\partial \boldsymbol{\theta}_C} \log Z(\boldsymbol{\theta}) \right] = \frac{1}{N} \sum_{i=1}^{N} \boldsymbol{\phi}_C(\mathbf{x}_C^i) - \sum_{\mathbf{C}} \boldsymbol{\phi}_C(\mathbf{x}_C) p(\mathbf{x}_C | \boldsymbol{\theta}_C).$$

The first term contains observed values in the sample of size N. The second term corresponds to the expected value for a given assignment of parameter $\boldsymbol{\theta}_C$ (its derivation is not shown). The intuition behind the expression of the derivative of the scaled log-likelihood is that the gradient attempts to make the potential counts in the empirical data equal to their expected counts relative to the learned model. The computation of this expectation requires inference in the Markov network model, which takes place once for every gradient step in the current model. This makes parameter estimation much slower in Markov networks than in BNs.

Several methods for alleviating this computational burden have been proposed in the literature. Some consist of using approximate inference techniques for computing the second term of the derivative of the scaled log-likelihood, such as **loopy belief propagation** (Yedidia et al., 2005) or **stochastic maximum likelihood** based on Monte Carlo sampling.

A different alternative is to maximize the **scaled pseudo-log-likelihood** (Besag, 1975), defined as follows:

$$\ell_{PL}(\boldsymbol{\theta}) = \frac{1}{N} \sum_{i=1}^{N} \sum_{j=1}^{n} \log p(x_j^i | \mathbf{x}_{-j}^i, \boldsymbol{\theta}),$$

where x_j^i denotes the jth component of the ith sample, and $\mathbf{x}_{-j}^i$ represents the $n-1$ components in the ith sample, different from the jth component. The pseudo-likelihood is faster to compute than the likelihood, as each element $p(x_j^i | \mathbf{x}_{-j}^i, \boldsymbol{\theta})$ only requires summing over the states of a single variable, X_j, in order to calculate the local normalization constant.

14.5.2.2 Structure Learning

As in BNs, the two main approaches for learning the structure of Markov networks from data are methods that recover the structure by detecting conditional independencies and score and search-based methods. Conditional independency detection methods are efficient, but raise some quality concerns, and score-and-search methods are intractable in practice.

Constraint-Based Methods. Constraint-based algorithms consider the problem of structure learning as an instance of the constraint satisfaction problem, where the constraints are the conditional independencies present in the input data set. **Independence-based** or constraint-based algorithms work by conducting a set of conditional independence tests on data, successively restricting the number of possible structures that are consistent with the test results to a singleton (if possible). Unlike score-and-search methods, a desirable characteristic of independence-based approaches is that they do not require the use of probabilistic inference during structure discovery. They are also amenable to proofs of correctness (under assumptions).

In a faithful domain (Section 14.1), it can be shown (Pearl and Paz, 1985) that there is an edge between two variables $X_i, X_j \in \mathbf{X}$ in the Markov network if and only if X_i and X_j are c.i. on all remaining variables in the domain, $\mathbf{X} \setminus \{X_i, X_j\}$, i.e., $e_{i,j} \in E \Leftrightarrow \neg I_P(X_i, X_j | \mathbf{X} \setminus \{X_i, X_j\})$, a property called pairwise Markov. Thus, it suffices, in theory, to perform only $n(n-1)/2$ tests to learn the structure: one test for each pair of variables given all the remaining variables. Unfortunately, this usually involves a test that conditions on a large number of variables in nontrivial domains. As in BNs (Section 13.3.2.1), large conditioning sets produce sparse contingency tables leading to unreliable estimates and tests.

A standard independence-based learning algorithm, called **grow-shrink inference-based Markov network** (GSIMN) (Bromberg et al., 2009) avoids this situation. GSIMN attempts to minimize the conditioning set size by choosing an order in which to examine the variables such that irrelevant variables are examined last. The main idea in GSIMN is to determine the set of variables $\mathbf{B}(X)$ that are adjacent to each variable $X \in \mathbf{X}$. This set is determined using an adaptation of the GS algorithm (Margaritis and Thrun, 2000), explained in Section 8.4.1.7. The Markov network structure is then constructed by connecting X with each variable in $\mathbf{B}(X)$.

GSIMN adapts GS in two ways. First, the examination order and the grow order of each variable is specified in the initialization phase. To determine the examination order, GSIMN computes the degree of dependence of each variable with respect to other variables, ranking variables showing stronger dependence higher. For the grow order of variable X, GSIMN prioritizes variables that are highly dependent on X. GSIMN fixes both orders heuristically. Second, the GSIMN algorithm is able to infer additional conditional independencies from tests conducted previously to improve its efficiency. This inference uses the **triangle theorem**. This theorem states that, for any variable X, Y, W and sets of variables $\mathbf{Z}_1$ and $\mathbf{Z}_2$ such that $\{X, Y, W\} \cap \mathbf{Z}_1 = \{X, Y, W\} \cap \mathbf{Z}_2 = \varnothing$, it holds that

$$\begin{aligned} \neg I_P(X, W | \mathbf{Z}_1) \ \wedge \ \neg I_P(W, Y | \mathbf{Z}_2) &\Rightarrow \neg I_P(X, Y | \mathbf{Z}_1 \cap \mathbf{Z}_2) \\ I_P(X, W | \mathbf{Z}_1) \ \wedge \ \neg I_P(W, Y | \mathbf{Z}_1 \cup \mathbf{Z}_2) &\Rightarrow I_P(X, Y | \mathbf{Z}_1). \end{aligned}$$

Note that the GSIMN algorithm is applicable to continuous Gaussian variables if an appropriate conditional independence test (such as partial correlation) is used.

Score-and-Search Methods. The basic approach for learning the structure of Markov networks from data was introduced by DellaPrieta et al. (1997). A greedy forward strategy is applied to learn the Markov network structure by inducing a set of potential functions from data. The initial model contains a set of n atomic potentials, one per variable. At each step, the algorithm creates a set of candidate potentials in two ways. First, each potential currently in the model is conjoined with every other potential in the model. Second, each potential in the current model is conjoined with each atomic potential not in the current model. In both cases, the parameters of the conjoined potentials are, for efficiency reasons, learned, assuming that the parameters of all other potentials remain unchanged. The inference process required to estimate the new parameters is enabled using Gibbs sampling (Section 14.3.2). For each candidate potential, the algorithm computes the improvement in the log-likelihood. The potential providing the highest improvement is added to the model. The algorithm ends when no candidate potential improves the log-likelihood.

The approach by DellaPrieta et al. (1997) uses a heuristic search over the combinatorial space of possible potential functions. An alternative perspective (Lee et al., 2007b) is to search the possible parameter vectors $\boldsymbol{\theta}$ with the same number of components as potential functions. Instead of maximizing the scaled log-likelihood of Equation (14.7), the idea is to solve the associated L_1-regularized problem, i.e.,

$$\boldsymbol{\theta}^* = \arg\max_{\boldsymbol{\theta}} \left[\sum_{i=1}^{N} \sum_{\mathbf{C} \in \mathcal{C}} \phi_{\mathbf{C}} \left(\mathbf{x}_{\mathbf{C}}^{(i)} \right)^T \boldsymbol{\theta}_{\mathbf{C}} - \sum_{\mathbf{C} \in \mathcal{C}} \beta_{\mathbf{C}} |\boldsymbol{\theta}_{\mathbf{C}}| \right],$$

where $\beta_{\mathbf{C}}$ is a parameter penalizing the size of the parameter vector $\boldsymbol{\theta}_{\mathbf{C}}$ associated with clique $\mathbf{C}$, and $|\boldsymbol{\theta}_{\mathbf{C}}|$ is the sum of its components. The above objective function is convex and can be optimized efficiently using methods like the conjugate gradient. The approach by Lee et al. (2007b) gradually selects potentials to add to the current model, enabling the optimization process to search for the optimal values for its parameters.

14.6   Conditional Random Fields

Probabilistic graphical models (BNs and Markov networks) have been used to provide a factorized representation of the JPD $p(\mathbf{y}, \mathbf{x})$, where the vector of variables $\mathbf{Y}$ represents the features of the entities that we wish to predict, and the vector of input variables $\mathbf{X}$ denotes our observed knowledge about the entities. One possibility to reduce the complexity of the modeling process is to not "waste resources" modeling observations, that is, the dependencies among the variables in $\mathbf{X}$. According to this approach, we can focus on modeling what we care about, namely, the distribution of entities to be predicted given the evidence, that is, $p(\mathbf{y}|\mathbf{x})$.

This is the approach taken by **conditional random fields** (CRFs) (Lafferty et al., 2001). A conditional random field is simply a conditional distribution $p(\mathbf{y}|\mathbf{x})$ with an associated graphical structure. Because the model is conditional, dependencies among the input variables $\mathbf{X}$ do not need to be explicitly represented, and the marginal distribution, $p(\mathbf{x})$, is not modeled.

Lafferty et al. (2001) defined a CRF on predictor variables $\mathbf{X}$ and variables $\mathbf{Y}$ to be predicted as follows: let $\mathcal{G} = (V,E)$ be a graph such that $\mathbf{Y} = (Y_v)_{v \in V}$, where $\mathbf{Y}$ is indexed by the vertices of $\mathcal{G}$. $(\mathbf{X}, \mathbf{Y})$ is a CRF with respect to $\mathcal{G}$ when the random variables Y_v conditioned on $\mathbf{X}$ obey the local Markov property with respect to the graph, that is, $p(y_v|\mathbf{x}, \mathbf{y} \setminus y_v) = p(y_v|\mathbf{x}, \mathbf{MB}(y_v))$, where $\mathbf{MB}(Y_v)$ denotes the Markov blanket of Y_v in $\mathcal{G}$.

$p(\mathbf{y}|\mathbf{x})$ modeling is highly interesting and applicable in different neuroscience scenarios. If $\mathbf{Y}$ is a discrete univariate variable, the model can be useful, for example, for discriminating between pyramidal and interneuron cells, as shown in Chapters 7–9, where $\mathbf{X}$ represents the set of morphological variables used as predictive features. The example shown in Chapter 10 concerning the simultaneous prediction of the five components of the quality of life for PD patients refers to the scenario when $\mathbf{Y}$ is a vector with five univariate components, the EQ-5D, and the predictive variables in $\mathbf{X}$ refer to the PDQ-39.

A CRF factorizes the conditional density in terms of clique potentials ψ_C conditioned on input feature values $\mathbf{x}$:

$$p(\mathbf{y}|\mathbf{x}, \boldsymbol{\theta}) = \frac{1}{Z(\mathbf{x}, \boldsymbol{\theta})} \prod_{C \in \mathcal{C}} \psi_C(\mathbf{y}_C|\mathbf{x}, \boldsymbol{\theta}).$$

Note that the partition function $Z(\mathbf{x}, \boldsymbol{\theta})$ also depends on $\mathbf{x}$. Usually the potentials are assumed to have a log-linear representation:

$$\psi_C(\mathbf{y}_C|\mathbf{x}, \boldsymbol{\theta}) = \exp(\phi_C(\mathbf{x}, \mathbf{y}_C)^T \boldsymbol{\theta}_C),$$

where $\phi_C(\mathbf{x}, \mathbf{y}_C)$ is a vector yielded by the global inputs $\mathbf{x}$, and the local outputs $\mathbf{y}_C$ that correspond to clique C.

A simple CRF, where each univariate output variable Y_k depends on Y_{k-1} and on $\mathbf{X}_k$ through a function $\psi_k(y_k, y_{k-1}, \mathbf{x}_k)$, is called a **linear-chain conditional random field** (linear-chain CRF). Like Equation (14.3), the distribution $p(\mathbf{y}|\mathbf{x}, \boldsymbol{\theta})$ takes the form

$$p(\mathbf{y}|\mathbf{x}, \boldsymbol{\theta}) = \frac{1}{Z(\mathbf{x}, \boldsymbol{\theta})} \exp\left\{ \sum_{k=1}^{K} \boldsymbol{\theta}_k \psi_k(y_k, y_{k-1}, \mathbf{x}_k) \right\},$$

for a linear-chain CRF with K components.

Figure 14.11 shows examples of structures for naive Bayes, hidden Markov models, and BNs as representatives of generative probabilistic graphical models and their corresponding logistic regression, linear-chain CRFs, and CRFs, represented as factor graphs, for discriminative approaches.

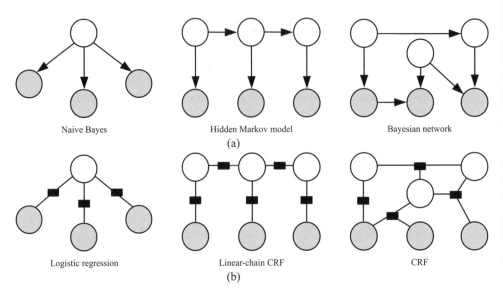

Figure 14.11 Examples of structures of some (a) generative and (b) discriminative probabilistic graphical models. Predictor variables are shaded.

CRFs have been extensively applied in neuroimaging, for example, with fMRI, as a label fusion method in a hippocampal segmentation problem into anatomical structures (Platero and Tobar, 2015) and for the detection of MS Gad-enhancing lesions with an adaptive CRF framework, capable of leveraging spatial and temporal information (Karimaghaloo et al., 2013). EEG signals were used to classify sleep recordings into sleep stages with the objective of having an accurate diagnosis and treatment of various sleep disorders (Luo and Min, 2007). In neuroanatomy, Funke et al. (2014) developed the automatic reconstruction of neurons from stacks of electron microscopy sections. French et al. (2009) used CRFs to automatically mine the neuroscience literature for mentions of brain regions.

14.7   Example: Functional Brain Connectivity of Alzheimer's Disease

AD is a neurodegenerative disorder characterized by progressive impairment of several cognitive functions, one of which is memory. Recent studies have demonstrated higher cognition as a result of the interaction among different brain regions. This issue leads to the hypothesis that patients suffering from AD can have abnormal functional brain connectivity patterns.

This section shows an example of the use of continuous Markov network learning algorithms for inducing the structures of functional brain connectivity for AD, MCI, and NC subjects. We will summarize the results reported by Huang et al. (2010), analyzing PET images of patients injected with fluorodeoxyglucose (FDG). The study included FDG-PET images from 49 AD, 116 MCI, and 67 NC subjects downloaded from the ADNI database, as described by Data Set 6 in Section 1.6.6. There are 42 variables extracted for frontal, parietal, occipital, and temporal lobes, see Table 1.12.

The structure of the Markov network was induced from data using a method for functional connectivity modeling, called **sparse inverse covariance estimation** (SICE), introduced by Huang et al. (2010). This method assumes that the n brain regions to be modeled, i.e., $\{X_1, \ldots, X_n\}$, represent random variables measuring the regional cerebral metabolic rate for glucose by FDG-PET. SICE also assumes a multivariate Gaussian distribution of the data and imposes a sparsity constraint on the maximum likelihood estimation of the inverse covariance matrix, $\mathbf{\Sigma}^{-1}$. More specifically, SICE uses Equation (14.6) to find an estimate for the inverse covariance matrix.

The elements of this matrix correspond with the partial correlation between pairs of brain regions given other regions (Section 14.4). SICE empirically proves which entries of the inverse covariance matrix are zero and which are nonzero. This structural information (i.e., zero and nonzero entries) was used to build the Markov network structure representing the brain connectivity model. This was carried out by adding an arc between nodes (i.e., brain regions) X_i and X_j if and only if $\hat{\mathbf{\Sigma}}_{i,j}^{-1} \neq 0$, where $\hat{\mathbf{\Sigma}}_{i,j}^{-1}$ is the entry at the ith row and jth column of $\hat{\mathbf{\Sigma}}^{-1}$.

To build a brain connectivity model for AD, Huang et al. (2010) first computed a sample covariance matrix, $\mathbf{S}$, of the 42 anatomical volumes of interest, based on the measurement data from the 49 AD patients. Then, SICE was applied to solve the optimization problem in Equation (14.6) based on $\mathbf{S}$ and a selected value for λ. The solution $\hat{\mathbf{\Sigma}}^{-1}$ is further converted to a graph consisting of nodes (those anatomical volumes) and edges (nonzero entries in $\hat{\mathbf{\Sigma}}^{-1}$). This is repeated for MCI and NC patient data. A matrix representation of the graphs yielded by SICE for three different values of λ and for the three types of subjects (AD, MCI, and NC) is shown in Figure 14.12, where gray squares are used to highlight the four lobes.

The analysis of these matrix representations leads to the following remarks:

1. Within-lobe connectivity:

    - The frontal lobe (X_1 to X_{12}) in AD has more direct connections than NC, for the three strength levels considered in the connectivity matrices. This can be explained by the fact that the frontal lobe regions are typically affected later in the course of AD (the data from Huang et al. (2010) are early AD), and the increased number of connections in the frontal lobe may help preserve some cognitive functions in AD patients.
    - The parietal (X_{13} to X_{20}) and occipital (X_{21} to X_{26}) lobes behave similarly in terms of the number of direct connections for AD, MCI, and NC patients.
    - The temporal lobe (variables X_{27} to X_{42}) in AD has fewer direct connections than NC. In particular, Hippocampus and ParaHippocampal regions (X_{39} to X_{42}) are much more isolated from other regions in AD than in NC. However, the number of direct connections in the temporal lobe of MCI patients is not a great deal smaller than for NC.

2. Between-lobe connectivity:

    - Humans brains tend to have fewer between-lobe connections than within-lobe connections. AD and MCI have more direct parietal-occipital connections than NC for the three analyzed values of λ. However, AD shows fewer temporal-occipital connections, fewer frontal-parietal connections, and more parietal-temporal connections than NC.

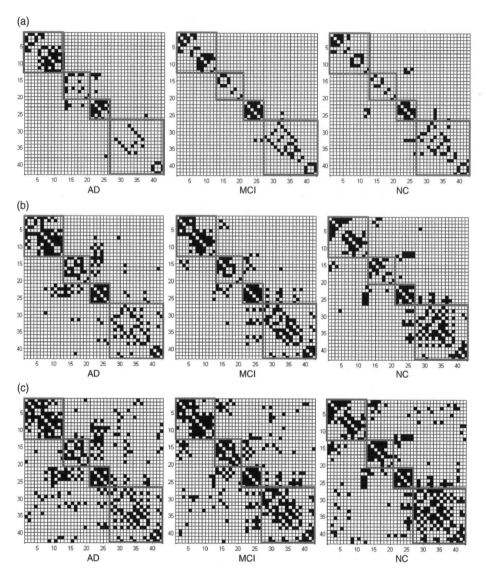

Figure 14.12 Inverse covariance matrix representation depicting the structure of the Markov networks induced by SICE for AD, MCI, and NC subjects (in columns) for brain connectivity models with three values of λ (in rows). (a) Total number of edges equal to 60. (b) Total number of edges equal to 120. (c) Total number of edges equal to 180. A black dot means a nonzero entry, that is, an edge in the Markov network structure. Gray squares highlight the four lobes (from top to bottom: frontal, parietal, occipital, and temporal). Reprinted with permission from Huang et al. (2010).

3. Between-hemisphere connectivity:

    • After counting the number of left-right pairs from the same regions in the connectivity models of AD, MCI, and NC, respectively, Huang et al. (2010) concluded that AD disrupts the strong connection between the same regions in the left and right hemispheres, whereas this disruption is smaller in MCI.

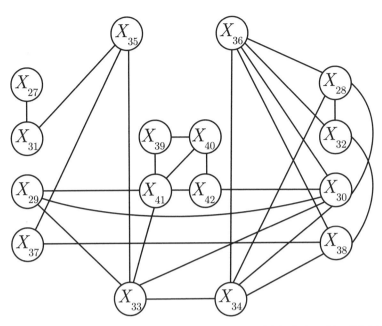

Figure 14.13 Markov network structure for the temporal lobe induced by SICE for AD subjects with a value $\lambda = \lambda_2$.

The structure of the Markov network for the temporal lobe (nodes X_{27} to X_{42}) for AD patients induced by SICE with $\lambda = \lambda_1$ was shown in Figure 14.2. Figure 14.13 displays the corresponding Markov network structure associated with $\lambda = \lambda_2$, and $\lambda_1 > \lambda_2$.

Comparing both figures, we appreciate the monotone property of SICE, that is, if two brain regions are not connected in the connectivity model at a certain λ, they will never become connected as λ grows. In other words, the subgraph representing the connectivity network for λ_1 is a subgraph of the connectivity network for λ_2 if $\lambda_1 > \lambda_2$. See Huang et al. (2010) for further details and analyses.

14.8   Bibliographic Notes

The analysis of spatial data has intrigued statisticians for nearly a century. On the methodological side, substantial progress is associated with the introduction of Markov random fields, as a class of parametric models for spatial data (Besag, 1974), see Chapter 15. The study of digital images is a prominent example in the field of neuroscience. The Hammersley–Clifford theorem has become important in the description of a dependence structure for log-linear models (Darroch et al., 1980).

The variable elimination algorithm is based on the idea of pushing sums inside products, which is something introduced for the first time in the context of genetic pedigree trees by Cannings et al. (1978) under the name of **peeling algorithm**. A variety of inference algorithms for Markov networks are explained in detail in the books by Darwiche (2009), Koller and Friedman (2009), and Murphy (2012).

Variational inference methods (Jordan et al., 1998), also mentioned in Section 13.6, is a kind of deterministic approximate inference algorithm that picks an approximation $q(\mathbf{x})$ to the true posterior from some tractable family, such as a multivariate Gaussian or a factored distribution. One of the most popular forms of variational inference is called **mean field approximation** (Opper and Saad, 2001). This form assumes $q(\mathbf{x})$ as a fully factorized approximation.

Loopy belief propagation (Weiss, 2000) is another simple approximate inference algorithm that consists of applying the belief propagation algorithm to any kind of directed or undirected graph, even if it has loops (i.e., even if it is not a tree). Expectation propagation (Minka, 2001) is a form of belief propagation where the messages are approximated only retaining expectations, such as mean and variance.

Dempster (1972) suggested to estimate the inverse covariance matrix of a multivariate Gaussian distribution by assuming some zero entries (called covariance selection models), without any graphical interpretation. Wermuth (1976) associated those zeros with missing edges in an undirected Gaussian Markov model (called Gaussian Markov networks later). For in-depth understanding of this topic, see Lauritzen and Wermuth (1989), Whittaker (1990) and more recently Córdoba et al. (2020).

Alternative edge exclusion proposals based on **limited-order partial correlations**, that is, q-**order partial correlations** with $q < n - 2$, were developed with the aim of improving the robustness of the hypothesis tests. In principle, q-order partial correlations can be computed for any $q < n - 2$; in practice, however, testing $\binom{n-2}{q}$ partial correlations for each of the $n(n-1)/2$ pairs of variables is computationally intensive unless q is small (Castelo and Roverato, 2006). For example, Wille and Bühlmann (2006) considered all q-order partial correlations for $q \leq 1$.

Several extensions of the graphical Lasso procedure have been proposed in the literature for the sparse estimation of the covariance matrix in Gaussian Markov networks. For example, Zhou et al. (2011) used a multi-step procedure combining L_1-norm regularization and a thresholding method in the first stage to infer a sparse undirected graphical model and then perform unpenalized maximum likelihood estimation for the covariance and its inverse based on the estimated graph.

Bayesian approaches for learning Gaussian Markov networks consider posterior distributions $p\left(\mathcal{G}, \boldsymbol{\Sigma} | \mathbf{x}^1, \ldots, \mathbf{x}^N\right)$ for specified priors $p(\mathcal{G}, \boldsymbol{\Sigma}) = p(\boldsymbol{\Sigma}|\mathcal{G})p(\mathcal{G})$. Giudici (1996) assumed that the **local prior**, $p(\boldsymbol{\Sigma}|\mathcal{G})$, is hyper-inverse Wishart, while Jones et al. (2005) considered a Bernoulli prior on each edge inclusion indicator variable with a parameter value inversely proportional to the number of nodes, thus encouraging sparse graphs, especially as dimension increases.

Apart from the Chow and Liu algorithm (Section 14.5), other proposals for learning Markov networks with a fixed dependency structure from data have been developed. These include the recovery of Markov networks of **bounded treewidth** (Srebro, 2003). The bounded treewidth Markov networks are reasonable, as this type of structures enable efficient inference computations. Meilă and Jordan (2000) studied distributions that are mixtures of tree-shaped Markov networks.

Alternative algorithms for learning the structure of general discrete Markov networks based on score-and-search approaches include research by Wainwright et al. (2007) on pairwise Markov networks based on training an L_1-regularized pseudo-likelihood logistic regression classifier for each variable given all the others. It then uses only the edges that are selected by these individual classifiers. A similar approach was proposed by Ravikumar et al. (2010) for estimating the graph associated with a binary Ising model.

The efficiency of the GSIMN algorithm (Bromberg et al., 2009), considered as the standard approach for conditional independence-based learning of discrete Markov networks, was improved by Margaritis and Bromberg (2009) by greedily selecting the statistical test that eliminates the highest number of inconsistent structures at each iteration. Bromberg and Margaritis (2009) reported an independence-based approach for dealing with unreliable tests. For a survey of independence-based algorithms for learning discrete Markov networks from data, see Schlüter (2014).

Part VI

Spatial Statistics

Part VI of this book deals with spatiality. **Spatial point processes** are mathematical models to describe how a set of objects (or points) randomly distributed in a region of the 2D plane, a surface or a 3D volume are arranged. The points may be molecules, cells, particles, or any other element. The data consist of point coordinates describing the spatial (and maybe temporal) location. For instance, epileptic seizure epicenter location and time for the same patient throughout his or her life. Sometimes additional information about their properties, e.g., size, type or shape, is attached. This information is usually referred to as **marks**. The mark variable can be categorical or continuous. Examples of a categorical mark variable (aka **multitype point pattern**) are species, age or disease status. Examples of a continuous mark variable are Feret diameter of a neuron or size and shape of a dendritic spine. Marks may be uni- or multi-variate. The data set may also include **covariates**, i.e., data that we treat as explanatory variables rather than as part of the response (like marks). For instance, the distance to soma in a pattern of synapsis locations.

15 Spatial Statistics

As a statistical methodology, point process analysis includes issues like sampling, exploratory data analysis, parameter estimation, model fitting, and hypothesis testing. Point process statistics is the most developed branch of spatial statistics.

To analyze spatial pattern data, a simple point map is useful as a preliminary visualization step to understand their properties. We may qualitatively characterize the pattern with vague terms: clustered, aggregated, clumped, patchy, regular, uniform... We can also identify correlations among marks. Nevertheless, hunches like these may be misleading and hide subtle differences. Hence, a precise quantification calls for an appropriate statistical methodology.

Also, unlike classical statistics, point process statistics identify and describe various types of pattern correlation: correlations between relative interpoint distances, correlation between the number of points in adjacent regions, and also spatial correlations between the characteristics of the objects represented by the points (marks). Therefore, typical point process statistical measures will describe correlations between the points relative to their distances, e.g., distances to nearest neighbors or numbers of neighbors within given distances.

Besides correlations between point locations, other correlations are interesting: correlations between marks, correlations between marks and point locations, and correlations with covariates.

In short, point process statistics should give an understanding and description of the short-range interaction between the points, thereby explain their mutual positions. This concerns the degree of clustering[1] or repulsion (inhibition) between points and also the spatial scale on which this occurs. For instance, Jinno et al. (2007) investigated the spatial patterns of Iba1-labeled microglia and S100β-labeled astrocyte distribution, each showing repulsive patterns, whereas a spatial attraction was revealed between microglia and astrocytes.

Although the probability theory of point processes is well developed, the corresponding statistical methodology is quite rudimentary. The practical techniques for the analysis of spatial point patterns have emerged from application areas (forestry, astronomy, ecology, geology...) rather than statistical science.

The chapter is organized as follows. Section 15.1 explains basic concepts of spatial point processes. Section 15.2 details essential analysis tools to investigate whether the process is devoid of any spatial structure. This is called complete spatial randomness. Section 15.3 contains general procedures based on simulation to perform goodness-of-fit tests, where

---

[1] In this context, cluster refers to aggregation or clumping or attraction and is not to be confused with the clustering methods explained in Chapters 11 and 12 to find groups or subsets of similar objects.

we check whether a specific model fits the data in the null hypothesis. Section 15.4 advises how to choose the study region and collect data that are representative of the underlying stochastic process. Section 15.5 presents some well-known models of spatial point processes that are more complex than complete spatial randomness. Section 15.6 illustrates the application of the ideas of this chapter to analyze the spatial distribution of synapses in the rat neocortex with Data Set 7 (Section 1.6.7). Finally, Section 15.7 addresses bibliographic notes.

15.1   Basic Concepts of Spatial Point Processes

A point pattern data set gives the locations of objects/events occurring in a study region. Thus, our data is the observed **point pattern** $\mathbf{x} = \{x_1, \dots, x_n\}^2$ (an unordered set of points). This is a realization of a random **point process** $\mathbf{X}$ that generated the pattern. x_i represents the 1D, 2D, or 3D coordinates of the location of point i. A point process $\mathbf{X}$ is a random set of points, with a random number N of points ($N = n$ in the observed $\mathbf{x}$) and random locations (x_i in the observed $\mathbf{x}$). It is assumed that $\mathbf{X}$ extends throughout the space (like stars in the galaxy), but is observed only inside an arbitrary fixed and known region W of any shape, the **sampling window** or **observation window**, see Figure 15.1. Thus, $x_i \in W, \forall i$. In a marked point process, we also have categorical or continuous values $\mathbf{m}_i$ associated with each x_i.

It is implicitly assumed that all points of $\mathbf{X}$ within W have been mapped. Likewise, it is assumed that there is no more than one point at each location. Moreover, most models assume that points could have been observed at any location in W, although this is not always realistic: some cells lie inside tissues, whereas spines lie along dendritic shafts. The goal is to determine the distribution of the random point process $\mathbf{X}$, estimate its parameters, and perform inferences.

A point process is called **stationary** if it is invariant to pattern translations, that is, the process and the translated process resulting from a shift of all points by the same vector

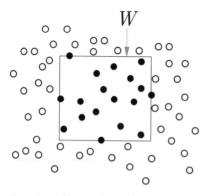

Figure 15.1 Observation window. The observed pattern (filled circles) is part of a much larger – supposedly infinite – structure, where points (open circles) are assumed to be distributed according to the same laws as in the observed pattern.

---

^{2} In this chapter, n (instead of N used in the remainder of the book) denotes the number of points because $N(\cdot)$ is used to signify a counting random variable.

have the same distribution. Stationary means that the chance of observing a particular point configuration at a specific location is independent of the location. Hence deviations from stationarity may occur if: (a) the point density (or intensity function, see Section 15.2.1) is not constant, or (b) the local point configurations are location-dependent (e.g., points may be aggregated within one subregion and random in another). A point process is **isotropic** if it is invariant to pattern rotations around the origin. Note that there are processes that are nonstationary but isotropic with respect to a fixed location, e.g., the locations of fungi around a tree.

The **point intensity** is the expected number of objects per unit area or volume, if point density can be considered constant across space. This resembles the sample mean in classical statistics. Intensity may be constant (uniform or homogeneous) across the study area or vary from location to location (nonuniform or inhomogeneous).

Interpoint interaction is statistical dependence between the points in a point pattern, which is expected to be strong between close points. An interesting question here is whether the spacing between points is greater than would be expected for a random pattern (for cells competing for resources).

For a point pattern data set with covariate data, it is worth investigating whether the intensity depends on the covariates. The degree of inhomogeneity of the point locations often reflects the influence of covariates. Intensity and marked point maps are useful and may be related to maps of values of covariates across space. If this dependence holds after accounting for point density variation due to covariates, we typically study the interaction between points. To investigate point process dependence on covariates, some observations of covariates at other non-data (or background) locations are necessary. Thus, covariate data may be of any kind, but are commonly a spatial function $Z(u)$ observable (potentially) at all spatial locations $u \in W$ and available in a fine grid. If there are only scattered observed locations, Z must be observed at all x_i of $\mathbf{x}$ and some other locations $u \notin \mathbf{x}$ at least. This function is usually a continuous regionalized variable, like terrain altitude or soil pH in forestry. These functions can be illustrated as a pixel image or a contour plot. Note, however, that marks are only given for the points x_i in the point pattern $\mathbf{x}$ and are therefore part of the response (the point pattern) rather than an explanatory variable.

An issue in marked point patterns is whether points with different mark values are segregated, i.e., the study region is divided into parts dominated by a single mark, or, else the different mark values are randomly interspersed.

Example. Amacrine Cells. A classic example in point process statistics is the marked pattern formed by cholinergic amacrine cells in rabbit retina (Diggle, 1986). These interneurons modulate the pattern of visual information as it passes through the retina and then play an important role in the detection of motion in particular directions. The retina is a flat sheet containing several layers of cells. Amacrine cells occupy two adjacent layers leading to two types of cells. Cells with somas within the inner nuclear layer are termed OFF cells, whereas cells with cell bodies in the ganglion cell layer are ON cells. ON cells and OFF cells are, respectively, excited by an increase or a decrease in illumination.

Figure 15.2 shows the pattern, i.e., locations of the ON and OFF cells in planar projection (294 points) within a $1,060 \times 662$ μm (small) section of the retina, taken from an area where the pattern continues similarly outside the observation window. The overall

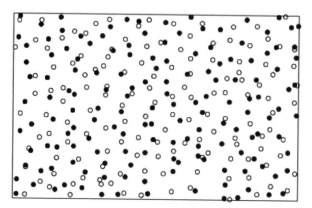

Figure 15.2 Amacrine cell data (Diggle, 1986). The points are marked as ON (open circles) or OFF (filled circles). The cells lie in different layers and are projected onto a plane. Thus, cells of different types may partially overlap, where cells of the same type cannot overlap. This data set comes with the spatstat R package installed (Baddeley and Turner, 2005).

distribution of cells varies, becoming less dense in the parafoveal regions and periphery of the retina. The points are marked as open circles (152 ON cells) or filled circles (142 OFF cells).

A marked point pattern can be regarded as either a superposition of single-type point patterns or a single point pattern with different types of labels indicating the type of points. We want to explore correlations between the different types of points and also the spatial scale and range of these correlations. Here there appears to be a slight trend in both subpatterns toward regularity with repulsion at a distance greater than cell size. The combined pattern looks weakly regular.

An interesting question is whether there is evidence that the ON and OFF cells grow independent of each other.   ∎

15.2   Complete Spatial Randomness

The final aim of spatial point pattern analysis is to quantify spatial structure. We have seen that the types of interaction between the points of a pattern may differ: they may be clustered, regular, or regularly clustered. If neither of the above interactions is found in a point pattern, it may be regarded as completely spatially random. In this case, the term random means that the n points $x_1, \dots, x_n$ are uniformly and independently distributed in W. This property of a pattern is termed **complete spatial randomness** (CSR).

15.2.1   Point Intensity

Investigating the intensity of a point process is one of the first steps in analyzing a point pattern. Let $N(\cdot)$ be a random counting measure denoting the random number of points in a region.

The simplest case is a uniform or homogeneous intensity. With CSR, the intensity is homogeneous. Thus, if the point process $\mathbf{X}$ is homogeneous, then $\mathbb{E}[N(\mathbf{X} \cap B)]$, the mean number of points in B, is $\lambda \cdot v(B)$ for any subregion B of the space. If we assume a 2D space, then $v(B)$ refers to its *area*, which is replaced by *volume* in three dimensions. λ is the intensity. Intensity units are numbers per unit area. To estimate λ from $\mathbf{x} = \{x_1, \dots, x_n\}$, we can use the empirical density of points, i.e.,

$$\hat{\lambda} = \frac{N(\mathbf{X} \cap W)}{v(W)}, \tag{15.1}$$

which is unbiased and the MLE. This is the standard estimator. Others are meant for when the number of points in W is very large, and they are too hard to count (i.e., counting cell nuclei in biology and medicine). These estimators only use counting in some systematically or randomly chosen regions or measure a small number of distances from test points instead of counting all points (see, e.g., Illian et al., 2008, Section 4.2.3).

In the case of inhomogeneous intensity, we will have an **intensity function** $\lambda(u)$ rather than a constant because the intensity varies from place to place. Assuming that the expected number of points falling in an infinitesimal region of area du around a location u is equal to $\lambda(u)du$, then

$$\mathbb{E}[N(\mathbf{X} \cap B)] = \int_B \lambda(u)du,$$

for any region B. $\lambda(u)$ is proportional to the **point density function** $f(u)$ around a location u, which loosely yields the probability of observing a point of the pattern in that infinitesimal region. In contrast, the intensity function provides the number of points expected per unit area. Thus, $f(u) = \lambda(u) / \int_B \lambda(u)du$.

In some cases, the intensity function $\lambda(u)$ does not exist when there are singular concentrations of intensity (like earthquake epicenters concentrated along a fault line). Then $\Lambda(B) = \mathbb{E}[N(\mathbf{X} \cap B)]$ is called **intensity measure**, assuming that the expectation is finite.

$\lambda(u)$ and $\Lambda(B)$ can be estimated nonparametrically. The two main estimation techniques are quadrat counting and kernel smoothing. In **quadrat counting**, W is divided into subregions (quadrats) $B_1, \dots, B_q$ of equal area and any shape. Then we count the number of points falling in each quadrat $n_j = N(\mathbf{x} \cap B_j), j = 1, \dots, q$. These counters are unbiased estimators of the corresponding intensity measure values $\Lambda(B_j)$. Counts should be approximately equal for a uniform density.

Kernel smoothing is the alternative option for estimating intensity. Remember that a kernel density estimator of a 1D density $f(x)$ from an i.i.d. sample $\{x_1, \dots, x_n\}$ is (see Section 8.4.2.2)

$$\tilde{f}(x) = \frac{1}{nh} \sum_{i=1}^{n} \kappa \left(\frac{x - x_i}{h} \right),$$

where $\kappa(u)$ is the kernel (an arbitrary probability density, e.g., Gaussian), and h is the smoothing parameter called the bandwidth. The higher the kernel standard deviation is, the smoother $\tilde{f}$ will be. Note that $\tilde{f}$ is calculated by adding together the heights of all kernels at any point along the x-axis. The idea may be extended to 2D and 3D density functions. Thus, for two dimensions and an i.i.d. sample $\{(x_1, y_1), \dots, (x_n, y_n)\}$,

$$\tilde{f}(x, y) = \frac{1}{nh_x h_y} \sum_{i=1}^{n} \kappa \left(\frac{x - x_i}{h_x} \right) \kappa \left(\frac{y - y_i}{h_y} \right).$$

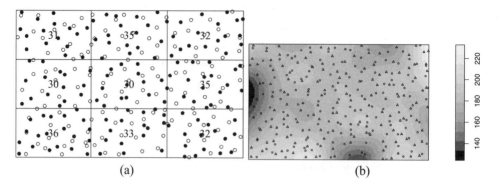

Figure 15.3 (a) Quadrat counting on the amacrine cell data set. (b) Kernel intensity estimation, where a gray scale shows the expected number of random points per unit area. All analyses were conducted using the `spatstat` R package: `quadratcount` function for (a) and `density` function for (b).

The result of estimating $\lambda(u)$ as $\tilde{f}$ for all $u = (x, y) \in W$ is a 2D smooth function or intensity surface, a valuable form of data analysis or regionalization that converts the point pattern into a function.

Example. Amacrine Cells (Quadrat Counting and Kernel Smoothing). In the amacrine cell data set, we can calculate $\hat{\lambda} = 183.61$ cells per square unit, where 1 unit is 662 μm. Figure 15.3(a) shows the result of quadrat counting with 3×3 quadrats.[3] The number of cells falling in each quadrat are displayed as figures in the center of each quadrat. For instance, the first quadrat has 31 cells.

Figure 15.3(b) illustrates an estimate of the intensity function of the point process that generated the point pattern. A kernel smoothed intensity function $\lambda(u)$ (gray tone regions) and the point pattern are superimposed. The kernel is an isotropic Gaussian kernel. The intensity values (gray tones), i.e., the expected number of random points per unit area, are computed at every spatial location u in a fine grid and are returned as a pixel image. The integral of the intensity function over a spatial region gives the expected number of points falling in this region.

Alternatively, the intensity function can be shown as a contour plot, see Figure 15.4. ■

The intensity can depend on covariates, i.e., there is a function ρ such that $\lambda(u) = \rho(Z(u))$, also estimated by kernel smoothing. In a pattern of synapse locations, for example, we want to investigate whether the synapses proliferate near to or far from the soma (the covariate is the distance from any point – synapse or not – to the soma).

There is a homogeneity test using Snedecor's F distribution to test whether the intensity function $\lambda(u)$ is really constant and decide between a homogeneous or inhomogeneous intensity. W is split into two subregions, and the null hypothesis is that the point densities are equal in both subregions (Illian et al., 2008, page 82). This test is formally correct only if the subregions are chosen a priori before data collection, for instance, to explore specific hypothesized trends in the point density. However, it is not appropriate for a given point pattern where we have already inspected subregions of very high/low point densities.

---

[3] All computations, models, and plots in this chapter were output using the `spatstat` R package.

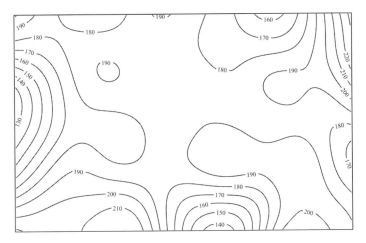

Figure 15.4 Intensity function shown as a contour plot of the pixel image in Figure 15.3(b).

15.2.2 Models of Complete Spatial Randomness

A theoretical model for patterns with the CSR property is an important null, benchmark, or reference model against which comparisons can be made and upon which more complicated models can be built. This model is the **homogenous** or **uniform Poisson point process** with intensity $\lambda > 0$.

A homogeneous Poisson process $\mathbf{X}$ is characterized by two properties:

P1. *Poisson distribution of counts*: the number of points $N(\mathbf{X} \cap B)$ falling in any region B follows a Poisson distribution (Section 3.2.5) with mean $\lambda \cdot v(B)$ points for some constant $\lambda > 0$. Therefore,

$$p(N(\mathbf{X} \cap B) = n) = \frac{(\lambda \cdot v(B))^n}{n!} \exp(-\lambda \cdot v(B)), \text{ for } n = 0, 1, \ldots$$

P2. *Independent scattering*: the number of points in k disjoint regions, $N(\mathbf{X} \cap B_1), \ldots, N(\mathbf{X} \cap B_k)$, are independent random variables for arbitrary k.

These properties imply that given n points inside region B (that is, $N(\mathbf{X} \cap B) = n$), their locations are i.i.d. and uniformly distributed in B. This represents the general concept of CSR, points that are uniformly distributed across the study area and independent of each other (and equally likely to be found at any location regardless of other points). The homogeneous Poisson process is sometimes simply called CSR. Moreover, this process is stationary and isotropic, that is, motion invariant.

If we restrict the homogeneous Poisson process to W conditional on $N(\mathbf{X} \cap B) = n$ (note that N is a count random variable and n is a possible value of N), this yields a new point process that is the **binomial point process** with n points, that is, the n points are uniformly (randomly scattered) and independently distributed in W. With a single point x uniformly distributed in W, $p(x \in A) = v(A)/v(W)$ for all subsets A of W. With n points, $x_1, \ldots, x_n$, we have the binomial point process, where

$$p(x_1 \in A_1, \ldots, x_n \in A_n) = p(x_1 \in A_1) \cdots p(x_n \in A_n) = \frac{v(A_1) \cdots v(A_n)}{v(W)^n},$$

for subsets $A_1, \ldots, A_n$ of W. For $A \in W$, the random number of points in A follows a binomial distribution (Section 3.2.3) and hence is referred to as binomial point process.

This process is close to the CSR model, although, despite the assumed independence, there are some spatial correlations in the pattern because the total number of points in W is fixed (equal to n). Only by assuming a random number of points and extending the approach to the whole space can we get the right definition of CSR. But this readily provides a method of simulating a homogeneous Poisson process as a two-step procedure: (i) the number of points in W is generated by simulating from a Poisson random variable (see Section 3.5.7), and (ii) the positions of the points in W are determined by simulating a binomial point process in W with the number of points found in the first step. A binomial process is easily enacted by superpositioning random points independently in the required region. If W is not rectangular, the smallest possible rectangle W^R containing W is found, and a sequence of independent uniform random points is simulated in W^R. These points are rejected if they are outside W, and the process is repeated until n points have fallen in W, and these n points form the sample of the binomial point process.

Figure 15.5 shows randomly generated homogenous Poisson process patterns with different intensities in the square unit. Note that visual assessment can often be misleading, and this is why statistical tools are required. In all (a)–(d), the patterns are apparently not uniformly spread, but there are gaps and clusters of points.

The homogeneous Poisson process may be generalized by introducing inhomogeneity but not interaction to yield the **inhomogeneous Poisson process**. Thus, the constant intensity λ is replaced by an intensity function $\lambda(u)$ whose value varies with the location u. Thus, property P1 is now

P1. *Poisson distribution of counts*: the number of points $N(\mathbf{X} \cap B)$ falling in any region B follows a Poisson distribution with mean $\int_B \lambda(u)du$,

whereas property P2 remains unchanged. Unlike homogeneity, given n points inside region B, their locations are still i.i.d. but not uniform. The n points form a sample of independent points with a probability density function proportional to $\lambda(u)$: $f(u) = \lambda(u)/\int_B \lambda(u)du$. Thus, we expect more (fewer) points in areas with higher (lower) values of $\lambda(u)$, that is, points are independent of one another, but clusters appear in areas of high intensity.

Inhomogenous Poisson models were used by Jammalamadaka et al. (2015) to analyze astrocyte locations in healthy mammalian retinas. They were found not to be random but more densely packed around blood vessels.

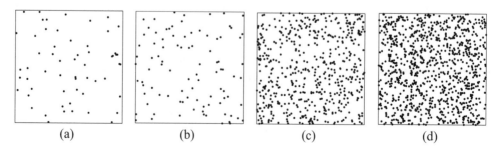

Figure 15.5 Random point patterns generated according to a homogeneous Poisson process of intensity λ points per square unit. (a) $\lambda = 50$. (b) $\lambda = 100$. (c) $\lambda = 500$. (d) $\lambda = 1,000$.

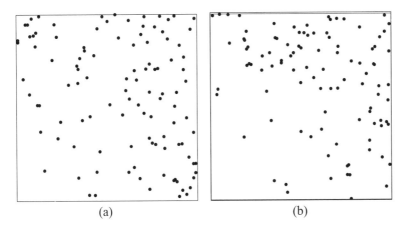

Figure 15.6 (a) and (b) Two random point patterns generated according to an inhomogeneous Poisson process with intensity function $\lambda(\mathbf{u}) = u_1 + u_2$ for a general point $\mathbf{u} = (u_1, u_2)$ in the square unit.

The inhomogeneous Poisson process is a plausible model under the following scenario of **random thinning**: a homogeneous Poisson process of intensity β is generated, and each point is either deleted or retained independent of other points. If the probability of retaining a point at location u is $p(u)$, then the resulting process of retained points is inhomogeneous Poisson with intensity $\lambda(u) = \beta p(u)$.

Figure 15.6 shows two replicates of an inhomogenous Poisson process randomly generated in the square unit. The intensity function is the sum of the coordinates of a point.

It is important to test the CSR hypothesis because, if not rejected, the simple Poisson process model can be used. This implies constant intensity and noninteraction between points. Points here are unpredictable, trendless, or unassociated with anything else. In contrast, if the CSR hypothesis is rejected, the (more interesting) search for spatial correlations in the given pattern begins. In this case, we can gain insights into the direction and cause of the deviation from CSR to guide further analysis.

A number of CSR hypothesis tests have been developed, each assessing particular aspects of CSR behavior. Many summary characteristics of point processes can be used to construct tests, as shown below in Section 15.2.3.2. The homogeneous Poisson null hypothesis is rejected if there is a large difference between the summary characteristic estimated from the data and the theoretical characteristic corresponding to a homogeneous Poisson process.

Because the point distribution of a homogeneous Poisson process is uniform, a natural approach is to apply goodness-of-fit tests for the uniformity hypothesis, like the chi-squared and Kolmogorov–Smirnov tests.

A popular check is the **quadrat counting test for CSR**. This is the Pearson chi-squared goodness-of-fit test (Section 4.2.2) based on quadrat counts n_j, which, under CSR, are Poisson random variables with the same expected value $\lambda \cdot v(B_j)$ (note that $v(B_j)$ are equal for all quadrats B_j). Also, counts in disjoint quadrats are independent. The test statistic is (see Equation (4.12))

$$X^2 = \sum_{j=1}^{q} \frac{\left(n_j - \frac{n}{q}\right)^2}{n/q},$$

where q is the number of quadrats, and $n = \sum_j n_j$ is the total number of points. The approximate distribution of X^2 under the null hypothesis is χ^2_{q-1}, and the critical region of the test is readily available without resorting to simulation. Also, X^2 coincides, up to a constant factor, with the sample variance-to-mean ratio of the counts n_j, that is, an index of their dispersion. Thus, for large X^2 values leading to the rejection of the CSR hypothesis, the process variability is stronger than for the Poisson process, i.e., there is aggregation. Likewise, for small X^2 values leading to the rejection of the CSR hypothesis, the process variability is smaller than for the Poisson process, i.e., there is regularity.

Some criticisms of this approach are that: (i) the scope of the negation of the CSR null hypothesis is too wide ("it is not a homogeneous Poisson process") and the point process may not satisfy the CSR property because its intensity is not uniform (violation of property P1 of a homogeneous Poisson process) or because points are interdependent and the counts are not independent (violation of property P2), and (ii) the statistical power of the test (Section 4.2.1) depends on the size of quadrats and is zero for very large or very small quadrats. The power also depends on the alternative hypothesis, specifically on the spatial scale of any departures from CSR, i.e., from the assumptions of constant intensity and independence of points. Note that the choice of quadrat size is implicitly related to the assumed spatial scale.

Example. Amacrine Cells (Quadrat Counting Test for CSR). Figure 15.3(a) used a quadrat counting with 3×3 quadrats. The expected count in each quadrat is 32.7 cells (i.e., 294/9). The result of the quadrat counting test for CSR is X-squared = 1.2245, df = 8, p-value = 0.0072, and the null hypothesis is rejected for $\alpha = 0.01$. For 7×7 quadrats (the χ^2 approximation may be inaccurate for more quadrats because some expected counts are small), the expected count in each quadrat is 6 cells (i.e., 294/49), and the test yields X-squared = 9.6667, df = 48, p-value = 8.386e-10. There is strong evidence for rejecting the CSR null hypothesis.   ∎

15.2.3 Interpoint Interaction

We now investigate dependence between the points in a point pattern, also called interpoint interaction. This describes their spacing relative to each other. As mentioned above, we expect dependence to be stronger between points that are close to one another.

If we assume a pattern has constant intensity and we wish to assess whether it is a homogeneous Poisson process, the alternative hypothesis is that the points are dependent. There are three basic classic patterns: (1) clustering (aka aggregation), attraction, or positive interactions, where points tend to be close together; (2) independence (Poisson process); and (3) regularity, inhibition, repulsion, or negative interactions, where points tend to avoid each other, and distances between points tend to be larger than expected when considering independent patterns. Clustered points do not imply that they are organized into identifiable clusters; they are closer to each other than expected for a Poisson process. Dependence is affected by, e.g., species traits such as territoriality, social behaviors, allelochemistry, emigration, immigration... and also distribution of resources, etc.

Figure 15.7 shows examples of the three cases.

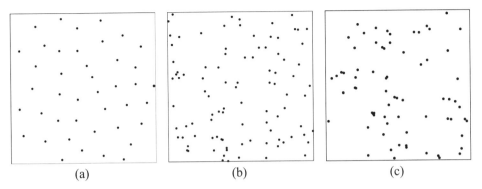

Figure 15.7 The three basic classic patterns of interpoint interaction. (a) Regular points. (b) Independent points (CSR). (c) Clustered points.

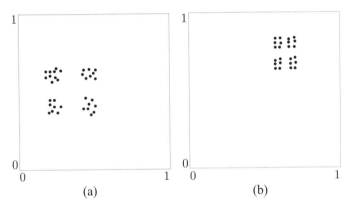

Figure 15.8 The spatial scale issue. (a) A regular pattern of clusters. (b) A cluster of regular patterns.

The behavior of a point process may differ on different spatial scales, not always behaving like one of the three basic patterns. Therefore, the spatial scale is a critical issue in the description of observed patterns. For instance, clustering and regularity may coexist in combination, each on different spatial scales or in different regions. The pattern in Figure 15.8(a) is regular on a large scale but the points are clustered at shorter distances, that is, we have a regular pattern of clusters. The opposite occurs in Figure 15.8(b) because we have a cluster of regular patterns, i.e., short-range regularity and long-range clustering.

15.2.3.1 Exploratory Data Analysis
Two simple diagnostics for dependence between points follow. Both are plots that must be used cautiously because they involve subjective interpretation.

The **Morisita index** (Morisita, 1959) measures the spatial aggregation of a point pattern based on quadrat counts. It is defined as

$$\text{MI} = q \frac{\sum_{j=1}^{q} n_j (n_j - 1)}{n(n-1)},$$

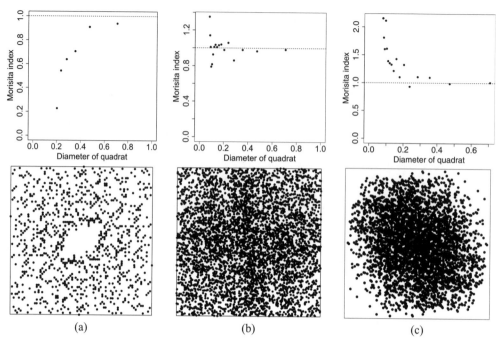

Figure 15.9 Respective diagnostics for interpoint interaction for the three patterns shown in Figure 15.7. The top row shows Morisita plots; the bottom row shows the corresponding Fry plots. (a) Regular, (b) independent, and (c) clustered. In the Morisita plot, W is normalized to have length 1 per side. With 2×2 quadrats, the diameter of the quadrats represented on the x-axis is $\sqrt{0.5^2 + 0.5^2} \approx 0.7$ (see the rightmost point); with 3×3 quadrats, the respective diameter is $\sqrt{(1/3)^2 + (1/3)^2} \approx 0.47$ (see the second rightmost point), etc.

for q quadrats and n_j points in quadrat j, $j = 1, \ldots, q$. MI is computed for each subdivision of the point pattern into quadrats (2×2 quadrats, 3×3 quadrats, etc.). The **Morisita plot** depicts MI on the y-axis against the diameter of the quadrats on the x-axis, see Figure 15.9, top. If the pattern is completely random, the MI values should be approximately equal to 1. Values greater than 1 suggest clustering, whereas MI values of less than 1 suggest regularity. With the quadrat subdivisions, the plot attempts to single out different scales of dependence in the point pattern data.

The **Fry plot** (Fry, 1979), also known as **Patterson plot** (Patterson, 1934), is more sophisticated, see Figure 15.9, bottom. This plot could be drawn manually using a transparent sheet with a mark in the middle. The sheet is then shifted so that the mark lies over one of the data points, and the positions of all the other data points are copied onto the transparent sheet. This procedure is repeated for each data point in turn. The resulting set of points on the transparent sheet is the Fry plot. In mathematical terms, the Fry plot is simply a scatterplot of the vector differences $x_i - x_j$ between all pairs of distinct points in $\mathbf{x}$.

The center bottom panel in Figure 15.9 represents a typical point of the point pattern, and the dots are the positions of other nearby points relative to the typical point. In (a), a void around the origin of the plot suggests regularity because data points come closer to each other as of a certain minimum distance only. In (b), there is no obvious pattern. In (c), there is a higher density of points near the origin, indicating a clustered pattern. Fry plots assume that the underlying process is stationary.

15.2.3.2 Distance Methods for Point Patterns and Functional Summary Characteristics

As mentioned above, a number of summary characteristics of point processes can be used to construct CSR tests. CSR serves as a boundary condition between processes that are more clustered or more regular than random. The tests are performed by comparing the empirical summary characteristics (estimated from the data) with theoretical characteristics for a homogeneous Poisson process. These characteristics are usually functions $S(r)$ of distance r, although some are numerical (a single value).

In general, let $\hat{S}(r)$ be an estimator of a functional summary characteristic $S(r)$, and let $S_{\text{Pois}}(r)$ be its theoretical Poisson counterpart. Then we reject the CSR hypothesis if

$$\max_{r \leq r^*} |\hat{S}(r) - S_{\text{Pois}}(r)| > S_\alpha, \tag{15.2}$$

where S_α is a critical value used to determine a large discrepancy between both $\hat{S}(r)$ and $S_{\text{Pois}}(r)$. The choice of the maximum r-value r^* is crucial and depends on the specific test. Very large values reduce the power of the tests. This is because as r is usually an interpoint distance, then $S(r)$ cannot be estimated for large r from a bounded window W of observation or is estimated from a few points with a large variance. Critical values S_α are sometimes known. Otherwise they have to be estimated using simulation tests (Section 15.3).

The alternative hypotheses are usually clustering or regularity, and some evidence or prior available knowledge may suggest which alternative is most suitable. This must be chosen prior to data collection. For instance, tumor cells may show clustering close to germ tumor cells, whereas they tend to be regular in dish-cultured cells. Other types of deviation from the CSR hypothesis are also possible alternative hypotheses: the combination of both clustering and regularity on different scales or in different regions, inhomogeneity, nonstationarity... Inhomogeneity often causes CSR tests to indicate (spurious) clustering.

Most summary functions are distances between points of the pattern and chosen test locations or between pairs of points of the pattern. The first distances are empty space (or void) distances: $d(u, \mathbf{x}) = d(u, \mathbf{X} \cap W) = \min\{\|u - x_i\| : x_i \in \mathbf{x}\}$, that is, the observed distance from a fixed reference location u in W (e.g., in a fine grid) to the nearest data point. Figure 15.10(a) shows the empty space distances for the amacrine cell pattern measured from every pixel. Their magnitudes are represented by a gray scale. The second distances are nearest neighbor distances: $t_i = \min_{j \neq i} \|x_i - x_j\|$, that is, the observed distance from each point x_i to its nearest neighbor. In Figure 15.10(b), the **Stienen diagram** draws a circle of diameter equal to the distance t_i to the its nearest neighbor around each data point x_i.

The following functional summary characteristics are then defined. All assume that $\mathbf{X}$ is stationary, and hence the definitions do not depend on the arbitrary reference location used (u or x_i). By moving the distance $r \geq 0$, they summarize the spatial dependence between points on a wide range of possible spatial scales.

1. **Empty space function** F (also called the spherical contact distribution or point-to-nearest event distribution): F is the cumulative distribution function of the empty space distance, that is,

$$F(r) = p(d(u, \mathbf{X}) \leq r),$$

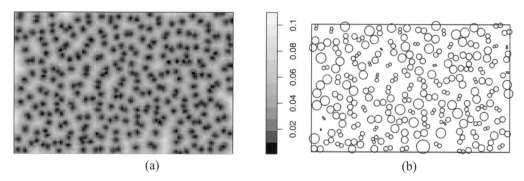

Figure 15.10 (a) Empty space distances to the amacrine cell pattern measured from every pixel and shown as a pixel image on a gray scale. (b) Stienen diagram where a circle of diameter equal to the distance to its nearest neighbor is drawn around each point of the amacrine cell pattern.

where u is an arbitrary reference location. Note that here the true distance $d(u, \mathbf{X})$ to the nearest point of the complete point process $\mathbf{X}$ is used. This may be different from the observed distance $d(u, \mathbf{x}) = d(u, \mathbf{X} \cap W)$, computed inside W.

2. **Nearest neighbor distance function** G (also called the event-to-event or inter-event distribution): G is the cumulative distribution function of the nearest neighbor distance for a typical point x_i in the pattern, that is,

$$G(r) = p(d(x_i, \mathbf{X} \setminus \{x_i\}) \leq r | x_i \in \mathbf{X}),$$

where $d(x_i, \mathbf{X} \setminus \{x_i\})$ is the (true) shortest distance from x_i to the point pattern $\mathbf{X}$ excluding x_i. Again, this may be different from the observed distance t_i, computed inside W.

3. The J **function** is a combination of F and G:

$$J(r) = \frac{1 - G(r)}{1 - F(r)}, \tag{15.3}$$

defined for all $r \geq 0$ such that $F(r) < 1$.

4. **Ripley's K function** or reduced second-order moment measure: Ripley (1977) defined the K function such that $\lambda K(r)$ is the expected number of points of the process (other than a typical point x_i of the process) within a distance r from the typical point, that is,

$$K(r) = \frac{1}{\lambda} \mathbb{E}[N(\mathbf{X} \cap b(x_i, r) \setminus \{x_i\}) | x_i \in \mathbf{X}],$$

where $b(x_i, r)$ is the disc of radius r centered on x_i. Dividing by λ, we eliminate the dependence on the intensity.

5. **Besag's L function** is a transformation of the K function (Besag, 1977). In the 2D space it is:

$$L(r) = \sqrt{\frac{K(r)}{\pi}}, \tag{15.4}$$

whereas in the 3D space, $L(r) = \sqrt[3]{\frac{K(r)}{\frac{4}{3}\pi}}.$

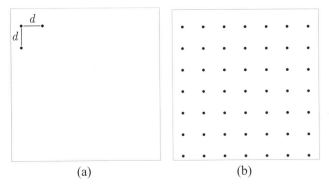

Figure 15.11 (a) A point process with isolated points with distance d. (b) A regular lattice with grid cells of side length d.

6. The **pair correlation function** g is also related to the K function. In the 2D space it is:

$$g(r) = \frac{K'(r)}{2\pi r}, \tag{15.5}$$

where $K'(r)$ is the derivative of $K(r)$. In the 3D version, the denominator is $4\pi r^2$.

Estimations of these functions are useful in exploratory data analysis. F and G both describe point-to-point distances. For G, the reference point is the typical point in the pattern, whereas a test location that is not a point in the pattern is the reference point for F. F summarizes the sizes of gaps in the pattern. G usually describes aspects of the geometry of the clusters only. For instance, if most of the points are arranged in tight clusters, there will be many nearest neighbors at short distances, and G will increase around such distances. Longer nearest neighbor distances will be unusual, and G will increase more slowly at such longer distances. However, G is not so good at reporting regular patterns. An extreme example is a point process with isolated points with distance d, see Figure 15.11(a). All nearest neighbor distances are d. Another pattern of a regular lattice with grid cells of side length d (Figure 15.11(b)) yields the same nearest neighbor distances. G does not distinguish between the first pattern and the lattice (it may help consider intensity as well as G).

F and G coincide for a Poisson process (Table 15.1). For a regular process, the interpoint distances tend to be larger than distances from test locations to points in the pattern. Hence if $d(x_i, \mathbf{X} \backslash \{x_i\}) \le r$, then $d(u, \mathbf{X}) \le r$, and, thus, $G(r) \le F(r)$ for $r \ge 0$. For a cluster process, the interpoint distances are mostly between points in the same clusters, and distances represented by G will be short. Distances from test locations to pattern points can be large. Then $G(r) \ge F(r)$ for $r \ge 0$.

The J function measures both the strength and range of interpoint interaction. For a Poisson process, $J(r) \equiv 1$, but this is not unique as there are other non-Poisson processes with the same J function. From the above discussion, we know that $J(r) \ge 1$ for regular processes and $J(r) \le 1$ for cluster processes. Note that, for large r, large fluctuations are expected for $J(r)$ because its denominator, $1 - F(r)$, is small. Figure 15.12 shows a hypothetical function J. We see short-range repulsion followed by clustering. The near

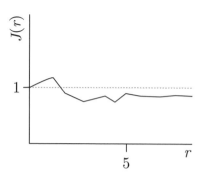

Figure 15.12 A hypothetical J function.

horizontal trend at the end suggests that the interaction between points is restricted to distances around 5 and shorter.

Second-order characteristics like K, L, g supplement the information provided by F and G. F and G are short-sighted as they do not provide information about points at larger distances beyond the nearest neighbor, that is, they ignore long-range spatial correlations.

K is a powerful function summarizing aspects of interpoint dependence and clustering. For clustered patterns, each point is likely to be surrounded by more points from the same cluster, and hence $K(r)$ will be large for small r. However, for regularly spaced patterns, each point is likely to be surrounded by empty space, and hence $K(r)$ will be small for small r. It has been shown that specifying $K(r)$ for all r is equivalent to specifying $Var[N(B)]$, the variance of the number of points occurring in a subregion B for any B. This is why $K(r)$ is referred to as the second-order moment.

The L function makes the K function easier to assess visually because the graph is compared to a line. Moreover, the fluctuations of estimated K functions increase with increasing r. The root transformation stabilizes these fluctuations (both means and variances) and can even make them independent of r.

The pair correlation function g is the most informative second-order summary characteristic and offers easily understandable information, although it is complicated to estimate statistically. It contains all the information necessary for describing the correlations of point locations (non-centered correlations). It characterizes the frequency of interpoint distances: if $g(r)$ is large for some r, then the interpoint distance r occurs frequently in the process. Function $g(r)$ always takes nonnegative values and approximates the value 1 for large r ($\lim_{r \to \infty} g(r) = 1$). If there is a finite distance r_{corr} with $g(r) = 1$ for $r \geq r_{corr}$, then there are no correlations between point positions at larger distances. r_{corr} is called **range of correlation**. It describes the size of the clusters (their diameter). Another interpretation of $g(r)$ is the probability of observing a pair of points separated by a distance r, divided by the corresponding probability for a Poisson process of the same intensity.

For inferential purposes, estimates of these functions from data are usually compared to their true value for a homogeneous Poisson process, which can be computed analytically. Table 15.1 includes the six functional summary characteristics explained above and their particular formulas for a homogeneous Poisson process. If a function $S(r)$ is lower (higher) than for the Poisson process $S_{Pois}(r)$, then another basic pattern (clustered, regular) is suggested. The situation differs depending on S.

Table 15.1 Relationship between the main functional summary characteristics of a generic spatial point process and a homogeneous Poisson process. The meaning of the last two columns is equivalent to the example for the first row: If $F(r) > F_{\text{Pois}}(r)$, it suggests a regular space pattern at distance r; otherwise it suggests a clustered space pattern at distance r

Characteristic $S(r)$	Homogeneous Poisson process, $S_{\text{Pois}}(r)$	$S(r) > S_{\text{Pois}}(r)$ suggests	$S(r) < S_{\text{Pois}}(r)$ suggests
$F(r)$	$F_{\text{Pois}}(r) = 1 - e^{-\lambda \pi r^2}$	Regular	Clustered
$G(r)$	$G_{\text{Pois}}(r) = 1 - e^{-\lambda \pi r^2}$	Clustered	Regular
$J(r)$	$J_{\text{Pois}}(r) = 1$	Regular	Clustered
$K(r)$	$K_{\text{Pois}}(r) = \pi r^2$	Clustered	Regular
$L(r)$	$L_{\text{Pois}}(r) = r$	Clustered	Regular
$g(r)$	$g_{\text{Pois}}(r) = 1$	Clustered	Regular

Derivations of functions in the second column are as follows. For a homogeneous Poisson process of intensity λ, the number of points falling in $b(u, r) \sim \text{Pois}(\lambda \cdot \text{area}(b(u, r)) = \lambda \pi r^2)$ and hence its distribution function $F_{\text{Pois}}(r)$ is readily derived: $F_{\text{Pois}}(r) = 1 - p(d(u, \mathbf{X}) > r) = 1 - p(N(\mathbf{X} \cap b(u, r)) = 0) = 1 - e^{-\lambda \pi r^2}$. It is not as straightforward to derive G for the Poisson process. For K in the homogeneous Poisson process, $x_i \in \mathbf{X}$ is known not to affect the other points of the process, and we still have a Poisson process. The expected number of points falling in $b(x_i, r)$ is $\lambda K_{\text{Pois}}(r) = \lambda \pi r^2$, and hence $K_{\text{Pois}}(r) = \pi r^2$. Hence, the derivation of J_{Pois}, L_{Pois}, and $g_{\text{Pois}}(r)$ is straightforward. The formulas are written for a 2D space; πr^2 is obviously replaced by $2r$ and by $\frac{4}{3}\pi r^3$ for 1D and 3D spaces, respectively.

The last two columns are explained as follows. Deviations of the functional summary characteristics from their respective homogeneous Poisson counterparts indicate deviations from CSR. When $F(r) > F_{\text{Pois}}(r)$, the empty space distances are shorter than for a Poisson process, thereby suggesting a regular pattern. For G, the reasoning is the opposite: when $G(r) > G_{\text{Pois}}(r)$, the nearest neighbor distances are shorter than for a Poisson process, and this suggests a clustered spatial pattern. Note that $F_{\text{Pois}}(r) = G_{\text{Pois}}(r)$ because, due to independence, x_i is a point of $\mathbf{X}$ that does not affect any other points of the process. Likewise, for K, $K(r) > K_{\text{Pois}}(r)$ suggests a clustered spatial pattern because we expect more points within distance r of an arbitrary point than under CSR.

For clustered processes, $g(r) \geq 1$ can take large values particularly for small r and is decreasing as r increases. For regular processes, $g(r) \leq 1$ for small r and can be greater than 1 with different shapes for large r.

Morales et al. (2014) tested spine distribution as a CSR model in apical and basal dendrites of layer III pyramidal neurons from the frontal, temporal, and cingulate cortex, discussing the relevance of these results for spine formation and plasticity and their functional impact on cortical circuits. The usual function G was used because the (necessary) spatial analysis *along* the dendrite (see Section 15.6) was translated into a traditional spatial analysis by straightening and unrolling transformations of the original data to analyze 3D points of insertion in a planar, unfolded arrangement. Schmitz et al. (2002) estimated the G function distribution of layer V pyramidal cells to analyze the effects of prenatal low-dose X-irradiation in the mouse brain. Jafari-Mamaghani et al. (2010) modeled the 3D spatial distribution also of layer V pyramidal neurons in mouse brain but using the

K function, where a new edge correction term was proposed (Section 15.2.3.3). In Cotter et al. (2002), the *K* function was used to test the hypothesis that glial cell deficit is more prominent close to neurons in major depressive disorder. Data from area 9 of the dorso-lateral prefrontal cortex, in both control and patient groups, provided no support for the hypothesis. Myllymäki et al. (2012) analyzed the spatial structure of epidermal nerve fiber entry points, the locations where the nerves enter the epidermis, in healthy subjects. The *K* function was used to investigate the effect of covariates (e.g., gender) on the degree of clustering of these entry points. Three diagnostic groups were used in Diggle et al. (1991): normal, schizoaffective, and schizophrenic people at the time of death. Departures from CSR between both subjects and groups of the spatial distribution of pyramidal neurons in the human cingulate cortex were investigated. They used the *K* function and replicated point patterns, i.e., several point patterns from the same process (Section 15.5.2).

Baddeley et al. (1993) examined the 3D locations of osteocyte lacunae in skull bones of Macaque monkeys observed using confocal microscopy. They used *F*, *G*, and *K* functions estimated by pooling replicates, and then the EM algorithm (Section 12.1) was applied for parameter estimation.

15.2.3.3 Edge Correction Methods

The summary characteristics have been introduced theoretically. However, we will now compute statistical estimates from an observed point pattern **x**. Thus, the characteristics for the Poisson process are calculated by plugging in the estimated intensity $\hat{\lambda}$ (Equation (15.1)). For instance, $\hat{F}_{\text{Pois}}(r) = 1 - e^{-\hat{\lambda}\pi r^2}$. But, most important, the window introduces a sampling bias because the observation of the process **X** only inside *W* leads to bias in the distance measurements. Thus, the observed distance $d(u, \mathbf{x}) = d(u, \mathbf{X} \cap W)$ to the nearest data point in *W* may be greater than the true distance $d(u, \mathbf{X})$ in the complete point process **X**. Beyond *W*, there may be closer neighbors, including the true nearest neighbor. For instance, the bottom left corner point in *W* of Figure 15.1 has a true distance to **X** (to the open circle below the point) shorter than in *W* (to the filled circle above to the right the point). The influence of the window boundaries is called the **edge effect** and has to be removed to avoid bias. If both *W* and the number of points *n* are large, edge effects have little influence and can simply be ignored.

When defining natural estimators of the summary characteristics (e.g., their empirical counterparts), we can correct the estimators by adding weights to unbias the measurements. Thus, in a grid of locations $u_j, j = 1, \ldots, m$, in *W*,

$$\hat{F}(r) = \sum_{j=1}^{m} e(u_j, r) \mathbb{I}(d(u_j, \mathbf{x}) \leq r), \qquad (15.6)$$

where $\mathbb{I}(\cdot)$ is the indicator function (Equation (3.3)), and $e(u, r)$ is an edge correction weight so that $\hat{F}(r)$ is an unbiased estimator of $F(r)$, and the influence of the window is reduced. Should we use $e(u_j, r) = 1/m$, for all *j*, then $\hat{F}(r)$ would be the empirical distribution function of the observed empty space distances, which is negatively biased for the reasons explained above (true distances cannot be accurately determined for points close to the window boundary).

Similarly,

$$\hat{G}(r) = \sum_{i=1}^{n} e(x_i, r) \mathbb{I}(t_i \leq r), \qquad (15.7)$$

where $e(x_i, r)$ is an edge correction, is an unbiased estimator of $G(r)$, and is better than using the empirical distribution function of the observed nearest neighbor distances (where $e(x_i, r) = 1/n$ for all i), a negatively biased estimator of $G(r)$. Finally,

$$\hat{K}(r) = \frac{1}{\hat{\lambda}^2 \text{area}(W)} \sum_i^n \sum_{j=1, j\neq i}^n e(x_i, x_j, r)\mathbb{I}(||x_i - x_j|| \leq r) \tag{15.8}$$

is an unbiased estimator of $K(r)$, where $e(x_i, x_j, r)$ is an edge correction. Without edge correction, the observed pairwise distances $||x_i - x_j||$ yield a biased sample of pairwise distances in the point process, favoring smaller distances (i.e., a pairwise distance greater than the diagonal or the diameter of W will never be observed). For points close to the border of W, the discs $b(x_i, r)$, used to calculate nearest neighbors, do not entirely lie within W, especially for large r, and it is impossible to determine the number of data points within distance r of point x_i with points in W only.

We now describe some general estimators. **Plus-sampling estimators** assume that natural empirical estimators can be applied. This implies that more information than is contained in W has to be available. Thus, if necessary, a forester (biologist) can determine nearest neighbors outside W for trees (cells) close to the border of the observed stand (tissue). If this is not possible, the simulation of new points outside W can yield an approximation.

When computing characteristics that assume that only the neighbors within a distance r are relevant for each point, **minus-sampling estimators** are the most popular. First, for each r, the window W is reduced to the smaller window W_r containing the points x in W such that $b(x, r) \subseteq W$, see Figure 15.13(a). Second, the estimators use the points in W_r only (i.e., points at a distance larger than r from the window boundary) as reference points

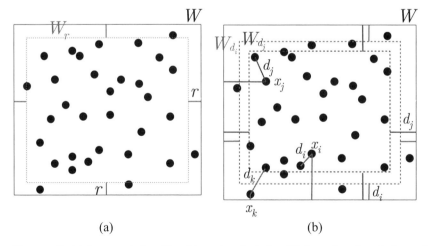

(a)   (b)

Figure 15.13 (a) Square window W and its reduced window W_r for r given in red when using minus sampling. The five points outside W_r are excluded as reference points, although they are used to compute distances from other reference points. (b) Nearest neighbor edge correction for points x_i (blue lines) and x_j (green lines). x_j is given a greater weight than x_i because $d_j > d_i$ means that window W_{d_j} is smaller than W_{d_i} and hence $v(W_{d_j}) < v(W_{d_i})$. Point x_k is excluded and not considered safe because d_k is longer than its distance to the boundary of W (in red). For the color version, please refer to the plate section.

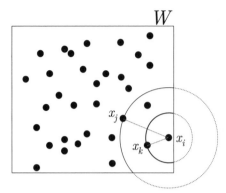

Figure 15.14 Second-order edge correction for point x_i. The relevant part (solid line) of the circumferences centered at x_i with radius $||x_i - x_j||$ and $||x_i - x_k||$ are used to calculate the weight.

(u and x_i), whereas all points in W are used to determine the nearest neighbor distances of these reference points and to determine the number of points within distance r from these reference points.

In other more refined edge-correction methods, *individual* points are weighted (as with the e expressions in Equations (15.6)–(15.8)) to compensate for the resulting loss of information due to point exclusion. For summary characteristics related to nearest neighbor distances, **nearest neighbor edge correction** is an option. Thus, a point x_i, whose nearest neighbor distance d_i is shorter than its distance to the boundary of W is considered "safe" in the estimation. Otherwise the point is excluded. When included, the point is assigned the weight $1/v(W_{d_i})$. Thus, this weight is low if d_i is small because W_{d_i} will be large. Likewise, this weight is large, if d_i is large. Figure 15.13(b) shows two examples x_i and x_j. For x_i, the weight is lower than for x_j, thereby receiving less edge correction. Point x_k is not safe and is excluded.

Other weights for the interpoint distance between x_i and x_j (as in the K function) are called **second-order edge correction** and are very common. For instance, in Ripley's isotropic correction (Ripley, 1988) (applicable only to stationary and isotropic point processes), we draw the circumference of radius $||x_i - x_j|| \leq r$ centered at x_i for a given point x_i and interpoint distance r, to compute the weight of the pair (x_i, x_j). Its length in W is divided by the total circumference length $2\pi||x_i - x_j||$. The weight is the inverse of this value. Thus, only about 2/5 of the circumference is inside W for the pair (x_i, x_j) in Figure 15.14, and therefore the weight is approximately 5/2, that is, because only 2/5 of the circumference is visible, we multiply the corresponding count by 5/2. However, for the pair (x_i, x_k), approximately half of the circumference lies inside W (a smaller proportion lies outside W than for x_j), yielding a smaller weight of 2.

Note that edge-effect problems become more serious in higher-dimensional spaces.

Example. Amacrine Cells (Functional Summary Characteristics). Figure 15.15 shows the $\hat{F}, \hat{G}, \hat{J}, \hat{K}, \hat{L}$, and $\hat{g}$ functions in the amacrine cell point pattern, all estimated with edge-correction methods. The benchmark functions of the homogeneous Poisson process are also shown (dashed lines) for comparison.[4] All summary functions except g consistently

---

[4] In spatstat, r^* must be larger than the radius of the largest disc contained in W.

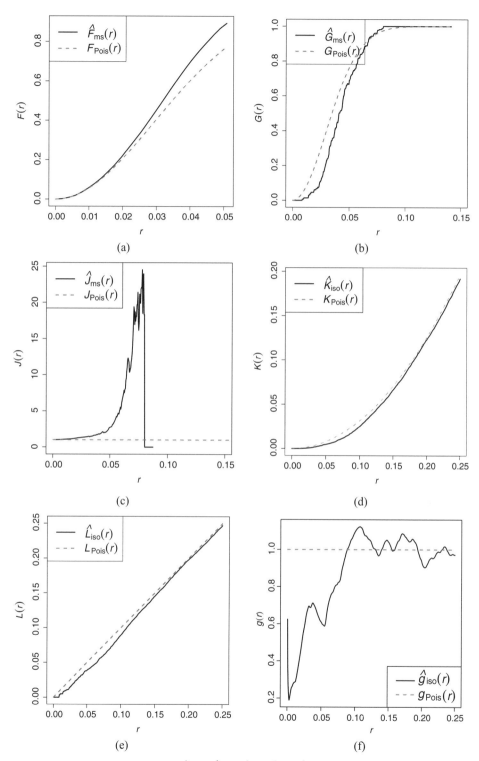

Figure 15.15 Estimated functions (a) $\hat{F}$, (b) $\hat{G}$, (c) $\hat{J}$, (d) $\hat{K}$, (e) $\hat{L}$, and (f) $\hat{g}$ for the amacrine cell pattern (black solid lines) versus their homogenous Poisson counterparts (with subindex "Pois" in dashed lines). Subindex "ms" denotes minus-sampling estimators, used for F, G, and J. Subindex "iso" is for the estimators calculated using Ripley's isotropic second-order edge correction, used for K, L, and g (they are second-order-related functions). One unit is equivalent to 662 microns in all plots.

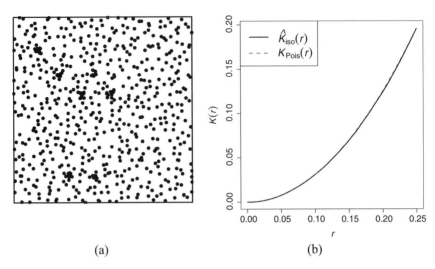

Figure 15.16 (a) A point pattern generated from the cell process. (b) $\hat{K}_{\text{iso}}(r)$ for this pattern (black solid line) versus $K_{\text{Pois}}(r)$ (dashed line). $\hat{K}_{\text{iso}}$ is calculated using Ripley's isotropic correction. Note that both functions match.

suggest a degree of regularity and a deviation from CSR. The g function approximately exhibits regularity, except for distances $r \in (0.08, 0.19)$. Note that not all functions always convey equivalent messages. ∎

There is a tendency to apply summary functions exclusively and uncritically. However, it is important to consider that they do not uniquely characterize the point process. Just as mean and variance in classical statistics do not uniquely determine the distribution of a random variable, different point processes can have the same intensity and K function in spatial statistics.

The points in Figure 15.16(a) were yielded by a simulated realization of the cell process (Baddeley and Silverman, 1984). This process is generated by dividing space into equal rectangular tiles or cells and by placing a random number of random points in each cell. The random number of points for different cells should be independent and are either 0, 1, or 10 points, with probabilities $1/10$, $8/9$, and $1/90$, respectively. Thus, most cells will contain 1 point, a few cells will be empty, and we will seldom find a tight cell including 10 points. Given a number of points, the points within a cell are independent and uniformly distributed. This inhomogeneous process exhibits exactly the same second-order characteristics (like K and g functions) as a homogeneous Poisson process (see Figure 15.16(b)). However, it is very different from such a process. Thus, the K function does not completely characterize a point pattern. Therefore, patterns cannot be singled out by first- or second-order methods.

Moreover, summary functions are defined and estimated under the stationarity assumption. This means that if the process is not stationary, deviations between the empirical and theoretical functions (e.g., between $\hat{F}(r)$ and $F_{\text{Pois}}(r)$) do not necessarily denote interpoint interaction but can be due to variations in intensity. Thus, the points in Figure 15.17(a) were generated from an inhomogeneous Poisson pattern with the same intensity function as in Figure 15.6. The corresponding estimated K functions in Figure 15.17(b) appear to be clustered, but this is an artifact of the spatial inhomogeneity.

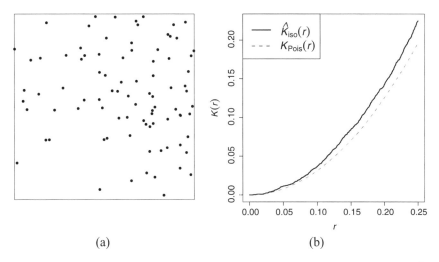

(a)   (b)

Figure 15.17 (a) A point pattern generated from an inhomogeneous Poisson pattern. (b) $\hat{K}_{iso}(r)$ for this pattern (black solid line) versus $K_{Pois}(r)$ (dashed line). The comparison suggests a clustered pattern, but this is due to the spatial inhomogeneity.

One solution is to reformulate the summary functions for inhomogeneity. There are modifications of the K, L, g functions that apply to inhomogeneous processes. For instance, if the true intensity function is $\lambda(u)$, then the **inhomogeneous K function** is defined as (Baddeley et al., 2000)

$$K_{inhom}(r) = \mathbb{E}\left[\sum_{x_i \in \mathbf{X}} \frac{1}{\lambda(x_i)} N((\mathbf{X} \cap b(x_i, r) \setminus \{x_i\}) | x_i \in \mathbf{X})\right],$$

where each point is now weighted by $1/\lambda(x_i)$. For the particular case of an inhomogeneous Poisson process with intensity function $\lambda(u)$, this function coincides with the homogeneous case, i.e., $K_{inhom,Pois}(r) = \pi r^2$. Like Equation (15.8), an estimator of the inhomogeneous K function is

$$\hat{K}_{inhom}(r) = \frac{1}{A} \sum_{i=1}^{n} \sum_{j=1, j \neq i}^{n} e(x_i, x_j, r) \frac{\mathbb{I}(||x_i - x_j|| \leq r)}{\hat{\lambda}(x_i)\hat{\lambda}(x_j)},$$

where A is either the area of W, area(W), as in Equation (15.8), or $\sum_i \frac{1}{\hat{\lambda}(x_i)}$, which is an unbiased estimator of the area of W if the intensity is correctly estimated. Because this introduces a data-dependent normalization, it is usually preferred to area(W). From this expression for the inhomogeneous K function, the inhomogeneous counterparts of the L function and the pair correlation function g are readily calculated using Equations (15.4) and (15.5). For an inhomogeneous Poisson process, $L_{inhom,Pois}(r) \equiv r$ and $g_{inhom,Pois}(r) \equiv 1$.

More sophisticated formulas are required for the F, G, and J functions (van Lieshout, 2011). Thus, under some conditions, the inhomogeneous F function is defined as

$$F_{inhom}(r) = 1 - \mathbb{E}\left[\prod_{x_i \in \mathbf{X} \cap b(u,r)} \left(1 - \frac{\lambda_{min}}{\lambda(x_i)}\right)\right],$$

and the inhomogeneous G function as

$$G_{\text{inhom}}(r) = 1 - \mathbb{E}\left[\prod_{x_i \in \mathbf{X} \cap b(u,r)} \left(1 - \frac{\lambda_{\min}}{\lambda(x_i)}\right) \,\middle|\, \mathbf{X} \text{ has a point at } u\right],$$

where u is an arbitrary location, and $\lambda(u) \geq \lambda_{\min} > 0$, for all u. The inhomogeneous J function is then derived using Equation (15.3). For an inhomogeneous Poisson process, $J_{\text{inhom,Pois}}(r) \equiv 1$.

15.3   Goodness-of-Fit Tests via Simulation

Many point process models are rather complicated, and no explicit analytical formulas have been found for even the simplest summary characteristics. These characteristics can be estimated based on simulated point patterns derived from these models. Simulation is often the only option and the standard approach in point process statistics. Goodness-of-fit tests, whose test statistics do not conform to the classical distributions, can also be performed as a simulation test. In these tests, simulations are employed to estimate both the null hypothesis model and the critical values for the test.

The null hypothesis H_0 of goodness-of-fit tests for point processes, equivalent to the Kolmogorov–Smirnov test in classical statistics (Section 4.2.2), states that the (specified) model fits the data. Two approaches for building goodness-of-fit tests are discussed: the envelope test and the deviation test. These tests are special cases of **Monte Carlo tests** based on simulations of the null hypothesis. The exploratory data analysis shown above with suggested deviations from CSR (as in Table 15.1) is now completed with these statistical tests.

First note that when comparing a functional summary characteristic $\hat{S}(r)$ with the theoretical $S_{\text{Pois}}(r)$, it can be hard to get a perfect fit between both functions even with a completely random pattern due to the inherent random variability. Figure 15.18 shows this variability for the K function of 20 simulated realizations of CSR with the same intensity.

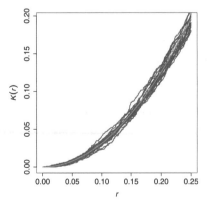

Figure 15.18 Estimated K functions of 20 simulated runs of CSR with the same intensity (blue) and exact K function of CSR (red), i.e., $K(r) = \pi r^2$. For the color version, please refer to the plate section.

This is the motivation for the first test. In the **envelope test**, we generate M independent simulations of the model (specified in H_0) inside W, and the estimate of $S_0(r)$, the theoretical summary function for the model in H_0 (its parameters are estimated from the data pattern), is computed for each realization, say $\hat{S}_0^j(r), j = 1, \dots, M$. Then the extreme values

$$S_0^{\min}(r) = \min_j \hat{S}_0^j(r)$$

$$S_0^{\max}(r) = \max_j \hat{S}_0^j(r)$$

are determined for each r. Three curves are plotted, showing $S_0^{\min}(r)$, $\hat{S}(r)$ (computed from the data pattern), and $S_0^{\max}(r)$. $S_0^{\min}(r)$ and $S_0^{\max}(r)$ form the envelope of $\hat{S}_0^j(r)$ from which the test takes its name.

For *any fixed* r chosen before the simulation, the probability of $\hat{S}(r)$ lying outside the envelope $[S_0^{\min}(r), S_0^{\max}(r)]$ for the simulated curves (type I error$= \alpha$) is equal to $2/(1+M)$. Thus $M = 39$ corresponds to $\alpha = 0.05$ and $M = 199$ corresponds to $\alpha = 0.01$. A test based on just a single r is expected to be conservative (the null hypothesis is unlikely to be rejected). This is because the model is simulated with parameters that have been estimated from the same data as used for the test.

These **pointwise envelopes** specify the critical values for a Monte Carlo test or significance bands (Ripley, 1981), but they should not be interpreted as confidence intervals for the true value of S. The test is applied by choosing a fixed r in advance and rejecting the null hypothesis if the observed function $\hat{S}$ lies outside the envelope at this value of r. However, checking whether $\hat{S}(r)$ is ever outside the envelope *for all* r is equivalent to the data-dependent choice of the value of r and the true significance level is higher (type I error is larger).

If there is no prior information about the range of spatial interaction, **global envelopes**, aka **simultaneous critical envelopes**, can solve the above problem. Again, we estimate $S(r)$ for each of the M simulations, denoted $\hat{S}_0^j(r), j = 1, \dots, M$. For each simulation j, equivalent to Equation (15.2), we compute the maximum deviations

$$\Delta_j = \max_{r \le r^*} |\hat{S}_0^j(r) - S_0(r)|.$$

When testing CSR, the theoretical $S_0(r)$ is known. For complex hypotheses where it is unknown, we can generate a separate set of M' simulations, compute the average estimated S functions of these M' simulations, and take this as an estimate of $S_0(r)$. Then, the maximum value $\Delta^{\max} = \max_{j=1,\dots,M} \Delta_j$ is calculated, and the lower and upper limits defining the global envelope are $S_0(r) - \Delta^{\max}$ and $S_0(r) + \Delta^{\max}$, respectively. Therefore, global envelopes have a constant width $2\Delta^{\max}$. These two limits and $\hat{S}$ are drawn for each r. Now if $\hat{S}(r)$ lies outside the global envelope at any value of r, the null hypothesis is rejected. The probability of this occurring under H_0 is $1/(M+1)$. Thus, a test of $\alpha = 0.05$ and $\alpha = 0.01$ is obtained by taking $M = 19$ and $M = 99$ simulations, respectively.

Example. Amacrine Cells (Envelope Test). We use the envelope test to assess the goodness of fit of a CSR model (i.e., H_0) to the amacrine cell pattern data.

Figure 15.19 shows the global envelope of the estimated L functions resulting from $M = 99$ simulations of CSR. The region between the envelopes is shaded. We use the L

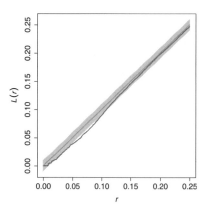

Figure 15.19 Envelope test with simultaneous critical envelopes of a CSR model applied to the amacrine cell data set. Ninety-nine simulated CSR realizations yield the envelopes $L_0^{\min}(r)$ and $L_0^{\max}(r)$ (defining the shaded area) for the L function. The curve $\hat{L}(r)$ computed from the amacrine cell pattern (blue) lies outside $[L_0^{\min}(r), L_0^{\max}(r)]$ for medium-low values of r, rejecting the CSR model. The theoretical curve of CSR, $L_0(r) = L_{\mathrm{Pois}}(r)$, is shown in red. For the color version, please refer to the plate section.

function because the test is more powerful. As mentioned above, the square root in its definition stabilizes the variance of the estimator so that L is more appropriate for use in simulation envelopes and hypothesis tests if we use the K function for the test. If we use the F or G functions, the recommended practice is to apply the test to a Fisher's variance-stabilizing transformation of F or G, defined as $\phi(\hat{S}(r)) = \sin^{-1}(\sqrt{\hat{S}(r)})$.

The red curve is the theoretical $L_0(r) = L_{\mathrm{Pois}}(r)$, used to compute the lower/upper limits. The blue curve is $\hat{L}(r)$, observed from the amacrine cell pattern. All L estimations were calculated with the Ripley's isotropic second-order edge correction. Observe the constant width of the global envelope. Notice that the L function estimated from the amacrine cell pattern lies outside the typical range of values of the L function for a completely random pattern. Therefore, the CSR hypothesis is rejected at $\alpha = 0.01$. ∎

The **deviation test** also starts by computing $\hat{S}_0^j(r)$ and $\Delta_j, j = 1, \ldots, M$, for each simulated pattern of the model specified in H_0. For the observed pattern, the deviation is also computed: $\Delta = \max_{r \le r^*} |\hat{S}(r) - S_0(r)|$. Now all $\Delta_1, \ldots, \Delta_M$ and Δ are arranged in increasing order. H_0 is rejected if Δ ranks extremely high among these values, i.e., if it is one of the $\alpha(M+1)$ highest values. Thus, for $\alpha = 0.01$ and $M = 999$, H_0 is rejected for a significance level α if Δ is in position 990 or higher (in one-sided testing). The p-value can be approximated as $\frac{1 + \sum_{j=1}^{M} \mathbb{I}(\Delta_j > \Delta)}{M+1}$.

The deviation test is a simultaneous Monte Carlo test, i.e., r does not need to be fixed in advance. The problem with the deviation test is that it is likely to be less powerful than the envelope test, as has been shown in practice.

Specifically, the deviation test for the J function for the CSR model is the J-test. This uses the $\max_{r \le r^*} |\hat{J}(r) - 1|$ statistic because $J_{\mathrm{Pois}}(r) = 1$ (Table 15.1). The power of this test has been shown to be strongly dependent on r^*: for large r^*, $1 - F(r)$ is close to zero and thus $J(r)$ may fluctuate largely. This complicates the test rather. On this ground, values of r^* such that $F(r) \ll 1$ are recommended. Trials can be run with different r^* values to compare results. Critical values for this test are calculated by simulation.

Similarly, the L-test of the CSR model uses the $\max_{r \leq r^*} |\hat{L}(r) - r|$ statistic because $L_{\text{Pois}}(r) = r$. As with the J-test, a Monte Carlo test based on simulations of the model to be tested, is commonly used. Recommendations with respect to the choice of r^* differ: half the diagonal length of W, less than or equal to $0.25h$ if W is a square of side length h, etc. Also, the test can be improved by introducing weight functions $w(r)$ to reduce the importance of a very small/large r, as $\max_{r \leq r^*} w(r) |\hat{L}(r) - r|$.

Stereological techniques for (approximately) counting objects, like neurons or synapses, that lie within a structure that has been sectioned, should be used in combination with spatial point process analysis. Stereological methods, like popular optical disector counting (Sterio, 1984), assume that objects are arranged in a completely random fashion, but this does not necessarily apply to the brain. When CSR holds, the choice of a small window size and a large number of disectors is reasonable. However, if CSR does not hold, the sampling plan should include a larger window size in order to get an accurate assessment of the spatial distributions of objects (Benes and Lange, 2001). Thus, trade-offs between window size, precision of neurobiological counts, and estimation of spatial distributions are key issues. The provision of representative tissue samples is a major concern, even if the tissue is heterogeneous. Stereology relies on the analysis of a limited number of single sections, and more modern methods, like the combination of focused ion beam milling and scanning electron microscopy (FIB/SEM), are possible, see Merchán-Pérez et al. (2009) for application to synapse counting.

15.3.1 Simulation of Point Process Models

It is evident how useful simulation based on point process models is, especially for hypothesis testing. Thus, we need procedures to simulate from a given model.

The procedure for simulations based on a homogeneous Poisson point process in window W is as follows:

1. Generate the total number of points: generate $N = n \sim \text{Pois}(\lambda \cdot \text{area}(W))$.
2. Place locations within W according to a uniform distribution: generate coordinates $x, y \sim \text{Unif}$ in the intervals corresponding with the width and height of W.
3. If W is not rectangular, embed W within a larger rectangle, and generate until there are n points within W.

The procedure for simulations based on an inhomogeneous Poisson point process in window W with a varying expected number of points $\lambda(u)$ per unit area is as follows:

1. Generate a sample of the homogeneous Poisson point process with $\lambda \equiv \lambda^* = \max_{u \in W} \lambda(u)$.
2. Retain or discard each generated point x_i with probability $p(x_i) = \lambda(x_i)/\lambda^*$ or $1 - p(x_i)$ (i.e., location-dependent thinning) respectively, regardless of what happens to the other points.

15.4 Data Collection Issues

Data collection methods depend on the objects, the objectives of the study, and the available resources. Important aspects are the spatial scale and the morphology, size, and density of objects. A good data set must be unbiased and representative, and the sampling strategy should account for this.

Mapping methods are the most commonly used data collection procedures for point patterns, where all object locations within a window are recorded. In contrast, **field methods** traditionally used in forestry and ecology only measure small fractions of the study area, usually randomly located regions or points. Other types of sampling units like strips and lines (transects) are also common. Field methods are tied to pre-fixed scales, whereas point patterns simultaneously can be analyzed on different spatial scales using mapping.

The size and shape of the observation window W are key issues. Typically, the researcher determines the size, shape, and positioning of W. In general, the larger the window, the better the statistical results. However, data collection resources and time may be limited, and the desired window may not be feasible. Nevertheless, chosen window size should be large enough to include all essential information. If W is very small, the observed point density trend may be spurious. If W is large, the density fluctuations observed on that spatial scale may be normal, and we conclude that the point distribution is globally homogeneous. The choice of window is related to the objective of the study. If we are looking for local interactions between points (relationships between neighbors), a window with a near homogeneous point distribution may be appropriate to avoid the influence of larger-scale inhomogeneity. If global fluctuations of points are the focus of the study, then larger windows will be more suitable.

An appropriate window size should ensure that the summary characteristics of interest achieve their asymptotic values in the window. There are measures for this purpose; they ensure that the variance of the statistic that estimates the characteristic (e.g., $Var[\hat{\lambda}]$ or $Var[\hat{g}(r)]$, see Illian et al., 2008, pages 266–267) is smaller than a predefined fixed value. The window size will depend on the variability of the point process and on the summary characteristics taken into account. For one and the same summary characteristic, larger windows are necessary to analyze cluster point processes, whereas smaller windows suffice for regular processes. Complex summary characteristics like the pair correlation function, require a larger window than simpler measures like intensity. With marked point processes, it must be ensured that all (discrete) marks are highly likely to be observed in W.

Usually some prior knowledge of the data is required to estimate the window size. This may be acquired in a pilot study, i.e., a preliminary statistical analysis of a small window. This is expected to yield basic information, like a rough estimate of the intensity and whether a pattern is regular or clustered. Based on this, the above-mentioned method can be used to calculate the variance of the statistic and then derive the window size.

An alternative approach is to generate a series of nested windows of increasing size and estimate the summary characteristics for each window. Then the window size is identified as representative when any further increase does essentially not change the statistical results further.

Equation (15.1) can be used in a Poisson process to build confidence intervals for λ because $\hat{\lambda} v(W) = N(\mathbf{X} \cap W)$ follows a Poisson distribution. For large $N(\mathbf{X} \cap W)$, using the normal approximation and a continuity correction, a $100(1 - \alpha)\%$ confidence interval for λ is

$$\left(\frac{z_{\alpha/2}}{2} - \sqrt{N(\mathbf{X} \cap W)}\right)^2 \leq \lambda v(W) \leq \left(\frac{z_{\alpha/2}}{2} + \sqrt{N(\mathbf{X} \cap W) + 1}\right)^2.$$

This is useful for determining the window size required for a given accuracy δ of estimation (say 10^{-5}). If δ is the desired (full) width of the confidence interval, then

$$\delta v(W) \approx \left(\frac{z_{\alpha/2}}{2} + \sqrt{\lambda v(W) + 1} \right)^2 - \left(\frac{z_{\alpha/2}}{2} - \sqrt{\lambda v(W)} \right)^2$$

yields the approximation

$$v(W) \approx \frac{4 \lambda z_{\alpha/2}^2}{\delta^2},$$

where λ is estimated from a pilot data set or using a priori information. If the true point process is not Poisson, this sample size may still be used as an approximation, although it may be slightly oversized.

The shape of the window is typically regular (rectangle, circle, polygon, parallelepiped), although more complex windows are also possible. In long rectangular windows, we can observe very long interpoint distances (interesting in some applications), albeit at the expense of serious problems with edge effects (Section 15.2.3.3).

In some cases, however, the window is naturally imposed by the physical limits of the environment in which objects exist. For instance, the distribution of trees in a city park is limited by its boundaries. The influence of the borders on the pattern geometry must be taken into account because we know the whole process. This kind of sampling area is termed **existence window**, and point patterns are considered finite, as opposed to the observation window, where point patterns are infinite. The approach for dealing with such finite point patterns is slightly different and closer to classical statistics.

15.5   Common Models of Spatial Point Processes

Beyond the simplest CSR model, the models for other point process statistics are more complicated. As in classical statistics, models are useful for formulating scientific hypotheses in terms of model parameters. Then we can check whether or not observed patterns support properties derived from these hypotheses.

Figure 15.20 shows the main models addressed in this section. Note the inclusion of some model families: Matérn cluster and Thomas processes are particular cases of Neyman–Scott processes, and the Gibbs hard-core is a Strauss process, a Gibbs process, and a hard-core process.

15.5.1   Cluster Processes

Clustered patterns (e.g., young trees, galaxies) are perhaps more common than regular or random patterns. Their point density varies strongly through space. In some areas, this density is very high, with groups of points surrounded by areas of low point density or empty space. The interpoint distance is below the average distance in the pattern. This is not simply due to random point density fluctuations. Note that it is not uncommon for inhomogeneity to be confused with clustering. Inhomogeneity refers to the spatial variation of the intensity function, whereas clustering refers to stochastic dependence among the points of the process, which are not easily distinguishable.

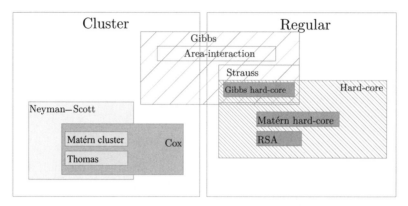

Figure 15.20 Main spatial point process models.

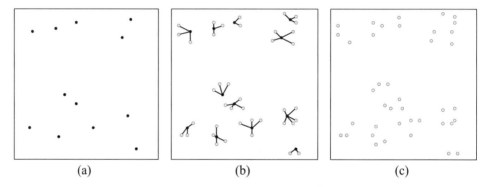

(a)   (b)   (c)

Figure 15.21 Mechanism of parent and daughter points to generate a clustered pattern. (a) Parent points (black) are the result of a homogenous Poisson process. (b) Each parent has a number of daughter points (open circles) according to a Poisson distribution, each placed independently and uniformly around the parent. (c) The resulting spatial pattern, formed by the daughter points.

When analyzing clustered patterns, clusters are hard to detect, if they are not clearly isolated. One approach is to count points within test circles of radii that are systematically varied, centered at lattice points or random points. Clusters are derived from extremely large numbers of points within a circle. MCMC approaches are also used.

Spatial clustering may have been caused by different processes, e.g., (i) a mechanism that involves parent points and daughter points, where the daughter points are scattered around the parent points (like insect egg masses and larvae distribution in fields, or target locations at bomb release and individual bomb impacts); (ii) points originally scattered across the whole space but remaining only in some irregularly distributed subregions (like wind-dispersed plant seeds germinating only where the environmental conditions are suitable); and (iii) a physical process making the points move in space (like galaxies).

A well-known example of (i) is the **Neyman–Scott model** (Neyman and Scott, 1952), where the parent points form a stationary Poisson process. Parent points are auxiliary rather than observable constructs (Figure 15.21(a)). The daughter points form the point pattern. In the typical cluster, they are random in number and scattered independently and distributed identically around the origin (Figures 15.21(b) and (c)). Thus, we start with a Poisson process $\mathbf{Y}$ of parent points. Then each parent point y_i in the point pattern $\mathbf{y}$ gives rise to a finite set of daughter points according to some stochastic mechanism. The Neyman–Scott process is stationary. Typical parameters for the Neyman–Scott process are the number of cluster points, which is an integer random variable, and the density function of the distances between a parent and a daughter point $\delta(r)$. Sometimes the density function of the distance $f_d(r)$ between two independent points in the same cluster is also considered. It is quite straightforward to derive formulas for the Neyman–Scott process due to its rather simple construction based on a Poisson process and independent clusters. Extensions of this idea may be based on non-Poisson parent processes, although it may be difficult to find closed-form expressions for summary characteristics.

Two examples of Neyman–Scott processes are the Matérn cluster process and the Thomas process. In the **Matérn cluster process** (Matérn, 1960), the number of points in the typical cluster has a Poisson distribution, and the points are independently uniformly scattered in a disc centered on the parent point and with radius R, a further model parameter. Densities $\delta(r), 0 \leq r \leq R$, and $f_d(r), 0 \leq r \leq 2R$ have specific formulas from which g is readily derived. Figure 15.7(c) shows a simulated realization of a Matérn cluster process. First, a homogeneous Poisson point process of parent points with intensity 10 is generated. Second, each parent point is replaced by a random cluster of daughter points with a random number of points following a Poisson distribution of parameter 5. Their positions are placed uniformly inside a disc of radius 0.3 centered on the parent point. The intensity of the point process is $10 \cdot 5 = 50$.

In the **Thomas process** (Thomas, 1949), each parent also has a Poisson number of daughters, and the distribution of the daughter points around the parent points is a Gaussian $\mathcal{N}(0, \sigma)$. g can also be derived from the expressions of $\delta(r)$ and $f_d(r), r \geq 0$. Matérn cluster and Thomas processes are also Cox processes (see below what is a Cox process and Figure 15.20). Moreover, they can be generalized by replacing the Poisson distribution of the random number of points per cluster by any other discrete distribution. Alternatively, there are nonstationary or inhomogeneous variations of Neyman–Scott processes. They are easily generated by making either the parent process or the daughter processes inhomogeneous, i.e., replacing the intensity of its Poisson process by an intensity function of location u or replacing the mean number of points per cluster by a function of location u, respectively.

Models suitable for (ii) are **Cox processes**, also called **doubly stochastic Poisson processes** (Cox, 1955). They describe clustering resulting from environmental variability. Cox processes are very general and flexible, with an elegant construction and yielding computationally tractable models. They are the best models for clustered point patterns.

Let $\Lambda(u) \geq 0$ be a stationary random function (called intensity field) defined at all locations $u \in \mathbb{R}^2$. Conditional on Λ, i.e., given that $\Lambda(u) = \lambda(u), \forall u$, let $\mathbf{X}$ be a Poisson process with intensity function Λ. Then $\mathbf{X}$ is a stationary Cox process. The realizations of this random function are treated as intensity functions of inhomogeneous Poisson processes and hence the points of the corresponding realization of the Cox process form an inhomogeneous Poisson process with intensity function $\lambda(u)$. A Cox process is a clever construction where independence (as in the Poisson process) is replaced by conditional independence.

This process is always overdispersed relative to a Poisson process, i.e., the variance of the number of points falling in a region is greater than the mean. Particular examples of Cox processes are the Matérn cluster process, the Thomas process, the mixed Poisson process, the log-Gaussian Cox process, the Poisson-gamma random field Cox process, the random-set-generated Cox process, the fiber-process-generated Cox process, and the thinning of Poisson processes. For instance, a random variable Λ is generated in the mixed Poisson process, and, conditional on Λ, a homogeneous Poisson process with intensity Λ is generated. An individual sample from this process looks like a sample from a stationary Poisson process, but the intensities differ from sample to sample. Poisson processes are thinned as mentioned above (Section 15.2.2), where points generated from a homogeneous Poisson process with intensity β are deleted at location u with probability $p(u)$, independent of other points. Note that independent thinning of a Cox process yields a new Cox process.

Because samples from a Cox process are samples from inhomogeneous Poisson processes given a realization of Λ, the main issue concerns the simulation of the intensity field model. Methods like maximum likelihood and minimum contrast can be used in order to estimate the parameters of these processes. In the **minimum contrast method**, we determine the values of the parameters θ to achieve the best match between the theoretical function $S_\theta(r)$ and the function $\hat{S}(r)$ estimated from data. This match is given as the discrepancy D between both functions over some range $[a, b]$:

$$D(\theta) = \int_a^b |\hat{S}(r) - S_\theta(r)|^q dr,$$

where q is an index and D has to be minimized with respect to θ. If the theoretical function is unknown, it may be approximated by simulation. Also, goodness-of-fit tests are based on the idea discussed in Section 15.3.

Finally, models for (iii) are beyond the scope of this book.

15.5.2   Regular Processes

The **hard-core process** is a typical example of a process with tendency toward regularity or repulsion between the points. In this process, there are no points at a distance smaller than a specific minimum distance r_0. A pattern of a hard-core process represents the locations of centers of nonoverlapping objects (like synaptic junctions whose volume has to be taken into account), typically circles/spheres with radius $R \leq r_0/2$. Consequently, $g(r) = G(r) = 0$ for $0 \leq r \leq r_0$. In fact, any object takes up some space, and there would be hard-core distances in all point patterns. However, the space around the objects is often large enough for object size to be ignored.

Some models of this process have been considered and can be simulated. However, summary function formulas have been derived for only the simplest (least interesting) cases. Hence, they have to be approximated by simulation. There are two main types of hard-core processes: (i) processes resulting from thinning operations, and (ii) processes resulting from the interaction of hard objects. In (i), the thinning operations remove points that are close to other points or points in clusters to produce a pattern of isolated points. For instance, dense patterns of seedlings develop into hard-core patterns as a consequence of competition. In (ii), the objects are hard and non-penetrable and cannot be closer than permitted by their sizes. They can exist from the beginning or can appear over time.

Some common hard-core models used in many applications are Matérn hard-core process (rather sparse); the **simple sequential inhibition** process, also called **random**

sequential adsorption (RSA) process (less sparse); the Gibbs hard-core process; and the packing models (rather dense).

The RSA process (Evans, 1993) is a finite point process model. The pattern is constructed by iteratively and randomly placing spheres with radii following a density function f in W. A new sphere is rejected if it intersects with an existing sphere, and another sphere, with a different center and radius, is generated. The process stops when either the required number of spheres have been placed or no new spheres can be added. The pattern of the sphere centers is an RSA process realization. Their radii may be considered as marks. Note that the spheres never touch. Summary functions are output by simulation.

Merchán-Pérez et al. (2014) modeled the 3D spatial distribution of synapses in layer III of the somatosensory neocortex (three male Wistar rats) as an RSA point process (see further details in Section 15.6). Anton-Sanchez et al. (2014) investigated whether there are statistical differences in both the synaptic density and spatial distribution of synapses between layers I to VI of the rat somatosensory cortex. The data were taken from several samples of each layer. Thus the analysis was conducted in the context of **replicated point patterns**, that is, a particular situation where different patterns are considered as instances of the same process (independent samples) to form a group. General summary characteristics are then determined by aggregating the statistical results for the single samples. The results showed that the synaptic distribution in layers II to VI was described by a common underlying RSA process with different densities per layer, whereas synapses in layer I had a slightly different spatial distribution.

15.5.3 Gibbs Processes

In Poisson processes, the points are independently distributed in W, whereas in Cox processes they are conditionally independent upon the intensity function. However, it is often useful in many cases to characterize the interpoint interaction, where this interaction can be a mutual repulsion (regular pattern) or a positive attraction (clustered pattern).

There are many ways of describing the interaction among the points (the so-called forces in physics) leading to the class of **Gibbs processes** (van Lieshout, 2000). These models are very versatile, especially for repulsion (as reviewed here), but they are mathematically complicated. They are constructed in terms of their location density functions. For each configuration $\mathbf{x} = \{x_1, \ldots, x_n\}$, the **location density** is a function $f(\mathbf{x})$, for any $n \geq 0$ (n is not fixed and may be zero, a peculiarity of this function), whose arguments are symmetric, that is, the values of the function are the same values regardless of the order of the points x_i. If we consider n infinitesimally small spheres $b_1, \ldots, b_n$ of volumes $dx_1, \ldots, dx_n$ centered on the different locations $x_1, \ldots, x_n$, then $f(x_1, \ldots, x_n)dx_1, \ldots, dx_n$ denotes the probability that the first point is in b_1, the second in b_2, and so on under the condition that the point process has exactly n points. Apart from this peculiarity, these densities for point processes behave much like probability densities in more familiar contexts.

The location density of a homogeneous Poisson process with intensity λ is $f(\mathbf{x}) \propto \lambda^{N(\mathbf{x})}$, where $N(\mathbf{x})$ is the number of points in configuration $\mathbf{x}$. For the inhomogeneous Poisson process with intensity function $\lambda(u)$, $f(\mathbf{x}) \propto \prod_{i=1}^{n} \lambda(x_i)$. Note that the densities are products of terms associated with individual points x_i, which is a reflection of the Poisson process independence property.

By introducing terms that depend on more than one point in the density, we can model interpoint interaction. Thus, pairwise interaction models have densities

$$f(\mathbf{x}) \propto \prod_{i=1}^{N(\mathbf{x})} b(x_i) \prod_{i<j} c(x_i, x_j),$$

where $b(x_i)$ is the first-order term and $c(x_i, x_j)$ is the second-order or pairwise interaction term that introduces dependence between points. Function c is also symmetric: $c(x_i, x_j) = c(x_j, x_i)$.

Two particular cases of pairwise interaction models are the Gibbs hard-core process and the Strauss process. In the **Gibbs hard-core process**, $b(x_i) \equiv \beta$ and $c(x_i, x_j) = 1$ if $\|x_i - x_j\| > r_0$ and 0 otherwise, where r_0 is the hard-core distance, which is fixed. Then the density is $f(\mathbf{x}) \propto \beta^{N(\mathbf{x})}$ if $\|x_i - x_j\| > r_0, \forall i \neq j$, and 0 otherwise. This is the density of the Poisson process of intensity β in W conditioned on the event that no two points of the pattern lie closer than r_0 units apart. This is known as the (classical) hard-core process. It is useful for points that are centers of spherical nonelastic particles of the same size, and r_0 is the diameter.

The **Strauss process** (Strauss, 1975) is more general: $b(x_i) \equiv \beta$, but

$$c(x_i, x_j) = \begin{cases} 1 & \text{if } \|x_i - x_j\| > r_0 \\ \gamma & \text{otherwise,} \end{cases}$$

where $0 \leq \gamma \leq 1$ is a parameter. Then the density is $f(\mathbf{x}) \propto \beta^{N(\mathbf{x})} \gamma^{M(\mathbf{x})}$, where $M(\mathbf{x})$ is the number of pairs $\{x_i, x_j\}$ in $\mathbf{x}$ that are less than r_0 units apart. The Strauss process is a model for spatial regularity, ranging from a strong hard-core inhibition (when $\gamma = 0$) to a random pattern (i.e., the Poisson process with intensity β when $\gamma = 1$). Thus, the parameter γ controls the strength of interaction between points.

Figure 15.22 shows two simulated realizations of the Strauss process. In (a), $\gamma = 0.2$ yielding a stronger interaction (inhibition) between points than in (b), where $\gamma = 0.7$.

The strength γ may vary in more general models, e.g., with the distance relative to an area of influence (in ecological or forestry models of competition).

Higher-order interactions are also possible. In the **area-interaction** or **Widom–Rowlinson process** (Baddeley and Lieshout, 1995), the density is $f(\mathbf{x}) \propto \beta^{N(\mathbf{x})} \gamma^{-A(\mathbf{x})}$,

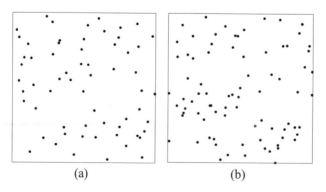

(a)   (b)

Figure 15.22 Two simulated realizations of the Strauss process. (a) The parameters are $\beta = 100, \gamma = 0.2, r_0 = 0.05$. (b) The parameters are $\beta = 100, \gamma = 0.7, r_0 = 0.05$. The model in (a) produces spatial patterns with a stronger inhibition than in (b).

where β and γ are again an intensity and an interaction parameter, respectively. $A(\mathbf{x})$ is the area of the union of all discs of radius r_0 centered at each point x_i. A value $\gamma < 1$ produces a regular process, and $\gamma > 1$ produces a clustered process. For $\gamma = 1$, we have a Poisson process. This process has interactions of all orders.

Gibbs models are simulated with MCMC algorithms (Section 13.2.3). In fact, MCMC algorithms were created to simulate Gibbs processes (Metropolis et al., 1953). Gibbs models are hard to fit with a maximum likelihood estimation, and a special pseudo-likelihood function is used instead (Baddeley and Turner, 2000).

15.6   Example: Spatial Location of Synapses in the Neocortex

Data Set 7 introduced in Section 1.6.7 includes 10 different samples of the neuropil in layer III of the somatosensory cortex in 3 different male 14-day-old Wistar rats (Table 1.13). The 3D brain tissue samples were obtained using combined FIB/SEM technology. These samples included 1,695 synaptic junctions, and the aim was to model their spatial distribution (Merchán-Pérez et al., 2014).

We compared the actual positions of the centroids of synaptic junctions with two theoretical models: CSR and RSA. As shown in Table 1.13, Feret's diameters of synaptic junctions are not negligible (417.06 ± 175.97 nm) when compared with the space around synaptic junctions (535.78 ± 166.81 nm). Therefore, junction size cannot be ignored, and a hard-core process that represents nonoverlapping objects makes sense as a candidate model. The minimum intersynaptic distances (measured between their centroids) must be limited by the sizes of the actual synaptic junctions.

Moreover, the observed Feret's diameters (as an estimate of synaptic junction sizes) were not constant but followed a probability density distribution. Using the Kolmogorov–Smirnov goodness-of-fit test (Section 4.2.2), we found that the distribution was log normal (Section 3.3.7) with parameters $\mu = 5.828$ nm and $\sigma = 0.446$ nm. As Feret's diameters follow a random distribution, the RSA model appears to be a good model choice.

For each of the 10 different experimental samples, we estimated the G, F, and K functions. They were compared against their respective theoretical functions under the CSR and RSA processes. The RSA process functions were approximated by simulation, following the procedure explained above. The number of placed spheres were the number of synaptic junctions observed for each original sample. The volume of the simulation region was the same as in the original sample. The number of simulated RSA realizations was 100.

Figure 15.23 shows the results of Sample 5 for the G functions (similar shapes were found in all 10 samples). In (a), the observed G function (blue) was closer to the RSA G curve (green) than to the CSR G curve (red), although they tended to be located slightly to the left of the RSA curves in most samples. A clear difference lies at short interpoint distances (marked by an arrow in Figure 15.23(a), where $\hat{G} = 0$ to its left due to the hard-core effect). All samples had an empty space around centroids due to the synaptic junction sizes (the synaptic junctions cannot overlap). This is captured by G because the fraction of centroids whose nearest neighbor is within such short distances is lower than expected for a CSR process. Note that the nearest neighbor of almost all centroids were placed at 1,000 nm or less, whereas the nearest neighbor of 20% was placed at 500 nm or less.

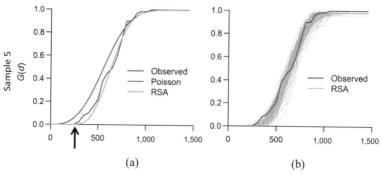

Figure 15.23 (a) $\hat{G}$ function (blue) estimated from the positions of the centroids of synaptic junctions in Sample 5 (see Table 1.13). The theoretical function G_{Pois} (red) and an approximation of G_{RSA} (green) are also shown. This approximation was computed as the mean of 100 $\hat{G}$ curves obtained from 100 simulated realizations of an RSA process shown in (b). The arrow points to the empty space around centroids due to the synaptic junction size. This is present in the experimentally observed function (blue) and for the RSA process (green). (b) Estimated individual $\hat{G}$ functions of 100 simulated RSA realizations (green) and the experimentally observed $\hat{G}$ function (blue). Image from Merchán-Pérez et al. (2014) reproduced with permission. For the color version, please refer to the plate section.

Figure 15.23(b) shows the individual G functions of 100 simulated RSA realizations (for performing an envelope test). Note that the experimental G functions overlapped with the simulated RSA functions. This was the general trend in most samples.

For the F (K) function, the CSR and RSA curves were very similar, and the experimentally observed curves either overlapped with RSA curves or tended to be located slightly to their right (left). These visual impressions were confirmed by two sample Kolmogorov–Smirnov tests (where instead of comparing a sample with a reference probability distribution, we check whether two samples come from the same distribution). When testing the goodness of fit of the experimentally observed functions in the 10 different samples with the respective RSA process function, the minimum p-value out of the 30 tests (10 samples and 3 functions, F, G, K) was 0.134, followed by 0.388, where the p-values were greater than 0.950 in 26 tests. Therefore, the RSA hypothesis is never rejected. For the CSR, the null hypothesis was only rejected ($p = 0.035$) for the G function in Sample 2, albeit without a clear deviation toward a clustered or regular pattern. In this case, 17 out of 30 tests yielded p-values over 0.950. Thus, RSA fitted better than CSR.

Therefore, the RSA model appears to be an appropriate model for the spatial distribution of synaptic junctions in this case. In fact, Feret's spheres occupy only 5.85% of the total volume, and this may explain why the CSR process also yields a good fit.

The fact that the nearest neighbor of 20–40% of synaptic junctions (in all samples) was of an intercentroid distance of <500 nm would mean that some synaptic functions are located side by side, and the neurotransmitter released by one synapse could perhaps reach its neighbor by diffusion and influence it, as discussed in Merchán-Pérez et al. (2014).

On the macroscopic and mesoscopic scales in mammals, it is well known that highly specific and ordered connections are established. This also applies even at the microscopic scale, where different areas/layers of the cortex receive specific inputs. However, the results on the ultrastructural scale appear to show that the synapse positions do not have any spatial preference. Thus, axon terminals first reach their destination (specific areas/layers) with a fine enough spatial resolution. Once there, they would randomly form synapses among their possible targets without a fine enough spatial resolution so as to reach a small target (like a specific dendritic branch or spine) within that area/layer. Spatial cues would not only be responsible for creating connections but also for other mechanisms such as molecular or activity-dependent cues. This implies that spatial specificity in the neocortex is scale-dependent.

In Merchán-Pérez et al. (2014), evidence was also found that symmetric synapses tend to be spatially segregated from asymmetric synapses. The number of symmetric synapses that had a nearest neighbor of the same type was over four times greater than would be expected if they were intermingled at random with asymmetric synapses.

Note that we have assumed that synaptic junctions can lie anywhere in the volume of tissue analyzed. More realistic is how **spatial analysis on linear networks** operates. This has been developed later (Okabe and Sugihara, 2012) and includes the equivalents of standard point process techniques. For example, Jammalamadaka et al. (2013) studied the spatial distribution of spines in rat hippocampal neurons along dendrites, i.e., spines are not free to lie anywhere but are constrained to lie on dendrites. The shortest path distances in the network are much harder to compute than Euclidean distances in traditional spatial statistics. The results suggested that dendritic spine densities were CSR, and spines had a tendency to cluster with other spines of the same type (a distinction was made between three types: mushroom, stubby, and thin).

Baddeley et al. (2014) also analyzed spines of these three types (a multitype pattern) on the dendrite network of a neuron. They used the linear network K and g functions, which were the counterparts of the standard functions adjusted for the network geometry. The dendrites investigated in these studies belonged to neurons in *in vitro* cell culture, which were almost flat. Hence, they omitted the third dimension and used a 2D projection.

With the same corrected K function, Anton-Sanchez et al. (2017) studied the spatial distribution of spines along both the basal and apical dendritic networks of human pyramidal neurons implementing for the first time methods to analyze 3D linear networks. They fitted an inhomogeneous Poisson model to account for the spatial variation in spine intensity dependent on the distance to the cell body. They found that there were no significant differences in spine distribution between basal trees of the same and different neurons. Moreover, they found that there were significant differences in the distribution of spines along basal and apical networks as of a certain distance from the cell body. The spines of apical dendrites were more clustered than basal spines.

15.7   Bibliographic Notes

Useful textbooks on spatial point processes are Ripley (1981), Diggle (2003), Moller and Waagepetersen (2003), Illian et al. (2008), and Baddeley et al. (2015). The analysis of spatial point process originated in application fields like forestry, medicine, ecology, and astronomy. One of the most influential papers to use summary functions in point pattern analysis is Ripley (1977).

Some issues have not been detailed in this chapter. Model selection in this setting is still under development. For Poisson nested models, differences of deviances between two models are calculated (as in Section 8.3.2.2), and a classical χ^2 test is performed (where H_0 represents the simplest model). For more general models (non-nested, non-Poisson), measures like AIC can be used for model scoring. So far, no one has systematically compared all CSR tests (Illian et al., 2008). This is an open issue.

The **Greig-Smith method** (Greig-Smith, 1964) improves the quadrat counting test by also using counts grouped by neighboring quadrats (number of points in a pair of quadrats, in a quartet of quadrats...). Accordingly, clustering/regularity can be detected on different scales.

The spatial pattern may be affected by differences in the properties of the objects (size, shape, age, species...), generally described as marks. The relationship between the two subprocesses formed by the two types of points in the amacrine data set was not analyzed here. Marked spatial point patterns have specificities that require further study (Illian et al., 2008). Locations and marks can be considered together in the process, but other approaches follow a marks conditioned on locations strategy or a locations conditioned on marks strategy. The possible influence of covariates on the spatial pattern was not covered here either.

In many cases, a single sample is sufficient for the statistical analysis, namely for i.i.d. clusters, inhomogeneous Poisson processes, and Gibbs processes with many points. However, if we want to explore the random number of points in the whole window, and analyze an inhomogeneous Cox process, or get a reliable estimation of intensity function trends, then more than one sample has to be analyzed.

Another data collection method is **repetitive mapping**, where the same sampling window is measured at several points in time. This is used in space-time analyses. Time instants can be used as marks. Illian et al. (2008) consider spatial-temporal processes, an area that is currently undergoing rapid development.

Bibliography

E. Abbe. *Über die Gesetzmässigkeit der Verheiling der Fehler bei Beobachtungrsreihen*. Habilitationsschrift Jena, 1836. [140]

P. Abbeel, D. Koller, and A. Y. Ng. Learning factor graphs in polynomial time and sample complexity. *Journal of Machine Learning Research*, 7:1743–1788, 2006. [545]

A. Abdullah, A. Hirayama, S. Yatsushiro, M. Matsumae, and K. Kuroda. Cerebrospinal fluid image segmentation using spatial fuzzy clustering method with improved evolutionary expectation maximization. In *35th Annual International Conference of the IEEE Engineering in Medicine and Biology Society*, pages 3359–3362, 2013. [448]

J. Abellán, A. Cano, A. R. Masegosa, and S. Moral. A semi-naive Bayes classifier with grouping of cases. In *Proceedings of the 9th European Conference in Symbolic and Quantitative Approaches to Reasoning with Uncertainty. Lecture Notes in Artificial Intelligence*, volume 4724, pages 477–488. Springer, 2007. [356]

J. Abellán, M. Gomez-Olmedo, and S. Moral. Some variations on the PC algorithm. In *Proceedings of the 3rd European Workshop on Probabilistic Graphical Models*, pages 1–8, 2006. [526]

M. Abramowitz and I. A. Stegun. *Handbook of Mathematical Functions with Formulas, Graphs, and Mathematical Tables*, chapter Modified Bessel functions I and K, pages 374–377. Dover, 1972. [113]

A. H. Abuzaid, I. B. Mohamed, and A. G. Hussin. Boxplot for circular variables. *Computational Statistics*, 27(3):381–392, 2012. [66]

U. R. Acharya, S. V. Sree, S. Chattopadhyay, W. Yu, and P. C. A. Ang. Application of recurrence quantification analysis for the automated identification of epileptic EEG signals. *International Journal of Neural Systems*, 21(3):199–211, 2011. [263]

D. H. Ackley, G. E. Hinton, and T. J. Sejnowski. A learning algorithm for Boltzmann machines. *Cognitive Science*, 9(1):147–169, 1985. [555]

C. C. Aggarwal and P. S. Yu. Finding generalized projected clusters in high dimensional space. In *Proceedings of the ACM SIGMOD International Conference on Management of Data*, pages 70–81, 2000. [460]

C. C. Aggarwal, C. M. Procopiuc, J. L. Wolf, P. S. Yu, and J. S. Park. Fast algorithms for projected clustering. In *Proceedings of the ACM SIGMOD International Conference on Management of Data*, pages 61–72, 1999. [459]

A. Agresti. *Categorical Data Analysis*. Wiley, 3rd edition, 2013. [341, 384]

D. W. Aha, D. Kibler, and M. K. Albert. Instance-based learning algorithms. *Machine Learning*, 6(1):37–66, 1991. [29, 227, 269]

M. A. Aizerman, E. M. Braverman, and L. I. Rozoner. Theoretical foundations of the potential function method in pattern recognition learning. *Automation and Remote Control*, 25:821–837, 1964. [319]

H. Akaike. A new look at the statistical model identification. *IEEE Transactions on Automatic Control*, 19(6):716–723, 1974. [532]

H. Akil, M. E. Martone, and D. C. van Essen. Challenges and opportunities in mining neuroscience data. *Science*, 331:708–711, 2011. [18, 19]

A. Al-Am. Ant colony optimization for feature subset selection. In *Proceedings of World Academy of Science, Engineering and Technology*, volume 4, pages 35–38, 2005. [241, 246]

A. Albert and J. A. Anderson. On the existence of maximum likelihood estimates in logistic models. *Biometrika*, 71:1–10, 1984. [339]

C. F. Aliferis, I. Tsamardinos, and M. S. Statnikov. HITON: A novel Markov blanket algorithm for optimal variable selection. In *AMIA Annual Symposium Proceedings*, pages 21–25, 2003. [364, 431]

H. Alikhanian, J. D. Crawford, J. F. Desouza, D. O. Cheyne, and G. Blohm. Adaptive cluster analysis approach for functional localization using magnetoencephalography. *Frontiers in Neuroscience*, 7:Article 73, 2013. [460]

H. Almuallim and T. G. Dietterich. Efficient algorithms for identifying relevant features. In *Proceedings of the 9th Canadian Conference on Artificial Intelligence*, pages 38–45. Morgan Kaufmann, 1992. [236]

J. I. Alonso-Barba, L. de la Ossa, J. A. Gámez, and J. M. Puerta. Scaling up the greedy equivalence search algorithm by constraining the search space of equivalence classes. *International Journal of Approximate Reasoning*, 54(4):429–451, 2013. [531]

E. Alpaydın. Combined 5x2cv F test for comparing supervised classification learning algorithms. *Neural Computation*, 11(8):1885–1892, 1999. [225]

K. H. Ambert, A. M. Cohen, G. A. Burns, E. Boudreau, and K. Sonmez. Virk: An active learning-based system for bootstrapping knowledge base development in the neurosciences. *Frontiers in Neuroinformatics*, 7:38, 2013. [314]

C. Ambroise and G. Govaert. Convergence of an EM-type algorithm for spatial clustering. *Pattern Recognition Letters*, 19(10):919–927, 1998. [486]

K. Amunts, C. Ebell, J. Muller, M. Telefont, A. Knoll, and T. Lippert. The Human Brain Project: Creating a European research infrastructure to decode the human brain. *Neuron*, 92:574–581, 2016. [9]

T. W. Anderson. *An Introduction to Multivariate Statistical Analysis*. Wiley, 2nd edition, 1984. [499]

S. Andjelic, T. Gallopin, B. Cauli, E. L. Hill, L. Roux, S. Badr, E. Hu, G. Tamás, and B. Lambolez. Glutamatergic nonpyramidal neurons from neocortical layer VI and their comparison with pyramidal and spiny stellate neurons. *Journal of Neurophysiology*, 101:641–654, 2009. [34]

M. Ankerst, M. M. Breunig, H. P. Kriegel, and J. Sander. OPTICS: Ordering points to identify the clustering structure. In *Proceedings of the International Conference on Management of Data*, pages 49–60. ACM Press, 1999. [467]

F. J. Anscombe and I. Guttman. Rejection of outliers. *Technometrics*, 2(2):123–147, 1960. [224]

L. Anton-Sanchez, C. Bielza, A. Merchán-Pérez, J. R. Rodríguez, J. DeFelipe, and P. Larrañaga. Three-dimensional distribution of cortical synapses: A replicated point pattern-based analysis. *Frontiers in Neuroanatomy*, 8:Article 85, 2014. [607]

L. Anton-Sanchez, P. Larrañaga, R. Benavides-Piccione, I. Fernaud-Espinosa, J. DeFelipe, and C. Bielza. Three-dimensional spatial modeling of spines along dendritic networks in human cortical pyramidal neurons. *PLoS ONE*, 12(6):e0180400, 2017. [611]

J. Arellano, R. Benavides-Piccione, J. DeFelipe, and R. Yuste. Ultrastructure of dendritic spines: Correlation between synaptic and spine morphologies. *Frontiers in Neuroscience*, 1:131–143, 2007. [38, 41, 469]

R. Armañanzas, C. Bielza, K. R. Chaudhuri, P. Martínez-Martín, and P. Larrañaga. Unveiling relevant non-motor Parkinson's disease severity symptoms using a machine learning approach. *Artificial Intelligence in Medicine*, 58(3):195–202, 2013. [239, 282]

S. Arnborg, D. G. Corneil, and A. Proskurowski. Complexity of finding embeddings in a *k*-tree. *SIAM Journal on Algebraic Discrete Methods*, 8(2):277–284, 1987. [510]

A. Arrigo, A. Calamuneri, E. Mormina, M. Gaeta, A. Quartarone, S. Marino, G. P. Anastasi, and P. Aragona. New insights in the optic radiations connectivity in the human brain. *Investigate Ophthalmology and Visual Science*, 57(1):1–5, 2016. [176]

G. A. Ascoli. Successes and rewards in sharing digital reconstructions of neuronal morphology. *Neuroinformatics*, 5:154–160, 2007. [44]

G. A. Ascoli. *Trees of the Brain, Roots of the Mind*. The MIT Press, 2015. [3]

G. A. Ascoli and J. L. Krichmar. L-Neuron: A modeling tool for the efficient generation and parsimonious description of dendritic morphology. *Neurocomputing*, 32-33:1003–1011, 2000. [540]

G. A. Ascoli, L. Alonso-Nanclares, S. A. Anderson, G. Barrionuevo, R. Benavides-Piccione, A. Burkhalter, G. Buzsaki, B. Cauli, J. DeFelipe, A. Fairen, D. Feldmeyer, G. Fishell, Y. Fregnac, T. F. Freund, D. Gardner, E. P. Gardner, J. H. Goldberg, M. Helmstaedter, S. Hestrin, F. Karube, Z. F. Kisvárday, B. Lambolez, D. A. Lewis, O. Marin, H. Markram, A. Muoz, A. Packer, C. C. Petersen, K. S. Rockland, J. Rossier, B. Rudy, P. Somogyi, J. F. Staiger, G. Tamas, A. M. Thomson, M. Toledo-Rodriguez, Y. Wang, D. C. West, and R. Yuste. Petilla terminology: Nomenclature of features of GABAergc interneurons of the cerebral cortex. *Nature Reviews Neuroscience*, 9:557–568, 2008. [34]

G. A. Ascoli, P. Maraver, S. Nanda, S. Polavaram, and R. Armañanzas. Win-win data sharing in neuroscience. *Nature Methods*, 14(2):112–116, 2017. [21, 417]

Z. A. Assis, J. Saini, M. Ranjan, A. K. Gupta, P. Sabharwal, and P. R. Naidu. Diffusion tensor imaging in evaluation of posterior fossa tumors in children on a 3T MRI scanner. *Indian Journal of Radiology and Imaging*, 25(4):445–452, 2015. [186]

P. Azimi, H. R. Mohammadi, E. C. Benzel, S. Shahzadi, S. Azhari, and A. Montazeri. Artificial neural networks in neurosurgery. *Journal of Neurology, Neurosurgery and Psychiatry*, 86(3):251–256, 2015. [293]

L. Babai. Monte-Carlo algorithms in graph isomorphism testing. Technical Report, Université de Montréal, 79-10, 1979. [244]

F. R. Bach and M. I. Jordan. Learning graphical models with Mercer kernels. In *Advances in Neural Information Processing Systems 15*, pages 1009–1016. The MIT Press, 2003. [502]

K. Bache and M. Lichman. UCI machine learning repository, 2013. URL `archive.ics.uci.edu/ml`. [366]

A. J. Baddeley and M. N. M. Lieshout. Area-interaction point processes. *Annals of the Institute of Statistical Mathematics*, 47(4):601–619, 1995. [608]

A. J. Baddeley and B. W. Silverman. A cautionary example on the use of second-order methods for analyzing point patterns. *Biometrics*, 40(4):1089–1093, 1984. [596]

A. J. Baddeley and R. Turner. Practical maximum pseudolikelihood for spatial point patterns. *Australian & New Zealand Journal of Statistics*, 42(3):283–322, 2000. [609]

A. J. Baddeley and R. Turner. spatstat: An R package for analyzing spatial point patterns. *Journal of Statistical Software*, 12(1), 2005. [578]

A. J. Baddeley, R. A. Moyeed, C. V. Howard, and A. Boyde. Analysis of a three-dimensional point pattern with replication. *Journal of the Royal Statistical Society, Series C*, 42(4):641–668, 1993. [592]

A. J. Baddeley, J. Møller, and R. P. Waagepetersen. Non- and semi-parametric estimation of interaction in inhomogeneous point patterns. *Statistica Neerlandica*, 54(3):329–350, 2000. [597]

A. J. Baddeley, A. Jammalamadaka, and G. Nair. Multitype point process analysis of spines on the dendrite network of a neuron. *Journal of the Royal Statistical Society, Series C*, 63(5):673–694, 2014. [611]

A. J. Baddeley, E. Rubak, and R. Turner. *Spatial Point Patterns: Methodology and Applications with R*. Chapman & Hall/CRC, 2015. [611]

T. C. Badea and J. Nathans. Quantitative analysis of neuronal morphologies in the mouse retina visualized by using a genetically directed reporter. *Journal of Comparative Neurology*, 480(4): 331–351, 2004. [445]

M. Bagheri, Z. Maghsoudi, S. Fayazi, N. Elahi, H. Tabesh, and N. Majdinasab. Several food items and multiple sclerosis: A case-control study in Ahvaz (Iran). *Iranian Journal of Nursing and Midwifery Research*, 19(6):659–665, 2014. [192]

G. H. Bakir, T. Hofmann, B. Schölkopf, A. Smola, and B. Taskar. *Predicting Structured Data*. The MIT Press, 2007. [434]

L. Bako. Real-time classification of datasets with hardware embedded neuromorphic neural networks. *Briefings in Bioinformatics*, 11(3):348–363, 2010. [300]

A. Banerjee, I. S. Dhillon, J. Ghosh, and S. Sra. Clustering on the unit hypersphere using von Mises–Fisher distributions. *Journal of Machine Learning Research*, 6:1345–1382, 2005. [475]

O. Banerjee, L. El Ghaoui, and A. D'Aspremont. Model selection through sparse maximum likelihood estimation for multivariate Gaussian or binary data. *Journal of Machine Learning Research*, 9:485–516, 2008. [561]

F. Barahona. On the computational complexity of Ising spin glass models. *Journal of Physics A: Mathematical and General*, 15(10):3241–3253, 1982. [562]

Y. Barash and N. Friedman. Context-specific Bayesian clustering for gene expression data. *Journal of Computational Biology*, 9(2):169–191, 2002. [481]

M. S. Bartlett. Properties of sufficiency and statistical tests. *Proceedings of the Royal Society of London*, 160:268–282, 1937. [197]

J. Barnes and P. Hut. A hierarchical $O(NlogN)$ force-calculation algorithm. *Nature*, 73:79–89, 1986. [84]

V. Barnett and T. Lewis. *Outliers in Statistical Data*. Wiley, 1994. [224]

S. Basaglia-Pappas, M. Laterza, C. Borg, A. Richard-Mornas, E. Favre, and C. Thomas-Antérion. Exploration of verbal and non-verbal semantic knowledge and autobiographical memories starting from popular songs in Alzheimer's disease. *International Psychogeriatrics*, 25(5):785–795, 2013. [183]

F. Baselice, L. Coppolino, S. D'Antonio, G. Ferraioli, and L. Sgaglione. A DBSCAN based approach for jointly segment and classify brain MR images. In *Proceedings of the 37th Annual International Conference of the IEEE Engineering in Medicine and Biology Society*, pages 2993–2996. IEEE Press, 2015. [456]

D. S. Bassett and M. S. Gazzaniga. Understanding complexity in the human brain. *Trends in Cognitive Sciences*, 15(5):200–209, 2011. [3]

D. Battaglia, A. Karagiannis, T. Gallopin, H. W. Gutch, and B. Cauli. Beyond the frontiers of neuronal types. *Frontiers in Neural Circuits*, 7(13), 2013. [34]

E. Bauer and R. Kohavi. An empirical comparison of voting classification algorithms: Bagging, boosting, and variants. *Machine Learning*, 36(1–2):105–139, 1999. [389, 402]

T. Bayes. An essay towards solving a problem in the doctrine of chances. *Philosophical Transactions*, 53:370–418, 1763. [140]

M. J. Beal. *Variational Algorithms for Approximate Bayesian Inference*. PhD thesis, University of London, 2003. [544]

C. Beeri, D. Maier, and M. Yannakakis. On the desirability of acyclic database schemes. *Journal of the ACM*, 30(3):479–513, 1983. [551]

R. E. Bellman. *Dynamic Programming*. Princeton University Press, 1957. [28]

A. Ben-Dor, L. Bruhn, N. Friedman, I. Nachman, M. Schummer, and Z. Yakhini. Tissue classification with gene expression profiles. *Journal of Computational Biology*, 7(3–4):559–584, 2000. [232, 235]

A. Ben-Hur and J. Weston. A user's guide to support vector machines. In *Data Mining Techniques for the Life Sciences*, volume 609, pages 223–239. Humana Press, 2010. [314]

A. Ben-Hur, D. Horn, H. T. Siegelmann, and V. Vapnik. Support vector clustering. *Journal of Machine Learning Research*, 2:125–137, 2002. [319]

R. Benavides-Piccione, F. Hamzei-Sichani, I. Ballesteros-Yáñez, J. DeFelipe, and R. Yuste. Dendritic size of pyramidal neurons differs among mouse cortical regions. *Cerebral Cortex*, 16(7):990–1001, 2006. [44, 82, 541]

R. Benavides-Piccione, I. Fernaud-Espinosa, V. Robles, R. Yuste, and J. DeFelipe. Age-based comparison of human dendritic spine structure using complete three-dimensional reconstructions. *Cerebral Cortex*, 23(8):1798–1810, 2013. [14, 41]

F. M. Benes and N. Lange. Two-dimensional versus three-dimensional cell counting: A practical perspective. *Trends in Neurosciences*, 24(1):11–17, 2001. [601]

Y. Bengio and Y. Grandvalet. No unbiased estimator of the variance of k-fold cross-validation. *Journal of Machine Learning Research*, 5:1089–1105, 2004. [225]

B. V. Benjamin, P. Gao, E. McQuinn, S. Choudhary, A. R. Chandrasekaran, J.-M. Bussat, R. Alvarez-Icaza, J. V. Arthur, P. A. Merolla, and K. Boahen. Neurogrid: A mixed-analog-digital multichip system for large-scale neural simulations. *Proceedings of the IEEE*, 102:699–716, 2014. [30]

Y. Benjamini and D. Yekutieli. The control of false discovery rate in multiple testing under dependency. *The Annals of Statistics*, 29:1165–1188, 2001. [559, 560]

M. Benjumeda, C. Bielza, and P. Larrañaga. Tractability of most probable explanations in multidimensional Bayesian network classifiers. *International Journal of Approaximate Reasoning*, 93:74–87, 2018. [430]

M. Benjumeda, C. Bielza, and P. Larrañaga. Learning tractable Bayesian networks in the space of elimination orders. *Artificial Intelligence*, 274:66–90, 2019. [546]

J. Benvenuto, Y. Jin, M. Casale, G. Lynch, and R. Granger. Identification of diagnostic evoked response potential segments in Alzheimer's disease. *Experimental Neurology*, 176(2):269–276, 2002. [263]

P. Berens. CircStat: A MATLAB toolbox for circular statistics. *Journal of Statistical Software*, 31(10):1–21, 2009. [151]

J. O. Berger. *Statistical Decision Theory and Bayesian Analysis*. Springer, New York, 1985. [196]

J. Berkson. Application of the logistic function to bio-assay. *Journal of the American Statistical Association*, 39(227):357–365, 1944. [384]

P. Bermejo, J. A. Gámez, and J. M. Puerta. A GRASP algorithm for fast hybrid (filter-wrapper) feature subset selection in high-dimensional datasets. *Pattern Recognition Letters*, 32:701–711, 2011. [241, 244]

J. M. Bernardo. Reference posterior distributions for Bayesian-inference. *Journal of the Royal Statistical Society, Series B*, 41(2):113–147, 1979. [196]

J. M. Bernardo and A. F. M. Smith. *Bayesian Theory*. Wiley, 2nd edition, 2007. [196]

J. Bernoulli. *Ars Conjectandi, Opus Posthumum. Accedit Tractatus de Seriebus Infinitis, et Epistola Gallice Scripta de Ludo Pilae Recticularis*. Impensis Thrurnisiorum, 1713a. [140]

J. Bernoulli. *Ars Conjectandi: Usum Applicationem Praecedentis Doctrinae in Civilibus, Moralibus, Oeconomicis*. Springer, 1713b. [196]

U. Bertelè and F. Brioschi. *Nonserial Dynamic Programming*. Academic Press, 1972. [507]

F. Berzal, J. C. Cubero, F. Cuenca, and M. J. Martín-Bautista. On the quest for easy-to-understand splitting rules. *Data & Knowledge Engineering*, 44(1):31–48, 2003. [279]

J. Besag. Statistical analysis of non-lattice data. *The Statistician*, 24:179–196, 1975. [563]

J. Besag. Discussion of "Modelling spatial patterns" by B. D. Ripley. *Journal of the Royal Statistical Society, Series B*, 39:193–195, 1977. [588]

J. E. Besag. Spatial interaction and the statistical analysis of lattice systems. *Journal of the Royal Statistical Society, Series B*, 36:192–236, 1974. [569]

J. C. Bezdek. *Pattern Recognition with Fuzzy Objective Function Algorithms*. Plenum Press, 1981. [447]

B. Bidyuk and R. Dechter. Cutset sampling for Bayesian networks. *Journal of Artificial Intelligence Research*, 28:1–48, 2007. [545]

C. Bielza and P. Larrañaga. Discrete Bayesian network classifiers: A survey. *ACM Computing Surveys*, 47(1):Article 5, 2014a. [348]

C. Bielza and P. Larrañaga. Bayesian networks in neuroscience: A survey. *Frontiers in Computational Neuroscience*, 8:Article 131, 2014b. [348, 489]

C. Bielza, M. Gómez, and P. P. Shenoy. Modelling challenges with influence diagrams: Constructing probability and utility models. *Decision Support Systems*, 49:354–364, 2010. [543]

C. Bielza, M. Gómez, and P. P. Shenoy. A review of representation issues and modelling challenges with influence diagrams. *Omega – The International Journal of Management Science*, 39:227–241, 2011a. [543]

C. Bielza, G. Li, and P. Larrañaga. Multi-dimensional classification with Bayesian networks. *International Journal of Approximate Reasoning*, 52:705–727, 2011b. [428, 429, 430]

C. Bielza, V. Robles, and P. Larrañaga. Regularized logistic regression without a penalty term: An application to cancer classification with microarray data. *Expert Systems with Applications*, 38(5): 5110–5118, 2011c. [385]

C. Bielza, R. Benavides-Piccione, P. L. López-Cruz, P. Larrañaga, and J. DeFelipe. Branching angles of pyramidal cell dendrites follow common geometrical design principles in different cortical areas. *Scientific Reports*, 4:5909, 2014. [113, 127, 169, 180]

C. M. Bishop. *Neural Networks for Pattern Recognition*. Oxford University Press, 1995. [318]

C. M. Bishop. *Pattern Recognition and Machine Learning*. Springer, 2006. [77, 95]

B. B. Biswal, M. Mennes, X.-N. Zuo, S. Gohel, C. Kelly, S. M. Smith, C. F. Beckmann, J. S. Adelstein, R. L. Buckner, S. Colcombe, A.-M. Dogonowski, M. Ernst, D. Fair, M. Hampson, M. J. Hoptman, J. S. Hyde, V. J. Kiviniemi, R. Kötter, S.-J. Li, C.-P. Lin, M. J. Lowe, C. Mackay, D. J. Madden, K. H. Madsen, D. S. Margulies, H. S. Mayberg, K. McMahon, C. S. Monk, S. H. Mostofsky, B. J. Nagel, J. J. Pekar, S. J. Peltier, S. E. Petersen, V. Riedl, S. A. R. B. Rombouts, B. Rypma, B. L. Schlaggar, S. Schmidt, R. D. Seidler, G. J. Siegle, C. Sorg, G.-J. Teng, J. Veijola, A. Villringer, M. Walter, L. Wang, X.-C. Weng, S. Whitfield-Gabrieli, P. Williamson, C. Windischberger, Y.-F. Zang, H.-Y. Zhang, F. X. Castellanos, and M. P. Milham. Toward discovery science of human brain function. *Proceedings of the National Academy of Sciences*, 107(10):4734–4739, 2010. [18]

R. Blagus and L. Lusa. SMOTE for high-dimensional class-imbalanced data. *BMC Bioinformatics*, 14:106, 2013. [224]

R. Blanco, I. Inza, and P. Larrañaga. Learning Bayesian networks in the space of structures by estimation of distribution algorithms. *International Journal of Intelligent Systems*, 18:205–220, 2003. [536]

R. Blanco, I. Inza, M. Merino, J. Quiroga, and P. Larrañaga. Feature selection in Bayesian classifiers for the prognosis of survival of cirrhotic patients treated with TIPS. *Journal of Biomedical Informatics*, 38(5):376–388, 2005. [232, 233, 254, 355, 356, 357, 358, 361]

D. D. Bock, W.-C. A. Lee, A. M. Kerlin, M. L. Andermann, G. Hood, A. W. Wetzel, S. Yurgenson, E. R. Soucy, H. S. Kim, and R. C. Reid. Network anatomy and in vivo physiology of visual cortical neurons. *Nature*, 471:177–182, 2011. [48]

R. Bonner. On some clustering techniques. *IBM Journal of Research and Development*, 8:22–32, 1964. [463]

T. Boogaerts, L. Tranchevent, G. A. Pavlopoulos, J. Aerts, and J. Vandewalle. Visualizing high dimensional datasets using parallel coordinates: Application to gene prioritization. In *Proceedings of the 2012 IEEE 12th International Conference on Bioinformatics & Bioengineering*, pages 52–57, 2012. [74]

H. Borchani, C. Bielza, and P. Larrañaga. Learning CB-decomposable multi-dimensional Bayesian network classifiers. In *Proceedings of the 5th European Workshop on Probabilistic Graphical Models*, pages 25–32, 2010. [430, 431]

H. Borchani, C. Bielza, P. Martínez-Martín, and P. Larrañaga. Markov blanket-based approach for learning multi-dimensional Bayesian network classifiers: An application to predict the European Quality of Life-5 Dimensions (EQ-5D) from the 39-item Parkinson's Disease Questionnaire (PDQ-39). *Journal of Biomedical Informatics*, 45:1175–1184, 2012. [38, 431, 432, 433]

G. T. Borujeny, M. Yazdi, A. Keshavarz-Haddad, and A. R. Borujeny. Detection of epileptic seizure using wireless sensor networks. *Journal of Medical Signals and Sensors*, 3(2):3–68, 2013. [263]

B. E. Boser, I. M. Guyon, and V. N. Vapnik. A training algorithm for optimal margin classifiers. In *Proceedings of the 5th Annual Workshop on Computational Learning Theory*, pages 144–152, 1992. ACM. [319]

S. G. Bøttcher. *Learning Bayesian Networks with Mixed Variables*. PhD thesis, Aalborg University, 2004. [503]

K. E. Bouchard, J. B. Aimone, M. Chun, T. Dean, M. Denker, M. Diesmann, D. D. Donofrio, L. M. Frank, N. Kasthuri, C. Koch, O. Ruebel, H. D. Simon, F. T. Sommer, and Prabhat. High-performance computing in neuroscience for data-driven discovery, integration, and dissemination. *Neuron*, 92(3):928–931, 2016. [20]

R. R. Bouckaert. Optimizing causal orderings for generating DAGs from data. In *Proceedings of the 8th Conference on Uncertainty in Artificial Intelligence*, pages 9–16. Morgan Kaufmann, 1992. [531]

R. R. Bouckaert. Choosing between two learning algorithms based on calibrated tests. In *Proceedings of the 20th International Conference on Machine Learning*, pages 51–58. AAAI Press, 2003. [215]

R. R. Bouckaert and E. Frank. Evaluating the replicability of significance tests for comparing learning algorithms. In *Proceedings of the 8th Pacific-Asia Conference on Advances in Knowledge Discovery and Data Mining*, pages 3–12. Springer, 2004. [219]

M. R. Boutell, J. Luo, X. Shen, C. M. Brown. Learning multi-label scene classification. *Pattern Recognition*, 37(9): 1757–1771, 2004. [424]

C. Boutilier, N. Friedman, M. Goldszmidt, and D. Koller. Context-specific independence in Bayesian networks. In *Proceedings of the 12th International Conference on Uncertainty in Artificial Intelligence*, pages 115–123. Morgan Kaufmann, 1996. [543]

C. Bowles, R. Gunn, A. Hammers, and D. Rueckert. Modelling the progression of Alzheimer's disease in MRI using generative adversarial networks. In *Proceedings of the SPIE Medical Imaging*, 2018. [319]

A. L. Bowley. Presidential address to the economic section of the British association. *Journal of the Royal Statistical Society*, 69:540–558, 1906. [196]

G. E. P. Box. Non-normality and test on variance. *Biometrika*, 40:318–335, 1953. [196]

E. R. Boykin, P. P. Khargonekar, P. R. Carney, W. O. Ogle, and S. S. Talathi. Detecting effective connectivity in networks of coupled neuronal oscillators. *Journal of Computational Neuroscience*, 32(3):521–538, 2012. [283]

A. P. Bradley. The use of the area under the ROC curve in the evaluation of machine learning algorithms. *Pattern Recognition*, 30(7):1145–1159, 1997. [224]

P. S. Bradley and O. L. Mangasarian. Feature selection via concave minimization and support vector machines. In *Proceedings of the 15th International Conference on Machine Learning*, pages 82–90. Morgan Kaufmann, 1988. [261]

P. S. Bradley and O. L. Mangasarian. k-plane clustering. *Journal of Global Optimization*, 16:23–32, 2000. [454]

U. M. Braga-Neto and E. Dougherty. Bolstered error estimation. *Pattern Recognition*, 37(6):1267–1281, 2004. [225]

P. B. Brazdil and C. Soares. A comparison of ranking methods for classification algorithm selection. In *Proceedings of the 11th European Conference on Machine Learning*, pages 63–74. Springer, 2000. [225]

P. B. Brazdil, C. Giraud-Carrier, C. Soares, and R. Vilalta. *Metalearning: Applications to Data Mining*. Springer, 2009. [414]

L. Breiman. Bagging predictors. *Machine Learning*, 24(2):123–140, 1996a. [401]

L. Breiman. Technical note: Some properties of splitting criteria. *Machine Learning*, 24(1):41–47, 1996b. [277]

L. Breiman. Arcing classifiers. *The Annals of Statistics*, 26(3):801–849, 1998. [407]

L. Breiman. Random forests. *Machine Learning*, 45(1):5–32, 2001a. [403]

L. Breiman. Statistical modeling: The two cultures. *Statistical Science*, 16(3):199–231, 2001b. [25, 28]

L. Breiman, J. H. Friedman, R. A. Olshen, and C. J. Stone. *Classification and Regression Trees*. Wadsworth Press, 1984. [29, 278, 282]

D. Bremmer, E. Demaine, J. Erickson, J. Iacono, S. Langerman, P. Morin, and G. Toussaint. Output-sensitive algorithms for computing nearest-neighbor decision boundaries. *Discrete and Computational Geometry*, 33(4):593–604, 2005. [265]

E. Brenner and D. Sontag. SparsityBoost: A new scoring function for learning Bayesian network structure. In *Proceedings of the 29th Conference on Uncertainty in Artificial Intelligence*, pages 112–121. AUAI Press, 2013. [546]

G. W. Brier. Verification of forecasts expressed in terms of probability. *Monthly Weather Review*, 78: 1–3, 1950. [206]

K. L. Briggman and W. Denk. Towards neural circuit reconstruction with volume electron microscopy techniques. *Current Opinion in Neurobiology*, 16:562–570, 2006. [48]

G. Bromberg and D. Margaritis. Improving the reliability of causal discovery from small data sets using argumentation. *Journal of Machine Learning Research*, 10:301–340, 2009. [571]

G. Bromberg, D. Margaritis, and V. Honavar. Efficient Markov network structure discovery using independence tests. *Journal of Artificial Intelligence Research*, 35:449–485, 2009. [563, 571]

S. Brooks, A. Gelman, G. Jones, and X. L. Meng. *Handbook of Markov Chain Monte Carlo*. Chapman & Hall/CRC, 2011. [545]

B. M. Broom, K.-A. Do, and D. Subramanian. Model averaging strategies for structure learning in Bayesian networks with limited data. *BMC Bioinformatics*, 13:S10, 2012. [546]

G. Brown, J. L. Wyattt, R. Harris, and X. Yao. Diversity creation methods: A survey and categorisation. *Information Fusion*, 6(1):5–20, 2005. [413]

W. Buntine and T. Niblett. A further comparison of splitting rules for decision-tree induction. *Machine Learning*, 8(1):75–85, 1992. [279]

W. L. Buntine. Theory refinement on Bayesian networks. In *Proceedings of the 7th Conference on Uncertainty in Artificial Intelligence*, pages 52–60. Morgan Kaufmann, 1991. [534, 536]

J. Burge and T. Lane. Learning class-discriminative dynamic Bayesian networks. In *Proceedings of the 22nd International Conference on Machine Learning*, pages 97–104. ACM, 2005. [385]

J. Burge, T. Lane, H. Link, S. Qiu, and V. P. Clark. Discrete dynamic Bayesian network analysis of fMRI data. *Human Brain Mapping*, 30:122–137, 2009. [492]

C. J. C. Burges. A tutorial on support vector machines for pattern recognition. *Data Mining and Knowledge Discovery*, 2(2):121–167, 1998. [319]

B. Burle, L. Spieser, C. Roger, L. Casini, T. Hasbroucq, and F. Vidal. Spatial and temporal resolutions of EEG: Is it really black and white? A scalp current density view. *International Journal of Psychophysiology*, 97(3):210–220, 2015. [15]

E. J. Burr. Small-sample distributions of the two-sample Cramer-von Mises' W^2 and Watson's U^2. *The Annals of Mathematical Statistics*, 35(3):1091–1098, 1964. [180]

C. J. Butz, J. S. Oliveira, and A. L. Madsen. Bayesian network inference using marginal trees. *International Journal of Approximate Reasoning*, 68:127–152, 2016. [544]

P. Buzás, K. Kovács, A. S. Ferecskó, J. M. Budd, U. T. Eysel, and Z. F. Kisvárday. Model-based analysis of excitatory lateral connections in the visual cortex. *Journal of Comparative Neurology*, 499(6):861–881, 2006. [113]

T. Calinski and J. Harabasz. A dendrite method for cluster analysis. *Communications in Statistics*, 3 (1):1–27, 1974. [458]

D. A. Cameron, F. A. Middleton, A. Chenn, and E. C. Olson. Hierarchical clustering of gene expression patterns in the Eomes + lineage of excitatory neurons during early neocortical development. *BMC Neuroscience*, 13:90, 2012. [440]

R. J. Campello, D. Moulavi, A. Zimek, and J. Sander Hierarchical density estimates for data clustering, visualization, and outlier detection. *ACM Transactions on Knowledge Discovery from Data*, 10(1):5, 2015. [456]

C. Cannings, E. A. Thompson, and M. H. Skolnick. Probability functions in complex pedigrees. *Advances in Applied Probability*, 10:26–61, 1978. [569]

A. Cano, M. Gómez-Olmedo, and S. Moral. Approximate inference in Bayesian networks using binary probability trees. *International Journal of Approximate Reasoning*, 52(1):49–62, 2011. [543]

J. E. Cano, L. D. Hernández, and S. Moral. Importance sampling algorithms for the propagation of probabilities in belief networks. *International Journal of Approximate Reasoning*, 15(1):77–92, 1996. [544]

I. Cantuti-Castelvetri, C. Keller-McGandy, B. Bouzou, G. Asteris, T. W. Clark, D. G. Frosch, and M. P. Standaert. Effects of gender on nigral gene expression and Parkinson disease. *Neurobiology of Disease*, 26(3):606–614, 2007. [104]

H. Cao, L. Peyrodie, S. Boudet, F. Cavillon, O. Agnani, P. Hautecoeur, and C. Donzé. Expanded disability status scale (EDSS) estimation in multiple sclerosis from posturographic data. *Gait Posture*, 37(2):242–245, 2013. [136]

A. Cappa, N. Ciccarelli, E. Baldonero, M. Martelli, and M. C. Silveri. Posterior AD-type pathology: Cognitive subtypes emerging from a cluster analysis. *Behavioural Neurology*, 2014:Article ID 259358, 2014. [440]

A. M. Carvalho, A. L. Oliveira, and M.-F. Sagot. Efficient learning of Bayesian network classifiers. In *Proceedings of the 20th Australian Joint Conference on Artificial Intelligence*, pages 16–25. Springer, 2007. [362]

A. M. Carvalho, T. Roos, A. L. Oliveira, and P. Myllymäki. Discriminative learning of Bayesian networks via factorized conditional log-likelihood. *Journal of Machine Learning Research*, 12: 2181–2210, 2011. [385]

G. Casella. An introduction to empirical Bayes data analysis. *The American Statistician*, 39(2):83–87, 1985. [197]

G. Casella, C. P. Robert, and M. T. Wells. Generalized accept-reject sampling schemes. In *A Festschrift for Herman Rubin*, volume 45, pages 342–347. Institute of Mathematical Statistics, 2004. [131]

R. Castelo and A. Roverato. A robust procedure for Gaussian graphical model search from microarray data with p larger than n. *Journal of Machine Learning Research*, 7:2621–2650, 2006. [570]

E. Castillo, J. Gutierrez, and A. Hadi. *Expert Systems and Probabilistic Network Models*. Springer, 1997. [493, 497, 543]

G. Castillo and J. Gama. Adaptive Bayesian network classifiers. *Intelligent Data Analysis*, 13(1): 39–59, 2009. [386]

J. Catlett. On changing continuous attributes into ordered discrete attributes. In *Proceedings of the European Working Session on Learning*, pages 164–178, 1991. [91]

R. B. Cattell. A note on correlation clusters and cluster search method. *Psychometrika*, 9:169–184, 1944. [467]

B. Cauli, J. T. Porter, K. Tsuzuki, B. Lambolez, J. Rossier, B. Quenet, and E. Audinat. Classification of fusiform neocortical interneurons based on unsupervised clustering. *Proceedings of the National Academy of Sciences*, 97(11):6144–6149, 2000. [34]

G. Celeux and J. Diebolt. The SEM algorithm: A probabilistic teacher derived from the EM algorithm for the mixture problem. *Computational Statistics Quarterly*, 2:73–82, 1985. [474]

G. Celeux and G. Govaert. A classification EM algorithm for clustering and two stochastic versions. *Computational Statistics & Data Analysis*, 14:315–332, 1992. [473]

G. Celeux and G. Govaert. Gaussian parsimonious clustering models. *Pattern Recognition*, 28:781–793, 1995. [482]

S.-H. Cha. Comprehensive survey on distance-similarity measures between probability density functions. *International Journal of Mathematical Models and Methods in Applied Sciences*, 14 (1):300–307, 2007. [236]

H. L. Chan, J. H. Chu, H. C. Fung, Y. T. Tsai, L. F. Meng, C. C. Huang, W. C. Hsu, P. K. Chao, J. J. Wang, J. D. Lee, Y. Y. Wai, and M. T. Tsai. Brain connectivity of patients with Alzheimer's disease by coherence and cross mutual information of electroencephalograms during photic stimulation. *Medical Engineering and Physics*, 35(2):241–252, 2013. [139]

V. Chandola, A. Banerjee, and V. Kumar. Anomaly detection: A survey. *ACM Computing Surveys*, 41(3):Article 15, 2009. [224]

G. Chandrashekar and F. Sahin. A survey on feature selection methods. *Computers and Electrical Engineering*, 40(1):16–28, 2013. [259]

J. Chang, H. Leung, and H. Poiner. Correlation among joint motions allows classification of Parkinsonian versus normal 3D reaching. *IEEE Transactions on Neural Systems and Rehabilitation*, 18 (2):142–149, 2010. [263]

R. Chaves, J. Ramírez, J. M. Górriz, M. López, D. Salas-González, I. Álvarez, and F. Segovia. Interpreting single trial data using groupwise regularisation. *NeuroImage*, 46:293–297, 2009. [234]

N. V. Chawla. *Data Mining and Knowledge Discovery Handbook*, chapter Data Mining for Imbalanced Datasets: An Overview, pages 875–886. Springer, 2009. [223]

N. V. Chawla, K. W. Bowyer, L. O. Hall, and W. P. Kegelmeyer. SMOTE: Synthetic minority oversampling technique. *Journal of Artificial Intelligence Research*, 16(1):321–357, 2002. [223]

P. Cheeseman, M. Self, J. Kelly, W., Taylor D. Freeman, and J. Stutz. Bayesian classification. In *Proceedings of the 6th National Conference on Artificial Intelligence*, pages 607–611. AAAI Press, 1988. [481]

J. Y. Chen. A simulation study investigating the impact of dendritic morphology and synaptic topology on neuronal firing patterns. *Neural Computation*, 22(4):1086–1111, 2009. [43]

T. Chen, N. L. Zhang, T. Liu, K. M. Poon, and Y. Wang. Model-based multidimensional clustering of categorical data. *Artificial Intelligence*, 176(1):2246–2269, 2012. [486]

J. Cheng and R. Greiner. Comparing Bayesian network classifiers. In *Proceedings of the 15th Conference on Uncertainty in Artificial Intelligence*, pages 101–108. Morgan Kaufmann Publishers, 1999. [362, 366]

J. Cheng and R. Greiner. Learning Bayesian belief networks classifiers: Algorithms and system. In *Proceedings of the 14th Biennial Conference of the Canadian Society for Computational Studies of Intelligence*, pages 141–151. Springer, 2001. [366]

M. R. Chernick. *Bootstrap Methods: A Guide for Practitioners and Researchers*. Wiley, 2007. [225]

H. Chernoff. The use of faces to represent points in k-dimensional space graphically. *Journal of the American Statistical Association*, 68(342):361–368, 1973. [73]

M. T. Chiang and B. Mirkin. Intelligent choice of the number of clusters in k-means clustering: An experimental study with different cluster spreads. *Journal of Classification*, 27(1):3–40, 2010. [458]

D. M. Chickering. A transformational characterization of equivalent Bayesian network structures. In *Proceedings of the 11th Conference on Uncertainty in Artificial Intelligence*, pages 87–98. Morgan Kaufmann, 1995. [498]

D. M. Chickering. Learning Bayesian networks is NP-complete. In *Learning from Data: Artificial Intelligence and Statistics V*, pages 121–130. Springer, 1996. [530]

D. M. Chickering. Learning equivalence classes of Bayesian-network structures. *Journal of Machine Learning Research*, 2:445–498, 2002a. [531]

D. M. Chickering. Optimal structure identification with greedy search. *Journal of Machine Learning Research*, 3:507–554, 2002b. [531]

D. M. Chickering and C. Meek. Selective greedy equivalence search: Finding optimal Bayesian networks using a polynomial number of score evaluations. In *Proceedings of the 31st Conference on Uncertainty in Artificial Intelligence*, pages 211–219. AUAI Press, 2015. [531]

D. M. Chickering, D. Heckerman, and C. Meek. A Bayesian approach to learning Bayesian networks with local structure. In *Proceedings of the 13th Conference on Uncertainty in Artificial Intelligence*, pages 80–89. Morgan Kaufmann, 1997. [543]

D. M. Chickering, D. Heckerman, and C. Meek. Large-sample learning of Bayesian networks is NP-hard. *Journal of Machine Learning Research*, 5:1287–1330, 2004. [364, 530]

C. K. Chow and C. N. Liu. Approximating discrete probability distributions with dependence trees. *IEEE Transactions on Information Theory*, 14(3):462–467, 1968. [357, 365, 366, 429, 561]

Y. J. Chu and T. H. Liu. On the shortest arborescence of a directed graph. *Scientia Sinica*, 14:1396–1400, 1965. [429]

C. Chubb, Y. Inagaki, P. Sheu, B. Cummings, A. Wasserman, E. Head, and C. Cotman. BioVision: An application for the automated image analysis of histological sections. *Neurobiology of Aging*, 27(10):1462–1476, 2006. [374]

A. Clare and R. D. King. Knowledge discovery in multi-label phenotype data. In *Proceedings of the 5th European Conference on Principles of Data Mining and Knowledge Discovery*, pages 42–53. Springer, 2001. [427]

P. Clark and T. Niblett. The CN2 induction algorithm. *Machine Learning*, 3:261–283, 1989. [287]

L. Clemmensen, T. Hastie, D. Witten, and B. Ersbøll. Sparse discriminant analysis. *Technometrics*, 53(4):406–413, 2011. [331]

B. R. Cobb and P. P. Shenoy. Inference in hybrid Bayesian networks with mixtures of truncated exponentials. *International Journal of Approximate Reasoning*, 41(3):257–286, 2006. [515]

B. R. Cobb, P. P. Shenoy, and R. Rumí. Approximating probability density functions in hybrid Bayesian networks with mixtures of truncated exponentials. *Statistics and Computing*, 16(3):293–308, 2006. [515]

W. G. Cochran. *Sampling Techniques*. Wiley, 1963. [195]

D. Codecasa and F. Stella. Learning continuous time Bayesian network classifiers. *International Journal of Approximate Reasoning*, 55(8):1728–1746, 2014. [386]

D. Codecasa and F. Stella. Classification and clustering with continuous time Bayesian network models. *Journal of Intelligent Information Systems*, 45(2):187–220, 2015. [486]

I. Cohen, F. G. Cozman, N. Sebe, M. C. Cirelo, and T. S. Huang. Semisupervised learning of classifiers: Theory, algorithms, and their application to human-computer interaction. *IEEE Transactions on Pattern Analysis and Machine Intelligence*, 26(12):1553–1567, 2004. [386]

J. Cohen. A coefficient of agreement for nominal scales. *Educational and Psychological Measurements*, 20:37–46, 1960. [205]

W. W. Cohen. Fast effective rule induction. In *Proceedings of the 12th International Conference on Machine Learning*, pages 115–123. Morgan Kaufmann, 1995. [288]

N. Coley, V. Gardette, C. Cantet, S. Gillette-Guyonnet, F. Nourhashemi, B. Vellas, and S. Andrieu. How should we deal with missing data in clinical trials involving Alzheimer's disease patients? *Current Alzheimer Research*, 8(4):421–433, 2011. [88]

M. Collins, R. E. Schapire, and Y. Singer. Logistic regression, AdaBoost and Bregman distances. *Machine Learning*, 48(1-3):253–285, 2002. [406]

D. Colombo and M. H. Maathuis. Order-independent constraint-based causal structure learning. *Journal of Machine Learning Research*, 15:3921–3962, 2014. [529]

D. Colombo, M. H. Maathuis, M. Kalisch, and T. S. Richardson. Learning high-dimensional directed acyclic graphs with latent and selection variables. *The Annals of Statistics*, 40(1):294–321, 2012. [529]

M. Colombo and P. Seriès. Bayes in the brain. On Bayesian modelling in neuroscience. *The British Journal for the Philosophy of Science*, 63:697–723, 2012. [159]

M. M. Conijn, M. I. Geerlings, G. J. Biessels, T. Takahara, T. D. Witkamp, J. J. Zwanenburg, P. R. Luijten, and J. Hendrikse. Cerebral microbleeds on MR imaging: Comparison between 1.5 and 7T. *American Journal of Neuroradiology*, 32(6):1043–1049, 2011. [176]

A. D. Coop, H. Cornelis, and F. Santamaria. Dendritic excitability modulates dendritic information processing in a Purkinje cell model. *Frontiers in Computational Neuroscience*, 4:Article 6, 2010. [139]

G. F. Cooper. The computational complexity of probabilistic inference using Bayesian belief networks. *Artificial Intelligence*, 42(2-3):393–405, 1990. [505]

G. F. Cooper and E. Herskovits. A Bayesian method for the induction of probabilistic networks from data. *Machine Learning*, 9:309–347, 1992. [362, 533, 534, 536]

I. Córdoba, C. Bielza, and P. Larrañaga. A review of Gaussian Markov models for conditional independence, *Journal of Statistical Planning and Inference*, 206:127–144, 2020.

C. Cortes and V. Vapnik. Support-vector networks. *Machine Learning*, 20(3):273–297, 1995. [306]

M. Cosottini, M. Giannelli, G. Siciliano, G. Lazzarotti, M. C. Michelassi, A. del Corona, C. Bartolozzi, and L. Murri. Diffusion-tensor MR imaging of corticospinal tract in amyotrophic lateral sclerosis and progressive muscular atrophy. *Radiology*, 237(1):258–264, 2005. [179]

M. A. Costa and A. P. Braga. Optimization of neural networks with multi-objective LASSO algorithm. In *International Joint Conference on Neural Networks*, pages 3312–3318. Morgan Kaufmann, 2006. [261]

D. Cotter, D. Mackay, G. Chana, C. Beasley, S. Landau, and I. P. Everall. Reduced neuronal size and glial cell density in area 9 of the dorsolateral prefrontal cortex in subjects with major depressive disorder. *Cerebral Cortex*, 12(4):386–394, 2002. [592]

T. M. Cover. Geometrical and statistical properties of systems of linear inequalities with applications in pattern recognition. *IEEE Transactions on Electronic Computers*, EC-14(3):326–334, 1965. [308]

T. M. Covert and P. E. Hart. Nearest neighbor pattern classification. *IEEE Transactions on Information Theory*, 13:21–27, 1967. [265, 268]

T. M. Cover and J. A. Thomas. *Elements of Information Theory*. Wiley, 1991. [137]

R. G. Cowell. Local propagation in conditional Gaussian Bayesian networks. *Journal of Machine Learning Research*, 6:1517–1550, 2005. [515]

R. G. Cowell, A. P. Dawid, S. L. Lauritzen, and D. J. Spiegelhalter. *Probabilistic Networks and Expert Systems*. Springer, 1999. [543]

D. R. Cox. Some statistical methods connected with series of events. *Journal of the Royal Statistical Society, Series B*, 17(2):129–164, 1955. [605]

T. F. Cox and M. A. A. Cox. *Multidimensional Scaling*. Chapman and Hall, 2nd edition, 2000. [95]

R. C. Craddock, G. A. James, P. E. Holtzheimer, X. P. Hu, and H. S. Mayberg. A whole brain fMRI atlas generated via spatially constrained spectral clustering. *Human Brain Mapping*, 33(8):1914–1918, 2012. [452]

A. Creswell, T. White, V. Dumoulin, K. Arulkumaran, B. Sengupta, and A. A. Bharath. Generative adversarial networks: An overview. *IEEE Signal Processing Magazine*, 35:53–65, 2018. [319]

N. Cristianini and J. Shawe-Taylor. *An Introduction to Support Vector Machines and Other Kernel-Based Learning Methods*. Cambridge University Press, 2000. [319]

P. Cunningham. A taxonomy of similarity mechanisms for case-based reasoning. *IEEE Transactions on Knowledge and Data Engineering*, 21(11):1532–1543, 2009. [317]

G. Cybenko. Approximation by superpositions of a sigmoidal function. *Mathematics of Control, Signals and Systems*, 2(4):303–314, 1989. [293]

P. Dagum and M. Luby. Approximating probabilistic inference in Bayesian belief networks is NP-hard. *Artificial Intelligence*, 60(1):141–153, 1993. [515]

R. Daly, Q. Shen, and J. S. Aitken. Learning Bayesian networks: Approaches and issues. *The Knowledge Engineering Review*, 26(2):99–157, 2011. [489]

J. N. Darroch, S. L. Lauritzen, and T. P. Speed. Markov fields and log-linear interaction for contingency tables. *The Annals of Statistics*, 8:522–539, 1980. [569]

A. Darwiche. A differential approach to inference in Bayesian networks. *Journal of the ACM*, 50(3): 280–305, 2003. [544]

A. Darwiche. *Modeling and Reasoning with Bayesian Networks*. Cambridge University Press, 2009. [543, 569]

C. Darwin. *On the Origin of Species by Means of Natural Selection*. John Murray, 1859. [247]

B. V. Dasarathy. *Nearest Neighbor (NN) Norms: NN Pattern Classification Techniques*. IEEE Computer Society Press, 1991. [317]

D. Dash and G. F. Cooper. Model averaging for prediction with discrete Bayesian networks. *Journal of Machine Learning Research*, 5:1177–1203, 2004. [481, 546]

M. Dash and H. Liu. Feature selection for classification. *Intelligent Data Analysis*, 1(3):131–156, 1997. [259]

R. N. Dave. Fuzzy shell-clustering and applications to circle detection in digital images. *International Journal of General Systems*, 16:343–355, 1990. [454]

R. N. Dave. Generalized fuzzy c-shells clustering and detection of circular and elliptical boundaries. *Pattern Recognition*, 25:713–721, 1992. [454]

J. Davis and M. Goadrich. The relationship between precision-recall and ROC curves. In *Proceedings of the 23rd International Workshop on Machine Learning*, pages 233–240. ACM Press, 2006. [224]

N. E. Day. Estimating the components of a mixture of normal distributions. *Biometrika*, 56(3):463–474, 1969. [373, 384, 475]

W. H. E. Day. Foreword: Comparison and consensus of classifications. *Journal of Classification*, 3: 183–185, 1986. [460]

R. de Boer, H. A. Vrooman, F. van der Lijn, M. W. Vernooij, M. A. Ikram, A. van der Lugt, M.M. Breteler, and W. J. Niessen. White matter lesion extension to automatic brain tissue segmentation on MRI. *NeuroImage*, 45(4):1151–1161, 2009. [263]

C. P. de Campos and Q. Ji. Efficient structure learning of Bayesian networks using constraints. *Journal of Machine Learning Research*, 12:663–689, 2011. [536]

L. M. de Campos. A scoring function for learning Bayesian networks based on mutual information and conditional independence tests. *Journal of Machine Learning Research*, 7:2149–2187, 2006. [546]

M. de Jongh. *Algorithms for Constraint-Based Learning of Bayesian Network Structures with Large Numbers of Variables*. PhD thesis, University of Pittsburgh, 2014. [545]

A. de Moivre. Approximatio ad summam terminorum binomii $(a+b)^n$, in seriem expansi. *Supplementum II to Miscellanae Analytica*, pages 1–7, 1733. [140, 196]

R. Lorente de Nó. La corteza cerebral del ratón. *Trabajos Laboratorio Investigaciones Biológicas*, 20:41–78, 1922. [31]

M. de Tommaso, F. De Carlo, O. Difruscolo, R. Massafra, V. Sciruicchio, and R. Bellotti. Detection of subclinical brain electrical activity changes in Huntington's disease using artificial neural networks. *Clinical Neurophysiology*, 114(7):1237–1245, 2003. [293]

T. Dean and K. Kanazawa. A model for reasoning about persistence and causation. *Computational Intelligence*, 5(3):142–150, 1989. [537]

R. Dechter and I. Rish. Mini-buckets: A general scheme for bounded inference. *Journal of the ACM*, 50(2):107–153, 2003. [544]

J. DeFelipe. The evolution of the brain, the human nature of cortical circuits, and intellectual creativity. *Frontiers in Neuroanatomy*, 5:Article 29, 2011. [7, 8, 97, 98, 99]

J. DeFelipe, G. N. Elston, I. Fujita, J. Fuster, K. H. Harrison, P. R. Hof, Y. Kawaguchi, K. A. C. Martin, K. S. Rockland, A. M. Thomson, S. S. H. Wang, E. L. White, and R. Yuste. Neocortical circuits: Evolutionary aspects and specificity versus non-specificity of synaptic connections. Remarks, main conclusions and general comments and discussion. *Journal of Neurocytology*, 31: 387–416, 2002. [48]

J. DeFelipe, P. L. López-Cruz, R. Benavides-Piccione, C. Bielza, P. Larrañaga, S. Anderson, A. Burkhalter, B. Cauli, A. Fairén, D. Feldmeyer, G. Fishell, D. Fitzpatrick, T. F. Freund, G. González-Burgos, S. Hestrin, S. Hill, P. R. Hof, J. Huang, E. G. Jones, Y. Kawaguchi, Z. Kisvárday, Y. Kubota, D. A. Lewis, O. Marín, H. Markram, C. J. McBain, H. S. Meyer, H. Monyer, S. B. Nelson, K. Rockland, J. Rossier, J. L. R. Rubenstein, B. Rudy, M. Scanziani, G. M. Shepherd, C. C. Sherwood, J. F. Staiger, G. Tamás, A. Thomson, Y. Wang, R. Yuste, and G. A. Ascoli. New insights into the classification and nomenclature of cortical GABAergic interneurons. *Nature Reviews Neuroscience*, 14(3):202–216, 2013. [34, 75, 214, 222, 238, 290, 293, 372]

S. DellaPrieta, V. DellaPrieta, and J. D. Lafferty. Inducing features of random fields. *IEEE Transactions on Pattern Analysis and Machine Intelligence*, 19(4):380–393, 1997. [564]

A. P. Dempster. Covariance selection. *Biometrics*, 28:157–175, 1972. [570]

A. P. Dempster, N. M. Laird, and D. B. Rubin. Maximum likelihood from incomplete data via the EM algorithm. *Journal of the Royal Statistical Society, Series B*, 39(1):1–38, 1977. [373, 470, 471, 472, 473, 485, 522]

J. Demšar. Statistical comparisons of classifiers over multiple data sets. *Journal of Machine Learning Research*, 7:1–30, 2006. [223, 225, 412]

X. Descombes, F. Kruggel, and D. Y. Cramon. Spatio-temporal fMRI analysis using Markov random fields. *IEEE Transactions on Medical Imaging*, 17(6):1028–1039, 1998. [547]

I. Despotović, I. Segers, L. Platiša, E. Vansteenkiste, A. Pizurica, K. Deblaere, and W. Philips. Automatic 3D graph cuts for brain cortex segmentation in patients with focal cortical dysplasia. In *International Conference of the IEEE Engineering in Medicine and Biology Society*, pages 7981–7984, 2011. [549]

P. A. Devijver and J. Kittler. *Pattern Recognition. A Statistical Approach*. Prentice Hall, 1982. [265, 269]

T. G. Dietterich. Approximate statistical tests for comparing supervised classification learning algorithms. *Neural Computation*, 10:1895–1924, 1998. [215, 225]

T. G. Dietterich. Ensemble methods in machine learning. In *Proceedings of the 1st International Workshop on Multiple Classifier Systems*, pages 1–15. Springer, 2000. [389]

F. J. Díez. Local conditioning in Bayesian networks. *Artificial Intelligence*, 87(1-2):1–20, 1996. [544]

P. J. Diggle. Displaced amacrine cells in the retina of a rabbit: Analysis of a bivariate spatial point pattern. *Journal of Neuroscience Methods*, 18(1–2):115–125, 1986. [577, 578]

P. J. Diggle. *Statistical Analysis of Spatial Point Patterns*. Hodder Arnold, 2nd edition, 2003. [611]

P. J. Diggle, N. Lange, and F. M. Benes. Analysis of variance for replicated spatial point patterns in clinical neuroanatomy. *Journal of the American Statistical Association*, 86(415):618–625, 1991. [592]

J. Doak. An evaluation of feature selection methods and their application to computer security. Technical Report, University of California at Davis, 1992. [241, 244]

M. d'Ocagne. *Coordonnées Parallèles et Axiales: Méthode de Transformation Géométrique et Procédé Nouveau de Calcul Graphique Déduits de la Considération des Coordonnées Parallèles.* Gauthier-Villars, 1885. [74]

P. Domingos. *The Master Algorithm: How to Quest for the Ultimate Learning Machine Will Remake Our World.* Basic Books, 2015. [24]

P. Domingos and M. Pazzani. On the optimality of the simple Bayesian classifier under zero-one loss. *Machine Learning*, 29:103–130, 1997. [351]

W. E. Donath and A. J. Hoffman. Lower bounds for the partitioning of graphs. *IBM Journal of Research and Development*, 17:420–425, 1973. [450, 467]

A. R. Donders, G. J. van der Heijden, T. Stijnen, and K. G. Moons. Review: A gentle introduction to imputation of missing values. *Journal of Clinical Epidemiology*, 59:1087–1091, 2006. [95]

D. E. Donohue and G. A. Ascoli. A comparative computer simulation of dendritic morphology. *PLoS Computational Biology*, 4(6):e1000089, 2008. [540]

M. Dorigo, V. Maniezzo, and A. Colorni. Ant colony: Optimization by a colony of cooperating agents. *IEEE Transactions on Systems, Man, and Cybernetics, Part B*, 1(1):53–66, 1996. [246]

J. Dougherty, R. Kohavi, and M. Sahami. Supervised and unsupervised discretization of continuous features. In *Proceedings of the 12th International Conference on Machine Learning*, pages 194–202. Morgan Kaufmann, 1995. [374]

K. Doya, S. Ishii, A. Pouget, and R. P. N. Rao. *Bayesian Brain*. The MIT Press, 2007. [159]

H. Drucker, C. J. C. Burges, L. Kaufman, A. J. Smola, and V. Vapnik. Support vector regression machines. In *Advances in Neural Information Processing Systems 9*, pages 155–161. The MIT Press, 1997. [319]

S. Druckmann, S. Hill, F. Schürmann, H. Markram, and I. Segev. A hierarchical structure of cortical interneuron electrical diversity revealed by automatic statistical analysis. *Cerebral Cortex*, 23(12): 2994–3006, 2013. [215]

M. M. Drugan and M. A. Wiering. Feature selection for Bayesian network classifiers using the MDL-FS score. *International Journal of Approximate Reasoning*, 51:695–717, 2010. [385]

P. Dua, S. Bais, and W. J. Lukiw. Analysis of network based co-expression modules for Alzheimer's disease. *Studies in Health Technology and Informatics*, 192:1227, 2013. [139]

R. Dubey, J. Zhou, Y. Wang, P. M. Thompson, and J. Ye. Analysis of sampling techniques for imbalanced data: An n=648 ADNI study. *NeuroImage*, 87:220–241, 2014. [223]

R. Duda and P. Hart. *Pattern Classification and Scene Analysis*. Wiley, 1973. [457]

R. Duda, P. Hart, and D. G. Stork. *Pattern Classification*. Wiley, 2nd edition, 2001. [167, 326, 351]

S. Dudoit, J. Fridlyand, and T. Speed. Comparison of discriminant methods for the classification of tumors using gene expression data. *Journal of the American Statistical Association*, 97(457): 77–87, 2002. [232, 235]

M. A. Dufour, A. Woodhouse, J. Amendola, and J. M. Coaillard. Non-linear developmental trajectory of electrical phenotype in rat substantia nigra pars compacta dopaminergic neurons. *eLife*, 3: e04059, 2014. [440]

D. Dumitriu, R. Cossart, J. Huang, and R. Yuste. Correlation between axonal morphologies and synaptic input kinetics of interneurons from mouse visual cortex. *Cerebral Cortex*, 17(1):81–91, 2007. [82]

A. Dunaevsky, A. Tashiro, A. Majewska, C. Mason, and R. Yuste. Developmental regulation of spine motility in the mammalian central nervous system. *Proceedings of the National Academy of Sciences*, 96(23):13438–13443, 1999. [41]

J. C. Dunn. A fuzzy relative of the ISODATA process and its use in detecting compact well-separated clusters. *Journal of Cybernetics*, 3(3):32–57, 1973. [447]

O. J. Dunn. Multiple comparisons among means. *Journal of the American Statistical Association*, 56 (293):52–64, 1961. [193]

K. Dunne, P. Cunningham, and F. Azuaje. Solutions to instability problems with sequential wrapper-based approaches to feature selection. Technical Report, Trinity College, 2002. [255]

A. Edwards. Note on the "correction for continuity" in testing the significance of the difference between correlated proportions. *Psychometrika*, 13:185–187, 1948. [220]

A. W. F. Edwards and L. L. Cavalli-Sforza. A method for cluster analysis. *Biometrics*, 21:363–375, 1965. [442]

B. Efron. Bootstrap methods: Another look at the jackknife. *The Annals of Statistics*, 7:1–26, 1979. [215]

B. Efron. Estimating the error rate of a prediction rule: Improvements on cross-validation. *Journal of the American Statistical Association*, 78:316–331, 1983. [225]

M. Ekdahl and T. Koski. Bounds for the loss in probability of correct classification under model based approximation. *Journal of Machine Learning Research*, 7:2449–2480, 2006. [351]

A. Eklund, T. E. Nichols, and H. Knutsson. Cluster failure: Why fMRI inferences for spatial extent have inflated false-positive rates. *Proceedings of the National Academy of Sciences*, 113:7900–7905, 2016. [20]

I. Eliasova, L. Anderkova, R. Marecek, and I. Rektorova. Non-invasive brain stimulation of the right inferior frontal gyrus may improve attention in early Alzheimer's disease: A pilot study. *Journal of Neurological Sciences*, 346(1–2):318–322, 2014. [177]

G. Elidan. Copula Bayesian networks. In *Advances in Neural Information Processing Systems 23*, pages 559–567. Curran Associates, Inc., 2011. [502]

A. Elisseeff and J. Weston. A kernel method for multi-labelled classification. In *Advances in Neural Information Processing Systems 14*, pages 681–687, 2002. [427]

C. Elkan. The foundations of cost-sensitive learning. In *Proceedings of the 17th International Joint Conference on Artificial Intelligence*, pages 973–978, 2001. [224]

B. Ellis and W. H. Wong. Learning causal Bayesian network structures from experimental data. *Journal of the American Statistical Association*, 103(482):778–789, 2008. [497]

G. N. Elston and M. G. Rosa. The occipitoparietal pathway of the macaque monkey: Comparison of pyramidal cell morphology in layer III of functionally related cortical visual areas. *Cerebral Cortex*, 7(5):432–452, 1997. [44]

S. Engelborghs, K. de Vreese, T. van de Casteele, H. Vanderstichele, B. van Everbroeck, P. Cras, J.-J. Martin, E. Vanmechelen, and P. P. de Deyn. Diagnostic performance of a CSF-biomarker panel in autopsy-confirmed dementia. *Neurobiology of Aging*, 29(8):1143–1159, 2008. [283]

S. H. Eriksson, S. L. Free, M. Thom, L. Martinian, M. R. Symms, T. M. Salmenpera, A. W. McEvoy, W. Harkness, J. S. Duncan, and S. M. Sisodiya. Correlation of quantitative MRI and neuropathology in epilepsy surgical resection specimens–T2 correlates with neuronal tissue in gray matter. *NeuroImage*, 37(1):48–55, 2007. [190]

F. Esposito, D. Malerba, and G. Semeraro. A comparative analysis of methods for pruning decision trees. *IEEE Transactions on Pattern Analysis and Machine Intelligence*, 19(5):476–491, 1997. [280]

M. Ester, H.-P. Kriegel, J. Sander, and X. Xu. A density-based algorithm for discovering clusters in large spatial databases with noise. In *Proceedings of the 2nd ACM International Conference on Knowledge Discovery and Data Mining*, pages 226–231. AAAI Press, 1996. [455]

J. W. Evans. Random and cooperative sequential adsorption. *Reviews of Modern Physics*, 65:1281–1329, 1993. [607]

B. Everitt, S. Landau, and M. Leese. *Cluster Analysis*. Arnold, 2001. [442]

K. J. Ezawa and S. W. Norton. Constructing Bayesian networks to predict uncollectible telecommunications accounts. *IEEE Expert*, 11(5):45–51, 1996. [362, 367]

J. Fan and J. Lv. A selective overview of variable selection in high dimensional feature space. *Statistica Sinica*, 220(1):101–148, 2010. [261]

A. Farzan, S. Mashohor, A. R. Ramli, and R. Mahmud. Boosting diagnosis accuracy of Alzheimer's disease using high dimensional recognition of longitudinal brain atrophy patterns. *Behavior Brain Research*, 290:124–130, 2015. [448]

T. Fawcett. An introduction to ROC analysis. *Pattern Recognition Letters*, 27(8):861–874, 2006. [209]

U. M. Fayyad and K. B. Irani. The attribute selection problem in decision tree generation. In *Proceedings of the 10th National Conference on Artificial Intelligence*, pages 104–110. AAAI Press, 1992. [278, 279]

U. M. Fayyad and K. B. Irani. Multi-interval discretization of continuous-valued attributes for classification learning. In *Proceedings of the 13th International Joint Conference on Artificial Intelligence*, pages 1022–1029, 1993. [92, 284]

A. J. Feelders and J. Ivanovs. Discriminative scoring of Bayesian network classifiers: A comparative study. In *Proceedings of the 3rd European Workshop on Probabilistic Graphical Models*, pages 75–82, 2006. [385]

T. A. Feo and M. G. C. Resende. Greedy randomized adaptive search procedures. *Journal of Global Optimization*, 6:109–133, 1995. [244]

A. R. Ferguson, J. L. Nielson, M. H. Cragin, A. E. Bandrowski, and M. E. Martone. Big data from small data: Data sharing in the "long tail" of neuroscience. *Nature Neuroscience*, 17(11):1442–1448, 2014. [20]

A. Fernández, J. A. Gámez, R. Rumí, and A. Salmerón. Data clustering using hidden variables in hybrid Bayesian networks. *Progress in Artificial Intelligence*, 2:141–152, 2014. [486]

A. Fernández, S. García, J. Luengo, E. Bernadó-Mansilla, and F. Herrera. Genetics-based machine learning for rule induction: State of the art, taxonomy, and comparative study. *IEEE Transactions on Evolutionary Computation*, 14(6):913–941, 2010. [318]

A. Fernández, R. Rumí, and A. Salmerón. Answering queries in hybrid Bayesian networks using importance sampling. *Decision Support Systems*, 53(3):580–590, 2012. [544]

P. Fernández-González, C. Bielza, and P. Larrañaga. Multidimensional classifiers for neuroanatomical data. In *ICML Workshop on Statistics, Machine Learning and Neuroscience*, volume 2837, 2015. [416]

P. Fernández-González, R. Benavides-Piccione, I. Leguey, C. Bielza, P. Larrañaga, and J. DeFelipe. Dendritic branching angles of pyramidal neurons of the human cerebral cortex. *Brain Structure and Function*, 222(4):1847–1859, 2017. [127, 181]

C. Ferri, P. A. Flach, and J. Hernández-Orallo. Learning decision trees using the area under the ROC curve. In *Proceedings of the 19th International Conference on Machine Learning*, pages 139–146. Morgan Kaufmann, 2002. [279]

C. Ferri, J. Hernández-Orallo, and M. A. Salido. Volume under the ROC surface for multi-class problems. In *Proceedings of the 14th European Conference on Machine Learning*, volume 2837, pages 108–120. Springer, 2003. [211]

C. Ferri, J. Hernández-Orallo, and R. Modroiu. An experimental comparison of performance measures for classification. *Pattern Recognition Letters*, 30(1):27–38, 2008. [224]

P. Feys, M. B. D'hooghe, G. Nagels, and W. F. Helsen. The effect of levetiracetam on tremor severity and functionality in patients with multiple sclerosis. *Multiple Sclerosis*, 15(3):371–378, 2009. [183]

M. Fiedler. Algebraic connectivity of graphs. *Czechoslovak Mathematical Journal*, 23(98):298–305, 1973. [467]

S. E. Fienberg. When did Bayesian inference become "Bayesian"? *Bayesian Analysis*, 1(1):1–40, 2006. [196]

M. A. Figueiredo and A. K. Jain. Unsupervised learning of finite mixture models. *IEEE Transactions on Pattern Analysis and Machine Intelligence*, 24(3):381–396, 2002. [473]

H. Firpi, E. Goodman, and L. Echauz. On prediction of epileptic seizures by means of genetic programming artificial features. *Annals of Biomedical Engineering*, 34(3):515–529, 2006. [263]

D. H. Fisher. Knowledge acquisition via incremental clustering. *Machine Learning*, 2(2):139–172, 1987. [468]

D. H. Fisher. Iterative optimization and simplification of hierarchical clusterings. *Journal of Artificial Intelligence Research*, 4:147–179, 1996. [467]

N. I. Fisher. *Statistical Analysis of Circular Data*. Cambridge University Press, 1993. [65]

R. A. Fisher. The use of multiple measurements in taxonomic problems. *Annals of Eugenics*, 7: 179–188, 1936. [384]

R. A. Fisher. *Statistical Methods for Research Workers*. Oliver and Boyd, 1925. [162, 197, 559]

R. A. Fisher. *The Design of Experiments*. Oliver and Boyd, 1935. [197]

R. A. Fisher. Dispersion on a sphere. *Proceedings of the Royal Society of London, Series A, Mathematical and Physical Sciences*, 217:295–305, 1953. [124]

E. Fix and J. L. Hodges. Discriminatory analysis–Nonparametric discrimination: Consistency properties. Technical Report 4, USAF School of Aviation Medicine, 1951. [29, 262]

E. Fix and J. L. Hodges. Discriminatory analysis–Nonparametric discrimination: Small sample performance. Technical Report 11, USAF School of Aviation Medicine, 1952. [262]

R. Fletcher. *Practical Methods of Optimization*. Wiley, 2nd edition, 2000. [305]

F. Fleuret. Fast binary feature selection with conditional mutual information. *Journal of Machine Learning Research*, 5:1531–1555, 2004. [236, 238]

K. Florek, J. Lukaszewicz, H. Perkal, H. Steinhaus, and S. Zubrzycki. Sur la liason et la division des points d'un ensemble fini. *Colloquium Mathematicum*, 2:282–285, 1951. [440, 441, 467]

M. J. Flores and J. A. Gámez. Triangulation of Bayesian networks by retriangulation. *International Journal of Intelligent Systems*, 18(2):153–164, 2003. [511]

M. J. Flores and J. A. Gámez. A review on distinct methods and approaches to perform triangulation for Bayesian networks. In *Advances in Probabilistic Graphical Models*, pages 127–152. Springer, 2007. [511]

M. J. Flores, J. A. Gámez, A. M. Martínez, and J. M. Puerta. HODE: Hidden one-dependence estimator. In *Proceedings of the 10th European Conference in Symbolic and Quantitative Approaches to Reasoning with Uncertainty*, pages 481–492. Springer, 2009. [360]

M. J. Flores, J. A. Gámez, A. M. Martínez, and A. Salmerón. Mixture of truncated exponentials in supervised classification: Case study for the naive Bayes and averaged one-dependence estimators classifiers. In *11th International Conference on Intelligent Systems Design and Applications*, pages 593–598. IEEE, 2011a. [377, 384]

M. J. Flores, J. A. Gámez, A. M. Martínez, and J. M. Puerta. Handling numeric attributes when comparing Bayesian network classifiers: Does the discretization method matter? *Applied Intelligence*, 34(3):372–385, 2011b. [374]

S. J. Foote, J. P. Rubio, M. Bahlo, T. J. Kilpatrick, T. P. Speed, J. Stankovich, R. Burfoot, H. Butzkueven, L. Johnson, C. Wilkinson, B. Taylor, M. Sale, I. A. van der Mei, J. L. Dickinson, and P. Groom. Multiple sclerosis: A haplotype association study. *Novartis Found Symposium*, 267: 31–39, 2005. [195]

E. W. Forgy. Cluster analysis of multivariate data: Efficiency versus interpretability of classifications. *Biometrics*, 21:768–769, 1965. [445]

G. Forman. An extensive empirical study of feature selection metrics for text classification. *Journal of Machine Learning Research*, 3:1289–1306, 2003. [232, 233, 234]

C. Fraley and A. E. Raftery. Bayesian regularization for normal mixture estimation and model-based clustering. *Journal of Classification*, 24:155–181, 2007. [474]

C. Fraley and A. E. Raftery. Model-based clustering, discriminant analysis and density estimation. *Journal of the American Ststistical Association*, 97:611–631, 2002. [374]

C. Fraley and A. E. Raftery. MCLUST version 3 for R: Normal mixture modeling and model-based clustering. Technical Report 504, University of Washington, 2006. [475]

C. A. Frantzidis, C. Bratsas, M. A. Klados, E. Konstantinidis, C. D. Lithari, A. B. Vivas, C. L. Papadelis, E. Kaldoudi, C. Pappas, and P. D. Bamidis. On the classification of emotional biosignals evoked while viewing affective pictures: An integrated data-mining-based approach for healthcare applications. *IEEE Transactions on Information Technology in Biomedicine*, 14(2):309–318, 2010. [282]

M. L. Fredman and R. E. Tarjan. Fibonacci heaps and their uses in improved network optimization algorithms. *Journal of the ACM*, 34(3):596–615, 1987. [358]

C. M. Freeman, F. J. Martinez, M. K. Han, T. M. Ames, S. W. Chensue, J. C. Todt, D. A. Arenberg, C. A. Meldrum, C. Getty, L. McCloskey, and J. L. Curtis. Lung dendritic cell expression of maturation molecules increases with worsening chronic obstructive pulmonary disease. *American Journal of Respiratory and Critical Care Medicine*, 180(12):1179–1188, 2009. [190]

L. French and P. Pavlidis. Informatics in neuroscience. *Briefings in Bioinformatics*, 8(6):446–456, 2007. [20]

L. French, S. Lane, L. Xu, and P. Pavlidis. Automated recognition of brain region mentions in neuroscience literature. *Frontiers in Neuroinformatics*, 3, Article 29, 2009. [566]

Y. Freund and R. E. Schapire. A decision-theoretic generalization of on-line learning and an application to boosting. *Journal of Computer and System Sciences*, 55(1):119–139, 1997. [405, 406]

B. J. Frey and D. Dueck. Clustering by passing messages between data points. *Science*, 315:972–976, 2007. [453]

J. Friedman. Regularized discriminant analysis. *Journal of the American Statistical Association*, 84: 165–175, 1989. [330]

J. Friedman, T. Hastie, and R. Tibshirani. Sparse inverse covariance estimation with the graphical lasso. *Biostatistics*, 9:432–441, 2007. [560]

J. H. Friedman. Multivariate adaptive regression splines. *The Annals of Statistics*, 19(1):1–67, 1991. [283]

J. H. Friedman. Flexible metric nearest neighbor classification. Technical Report, Stanford University, 1994. [317]

N. Friedman. The Bayesian structural EM algorithm. In *Proceedings of the 14th Conference on Uncertainty in Artificial Intelligence*, pages 129–138. Morgan Kaufmann, 1998. [479, 522]

N. Friedman and M. Goldszmidt. Discretizing continuous attributes while learning Bayesian networks. In *Proceedings of the 13th International Conference on Machine Learning*, pages 157–165. Morgan Kaufmann, 1996. [499]

N. Friedman and D. Koller. Being Bayesian about network structure: A Bayesian approach to structure discovery in Bayesian networks. *Machine Learning*, 50(1–2):95–125, 2003. [536]

N. Friedman and I. Nachman. Gaussian process networks. In *Proceedings of the 16th Conference on Uncertainty in Artificial Intelligence*, pages 211–219. Morgan Kaufmann, 2000. [502]

N. Friedman and Z. Yakhini. On the sample complexity of learning Bayesian networks. In *Proceedings of the 12th Conference on Uncertainty in Artificial Intelligence*, pages 274–282. Morgan Kaufmann, 1996. [545]

N. Friedman, D. Geiger, and M. Goldszmidt. Bayesian network classifiers. *Machine Learning*, 29: 131–163, 1997. [348, 356, 362, 366, 367, 372]

N. Friedman, M. Goldszmidt, and T. Lee. Bayesian network classification with continuous attributes: Getting the best of both discretization and parametric fitting. In *Proceedings of the 15th National Conference on Machine Learning*, pages 179–187, 1998a. [371, 384]

N. Friedman, K. Murphy, and S. Russell. Learning the structure of dynamic probabilistic networks. In *Proceedings of the 14th Conference on Uncertainty in Artificial Intelligence*, pages 139–147. Morgan Kaufmann, 1998b. [538]

N. Friedman, M. Goldszmidt, and A. Wyner. Data analysis with Bayesian networks: A bootstrap approach. In *Proceedings of the 15th Conference on Uncertainty in Artificial Intelligence*, pages 196–205. Morgan Kaufmann, 1999a. [364]

N. Friedman, I. Nachman, and D. Pe'er. Learning Bayesian network structure from massive datasets: The "sparse candidate" algorithm. In *Proceedings of the 15th Conference on Uncertainty in Artificial Intelligence*, pages 206–215. Morgan Kaufmann, 1999b. [536]

K. Friston. The history of the future of the Bayesian brain. *NeuroImage*, 62(2):1230–1233, 2012. [159]

N. Fry. Random point distributions and strain measurement in rocks. *Tectonophysics*, 60:89–105, 1979. [586]

M. Frydenberg. The chain graph Markov property. *Scandinavian Journal of Statistics*, 17(4):333–353, 1990. [498]

K. S. Fu. *Sequential Methods in Pattern Recognition and Machine Learning*. Academic Press, 1968. [240, 241]

L. D. Fu. A Comparison of State-of-the-Art Algorithms for Learning Bayesian Network Structure from Continuous Data. Master's thesis, Vanderbilt University, 2005. [499]

A. Fujino, N. Ueda, and K. Saito. A hybrid generative/discriminative approach to text classification with additional information. *Information Processing and Management*, 43(2):379–392, 2007. [385]

R. M. Fung and K.-C. Chang. Weighing and integrating evidence for stochastic simulation in Bayesian networks. In *Proceedings of the 6th Conference on Uncertainty in Artificial Intelligence*, pages 209–220. Elsevier, 1990. [516]

J. Funke, J. N. Martel, S. Gerhard, B. Andres, D. C. Cireşan, A. Giusti, L. M. Gambardella, J. Schmidhuber, H. Pfister, A. Cardona, and M. Cook. Candidate sampling for neuron reconstruction from anisotropic electron microscopy volumes. *Medical Image Computing and Computer-Assisted Intervention*, 17(1):17–24, 2014. [566]

S. B. Furber, F. Galluppi, S. Temple, and L. A. Plana. The SpiNNaker project. *Proceedings of the IEEE*, 102:652–665, 2014. [30]

J. Fürnkranz and G. Widmer. Incremental reduced error pruning. In *Machine Learning: Proceedings of the 11th Annual Conference*, pages 70–77. Morgan Kaufmann, 1994. [253, 288]

J. Fürnkranz, E. Hüllermeier, and W. Cheng. Multi-label classification via calibrated label ranking. *Machine Learning*, 73(2):133–153, 2008. [424]

Z. Galaz, J. Mekyska, Z. Mzourek, Z. Smekal, I. Rektorova, I. Eliasova, M. Kostalova, M. Mrackova, and D. Berankova. Prosodic analysis of neutral, stress-modified and rhymed speech in patients with Parkinson's disease. *Computer Methods and Programs in Biomedicine*, 27:301–317, 2016. [195]

F. Galton. The geometric mean in vital and social statistics. *Proceedings of the Royal Society of London*, 29:365–367, 1879. [140]

J. A. Gámez and J. M. Puerta. Searching for the best elimination sequence in Bayesian networks by using ant colony optimization. *Pattern Recognition Letters*, 23(1-3):261–277, 2002. [511]

J. A. Gámez, J. L. Mateo, T. D. Nielsen, and J. M. Puerta. Robust classification using mixtures of dependency networks. In *Proceedings of the 4th European Workshop on Probabilistic Graphical Models*, pages 129–136, 2008. [386]

S. García and F. Herrera. An extension of "Statistical comparisons of classifiers over multiple data sets" for all pairwise comparisons. *Journal of Machine Learning Research*, 9:2677–2694, 2008. [225]

S. García, J. Derrac, J. R. Cano, and F. Herrera. Prototype selection for nearest neighbor classification: Taxonomy and empirical study. *IEEE Transactions on Pattern Analysis and Machine Intelligence*, 34(3):417–435, 2012. [268]

S. García, J. Luengo, J. A. Saez, V. López, and F. Herrera. A survey of discretization techniques: Taxonomy and empirical analysis in supervised learning. *IEEE Transactions on Knowledge and Data Engineering*, 25(4):734–750, 2013. [90]

F. García-López, M. García-Torres, B. Melián-Batista, J. A. Moreno-Pérez, and J. M. Moreno-Vega. Solving feature subset selection problem by a parallel scatter search. *European Journal of Operational Research*, 169:477–489, 2006. [241, 246]

E. Garcia-Martin, L. E. Pablo, R. Herrero, J. R. Ara, J. Martin, J. M. Larrosa, V. Polo, J. Garcia-Feijoo, and J. Fernandez. Neural networks to identify multiple sclerosis with optical coherence tomography. *Acta Ophthalmologica*, 91(8):628–634, 2013. [293]

M. García-Torres, B. Melián-Batista, J. A. Moreno-Pérez, and J. M. Moreno-Vega. Variable neighborhood search for the feature subset selection problem. In *The 6th Metaheuristics International Conference*, pages 1–6, 2005. [241, 245]

S. Garg, R. Sharma, S. Mittal, and S. Thapar. Alterations in brain-stem auditory evoked potentials among drug addicts. A cross-sectional study. *Neurosciences*, 20(3):253–258, 2015. [178]

G. W. Gates. The reduced nearest neighbor rule. *IEEE Transactions on Information Theory*, 18(3):431–433, 1972. [268]

C. F. Gauss. *Theoria Motus Corporum*. Werke, 1809. [140]

C. F. Gauss. Theoria Combinationis Observationum Erroribus Minimis Obnoxiae. *Werke*, 4:1–108, 1821. [196]

M. Gazzaniga. *Human: The Science Behind What Makes Us Unique*. Harper Collins, 2008. [7]

B. Ge, L. Guo, J. Lv, J. Han, T. Zhang, and T. Liu. Resting state fMRI-guided fiber clustering: Methods and applications. *Neuroinformatics*, 11(1):119–133, 2013. [454]

D. Geiger and D. Heckerman. Learning Gaussian networks. In *Proceedings of the 10th International Conference on Uncertainty in Artificial Intelligence*, pages 235–243. Morgan Kaufmann, 1994. [499, 500, 524, 535]

D. Geiger and D. Heckerman. Knowledge representation and inference in similarity networks and Bayesian multinets. *Artificial Intelligence*, 82:45–74, 1996. [357, 365, 367]

A. Gelman. Objections to Bayesian statistics. *Bayesian Analysis*, 3(3):445–449, 2008. [196]

A. Gelman and D. B. Rubin. Inference from iterative simulation using multiple sequences. *Statistical Science*, 7(4):457–472, 1992. [545]

A. Gelman, J. B. Carlin, H. S. Stern, and D. B. Rubin. *Bayesian Data Analysis*. Chapman & Hall, London, 1995. [196]

S. Geman and D. Geman. Stochastic relaxation, Gibbs distributions, and the Bayesian restoration of images. *IEEE Transactions on Pattern Analysis and Machine Intelligence*, 6(6):721–741, 1984. [545, 557]

S. Geman, E. Bienenstock, and R. Doursat. Neural networks and the bias/variance dilemma. *Neural Computation*, 4(1):1–58, 1992. [392]

S. Gey and J.-M. Poggi. Boosting and instability for regression trees. *Computational Statistics & Data Analysis*, 50(2):533–550, 2006. [414]

Z. Ghahramani. An introduction to hidden Markov models and Bayesian networks. *International Journal of Pattern Recognition and Artificial Intelligence*, 15(1):9–42, 2001. [538]

A. K. Ghosh. On optimum choice of k in nearest neighbor classification. *Computational Statistics & Data Analysis*, 50(11):3113–3123, 2006. [268]

J. Ghosh and A. Achraya. Cluster ensembles. *WIREs Data Mining and Knowledge Discovery*, 1:305–315, 2011. [460]

E. Gibaja and S. Ventura. A tutorial on multi-label learning. *ACM Computing Surveys*, 47(3):Article 52, 2015. [416]

J. W. Gibbs. *Elementary Principles in Statistical Mechanics*. Charles Scribner's Sons, 1902. [554]

A. Gifi. *Nonlinear Multivariate Analysis*. Wiley, 1990. [95]

L. M. Giil, E. K. Kristoffersen, C. A. Vedeler, D. Aarsland, J. E. Nordrehaug, B. Winblad, A. Cedazo-Minguez, A. Lund, and T. R. Reksten. Autoantibodies toward the angiotensin 2 type 1 receptor: A novel autoantibody in Alzheimer's disease. *Journal of Alzheimer's Disease*, 47(2):523–529, 2015. [190]

S. Gil-Begue, C. Bielza, and P. Larrañaga. Multi-dimensional Bayesian network classifier trees. In *Proceedings of the 19th International Conference on Intelligent Data Engineering and Automatic Learning*, pages 354–363, 2018. [432]

S. Gil-Begue, C. Bielza, and P. Larrañaga. Multi-dimensional Bayesian network classifiers: A survey. *Artificial Intelligence Review*, 53, in press 2020. [432]

W. R. Gilks and P. Wild. Adaptive rejection sampling for Gibbs sampling. *Journal of the Royal Statistical Society, Series C*, 41(2):337–48, 1992. [131]

W. R. Gilks, S. Richardson, and D. Spiegelhalter. *Markov Chain Monte Carlo in Practice*. Chapman & Hall/CRC, 1995. [545]

S. B. Gillispie and M. D. Perlman. The size distribution for Markov equivalence classes of acyclic digraph models. *Artificial Intelligence*, 141(1/2):137–155, 2002. [530]

P. Giudici. *Bayesian Statistics*, volume 5, chapter Learning in graphical Gaussian models, pages 621–628. Oxford University Press, 1996. [570]

P. Giudici and R. Castelo. Improving Markov chain Monte Carlo model search for data mining. *Machine Learning*, 50(1):127–158, 2003. [519]

P. Giudici and P. J. Green. Decomposable graphical Gaussian model determination. *Biometrika*, 86 (4):785–801, 1999. [536]

J. Glaser and E. Glaser. Neuron imaging with Neurolucida – A PC-based system for image combining microscopy. *Computerized Medical Imaging and Graphics*, 14(5):307–317, 1990. [31, 44, 417]

F. Glover. Heuristics for integer programming using surrogate constraints. *Decision Sciences*, 8:156–166, 1977. [245]

F. Glover. Future paths for integer programming and links to artificial intelligence. *Computers & Operation Research*, 13(5):533–549, 1986. [228]

F. Glover. Tabu search, Part I. *ORSA Journal on Computing*, 1(3):190–206, 1989. [241]

G. H. Glover. Overview of functional magnetic resonance imaging. *Neurosurgery Clinics of North America*, 22(2):133–139, 2011. [16]

S. Godbole and S. Sarawagi. Discriminative methods for multi-labeled classification. In *Proceedings of the 8th Pacific-Asia Conference on Knowledge Discovery and Data Mining*, pages 22–30. Springer, 2004. [422]

E. Gokgoz and A. Subasi. Effect of multiscale PCA de-noising on EMG signal classification for diagnosis of neuromuscular disorders. *Journal of Medical Systems*, 38(4), 2014. [263]

J. I. Gold and M. N. Shadlen. Banburismus and the brain: Decoding the relationship between sensory stimuli, decisions, and reward. *Neuron*, 36(2):299–308, 2002. [159]

D. E. Goldberg. *Genetic Algorithms in Search, Optimization, and Machine Learning*. Addison Wesley, 1989. [247]

G. H. Golub and C. F. van Loan. *Matrix Computations*. Johns Hopkins University Press, 4th edition, 2012. [78]

I. J. Good. Studies in the history of probability and statistics. XXXVII A. M. Turing's statistical work in World War II. *Biometrika*, 66(2):393–396, 1979. [159]

I. Goodfellow, Y. Bengio, and A. Courville. *Deep Learning*. The MIT Press, 2016. [319]

I. J. Goodfellow, J. Pouget-Abadie, M. Mirza, B. Xu, D. Warde-Farley, S. Ozair, A. Courville, and Y. Bengio. Generative adversarial nets. In *Advances in Neural Information Processing Systems 27*, pages 2672–2680, 2014. [319]

A. D. Gordon. A review of hierarchical classification. *Journal of the Royal Statistical Society, Series A*, 150(2):119–137, 1987. [439]

S. W. Gosset. "Student": The probable error of a mean. *Biometrika*, 6:1–25, 1908. [140]

R. L. Gould, B. Arroyo, R. G. Brown, A. M. Owen, E. T. Bullmore, and R. J. Howard. Brain mechanisms of successful compensation during learning in Alzheimer disease. *Neurology*, 67(6): 1011–1017, 2006. [46]

C. L. Grady, M. L. Furey, P. Pietrini, B. Horwitz, and S. I. Rapoport. Altered brain functional connectivity and impaired short-term memory in Alzheimer's disease. *Brain*, 124(4):739–756, 2001. [46]

E. G. Gray. Axo-somatic and axo-dendritic synapses of the cerebral cortex: An electron microscope study. *Journal of Anatomy*, 93:420–433, 1959. [48]

D. M. Green and J. A. Swets. *Signal Detection Theory and Psychophysics*. Wiley, 1966. [208]

P. Greig-Smith. *Quantitative Plant Ecology*. Butterworths, 1964. [612]

R. Greiner, X. Su, B. Shen, and W. Zhou. Structural extension to logistic regression: Discriminative parameter learning of belief net classifiers. *Machine Learning*, 59(3):297–322, 2005. [385]

D. Grossman and P. Domingos. Learning Bayesian network classifiers by maximizing conditional likelihood. In *Proceedings of the 21st International Conference on Machine Learning*, pages 361–368, 2004. [385]

A. Grover, S. Bhartia, A. Yadav, and Seeja K. R. Predicting severity of Parkinson's disease using deep learning. *Procedia Computer Science*, 132:1788–1794, 2018. [299]

M. Grzegorczyk and D. Husmeier. Improving the structure MCMC sampler for Bayesian networks by introducing a new edge reversal move. *Machine Learning*, 71(2):265–305, 2008. [536]

H. Gudbjartsson and S. Patz. The Rician distribution of noisy MRI data. *Magnetic Resonance in Medicine*, 34(6):910–914, 1995. [535]

L. Guerra, L. McGarry, V. Robles, C. Bielza, P. Larrañaga, and R. Yuste. Comparison between supervised and unsupervised classification of neuronal cell types: A case study. *Developmental Neurobiology*, 71(1):71–82, 2011. [31, 32, 82, 214, 222, 239, 293, 345, 440]

L. Guerra, V. Robles, C. Bielza, and P. Larrañaga. A comparison of clustering quality indices using outliers and noise. *Intelligent Data Analysis*, 16(4):703–715, 2012. [468]

H. Guo and W. Hsu. A survey of algorithms for real-time Bayesian network inference. In *Proceedings of the AAAI Workshop on Real-Time Decision Support and Diagnosis Systems*, pages 1–12. AAAI Press, 2002. [545]

Y. Guo and R. Greiner. Discriminative model selection for belief net structures. In *Proceedings of the 20th National Conference on Artificial Intelligence*, pages 770–776. AAAI Press, 2005. [385]

Y. Guo, D. F. Wilkinson, and D. Schuurmans. Maximum margin Bayesian networks. In *Proceedings of the 21st Conference on Uncertainty in Artificial Intelligence*, pages 233–242. AUAI Press, 2005. [385]

A. R. Gupta, M. Pirruccello, F. Cheng, H. J. Kang, T. V. Fernandez, J. M. Baskin, M. Choi, L. Liu, A. G. Ercan-Sencicek, J. D. Murdoch, L. Klei, B. M. Neale, D. Franjic, M. J. Daly, R. P. Lifton, P. de Camilli, H. Zhao, N. Sestan, and M. W. State. Rare deleterious mutations of the gene EFR3A in autism spectrum disorders. *Molecular Autism*, 5:31, 2014. [195]

M. R. Gupta and Y. Chen. Theory and use of the EM algorithm. *Foundations and Trends in Signal Processing*, 4(3):223–296, 2010. [486]

K. N. Gurney. Information processing in dendrites. II. Information theoretic complexity. *Neural Networks*, 14(8):1005–1022, 2001. [138]

Y. Gurwicz and B. Lerner. Bayesian class-matched multinet classifier. In *Proceedings of the 2006 Joint IAPR International Conference on Structural, Syntactic, and Statistical Pattern Recognition*, pages 145–153. Springer, 2006. [365]

I. Guyon, J. Weston, S. Barnhill, and V. Vapnik. Gene selection for cancer classification using support vector machines. *Machine Learning*, 46(1-3):389–422, 2002. [253]

J. D. F. Habbema and J. Hermans. Selection of variables in discriminant analysis by F-statistic and error rate. *Technometrics*, 19(4):487–493, 1977. [261]

L. Hagen and A. Kahng. New spectral methods for ratio cut partitioning and clustering. *IEEE Transactions on Computer-Aided Design*, 11(9):1074–1085, 1992. [452]

M. A. Hall. A decision tree-based attribute weighting filter for naive Bayes. *Knowledge-Based Systems*, 20(2):120–126, 2007. [351]

M. A. Hall. *Correlation-Based Feature Selection for Machine Learning*. PhD thesis, University of Waikato, 1999. [232, 233, 236, 237, 238]

M. A. Hall and L. A. Smith. Practical feature subset selection for machine learning. In *Proceedings of the 21st Australian Computer Science Conference*, pages 181–191, 1998. [232, 233]

M. A. Hall, E. Frank, G. Holmes, B. Pfahringer, P. Reutemann, and I. H. Witten. The WEKA data mining software: An update. *SIGKDD Explorations*, 11(1):10–18, 2009. [256, 269, 273, 284, 315, 345, 368, 410]

J. M. Hammersley and P. Clifford. Markov fields on finite graphs and lattices. Unpublished manuscript, 1971. [552]

D. J. Hand. Statistics and computing: The genesis of data science. *Statistics and Computing*, 25: 705–711, 2015. [22]

D. J. Hand and R. J. Till. A simple generalization of the area under the ROC curve for multiple class classification problems. *Machine Learning*, 45:171–186, 2001. [211]

D. J. Hand and K. Yu. Idiot's Bayes – not so stupid after all? *International Statistical Review*, 69(3): 385–398, 2001. [351]

T. E. Handley, S. A. Hiles, K. J. Inder, F. J. Kay-Lambkin, B. J. Kelly, T. J. Lewin, M. McEvoy, R. Peel, and J. R. Attia. Predictors of suicidal ideation in older people: A decision tree analysis. *American Journal of Geriatric Psychiatry*, 22(11):1325–1335, 2014. [283]

D. Hardin, I. Tsamardinos, and C. F. Aliferis. A theoretical characterization of linear SVM-based feature selection. In *Proceedings of the 21st International Conference on Machine Learning*, pages 48–55. ACM, 2004. [319]

O. Harel and X.-H. Zhou. Multiple imputation: Review of theory, implementation and software. *Statistics in Medicine*, 26:3057–3077, 2007. [95]

M. H. Harirchian, N. Karimi, S. Nafisi, S. Akrami, D. Ghanbarian, and S. Gharibzadeh. Vestibular evoked myogenic potential for diagnoses of multiple sclerosis: Is it beneficial? *Medicinski Glasnik*, 10(2):321–326, 2013. [171]

R. Harmouche, N. K. Subbanna, D. L. Collins, D. L. Arnold, and T. Arbel. Probabilistic multiple sclerosis lesion classification based on modelling regional intensity variability and local neighbourhood information. *IEEE Transactions on Biomedical Engineering*, 62(5):1281–1292, 2014. [549]

K. M. Harris and J. K. Stevens. Dendritic spines of CA1 pyramidal cells in the rat hippocampus: Serial electron microscopy with reference to their biophysical characteristics. *Journal of Neuroscience*, 9:2982–2997, 1989. [39]

P. E. Hart. The condensed nearest neighbor rule. *IEEE Transactions on Information Theory*, 14(3): 515–516, 1968. [268]

J. A. Hartigan. Direct clustering of a data matrix. *Journal of the American Statistical Association*, 67:123–129, 1972. [468]

J. A. Hartigan. *Clustering Algorithms*. Wiley, 1975. [458, 467, 468]

H. O. Hartley. Maximum likelihood estimation for incomplete data. *Biometrics*, 14(2):174–194, 1958. [486]

T. Hastie and R. Tibshirani. Discriminant adaptive nearest-neighbor classification. *IEEE Pattern Analysis and Machine Intelligence*, 18:607–616, 1996. [317]

T. Hastie, R. Tibshirani, and A. Buja. Flexible discriminant analysis by optimal scoring. *Journal of the American Statistical Association*, 89(428):1255–1270, 1994. [330]

T. Hastie, A. Buja, and R. Tibshirani. Penalized discriminant analysis. *The Annals of Statistics*, 23(1): 73–102, 1995. [331]

T. Hastie, R. Tibshirani, and J. Friedman. *The Elements of Statistical Learning: Data Mining, Inference, and Predictions*. Springer, 2nd edition, 2008. [384]

A.-C. Haury, P. Gestraud, and J.-P. Vert. The influence of feature selection methods on accuracy, stability and interpretability of molecular signatures. *PLoS ONE*, 6(12):e28210, 2011. [255]

A. Hauser and P. Bühlmann. Jointly interventional and observational data: Estimation of interventional Markov equivalence classes of directed acyclic graphs. *Journal of the Royal Statistical Society, Series B*, 77(1):291–318, 2015. [497]

M. Häusser and B. Mel. Dendrites: Bug or feature? *Current Opinion in Neurobiology*, 13(3):372–383, 2003. [43]

J.-D. Haynes and G. Rees. Decoding mental states from brain activity in humans. *Nature Reviews Neuroscience*, 7:523–534, 2006. [226]

K. He, H. Wang, G.-H. Lee, and Y. Tian. ProbGAN: Towards probabilistic GAN with theoretical guarantees. In *Proceedings of the 7th International Conference on Learning Representations*, 2019. [544]

D. O. Hebb. *The Organization of Behavior*. Wiley, 1949. [318]

D. Heckerman. A tutorial on learning with Bayesian networks. Technical Report MSR-TR-95-06, Microsoft Research, 1995. [536]

D. Heckerman, D. Geiger, and D. M. Chickering. Learning Bayesian networks: The combination of knowledge and statistical data. *Machine Learning*, 20:197–243, 1995. [533, 534, 535, 536, 546]

J. Helm, G. Akgul, and L. P. Wollmuth. Subgroups of parvalbumin-expressing interneurons in layers 2/3 of the visual cortex. *Journal of Neurophysiology*, 109(6):1600–1613, 2013. [34, 445]

M. Helmstaedter, B. Sakmann, and D. Feldmeyer. Neuronal correlates of local, lateral, and translaminar inhibition with reference to cortical columns. *Cerebral Cortex*, 19(4):926–937, 2009a. [34]

M. Helmstaedter, B. Sakmann, and D. Feldmeyer. L2/3 interneuron groups defined by multiparameter analysis of axonal projection, dendritic geometry and electrical excitability. *Cerebral Cortex*, 19(4):951–962, 2009b. [34]

M. Helmstaedter, K. L. Briggman, S. C. Turaga, V. Jain, H. S. Seung, and W. Denk. Connectomic reconstruction of the inner plexiform layer in the mouse retina. *Nature*, 500:168–174, 2013. [21]

M. Henrion. Propagating uncertainty in Bayesian networks by probabilistic logic sampling. In *Uncertainty in Artificial Intelligence 2*, pages 149–163. Elsevier Science, 1988. [516]

S. Herculano-Houzal. The human brain in numbers: A linearly scaled-up primate brain. *Frontiers in Human Neuroscience*, 3:Article 31, 2009. [142]

S. Herculano-Houzel and C. Lent. Isotropic fractionator: A simple, rapid method for the quantification of total cell and neuron numbers in the brain. *Journal of Neuroscience*, 25:2518–2521, 2005. [6]

I. Hernández, A. Mauleón, M. Rosense-Roca, M. Alegret, G. Vinyes, A. Espinosa, O. Sotolongo-Grau, J. T. Becker, S. Valero, L. Tarraga, O. L. López, A. Ruiz, and M. Boada. Identification of misdiagnosed fronto-temporal dementia using APOE genotype and phenotype-genotype correlation analyses. *Current Alzheimer Research*, 11(2):182–191, 2014. [344]

L. Hernández and S. Moral. Mixing exact and importance sampling propagation algorithms in dependence graphs. *International Journal of Intelligent Systems*, 12:553–576, 1997. [544]

F. Herrera, F. Charte, A. J. Rivera, and M. J. del Jesus. *Multilabel Classification: Problem Analysis, Metrics and Techniques*. Springer, 2016. [416]

T. Hesterberg, N. M. Choi, L. Meier, and C. Fraley. Least angle and l_1 penalized regression: A review. *Statistics Surveys*, 2(1):61–93, 2008. [385]

J. Hilden and B. Bjerregaard. Computer-aided diagnosis and the atypical case. In *Decision Making and Medical Care. Can Information Science Help?*, pages 365–378. Elsevier, 1976. [351]

D. V. Hinkley. Bootstrap methods. *Journal of the Royal Statistical Society, Series B*, 50(3):321–337, 1988. [225]

G. E. Hinton. Machine learning for neuroscience. *Neural Systems and Circuits*, 1:12–13, 2011. [23]

T. K. Ho. The random subspace method for constructing decision forests. *IEEE Transactions on Pattern Analysis and Machine Intelligence*, 20(8):832–844, 1998. [403]

T. K. Ho. Multiple classifier combination: Lessons and next steps. In *Hybrid Methods in Pattern Recognition*, volume 47, pages 171–198. World Scientific, 2002. [413]

M. Hoehn and M. Yahr. Parkinsonism: Onset, progression and mortality. *Neurology*, 17(5):427–442, 1967. [174]

J. A. Hoeting, D. Madigan, A. E. Raftery, and C. T. Volinsky. Bayesian model averaging: A tutorial. *Statistical Science*, 14(4):382–417, 1999. [546]

R. Hofmann and V. Tresp. Discovering structure in continuous variables using Bayesian networks. In *Advances in Neural Information Processing Systems 8*, pages 500–506. The MIT Press, 1996. [502]

J. H. Holland. *Adaptation in Natural and Artificial Systems*. University of Michigan Press, 1975. [248]

J. H. Holland. *Progress in Theoretical Biology*, volume 4, chapter Adaptation, pages 263–293. Academic Press, 1976. [318]

Y. Höller, J. Bergmann, A. Thomschewski, P. Höller, J. S. Crone, E. V. Schmid, K. Butz, R. Nardone, and E. Trinka. Comparison of EEG-features and classification methods for motor imagery in patients with disorders of consciousness. *PLoS ONE*, 25(8):e80479, 2013. [263]

S. Holm. A simple sequentially rejective multiple test procedure. *Scandinavian Journal of Statistics*, 6:65–70, 1979. [193]

D. E. Holmes and L. C. Jain. *Innovations in Bayesian Networks. Theory and Applications*. Springer, 2008. [543]

R. C. Holte. Very simple classification rules perform well. *Machine Learning*, 11:63–91, 1993. [286]

J. J. Hopfield. Neural networks and physical systems with emergent collective computational abilities. *Proceedings of the National Academy of Sciences*, 79(8):2554–2558, 1982. [319, 555]

K. Hornik, M. Stinchcombe, and H. White. Multilayer feedforward networks are universal approximators. *Neural Networks*, 2:359–366, 1989. [293]

A. Horváth, G. Perlaki, A. Tóth, G. Orsi, S. Nagy, T. Dóczi, Z. Horváth, and P. Bogner. Increased diffusion in the normal appearing white matter of brain tumor patients: Is this just tumor infiltration? *Journal of Neuro-Oncology*, 127(1):83–990, 2016. [179]

E. Horvitz, J. Suermondt, and G. F. Cooper. Bounded conditioning: Flexible inference for decisions under scarce resources. In *Proceedings of the 5th Conference on Uncertainty in Artificial Intelligence*, pages 182–193. Elsevier, 1989. [544]

B. Horwitz. The elusive concept of brain connectivity. *NeuroImage*, 19:466–470, 2003. [46]

D. W. Hosmer and S. Lemeshow. *Applied Logistic Regression*. Wiley, 2nd edition, 2000. [253, 339, 384]

A. Hossen. A neural network approach for feature extraction and discrimination between Parkinsonian tremor and essential tremor. *Technology and Health Care*, 21(4):345–356, 2013. [293]

H. Hotelling. Analysis of a complex of statistical variables into principal components. *Journal of Educational Psychology*, 24:417–441, 1933. [94]

R. Howard and J. Matheson. *Readings on the Principles and Applications of Decision Analysis*, chapter Influence diagrams, pages 719–762. Strategic Decisions Group, 1984. [543]

E. R. Hruschka and N. F. F. Ebecken. Towards efficient variables ordering for Bayesian network classifiers. *Data and Knowledge Engineering*, 63:258–269, 2007. [365]

C.-W. Hsu and C.-J. Lin. A comparison of methods for multiclass support vector machines. *IEEE Transactions on Neural Networks*, 13(2):415–425, 2002. [317]

C.-N. Hsu, H.-J. Huang, and T.-T. Wong. Why discretization works for naive Bayesian classifiers. In *Proceedings of the 17th International Conference on Machine Learning*, pages 399–406. Morgan Kaufmann, 2000. [374]

C.-N. Hsu, H.-J. Huang, and T.-T. Wong. Implications of the Dirichlet assumption for discretization of continuous variables in naive Bayesian classifiers. *Machine Learning*, 53(3):235–263, 2003. [374]

J. J. Huang, C. T. Yen, H. W. Tsao, M. L. Tsai, and C. Huang. Neuronal oscillations in Golgi cells and Purkinje cells are accompanied by decreases in Shannon information entropy. *Cerebellum*, 13 (1):97–108, 2014. [136]

J. Z. Huang, M. K. Ng, H. Rong, and Z. Li. Automated variable weighting in k-means type clustering. *IEEE Transactions on Pattern Analysis and Machine Intelligence*, 27(5):657–668, 2005. [467]

K. Huang, I. King, and M. R. Lyu. Discriminative training of Bayesian Chow-Liu multinet classifiers. In *Proceedings of the International Joint Conference on Neural Networks*, pages 484–488, 2003. [365]

S. Huang, J. Li, L. Sun, J. Ye, A. Fleisher, T. Wu, K. Chen, and E. Reiman. Learning brain connectivity of Alzheimer's disease by sparse inverse covariance estimation. *NeuroImage*, 50(3): 935–949, 2010. [46, 547, 548, 566, 567, 568, 569]

Z. Huang. Extensions to the k-means algorithm for clustering large data sets with categorical values. *Data Mining and Knowledge Discovery*, 2:283–304, 1998. [446, 467]

L. Hubert. Monotone invariant clustering procedures. *Psychometrika*, 38:47–62, 1973. [442]

L. Hubert and P. Arabie. Comparing partitions. *Journal of Classification*, 2:193–218, 1985. [461]

D. A. Hull. *Information Retrieval Using Statistical Classification*. PhD thesis, Stanford University, 1994. [225]

T. E. Hull and A. R. Dobell. Random number generators. *SIAM Review*, 4(3):230–254, 1962. [125]

E. Hüllermeier, J. Fürnkranz, and W. Cheng. Label ranking by learning pairwise preferences. *Artificial Intelligence*, 172:1897–1916, 2008. [423]

A. Hussein and E. Santos. Exploring case-based Bayesian networks and Bayesian multi-nets for classification. In *Proceedings of the 17th Conference of the Canadian Society for Computational Studies of Intelligence*, pages 485–492. Springer, 2004. [366]

C. Huygens. *De Ratiociniis in Ludo Aleae*. Elsevirii, 1657. [140, 195]

L. Hyafil and R. L. Rivest. Constructing optimal binary decision trees is NP-complete. *Information Processing Letters*, 5(1):15–17, 1976. [273]

J. Illian, A. Penttinen, H. Stoyan, and D. Stoyan. *Statistical Analysis and Modelling of Spatial Point Patterns*. Wiley, 2008. [579, 580, 602, 611, 612]

S. Imoto, S. Kim, T. Goto, S. Aburatani, K. Tashiro, S. Kuhara, and S. Miyano. Bayesian network and nonparametric heteroscedastic regression for nonlinear modeling of genetic network. In *Proceedings of the 1st IEEE Bioinformatics Conference of the Computer Society*, pages 219–227. IEEE, 2002. [502]

M. Inglese, G. Madelin, N. Oesingmann, J. S. Babb, W. Wu, B. Stoeckel, G. Herbert, and J. Johnson. Brain tissue sodium concentration in multiple sclerosis: A sodium imaging study at 3 tesla. *Brain*, 133:847–857, 2010. [190]

M. Inoue and N. Ueda. Exploitation of unlabeled sequences in hidden Markov models. *IEEE Transactions on Pattern Analysis and Machine Intelligence*, 25:1570–1581, 2003. [486]

A. Inselberg. The plane with parallel coordinates. *Visual Computer*, 1(4):69–91, 1985. [74]

I. Inza, P. Larrañaga, B. Sierra, R. Etxeberria, J. A. Lozano, and J. M. Peña. Representing the behaviour of supervised classification learning algorithms by Bayesian networks. *Pattern Recognition Letters*, 20(11–13):1201–1209, 1999. [413]

I. Inza, P. Larrañaga, R. Etxeberria, and B. Sierra. Feature subset selection by Bayesian network-based optimization. *Artificial Intelligence*, 123(1–2):157–184, 2000. [241, 249, 353]

I. Inza, P. Larrañaga, R. Blanco, and A. J. Cerrolaza. Filter versus wrapper gene selection approaches in DNA microarray domains. *Artificial Intelligence in Medicine*, 31(2):91–103, 2004. [232, 235, 353]

E. Ising. Beitrag zur theorie des ferromagnetismus. *Zeitschrift fur Physik*, 31:253–258, 1925. [554]

T. Jaakkola, D. Sontag, A. Globerson, and M. Meilă. Learning Bayesian network structure using LP relaxations. In *Proceedings of the 13th International Conference on Artificial Intelligence and Statistics*, pages 358–365, 2010. [536]

I. Jabalpurwala. Brain Canada: One brain one community. *Neuron*, 92:601–606, 2016. [11]

M. Jaeger, J. D. Nielsen, and T. Silander. Learning probabilistic decision graphs. *International Journal of Approximate Reasoning*, 42(1-2):84–100, 2006. [543]

P. Jafari and F. Azuaje. An assessment of recently published gene expression data analyses: Reporting experimental design and statistical factors. *BMC Medical Informatics and Decision Making*, 6(1): 27, 2006. [232, 234]

M. Jafari-Mamaghani, M. Anderson, and P. Krieger. Spatial point pattern analysis of neurons using Ripley's K-function in *3D*. *Frontiers in Neuroscience*, 4:Article 9, 2010. [591]

A. K. Jain. Data clustering: 50 years beyond K-means. *Pattern Recognition Letters*, 31(8):651–666, 2010. [467]

A. K. Jain and R. C. Dubes. *Algorithms for Clustering Data*. Prentice-Hall, 1988. [446]

A. K. Jain, R. C. Dubes, and C.-C. Chen. Bootstrap techniques for error estimation. *IEEE Transactions on Pattern Analysis and Machine Intelligence*, 9(5):628–633, 1987. [225]

A. Jammalamadaka, S. Banerjee, B. S. Manjunath, and K. S. Kosik. Statistical analysis of dendritic spine distributions in rat hippocampal cultures. *BMC Bioinformatics*, 14:287, 2013. [343, 611]

A. Jammalamadaka, P. Suwannat, S. K. Fisher, B. S. Manjunath, T. Hollerer, and G. Luna. Characterizing spatial distributions of astrocytes in the mammalian retina. *Bioinformatics*, 31(12): 2024–2031, 2015. [582]

S. R. Jammalamadaka and A. SenGupta. *Topics in Circular Statistics*. World Scientific, 2001. [62]

D. Jansson, A. Medvedev, H. Axelson, and D. Nyholm. *Signal and Image Analysis for Biomedical and Life Sciences*, chapter Stochastic anomaly detection in eye-tracking data for quantification of motor symptoms in Parkinson's disease, pages 63–82. Springer, 2015. [224]

N. Japkowicz. The class imbalance problem: Significance and strategies. *Complexity*, 1:111–117, 2000. [223]

N. Japkowicz and S. Mohak. *Evaluating Learning Algorithms. A Classification Perspective*. Cambridge University Press, 2011. [211, 224]

H. (Sir) Jeffreys. *Theory of Probability*. Oxford University Press, 3rd edition, 1961. [196]

F. V. Jensen and T. D. Nielsen. *Bayesian Networks and Decision Graphs*. Springer, 2nd edition, 2007. [498, 543]

S.-J. Jeong, H. Lee, E.-M. Hur, Y. Choe, J. W. Koo, K. J. Lee J.-C. Rah, H.-H. Lim, W. Sun, C. Moon, and K. Kim. Korea Brain Initiative: Integration and control of brain functions. *Neuron*, 92:607–611, 2016. [11]

L. Jiang and H. Zhang. Lazy averaged one-dependence estimators. In *Proceedings of the 19th Canadian Conference on Computational Studies of Intelligence*, volume 4013, pages 515–525. Springer, 2006. [359]

B. Jin, A. Strasburger, S. J. Laken, F. A. Kozel, K. A. Johnson, M. S. George, and X. Lu. Feature selection for fMRI-based deception detection. *BMC Bioinformatics*, 10:S15, 2009. [240]

S. Jinno, F. Fleischer, S. Eckel, V. Schmidt, and T. Kosaka. Spatial arrangement of microglia in the mouse hippocampus: A stereological study in comparison with astrocytes. *Glia*, 55:1334–1347, 2007. [575]

G. H. John and P. Langley. Estimating continuous distributions in Bayesian classifiers. In *Proceedings of the 11th Annual Conference on Uncertainty in Artificial Intelligence*, pages 338–345. Morgan Kaufmann, 1995. [376, 384]

G. H. John, R. Kohavi, and P. Pfleger. Irrelevant features and the subset selection problem. In *Proceedings of the 11th International Conference in Machine Learning*, pages 121–129. Morgan Kaufmann, 1994. [238, 240, 241, 261]

J. Jolliffe. *Principal Component Analysis*. Springer, 1986. [75]

B. Jones, C. Carvalho, A. Dobra, C. Hans, C. Carter, and M. West. Experiments in stochastic computation for high-dimensional graphical models. *Statistical Science*, 20(4):383–400, 2005. [570]

E. Jones and A. Peters. *Cerebral Cortex: Volume 1. Cellular Components of the Cerebral Cortex*. Plenum Press, 1984. [35]

M. I. Jordan and T. M. Mitchell. Machine learning: Trends, perspectives, and prospects. *Science*, 349 (6245):255–260, 2015. [24]

M. I. Jordan, Z. Ghahramani, T. S. Jaakola, and L. K. Saul. *Learning in Graphical Models*, chapter An introduction to variational methods for graphical models, pages 105–162. The MIT Press, 1998. [570]

P. E. Jupp and K. V. Mardia. Maximum likelihood estimators for the matrix von Mises–Fisher and Bingham distributions. *The Annals of Statistics*, 7:599–606, 1979. [124]

D. Kahneman, P. Slovic, and A. Tversky. *Judgment under Uncertainty: Heuristics and Biases*. Cambridge University Press, 1982. [498]

M. Kalisch and P. Bühlmann. Estimating high-dimensional directed acyclic graphs with the PC algorithm. *Journal of Machine Learning Research*, 8:613–636, 2007. [529, 545]

R. E. Kalman. A new approach to linear filtering and prediction problems. *Transactions of the ASME – Journal of Basic Engineering*, 82:35–45, 1960. [539]

A. Kalousis, J. Prados, and M. Hilario. Stability of feature selection algorithms: A study on high dimensional spaces. *Knowledge and Information Systems*, 12(1):95–116, 2007. [255]

C. Kang and J. Tian. A hybrid generative/discriminative Bayesian classifier. In *Proceedings of the 19th International Florida Artificial Intelligence Research Society Conference*, pages 562–567. AAAI Press, 2006. [385]

A. Karagiannis, T. Gallopin, D. Csaba, D. Battaglia, H. Geoffroy, J. Rossier, E. Hillman, J. Staiger, and B. Cauli. Classification of NPY-expressing neocortical interneurons. *The Journal of Neuroscience*, 29(11):3642–3659, 2009. [34]

Z. Karimaghaloo, H. Rivaz, D. L. Arnold, D. L. Collins, and T. Arbel. Adaptive voxel, texture and temporal conditional random fields for detection of Gad-enhancing multiple sclerosis lesions in brain MRI. *Medical Image Computing and Computer-Assisted Intervention*, 16(3):543–550, 2013. [566]

W. Karush. Minima of functions of several variables with inequalities as side constraints. Master's thesis, University of Chicago, 1939. [319]

H. Kasai, M. Fukuda, S. Watanabe, A. Hayashi-Takagi, and J. Noguchi. Structural dynamics of dendritic spines in memory and cognition. *Trends in Neuroscience*, 33:121–129, 2010. [41]

G. V. Kass. An exploratory technique for investigating large quantities of categorical data. *Applied Statistics*, 29(2):119–127, 1980. [283]

L. Kaufman and P. J. Rousseeuw. *Finding Groups in Data: An Introduction to Cluster Analysis*. Wiley, 1990. [447, 453, 467]

L. Kaufman and P. J. Rousseeuw. *Statistical Data Analysis Based on the l_1 Norm and Related Methods*, chapter Clustering by means of medoids, pages 405–416. North-Holland, 1997. [452]

M. Kayaalp and G. F. Cooper. A Bayesian network scoring metric that is based on globally uniform parameter priors. In *Proceedings of the 18th Conference on Uncertainty in Artificial Intelligence*, pages 251–258. Morgan Kaufmann, 2002. [546]

C. Kaynak and E. Alpaydın. Multistage cascading of multiple classifiers: One man's noise is another man's data. In *Proceedings of the 17th International Conference on Machine Learning*, pages 455–462. Morgan Kaufmann, 2000. [400]

O. Keivani and J. M. Peña. *Unsupervised Learning Algorithms*, chapter Uni- and multi-dimensional clustering via Bayesian networks, pages 163–192. Springer, 2016. [486]

M. G. Kendall and B. B. Smith. Randomness and random sampling numbers. *Journal of the Royal Statistical Society*, 101(1):147–166, 1938. [125]

J. Kennedy and R. C. Eberhart. Particle swarm optimization. In *Proceedings of the International Conference on Neural Networks*, volume 4, pages 1942–1948, 1995. [247]

E. J. Keogh and M. J. Pazzani. Learning the structure of augmented Bayesian classifiers. *International Journal on Artificial Intelligence Tools*, 11(4):587–601, 2002. [358, 366, 367, 368, 373]

M. I. Kester, C. E. Teunissen, C. Sutphen, E. M. Herries, J. H. Ladenson, C. Xiong, P. Scheltens, W. M. van der Flier, J. C. Morris, D. M. Holtzman, and A. M. Fagan. Cerebrospinal fluid VILIP-1 and YKL-40, candidate biomarkers to diagnose, predict and monitor Alzheimer's disease in a memory clinic cohort. *Alzheimer's Research and Therapy*, 7(1):59, 2015. [186]

A. Khan, A. R. Baig, and K. Zafar. Comparative analysis of multi-objective feature subset selection using meta-heuristic techniques. *Journal of Basic and Applied Scientific Research*, 3(12):210–217, 2013. [251]

T. Khan, D. Nyholm, J. Westin, and M. Dougherty. A computer vision framework for finger-tapping evaluation in Parkinson's disease. *Artificial Intelligence in Medicine*, 60(1):27–40, 2014. [314]

N. Khoury, F. Attal, Y. Amirat, L. Oukhellou, and S. Mohammed. Data-driven based approach to aid Parkinson's disease diagnosis. *Sensors*, 19(2):242, 2019. [223]

R. N. Khushaba, A. Al-Ani, and A. Al-Jumaily. Feature subset selection using differential evolution. In *Proceedings of the 15th International Conference on Neural Information Processing*, pages 103–110. Springer, 2009. [241, 250]

J. H. Kim. Estimating classification error rate: Repeated cross-validation, repeated hold-out and bootstrap. *Computational Statistics & Data Analysis*, 53:3735–3745, 2009. [225]

J. H. Kim and J. Pearl. A computational model for combined causal and diagnostic reasoning in inference systems. In *Proceedings of the 8th International Joint Conference on Artificial Intelligence*, volume 1, pages 190–193, 1983. [509]

R. Kindermann and J. L Snell. *Markov Random Fields and Their Applications*. American Mathematical Society, 1980. [547]

L. Kipinski, R. König, C. Sieluzycki, and W. Kordecki. Application of modern tests for stationarity to single-trial MEG data: Transferring powerful statistical tools from econometrics to neuroscience. *Biological Cybernetics*, 105(3–4):183–195, 2011. [167]

K. Kira and L. A. Rendell. The feature selection problem: Traditional methods and a new algorithm. In *Proceedings of the 10th National Conference on Artificial Intelligence*, pages 129–134, 1992. [236]

S. Kirkpatrick, C. D. Gelatt, and M. P. Vecchi. Optimization by simulated annealing. *Science*, 220 (4598):671–680, 1983. [242]

S. L. Kirvell, M. S. Elliott, R. N. Kalaria, T. Hortobágyi, C. G. Ballard, and P. T. Francis. Vesicular glutamate transporter and cognition in stroke: A case-control autopsy study. *Neurology*, 75(20): 1803–1809, 2010. [193]

U. Kjærulff. Optimal decomposition of probabilistic networks by simulated annealing. *Statistics and Computing*, 2(1):7–17, 1992. [511]

U. Kjærulff. HUGS: Combining exact inference and Gibbs sampling in junction trees. In *Proceedings of the 11th Conference on Uncertainty in Artificial Intelligence*, pages 368–375. Morgan Kaufmann, 1995. [544]

U. Kjaerulff and A. L. Madsen. *Bayesian Networks and Influence Diagrams – A Guide to Construction and Analysis.* Springer, 2008. [495]

T. H. Kjeldsen. A contextualized historical analysis of the Kuhn–Tucker theorem in nonlinear programming: The impact of World War II. *Historia Mathematica*, 27(4):331–361, 2000. [319]

D. G. Kleinbaum. *Logistic Regression.* Springer, 1994. [342]

E. M. Kleinberg. Stochastic discrimination. *Annals of Mathematics and Artificial Intelligence*, 1(1): 207–239, 1990. [413]

M. A. Kłopotek. Very large Bayesian multinets for text classification. *Future Generation Computer Systems*, 21(7):1068–1082, 2005. [365]

S. Kloppel, C. Chu, G. C. Tan, B. Draganski, H. Johnson, J. S. Paulsen, W. Kienzle, S. J. Tabrizi, J. Ashburner, and R. S. Frackowiak. Automatic detection of preclinical neurodegeneration: Presymptomatic Huntington disease. *Neurology*, 72(5):426–431, 2009. [306]

D. C. Knill and W. Richards, editors. *Perception as Bayesian Inference.* Cambridge University Press, 1996. [159]

C. Koch. *Biophysics of Computation: Information Processing in Single Neurons.* Oxford University Press, 1999. [7]

C. Koch and A. Jones. Big science, team science, and open science for neuroscience. *Neuron*, 92: 612–616, 2016. [21]

C. Koch and I. Segev. The role of single neurons in information processing. *Nature Neuroscience*, 3: 1171–1177, 2000. [43]

R. Kohavi. Scaling up the accuracy of naive-Bayes classifiers: A decision-tree hybrid. In *Proceedings of the 2nd International Conference on Knowledge Discovery and Data Mining*, pages 202–207, 1996. [409]

R. Kohavi and G. H. John. Wrappers for feature subset selection. *Artificial Intelligence*, 97(1):273–324, 1997. [242]

T. Kohonen. Self-organized formation of topologically correct feature maps. *Biological Cybernetics*, 43:59–69, 1982. [319, 448]

T. Kohonen. *Self-Organizing Maps.* Springer, 1997. [448]

M. Koivisto and K. Sood. Exact Bayesian structure discovery in Bayesian networks. *Journal of Machine Learning Research*, 5:549–573, 2004. [536, 546]

D. Koller and N. Friedman. *Probabilistic Graphical Models: Principles and Techniques.* The MIT Press, 2009. [29, 490, 515, 543, 544, 550, 562, 569]

D. Koller and A. Pfeffer. Object-oriented Bayesian networks. In *Proceedings of the 13th Conference on Uncertainty in Artificial Intelligence*, pages 302–313. Morgan Kaufmann, 1997. [543]

D. Koller and M. Sahami. Toward optimal feature selection. In *Proceedings of the 13th International Conference on Machine Learning*, pages 284–292, 1996. [363, 367]

A. N. Kolmogorov. Sulla determinazione empirica di una lege di distribuzione. *Giornale dell'Instituto Italiano degli Attuari*, 4:83–91, 1933a. [197]

A. N. Kolmogorov. *Grundbegriffe der Wahrscheinlichkeitsrechnung.* Springer, 1933b. [140]

J. Kolodner. *Case-based Reasoning.* Morgan Kaufmann, 1993. [29]

P. Kontkanen, P. Myllymäki, and H. Tirri. Constructing Bayesian finite mixture models by the EM algorithm. Technical Report C-1996-9, University of Helsinki, 1996. [351, 352]

K. Körding. Decision theory: What "should" the nervous system do? *Science*, 318:606–610, 2007. [159]

P. Kosa, M. Komori, R. Waters, T. Wu, I. Cortese, J. Ohayon, K. Fenton, J. Cherup, T. Gedeon, and B. Bielekova. Novel composite MRI scale correlates highly with disability in multiple sclerosis patients. *Multiple Sclerosis and Related Disorders*, 4(6):526–535, 2015. [190]

S. B. Kotsiantis. Decision trees: A recent overview. *Artificial Intelligence Review*, 39(4):261–283, 2013. [318]

J. R. Koza. *Genetic Programming*. The MIT Press, 1992. [250]

J. Kozloski, F. Hamzei-Sichani, and R. Yuste. Stereotyped position of local synaptic targets in neocortex. *Science*, 293:868–872, 2001. [34]

A. V. Kozlov and D. Koller. Nonuniform dynamic discretization in hybrid networks. In *Proceedings of the 13th Conference on Uncertainty in Artificial Intelligence*, pages 314–325. Morgan Kaufmann, 1997. [499]

H.-P. Kriegel, P. Kröger, and A. Zimek. Clustering high dimensional data: A survey on subspace clustering, pattern-based clustering, and correlation clustering. *ACM Transactions on Knowledge Discovery from Data*, 3:1–58, 2009. [458]

H.-P. Kriegel, P. Kröger, J. Sander, and A. Zimek. Density-based clustering. *WIRES Data Mining and Knowledge Discovery*, 1:231–240, 2011. [454]

R. Krishnapuram and J. M. Keller. The possibilistic C-means algorithm. Insights and recommendations. *IEEE Transactions on Fuzzy Systems*, 4:385–393, 1996. [467]

R. Krishnapuraxa, O. Nasraoui, and H. Frigui. The fuzzy c spherical shells algorithm, a new approach. *IEEE Transactions on Neural Networks*, 16:663–671, 1992. [454]

J. B. Kruskal. On the shortest spanning subtree of a graph and the traveling salesman problem. *Proceedings of the American Mathematical Society*, 7(1):48–50, 1956. [356, 562]

W. H. Kruskal and W. A. Wallis. Use of ranks in one-criterion variance analysis. *Journal of the American Statistical Association*, 47:583–621, 1952. [187]

F. R. Kschischang, B. J. Frey, and H. A. Loeliger. Factor graphs and the sum-product algorithm. *IEEE Transactions on Information Theory*, 47(2):498–519, 2001. [553]

R. Küffner, N. Zach, R. Norel, J. Hawe, D. Schoenfeld, L. Wang, G. Li, L. Fang, L. Mackey, O. Hardiman, M. Cudkowicz, A. Sherman, G. Ertaylan, M. Grosse-Wentrup, T. Hothorn, J. van Ligtenberg, J. H. Macke, T. Meyer, B. Schölkopf, L. Tran, R. Vaughan, G. Stolovitzky, and M. L. Leitner. Crowdsourced analysis of clinical trial data to predict amyotrophic lateral sclerosis progression. *Nature Biotechnology*, 33:51–57, 2015. [21]

H. W. Kuhn and A. W. Tucker. Nonlinear programming. In *Proceedings of the 2nd Berkeley Symposium on Mathematical Statistics and Probability*, pages 481–492. University of California Press, Berkeley and Los Angeles, 1951. [319]

J. Kuipers, G. Moffa, and D. Heckerman. Addendum on the scoring of Gaussian directed acyclic graphical models. *The Annals of Statistics*, 42(4):1689–1691, 2014. [535]

S. Kullback and R. A. Leibler. On information and sufficiency. *Annals of Mathematical Statistics*, 22 (1):79–86, 1951. [139]

L. I. Kuncheva. *Combining Pattern Classifiers: Methods and Algorithms*. Wiley, 2004. [390, 394, 413]

L. I. Kuncheva. A stability index for feature selection. In *Proceedings of the 25th International Multi-Conference on Artificial Intelligence and Applications*, pages 421–427. ACTA Press Anaheim, 2007. [256]

L. Kurgan and K. J. Cios. CAIM discretization algorithm. *IEEE Transactions on Knowledge and Data Engineering*, 16(2):145–153, 2004. [92]

A. K. Kurtz. A research test of Rorschach test. *Personnel Psychology*, 1:41–53, 1948. [213]

C. K. Kwoh and D. Gillies. Using hidden nodes in Bayesian networks. *Artificial Intelligence*, 88: 1–38, 1996. [351, 352]

P. A. Lachenbruch and M. R. Mickey. Estimation of error rates in discriminant analysis. *Technometrics*, 10(1):1–11, 1968. [268]

J. Lafferty, A. McCallum, and F. Pereira. Conditional random fields: Probabilistic models for segmenting and labelling sequence data. In *Proceedings of the 19th International Conference on Machine Learning*, pages 282–289. Morgan Kaufmann, 2001. [565]

W. Lam and F. Bacchus. Learning Bayesian belief networks: An approach based on the MDL principle. *Computational Intelligence*, 10:269–293, 1994. [532]

L. Lan and S. Vucetic. Improving accuracy of microarray classification by a simple multi-task feature selection filter. *International Journal of Data Mining and Bioinformatics*, 5(2):189–208, 2011. [232, 235]

N. Landwehr, M. Hall, and E. Frank. Logistic model trees. *Machine Learning*, 59(1–2):161–205, 2003. [410]

D. D. Langleben, J. W. Loughead, W. B. Bilker, K. Ruparel, A. R. Childress, S. I. Busch, and R. C. Gur. Telling truth from lie in individual subjects with fast event-related fMRI. *Human Brain Mapping*, 26(4):262–272, 2005. [332]

P. Langley and S. Sage. *Computational Learning Theory and Natural Learning Systems*, chapter Scaling to domains with irrelevant features, pages 51–63. The MIT Press, 1994a. [238, 261]

P. Langley and S. Sage. Induction of selective Bayesian classifiers. In *Proceedings of the 10th Conference on Uncertainty in Artificial Intelligence*, pages 399–406. Morgan Kaufmann, 1994b. [227, 261, 351, 353, 367]

H. Langseth and T. D. Nielsen. Classification using hierarchical naïve Bayes models. *Machine Learning*, 63(2):135–159, 2006. [351, 352]

H. Langseth, T. D. Nielsen, R. Rumí, and A. Salmerón. Parameter estimation and model selection for mixtures of truncated exponentials. *International Journal of Approximate Reasoning*, 51:485–498, 2010. [376, 537]

H. Langseth, T. D. Nielsen, R. Rumí, and A. Salmerón. Mixtures of truncated basis functions. *International Journal of Approximate Reasoning*, 53(2):212–227, 2012. [502, 503]

P. S. Laplace. Mémorie sur la probabilité des causes par les événements. *Mémoires de l'Académie Royale des Sciences de Paris*, 6:621–656, 1774. [140]

P. S. Laplace. *Théorie Analytique des Probabilités*. Courcier, 1836. [140]

A. U. Larkman. Dendritic morphology of pyramidal neurones of the visual cortex of the rat: I. Branching patterns. *Journal of Comparative Neurology*, 306:307–319, 1991. [44]

P. Larrañaga and C. Bielza. Alan Turing and Bayesian statistics. *Mathware & Soft Computing Magazine*, 19(2):23–24, 2012. [159]

P. Larrañaga and J. A. Lozano, editors. *Estimation of Distribution Algorithms. A New Tool for Evolutionary Computation*. Kluwer Academic Publishers, 2002. [249]

P. Larrañaga, C. M. H. Kuijpers, R. H. Murga, and Y. Yurramendi. Learning Bayesian network structures by searching for the best ordering with genetic algorithms. *IEEE Transactions on Systems, Man and Cybernetics, Part A*, 26(4):487–493, 1996a. [531]

P. Larrañaga, M. Poza, Y. Yurramendi, R. H. Murga, and C. M. H. Kuijpers. Structure learning of Bayesian networks by genetic algorithms: A performance analysis of control parameters. *IEEE Transactions on Pattern Analysis and Machine Intelligence*, 18(9):912–926, 1996b. [536]

P. Larrañaga, C. M. H. Kuijpers, M. Poza, and R. H. Murga. Decomposing Bayesian networks: Triangulation of the moral graph with genetic algorithms. *Statistics and Computing*, 7(1):19–34, 1997. [511]

P. Larrañaga, R. Etxeberria, J. A. Lozano, and J. M. Peña. Optimization in continuous domains by learning and simulation of Gaussian networks. In *Proceedings of the 2000 Genetic and Evolutionary Computation Conference*, pages 201–204. Morgan Kaufmann, 2000. [536]

M. Laubach. Wavelet-based processing of neuronal spike trains prior to discriminant analysis. *Journal of Neuroscience Methods*, 134:159–168, 2004. [326]

M. Laubach, M. Shuler, and M. A. L. Nicolelis. Independent component analyses for quantifying neuronal ensemble interactions. *Journal of Neuroscience Methods*, 94(1):141–154, 1999. [82]

S. L. Lauritzen. Propagation of probabilities, means and variances in mixed graphical association models. *Journal of the American Statistical Association*, 87:1098–1108, 1992. [503, 515]

S. L. Lauritzen. The EM algorithm for graphical association models with missing data. *Computational Statistics & Data Analysis*, 19:191–201, 1995. [479, 522]

S. L. Lauritzen. *Graphical Models*. Oxford University Press, 1996. [529, 543]

S. L. Lauritzen and F. V. Jensen. Stable local computation with conditional Gaussian distributions. *Statistics and Computing*, 11(2):191–203, 2001. [503, 515]

S. L. Lauritzen and D. J. Spiegelhalter. Local computations with probabilities on graphical structures and their application to expert systems. *Journal of the Royal Statistical Society, Series B*, 50(2): 157–224, 1988. [479, 509]

S. L. Lauritzen and N. Wermuth. Graphical models for associations between variables, some of which are qualitative and some quantitative. *The Annals of Statistics*, 17(1):31–57, 1989. [502, 570]

S. L. Lauritzen, A. P. Dawid, B. N. Larsen, and H.-G. Leimer. Independence properties of directed Markov fields. *Networks*, 20(5):491–505, 1990. [494]

E. L. Lawler and D. E. Wood. Branch-and-bound methods. A survey. *Operations Research*, 149(4), 1966. [242]

M. Lawton, F. Baig, M. Rolinski, C. Ruffman, K. Nithi, M. T. May, Y. Ben-Shlomo, and M. T. Hu. Parkinson's disease subtypes in the Oxford Parkinson disease center (OPDC) discovery cohort. *Journal of Parkinson's Disease*, 5(2):269–279, 2015. [88]

C. Lazar, J. Taminau, S. Meganck, D. Steenhoff, A. Coletta, C. Molter, V. de Schaetzen, R. Duque, H. Bersini, and A. Nowé. A survey on filter techniques for feature selection in gene expression microarray analysis. *IEEE/ACM Transactions on Computational Biology and Bioinformatics*, 9 (4):1106–1119, 2012. [261]

P. F. Lazarsfeld and N. W. Henry. *Latent Structure Analysis*. Houghton Mifflin, 1968. [478]

L. Le Cam. The central limit theorem around 1935. *Statistical Science*, 1(1):78–91, 1986. [196]

C. Le Mouel, K. D. Harris, and P. Yger. Supervised learning with decision margins in pools of spiking neurons. *Journal of Computational Neuroscience*, 37(2):333–344, 2014. [302]

G. Lee, K. Nho, B. Kang, K.-A. Sohn, and D. Kim. Predicting Alzheimer's disease progression using multi-modal deep learning approach. *Scientific Reports*, 9:1952, 2019. [300]

J. Lee and D.-W. Kim. Feature selection for multi-label classification using multivariate mutual information. *Pattern Recognition Letters*, 34(3):349–357, 2013. [434]

K. Lee and J. J. Koval. Determination of the best significance level in forward stepwise logistic regression. *Communications in Statistics – Simulation and Computation*, 26:559–575, 1997. [261]

P. W. Lee, Z. Wang, S. J. Palmer, and M. J. McKeown. Spectral clustering of fMRI data within regions of interest: Clarification of L-dopa effects in Parkinson's disease. In *Proceedings of the 29th Annual International Conference of the IEEE Engineering in Medicine and Biology Society*, pages 5235–5238. IEEE Press, 2007a. [452]

S.-I. Lee, V. Ganapathi, and D. Koller. Efficient structure learning of Markov networks using l_1-regularization. In *Advances in Neural Information Processing Systems 19*, pages 817–824, 2007b. [564]

A. J. Lees, J. Hardy, and T. Revesz. Parkinson's disease. *Lancet*, 373:2055–2066, 2009. [433]

I. Leguey, C. Bielza, P. Larrañaga, A. Kastanauskaite, C. Rojo, R. Benavides-Piccione, and J. DeFelipe. Dendritic branching angles of pyramidal cells across layers of the juvenile rat somatosensory cortex. *Journal of Comparative Neurology*, 524(13):2567–2576, 2016. [63, 66, 67, 113, 127, 169, 181]

I. Leguey, C. Bielza, and P. Larrañaga. Circular Bayesian classifiers using wrapped Cauchy distributions. *Data and Knowledge Engineering*, 122, 101–115, 2019. [148]

F. Leitner, C. Bielza, S. L. Hill, and P. Larrañaga. Data publications correlate with citation impact. *Frontiers in Neuroscience*, 10:Article 419, 2016. [21]

B. Lenne, J. L. Blanc, J. L. Nandrino, P. Gallois, P. Hautecur, and L. Pezard. Decrease of mutual information in brain electrical activity of patients with relapsing-remitting multiple sclerosis. *Behavioural Neurology*, 27(2):201–212, 2013. [139]

C. Léon, S. Pin, C. Kreft-Jaïs, and P. Arwidson. Perceptions of Alzheimer's disease in the French population: Evolutions between 2008 and 2013 and associated factors in 2013. *Journal of Alzheimer's Disease*, 47(2):467–478, 2015. [192]

U. Lerner and R. Parr. Inference in hybrid networks: Theoretical limits and practical algorithms. In *Proceedings of the 17th Conference on Uncertainty in Artificial Intelligence*, pages 310–318. Morgan Kaufmann, 2001. [515]

U. Lerner, E. Segal, and D. Koller. Exact inference in networks with discrete children of continuous parents. In *Proceedings of the 17th Conference on Uncertainty in Artificial Intelligence*, pages 319–328. Morgan Kaufmann, 2001. [503]

P. M. Lewis. The characteristic selection problem in recognition systems. *IRE Transactions on Information Theory*, 8:171–178, 1962. [227]

C. Li and M. Ueno. An extended depth-first search algorithm for optimal triangulation of Bayesian networks. *International Journal of Approximate Reasoning*, 80:294–312, 2017. [511]

C. Li, M. Welling, J. Zhu, and B. Zhang. Graphical generative adversarial networks. In *Proceedings of the 32nd Conference on Neural Information Processing Systems*, pages 6072–6083, 2018. [544]

J. Li and Z. J. Wang. Controlling the false discovery rate of the association/causality structure learned with the PC algorithm. *Journal of Machine Learning Research*, 10:475–514, 2009. [529]

J. Li, S. Ray, and B. Lindsay. A nonparametric statistical approach to clustering via mode identification. *Journal of Machine Learning Research*, 8:1687–1723, 2007. [486]

R.-H. Li and G. G. Belford. Instability of decision tree classification algorithms. In *Proceedings of the 8th ACM SIGKDD International Conference on Knowledge Discovery and Data Mining*, pages 570–575. ACM, 2002. [318]

F. Liang, C. Liu, and R. Carroll. *Advanced Markov Chain Monte Carlo Methods: Learning from Past Samples*. Wiley, 2010. [545]

X. X. Liao, Z. X. Zhan, Y. Y. Luo, K. Li, J. L. Wang, J. F. Guo, X. X. Yan, K. Xia, B. S. Tang, and L. Shen. Association study between SNP rs150689919 in the DNA demethylation gene, TET1, and Parkinson's disease in Chinese Han population. *BMC Neurology*, 13(196), 2013. [192]

J. W. Lichtman, H. Pfister, and N. Shavit. The big data challenges of connectomics. *Nature Neuroscience*, 17:1448–1454, 2014. [19]

T.-S. Lim, W.-Y. Loh, and Y.-S. Shih. A comparison of prediction accuracy, complexity, and training time of thirty-three old and new classification algorithms. *Machine Learning*, 40(3):203-228, 2000. [318]

S. W. Lin, K. C. Ying, S. C. Chen, and Z. J. Lee. Particle swarm optimization for parameter determination and feature selection of support vector machines. *Expert Systems with Applications*, 35:1817-1824, 2008. [241, 247]

I. Lipkovich, L. Citrome, R. Perlis, W. Deberdt, J. P. Houston, J. Ahl, and T. Hardy. Early predictors of substantial weight gain in bipolar patients treated with olanzapine. *Journal of Clinical Psychopharmacology*, 26(3):316–320, 2006. [283]

R. J. A. Little and D. B. Rubin. *Statistical Analysis with Missing Data*. Wiley, 1987. [95]

H. Liu and H. Motoda. *Feature Selection for Knowledge Discovery and Data Mining*. Kluwer Academic Publishers, 1998. [241, 244, 259]

H. Liu and H. Motoda. *Computational Methods of Feature Selection*. Chapman and Hall, 2008. [259]

H. Liu and R. Setiono. A probabilistic approach to feature selection: A filter solution. In *Proceedings of the 13th International Conference on Machine Learning*. Morgan Kaufmann, pages 319–327, 1996. [236, 237]

H. Liu, F. Hussain, C. L. Tan, and M. Dash. Discretization: An enabling technique. *Data Mining and Knowledge Discovery*, 6(4):393–423, 2002. [90]

J. N. K. Liu, N. L. Li, and T. S. Dillon. An improved naive Bayes classifier technique coupled with a novel input solution method. *IEEE Transactions on Systems, Man, and Cybernetics, Part C*, 31: 249–256, 2001. [353]

M. Liu, A. Hommersom, M. van der Heijden, and P. J. F. Lucas. Hybrid time Bayesian networks. In *Proceedings of the 13th European Conference in Symbolic and Quantitative Approaches to Reasoning with Uncertainty*, pages 376–386. Springer, 2015. [546]

W. Liu, P. Zhu, J. S. Anderson, D. Yurgelun-Todd, and P. T. Fletcher. Spatial regularization of functional connectivity using high-dimensional Markov random fields. In *International Conference on Medical Image Computing and Computer-Assisted Intervention*, pages 363–370, 2010. [547]

Z. Liu, B. Malone, and C. Yuan. Empirical evaluation of scoring functions for Bayesian network model selection. *BMC Bioinformatics*, 13(Suppl 15):S14, 2012. [546]

S. P. Lloyd. Least squares quantization in PCM. *IEEE Transactions on Information Theory*, 28(2): 129–137, 1982. [467]

R. A. Lockhart and M. A. Stephens. Tests of fit for the von Mises distribution. *Biometrika*, 72(3): 647–652, 1985. [169]

D. O. Loftsgaarden and C. P. Quesenberry. A nonparametric estimate of multivariate density function. *The Annals of Mathematical Statistics*, 36:1049–1051, 1965. [268]

W.-Y. Loh. Fifty years of classification and regression trees. *International Statistical Review*, 82(3): 329–348, 2014. [318]

W.-Y. Loh and Y.-S. Shih. Split selection methods for classification trees. *Statistica Sinica*, 7:815–840, 1997. [283]

M. London, A. Schreibman, M. Häusser, M. E. Larkum, and I. Segev. The information efficacy of a synapse. *Nature Reviews Neuroscience*, 5(4):332–340, 2002. [139]

P. L. López-Cruz, C. Bielza, P. Larrañaga, R. Benavides-Piccione, and J. DeFelipe. Models and simulation of 3D neuronal dendritic trees using Bayesian networks. *Neuroinformatics*, 9:347–369, 2011. [44, 46, 129, 139, 539, 541]

P. L. López-Cruz, C. Bielza, and P. Larrañaga. Learning conditional linear Gaussian classifiers with probabilistic class labels. In *Proceedings of the 15th MultiConference of the Spanish Association for Artificial Intelligence*, pages 139–148. Springer, 2013. [386]

P. L. López-Cruz, C. Bielza, and P. Larrañaga. Learning mixtures of polynomials of multidimensional probability densities from data using B-spline interpolation. *International Journal of Approximate Reasoning*, 55(4):989–1010, 2014a. [379, 380, 384]

P. L. López-Cruz, P. Larrañaga, J. DeFelipe, and C. Bielza. Bayesian network modeling of the consensus between experts: An application to neuron classification. *International Journal of Approximate Reasoning*, 55(1):3–22, 2014b. [546]

P. L. López-Cruz, C. Bielza, and P. Larrañaga. Directional naive Bayes classifiers. *Pattern Analysis and Applications*, 18:225–246, 2015. [380, 381, 382, 383, 384]

R. López de Mántaras. A distance-based attribute selection measure for decision tree induction. *Machine Learning*, 6(1):81–92, 1991. [278]

F. M. Lu and Z. Yuan. PET/SPECT molecular imaging in clinical neuroscience: Recent advances in the investigation of CNS diseases. *Quantitative Imaging in Medicine and Surgery*, 5(3):433–447, 2015. [16]

Z. Lu, H. Pu, F. Wang, Z. Hu, and L. Wang. The expressive power of neural networks: A view from the width. In *Proceedings of the 31st Conference on Neural Information Processing Systems*, 2017. [299]

P. Lucas. *Advances in Bayesian Networks*, chapter Restricted Bayesian network structure learning, pages 217–232. Springer, 2004. [358, 359, 367]

R. D. Luce and A. D. Perry. A method of matrix analysis of group structure. *Psychometrika*, 14(2): 95–116, 1949. [544]

S. Luengo-Sanchez, C. Bielza, and P. Larrañaga. Hybrid Gaussian and von Mises model-based clustering. In *22nd European Conference on Artificial Intelligence*, pages 855–862. IOS Press, 2016. [484]

S. Luengo-Sanchez, I. Fernaud-Espinosa, C. Bielza, R. Benavides-Piccione, P. Larrañaga, and J. DeFelipe. 3D morphology-based clustering and simulation of human pyramidal cell dendritic spines. *PLoS Computational Biology*, 14(6):Article e1006221, 2018. [41, 42, 465, 475, 484]

S. Luengo-Sanchez, P. Larrañaga, and C. Bielza. A directional-linear Bayesian network for clustering and simulation of neural somas. *IEEE Access*, 7:69907–69921, 2019. [484]

D. Lunn, C. Jackson, N. Best, A. Thomas, and D. Spiegelhalter. *The BUGS Book: A Practical Introduction to Bayesian Analysis*. Chapman & Hall/CRC, 2012. [545]

G. Luo and W. Min. Subject-adaptive real-time sleep stage classification based on conditional random fields. In *AMIA Annual Symposium Proceedings*, pages 488–492, 2007. [566]

L. B. Lusted. Logical analysis in roentgen diagnosis. *Radiology*, 74:178–193, 1960. [208]

U. V. Luxburg. A tutorial on spectral clustering. *Statistics and Computing*, 17:395–416, 2007. [450, 467]

A. I. R. Maas, C. L. Harrison-Felix, D. Menon, P. D. Adelson, T. Balkin, R. Bullock, D. C. Engel, W. Gordon, J. Langlois-Orman, H. L. Lew, C. Robertson, N. Temkin, A. Valadka, M. Verfaellie, M. Wainwright, D. W. Wright, and K. Schwab. Standardizing data collection in traumatic brain injury. *Journal of Neurotrauma*, 28(2):177–187, 2011. [20]

W. Maas. Networks of spiking neurons: The third generation of neural network models. *Neural Networks*, 10:1659–1671, 1997. [300]

V. MacDonald, G. M. Halliday, R. J. Trent, and E. A. McCusker. Significant loss of pyramidal neurons in the angular gyrus of patients with Huntington's disease. *Neuropathology and Applied Neurobiology*, 23(6):492–495, 1997. [179]

P. Macnaughton-Smith, W. T. Williams, M. B. Dale, and L. G. Mockett. Dissimilarity analysis: A new technique of hierarchical sub-division. *Nature*, 202:1034–1035, 1964. [442]

J. MacQueen. Some methods for classification and analyisis of multivariate observations. In *Proceedings of 5th Berkeley Symposium on Mathematical Statistics and Probability*, pages 281–297, 1967. [444, 445, 467]

M. G. Madden. On the classification performance of TAN and general Bayesian networks. *Knowledge-Based Systems*, 22(7):489–495, 2009. [366]

S. C. Madeira and A. L. Oliveira. Biclustering algorithms for biological data analysis: A survey. *IEEE Transaction on Computational Biology and Bioinformatics*, 1(1):24–45, 2004. [468]

D. Madigan and J. York. Bayesian graphical models for discrete data. *International Statistical Review*, 63(2):215–232, 1995. [519]

D. Madigan, S. A. Andersson, M. D. Perlman, and C. T. Volinsky. Bayesian model averaging and model selection for Markov equivalence classes of acyclic digraphs. *Communications in Statistics – Theory and Methods*, 25:2493–2519, 1996. [546]

G. Madjarov, D. Kocev, D. Gjorgjevikj, and S. Džeroski. An extensive experimental comparison of methods for multi-label learning. *Pattern Recognition*, 45(9):3084–3104, 2012. [427]

A. Mahfouz, M. van de Giessen, L. van der Maaten, S. Huisman, M. Reinders, M. J. Hawrylycz, and B. P. F. Lelieveldt. Visualizing the spatial gene expression organization in the brain through non-linear similarity embeddings. *Methods*, 73:79–89, 2015. [84]

Z. F. Mainen and T. J. Sejnowski. Influence of dendritic structure on firing pattern in model neocortical neurons. *Nature*, 382(6589):363–366, 1996. [43]

R. Maitra. Clustering massive datasets with applications to software metrics and tomography. *Technometrics*, 43(3):336–346, 2001. [486]

N. Malek, D. M. Swallow, K. A. Grosset, M. A. Lawton, C. R. Smith, N. P. Bajaj, R. A. Barker, Y. Ben-Shlomo, C. Bresner, D. J. Burn, T. Foltynie, H. R. Morris, N. Williams, N. W. Wood, D. G. Grosset, and PRoBaND Investigators. Olfaction in Parkin single and compound heterozygotes in a cohort of young onset Parkinson's disease patients. *Acta Neurologica Scandinavica*, 134(4): 271–276, 2016. [186]

B. Malone, C. Yuan, and E. A. Hansen. Memory-efficient dynamic programming for learning optimal Bayesian networks. In *Proceedings of the 25th AAAI Conference on Artificial Intelligence*, pages 1057–1062. AAAI Press, 2011. [536]

M. Manca, G. Ferraresi, M. Cosma, L. Cavazzuti, M. Morelli, and M. G. Benedetti. Gait patterns in hemiplegic patients with equinus foot deformity. *BioMed Research International*, 2014:Article 939316, 2014. [440]

B. Mandelbrot. *The Fractal Geometry of Nature*. Freeman, 1982. [36]

H. B. Mann and D. R. Whitney. On a test of whether one of two random variables is stochastically larger than the other. *Annals of Mathematical Statistics*, 18(1):50–60, 1947. [178]

K. V. Mardia and P. E. Jupp. *Directional Statistics*. Wiley, 2000. [62]

K. V. Mardia, J. T. Kent, and J. M. Bibby. *Multivariate Analysis*. Academic Press, 1979. [457]

K. V. Mardia, G. Hughes, C. C. Taylor, and H. Singh. A multivariate von Mises distribution with applications to bioinformatics. *The Canadian Journal of Statistics*, 36(1):99–109, 2008. [122]

D. Margaritis and G. Bromberg. Efficient Markov network structure discovery using particle filter. *Computational Intelligence*, 25(4):367–394, 2009. [571]

D. Margaritis and V. Thrun. Bayesian network induction via local neighborhoods. In *Advances in Neural Information Processing Systems 12*, volume 12, pages 505–511. The MIT Press, 2000. [363, 529, 563]

T. Marill and D. M. Green. On the effectiveness of receptors in recognition systems. *IEEE Transactions on Information Theory*, 9:11–17, 1963. [240, 241]

E. C. Marin, T. Jefferis, G. S. Komiyama, H. Zhu, and L. Luo. Representation of the glomerular olfactory map in the drosophila brain. *Cell*, 109:243–255, 2002. [82, 215, 326]

M. Markatou, H. Tian, G. Biswas, and S. Hripcsak. Analysis of variance of cross-validation estimators of the generalization error. *Journal of Machine Learning Research*, 6:1127–1168, 2005. [225]

M. Maron and J. Kuhns. On relevance, probabilistic indexing, and information retrieval. *Journal of the Association for Computing Machinery*, 7:216–244, 1960. [350, 367]

C. L. Martin and M. Chun. The BRAIN Initiative: Building, strengthening, and sustaining. *Neuron*, 92:570–573, 2016. [9]

P. Martin-Lof. The notion of redundancy and its use as a quantitative measure of the discrepancy between a statistical hypothesis and a set of observational data. *Scandinavian Journal of Statistics*, 1:3–18, 1974. [485]

M. Martínez-Ramón, V. Koltchinskii, G. L. Heileman, and S. Posse. fMRI pattern classification using neuroanatomically constrained boosting. *NeuroImage*, 31(3):1129–1141, 2006. [406]

A. M. Martínez-Rodríguez, J. H. May, and L. G. Vargas. An optimization-based approach for the design of Bayesian networks. *Mathematical and Computer Modelling*, 48(7-8):1265–1278, 2008. [536]

A. R. Masegosa and S. Moral. An interactive approach for Bayesian network learning using domain/expert knowledge. *International Journal of Approximate Reasoning*, 54(8):1168–1181, 2013. [546]

M. S. Matell, E. Shea-Brown, C. Gooch, A. G. Wilson, and J. Rinzel. A heterogeneous population code for elapsed time in rat medial agranular cortex. *Behavioral Neuroscience*, 125(1):54–73, 2011. [326]

B. Matérn. *Spatial Variation: Stochastic Models and Their Application to Some Problems in Forest Surveys and Other Sampling Investigations*. PhD thesis, Meddelanden från Statens Skogsforskningsinstitut, 1960. [605]

M. Matsuzaki, N. Honkura, G. C. Ellis-Davies, and H. Kasai. Structural basis of long-term potentiation in single dendritic spines. *Nature*, 429:761–766, 2004. [41]

A. Matus. Actin-based plasticity in dendritic spines. *Science*, 290:754–758, 2000. [41]

I. Matzkevich and B. Abramson. The topological fusion of Bayes nets. In *Proceedings of the 8th Conference on Uncertainty in Artificial Intelligence*, pages 191–198. Morgan Kaufmann, 1992. [546]

P. McCullagh and J. A. Nelder. *Generalized Linear Models*. Chapman & Hall/CRC, 2nd edition, 1989. [385]

W. McCulloch and W. Pitts. A logical calculus of the ideas immanent in nervous activity. *Bulletin of Mathematical Biophysics*, 5:115–133, 1943. [318]

L. M. McGarry, A. M. Packer, E. Fino, V. Nikolenko, T. Sippy, and R. Yuste. Quantitative classification of somatostatin-positive neocortical interneurons identifies three interneuron subtypes. *Frontiers in Neural Circuits*, 4:Article 12, 2010. [34]

G. J. McLachlan and T. Krishnan. *The EM Algorithm and Extensions*. Wiley, 1997. [473, 475, 486]

G. J. McLachlan and D. Peel. *Finite Mixture Models*. Wiley, 2000. [373, 486]

Q. McNemar. Note on the sampling error of the difference between correlated proportions or percentages. *Psychometrika*, 12(2):153–157, 1947. [219]

C. Mead. *Analog VLSI and Neural Systems*. Addison-Wesley, 1989. [30]

C. Meek. *Graphical Models: Selecting Causal and Statistical Models*. PhD thesis, Carnegie Mellon University, 1997. [531]

L. Meier, S. van de Geer, and P. Bühlmann. The group lasso for logistic regression. *Journal of the Royal Statistical Society, Series B*, 70(1):53–71, 2008. [341]

M. Meilă. Comparing clustering by the variation of information. In *16th Annual Conference on Learning Theory*, pages 173–187, 2003. [462]

M. Meilă and M. I. Jordan. Learning with mixtures of trees. *Journal of Machine Learning Research*, 1:1–48, 2000. [570]

V. Melnykov and R. Maitra. Finite mixture models and model-based clustering. *Statistics Surveys*, 4:80–116, 2010. [478, 486]

P. Melville and R. J. Mooney. Creating diversity in ensembles using artificial data. *Information Fusion*, 6(1):99–111, 2005. [413]

X. L. Meng and D. Rubin. Maximum likelihood estimation via the ECM algorithm: A general framework. *Biometrika*, 80(2):267–278, 1993. [473]

J. Mercer. Functions of positive and negative type, and their connection with the theory of integral equations. *Philosophical Transactions of the Royal Society of London*, 83(559):69–70, 1909. [312]

A. Merchán-Pérez, J.-R. Rodríguez, L. Alonso-Nanclares, A. Schertel, and J. DeFelipe. Counting synapses using FIB/SEM microscopy: A true revolution for ultrastructural volume reconstruction. *Frontiers in Neuroanatomy*, 3:Article 18, 2009. [48, 601]

A. Merchán-Pérez, J.-R. Rodríguez, S. González, V. Robles, J. DeFelipe, P. Larrañaga, and C. Bielza. Three-dimensional spatial distribution of synapses in the neocortex: A dual-beam electron microscopy study. *Cerebral Cortex*, 24(6):1579–1588, 2014. [48, 49, 607, 610, 611]

P. A. Merolla, J. V. Arthur, R. Alvarez-Icaza, A. S. Cassidy, J. Sawada, F. Akopyand B. L. Jackson, N. Imam, C. Guo, Y. Nakamura, B. Brezzo, I. Vo, S. K. Esser, R. Appuswamy, B. Taba, A. Amir, M. D. Flickner, W. P. Risk, R. Manohar, and D. S. Modha. A million spiking-neuron integrated circuit with a scalable communication network and interface. *Science*, 345:668–673, 2014. [30]

N. Metropolis, A. W. Rosenbluth, M. N. Rosenbluth, A. H. Teller, and E. Teller. Equation of state calculations by fast computing machines. *The Journal of Chemical Physics*, 21(6):1087–1092, 1953. [519, 545, 609]

R. S. Michalski. On the quasi-minimal solution of the general covering problem. In *Proceedings of the 5th International Symposium on Information Processing*, pages 125–128, 1969. [287]

R. S. Michalski and R. Chilausky. Learning by being told and learning from examples: An experimental comparison of the two methods of knowledge acquisition in the context of developing an expert system for soybean disease diagnosis. *International Journal of Policy Analysis and Information Systems*, 4:125–160, 1980. [287]

R. S. Michalski and R. E. Stepp. Automated construction of classifications: Conceptual clustering versus numerical taxonomy. *IEEE Transactions on Pattern Analysis and Machine Intelligence*, 5 (4):396–410, 1983. [468]

D. Michie, D. J. Spiegelhalter, and C. C. Taylor. *Machine Learning, Neural and Statistical Classification*. Ellis Horwood, 1994. [29]

M. M. Mielke, J. M. Leoutsakos, J. T. Tschanz, R. C. Green, Y. Tripodis, C. D. Corcoran, M. C. Norton, and C. G. Lyketsos. Interaction between vascular factors and the APOE $\varepsilon 4$ allele in predicting rate of progression in Alzheimer's disease. *Journal of Alzheimer's Disease*, 26(1):127–134, 2011. [194]

B. Mihaljević, C. Bielza, R. Benavides-Piccione, J. DeFelipe, and P. Larrañaga. Multi-dimensional classification of GABAergic interneurons with Bayesian network-modeled label uncertainty. *Frontiers in Computational Neuroscience*, 8:Article 150, 2014. [417]

B. Mihaljević, R. Benavides-Piccione, L. Guerra, J. DeFelipe, P. Larrañaga, and C. Bielza. Classifying GABAergic interneurons with semi-supervised projected model-based clustering. *Artificial Intelligence Medicine*, 65(1):49–59, 2015. [475, 486]

E. Miller. Effectiveness of rehabilitation in multiple sclerosis. *Polski Merkuriusz Lekarski*, 26(153): 205–207, 2009. [175]

G. W. Milligan. An examination of the effect of six types of error perturbation on fifteen clustering algorithms. *Psychometrika*, 45:325–342, 1980. [467]

G. W. Milligan. A Monte-Carlo study of thirty internal criterion measures for cluster analysis. *Psychometrika*, 46:187–199, 1981. [458]

G. W. Milligan and M. C. Cooper. An examination of procedures for determining the number of clusters in a data set. *Psychometrica*, 50:159–179, 1985. [458, 468]

T. Minka. Expectation propagation for approximate Bayesian inference. In *Proceedings of the 17th Conference in Uncertainty in Artificial Intelligence*, pages 362–369. AUAI Press, 2001. [544, 570]

M. L. Minsky. Steps toward artificial intelligence. *Transactions on Institute of Radio Engineers*, 49: 8–30, 1961. [299, 350]

M. L. Minsky. Memoir on inventing the confocal scanning microscope. *Scanning*, 10:128–138, 1988. [13]

M. L. Minsky and S. A. Papert. *Perceptrons*. The MIT Press, 1969. [318]

B. Mirkin. Choosing the number of clusters. *WIREs Data Mining and Knowledge Discovery*, 1: 252–260, 2011. [456]

T. M. Mitchell, R. Hutchinson, R. S. Niculescu, F. Pereira, X. Wang, M. Just, and S. Newman. Learning to decode cognitive states from brain images. *Machine Learning*, 57(1–2):145–175, 2004. [239, 372]

D. Mladenic and M. Grobelnik. Feature selection for unbalanced class distribution and naive Bayes. In *Proceedings of the 16th International Conference on Machine Learning*, pages 258–267. Morgan Kaufmann, 1999. [232, 234, 352]

M. Mladenovic and P. Hansen. Variable neighborhood search. *Computers & Operations Research*, 24:1097–1100, 1997. [244]

F. B. Mohamed, S. Vinitski, C. F. Gonzalez, S. H. Faro, F. A. Lublin, R. Knobler, and J. E. Gutierrez. Increased differentiation of intracranial white matter lesions by multispectral 3D-tissue segmentation: Preliminary results. *Magnetic Resonance Imaging*, 19(2):207–218, 2001. [263]

R. Mojena. Hierarchical grouping methods and stopping rules. An evaluation. *The Computer Journal*, 20:359–363, 1977. [458, 465]

T. Moldwin and I. Segev. Perceptron learning and classification in a modeled cortical pyramidal cell. *Frontiers in Computional Neuroscience*, 14:Article 33, 2020. [297]

T. Mollayeva, B. Pratt, S. Mollayeva, C. M. Shapiro, J. D. Cassidy, and A. Colantonio. The relationship between insomnia and disability in workers with mild traumatic brain injury/concussion: Insomnia and disability in chronic mild traumatic brain injury. *Sleep Medicine*, 20:157–166, 2015. [192]

J. Moller and R. P. Waagepetersen. *Statistical Inference and Simulation for Spatial Point Processes.* Chapman & Hall/CRC, 2003. [611]

S. Monti and G. F. Cooper. A multivariate discretization method for learning Bayesian networks from mixed data. In *Proceedings of the 14th Conference on Uncertainty in Artificial Intelligence*, pages 404–413. Morgan Kaufmann, 1998. [499]

S. Monti and G. F. Cooper. A Bayesian network classifier that combines a finite mixture model and a naïve Bayes model. In *Proceedings of the 15th Conference on Uncertainty in Artificial Intelligence*, pages 447–456, 1999. [352]

S. Moral, R. Rumí, and A. Salmerón. Mixtures of truncated exponentials in hybrid Bayesian networks. In *Proceedings of the 6th European Conference in Symbolic and Quantitative Approaches to Reasoning with Uncertainty*, pages 156–167. Springer, 2001. [385, 502, 503]

D. Morales, Y. Vives-Gilabert, B. Gómez-Ansón, E. Bengoetxea, P. Larrañaga, C. Bielza, J. Pagonabarraga, J. Kulisevsky, I. Corcuera-Solano, and M. Delfino. Predicting dementia development in Parkinson's disease using Bayesian network classifiers. *Psychiatry Research: NeuroImaging*, 213:92–98, 2013. [238, 353]

J. Morales, L. Alonso-Nanclares, J.-R. Rodríguez, J. DeFelipe, A. Rodríguez, and A. Merchán-Pérez. Espina: A tool for the automated segmentation and counting of synapses in large stacks of electron microscopy images. *Frontiers in Neuroanatomy*, 5:Article 18, 2011. [14, 49]

J. Morales, R. Benavides-Piccione, M. Dar, I. Fernaud, A. Rodríguez, L. Anton-Sanchez, C. Bielza, P. Larrañaga, J. DeFelipe, and R. Yuste. Random positions of dendritic spines in human cerebral cortex. *Journal of Neuroscience*, 34(30):10078–10084, 2014. [591]

D. Moreno-Dominguez, A. Anwander, and T. R. Knösche. A hierarchical method for whole-brain connectivity-based parcellation. *Human Brain Mapping*, 35(10):5000–5025, 2014. [440]

E. Mori, M. Ikeda, R. Nagai, K. Matsuo, M. Nakagawa, and K. Kosaka. Long-term donepezil use for dementia with Lewy bodies: Results from an open-label extension of phase III trial. *Alzheimer's Research and Theraphy*, 7(1):5, 2015. [175]

M. Morisita. *Memoires of the Faculty of Science*, volume 185 of *Series E Biology*, chapter Measuring of the dispersion and analysis of distribution patterns, pages 215–235. Kyushu University, 1959. [585]

Z. Mortezapouraghdam, R. C. Wilson, L. Schwabe, and D. J. Strauss. Bayesian modeling of the dynamics of phase modulations and their application to auditory event related potentials at different loudness scales. *Frontiers in Computational Neuroscience*, 10:Article 2, 2016. [113]

J. Mu, K. R. Chaudhuri, C. Bielza, J. De Pedro, P. Larrañaga, and P. Martínez-Martín. Parkinson's disease subtypes identified from cluster analysis of motor and non-motor symptoms. *Frontiers in Aging Neuroscience*, 9:Article 301, 2017. [445]

K. Muata and O. Bryson. Post-pruning in decision tree induction using multiple performance measures. *Computers & Operations Research*, 34(11):3331–3345, 2007. [280]

I. Mukherjee and R. E. Schapire. A theory of multiclass boosting. *Journal of Machine Learning Research*, 14(1):437–497, 2013. [414]

J. A. Mumford and J. D. Ramsey. Bayesian networks for fMRI: A primer. *NeuroImage*, 86:573–582, 2014. [535]

D. P. Muni, N. R. Pal, and J. Das. A novel approach to design classifiers using genetic programming. *IEEE Transactions on Evolutionary Computation*, 8(2):183–196, 2004. [241, 250]

H. Mure, C. C. Tang, M. Argyelan, M. F. Ghilardi, M. G. Kaplitt, V. Dhawan, and D. Eidelberg. Improved sequence learning with subthalamic nucleus deep brain stimulation: Evidence for treatment-specific network modulation. *The Journal of Neuroscience*, 32(8):2804–2813, 2012. [195]

K. P. Murphy. *Dynamic Bayesian Networks: Representation, Inference and Learning*. PhD thesis, University of California at Berkeley, 2002. [537]

K. P. Murphy. *Machine Learning: A Probabilistic Perspective*. The MIT Press, 2012. [384, 569]

K. P. Murphy, Y. Weiss, and M. I. Jordan. Loopy belief propagation for approximate inference: An empirical study. In *Proceedings of the 15th Conference on Uncertainty in Artificial Intelligence*, pages 467–475. Morgan Kaufmann, 1999. [544]

F. Murtagh and P. Contreras. Algorithms for hierarchical clustering: An overview. *WIREs Data Mining and Knowledge Discovery*, 2:86–97, 2012. [439]

S. B. Murthy, Y. Moradiya, D. F. Hanley, and W. C. Ziai. Palliative care utilization in nontraumatic intracerebral hemorrhage in the United States. *Critical Care Medicine*, 44(3):575–582, 2016. [179, 192]

B. Mwangi, S. Tian, and J. C. Soares. A review of feature reduction techniques in neuroimaging. *Neuroinformatics*, 12:229–244, 2014. [226]

M. Myllymäki, I. G. Panoutsopoulou, and A. Särkkä. Analysis of spatial structure of epidermal nerve entry point patterns based on replicated data. *Journal of Microscopy*, 247:228–239, 2012. [592]

C. Nadeau and Y. Bengio. Inference for the generalization error. *Machine Learning*, 52(3):239–281, 2003. [218]

M. Narasimhan and J. A. Bilmes. A submodular-supermodular procedure with applications to discriminative structure learning. In *Proceedings of the 21st Conference on Uncertainty in Artificial Intelligence*, pages 404–412. AUAI Press, 2005. [385]

P. Narendra and K. Fukunaga. A branch and bound algorithm for feature subset selection. *IEEE Transactions on Computers*, 26:917–922, 1977. [241, 242]

Nature Neuroscience Editorial. Running the numbers. *Nature Neuroscience*, 8(2):123–123, 2005. [22]

C. S. Nayak, S. Sinha, M. Nagappa, T. Kandavel, and A. B. Taly. Effect of valproate on the sleep microstructure of juvenile myoclonic epilepsy patients – A cross-sectional CAP based study. *Sleep Medicine*, 17:129–133, 2016. [186]

R. M. Neal and G. E. Hinton. *Learning in Graphical Models*, chapter A view of the EM algorithm that justifies incremental, sparse, and other variants, pages 355–368. NATO Science Series, 1999. [473]

R. Neapolitan. *Learning Bayesian Networks*. Prentice Hall, 2003. [543]

P. B. Nemenyi. *Distribution-free Multiple Comparisons*. PhD thesis, Princeton University, 1963. [194]

Neuro Cloud Consortium. To the cloud! A grassroots proposal to accelerate brain science discovery. *Neuron*, 92:622–627, 2016. [18]

S. Newcomb. A generalized theory of the combination of observations so as to obtain the best results. *American Journal of Mathematics*, 8:343–366, 1886. [486]

M. Newton, C. Kendziorski, C. Richmond, C. Blattner, and K. Tsui. On differential variability of expression ratios: Improving statistical inference about gene expression changes from microarray data. *Journal of Computational Biology*, 8:37–52, 2001. [233]

J. Neyman and E. S. Pearson. On the use and interpretation of certain criteria for purposes of statistical inference. Part I. *Biometrika*, 20:175–240, 1928a. [197]

J. Neyman and E. S. Pearson. On the use and interpretation of certain criteria for purposes of statistical inference. Part II. *Biometrika*, 20:263–294, 1928b. [197]

J. Neyman and E. L. Scott. A theory of the spatial distribution of galaxies. *The Astrophysical Journal*, 116:144–163, 1952. [604]

A. Ng and M. Jordan. On discriminative vs. generative classifiers: A comparison of logistic regression and naïve Bayes. In *Advances in Neural Information Processing Systems 14*, pages 841–848. The MIT Press, 2002. [385]

J. D. Nielsen, T. Kočka, and J. M. Peña. On local optima in learning Bayesian networks. In *Proceedings of the 19th Conference on Uncertainty in Artificial Intelligence*, pages 435–442. Morgan Kaufmann, 2003. [531]

J. D. Nielsen, J. A. Gámez, and A. Salmerón. Modelling and inference with conditional Gaussian probabilistic decision graphs. *International Journal of Approximate Reasoning*, 53(7):929–945, 2012. [543]

J. L. Nielson, C. F. Guandique, A. W. Liu, D. A. Burke, A. T. Lash, R. Moseanko, S. Hawbecker, S. C. Strand, S. Zdunowski, K. A. Irvine, J. H. Brock, Y. S. Nout-Lomas, J. C. Gensel, K. D. Anderson, M. R. Segal, E. S. Rosenzweig, D. S. Magnuson, S. R. Whittemore, D. M. McTigue, P. G. Popovich, A. G. Rabchevsky, S. W. Scheff, O. Steward, G. Courtine, V. R. Edgerton, M. H. Tuszynski, M. S. Beattie, J. C. Bresnahan, and A. R. Ferguson. Development of a database for translational spinal cord injury research. *Journal of Neurotrauma*, 31(21):1789–1799, 2014. [20]

S. Nieuwenhuis, B. U. Forstmann, and E.-J. Wagenmakers. Erroneous analyses of interactions in neuroscience: A problem of significance. *Nature Neuroscience*, 14(9):1105–1107, 2011. [22]

J. B. Nikas and W. C. Low. Application of clustering analysis to the diagnosis of Huntington disease in mice and other diseases with well-defined group boundaries. *Computer Methods and Programs in Biomedicine*, 104(3):133–147, 2011. [453]

G. Niso, S. Carrasco, M. Gudín, F. Maestú, F. Del-Pozo, and F. Pereda. What graph theory actually tells us about resting state interictal MEG epileptic activity. *NeuroImage: Clinical*, 23(8):503–515, 2015. [454]

U. Nodelman, C. R. Shelton, and D. Koller. Continuous time Bayesian networks. In *Proceedings of the 18th Conference on Uncertainty in Artificial Intelligence*, pages 378–387, 2002. [546]

U. Nodelman, C. R. Shelton, and D. Koller. Learning continuous time Bayesian networks. In *Proceedings of the 19th Conference on Uncertainty in Artificial Intelligence*, pages 451–458, 2003. [546]

J. A. Nordin. Determining sample size. *Journal of the American Statistical Association*, 39:497–506, 1944. [195]

C. Nunes, D. Silva, M. Guerreiro, A. de Mendonca, A. M. Carvalho, and S. C Madeira. Class imbalance in the prediction of dementia from neuropsychological data. In *Proceedings of the 16th Portuguese Conference on Artificial Intelligence*, pages 138–151, 2013. [223]

Z. Nusser, R. Lujan, G. Laube, J. Roberts, E. Molnar, and P. Somogyi. Cell type and pathway dependence of synaptic AMPA receptor number and variability in the hippocampus. *Neuron*, 21:545–559, 1998. [39]

M. Ojala and G. C. Garriga. Permutation tests for studying classifier performance. *Journal of Machine Learning Research*, 11:1833–1863, 2010. [225]

A. Okabe and K. Sugihara. *Spatial Analysis Along Networks*. Wiley, 2012. [611]

H. Okano, E. Sasaki, T. Yamamori, A. Iriki, T. Shimogori, Y. Yamaguchi, K. Kasai, and A. Miyawaki. Brain/MINDS: A Japanese national brain project for marmoset neuroscience. *Neuron*, 92:582–590, 2016. [10]

K. G. Olesen. Causal probabilistic networks with both discrete and continuous variables. *IEEE Transactions on Pattern Analysis and Machine Intelligence*, 15(3):275–279, 1993. [502]

F. H. M. Oliveira, A. R. P. Machado, and A. O. Andrade. On the use of *t*-distributed stochastic neighbor embedding for data visualization and classification of individuals with Parkinson's disease. *Computational Mathematical Methods in Medicine*, 2018:Article 8019232, 2018. [84]

C. Olson. Parallel algorithms for hierarchical clustering. *Parallel Computing*, 21:1313–1325, 1995. [467]

M. A. Olude, O. A. Mustapha, O. A. Aderounmu, J. O. Olopade, and A. O. Ihunwo. Astrocyte morphology, heterogeneity, and density in the developing African giant rat (*Cricetomys gambianus*). *Frontiers in Neuroanatomy*, 9:Article 67, 2015. [178]

W. G. Ondo, R. Tintner, M. Thomas, and J. Jankovic. Tetrabenazine treatment for Huntington's disease-associated chorea. *Clinical Neuropharmacology*, 25(6):300–302, 2002. [176]

D. W. Opitz and R. Maclin. Popular ensemble methods: An empirical study. *Journal of Artificial Intelligence Research*, 11:169–198, 1999. [389]

M. Opper and D. Saad. *Advanced Mean Field Methods: Theory and Practice*. The MIT Press, 2001. [570]

A. Ortiz, J. M. Górriz, J. Ramírez, F. J. Martinez-Murcia, and Alzheimer's Disease Neuroimaging Initiative. Automatic ROI selection in structural brain MRI using SOM 3D projection. *PLoS ONE*, 9(4):e93851, 2014. [449]

M. Osborne, B. Presnell, and B. Turlach. On the LASSO and its dual. *Journal of Computational and Graphical Statistics*, 9(2):319–337, 2000. [341]

K.-M. Osei-Bryson and K. Giles. Splitting methods for decision tree induction: An exploration of the relative performance of two entropy-based families. *Information Systems Frontiers*, 8(3):195–209, 2006. [279]

M. Ota, N. Sato, M. Ishikawa, H. Hori, D. Sasayama, K. Hattori, T. Teraishi, S. Obu, Y. Nakata, K. Nemoto, Y. Moriguchi, R. Hashimoto, and H. Kunugi. Discrimination of female schizophrenia patients from healthy women using multiple structural brain measures obtained with voxel-based morphometry. *Psychiatry and Clinical Neurosciences*, 66:611–617, 2012. [326]

T. J. Ottosen and J. Vomlel. All roads lead to Rome – New search methods for the optimal triangulation problem. *International Journal of Approximate Reasoning*, 53(9):1350–1366, 2012. [511]

A. Ozcift. SVM feature selection based rotation forest ensemble classifiers to improve computer-aided diagnosis of Parkinson disease. *Journal of Medical Systems*, 36(4):2141–2147, 2011.

B. Ozenne, F. Subtil, L. Østergaard, and D. Maucort-Boulch. Spatially regularized mixture model for lesion segmentation with application to stroke patients. *Biostatistics*, 16(3):580–595, 2015. [475]

G. Pagallo and D. Hausler. Boolean feature discovery in empirical learning. *Machine Learning*, 9(1): 71–99, 1990. [288]

A. Painold, P. Anderer, A. K. Holl, M. Letmaier, G. M. Saletu-Zyhlarz, B. Saletu, and R. M. Bonelli. EEG low-resolution brain electromagnetic tomography (LORETA) in Huntington's disease. *Journal of Neurology*, 285(5):840–854, 2011. [190]

W. Pan. On the use of permutation in and the performance of a class of nonparametric methods to detect differential gene expression. *Bioinformatics*, 19(11):1333–1340, 2003. [232, 236]

W. Pan and X. Shen. Penalized model-based clustering with application to variable selection. *Journal of Machine Learning Research*, 8:1145–1164, 2006. [478]

Y. Pan, M. Liu, C. Lian, T. Zhou, Y. Xia, and S. Shen. Synthesizing missing PET from MRI with cycle-consistent generative adversarial networks for Alzheimer disease diagnosis. In *21st International Conference on Medical Image Computing and Computer Assisted Intervention*, pages 455–463. Springer, 2018. [319]

J. D. Park and A. Darwiche. A differential semantics for jointree algorithms. *Artificial Intelligence*, 156(2):197–216, 2004. [544]

M. Y. Park and T. Hastie. Penalized logistic regression for detecting gene interactions. *Biostatistics*, 9(1):30–50, 2008. [343]

L. Parsons, E. Haque, and H. Liu. Subspace clustering for high dimensional data: A review. *SIGKDD Explorations*, 6:90–105, 2004. [458]

E. Parzen. On estimation of a probability density function and mode. *Annals of Mathematical Statistics*, 33(3):1065–1076, 1962. [376]

B. Pascal. *Varia Opera Mathematica. D. Petri De Fermat, Senatoris Tolosani*. Tolosae, 1679. [140]

R. B. Patil and S. Ramakrishnan. Analysis of sub-anatomic diffusion tensor imaging indices in white matter regions of Alzheimer with MMSE score. *Computer Methods and Programs in Biomedicine*, 117(1):13–19, 2014. [314]

A. L. Patterson. A Fourier series method for the determination of the component of inter-atomic distances in crystals. *Physics Reviews*, 46:372–376, 1934. [586]

M. Pazzani. Constructive induction of Cartesian product attributes. In *Proceedings of the Information, Statistics and Induction in Science Conference*, pages 66–77, 1996. [354, 355, 367, 482]

M. Pazzani and D. Billsus. Learning and revising user profiles: The identification of interesting web sites. *Machine Learning*, 27:313–331, 1997. [352]

J. Pearl. Reverend Bayes on inference engines: A distributed hierarchical approach. In *Proceedings of the 2nd National Conference on Artificial Intelligence*, pages 133–136. AAAI Press, 1982. [509]

J. Pearl. *Uncertainty in Artificial Intelligence*, chapter A constraint propagation approach to probabilistic reasoning, pages 357–370. Elsevier, 1986. [544]

J. Pearl. Evidential reasoning using stochastic simulation of causal models. *Artificial Intelligence*, 32 (2):245–257, 1987. [518, 545]

J. Pearl. *Probabilistic Reasoning in Intelligent Systems*. Morgan Kaufmann, 1988. [348, 349, 490, 543, 551, 561]

J. Pearl. *Causality: Models, Reasoning, and Inference*. Cambridge University Press, 2000. [497, 545]

J. Pearl, M. Glymour, N. P. Jewell. *Causal Inference in Statistics*. Wiley, 2016. [497]

J. Pearl and A. Paz. Graphoids: A graph-based logic for reasoning about relevance relations. Technical Report 850038, University of California, 1985. [563]

K. Pearson. Contribution to the mathematical theory of evolution. *Philosophical Transactions of the Royal Society, Series A*, 185:71–110, 1894. [486]

K. Pearson. On lines and planes of closest fit to systems of points in space. *Philosophical Magazine*, 2(11):559–572, 1901. [94]

D. Pecevski, L. Buesing, and W. Maass. Probabilistic inference in general graphical models through sampling in stochastic networks of spiking neurons. *PLoS Computational Biology*, 7:e1002294, 2011. [300]

E. Pellicano and D. Burr. When the world becomes "too real": A Bayesian explanation of autistic perception. *Trends in Cognitive Sciences*, 16(10):504–510, 2012. [159]

O. Pelykh, A. M. Klein, K. Bötzel, and Z. Kosutzka, and J. Ilmberger. Dynamics of postural control in Parkinson patients with and without symptoms of freezing of gait. *Gait Posture*, 42(3):246–250, 2015. [136]

J. M. Peña. Learning Gaussian graphical models of gene networks with false discovery rate control. In *Proceedings of the 6th European Conference on Evolutionary Computation, Machine Learning and Data Mining in Bioinformatics*, pages 165–176. Springer, 2008. [560]

J. M. Peña. Finding consensus Bayesian network structures. *Journal of Artificial Intelligence Research*, 42(1):661–687, 2011. [546]

J. M. Peña, J. A. Lozano, and P. Larrañaga. An empirical comparison of four initialization methods for the K-means algorithm. *Pattern Recognition Letters*, 20:1027–1040, 1999a. [467]

J. M. Peña, J. A. Lozano, and P. Larrañaga. Learning Bayesian networks for clustering by means of constructive induction. *Pattern Recognition Letters*, 20:1219–1230, 1999b. [482]

J. M. Peña, J. A. Lozano, and P. Larrañaga. Performance evaluation of compromise conditional Gaussian networks for data clustering. *International Journal of Approximate Reasoning*, 28:23–50, 2001a. [483]

J. M. Peña, J. A. Lozano, P. Larrañaga, and I. Inza. Dimensionality reduction in unsupervised learning of conditional Gaussian networks. *IEEE Transactions on Pattern Analysis and Machine Intelligence*, 23(6):590–603, 2001b. [483]

J. M. Peña, J. A. Lozano, and P. Larrañaga. Learning recursive Bayesian multinets for clustering by means of constructive induction. *Machine Learning*, 47:63–89, 2002. [483]

J. M. Peña, J. A. Lozano, and P. Larrañaga. Unsupervised learning of Bayesian networks via estimation of distribution algorithms: An application to gene expression data clustering. *International Journal of Uncertainty, Fuzziness and Knowledge-Based Systems*, 12(1):63–82, 2004. [482]

J. M. Peña, R. Nilsson, J. Björkegren, and J. Tegnér. Towards scalable and data efficient learning of Markov boundaries. *International Journal of Approximate Reasoning*, 45(2):211–232, 2007. [364]

H. Peng, F. Long, and C. Ding. Feature selection based on mutual information: Criteria of max-dependency, max-relevance, and min-redundancy. *IEEE Transactions on Pattern Analysis and Machine Intelligence*, 27(8):1226–1238, 2005. [254]

H. Peng, M. Hawrylycz, J. Roskams, S. Hill, N. Spruston, E. Meijering, and G. A. Ascoli. BigNeuron: Large-scale 3D neuron reconstruction from optical microscopy images. *Neuron*, 87: 252–256, 2015. [21]

Y. Peng and J. A. Reggia. A probabilistic causal model for diagnosis problem solving – Part I: Integrating symbolic causal inference with numeric probabilistic inference. *IEEE Transactions on Systems, Man, and Cybernetics*, 17(2):146–162, 1987a. [434]

Y. Peng and J. A. Reggia. A probabilistic causal model for diagnosis problem solving – Part II: Diagnostic strategy. *IEEE Transactions on Systems, Man, and Cybernetics*, 17(3):395–406, 1987b. [434]

J. Pensar, H. Nyman, J. Lintusaari, and J. Corander. The role of local partial independence in learning of Bayesian networks. *International Journal of Approximate Reasoning*, 69:91–105, 2016. [543]

M. S. Pepe. *The Statistical Evaluation of Medical Tests for Classification and Prediction*. Oxford University Press, 2003. [224]

A. Pérez, P. Larrañaga, and I. Inza. Supervised classification with conditional Gaussian networks: Increasing the structure complexity from naive Bayes. *International Journal of Approximate Reasoning*, 43:1–25, 2006. [371, 372, 373, 384]

A. Pérez, P. Larrañaga, and I. Inza. Bayesian classifiers based on kernel density estimation: Flexible classifiers. *International Journal of Approximate Reasoning*, 50:341–362, 2009. [375, 376]

S. Pérez de la Cruz, A. V. García-Luengo, and J. Lambeck. Effects of an Ai Chi fall prevention programme for patients with Parkinson's disease. *Neurología (English Edition)*, 31(3):176–182, 2016. [183]

R. Perneczky, P. Alexopoulos, and Alzheimer's Disease Euroimaging Initiative. Cerebrospinal fluid BACE1 activity and markers of amyloid precursor protein metabolism and axonal degeneration in Alzheimer's disease. *Alzheimer's & Dementia*, 10(5):S425–S429, 2014. [193]

F. Pernkopf. Bayesian network classifiers versus selective *k*-NN classifier. *Pattern Recognition*, 38: 1–10, 2005. [366]

F. Pernkopf and J. A. Bilmes. Efficient heuristics for discriminative structure learning of Bayesian network classifiers. *Journal of Machine Learning Research*, 11:2323–2360, 2010. [362]

F. Pernkopf and P. O'Leary. Floating search algorithm for structure learning of Bayesian network classifiers. *Pattern Recognition Letters*, 24:2839–2848, 2003. [353, 358, 362]

F. Pernkopf and M. Wohlmayr. On discriminative parameter learning of Bayesian network classifiers. In *Proceedings of the 20th European Conference on Machine Learning and Principles and Practice of Knowledge Discovery in Databases*, volume 5782, pages 221–237. Springer, 2009. [385]

Q. Perrenoud, J. Rossier, H. Geoffroy, T. Vitalis, and T. Gallopin. Diversity of GABAergic interneurons in layer VIa and VIb of mouse barrel cortex. *Cerebral Cortex*, 23(2):423–441, 2013. [34]

T. Persson. A new way to obtain Watson's U^2. *Scandinavian Journal of Statistics*, 6(3):119–122, 1979. [180]

A. Peters and E. G. Jones. *Cerebral Cortex: Cellular Components of the Cerebral Cortex*. Plenum, 1984. [6]

A. Peters and I. R. Kaiserman-Abramof. The small pyramidal neuron of the rat cerebral cortex. The perikaryon, dendrites and spines. *American Journal of Anatomy*, 127(4):321–355, 1970. [41, 469]

J. Peters, D. Janzing, B. Schölkopf. *Elements of Causal Inference*. The MIT Press. 2017. [497]

J. Peters, J. M. Mooij, D. Janzing, and B. Schölkopf. Causal discovery with continuous additive noise models. *Journal of Machine Learning Research*, 15(1):2009–2053, 2014. [545]

A. Pham, M. Z. Yondorf, B. Parashar, R. J. Scheff, S. C. Pannullo, R. Ramakrishna, P. E. Stieg, T. H. Schwartz, and A. G. Wernicke. Neurocognitive function and quality of life in patients with newly diagnosed brain metastasis after treatment with intra-operative cesium-131 brachytherapy: A prospective trial. *Journal of Neuro-Oncology*, 127(1):63–71, 2015. [176]

D. T. Pham and G. A. Ruz. Unsupervised training of Bayesian networks for data clustering. *Proceedings of the Royal Society A: Mathematical, Physical and Engineering Sciences*, 465:2927–2948, 2009. [482]

T. T. Pham, T. S. Moore, S. J. G. Lewis, D. N. Nguyen, E. Dutkiewicz, A. J. Fuglevand, A. L. McEwan, and P. H. W. Leong. Freezing of gait detection in Parkinson's disease: A subject-independent detector using anomaly scores. *IEEE Transactions on Biomedical Engineering*, 64 (11):2719–2728, 2017. [224]

T. V. Pham, M. Worring, and A. W. M. Smeulders. Face detection by aggregated Bayesian network classifiers. *Pattern Recognition Letters*, 23(4):451–461, 2002.. [365, 366]

T. D. Pigott. A review of methods for missing data. *Educational Research and Evaluation*, 7(4): 353–383, 2001. [95]

O. Piguet, C. E. Leyton, L. D. Gleeson, C. Hoon, and J. R. Hodges. Memory and emotion processing performance contributes to the diagnosis of non-semantic primary progressive aphasia syndromes. *Journal of Alzheimer's Disease*, 2014. [333]

R. Pique-Regi and A. Ortega. Block diagonal linear discriminant analysis with sequential embedded feature selection. In *2006 IEEE International Conference on Acoustics Speech and Signal Processing Proceedings*, volume 5, pages 729–732, 2006. [253]

E. Pitman and J. Wishart. Sufficient statistics and intrinsic accuracy. *Mathematical Proceedings of the Cambridge Philosophical Society*, 32(4):567–578, 1936. [485]

J. Pizarro, E. Guerrero, and Galindo P. L. Multiple comparison procedures applied to model selection. *Neurocomputing*, 48:155–173, 2002. [222]

C. Plant, S. J. Teipel, A. Oswald, C. Böhm, T. Meindl, J. Mourao-Miranda, A. W. Bokde, H. Hampel, and M. Ewers. Automated detection of brain atrophy patterns based on MRI for the prediction of Alzheimer's disease. *NeuroImage*, 50:162–174, 2010. [234]

C. Platero and M. C. Tobar. A label fusion method using conditional random fields with higher-order potentials: Application to hippocampal segmentation. *Artificial Intelligence in Medicine*, 64(2): 117–129, 2015. [566]

J. C. Platt. Fast training of support vector machines using sequential minimal optimization. In *Advances in Kernel Methods – Support Vector Learning*, pages 185–208. The MIT Press, 1999a. [305, 315]

J. C. Platt. *Advances in Large Margin Classifiers*, chapter Probabilistic outputs for support vector machines and comparisons to regularized likelihood methods, pages 61–74. The MIT Press, 1999b. [393]

C. O. Plumpton, L. I. Kuncheva, N. N. Oosterhof, and S. J. Johnston. Naive random subspace ensemble with linear classifiers for real-time classification of fMRI data. *Pattern Recognition*, 45(6):2101–2108, 2012. [403]

S. S. Poil, S. Bollmann, C. Ghisleni, R. L. O'Gorman, P. Klaver, J. Ball, D. Eich-Hochli, D. Brandeis, and L. Michels. Age dependent electroencephalographic changes in attention-deficit/hyperactivity disorder (ADHD). *Clinical Neurophysiology*, 125(8):1626–1638, 2014. [314]

S. D. Poisson. *Recherches sur la Probabilité des Jugements en Matière Criminelle et en Matière Civile, Précédées des Règles Générales du Calcul des Probabilitiés*. Bachelier, 1837. [140, 196]

D. Pokrajac, V. Megalooikonomou, A. Lazarevic, D. Kontos, and Z. Obradovic. Applying spatial distribution analysis techniques to classification of 3D medical images. *Artificial Intelligence in Medicine*, 33(3):261–280, 2005. [139]

R. Polikar, A. Topalis, D. Parikh, D. Green, J. Frymiare, J. Kounios, and C. M. Clark. An ensemble based data fusion approach for early diagnosis of Alzheimer's disease. *Information Fusion*, 9(1): 83–95, 2008. [407]

G. Pólya. ber den zentralen Grenzwertsatz der Wahrscheinlichkeitsrechnung und das Momentenproblem. *Mathematische Zeitschrift*, 8(3-4):171–181, 1920. [196]

M. Poo, J. Du, N. Y. Ip, Z. Xiong, B. Xu, and T. Tan. China Brain project: Basic neuroscience, brain diseases, and brain-inspired computing. *Neuron*, 92:591–596, 2016. [10]

D. Poole. Average-case analysis of a search algorithm for estimating prior and posterior probabilities in Bayesian networks with extreme probabilities. In *Proceedings of the 13th International Joint Conference on Artificial Intelligence*, pages 606–612, 1993. [545]

D. Poole. Probabilistic partial evaluation: Exploiting rule structure in probabilistic inference. In *Proceedings of the 17th International Joint Conference in Artificial Intelligence*, pages 1284–1291. Morgan Kaufmann, 1997. [544]

H. Prautzsch, W. Boehm, and M. Paluszny. *Bèzier and B-Spline Techniques*. Springer, 2002. [378]

A. Proddutur, J. Yu, F. S. Elgammal, and V. Santhakumar. Seizure-induced alterations in fast-spiking basket cell GABA currents modulate frequency and coherence of gamma oscillation in network simulations. *Chaos*, 23(4), 2013. [103]

G. M. Provan and M. Singh. Learning Bayesian networks using feature selection. In *Proceedings of the 5th International Workshop on Artificial Intelligence and Statistics*, pages 450–456, 1995. [364, 367]

P. Pudil, J. Novovicova, and J. Kittler. Floating search methods in feature selection. *Pattern Recognition Letters*, 15:1119–1125, 1994. [241]

S. R. Quartz and T. J. Sejnowski. The neural basis of cognitive development: A constructivist manifesto. *Behavioral and Brain Sciences*, 20(4):537–556, 1997. [298]

J. R. Quinlan. Induction of decision trees. *Machine Learning*, 1(1):81–106, 1986. [29, 274]

J. R. Quinlan. Simplifying decision trees. *International Journal of Man-Machine Studies*, 27(3): 221–234, 1987. [280]

J. R. Quinlan. Learning logical definitions from relations. *Machine Learning*, 5(3):239–266, 1990. [289]

J. R. Quinlan. *C4.5: Programs for Machine Learning*. Morgan Kaufmann, 1993. [252, 282]

P. R. Raamana, M. W. Weiner, L. Wang, M. F. Beg, and Alzheimer's Disease Neuroimaging Initiative. Thickness network features for prognostic applications in dementia. *Neurobiology of Aging*, 36:S91–S102, 2015. [445]

L. Rabiner and B. Juang. An introduction to hidden Markov models. *IEEE ASSP Magazine*, 3(1): 4–16, 1986. [538]

A. E. Raftery and N. Dean. Variable selection for model-based clustering. *Journal of the American Statistical Association*, 101:168–178, 2006. [478]

R. Raina, Y. Shen, A. Y. Ng, and A. McCallum. Classification with hybrid generative/discriminative models. In *Advances in Neural Information Processing Systems 16*, pages 545–552. The MIT Press, 2004. [385]

S. Ramón y Cajal. *Textura del Sistema Nervioso del Hombre y de los Vertebrados*. Moya, 1899. [31]

J. D. Ramsey, S. J. Hanson, C. Hanson, Y. O. Halchenko, R. A. Poldrack, and C. Glymour. Six problems for causal inference from fMRI. *NeuroImage*, 49(2):1545–1558, 2010. [536]

W. M. Rand. Objective criteria for the evaluation of clustering methods. *Journal of the American Statistical Association*, 66:846–850, 1971. [465]

R. P. N. Rao, B. A. Olshausen, and M. S. Lewicki. *Probabilistic Models of the Brain*. The MIT Press, 2002. [159]

P. M. Rasmussen, L. K. Hansen, K. H. Madsen, N. W. Churchill, and S. C. Strother. Model sparsity and brain pattern interpretation of classification models in neuroimaging. *Pattern Recognition*, 25 (6):2085–2100, 2012. [252]

S. Rässler, D. B. Rubin, and E. R. Zell. Imputation. *WIREs Computational Statistics*, 5:20–29, 2013. [95]

Ch.A. Ratanamahatana and D. Gunopulos. Feature selection for the naive Bayesian classifier using decision trees. *Applied Artificial Intelligence*, 17(5–6):475–487, 2003. [353]

N. Ratnarajah, A. Simmons, and A. Hojjatoleslami. Probabilistic clustering and shape modelling of white matter fibre bundles using regression mixtures. *Medical Image Computing and Computer-Assisted Intervention*, 14:25–32, 2011. [475]

P. Ravikumar, J. Lafferty, H. Liu, and L. Wasserman. Sparse additive models. *Journal of the Royal Statistical Society, Series B*, 71(5):1009–1030, 2009. [342]

P. Ravikumar, M. J. Wainwright, and J. D. Lafferty. High-dimensional Ising model selection using l_1-regularized logistic regression. *The Annals of Statistics*, 38(3):1287–1319, 2010. [571]

H. RaviPrakash, M. Korostenskaja, E. M. Castillo, K. H. Leed, C. M. Salinas, J. Baumgartner, S. M. Anwar, C. Spampinato, and U. Bagci. Deep learning provides exceptional accuracy to ECoG-based functional language mapping for epilepsy surgery. *Frontiers in Neuroscience*, 14:Article 409, 2020. [300]

J. Read, B. Pfahringer, G. Homes, and E. Frank. Classifier chains for multi-label classification. *Machine Learning*, 85(3):333–359, 2011. [423, 427]

S. Reardon. Global brain project sparks concern. *Nature*, 537:597–597, 2016a. [12]

S. Reardon. Public-health goal for brain mappers. *Nature*, 539:151, 2016b. [12]

I. Rechenberg. *Evolutionstrategie: Optimierung technischer Systeme nach Prinzipien der biologischen Evolution*. Frommann-Holzboog, 1973. [250]

H. Reichenbach. *The Direction of Time*. University of California Press, 1956. [543]

J. Remington. *Distributed Systems in Small Scale Research Environments: Hadoop and the EM Algorithm*. PhD thesis, Colorado State University, 2011. [486]

H. Rickards, J. De Souza, J. Crooks, M. R. van Walsem, E. van Duijn, B. Landwehrmeyer, F. Squitieri, and S. A. Simpson. Discriminant analysis of Beck depression inventory and Hamilton rating scale for depression in Huntington's disease. *The Journal of Neuropsychiatry and Clinical Neurosciences*, 23:399–402, 2011. [326]

G. Ridgeway. Looking for lumps: Boosting and bagging for density estimation. *Computational Statistics & Data Analysis*, 38(4):379–392, 2002. [414]

G. R. Ridgway, M. Lehmann, J. Barnes, J. D. Rohrer, J. D. Warren, S. J. Crutch, and N. C. Fox. Early-onset Alzheimer disease clinical variants: Multivariate analyses of cortical thickness. *Neurology*, 79(1):80–84, 2012. [84]

B. D. Ripley. Modelling spatial patterns (with discussion). *Journal of the Royal Statistical Society, Series B*, 39:172–212, 1977. [588, 611]

B. D. Ripley. *Spatial Statistics*. Wiley, 1981. [599, 611]

B. D. Ripley. *Statistical Inference for Spatial Processes*. Cambridge University Press, 2nd edition, 1988. [594]

B. D. Ripley. *Pattern Recognition and Neural Networks*. Cambridge University Press, 1996. [318]

R. L. Rivest. Learning decision lists. *Machine Learning*, 2:229–246, 1987. [287]

C. P. Robert. *The Bayesian Choice: A Decision-Theoretic Motivation*. Springer, 1994. [196]

C. P. Robert and G. Casella. *Introducing Monte Carlo Methods with R*. Springer, 2009. [545]

C. P. Robert, N. Chopin, and J. Rousseau. Harold Jeffreys's theory of probability revisited. *Statistical Science*, 24(2):141–172, 2009. [196]

R. Robinson. Counting unlabeled acyclic digraphs. In *Combinatorial Mathematics V*, volume 622, pages 28–43. Springer, 1977. [529]

V. Robles, P. Larrañaga, J. M. Peña, M. S. Pérez, E. Menasalvas, and V. Herves. Learning semi naïve Bayes structures by estimation of distribution algorithms. In *Proceedings of the 11th Portuguese Conference on Artificial Intelligence*, pages 244–258, 2003. [355]

V. Robles, C. Bielza, P. Larrañaga, S. González, and L. Ohno-Machado. Optimizing logistic regression coefficients for discrimination and calibration using estimation of distribution algorithms. *TOP*, 16(2):345–366, 2008. [385]

J. J. Rodriguez, L. I. Kuncheva, and C. J. Alonso. Rotation forest: A new classifier ensemble method. *IEEE Transactions on Pattern Analysis and Machine Intelligence*, 28(10):1619–1630, 2006. [404]

L. Rodriguez-Lujan, P. Larrañaga, and C. Bielza. Frobenius norm regularization for the multivariate von Mises distribution. *International Journal of Intelligent Systems*, 32(2):153–176, 2017. [122]

R. Y. Rohekar, S. Nisimov, Y. Gurwicz, G. Koren, and G. Novik. Constructing deep neural networks by Bayesian network structure learning. In *Proceedings of the 32nd Conference on Neural Information Processing Systems*, pages 3051–3062, 2018. [299]

L. Rokach. Taxonomy for characterizing ensemble methods in classification tasks: A review and annotated bibliography. *Computational Statistics & Data Analysis*, 53(12):4046–4072, 2009. [413]

L. Rokach and O. Maimon. *The Data Mining and Knowledge Discovery Handbook*, chapter Cluster analysis, pages 321–352. Springer, 2005a. [438]

L. Rokach and O. Maimon. Top-down induction of decision trees classifiers – A survey. *IEEE Transactions on Systems, Man, and Cybernetics, Part C*, 35(4):476–487, 2005b. [279]

T. Romero and P. Larrañaga. Triangulation of Bayesian networks with recursive estimation of distribution algorithms. *International Journal of Approximate Reasoning*, 50(3):472–484, 2009. [511]

T. Romero, P. Larrañaga, and B. Sierra. Learning Bayesian networks in the space of orderings with estimation of distribution algorithms. *International Journal of Pattern Recognition and Artificial Intelligence*, 18(4):607–625, 2004. [531]

V. Romero, R. Rumí, and A. Salmerón. Learning hybrid Bayesian networks using mixtures of truncated exponentials. *International Journal of Approximate Reasoning*, 42(1):54–68, 2006. [537]

T. Roos, H. Wettig, P. Grünwald, P. Myllymäki, and H. Tirri. On discriminative Bayesian network classifiers and logistic regression. *Machine Learning*, 59(3):267–296, 2005. [385]

F. Rosenblatt. The perceptron: A probabilistic model for information storage and organization in the brain. *Psychological Review*, 65:386–408, 1958. [318]

J. Roskams and Z. Popovic. Power to the people: Addressing big data challenges in neuroscience by creating a new cadre of citizen neuroscientists. *Neuron*, 92:658–664, 2016. [21]

V. Roth. The generalized LASSO. *IEEE Transactions in Neural Networks*, 15(1):16–28, 2004. [341]

D. B. Rubin. Inference and missing data. *Biometrika*, 63:581–590, 1976. [87, 95]

D. B. Rubin. *Multiple Imputation for Nonresponse in Surveys*. Wiley, 1987. [95]

L. H. Rubin, K. Witiewitz, J. S. Andre, and S. Reilly. Methods for handling missing data in the behavioral neurosciences: Don't throw the baby rat out with the bath water. *The Journal of Undergraduate Neouroscience Education*, 5(2):71–77, 2007. [88]

C. Rudin. Stop explaining black box machine learning models for high stakes decisions and use interpretable models instead. *Nature Machine Intelligence*, 1:206–215, 2019. [25]

D. E. Rumelhart, G. R. Hinton, and R. J. Williams. Learning representation by back-propagation errors. *Nature*, 323:533–536, 1986. [318]

R. Rumí and A. Salmerón. Approximate probability propagation with mixtures of truncated exponentials. *International Journal of Approximate Reasoning*, 45(2):191–210, 2007. [515]

R. Rumí, A. Salmerón, and S. Moral. Estimating mixtures of truncated exponentials in hybrid Bayesian networks. *TEST*, 15:397–421, 2006. [376, 377, 384, 537]

V. Ruonala, A. Meigal, S. M. Rissanen, O. Airaksinen, M. Kankaanpä, and P. A. Karjalainen. EMG signal morphology and kinematic parameters in essential tremor and Parkinson's disease patients. *Journal of Electromyography and Kinesiology*, 24(2):300–306, 2014. [136]

S. Ryali, T. Chen, K. Supekar, and V. Menon. A parcellation scheme based on von Mises-Fisher distributions and Markov random fields for segmenting brain regions using resting-state fMRI. *NeuroImage*, 65:83–96, 2013. [547]

S. Ryali, T. Chen, A. Padmanabhan, W. Cai, and V. Menon. Development and validation of consensus clustering-based framework for brain segmentation using resting fMRI. *Journal of Neuroscience Methods*, 240:128–140, 2015. [460]

T. P. Ryan. *Modern Regression Methods*. Wiley, 1997. [339, 384]

E. Ryzhikova, O. Kazakov, L. Halamkova, D. Celmins, P. Malone, E. Molho, E. A. Zimmerman, and I. K. Lednev. Raman spectroscopy of blood serum for Alzheimer's disease diagnostics: Specificity relative to other types of dementia. *Journal of Biophotonics*, 8(7):584–596, 2015. [293]

S. Šabanagić-Hajrić and A. Alajbegović. Impacts of education level and employment status on health-related quality of life in multiple sclerosis patients. *Medicinski Glasnik*, 12(1):61–67, 2015. [187]

Y. Saeys, I. Inza, and P. Larrañaga. A review of feature selection techniques in bioinformatics. *Bioinformatics*, 23(19):2507–2517, 2007. [261]

S. R. Safavian and D. Landgrebe. A survey of decision tree classifier methodology. *IEEE Transactions on Systems, Man and Cybernetics*, 21(3):660–674, 1991. [318]

M. Sahami. Learning limited dependence Bayesian classifiers. In *Proceedings of the 2nd International Conference on Knowledge Discovery and Data Mining*, pages 335–338, 1996. [360, 362, 367, 373]

C. O. Sakar and O. Kursun. Telediagnosis of Parkinson's disease using measurements of dysphonia. *Journal of Medical Systems*, 34(4):591–599, 2010. [139]

W. Sako, T. Abe, Y. Izumi, M. Harada, and R. Kaji. Fractional anisotropy in the supplementary motor area correlates with disease duration and severity of amyotrophic lateral sclerosis. *Neurological Sciences*, 37(4):573–577, 2016. [190]

R. Salakhutdinov and S. Roweis. Adaptive overrelaxed bound optimization methods. In *Proceedings of the 20th International Conference on Machine Learning*, pages 664–671, 2003. [474]

R. Salza, J. B. Oudart, L. Ramont, F. X. Maquart, S. Bakchine, H. Thoannès, and S. Ricard-Blum. Endostatin level in cerebrospinal fluid of patients with Alzheimer's disease. *Journal of Alzheimer's Disease*, 44(4):1253–1261, 2015. [187]

S. L. Salzberg. On comparing classifiers: Pitfalls to avoid and a recommended approach. *Data Mining and Knowledge Discovery*, 1:317–328, 1997. [225]

M. P. Sampat, A. M. Berger, B. C. Healy, P. Hildenbrand, J. Vass, D. S. Meier, T. Chitnis, H. L. Weiner, R. Bakshi, and C. R. Guttmann. Regional white matter atrophy–based classification of multiple sclerosis in cross-sectional and longitudinal data. *American Journal of Neuroradiology*, 30(9):1731–1739, 2009. [273]

B. Sangelaji, F. Estebsari, S. M. Nabavi, E. Jamshidi, D. Morsali, and M. Dastoorpoor. The effect of exercise therapy on cognitive functions in multiple sclerosis patients: A pilot study. *Medical Journal of the Islamic Republic of Iran*, 29:205, 2015. [176]

G. Santafé, J. A. Lozano, and P. Larrañaga. Bayesian model averaging of naive Bayes for clustering. *IEEE Transactions on Systems, Man, and Cybernetics, Part B*, 35(5):1149–1161, 2006a. [481]

G. Santafé, J. A. Lozano, and P. Larrañaga. Bayesian model averaging of TAN models for clustering. In *Proceedings of the 3rd European Workshop on Probabilistic Graphical Models*, pages 271–278, 2006b. [482]

R. Santana, C. Bielza, and P. Larrañaga. Regularized logistic regression and multi-objective variable selection for classifying MEG data. *Biological Cybernetics*, 106(6–7):389–405, 2012. [252, 343]

R. Santana, L. M. McGarry, C. Bielza, P. Larrañaga, and R. Yuste. Classification of neocortical interneurons using affinity propagation. *Frontiers in Neural Circuits*, 7:Article 185, 2013. [454]

J. L. Schafer. *Analysis of Incomplete Multivariate Data*. Chapman and Hall, 1997. [95]

J. L. Schafer and J. W. Graham. Missing data: Our view of the state of the art. *Psychological Methods*, 7(2):147–177, 2002. [95]

R. E. Schapire and Y. Singer. Improved boosting algorithms using confidence-rated predictions. *Machine Learning*, 37(3):297–336, 1999. [427]

R. E. Schapire, Y. Freund, P. Bartlett, and W. S. Lee. Boosting the margin: A new explanation for the effectiveness of voting methods. *The Annals of Statistics*, 26(5):1651–1686, 1998. [406]

J. Schemmel, D. Brüderle, A. Grübl, M. Hock, K. Meier, and S. Millner. A wafer-scale neuromorphic hardware system for large-scale neural modeling. In *Proceedings of the 2010 International Symposium on Circuits and Systems*, pages 1947–1950. IEEE, 2010. [30]

L. Scheubert, M. Luštrek, R. Schmidt, D. Repsilber, and G. Fuellen. Tissue-based Alzheimer gene expression markers-comparison of multiple machine learning approaches and investigation of redundancy in small biomarker sets. *BMC Bioinformatics*, 13:266, 2012. [314]

F. Schlüter. A survey on independence-based Markov networks learning. *Artificial Intelligence Review*, 42(4):1069–1093, 2014. [571]

J. Schmidhuber. Deep learning in neural networks: An overview. *Neural Networks*, 61:85–117, 2015. [319]

C. Schmitz, N. Grolms, P. R. Hof, R. Bochringer, J. Glaser, and H. Korr. Altered spatial arrangement of layer V pyramidal cells in the mouse brain following prenatal low-dose X-irradiation. A stereological study using a novel three-dimensional analysis method to estimate the nearest neighbor distance distributions of cells in thick sections. *Cerebral Cortex*, 12(9):954–960, 2002. [591]

I. J. Schoenberg. Contributions to the problem of approximation of equidistant data by analytic functions. Part B: On the problem of osculatory formulae. *Quarterly of Applied Mathematics*, 4:112–141, 1946. [378]

S. J. Schreiner, X. Liu, A. F. Gietl, M. Wyss, S. C. Steininger, E. Gruber, V. Treyer, I. B. Meier, A. M. Kälin, S. E. Leh, A. Buck, R. M. Nitsch, K. P. Pruessmann, C. Hock, and P. G. Unschuld. Regional fluid-attenuated inversion recovery (FLAIR) at 7 Tesla correlates with amyloid beta in hippocampus and brainstem of cognitively normal elderly subjects. *Frontiers in Aging Neuroscience*, 6:Article 240, 2014. [194]

G. Schwarz. Estimating the dimension of a model. *The Annals of Statistics*, 6(2):461–464, 1978. [532]

E. K. Scott and L. Luo. How do dendrites take their shape? *Nature Neuroscience*, 4(4):359–365, 2001. [539]

G. Sebestyen. *Decision-Making Processes in Pattern Recognition*. MacMillan, 1962. [227, 413]

K. Sechidis, G. Tsoumakas, and I. Vlahavas. On the stratification of multi-label data. In *Proceedings of the 14th European Conference on Machine Learning and Principles and Practice of Knowledge Discovery in Databases*, volume 6913, pages 145–158. Springer, 2011. [434]

K. Seeliger, U. Güçlü, L. Ambrogioni, Y. Güçlütürk, and M. A. J. van Gerven. Generative adversarial networks for reconstructing natural images from brain activity. *NeuroImage*, 181:775–785, 2018. [319]

T. J. Sejnowski, P. S. Churchland, and J. A. Movshon. Putting big data to good use in neuroscience. *Nature Neuroscience*, 17(11):1440–1441, 2014. [20]

D. Sengupta, I. Aich, and S. Bandyopadhyay. Feature selection using feature dissimilarity measure and density-based clustering: Application to biological data. *Journal of Biosciences*, 40:721–730, 2015. [456]

H. Sepehri and F. Ganji. The protective role of ascorbic acid on hippocampal CA1 pyramidal neurons in a rat model of maternal lead exposure. *Journal of Chemical Neuroanatomy*, 74:5–10, 2016. [186]

R. Setiono and H. Liu. Neural-network feature selector. *IEEE Transactions on Neural Networks*, 8 (3):654–662, 1997. [253]

R. D. Shachter. Evaluating influence diagrams. *Operations Research*, 34:871–882, 1986. [543]

R. D. Shachter and C. R. Kenley. Gaussian influence diagrams. *Management Science*, 35(5):527–550, 1989. [499, 500]

R. D. Shachter and M. A. Peot. Simulation approaches to general probabilistic inference on belief networks. In *Proceedings of the 5th Annual Conference on Uncertainty in Artificial Intelligence*, pages 221–234. Elsevier, 1989. [516, 544]

G. Shafer and P. P. Shenoy. Probability propagation. *Annals of Mathematics and Artificial Intelligence*, 2:327–352, 1990. [509]

S. Shahrbanian, P. Duquette, A. Kuspinar, and N. E. Mayo. Contribution of symptom clusters to multiple sclerosis consequences. *Quality of Life Research*, 24(3):617–629, 2015. [446]

C. E. Shannon. A mathematical theory of communication. *The Bell System Technical Journal*, 27(3): 379–423 and 623–656, 1948. [136]

S. S. Shapiro and M. B. Wilk. An analysis of variance test for normality (complete samples). *Biometrika*, 52(3-4):591–611, 1965. [167]

A. A. Sharief, A. Badea, A. M. Dale, and G. A. Johnson. Automated segmentation of the actively stained mouse brain using multi-spectral MR microscopy. *NeuroImage*, 39(1):136–145, 2008. [549]

S. Sharma. *Applied Multivariate Techniques*. Wiley, 1996. [384]

H. Sharp. Cardinality of finite topologies. *Journal of Combinatorial Theory*, 5:82–86, 1968. [444]

V. Shaygannejad, S. R. Dehnavi, F. Ashtari, S. Karimi, L. Dehghani, R. Meamar, and Z. Tolou-Ghamari. Study of type A and B behavior patterns in patients with multiple sclerosis in an Iranian population. *International Journal of Preventive Medicine*, 4:279–283, 2013. [178]

P. P. Shenoy. Inference in hybrid Bayesian networks using mixtures of Gaussians. In *Proceedings of the 22nd Conference on Uncertainty in Artificial Intelligence*, pages 428–436. AUAI Press, 2006. [503]

P. P. Shenoy. Two issues in using mixtures of polynomials for inference in hybrid Bayesian networks. *International Journal of Approximate Reasoning*, 53(5):847–866, 2012. [378, 385]

P. P. Shenoy and G. Shafer. Axioms for probability and belief-function propagation. In *Proceedings of the 6th Conference on Uncertainty in Artificial Intelligence*, pages 169–198. Elsevier, 1990. [509]

P. P. Shenoy and J. C. West. Inference in hybrid Bayesian networks using mixtures of polynomials. *International Journal of Approximate Reasoning*, 52(5):641–657, 2011. [377, 378, 385, 502, 503, 515]

D. J. Sheskin. *Handbook of Parametric and Nonparametric Statistical Procedures*. Chapman and Hall/CRC, 2000. [165]

S. Shevade and S. Keerthi. A simple and efficient algorithm for gene selection using sparse logistic regression. *Bioinformatics*, 19(17):2246–2253, 2003. [341]

J. Shi and J. Malik. Normalized cuts and image segmentation. *IEEE Transactions on Pattern Analysis and Machine Intelligence*, 22(8):888–905, 2000. [452]

J. Shi, W. Yin, S. Osher, and P. Sajda. A fast hybrid algorithm for large-scale ℓ_1-regularized logistic regression. *Journal of Machine Learning Research*, 11(1):713–741, 2010. [341]

Y.-S. Shih. Families of splitting criteria for classification trees. *Statistics and Computing*, 9(4):309–315, 1999. [279]

S. E. Shimony. Explanation, irrelevance and statistical independence. In *Proceedings of the 9th National Conference on Artificial Intelligence*, pages 482–487. AAAI Press, 1991. [543]

D. A. Sholl. Dendritic organization in the neurons of the visual and motor cortices of the cat. *Journal of Anatomy*, 87:387–406, 1953. [32]

Z. Šidák. Rectangular confidence regions for the means of multivariate normal distributions. *Journal of the American Statistical Association*, 62(31):626–633, 1967. [193]

W. Siedlecki and J. Sklansky. A note on genetic algorithms for large-scale feature selection. *Pattern Recognition Letters*, 10:335–347, 1989. [241, 249]

S. Siegel. *Nonparametric Statistics for the Behavioral Sciences*. McGraw-Hill, 1956. [165]

B. Sierra and P. Larrañaga. Predicting the survival in malignant skin melanoma using Bayesian networks automatically induced by genetic algorithms. An empirical comparison between different approaches. *Artificial Intelligence in Medicine*, 14:215–230, 1998. [364]

J. Sietsma and R. J. F. Dow. Creating artificial neural networks that generalize. *Neural Networks*, 4(1):67–69, 1991. [261]

T. Silander and P. Myllymäki. A simple approach for finding the globally optimal Bayesian network structure. In *Proceedings of the 22nd Conference on Uncertainty in Artificial Intelligence*, pages 445–452. AUAI Press, 2006. [536]

T. Silander, P. Kontkanen, and P. Myllymäki. On sensitivity of the MAP Bayesian network structure to the equivalent sample size parameter. In *Proceedings of the 23rd Conference on Uncertainty in Artificial Intelligence*, pages 360–367. AUAI Press, 2007. [534]

T. Silander, T. Roos, P. Kontkanen, and P. Myllymäki. Factorized normalized maximum likelihood criterion for learning Bayesian network structures. In *Proceedings of the 4th European Workshop on Probabilistic Graphical Models*, pages 257–264, 2008. [546]

B. W. Silverman. *Density Estimation for Statistics and Data Analysis*. Chapman and Hall, 1986. [268, 374, 375]

B. W. Silverman and M. C. Jones. E. Fix and J. L. Hodges (1951): An important contribution to nonparametric discriminant analysis and density estimation. *International Statistical Review*, 57:233–247, 1989. [263]

D. Simon. *Evolutionary Optimization Algorithms*. Wiley, 2013. [247]

J. S. Simonoff. *Smoothing Methods in Statistics*. Springer, 1996. [375]

T. Sing, O. Sander, N. Beerenwinkel, and T. Lengauer. ROCR: Visualizing classifier performance in R. *Bioinformatics*, 21:3940–3941, 2005. [210]

G. Singh and L. Samavedham. Unsupervised learning based feature extraction for differential diagnosis of neurodegenerative diseases: A case study on early-stage diagnosis of Parkinson disease. *Journal of Neuroscience Methods*, 256:30–40, 2015. [449]

M. Singh and G. Provan. Efficient learning of selective Bayesian network classifiers. In *Proceedings of the 13th International Conference on Machine Learning*, pages 453–461, 1996. [365]

M. Singh and M. Valtorta. Construction of Bayesian network structures from data: A brief survey and an efficient algorithm. *International Journal of Approximate Reasoning*, 12(2):111–131, 1995. [365, 531]

H. Skirton, J. K. Williams, J. Jackson-Barnette, and J. S. Paulsen. Huntington disease: Families' experiences of healthcare services. *Journal of Advanced Nursing*, 66(3):500–510, 2010. [192]

M. Skurichina. *Stabilizing Weak Classifiers: Regularization and Combining Techniques in Discriminant Analysis*. PhD thesis, Delft University of Technology, 2001. [402]

S. Slaets, N. Le Bastard, J. J. Martin, K. Sleegers, C. Van Broeckhoven, P. P. De Deyn, and S. Engelborghs. Cerebrospinal fluid Aβ1-40 improves differential dementia diagnosis in patients with intermediate P-tau181P levels. *Journal of Alzheimer's Disease*, 36(4):759–767, 2013. [283]

D. K. Slonim, P. Tamayo, J. P. Mesirov, T. R. Golub, and E. S. Lander. Class prediction and discovery using gene expression data. In *Proceedings of the 4th Annual International Conference on Computational Molecular Biology*, pages 263–272, 2000. [232, 235]

S. Small, K. Kent, A. Pierce, C. Leung, M. S. Kang, H. Okada, L. Honig, J. P. Vonsattel, and T. W. Kim. Model-guided microarray implicates the retromer complex in Alzheimer's disease. *Annals of Neurology*, 58(6):909–919, 2005. [193]

F. Smeraldi, M. Bicego, M. Cristani, and V. Murino. CLOOSTING: CLustering data with bOOST-ING. In *Proceedings of the 10th International Workshop on Multiple Classifier Systems*, volume 6713, pages 289–298. Springer, 2011. [414]

P. Smialowski, D. Frishman, and S. Kramer. Pitfalls of supervised feature selection. *Bioinformatics*, 26(3):440–443, 2010. [230]

N. V. Smirnov. Estimate of deviation between empirical distribution functions in two independent samples. *Bulletin Moscow University*, 2:3–16, 1939. [197]

P. W. F. Smith and J. Whittaker. Edge exclusion tests for graphical Gaussian models. In *Learning in Graphical Models*, pages 555–574. Kluwer Academic Publishers, 1998. [484, 529, 559]

S. F. Smith. *A Learning System Based on Genetic Adaptive Algorithms*. PhD thesis, University of Pittsburgh, 1980. [318]

S. M. Smith, K. L. Miller, G. Salimi-Khorshidi, M. Webster, C. F. Beckmann, T. E. Nichols, J. D. Ramsey, and M. W. Woolrich. Network modelling methods for fMRI. *NeuroImage*, 54(2):875–891, 2011. [535]

P. Smolensky. *Parallel Distributed Processing: Explorations in the Microstructure of Cognition, Volume 1: Foundations*, chapter Information processing in dynamical systems: Foundations of harmony theory, pages 194–281. The MIT Press, 1986. [555]

P. H. A. Sneath and R. R. Sokal. *Numerical Taxonomy*. Freeman, 1973. [467]

M. Sobstyl, M. Zabek, W. Górecki, and Z. Mossakowski. Quality of life in advanced Parkinson's disease after bilateral subthalamic stimulation: 2 years follow-up study. *Clinical Neurology and Neurosurgery*, 124:161–165, 2014. [177]

R. R. Sokal and C. D. Michener. A statistical method for evaluating systematic relationships. *University of Kansas Scientific Bulletin*, 38:1409–1438, 1958. [441]

M. Sokolova and G. Lapalme. A systematic analysis of performance measures for classification tasks. *Information Processing and Management*, 45:427–437, 2009. [224]

P. Somol and J. Novovicová. Evaluating stability and comparing output of feature selectors that optimize feature subset cardinality. *IEEE Transactions on Pattern Analysis and Machine Intelligence*, 32(11):1921–1939, 2010. [255]

D. Sonntag, J. M. Peña, and M. Gómez-Olmedo. Approximate counting of graphical models via MCMC revisited. *International Journal of Intelligent Systems*, 30(3):384–420, 2015. [530]

J. A. Sonquist and J. N. Morgan. The detection of interaction effects. Technical Report 35, University of Michigan, 1964. [467]

T. Sørensen. A method for establishing groups of equal amplitude in plant sociology based on similarity of species contents and its application to analyses of the vegetation on Danish commons. *Biologiske Skrifter*, 5:1–34, 1948. [440, 441]

K. A. Spackman. Signal detection theory: Valuable tools for evaluating inductive learning. In *Proceedings of the 6th International Workshop on Machine Learning*, pages 160–163. Morgan Kaufmann, 1989. [224]

T. P. Speed and H. Kiiveri. Gaussian Markov distributions over finite graphs. *The Annals of Statistics*, 14:138–150, 1986. [558]

D. J. Spiegelhalter and S. L. Lauritzen. Sequential updating of conditional probabilities on directed graphical structures. *Networks*, 20:579–605, 1990. [521, 522]

P. Spirtes and C. Glymour. An algorithm for fast recovery of sparse causal graphs. *Social Science Computer Review*, 90(1):62–72, 1991. [525]

P. Spirtes, C. Glymour, and R. Scheines. *Causation, Prediction, and Search*. Springer, 1993. [362, 497, 525, 551]

P. Spirtes, C. Meek, and T. Richardson. Causal inference in the presence of latent variables and selection bias. In *Proceedings of the 15th Conference on Uncertainty in Artificial Intelligence*, pages 499–506. Morgan Kaufmann, 1999. [529]

K. Spisak, A. Klimkowicz-Mrowiec, J. Pera, T. Dziedzic, G. Aleksandra, and A. Slowik. rs2070424 of the SOD1 gene is associated with risk of Alzheimer's disease. *Neurologia i Neurochirurgia Polska*, 48(5):342–345, 2014. [178]

E. A. Spitzka. A study of the brains of six eminent scientist and scholars belonging to the American anthropometric society, together with a description of the skull of professor E. D. Cope. *Transactions of the American Philosophical Society*, 21:175–308, 1907. [7]

O. Sporns. *Networks of the Brain*. The MIT Press, 2010. [5]

S. Sra. A short note on parameter approximation for von Mises–Fisher distributions: And a fast implementation of $I_s(x)$. *Computational Statistics*, 27(1):177–190, 2012. [151]

N. Srebro. Maximum likelihood bounded tree-width Markov networks. *Artificial Intelligence*, 143:123–138, 2003. [570]

S. Srinivas. A probabilistic approach to hierarchical model-based diagnosis. In *Proceedings of the 10th International Conference on Uncertainty in Artificial Intelligence*, pages 538–545. Morgan Kaufmann, 1994. [543]

S. D. Stearns. On selecting features for pattern recognition. In *Proceedings of the 3rd International Conference on Pattern Recognition*, pages 71–75, 1976. [241]

H. Steck and T. S. Jaakkola. Predictive discretization during model selection. In *Proceedings of the 26th Symposium of the German Association for Pattern Recognition*, pages 1–8. Springer, 2004. [499]

H. Steinhaus. Sur la division des corps matériels en parties. *Bulletin de L'Academie Polonaise des Sciences*, IV(12):801–804, 1956. [467]

F. Stella and Y. Amer. Continuous time Bayesian network classifiers. *Journal of Biomedical Informatics*, 45(6):1108–1119, 2012. [386]

F. Stella, C. E. Banzato, E. M. Barasnevicius-Quagliato, and M. A. Viana. Depression in patients with Parkinson's disease: Impact on functioning. *Journal of Neurological Sciences*, 272(1–2):158–163, 2008. [178]

W. Stephenson. Introduction of inverted factor analysis with some applications to studies in orexis. *Journal of Educational Psychology*, 5:553–567, 1936. [467]

D. C. Sterio. The unbiased estimation of number and sizes of arbitrary particles using the disector. *Journal of Microscopy*, 134(2):127–136, 1984. [601]

S. M. Stigler. Who discovered Bayes's theorem? *The American Statistician*, 37(4):290–296, 1983. [196]

M. Stone. Asymptotics for and against cross-validation. *Biometrika*, 64(1):29–35, 1977. [213, 268]

R. Storn and K. Price. Differential evolution. A simple and efficient heuristic for global optimization over continuous spaces. *Journal of Global Optimization*, 11(4):341–359, 1997. [249]

D. J. Strauss. A model for clustering. *Biometrika*, 62:467–475, 1975. [608]

M. E. Strauss and J. Brandt. Attempt at preclinical identification of Huntington's disease using the WAIS. *Journal of Clinical and Experimental Neuropsychology*, 8(3):210–218, 1986. [440]

A. Strehl and J. Ghosh. Combining multiple clusterings using evidence accumulation. *Journal of Machine Learning Research*, 3:583–617, 2002. [462]

C. Strobl, A.-L. Boulesteix, T. Kneib, T. Augustin, and A. Zeileis. Conditional variable importance for random forests. *BMC Bioinformatics*, 9(1):307, 2008. [403]

A. Sturrock, C. Laule, K. Wyper, R. A. Milner, J. Decolongon, R. Dar Santos, A. J. Coleman, K. Carter, S. Creighton, N. Bechtel, S. Bohlen, R. Reilmann, H. J. Johnson, M. R. Hayden, S. J. Tabrizi, A. L. Mackay, and B. R. Leavitt. A longitudinal study of magnetic resonance spectroscopy Huntington's disease biomarkers. *Movement Disorders*, 30(3):393–401, 2015. [186]

J. Su, H. Zhang, C. X. Ling, and S. Matwin. Discriminative parameter learning for Bayesian networks. In *Proceedings of the 25th International Conference on Machine Learning*, volume 307, pages 1016–1023. ACM, 2008. [385]

L. Su, L. Wang, H. Shen, G. Feng, and D. Hu. Discriminative analysis of nonlinear brain connectivity in schizophrenia: An fMRI study. *Frontiers in Human Neuroscience*, 7:Article 702, 2013. [314]

L. E. Sucar. *Probabilistic Graphical Models: Principles and Applications*. Springer, 2015. [543]

H. J. Suermondt and G. F. Cooper. Probabilistic inference in multiply connected belief networks using loop cutsets. *International Journal of Approximate Reasoning*, 4(4):283–306, 1990. [544]

D. C. Suh, R. Pahwa, and U. Mallya. Treatment patterns and associated costs with Parkinson's disease levodopa induced dyskinesia. *Journal of Neurological Sciences*, 319(1-2):24–31, 2012. [108]

R. Sundberg. Maximum likelihood theory for incomplete data from an exponential family. *Scandinavian Journal of Statistics*, 1(2):49–58, 1974. [485]

R. Sundberg. An iterative method for solution of the likelihood equations for incomplete data from exponential families. *Communications in Statistics–Simulation and Computation*, 5(1):55–64, 1976. [485]

K. Supekar, V. Menon, D. Rubin, M. Musen, and M. D. Greicius. Network analysis of intrinsic functional brain connectivity in Alzheimer's disease. *PLoS Computational Biology*, 4(6):1–11, 2008. [46]

T. Tandrup. Unbiased estimates of number and size of rat dorsal root ganglion cells in studies of structure and cell survival. *Journal of Neurocytology*, 33(2):173–192, 2004. [57]

J. W. H. Tangelder and R. C. Veltkamp. A survey of content based 3D shape retrieval methods. *Multimedia Tools and Applications*, 39:441–471, 2008. [41]

C. L. Tardif, D. L. Collins, S. F. Eskildsen, J. B. Richardson, and G. B. Pike. *Medical Image Computing and Computer-Assisted Intervention*, chapter Segmentation of cortical MS lesions on MRI using automated laminar profile shape analysis, pages 181–188. Springer, 2010. [445]

R. E. Tarjan and M. Yannakakis. Simple linear-time algorithms to test chordality of graphs, test acyclicity of hypergraphs, and selectively reduce acyclic hypergraphs. *SIAM Journal on Computing*, 13(3):566–579, 1984. [511]

D. M. J. Tax and R. P. W. Duin. Support vector domain description. *Pattern Recognition Letters*, 20 (11):1191–1199, 1999. [319]

L. Tenenboim, L. Rokach, and B. Shapira. Identification of label dependencies for multi-label classification. In *Proceedings of the 2nd International Workshop on Learning from Multi-Label Data*, pages 53–60, 2010. [426]

C. Tenopir, S. Allard, K. Douglass, A. U. Aydinoglu, L. Wu, E. Read, M. Manoff, and M. Frame. Data sharing by scientists: Practices and perceptions. *PLoS ONE*, 6(6):e21101, 2011. [20]

H. Teramoto, A. Morita, S. Ninomiya, H. Shiota, and S. Kamei. Relation between freezing of gait and frontal function in Parkinson's disease. *Parkinsonism & Related Disorders*, 20(10):1046–1069, 2014. [179]

C. Teufel, N. Subramaniam, and P. Fletcher. The role of priors in Bayesian models of perception. *Frontiers in Computational Neuroscience*, 7:Article 25, 2013. [159]

M. Teyssier and D. Koller. Ordering-based search: A simple and effective algorithm for learning Bayesian networks. In *Proceedings of the 21st Conference on Uncertainty in Artificial Intelligence*, pages 584–590. AUAI Press, 2005. [531]

B. Thiesson, C. Meek, D. M. Chickering, and D. Heckerman. Learning mixtures of DAG models. In *Proceedings of the 14th Conference in Uncertainty in Artificial Intelligence*, pages 504–513. AUAI Press, 1998. [483]

J. Thomas, J. Olson, S. Tapscott, and L. Zhao. An efficient and robust statistical modeling approach to discover differentially expressed genes using genomic expression profiles. *Genome Research*, 11:1227–1236, 2001. [232, 235]

M. Thomas. A generalization of Poisson's binomial limit for use in ecology. *Biometrika*, 36(1/2): 18–25, 1949. [605]

W. M. Thorburn. Occam's razor. *Mind*, 24:287–288, 1915. [28]

R. L Thorndike. Who belongs in the family? *Psychometrika*, 18(4):267–276, 1953. [457, 466]

G. L. Tian, M. L. Tang, H. B. Fang, and M. Tan. Efficient methods for estimating constrained parameters with applications to regularized (lasso) logistic regression. *Computational Statistics & Data Analysis*, 52(7):3528–3542, 2008. [343]

R. Tibshirani. Regression shrinkage and selection via the lasso. *Journal of the Royal Statistical Society, Series B*, 58(1):267–288, 1996. [252, 261, 341]

R. Tibshirani, G. Walther, and T. Hastie. Estimating the number of clusters in a dataset via the gap statistics. *Journal of the Royal Statistical Society, Series B*, 63:411–423, 2001. [458]

A. N. Tikhonov. On the stability of inverse problems. *Doklady Akademii Nauk SSSR*, 39(5):176–179, 1943. [252]

D. Titterington, A. Smith, and U. Makov. *Statistical Analysis of Finite Mixture Distributions*. Wiley, 1985. [486]

S. N. Tomson, M. Narayan, G. I. Allen, and D. M. Eagleman. Neural networks of colored sequence synesthesia. *Journal of Neuroscience*, 33(35):14098–14106, 2013. [548]

B. Torben-Nielsen, S. Vanderlooy, and E. O. Postma. Non-parametric algorithmic generation of neuronal morphologies. *Neuroinformatics*, 6:257–277, 2008. [540]

W. S. Torgerson. Multidimensional scaling: I. Theory and method. *Psychometrika*, 17(4):401–419, 1952. [95]

E. B. Torres. The rates of change of the stochastic trajectories of acceleration variability are a good predictor of normal aging and of the stage of Parkinson's disease. *Frontiers in Integrative Neuroscience*, 7:Article 50, 2013. [108]

G. Trabelsi. *New Structure Learning Algorithms and Evaluation Methods for Large Dynamic Bayesian Networks*. PhD thesis, Université de Nantes, 2013. [538]

E. Triantaphyllou and G. Felici, editors. *Data Mining and Knowledge Discovery Approaches Based on Rule Induction Techniques*. Springer, 2006. [318]

E. E. Tripoliti, A. T. Tzallas, M. G. Tsipouras, G. Rigas, P. Bougia, M. Leontiou, S. Konitsiotis, M. Chondrogiorgi, S. Tsouli, and D. I. Fotiadis. Automatic detection of freezing of gait events in patients with Parkinson's disease. *Computer Methods and Programs in Biomedicine*, 110(1): 12–26, 2013. [282]

R. C. Tryon. *Cluster Analysis*. Edwards Bros, 1939. [467]

A. Tsai, M. Malek-Ahmadi, V. Kahlon, and M. N. Sabbagh. Differences in cerebrospinal fluid biomarkers between clinically diagnosed idiopathic normal pressure hydrocephalus and Alzheimer's disease. *Journal of Alzheimer's Disease & Parkinsonism*, 4(4), 2014. [179]

I. Tsamardinos and C. F. Aliferis. Towards principled feature selection: Relevancy, filters and wrappers. In *Proceedings of the 9th International Workshop on Artificial Intelligence and Statistics*, 2003. [364, 560]

I. Tsamardinos, C. F. Aliferis, and A. R. Statnikov. Algorithms for large scale Markov blanket discovery. In *Proceedings of the 16th International Florida Artificial Intelligence Research Society Conference*, pages 376–381. AAAI Press, 2003a. [364]

I. Tsamardinos, C. F. Aliferis, and A. R. Statnikov. Time and sample efficient discovery of Markov blankets and direct causal relations. In *Proceedings of the 9th ACM SIGKDD International Conference on Knowledge Discovery and Data Mining*, pages 673–678, 2003b. [364]

I. Tsamardinos, L. E. Brown, and C. F. Aliferis. The max-min hill-climbing Bayesian network structure learning algorithm. *Machine Learning*, 65(1):31–78, 2006. [538, 546]

A. Tsiola, F. Hamzei-Sichani, Z. Peterlin, and R. Yuste. Quantitative morphological classification of layer 5 neurons from mouse primary visual cortex. *The Journal of Comparative Neurology*, 461: 415–428, 2003. [34]

G. Tsoumakas and I. Katakis. Multi-label classification: An overview. *International Journal of Data Warehousing and Mining*, 3:1–13, 2007. [416]

G. Tsoumakas, A. Dimou, E. Spyromitros, V. Mezaris, I. Kompatsiaris, and I. Vlahavas. Correlation-based pruning of stacked binary relevance models for multi-label learning. In *Proceedings of the 1st International Workshop on Learning from Multi-Label Data*, pages 101–116, 2009. [426]

G. Tsoumakas, I. Katakis, and I. Vlahavas. Random k-labelsets for multi-label classification. *IEEE Transactions on Knowledge and Data Engineering*, 23(7):1079–1089, 2010. [425]

R. Tsurusawa, Y. Goto, A. Mitsudome, T. Nakashima, and S. Tobimatsu. Different perceptual sensitivities for Chernoff's face between children and adults. *Neuroscience Research*, 60(2):176–183, 2008. [73]

J. W. Tukey. *Exploratory Data Analysis*. Addison-Wesley, 1977. [53, 89, 94, 413]

M. Turner, C. Chakrabarti, T. B. Jones, J. F. Xu, P. T. Fox, G. F. Luger, A. R. Laird, and J. A. Turner. Automated annotation of functional imaging experiments via multi-label classification. *Frontiers in Neuroscience*, 7:Article 240, 2013. [417]

G. Tutz and H. Binder. Boosting ridge regression. *Computational Statistics & Data Analysis*, 51(12): 6044–6059, 2007. [414]

A. Tversky and D. Kahneman. Judgment under uncertainty: Heuristics and biases. *Science*, 185 (4157):1124–1131, 1974. [498]

M. Uhring, C. Ittrich, V. Wiedmann, Y. Knyazev, A. Weninger, M. Riemenschneider, and T. Hartmann. New Alzheimer amyloid β responsive genes identified in human neuroblastoma cells by hierarchical clustering. *PLoS ONE*, 4(8):e6779, 2009. [440]

K. Uludağ and A. Roebroeck. General overview on the merits of multimodal neuroimaging data fusion. *NeuroImage*, 102:3–10, 2014. [16]

M. Uszynski, H. Purtill, and S. Coote. Relationship between foot vibration threshold and walking and balance functions in people with multiple sclerosis (PwMS). *Gait Posture*, 41(1):228–232, 2015. [179]

H. Vafaie and K. De Jong. Improving the performance of a rule induction system using genetic algorithms. In *Proceedings of the 1st International Workshop on Multistrategy Learning*, pages 8–11, 1991. [261]

I. Valtokin, W. Theimer, and G. Rudolph. Design and comparison of differential evolution strategies for feature selection and consolidation in music classification. In 2009 *Congress on Evolutionary Computation*, pages 174–181. IEEE Conference Publications, 2009. [241, 250]

S. van Buuren. *Flexible Imputation of Missing Data*. Chapman and Hall, 2012. [95]

T. N. van den Kommer, H. C. Comijs, K. J. Rijs, M. W. Heymans, M. P. J. van Boxtel, and D. J. H. Deeg. Classification models for identification of at-risk groups for incident memory complaints. *International Psychogeriatrics*, 26(2):257–271, 2014. [88]

A. W. van der Eerden, O. Khalilzadeh, V. Perlbarg, J. Dinkel, P. Sanchez, P. E. Vos, C. E. Luyt, R. D. Stevens, N. Menjot de Champfleur, C. Delmaire, E. Tollard, R. Gupta, D. Dormont, S. Laureys, H. Benali, A. Vanhaudenhuyse, D. Galanaud, L. Puybasset, and NICER (Neuro Imaging for

Coma Emergence and Recovery) Consortium. White matter changes in comatose survivors of anoxic ischemic encephalopathy and traumatic brain injury: Comparative diffusion-tensor imaging study. *Radiology*, 270(2):506–516, 2014. [193]

L. C. van der Gaag and P. R. de Waal. Multi-dimensional Bayesian network classifiers. In *Proceedings of the 3rd European Workshop on Probabilistic Graphical Models*, pages 107–114, 2006. [428, 429]

M. van der Heijden, M. Velikova, and P. J. F. Lucas. Learning Bayesian networks for clinical time series analysis. *Journal of Biomedical Informatics*, 48:94–105, 2014. [386]

L. J. P. van der Maaten and G. E. Hinton. Visualizing high-dimensional data using t-SNE. *Journal of Machine Learning Research*, 9:2579–2605, 2008. [83]

M. van Eeden, J. A. Kootker, S. M. Evers, C. M. van Heugten, A. C. Geurts, and G. A. van Mastrigt. An economic evaluation of an augmented cognitive behavioral intervention vs. computerized cognitive training for post-stroke depressive symptoms. *BMC Neurology*, 15(1):266, 2015. [88]

M. van Gerven and P. J. F. Lucas. Employing maximum mutual information for Bayesian classification. In *Proceedings of the 5th International Symposium on Biological and Medical Data Analysis*, pages 188–199. Springer, 2004. [362]

M. van Gerven, C. Hesse, O. Jensen, and T. Heskes. Interpreting single trial data using groupwise regularisation. *NeuroImage*, 46:665–676, 2009. [252]

M. van Gerven, B. Cseke, F. P. de Lange, and T. Heskes. Efficient Bayesian multivariate fMRI analysis using a sparsifying spatio-temporal prior. *NeuroImage*, 50(1):150–161, 2010. [341]

M. N. M. van Lieshout. *Markov Point Processes and Their Applications*. Imperial College Press, 2000. [607]

M. N. M. van Lieshout. A J-function for inhomogeneous point processes. *Statistica Neerlandica*, 65 (2):183–201, 2011. [597]

C. J. Van Rijsbergen. *Information Retrieval*. Butterworth, 1979. [205]

V. N. Vapnik. *Statistical Learning Theory*. Wiley, 1998. [300, 314]

G. Varando, C. Bielza, and P. Larrañaga. Decision boundary for discrete Bayesian network classifiers. *Journal of Machine Learning Research*, 16:2725–2749, 2015. [362]

Y. Vardi, L. A. Shepp, and L. A. Kaufman. A statistical model for positron emission tomography. *Journal of the American Statistical Association*, 80:8–37, 2006. [475]

B. E. Varga, W. Gao, K. L. Laurik, E. Tátrai, M. Simó, G. M. Somfai, and D. Cabrera DeBuc. Investigating tissue optical properties and texture descriptors of the retina in patients with multiple sclerosis. *PLoS ONE*, 10(11):e0143711, 2015. [186]

S. Vega-Pons and J. Ruiz-Shulcloper. A survey of clustering ensemble algorithms. *International Journal of Pattern Recognition and Artificial Intelligence*, 25(3):337–372, 2011. [414]

J. R. Vergara and P. A. Estévez. A review of feature selection methods based on mutual information. *Neural Computation and Applications*, 24(1):175–186, 2013. [261]

T. Verma and J. Pearl. Equivalence and synthesis of causal models. In *Proceedings of the 6th Conference on Uncertainty in Artificial Intelligence*, pages 255–270. Elsevier, 1990a. [498]

T. Verma and J. Pearl. Causal networks: Semantics and expressiveness. In *Proceedings of the 4th Annual Conference on Uncertainty in Artificial Intelligence*, pages 69–78. North-Holland, 1990b. [493]

P. Vetter, A. Roth, and M. Häusser. Propagation of action potentials in dendrites depends on dendritic morphology. *Journal of Neurophysiology*, 85(2):926–937, 2001. [43]

R. Vidal. Subspace clustering. *IEEE Signal Processing Magazine*, 28:52–68, 2011. [458]

D. Vidaurre, C. Bielza, and P. Larrañaga. Learning an L1-regularized Gaussian Bayesian network in the equivalence class space. *IEEE Transactions on Systems, Man and Cybernetics, Part B*, 40(5): 1231–1242, 2010. [531]

D. Vidaurre, C. Bielza, and P. Larrañaga. Forward stagewise naive Bayes. *Progress in Artificial Intelligence*, 1:57–69, 2012. [353, 354]

D. Vidaurre, C. Bielza, and P. Larrañaga. An L_1-regularized naive Bayes-inspired classifier for discarding redundant predictors. *International Journal on Artificial Intelligence Tools*, 22(4): 1350019, 2013a. [261, 354]

D. Vidaurre, C. Bielza, and P. Larrañaga. A survey on L_1-regression. *International Statistical Review*, 81(3):361–387, 2013b. [385]

D. Viggiano, D. P. Srivastava, L. Speranza, C. Perrone-Capano, G. C. Bellenchi, U. di Porzio, and N. J. Buckley. Quantifying barcodes of dendritic spines using entropy-based metrics. *Scientific Reports*, 5:14622, 2015. [136]

T. M. Vital, S. S. Hernandez, A. M. Stein, M. Garuffi, D. I. Corazza, L. P. de Andrade, J. L. Costa, and F. Stella. Depressive symptoms and level of physical activity in patients with Alzheimer's disease. *Geriatrics and Gerontology International Journal*, 12(4):67–642, 2012. [167]

P. T. von Hippel. Mean, median, and skew: Correcting a textbook rule. *Journal of Statistics Education*, 13(2), 2005. [59]

R. von Mises. Uber die "Ganzzahligkeit" der Atomgewichte und verwandte Fragen. *Physikalische Zeitschrift*, 19:490–500, 1918. [113]

J. von Neumann. Various techniques used in connection with random digits. *National Bureau of Standards Applied Math Series*, 12:36–38, 1951. [130]

M. J. Wainwright, P. Ravikumar, and J. D. Lafferty. High-dimensional graphical model selection using ℓ_1-regularized logistic regression. In *Advances in Neural Information Processing Systems 19*, pages 1465–1472. The MIT Press, 2007. [570]

K. Wang, M. Liang, L. Wang, L. Tian, X. Zhang, K. Li, and T. Jiang. Altered functional connectivity in early Alzheimer's disease: A resting-state fMRI study. *Human Brain Mapping*, 28:967–978, 2007. [46]

S. Wang and J. Zhu. Variable selection for model-based high-dimensional clustering and its application to microarray data. *Biometrics*, 64:440–448, 2008. [478]

S. Wang, M. Chopp, M. R. Nazem-Zadeh, G. Ding, S. P. Nejad-Davarani, C. Qu, M. Lu, L. Li, E. Davoodi-Bojd, J. Hu, Q. Li, A. Mahmood, and Q. Jiang. Comparison of neurite density measured by MRI and histology after TBI. *PLoS ONE*, 8(5):e63511, 2013. [190]

J. H. Ward. Hierarchical grouping to optimize an objective function. *Journal of the American Statistical Association*, 58:236–244, 1963. [441]

G. S. Watson. Goodness-of-fit tests on a circle. *Biometrika*, 48:109–114, 1961. [168]

G. S. Watson. *Statistics on Spheres*. Wiley, 1983. [179]

G. I. Webb and M. J. Pazzani. Adjusted probability naïve Bayesian induction. In *Proceedings of the 11th Australian Joint Conference on Artificial Intelligence*, pages 285–295. Springer, 1998. [351]

G. I. Webb, J. Boughton, and Z. Wang. Not so naive Bayes: Aggregating one-dependence estimators. *Machine Learning*, 58:5–24, 2005. [359]

G. Wei and M. Tanner. A Monte Carlo implementation of the EM algorithm and the poor man's data augmentation algorithms. *Journal of the American Statistical Association*, 85(411):699–704, 1990. [474]

S. M. Weiss and C. A. Kulikowski. *Computer Systems that Learn: Classification and Prediction Methods from Statistics, Neural Nets, Machine Learning, and Expert Systems*. Morgan Kaufmann, 1991. [29]

S. M. Weiss, R. S. Galen, and P. V. Tadepalli. Maximizing the predictive value of production rules. *Artificial Intelligence*, 45:47–71, 1990. [286]

Y. Weiss. Correctness of local probability propagation in graphical models with loops. *Neural Computation*, 12(1):1–41, 2000. [570]

Y. Weiss, E. P. Simoncelli, and E. H. Adelson. Motion illusions as optimal percepts. *Nature Neuroscience*, 5(6):598–604, 2002. [159]

H. G. Wells. *World Brain*. Methuen & Co, 1938. [23]

Q. Wen, A. Stepanyants, G. Elston, A. Grosberg, and D. Chklovskii. Maximization of the connectivity repertoire as a statistical principle governing the shapes of dendritic arbors. *Proceedings of the National Academy of Sciences*, 106(30):12536–12541, 2009. [43]

P. J. Werbos. *Beyond Regression: New Tools for Prediction and Analysis in the Behavioral Sciences*. PhD thesis, Harvard University, 1974. [318]

N. Wermuth. Analogies between multiplicative models in contingency tables and covariance selection. *Biometrics*, 32:95–108, 1976. [570]

N. Wermuth. Linear recursive equations, covariance selection, and path analysis. *Journal of the American Statistical Association*, 75(372):963–972, 1980. [500]

J. Weston, S. Mukherjee, O. Chapelle, M. Pontil, T. Poggio, and V. Vapnik. Feature selection for SVMs. In *Advances in Neural Information Processing Systems 13*, pages 51–63. The MIT Press, 2001. [261, 319]

J. Whittaker. *Graphical Models in Applied Multivariate Statistics*. Wiley, 1990. [484, 559, 570]

J. M. Wicherts, M. Bakker, and D. Molenaar. Willingness to share research data is related to the strength of the evidence and the quality of reporting of statistical results. *PLoS ONE*, 6(11):e26828, 2011. [20]

B. Widrow and M. E. Hoff. Adaptive switching circuits. In *1960 IRE WESCON Convention Record*, pages 96–104, 1960. [318]

R. Wiest, Y. Burren, M. Hauf, G. Schroth, J. Pruessner, M. Zbinden, K. Cattapan-Ludewig, and C. Kiefer. Classification of mild cognitive impairment and Alzheimer disease using model-based MR and magnetization transfer imaging. *American Journal of Neuroradiology*, 34(4):740–746, 2013. [448]

F. Wilcoxon. Individual comparisons by ranking methods. *Biometrics Bulletin*, 1(6):80–83, 1945. [176]

A. Wille and P. Bühlmann. Low-order conditional independence graphs for inferring genetic networks. *Statistical Applications in Genetics and Molecular Biology*, 5:Article 1, 2006. [570]

W. T. Williams and J. M. Lambert. Multivariate methods in plant ecology I. Association analysis in plant communities. *The Journal of Ecology*, 47:83–101, 1959. [442]

D. L. Wilson. Asympotic properties of nearest neighbor rules using edited data. *IEEE Transactions on Systems, Man, and Cybernetics*, 2(3):408–421, 1972. [269]

B. A. Wilt, L. D. Burns, E. Tatt Wei Ho, K. K. Ghosh, E. A. Mukamel, and M. J. Schnitzer. Advances in light microscopy for neuroscience. *Annual Review of Neuroscience*, 32:435–506, 2009. [13]

J. Winn, C. M. Bishop, and T. Jaakkola. Variational message passing. *Journal of Machine Learning Research*, 6:661–694, 2005. [544]

D. M. Witten and R. Tibshirani. Penalized classification using Fisher's linear discriminant. *Journal of the Royal Statistical Society, Series B*, 73(5):753–772, 2011. [261]

J. H. Wolfe. NORMIX: Computational methods for estimating the parameters of multivariate normal mixture distributions. *Technical Bulletin USNPRA*, 68(2), 1967. [475]

D. H. Wolpert. Stacked generalization. *Neural Networks*, 5:241–259, 1992. [399, 426]

D. H. Wolpert and W. G. Macready. No free lunch theorems for optimization. *IEEE Transactions on Evolutionary Computation*, 1(1):67–82, 1997. [388]

A. M. Wong, J. W. Wang, and R. Axel. Spatial representation of the glomerular map in the drosophila protocerebrum. *Cell*, 109:229–241, 2002. [34]

A. T. A. Wood. Simulation of the von Mises–Fisher distribution. *Communications in Statistics – Simulation and Computation*, 23(1):157–164, 1994. [152]

M. W. Woolrich, T. E. Behrens, C. F. Beckmann, and S. M. Smith. Mixture models with adaptive spatial regularization for segmentation with an application to fMRI data. *IEEE Transactions on Medical Imaging*, 24(1):1–11, 2005. [547]

M. Wozniak, M. Graña, and E. Corchado. A survey of multiple classifier systems as hybrid systems. *Information Fusion*, 16(0):3–17, 2014. [413]

C. F. J. Wu. On the convergence properties of the EM algorithm. *The Annals of Statistics*, 11:95–103, 1983. [473]

J. Wu, J. Chen, H. Xiong, and M. Xie. External validation measures for k-means clustering: A data distribution perspective. *Expert Systems with Applications*, 36:6050–6061, 2009. [462]

Y. Wu, S. K. Warfiled, I. L. Tan, W. M. Wells, D. S. Meier, R. A. van Schijndel, F. Barkhof, and C. R. Guttmann. Automated segmentation of multiple sclerosis lesion subtypes with multichannel MRI. *NeuroImage*, 32(3):1205–1215, 2006. [263]

J. Xiao, C. He, and X. Jiang. Structure identification of Bayesian classifiers based on GMDH. *Knowledge-Based Systems*, 22:461–470, 2009. [362]

B. Xie, W. Pan, and X. Shen. Variable selection in penalized model-based clustering via regularization on grouped parameters. *Bioinformatics*, 64:921–930, 2008. [478]

L. Xu, P. Yan, and T. Chang. Best first strategy for feature selection. In *Proceedings of the 9th International Conference on Pattern Recognition*, pages 706–708, IEEE, 1988. [240, 241]

X. L. Xu, J. M. Olson, and L. P. Zhao. A regression-based method to identify differentially expressed genes in microarray time course studies and its application in an inducible Huntington's disease transgenic model. *Human Molecular Genetics*, 11(17):1977–1985, 2002. [195]

J.-H. Xue and D. M. Titterington. Joint discriminative-generative modelling based on statistical tests for classification. *Pattern Recognition Letters*, 31(9):1048–1055, 2010. [385]

G. Yang, P. C. Chang, A. Bekker, T. J. Blanck, and W. B. Gan. Transient effects of anesthetics on dendritic spines and filopodia in the living mouse cortex. *Anesthesiology*, 115(4):718–726, 2011. [175]

G. Yang, F. Raschke, T. R. Barrick, and F. A. Howe. Manifold learning in MR spectroscopy using nonlinear dimensionality reduction and unsupervised clustering. *Magnetic Resonance in Medicine*, 74(3):868–878, 2015. [440]

H. Yang, J. Liu, J. Sui, G. Pearlson, and V. D. Calhoun. A hybrid machine learning method for fusing fMRI and genetic data: Combining both improves classification of schizophrenia. *Frontiers in Human Neuroscience*, 4:Article 192, 2010a. [406]

J. Yang, W. Peng, M. O. Ward, and E. A. Rundensteiner. Interactive hierarchical dimension ordering, spacing and filtering for exploration of high dimensional datasets. In *Proceedings of the 9th Annual IEEE Conference on Information Visualization*, pages 105–112. IEEE, 2003. [74]

Y. Yang and G. I. Webb. On why discretization works for naive-Bayes classifiers. In *Proceedings of the 16th Australian Conference on Artificial Intelligence*, volume 2903, pages 440–452, 2003. [374]

Y. Yang and G. I. Webb. Discretization for naive-Bayes learning: Managing discretization bias and variance. *Machine Learning*, 74(1):39–74, 2009. [91]

Y. Yang, K. B. Korb, K. M. Ting, and G. I. Webb. Ensemble selection for superparent-one-dependence estimators. In *Proceedings of the 18th Australian Conference on Artificial Intelligence*, pages 102–112, 2005. [359]

Y. Yang, G. I. Webb, J. Cerquides, K. B. Korb, J. Boughton, and K. M. Ting. To select or to weigh: A comparative study of linear combination schemes for superparent-one-dependence estimators. *IEEE Transactions on Knowledge and Data Engineering*, 19:1652–1665, 2007. [360]

Y. Yang, G. I. Webb, and X. Wu. *Data Mining and Knowledge Discovery Handbook*, chapter Discretization methods, pages 101–116. Springer, 2010b. [90]

S. Yanmin, A. K. C. Wong, and M. S. Kamel. Classification of imbalanced data: A review. *International Journal of Pattern Recognition and Artificial Intelligence*, 23(4):687–719, 2009. [223]

S. Yaramakala and D. Margaritis. Speculative Markov blanket discovery for optimal feature selection. In *Proceedings of the 5th IEEE International Conference on Data Mining*, pages 809–812. IEEE, 2005. [364]

F. Yates. Contingency table involving small numbers and the χ^2 test. *Journal of the Royal Statistical Society*, 1(2):217–235, 1934. [220]

J. S. Yedidia, W. T. Freeman, and Y. Weiss. Constructing free-energy approximations and generalized belief propagation algorithms. *IEEE Transactions on Information Theory*, 51(7):2282–2312, 2005. [562]

C. T. Yildiz and E. Alpaydın. Omnivariate decision trees. *IEEE Transactions on Neural Networks*, 12(6):1539–1546, 2001. [276]

J. Yu, Q. Cheng, and M. Huang. Analysis of the weighting exponent in the FCM. *IEEE Transactions on Systems, Man, and Cybernetics, Part B*, 34:634–639, 2004. [447]

C. Yuan and M. J. Druzdzel. Importance sampling algorithms for Bayesian networks: Principles and performance. *Mathematical and Computer Modelling*, 43(9-10):1189–1207, 2006. [544]

J. Yuan, G. Cui, W. Li, X. Zhang, X. Wang, H. Zheng, J. Zhang, S. Xiang, and Z. Xie. Propofol enhances hemoglobin-induced cytotoxicity in neurons. *Anesthesia and Analgesia Journal*, 122 (4):1024–1030, 2016. [179]

M. Yuan and Y. Lin. Model selection and estimation in regression with grouped variables. *Journal of the Royal Statistical Society, Series B*, 70(1):53–71, 2006. [341]

R. Yuste. *Dendritic Spines*. The MIT Press, 2010. [38]

R. Yuste and G. M. Church. The new century of the brain. *Scientific American*, 310(3):38–45, 2014. [13, 19]

R. Yuste, E. Lein, M. Hawrylycz, and Copenhagen Convention Group. A community-based transcriptomics classification and nomenclature of neocortical cell types, *Nature Neuroscience*, 23, in press 2020. [34]

R. Yuste, A. Majewska, and K. Holthoff. From form to function: Calcium compartmentalization in dendritic spines. *Nature Neuroscience*, 3:653–659, 2000. [39]

N. A. Zaidi, J. Cerquides, M. J. Carman, and G. I. Webb. Alleviating naive Bayes attribute independence assumption by attribute weighting. *Journal of Machine Learning Research*, 14: 1947–1988, 2013. [385]

H. Zhang and G. Sun. Feature selection using tabu search method. *Pattern Recognition*, 35:701–711, 2002. [241, 242]

J. Zhang. On the completeness of orientation rules for causal discovery in the presence of latent confounders and selection bias. *Artificial Intelligence*, 172(16-17):1873–1896, 2008. [545]

M.-L. Zhang, J. M. Peña, and V. Robles. Feature selection for multi-label naive Bayes classification. *Information Sciences*, 179(19):3218–3229, 2009. [429]

M.-L. Zhang and Z.-H. Zhou. Multilabel neural networks with applications to functional genomics and text categorization. *IEEE Transactions on Knowledge and Data Engineering*, 18(10):1338–1351, 2006. [427]

M.-L. Zhang and Z.-H. Zhou. ML-KNN: A lazy learning approach to multi-label learning. *Pattern Recognition*, 40(7):2038–2048, 2007. [427]

M.-L. Zhang and Z.-H. Zhou. A review on multi-label learning algorithms. *IEEE Transactions on Knowledge and Data Engineering*, 26(8):1819–1837, 2014. [416]

N. Zhang and D. Poole. A simple approach to Bayesian network computations. In *Proceedings of the 10th Biennial Canadian Conference on Artificial Intelligence*, pages 171–178, 1994. [507]

N. L. Zhang. Hierarchical latent class models for cluster analysis. *Journal of Machine Learning Research*, 5:697–723, 2004. [486]

N. L. Zhang, T. D. Nielsen, and F. V. Jensen. Latent variable discovery in classification models. *Artificial Intelligence in Medicine*, 30(3):283–299, 2004. [351, 352]

T. Zhang, R. Ramakrishnan, and M. Livny. BIRCH: An efficient data clustering method for very large databases. In *Proceedings of the ACM SIGMOD Conference on Management of Data*, pages 103–114, 1996. [467]

X. Zhang, C. Henriquez, and S. Ferrari. Spike-based indirect training of a spiking neural network-controlled virtual insect. In *52nd IEEE Conference on Decision and Control*, pages 6798–6805, 2013a. [300]

Y. Zhang, S. Wang, G. Ji, and Z. Dong. An MR brain images classifier system via particle swarm optimization and kernel support vector machine. *The Scientific World Journal*, 2013:Article 130134, 2013b. [314]

Y. N. Zhang. Can a smartphone diagnose Parkinson disease? A deep neural network method and telediagnosis system implementation. *Parkinson's Disease*, 2017: Article 6209703, 2017. [299]

M. Zhao, A. Batista, J. P. Cunningham, C. Chestek, Z. Rivera-Alvidrez, R. Kalmar, S. Ryu, K. Shenoy, and S. Iyengar. An L_1-regularized logistic model for detecting short-term neuronal interactions. *Journal of Computational Neuroscience*, 32(3):479–497, 2012. [341]

Z. Zheng and G. I. Webb. Lazy learning of Bayesian rules. *Machine Learning*, 41(1):53–84, 2000. [409]

A. B. Zheutlin, R. W. Viehman, R. Fortgang, J. Borg, D. J. Smith, J. Suvisaari, S. Therman, C. M. Hultman, and T. D. Cannon. Cognitive endophenotypes inform genome-wide expression profiling in schizophrenia. *Neuropsychology*, 30(1):40–52, 2016. [193]

S. Zhou, P. Rütimann, M. Xu, and P. Bühlmann. High-dimensional covariance estimation based on Gaussian graphical models. *Journal of Machine Learning Research*, 12:2975–3026, 2011. [570]

Z.-H. Zhou. *Ensemble Methods. Foundations and Algorithms*. Chapman & Hall/CRC, 2012. [413, 414]

Z.-H. Zhou, M. L. Zhang, S. J. Huang, and Y. F. Li. Multi-instance multi-label learning. *Artificial Intelligence*, 176:2291–2320, 2012. [434]

G. Zhu, Y. Li, P. P Wen, and S. Wang. *Signal and Image Analysis for Biomedical and Life Sciences. Advances in Experimental Medicine and Biology*, chapter Classifying epileptic EEG signals with delay permutation entropy and multi-scale K-means, pages 143–157. Springer, 2015. [445]

B. Ziebart, A. K. Dey, and J. A. Bagnell. Learning selectively conditioned forest structures with applications to DBNs and classification. In *Proceedings of the 23rd Conference Annual Conference on Uncertainty in Artificial Intelligence*, pages 458–465. AUAI Press, 2007. [358, 359]

Z. Zong. *Information-Theoretic Methods for Estimating Complicated Probability Distributions*. Elsevier, 2006. [378, 379]

O. Zuk, S. Margel, and E. Domany. On the number of samples needed to learn the correct structure of a Bayesian network. In *Proceedings of the 22nd Conference on Uncertainty in Artificial Intelligence*, pages 560–567. AUAI Press, 2006. [545]

Subject Index